Western Civilization
Beyond Boundaries

Western Civilization

Beyond Boundaries

Fifth Edition

Thomas F. X. Noble
University of Notre Dame

Barry Strauss
Cornell University

Duane J. Osheim
University of Virginia

Kristen B. Neuschel
Duke University

Elinor A. Accampo
University of Southern California

David D. Roberts
University of Georgia

William B. Cohen
Late of Indiana University

Houghton Mifflin Company   Boston   New York

Publisher: Suzanne Jeans
Senior Sponsoring Editor: Nancy Blaine
Senior Marketing Manager: Katherine Bates
Marketing Assistant: Lauren Bussard
Senior Development Editor: Julie Swasey
Editorial Assistant: Adrienne Zicht
Senior Project Editor: Christina Horn
Editorial Assistant: Carrie Parker
Art and Design Coordinator: Jill Haber
Cover Design Director: Tony Saizon
Senior Photo Editor: Jennifer Meyer Dare
Composition Buyer: Chuck Dutton
New Title Project Manager: James Lonergan

Cover image: Louise Elizabeth Vigée-LeBrun (1755–1842), *Madame Molé-Raymond* (1759–1833), actress with the company of the Comédie italienne in Paris, 1786. Photograph: Louvre, Paris/Erich Lessing/Art Resource, NY.

Text credits: Page 71: Quotation by Sappho from *Ancient Greek Literature and Society,* 2d ed., by Charles Rowan Beye. Copyright © 1987 by Cornell University Press. Reprinted by permission. **Page 121:** Excerpt from *The Aeneid of Virgil,* trans. Allen Mandelbaum. Copyright © 1971 by Allen Mandelbaum. Reprinted by permission of Bantam Books, a division of Bantam, Doubleday, Dell Publishing Group, Inc. **Page 305:** "Down there, around Ventadorn" from *The Lyrics of the Troubadour and Trouvères,* trans. Frederick Goldin. Copyright © 1973 by Frederick Goldin. Used by permission of Doubleday, a division of Random House, Inc. **Page 305:** "Friend, if you had shown consideration" from lyrics by Castellozza, in *The Women Troubadours* by Meg Bogin (W. W. Norton, 1976). Copyright © 1976 by Magda Bogin. Reprinted by permission of Magda Bogin. **Page 831:** Excerpts from *A Room of One's Own* by Virginia Woolf. Copyright © 1929 by Harcourt, Inc., and renewed 1957 by Leonard Woolf. Reprinted by permission of the publisher.

Printed in the U.S.A.

Library of Congress Control Number: 2006935032

Instructor's Exam Copy:
ISBN-13: 978-0-618-83423-5
ISBN-10: 0-618-83423-0

For orders, use Student Text ISBNs:
ISBN-13: 978-0-618-79424-9
ISBN-10: 0-618-79424-7

3456789-VH-10 09 08 07

BRIEF CONTENTS

CONTENTS

MAPS

Documents

THE VISUAL RECORD

PREFACE

An old adage says that each generation must write history for itself. If the adage is true, then it would also be true that each generation must teach and learn history for itself. The history, of course, does not change, although new discoveries come to light all the time. What does change is us, each succeeding generation of us. What causes us to change, and thus to experience and understand history in ever new ways, are the great developments of our own times. Think of the world-changing events of the last century: two world wars, the Great Depression, the cold war, nuclear weapons, the civil rights movement, the women's movement, the explosion in scientific knowledge, and the media revolutions involving radio and television, the computer, and the Internet. The pace of change has accelerated in our time, but the process of change always affects people's view of their world.

As we launch the fifth edition for this book we are once again acutely aware of the need to address big questions in ways that make sense to teachers and students right now, in the world we live in today. As these words are being written, the news is full of reports from Afghanistan, Iraq, Iran, and Darfur. In such circumstances we might well ask, What is the West; what is Western? Some believe that we are engaged in a "Clash of Civilizations." Is one of these Western Civilization? If so, who or what is its adversary? The West is sometimes understood geographically and sometimes culturally. For most people, the West means western Europe. And yet western Europe itself is the heir of the peoples and cultures of antiquity, including the Sumerians, Egyptians, Persians, Greeks, Romans, Jews, Christians, and Muslims. In fact, Europe is the heir of even earlier civilizations in Asia and Africa. As a cultural phenomenon, "Western" implies many things: freedom and free, participatory political institutions; economic initiative and opportunity; monotheistic religious faiths (Judaism, Christianity, and Islam); rationalism and ordered thought in the social, political, and philosophical realms; an aesthetic sensibility that aspires to a universal sense of beauty. But the West has felt free to evoke tradition as its guiding light and also to innovate brilliantly, to accommodate slavery and freedom simultaneously, and to esteem original thought and persecute people who deviate from the norm. "Western" indeed has meant many things in various places at different times. This book constantly and explicitly attempts to situate its readers in place, time, and tradition.

Another big question is this: What exactly is civilization? No definition can win universal acceptance, but certain elements of a definition are widely accepted.

Cities are crucial; with cities emerge complex social organizations that involve at least a minimal division of labor. Some people work in the fields, some in the home. Soldiers defend the city, and artisans provide its daily goods. Governing institutions have a wide measure of acceptance and have the ability to enforce their will. Complex cultures also develop religious ideas and authorities; a literature and law that may be oral or written; monumental architecture, especially fortifications, palaces, and temples; and arts such as music, painting, and sculpture.

Western Civilization has had an influence on almost every person alive today. The West deserves to be studied because its tale is compelling, but it demands to be studied because its story has been so central to the development of the world in which we live. Many of the world's dominant institutions are Western in their origin and in their contemporary manifestations—most notably parliamentary democracy. Commercial capitalism, a Western construct, is the world's dominant form of economic organization, and even its greatest rival, communism, is fundamentally Western: its theoreticians were Europeans who drew on utopian ideals, classical economics, Enlightenment doctrines, and the ideologies of the French Revolution.

Until a generation or so ago, Western Civilization was a staple of college and university curricula and was generally studied in isolation. Although it was, and is, important for us to know who we are, it is also important for us to see that we have changed in dramatic ways and that we can no longer understand ourselves in isolation from the world around us. Accordingly, this book repeatedly sets the experience of the West into its global context. This is not a World History book. But it is a book that sees Western Civilization as one significant segment of the world's history.

BASIC APPROACH

Nearly two decades ago the six original authors of *Western Civilization: Beyond Boundaries* set out to create a textbook for a course that would, as a total effort, inform students about essential developments within a tradition that has powerfully, though not always positively, affected everyone in the contemporary world. Although each of us found something to admire in all of the existing textbooks, none of us was fully happy with any of them. We were disappointed with books that claimed "balance," but actually stressed a single kind of history. We regretted that so many texts were uneven in their command of recent scholarship. Although we were convinced of both the inherent interest of Western Civilization and the importance of teaching the subject, we were disconcerted by the celebratory tone of some books, which portrayed the West as resting on its laurels instead of creatively facing its future.

We decided to produce a book that is balanced and coherent; that addresses the full range of subjects that a Western Civilization book needs to address; that provides the student reader with interesting, timely material; that is up-to-date in terms of scholarship and approach; and that is handsome to look at—in short, a book that helps the instructor to teach and the student to learn. We have kept our common vision fresh through frequent meetings, correspondence, critical mutual readings, and expert editorial guidance. The misfortune of the untimely death of one member of our team has brought us the fortune of a new colleague who has inspired and challenged the rest of us in new ways. Because each of us has focused on his or her own area of specialization, we believe that we have attained a rare blend of competence, confidence, and enthusiasm. Moreover, in moving from plans for a first edition to the preparation of a fifth, we have been able to profit from the experience of using the book, the advice and criticism of dozens of colleagues, and the reactions of thousands of students.

Western Civilization is a story. Therefore, we aimed at a strong chronological narrative line. Our experience as teachers tells us that students appreciate this clear but gentle orientation. Our experience tells us, too, that an approach that is broadly chronological will leave instructors plenty of room to adapt our narrative to their preferred organization, or to supplement our narrative with one of their own.

Although we maintain the familiar, large-scale divisions of a Western Civilization book, we also present some innovative adjustments in arrangement. For instance, Chapter 2 treats early Greece together with the whole eastern Mediterranean region in the period from about 1500 to 750 B.C. This approach both links kindred cultures and respects chronological flow better than customary treatments, which take western Asia to a certain point and then backtrack to deal with early Greece. We incorporate a single chapter on Late Antiquity, the tumultuous and fascinating period from about A.D. 300 to 600 that witnessed the transformation of the Roman Empire into three successors: Byzantine, Islamic, and European. One chapter studies those three successors, thereby permitting careful comparisons. But we also assign chapters to some of the greatest issues in Western Civilization, such as the Renaissance, the age of European exploration and conquest, the Scientific Revolution, and the industrial transformation. Our twentieth-century chapters reflect an understanding of the last century formed in its clos-

ing years rather than in its middle decades. What is new in our organization represents adjustments grounded in the best scholarship, and what is old represents time-tested approaches.

In fashioning our picture of the West, we took two unusual steps. First, our West is itself bigger than the one found in most textbooks. We treat the Celtic world, Scandinavia, and the Slavic world as integral parts of the story. We look often at the lands that border the West—Anatolia/Turkey, western Asia, North Africa, the Eurasian steppes—in order to show the to-and-fro of peoples, ideas, technologies, and products. Second, we continually situate the West in its global context. Just as we recognize that the West has influenced the rest of the world, we also carefully acknowledge how the rest of the world has influenced the West. We begin this story of mutual interaction with the Greeks and Romans, carry it through the European Middle Ages, focus on it in the age of European exploration and conquest, and analyze it closely in the modern world of industry, diplomacy, empire, immigration, and questions of citizenship and identity.

Another approach that runs like a ribbon throughout this textbook involves balance and integration. Teachers and students, just like the authors of this book, have their particular interests and emphases. In the large and diverse American academy, that is as it should be. But a textbook, if it is to be helpful and useful, should incorporate as many interests and emphases as possible. For a long time, some said, Western Civilization books devoted excessive coverage to high politics—"the public deeds of great men," as an ancient Greek writer defined the historian's subject. Others felt that high culture—all the Aristotles and Mozarts—were included to the exclusion of supposedly lesser figures and ordinary men and women. In the 1970s books began to emphasize social history. Some applauded this new emphasis even as they debated fiercely over what to include under this heading.

In this book, we attempt to capture the Western tradition in its full contours, to hear the voices of all those who have made durable contributions. But because we cannot say everything about everybody at every moment, we have had to make choices about how and where to array key topics within our narrative. Above all, we have tried to be integrative. For example, when we talk about government and politics, we present the institutional structures through which power was exercised, the people who possessed power as well as the people who did not, the ideological foundations for the use of power, and the material conditions that fostered or hindered the real or the would-be powerful. In other words, instead of treating old-fashioned "high politics" in abstract and descriptive ways, we take an approach that is organic and analytical: How did things work? Our approach to the history of women is another example. A glance at this book's table of contents and then at its index is revealing. The former reveals very few sections devoted explicitly and exclusively to women. The latter shows that women appear constantly in every section of this book. Is there a contradiction here? Not at all. Women and men have not been historical actors in isolation from one another. Yet gender, which is relational, reciprocal, and mutual, is an important variable that has shaped individual and collective experience. Hence we seek to explain why certain political, economic, or social circumstances had differing impacts on men and women, and how such conditions led them to make different choices.

Similarly, when we talk of great ideas, we describe the antecedent ideas from which seemingly new ones were built up, and we ask about the consequences of those ideas. We explore the social positions of the authors of those ideas to see if this helps us explain the ideas themselves or gauge their influence. We try to understand how ideas in one field of human endeavor prove to be influential in other fields. For instance, gender is viewed as connected to and part of the larger fabric of ideas including power, culture, and piety.

We invite the reader to look at our narrative as if it were a mosaic. Taken as a whole, our narrative contains a coherent picture. Viewed more closely, it is made up of countless tiny bits that may have their individual interest but do not even hint at the larger picture of which they are parts. Finally, just as the viewer of a mosaic may find his or her eye drawn especially to one area, feature, color, or style, so too the reader of this book will find some parts more engaging or compelling than others. But it is only because there is, in this book as in a mosaic, a complete picture that the individual sections make sense, command our attention, excite our interest.

One word sums up our approach in this book: "balance." We tell a good story, but we pause often to reflect on that story, to analyze it. We devote substantial coverage to the typical areas of Greece, Rome, Italy, France, Great Britain, and so forth, but we say more about western Europe's frontiers than any other book. We do not try to disguise our Western Civilization book as a World History book, but we take great pains to locate the West within its global context. And we always assume that context means mutuality and reciprocity. We have high politics and big ideas alongside household management and popular culture. We think that part of the fascination of the past lies in its capacity to suggest understandings of the present and possibilities for the future.

Our subtitle, "Beyond Boundaries," is intended to suggest growth, challenge, and opportunity. The West began in Mesopotamia but soon spread to all of western Asia. Gradually the Greeks entered the scene and disseminated their ideas throughout the Mediterranean world. The Romans, always heirs of the Greeks, carried ideas and institutions from Britain to Mesopotamia. As the Roman order collapsed, Rome's imprint was left on a small segment of Europe lying west of the Rhine and south of the Danube. Europeans then crashed through those boundaries to create a culture that extended from Iceland to the Russian steppes. At the dawn of the modern age Europe entered into a complex set of commercial, colonial, military, and political relations with the rest of the globe. Our contemporary world sees Western influences everywhere. No western "boundary" has ever been more than temporary, provisional.

DISTINCTIVE FEATURES

To make this book as accessible as possible to students, we have constantly been aware of its place in a program of teaching and learning. In the preceding paragraphs something has been said about this book's distinctive substantive features and how, we believe, they will contribute to the attainment of a deeper understanding of Western Civilization, as well as of its importance and place in the wider history of the earth's peoples. Teaching and learning also involves pedagogical techniques and innovations. We have attended conscientiously to pedagogical issues from the start, and we have made some significant changes in this edition.

Our chapters have always begun with a vignette that is directly tied to an accompanying picture. These vignettes alert the reader to one or more of the key aspects of the chapter. Thus the readers have encountered a thematic introduction that evokes interest while pointing clearly and in some detail to what follows.

To make our chapter introductions more effective, which means to give students greater confidence as they proceed through the book, we have taken numerous steps. First, as in past editions, we reviewed and revised our opening vignettes to connect text and picture more closely and to use both to invite the reader into the chapter.

Second, the first page of each chapter contains a succinct Outline that immediately and dramatically tells the reader what he or she is going to encounter in the following pages. Third, a list of Key Terms is designed to work with the introduction and Outline to give the student a clear orientation to what will follow. Fourth, the chapter introductions conclude with a list of Focus Questions that both echo the introduction and set the reader off on the right path into the following pages. Fifth, as the student begins to read the chapter proper, a Chronology serves as yet another orientation to the material contained in the chapter. Subject-specific chronologies still appear in various parts of the book, but we felt readers would benefit from a chronological guide at the beginning of each chapter.

In this edition we have repeated each Focus Question at the head of the section to which it pertains. At the end of each major section, we provide succinct Section Summaries. Each chapter concludes with a Chapter Summary that reiterates the Focus Questions and then briefly answers them once again.

As a complement to text coverage, a ready reference, and a potential study guide, all of the Key Terms have always been gathered into a Glossary at the back of the book. For this edition, we have also placed definitions on the pages where the Key Terms first appear.

In addition to this fundamental attention to chapter themes and contents, we have sought to improve the book's teachability by adding a pronunciation guide. Whenever we use an unfamiliar name or term, we show the reader how to pronounce it. Instead of using the intricate rules of phonetics, we provide commonsense guides to pronunciation in parentheses directly following the word.

This edition is a bit shorter than its predecessors. Relevance, "teachability," and "learnability" were our guides in streamlining our coverage at many points. Virtually every chapter experienced some slimming in the interest of keeping major points and themes front and center.

We have been conscious of how the book *looks* to the reader from the very beginning. Attractively laid-out pages, a handsome full-color design, engaging maps, and beautifully reproduced pictures enhance the book's appearance. In keeping with our desire to integrate the components of the book into a coherent whole, we carefully anchor the maps and pictures into the volume. The authors designed the content of the maps in this book, labeled them to complement its text, and captioned them to advance its teaching role. The same is true of the pictures: the authors selected them, worked with the book's designers to place them advantageously (and not just decoratively), and wrote all the captions. For this edition, we paid particular attention to reviewing all the captions and to revising many of them. All of the maps are cross-referenced in the text, some of them several times, and the text often refers directly to the pictures.

From the start, every chapter in this book has had boxed documents, one of which treated a "global" theme, as well as a two-page feature entitled "Weighing the Evidence." For this edition, we thought hard about our features and decided to take some decisive steps to make them work better for teachers and students. First, we reduced the number of features to three per chapter. Second, we introduced a uniform structure and format. One feature, entitled "The Global Record," presents a significant document that sets some aspect of Western Civilization within the global perspective.

These documents are substantial, are carefully introduced, and conclude with study questions. Another feature is called "The Written Record." This feature contains a significant document relevant to the text materials then under discussion with a careful introduction and study questions. The third feature is called "The Visual Record." This feature represents a reconceptualization of our former "Weighing the Evidence" feature. Most of those features did focus on visual evidence, but now the Visual Record features all do so. As with the Global Record and Written Record features, the Visual Records have helpful questions. Whereas the Weighing the Evidence features always concluded our chapters, now the Visual Records are placed into the chapters at the most appropriate position. For this edition, we cast a careful eye over all the Visual Record features and prepared eight new ones.

ORGANIZATION AND CONTENT CHANGES

As always, we have paid close attention to how our chapters "work." Accordingly, Chapter 1 contains new material on ancient treaty making, Chapter 2 incorporates new archaeological findings, Chapter 3 has fresh material on Greek politics, and Chapter 5 includes revised material on Roman politics and the conflict of the orders, as well as material on the Roman household and the connection between family and government. Chapter 7 has reorganized material on the Catholic Church, and Chapter 9 has expanded coverage of the Crusades. Chapters 9 and 10 have been shortened and streamlined. Chapter 13 has new material, as do Chapters 15 and 17, both of which were significantly reorganized. The material on the Thirty Years' War in Chapter 15 has been fully reworked and now includes a section on the developments in eastern and central Europe. New material on the slave trade has been added to Chapter 18. The treatment of industrialization in Chapter 20 has been recast. In Chapter 23, a new discussion of women and charity has been added, focusing on Josephine Grey Butler, Annie Wood Besant, and others. Chapter 24 has exciting new material on communications and propaganda. Chapter 28 incorporates new scholarship on the role of Pope Pius XII during the Holocaust, as well as an expanded account of the Warsaw uprising. Finally, in light of the drastic changes in the world since this book was last revised, Chapter 30 has been thoroughly rewritten to include coverage of the Iraq War, recent environmental issues, the expanding European Union, the changing demographics of Europe, the issues of unilateralism and Western responsibility in an increasingly global community, and the outrage provoked in the Muslim world over certain Danish political cartoons.

ANCILLARIES

A wide array of supplements accompany this text to help students better master the material and to help instructors in teaching from the book:

▶ *Online Study Center student website* ⟨Online Study Center⟩

▶ *Online Teaching Center instructor website*
⟨Online Teaching Center⟩

▶ *HM Testing CD-ROM (powered by Diploma)*

▶ *Online Instructor's Resource Manual*

▶ *PowerPoint maps, images, and lecture outlines*

▶ *PowerPoint questions for personal response systems*

▶ *Blackboard™ and WebCT™ course cartridges*

▶ *Eduspace™ (powered by Blackboard™)*

▶ *Interactive ebook*

The *Online Study Center* is a companion website for students that features a wide assortment of resources to help students master the subject matter. The website, prepared by Jacqueline Cavalier of Community College of Allegheny County and Douglas Keith, is divided into three major sections:

▶ **"Prepare for Class"** includes material such as learning objectives, chapter outlines, and pre-class quizzes for a student to consult before going to class.

▶ **"Improve Your Grade"** includes practice review material like interactive flashcards, chronological ordering exercises, primary sources, and interactive map exercises.

▶ **"ACE the Test"** features our successful ACE brand of practice tests as well as other self-testing materials.

Students can find additional text resources such as an online glossary, audio MP3 files of chapter summaries, and material on how to study more effectively in the **"General Resources"** section. Throughout the text, icons direct students to relevant exercises and self-testing material located on the *Online Study Center*. Access the *Online Study Center* for this text by visiting **college.hmco.com/pic/noble5e.**

The *Online Teaching Center* is a companion website for instructors. It features all of the material on the student site plus additional password-protected resources that help instructors teach the course, such as an electronic version of the *Instructor's Resource Manual* and *PowerPoint* slides. Access the *Online Teaching Center* for this text by visiting **college.hmco.com/pic/noble5e.**

The *Instructor's Resource Manual,* prepared by William A. Paquette of Tidewater Community College, contains instructional objectives, chapter outlines and summaries, lecture suggestions, suggested debate and research topics, cooperative learning activities, and suggested readings and resources.

HM Testing (powered by *Diploma*) offers instructors a flexible and powerful tool for test generation and test management. Now supported by the Brownstone Research Group's market-leading *Diploma* software, this new version of *HM Testing* significantly improves on functionality and ease of use by offering all the tools needed to create, author, deliver, and customize multiple types of tests. *Diploma* is currently in use at thousands of college and university campuses throughout the United States and Canada. The *HM Testing* content for this text was developed by Janusz Duzinkiewicz of Purdue University North Central and offers key term identification, multiple-choice questions (with page references to the correct response), short answer, essay questions (with sample answers), and map questions that refer to maps in the text, as well as final exams for both volumes.

We are pleased to offer a collection of Western Civilization *PowerPoint* lecture outlines, maps, and images for use in classroom presentations. Detailed lecture outlines correspond to the book's chapters and make it easier for instructors to cover the major topics in class. The art collection includes all of the photos and maps in the text, as well as numerous other images from our Western Civilization titles. *PowerPoint* questions and answers for use with personal response system software are also offered to adopters free of charge.

A variety of assignable homework and testing material has been developed to work with the *Blackboard™* and *WebCT™* course management systems, as well as with *Eduspace™,* Houghton Mifflin's Online Learning Tool (powered by Blackboard™). *Eduspace™* is a web-based online learning environment that provides instructors with a gradebook and communication capabilities, such as synchronous and asynchronous chats and announcement postings. It offers access to assignments such as over 650 gradable homework exercises, writing assignments, interactive maps with questions, primary sources, discussion questions for online discussion boards, and tests, which all come ready-to-use. Instructors can choose to use the content as is, modify it, or even add their own material. *Eduspace™* also contains an interactive ebook, which contains in-text links to interactive maps, primary sources, and audio pronunciation files, as well as review and self-testing material for students.

ACKNOWLEDGMENTS

The authors have benefited throughout the process of revision from the acute and helpful criticisms of numerous colleagues. We thank in particular: **Daniel Brown,** Moorpark College; **Elizabeth Carney,** Clemson University; **Jacqueline Cavalier,** Community College of Allegheny County; **Janusz Duzinkiewicz,** Purdue University North Central; **Lisa Lane,** Mira Costa College; **Clementine Oliver,** California State Northridge; **William Paquette,** Tidewater Community College; **Rick Parrish,** Brevard Community College; and **Stuart Smyth,** SUNY Albany.

Each of us has benefited from the close readings and careful criticisms of our coauthors, although we all assume responsibility for our own chapters. Barry Strauss has written Chapters 1–6; Thomas Noble, 7–10; Duane Osheim, 11–14; Kristen Neuschel, 15–19; and David Roberts, 25–30. William Cohen originally wrote Chapters 20–24, and these have now been thoroughly reviewed by Elinor Accampo.

Many colleagues, friends, and family members have helped us develop this work as well. Thomas Noble continues to be grateful for Linda Noble's patience and good humor. He is also grateful to John Contreni, Thomas Head, Elizabeth Meyer, Julia Smith, the late Richard E. Sullivan, John Van Engen, and Robert Wilken. He also thanks some two dozen teaching assistants who have helped him to think through the Western Civilization experience.

Barry Strauss is grateful to colleagues at Cornell and at other universities who offered advice and encouragement and responded to scholarly questions. He would also like to thank the people at Cornell who provided technical assistance and support. Most important have been the support and forbearance of his family. His daughter, Sylvie; his son, Michael; and, above all, his wife, Marcia, have truly been sources of inspiration.

Duane Osheim thanks family and friends who continue to support and comment on the text. He would especially like to thank colleagues at the University of Virginia who have engaged him in a long and fruitful discussion of Western Civilization and its relationship to other cultures. They make clear the mutual interdependence of the cultures of the wider world. He particularly wishes to thank H. C. Erik Midelfort, Arthur Field, Brian Owensby, Joseph C. Miller, Chris Carlsmith, Beth Plummer, and David D'Andrea for information and clarification on a host of topics.

Kristen Neuschel thanks her colleagues at Duke University for sharing their expertise. She is especially grateful to Sy Mauskopf, Bill Reddy, John Richards, Tom Robisheaux, Alex Roland, Barry Gaspar, and Peter Wood. She also thanks her husband and fellow historian, Alan Williams, for his wisdom about Western Civilization and his support throughout the project, and her children, Jesse and Rachel, for their patience, joy, and curiosity.

Elinor Accampo is deeply indebted to the late Bill Cohen, whose work she edited, revised, and added to. His original chapters offered a model of expertise and prose, and it is with great pride, respect, and humility that she carries on what he originated. She also wishes to thank the coauthors—Thomas Noble, Barry Strauss, Duane Osheim, Kristen Neuschel, and David Roberts for their warm welcome to the team, and for the advice and expertise they offered. She owes special thanks to Kristen Neuschel and Rachel Fuchs (who contributed to an earlier edition) for friendship, support, and advice, as well as to Nancy Blaine and Julie Swasey for graciously responding to the persistent questions of a novice on this long-standing project.

David Roberts wishes to thank Bonnie Cary, Vici Payne, and Brenda Luke for their able assistance and Walter Adamson, Timothy Cleaveland, Karl Friday, Michael Kwass, John Morrow, Miranda Pollard, Judith Rohrer, William Steuck, and Kirk Willis for sharing their expertise in response to questions. He also thanks Beth Roberts for her constant support and interest and her exceedingly critical eye.

The first plans for this book were laid in 1988, and over the course of eighteen years there has been remarkable stability in the core group of people responsible for its development. The author team lost a member, Bill Cohen, but Elinor Accampo stepped into Bill's place with such skill and grace that it seemed as though she had been with us from the start. Our original sponsoring editor, Jean Woy, moved up the corporate ladder but never missed an author meeting with us. Christina Horn, our senior project editor, has been the wizard behind the curtain for all five editions. More than anyone else, she has taught us how to *make* a book. Carole Frohlich, our picture researcher, has also been with us from the beginning, and she has been masterful at fulfilling and enhancing our picture requests. Our sponsoring editor for most of a decade, Nancy Blaine, has been a tower of strength. She believes in us, as we believe in her. We have been fortunate in our editors, Elizabeth Welch, Jennifer Sutherland, and Julie Swasey. All these kind and skillful people have elicited from us authors a level of achievement that fills us at once with pride and humility.

Thomas F. X. Noble

ABOUT THE AUTHORS

Thomas F. X. Noble   After receiving his Ph.D. from Michigan State University, Thomas Noble taught at Albion College, Michigan State University, Texas Tech University, and the University of Virginia. In 1999 he received the University of Virginia's highest award for teaching excellence. In 2001 he became Robert M. Conway Director of the Medieval Institute at the University of Notre Dame. He is the author of *The Republic of St. Peter: The Birth of the Papal State, 680–825; Religion, Culture and Society in the Early Middle Ages; Soldiers of Christ: Saints and Saints' Lives from Late Antiquity and the Early Middle Ages; Images and the Carolingians: Tradition, Order, and Worship;* and *From Roman Provinces to Medieval Kingdoms.* Noble's articles and reviews have appeared in many leading journals, including the *American Historical Review, Byzantinische Zeitschrift, Catholic Historical Review, Revue d'histoire ecclésiastique, Speculum,* and *Studi medievali.* He has also contributed chapters to several books and articles to three encyclopedias. He was a member of the Institute for Advanced Study in 1994 and the Netherlands Institute for Advanced Study in 1999–2000. He has been awarded fellowships by the National Endowment for the Humanities (twice) and the American Philosophical Society. He was elected a Fellow of the Medieval Academy of America in 2004.

Barry Strauss   Professor of history and Classics at Cornell University, Barry Strauss holds a Ph.D. from Yale. He has been awarded fellowships by the National Endowment for the Humanities, the American School of Classical Studies at Athens, the MacDowell Colony for the Arts, the Korea Foundation, and the Killam Foundation of Canada. He is the recipient of the Clark Award for excellence in teaching from Cornell. He served as Director of Cornell's Peace Studies Program. His many publications include *Athens After the Peloponnesian War: Class, Faction, and Policy, 403–386 B.C.; Fathers and Sons in Athens: Ideology and Society in the Era of the Peloponnesian War; The Anatomy of Error: Ancient Military Disasters and Their Lessons for Modern Strategists* (with Josiah Ober); *Hegemonic Rivalry from Thucydides to the Nuclear Age* (co-edited with R. Ned Lebow); *War and Democracy: A Comparative Study of the Korean War and the Peloponnesian War* (co-edited with David R. McCann); *Rowing Against the Current: On Learning to Scull at Forty; The Battle of Salamis, the Naval Encounter That Saved Greece—and Western Civilization;* and *The Trojan War: A New History.* His book *The Battle of Salamis* has been translated into five languages and was named one of the best books of 2004 by the Washington Post.

Duane J. Osheim   A Fellow of the American Academy in Rome with a Ph.D. in history from the University of California at Davis, Duane Osheim is department chair and professor of history at the University of Virginia. He is the author and editor of numerous books on the social and cultural history of late medieval and Renaissance Italy, including *A Tuscan Monastery and Its Social World; An Italian Lordship: The Bishopric of Lucca in the Late Middle Ages;* and *Beyond Florence: The Contours of Medieval and Early Modern Italy.* To appear shortly is *Chronicling History: Chroniclers and Historians in Medieval and Renaissance Italy.*

Kristen B. Neuschel   After receiving her Ph.D. from Brown University, Kristen Neuschel taught at Denison University and Duke University, where she is currently associate professor of history. She is a specialist in early modern French history and is the author of *Word of Honor: Interpreting Noble Culture in Sixteenth-Century France* and articles on French social history and European women's history. She has received grants from the National Endowment for the Humanities and the American Council of Learned Societies. She has also received the Alumni Distinguished Undergraduate Teaching Award, which is awarded annually on the basis of student nominations for excellence in teaching at Duke.

Elinor A. Accampo   Professor of history and gender studies at the University of Southern California, Elinor Accampo completed her Ph.D. at the University of California, Berkeley. Prior to her career at USC, she taught at Colorado College and Denison University. She specializes in modern France and is the author of *Blessed Motherhood; Bitter Fruit: Nelly Roussel and the Politics of Female Pain in Third Republic France;* and *Industrialization, Family, and Class Relations: Saint Chamond, 1815–1914.* She has also published *Gender and the Politics of Social Reform in France* (co-edited with Rachel Fuchs and Mary Lynn Stewart) and articles and book chapters on the history of reproductive rights and birth control movements. She has received fellowships and travel grants from the German Marshall Fund, the Haynes Foundation, the American

Council of Learned Societies, and the National Endowment for the Humanities, as well as an award for Innovative Undergraduate Teaching at USC.

David D. Roberts   After taking his Ph.D. in modern European history at the University of California, Berkeley, David Roberts taught at the Universities of Virginia and Rochester before becoming professor of history at the University of Georgia in 1988. At Rochester he chaired the Humanities Department of the Eastman School of Music, and he chaired the History Department at Georgia from 1993 to 1998. A recipient of Woodrow Wilson and Rockefeller Foundation fellowships, he is the author of *The Syndicalist Tradition and Italian Fascism; Benedetto Croce and the Uses of Historicism; Nothing but History: Reconstruction and Extremity After Metaphysics*; and *The Totalitarian Experiment in Twentieth-Century Europe: Rethinking the Poverty of Great Politics,* as well as two books in Italian and numerous articles and reviews. He is currently the Albert Berry Saye Professor of History at Georgia.

Western
Civilization
Beyond
Boundaries

THE ANCESTORS
OF THE WEST

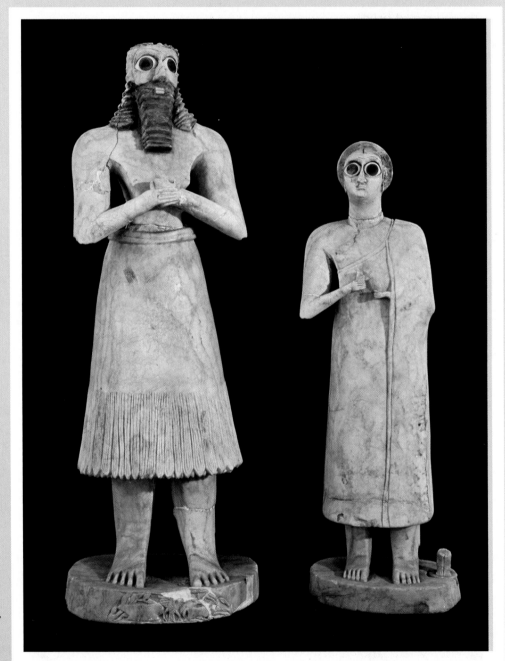

**Male and Female
Statuettes**
Early Dynastic Period,
Mesopotamia. *(Iraq Museum,
Baghdad/Scala/Art Resource, NY)*

The powerful gaze of their inlaid alabaster

heir huge staring eyes peer out across the centuries. He has long hair, a flowing beard, and a pleated skirt. She has short black hair and wears a simple dress and cloak that go down to her ankles. The man is taller and broader and grabs our attention with his big hair and his hands clasped in prayer. The woman seems modest and may originally have had a child beside her. They represent one of history's oldest couples, dating back to about 2500 B.C.

The powerful gaze of their inlaid alabaster eyes is a way of looking toward heaven. In fact, the couple may have represented gods. Certainly, they did not lack for company, to judge from the dozen other figurines and busts found with them, most of them smaller than the couple and so probably priests and worshipers. One is inscribed with a name, no doubt of an important person. They all come from a temple in the ancient Mesopotamian city of Eshnunna (modern Tell Asmar in Iraq), where they had been placed as an offering to the gods. The statuettes show us that early civilization was religious, artistic, literate, structured by rank and status, and fascinated by the relationship between men and women.

The world of 2500 B.C. had already seen the most momentous inventions in human history. They began approximately 100,000 years ago, when the first modern humans evolved from humanlike ancestors. Human beings wrestled with an often-hostile environment, engaging in a continuing series of experiments, until beginning about 10,000 B.C. they learned how to plant crops and tame animals. The shift from a food-collecting to a food-producing economy dramatically increased the amount of human life that the earth could support. Between 3500 and 3000 B.C., human society became well organized in urban centers, supported by farmers in the surrounding territories, and able to keep written records: it had, in short, achieved civilization.

What we call Western civilization, however, was still more than two thousand years away. As a term, *Western civilization* is imprecise, inviting disagreement about its definition and about the lands, peoples, and cultures that it embraces at any given time. In the strictest sense, Western civilization means the "West," and that, in turn, has traditionally meant the lands and peoples of western Europe.

CHAPTER OUTLINE

ORIGINS, TO CA. 3000 B.C.

MESOPOTAMIA, TO CA. 1600 B.C.

EGYPT, TO CA. 1100 B.C.

WIDENING HORIZONS: THE LEVANT
  AND ANATOLIA, 2500–1150 B.C.

KEY TERMS

hominids

hunter-gatherers

Neolithic Revolution

cuneiform

papyrus

Sumerians

city-state

pharaoh

Amarna reform

Hittites

Online Study Center

This icon will direct you to interactive map and primary source activities on the website **college.hmco.com/ pic/noble5e**

3

Initially, however, the West embraced the Greek and Roman peoples, plus the foundational monotheistic religions of Judaism and Christianity. These first Westerners in turn borrowed many ideas and institutions from the earlier civilizations of western Asia and Egypt. (These civilizations are sometimes referred to as the ancient Near East.) Indeed, civilization began in those lands and came only relatively late to Europe.

Western Asia and Egypt contributed greatly to the cultures of Greece and Rome and to the religious visions of the Jews and Christians. Yet those earlier civilizations are sufficiently different from the West and its society, politics, and religion that they are better considered as ancestors or forerunners of the West rather than as its founders. (For a longer discussion of the definition of Western civilization, see the Preface.)

So, after briefly surveying the origins of the human species, the historian of the West must begin with the emergence of civilizations after 3500 B.C. in two great river valleys: the valley of the Tigris (TY-gris) and Euphrates (yoo-FRAY-tees) in Mesopotamia (today, Iraq and Syria), and the valley of the Nile in Egypt. Impressive in their own right, Mesopotamia and Egypt influenced a wide range of other early civilizations in western Asia and northern Africa. Among them were the Hittites and the Syro-Palestinian city-states, whose own cultural contributions make them ancestors of the West as well. They are studied in this chapter. The Hebrews and the Greeks were also influenced by Mesopotamia and Egypt, but with the Hebrews and the Greeks, Western civilization begins, and so they are covered in Chapter 2.

FOCUS QUESTIONS

How did the earliest human beings adapt to their environments and create the first civilizations?

What were the Mesopotamians' major contributions to government, religion, and art and culture?

How did the king's power affect various aspects of Egyptian society?

What were the contributions of the Levant and Anatolia to the West and why did these early states eventually collapse?

ORIGINS, TO CA. 3000 B.C.

How did the earliest human beings adapt to their environments and create the first civilizations?

The earth is old; modern human beings are young; and civilization is a recent innovation. Scientists have made great strides in explaining human origins, but great disagreement still reigns. Each decade seems to bring an exciting new discovery that calls for the reassessment of previous theories.

We can be more certain about the series of processes, beginning around 10,000 B.C., that led to the emergence of civilization by 3500 to 3000 B.C. The period studied in this chapter includes both prehistory—the term often used for time before the invention of writing—and recorded history. Writing appeared last among the complex of characteristics that marks the emergence of civilization. Over a period of several thousand years, humans abandoned a mobile existence for a sedentary one. They learned to domesticate animals and to cultivate plants. They shifted from a food-collecting economy to a predominantly food-producing economy. They developed the first towns, from which, over several millennia, the first urban societies slowly evolved. The result--the first civilizations, found in western Asia and Egypt—laid the groundwork on which later would be built the founding civilizations of the West: the Greeks, Romans, and Hebrews.

THE FIRST HUMAN BEINGS

Anatomically modern human beings, *Homo sapiens sapiens*—genus *Homo,* species *sapiens,* subspecies *sapiens*—first appeared about 100,000 years ago. But the human family is much older. Also known as **hominids,** the human family includes many ancient and extinct species.

> **hominids**   The primate family *Hominidae,* which includes humans. The modern human being, *Homo sapiens sapiens,* is the only species of this family still in existence.

Africa is the cradle of humanity. The first hominids appeared in Africa's tropics and subtropics over 4 million years ago. By 2.5 million years ago they had evolved into creatures who invented the first technology, simple stone tools. Prehistory is traditionally referred to as the Stone Age because stone was the primary medium from which hominids made tools. The hominids were migratory: not less than 1.6 million years ago and perhaps much earlier, they appeared in East Asia and the eastern edge of Europe. The next important stage in human evolution is *Homo erectus* ("upright person"), a hominid with a large brain who used more complex stone tools and may have acquired language. The appearance of *Homo erectus* is usually dated to 1.8 million years ago, but a recent discovery in China may date *Homo erectus* as early as 2.25 million years ago.

But the most recent research suggests that all anatomically modern humans are descended from a single African ancestor. About 89,000 years ago, the *Homo sapiens sapiens* from whom we are all descended was born in Africa. About 70,000 years ago, descendants of that man left Africa for the other continents.

For many millennia humans struggled with the ebb and flow of glaciers. They lived during the Ice Age, as scholars refer to the period of fluctuating cycles of warm and cold, beginning about 730,000 years ago and ending only about 10,000 years ago. Early humans existed amid great contrasts in temperature, seasons, and landscapes, requiring considerable adaptation—but adapt they did.

Archaic humans first appeared in Europe about 800,000 years ago. Beginning about 400,000 years ago, Europe was home to the ancestors of the best-known archaic people, the Neandertals. Neandertals lived in Europe and western Asia until about 30,000 years ago. They had strong and stocky physiques, which were perhaps an adaptation to the rugged climate of the Ice Age, but the Neandertals were no brutes, as they are usually imagined to be. They were, for example, among the first people to bury their dead, often with grave offerings—for example, flint, animal bones, or flowers—a practice that suggests they were sensitive enough to mourn their losses. Recent research shows that Neandertals were both clever enough to use tools to attack one another and caring enough to nurse their wounded back to health.

Neandertals, however, were not modern humans. Modern humans entered Europe about 35,000 years ago, having originated in Africa. Within 5,000 years Neandertals had disappeared—whether through war, disease, or an inability to compete with modern humans, we do not know. The first modern humans tended to be taller and less muscular than Neandertals. They also used their hands more precisely and walked more efficiently, and they lived longer. The modern human skull, with its high forehead and tucked-in face, is dis-

ca. 4.4 million years ago	Earliest hominids
800,000 years ago	First humans in Europe
ca. 100,000 years ago	*Homo sapiens sapiens*
40,000–10,000 B.C.	Upper Paleolithic era
10,000–2500 B.C.	Neolithic era
3500–3000 B.C.	First civilizations
3500–3100 B.C.	First writing in Mesopotamia
3300–3200 B.C.	First writing in Egypt
ca. 3200 B.C.	Unification of Nile Valley
2800–2350 B.C.	Early Dynastic Period
2695–2160 B.C.	Egyptian Old Kingdom
2500–2350 B.C.	Cuneiform texts from Ebla
2025–1786 B.C.	Egyptian Middle Kingdom
1650–1180 B.C.	Hittite Old, Middle, and New Kingdoms
1550–1075 B.C.	Egyptian New Kingdom
1450–1300 B.C.	First international system
1400–1200 B.C.	Height of prosperity at Ugarit
1250–1150 B.C.	Sea Peoples invade

(All dates in this chapter are approximate.)

tinctive, but differences between the modern and archaic human brain are a matter of scholarly debate. What no one debates, however, is that, with the disappearance of Neandertals, modern humans put into effect a revolution in culture.

THE REVOLUTION IN HUMAN CULTURE, CA. 70,000–10,000 B.C.

Before the emergence of modern humans, people had relatively little ability to change the natural environment. Modern humans changed that. They exploited natural resources largely by means of technology and organization. Thus they began the process of human manipulation of the environment that—sometimes brilliantly, sometimes disastrously—has remained a leading theme of the human experience ever since. The key to this change was a dramatic increase in the amount and complexity of information being communicated—what might be called the first information revolution. The twin symbols of the revolution are cave paintings and

Chauvet Cave Art
This black-painted panel shows horses, rhinoceroses, and wild oxen. The purpose of cave paintings is unknown, but perhaps they served as illustrations of myths or as attempts to control the environment through magic.   *(Courtesy, Jean Cottes/Ministère de la Culture)*

notations made on bone, signs that humans were thinking about their environment and their experiences.

It was long thought that these dramatic changes began in Europe about 40,000 B.C.* Recently, however, they have been traced to southern Africa, probably more than 70,000 years ago. The discovery there of carefully worked bone tools and stone spearheads pinpoints the dawn of modern human technology. Still, it is not in Africa but elsewhere that we can best trace the early evolution of the modern human mind. Europe from about 40,000 to about 10,000 B.C. provides reliable evidence of the way of life and the culture of early human hunter-gatherer societies, complex organiza-

tions that survived by a food-collecting economy of hunting, fishing, and gathering fruits and nuts. This period is sometimes called the Upper Paleolithic (Greek for "Old Stone") era. Then, around 10,000 B.C., western Asia offers evidence of a second revolution: the invention of a food-producing economy, consisting of the domestication of animals and the cultivation of crops. The period from about 10,000 to 3000 B.C. is sometimes called the Neolithic (Greek for "New Stone") era.

Archaeology tells us something about early people's way of life. So do analogies from contemporary anthropology, for even today a tiny number of people still exist in hunter-gatherer societies in isolated corners of the globe—for example, in the Kalahari Desert of Africa and in the Arctic. An educated guess is that early humans lived in small groups, of maybe twenty-five to fifty persons, related by kinship or marriage. Early **hunter-gatherers** moved from place to place, following the seasonal migration of game, but by the eve of the invention of agriculture, some hunter-gatherers

---

*We follow the traditional practice in the West of expressing historical dates in relation to the birth of Jesus Christ (actually, to a now discredited calculation of his birth date, because in fact Jesus was not born in A.D. 1; see page 172). Dates before his birth are labeled B.C. (which stands for "before Christ"), and dates after his birth are labeled A.D. (*anno Domini*, Latin for "in the year of the Lord"). A widely used alternative refers to these dates as B.C.E. ("before the common era") and C.E. ("of the common era").

hunter-gatherers   Food-collecting society in which people live by hunting, fishing, and gathering fruits and nuts, with no crops or livestock being raised for food.

had settled down in villages. Hunting was largely a male preserve, while gathering nuts and berries fell into the female domain. Perhaps women brought their children with them as they worked or relied on kin or friends for child-care.

It was probably common for men and women to pair off, have children, and establish a family, much as marriage is a near-universal practice among humans today. Compared with other animals, humans produce extremely dependent infants requiring years of attention. To ensure the survival of the young to adulthood, men as well as women need to play a role in child rearing.

Early people found shelter by building huts or, frequently, by living in caves or rock shelters—hence our notion of the "caveman." Caves offered shelter, could be heated, and made a naturally good vantage point for observing prey and hostile humans. In the Upper Paleolithic era, about 30,000 years ago, caves were the site of the earliest representational art. The most spectacular Upper Paleolithic paintings discovered so far have been found in caves in southern France (for example, at Lascaux [lass-CO] and at Chauvet [show-VAY] Cave) and in Spain (at Altamira). European cave paintings of animals such as the bison, horse, reindeer, and woolly mammoth (a huge, extinct member of the elephant family with hairy skin and long, upward-curving tusks) attest to early human artistic skill.

Other early art includes engravings on stone of animals, birds, and stylized human females, as well as female figurines carved from ivory or bone. Usually represented with exaggerated breasts or buttocks, the carvings are called Venus figurines, after Venus, the Roman goddess of love. They may represent an attempt to control fertility through magic.

Upper Paleolithic craftsmanship is as impressive as the art. The early human tool kit included the first utensils in such easily worked materials as antler and ivory. Stone tools became longer and more varied. The first stone and bone spear points, the first bows and arrows, and the first bone needles and awls (probably for sewing animal skins) all appeared.

Hunting was a communal enterprise. Related families are likely to have joined together in clans, which in turn may have formed tribes. It is often thought that each of these groups was patriarchal (literally, "ruled by the father"); that is, the family was governed by the father, the tribe by a male headman or chief. To be sure, some later myths (for example, among the ancient Greeks) argue that women were the rulers of prehistoric society. Today some historians see the possibility of matriarchy (literally, "rule by the mother") in the Venus figurines. There is, however, no firm evidence of matriarchy. Male chiefs probably did exist, as in later periods, but some tribes may have had no chief at all, following the decision of the community rather than an individual leader.

THE COMING OF AGRICULTURE, CA. 10,000–5000 B.C.

The human invention of agriculture was dramatic, meriting the name **Neolithic Revolution** that scholars sometimes give it. Yet if dramatic, the invention spread slowly and unevenly. In most areas, hunting and fishing continued to be a major source of food, even though agriculture fed more people. Agriculture was first invented sometime after 10,000 B.C. in western Asia, then discovered again independently in other parts of the world. By 5000 B.C. information about the new practices had spread so widely that farming could be found in many places around the world.

The story begins about 13,000 B.C., when humans began to specialize in the wild plants they collected and the animals they hunted. They had good reason to do so because hunter-gatherer society had become increasingly complex, and in some places permanent settlements had appeared. There were now probably more mouths to feed, stimulating the need for more food. The next step is not surprising: learning how to domesticate plants and animals.

The first animals to be domesticated were probably dogs because they were useful in hunting. Then came sheep, goats, and cattle. As for plants, wheat and barley were the first that humans learned to grow, followed by legumes (beans). With males occupied in hunting, it may well have been females who first unraveled the secrets of agriculture.

Domestication began in a crescent-shaped zone of land of dependable annual rainfall. The region stretches west to east from what is today southern Jordan to southern Iran: scholars call it the Fertile Crescent (see **MAP 1.1**). With domestication came small agricultural settlements, which were increasingly common after 7000 B.C. Thus was born the farming village, probably the place that most people have called home since the spread of agriculture around the world.

Scholars once thought of Neolithic villages as simple places devoted to subsistence agriculture, with no craft specialization, and as egalitarian societies lacking social hierarchies. In recent years, new evidence and a rethinking of older information have altered this picture considerably. The Neolithic village site of Çayönü Tepesi (CHAH-yer-ner THE-peh-see) in eastern Anatolia, for example, provides evidence of metalworking (of copper) and specialization of labor (in beadmaking) from approximately 7000 to 6000 B.C. The site also contains the world's earliest known example of cloth, probably linen, woven around 7000 B.C. Artwork shows men wearing loincloths and headdresses, women wearing pants and halter tops, and both sexes wearing jewelry.

> **Neolithic Revolution** Human discovery and spread of agriculture, between about 10,000 and 5000 B.C. People first domesticated dogs and other animals and then learned how to cultivate crops.

MAP 1.1   Western Asia

The Neolithic Revolution began after 10,000 B.C. in the Fertile Crescent, an arc-shaped region of dependable annual rainfall. In this area between the Tigris and Euphrates Rivers known as Mesopotamia, the world's first urban civilization took root about 3500 to 3000 B.C.

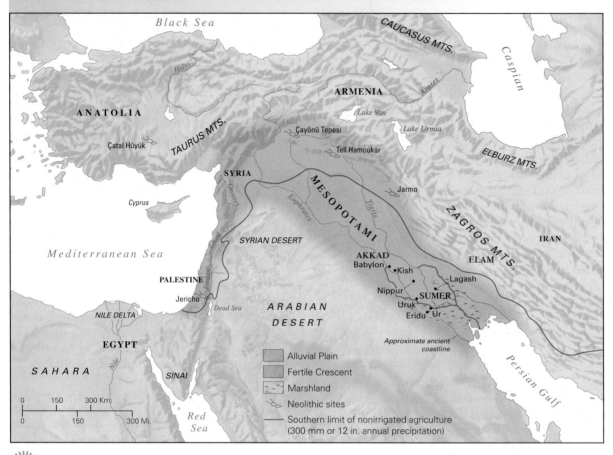

Online Study Center **Improve Your Grade**   Interactive Map: Western Asia

Consider the case of Jericho (JEH-rih-co), in Palestine near the Dead Sea (see Map 1.1), perhaps the oldest settled community on earth. Jericho around 7000 B.C. was a town surrounded by massive walls 10 feet thick and 13 or more feet high, about 765 yards long, and probably enclosing an area of about 10 acres. The most prominent feature of the walls was a great tower 33 feet in diameter and 28 feet high with an interior stairway. Inside the walls lived a densely packed population of about two thousand people.

An even larger Neolithic town was Çatal Hüyük (CHAH-tal Her-yerk) in south-central Anatolia (see Map 1.1). Its population of six thousand people in 6000 B.C. made it by far the largest settlement of the era. It was probably a trading center and perhaps a religious shrine. Carbonization from fire has preserved many objects showing Çatal Hüyük's sophistication, including woven fabrics, obsidian (a sharp volcanic glass used in tools) mirrors, wooden vessels, and makeup applicators.

Agriculture made human populations richer and more numerous, but it also bred disease and probably increased the scale of war. More men than ever before were available to fight because agriculture proved to be so efficient a source of food that it freed people for specialized labor—including war.

This is not to say that war in Neolithic times was sophisticated. Indeed, it was probably more a matter of group skirmishes and sporadic raids than of systematic warfare. Spanish rock art shows a confrontation between two groups of archers, one following what seems to be a leader. The scene may be a ritual rather than a violent conflict, but we have physical cases of actual bloodshed. The earliest known evidence of what may have been organized warfare comes from a cemetery in Sudan dating from 12,000 to 4500 B.C. Of fifty-nine human skeletons there, nearly half died violently, including women and children.

NEOLITHIC AND COPPER AGE EUROPE, 7000–2500 B.C.

Europe was one day to become the center of Western civilization, but the region lagged behind its neighbors at first. Innovations from the east reached Europe after 7000 B.C. and slowly transformed it. At the same time, Europeans developed their own unique culture.

The term *Europe* refers to a vast peninsula of the Eurasian continent with several distinct regions. Southern Europe is made up of a rugged and hilly Mediterranean coastal strip, linked to northern Africa and western Asia by the sea and by similarities in climate and landscape. High mountains are found in the Alps of south-central Europe, from which chains of lower mountains radiate toward the southwest and southeast. Northern Europe, by contrast, consists in large part of a forested plain, indented here and there by great rivers. In the southeast the plain, or steppe, becomes open and mostly treeless. The eastern boundaries of Europe are, in the north, the Ural Mountains and, in the south, the Caucasus Mountains. Georgia, Armenia, and Azerbaijan are all considered parts of Europe.

Before 7000 B.C. Europeans lived a traditional hunter-gatherer existence. Then came farming, which was introduced in southeastern Europe around 7000 B.C. by migrants from western Asia. Agriculture expanded across Europe between about 6000 and 4500 B.C., but not until 2500 B.C. did the majority of Europeans adopt a food-producing way of life. Yet Europe was hardly static in the meantime. The era of European prehistory from 4500 to 2500 B.C. is known as the Late Neolithic Age, or the Copper Age, because copper came into use on the Continent during this time, as did gold.

Between about 3500 and 2500 B.C., Copper Age Europe grew in sophistication. The urbanization of Mesopotamia (in modern-day Iraq; see Map 1.1) had an impact on southeastern Europe, which supplied raw materials for western Asia. Greece underwent the greatest transformation, to the extent that it developed its own urban civilization by about 2000 B.C. (see Chapter 2). The recent discovery of a Copper Age corpse preserved in the ice of the Italian Alps opens a window into northern Italian society of about 3200 B.C. (See the feature "The Visual Record: The Iceman and His World.")

On Europe's northern and western edges people began to set up megaliths—stone tombs and monuments—often of huge blocks. Such monuments may illustrate an awareness of time created by the spread of agriculture, with its seasonal rhythms. In Britain megalithic architecture reached its peak with Stonehenge, built in stages from about 2800 to 1500 B.C. This famous monument consists of a circle of stones oriented precisely on the rising sun of midsummer—a sign both of early Europeans' interest in the calendar and of their skill in technology.

THE EMERGENCE OF CIVILIZATION, 3500–3000 B.C.

Civilization comes from the Latin word *civitas,* meaning "commonwealth" or "city." The first civilizations, beginning in Mesopotamia and Egypt between 3500 and 3000 B.C., probably contained the first cities. What differentiated them from their predecessors, however, was not so much size (a city versus a town) as complexity. Civilization allowed human beings to think big. A large

The Maltese Female
The "Sleeping Lady," a terracotta statuette of the late fourth millennium B.C. from Malta, shows a reclining woman, perhaps a goddess or priestess. Her double-egg-shaped buttocks are thought to symbolize fertility or regeneration.
(Erich Lessing/Art Resource, NY)

The Iceman and His World

On September 19, 1991, a German couple went hiking in the Italian Alps. At 10,530 feet above sea level, in a mountain pass, they thought they had left civilization and its problems behind until they stumbled on an unexpected sight: the body of a dead man lying in the melting ice. Nor was that their only surprise. At first they thought the corpse was the victim of a recent accident. When the authorities arrived, however, the body was discovered to be very old. A helicopter was ordered, and the body was brought to a research institute in Innsbruck, Austria. When the investigators were through, it was clear that the hikers had chanced upon one of the most remarkable archaeological discoveries of the century.*

He was 5,300 years old. The Iceman—as the corpse has become known—is a natural mummy, preserved under the snow: the oldest known remains of human flesh. If that weren't striking enough, consider the clothes and extensive gear that survived with him—they are a window into the European world of about 3200 B.C. The most difficult and most fascinating question is this: Who was the Iceman?

His body offers an introduction. The Iceman stood 5 feet 2 inches tall. He was in his mid-40s and probably had a beard. Genetic testing shows that he was a European, a close relative of modern northern and alpine Europeans. Other tests indicate a difficult life. His growth was arrested by periods of illness, grave hunger, or metal poisoning. His teeth are badly worn, the result perhaps of chewing dried meat or, alternatively, of working leather. He may have undergone a kind of acupuncture; at any rate, he is tattooed, which in some cultures is a medical treatment rather than a form of decoration. He has several broken ribs, which indicates either damage under the ice, mishandling when the body was discovered, or an ancient accident or fight.

And it was a fight—a hand-to-hand combat—that killed him. Blood tests indicate a long fight involving four people besides the Iceman. The Iceman was shot through the chest with an arrow and cut severely by a rough blade on his right hand. The arrow caused a very painful death. After the fight, he might have managed to escape up the mountain until he fell down and died in the snow.

Not long before he died, the Iceman was in the valley to the south. There he ate his last meal, which consisted of goat meat and bread cooked in a charcoal oven. We might guess that the Iceman's fatal struggle took place in a farming village in the valley.

But his enemies did not find him on the mountain; otherwise they would have stripped the gear

Mummy of Iceman   (Copyright Photo Archives, South Tyrol Museum of Archaeology)

found with him. Today that gear provides tantalizing clues to his social status. Look at the artist's drawing. A woven grass or reed cape lies over the Iceman's deerskin coat, which in turn covers a leather loincloth and garter, held in place by a leather belt. A bearskin hat, skin leggings, and calfskin shoes, stuffed with grass for insulation, complete his wardrobe. The Iceman and his contemporaries knew how to dress for the cold weather of the mountains.

The Iceman carries a rich tool kit. Notice his copper ax and 6-foot-long bow, made of yew, the best wood then available for making bows. A quiver (arrow case), two birch-bark containers, a waist pouch, and a frame—probably part of a backpack—hang from his body. Among his items of equipment are flint tools (including a dagger, a retouching tool, and a scraper); a piece of net; two birch-fungus-like "polypores" threaded on a leather thong, probably used as a natural antibiotic; and fourteen arrows, all, oddly, broken. In short, it appears that the Iceman was equipped with a state-of-the-art mountain survival kit of his day. It is not clear why he carried broken arrows, but he would not have had time to change his gear before he fled.

Scholars differ about the Iceman's occupation. Guesses range from a hunter to a trader to a warrior to an outlaw to a shaman (a priest who uses magic). The Iceman's complex weapons and well-made clothing point to a sophisticated culture. The copper ax is the key to that culture and its relationship with the wider world. Similar axes have been found in northern Italian tombs in Remedello, about 240 miles south of the Alps. Before the discovery of the Iceman, archaeologists believed that Italians learned the metalwork technology needed for such an ax from Anatolia, where similar pieces of metalwork are dated to approximately 2700 to 2400 B.C. Hence the Remedello culture was usually also dated to that period. The discovery of the Iceman means that Remedello must be backdated by about five hundred years. It is clear, then, that by about 3200 B.C. northern Italians not only borrowed from the more advanced eastern Mediterranean areas but also created their own original technology and culture. Thus a small object (a copper ax), placed within a larger body of evidence (Italian and Anatolian metalwork), permits broad generalization about the interaction and independence of ancient cultures.

Artist's Rendition of the Iceman   *(© Michael Rothman)*

QUESTIONS

1. What do the Iceman's clothing, tools, and weapons tell us about his society?

2. How do modern, scientific tests add to our knowledge of the Iceman?

3. How does the discovery of the Iceman change our understanding of the relationship between Europe and Anatolia about five thousand years ago?

4. How skilled at technology was Copper Age Europe?

5. What role did violence play in prehistoric human relations?

---

*For an introduction to the Iceman, see Brenda Fowler, *Iceman: Uncovering the Life and Times of a Prehistoric Man Found in an Alpine Glacier* (Chicago: University of Chicago Press, 2001); James H. Dickson, Klaus Oeggl, and Linda L. Handley, "The Iceman Reconsidered," *Scientific American* (May 2003); and <http://www.mummytombs.com/mummylocator/featured/otzi.htm>.

Online Study Center
Improve Your Grade Visual Record Activities

and specialized labor force, organized by a strong government, made it possible to expand control over nature, improve technology, and trade and compete over ever widening areas. An elite class emerged that was able to pursue ever more ambitious projects in art and thought and to invent systems of writing. In short, the advent of civilization in the fourth millennium B.C. marked a major turning point. Thereafter, the human horizon expanded forever.

Civilization arose in Iraq, in the valley between the Tigris and Euphrates Rivers (see Map 1.1), a region that the Greeks named Mesopotamia (literally, "between the rivers"). At around the same time or shortly afterward, civilization also began in the valley of the Nile River in Egypt. Both Mesopotamia and Egypt are home to valleys containing alluvial land—that is, a relatively flat tract where fertile soil is deposited by a river. Although these civilizations each developed largely independently, some borrowing between the two took place.

The First Cities   It was long thought that the first cities developed in southern Mesopotamia. But a recent discovery suggests that cities were found in northern Mesopotamia around the same time—that is, during the Uruk (OO-rook) Period (3800–3200 B.C.). An excavation at Tell Hamoukar (tell ha-moo-CAR) in northeastern Syria, near the Iraqi border, uncovered what appears to be a city from around 3500 B.C. The excavators found ovens and pottery, apparently used for large-scale food production, and they unearthed stamp seals and clay seal impressions, which may indicate a bureaucracy. A mud-brick fortification wall has tentatively been identified. In short, several signs point to a city.

If cities developed simultaneously in northern and southern Mesopotamia in the mid-fourth millennium B.C. they may share a common, earlier source: the Ubaid (oo-BA-id) culture of mid-fifth-millennium B.C. Mesopotamia. Many questions arise, among them whether Ubaid cities existed as early as 4500 B.C., a thousand years earlier than cities were thought to have first appeared. We will have to wait for future excavation and study to know.

The first cities emerged through a process of action and reaction. In order to feed cities, Mesopotamian farmers worked harder, used better techniques, and increased the amount of land under cultivation. Meanwhile, both the number and variety of settlements increased.

The Development of Writing   Along with cities came writing, which developed between about 3500 and 3100 B.C. in Mesopotamia. The growth of writing from simple recordkeeping can be traced step by step. Before writing, Mesopotamian people used tiny clay or stone tokens to represent objects being counted or traded. By 3500 B.C., with 250 different types of tokens in play, the system had grown unwieldy enough for people to start using signs to indicate tokens. It was a short step to dispensing with the tokens and placing the signs on a clay tablet by making indentations in the clay with a reed stylus: writing. New words were soon added through pictographs (pictures that stand for particular objects). In time the pictographs evolved into ideograms—that is, abstract symbols that are no longer recognizable as specific objects and thus can be used to denote ideas as well as things.

In the centuries following its introduction, Mesopotamian writing became standardized. Scholars call the signs **cuneiform,** from the Latin for "wedge-shaped," a good description of what early writing looks like (see **FIGURE 1.1**). In its first centuries, cuneiform was used almost entirely for economic records or commercial transactions. Then it was used to record offerings to the gods. By 2350 B.C. cuneiform had evolved into a mixed system of about six hundred signs, most of them phonetic (syllabic), with relatively few ideograms.

Experts used to think that writing began in Mesopotamia and spread to Egypt. Recent excavations, however, have found examples of early Egyptian writing securely dated to 3300 to 3200 B.C. In other words, Egyptian writing was independent: it was not derived from or related to cuneiform. Whether writing began in Egypt or Mesopotamia, therefore, is now an open question. What is clear, however, is that writing was invented to meet economic rather than creative needs. In Egypt the earliest writing includes records of the delivery of linen and oil as taxes to King Scorpion I. The writing consists of early *hieroglyphs* (literally, "sacred carvings"), a system of pictures and abstract signs that represent sounds or ideas, later to become more formal and standardized.

Incising cuneiform on clay was much clumsier than writing with pen and ink on **papyrus,** as became possible in Egypt. The papyrus plant grew in the Nile marshes and it was the source of the ancient world's favorite writing material. (Our word *paper* comes from "papyrus," although modern paper comes from a different source, trees.) Nonetheless, cuneiform was flexible enough to record the spoken language and to be used for poetry as well as for bookkeeping. Moreover,

cuneiform   First writing system in Mesopotamia, consisting of wedge-shaped impressions in soft clay. Named from the Latin word for "wedge-shaped," it was developed about 3500–3100 B.C.

papyrus   Paperlike writing material used by the ancient Egyptians, Greeks, and Romans. Made primarily in Egypt from the papyrus plant, it was durable, flexible, and easy to write on.

FIGURE 1.1   Early Mesopotamian Writing

The pictographs of early writing evolved into a system of phonetic syllables and abstract symbols. Simplified and standardized, this writing was *cuneiform*, or "wedge-shaped." Over time, it was adapted from Sumerian to Babylonian and other languages throughout western Asia.   *(Source: From* Babylon, *by Joan Oates. Published by Thames and Hudson Ltd., 1978. Reprinted by permission of the publisher.)*

Uruk IV ca. 3100 B.C.	Sumerian ca. 2500 B.C.	Old Babylonian ca. 1800 B.C.	Neo-Babylonian ca. 600 B.C.	SUMERIAN Babylonian
				APIN epinnu plow
				ŠE še'u grain
				ŠAR kirû orchard
				KUR šadû mountain
				GUD alpu ox
				KU(A) nunu fish
				DUG karpatu jar

cuneiform became the standard script of various languages of western Asia for several thousand years. Clumsy it may have been, but cuneiform was writing, and writing is both a catalyst for change and the historian's best friend. Mesopotamia after 3000 B.C. was dynamic, sophisticated, and, best of all, intelligible to us.

SECTION SUMMARY

- Anatomically modern human beings are called *homo sapiens sapiens* and first appeared about 100,000 years ago.

- Humans lived by hunting animals and gathering nuts and berries until agriculture was invented shortly after 10,000 B.C. in western Asia.

- Early Europeans were skilled metalworkers and architects, but they lagged behind the more advanced regions, Egypt and Mesopotamia.

- The first civilizations in Mesopotamia and Egypt emerged between 3500 and 3000 B.C. and probably contained the first cities.

- Civilization meant bigger and more complex societies, with specialized labor forces, strong governments, and well-structured armies.

- Along with cities came writing, which developed independently in Egypt and Mesopotamia between about 3500 and about 3100 B.C.

MESOPOTAMIA, TO CA. 1600 B.C.

What were the Mesopotamians' major contributions to government, religion, and art and culture?

After 3000 B.C. the people of Mesopotamia flourished. They experimented in government, in cooperation and conflict among different ethnic groups, in law, and in the working out of class and gender relations. Keenly aware of human limitations and vanity, they sought divine justice, as their literary and religious texts show. Their engineering skill, mathematics, and astronomy set ancient science on an upward path. In later centuries, Western civilization would build on these foundations, and then take off in new directions.

The fertile Tigris-Euphrates plain had to be tamed by would-be farmers. Most of the soil was in turn so dry or so marshy that agriculture required considerable irrigation and drainage—that is, the use of channels, dikes, or dams to control floodwaters and improve the fertility of the land. Making matters worse, Mesopotamia was given to extreme heat and scorching winds. Some scholars argue that the very hostility of Mesopotamia's environment generated the cooperation and control that civilization requires.

Archaeologists sometimes refer to the third and second millennia in the eastern Mediterranean and western Asia as the Bronze Age. In this period people mastered the technology of making bronze, an alloy of copper and tin, and bronze frequently replaced stone as a primary material for everyday use.

THE CITY-STATES OF SUMER

Though their culture is long dead, the Sumerians live on. Whenever someone today counts the minutes, debates politics, or quotes the law, the Sumerians live, for these are all legacies of that ingenious society.

The dominant inhabitants of Mesopotamian civilization in its first flowering are named **Sumerians.** Present in southern Mesopotamia by 3200 B.C. and probably earlier, the Sumerians entered their great age in the third millennium B.C., when their **city-states** enjoyed a proud independence (see Map 1.1).

The formative era of Mesopotamian civilization is known as the Uruk Period (ca. 3800–3200 B.C.), after one of its major archaeological sites. During the Uruk Period the Sumerians invented the wheel and the plow, planted the first orchards—of dates, figs, or olives— and developed the first sophisticated metal-casting processes. They built some of the first cities, for example, Uruk. They expanded the size of territories and populations, the scale of war, the complexity of society, and the power of government. Finally, as if to cap a period of remarkable change, at the end of the Uruk Period the Sumerians invented cuneiform writing.

Mesopotamian cities flourished in this era. By the period that scholars have named the Early Dynastic Period (2800–2350 B.C.), named for the first royal dynasties (ruling families), a large Mesopotamian city had grown to the point where it might cover 1,000 acres surrounded by more than 5 miles of walls, within which lived about fifty thousand people. Such a city was part of a network of thirty such city-states with a common culture, commerce, and propensity to make war on one another. Hence the city-states of Mesopotamia may be called the first civilization.

It was a land of cooperation and conflict. The Sumerian cities had much in common: language, literature, arts and sciences, and religion. Yet the cities often quarreled, often over farmland boundaries or water rights. Each city had its own urbanized area and a larger agricultural hinterland irrigated by canals. Cities traded with one another and with the outside world. The primary political units of southern Mesopotamia for most of the third millennium B.C., Sumerian city-states were an incubator of civilization.

A history of Sumerian government begins in the Early Dynastic Period, because good evidence for earlier times is lacking. Certainly the first Sumerian temples were wealthy and powerful. Each city had at least one temple, the house of its patron god and the common symbol of the community. But there is no proof that the early Sumerian cities were temple-states governed by priests, as historians once thought.

By the Early Dynastic Period, around 2800 B.C., political power in a Sumerian city rested largely with its Council of Elders, whose members were probably wealthy landowners. Some scholars argue that the council shared power with a popular assembly, creating, in effect, a bicameral legislature and perhaps even a primitive democracy. But this is just a theory.

As for ordinary people, they enjoyed only limited

Sumerians Dominant inhabitants of Mesopotamia in the third millennium B.C. They established the world's first civilization, thirty flourishing city-states with a common culture, commerce, and tendency to make war on one another.

city-state State consisting of an independent city and the surrounding territory under its control. Early examples were the Sumerian city-states in the third millennium B.C.

freedom. Even if they owned their own land, farmers often had to provide forced labor for the state as a kind of taxation—maintaining the vast Mesopotamian irrigation system, for example. There was also apparently a large group of semi-free people who owned no land of their own but worked others' land. Finally, there were slaves—that is, people who could be bought and sold. Slaves were not numerous because there was no policing system to stop runaways from the fields. Still, wealthy people usually had a few slaves in the household. Slaves were usually foreign prisoners of war, but some were local people who had been sold into slavery to pay off a debt; often parents sold their own children (especially daughters).

By about 2700 B.C. political power shifted. War between cities was chronic and the times demanded a strong hand. The new ruler was not a Council of Elders but rather a "big man" (*lugal*) or, less often, a "governor" (*ensi*)—that is, a king or, occasionally, a queen. Kings sponsored irrigation works, raised fortification walls, restored temples, and built palaces. But the monarch was first and foremost a warrior.

One of the earliest Sumerian kings, dating from the period 2700 to 2600 B.C., was Gilgamesh (GIL-ga-mesh) of Uruk, a hero of epic poetry whom many scholars consider a genuine historical personage. In the cities of Ur and Lagash, the king's wife was often a power in her own right. Kish was ruled by Ku-baba (r. ca. 2450 B.C.), the first reigning queen of recorded history.

Though warriors, Sumerian monarchs also recognized a responsibility for promoting justice. History's earliest known reformer of law and society was Uru-inim-gina, king of Lagash around 2400 B.C. Surviving documents describe Lagash as a society in which wealthy landowners interfered with the temples and oppressed the poor, and in which royal administrators mistreated ordinary people. Uru-inim-gina attempted to manage the bureaucracy, protect the property of humble people, and guard the temples. He also put into effect the first known wage and price controls. Uru-inim-gina's proclaimed intention was to promote impartial justice, a goal that he expressed in the formula "[the king] will protect the mother that is in distress, the mighty man shall not oppress the naked and the widow." No doubt he also wanted to weaken independent sources of power threatening royal authority. As it turned out, Lagash was conquered only a few years after Uru-inim-gina's reign. His reforms nonetheless survived as the precedent for a long Mesopotamian tradition of royal lawgiving.

CONQUEST AND ASSIMILATION, CA. 2350–1900 B.C.

The poor and tough peoples of the desert and the mountains coveted Mesopotamia's wealth. They at-

tacked: some from without, by raising armies and assaulting cities, while others climbed to power from within the Sumerian city-states. The attackers were sufficiently impressed by Sumerian culture to adopt a great many Sumerian customs and ideas. The most successful attacker was Sargon (r. 2371–2316 B.C.), who rose from nowhere to a high position under the king of Kish before founding his own capital city, Agade (ah-GAH-day). Notice that Sargon was a native speaker not of Sumerian but of Akkadian.

The Akkadians were originally a seminomadic people who lived on the edge of the desert. Shepherds, they moved their flocks with the seasons. They had begun settling in the northern cities of southern Mesopotamia by the end of the Uruk Period, in a part of southern Mesopotamia known as Akkad. Their language, Akkadian, belongs to the Semitic group of languages, which also includes Arabic and Hebrew.

As commander of one of history's first professional armies, Sargon conquered all of Mesopotamia, and his power extended westward along the Euphrates and

Akkadian Bronze
This stern-faced, life-size cast-bronze head, with its stylized ringleted beard and carefully arranged hair, shows Mesopotamian craftsmanship at its finest. Thought by some to be Sargon (r. 2371–2316 B.C.) or Naramsin (r. ca. 2250–2220 B.C.), it was deliberately mutilated in ancient times. *(Claus Hansmann, München)*

eastward into Iran. Rather than rule conquered peoples directly, the Akkadians generally were satisfied with loose control, as long as they could monopolize trade. They adopted Sumerian religion and wrote Akkadian in cuneiform.

Sargon's son inherited his throne. His dynasty boasted that it reigned over "the peoples of all lands" or "the four quarters of the earth." Sargon proved to be one of western Asia's most influential figures. His dynasty's ideal of universal rule was one to which future conquerors would lay claim.

Assimilation was another lasting Akkadian legacy. Although Sargon made Akkadian the official language of administration, he made politic concessions to Sumerian sensibilities. For instance, his daughter Enkheduanna (en-khe-du-AN-na), whom he appointed high priestess at Ur and Uruk, wrote poetry in Sumerian, poetry powerful enough to be quoted often in later Sumerian texts. The first known woman poet, Enkheduanna described the union of Sumerians and Akkadians.

Around 2200 B.C. the Akkadian kingdom broke up into a series of smaller successor states. Then, after a century of rule by invaders from the east, the Sumerians returned to power under the Third Dynasty of Ur (2112–2004 B.C.). Far from stripping away all Akkadian influence, the revived Sumerian rulers spoke of themselves as "kings of Sumer and Akkad." It was a title that would have a long and potent history: for the next fifteen hundred years, many of the great kings of western Asia would use this label, in recognition of a composite, common Mesopotamian society.

After renewed political turmoil in Mesopotamia around 2000 B.C., a new kingdom emerged in the south under the rule of the Amorites around 1900 B.C. The Amorites were Semitic speakers and shared Mesopotamian culture and traditions. Babylon, northwest of Ur in the central part of Mesopotamia, became the Amorite capital. From Babylon, Amorite kings issued cuneiform decrees that, although written in a Semitic language, drew heavily on Sumerian material.

HAMMURABI'S CODE

The most famous Amorite king, Hammurabi (r. 1792–1750 B.C.) ruled in Babylon about six hundred years after Sargon. Much of his forty-two-year reign was devoted to creating a Mesopotamian empire. A careful administrator who ushered in an era of prosperity and cultural flowering, Hammurabi is most famous for the text known as Hammurabi's Code. Although the work was less a "code" than a collection listing various crimes and their punishments—a kind of treatise on justice glorifying Hammurabi's qualities as a judge—we shall use the familiar name. Hammurabi's Code became both a legal and a literary classic, much copied in later times.

Hammurabi's Code offers a portrait of Mesopotamian society. The document contains nearly three hundred rulings in cases ranging from family to commercial law, from wage rates to murder. The administration of justice in Mesopotamia was entirely practical: we find no notion of abstract absolutes or universal principles, not even a word for "law."

Though occasionally less harsh than earlier law codes, which date as far back as around 2100 B.C., Hammurabi's Code was by no means lenient. Whereas earlier codes were satisfied with payment in silver as recompense for crime, Hammurabi's Code was the first to stipulate such ruthless penalties as mutilation, drowning, and impaling. It also introduced the law of retaliation for wounds: "If a man has destroyed the eye of a member of the aristocracy: they shall destroy his eye. If he has broken his limb: they shall break the (same) limb." Moreover, children could be punished for the crimes of their fathers.

Inscribed in forty-nine vertical columns on a stone stele about 7½ feet high and displayed in a prominent public place, Hammurabi's Code symbolized the notion that the law belonged to everyone. Although ordinary people could not read, it was possible for them to find a patron who could. Yet the societies of western Asia and Egypt were anything but egalitarian, and Hammurabi's society was no exception. Punishments were class-based: crimes against a free person, for example, received harsher treatment than crimes against a slave or a semi-free person. Debt seems to have been a serious and widespread problem, frequently leading to debt slavery. Women could own and inherit property and testify in court. The overall direction of the code, however, was patriarchal: it enshrined the power of the male head of the family.

Online Study Center **Improve Your Grade**
Primary Source: The State Regulates Health Care: Hammurabi's Code and Surgeons

DIVINE MASTERS

The Sumerians were polytheists—that is, they had many gods—and their gods (like the later gods of Greece) were anthropomorphic, or human in form. Indeed, Sumerian (and Greek) gods were thought to be much like human beings, by turns wise and foolish, except that they were immortal and superpowerful. Many Sumerian gods arose out of the forces of nature: An, the sky-god; Enki, the earth-god and freshwater-god; Enlil, the air-god; Nanna, the moon-god; and Utu (Semitic, Shamash), the sun-god. Other Sumerian gods embodied human passions or notions about the afterlife: Inanna (Semitic, Ishtar), goddess of love and war; and Ereshkigal, goddess of the underworld.

The Sumerians sometimes envisioned their gods holding an assembly, much like a boisterous Sumerian prototype. The Sumerians and Akkadians considered Enlil, city-god of Nippur, to be the chief god. The Babylonians replaced him with Marduk, city-god of Babylon.

Every Mesopotamian city had its main temple complex, the most striking feature of which was a *ziggurat,* or stepped tower. Constructed originally as simple raised terraces, ziggurats eventually became seven-stage structures. Unlike the pyramids of Egypt, ziggurats were not tombs but "stairways" connecting humans and the gods.

The keynote of Mesopotamian religion was pessimism. It is not surprising that the Mesopotamians, living in a difficult natural environment, regarded the gods with fear and awe. Although the gods communicated with humans, their language was mysterious. To understand the divine will, the Mesopotamians engaged in various kinds of divination: they interpreted dreams, examined the entrails of slaughtered animals, and studied the stars (which stimulated great advances in astronomy, as we will see).

Most people expected nothing glorious in the afterlife, merely a shadowy existence. It was thought that with a person's last breath, his or her spirit embarked on a long journey to the Netherworld, a place under the earth. More than one Mesopotamian text describes the Netherworld as the "Land-of-no-return" and "the house wherein the dwellers are bereft of light, / Where dust is their fare and clay their food, / Where they see no light, residing in darkness."[1] The dead resided there permanently, though in some texts their spirits return to earth, often with hostile intent toward the living.

Archaeological evidence indicates a possible shift in such attitudes toward death, at least on the part of the Mesopotamian upper classes, by the late third millennium B.C. The kings and nobles of the Third Dynasty of Ur were buried with rich grave goods and with their servants, who were apparently the victims of human sacrifice following the master's death. Perhaps the rulers now expected to have the opportunity to use their wealth again in a comfortable immortality, possibly influenced by Egyptian ideas (see pages 21–22).

ARTS AND SCIENCES

The people of Mesopotamia were deeply inquisitive. They focused on the beginning and the end of things. "How did the world come into being?" and "What happens to us when we die?" are perhaps the two basic questions of their literature. Consider, for example, the Babylonian creation epic known from its first line as *Enuma Elish* ("When on high"). An epic poem is the story of heroic deeds, in this case the deeds of the gods of order, who triumphed over the forces of chaos. Another important Babylonian literary form, known as wisdom literature, responded to life's ups and downs with teachings that are sometimes simple, sometimes sophisticated. It proved eventually to influence the wisdom literature of the Hebrew Bible.

The best-known example of Mesopotamian literature is the *Epic of Gilgamesh.* Frequently translated and adapted by various western Asian peoples, *Gilgamesh* may be a Sumerian work dating to about 2500 B.C. Gilgamesh, king of Uruk, was probably a real historical person, but the poem concerns his fictionalized personal life. The main themes are friendship, loss, and the inevitability of death. As king, Gilgamesh is a tyrant; Enkidu arrives and puts him in his place, and then the two become close friends and comrades in arms. Enkidu's untimely death makes Gilgamesh aware of his own mortality. Distraught by his friend's passing, Gilgamesh goes on a vain quest for immortality. The *Epic of Gilgamesh* contains stories that presage the later biblical Eden and Flood narratives; there is little doubt but that those narratives found their way from Mesopotamia to the Hebrew Bible. (See the box "The Written Record: Heroism and Death in Mesopotamia.")

Online Study Center   **Improve Your Grade**
Primary Source: The Epic of Gilgamesh Describes a Great Flood

The Mesopotamians made advances in mathematics, astronomy, medicine, and engineering. The Sumerians had two systems of numbers: a decimal system (powers of ten) for administration and business and a sexagesimal system (powers of sixty) for weights and mathematical or astronomical calculations. Like the Babylonians, we still divide hours by sixty today. Furthermore, our modern system of numerical place-value notation—for example, the difference between 42 and 24—is derived, through Hindu-Arabic intermediaries, from the Babylonian system. The Babylonians were adept at arithmetic and could solve problems for which we would use algebra. A millennium before the Greek mathematician Pythagoras (who claimed to have studied the Mesopotamian tradition) proved the validity of the theorem that bears his name, they were familiar with the proposition that in a right triangle the square of the longest side is equal to the sum of the squares of the other two sides. In the first millennium B.C. the Babylonians developed a sophisticated mathematical astronomy (see page 35). As early as the seventeenth century B.C., they made systematic, if not always accurate, recordings of the movements of the planet Venus.

In medical matters they demonstrated considerable critical ability. Physicians made advances in the use of plant products for medicines and in very rudimentary surgery. The Babylonians had a simple pregnancy test of moderate accuracy, for example, and their surgeons were experienced at setting broken bones. When they became ill, however, most people in Mesopotamia set more store by magic and incantations than by surgery or herbal medicine.

THE WRITTEN RECORD

HEROISM AND DEATH IN MESOPOTAMIA

The Epic of Gilgamesh *sheds light on categories of gender and power in Mesopotamia. Men such as King Gilgamesh and his friend Enkidu have heroic adventures and risk death. Women lead quieter lives but are wiser and more realistic, as the following excerpts show. Here Gilgamesh, who wanders in his grief over the death of Enkidu, comes to the cottage of the barmaid Siduri.*

Who are you? You are no one that I know. / I am Gilgamesh, who killed Humbaba / And the bull of heaven with my friend.

If you are Gilgamesh and did those things, why / Are you so emaciated and your face half-crazed?

I have grieved! Is it so impossible / To believe? He pleaded. / My friend who went through everything with me / Is dead!

No one grieves that much, she said. / Your friend is gone. Forget him. / No one remembers him. He is dead Enkidu. Enkidu. Gilgamesh called out:

Help me. They do not know you as I know you?

Then she took pity on him / And let him enter and lie down and rest. / She gave him her bed to fall into and sleep / And rubbed his back and neck and legs and arms / When he was coming out of sleep, still muttering / About the one "who went with me through everything." / Like those old people who forget their listeners / Have not lived through their past with them, / Mentioning names that no one knows. / Enkidu, whom I loved so much, / Who went through everything with me / He died—like any ordinary man. / I have cried both day and night. / I did not want to put him in a grave. / He will rise, I know, one day. /

But then I saw that he *was* dead. / His face collapsed within / After several days, / Like cobwebs I have touched / With my finger.

She wiped his face with a moist cloth / Saying: Yes yes yes yes, / As she made him cooler / Trying to help him forget / By the steady softness of her flesh. / She moved her lips across his chest / And caressed the length of his tired body / And lay over him at night until he slept.

You will never find an end to grief by going on, / She said to the one half sleeping at her side, / Leaning forward to wipe the perspiration from his face. / His eyes were open though his whole self felt asleep / Far off alone in some deep forest / Planted in his flesh / Through which he felt his way in pain / Without the help / Of friends. / She spoke as to a child who could not understand / All the futility that lay ahead / Yet who she knew would go on to repeat / Repeat repeat the things men had to learn. The gods gave death to man and kept life for / Themselves. That is the only way it is. / Cherish your rests; the children you might have; / You are a thing that carries so much tiredness.

QUESTIONS

1. What differences between men and women appear in this excerpt?

2. Why is it so hard for Gilgamesh to accept Enkidu's death?

3. Is Siduri's view of the gods pessimistic or realistic?

Source: Herbert Mason, *Gilgamesh: A Verse Narrative.* Copyright © 1970 by Herbert Mason. Reprinted by permission of Houghton Mifflin Company. All rights reserved.

S E C T I O N   S U M M A R Y

- Approximately thirty city-states of southern Mesopotamia spoke Sumerian and flourished in the third millennium B.C.

- Sargon, an Akkadian, conquered the Sumerian cities of Mesopotamia and united them in one kingdom.

- Hammurabi's Code (1792–1750 B.C.), one of the earliest collections of laws, reveals the inequality and harshness of Mesopotamian society.

- Mesopotamians were religious, believed in many gods, and expected only a grim and shadowy Netherworld after death.

- Mesopotamia's rich culture excelled in mathematics, astronomy, and epic poetry.

EGYPT, TO CA. 1100 B.C.

How did the king's power affect various aspects of Egyptian society?

From Babylon to the valley of the Nile River was about 750 miles by way of the caravan routes through Syria southward—close enough to exchange goods and customs but far enough for a distinct Egyptian civilization to emerge. As in Sumer, civilization in Egypt arose in a river valley, but Egypt was much earlier than Mesopotamia in becoming a unified kingdom under one ruler. Moreover, ancient Egypt survived as a united and independent kingdom for over two thousand years (to be sure, with some periods of civil war and foreign rule). Egypt made great strides in a variety of areas of human achievement, from the arts to warfare. Western civilization borrowed much from Egypt, especially in technology and religion.

Ancient Egypt is a product of the unique characteristics of the Nile River (see **MAP 1.2**). Yet most of Egypt is desert. Today only about 5 percent is habitable by humans, including a few oases, the Nile Delta, and the Nile Valley itself, which extends about 760 miles from Cairo to Egypt's modern southern border: Upper Egypt, a long and narrow valley never more than about 14 miles wide. North of Cairo, in Lower Egypt, the Nile branches out into the wide, low-lying delta before flowing into the Mediterranean Sea.

DIVINE KINGSHIP

The fertility of the Nile River gave ancient Egypt a prosperous economy and optimistic culture. The river's annual floods, which took place during late summer and autumn, were generally benign. With less human effort than was required in Mesopotamia, the floodwaters could be used to irrigate most of the farmland in the Nile Valley. As a result, Egyptian agriculture was one of the wealthiest in the ancient world.

No wonder many Egyptians considered change as undesirable. Even death appeared to be a minor event compared with the eternal regularity of the Nile, which may help explain the prominence in Egyptian religion of belief in the afterlife. In addition, the static outlook helped promote the idea of an absolute, all-powerful, and all-providing king—namely, **pharaoh.**

Agriculture and settled village life emerged in Egypt around 5000 B.C. By 4000 B.C. villages had grown into towns, each controlling a strip of territory. By about 3100 B.C., Egyptian communities up and down the Nile Valley had cleared marshes and expanded the amount of land under cultivation, which in turn could support a larger population. The Nile Valley became

MAP 1.2   Ancient Egypt and the Levant
The unique geography of the Nile Valley and its fertile soil left a stamp on ancient Egypt. Egypt enjoyed trade and cultural contact—and sometimes went to war—with nearby lands such as Nubia and the Levant.

Online Study Center **Improve Your Grade**
Interactive Map: Ancient Egypt and the Levant

pharaoh   Ancient Egyptians' title for their king, an absolute, all-powerful, and all-providing ruler.

one unified kingdom of Egypt, with a capital city perhaps at Memphis.

The new kingdom had monumental architecture, writing, and a king. For several centuries Egyptians consolidated their institutions. Although few specifics are known about this Archaic Period (3200–2695 B.C.), it clearly laid the groundwork for the next era. Around 2700 B.C., a remarkable, distinctive, and relatively well-documented period of creativity began, the Third (2695–2600 B.C.) and Fourth (2600–2500 B.C.) Dynasties (that is, ruling families) of the Old Kingdom.

The history of third- and second-millennium B.C. Egypt is usually divided into three distinct eras of great prosperity: the Old Kingdom (2695–2160 B.C.), the Middle Kingdom (2025–1786 B.C.), and the New Kingdom (1550–1075 B.C.). Between the kingdoms, central authority broke down in the Intermediate Periods. Broadly speaking, the Old Kingdom was an era of spectacular creativity and originality, symbolized by the building of the Great Pyramids; the Middle Kingdom, an era of introspection and literary production; and the New Kingdom, an era in which Egypt's traditional isolation gave way to international diplomacy and expansion.

Egypt's was the first government in recorded history to govern a large territory. Indeed, a chart of Egypt's power structure would look like a pyramid, with a broad base of laborers and artisans supporting a small commanding elite. The holder of the highest point of power was considered so important that for centuries Egyptians referred to the office rather than to the person, calling it "the Great House"—in Egyptian, *per-aa,* or "pharaoh," as the ruler himself (or occasionally herself) was eventually called.

Egyptian kingship was sacred monarchy. In Mesopotamia, the king generally claimed to have been appointed by the gods. In Egypt, pharaoh was deemed to *be* a god. The most dramatic symbol of the king's divinity was a building—or, rather, a series of buildings—the pyramids. The ancients built thirty-five major and many smaller pyramids, of which the best known are

Great Pyramids of Giza
Royal funerary monuments of three Egyptian kings of the twenty-sixth century B.C., the pyramids symbolize the power and ambition of the Old Kingdom. The pyramid of King Khufu (or Cheops, rearmost in the photo) is still the largest all-stone building in human history. *(Michael Holford)*

the Great Pyramids of Giza—three gigantic, perfectly symmetrical limestone tombs. They were constructed during the Fourth Dynasty. Now, nearly five thousand years later, the pyramid of King Khufu (r. 2589–2566 B.C., better known by his Greek name, Cheops) is still the largest all-stone building in human history. Near the Great Pyramids stands the Great Sphinx, a human-headed lion carved out of a rock outcropping, perhaps representing Khufu's son, King Khafre (r. 2558–2532 B.C.; Greek name, Chephren), for whom the second pyramid at Giza was built.

The pyramids were not just monuments to an ego but also temples where the king would continue to be worshiped and served in the afterlife. The structures served a political purpose as well. When the Great Pyramids were constructed, the kingdom of Egypt was still young and fragile. By building the pyramids, the king made a statement of his power—an eloquent, simple, and irrefutable statement. The sheer size of the Great Pyramids demonstrated the king's ability to organize a vast labor force. Indeed, the encampment of workers at Giza may have been the largest gathering of human beings to that date.

In theory, the king owned all the land, but in practice Egypt's economy was a mixture of private enterprise and centralized control. The king delegated authority to a large group of officials, including governors, mayors, military commanders, judges, treasurers, engineers, agricultural overseers, scribes, and others. The highest official was the vizier, a sort of prime minister who had more day-to-day power than pharaoh himself.

The essence of good government was what the Egyptians called *ma'at*, whose basic meaning is "order"—in government, society, or the universe. *Ma'at* can also mean "truth" or "justice." Egypt had a well-functioning system of judges who heard lawsuits, and it probably also had a detailed law code, although few written laws survive.

LIFE AND AFTERLIFE

Egyptian life was full of religious practices, from daily rituals and seasonal festivals to ethical teachings and magic. Egyptian religion tended toward *syncretism*—that is, the blending of mutually opposed beliefs, principles, or practices. For example, Egyptian mythology taught variously that the sky was a cow, was held up by a god or by a post, or was a goddess stretched over the earth. No one was troubled by such inconsistencies, as a modern worshiper might be, because Egyptians believed that a fundamental unity underlay the varieties of nature.

Egypt's religion had many greater and lesser deities, including human, animal, and composite gods. Various animals, from cats and dogs to crocodiles and serpents, were thought to represent the divine. Important deities included Thoth, the moon-god and god of wisdom; Nut, goddess of the sky; Ptah, a creator-god; Osiris, who invented agriculture and became lord of the dead; Horus, son of Osiris, a sky-god imagined as a giant falcon; and Isis, wife of Osiris and mother of Horus, a mother-goddess. Temples were numerous and lavish.

Egyptian religion focused on the afterlife. Unlike the Mesopotamians, the Egyptians believed that death could be a pleasant continuation of life on earth. Hence, they actively sought immortality. The wealthy built tombs that were decorated with paintings and inscriptions and stocked with cherished possessions

Egyptian Book of the Dead
This scene from a lavishly illustrated papyrus shows a dead person's appearance before a divine court of judgment. His heart is being weighed in the balance to determine his fate in the afterlife. *(Courtesy of the Trustees of the British Museum)*

for use after death. The most cherished possession of all was the body, and the Egyptians provided for its preservation through their mastery of the science of embalming—thus the Egyptian mummies.

Reserved for the king and his officials in the Old Kingdom, the afterlife became, as it were, democratized by the Middle Kingdom. By the Middle Kingdom, even ordinary Egyptians believed they could enjoy immortality after death, as gods, as long as they could purchase for their graves funerary texts containing the relevant prayers. The texts emphasize ritual—incantations, magic spells, prayers—as the key to eternal life. Yet from time to time we find other texts, especially from the Middle Kingdom, that say that ritual is not enough; ethical behavior also is required. New Kingdom texts describe the details of a dead person's appearance before a divine court for judgment. The sinless are admitted into eternal life in the kingdom of the blessed. The guilty, their heavy hearts devoured by a beast, suffer a second, final death.

Online Study Center **Improve Your Grade**
Primary Source: The Egyptian Book of the Dead's Declaration of Independence

Such absolute judgments were not found in daily life. Consider relations between the sexes. Egyptian women did not enjoy equal status with men, but they had more freedom than women in other ancient societies, particularly in legal matters. As in Mesopotamia, so in Egypt a woman could buy or sell, bequeath or inherit, sue or testify in court, but a married Egyptian woman, unlike her eastern sisters, could do so without a male guardian's approval. A married woman in Egypt retained the status of complete legal independence. She could even own property without her husband's involvement. But how often did women exercise such privileges? Egyptian women worked in agriculture and trade, in the textile and perfume industries, in dining halls, and in entertainment, but they were rarely managers. Women also served as priestesses of various kinds. Yet in Egypt, as elsewhere, women were expected to make the home the focus of their activities. So although Egyptian women had more freedom outside the home than most ancient women, they exercised nothing like the freedom enjoyed by some women today.

WAR ABROAD, REFORM AT HOME, 1786–1075 B.C.

The humane attitudes of the Middle Kingdom were swept away after about 1700 B.C., when Semitic-speaking immigrants from Canaan*—the Hyksos (HICK-sos)—conquered much of Egypt. In many ways gentle conquerors, the Hyksos worshiped Egyptian gods, built

---

*Canaan is an ancient name for the lands currently called Israel, Palestine, and coastal Syria and Lebanon.

and restored Egyptian temples, and intermarried with natives. As foreigners, however, the Hyksos were unpopular. Eventually a war launched from Upper Egypt, which had retained a loose independence, drove the Hyksos out.

The first restored Egyptian ruler of the New Kingdom was Ahmose I (r. 1550–1525 B.C.). His proved to be a new Egypt indeed. The Hyksos had brought advanced military technology to Egypt, including the horse-drawn war chariot, new kinds of daggers and swords, and the composite bow. Made of laminated materials including wood, leather, and horn, the composite bow could hit a target at 600 yards.

Warlike, expansionist, and marked by a daring attempt at religious reform, the New Kingdom's Eighteenth Dynasty (1540–1293 B.C.) has long held a special fascination for historians. One of the dynasty's memorable names is that of Queen Hatshepsut (HAT-shep-soot). Widow of Thutmose II (r. 1491–1479 B.C.), Hatshepsut first served as regent for her young stepson and then assumed the kingship herself (r. 1479–1457 B.C.). Other Egyptian queens had exercised royal power before, but Hatshepsut was the first to call herself king. Although Hatshepsut dispatched Egyptian armies to fight, her reign is best known for peaceful activities: at home, public works and temple rebuilding; abroad, a commercial expedition over the Red Sea to the "Land of Punt" (perhaps modern Somalia, in eastern Africa).

After her death Hatshepsut was succeeded by her stepson, Thutmose III (r. 1479–1425 B.C.). Late in his reign, he tried to erase his stepmother's memory by having Hatshepsut's statues destroyed and her name expunged from records—an attempt, perhaps, to cut off a claim to the throne by her supporters. A warrior-pharaoh, Thutmose III led his dynasty's armed expansion in western Asia and northern Africa. Thutmose won his greatest victory during his first campaign, at the Battle of Megiddo in Canaan in 1457 B.C. (see Map 1.2), where Egypt's triumph prevented the kingdom of Mitanni from expanding southward. Egypt now ruled an empire with territory in Nubia and Canaan.

Empire brings power, and power often causes conflict. In imperial Egypt during the fourteenth century B.C., kings and priests struggled over authority. Consider the Amarna (a-MAR-na) reform, named for a major archaeological site at the modern town of Tell el-Amarna.

The **Amarna reform** was carried out by Thutmose III's great-great-grandson, King Amenhotep IV (r. 1352–1336 B.C.). Earlier, the god Amun-Re had become the chief deity of the New Kingdom. As supporters of imperialism, his temple priests had been rewarded with enough land and wealth that their power now rivaled

Amarna reform   Term for the ancient Egyptian king Amenhotep IV's seizure of power from temple priests by replacing the god Amun-Re with Aten and renaming himself Akhenaten.

pharaoh's own. Amenhotep IV responded by forbidding the worship of Amun-Re and replacing him with the god Aten, the solar disk. The king changed his own name to Akhenaten ("pleasing to Aten"). He also created a new capital city: Akhetaten (modern Amarna). Akhenaten's wife, Nefertiti, figures prominently in Amarna art, and she too may have played an important role in the reform.

The reformers gained power, but we need not doubt their sincerity. Contemporary literature suggests intense religious conviction in Aten as a benevolent god and one who nurtured not only Egypt but all countries. Although the Aten cult focuses on one god, only Akhenaten and his family were permitted to worship Aten directly; the rest of the Egyptian population was expected to worship the god through pharaoh.

Bold as the reform was, it was too radical to last. After Akhenaten's death his son-in-law and successor, Tutankhaten (r. 1336–1327 B.C.) restored good relations with the priests of Amun-Re, which he signaled by changing his name to Tutankhamun. The Amun-Re cult was revived, the Aten cult was abolished, and the city of Akhetaten was abandoned. After Tutankhamun's death the military exercised great influence over the remaining pharaohs of the Eighteenth Dynasty. Then, in 1291 B.C., a military officer founded a new dynasty as Ramesses (RAM-zeez) I (r. 1291–1289 B.C.).

The Nineteenth (ca. 1291–1185 B.C.) and Twentieth (ca. 1185–1075 B.C.) Dynasties are known as the Ramesside Era, from the most common name of the pharaohs. Although there were great warrior-pharaohs and builder-pharaohs, over time the kings lost power to the priests of Amun. When the Twentieth Dynasty ended in 1075 B.C., the New Kingdom ended with it, and regional conflict between the Nile Delta and Upper Egypt broke out.

ARTS AND SCIENCES IN THE NEW KINGDOM

The Egyptians were superb builders, architects, and engineers. In addition to pyramids and irrigation works, they constructed monumental royal tombs, palaces, forts, and temples, and they erected looming obelisks.

At their best, Egyptian architects designed buildings in harmony with the unique landscape—one of the reasons for the structures' lasting appeal. Their most original and enduring work was done in stone. Stone temples, for example, culminated in the imposing pillared structures of the New Kingdom. That period also saw the construction of rock-cut temples, the most famous of which is Ramesses II's (r. 1279–1213 B.C.) project at Abu Simbel (see Map 1.2). In front of the temples sit four colossal statues of Ramesses, also carved out of rock. Obelisks were slender, tapering pillars carved of a single piece of stone. Inscribed with figures and hieroglyphs, and usually erected in pairs in front of a temple, obelisks were meant to glorify the sun-god.

Throughout history royal courts have excelled as patrons of the arts; the Egyptian court was one of the first and greatest. Egyptian craftsmen were master goldsmiths, glassmakers, and woodworkers. The major arts are well represented in tombs, which were decorated with rich, multicolored wall paintings, the first narrative depictions.

Sculpture was another art form in which Egyptians excelled. Carved in stone, wood, or metal, Egyptian sculpture is a study in contrasts. The body posture is usually rigid and stiff, the musculature only sketchy; the face, in contrast, is often individualistic, the expression full of character and drawn from life. Statues represent kings and queens, gods and goddesses, husbands and wives, adults and children, officials, priests, scribes, animals.

Ancient Egyptian literature is notable for its variety. Religious subjects, historical and commemorative records, technical treatises in mathematics and medicine, and secular stories survive alongside business contracts and royal proclamations. Egyptian writing is best known for hieroglyphs. Elaborate and formal, hieroglyphs were generally used after the Archaic Period only for monuments and ornamentation. Two simplified scripts served for everyday use.

The people who built the pyramids had to be skilled at arithmetic and geometry. Egyptians were able to approximate pi (the ratio of the circumference of a circle to its diameter) and to solve equations containing one or two unknowns. Mathematical astronomy never reached the heights in Egypt that it reached in Babylon (see page 35), but the Egyptian calendar was a remarkable achievement. Based on observation of the star Sirius, the Egyptian calendar, with its 365-day year, approximates the solar calendar. Corrected to 365¼ days, it survives to this day as the calendar of Europe, the Americas, and much of the rest of the world.

Egyptian medical doctors were admired in antiquity and in demand abroad. They knew how to set a dislocated shoulder and used a full battery of splints, sutures, adhesive plasters, elementary disinfectants (from tree leaves), and burn treatments (fatty substances). One Egyptian treatise offers something like modern triage, dividing diseases into three categories: treatable, possibly treatable, and untreatable. Egyptian doctors may have done postmortem dissection in order to understand the human body better.

SECTION SUMMARY

- The Nile River, with its dependable annual flooding, gave ancient Egypt fertile soil, economic prosperity, and an optimistic worldview.

- Egypt invented the idea of worshiping the king as a god; eventually, the king became known as pharaoh.

- Egyptians believed in a happy afterlife after death, as long as the gods judged that the dead person had led a life without sin.

- Egypt's New Kingdom was a great military power that expanded into southwest Asia.

- The Amarna reform of the 1300s was history's first great struggle between church and state.

- The Egyptians excelled at architecture, such as the pyramids, as well as at sculpture and medicine, and they invented the solar calendar that we still use (in revised form) today.

WIDENING HORIZONS: THE LEVANT AND ANATOLIA, 2500–1150 B.C.

What were the contributions of the Levant and Anatolia to the West and why did these early states eventually collapse?

Egypt and Mesopotamia tend to capture our attention, but other early, nearby civilizations are, if less important, also significant contributors to the West. Not only were they the cradle of Western languages and writing systems, but they took part in the first international system of states, a forerunner of later international relations between the West and its neighbors. Let us look in particular at the city-states of the Levant (le-VANT)—the geographic region known today as Syria and Palestine or Israel—and at a kingdom in Anatolia, today's Turkey.

THE CANAANITE CITY-STATES, CA. 2500–1200 B.C.

The discovery in 1974 of a huge cuneiform archive at Ebla (EH-bla) (modern Tell Mardikh) in northern Syria revolutionized our knowledge of one such city-state in the mid-third millennium B.C. Another Levantine city-state, Ugarit (OO-ga-rit) (modern Ras Shamra), a cosmopolitan port, flourished in the second millennium B.C.

A prosperous city, Ebla was known for commerce and artisanry as well as scholarship. Its extensive cunei-

MAP 1.3   The International System, ca. 1500–1250 B.C.

This era of competing kingdoms and city-states witnessed considerable war, especially between Egypt and the Hittites for control of the Canaanite states. Yet it was also a period of international trade, diplomacy, and, from 1450 to 1300 B.C., peace.

form archives include the world's earliest known dictionaries. Sometime between 2500 and 2300 B.C., Ebla ruled a large kingdom, extending over much of Syria and possibly containing as many as 250,000 people, of whom perhaps 30,000 lived in the city (see **MAP 1.3**). Ebla's government fostered trade by negotiating commercial treaties, arranging dynastic marriages and, when necessary, making war. Ebla conquered Mari, a commercial competitor 300 miles downstream on the Euphrates.

Ebla was ruled by an oligarchy (a small, elite group) headed by fourteen regional governors who were probably also clan elders. The king, a sort of first among equals, was chosen by election rather than inheritance; his power was limited by the oligarchic council. The queen and queen mother had significant government authority. The queen had her own properties, administered by officials who answered to her. If she was still alive, the queen mother, officially addressed as "the honored mother of the king," had considerable say in the succession.

Ebla fell to the Amorites around 2000 B.C. It remained a wealthy city, though much diminished in power. To find a much more vibrant city in Syria after 2000 B.C., we need only look at the coast and the city of Ugarit (see Map 1.3). Ugarit was a thriving Mediter-

ranean port, especially around 1400 to 1200 B.C. Its cosmopolitanism made Ugarit distinctive among western Asian city-states. As a trading center, it linked ships coming from the eastern Mediterranean island of Cyprus or the Anatolian ports with land caravans heading to Babylonia. The native inhabitants of Ugarit spoke a Semitic language. The merchants of Ugarit, however, were often foreigners, and the bazaars echoed with a multitude of languages.

Ugarit played an important role in the spread of one of history's most important writing systems: the alphabet. Unlike the pictographic or syllabic systems of Mesopotamia, Egypt, and China, in an alphabet each sign stands for one and only one sound. In the 1300s B.C. scribes in Ugarit developed an alphabet. It was not the first alphabet, however. In Egypt, in the desert west of the Nile, limestone inscriptions have recently been found in a Semitic script with Egyptian influences. Dated to about 1900 to 1800 B.C., during the Middle Kingdom, the writing is now recognized as the earliest known example of an alphabet.

We do not know whether that alphabet was invented by Egyptians or by speakers of a Semitic language who were visiting Egypt. Nor do we know if that alphabet influenced Ugarit. What is clear is that Ugaritic scribes invented thirty cuneiform signs as an alphabet to write their Semitic language. Later adapted by the Phoenicians and, through them, the Greeks, the Ugaritic alphabet is the source of the Roman alphabet, used today by English and many other languages around the world.

THE HITTITES, 1650–1180 B.C.

Almost all the peoples of western Asia and Egypt whom we have discussed so far spoke a language belonging to the large Afro-Asiatic language family. But none of these languages survived antiquity in Europe. Instead, virtually every modern European language—as well as the dominant languages of Iran and India—are descendants of the long-lost proto–Indo-European language. These languages, from English and Russian to Iranian and Hindi, are said to belong to the Indo-European language family.

Indo-European speakers probably originated between 4500 and 2500 B.C. in southern Russia. A warlike, mobile people, they emigrated east and west. The first speakers of an Indo-European language to establish a civilization in western Asia were the **Hittites,** who came to Anatolia sometime before 1800 B.C. The Hittites were great warriors and intelligent administrators. They absorbed Anatolia's sophisticated culture and made it their own. The Hittites were masters of the horse and rank among the leading charioteers of what was the golden age of chariot battle. They made full use of Anatolia's mineral wealth and made a limited number of iron weapons as well as the more usual bronze. They ruled Anatolia from their city of Hattusa, in what is today central Turkey.

Hittite history is divided into several periods. After conquest and consolidation in the Old Kingdom (ca. 1650–1450 B.C.) came a period of retrenchment and loss of territory known as the Middle Kingdom (ca. 1450–1380 B.C.). During the New Kingdom (ca. 1380–1180 B.C.), the Hittites' power extended into Syria and northern Mesopotamia (see Map 1.3). Afterward came the Neo-Hittite era (ca. 1180–700 B.C.), when the Hittite kingdom had disintegrated into small successor states.

The Hittite kingdom was a warrior society whose strong nobility competed for power with the king. Hittite queens and queen mothers often had considerable power, as at Ebla. Puduhepa (pu-du-HE-pa), wife of King Hattusilis (hat-tu-SIL-is) III (r. 1278–1250 B.C.), played a memorable role in state affairs. Some of her prayers were written down and survive to this day. Puduhepa seems to have been the prime mover in mak-

Hittites   Builders of a great empire in Anatolia in the Late Bronze Age, the Hittites fought Egypt to a standstill and made history's first peace treaty between equals. Hittite is the oldest recorded Indo-European language, the language group to which English belongs.

Hittite God
This figurine in gold, standing only 1.5 inches high, represents Hittite art of the Old Kingdom (ca. 1650–1450 B.C.). The clothes, shoes, and conical hat are typical of Hittite depictions of gods.   *(Louvre/R.M.N./Art Resource, NY)*

ing the Hurrian sun-goddess of Arinna (a shrine near Hattusas) the chief deity of the Hittite state. Hattusilis publicly declared that he would not have rebelled against the previous king had Puduhepa not first dreamed of divine support for the coup.

The Hittites had a genuine and original sense of history. Earlier peoples had kept lists and chronicles; Hittite annals are livelier and better argued. The royal annals of King Hattusilis III, for example, read in parts like a lawsuit, carefully pleading a justification of the king's actions. Hattusilis excused his usurpation of the throne by stating that the former king had unjustly stripped him of territory; furthermore, Hattusilis rebelled openly. Hittite treaties with lesser states similarly argue their cases: each begins with an introduction providing historical background and justifying the relationship sworn to in the body of the text.

THE FIRST INTERNATIONAL PEACE, CA. 1500–1150 B.C.

The Hittites and New Kingdom Egyptians exercised great military power, yet what is even more remarkable about these states and others is their ability to make and maintain peace. The years from about 1450 to about 1300 B.C. marked a period of peace among the great powers from Egypt to Anatolia and Mesopotamia—what historians call the first international system. The arts of peace are illustrated in surviving treaties and letters between monarchs, many of which come from Amarna.

The Amarna Archives (mid-fourteenth century B.C.), written in Akkadian cuneiform, illustrate formal communication among states. Rulers of great powers addressed each other as "brother," while Canaanite princes called pharaoh "my lord and my Sun-god" and assured him that they were "thy servant and the dirt on which thou dost tread." The texts reveal a system of gift exchange and commerce, politeness and formality, alliance and dynastic marriage, subjects and governors, rebels and garrisons. Because of a rough equality of power, no king was likely to defeat the others, so the

PEACE AND BROTHERHOOD

After the stalemate at Qadesh (1274 B.C.) the kings of Egypt and the Hittites (referred to below as Hatti) agreed to make peace permanently. The result was a landmark of history, the first peace treaty between equals. A copy of this treaty is displayed in the United Nations building in New York City.

Preamble

P1 (A obv. 1-3) [The treaty which] Ramses, [Beloved] of Amon, Great King, King [of Egypt, Hero, concluded] on [a tablet of silver] with Hattusili, [Great King], King of Hatti, his brother, in order to establish [great] peace and great [brotherhood] between them forever. . . .

Purpose of Treaty; Previous Relations

P3 (A obv. 7-13) I have now established good brotherhood and good peace between us forever, in order likewise to establish good peace and good brotherhood in [the relations] of Egypt with Hatti forever. As far as the relations of the Great King, King of Egypt, [and] the Great King, King of Hatti, are concerned, from the beginning of time and forever [by means of a treaty] the god has not allowed the making of war between them. . . .

Future Relations

P4 (A obv. 13-18) And Ramses, Beloved of Amon, Great King, King [of Egypt], has indeed created <it> (the relationship) [on] this [day] by means of a treaty upon a tablet of silver, with [Hattusili], Great King, King of Hatti, his brother, in order to establish good peace and good brotherhood [between them] forever. He is [my] brother, and I am his brother. <He is at peace with me>, and I am at peace with him [forever. And] we will create our brotherhood and our [peace], and they will be better than the former brotherhood and peace of [Egypt with] Hatti.

P5 (A obv. 19-21) Ramses, Great King, King of Egypt, is in good peace and good brotherhood with [Hattusili], Great King of Hatti. The sons of Ramses, Beloved of Amon, <Great King>, King of Egypt, will be at peace and [brothers with] the sons of Hattusili, Great King, King of Hatti, forever.

And they will remain as in our relationship of brotherhood [and of] peace, so that Egypt will be at peace with Hatti and they will be brothers like us forever.

Non-aggression

P6 (A obv. 22-27) And Ramses, Beloved of Amon, Great King, King of Egypt, for all time shall not open hostilities against Hatti in order to take anything from it. And Hattusili, Great King, King of Hatti, for all time shall not open hostilities against Egypt in order to take [anything] from it. The eternal regulation which the Sun-god and the Storm-god made for Egypt with Hatti is intended <to provide> peace and brotherhood and to prohibit hostilities between them. . . .

Defensive Alliance

P7 (A obv. 27-30) And if someone else, an enemy, comes against Hatti, and Hattusili, [Great King, King of Hatti], sends to me: "Come to me to my aid against him," then [Ramses, Beloved] of Amon, Great King, King of Egypt, must send his infantry and his chariotry and they will defeat [his enemy and] take revenge for Hatti.

P8 (A obv. 31-33) And if Hattusili, Great King, King of Hatti, [becomes angry] with his own [subjects], after they have offended against him, and he sends to Ramses, Great King, King of Egypt, on account of this, then Ramses, Beloved of Amon, must send his infantry and his chariotry, [and] they will destroy all with whom he is angry. . . .

[The next two paragraphs repeat these obligations but with the roles of the two kings reversed.]

Fugitives

. . . P18 (A obv. 60-64) [And if] a single man flees from [Hatti, or] two men, [or three men, and they come to] Ramses, Beloved [of Amon, Great King, King] of Egypt, his brother, [then Ramses], Beloved of Amon, Great King, [King of Egypt, must seize them and send them] to Hattusili, his brother [. . .]—for they are brothers. But [they shall not punish them for] their offenses. They shall [not] tear out [their tongues or their eyes]. And [they shall not mutilate(?) their ears or [their] feet. [And they shall not destroy(?) their households, together with their wives] and their sons.

QUESTIONS

1. What does the treaty mean by "good brotherhood and good peace"?
2. In what ways does the treaty display more concern for kings than for their subjects?
3. What punishments were usually given to fugitives from justice?

Source: Gary Beckman, *Hittite Diplomatic Texts*, 2d ed. (Atlanta: Scholar's Press, 1999), pp. 96–99.

parties avoided all-out war. They preferred instead to compete by jockeying for allies among the small Canaanite border states.

Sometimes the competition turned into war. By the late fourteenth century B.C., Egypt and the Hittites were fighting again. The most dramatic episode was the Battle of Qadesh in northern Syria in 1274 B.C., where twenty thousand Egyptian troops faced seventeen thousand Hittites. Qadesh is the first well-documented battle in history. Since neither of the two evenly matched powers managed to conquer the other, they made peace. The treaty between them still survives, and it is the oldest surviving peace treaty between equals. (See the box "The Global Record: Peace and Brotherhood.")

But peace was temporary. Between about 1200 and 1150 B.C., the international system came to a crashing end. From Mesopotamia to Greece, from Anatolia to Egypt, one state after another collapsed. Surviving evidence is fragmentary, but it suggests that both foreign and domestic problems were devastating. Raiders and invaders beset the eastern Mediterranean in this period. Called "Sea Peoples" by the Egyptians, they attacked both on land and at sea. We do not know precisely who they were. In addition, some evidence of regional famine and climatic change indicates that natural causes may have led to disruption and rebellion.

Whatever the cause, what followed would prove to be a different world. Yet the end of the international system did not result in the disappearance of ancient cultures. Although new peoples appeared and old peoples changed, both continued to borrow from the cultures that had flowered before 1200 B.C.

SECTION SUMMARY

- Our alphabet dates back to an alphabet invented in the 1300s B.C. in the cosmopolitan city-state of Ugarit, a Mediterranean port in today's Syria.

- The first alphabet is even earlier (ca. 1900–1800 B.C.) and has been discovered in Egypt.

- English as well as most of the languages of Europe, Iran, and India, date back to a common source in an ancient and now-lost language called Indo-European.

- The earliest known Indo-European civilization is that of the Hittites, who established a great kingdom in today's Turkey and left thousands of documents.

- The conflicts between Hittites and Egyptians led to history's first great system of diplomacy, its first well-documented battle (Qadesh), and its first peace treaty between equals.

- We are not sure why, but the great civilizations of the ancient Near East all either declined, split apart, or collapsed not long after 1200 B.C.

 # CHAPTER SUMMARY

Online Study Center **ACE the Test**

How did the earliest human beings adapt to their environments and create the first civilizations?

What were the Mesopotamians' major contributions to government, religion, and art and culture?

How did the king's power affect various aspects of Egyptian society?

What were the contributions of the Levant and Anatolia to the West and why did these early states eventually collapse?

The earliest human beings, probably beginning before 70,000 B.C., invented human culture—that is, they developed communications enough that people could cooperate and exploit their natural environment by means of technology. Next came the move from a food-collecting to a food-producing economy. After beginning in the Fertile Crescent region of western Asia shortly after 10,000 B.C., food production spread to Europe beginning around 7000 B.C. Over the thousands of years following the invention of agriculture, human society became more complex and won increasing control of the natural environment. The result was the emergence of civilization in Egypt and

Mesopotamia after 3500 B.C. The first cities appeared in Mesopotamia about 3500 B.C. and maybe even earlier. Writing was invented independently in Mesopotamia and Egypt between 3500 and 3000 B.C. In Mesopotamia the Sumerians and Akkadians flourished in city-states, which were eventually conquered and united into a kingdom. The Mesopotamians wrote the first law codes, including the famous Hammurabi's Code (1792–1750 B.C.). Mesopotamians were religious, believed in many gods, and expected only a grim and shadowy Netherworld after death. Mesopotamia's rich culture excelled in mathematics, astronomy, and epic poetry.

Egyptian society and culture was focused on the king. Egypt invented the idea of worshipping the king as a god; eventually, the king became known as pharaoh. Early Egypt was relatively peaceful and inward-looking, but after a period of foreign rule, the newly liberated Egypt of the New Kingdom was a great military power

that expanded into southwest Asia. The Egyptians excelled at architecture, such as the pyramids, as well as at sculpture and medicine, and they invented the solar calendar that we still use (in revised form) today.

Our alphabet dates back to an alphabet invented in the 1300s B.C. in the cosmopolitan city-state of Ugarit, a Mediterranean port in today's Syria. Our language, English, belongs to the Indo-European language group; the first known Indo-European civilization is that of the Hittites, the dominant power in Anatolia from 1650 to 1180 B.C. The conflicts between Hittites and Egyptians led to history's first great system of diplomacy, its first well-documented battle (Qadesh), and its first peace treaty between equals. The great civilizations of the ancient Near East all either declined, split apart, or collapsed not long after 1200 B.C. Although this destruction is often attributed to the Sea Peoples, the cause is still uncertain.

LOOKING AHEAD

The states of Egypt and western Asia were the ancestors of the West. The West itself begins with the Hebrews, Greeks, and Romans. Ancient Israel was one of the new states to emerge after the post-1200 B.C. collapse, while the Greeks rose to far greater heights after 1200 than before—although their first achievements are noteworthy. Important developments for the West also took place after 1200 in Assyria (northern Mesopotamia) and Persia. We turn to these places in the next chapter.

KEY TERMS

hominids (p. 4)

hunter-gatherers (p. 6)

Neolithic Revolution (p. 7)

cuneiform (p. 12)

papyrus (p. 12)

Sumerians (p. 14)

city-state (p. 14)

pharaoh (p. 19)

Amarna reform (p. 22)

Hittites (p. 26)

Online Study Center
Improve Your Grade Flashcards

SUGGESTED READING

Bertman, Stephen. *Handbook to Life in Ancient Mesopotamia.* 2003. A useful and informative introduction, offering thumbnail sketches, in encyclopedia form, of a wide variety of subjects from archaeology to ziggurats.

Bottéro, Jean, et al. *Everyday Life in Ancient Mesopotamia.* 2001. One of the most readable introductions.

Bryce, Trevor. *The Kingdom of the Hittites.* 2006. One of the best and most up-to-date introductions.

Cunliffe, Barry, ed. *The Oxford Illustrated Prehistory of Europe.* New edition, 2001. A guide to European material culture from the Paleolithic era to the early medieval period, written by a dozen archaeologists.

Johanson, D. C., and Edgar B. Johanson. *From Lucy to Language.* Revised and updated edition, 2006. Excellent and relatively up-to-date introduction to human evolution, with outstanding photographs.

Murnane, William J. *The Penguin Guide to Ancient Egypt.* Second edition, 1997. Both a well-illustrated travel guide and a scholarly, basic introduction.

Van de Mieroop, Marc. *History of the Ancient Near East: ca. 3000–323 B.C.* (Blackwell History of the Ancient World, 1). 2003. A thorough and clear account.

NOTES

1. James B. Pritchard, ed., *Ancient Near Eastern Texts Relating to the Old Testament,* 3d ed., with Supplement (Princeton, N.J.: Princeton University Press, 1969), p. 107.

2

THE SWORD, THE BOOK, AND THE MYTHS: WESTERN ASIA AND EARLY GREECE

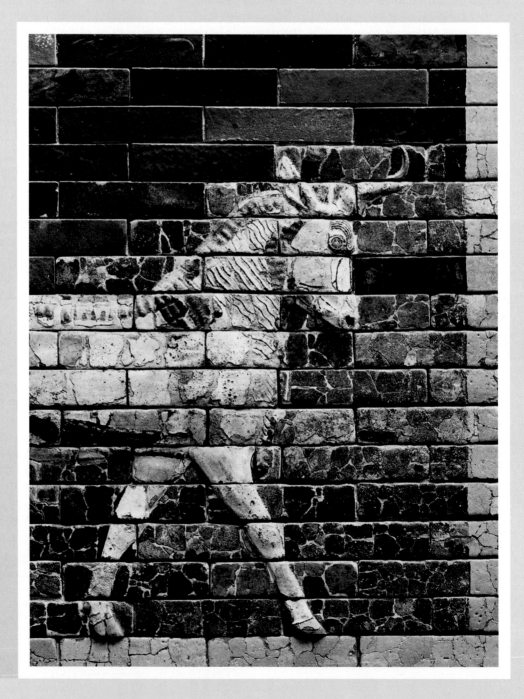

Bull from Ishtar Gate, Babylon
(Bildarchiv Preussischer Kulturbesitz/Art Resource, NY)

The bull in brick relief shown on the left symbolizes power even today, twenty-six hundred years after it was molded and glazed. About 4 feet high, this bull was one of several dozen figures of bulls and dragons that decorated the massive Ishtar Gate, which led through the inner town wall of Babylon (BAB-eh-lon) into the palace. The gate represents only a small part of a magnificent reconstruction of the city by the Neo-Babylonian kings who ruled western Asia around 600 to 539 B.C.

Imagine the king's surprise had he known that under his nose an obscure prophet—we know him only as "Second Isaiah" (eye-ZAY-ah)—was preaching a bold message to his compatriots, a conquered people living in exile in Babylon. Isaiah reminded them that Yahweh (YAH-way), their god, was a god of justice and mercy—the one and only true god of the entire world—and that Yahweh had chosen the king of mountainous, backward Persia to conquer western Asia and redeem Yahweh's people. The Neo-Babylonian king might have laughed at the idea. Yet the Persians under Cyrus the Great conquered Babylon in 539 B.C. and proclaimed the freedom of Yahweh's people—the Jews—to return to Palestine and re-establish the Temple to their god in the city of Jerusalem (juh-ROO-suh-lem). They did so, and around this time they wrote down their religious and historical traditions in large sections of what would become the Hebrew Bible, or Old Testament.

Also in the sixth century B.C., Pisistratus (pie-SIS-trah-tus), the ambitious ruler of Athens, a tiny city-state a thousand miles northwest of Babylon, sponsored a literary project to preserve the religious and historical traditions of his people. The literary works whose texts were standardized under his patronage are the *Iliad* and *Odyssey,* the epic poems of Homer, who had composed them about two centuries before.

Both the Hebrew Bible and the Homeric poems are deeply religious in outlook, but there the similarities end. The Hebrew Bible is monotheistic and focuses on the individual's subordination to God. Homer is polytheistic and glorifies the hero, who, though doomed to fail, aspires to godlike achievement. For most scholars the Bible and Homer represent two poles of Western civilization: the sacred and the worldly, the reverent and the heroic, holy writ and poetic craftsmanship.

Israel and Greece are, along with Rome, the founders of the West. Israel's holy book, the Hebrew Bible, founded the Western religious tradition. Greece, which founded the Western tradition of philosophy and politics, had its first

CHAPTER OUTLINE

ASSYRIANS, NEO-BABYLONIANS, AND PERSIANS, CA. 1200–330 B.C.

ISRAEL, CA. 1500–400 B.C.

EARLY GREECE, TO CA. 725 B.C.

KEY TERMS

Assyrians	covenant
Neo-Babylonians	Israelites
Phoenicians	monotheism
Persian Empire	Minoans
Zoroastrianism	Mycenaeans
Torah	Homer

Online Study Center

This icon will direct you to interactive map and primary source activities on the website **college.hmco.com/pic/noble5e**

great literary flowering in the works of Homer, whose epic poems are based on Greek myths.

The Neo-Babylonians, along with the other great empires of the era, the Assyrians and Persians, are ancestors of the West. Conquerors, they came to power by the sword, but once in power they spread civilization, serving as conduits through which the achievements of Mesopotamia were transmitted. They built great empires whose institutions were eventually transformed into notions of mass citizenship under law and justice in a universal empire by the third founder of the West, Rome.

The first half of the first millennium B.C., therefore, left a divergent legacy to the West. On the one hand, new empires arose that were more systematically organized, farther-flung, and more diverse ethnically than those created before. On the other hand, prophets, philosophers, and poets looked in new and deeper ways into the human soul.

In this chapter we look at the deeply influential developments in empire, religion, and thought forged in the first half of the first millennium B.C. At the same time, we consider the peaceful expansion in this era, through trade and colonization, particularly under the Phoenicians. Finally, we examine the material innovation that has earned the period the title "Iron Age."

FOCUS QUESTIONS

What made the first-millennium B.C. empires of the Assyrians, Neo-Babylonians, and Persians so much more effective than earlier empires?

What was the religious experience of ancient Israel, and what is its legacy today?

What are the Homeric poems, and what light do they shed on the history of early Greece?

ASSYRIANS, NEO-BABYLONIANS, AND PERSIANS, CA. 1200–330 B.C.

What made the first-millennium B.C. empires of the Assyrians, Neo-Babylonians, and Persians so much more effective than earlier empires?

Ancestors of the West, three great multiethnic empires emerged between the 800s and 500s B.C. Ruthless soldiers, brutal conquerors, and innovative administrators, the Assyrians established an empire in western Asia and Egypt during the ninth through seventh centuries B.C. They were followed in turn by a Neo-Babylonian empire in the late seventh and sixth centuries. However, neither of these was as successful or as durable as the empire of the Persians (ca. 550–330 B.C.). At its height the Persian Empire stretched from central Asia and northwest India in the east to Macedonia and Libya in the west (see **MAP 2.1**). Persia's vast empire was loosely governed by a Persian ruling elite and its native helpers. Unlike the ironfisted Assyrians, the Persians were relatively tolerant and respectful of their subjects' customs. Many of Persia's kings were followers of Zoroastrianism, an ethical and forceful religion. A period of relative peace in most of Persia's domains from the 530s to the 330s B.C. fostered widespread economic prosperity.

Borrowing the administrative methods of the Assyrians and Medes (meedz) and the long-established officialdom of Babylon, the Persians built a new and durable imperial government. Their official art stressed the unity of the peoples of the empire under Persian leadership. Persian rule represented the greatest success yet in implementing the notions of universal kingship that dated back to Sargon of Agade (r. 2371–2316 B.C.) (see page 15). In turn, Persia transmitted the trappings of absolute kingship to later ambitious rulers, from Alexander the Great to the caesars of Rome and from the Byzantine emperors to the Muslim caliphs.

ASSYRIANS AND NEO-BABYLONIANS

The **Assyrians** already had a long history as a military and commercial power in the Bronze Age. They lived in what is today northern Iraq and spoke a Semitic language. Around 1200 B.C. their state collapsed during that era of international crisis (see page 28), but they held on to a small homeland of about 5,000 square miles, roughly the size of Connecticut. The toughened survivors emerged with an aggressive, expansionist ideology.

Assyria's greatest successes came in the eighth and seventh centuries. One by one, states large and small fell—Babylonia, Syria, the kingdom of Israel, Cilicia in southern Anatolia, even Egypt (though Assyrian rule there lasted only a generation). Assyria became the first state to rule the two great river valleys of the ancient Near East, the Nile and the Tigris-Euphrates (see Map 2.1).

The Assyrians were warriors. Ashur, their main deity, was a war-god. Theirs was an ideology of power, conquest, and control. The key to Assyria's success was its army—100,000 to 200,000 men strong—which made an unforgettable impression on observers and foes. The Israelite prophet Isaiah of Jerusalem ("First Isaiah") said of Assyrian soldiers: "[Their] arrows are sharpened, and all their bows bent, their horses' hoofs are like flint, their chariot wheels like the whirlwind. Their growling is like that of a lion" (Isaiah 5:28–29). He might have added that Assyrian spearmen, archers, and cavalrymen were equipped with weapons and armor of iron.

Thanks to new heating and cooling techniques, metal smiths in the ancient world produced an alloy of carbon and iron that was harder and more durable than bronze. It was also easier to obtain since iron ore is widespread—unlike tin, an essential element of bronze. Iron tools and weapons were often stronger and cheaper than their bronze predecessors, which opened up new technical and military possibilities.

Adding to its might, Assyria was the first major state to employ regular cavalry units (rather than charioteers) as the main strike force. The Assyrians were also excellent engineers, adept at taking walled cities by siege.

In addition, the Assyrians displayed superb organizational skills. The central standing army was supplemented with draftees conscripted from around the empire. Provinces were kept small to prevent the emergence of separate power bases, and independent-minded nobles were regularly checked by the kings.

To control the restive subjects of their far-flung empire, the Assyrians met rebellion with ferocious reprisals. Disloyal cities were attacked and, if need be, destroyed. Sculptured reliefs and inscriptions were set up to show, often in gruesome detail, the fate awaiting Assyria's

Assyrians Warlike people who ruled the ancient Near East during the first millennium B.C. Their innovations included using cavalry as their main striking force and having weapons and armor made of iron.

CHRONOLOGY

2000 B.C.	First Minoan palaces on Crete
1800–1490 B.C.	Height of Minoan civilization
Late 1600s B.C.	Eruption of Thera volcano
1490 B.C.	Mycenaeans conquer Crete
1375 B.C.	Palace at Knossos destroyed
1400–1180 B.C.	Height of Mycenaean civilization
1250–1150 B.C.	Sea Peoples invade Palestine
1180 B.C.	Mycenaean palaces destroyed
ca. 1200–1000 B.C.	Israelites settle Canaanite hill country
ca. 1050–750 B.C.	Height of Phoenician city-states
1004–928 B.C.	Reigns of David and Solomon
ca. 725 B.C.	Homer
722 B.C.	Assyrians conquer kingdom of Israel
612 B.C.	Conquest of Nineveh ends Assyrian power
598 B.C.	Neo-Babylonians conquer kingdom of Judah
559–530 B.C.	Reign of Cyrus the Great
550–330 B.C.	Achaemenid Persian Empire
539 B.C.	Cyrus conquers Babylon; permits Jews to return to Palestine
ca. 425 B.C.	Judean assembly accepts the Torah

enemies. We see or read of cities burned to the ground; of men flayed alive, even though they had surrendered, and walls covered with their skin; and of piles of human skulls.

The Assyrians also engaged in mass deportations. They uprooted the people of a conquered country, resettled them far away—often in Assyria itself—and colonized their land with Assyrian loyalists. The so-called Ten Lost Tribes of Israel—the people of the northern Israelite kingdom (see page 43)—were conquered by Assyria in 722 B.C., and many of them were transported to Mesopotamia, where they disappeared from history. (Those who remained in Israel mixed with colonists, and the new group became known, and scorned, as Samaritans.)

Assyrian policy was the result of careful calculation. The political goal was to punish rebellion, the economic goal to create a varied labor force. For example, although it is estimated that the Assyrians deported

MAP 2.1   The Assyrian and Persian Empires

In the 660s B.C. the Assyrians ruled the largest empire the ancient world had seen, extending from the Tigris to the Nile. The Persian Empire was even greater. Around 500 B.C. it reached from its heartland in southwestern Iran westward to Macedonia and eastward to India.

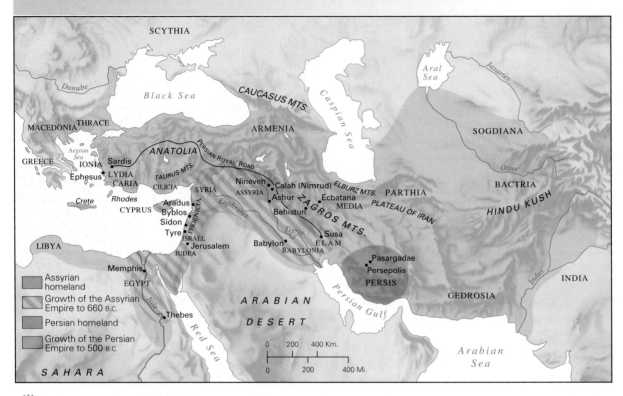

Online Study Center **Improve Your Grade**
Interactive Map: The Assyrian and Persian Empires

several million people, they deported not whole populations but a carefully chosen cross section of professions. They also deported entire families together, to weaken deportees' emotional ties to their former homes.

Assyria's success also was due in part to the relative weakness of other powers. Egypt had been at the mercy of factions and invaders for much of the Third Intermediate Period (1075–656 B.C.). Around 950, for example, the kingship came into the hands of Libyan mercenaries. From the eighth century on, their rule was challenged in turn by invaders from the south, rulers of a new Nubian kingdom called Kush (see Map 1.2 on page 19). Kushite pharaohs governed Egypt from around 719 until 656, when they withdrew back south. It was they who faced the Assyrian attacks in 671 and 667.

The conquest of Egypt marked imperial Assyria's greatest extent—and its overextension (see Map 2.1). A coalition army consisting of soldiers from a revived Babylonian kingdom and of Medes (who had formed a powerful state in Iran; see page 36) conquered Nineveh (NIN-eh-veh), the Assyrian capital, in 612 B.C. and de-

feated the remnants of the Assyrian army in battles in 609 and 605. Few of its subjects mourned the empire's passing.

The destruction of Assyria led to revival for Babylon, whose rulers attempted to recapture the glories of Hammurabi's day (see page 16). For a short period, until the Persian conquest in 539 B.C., the **Neo-Babylonian** dynasty (founded in 626 B.C.) and the Medes of Iran were the dominant military forces in western Asia. The Neo-Babylonian king Nebuchadrezzar II (neh-boo-khad-REZ-zar) conquered the kingdom of Judah (in southern Palestine) in 598 and destroyed Jerusalem, its capital, in 586. He deported many thousands of Judeans to Babylon, an event remembered by Christians and Jews as the Babylonian Captivity. Most of the rest of western Asia also fell to Nebuchadrezzar's troops. His most enduring achievement was rebuilding Babylon on a grand scale. In addition to the city's numerous temples, shrines,

Neo-Babylonians   Rulers of western Asia between 612 and 539 B.C. who elaborately rebuilt Babylon, creating the famous Hanging Gardens. They destroyed Jerusalem, deporting many Judeans in what is known as the Babylonian Captivity.

and altars, he created the so-called Hanging Gardens celebrated by later Greek writers. They describe the structure as a large terraced complex that Nebuchadrezzar built for his queen, although it may have been a plant-covered ziggurat.

The Neo-Babylonians and Assyrians both made great strides in astronomy. Their primary motive was not scientific but religious—that is, a belief in astrology (the study of the movements of heavenly bodies in the belief that they influence human affairs). Astrology led to advances in the scientific observation of the heavens. Assyrian priests had produced relatively accurate circular diagrams (astrolabes) that showed the positions of the major constellations, stars, and planets over the course of the year. By 600 B.C. Assyrian and Neo-Babylonian astronomers could predict solstices, equinoxes, and lunar eclipses.

Astronomy in Mesopotamia reached its heights in the centuries after 500 B.C. The zodiac, a diagram showing the movement of the sun and planets relative to the constellations, was invented in Persian-ruled Babylon in the fourth century B.C. In the third and second centuries B.C., when Babylonia was under Hellenistic Greek rule, native scientists made impressive advances in mathematical astronomy, composing tables that could be used to calculate movements of the moon and planets. More sophisticated mathematical astronomy would not be produced in the West until the Scientific Revolution of the sixteenth century A.D.

Another western Asian society during this period was created by trade, not war. In both the Hebrew Bible and Homer, the **Phoenicians** (fuh-NEESH-anz) loom large as merchants and seamen, as "traders the world honored" (Isaiah 23:8). Phoenicians were Canaanites (CAY-nan-ites), speakers of a Semitic language and heirs to the civilization that had prospered in Ugarit around 1400 B.C. (see page 25). After the invasions of the Sea Peoples and others around 1200 B.C., the Canaanites' once-large territory was reduced to a narrow strip along the Mediterranean in the area of modern Lebanon and northern Israel (see Map 2.2 on page 43).

Phoenicians Canaanites whose civilization flourished about 1050–750 B.C. in present-day coastal Syria, where they established major trading ports. Master sailors, they planted colonies around the Mediterranean, many of which, including Carthage, became independent states.

Between 1050 and 750 B.C., the inhabitants of the area flourished; historians call them, as did the ancient Greeks, "Phoenicians." Their purple-dyed textiles gave the Greeks their word for the color purple: *Phoenician.*

The Phoenicians were master shipbuilders and sailors. Around 600 B.C. their ships accomplished the first known circumnavigation of Africa. Around 450 B.C. they made the first known commercial sailing trip to the British Isles. Some scholars think they even reached Brazil. The most lasting Phoenician achievement at sea, however, was the planting of colonies in the Mediterranean, probably beginning in the ninth century B.C. Many of their colonies eventually became independent states. The greatest Phoenician colony was Carthage (CAR-thidge), founded by the city of Tyre around 750 B.C. It was the major port city of the western Mediterranean for much of the next thousand years.

Phoenician culture was open to outside influences. Phoenician religious art is full of Egyptian sphinxes, coffins that look like mummy cases, and women wearing wigs in the style of Egypt's New Kingdom. But Phoenician art also contains Near Eastern seals and figures out of Greek myths.

Phoenician Ivory
This delicately carved plaque of a cow and calf, just 3 inches high, illustrates the wealth of artistic talent at the disposal of the Phoenicians, whose civilization reached its peak between 1050 and 750 B.C.
(Iraq Antiquities Department)

Phoenician traders introduced advanced material goods, slaves, and possibly law codes to the Greeks. It was probably from the Phoenicians, whose alphabet derived from Ugarit, that the Greeks adapted their alphabet.

Around 750 B.C. the Phoenician city-states lost their independence to the Assyrians, and in later years Neo-Babylonians, Persians, and other foreign conquerors followed. But Phoenician culture survived—at home, in the colonies, and among the many Mediterranean peoples influenced by it. The result, though unintended, was that Phoenician colonists exported the civilization of western Asia to the western Mediterranean.

BUILDING THE PERSIAN EMPIRE

A thousand miles east of Phoenicia, a great empire took root. Indo-European–speaking peoples, the Medes and Persians arrived in western Iran probably around 1500 B.C. but perhaps not until 900 B.C. The two peoples were closely related in language and customs. The Medes lived in the central Zagros Mountains. The Persians made their homeland farther south in Anshan (modern Fars). At first the Medes ruled the Persians, but in 550 B.C. the tables were turned when the Medes were

suddenly conquered by the young Persian king Cyrus the Great (r. 559–530 B.C.).

It took Cyrus only twenty years to conquer most of western Asia and much of central Asia. Within five years of his death in 530 B.C., his son and successor, Cambyses (kam-BYE-seez) (r. 530–525 B.C.), added Egypt and Libya. Cambyses' successor, Darius (dah-RYE-us) (r. 521–486 B.C.), corralled northwestern India and Thrace. The frontier regions, especially Egypt, were often in revolt, and the attempt of Darius and his successor, Xerxes (ZURK-seez) (r. 486–465 B.C.), to extend Persian rule to Greece ended in failure (see pages 77–79). The Achaemenid **Persian Empire** (named after a legendary founder, Achaemenes) survived for two hundred years, until a Greco-Macedonian army under Alexander the Great, king of Macedon (r. 336–323 B.C.), destroyed it.

Let us consider several reasons for the success of Achaemenid (ah-KEE-men-id) Persia. The first was military prowess. Persia was ruled by a warrior-aristocracy whose traditional values, according to the Greek historian Herodotus, were "riding, hunting, and telling the truth." The state was able to field a huge army of about 300,000 men, conscripted from the various subject peoples. Although the resultant hodgepodge of soldiers from across the empire did not always fight as a unit, a crack infantry group, the 10,000 Immortals, provided a solid core. The Persians excelled as bowmen and cavalrymen. Following the Assyrians, they made cavalry into the decisive strike force of the battlefield, assigning a more minor role to chariotry. Persia was even more innovative at sea, where it had its subjects build the first great navy. Although Persians served as marines and sometimes as commanders, the rowers and seamen were usually Phoenicians or Greeks.

The second reason for Persia's success was political. Unlike the Assyrians, the Persians considered generosity and tolerance to be more effective than terrorism and brutality. As Cyrus prepared to attack Babylon, he portrayed himself as the champion of the traditional Babylonian religion, and Babylon surrendered to him without a fight. Cyrus also emphasized his continuity with earlier Mesopotamian history by adopting the traditional title of "King of Sumer and Akkad." Nor did he hesitate to break with Assyrian and Neo-Babylonian population transfers, as witnessed in his edict permitting the Jewish exiles in Babylon to return to Judea.

The third reason for Persia's success was its skill at administration and organization. Darius played a crucial role in reorganizing the imperial administration and finances. Like the Assyrian Empire, the Persian domain was divided into provinces, called *satrapies* (SAY-truh-peez). Each of the twenty satrapies was a unit of

Persian Empire   Vast, prosperous, and law-abiding West Asian empire, from about 550 to 330 B.C., it represented the greatest success yet of a universal kingship. The Persians also built the first great navy.

administration and tax collection. For the first time, taxes could be paid with a stable, official coinage: the gold daric (named after Darius) and the silver shekel. Coins had been invented in the kingdom of Lydia in western Asia Minor in the seventh century B.C. Croesus (r. 560–547 B.C.), Lydia's king, was known for his wealth—hence the expression "rich as Croesus"—before Cyrus conquered him in 547 B.C.

The provincial governors, or *satraps,* were powerful, often quasi-independent figures. But the king tried to keep a firm hand on them. Each province had a royal secretary and was visited regularly by traveling inspectors called "the king's eyes." A network of good roads radiated from the capital cities of Susa and Persepolis. The most famous road, the so-called Royal Road, stretched 1,600 miles from western Iran to western Anatolia (see Map 2.1). Covering the whole distance took most travelers three months, but the king's relay messenger corps could make the trip in a week, thanks to a series of staging posts furnished with fresh horses.

Another unifying element was a society that was law-abiding and prosperous. Darius proclaimed in an inscription that he had fostered the rule of law: "These countries [of the empire] showed respect toward my law; as was said to them by me, thus it was done." Darius and other Persian kings helped create the conditions for compliance and security by taking an interest in the economy. For example, they opened to commercial traffic Persian roads and a canal connecting the Red Sea and the Nile.

Language, too, built unity. Not Persian, which relatively few people spoke, but Aramaic, the most widespread language of western Asia, became the empire's basic language of commerce and administration. A Semitic language related to Hebrew, Aramaic was first used by the Aramaeans (air-uh-MAY-unz), a nomadic people who settled in northern Syria about 1100 B.C. and ruled an area extending into Mesopotamia before succumbing to Assyrian conquest about 725 B.C. The Aramaeans dominated the overland trade routes, which, combined with the simple and easily learned Aramaic alphabet, contributed to the spread of their language. Aramaic facilitated the development of literacy and recordkeeping. Aramaic would become the common language of western Asia for over a thousand years, until Arabic replaced it; Jesus Christ was to be its most famous native speaker.

THE KING OF KINGS

Persia's empire had several weaknesses. First, Cyrus had bequeathed a legacy as a charismatic war leader. Feeling the need to live up to his example, his successors sometimes undertook ambitious and expensive expeditions that failed, such as wars with the Scythians (a tough nomadic people in Ukraine) and the Greeks. Second, however mild Persian rule, however peaceful and prosperous, it was still ruled by foreigners and it still involved taxation. Persian officials, military garrisons, and colonists were found—and were resented—in every corner of the empire. Native resentment, particularly in Egypt, and the independence of certain satraps led to intermittent provincial revolts.

The exaltation of the Persian king served as a counterweight to rebellious tendencies. From Darius on, the Persian monarch tried to overawe his officials with his majesty and might. The "King of Kings," as the monarch called himself, sat on a high, gold and blue throne, dressed in purple, decked out in gold jewelry, wearing fragrant oils and cosmetics, and attended by corps of slaves and eunuchs (castrated men employed in high positions). Although he was not considered a god, he had to be treated with reverence. Persians spoke of the king's *khvarna,* his "kingly glory," a mysterious aura of power. Anyone who came into the royal presence had to approach him with a bow to the ground, face-down.

Impressive as the court ceremonial was, Persian kings were not all-powerful. They were bound by the rule of law and by the considerable power of Persia's

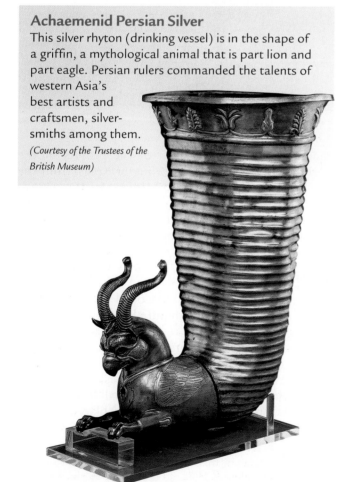

Achaemenid Persian Silver

This silver rhyton (drinking vessel) is in the shape of a griffin, a mythological animal that is part lion and part eagle. Persian rulers commanded the talents of western Asia's best artists and craftsmen, silversmiths among them.
(Courtesy of the Trustees of the British Museum)

Frieze at Persepolis
This sculptured relief lines the stairway to the audience hall of King Darius (r. 521–486 B.C.).
It depicts Persian nobles, well groomed and formally dressed, carrying flowers for the New
Year's feast.   *(Rony Jaques/Photo Researchers)*

proud nobility, on whom they relied to fill the top administrative positions. Competing factions of ministers, wives, concubines, eunuchs, and sons often brought intrigue and discord to court, especially in the fourth century B.C., a time of frequent rebellion.

Royal authority was symbolized in the decoration of the great palaces at Susa and Persepolis, a project begun by Darius I and completed by his son and successor, Xerxes. The Susa palace, the larger of the two, reflected the universality of the empire in the variety of hands that built it. Craftsmen from east and west took part in the construction. (See the box "The Global Record: The Subject Peoples of a Multicultural Empire.") The Persepolis palace, too, displayed the heterogeneity of the empire in its architecture. The palace was placed on a terrace, as in Mesopotamia, but contained columned halls as in Egypt, with Assyrian-style column capitals or tops. In Persepolis, a frieze of sculpted relief panels lining a monumental stairway leading to the palace emphasized the king's vast power. The panels

depict an endless procession of the peoples of the world paying homage to the King of Kings: from the nobility to the Immortals, to Median and Persian soldiers, to tribute-bearing subjects from the ends of the earth. The overall feeling of the scene is static, as if the Persian Empire would last forever.

ZOROASTRIANISM

Like ancient Israel, Persia developed a highly ethical religion in the first millennium B.C. From obscure beginnings, **Zoroastrianism** (zoh-roh-AS-tree-un-izm) became the religion of Persia that persisted until the Muslim conquest in the seventh century A.D. Although largely extinct in today's Iran, an Islamic country, Zoroastrianism still survives in small communities elsewhere, primarily in India. Some scholars argue that

Zoroastrianism   Religion founded about
1000–550 B.C. by the Persian prophet Zarathustra
(*Zoroaster* in Greek). Zoroastrians believe in a supreme
deity and a cosmic contest between good and evil
within each individual.

THE SUBJECT PEOPLES OF A MULTICULTURAL EMPIRE

The Persian Empire ruled more people than ever before, and the kings were proud of that. This inscription from the capital city of Susa, dated probably about 520 B.C., emphasizes the participation of a variety of peoples, from India to Egypt and the Aegean Sea, in the construction of King Darius's palace.

§2. I am Darius, the Great King, the king of kings, king of the lands, king of this earth, son of Hystaspes, an Achaemenid. And Darius the king says: "Ahura Mazda, who is the greatest of the gods, has created me, has made me king, has given me this kingdom, which is great, and which has good horses and good men. By the favor of Ahura Mazda, my father Hystaspes and Arsames, my grandfather, were both alive when Ahura Mazda made me king on this earth. Thus it was the desire of Ahura Mazda to choose me as his man on this entire earth, he made me king on this earth. I worshipped Ahura Mazda. Ahura Mazda brought me aid. What I ordered (to be done), this he accomplished for me. I achieved all of what I did by the grace of Ahura Mazda.

§3. "This palace which I built at Susa: its materials were brought from afar. The earth was dug down deep, until the rock was reached in the earth. When the excavation had been made, then rubble was packed down, some 40 cubits (ca. 65 feet) deep, another (part) 20 cubits deep. On that rubble the palace was constructed. And that earth, which was dug deep, and that rubble, which was packed down, and the sundried bricks, which were molded, the Babylonian people—they performed (these tasks).

§4. "The cedar timber was brought from a mountain called Lebanon. The Assyrian people brought it to Babylon. From Babylon the Carians and Ionians brought it to Susa. The sissoo-timber was brought from Gandara and from Carmania. The gold which was worked here was brought from Sardis and from Bactria. The precious stone lapis lazuli and carnelian which was worked here was brought from Sogdiana. The precious stone turquoise, which was worked here, this was brought from Chorasmia. The silver and the ebony were brought from Egypt. The ornamentation with which the wall was adorned was brought from Ionia. The ivory which was worked here was brought from Ethiopia, and from India and from Arachosia. The stone columns which were worked here were brought from a village called Abiradu, in Elam. The stonecutters who worked the stone were Ionians and Sardians. The goldsmiths who worked the gold were Medes and Egyptians. The men who worked the wood were Sardians and Egyptians. The men who worked the baked brick were Babylonians. The men who adorned the wall were Medes and Egyptians."

§5. Darius the king says: "At Susa a very excellent work was ordered, a very excellent work was brought to completion. May Ahura Mazda protect me, and Hystaspes my father and my country."

QUESTIONS

1. What does Darius consider to be special signs that heaven favored him? Why does he choose these signs?

2. List all the different materials in the palace and all the different ethnic groups that brought them to Susa. What do you think was the most valuable material? Least valuable?

3. How does the variety of peoples and materials demonstrate Darius's power?

Source: LACTOR 16, *The Persian Empire from Cyrus II to Artaxerxes I,* translated and edited by Maria Brosius. Copyright 2000. Reprinted by permission of L.A.C.T. For more information, contact http://www.kcl.ac.uk/humanities/cch/lactor.

Zoroastrian beliefs eventually influenced Judaism and Christianity, as well as Roman paganism and Indian Buddhism.

It is easier to describe ancient Zoroastrianism in broad strokes than in detail, partly because the religion changed radically over the course of its ancient history, and partly because relatively little information survives before A.D. 300. This much is clear: The religion was founded by a great reformer and prophet named Zarathustra (*Zoroaster* in Greek). Zarathustra (zah-ruh-THOOS-truh) lived in eastern Iran. His teachings survive in the *Gathas* ("Songs"), a portion of the Zoroastrian holy book called the *Avesta*. Some scholars date Zarathustra as late as 550 B.C.; others prefer an earlier date, 750 or even 1000 B.C.

Zarathustra's society was dominated by warriors whose religion consisted of blood cults, violent gods, animal sacrifice, and ecstatic rituals in which hallucinogens were eaten. Zarathustra rejected such violent practices in favor of an inward-looking, intellectual, and ethical religion. He favored ceremonies involving fire, considered a symbol of purity. Zarathustra was not a strict monotheist like the Jews, but he did emphasize the power of one god over all people, the supremely good and wise creator of the universe, whom he called Ahura Mazda ("Wise Lord"). Unlike the Jews, Zarathustra considered the problem of evil to be the central question of religion. If god was one, good, and omnipotent, how could evil exist?

Zarathustra's answer might be called *ethical dualism* (dualism is the notion of a grand conflict between good and evil). Ahura Mazda had twin children: the Beneficent Spirit and the Hostile Spirit. Each spirit had made a free choice: one for the "truth" and the other for the "lie"—that is, one for good and the other for evil. Every human being faces a similar choice between good and evil. "Reflect with a clear mind—man by man for himself—upon the two choices of decision, being aware to declare yourselves to Him before the great retribution," says Zarathustra.[1] Indeed, humanity is caught in a great cosmic struggle in which individuals are free to make a momentous choice. Zarathustra distinguished between two states of being: the spiritual and the material. The more a person pursued spiritual purity, the greater was the person's ability to choose good rather than evil.

Zarathustra held a linear conception of history, similar to that in the Hebrew Bible. His religion is marked by a strong *eschatology* (interest in the end of the world) as well as *soteriology* (belief in a savior). He believed that one day, through an ordeal by fire, Ahura Mazda would judge all the people who had ever lived.

Those who had chosen good would be rewarded, and those who had chosen evil would be punished. Then would follow a Last Judgment in which the dead would be transfigured and restored to a glorious bodily existence. There would be, Zarathustra promised, "long destruction for the deceitful but salvation for the truthful." The notion of a savior who would initiate the Last Judgment is an early Zoroastrian belief, if perhaps not a doctrine of Zarathustra himself.

In later centuries, Zarathustra's followers eased his uncompromising rejection of Iranian paganism. Under the leadership of priests, known as *magi* (MAY-jye) in western Iran, the religion changed considerably. Lesser deities beneath Ahura Mazda were added to the Zoroastrian pantheon, in part to suit the religion to the needs of the huge, multicultural Persian Empire.

It is tempting to attribute Cyrus's policy of toleration to the ethical teachings of Zarathustra, but it is uncertain whether Cyrus was Zoroastrian. We are on firmer ground with later Persian kings, particularly Darius I, who had an image of himself alongside Ahura Mazda carved on the face of an Iranian cliff. In an accompanying inscription Darius announces: "For this reason Ahura Mazda bore aid, and the other gods who . . . [exist], because I was not hostile, I was not a Lie-follower, I was not a doer of wrong—neither I nor my family. According to righteousness I conducted myself."[2]

═══════════ S E C T I O N   S U M M A R Y ═══════════

- Iron arms and armor, engineering skill, organizing ability, and brutality all helped build Assyria's empire, at its height in the 660s B.C.

- The Neo-Babylonian kingdom (626–539 B.C.) was famous for its Hanging Gardens and astronomers.

- Phoenicia's outstanding sailors spread the alphabet and established the great city of Carthage.

- From their homeland in Iran, the Persians built the ancient world's largest empire yet, the Achaemenid Empire (ca. 550–330 B.C.).

- Rather than try to "Persianize" the empire, the Persian kings emphasized the variety of peoples under their rule.

- Zoroastrianism, an ethical religion emphasizing the struggle between good and evil, flourished in Achaemenid Persia.

ISRAEL, CA. 1500–400 B.C.

What was the religious experience of ancient Israel, and what is its legacy today?

In the first millennium B.C. a small, often-conquered people turned imperialism on its head. Human achievement is meaningless, they argued; only the power of divinity matters. There is only one god, they said; all other gods are false. The one true god had revealed himself not to the awesome, imperialistic Assyrians but to the less powerful Hebrews—ancient Jews.

They founded the Western tradition of religion. The God of ancient Israel eventually gave rise to the God of Christianity and of Islam as well as of modern Judaism.

The Hebrews, also known as Israelites, had existed as a people since about 1200 B.C. and perhaps for centuries earlier. They spoke a Semitic language.

Israelite Seal
This seal stone, which shows a roaring lion, was used by a man named Shema, an official of King Jeroboam of Israel. The stone was used to make an impression in hot wax, creating a seal on a document. *(Reuben and Edith Hecht Collection, University of Haifa, Israel/Erich Lessing/Art Resource, NY)*

THE HEBREW BIBLE

As literature and as religious teaching, the Bible is the most influential single text in the history of Western civilization. As a source of history, however, it presents difficulties. Much of the Hebrew Bible (called the Old Testament by Christians) is based on written sources that probably date back at least as far as the early Israelite monarchy of about 1000 B.C. Other parts of the Hebrew Bible are probably the product of an oral tradition, and the nature, antiquity, and reliability of that tradition are the subject of much scholarly debate.

Archaeological evidence from the area of ancient Israel, a small number of inscriptions (almost all after 800 B.C.), and some information in Greek and Roman writings provide an alternative source of information. Yet little of that alternative evidence sheds light on the period before about 1200 B.C., and it offers only partial insight into the later period. The historian needs both to pay attention to the Bible and to consider its nature.

The Hebrew Bible reached something close to its current form a century or two before the birth of Christ. It consists of three main sections: (1) the **Torah** (TOE-rah), also known as the Pentateuch, or five books of Moses (that is, the first five books of the Bible); (2) the Prophets, that is, the "historical" books of the early prophets (Joshua, Judges, Kings, and Chronicles) and the books of the later prophets (Isaiah, Jeremiah, Ezekiel, and the twelve "minor prophets"); and (3) the Writings, various books of poetry, proverbs, and wisdom literature.

The books of the Hebrew (and Christian) Bible are canonical: one by one, each was accepted by established authority as sacred. Two key dates stand out in the canonization of the Hebrew Bible: 622 B.C. and about 425 B.C. On the first date, Josiah, king of Judah (see page 44), assembled "the entire population, high and low" to swear to obey "the scroll of the covenant which had been discovered in the house of the Lord" (the scroll probably was Deuteronomy, now the fifth book of the Torah). On the second date, a similar assembly of the people, called by the religious leader Ezra, swore to accept the five books of the Torah that had by then been assembled. The introduction of the Torah (literally, "teaching") made its worshipers into what they have been ever since: "a people of the Book," as the Muslims would put it many years later. The written tradition and literacy became central to the Hebrews.

The Hebrews are the first people we know of to have a single national history book. That book was written not as secular history but as sacred history. It is the story of the working out of God's pact, or **covenant,** with the Hebrews, his chosen people. All ancient peoples told stories of their semidivine foundation. Only the Hebrews imagined the nation created by an actual treaty between the people and their God.

The central fact of human existence in the Hebrew Bible is God's covenant with the Hebrews. Because of the covenant, history has meaning. History is the story of the success or failure of the Hebrew people in carrying out God's commandments. The emphatic focus is on the individual: on individual people taking actions that have not just moral but military and political consequences that unfold over time.

Many of the themes, narrative details, and styles of writing in the Hebrew Bible derive from earlier cultures. The biblical Flood story, for example, seems to have been modeled on a similar flood in the *Epic of Gilgamesh* (see page 17). Biblical poems in praise of God are often similar to Egyptian poems in praise of pagan gods, and biblical wisdom literature (that is, works containing proverbs and rules of conduct) often recalls

Torah   First five books of the Bible. Accepted as sacred by the Hebrews around 425 B.C., it relates the working out of God's pact, or covenant, with the Hebrews, his chosen people.

covenant   As told in the Hebrew Bible, the pact God made with Abraham, the first patriarch of Israel. In return for the land of Canaan and the promise of becoming a great nation, the Israelites agreed to worship no other gods.

Egyptian or Babylonian parallels. In spite of such borrowings, the Hebrew Bible is dramatically different from its predecessors because it subordinates everything to one central theme: God's plan for humanity and, in particular, for his chosen people—the Hebrews.

THE EMERGENCE OF HEBREW MONOTHEISM, CA. 1500–600 B.C.

We first hear of the Hebrews, outside of the Bible, in an inscribed monument of the New Kingdom Egyptian pharaoh Merneptah (r. 1224–1214 B.C.). After a military expedition into Canaan (KAY-nan), pharaoh declared triumphantly that "Israel is laid waste." Most scholars accept this as evidence of an Israelite presence in Canaan, but the question is, how did they get there? The Bible says that the **Israelites** settled Palestine by conquering its earlier inhabitants. Most scholars now reject that account. Archaeological evidence suggests, rather, a more complex process. Perhaps the Israelites were a combination of three groups: armed conquerors, shepherds who gradually entered the country and later settled down to farming, and dispossessed and oppressed Canaanites who rebelled against their masters.

From such sources the Israelites may have emerged. The Bible, however, tells a different story of Israelite origins. Although much of it is credible, none of it is confirmed by nonbiblical sources. Still, the biblical story of Israelite origins has been so influential in later Western culture that we must examine it. If one follows the Bible, Hebrew history began sometime during the period 2000 to 1500 B.C. with the patriarchs, or founding fathers. Abraham, the first patriarch, migrated to Canaan from the city of Haran in northern Mesopotamia. A seminomadic chieftain, Abraham settled on territory north and west of the Dead Sea, where he grazed his herds. Seminomadic clans in the region frequently made long migrations in antiquity, so the biblical account of Abraham and his descendants, Isaac and Jacob, is plausible.

The Bible, however, emphasizes the implausible: Abraham's extraordinary decision to give up Mesopotamian polytheism for belief in one god. This god commanded Abraham to leave Haran; indeed, he made a treaty, or covenant, with Abraham. In return for Abraham's faith, said the god, "As a possession for all time I shall give you and your descendants after you the land in which you are now aliens, the whole of Canaan, and I shall be their God" (Genesis 17:8). Abraham was not a strict monotheist: although he worshiped only one god, he did not deny the existence of other gods. (See, for a comparison, the discussion of Akhenaten on pages 22–23.) Nevertheless, he took a giant step on the road

to pure **monotheism** by coming to believe that only one god rules *all* peoples.

According to the Bible, the next important step took place several hundred years later. In a time of famine in Canaan, many of Abraham's descendants left for prosperous Egypt. At first they thrived there, but in time they were enslaved and forced to build cities in the Nile Delta. Eventually, Moses, a divinely appointed leader, released the Hebrews from bondage in Egypt and led them back toward Canaan and freedom.

The Exodus ("journey out," in Greek), as this movement has been called, is a rare example of a successful national liberation movement in antiquity. Among those who accept its historicity, a date in the thirteenth century B.C. is frequently assigned to the Exodus. According to the Bible, the Exodus marked the key moment of another covenant, this time between the god of Abraham and the entire Israelite people. At Mount Sinai (SYE-nye), traditionally located on the rugged Sinai Peninsula between Egypt and Palestine, the Israelites are said to have first accepted as their one god a deity whose name is represented in Hebrew by the letters corresponding to YHWH. YHWH is traditionally rendered in English as "Jehovah," but "Yahweh" is more likely to be accurate. The Israelites accepted Yahweh's laws, summarized by the Ten Commandments. In return for obedience to Yahweh's commandments, they would be God's chosen people, his "special possession; . . . a kingdom of priests, . . . [his] holy nation."

The Ten Commandments are both more general and more personal than the laws of Hammurabi's Code. They are addressed to the individual, whom they commit to a universal standard. They emphasize prohibitions, saying more about what one should *not* do than about what one should do. The first three commandments establish Yahweh as the sole god of Israel, prohibit any sculpture or image of God, and forbid misuse of the divine name. The next two commandments are injunctions to observe the seventh day of the week (the Sabbath) as a day free of work and to honor one's parents. The sixth and seventh prohibit destructive or violent acts against neighbors, in particular adultery and killing. The final three commandments regulate community life by prohibiting stealing, testifying falsely, and coveting another man's wife or goods. In contrast to the starkness of the Ten Commandments, an enormous amount of detailed legal material is also found in the Hebrew Bible.

Online Study Center **Improve Your Grade**
Primary Source: Moses Descends Mount Sinai
with the Ten Commandments

Israelites   People who settled on the eastern shore of the Mediterranean around 1200 B.C., or perhaps earlier. Their belief in one God directly influenced the faith of Christians, Muslims, and modern Jews.

monotheism   Belief that there is only one God. The Hebrew Bible places this belief as originating about 2000–1500 B.C., when God commanded Abraham to give up Mesopotamian polytheism for belief in one God.

MAP 2.2   Ancient Israel

The Israelites settled in the Canaanite hill country west of the Jordan River and the Dead Sea after 1200 B.C. (*top map*). Control of Israelite territory after 928 B.C. was shared between two monarchies (*bottom map*): the kingdoms of Israel (conquered by the Assyrians in 722 B.C.) and Judah (conquered by the Babylonians in 598 B.C.).

Many scholars doubt whether Hebrew monotheism emerged as early as the thirteenth century. In any case, the Bible makes clear that many ordinary Hebrews remained unconvinced. For centuries afterward, many Israelite worshipers deemed Yahweh their greatest god but not their only god. Unready for the radical innovation that monotheism represented, they carried out the rituals of various Canaanite deities, whom they worshiped on hilltop altars. Forging a national consensus for monotheism took centuries.

From the thirteenth to the late eleventh century B.C., the Hebrews were governed by a series of tribal leaders, referred to as "judges" in the Bible, but eventually the military threat posed by the Philistines (FILL-uh-steenz) persuaded the tribes to accept a centralized monarchy. The Philistines, one of the Sea Peoples, had captured the Palestinian coast in the twelfth and eleventh centuries and seriously endangered Israel. The first Israelite king, Saul (r. ca. 1020–1004 B.C.), had some success against them but eventually fell in battle along with his son, Jonathan. The next king, David (r. 1004–965 B.C.), a former mercenary captain for the Philistines, defeated them decisively.

David was Israel's greatest king. He extended the kingdom into parts of modern Jordan, Lebanon, and Syria and conquered the Canaanite city of Jerusalem, which he made Israel's capital. David's son and successor, Solomon (r. 965–928 B.C.), was also a great king, a centralizer who moved from a loose kingship toward a tightly organized monarchy. His most famous accomplishment was the construction of the magnificent Temple in Jerusalem. The Temple priesthood and sacrifices became the focus of the national cult of Yahweh. Previously, that focus had been a humble, movable wooden chest known as the Ark of the Covenant.

Online Study Center Improve Your Grade
Primary Source: The Wealth, Power, Wisdom, and Weakness of Solomon

Solomon's reign represented the high-water mark of the power of the Israelite monarchy. Under his successors the monarchy was split into a large northern kingdom of Israel with a capital at Samaria and a smaller southern kingdom of Judah (JOO-duh) centered on Jerusalem (see **MAP 2.2**). In 722 B.C., the Assyrians conquered the kingdom of Israel and deported its inhabitants. Judah survived, first as a state controlled by Assyria and then as an independent power.

The religious history of the period of the two kingdoms (928–722 B.C.) and the Judean survivor-state

(722–587 B.C.) is marked by an intense drive toward monotheism. The kings of Judah in the seventh century B.C., especially Hezekiah (r. 715–686 B.C.) and Josiah (r. 640–609 B.C.), aggressively attacked the worship of all gods other than Yahweh and all centers of Yahweh worship other than the Temple in Jerusalem. The kings also began the process of canonizing the Hebrew Bible. Ambitious and independent, Hezekiah joined in a revolt against Assyria that was brutally suppressed in 701 B.C. and almost cost him his kingdom.

The Judean kings could not have succeeded without the help of the prophets, who were prominent from approximately 900 to 500 B.C. Seers uttering divinely inspired predictions were universal figures in ancient religion. No other culture of antiquity, however, has anything like the Hebrew prophets: charismatic, uncompromising, terrible figures who announced God's anger and ultimate forgiveness. The prophets remind us of the most radical spiritual teachings of Israel: absolute monotheism, an insistence on righteousness, contempt for materialism and worldly power, love of the powerless. They often supported the kings but did not shrink from confronting authority and insisting on uncompromising justice. Among them were Amos, a humble shepherd who preached the superiority of righteousness to ritual; Jeremiah, who prophesied the destruction of Jerusalem as punishment for the people's idolatry; and Isaiah, who predicted the coming of a savior who would inaugurate a new day of universal peace and justice.

A characteristic story of the prophets is the confrontation between Elijah, perhaps the most famous prophet, and Ahab, king of Israel (r. 871–852 B.C.). Ahab coveted the vineyard of one Naboth, but Naboth refused Ahab's offer to buy it. Spurred on by his wife, Jezebel, Ahab trumped up charges against Naboth, who was unjustly stoned to death. Ahab then confiscated the vineyard. God sent Elijah to declare to Ahab that, as punishment for committing murder, "dogs will lick [Ahab's] blood" and that of his family (1 Kings 21:19). In a remarkable scene, we witness not only Elijah's courage in confronting the king but also the king's surrender and repentance before Elijah's spiritual authority. Ahab (though not Jezebel) humbles himself and is spared, but his son and successor, King Ahaziah, who is equally wicked, is punished with a fatal injury. The Western tradition of civil disobedience owes much to the courage of the Hebrew prophets.

EXILE AND RETURN, 598–CA. 400 B.C.

The prophets taught the people of Judah how to survive. They correctly predicted ruin and exile and the promise that divine providence would guarantee return. The Judeans clung to this message with remark-

able tenacity. Indeed, they had to, for between 598 and 586 B.C. the Neo-Babylonians conquered Judah, destroying Jerusalem and the Temple. The cultural, political, and economic elite were deported to Babylon. Those who could, fled for Egypt. The dispirited remnant in Palestine shared their land with colonists from neighboring regions, with whom they intermarried and among whom their religion all but disappeared.

And that, given the usual fate of exiled and uprooted peoples in antiquity, should have been that. Yet not only did the Judeans in the Babylonian Captivity persevere in their religious loyalty; they actually returned to Palestine in large numbers.

The Neo-Babylonian rulers allowed Jewish deportees to continue to practice their religion. Jews* in Babylon were not slaves; rather they rented land on royal estates, and some became prosperous. Although some Babylonian Jews assimilated to local ways, many continued a Jewish religious life. Communal worship was observed in open places, perhaps with associated buildings. Some scholars argue that synagogues ("gatherings" in Greek), modest centers of prayer and study that have been the focus of Jewish worship ever since, first emerged in Babylon. It is also possible that the exiles put together the Torah in something like its current form. Elders led the community, while prophets continued to speak out: two examples are Ezekiel, who preached the restoration of the Temple, and the man known to us only as "Second Isaiah" (Isaiah 40–66). Second Isaiah emphasized the universal aspect of the god of Israel, who made empires rise and fall and would bring the exiles home from far-off Babylon.

The Temple in Jerusalem was rebuilt around 515 B.C., only seventy years after its destruction. This remarkable turn of events was possible partly because of the Persians, who conquered Babylon in 539 B.C. and proclaimed the freedom of the Jews to rebuild their Temple in Jerusalem. Still, Persian benevolence would not have been enough if the Judean elite had not kept the faith burning among the exiles.

Second Isaiah's message points to a second important development among the exiles of Judah. As striking as the return to Palestine was the survival of large numbers of Judeans as an unassimilated people outside of Judah—in other words, as Jews. For the first time, membership in a community of worship was divorced from residence. Jewish communities flourished in Babylon, Persia, and Egypt, but the members often chose not to become Babylonians, Persians, or Egyptians. From the sixth century B.C. on, a majority of Jews were living outside Palestine, and the Jewish Diaspora ("dispersion") became a permanent fact of history.

_____

*Strictly speaking, the terms *Jew* and *Jewish* are anachronistic before the fifth century B.C.

THE PEOPLE OF THE COVENANT

Equality, limited government, and the rule of law under God were basic Israelite political principles. Eventually, they would become fundamental political ideals for many in the West, and they would be applied not only to Israelites but to all people.

According to Israelite belief, God made humans in his own image. Thus all individuals were equal in a fundamental sense; all were bound by God's law. A king who disobeyed this law was illegitimate. Indeed, Israel was ambivalent at best about the institution of kingship, which was tolerated as an evil made necessary only by the country's many armed enemies. God's covenant with the Hebrews was a religious contract with political consequences, rendering God the only true king of Israel. Far from being gods themselves or even God's representatives, Israel's kings were merely God's humble servants.

Israelite egalitarianism was restricted to men. Israelite women usually could not own or inherit property, as women could in Hammurabi's Babylon; or sue in court, as women could in pharaonic Egypt; or initiate a divorce, as women could in Classical Athens (see page 76). The powerful goddesses of other ancient cultures were absent in Israel. Women participated in the rituals of early Israelite religion and the original Temple (ca. 940–586 B.C.) but were segregated in a separate women's courtyard in the rebuilt Temple (ca. 515 B.C.–A.D. 79) and absent from Temple ritual. Indeed, the perspective of the Hebrew Bible is predominantly male. Consider just two examples. First, of the 1,426 names in the Hebrew Bible, 1,315 are male; only 111 women's names appear, about 9 percent of the total.[3] Second, only men and boys can bear the sign of the Lord's covenant with Israel—that is, circumcision.

Nevertheless, Israelite women enjoyed honor as mothers and partners in running the household. The Hebrew Bible states that woman (as exemplified by Eve, the first woman) was created as "a suitable partner" for man (Genesis 2:18, 20). Reproduction and hence motherhood assume great importance in the Hebrew Bible; the Lord enjoins humans to "be fruitful and multiply" (Genesis 1:28). The Bible also commands that children honor both their father and their mother: the two parents are equal in parental authority (Exodus 20:12).

The Hebrew Bible sometimes displays sympathy for and insights into the strategies that women used to counter the abuses of male power. Rebecca, for instance, thwarts her husband Isaac's plan to give his blessing to their son Esau. As the eldest, Esau was entitled to this honor, but Rebecca preferred her younger son Jacob, and she saw to it that he and not Esau obtained her husband's blessing.

Only about a half dozen women in the Hebrew Bible served as leaders of Israel, but that is more than in the literature of most other ancient cultures. Deborah (ca. 1125 B.C.), for example, a charismatic Israelite prophet, organizes an army that destroys the forces of a Canaanite commander. In a later book Esther, a Hebrew woman, becomes the wife of a Persian king whom the Bible calls Ahasuerus (probably Xerxes, r. 485–465 B.C.). Esther works ferociously at the Persian court to defeat a conspiracy to wipe out her people, and she saves them. The Book of Ruth (date uncertain) tells the story of a selfless and loyal woman, Ruth, who rescues her mother-in-law, Naomi, from ruin and poverty. The Bible celebrates Ruth as Naomi's "devoted daughter-in-law, who has proved better to you [Naomi] than seven sons." (See the box "The Written Record: Ruth.")

Israelite culture prized women for their cunning, courage, and perseverance—qualities that allowed the people to survive. Military prowess was highly valued in men, but their inner qualities were appreciated as well. Schooled in defeat and exile, many Israelites came to the conclusion that "wisdom is better than weapons of war" (Ecclesiastes 9:18). Thus the Hebrew Bible stresses God's primary interest in goodness of soul: "The Lord does not see as man sees; men judge by appearances, but the Lord judges by the heart" (1 Samuel 16:7). The God of Israel prized righteousness above wealth, might, sacrifice, or ritual.

One might say that Israelite law reflected a similar tension between power and righteousness. On the one hand, just as the God of Israel was omnipotent and jealous, so the law of Israel was meant to be comprehensive and forceful. Capital punishment existed for murder, rape, incorrigible rebelliousness of a son against his parents, adultery by a married woman (both she and her lover were to be executed), a woman's loss of her virginity before marriage, and other offenses. Harsh punishment was mandated for Canaanite towns taken by siege: the entire population was to be killed so as not to corrupt Israel with their religious practices.

On the other hand, by taking intention into account, Israelite law echoed a note already present in Mesopotamia. The so-called Law of the Goring Ox, for instance, allowed a person to go unpunished for owning an ox that gores a person to death, unless the owner knew beforehand that the animal was dangerous. If the owner did know, however, the owner had to be put to death. Israelite law, moreover, demonstrated a belief in the sanctity of human life by prohibiting human sacrifice. An Israelite had to be ready in his or her heart (but *only* in his or her heart) to sacrifice his or her child to Yahweh, as Abraham was willing to sacrifice Isaac when Yahweh so commanded. After ascertaining Abraham's willingness to obey even to the point of sacrificing his son, Yahweh freed Isaac from the altar and supplied a ram as a substitute offering. Israelite monotheism thus rejected human sacrifice, as did the religions later derived from it.

RUTH

Some parts of the Hebrew Bible prohibit intermarriage. The Book of Ruth, however, praises marriage between Judean men and women from neighboring Moab (modern Jordan; see Map 2.2). This excerpt illustrates such unions, as it does the problem of food shortages, which were a special burden for widows.

Once, in the time of the Judges when there was a famine in the land, a man [Elimelech] from Bethlehem in Judah went with his wife [Naomi] to live in Moabite territory. . . .

Elimelech died, and Naomi was left a widow with her two sons. The sons married Moabite women, one of whom was called Orpah and the other Ruth. [After ten years the sons died.] . . . Then Naomi, bereaved of her two sons as well as of her husband, got ready to return to her own country with her daughters-in-law, because she had heard in Moab that the Lord had shown his care for his people by giving them food. Accompanied by her two daughters-in-law she left the place where she had been living and they took the road leading back to Judah.

Naomi said to her daughters-in-law, "Go back, both of you, home to your own mothers. May the Lord keep faith with you, as you have kept faith with the dead and with me; and may he grant each of you the security of a home with a new husband." And she kissed them goodbye. They wept aloud and said, "No, we shall return with you to your people." But Naomi insisted, "Go back, my daughters, go; for I am too old to marry again. But if I could say that I had hope of a child, even if I were to be married tonight and were to bear sons, would you, then, wait until they grew up? Would you on their account remain unmarried? No, my daughters! For your sakes I feel bitter that the Lord has inflicted such misfortune on me." At this they wept still more. Then Orpah kissed her mother-in-law and took her leave, but Ruth clung to her.

"Look," said Naomi, "your sister-in-law has gone back to her people and her God. Go, follow her." Ruth answered, "Do not urge me to go back and desert you. Where you go, I shall go, and where you stay, I shall stay. Your people will be my people, and your God my God. Where you die, I shall die, and there be buried. I solemnly declare before the Lord that nothing but death will part me from you." When Naomi saw that Ruth was determined to go with her, she said no more.

[They returned to Naomi's hometown, Bethlehem, in Judah.]

Naomi had a relative on her husband's side, a prominent and well-to-do . . . [man named] Boaz. One day Ruth the Moabite asked Naomi, "May I go to the harvest fields and glean [collect excess grain] behind anyone who will allow me?" "Yes, go my daughter," she replied. So Ruth went gleaning in the fields behind the reapers. [She met Boaz in his fields.] . . .

Boaz said to Ruth, "Listen, my daughter: do not go to glean in any other field. Do not look any farther, but stay close to my servant-girls. Watch where the men reap, and follow the gleaners; I have told the men not to molest you. Any time you are thirsty, go and drink from the jars they have filled." She bowed to the ground and said, "Why are you so kind as to take notice of me, when I am just a foreigner?" Boaz answered, "I have been told the whole story of what you have done for your mother-in-law since the death of your husband, how you left father and mother and homeland and came among a people you didn't know before. The Lord reward you for what you have done. . . ."

[Eventually, Boaz marries Ruth; their great-grandson would be Israel's greatest king, David.]

QUESTIONS

1. In this excerpt, what are the various ways in which people cope with hunger and famine?
2. Why does Ruth, a foreign widow, stay with her mother-in-law and go to Judah?
3. Why does Boaz admire and eventually marry Ruth?

Source: Ruth 1:1, 3–7, 8–18; 2:1–3, 8–12, in *The Oxford Study Bible: Revised English Bible with the Apocrypha.* © Oxford University Press and Cambridge University Press, 1989. Reprinted by permission of Cambridge University Press, Ltd., England.

SECTION SUMMARY

- The Bible, including the Hebrew Bible (called Old Testament by Christians) and the Christian New Testament, is the single most influential text in Western civilization.

- The central theme of the Hebrew Bible is God's covenant with his chosen people—the Hebrews.

- Hebrew monotheism evolved between the 1200s and 600 B.C. with tribal leaders, kings, and prophets each playing a major role.

● Jews deported to Babylon after 598 B.C. maintained their religion and some returned home after the Persians conquered Babylon in 539 B.C.

● Equality, limited government, and the rule of law under God were Israelite political notions that have greatly influenced the later West.

EARLY GREECE, TO CA. 725 B.C.

What are the Homeric poems, and what light do they shed on the history of early Greece?

The Greeks founded the Western tradition in politics and philosophy. The ancient Greek genius was at its height in the era of the Greek city-states (ca. 700–300 B.C.), but it is already visible in the *Iliad* (IL-ee-ud) and the *Odyssey* (ODD-uh-see), the epic poems of Homer (ca. 725 B.C.). Both are products of the first millennium B.C. Civilization, however, flourished in Greece a thousand years earlier, and Homer's works have roots in this earlier era. Most of what we know of this earlier period, called "Aegean (ih-JEE-un) Greece" by scholars, is based on the discoveries of archaeologists. In particular, archaeology provides the evidence for the rise and fall of two monument-building, literate civilizations: the Minoans on the island of Crete and the Mycenaeans on the Greek mainland (see Map 2.3).

THE MINOANS AND EARLY GREECE, 3000–1375 B.C.

Europe's first civilization appeared in Greece, on the Aegean island of Crete (KREET) around 2000 B.C. From there, civilization spread to the Greek mainland.

Civilization came relatively late to Greece, but in comparison with Egypt and even western Asia, Greece is not a hospitable land. Mountainous, and watered by few rivers, it contains little cultivable farmland. Although pastureland and forest are more abundant, one-third of the country is entirely unproductive. And most of the farmland is to be found in upland plains, which are divided by mountains, making it difficult to work the land efficiently. The south enjoys a mild Mediterranean climate but is very dry. The north has a Balkan climate of hot summers and cold winters. The indented seacoast provides Greece with many harbors. Greece's geography influenced several recurring features of its history: contrasts between seafarers and mountaineers and between north and south, and the challenge of unifying so mountainous a land.

Agriculture preceded civilization in Greece. The first agricultural villages appeared shortly after 7000 B.C., bronze-making skills after 3000 B.C. After 3500 B.C.

"La Parisienne"
This masterpiece of Minoan art shows a priestess in a long robe, with her hair tied in a special knot. A fresco from Knossos, it was dubbed "the Parisian lady" because of its elegance.
(Historical Museum of Crete, Herakleion/Archaeological Receipts Fund)

MAP 2.3   Aegean Greece

The Minoan civilization (height: ca. 1800–1490 B.C.) and Mycenaean civilization (height: ca. 1400–1180 B.C.) flourished in turn in the Aegean region during the second millennium B.C. The center of Minoan civilization was the island of Crete. A mainland people, the Mycenaeans conquered Minoan Crete around 1490 B.C.

Online Study Center **Improve Your Grade**
Interactive Map: Ancient Greece from the Aegean Through the Classical Period

Greece became a supplier of raw materials for the new cities of western Asia. Both on the islands and the mainland, small towns appeared, sometimes fortified with stone walls, occasionally containing substantial stone and mud-brick structures. Between 3000 and 2400 B.C., people living on the Cycladic islands of the Aegean Sea produced exquisite marble sculptures and incised terra-cotta dishes.

Around 2000 B.C. civilization appeared on Crete. Its origins are hotly debated, but we know that it was literate because Cretan writing has survived. It consists of a syllabary, or system of simple syllables that form words, known as "Linear A." Although we know its language is not Greek, we do not know what it is. The island of Crete is located on the sea routes between the Greek mainland, Egypt, and Anatolia. The archaeological record contains many signs of trade and cultural con-

tact between Cretans and nearby peoples, from one of whom, perhaps, the **Minoans** were descended. The evidence for Minoan civilization is concentrated in Crete's palaces—monumental structures that first appeared at various locations on the island around 2000 B.C. After destruction by earthquake, the palaces were rebuilt on an even grander scale, to flourish especially during the period from 1800 to 1490 B.C. Scholars call the palace-builders and their civilization "Minoan (mih-NO-un)," after King Minos of later Greek myth. He was supposed to have ruled a great sea empire from his palace at Knossos (see **MAP 2.3**). What the Minoans called themselves remains a mystery.

Minoans   Society that flourished between 2000 and 1490 B.C. on the Aegean island of Crete, where Greece's first civilization appeared. Their sophisticated culture and economy were administered from their magnificent palaces.

The Minoan palaces were not merely royal residences but centers of administration, religion, politics, and economics. Minoan palace bureaucrats supervised a large sector of the economy, just as their counterparts did in Ugarit, Egypt, the Hittite kingdom, and other ancient societies. The largest Cretan palace, as well as the first to be excavated, Knossos offers a striking example of Minoan civilization. The main building at Knossos covers 3 acres, the associated structures an additional 2 acres. The palace was built around a large central court, 180 feet long by 82 feet wide, probably used for public ceremonies. A mazelike structure surrounded the court. The palace had enormous staterooms, residence quarters, storage rooms, artisans' workshops, and bathrooms, interconnected by corridors, ramps, and stairways. Light wells admitted daylight, and brightly colored frescoes decorated the walls. Cretan architects were aware of palace architecture elsewhere in the eastern Mediterranean and may have borrowed from it, but precisely who influenced whom remains an open question.

The palaces make clear that the Minoans exploited Crete's considerable natural wealth in agriculture and timber. Archaeological and linguistic evidence indicates a widespread Minoan trading network from the Levant to Sicily. A Minoan settlement flourished on the Aegean island of Thera, 70 miles north of Crete (see Map 2.3). This settlement was destroyed sometime in the late 1600s B.C. by one of the most violent volcanic eruptions in history. So huge a catastrophe produced climate changes for several years, which may be evident in the pattern of tree rings in ancient wood as well as in ancient ice preserved in glaciers in Greenland. Future research may allow scholars to offer a specific date for Thera's eruption.

From the lack of fortifications around Cretan palaces and the small amount of arms and armor found in burial sites, it appears that the Minoans lived in relative peace. Minoan frescoes show that women as well as men played important roles in cult and ritual. The women portrayed by Cretan artists are often beautiful, bejeweled, and elegant, the men often graceful and athletic. We see, for example, acrobats practicing the sport of bull jumping. Landscapes and animals are frequently illustrated. A statuette of a priestess holding a snake in either hand depicts Minoan interest in the relationship between humans and the natural world. In short, Minoan civilization gives an impression of peace, prosperity, and happiness. No wonder we sense a somewhat lost-Eden quality about the violent and relatively sudden destruction of Minoan civilization. All of the palaces except Knossos were destroyed around 1490 B.C.; Knossos fell around 1375 B.C.

No shortage of theories has surfaced about the cause of the destruction, but the archaeological evidence strongly supports the notion of an invasion. But by whom? To find the answer, let us look to the Greek mainland.

THE MYCENAEANS, TO CA. 1180 B.C.

A wave of destruction put an end to the Greek mainland's vigorous Copper Age (see page 9) around 2300 B.C. Centuries of relative poverty followed until, around 1700 B.C., signs of power and prosperity appear at a series of burial sites in central Greece and the Peloponnesus. The most dramatic are at Mycenae (see Map 2.3), where the royal burials contain a treasure house of objects in gold and other precious metals. Many of the other cities in Greece that would later become famous, such as Athens and Thebes, were also thriving cities in this period.

The inhabitants of Mycenae (my-SEE-ne), unlike the earlier inhabitants of the Greek peninsula, were Greek-speakers. They and the wider civilization they represent are called Mycenaean (My-suh-NEE-un). Just when and how the **Mycenaeans** got to Greece are tangled questions. Some scholars imagine migration, others invasion. Some believe the Mycenaeans' ancestors arrived as early as 2300 B.C., whereas others think it was not until 1700 B.C., more than half a millennium later.

The Mycenaeans adopted and adapted technology, ideas, and art from their advanced neighbors in Crete, Egypt, Anatolia, and the Levant. The Mycenaeans traded with these neighbors. They also fought with them, for Mycenaean society was dominated by warrior-kings, raiders who exchanged booty to show off their wealth.

Around 1490 B.C. the mainland warriors achieved their greatest feat: the conquest of Crete. They destroyed most of the palaces but spared Knossos, which did not fall until about 1375 B.C. (we do not know the cause of that destruction). The warlike Mycenaeans had conquered the sophisticated Minoans. In turn, the Mycenaeans learned from their subjects and adopted a Minoan-style palace economy.

The Mycenaeans were warriors and sailors. Mycenaean pottery was exported from Sicily to the Levant, but it is not clear if the Mycenaeans themselves were merchants; they may have left trading to others. The Mycenaeans took over a Minoan colony at Miletus and used it as a base for raids. They conquered many Aegean islands and launched shipborne attacks on Anatolia, often in large numbers. Perhaps one such attack was the Trojan War. (See the feature "The Visual Record: The Trojan War.")

Mycenaean civilization was at its height between about 1400 and 1180 B.C. Kings lived in palaces whose

Mycenaeans Militaristic people from the Greek mainland who conquered the Minoans around 1490–1375 B.C. Mycenaean civilization was a center of Bronze Age culture until its destruction around 1100 B.C.

The Trojan War

The "Homeric question," that is, who wrote the *Iliad* and the *Odyssey* and whether the poems are history or myth, is one of the oldest problems in Western scholarship. Archaeology has played a key part in the debate, ever since Heinrich Schliemann started digging in northwestern Anatolia in 1871. He excavated a large man-made mound about three miles from the Hellespont (Dardanelles) and about four miles from the Aegean Sea. Today, almost all scholars agree that he found Troy.

But the results were disappointing even so, especially after new excavations in the 1890s and 1930s. These showed that ancient Troy had a very long history dating back to about 3000 B.C., but it appeared that Troy was a small fort rather than a city. Troy had impressive walls but it was a citadel only of about one half-acre in size. Although it had enjoyed periods of wealth, Troy was apparently poor and unimpressive when it was destroyed by war about 1225 B.C. Contrary to Homer, Troy was neither big nor wealthy.

Now, new excavations at the site of Troy since 1988 have changed the picture. An international team under the direction of the late German archaeologist Manfred Korfmann found evidence that Troy was a large, wealthy, and important city when it was sacked—an event that they redate to about 1210–1180 B.C. We always knew that some houses at Troy were outside the citadel but not how many. Now the archaeologists were able to trace the extent of the Lower Town, thanks in large part to new technology. Electromagnetic prospecting, a technique for identifying underground structures without digging, played a big rule. And the archaeologists dug, too: in particular, they excavated the remains of a defensive ditch outside the Lower Town as well as evidence of a wooden palisade and a wall to go along with the ditch.

The excavators also found important new objects, including the first writing from Bronze Age Troy. This is a scribe's seal stone, writing in Luwian, a language closely related to Hittite. Meanwhile, other evidence, particularly new or newly deciphered Hittite inscriptions, suggests strongly that what Homer called Troy or Ilion was in fact the kingdom called Taruisa or Wilusa. This kingdom was a Hittite ally. Like its neighbors, it lived with the threat of attack from a place that the Hittites called Ahhiyawa. Many scholars say that Ahhiyawa is none other than Homer's land of the Achaeans, that is, Greece.

Look at the bronze figurine pictured here. It is one of the recent discoveries from Troy. Standing about 4 inches high, it shows a man whose right hand is closed in a fist while his left hand is placed on his breast, probably a gesture of prayer. His face is composed of big eyes; a long, straight nose; and oversized ears, all signs of Hittite style. Like other evidence, it suggests Troy's Hittite connections.

The figurine was found in a house in the Lower City, just outside the citadel wall. The house had

Bronze Figurine, Troy   *(Courtesy, Dogan Burda Dergi, Istanbul)*

Arrowheads and Spearheads, Troy
(Courtesy, Dogan Burda Dergi, Istanbul)

painted plaster walls and a separate kitchen wing with a dozen large vases sunk into the earth to provide a kind of refrigerated storage. Finds in this and similar dwellings include imported jewelry and seal stones, fine pottery and silver bowls, as well as textiles and ivories. Clearly, wealthy people lived here. We might imagine that they left their valuables behind because the fire that destroyed Troy left them no choice but to run for their lives.

Hence the new evidence brings us closer to the history behind Homer's poems. Or does it? If the evidence is strong, it is not absolute proof. And skeptical scholars deny even that the evidence is strong. If Troy was a big city, then it should have yielded more buildings and more artifacts, they say. The so-called defensive ditch is too narrow to protect the city and was probably just a drainage canal. And they consider the evidence to be much more ambiguous than the excavators claim.

For example, look at the arrowheads and spearheads recently found outside the citadel walls. One of the weapons is made of bone and the others are bronze. The arrowheads are barbed, which would have made removing them difficult and painful as well as dangerous, because of the possibility of shock or infection. Arrows were important weapons in Bronze Age Anatolia and on Crete, but they were less common on the Greek mainland. Homer emphasizes spears as the main weapon in the *Iliad*.

Everyone agrees that Troy was destroyed by fire, but the skeptics point to lightning or accident as the cause and not to war. Are these weapons evidence of fighting? Some say yes, and they cite as well some 150 sling stones recently found in the Lower Town, which they speculate were used by Troy's defenders. Others are unimpressed, because some ancient cities have yielded much more evidence of war, including hundreds of arrowheads. But Troy is not a virgin site. In antiquity it was destroyed and rebuilt several times after 1180 B.C. Troy became the premier tourist site of the Greco-Roman world, and relics of the Trojan War were highly prized.

The excavations at Troy continue, and archaeologists are hoping to find the city's Bronze Age cemetery. The controversy continues, too, but we can be certain that Homer and Troy will continue to fascinate us.

QUESTIONS

1. Did the Trojan War really happen? What are the arguments for and against?

2. What evidence do the arrowheads offer about Troy?

3. What information does the bronze figurine provide about Troy?

Online Study Center
Improve Your Grade Visual Record Activities

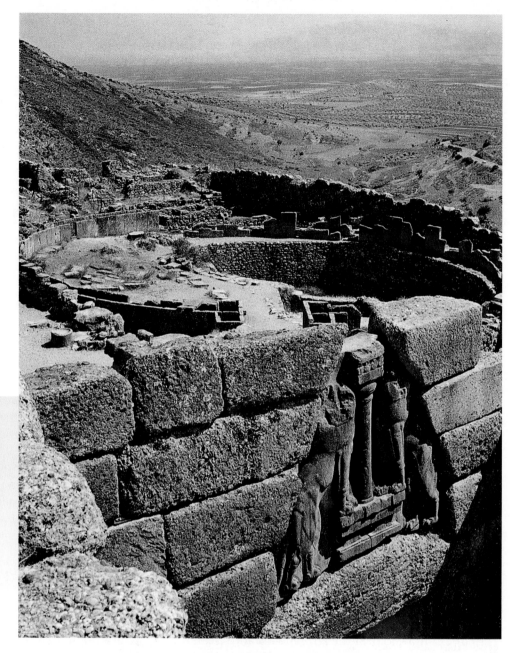

Lion Gate at Mycenae
Carved about 1250 B.C. above the main gate of the citadel's massive walls, the lions—flanking a column, their front paws resting on altars—probably represent royal authority. Inside the walls is Grave Circle B, a royal burial site. *(Dmitrios Harissiadis/Benaki Museum)*

storerooms were crammed with treasures. They traveled through their kingdoms on a network of good roads and could muster rowers and ships. Mycenaean artists excelled at pottery making and fresco painting, gold inlay work and ivory carving. Mycenaean builders constructed palaces, fortifications, bridges, huge vaulted tombs, and sophisticated drainage works.

A Mycenaean kingdom represented a mixed economy and shared power. The king was strong but nobles controlled their own power bases. The royal household was organized to produce textiles, arms, and armor, with raw materials provided by the common people. They furnished some labor as well, but much of the la-

bor force consisted of slaves captured in raids on Anatolia. Our knowledge of the palace economy comes primarily from thousands of clay tablets inscribed by palace scribes around 1200 B.C. They are written in a script scholars call "Linear B," mostly an early form of Greek consisting of a combination of syllabary and ideograms (a system of symbols that stand for words or ideas).

In the thirteenth century B.C., at the height of Mycenaean power, some unknown threat prompted the Mycenaean kings to fortify the palaces at Mycenae and elsewhere with stone walls. By 1180 B.C. most of the fortified sites had been destroyed. Afterward, only a few people continued to live in the old towns. It appears likely that Mycenaean Greece suffered from a combination of internal weakness and foreign invasion similar to that experienced by most of the eastern Mediterranean around 1250 to 1150 B.C., the era of the Sea Peoples (see page 28).

BETWEEN MYCENAE AND THE CITY-STATES, CA. 1100–725 B.C.

The era from the fall of Mycenae to the rise of the Greek city-states was long referred to as the Greek Dark Ages. But that gloomy term is used less often as archaeology increases our knowledge of the period from roughly 1100 to 800 B.C. The evidence does, however, suggest a considerable depopulation in Greece from the twelfth through the ninth century B.C. It seems that rich and poor alike were worse off than in Mycenaean times.

After the destruction of the palaces around 1180 B.C., Mycenaean culture continued to flicker before finally fading in the early eleventh century B.C. New peoples began to move into central and southern Greece around this time. They probably were the Dorians, speakers of a Greek dialect who came from northern Greece. Their material culture was rougher and ruder than that of Mycenae's descendants; it boasts few distinctions besides the iron slashing sword and the long bronze fastener. The Dorians drove out or dominated the Mycenaean Greeks, turning much of central and southern Greece, including Crete, into Dorian centers. Among major settlements, only Athens maintained its independence. The city served as an asylum for Mycenaean refugees, many of whom migrated eastward around 1000 B.C. to the Aegean coast of Anatolia, which was destined to become an important center of Greek culture.

Greece from roughly 1100 to 800 B.C. was largely a poor and illiterate society of small towns and low-level agriculture and trade. Nevertheless, it produced notable painted pottery and preserved an oral tradition of poetry handed down from the Mycenaean era. After 800 B.C. a huge change came over Greece.

First of all, peace contributed to a sharp population rise, and the economy shifted from herding to farming, a more efficient source of food. Greek commerce, too, expanded, thanks in part to the impact of Phoenician traders.

Under pressure from rising population, Greeks founded colonies around the Mediterranean and the Black Sea beginning around 750 B.C. Meanwhile, trade and colonization inspired change at home. Dramatic new experiments in politics, warfare, and culture were attempted. It was the dawn of the era of the Greek city-state. We look at these changes in detail in Chapter 3. Here we focus on a milestone in literary artistry that heralded a new age: the epic poetry of Homer.

HOMER AND HISTORY

Had ancient Greece produced a Bible, the *Iliad* and the *Odyssey* of **Homer** would have been its two Testaments. Only Hesiod (HEE-see-ud), a poet who lived around 700 B.C., had as much influence on later generations, but his poems (*Theogony* and *Works and Days*), though composed in the epic tradition, were shorter than Homer's and arguably less dramatic. But Greece did not have a Bible. Homer and Hesiod were poets, not priests. (As far as we know, the Greek world never had a priestly class comparable to that of Egypt or western Asia.) Although their poems inspired, moved, and educated the Greeks—a large part of a Greek boy's education consisted of learning to recite Homer from memory—they were not divine writ.

Homer was not a historian either. He was a bard, a professional singer of heroic poetry—of songs praising the deeds of the great. Heroic poetry consciously glorifies and magnifies the actions of its subjects.

Yet both archaeology and the evidence of inscriptions suggest that the story of the Trojan War is based on a kernel of truth. Troy really existed: it was a big, wealthy city, strategically located near the entrance to the Hellespont (or Dardanelles), the straits that lead toward the Black Sea. The king of Troy was attached politically to the Hittite empire, and his city had strong trading relations with the Mycenaean Greeks. The people of Troy possibly spoke Luwian, a language closely related to Hittite. Troy was destroyed violently in the period 1210–1180 B.C., possibly by Mycenaean warriors.

Most scholars today would date Homer to about 725 B.C. or later. Although Homer lived centuries after the end of Troy, he resided in an area whose culture had been affected by Troy and its neighbors. Homer lived in Ionia, a region of the central western coast of Anatolia, perhaps in the city of Smyrna. Homer was influenced by the earlier pre-Greek poets of Anatolia. A Luwian poem about Troy may have existed, and Homer could have drawn some of his material from it. In short, there might be more than a little history in Homer.

The author (or possibly authors) of the *Iliad* and the *Odyssey* worked in a continuous poetic tradition going back to the Mycenaean Age. Most scholars accept the theory that this tradition was oral, not written. Like oral poets elsewhere, Homer and his predecessors composed their poems as they sang them, making use

Homer   Greatest ancient Greek poet, credited as the author of the epics the *Iliad* and the *Odyssey,* both written during the eighth century B.C. His dramatic stories inspired, moved, and educated the Greeks.

of a stock of stories and formulaic expressions (such as the Greek equivalents of "swift-footed Achilles" and "grey-eyed goddess Athena"). In fact, Homer may have been illiterate.

Oral tradition gave Homer knowledge of a society that was long gone by his day. His poems are a combination of accurate details of Mycenaean palace life, historical fiction, and details of his own, post-Mycenaean society.

Both in Mycenaean times and in Homer's day, the Greeks were polytheists. The gods of Greece are similar in many ways to the gods of Sumer. They share the foibles and foolishness of humanity but are immortal and far more powerful than humans. The gods figure prominently in early Greek poetry, but they are less powerful than Yahweh, less immediate, and less interested in the inner life of men and women. Already emerging at the beginning of the Greek cultural tradition was the belief that became the hallmark of ancient Greece: that "man is the measure of all things," as the thinker Protagoras would declare in the fifth century B.C.

The Greek gods of the first millennium B.C. were worshiped in Mycenaean times—offerings to them are recorded on Linear B tablets. Because they were thought to live on Mount Olympus, a 9,500-foot-high peak in northern Greece (see Map 2.3), the gods were called the Olympians. Hesiod's *Theogony* tells the story of the Olympians' birth and their triumph over an older generation of deities. The "household" of the Olympians—the early Greek pantheon was conceived of as a noble's household—included Zeus (ZOOS), a skygod and the "father of gods and men," and his consort, Hera; Zeus's brother, Poseidon, god of the sea, earthquakes, and horses; Ares, god of war; and Aphrodite, goddess of love. Also in the "household" were Zeus's children: Athena, goddess of wisdom and cunning; Hephaestus, god of craftsmen; Hermes, god of travelers and thieves; Apollo, god of disease and healing; and Artemis, goddess of the hunt, of maidens, and of childbirth.

Flawed and sometimes unpredictable, the Greek gods often seem childish, but the natural world they symbolized seemed equally inconstant to the ancients. The gods embody the values of a warrior society that put a premium on *aretê* (ah-reh-TAY), or excellence, especially excellence in battle. The heroes in the *Iliad* and the *Odyssey* seek glory through military exploits. Homer's gods reward great warriors, but the gods insist on justice as well. Zeus punishes those who do evil—those who, for example, break oaths or give false judgments or violate the laws of hospitality. In the *Iliad,* the Trojan prince Paris sparks the Trojan War by abducting the beautiful Helen from her husband, the Greek king Menelaus, while he is a guest in Menelaus's household.

In return, the Greeks attack Troy, a wealthy city in northwestern Anatolia. The gods destroy Troy as punishment for Paris's crime.

The *Iliad* and the *Odyssey* focus on the Trojan War and its aftermath. The *Iliad* is set in the tenth year of the conflict. The strain of fighting leads to a quarrel between Greek chieftains: Agamemnon, king of Mycenae and the leader of the expedition, and Achilles (uh-KIL-eez), the greatest Greek warrior. The most prominent Trojans, King Priam and his eldest son, Hector, are less petty but will suffer the greater ruin. The *Odyssey* tells the story of the struggle of the Greek hero Odysseus (oh-DIS-ee-us) to return to Ithaca and to regain his kingship after a twenty-year absence, ten years in the war at Troy and ten years wandering homeward. It also focuses on the loyalty and ingenuity of Odysseus's wife, Penelope, who saves the household in her husband's absence, and the maturation of their son, Telemachus (te-LEH-muh-kus), who helps his father regain his kingdom.

Online Study Center   **Improve Your Grade**
Primary Source: Odysseus Is Rescued by the Princess Nausicaa

Homer puts as much emphasis on brains as on brawn; Odysseus, for example, is not just strong but also smart and cunning. And Homer's gods are no brutes; they believe in justice, hospitality, and respect for parents. Finally, although the Homeric poems focus on the upper classes—and primarily on men—the poems have a strain of sympathy for ordinary people and for women. Indeed, they show sympathy for failure. Homer's heroes court death and often obtain it. Unlike the psalmist of the Hebrew Bible, a Homeric hero walks alone "through the valley of the shadow of death" (Psalm 23:4); he has no god to comfort or redeem him. He knows that the gods make human life hard and full of suffering. Human frailty, however, ennobles Homer's heroes.

Homer's princes are proud and jealous. In the *Iliad,* when Agamemnon is forced by divine command to return his "prize"—a girl captured in a raid—he demands in return the "prize" of Achilles, his greatest warrior—that is, Achilles' girl. Achilles' response is to sulk in his tent while the Trojans nearly defeat his fellow Greeks. In the *Odyssey,* a group of nobles live off the absent Odysseus's estate, waiting to see which of them Odysseus's wife (and supposed widow) might marry. Odysseus's honor demands that he punish them by killing every last one. In both cases, Homer recognizes that the hero goes too far: Achilles' inaction leads to the death of his best friend, and ultimately to his own death; Odysseus's thirst for revenge leads to civil war.

WORLD OF THE HEROES

Homer focuses on the elite. Homeric warriors and their women hold aristocratic values and tend to look down on ordinary people. But society in Homer's day was more level and egalitarian. Except for a small number of traders and craft specialists who lived in towns, most people in the Greece of 725 B.C. lived in villages and hamlets. Most farmed or herded pigs, goats, or sheep, and most were free. The people of each community were called the *demos* (DEE-mus); the leading men, *basileis* (bah-see-LAYS). *Basileis* means "kings," but it is more accurate to understand them as chiefs. No great difference of wealth existed between the basileis and ordinary free farmers.

Although the basileis took the lead in both government and war, the demos played a crucial role. Homer spotlights contests between aristocratic champions, but his vivid battle scenes also include large companies of ordinary men fighting in mass combat in close formation. And if the basileis dominated Homeric government, the demos had at least a small say.[4]

The basic instruments of government that would exist for centuries in Greece appear in the *Iliad* and the *Odyssey:* generals, orators, judges, a council, and an assembly. When making decisions about war and peace, a council of elder basileis consults an assembly of the warriors. In this arrangement we see a fundamental principle of Greek government: the political community should be composed of the warriors.

Let us turn now to the ideology of Homer's basileis, which would greatly influence later generations in antiquity. In the epics, the chiefs make friendships and exchange goods across international boundaries. Greek and Trojan chiefs kill each other on the battlefield but rarely hate each other. Indeed, some are bound by hereditary ties of guest-friendship and so decline to fight each other.

The main activity of Homer's basileis is warfare. The *Iliad* consists largely of a series of battlefield contests. Since women did not take part in battle, they are not presented as men's equals. Yet Homer rarely criticizes women in general, as some ancient Greek writers would in later centuries. Homer's women are weaker than men, but they are neither timid nor helpless. Penelope, for example, personifies female resourcefulness: by refusing to marry until she has finished weaving a shroud for Odysseus's elderly father, and then by unraveling every night what she has woven during the day, she puts the noble suitors off for years. She is as concerned with honor as any Homeric man. By refusing to accept an offer of marriage while Odysseus might still be alive, Penelope does honor to her own good name and to her husband's.

Homeric women play important roles in encouraging men or in bolstering men's courage by playing the foils to their doubts and dreads. In the *Iliad,* Hector overcomes his own fears of battle by hearing his wife, Andromache (an-DROM-eh-kee), express *her* terror at the thought of his dying and leaving her a widow and their infant son an orphan. Moreover, by taking the burden of hearth and home on herself, Andromache allows Hector to define masculinity as making war.

Loyalty to the family played an important role in social relations. A person's obligations to kin included the duty to avenge crime or murder. Friendship, cemented by an exchange of gifts, was another important social institution. Even humble peasants prided themselves on hospitality.

Such values served Homeric society well. Although they would survive in later centuries, they would be challenged after 700 B.C. by the increasing emphasis on public life as the Greek city-state evolved.

SECTION SUMMARY

- The Minoans built Greece's first civilization, centered on the island of Crete around 2000–1375 B.C.

- Greek-speakers arrived in Greece about 2300–1700 B.C. and established the wealthy and warlike Mycenaean civilization on the mainland, at its height about 1400–1180 B.C.

- From 1100 to 800 B.C., between the fall of Mycenaean civilization and the rise of the city-states, Greece was largely poor and illiterate.

- Homer did not live until 725 B.C. or later but an oral tradition of poetry going back to Mycenaean times means that the *Iliad* and *Odyssey* are based on a kernel of historical truth.

- Homer expresses the heroic and aristocratic values of elite men and women that would influence Greek antiquity for centuries.

CHAPTER SUMMARY

What made the first-millennium B.C. empires of the Assyrians, Neo-Babylonians, and Persians so much more effective than earlier empires?

What was the religious experience of ancient Israel, and what is its legacy today?

What are the Homeric poems, and what light do they shed on the history of early Greece?

The first half of the first millennium B.C. witnessed dramatic developments among both the ancestors of the West and its founders. A new form of empire appeared. New military technology, the frank adoption of brutal and inhumane methods, and improvements in administration led to the creation of the Assyrian Empire, stretching from western Iran to Palestine and briefly even to Egypt. After short-lived hegemonies by Neo-Babylonians and Medes, the Persians established an empire that was larger, better organized, and more tolerant than the empire of the Assyrians. Multi-ethnic, far-flung, and claiming to be universal, such an empire would one day be brought into the Western tradition of Rome.

The most important developments of the era, however, were not in commerce, weaponry, or imperialism but in new conceptions of the nature and meaning of human life. The Israelites conquered Palestine and, even after losing it, held on to their identity by means of a tenacious belief in one god. They broke with tradition by insisting that their god was merciful and just. Omnipotent, God gave history meaning and direction. The purpose of life, in the Israelite view, was to serve God by acting righteously. The new religion laid the foundation for Judaism as well as Christianity and Islam. The Jews wrote down their religious and historical traditions in a book that, along with the Christian New Testament, proved to be the most influential single text in the history of the West: the Hebrew Bible.

Homer's epic poems, the *Iliad* and *Odyssey,* which took shape around 725 B.C., would promote heroic and aristocratic ideals throughout ancient Greek civilization. Because he represented an unbroken oral poetic tradition that dated back to Mycenaean times, Homer based his poems on a kernel of truth. The Mycenaean Greek kingdoms were run by the king's household and engaged in military expeditions and raids across the Aegean Sea. Although he was an original genius, Homer borrowed themes and stories from Near Eastern poetry and myth.

LOOKING AHEAD

Homer's poems are splendid but they only hint at the achievements of the Greek city-states in the centuries that followed. As we will see in the next chapter, their successes and failures in such diverse activities as politics and philosophy, war and art, literature and history were so important that they have been the basis ever since for much of Western civilization.

KEY TERMS

Assyrians (p. 33)

Neo-Babylonians (p. 34)

Phoenicians (p. 35)

Persian Empire (p. 36)

Zoroastrianism (p. 38)

Torah (p. 41)

covenant (p. 41)

Israelites (p. 42)

monotheism (p. 42)

Minoans (p. 48)

Mycenaeans (p. 49)

Homer (p. 53)

Online Study Center
Improve Your Grade Flashcards

SUGGESTED READING

Briant, Pierre. *From Cyrus to Alexander: The Persian Empire.* Trans. Peter T. Daniels. 2002. The fundamental introduction to the subject. Essential reading.

Finkelstein, Israel, and Neil Asher Silberman. *The Bible Unearthed: Archaeology's New Vision of Ancient Israel and the Origin of Its Sacred Texts.* 2002. A fascinating overview of what we do and do not know about Bible history to about 440 B.C.

Latacz, Joachim. *Troy and Homer, Towards a Solution of an Old Mystery.* 2005. A thorough discussion of the new evidence that concludes that the Trojan War is likely to have really happened.

Markoe, Glenn. *Phoenicians.* 2001. A concise introduction.

Oates, J. *Babylon.* Rev. ed. 1986. A well-illustrated survey, from the period of Sargon to the Hellenistic Greeks, with a section on Babylon's cultural legacy.

Preziosi, Donald, and Louise A. Hitchcock. *Aegean Art and Archaeology (Oxford History of Art).* 2000. A readable introduction that puts art and architecture in their historical context.

Saggs, H. W. F. *The Might That Was Assyria.* 1990. A readable introductory history celebrating the Assyrians' achievements.

Strauss, Barry. *The Trojan War: A New History.* 2006. The story of how the war is likely to have been fought, based on the latest discoveries.

Taylour, William. *The Mycenaeans (Ancient Peoples and Places).* Rev. and enlarged ed. 1990. A succinct and readable introduction.

NOTES

1. S. Insler, *The Gāthās of Zarathustra: Acta Iranica,* 8 (Leiden: E. J. Brill, 1975), p. 33.

2. Roland G. Kent, *Old Persian: Grammar, Texts, Lexicon* (New Haven, Conn.: American Oriental Society, 1950), p. 132.

3. Carol L. Meyers, "Everyday Life: Women in the Period of the Hebrew Bible," in *The Women's Bible Commentary,* ed. Carol A. Newsom and Sharon H. Ringe (Louisville, Ky.: Westminster/John Knox Press, 1992), p. 245.

4. Kurt A. Raaflaub, "Homer to Solon. The Rise of the Polis: The Written Sources," in The Ancient Greek City-State: Symposium on the Occasion of the 250th Anniversary of the Royal Danish Academy of Sciences and Letters, July 1–4, 1992, Historisk-filosofiske Meddelelser 67, The Royal Danish Academy of Sciences and Letters, ed. Mogens Herman Hansen (Copenhagen: Munksgaard, 1993), pp. 41–105.

3

THE AGE OF THE POLIS IN GREECE, CA. 750–350 B.C.

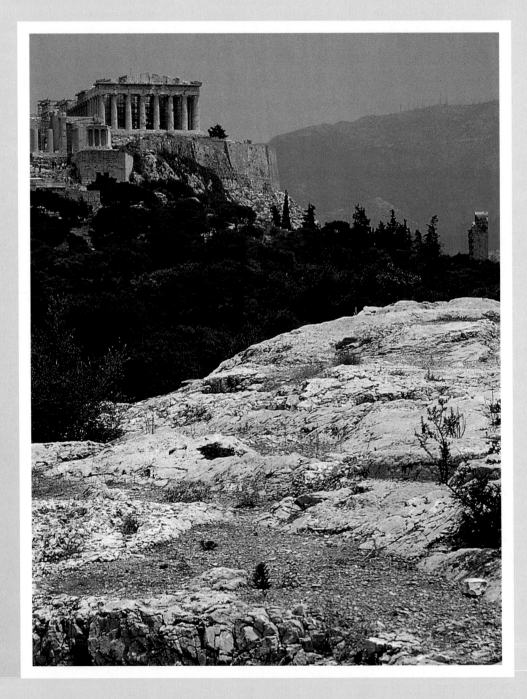

Athenian Acropolis,
with Pnyx Hill in
Foreground
(Photo: Julia M. Fair)

It is dawn. The light reveals a hillside in the city of Athens, a natural auditorium. Its rocky slopes, visible in the photograph opposite, would have been covered, beginning about 500 B.C., with wooden benches facing a platform cut into the rock. The six thousand men gathered there constitute a diverse group, ranging from farmers to philosophers, from dockyard workers to aristocrats. As they take their seats, these, the citizens of Athens, watch priests conducting prayers and offering a sacrifice. Then all eyes turn to the individual who mounts the platform—a herald. His booming voice asks the question that marks the start of business: "Who wishes to speak?" Someone rises to address the assembly. It is the first democracy in history—and the central laboratory in this great experiment in participation.

The assembly meeting recalls the defining features of what was, in its era, the characteristic political institution in much of Greece: the *polis* (plural, *poleis*). Usually translated as "city-state," the polis is better understood as "citizen-state." The polis was the product of communal activities—whether in the assembly, the military, or the theater—undertaken by its members: its citizens. Not every polis was a democracy, but every polis emphasized cooperative activities whose participants enjoyed at least a measure of equality. Every polis also sought a balance between the group and the individual, be that person the speaker, a military hero, or a freethinker.

Balance is a difficult state to achieve, however, and the equilibrium of the polis was frequently disturbed by tension and exclusion. Paradox marked the polis. Greek democracy failed to grant equal rights to women or immigrants, and it depended on slave labor. Relations among poleis were less often a matter of cooperation than of war. Although the Greeks created magnificent religious architecture, a portion of their intellectual elite came to the conclusion that the gods were of little importance in explaining the universe. Whereas one leading polis, Sparta, was a paragon of militarism, obedience, and austerity, scorning the life of the mind, another, Athens, prided itself on freedom and cultural attainments. Yet the Greeks made the most even of such tensions, exploring them in literary genres—tragedy, comedy, history, and philosophy—that focused on the polis as a central theme. Creative tensions also marked Greek achievements in sculpture, painting, and architecture.

CHAPTER OUTLINE

SOCIETY AND POLITICS IN ARCHAIC GREECE, CA. 750–500 B.C.

THE CULTURE OF ARCHAIC GREECE

CLASSICAL GREECE

THE PUBLIC CULTURE OF CLASSICAL GREECE

KEY TERMS

Archaic Greece	Pericles
polis	Socrates
hoplite phalanx	Plato
Solon	Aristotle
Sappho	tragedy
Classical Greece	Herodotus
demokratia	Thucydides

Online Study Center

This icon will direct you to interactive map and primary source activities on the website **college.hmco.com/pic/noble5e**

The era of the polis proved to be a defining moment in Western history. Although the Greeks of this era borrowed much from neighboring cultures, they were remarkably original. In the mid-first millennium B.C., the monotheistic religious heritage of the West first emerged among the Jews. During that same era, the Greeks founded the Western tradition in a broad range of culture, including politics; philosophy; literary genres such as comedy, tragedy, and history; and the visual and plastic arts of painting, sculpture, and architecture.

FOCUS QUESTIONS

What was the Greek polis, and how did it develop in Sparta, Athens, and Corinth in Archaic Greece?

How did Western individualism and rationalism take root in Archaic Greece?

What was Athenian democracy and how did it clash with Sparta in the Peloponnesian War?

How did tragedy, comedy, philosophy, and history all begin and develop in the culture of Classical Greece?

SOCIETY AND POLITICS IN ARCHAIC GREECE, CA. 750–500 B.C.

What was the Greek polis, and how did it develop in Sparta, Athens, and Corinth in Archaic Greece?

Historians usually call the era in Greek history from roughly 750 to 500 B.C. the "Archaic period." In this context *archaic* refers to the style of sculpture in the two centuries before the "Classical period" (480–323 B.C.). **Archaic Greece** was a patchwork of hundreds of separate city-states, tribal leagues, and monarchies (see **MAP 3.1**). Nevertheless, it displayed a distinctive style and outlook not only in art but also in politics, military arrangements, technology, economics, literature, and religion.

Although it was a period of paradox, the Archaic era laid the groundwork for much of lasting importance in Western civilization. Archaic Greece witnessed the simultaneous growth of individualism and a tight community spirit, the emergence of social cohesion despite a continual state of war, and the coexistence of deep religious piety and the West's first nontheistic philosophy. The Archaic period also saw the origin of characteristic Western types of governmental regimes—tyranny, oligarchy, and the first steps toward democracy—and of fundamental Western notions of citizenship and the rule of law.

AGRICULTURE, TRADE, COLONIZATION, AND WARFARE

An observer of ninth-century B.C. Greece would hardly have predicted greatness of that poor, illiterate society of small settlements and low-level trade. Yet, as we saw in the discussion of Homer in Chapter 2, everything began to change in Greece in the eighth century B.C. It was out of these changes that a new communal institution emerged: the **polis** (PO-liss).

Change was a product of peace, which stimulated a sharp population rise. In response, the economy shifted from herding to farming, a more efficient source of food. Seeking new agricultural land in the rocky Greek peninsula, farmers terraced hillsides and drained marshes. The typical agricultural unit was the family farm. Most farms were small and roughly equal in size, apparently a stimulus of social and political equality in Greece.

Greek commerce, too, was expanding. Shortly before 800 B.C., Greeks from the island of Euboea, perhaps following the example of Phoenician merchants and seafarers who had been casual traders in Greece for a century (see page 35), established a trading post in Syria at Al-Mina on the mouth of the Orontes River, at the end of the chief caravan route from Mesopotamia (see **MAP 3.2**). Shortly afterward, Euboeans established another trading post in the west, on an island in the Bay of Naples in Italy. In both east and west, Greek merchants sought iron and luxury goods. What they offered in return was probably silver, of which ancient Greece had rich deposits, and slaves.

From commerce it was but a short step to colonization in order to siphon off the extra mouths created by population growth. In colonization as in trade, the Greeks may have followed the example of the Phoeni-

---

Archaic Greece Period of ancient Greek history from around 700 to 500 B.C.

polis Term for an ancient Greek city-state, a system that reached its height around 700–300 B.C.

cians, who had begun establishing colonies probably in the ninth century B.C. Between about 750 and 500 B.C., the Greeks founded colonies throughout the Mediterranean and the Black Sea, planting nearly as many cities as already existed in Greece (see Map 3.2). Colonization in Italy and Sicily began in earnest around 750 B.C.; in the Chalcidice (kal-SID-uh-see) in the northeast Aegean perhaps a generation later; in the Sea of Marmara about 680 B.C.; in North Africa around 630 B.C.; and in the Black Sea about 610 B.C. In the far west, Massalia (modern Marseilles) was established about 600 B.C. Southern Italy and Sicily, whose climate and landscape recalled the Aegean, were especially intense areas of Greek settlement, so much so that the Romans later called the region *Magna Graecia* ("Great Greece"). In the long run, Greek colonization proved to be of great importance for the spread of urban civilization westward, especially into Italy.

One important consequence of foreign contact was the introduction to Greece of the alphabet, borrowed from the Phoenicians. The first datable examples of the Greek alphabet were inscribed on pots in about 750 B.C. The alphabet spread rapidly and widely in the next century. Literacy underlay the achievements in poetry, philosophy, and the law that Archaic Greece has left behind. However, so few people at the time could read and write well that ancient Greek culture remained primarily an oral culture.

Another consequence of foreign contact was the introduction of new military technology, which the increase in wealth allowed the Greeks to adopt. Social changes, furthermore, fostered new tactics on the battlefield. The result was the **hoplite phalanx** (HOP-lite FAY-lanks), a tightly ordered unit of heavily armed, pike-bearing infantrymen. The phalanx not only became the dominant military force in Archaic Greece, but, with relatively few changes in equipment and tactics, it remained supreme on land in Greece, western Asia, and other Mediterranean regions for centuries, until its defeat by a Roman army in 197 B.C.

The phalanx emerged through a process of evolution rather than in a revolutionary leap. Before 800 B.C., single combat among the *basileis* (elite) appears to have decided battles. Around 800 to 750 B.C. armies began to include more men, fighting in close formation. Around 700 B.C. came new armaments. The result was the phalanx. The heavily armed infantryman (hoplite) of the fighting unit (phalanx) wore bronze armor on his shins and chest and a bronze helmet slit with a narrow opening for eyes and mouth. He carried a heavy wooden shield in his left hand. His weapons were a pike—a heavy, wooden, iron-tipped thrusting spear at least 9 feet long—and a short, iron stabbing sword.

hoplite phalanx   Battlefield tactic of Archaic Greece that relied on a tightly ordered unit of heavily armed, pike-bearing infantrymen.

ca. 750 B.C.	Greek colonization of Magna Graecia begins
ca. 725 B.C.	Sparta conquers Messenia
ca. 675 B.C.	Pheidon becomes tyrant of Argos
ca. 625 B.C.	Sappho active as poet
594 B.C.	Solon is archon in Athens
ca. 560 B.C.	Pisistratus becomes tyrant of Athens
508 B.C.	Cleisthenes begins reforms in Athens
499 B.C.	Ionians revolt against Persia
490 B.C.	Battle of Marathon
480–479 B.C.	Persia invades Greece
477 B.C.	Delian League founded
460–429 B.C.	Pericles at peak of power
458 B.C.	Aeschylus's *Oresteia* first performed in Athens
431–404 B.C.	Peloponnesian War
399 B.C.	Trial of Socrates
395–386 B.C.	Corinthian War
371 B.C.	Battle of Leuctra

The men of the phalanx were arranged in close ranks, normally four to eight deep. Soldiers stood together in line, each man's shield overlapping his neighbor's. Hoplite combat involved set battles—head-to-head, army-against-army, all-or-nothing affairs—rather than individual skirmishes or guerrilla raids. Too unwieldy for Greece's mountains, the phalanx fought only in the plains. Battle usually consisted of an initial charge, followed by a grueling contest. The men in the front line pounded the enemy with their pikes, while the men in the rear pushed forward. Finally, one side would give way and run. The victors stayed and erected a trophy.

Greek hoplite warfare rested on deep societal roots. Only independent men of means could afford hoplite armor. Thanks to the spread of the family farm, such men were common in Greece by around 700 B.C. Hoplites were amateur soldiers. Most were full-time farmers outside the fighting season, which lasted only for the summer months. The notion of the farmer-soldier, independent and free, would have a lasting impact on Western political thought. So would the warrior values of what became a way of life in Greece.

Aretê, now translated as "excellence" or "virtue" but originally meaning "warrior prowess," was a central concept for the Greeks. In Homer a warrior fought mainly for personal and familial honor (see page 55). By around 650 B.C. aretê referred also to the community. According to the poet Tyrtaeus (ca. 650 B.C.), the

MAP 3.2 Phoenician and Greek Colonization

Both the Phoenicians (beginning perhaps after 900 B.C.) and the Greeks (beginning around 750 B.C.) established numerous colonies on the coasts of the Mediterranean and Black Seas.

Online Study Center **Improve Your Grade**
Interactive Map: Phoenician and Greek Colonization

ideal soldier not only fights bravely but "heartens his neighbor by his words." Should he die, his death brings glory not only to his father but also to his city and his countrymen. Although the battlefield remained the favored arena for displays of aretê, the assembly or the council house became increasingly acceptable as an alternative.

Greek women did not serve as soldiers, but they were expected to encourage their men to fight and die for the city. Women were praised for bearing and raising sons to serve as future soldiers.

MAP 3.1 Archaic and Classical Greece

The region of the Aegean Sea was the heartland of Greek civilization around 750 to 350 B.C. The mountainous terrain, rugged coastline, and numerous islands encouraged political fragmentation.

Online Study Center **Improve Your Grade**
Interactive Map: Ancient Greece

EMERGENCE OF THE POLIS

Paradoxes abound in the origins of the polis. The polis was both a product of the changes of the eighth century B.C. and a stimulus for change. As an urban settlement, the polis existed as early as the ninth or even the tenth century B.C., but its intense communal spirit did not emerge until around 700 B.C. In agriculture, the most important single profession, the prevalence of the family farm created a kind of rough social equality, which was reflected in a cultural emphasis on equality. Yet the polis was marked by social inequality as some grew rich on the profits of trade.

Polis came to denote not just a city but the community as a whole, corresponding roughly to a country or nation. One crude gauge of the centrality of the polis is the number, not to mention the significance, of words the Greeks derived from it: among them, *polites* (citizen), *politeia* (constitution), *politeô* (to govern), *ta politika* (politics), and *politikos* (politician).

Most poleis (PO-lays) were small, many less than 100 square miles in size. Athens was one of the largest.

Hoplites
A detail from a Corinthian vase of 625 to 600 B.C. shows pike-wielding hoplites closed in battle over a fallen comrade. In this image as elsewhere, Greek artists rendered warriors seminude and fighting in small groups, but in reality hoplites went into battle wearing heavy armor and fought in large units.
(Louvre/R.M.N./Art Resource, NY)

Its territory, known as Attica (see Map 3.3), covered 1,000 square miles (approximately the size of Rhode Island). At its height (ca. 430 B.C.) the population of Athens was about 400,000, but a typical polis contained only between 5,000 and 10,000 people. The philosopher Aristotle (AR-is-tot-il) (384–322 B.C.) wrote that an ideal polis should be small enough that the citizens know one another personally.

The polis consisted of two parts: the urban area, which usually was tiny, and the surrounding countryside, where most people lived. From the earliest times, the urban public space included both a defensible hill (preferably with a water supply), called a "high city" (*acropolis* [uh-CROP-uh-liss]), and a "gathering place" (*agora* [AH-go-rah]), used as a marketplace and meeting place. At least one temple usually served as a focal point. After around 500 B.C. stone buildings, including council houses, theaters, covered porticoes, gymnasia, and baths, became increasingly common.

What distinguished the early polis, however, was not its buildings but its spirit. As the poet Alcaeus (b. ca. 630 B.C.) puts it, "Not houses finely roofed or the stones of walls well-built, nay nor canals and dockyards, make the polis, but men able to use their opportunity."

The Greeks came to call the polis a "common thing" (*koinon*). It was a shared commonwealth. It belonged to its people, not to a few nobles or to a king or a god. As early as about 700 B.C., important public documents were inscribed in stone. Acts of state were attributed not to a personified polis but to the community—for example, not to Thera but to "the Thereans," not to Sybaris but to "the Sybarites." The emphasis is on the plurality.

The emphasis was on equality as well. The early polis developed an ethos of measure and moderation. The ideal citizen was thought to be neither rich nor poor but of moderate means. Women were generally not considered citizens and were excluded from taking part in politics. Yet women's behavior was considered important to the polis. Laws against extravagant jewelry or unrestrained mourning (mourning the dead was considered women's work), for example, were put into place in some poleis.

In theory, all citizens were supposed to be roughly similar, but this was not always true in practice, as the politics of the early polis makes clear.

CORINTH AND TYRANNY

Trade and colonization inspired change at home, for one thing, making increasing numbers of Greeks into seafarers. In antiquity, ships moved more quickly and cheaply than land transport; thus seafaring usually accelerated the rate of change. One such change was Greece's growing wealth. Corinth became the wealthiest city in mainland Greece. With its location in central Greece near both the Corinthian Gulf and the Saronic Gulf, Corinth became a great seaport. Its rich farmland offered agricultural produce for export. Its luxuries made it a tourist destination. And Corinth was in the forefront of political change.

Political change followed economic trends. Although some Greeks shot to the top of the economic ladder, many of these newly rich lacked the status of the *basileis,* the elite of landowning families who monopolized political power and honor. In order to claim a share, the newly rich seem to have made common cause with the independent farmers who staffed the hoplite phalanx. The result was tyranny.

Tyrant, a term borrowed from the East, possibly from Lydia (a wealthy kingdom in Anatolia), originally referred not to an arbitrary and oppressive ruler but rather to a champion of the people. Having overthrown a narrow and entrenched aristocracy, tyrants were popular at first. *Tyrant* did not become a pejorative word before roughly 550 B.C., when the people soured on the second and third generation of tyrants.

Greek tyranny began in Argos, a polis in the northeastern Peloponnesus (pel-uh-puh-NEE-suss), around 675 B.C. (see Map 3.1). The first tyrant was an Argive named Pheidon. By 660 B.C. tyranny had spread to nearby Corinth. Over the course of the seventh and sixth centuries B.C., all the major Greek poleis except Sparta became tyrannies.

Sources of evidence for the first tyrannies are poor, and much about the tyrants is debated by scholars. Yet it does seem that in the seventh century B.C., wealthy men who had been denied political power rose on the shoulders of the hoplites and overthrew a narrow elite. They set up one-man rule, not in the name of the basileis, but on behalf of a much broader group: the prosperous farmers who fought in the phalanx.

Much of what the tyrants did, especially in the first generation, was popular and progressive. They stimulated the economy by founding colonies on trade routes, standardizing weights and measures, and encouraging the immigration of skilled craftsmen from other poleis. Corinth under the tyrant Cypselus (r. ca. 657–625 B.C.), for example, reached a peak of prosperity. Tyrants built temples and instituted festivals, providing both jobs and leisure-time activities.

When tyrants passed power on to their sons, however, the second generation tended to rule oppressively. Buoyed by the discontent of the demos, the basileis regrouped and tried to take back power. Thrasybulus of Miletus (ca. 600 B.C.), one second-generation tyrant, advised accordingly: to maintain power, a tyrant should "lop off the tallest ears of grain"—that is, execute or exile aristocrats in order to deny leaders to the opposition. But the tide of discontent was not to be stopped. Few tyrannies lasted beyond the third generation, when they were overthrown and replaced by oligarchy (literally, "rule by the few") or, less often, by democracy (literally, "power of the people"). By 500 B.C. tyranny had disappeared from most of Greece.

SPARTA

Located in Laconia, a fertile valley in the south-central Peloponnesus, in the southern part of mainland Greece, Sparta seemed destined by geography for prosperity but not for glory. It was positioned not at a crossroads or beside a great harbor but rather by rugged mountains that might have left it isolated (see Map 3.1). Yet Sparta proved to be a powerful model of citizenship and constitutionalism, virtue and community, austerity and militarism.

The history of Sparta is not easy to write. Sparta was a closed military society, contemptuous of book learning, suspicious of foreigners, and secretive toward the outside world. Scholarship has lifted the veil a little, however. For example, Spartans believed that their unique system had been created at a stroke by the legendary lawgiver Lycurgus, who is supposed to have lived (according to the most common version) in the eighth century B.C. and whose charter for Sparta was a divine command. Nowadays, scholars argue for gradual innovations in Sparta rather than revolutionary change, for a process beginning around 650 B.C. and continuing for generations. And it is by no means clear that there ever was a Lycurgus. Let us consider the question of origins.

Government The foundations of the Spartan regime were laid around 650 B.C., when a three-part class system emerged. Helots (HEL-uts), unfree laborers who worked the land for their masters, were at the lowest level. In the middle ranks were *perioikoi* (roughly, "neighbors"), who were free but under the thumb of the highest class. At the top stood Similars, who were the only full citizens. We do not know the number of helots, but we do know that they vastly outnumbered the other two classes.

Compared with individuals of the other classes, a Similar had a good life. If male and over age 30, he had the right to attend the assembly and to hold public office. Each male Similar, moreover, was given a basic allotment of land worked by helots, which freed him to fight. As the name implies, Similars were alike but not equal. Wealthy Similars owned more land than the basic allotment.

Although Sparta is remembered as a conservative society, the idea of a large group of men sharing power was radical in its day. When the system began around 650 B.C., Similars numbered about nine thousand. What gave them their clout and prestige? The Similars were probably hoplites, the backbone of Sparta's army.

In the mid-seventh century B.C., Sparta was even more dependent on its army than was the average polis; the reason is the helots. Most helots were Messenians, whose fertile territory had been conquered by Sparta in about 725 B.C. Although the Messenians were Greeks, they were forced to work for the conquerors. Sparta profited, but it now faced a security problem. The restive Messenian helots had to be policed, and a dramatic revolt sometime between 675 and 650 B.C. almost succeeded in expelling the Spartans. To keep Messenia, Sparta needed a crack army; to get that, it needed to train, support, and glorify its soldiers. The political and economic result was to make all Spartan hoplites into Similars.

Sparta was no democracy, however. The ancients classified the Spartan government as "mixed" because it distributed power among the Similars through a combination of monarchy, oligarchy (that is, rule by an elite few), and popular government. The assembly of Similars was the popular element in the regime, but its powers were limited. Real power was shared among those Similars who were kings, elders, and *ephors* (overseers), men generally belonging to a few wealthy families.

Society The elite did not lead lives of luxury, however, at least not after around 550 B.C., when austerity became the order of the day. Society was reordered to promote the discipline needed to keep control of the helots. For example, the Spartans' diet was famous for its simplicity. The preferred food was a black broth of pork cooked in its own blood and spiced with salt and vinegar. To discourage consumption, Sparta issued no coins; the official "currency" consisted of heavy and clumsy iron skewers. Since the outside world was considered corrupt, Sparta engaged in little trade and admitted few foreigners to its territory—and those who were admitted were subject to periodic expulsion.

Whereas other poleis offered little or no formal public education, Sparta schooled its sons from childhood to be soldiers—a system known as the *agoge* (ah-go-GAY) ("upbringing"). Limited to male Similars, the agoge created a life cycle unique in Greece. At birth babies were examined by public inspectors. Those who were considered deformed or unfit were "exposed"—that is, they were abandoned without food or shelter. The victims might die, but they might also be sold into slavery or even secretly adopted. (Other Greeks also practiced exposure of infants, but the choice was a family matter, not public policy.) Surviving children were raised at home up to the age of 7, at which point boys left the family to be boarded with a "herd" of their age-mates. For the eleven years from age 7 to age 18, a boy went through rigorous training. On the theory that good soldiers should be strong and silent, boys learned only enough reading and writing for practical ends—for example, to transmit messages to and from military headquarters.

Many boys between the ages of 18 and 20 served in the *krypteia* (secret service), living secretly in the hills of Messenia, where they survived by hunting, foraging, and stealing. They spied on the ever rebellious Messenian helots, whom they could kill freely because every year Sparta declared war on helots. By age 20 all Similars had become hoplites, and they continued to serve in the army until age 60. Supported by helot labor, they devoted all their time to fighting and training the next generation.

Ironically, Sparta offered more opportunities outside the home to elite women than did other Greek states. For example, unlike most Greek girls, Spartan girls received a public education—limited, however, to physical training, which was thought to strengthen females for childbearing. Still, the sight of girls running, wrestling, and throwing the discus and javelin, which was common in Sparta, was unthinkable elsewhere in Greece. So was Sparta's unique recognition of the risks of maternity. Like Spartan men who died in battle, Spartan women who died in childbirth were allowed to have their names inscribed on their tombstones. All other Spartan burials were anonymous.

Spartan women were relatively more independent than women elsewhere in Greece. With the men consumed by military training or warfare, women ran the day-to-day operations of life, controlling the helot farmworkers and servants, and raising the girls and the very small boys. Women married around age 20, men around

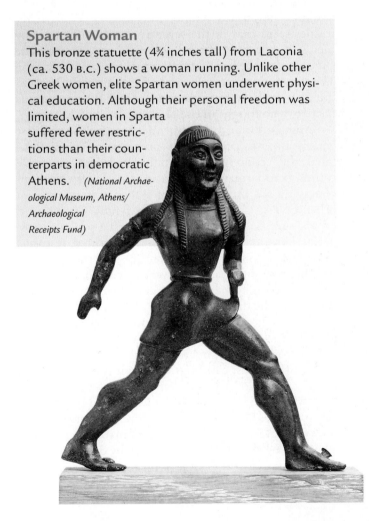

Spartan Woman
This bronze statuette (4¾ inches tall) from Laconia (ca. 530 B.C.) shows a woman running. Unlike other Greek women, elite Spartan women underwent physical education. Although their personal freedom was limited, women in Sparta suffered fewer restrictions than their counterparts in democratic Athens. *(National Archaeological Museum, Athens/ Archaeological Receipts Fund)*

SPARTAN WOMEN

Spartan women were famous in antiquity for their remarkable freedom, but male observers differed as to whether the results were good or bad. In the following excerpts, Aristotle (384–322 B.C.) criticizes Spartan women, whereas Plutarch (ca. A.D. 50–120), a Greek scholar living in the Roman Empire, praises them.

Aristotle Complains

. . . The legislator [Lycurgus] wished the city as a whole to be hardy, and this is manifest in terms of the men; but he thoroughly neglected it in the case of the women, who live licentiously in every respect and in luxury. Wealth will necessarily be honored in a regime of this sort, particularly if they are dominated by women, as is the case of most stocks that are fond of soldiering and war. . . . This was the case with the Spartans, and many matters were administered by the women during the period of their [imperial] rule [405–371 B.C.]. And yet what difference is there between women ruling and rulers who are ruled by women? For the result is the same. . . .

Now this laxness concerning women appears to have arisen among the Spartans in a way that is quite reasonable. They spent much time away from their own land when they were at war. . . . As for the women, they say Lycurgus attempted to lead them toward the laws, but they were resistant, and he gave it up. . . . That what is connected with the women is not finely handled would seem not only to create an inappropriateness in the regime in its own terms, as was said earlier, but to contribute to their greed. For next to what has just been said, one must censure what pertains to the disparity in possessions. For it has happened that some of them possess too much property, and others very little; hence the territory has come into the hands of a few. . . . Indeed, nearly two fifths of the entire territory belongs to women, both because many have become heiresses and because large dowries are given.

Plutarch Counters

Aristotle claims wrongly that he [Lycurgus] tried to discipline the women but gave up when he could not control the considerable degree of license and power attained by women because of their husbands' frequent campaigning. . . . Lycurgus rather showed all possible concern for . . . [women] too. First he toughened the girls physically by making them run and wrestle and throw the discus and javelin. Thereby their children in embryo would make a strong start in strong bodies and would develop better, while the women themselves would also bear their pregnancies with vigour and would meet the challenge of childbirth in a successful, relaxed way. He did away with prudery, sheltered upbringing and effeminacy of any kind. He made young girls no less than young men grow used to walking nude in processions, as well as to dancing and singing at certain festivals with the young men present and looking on. . . .

There was nothing disreputable about the girls' nudity. It was altogether modest, and there was no hint of immorality. Instead it encouraged simple habits and an enthusiasm for physical fitness, as well as giving the female sex a taste of masculine gallantry, since it too was granted equal participation in both excellence and ambition.

QUESTIONS

1. According to Aristotle, how and why do Spartan women misbehave?

2. How does Plutarch defend Spartan women?

3. Which author is more convincing? Why?

Sources: Aristotle, *The Politics,* trans. Carnes Lord. Reprinted by permission of the publisher, The University of Chicago Press; Plutarch, "Life of Lycurgus," in *Plutarch on Sparta,* trans. Richard J. A. Talbert (Harmondsworth, England: Penguin, 1988), p. 24. Translation copyright © Richard J. A. Talbert. Reproduced by permission of Penguin Books Ltd.

---

30. Newlyweds were supposed to spend only enough time together to produce offspring. Often left on their own without a husband's interference, and having been schooled in assertiveness by youthful physical training outdoors, Spartan women also had the advantage of being able to inherit property, unlike Athenian women. (See the box "The Written Record: Spartan Women.")

Beginning around 550 B.C., Sparta used its military might to build up a network of alliances (dubbed the "Peloponnesian League" by scholars) in the Peloponnesus and central Greece. It may seem paradoxical that a society that feared foreigners, as Sparta did, became the *hegemon* (HEJ-uh-mahn) (literally, "leader") of an extensive alliance system, but Sparta's fear made its leadership slow and careful. Sparta intervened in the wider world only to prevent threats from arising on the horizon, and usually only after a great deal of debate and with the utmost caution.

By around 500 B.C. all of the Peloponnesian poleis except Argos had alliances with Sparta, and in central

Greece Thebes came aboard shortly thereafter. Allies swore "to follow Sparta wherever it may lead and to have the same friends and enemies." Until its breakup in the aftermath of the Peloponnesian War (431–404 B.C.; see page 79), the Peloponnesian League was the dominant land power in Greece and, after the defeat of Persia in 480 B.C., in the entire eastern Mediterranean.

Sparta exemplified community spirit and respect for law. The people of Sparta, as the historian Herodotus (he-ROD-uh-tus) (ca. 485–425 B.C.) quotes a Spartan king, "are free . . . , but not entirely free; for they have a master, and that master is Law, which they fear." Sparta was also an exemplar of equality—limited equality, to be sure, but equality extended to a wider group than ever before in Greece. The notion of the Similars, moreover, contains the germ of the idea of the citizen: a free member of the political community who, unlike a subject, has rights as well as duties. Few other poleis could match the stability and sense of civic duty fostered by Sparta. In the realms of equality and citizenship, however, Sparta was eventually outstripped by Athens. In the realm of liberty, Athens wrote a new chapter in Western history.

EARLY ATHENS

Around 650 B.C. the basileis of the Pedion, or Attic, Plain, who proudly called themselves the Eupatrids ("well-fathered men"), ruled Athens (see **MAP 3.3**). They served in one-year magistracies and afterward became life members of the Areopagus (ar-ee-OP-uh-gus), a council of elders named for its meeting place on the "hill of Ares." By its prestige, this aristocratic council held the lion's share of power, both in politics and in justice, for it also served as a court. The demos (DEE-mus) (the people) met in an assembly. Probably from early times on, the assembly had, in theory, supreme lawmaking power as well as authority over war and peace, but voting was by shouting, and few people challenged Eupatrid wishes.

By 632 B.C. the aristocrats faced trouble in Athens as elsewhere because of corruption, economic change, and assertive hoplites. A failed attempt that year to establish a tyranny left the forces for change eager. In 621 B.C. a loose coalition opposed to Eupatrid rule forced a codification of the laws, which were then issued in writing. This Code of Draco (DRAY-co), named for its main drafter, was infamous for its harsh provisions (hence the adjective *draconian*); it was written, a later commentator suggested, "not in ink but blood." Yet Draco's Code seems only to have whetted an appetite for change. A wealthy non-Eupatrid elite of hoplites was emerging, grown rich exporting olive oil. Some were merchants; most were prosperous farmers. They now wanted political power. As for ordinary Athe-

nians, they typically worked small family farms. Over the years, bad harvests and soil exhaustion had sent many into debt. Those who had pledged their land as collateral became known as *hektemoroi* ("sixth-parters"), probably because they owed one-sixth of their crops to their creditors. Other farmers sank even further into debt and had only themselves or their children as collateral. Some ended up as slaves, sometimes sold abroad. Because both rich and poor Athenians had grievances against the Eupatrids, revolution was in the air.

Online Study Center **Improve Your Grade**
Primary Source: A Draconian Response to Homicide

Enter **Solon** (ca. 630–560 B.C.), who was appointed to the emergency position of sole *archon* (chief officer) for one year, probably 594 B.C. A Eupatrid who had become a merchant, Solon (SO-lun) understood both the old and the new elite, and he was sympathetic to ordinary Athenians as well. As his surviving writings show, Solon was a moderate. He could have become tyrant, but he preferred to be a mediator; as such, he said, he "stood with a strong shield before both parties [the common people and the powerful] and allowed neither one to win an unfair victory."[1]

Solon's reforms were comprehensive, spanning both economics and politics. Many of his measures were aimed at encouraging Athenian trade, and they led to a commercial boom. More important, Solon helped ordinary people by the "shaking off of burdens," measures that abolished the institution of *hektemorage* and probably canceled some debts. He also abolished the practice of making loans on personal surety and set up a fund to redeem Athenians who had been sold into slavery abroad. By freeing the hektemoroi, Solon ensured Athens a large class of independent small farmers.

Solon made fundamental changes in Athenian government, too. He changed qualifications for office from birth to wealth, a boon to the non-Eupatrid elite. He established four census classes based on agricultural production. Most offices were reserved for men of property, but the poorest class, known as *thetes,* could participate in the assembly and courts. Solon probably established the Council of 400, which prepared the assembly's agenda. He is probably also responsible for regularizing council and assembly meetings and replacing the assembly's voice votes with the counting of hands.

Solon's moderation, respect for law, and liberation of the poor and downtrodden are milestones in Greek history. Without his reforms it is doubtful that democracy could have later taken root in Athens. Yet Solon's work had an unexpected byproduct: the growth of slavery in Athens. Though booming, the Athenian

Solon Statesman of early Athens, he transformed Greek society through mediation, moderation, respect for law, and measures that liberated the poor and downtrodden.

MAP 3.3 Attica

Mountains and plains alternate in the 1,000-square-mile area of ancient Attica. The Long Walls connecting Athens with the port city of Piraeus were built around 450 B.C.

economy lost its cheap labor when Solon freed debt slaves and hektemoroi. The solution was to buy slaves abroad and import them to Athens. At the time, the island city-state of Chios was the center of the slave trade in Greece (see Map 3.1). After Solon, Athens along with Chios developed one of history's first large-scale slave systems. Slaves worked in agriculture, crafts, trade, and elsewhere in the economy. Unlike helots, slaves could be bought and sold and were often uprooted, and the system was better policed than in earlier societies.

In the centuries after Solon, slavery grew widespread in Athens. Some slaves served in agriculture, some labored under miserable conditions in Athenian silver mines, and some were engaged in commerce or the military (where some rowers were slaves). Most, however, worked as domestics or in small workshops as, for example, metalworkers or furniture makers. The vast majority of slaves were non-Greek. Most were pris-

oners of war; some were victims of pirates or debtors from states where, unlike Athens, citizens might end up in debt slavery. Thrace (roughly, modern Bulgaria) and Anatolia were the main sources of slaves, but some slaves came from North Africa and other Mediterranean regions.

Living conditions for slaves were usually poor and those in the silver mines abysmal. Emancipation, however, was more common in Athens than in the American South before 1865. A few ex-slaves even rose to positions of wealth and power in Athens. A striking and unusual case is that of Pasion (d. 370 B.C.). Originally a slave employee of a banking firm, he bought his freedom and became the wealthiest Athenian banker of his day, as well as an Athenian citizen.

If free Athenians had any moral doubts about slavery, they went unrecorded. Yet there was much dissatisfaction with Solon's reforms, since his middle way satisfied neither Eupatrids nor champions of the free poor. After years of conflict, around 560 B.C. advocates of radical reform established a tyranny under Pisistratus (pie-SIS-trah-tus) (ca. 600–528 B.C.). He and his sons held power for forty of the next fifty years.

Supported by the thetes, the Pisistratids exiled many Eupatrids and confiscated and redistributed their land. Pisistratus kept the façade of Solon's reforms while ensuring that loyal supporters held all key offices.

A stable regime, the tyranny witnessed prosperity at home and the expansion of Athenian influence abroad. Yet Pisistratus's dynasty lasted only two generations. A steadfast opponent of tyrants, Sparta deposed his son, Hippias, in 510 B.C. Athens's elites by birth and wealth were ready to establish an oligarchy, but the way was open for an unexpected development: the emergence of popular government.

═══════════ S E C T I O N ═════ S U M M A R Y ═══════════

- Trade, colonization, and the invention of the Greek alphabet and of the hoplite phalanx all contributed to the emergence of the polis around 700 B.C.

- The polis was a community of citizens that emphasized participation and equality.

- Corinth is the best example of a polis where new wealth led to the emergence of the first tyrants—originally, popular champions.

- Sparta's austere and militaristic society turned boys into soldiers and trained girls to be tough and assertive wives and mothers.

- Solon's reforms freed the poor, but unintentionally laid the foundations for the growth of slavery.

THE CULTURE OF ARCHAIC GREECE

How did Western individualism and rationalism take root in Archaic Greece?

While one trend in Archaic culture was communal solidarity, as reflected in the hoplite phalanx, another was the opposite: a growing elevation of individualism. Increased prosperity and mobility (social, geographic, and political) during the Archaic period encouraged the breakdown of old ties and left some people with a sense of their uniqueness. Archaic poetry and sculpture both demonstrate this new consciousness of the self.

Meanwhile, although most Archaic Greeks celebrated religion, a small group of thinkers expressed religious doubts. While monumental stone temples and international centers for divination were being erected to honor the pantheon of gods, Greek thinkers began to move away from divine and toward abstract and mechanistic explanations of the universe. Their defection marked the start of the Western philosophical tradition.

REVEALING THE SELF: LYRIC POETRY AND SCULPTURE

Between approximately 675 and 500 B.C., the dominant Greek literary form was lyric poetry. This genre consisted of short poems written in a variety of styles but sharing a willingness to experiment, sometimes by revealing private feelings, sometimes by commenting on contemporary politics (as in the poetry of Tyrtaeus). Epic poetry, by contrast, was longer, grander in theme and tone, and less personal.

Homer never speaks directly about himself, and Hesiod reveals only a few personal details. In contrast, Archilochus (ar-KIL-uh-kus) of Paros (ca. 700–650 B.C.), the earliest known of the lyric poets, flaunts the self. Born on the Cycladic island of Paros, Archilochus was the son, perhaps the illegitimate son, of a noble. He was a mercenary soldier (that is, he fought for pay for a foreign country) and a colonist before returning home and dying in a hoplite battle against a neighboring island. The varied subjects of Archilochus's poetry include love, travel, and war. Much of his poetry is satire, sometimes mocking and ironic, sometimes vicious and abusive. Archilochus takes a cynical and detached view of hoplite ideals, freely admitting that he once tossed away his shield to escape the battlefield: "And that shield, to hell with it! Tomorrow I'll get me another one no worse."[2]

Sappho of Lesbos (ca. 625 B.C.) is also famous as a private poet, one who composed unmatched descriptions of intimate feelings, among them love for other women. Sappho (SAF-foh) is one of the few

Sappho Ancient Greek poet from the island of Lesbos, she wrote odes, wedding songs, and hymns expressing intimate feelings, including love for other women.

Athenian Kore
This statue of a young woman (*kore*) exemplifies Archaic Greek sculpture's interest in the idealized human form. Note the slight smile, the carefully coifed hair, and the elaborate clothes. Influenced by contemporary Egyptian statues, Greek sculptors nonetheless created a new and original style. *(Robert Frerck/Odyssey Productions)*

women poets of antiquity whose work has survived—very little, unfortunately, but enough to show that she was educated, worldly, and versed in politics. Like a modern experimental poet, she uses language self-consciously. Sappho's sensuality comes through in a description of her feelings at seeing a woman whose company she desires talking with a man: her heart shakes, her tongue is stuck, her eyes cannot see, her skin is on fire. "I am greener than grass," Sappho writes. "I feel nearly as if I could die."[3]

Online Study Center **Improve Your Grade**
Primary Source: A Lyric Poem Laments an Absent Lover

Sappho discusses female sexuality, a subject that Greek elite culture, dominated by males, tended to ignore. We know little about the sexuality of Greek women or of non-elite males. Among the male elite, romantic love in Archaic and **Classical Greece** was homosexual love or, to be precise, *pederasty* ("boy love"). The ideal relationship was supposed to involve a man in his twenties and a boy in his teens. The male elite was, strictly speaking, bisexual. By age 30, a man was expected to marry and raise a family. Perhaps bisexuality prevailed among elite females as well; Sappho, for example, eventually married and had a child.

Another sign of Archaic Greece's interest in the personal is the growing attention paid to the depiction of the human body, both in painting (most of the surviving examples are painted pottery) and in sculpture. Archaic artists displayed increasing skill and sensitivity in depicting the human form. The rich marble deposits in Greek soil gave sculptors promising material; baked clay (terra cotta) and bronze were other common sculptural media.

Early Archaic marble sculpture (seventh century B.C.) was strongly influenced by the way Egyptian sculpture represented the human body. Like Egyptian statuary, early Greek sculpture tended to be formal and frontal. But over the course of the seventh and sixth

centuries B.C., Greek sculptors experimented with a greater variety of poses and with increasing realism in showing musculature and motion. This realism, however, was expressed within limits, for the favorite subject of Archaic sculptors was not ordinary people but idealized, beautiful youth. Typical sculptural forms were the naked young man (*kouros*) and clothed young woman (*kore*), which often served as grave markers or monuments. The goal was to show people not as they were but as they might be.

RELIGIOUS FAITH AND PRACTICE

The Olympian gods who had been worshiped in the Mycenaean era survived in later ages, adapted to fit new political and social conditions. In the Archaic period, accordingly, the Olympian gods became gods of the polis.

Although the Olympians were revered throughout Greece, each polis had its patron deity: Apollo at Corinth, Hera at Argos and Samos, Athena at Athens and Sparta. Each polis also had its favorite heroes or demigods—for

Classical Greece Period of ancient Greek history from about 480 to 323 B.C.

example, Theseus, the legendary founder of Athens, and Heracles (Hercules), a favorite of Dorian cities such as Sparta and Thebes. Devotees considered it important to build a "house"—that is, a temple—for the local patron god or at least for his or her statue. The first temples were built of wood; the earliest stone temple, a temple of Apollo at Corinth, was built around 550 B.C.

Temples were rectangular structures with long sides on the north and south, short sides on the east and west, a colonnade around all four sides, and a pitched roof. The columns were based loosely on those of Egyptian architecture. Greek temples faced east so sunlight would illuminate the interior, which consisted of two rooms: a small treasury, open to the west, and a larger main chamber, in which a statue of the deity stood. The interior decoration of the temple was simple. Outside, however, brownish red roof tiles, painted sculpture above the colonnade and in the pediments (the area between the gables and the front and rear doorways), and terra-cotta roof ornaments created a festive and lively effect. The bare white ruins seen today are misleading.

The emphasis on exterior rather than interior decoration in a Greek temple reflects the way the building was used. The main ceremony took place outside. A long altar stood in front of the temple and parallel to it. On feast days—and under the tyrants the number of such days was increased greatly, as a concession to the common people—temple priests would sacrifice animals (pigs, goats, lambs, and, less often, bulls) on the altar. Only the thighs would be burned for the gods. The rest of the meat would be boiled and distributed to worshipers.

As in other ancient cultures, so in Greece divination was an important element of religion. Divination was institutionalized in *oracles*, places where, it was believed, a god or hero might be consulted for advice. Of the various Greek oracles, that of Apollo at Delphi (DEL-fye) in central Greece became the most prestigious and respected. At Delphi, Apollo spoke through the Pythia, a priestess who went into a trance. The utterances of Apollo at Delphi were famous among the Greeks for being ambiguous. Because different people might interpret them in different ways, Apollo could always be absolved after the fact if things did not turn out as the listener expected.

The oracle of Delphi was regularly consulted by poleis wishing to establish colonies. The oracle gave advice about the choice of location and the appropriate patron god or goddess, and it helped settlers draft new law codes. Delphi was also active in the search for new constitutions in the old poleis of Greece. Tradition says that Sparta based its government on a pronouncement of the Delphic oracle.

Archaic thinkers pondered the theme of divine justice. In Archaic literature we see less of the petty squabbling among the gods than in Homer and more of Zeus's majesty and justice. Although the wicked might seem to prosper, Zeus eventually punishes them or their descendants. "It never escapes him all the way when a man has a sinful spirit; and always, in the end, his judgment is plain," says Solon.[4]

Archaic writers delighted in portraying human emotions, but they had no confidence about the human ability to master emotions. In Archaic literature, people are weak and insignificant; their fortune is uncertain and mutable. Further, the gods are jealous of human success. People who aim too high are guilty of *hubris*—arrogance with overtones of violence and transgression. Hubris inevitably brings *nemesis,* "punishment" or "allotment." The safest course is for a person to be pious and humble.

So Archaic religion taught a humbling, even pessimistic, lesson. Yet religious teachings were not always heeded. The pages of Archaic history are full of people who aimed high and sought success with seemingly little worry and no dire consequences. In Ionia (eye-OH-nee-uh), the territory of the Greek cities along the central western Anatolian coast (see Map 3.1), one group of Greek thinkers made a radical break with Archaic religion and invented speculative philosophy.

THE ORIGINS OF WESTERN PHILOSOPHY

Abstract, rationalistic, speculative thinking emerged in Greece during the sixth century B.C. The first developments took place in Miletus (my-LEE-tus), an Ionian city. It is often said that the thinkers of Miletus (the Milesians) and their followers in other parts of Ionia invented philosophy. So they did, but we must be precise about what this means.

The Ionians were not the first to ask questions or tell stories about the nature and origins of the universe; virtually every ancient people did so. Nor did the Ionians invent science. They conducted no experiments. By 600 B.C., moreover, science—including mathematics, astronomy, medicine, and engineering—had been thriving for over two thousand years in Egypt and Mesopotamia, a heritage with which the Ionians were familiar and from which they borrowed.

The real importance of the Ionians is as pioneers of rationalism. They began the movement away from anthropomorphic or divine explanations and toward an abstract and mechanistic explanation of the universe. They themselves did not make a clear distinction between reason and revelation, but they made it possible for later Greek thinkers to do so. Later Greek philosophers were rarely (if ever) atheists, but they took for granted what the Ionians labored to establish: the primacy of human reason.

The Ionians saw themselves as students of nature—*physis* (from which the word *physics* is derived). Although they also commented on morality and politics, their interest in natural phenomena is what makes the Ionians significant. In their own day, the Ionians were called "wise men" (*sophoi*); to a later generation, they were "lovers of wisdom," *philosophoi* (from which *philosopher* comes).

Thales (THAY-leez), the first Milesian thinker, made a name for himself by successfully predicting a solar eclipse in 585 B.C. He is credited with founding Greek geometry and astronomy. Little survives of his writings or those of the other Milesians, but it is clear that he created the first general and systematic theory about the nature of the universe. According to Thales, the primary substance, the element from which all of nature was created, was water. He emphasized the mobility of water and its ability to nourish life.

A reply was not long in coming. Around 550 B.C. Anaximander of Miletus wrote the first known book of prose in Greek, expounding his own philosophy of nature. He attacked Thales for oversimplifying and for failing to do justice to the dynamism of nature. Anaximander accepted Thales' monist assumption—that all matter originated from one primary substance—but he called the substance "the unlimited" or "the undefined" rather than water. A third Milesian, Anaximenes, replied that the primary substance might be unlimited but it was not undefined. It was air, whose properties of condensation and rarefaction symbolized the dynamic and changing nature of things.

Humble as these theories might seem today, they represent a dramatic development: an open and critical debate among thinkers, each of whom was proposing an abstract and rational model of the universe. Many scholars have speculated about the origins of this development. Why Miletus? Why the sixth century B.C.? There are no sure answers, although certain influences have been suggested. Among them are Miletus's contacts on the trade routes with sophisticated Babylon, the proximity of Ionia to non-Greek peoples and the resulting Milesian appreciation of variety and complexity, and the search for law and order in contemporary Greek political life and its extension to the philosophical plane.

In its second generation early Greek philosophy moved to other Ionian cities and then migrated westward across the Mediterranean. Heracleitus (her-uh-CLY-tus) of Ephesus (ca. 500 B.C.) proposed fire as the primary substance. Although fire was ever changing, it had an underlying coherence. According to Heracleitus, this paradox nicely symbolized the nature of the universe. He summed up the importance of change by

the aphorisms "All things flow" and "You cannot step into the same river twice." The universe witnessed a constant struggle of opposites, yet an essential unity and order prevailed. To describe this order, Heracleitus used the term *logos*. This key concept of Greek philosophy is difficult to translate; among other definitions, *logos* can mean "word," "thought," "reason," "story," or "calculation."

Heracleitus's contemporary, Pythagoras (py-THAG-uh-russ) of Samos, was both a rationalist and a religious thinker. On the one hand, Pythagoras was a mathematician who discovered the numerical ratios determining the major intervals of the musical scale—that is, the range of sound between high and low. It is less certain if, as tradition has it, he discovered the so-called Pythagorean theorem—that in a right triangle the hypotenuse squared is equal to the sum of the squares of the other two sides.

On the other hand, Pythagoras believed that the purity of mathematics would improve the human soul. Just as he had imposed numerical order on the musical scale, so could philosophers understand the entire universe through number and proportion. The resulting knowledge was no mere academic exercise but a way of life. Pythagoras devoted himself to "observation" or "contemplation"—to *theoria* (from which *theory* comes).

In Croton in Magna Graecia (southern Italy), Pythagoras founded a religious community. Its members observed strict secrecy, but it appears that they abstained from meat because they believed in the kinship of all living things. They also believed in the reincarnation of the human soul, though not necessarily into a human body. Pythagoras is said to have stopped a man from beating a dog because he recognized from the barking that the dog was the reincarnation of a friend who had died.

The early Greek philosopher whose work is most fully preserved is Parmenides (par-MEN-uh-deez) of Elea in Magna Graecia. Parmenides (b. ca. 515 B.C.) completely distrusted the senses. He believed that reality was a world of pure being: eternal, unchanging, and indivisible, comparable to a sphere. To Parmenides, change was a mere illusion. Parmenides, therefore, is the first Western philosopher to propose a radical difference between the world of the senses and reality. This fundamental strain of Western thought would be taken up by Plato and his followers and then passed to Christianity.

To sum up, in philosophy as in so many other endeavors, the Archaic Greeks were great borrowers and even greater innovators who left a profound mark on later ages. By the late sixth century B.C., Archaic Greece was poised on the brink of a revolution that would give birth to the Classical period of Greek civilization.

═══════════════════ S E C T I O N   S U M M A R Y ═══════════════════

- Lyric poetry and Archaic sculpture display a groundbreaking interest in individual feelings and the human body.

- Archaic Greek religion was pessimistic. It feared human arrogance (*hubris*) and divine punishment (*nemesis*).

- Western philosophy began in Ionia in the 500s B.C.

- The first philosophers were rationalists who offered abstract and mechanistic explanations of nature.

CLASSICAL GREECE

What was Athenian democracy and how did it clash with Sparta in the Peloponnesian War?

The word *democracy* comes from the Greek word *demokratia* (deh-mo-kra-TEE-uh), coined in Athens early in the fifth century B.C. *Demokratia* literally means "the power (*kratos*) of the people (*demos*)." A modern democracy is characterized by mass citizenship, elections, and representative government. Athenian *demokratia*, in contrast, was a direct democracy in which elections mattered less than direct participation, citizenship was narrowly restricted, women were excluded from politics, resident aliens could almost never become citizens, and citizens owned slaves and ruled an empire. Modern democracies may cover a huge territory, but Athens encompassed only 1,000 square miles. Modern democracies tend to emphasize individual rights. Athens, in contrast, often placed the community first. In spite of these differences, Athenian *demokratia* established principles that are enshrined in democracy today: freedom, equality, citizenship without property qualifications, the right of most citizens to hold public office, and the rule of law.

The young democracy's greatest achievement was to spearhead Greece's victory over the Persian invaders in 480 B.C. After that victory, Athens became Greece's leading sea power. Yet Sparta remained the superior land power, and the two poleis were soon locked in a cycle of competition and war. The result nearly destroyed Athenian democracy. Even more serious, it undermined Greece's very independence.

THE DEVELOPMENT OF DEMOKRATIA, 508–322 B.C.

Tyranny often gave way to oligarchy—to government by wealthy men, both Eupatrids and non-Eupatrids. In Athens after Pisistratid rule, however, conditions were ripe for revolution. Solon had left a society of independent small farmers, while the Pisistratids had strengthened the ranks of immigrants and weakened the Eupatrids. Elite leaders nonetheless tried to establish an Athenian oligarchy. We may imagine strong popular opposition.

Ironically, a Eupatrid, a member of the Alcmeonid clan by the name of Cleisthenes (KLICE-the-neez) (d. ca. 500 B.C.), led the revolution. Originally Cleisthenes aimed to head the oligarchy, but his rivals shut him out of power. He turned then to the demos, whose leader he became. The watchwords of the day were *equality* and *mixing* (that is, mixing people from different regions of Attica in order to break down local, aristocratic power bases).

Frightened by the assertive populace, the oligarchs called for Spartan military assistance, but to no avail: Cleisthenes rallied the people to victory. The Athenian triumph proved, in Herodotus's opinion, "that equality is an excellent thing, not in one way only but in many. For while they were under a tyranny, [Athenians] were no better at fighting than any of their neighbors, but once they were rid of tyrants they became by far the best."[5]

Cleisthenes extinguished Eupatrid power once and for all by attacking its local bases of support. For example, he abolished the four traditional tribes and apportioned the people among ten new tribes. Immigrants and their descendants, who had been excluded from the old tribes, now joined natives in the new tribes. The tribes formed the basis of a new Council of 500 to replace Solon's Council of 400. The council was divided into ten tribal units, each serving as a kind of executive committee for one of the ten months of the civic year.

The centerpiece of the government was the assembly, some of whose members, emboldened by the new spirit of equality, now spoke up for the first time. The new Council of 500, like its predecessor, prepared the assembly's agenda, but assemblymen felt free to amend it. Only the Areopagus council remained a privileged preserve.

demokratia   Term coined in Athens in the fifth century B.C. to describe the city's system of direct government.

Greek Trireme

Olympias is a hypothetical reconstruction of an Athenian war galley of about 400 B.C. Rowed by 170 oarsmen arranged on three decks, the trireme fought by ramming an enemy ship with the bronze ram attached to its bow. *(Courtesy of the Trireme Trust)*

The last and most unusual part of the Cleisthenic system was ostracism, a sort of annual *un*popularity contest that received its name from the pieces of broken pottery (*ostraka*) on which the names of victims were chiseled. The "winner" was forced into ten years of exile, although his property would not be confiscated. Ostracism was meant to protect the regime by defusing factionalism and discouraging tyrants. Judging by Athens's consequent political stability, it worked.

In 508 B.C. the poorest Athenians had relatively little power in Cleisthenic government. But a change in conditions by the 450s made Athens even more democratic. During that period the oldest principle of Greek politics came to the fore: Whoever fights for the state governs it. To counter the Persian threat against Greece in the 480s (see page 77), Athens built a great navy. The standard ship was a trireme (TRY-reem), an oared warship rowed by 170 men on three decks. The core of the rowers consisted of Athenian thetes. Just as hoplites supported new regimes in Greece after 700 B.C., so rowers supported new regimes in Greece after 500 B.C.

A second revolution occurred around 461 B.C., when Ephialtes (d. ca. 460 B.C.) and his young associate **Pericles** (ca. 495–429 B.C.) targeted the last bulwark of privilege, the Areopagus. They stripped away the council's long-standing supervisory powers over the regime and redistributed those powers to the Council of 500 and the people's court. The decade of the 450s B.C. saw another innovation: payment for public service, specifically for jurors, who received a half-drachma (perhaps half a day's wages) for a day of jury duty. Eventually other public servants also received pay. Conservatives complained bitterly because they perceived, rightly, that state pay made political activity by poor people possible. State pay was, an Athenian said, "the glue of demokratia."

Demokratia became closely connected with Pericles (PAIR-ih-kleez), who inherited the constituency of Ephialtes after his assassination around 460 B.C. For much of the next thirty years, Pericles dominated Athenian politics. An aristocrat who respected the common people, an excellent orator who benefited from an education in philosophy, an honest and tireless worker, and a general who led in peace as well as war, Pericles was a political giant. Under his leadership, demokratia became firmly entrenched as the government and way of life in Athens.

Athenian democracy survived, with occasional oligarchic intrusions, for 150 years after Pericles' death. During those years it became more institutionalized and cautious, but it also became more thoroughly egalitarian.

Pericles Leader of fifth-century B.C. Athens, he established Athens as a great center of art and literature as well as a great empire.

HOW DEMOKRATIA WORKED

Unlike most modern democracies, Athenian demokratia was direct and participatory. Pericles once claimed that in Athens "people pay attention both to their own household and to politics. Even those occupied with other activities are no less knowledgeable about politics."[6] This is part boast, but only part. Large numbers of ordinary citizens attended the assembly from time to time and held public office or served on the Council of 500 for a year or two.

Government   The instruments of government are easily sketched. The central institution was the assembly. Open to all male citizens over age 20, assembly meetings were held in the open air, on a hillside seating several thousand on benches (see the photograph on page 58). In the fourth century B.C. the assembly gathered a minimum of forty times per year, about once every ten days.

The assembly heard the great debates of the day. It made decisions about war and peace, alliance and friendship; it conferred honors and issued condemnations; it passed decrees relating to current issues and set up commissions to revise fundamental laws. In the assembly top orators addressed the people, but everyone, however humble, was theoretically entitled to speak.

The judicial branch consisted of courts, which, with a few exceptions, were open to all citizens, no matter how poor. Aristotle or a member of his school comments that "when the people have the right to vote in the courts, they control the constitution." Juries were large, commonly consisting of several hundred men chosen by lottery; small juries, it was felt, were easily bribed. After a preliminary hearing, cases were decided in a single day.

The executive consisted of the Council of 500 and some seven hundred public officials (also, under Athens's empire in the fifth century B.C., several hundred others living abroad). All male citizens over age 30 were eligible to serve. Most public officials were chosen by lottery, which put rich and poor, talented and untalented, on an equal footing. To guard against installing incompetents or criminals, all officials had to undergo a scrutiny by the council before taking office and an audit after the term. Most magistracies, moreover, were boards, usually of ten men, so even if a bad man managed to pass this scrutiny, he would be counterbalanced by his colleagues. Only generals and treasurers were chosen by election.

Athens had a relatively weak executive and no chief executive such as a president or prime minister. Generals and orators led assembly debates and sometimes exercised great influence, but ordinary people set the agenda and made the decisions by taking votes at each assembly meeting. On the local level, every deme (county) had an annually chosen executive and a deme assembly of all citizens.

So novel and populist a system of government has not been without critics, either in antiquity or today. Some have charged that the Athenian people were uneducated, emotional, and easily swayed by oratorical tricks. Others say that demokratia degenerated into mob rule after the death of Pericles. Still others complain about the lack of a system of formal public education, which denied many citizens equality of opportunity.

Women and Resident Aliens   Another serious charge against Athenian demokratia is that it was democracy for a small elite only. Adult male citizens never accounted for more than one-tenth of the population, approximately 40,000 out of a total population—men, women and children, resident aliens, and slaves—of about 400,000. To become a citizen, a boy at age 18 had to prove that he was the legitimate son of a citizen father and a citizen maternal grandfather. Girls were never officially registered as citizens. Although the term *citizeness* existed, Athenian citizen women were usually referred to as "city women." As for resident aliens, whether male or female, they rarely attained citizenship.

In the fifth and fourth centuries B.C., Athens had a large population of foreigners. Some were transient. Others were officially registered resident aliens, or *metics* (MEH-tiks). Metics came by the thousands from all over the Greek world and beyond. Some, like Aristotle (a native of a Greek colony in Macedonia (mah-suh-DOE-nee-uh), were attracted by the city's schools of philosophy, but most came because of its unparalleled economic opportunities. Metics could not own land in Athens, and they had to pay extra taxes and serve in the Athenian military. Nevertheless, they prospered in Athenian commerce and crafts.

Athenian women were excluded from politics and played only a modest role in commerce as small retailers. In legal matters women were almost always required to be represented by a male guardian. Demokratia also promoted an ideal of the male as master of his household. Women were expected to be obedient and remain indoors.

Practice, however, was another matter. As Aristotle asks rhetorically, "How is it possible to prevent the wives of the poor from going out?" *Poor* is a synonym for *ordinary* in ancient Greek. Ordinary women could not stay at home because they had to run errands, draw water, and sometimes even help make ends meet. Ordinary houses, moreover, were small and cramped, and in the Mediterranean heat women could not stay inside all the time.

We occasionally get glimpses, sometimes more, of Athenian women resisting or working behind the scenes to correct male mistakes. An inheritance case reveals a woman go-between interceding among her quarreling male relations. Greek comedy shows women mocking male pretensions and establishing sisterly friendships. A woman who brought a large dowry into a marriage could use it and the threat of divorce to influence her husband (the dowry had to be returned to the woman's father or guardian if there was a divorce). In short, Athenian women had some access to the world outside the household and some influence within the household. There existed, nonetheless, a real disparity in power between men and women.

Athenian demokratia lacked many features of modern democracy, including a notion of universal human rights, the possibility for immigrants to become citizens, gender equality, the abolition of slavery, and public education. To its small citizen body, however, Athenian demokratia offered extraordinary freedom, equality, and responsibility, as well as a degree of participation in public life seldom equaled. Demokratia was a model of what democracy could be but not of who could take part.

THE PERSIAN WARS, 499–479 B.C.

In 500 B.C. Sparta, hegemon of the Peloponnesian League, was the most prominent power of the Greek mainland. Across the Aegean Sea in Anatolia, the Greek city-states had been under Persian rule for two generations, since Cyrus the Great's conquest in the 540s B.C. In 499 B.C., however, events began to unfold that not only would revolutionize that balance of power but also would throw the entire eastern Mediterranean into two hundred years of turmoil.

Led by Miletus, the Ionian Greek city-states rose in revolt against Persia in 499 B.C. Athens sent troops to help, but despite initial successes, Athens reconsidered the alliance and withdrew its forces. The Ionian coalition broke down thereafter and was

crushed by Persia. Miletus was besieged and destroyed, but otherwise Persia was relatively lenient in Ionia.

Upstart Athens, however, could not go unpunished. In 490 B.C. Darius I sent a large naval expedition to Athens. About 25,000 infantrymen and 1,200 cavalrymen (with horses) landed at Marathon, some 24 miles from the city of Athens (see Map 3.3). Athens sent 10,000 men (including 1,000 allies) to defend Marathon, and a great battle ensued.

Persian overconfidence and the superiority of the Greek phalanx over Persia's loosely organized infantrymen won Athens a smashing victory. Persia suffered 6,400 casualties, Athens only 192. (The story, unconfirmed, that a messenger ran from the battlefield to the city of Athens with the news, "Rejoice, we conquer!" is the inspiration for the modern marathon race, a slightly longer distance of about 26 miles.) After the battle, Athens experienced a burst of confidence that propelled it to power and glory.

Meanwhile, Persia sought a rematch. After Darius's death in 486, his son and successor, Xerxes, amassed a huge force of about a thousand ships and several hundred thousand soldiers and rowers, vastly outnumbering potential Greek opposition. Athens, under the leadership of Themistocles (ca. 525–460 B.C.), prepared by building a fleet of two hundred ships. Athens joined Sparta and twenty-nine other Peloponnesian poleis in the Hellenic League of defense, with Sparta in overall command. Most poleis either stayed neutral or, like Thebes and Argos, collaborated with Persia. The Greeks had over three hundred ships and about fifty thousand infantrymen.

Persia invaded Greece in 480 B.C. and won the opening moves. At the narrow pass of Thermopylae in central Greece (see Map 3.1), the Persians outflanked and crushed a small Spartan army, who died fighting to the last man, including their king,

Amazon Queen
This red-figure Athenian cup (ca. 440 B.C.) shows the Greek warrior Achilles about to slay the Amazon queen Penthesilea during the Trojan War, in which she fought on Troy's side. She was a symbol of feminine courage and beauty.
(Staatliche Antikensammlungen und Glyptothek, Munich)

THE ENEMY AS BARBARIAN

Classical Greeks no longer regarded the enemy as honored rivals, as Homer's heroes had regarded Trojans. Rather, they looked down on the enemy as a barbarian. Greece's archenemies, the Persians, were portrayed as indulgent, effeminate, emotional, slavish, cruel, and dangerous. Consider the contrasting portraits of Persians and Greeks in these excerpts from the historian Herodotus's account of Persia's invasion of Greece in 480 B.C.

The Persians

He [King Xerxes of Persia] then prepared to move forward to Abydos, where a bridge had already been constructed across the Hellespont from Europe to Asia. . . . It was here not long afterwards that the Greeks under Xanthippus the son of Ariphron took Artayctes the Persian governor of Sestos, and nailed him alive to a plank—he was the man who collected women in the temple of Protesilaus at Elaeus and committed various acts of sacrilege. This headland was the point to which Xerxes' engineers carried their two bridges from Abydos—a distance of seven furlongs. . . . The work was successfully completed, but a subsequent storm of great violence smashed it up and carried everything away. Xerxes was very angry when he learned of the disaster, and gave orders that the Hellespont should receive three hundred lashes and have a pair of fetters thrown into it. And I have heard before now that he also sent people to brand it with hot irons. He certainly instructed the men with the whips to utter, as they wielded them, the following words: "You salt and bitter stream, your master lays this punishment upon you for injuring him, who never injured you. But Xerxes the King will cross you, with or without your permission. No man sacrifices to you, and you deserve the neglect by your acrid and muddy waters"—a highly presumptuous way of addressing the Hellespont, and typical of a barbarous nation. In addition to punishing the Hellespont Xerxes gave orders that the men responsible for building the bridge should have their heads cut off. This unseemly order was duly carried out. . . .

The Greeks

To the Spartan envoys . . . [the Athenians] said: "No doubt it was natural that the Lacedaemonians [Spartans] should dread the possibility of our making terms with Persia; nonetheless it shows a poor estimate of the spirit of Athens. Were we offered all the gold in the world, and the fairest and richest country the earth contains, we should never consent to join the common enemy and bring Greece into submission. There are many compelling reasons to prevent our taking such a course, even if we wish to do so: the first and greatest is the burning of the temples and images of our gods—now mere heaps of rubble. It is our bounden duty to avenge this desecration with all the power we possess—not to clasp in friendship the hand that wrought it. Again, there is the Greek nation—the common blood, the common language; the temples and religious ritual; the whole way of life we understand and share together—indeed, if Athens were to betray all this it would not be well done. We would have you know, therefore, if you did not already know it, that we will never make peace with Xerxes so long as a single Athenian remains alive."

QUESTIONS

1. Find at least three examples in these passages of Persian barbarism.

2. By deciding to make war instead of negotiating peace, are the Athenians barbarians or civilized people?

3. Does Herodotus offer convincing proof that the Persians are more barbarous than the Greeks? Is he fair?

Leonidas. This sacrifice added to the Spartan reputation for courage but left the road south open. Abandoned by its defenders, Athens was sacked.

The tide then turned. The Greeks lured the Persian fleet into the narrow straits between Athens and Salamis. The Persians could not use their numerical superiority in this confined space, and the Greeks had the home advantage. The result was a crushing Persian defeat under the eyes of Xerxes himself, who watched the battle from a throne on a hillside near the shore.

Because their sea links to the Levant had been cut, Xerxes and the remainder of the Persian fleet left for home. Soon afterward the united Greek army under Spartan leadership defeated Persian forces on land at Plataea (just north of Attica; see Map 3.1) in 479 B.C. At about the same time, the Greek fleet defeated a reorganized Persian fleet off the Anatolian coast near Mycale. The victorious Greeks sailed the coast and liberated the Ionians. Not only did Persia fail to conquer the Greek mainland, but it also lost its eastern Aegean empire.

MAP 3.4 Greece in the Peloponnesian War

During the long and bloody Peloponnesian War (431–404 B.C.), much of the Greek world was divided into two camps: one led by Sparta, the other by Athens.

Greeks did not remember the invader fondly. After 480 they thought of Persians not merely as enemies but as barbarians—that is, cultural inferiors. (See the box "The Global Record: The Enemy as Barbarian.") At the same time, Greeks became more conscious of their own common culture.

STRUGGLES TO DOMINATE GREECE, 478–362 B.C.

The Greek unity forged by the struggle against Persia was fragile and short-lived. What followed was a constant struggle in diplomacy and war among city-states, usually arranged in leagues under hegemons.

Following the Greek victory over Persia, Athens expanded its power as hegemon of a new security organization. Founded on the island of Delos in the Aegean Sea, the so-called Delian League aimed both at protecting Greek lands and at plundering Persian territory. The number of allies grew from about 150 in 477 B.C. to about 250 in 431 B.C. at the height of the league.

Because they feared entanglement outside the Peloponnesus, most Spartans preferred to leave the Aegean to Athens. Some Spartans nonetheless watched with unease and jealousy as Athenian power boomed.

Afraid of the new titan, the major allied states rebelled, one by one, beginning with Thasos in 465 B.C., but Athens crushed each rebellion. Sometimes after surrender, rebels were executed and their wives and children sold into slavery. Allied complaints began to stir Sparta. A conflict between Greece's greatest land power, Sparta, and Greece's greatest sea power, Athens, started to look all but inevitable.

The Peloponnesian War, as this conflict is known today, came in 431 B.C. and lasted intermittently until 404 B.C. The war proved bloody and bitter. Battles between huge fleets, economic warfare, protracted sieges, epidemic disease, and ideological struggle produced a devastating war. It was clear that the Greeks could not maintain their unity against Persia; indeed, they appeared to be destroying themselves.

In this era both democratic Athens and oligarchic Sparta sought to promote their respective ideologies. Some unfortunate states became ideological battlegrounds, often at great cost of life. In Corcyra (modern Corfu; see **MAP 3.4**), for example, bloody civil war marked a series of coups and countercoups in the 420s B.C.

Given Spartan supremacy on land and Athenian mastery of the sea, it is not surprising that the Peloponnesian War remained undecided for a decade and a half. The balance of power shifted only after an Athenian blunder, an expedition to conquer Sicily (415–413 B.C.) that became a quagmire and then a disaster, leading to total defeat and thousands of Athenian casualties. In the aftermath most of the Athenian empire rose in revolt. Persia re-emerged and intervened on Sparta's side—in return for Sparta's restoration of Ionia to Persia, an ironic counterpoint to Sparta's role in driving Persia from Greece in 479. Athens, nevertheless, was sufficiently wealthy and plucky to hold out until 404 B.C.

Sparta won the Peloponnesian War, but establishing a new Greek order proved beyond its grasp. Spartans were soldiers, not diplomats; infantrymen, not sailors; and commanders, not public speakers. They made poor leaders. Sparta took over Athens's former empire and quickly had a falling-out with its allies, Persia, Corinth, and the Boeotian (bee-O-shun) city-states, especially Thebes.

In addition, Sparta suffered a vast decline in the number of citizens. The original nine thousand Similars of the seventh century B.C. had dropped to only about fifteen hundred in 371 B.C. The main problem seems to have been greed. Rich Spartans preferred to get richer by concentrating wealth in fewer hands rather than open the elite to new blood. Thousands of men could no longer afford to live as elite soldiers.

The result was military disaster. In 371 B.C. the Boeotian army crushed the Spartans at the Battle of Leuctra, killing a thousand men (including four hundred Similars) and a Spartan king. In the next few years Boeotia invaded the Peloponnesus, freed the Messenian helots, and restored Messenia to independence, after some 350 years of bondage. It was a fatal blow to Spartan power, but Boeotia, too, was exhausted and its main leaders, Epaminondas (d. 362 B.C.) and Pelopidas (403–364 B.C.), were dead. None of the Greek city-states had been able to maintain hegemony.

Nothing better demonstrates the fatal excess of individualism in Classical Greece and the absence of cooperative virtues than the wars of the city-states in the fourth century B.C. They accomplished nothing but leaving a weakened Greece prey to outsiders.

━━━━━━━━━ S E C T I O N   S U M M A R Y ━━━━━━━━━

- Democracy or "people power" (*demokratia*) began in ancient Greece, and Athens was the most influential Greek democracy.

- Athenian democracy was direct and participatory for adult male citizens, but women, resident aliens, and slaves were all denied citizen rights.

- Persia's massive invasion of mainland Greece in 480–479 B.C. was defeated by a coalition led by Sparta and Athens.

- The Greek *poleis* then turned on each other in a series of wars that lasted about a century.

- Sparta defeated Athens in the most intense phase of these conflicts, known today as the Peloponnesian War (431–404 B.C.).

THE PUBLIC CULTURE OF CLASSICAL GREECE

How did tragedy, comedy, philosophy, and history all begin and develop in the culture of Classical Greece?

The word *classical* means "to set a standard." The culture of Greece between 480 and 322 B.C. proved so influential in the later West that it may justly be called classical. Classical Greek culture was public culture. Poets were not inward-looking or alienated figures. Rather, to quote the Athenian playwright Aristophanes (air-ih-STOF-uh-neez) (ca. 455–385 B.C.), they were "the teachers of men," who commented on contemporary public debate. (As the quota-

tion might also suggest, men, especially citizens, dominated public life.) Dramas were performed in a state theater at state religious festivals. The philosopher Socrates (sock-ruh-TEEZ) (469–399 B.C.) discussed philosophy in marketplaces and gymnasia. It was not private individuals but the public that was the major patron of sculpture and architecture.

Public life, accordingly, is the central theme of Classical Greek art and literature. In tragedy, for example, regardless of the particular hero or plot, the same character always looms in the background: the polis. The Classical historians Herodotus, Xenophon, and especially Thucydides focus on public affairs rather than private life. Classical philosophy ranged from biology to metaphysics, but politics was undoubtedly its central focus.

RELIGION AND ART

A hallmark of Classical culture is the tension between the religious heritage of the Archaic period and the worldly spirit of the Classical age. The Classical period was a time of prosperity, political debate, and military conflict. "Wonders are many on earth, and none more wondrous than man," said the Athenian tragedian Sophocles (sof-uh-KLEEZ) (ca. 495–406 B.C.). Yet Sophocles was a deeply religious man who also believed that people were doomed to disaster unless they obeyed the laws of the gods. Sophocles mirrored a widespread debate, for he knew his countrymen well. He was not only a popular playwright but also a general, state treasurer, priest, and friend of Pericles.

Classical religion was less sure of itself than its Archaic predecessor. A few people even questioned the very existence of the gods, although most Greeks wanted religion to be adapted to the new age, not discarded altogether. Thus Athenian religion was tailored to the needs of a democratic and imperial city. In the 440s B.C., under Pericles' leadership, Athens embarked on a vast, ambitious, and expensive temple-building project, using Delian League funds and serving as a large public employment program. Temples were built in and around the city, most notably on the Athenian Acropolis. (See the feature "The Visual Record: The Parthenon.")

To adapt religion to a new age, new cults also were introduced. The most popular was the worship of

The Parthenon
The temple of Athena Parthenos ("the Maiden") on the Athenian Acropolis, the Parthenon was dedicated in 438 B.C. One of the largest and most complex Greek temples, it was built of fine marble. The partially restored ruins symbolize the wealth, power, and greatness of Classical Greece. *(William Katz/Photo Researchers)*

The Parthenon

The Parthenon, completed in 432 B.C., dominates both the skyline of Athens and the historical imagination of the West. The building's fine marble and Classical proportions symbolize the free, confident, and united society that one might expect of Periclean Athens, the world's first democracy (see the photograph on page 81). A close look, however, suggests a more complex story. The Parthenon's sculpture offers glimpses of the tensions behind the Classical façade.

The temple of Athena Parthenos ("the Maiden"), as the Parthenon is formally known, was a public project of Greece's wealthiest city-state, leading naval power, and premier democracy. Athenians spared no expense on its construction. Sculpture included a gold and ivory statue of the goddess Athena inside the temple and, on the outside, statuary in each pediment (the triangular space under the eaves) and sculptured reliefs running around the building above the exterior and interior colonnades.

So lavish a program of art demonstrated Athenian wealth but also served an educational purpose: to illustrate basic Athenian values. Because every Athenian male was expected to fight for the city when called on, militant competition is a central theme. Above the exterior colonnade, for example, ninety-two separate panels of relief sculpture depict gods and heroes fighting foes such as giants and centaurs.

See the detail from the south wall. It shows a fight between a human male and a centaur, a mythological creature who was half-man, half-beast. Both the man and the centaur are powerful, but the centaur is old and ugly, while the man is young and handsome. The man fights fairly, while the centaur makes a savage attack with arm and forelegs. The man belongs to a Greek people known as the Lapiths. According to myth, the centaurs attacked the Lapiths during a wedding celebration, but they were driven off by the Lapith men, led by the bridegroom and his Athenian friend, the hero Theseus.

To a real-life Athenian observer, the triumph of the Lapiths might have symbolized Athens's victory over the Persians. It was easy to make the connection because the Parthenon was in effect a war memorial as well as a temple. When the Persians invaded Athens in 480 B.C. they destroyed the temples on the Acropolis. For forty years after Greece's victory, Athens left the Acropolis empty as a reminder of Persian barbarism. Then Pericles sponsored a building program of new temples, of which the Parthenon was the grandest.

Delian League funds were diverted to pay for the new buildings, which raised controversy. Ironically, democratic Athens used allied money, earmarked for defense, to glorify itself. Some people considered that oppressive.

The sculpture above the interior colonnade is a continuous band, or frieze, around the four sides of the building, and it illustrates a procession. Warriors aplenty, primarily cavalrymen but also hoplites and charioteers, compose the lineup. Like the Lapith, the cavalrymen are depicted without clothes, and so they embody the ideal of strong bodies in the service of the polis.

Centaur Struggling with Lapith, Parthenon Metope, South Side
(Courtesy of the Trustees of the British Museum)

Four Women in Procession,
Parthenon Frieze, East Wall
(Louvre/R.M.N./Art Resource, NY)

Not all of the men in the interior frieze are warriors, though. Women, too, are depicted. See the detail from the east wall. Look at the four women shown here. The women are on foot, clothed and in solemn procession. The heavy folds of their robes, the hands held at their sides, and the expression on the one visible face all suggest calm and decorum.

From both of these pieces we may detect Athenian commonplaces about gender. Young women were expected to be maidenly, reserved, and modest. Their bodies were to be kept private. Young men were expected to be outgoing and assertive. Although men wore clothes in public, they exercised naked in gymnasia, wrestling grounds, and stadiums, competing in a healthy activity considered to be effective preparation for war.

The historian finds subtler messages in the two scenes. For example, however constrained the role of women, their very presence in the frieze is significant. Women were not permitted to attend the Athenian assembly, but they participated in the rituals and festivals that played so large a role in Athenian public life. Notice, for instance, the two girls shown in the back who are carrying ritual vessels.

Scholars disagree about the subject of the procession in the frieze. Most scholars argue that the subject is the Pan-Athenaic procession, held once every four years to honor Athena. The people depicted are said to be the people of Athens—a daring novelty, considering that all previous Greek temple sculpture was restricted to gods, heroes, and mythological figures. Some scholars view the scene as an illustration of a legend from the early history of Athens. In either case, one thing is clear: the Parthenon sculptures depict the Athenians the way they wanted to see themselves—as courageous, pious, and public-spirited.

QUESTIONS

1. In what sense is the Parthenon an example of public education in democratic Athens?

2. What does the Parthenon have to say about gender in Athens?

3. What does the Parthenon have to say about Greek-Persian relations?

Online Study Center
Improve Your Grade Visual Record Activities

Asclipius, god of healing. Traditionally a minor figure and considered a son of Apollo, Asclipius became enormously popular in his own right beginning in the late fifth century B.C., perhaps in response to the high mortality of the Peloponnesian War. Outside Athens, large shrines to Asclipius at Epidauros (in the Peloponnesus) and Cos (an island off the Anatolian coast) became pilgrimage centers in the fourth century B.C. for ailing people in search of a cure.

Women played a major role in Classical Athenian religion. They were priestesses in more than forty major cults. They participated each year in many festivals, including several reserved only for women. One such festival, the Thesmophoria, a celebration of fertility held each autumn, featured a three-day encampment of women on a hillside in the city, right beside the Athenian assembly amphitheater. Women also attended public funeral orations in honor of soldiers who had died in battle. They probably attended plays as well.

Pericles was very much influenced by a woman, Aspasia (uh-SPAY-see-uh). She belonged to the small group of noncitizen women called *hetairai*, or courtesans (that is, prostitutes patronized by men of wealth and status). An educated woman from Miletus, Aspasia was for many years Pericles' mistress and bore him a son. Aspasia and Pericles gathered around them a glittering circle of thinkers and artists. Some say that Aspasia even influenced Pericles' political decisions.

In art, Classical sculptors completed the process begun by their Archaic forebears of mastering the accurate representation of the human body. In anatomical precision, Classical Greek sculpture was the most technically proficient sculpture the world had seen. Like Archaic sculpture, it was not, however, an attempt to portray humans "warts and all" but rather an idealization of the human form.

THE SOPHISTS AND SOCRATES

Success in democratic politics required a knowledge of oratory. This demand was met in the late fifth century B.C. by the arrival in Athens of itinerant professional teachers of *rhetoric*, the art of speaking. They were known as Sophists (SOF-ists) (from a word meaning "instruct" or "make wise"). Sicilian Greeks invented rhetoric around 465 B.C. by drawing up the rules of argument. For a fee—rarely small and sometimes astronomical—Sophists taught young Athenians the art of speaking. Their curriculum consisted not only of rhetoric but also of the rudiments of linguistics, ethics, psychology, history, and anthropology—in other words, any aspect of "human nature" that might help an aspiring politician. Within a few years most ambitious young Athenians of prosperous families were studying with Sophists.

At their best, Sophists sharpened young minds. Athenian tragedians, historians, and philosophers all benefited from sophistic teaching. Protagoras (b. ca. 485 B.C.), perhaps the best-known Sophist, summed up the spirit of the age in his famous dictum "Man is the measure of all things"—an appropriate credo for the interest in all things human that is apparent in Classical literature and art. There is, however, a more troubling side to the Sophists. As teachers of rhetoric, they taught respect for success, not for truth. Thus they acquired a reputation as word-twisters who taught men how to make "the weaker argument defeat the stronger."

Much to the distress of conservatives, Sophists drew a distinction between *nomos,* a word that means "law" or "convention," and *physis,* which means "nature." The distinction had revolutionary potential. In general, Sophists had little respect for the established order, or nomos. They considered it mere convention. A great man trained by a Sophist might rise above convention to realize the limitless potential of his nature, or physis. If he used his skill to overturn democracy and establish a tyranny, so much the worse for democracy. Indeed, the Sophists trained both unscrupulous democratic politicians and many of the oligarchs who launched coups d'état against Athenian democracy at the end of the fifth century B.C. As a result, *sophist* became a term of abuse in Athens and remains so to this day.

Classical Greek advances in rhetoric, therefore, were as problematic as they were brilliant. The Sophists had a wide-ranging effect on many different branches of thought. Consider, for example, the work of the philosopher Democritus (dee-MOCK-ruh-tus) (b. ca. 460 B.C.), a native of the northern Greek polis of Abdera but a visitor to Athens. Democritus was not a Sophist, but he shared the common Sophistic notion that the reality of nature was far more radical than conventionally thought. He concluded that all things consisted of tiny, indivisible particles, which could be arranged and rearranged in an infinite variety of configurations. He called these particles *atoma,* "uncuttable" (from which the word *atom* is derived).

The physicians of the Aegean island of Cos are known as Hippocratics, from Hippocrates (hih-POK-ruh-teez) (b. ca. 460 B.C.), the first great thinker of their school. If they were not directly influenced by the Sophists, they shared similar habits of thought. Like the Sophists, the Hippocratics were religious skeptics. They considered disease to be strictly a natural phenomenon in which the gods played no part. Hippocratic medicine was noteworthy for its methodology, which emphasized observation and prognosis (the reasoned prediction of future developments). The Hippocratics were the most rigorously naturalistic physicians to date, although no more successful in healing illness than earlier practitioners.

In the fifth century B.C. not all thinkers welcomed the conclusions of the Sophists. Perhaps their most notable critic, and the greatest of all fifth-century B.C. philosophers, was **Socrates** (469–399 B.C.). Unlike the Sophists, he charged no fees, had no formal students, and did not claim to teach any positive body of knowledge. His main virtue, he believed, was his awareness of his ignorance. Unlike the Sophists, most of whom were metics, Socrates was an Athenian citizen.

Socrates, however, resembled the Sophists in his intense interest in political theory. Like any good Athenian citizen, Socrates served in the military—as a hoplite during the Peloponnesian War. He had his doubts about democracy, which he criticized for inefficiency and for giving an equal voice to the uneducated. He preferred rule by a wise elite. Nonetheless, Socrates was too loyal an Athenian to advocate revolution.

Yet Socrates made many enemies because of his role as a self-styled "gadfly." He stung the pride of Athens's leaders by demonstrating their ignorance. Mistakenly considered a Sophist by the public because of his unconventional opinions, Socrates was tried, convicted, and executed in 399 B.C. by an Athenian court for alleged atheism and "corrupting the young." The Athenian public soon had second thoughts, and the trial of Socrates is usually considered one of history's great miscarriages of justice, as well as one of Athenian democracy's greatest blunders.

Socrates was trained in the Ionian natural philosophy tradition. He went beyond it, as the Roman thinker Cicero later said, by bringing philosophy "down from the heavens into the streets"; he changed the emphasis from the natural world to human ethics. Like most Greeks, Socrates believed that the purpose of life was the pursuit of aretê. Unlike his contemporaries, however, he did not consider aretê to be primarily excellence in battle or in public life but rather excellence in philosophy. One became good by studying the truth, which is part of what Socrates meant by his saying "Virtue (aretê) is knowledge." He also meant that no one who truly understood goodness would ever choose to do evil.

Teach people well, Socrates says, and they will behave morally. Socrates has gone down in history as an inspiring teacher despite his protestations of not teaching anything. His emphasis was not on research or writing, and in fact he refused to write anything down. He believed that truth can be found only in persons, not through books—that philosophy requires a thoughtful verbal exchange. His favorite technique was to ask people difficult questions. Pedagogy that relies on inquiry is still called the "Socratic method."

PLATO AND ARISTOTLE

Because Socrates never wrote anything down, we are dependent on others for our knowledge of him. Fortunately for us, he inspired students who committed his words and ideas to paper. Socrates' most distinguished student, and our most important source for his thought, was Plato (427–348 B.C.), who in turn was the teacher of Aristotle (384–322 B.C.). Together, these three men laid the foundations of the Western philosophical tradition. They were thinkers for the ages, but each was also a man of his times.

Socrates grew up in confident Periclean days. **Plato** (PLAY-toe) came of age during the Peloponnesian War, a period culminating in the execution of Socrates. Shocked and disillusioned, Plato turned his back on public life, although he was an Athenian citizen. Instead of discussing philosophy in public, Plato founded a private school in an Athenian suburb, the Academy. Plato held a low opinion of democracy, and when he did intervene in politics, it was not in Athens but in far-off Syracuse (in Sicily). Syracuse was governed by a tyranny, and Plato hoped to educate the tyrant's heir in philosophy—a vain hope, as it turned out.

In an attempt to recapture the stimulating give-and-take of a conversation with Socrates, Plato did not write straightforward philosophical treatises but instead dialogues or speeches. All of Plato's dialogues have more than one speaker, and in most the main speaker is named "Socrates." Sometimes this figure is the historical Socrates, sometimes merely a mouthpiece for ideas Plato wished to explore.

A voluminous writer, Plato is not easily summarized. The word that best characterizes his legacy, though, is *idealism,* of which Plato is one of Western philosophy's greatest exponents. Like Parmenides, Plato believed that the senses are misleading. Truth exists but is attained only by training the mind to overcome commonsense evidence. The model for Plato's philosophical method is geometry. Just as geometry deals not with this or that triangle or rectangle but with ideal forms—with a pure triangle, a pure rectangle—so the philosopher could learn to recognize purity. A philosopher would not be misled by, for example, comparing aretê in Athens, Sparta, and Persia; a philosopher would understand the meaning of pure, ideal aretê. No relativist, Plato believed in absolute good and evil.

Philosophy is not for everyone, according to Plato. Only a few people have the necessary intelligence and discipline. In the *Republic,* a dialogue that is perhaps his best-known work, Plato demonstrates the nature of his idealism and its political consequences. He envisioned a society whose elite would study philosophy and

---

Socrates Ancient Greek philosopher, he was a founder of the Western philosophical tradition and is credited with the "Socratic method" of learning.

Plato Ancient Greek philosopher and student of Socrates, he is best known for his work, the *Republic*.

attain enlightenment. They would understand the vanity of political ambition but would nonetheless accept the responsibility of governing the masses. Plato never makes clear precisely why they should assume this burden. It is possible he was enough of a traditionalist, in spite of himself, to consider a citizen's responsibility to the polis to be obvious. In any case, Plato's ideal state was one in which philosophers would rule as kings, benevolently and unselfishly.

Plato explored the details of such a state in the *Republic* and in other dialogues, particularly the *Laws*. It is not clear how wedded he was to specific details; indeed, some of them may have been meant merely to shock or to satirize. An overall picture emerges, however. The ideal state would be like a small polis: self-sufficient and closed to outside corrupt influences like Sparta, but committed to the pursuit of things intellectual like Athens. Society would be sharply divided into three classes—philosophers, soldiers, and farmers—with admission to each class based on merit rather than heredity. Poetry and drama would be strictly censored. Plato advocated public education and toyed with more radical notions: not only gender equality but also the abolition of the family and private property, institutions that he felt led to disunity and dissension.

Plato's ideas have always been controversial but almost never ignored. Even in his own day, most people considered Plato far too radical. The writings of his great student Aristotle were more to contemporary tastes. Originally from Macedonia, **Aristotle** spent most of his life in Athens, first as a student at the Academy, then as the founder of his own school, the Lyceum (lie-SEE-um). Like Plato, Aristotle wrote dialogues, but none has survived. His main extant works are treatises, largely compilations by students of his lecture notes. One of the most wide-ranging intellectuals, Aristotle had a voracious appetite for knowledge and for writing. His treatises embrace politics, ethics, poetry, botany, physics, metaphysics, astronomy, rhetoric, zoology, logic, and psychology.

Though influenced by Plato's idealism, Aristotle was a far more practical, down-to-earth thinker. His father had been a doctor, which may account for Aristotle's interest in applied science and in biology and the biological method. Unlike Plato, Aristotle placed great emphasis on observation and fieldwork and on classification and systemization.

Aristotle agreed with Plato about the existence of absolute standards of good and evil, but he emphasized the relevance of such standards to everyday life. Unlike Plato, Aristotle considered the senses important guides. Change, he believed, was not an illusion but rather an

Aristotle Ancient Greek philosopher, student of Plato and tutor of Alexander the Great. His scientific writings were the most influential philosophical classics of Greek and Roman civilization and remained so during the Middle Ages.

important phenomenon. Aristotle's view of change was teleological—that is, he emphasized the goal (*telos* in Greek) of change. According to Aristotle, every organism changes and grows toward a particular end and is an integral and harmonious part of a larger whole. The entire cosmos is teleological, and each and every one of its parts has a purpose. Behind the cosmos was a principle that Aristotle called "the unmoved mover," the supreme cause of existence.

Aristotle defined an object's aretê as the fulfillment of its inherent function in the cosmos. The aretê of a horse, for example, was to be strong, fast, and obedient; the aretê of a rose was to look beautiful and smell sweet. As for the aretê of a human being, Aristotle agreed with Plato: only the philosopher achieved true aretê. As a pragmatist, however, Aristotle did not imagine philosophers becoming kings. Even so, he did not advocate democracy, which he considered mob rule. Instead, he advocated a government of wealthy gentlemen who had been trained by philosophers—not the best regime imaginable but, in Aristotle's opinion, the best one possible.

Aristotle believed that men had stronger capacities to make judgments than women and so should rule over them. He condemned states like Sparta that accorded power to women. (See the box "The Written Record: Spartan Women" on page 67.) Hence Aristotle would be cited in later centuries to justify male dominance. Ironically, however, Aristotle was more enlightened on gender issues than most of his contemporaries. For example, he believed that since women played a crucial role in the family, they should receive education in morality.

Online Study Center **Improve Your Grade**
Primary Source: Aristotle's Politics Offers a Conservative Commentary on Social and Gender Equality

Aristotle may be the single most influential thinker in Western history. His scientific writings not only were the most influential philosophical classics of Greek civilization, and of Roman civilization as well, but they remained so during the Middle Ages in the Arabic and Latin worlds. It took nearly two thousand years for serious rivals to challenge Aristotle's intellectual supremacy.

ATHENIAN DRAMA

Perhaps the greatest art form that emerged in the polis was drama. Modern comedy and tragedy find distant ancestors in the productions of Athens's theater of Dionysus, named for the god of unrestraint, liberation, and wine. Comedy and tragedy began in religious festivals honoring Dionysus (also known as Bacchus) but quickly became an independent forum for comment on public life. Ancient drama was poetry, not prose. Because it highlighted the relation of the individual to

Theater at Delphi
Open to the air, an ancient Greek theater contained tiers of stone benches above a circular area where the action took place, behind which backdrops could be erected. The audience often had a view of stirring scenery that, at Delphi, included the temple of Apollo and the valley below. *(Vanni/Art Resource, NY)*

the community, drama proved to be the most suitable poetic medium for the ideology of the polis.

According to ancient tradition, **tragedy** was first presented at the Dionysian festival in Athens by Thespis in the 530s B.C. (hence the word *thespian* for "actor"). The first surviving tragedy dates from the 470s B.C., the first surviving comedy from the 420s B.C. A play in the fifth century B.C. consisted of a chorus (a group of performers working in unison) and three individual actors, who played all the various individual speaking parts. Plays were performed in an open-air theater on the south hillside of the Acropolis. Enormously popular, drama spread all over Greece, and eventually most poleis had a theater.

Classical Athenian tragedy was performed at the annual Dionysia in March. Each playwright would submit a trilogy of plays on a central theme, plus a raucous farce to break the tension afterward. Comedies, which were independent plays rather than trilogies, were performed both at the Dionysia and at a separate festival held in winter. Wealthy producers competed to outfit the most lavish and impressive productions. Judges would award prizes for the best plays—a typical reflection of Greek competitiveness.

Tragedy is not easy to define, except generally: a serious play with an unhappy ending. Perhaps a short tag from the playwright Aeschylus (ESS-kih-luhs) can be said to sum up tragedy: *pathos mathei*, "suffering teaches." The essence of tragedy is what has been called the tragic sense of life: the nobility in the spectacle of a great man or woman failing but learning from failure. In *Oedipus the Tyrant* (ca. 428 B.C.) by Sophocles, for example, the hero unknowingly kills his father and unknowingly marries his mother. Oedipus cannot escape the consequences of his deeds, but he can react to his fate with dignity and heroism; he can try to understand it. Oedipus loses his power as tyrant and goes into exile, but he retains a degree of honor. He carries out his own punishment by blinding himself. As Aristotle observed, tragedy derives its emotional power from the fear and pity that it evokes and from the purification of the senses (*katharsis*) that it leaves in its aftermath.

The great period of Attic tragedy began and ended in the fifth century B.C. Aeschylus (525–456 B.C.), Sopho-

tragedy Serious play with an unhappy ending. Greek tragedy emerged and reached its height in the fifth century B.C. in the works of Aeschylus, Sophocles, and Euripides.

cles (ca. 495–406 B.C.), and Euripides (ca. 485–406 B.C.) were and are considered the three giant playwrights. Although other tragedians wrote plays, only the works of these three men (or, rather, a small fraction of their works) have survived. Aeschylus was perhaps the most pious of the three. His plays—notably the trilogy of the *Oresteia* (the *Agamemnon,* the *Libation Bearers,* and the *Eumenides*), the only surviving tragic trilogy, dating from 458 B.C.—take as their central question the justice of Zeus. The subject is the myth of the House of Atreus—in particular, the murder of King Agamemnon by his much-wronged wife, Clytemnestra, and her murder in turn by their son, Orestes, avenging his father. Aeschylus casts this primitive saga into an epic of the discovery of justice. In fulfillment of the will of Zeus, Athena puts an end to vengeance killings and institutes the supposed first court of law: the court of the Areopagus in Athens.

Sophocles, too, was interested in divine justice. His tragedies focus on the relationship between the individual and the community. Heroic individuals have a spark of the divine in them, but their towering virtues are threats to ordinary people. In *Antigone* (ca. 442 B.C.), for example, the heroine refuses to compromise with injustice. Her late brother had committed treason, for which his corpse is denied burial—the standard Greek punishment. Antigone, however, insists on following a higher law, Zeus's law, which demands that all bodies be buried. Turmoil, disorder, and death ensue, but Antigone stays true to principle.

Of the three tragedians, Euripides (yoo-RIP-uh-deez) is the least traditional and the most influenced by the Sophists. His plays reflect the disillusionment of the Peloponnesian War era. Euripides was more impressed by divine power than by divine justice. The central gods of Aeschylean drama are Zeus the father and Apollo the lawgiver, while Sophocles focuses on semidivine heroes, but Euripides' major deities are Dionysus and Aphrodite, goddess of erotic passion. In the *Bacchae* (406 B.C.), for example, an arrogant young king named Pentheus is punished for refusing to recognize the power of Dionysus (Bacchus). When he goes to the hills to spy on drunken women, called "Bacchae," who are worshiping the god, he ends up as their prisoner. Driven to frenzy by Dionysus, the women do not recognize the king. Indeed, Pentheus's own mother, one of the Bacchae, mistakes him for an animal and kills him.

The changes in tragedy from Aeschylus to Euripides reflect the changes in Athens as first imperial arrogance and then the Peloponnesian War took their moral toll. Aeschylus's confidence in the goodness of the community gives way first to a focus on the individual struggling to be good and then to a fundamental doubt about the possibility of goodness. The civic order, celebrated so confidently at the end of the *Oresteia* (458 B.C.), looks less certain in Sophocles' *Oedipus*

(ca. 428 B.C.) and by the time of Euripides' *Bacchae* (406 B.C.) seems terrifyingly weak.

Comedy, too, was invented in Athens in the Classical period. Like tragedy, comedy offers a moral commentary on contemporary Athenian life. Unlike tragedy, which is usually set in the past and takes its characters from mythology, Athenian comedy (the so-called Old Comedy) is set in the present and pokes fun at politicians and public figures. Whereas tragedy is generally serious and sad, comedy is light, biting, and humorous.

The greatest writer of comedy in the fifth century B.C. was Aristophanes (ca. 455–385 B.C.). His extant plays are lively, ribald, even scatological, and full of allusions to contemporary politics. Aristophanes loved to show the "little guy" getting the better of the powerful and women deflating the pretensions of men. In *Lysistrata* (411 B.C.), his best-known play, he imagines the women of Greece stopping the Peloponnesian War by going on a sex strike, which forces the men to make peace.

HISTORICAL THOUGHT AND WRITING

Like drama, history flourished in the exciting intellectual atmosphere of classical Athens. Indeed, its two greatest historians, **Herodotus** (ca. 485–425 B.C.) and **Thucydides** (ca. 455–397 B.C.), are among the founders of history-writing in the West. This judgment is not meant to discount the contributions of, for example, the Hittites or Hebrews, or the chronicles, inventories, and genealogies of early Greece. Herodotus and Thucydides, however, are more rationalistic than their predecessors, and their subject matter is war, politics, peoples, and customs—what we think of as the stuff of history-writing today. Indeed, the word *history* comes from a word used by Herodotus, *historiai,* meaning "inquiries" or "research."

The works of Herodotus (*The Histories*) and Thucydides (*The Peloponnesian War*) have unifying themes. The thread through *The Histories* is the cyclical rise and fall of empires. Herodotus sees the Persian Wars as merely one episode in a vast historical drama. Again and again, hardy, disciplined peoples conquered their neighbors, grew wealthy, were corrupted by a life of luxury, and were eventually conquered in turn. Success made people arrogant, driving them to commit injustices, which were eventually punished by Zeus. The breadth of Herodotus's vision is noteworthy. A native of Halicarnassus (a polis on the southwestern coast of Anatolia; see Map 3.4), Herodotus traveled widely, eventually settling in Athens. He wrote not only about Greeks but also about Persians, Egyptians, and a host of other

Herodotus Credited, along with Thucydides, of founding history-writing in the West. The word *history* comes from the word *historiai* used by Herodotus.

Thucydides Ancient Greek historian; with Herodotus, a founder of history-writing in the West.

peoples in Europe, Asia, and Africa. (See the box "The Global Record: The Enemy as Barbarian" on page 78.)

Only a child at the time of the Persian Wars, Herodotus gathered information by interviewing older people in various countries as well as by checking what limited written public records existed. Herodotus also wrote about previous centuries and places he had not visited, but with uneven accuracy. He could rarely resist a good story, and alongside solid research are tall tales, unconfirmed accounts, and myths.

Thucydides, by contrast, prided himself on accuracy. He confined himself mainly to writing about an event that he had lived through and participated in: the Peloponnesian War. A failed Athenian general, Thucy-dides spent most of the Peloponnesian War in exile, carefully observing, taking notes, and writing.

Like Herodotus, Thucydides was influenced by the grandeur of Classical tragedy. He also shows the signs of the Sophist movement, especially in the finely crafted speeches he includes in his writing. Thucydides' great theme is the disastrous effect of war on the human soul. His case study, the Peloponnesian War, proved that war is a harsh teacher: it strips away the veneer of civilization and reveals the savagery of human nature. In Thucydides' opinion, Periclean Athens was a high point in the history of civilization. The strain of prolonged war, however, destroyed Athens's moral fiber as well as its empire.

SECTION SUMMARY

- The culture of Greece during 480–322 B.C. is called classical because it has proved influential throughout the history of the West.

- Classical Greek sculpture was the most technically proficient sculpture seen yet, and it set a standard for all future work.

- The Athenian Socrates changed the emphasis of Greek philosophy from nature to human ethics.

- The idealist philosopher Plato and his more practical student, Aristotle, are the most influential philosophers of the West.

- Comedy and tragedy were invented in Athens, flourished in public festivals, and offered a moral commentary on contemporary life.

- Herodotus and Thucydides are among the founders of history-writing in the West.

 # CHAPTER SUMMARY

Online Study Center **ACE the Test**

What was the Greek polis, and how did it develop in Sparta, Athens, and Corinth in Archaic Greece?

How did Western individualism and rationalism take root in Archaic Greece?

What was Athenian democracy and how did it clash with Sparta in the Peloponnesian War?

How did tragedy, comedy, philosophy, and history all begin and develop in the culture of Classical Greece?

Western philosophy, science, politics, sculpture, painting, and literary genres such as comedy, tragedy, and history all emerged in Archaic and Classical Greece.

The focus of ancient Greek life was the polis. The polis was a city-state that emphasized participation and equality and invented the idea of the citizen. Trade, colonization, and the invention of the Greek alphabet and of the hoplite phalanx all contributed to the emergence of the polis around 700 B.C.

Archaic Sparta developed Greece's best citizen-army whose job was to prevent helot uprisings or attacks from abroad. Sparta's stable government and austere culture fostered the idea that public duty is more important than private advantage. Archaic Corinth is the prime example of tyranny, a widespread form of government in Greece in which new wealth led to the emergence of popular champions. Archaic Athens developed, thanks to Solon's reforms, a large class of independent small farmers. They later turned out to be the backbone of democracy. Solon unintentionally created conditions for the growth of slavery.

The culture of Archaic Greece was the seedbed of Western individualism and rationalism. Lyric poetry emphasized individual emotion, and Archaic sculpture focused on the human body. Although Archaic Greece was a religious society, it also gave rise to the first philosophers. They lived in Ionia in the 500s B.C. and offered a nontheological explanation of nature.

Democracy or "people power" (*demokratia*) began in ancient Greece, and the Athenian version is best known.

Athenian democracy was direct and participatory but limited to adult males. Classical Greece was a period of intense war. Athens and Sparta united to lead a Greek coalition that defeated Persia's invasion in 480–479 B.C. Afterward, the two poleis turned on each other, most violently in the Peloponnesian War (431–404 B.C.). With its democracy, freedom, and high culture, Athens stands for one aspect of the achievement of the polis; with its hierarchy, militarism, and citizen virtue, Sparta stands for another.

Classical Greek culture has proved influential again and again in the history of the West. Athens became Greece's cultural center. Here, comedy and tragedy were invented, history-writing was founded, sculpture reached a peak of proficiency in showing the human body, and philosophy changed its emphasis from nature to human ethics. The philosophers Socrates, Plato, and Aristotle are among the West's greatest thinkers.

LOOKING AHEAD

The outbreak of the Peloponnesian War in 431 B.C. marked the beginning of a century in which Greek warfare was more brutal than before. By the end of the fourth century B.C., as we shall see in Chapter 4, the polis would lose its independence to a powerful monarchy. In succeeding years, new cities in western Asia and Egypt would amass the wealth and power to challenge such old centers as Athens as cultural capitals. Yet the culture that flourished in the new sites was Greek culture. The polis lost its freedom but gained a central place in the legacy of the West.

KEY TERMS

Archaic Greece (p. 60)

polis (p. 60)

hoplite phalanx (p. 61)

Solon (p. 68)

Sappho (p. 70)

Classical Greece (p. 71)

demokratia (p. 74)

Pericles (p. 75)

Socrates (p. 85)

Plato (p. 85)

Aristotle (p. 86)

tragedy (p. 87)

Herodotus (p. 88)

Thucydides (p. 88)

Online Study Center
Improve Your Grade Flashcards

SUGGESTED READING

Beard, Mary. *The Parthenon.* An elegant and erudite short history.

Biers, W. *The Archaeology of Ancient Greece: An Introduction.* 2d ed. 1996. A clear presentation of the achievements and variety of archaeological excavation in Greece.

Boardman, John. *The Greeks Overseas: Their Early Colonies and Trade.* 4th ed. 1999. The standard introduction; authoritative, vivid, updated, and beautifully illustrated.

Cartledge, Paul. *The Spartans: The World of the Warrior-Heroes of Ancient Greece.* 2003. A lively and reliable introduction by a great expert on ancient Sparta.

Connolly, Peter, and Hazel Dodge. *The Ancient City: Life in Classical Athens and Rome.* 1998. Connolly's gorgeous illustrations and outstanding reconstructions distinguish this introduction to daily life in the two cities.

Hanson, Victor Davis. *A War Like No Other: How the Athenians and Spartans Fought the Peloponnesian War.* 2005. New insight into the brutal reality of the war, by a leading military historian.

Martin, Thomas. *Ancient Greece from Prehistoric to Hellenistic Times.* 2000. A readable and scholarly introduction emphasizing politics and war.

Pomeroy, Sarah B. *Goddesses, Whores, Wives, and Slaves: Women in Classical Antiquity.* 1975. An overview of women in politics and society in Greece, the Hellenistic world, and Rome; still the best introduction to the subject.

Strauss, Barry S. *The Battle of Salamis: The Naval Encounter That Saved Ancient Greece.* 2004. Opens a window onto Greece and Persia while telling a gripping story.

NOTES

1. Excerpt from a poem by Solon, quoted in Aristotle, *Constitution of Athens,* trans. Barry S. Strauss.

2. Charles Rowan Beye, *Ancient Greek Literature and Society,* 2d ed. (Ithaca, N.Y.: Cornell University Press, 1987), p. 78.

3. Ibid., p. 79.

4. Adapted from Richmond Lattimore, trans., *Greek Lyrics,* 2d ed. (Chicago: University of Chicago Press, 1960), p. 19.

5. Herodotus, *The Histories,* trans. Barry S. Strauss.

6. Thucydides, *The Peloponnesian War,* trans. Barry S. Strauss.

4

ALEXANDER THE GREAT AND THE SPREAD OF GREEK CIVILIZATION, CA. 350–30 B.C.

Stag Hunt
Pebble mosaic from Pella.
(Pella Museum/Archaeological Receipts Fund)

The young men in the pebble mosaic shown opposite wield ax and sword against the stag whom they are hunting. The artist, named Gnosis, was a master at rendering perspective and drama. Clearly, no expense was spared on the work, dated around 325 B.C. Both the vigor of the scene and the quality of the craftsmanship symbolize the spirit of a young man who was born in Pella, the Macedonian (mah-seh-DOE-nee-un) capital where the mosaic was displayed: that man was Alexander the Great. Alexander was a fearless warrior and one of the most brilliant generals in the history of the world. In just twelve years he conquered all the territory between Greece and India, as well as Egypt.

Alexander created new realities of power as king of Macedon (r. 336–323 B.C.). A northeastern Greek kingdom that had previously been only a fringe power, Macedon rose meteorically under Alexander's father, Philip II (r. 359–336 B.C.), to become the leading military power in Greece. Philip was a brilliant and ambitious general, but Alexander outstripped him.

Alexander laid the foundations of a new Greek world: the world of the Hellenistic (hel-len-IS-tik) period (323–30 B.C.), in which Hellenic, or Greek, language and civilization spread and were transformed. This era was distinct in many ways from the preceding Hellenic period (ca. 750–323 B.C.). In Hellenistic times, Macedonians and Greeks replaced Persians as the ruling people of Egypt and western Asia. Large numbers of Greek-speaking colonists moved south and east. Governed by Macedonian dynasties, Egypt and the Levant became integral parts of the Greek world and remained so until the Arab conquest in the seventh century A.D. Greek-speaking kingdoms thrived briefly as far east as modern Afghanistan and Pakistan. At times the new ruling elite was open to natives who learned Greek and adopted Greek ways, but more often natives were excluded and exploited.

Conquest put huge amounts of wealth into Greek hands. Alexander and his successors built great new cities: Antioch (AN-tee-ock) in Syria, Pergamum in Anatolia, Seleucia (seh-LOO-she-uh) in Mesopotamia, and, greatest of all, Alexandria in Egypt. Trade increased and expanded southward and eastward. In political life, individual cities continued to be important, but federal leagues (that is, unions of city-states) and monarchies ruled most of the Greek-speaking world.

CHAPTER OUTLINE

PHILIP AND ALEXANDER

THE HELLENISTIC KINGDOMS, 323–30 B.C.

ALEXANDRIAN CULTURE

THE TURN INWARD: NEW PHILOSOPHIES, NEW FAITHS

KEY TERMS

Macedon	Alexandria
Philip II	Antioch
Alexander the Great	Stoics
Hellenism	Epicureans
Ptolemies	mystery religions
Seleucids	Maccabees
Antigonids	

Online Study Center

This icon will direct you to interactive map and primary source activities on the website **college.hmco.com/pic/noble5e**

Material and political expansion led to unanticipated cultural changes, which may be summarized as a turn inward. Frequently finding themselves among strange peoples, the Greeks sought comfort in new philosophies, religions, and modes of literary and artistic expression. Many of these new cultural forms emphasized people's emotions and intentions, not simply their actions. Science, meanwhile, flourished under royal patronage, as did the emerging discipline of literary criticism. The prestige of royal women tended to promote improvements in the overall status of Greek women.

Hellenistic Greeks boasted of having created one world—a common, or ecumenical (from the Greek *oikoumene* [oy-koo-men-AY], "inhabited"), region. In truth, that world was complex. Native cultures flourished, while Greeks adapted and Hellenized a number of Egyptian and Asian deities.

Hellenistic Greek contact with one native culture in particular—Judaism—proved to have a lasting impact on the West. Under the impact of the Greeks, Judaism became more self-conscious and placed a greater emphasis on salvation, martyrdom, and individual study and prayer. Some Jews resisted Greek culture, others adopted it, and still others resolved to convert Greeks to Judaism. Reshaped by its contacts with the Greeks, Hellenistic Judaism was poised to transform Western religion.

FOCUS QUESTIONS

How did Macedon under Philip and Alexander conquer both the Greek city-states and the Persian Empire?

What new states emerged as a result of Alexander's conquests and how did they integrate Greek settlers with native peoples?

How did Greek civilization spread during the Hellenistic era, and what were the main trends in literature, science, and art?

What new philosophies and religions emerged in the Hellenistic period?

PHILIP AND ALEXANDER

How did Macedon under Philip and Alexander conquer both the Greek city-states and the Persian Empire?

The Hellenistic world was founded by two conquerors: Philip II of Macedon (382–336 B.C.) and his son, Alexander III, known as Alexander the Great (356–323 B.C.). After a century of indecisive warfare among the Greek city-states, Philip swept south and conquered them in twenty years. In even less time Alexander conquered Egypt and all of western Asia as far east as modern India. The legacy of these impressive conquests was to spread Greek civilization and to change it, both of which consequences were revolutionary developments.

THE RISE OF MACEDON

Macedon was a border state, long weaker than its more advanced neighbors but capable of learning from them and ultimately of conquering them. Though rich in resources and manpower, Macedon lacked the relatively efficient organization of the polis. Several dialects of Greek were spoken, some unintelligible to southern Greeks, who considered Macedonians "barbarians" (from the Greek *barbaros,* meaning "a person who does not speak Greek"). Ordinary Macedonians lived rough, sturdy lives, while the king and the royal court inhabited a sophisticated capital city, Pella, where they sponsored visits by leading Greek artists and writers. **Philip II** confounded Greek stereotypes of Macedonian barbarism by turning out to be a brilliant soldier and statesman—a man of vast ambition, appetite, and energy. A hard drinker, vain, and a man with numerous wives and lovers, he was also an excellent orator and general. Philip's goals were to make himself dominant in Macedon and then, after neutralizing opposition in Greece, to conquer the Persian Empire, or at

---

Macedon   Weaker, less culturally advanced state on Greece's northern border that was unified and led to power by Philip II and Alexander the Great.

Philip II   King of Macedon and father of Alexander the Great, he was a brilliant soldier and statesman who conquered the Greek world.

least its holdings in Anatolia. He accomplished all but the last.

The instrument of Philip's success was his army, a well-trained, professional, year-round force. Macedon, with its plains and horses, was cavalry country, and Philip raised cavalry to a new level of importance. In battle, the Macedonian phalanx would first hold the enemy phalanx until the cavalry could find a weak spot and break the enemy line. Then the phalanx would attack and finish the job. Macedonian hoplites carried extra-long pikes to keep the enemy at a distance. Philip also mastered the technology of siegecraft, raising it to a level unseen since Assyrian days (see page 33).

Philip used his army effectively. After capturing a gold mine in Thrace (the region east of Macedon), he turned to the Greek city-states nearby. Olynthus, the most important, fell in 348 B.C. Led by the Athenian Demosthenes (de-MOSS-thuh-neez) (ca. 385–322 B.C.), the main Greek city-states prepared to make a stand. Demosthenes was a superb orator, but his attempts to forge a unified force came too late. By 338 B.C., when an Atheno-Theban army met the Macedonians, Philip had already won over much of the Greek world through diplomacy, bribes, and threats. His complete military victory at Chaeronea in Boeotia was followed up with a lenient settlement in which all the Greeks except Sparta acknowledged Philip's hegemony (see **MAP 4.1**). The Greeks would rebel against Macedon more than once but always in vain, until they fell under the even greater power of Rome. The polis would no longer decide the fate of the eastern Mediterranean.

In 336 B.C. Philip was murdered by a disgruntled courtier, and the invasion of the Persian Empire fell to his 20-year-old son, Alexander, the new king.

ALEXANDER THE CONQUEROR

Alexander III of Macedon (r. 336–323 B.C.), better known as **Alexander the Great,** is as famous in art as in literature, in romance as in history, in Iran and India as in Europe and America. Yet the evidence for the historical Alexander is almost as problematic as that for the historical Socrates or Jesus. After Alexander's untimely death at age 32, contemporaries wrote histories and memoirs, but none has survived. Several good historical accounts, based on earlier texts, are extant, but none was written less than three hundred years after Alexander's day. (See the box "The Written Record: Virtues and Vices of Alexander the Great.") Alexander, moreover, was not only a legend in his own time but also a master propagandist. Many of the incidents of his life took place in remote regions or among a few individuals, and they tended to grow with the telling.

Alexander the Great   King of Macedon and conqueror of the Persian Empire, he spread Greek civilization to western Asia, Egypt, and India.

359–336 B.C.	Reign of Philip II of Macedon
ca. 342–292 B.C.	Life of playwright Menander
338 B.C.	Greece falls to Philip at Battle of Chaeronea
336–323 B.C.	Reign of Alexander the Great
331 B.C.	Battle of Gaugamela completes Persian defeat
323–275 B.C.	Wars of the Successors
313 B.C.	Zeno founds Stoic philosophy in Athens
312 B.C.	Seleucus I conquers Babylon
304 B.C.	Ptolemy I king of Egypt
294 B.C.	Museum founded in Alexandria
276 B.C.	Antigonus Gonatas king of Macedon
263 B.C.	Kingdom of Pergamum founded
ca. 246 B.C.	Parthia revolts from Seleucids
ca. 245 B.C.	Bactria gains independence
244–222 B.C.	Reforms of Agis and Cleomenes in Sparta
ca. 225 B.C.	Eratosthenes of Cyrene calculates earth's circumference
217 B.C.	Battle of Raphia brings Palestine under Ptolemies
167–142 B.C.	Maccabean revolt in Judea
146 B.C.	Antigonid Macedonia becomes a Roman province
64 B.C.	Seleucid Syria becomes a Roman province
30 B.C.	Ptolemaic Egypt becomes a Roman province

Still, Alexander's virtues are clear. He was charismatic, handsome, intelligent, and well educated; as a teenager he had Aristotle himself as a private tutor. Alexander was ruthless as well as cultured. He began his reign with a massacre of his male relatives, but he brought a team of Greek scientists along with him on his expedition through the Persian Empire. Although he destroyed peoples and places, Alexander founded twenty cities. One of those cities was born in 331 B.C., at the site of a fishing village in the northwestern part of Egypt's delta. Alexander and his advisers planned a great trading center to replace Tyre, whose inhabitants had been killed

MAP 4.1   Conquests of Philip and Alexander

Between 359 and 323 B.C., the armies of Macedon conquered first the Greek city-states and then the Persian Empire. Macedonian power extended from Greece and Egypt eastward to modern India.

Online Study Center   **Improve Your Grade**
Interactive Map: Conquests of Philip and Alexander

or enslaved by the Macedonians who had stormed the town in 332 B.C. The new city, called Alexandria, later grew into the largest city in the Mediterranean.

For all his varied interests, Alexander was first and foremost a warrior. Battlefield commander of the Macedonian cavalry at age 18, he devoted most of the rest of his life to warfare. As a leader of men, Alexander was popular and inspiring, and he shared risks with his troops. He knew the value of propaganda and took pains to depict his expedition to the Greek city-states as a war of revenge for Persia's invasion of Greece in 480 B.C.

On the eve of invasion, Persia vastly outnumbered Macedon on both land and sea. Darius III of Persia was rich; Alexander's treasury was virtually empty. The Macedonian expeditionary force was short on supplies. The peoples in Persia's multi-ethnic empire were restive, but

so too were Alexander's Greek allies, the mainstay of his fleet. One of Darius's advisers proposed a naval campaign to raise a revolt in Greece and force the Macedonians home. How, then, did Alexander propose to conquer Persia?

The answer was the Macedonian army. Although Alexander invaded Anatolia with only about thirty-five thousand men, they were the fastest-marching, most experienced, and most skilled army in the eastern Mediterranean. If Persia would fight the Macedonians in a set battle, Alexander might be confident of victory—and proud Persia insisted on fighting. As expected, Macedon won the war in three great battles (see Map 4.1): at the Granicus River in Anatolia (334 B.C.), at Issus in Syria (333 B.C.), and at Gaugamela in Mesopotamia (331 B.C.). By 328 B.C. Alexander's claim to be king of Persia was sealed with blood and iron.

Having conquered the Persian heartland, Alexander turned eastward. The last seven years of his career are marked by three themes. First is the continuing military campaign. Alexander pushed his army not only into the eastern parts of the Persian Empire but beyond, into India, which had not been controlled by Persia since the early fifth century B.C. The Macedonians won a big victory there in 326 B.C. near the Hydaspes River (modern Jhelum River) over the army of King Porus, which had as many as two hundred elephants (see Map 4.1). Alexander's infantry suffered heavy casualties before inflicting enough wounds on the elephants to make them uncontrollable. Alexander wanted to continue eastward, perhaps as far as the Bay of Bengal, but his exhausted and homesick men had other plans. They mutinied and forced Alexander finally to turn back. He reached Persia in late 325 B.C.

The second theme of Alexander's later career is his increasing despotism. The king turned on the Macedonian nobility, which had a tradition of rebelling against strong rulers. The years after 330 B.C. were marked by conspiracy trials, purges, and assassinations. Alexander offended independent-minded Macedonians by demanding that they bow down to him, Persian style. He offended Greek city-states by insisting that they deify him. "If Alexander wishes to be a god, let him be" was the concise reply of the Spartans, but Alexander had set a precedent for both Hellenistic monarchs and Roman emperors.

The third theme of Alexander's later career is his policy of fusion. In 325 B.C. Alexander began training an army of thirty thousand Persians and dismissed a large number of Macedonian troops. He forced his commanders to marry Persian women, just as he himself did. He publicly prayed for "concord and a partnership in rule between Greeks and Persians." It was all a sharp break with traditional Greek nationalism but it was not entirely idealistic, since it would give Alexander a new power base independent of the Macedonian nobility.

Alexander died in Babylon in June 323 B.C., a month before he turned 33, probably of malarial fever, although some contemporaries suspected poison and some historians have suggested drunkenness. Alexander did not name a successor. The Macedonian generals fought a long and bloody round of wars over the spoils of empire. Not until 275 B.C. was it clear that three large kingdoms—Macedon (under the Antigonid dynasty), Ptolemaic (tol-eh-MAY-ik) Egypt, and the Seleucid (seh-LOO-sid) realm—would inherit most of Alexander's empire. The rest was divided among small kingdoms, federal leagues, and independent city-states (see **MAP 4.2**).

Alexander Mosaic

This detail of a Roman-era mosaic from Pompeii shows Alexander the Great in battle, probably at Issus. Shining in his battle armor, Alexander is bareheaded, with a wide-eyed, intense gaze betokening his power. The larger scene includes the Persian king Darius, fleeing in his chariot. *(Scala/Art Resource, NY)*

MAP 4.2   **Hellenistic Kingdoms, Leagues, and City-States, ca. 240 B.C.**
After Alexander's death, his empire lost its political unity. Great new cities and kingdoms arose in the lands he had conquered.

In the long run, Alexander's life was far more influential than his death. His conquests did nothing less than lay the foundations of the Hellenistic world. It is ironic to measure in such impersonal terms the achievements of one who, more than most people in history, exemplifies individual success. Whether it was exalting a savior or debunking a hero, much of Hellenistic culture centered on the myth of heroism that

Alexander had engendered. Historians who insist that the individual is insignificant will rarely have a more challenging refutation than Alexander.

Online Study Center **Improve Your Grade**
Primary Source: Alexander the Great Remembered: Visions of Divinity

━━━━━━ S E C T I O N   S U M M A R Y ━━━━━━

- Macedon rose to power under King Philip and conquered the Greek city-states.

- Alexander was a brilliant soldier and leader of the most skilled army in the eastern Mediterranean, created by his father Philip.

- Alexander and the Macedonians won thanks to Persia's proud but foolish decision to fight the enemy in pitched battles.

- A march into India, increasing despotism, and a policy of fusion of Greeks and Macedonians all marked Alexander's last years.

- By conquering the Persian Empire, Alexander ushered in a new age in Greek history: the Hellenistic era.

VIRTUES AND VICES OF ALEXANDER THE GREAT

Writing in the second century A.D., four centuries after Alexander's death, the historian Arrian composed from earlier accounts what is now the best surviving history of Alexander. A military man himself, Arrian appreciated Alexander's skills but was not blind to his flaws.

Alexander died in the 114th Olympiad, in the archonship of Hegesias at Athens [June 323 B.C.]. He lived, as Aristobulus tells us, thirty-two years and eight months, and reigned twelve years and eight months. He had great personal beauty, invincible power of endurance, and a keen intellect; he was brave and adventurous, strict in the observance of his religious duties, and hungry for fame. Most temperate in the pleasures of the body, his passion was for glory only, and in that he was insatiable. He had an uncanny instinct for the right course in a difficult and complex situation, and was most happy in his deductions from observed facts. In arming and equipping troops and in his military dispositions he was always masterly. Noble indeed was his power of inspiring his men, of filling them with confidence, and, in the moment of danger, of sweeping away their fear by the spectacle of his own fearlessness. When risks had to be taken, he took them with the utmost boldness, and his ability to seize the moment for a swift blow, before the enemy had any suspicion of what was coming, was beyond praise. No cheat or liar ever caught him off guard, and both his word and his bond were inviolable. Spending but little on his own pleas-ures, he poured out his money without stint for the benefit of his friends.

Doubtless, in the passion of the moment Alexander sometimes erred; it is true he took some steps towards the pomp and arrogance of the Asiatic kings: but I, at least, cannot feel that such errors were very heinous, if the circumstances are taken fairly into consideration. For, after all, he was young; the chain of his successes was unbroken, and, like all kings, past, present, and to come, he was surrounded by courtiers who spoke to please, regardless of what evil their word might do. On the other hand, I do indeed know that Alexander, of all the monarchs of old, was the only one who had the nobility of heart to be sorry for his mistakes. . . .

In the course of this book I have, admittedly, found fault with some of the things which Alexander did, but of the man himself I am not ashamed to express ungrudging admiration.

QUESTIONS

1. What are Alexander's main virtues, according to Arrian?

2. In what way does Arrian find fault with Alexander?

3. For Arrian, what is the "bottom line" about Alexander?

Source: Arrian, *The Campaigns of Alexander,* trans. Aubrey de Sélin-court, rev. J. R. Hamilton (Harmondsworth, U.K.: Penguin, 1971), pp. 395–396. Reproduced by permission of Penguin Books Ltd.

THE HELLENISTIC KINGDOMS, 323–30 B.C.

What new states emerged as a result of Alexander's conquests and how did they integrate Greek settlers with native peoples?

Variety, flexibility, and the creation of a new elite to transmit Greek culture compose the Hellenistic political legacy. Hellenistic political units ranged from multi-ethnic kingdoms to small, ethnically homogeneous city-states (see Map 4.2). The Greek peninsula saw both a monarchy with republican leanings as well as experiments in federalism and social revolution. In Asia and Egypt, a new ruling elite emerged consisting both of Greeks and Macedonians and of natives. Although the first group tended to dominate high office, natives were by no means excluded. The immigrants wanted land, wealth, or adventure. Their paths were smoothed by a new ideology that identified being Greek less with loyalty to an individual city than with participation in a common Greek civilization.

Although the Hellenistic world became relatively peaceful after 275 B.C., conflict among the kingdoms continued. Generally waged at a low level of intensity, with bribes and diplomacy as weapons, the conflict nonetheless sometimes broke out into major battles. A number of small states emerged in Anatolia, notably Pergamum, whose wealthy rulers were patrons of literature and art, and Galatia (guh-LAY-shuh), carved out by Celtic invaders from Europe.

COLONIALISM, GREEK STYLE

Many Greeks and Macedonians emigrated from home during the fourth and third centuries B.C., but we do not know how many. The few available statistics indicate a significant migration but not a mass exodus. By the second century B.C. the colonizing impulse had diminished in Greece and Macedon, but a large number of Jews left war-torn Palestine, particularly for Egypt. Ptolemaic Egypt and the Seleucid realm were also the most common destinations for Greek and Macedonian migrants.

Greek migrants could take advantage of a new definition of being Greek that had begun to emerge even before Alexander's conquests. Isocrates (eye-SOCK-rah-teez) (428–338 B.C.), an Athenian teacher of rhetoric, redefined Greek identity by promoting the idea that Greece was not a collection of city-states but a civilization. "The people we call Hellenes"—that is, Greeks—he wrote, "are those who have the same culture as us, not the same blood."[1]

The ideal of Greek culture made it easier for the migrants to maintain a Greek identity. For that matter, it was now possible for foreigners to become Greek by learning the Greek language and literature. The number of Hellenized foreigners was relatively small, yet their very existence marked a break from the Classical polis, where even a resident genius such as Aristotle could not obtain Athenian citizenship because he was not of Athenian descent.

The Greek language also served as a common denominator, along with Aramaic, both of which became the languages of trade in the eastern Mediterranean. To get a sense of the importance of Isocrates' redefinition of **Hellenism,** consider that one of the most famous Greek-speakers of all antiquity was Paul, the Christian apostle who was born a Jew in Tarsus, a city in southern Anatolia.

Immigrants sought to realize dreams of prosperity or adventure. Although agriculture was the main economic pursuit, trade, industry, finance, administration, and military service also offered opportunities.

In the Ptolemaic and Seleucid realms, administration was a joint effort of both immigrants and natives. The upper ranks of government were dominated by Greeks and Macedonians while native elites usually held low- or midlevel government positions. Especially after about 200 B.C., some natives even reached high of-

fice. Others worked in the traditional native administrative structures that survived largely intact in the new kingdoms—for example, as judges or village headmen or priests.

Consider, for example, soldiers. To create a hereditary military group in the countryside, Ptolemy (TOL-eh-mee) I settled his soldiers on land allotments. Native Egyptians were excluded from the army at first but served as policemen. By the second century B.C., however, the dynasty turned to native Egyptians as a new source of soldiers. In return for military service, natives now received land, tax breaks, and the right to call themselves Hellenes. Their Hellenism sometimes merely scratched the surface, but other times it went deeper.

An Egyptian named Plenis, a villager in Middle Egypt in the late second century B.C., is a good example. Plenis was a tenant farmer on a royal estate and a priest in a local Egyptian cult. Like his father before him, Plenis served as a soldier in the Ptolemaic army. Plenis could write Greek as well as Egyptian, and he even used a Greek name: Dionysius, son of Kephalas.

Temples, which often administered large estates, represented important sources of native power. Priests shaped local opinion and were in a position, therefore, both to enjoy autonomy and to demand royal patronage. Both **Ptolemies** and **Seleucids** complied: from Babylon to Edfu, money poured into temple-building and renovation.

The Seleucids addressed the security needs of their far-flung realms by establishing over seventy colonies extending to central Asia. Some colonies were civilian, but most were military, composed of retired or reserve soldiers, mostly Greeks or Macedonians, but also Jews and other non-Greek peoples. Colonists received land allotments. Greek-style public buildings were erected, and some cities were laid out according to a rectilinear grid reminiscent of the Classical polis. The gymnasium attained a great practical and symbolic importance as both the center of Greek culture and the preparatory school for entry into the elite. The Hellenistic gymnasium offered education in literature, philosophy, and oratory as well as athletics.

Some Seleucid colonies developed into flourishing cities. For example, Greek cities dominated the Syrian coastline and much of Anatolia until the coming of Islam in the seventh century A.D. Greek urbanization should not create the false impression, however, that the Seleucids were motivated by some civilizing mission. They were not. They established colonies to increase their power.

Ptolemies Dynasty founded by Ptolemy I and ruled by Egyptian kings, it was the wealthiest, most sophisticated, and longest lasting of the Hellenistic kingdoms.

Seleucids Dynasty founded by Seleucus and governed by rulers of Asia Minor from 312 to 64 B.C., it established seventy colonies throughout the Near East.

Hellenism Term used to designate ancient Greece's language, culture, and civilization.

ECONOMIC EXPANSION

Immigration and colonization were not the only sources of new economic opportunities. At the beginning of the Hellenistic era, Alexander turned the huge gold and silver reserves of Persia into coinage and released it onto the market virtually all at once. The result was about seventy-five years of inflation but also a commercial boom. In particular, money largely replaced barter in Egypt, which increased production and trade, helping to render Egypt an economic powerhouse. Another stimulus to trade was the creation of thriving new Hellenistic cities, especially Alexandria with its great harbors, canals, marketplaces, and infrastructure of banks, inns, courts, and shipbuilding facilities.

During Hellenistic times, commerce tended to shift from Greece proper to Anatolia and Egypt (see **MAP 4.3**).

The island of Rhodes, located off the southwest tip of Anatolia, grew into a major trading center, especially for grain. The Rhodian aristocracy grew rich off taxes and duties, wisely reinvesting a portion of the profits in naval infrastructure (such as arsenals and dockyards) and in campaigns against pirates. Egypt, too, had many products to trade. Grain was the most important, but textiles, glass, papyrus, and luxury goods were also significant. A network of canals connecting Alexandria to the Nile and the Red Sea beyond made trading possible with Sudan, Arabia, and India.

The Seleucid kingdoms controlled rich trade routes to the east. Commerce was facilitated by good roads, safe sea travel between the Persian Gulf and India, and a unified royal coinage. The Seleucids traded agricultural goods and manufactured products such as textiles, glassware, and metalwork for spices from India and Arabia. In

MAP 4.3   The Eastern Mediterranean, ca. 200 B.C.

The great Hellenistic powers contended for control of this vibrant, turbulent, and prosperous region. Conflict centered on Palestine and the Aegean islands, the rulership of which frequently changed hands.

Seleucid Monarchy
Ptolemaic Monarchy
Antigonid Monarchy
Pergamene Monarchy
Other Greek states and Hellenized kingdoms
Roman allies and dependents

Online Study Center **Improve Your Grade**
Interactive Map: The Eastern Mediterranean, ca. 200 B.C.

Tanagra Figurine
A terra-cotta (baked clay) statuette of around 320 B.C. shows a modestly dressed woman wearing a hat and carrying a fan. Named for its place of manufacture in Greece, this popular style of figure demonstrates the Hellenistic taste for ordinary, house-hold themes.
(Bildarchiv Preussischer Kulturbesitz/Art Resource, NY)

the first century B.C. they even had trade contacts with China, whose silk garments reached the Mediterranean. The kingdom of Pergamum, which stretched inland from Anatolia's northwest coast, exported the agricultural products of the rich hinterland it controlled, as well as the local gray-blue building stone and, as an alternative to Egyptian papyrus, parchment.

Slavery was an important part of the Hellenistic social and economic scene. Although war and piracy were the main sources of enslavement, some people were born into slavery. In Sicily and southern Italy, slaves worked huge plantations, but eastern Mediterranean slaves were commonly found in the household or in administration, and in cities rather than in the countryside. Many unfree laborers worked on farms in Egypt and western Asia. Following the pre-Greek traditions of those regions, they were generally tenant farmers tied to kings or potentates rather than outright slaves.

On some plantations conditions for slaves were harsh enough to lead to mass uprisings. It was not unusual, however, for domestic or administrative slaves to buy their freedom, sometimes using savings they were allowed to keep, sometimes borrowing money from the master or from friends. Greeks enslaved fellow Greeks, but often, it seems, with guilty consciences; they frequently made special efforts to help Greek slaves win their freedom. Even in bondage, therefore, Greeks had special privileges.

MACEDON AND GREECE

Macedon was the last of the three great Hellenistic kingdoms to emerge from civil war after Alexander's death. Not until 276 B.C. was Antigonus Gonatas, grandson of Alexander's general Antigonus the One-Eyed, established firmly on the throne. His Antigonid (an-TIG-on-id) dynasty lasted about a century, when the conquering Romans made Macedon first a republic and then a Roman province.

True to the traditions of Macedon, the **Antigonids** projected an image of simplicity and toughness. As a young man, Antigonus had studied the new school of Stoic philosophy in Athens (see page 174). As king, he devoted himself to the Stoic dictates of duty, describing his office as "noble servitude" and his diadem as a mere "rag." Antigonus shared the traditional Macedonian ambition to dominate the Greek city-states, but he faced rival powers. Besides Ptolemaic Egypt, there was the kingdom of Epirus in northwestern Greece and two new federal leagues in the south, the Aetolians (ay-TOL-ee-unz) (north of the Corinthian Gulf) and the Achaeans (uh-KEE-unz) (in the Peloponnesus; see Map 4.3).

Antigonids Dynasty founded by Antigonus Gonatas in 276 B.C. and governed by Macedonian rulers for about 140 years, until the Roman conquest.

The new leagues were dominated by the wealthy; they were not democracies. Yet the leagues interest us as models of federalism that would one day influence the founders of the United States. The Achaeans, for example, successfully balanced local and federal authorities. Constituent cities kept their own constitutions while recognizing federal jurisdiction. The federal government consisted of a governing general (both president and commander-in-chief) and ten subordinate magistrates, an executive council, and a general assembly.

Extremes of wealth and poverty, problems of debt, and class conflict challenged Hellenistic Greece. Athens remained a vibrant democracy until the late third century B.C., when the oligarchic upper classes finally won the upper hand for good. The decline of democracy enabled the wealthy to contribute less to the public good in taxes and to amass private fortunes. The result was sometimes class conflict, but the elite usually made just enough concessions to avoid full-scale revolution.

Sparta was an exception. In the late third century B.C. a social revolution was launched from above by Agis and Cleomenes, two Spartan kings working together. After defeat in the fourth century B.C., Sparta had become impoverished (see page 80). The reformers now offered debt relief, redistribution of land, and restoration of Classical Spartan austerity and equality. Popular in Sparta, the revolution threatened to spread elsewhere. Peloponnesian oligarchs called in Macedonian forces, which crushed Sparta in 222 B.C. and ended the revolution.

PTOLEMAIC EGYPT

The wealthiest, most sophisticated, and longest-lasting Hellenistic kingdom was Ptolemaic Egypt. One of Alexander's great generals, Ptolemy (d. 283 B.C.), founded a dynasty that lasted until Rome annexed Egypt in 30 B.C., after the suicide of the last of the line, Queen Cleopatra (see page 149). By then, Rome had already conquered or annexed all the other Hellenistic kingdoms.

Unlike the Antigonids, the Ptolemies gloried in wealth and grandeur. Ptolemy I showed the way to his successors when he had Alexander's funeral procession hijacked on its way to Macedonia and established a tomb and then a cult in the capital city, **Alexandria**—a Greek hero-shrine in the land of the pyramids. Ptolemy I made arrangements to have himself proclaimed "savior-god" after his death; his successors, less reticent, took divine honors while still alive.

Like the pharaohs the Ptolemies intervened in the Egyptian economy on a massive scale. Putting to use the science of the Museum, the great institute in Alexandria (see page 109), the Ptolemies sponsored irrigation and land reclamation projects, the introduction of new crops (for example, new varieties of wheat), and the greatly expanded cultivation of old ones (such as grapes for wine).

Most of the people of Egypt made their living in agriculture, either as independent small farmers or as tenants on large estates. Government enriched itself through taxes, rents, demands for compulsory labor, state monopolies (on such diverse items as oils, textiles, and beer), and various internal tolls and customs duties. The result was boom times under strong kings and queens in the third century B.C. Egypt became the most prosperous part of the Hellenistic world, and Alexandria became the wealthiest, most populous city in the Mediterranean, as well as its literary capital (see Map 4.3). In the second century B.C., however, continued economic prosperity was derailed by decline, which created conditions for revolt.

To defeat the Seleucids at the Battle of Raphia in Gaza in 217 B.C., the Ptolemies had to enroll thousands of Egyptians in the Macedonian phalanx, because of a shortage of Greek mercenaries. Emboldened by their new military power, people in Upper Egypt soon broke into armed revolt against the government in far-off Alexandria. Rival kings appeared in the south, and unrest continued for about a century.

To advance their cause, the rebels inflamed anti-Greek sentiment. High taxes and regional rivalries, however, probably carried more weight than nationalism in the minds of most people. Although friction between immigrants and natives sparked from time to time, most Egyptians accepted the Ptolemies as pharaohs as long as they brought peace and prosperity. (See the box "The Global Record: Egyptians Versus Greeks in a Temple.")

And the Ptolemies reasserted their power. In 196 B.C., for example, Ptolemy V Epiphanes celebrated his coronation in full pharaonic ceremonial in Memphis. Egyptian priests commemorated the occasion in a decree written in Egypt's traditional language of kingship in a trilingual inscription (Greek, hieroglyphic, and demotic—ordinary—Egyptian). This inscription, discovered by French soldiers in 1799 and dubbed the Rosetta stone (named for the place where it was found), led to the modern European deciphering of hieroglyphics.

Despite the frictions, evidence points to native-settler cooperation, especially in the countryside, where intermarriage and bilingualism became common. Many an ordinary Greek became fully assimilated to Egyptian ways, and even wealthy, sophisticated, urban Greeks adopted a smattering of Egyptian customs. By 98 B.C. assimilation was evident in the cultural hybrid of a group of 18- and 19-year-old male youths who received traditional Greek military and literary training but prayed to Egypt's crocodile-god.

Alexandria Thriving Hellenistic city in northern Egypt founded by Alexander the Great in 332 B.C.

EGYPTIANS VERSUS GREEKS IN A TEMPLE

This second-century B.C. papyrus, a petition to the authorities from a Greek worshiper of Serapis, provides insight into relations between Greeks and Egyptians in Hellenistic Egypt. It shows how Greeks lived in the temple at Memphis in order to worship Serapis, a Hellenized Egyptian god (see page 116). It also depicts violence and hostility across ethnic lines.

To Dionysius, general and one of the "friends" [of the king], from Ptolemy son of Glaucias, a Macedonian, one of those "held in detention" [that is, on a voluntary, religious retreat] for twelve years in the great Temple of Serapis in Memphis. As I have suffered grave injustice and my life has been frequently endangered by the temple cleaners whose names are listed below, I am taking refuge with you in the belief that in this way I would best secure justice. For on . . . [November 9, 161 B.C.] they came to the temple of Astarte, which is in the sanctuary, and in which I have been living "in detention" for the number of years mentioned above; some of them had stones in their hand and others sticks, and they tried to force their way in, in order to seize the opportunity to plunder the temple and to put me to death because I am a Greek, like men laying a plot against my life. But when I anticipated them and shut the door of the temple, and shouted to them to withdraw in peace, they did not go away even so. When Diphilus, one of the worshipers held "in detention" by Serapis besides me, expressed indignation at their conduct in such a temple, they pushed him back, handled him very roughly and beat him up, so that their lawless brutality was clear for all to see. When these same men treated me in the same way in . . . [November 163 B.C.], I immediately addressed a petition to you, but as I had no one to look after the matter further, they were let off scot-free and became even more arrogant. I therefore ask you, if you please, to order them to be brought before you, so that they may receive the punishment they deserve for all these misdeeds. Farewell.

QUESTIONS

1. What is the complaint of Ptolemy, son of Glaucias, about? Is this the first time he has made such a complaint?

2. Why was Ptolemy unable to get justice before? What does this tell us about the way petitions were handled by the government?

3. Why were Ptolemy and Diphilus attacked? What does the attack indicate about Greek-Egyptian relations in second-century B.C. Egypt?

Source: Adapted from M. M. Austin, *The Hellenistic World from Alexander to the Roman Conquest: A Selection of Ancient Sources in Translation* (Cambridge: Cambridge University Press, 1981), pp. 434–435. Reprinted with the permission of Cambridge University Press.

SELEUCIDS AND ATTALIDS

The kingdom founded by Alexander's general Seleucus (suh-LOO-kus) (ca. 358–281 B.C.) experienced shifting borders and inhabitants. The Seleucid kingdom began when Seleucus took Babylon in 312 B.C. and ended in 64 B.C. when Syria became a Roman province. Many territorial changes occurred in between. The first three kings ruled a domain stretching from the Aegean to Bactria (BACK-tree-uh) (modern Afghanistan), but by the early second century B.C. most of the Iranian Plateau and lands eastward had been lost. At its height, in the third century B.C., the Seleucid kingdom had three nerve centers: Ionia (in western Anatolia), with a capital at Sardis; Syria, with a capital at Antioch; and Babylonia, whose capital was Seleucia-on-the-Tigris (near modern Baghdad; see Map 4.2).

The far-flung and multi-ethnic Seleucid lands presented an enormous administrative challenge. The kings took over the Persian system of satraps (provincial governors), taxes, and royal roads and post (see page 37), to which they added a Macedonian-style army, a common coinage, and a Hellenistic ruler cult. The chief Seleucid innovation was the establishment of colonies. Greek and Macedonian soldiers and administrators dominated, but natives also filled bureaucratic slots.

The greatest Seleucid city was **Antioch,** which became one of the wealthiest and most luxurious of all eastern Mediterranean cities; only Ptolemaic Alexandria outstripped it. The intellectual and artistic capital of Greek Asia in Hellenistic times, however, was not Antioch but Pergamum, in northwestern Anatolia (see Map 4.3).

The rulers of Pergamum, the Attalid dynasty of kings, carved out a small kingdom that became independent of the Seleucids in 263 B.C. and fell into Roman hands in 133 B.C. The Attalids made Pergamum into a showplace of Greek civilization, a would-be second Athens. As in Athens, public building was focused on a steep acropolis. The upper city of Pergamum was laid

Antioch Located near the present-day Turkish-Syrian border, it is the greatest of the cities founded by Seleucus, a general of Alexander the Great.

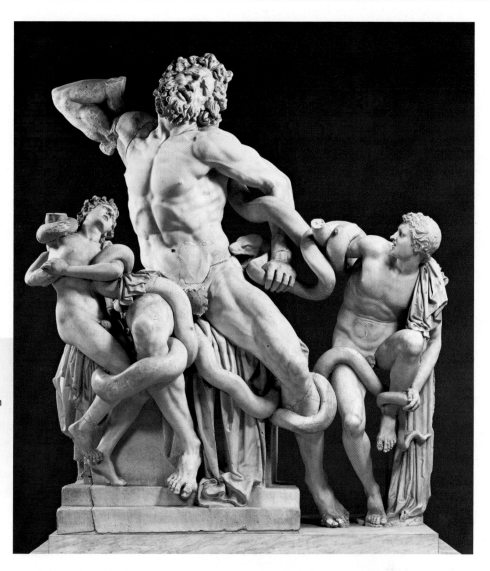

Laocoön
This famous statue group of the second or first century B.C. shows the Trojan priest Laocoön and his sons being strangled by snakes sent by the gods. The scene's emphasis on extreme emotion is typical of Hellenistic art.   *(Scala/Art Resource, NY)*

out on hillside terraces rising to a palace and fortified citadel. One of the terraces housed the famous Pergamum Altar, a huge monument to an Attalid victory over the Celts, who first invaded Anatolia in 278 B.C. and whose advance the Attalids checked. They could not, however, stop the Celts from settling in central Anatolia, where they created their kingdom of Galatia.

Pergamum was famous for its sculptors and for a library second only to Alexandria's. Pergamene writers focused on scholarship, to the exclusion of poetry, perhaps as a result of the influence of Stoic philosophers, who disapproved of poetry's emotionalism.

THE GRECO-INDIAN INTERACTION

The Seleucids' hold on Alexander's vast eastern domains turned out to be temporary. A new Persian dynasty, the Parthians (PAR-thee-unz), achieved independence in the mid-third century B.C. and over the next century carved out an empire extending westward into Mesopotamia. But to the east, Bactria remained Greek, if not Seleucid. From the mid-third century B.C. an independent Greek Bactria prospered (see Map 4.2).

Vivid evidence of Greek colonization in Bactria comes from the site of Aï Khanum (its ancient name is unknown) in northern Afghanistan. This prosperous and populous city contained many reminders of Greece, among them a gymnasium, theater, and library. A pillar in the gymnasium was inscribed in the mid-third century B.C. with 140 moral maxims from Delphi in Greece, over 3,000 miles away.

In the second century B.C. Bactrian kings extended their rule into the Indus River valley and the Punjab, a region with a modest Greek presence since the fifth century B.C., when the Persians settled Greek mercenaries there. Virtually no literary evidence survives, but monuments and, particularly, coins demonstrate Greco-Indian cultural interaction. For example, some coins from the second century B.C. show bilingual inscriptions in Greek and Indian languages. Their designs include a variety of Indian religious motifs, such as the lotus plant, symbol of Lakshmi, goddess of wealth and good fortune. Indians admired Hellenistic astronomy; one text goes so far as to say that Greek scientists should be "revenced like gods."

The Hellenistic world seems to have intrigued King Asoka (uh-SO-kuh) (r. ca. 270–230 B.C.), who ruled al-

A Greek-Influenced Indian Statue

This figure of a *bodhisattva* ("enlightened one") belongs to the Gandharan school, which was heavily influenced by Hellenistic sculpture. The statue's proportions, facial features, and draped clothing particularly recall Hellenistic motifs, suggesting that it may be the work of a Greek sculptor.

(Photograph courtesy of the Royal Ontario Museum, © ROM)

most the entire subcontinent, the largest empire in India to date. Asoka is best remembered as a religious reformer. A convert to Buddhism, he played a major role in its spread, which proceeded under the slogan of *dhamma*—that is, "morality" or "righteousness." One of his inscriptions records "victory" by dhamma, "where reigns the Greek king named Antiochus, and beyond the realm of Antiochus in the lands of the four kings named Ptolemy, Antigonus, Magas, and Alexander," which is generally thought to refer to embassies to the Hellenistic kingdoms.[2]

The envoys apparently found few converts, for it is difficult to find any trace of Buddhism in Hellenistic Greek culture, at least outside the Greco-Indian kingdoms. There one of the most powerful Greek rulers, Menander Soter Dikaios (r. ca. 155–130 B.C.), may have converted to Buddhism in the mid-second century B.C. But certain aspects of Indian religion—especially India's powerful currents of asceticism, mysticism, and monasticism—interested Greek intellectuals around the Mediterranean in Hellenistic and Roman times. Observers on Alexander's expedition, Hellenistic envoys, merchants, and philosophers in search of Eastern wisdom all served as conduits between East and West. One of the most influential was Megasthenes, a Seleucid ambassador to the court of Asoka's grandfather, who published his *Indika,* a description of India, around 300 B.C.

Yet the degree to which this interest influenced Greek and Roman culture is debatable. Although ancient writers mention Greek or Roman philosophers who were attracted by Indian culture, modern scholars tend to be cautious. The ancients had a weakness for tall tales and stories of exotic inspiration. Consider, for example, the following reports. Pyrrho of Elis, founder of the Hellenistic philosophical school of skepticism (see page 115), supposedly based his notion of the imperturbable sage on one Calanos, an Indian whom Pyrrho saw step calmly on a funeral pyre when Pyrrho was part of Alexander's expedition. Around A.D. 40 Apollonius of Tyana, a pagan religious thinker, is supposed to have traveled to India to study with its sages. Two centuries later the great Neo-Platonic philosopher Plotinus (A.D. 235–270) is reported to have traveled with the Roman emperor Gordian's army eastward, hoping in vain to reach India. Some scholars see Indian influence in Plotinus's mysticism and pantheism, but others dismiss these various reports.

Central Asian nomads overran Bactria in the late second century B.C. The Hellenistic kingdoms of India and Pakistan, however, survived until about the time of Christ, and some Greek communities lasted until the fifth century A.D. The Gandharan sculptors who flourished in a formerly Greek-ruled region in about A.D. 200 used Greek artistic techniques to depict Buddhist subjects, which might suggest the impact of Indian culture on the remaining Greek population.

━━━━━━━━━━━ S E C T I O N   S U M M A R Y ━━━━━━━━━━━

- Greek and Macedonian colonists and their descendants dominated the army and administration in the Ptolemaic and Seleucid kingdoms, but natives played a role as well.

- Greek culture made only a small impact in the multi-ethnic kingdoms of the Ptolemies and Seleucids; native cultures flourished.

- The Antigonid dynasty of Macedon and federal leagues joined city-states as prominent features of Hellenistic Greek political life.

- Ptolemaic Egypt, with its capital of Alexandria, was the wealthiest, most sophisticated, and longest-lasting Hellenistic kingdom.

- Seleucid Antioch and Attalid Pergamum were new and thriving cities of Hellenistic southwest Asia.

- Hellenistic Greek kingdoms prospered for centuries in parts of Afghanistan, India, and Pakistan.

ALEXANDRIAN CULTURE

How did Greek civilization spread during the Hellenistic era, and what were the main trends in literature, science, and art?

By the first century B.C. Alexandria was a city of half a million or more inhabitants. It was one of the largest and wealthiest cities in the world. The bulk of the people were Egyptian, but Greeks and Jews made up large minorities, and no one would have been surprised, in this cosmopolitan center, to see an Indian or a Celt, an Italian or a Persian.

The capital of Egypt, Alexandria was also perhaps the most important place where Greek culture was spread and transformed in the Hellenistic era. At the same time, it was a mix of ethnic cooperation and conflict. Underwater archaeologists, for example, looking for submerged parts of the city in Alexandria harbor, have found Egyptian sphinxes and obelisks as well as Greek statues. Written sources portray a picture of social change in the elite, an increase in leisure time, a growth in educational opportunities for both sexes, royal patronage of culture, and the value of even a limited knowledge of Greek literature as the ticket to advancement.

THE MUSEUM AND ALEXANDRIAN CULTURE

In 294 B.C. King Ptolemy I invited the deposed tyrant of Athens, Demetrius of Phalerum, to found an institution of culture in Alexandria. Demetrius had studied with Aristotle's successor at the Lyceum, Theophrastus (the-uh-FRAS-tus) (ca. 370–288 B.C.), a practical man interested in compiling and cataloging knowledge.

The new institution was called the Museum (literally, "House of the Muses," or the home of the female deities who inspired creativity). The Museum was a res-

idence, study, and lecture hall for scholars, scientists, and poets. It was also a research center to keep the king's engineers up to date on new technology for warfare and agriculture. One of the Museum's key components was the Library, in its day the largest collection of Greek writing in the world. In the third century B.C.—at the height of the Ptolemaic kingdom—the Library contained 700,000 papyrus rolls, the equivalent of roughly 50,000 modern books. Its nearest competitor, at Pergamum, contained less than a third as many rolls. The Library reflects the growth of the Hellenistic reading and writing public. The names of over a thousand writers of the Hellenistic era survive, and after 300 B.C. anthologies, abridgments, and school texts multiplied.

Online Study Center **Improve Your Grade**
Primary Source: A New Acquisition for the Library at Alexandria: Hebrew Scripture

Though modeled on Athens's Lyceum, the Museum represented a break from the public culture of the Classical period. The denizens of the Museum were an elite, dependent on royal patronage and self-consciously Greek and not Egyptian. A clever remark of Timon, a philosopher from the Peloponnesus who lived in the third century B.C., rings true: "In Egypt, land of diverse tribes, graze many pedants, fatted fowls that quarrel without end in the hen coop of the Muses."

Before we examine Alexandrian literature further, it is worth noting how greatly Hellenistic Athenian literature diverged from Classical culture. The greatest Hellenistic Athenian writer, a man famous throughout the ancient world, was Menander (ca. 342–292 B.C.). He was the master of a style of comedy called "New

Comedy," as distinguished from the "Old Comedy" of Aristophanes, which had flourished a century earlier (see page 88). Where Old Comedy was raucous and ribald, New Comedy was restrained; where Old Comedy focused on public matters such as war and politics, New Comedy was domestic and private. New Comedy was typical of the turn away from public life in Hellenistic times.

Menander wrote over seventy plays, but only one complete work has survived, *Dyskolos* (*The Grouch*). There are also large excerpts from several other comedies as well as Roman imitations. Witty and fluent, Menander favored stock plots and stock characters: the boastful soldier, the clever slave, the dashing but inept young man, the sweet maiden, and the old miser. Within those limitations, Menander created realistic and idiosyncratic characters. As a Hellenistic critic asked rhetorically: "O Menander and Life, which of you imitated the other?"

Like Menander, Alexandrian writers spurned public themes, but in Alexandria the characteristic literary figure was not the playwright but the critic: a professional man of letters. Adopted by the Romans, Alexandrian critical standards have influenced the West to this day.

Of the three greatest Alexandrian writers, two—Callimachus (305–240 B.C.) and Apollonius of Rhodes (b. ca. 295 B.C.)—worked at the Library; the third, Theocritus (ca. 300–260 B.C.), probably lived on a stipend from the Ptolemies. Popular for centuries, Callimachus was probably the most influential, the complete Hellenistic poet. A native of Cyrene (see Map 4.2) who came to Alexandria as a schoolteacher, Callimachus found a position in the Library. There he composed a virtually universal history of all recorded Greek (and much non-Greek) knowledge.

A prolific writer, Callimachus generally preferred short to long poems: "Big book, big evil" was his maxim. Earlier Greek poets were usually austere and public-minded; Callimachus preferred the private, the light, and the exotic. "Don't expect from me a big-sounding

Street Musicians

The lively scene of a mixed group of young and old, male and female, recalls the jaunty mimes popular with the Hellenistic public. A mosaic from about 100 B.C., the artwork comes from a private villa in the Greco-Italian city of Pompeii. *(Museo Nazionale, Naples)*

poem," he writes. "Zeus thunders, not I."[3] Callimachus was expert at the pithy statement in verse—the epigram.

Another major Alexandrian writer was Callimachus's student Apollonius of Rhodes. His major work was the epic poem *Argonautica* (ar-go-NAW-tih-kuh) (*Voyage of the Argo*). The subject is the legend of Jason and the heroes who travel on the ship *Argo* to the Black Sea, in pursuit of the Golden Fleece (the skin of a winged ram). With the help of the princess Medea, who falls in love with Jason, the heroes succeed and return home safely after numerous adventures.

The most striking thing about Apollonius is his doubt about the very possibility of heroism. Apollonius's Jason is no hero of old. Whereas Homer describes Odysseus as "never at a loss," Apollonius describes Jason as "helpless." Men move the action in the *Iliad* and the *Odyssey*; Jason depends on a woman, Medea, for his success. Indeed, much of the *Argonautica* focuses on Medea and in particular on her love for Jason. All in all, the *Argonautica* is less a traditional epic than an anti-epic.

Like Callimachus, Theocritus, a native of Syracuse, wrote short, polished poetry. He composed thirty-one subtle and refined poems, conventionally known as idylls. The best known of the poems focus on country life. They are the first known pastoral poems; indeed, Theocritus probably invented the genre. Through his Roman admirers, Theocritus's love of nature has exerted a powerful hold on the Western literary imagination.

Outside the Museum, Alexandria had a lively popular culture, much of it Egyptian or influenced by Egyptian models. A glimpse of this culture is offered in the seven surviving mimes, or farces, of an obscure writer named Herondas or Herodas. Though written in literary Greek, they discuss commonplace subjects—shopping for shoes, tourism, lawsuits, and beatings at school—and titillating themes such as adultery and prostitution. Lively, bawdy, funny, and filled with the grit of everyday life in the third century B.C., they are a reminder of just how specialized the culture of the Museum was.

ADVANCES IN SCIENCE AND MEDICINE

The Ptolemies not only reaped practical benefits in military and agricultural technology from their Museum, but also became the patrons of a flourishing period in the history of pure scientific inquiry. They unwittingly promoted a split between philosophy and science that has characterized much of Western culture since. Antigonid patronage of ethical and political philosophy helped keep Athens pre-eminent in those fields. In contrast, the study of science tended to shift to Alexandria. The rulers of Pergamum and, far to the west, Syracuse, a flourishing Hellenistic city in Sicily, were great patrons of science as well. Wealth, improved communi-cations and literacy, continued warfare, and cross-fertilization between Greek and non-Greek traditions, especially Greek and Babylonian astronomy, were all catalysts of Hellenistic science.

Mathematics   Some of the best-known figures of Hellenistic science were mathematicians. In his *Elements,* the Alexandrian Euclid (active ca. 300 B.C.) produced a systematic study of geometry that was hugely influential in both Western and Islamic civilizations.

But the greatest mathematician of Greek antiquity was a Sicilian Greek, Archimedes (ar-kuh-MEE-deez) of Syracuse (287–212 B.C.). He was also a notable inventor. Among other things, Archimedes calculated the approximate value of pi (the ratio of a circle's circumference to its diameter) and made important discoveries in astronomy, engineering, optics, and other fields. One of the most important of his inventions was the water snail, also known as Archimedes' screw—a device to raise water for irrigation. Invented by Archimedes during a stay in Egypt, the screw made it possible to irrigate previously barren land, as did the ox-driven water wheel, another Ptolemaic invention.

Advances in mathematics promoted advances in astronomy. Aristarchus of Samos (active ca. 275 B.C.) is known for his heliocentric hypothesis, which confounded tradition by having the earth revolve around the sun, instead of the sun around the earth. He was right, but Hellenistic astronomy lacked the data to prove his theory, so its rejection was not unreasonable at the time. Eratosthenes (er-uh-TOSS-the-neez) of Cyrene (active ca. 225 B.C.) was saddled with the frustrating nickname of "Beta" (the second letter of the Greek alphabet) because he was considered second best in every branch of study. This "second best" nonetheless calculated through simple geometry an extraordinarily accurate measurement of the earth's circumference.

Medicine   Hellenistic medicine thrived in Alexandria. Both Greece and Egypt had long-established medical traditions but the key to medical advance was the dissection of human cadavers in Alexandria, a first in the history of science. In Greece, as in many ancient societies, religious tradition demanded that dead bodies not be mutilated. But in the frontier atmosphere of early Alexandria, this traditional taboo lost much of its force. Although Egyptians did not practice dissection, they did practice embalming, which may have helped Alexandrian Greeks overcome the prohibition against cutting open the human body. Ever supportive of research, the Ptolemies provided corpses to Greek scientists for dissection. Indeed, they had condemned criminals sent from prison for live dissection by scientists. The practice, only a short-lived experiment in the early third century B.C., outraged many writers in antiquity, just as today it would be considered an atrocity.

The leading scientific beneficiary was Herophilus (her-AH-fih-lus) of Chalcedon (ca. 320–250 B.C.), a practicing physician in Alexandria. Among his achievements was the recognition (against Aristotle) that the brain is the center of the nervous system, a careful dissection of the eye, the discovery of the ovaries, and the description of the duodenum, which he named (*duodenum* is a Latin translation of a Greek word meaning "twelve fingers," describing the organ's length). In addition, Herophilus developed a detailed theory of the diagnostic value of measuring pulse rates.

Engineering Hellenistic technology has long fascinated and frustrated scholars. The great engineers invented both numerous engines of war and various "wonderworks" to amuse the royal court. Among the latter were mechanical puppets and steam-run toys. Given these advances, why did the Greeks achieve neither a scientific revolution, along the lines of the one begun in the early modern era by thinkers such as Copernicus and Galileo, nor an industrial transformation, such as was ushered in by the steam engine around A.D. 1800? Historians are not entirely sure but can venture a guess. Greek machine-making technology was not as sophisticated as that of eighteenth-century Europe. The prevalence of slavery in antiquity discouraged laborsaving machines; steam was used only for playthings and gadgets. A related point is the elitist bias of Greek intellectual life. After Archimedes' death, for example, it was claimed that although he had written copiously on theoretical matters, he never bothered to write about his mechanical inventions because he considered them "ignoble and vulgar."

Perhaps the most important point is the Greek attitude toward nature. Whereas Jews and Christians learned from the Bible that human beings have dominion over nature, thereby making possible the conclusion that it is appropriate to conquer nature, the Greeks thought in more restricted terms. They believed that nature set limits, that a virtuous person tried to follow nature, not subdue it. Thus Greek engineers were not inclined to make the revolutionary changes that their modern counterparts have promoted.

MEN AND WOMEN IN ART AND SOCIETY

Like Hellenistic literature, Hellenistic art attests to changing male attitudes toward women and toward gender issues. The portrait of Jason and Medea in Apollonius's *Argonautica* makes fun of masculine pretensions and celebrates the triumph of female intelligence. It also presents a sympathetic portrait of a woman's romantic desire for a man, as does Theocritus's work. In the Classical period, depictions of romantic love were generally restricted to male homoeroticism. Accordingly, statues of naked males were common, but women were almost always depicted clothed. Hellenistic sculpture, by contrast, affords many erotic examples of the female nude.

There are indications that the Hellenistic Greek male of the elite was much more willing than his Classical predecessor to see lovemaking as a matter of mutuality and respect. Classical vase-painting often depicts heterosexual lovemaking with a lusty and explicit mood. In contrast, in Hellenistic vase-painting the emphasis is more often on tenderness and domesticity. Hellenistic men wrote with sensitivity about satisfying a woman's needs and desires. The vogue for representations of Hermaphrodite (her-MAF-ro-dyte), the mythical creature who was half-female and half-male, may suggest a belief that the feminine was as important a part of human nature as the masculine.

Many a Hellenistic artist or writer seems to be as interested in emotion as in action and to focus on the inner as much as on the outer life. Hellenistic art often depicts women, children, and domestic scenes. Representations of warriors are as likely to focus on their unrestrained emotions as on their soldierly self-control.

Hellenistic women enjoyed small improvements in political and legal status and bigger improvements in economic and ideological status. Greek women, particularly in the elite, benefited from the spread of monarchy. Queens and princesses had more power than female commoners in city-states. Also, in the new cities, as in many a frontier society, women were permitted to inherit and use property more often than in old Greece.

It was an era of powerful queens: Olympias, Alexander the Great's mother, played kingmaker after her son's death. Arsinoe II Philadelphus was co-ruler of Egypt with her husband (who was also her brother) for five years at the height of Ptolemaic prosperity around 275 B.C. The most famous Hellenistic woman, Cleopatra VII, was queen of Egypt from 51 to 30 B.C. Although she was the lover of two of the most powerful men in the world, the Romans Julius Caesar and Mark Antony, Cleopatra was no exotic plaything. Rather, she was a brilliant and ambitious strategist who nearly succeeded in winning a world empire for her family. (See the feature "The Visual Record: Images of Cleopatra.")

Writers in the new Hellenistic cities often described freedom of movement for women. Theocritus and Herondas, for example, show women visiting a temple or a show. In Hellenistic Athens, aristocratic fathers put up inscriptions in honor of their daughters who had participated in the cult of Athena. Although women generally continued to need a male guardian to represent them in public, in some situations, at least in Egypt (where the evidence is most plentiful), a woman could represent herself. A woman could petition the government on her own behalf. Widows and mothers of illegitimate children could give their daughters in marriage or apprentice their sons. A few cities granted women citizenship and even permitted them to hold public office.

Aphrodite of Cnidos
This 7½-foot-tall marble statue is a Roman copy of an original by Praxiteles (ca. 350–330 B.C.). Perhaps the most famous of Hellenistic female nudes, the statue was housed in a special shrine where it could be viewed in the round to accommodate all the interest it generated. *(Vatican Museums)*

Some Hellenistic cities admitted women to the gymnasium, previously a male preserve. Heretofore only Sparta had promoted physical education for women, but by the first century A.D. women were even competing in the great Pan-Hellenic games. Gymnasia were also centers of education in music and reading. One consequence of growing literacy was the re-emergence of women poets and the first appearance of women philosophers in the West. Before dying at age 19, Erinna, who lived on the Aegean island of Telos during the late fourth century B.C., wrote the *Distaff,* a poem in memory of her childhood friend Baucis. This three-hundred-line poem, famous in antiquity, describes the shared experiences of girlhood. Hipparchia (hih-PAR-kee-uh) of Maroneia (b. ca. 350 B.C.), like her husband, Crates of Thebes, studied Cynic philosophy. The Cynics, like another philosophical school, the Epicureans, supported a measure of equality between women and men. Hipparchia and Crates led an itinerant life as popular teachers and the Hellenistic equivalent of counselors or psychologists.

Much of the explanation for the relative freedom of elite women lies in the new economic power of this group. The new cities generally imposed fewer restrictions on women's economic roles than had Classical poleis such as Athens. In many cities women could sell land, borrow money, and decide whether their husbands could make loans or contracts on the strength of their dowries. Free women could manumit slaves as well.

Hellenistic women never attained the equality that sometimes exists between men and women today, but they did enjoy genuine though limited improvements in status. Men and women played new roles in a changed, complex world. The new Hellenistic philosophies and religions attempted to address that complexity.

SECTION SUMMARY

- Alexandria's Museum (a research institute) and Library were the focal point of much of Hellenistic literature and science.

- The playwright Menander and the poets Callimachus, Apollonius of Rhodes, and Theocritus represent the Hellenistic era's turn away from civic and heroic themes.

- Mathematics, astronomy, and medicine are all fields in which notable advances were made in the Hellenistic era, thanks in part to royal patronage.

- Philosophy and science first became separate disciplines, as they are today.

- Hellenistic women experienced real though limited improvements in status and power.

Images of Cleopatra

Cleopatra's nose: if it had been shorter, the whole face of the earth would have changed," wrote the French philosopher Blaise Pascal (1623–1662). He does Cleopatra an injustice. It was not a pretty face and classical features that enabled her to win the throne of Egypt (r. 51–30 B.C.), to obtain first Julius Caesar and then Mark Antony as ally and lover, and finally to come close to gaining control of the Roman Empire. Intelligence, daring, charm, and extraordinary diplomatic skill account for Cleopatra's success.

Let us consider the queen's manipulation of her public image—no mean task, given the fragility of Ptolemaic power in the first century B.C. Within Egypt the monarch had to satisfy several different ethnic groups. Most important were the Greeks and Macedonians—who dominated government, the military, and the economy—and the native Egyptian majority. Daughter of Ptolemy XII (r. 80–51 B.C.), Cleopatra was supposed to rule jointly with her brother, but they had a falling-out. She grabbed the throne from him and then from another brother and thus had to assert her legitimacy. Also, Ptolemaic Egypt had to project an image of unity to the Romans, who were threatening to annex it as they had the other Hellenistic monarchies.

Cleopatra, like earlier Ptolemaic monarchs, met these challenges by presenting two faces to the world. To the Greeks and Romans she was a Hellenistic monarch; to the Egyptians she was an ancient pharaonic queen. Look first at the bronze coin of Cleopatra issued at Alexandria probably in the 30s B.C. The queen is shown as a young woman. Her hair, tied in a bun at the nape of her neck, is in the so-called melon style often seen in Hellenistic female portraits. She wears a diadem (royal headband), its ends hanging behind her neck. More commonly worn by Hellenistic kings than by queens, the diadem signifies Cleopatra's claim to authority.

So does the queen's profile. She is portrayed with a prominent chin, a large mouth, and a rugged nose. These features may not be the standard attributes of beauty, but they are precisely the features that mark coin portraits of Cleopatra's father. By emphasizing Cleopatra's physical similarity to her father, the portrait artist perhaps subtly suggests her right to sit on his throne.

The side of the coin not shown here is far from subtle: its legend states clearly in Greek, "Queen Cleopatra." The illustration is of an eagle and thunderbolt and a double cornucopia (horn of plenty) entwined with a diadem. The eagle and thunderbolt recall the Greek god Zeus, and the two cornucopias suggest fertility and prosperity. All are recurrent symbols of Ptolemaic royalty. The coin thus portrays Cleopatra as a Greek monarch, the worthy heir of her father. It would have been an effective image in Alexandria, a city dominated by Greeks and visited by Romans, but not in the countryside, especially south of the Nile Delta, in Upper Egypt, an area that was primarily Egyptian. Following dynastic custom, Cleopatra changed her image there.

In Upper Egypt earlier Ptolemies frequently had been represented in stone in traditional pharaonic style, and they were great restorers of ancient Egyptian temples and builders of new ones. Look at the sculptural relief from the temple of the Egyptian cow-goddess Hathor at Dendera in Upper Egypt. The temple was a monumental structure initiated and underwritten by Ptolemy XII. Cleopatra, his daughter, added an enormous relief on the outside of the rear wall. Carved into the stone are two persons carrying offerings for Egyptian deities. The persons are Cleopatra (*left*) and her son Ptolemy

Bronze Coin of Cleopatra *(Courtesy of the Trustees of the British Museum)*

Relief of Cleopatra and Caesarion
(Erich Lessing/Art Resource, NY)

Cleopatra's face is in profile but otherwise has very little in common with her portrait on the Alexandrian coin. Although the features are stylized pharaonic commonplaces, the shape of her head perhaps echoes the elegant and graceful relief portraits of Hatshepsut (r. 1479–1457 B.C.), the most famous female pharaoh before Cleopatra.

Cleopatra commissioned other artworks and monuments in the native style in the Nile Valley. This was the custom of her dynasty, and Cleopatra had absorbed its traditions, but she stands second to none of the Ptolemies in shrewdness and subtlety. She was the only Ptolemaic monarch to learn to speak Egyptian, and she was the only one to come even close to gaining the upper hand over Rome. As the artifacts shown here indicate, she was able to put on an Egyptian face as easily as a Greek one, but she never lost sight of her true interests.

XV Caesar, who ruled with his mother from 44 to 30 B.C. Alleged to be the illegitimate son of Julius Caesar, Ptolemy XV was commonly known as Caesarion, or "little Caesar." At Dendera, however, he and his mother are shown neither as Romans nor as Greeks but as Egyptians.

Look closely at Cleopatra. She wears a long body-hugging robe. On her head is a royal headdress with symbols of the Egyptian gods: the lyre-shaped cow horns and sun-disk of Hathor, the tall plumes of Isis, and the ram's horn of Amon. Caesarion is shown as a pharaoh, wearing the double crown of Upper and Lower Egypt. Mother and son offer incense to the local deities. The small figure between Caesarion and Cleopatra is his *ka,* or soul.

QUESTIONS

1. Why did Cleopatra need to show two faces to the world?

2. Does Cleopatra's coin emphasize her good looks? Why or why not?

3. What image of herself does Cleopatra present at the Temple of Hathor at Dendera? Why?

Online Study Center
Improve Your Grade Visual Record Activities

THE TURN INWARD:
NEW PHILOSOPHIES, NEW FAITHS

What new philosophies and religions emerged in the Hellenistic period?

The events of the Hellenistic era—emigration, a trend from independent city-states to monarchies and federal leagues, new extremes of wealth and poverty, and contact with foreign peoples and customs—all generated uncertainty. In response, Greek culture was spread and transformed. As literacy expanded, more Greeks than ever before could participate in cultural debate. New philosophies and religions arose to meet new spiritual concerns, generating ideas that would be influential for centuries.

The meeting of Jews and Greeks proved to be just as significant. Challenged by Greek conquest, Greek colonization, and their own migration to Greek lands, Jews alternately embraced Hellenism and engaged in resistance, both cultural and armed. In the process, first Judaism and then Hellenism were changed forever.

HELLENISTIC PHILOSOPHY

Although the polis lost its military and political preeminence in the fourth century B.C., philosophy continued to thrive. It was, however, much changed. With the city-state losing significance as a focus of loyalty, and with the Greek-reading public growing in size and geographic extent, Hellenistic philosophy paid less and less attention to politics. Since Hellenistic science tended to become a separate discipline from philosophy, philosophers focused on ethics, the discovery of the best way to live. The essence of the good life, most philosophers agreed, was peace of mind, or freedom from troubles. Hellenistic philosophy won a wide following; indeed, for many people, primarily in the elite, philosophy became a way of life, even a religion.

Cynicism   Several competing philosophical schools emerged, beginning with Cynicism (SIN-uh-sizm). Never a widespread philosophy, Cynicism is nonetheless important as a precursor of the two most popular doctrines, Stoicism and Epicureanism. Skepticism rejected the main philosophies as mere dogmatism and proposed instead a commonsense attitude toward ethics.

The first Cynic was Diogenes (dye-AH-juh-neez) of Sinope (ca. 400–325 B.C.). An exile in Athens, Diogenes developed a philosophy that rejected all conventions. People find happiness, he decided, by satisfying their natural needs with simplicity. Accordingly, Diogenes chose a life of poverty. A beggar in rags, he delighted in shocking conventional morality. Famous for wit and

shamelessness, he was nicknamed "Dog" (*kuon*) because the Greeks considered dogs to be shameless animals; his followers were called "Doglike" (*kunikoi*, whence the name *Cynic*).

Stoicism   Although he founded no school, Diogenes cast a wide shadow. Among those whom he indirectly influenced was Zeno (335–263 B.C.), who began one of the most important philosophical systems of antiquity: Stoicism (STO-ih-sizm). Zeno came to Athens in 313 B.C. from Citium in Cyprus, a multi-ethnic city; he was possibly of Phoenician origin. Influenced by both Cynicism and Socratic philosophy, Zeno developed his own doctrines, which he taught in the *Stoa Poikile* ("Painted Porch," whence the name *Stoic*), a public building.

Like Plato and Aristotle, Zeno sought an absolute standard of good on which to base philosophical decisions. He found it in the divine reason (*logos*), which he considered the principle of the universe and the guide to human behavior. The best life was spent in pursuit of wisdom—that is, a life of philosophy. Only that rare and forbidding figure, the Sage, could truly attain wisdom; ordinary people could merely progress toward it through study and the attempt to be free from all passion.

Stoicism may seem harsh. It is not surprising that *stoical* has come to describe austere indifference to pain. In some ways, however, Stoicism was comforting. The **Stoics** were empiricists—that is, they trusted the evidence of the senses, an attitude that they thought would inspire confidence and security. They believed in human brotherhood—led, to be sure, by a Greek-speaking elite. Since brothers have a duty to one another, the Stoics argued that a good person should play an active role in public life.

The Stoics emphasized the inner life. They believed that intentions matter. This was an important departure from Greek tradition, which tended to emphasize the outcome of an action, not its motivation. Stoicism also departed from traditional Greek localism, embracing a more cosmopolitan outlook. "This world is a great city, [and] has one constitution and one law," wrote Philo of Alexandria (30 B.C.–A.D. 45), a Stoic and a Jew. Many Stoics believed in a natural law or law of

Stoics   Believers in a philosophical system begun in Athens by Zeno, which emphasized the pursuit of wisdom, the reliability of sensory experience, and freedom from all passion.

nations—that is, that overarching and common principles governed international relations.

With its emphasis on duty and order, Stoicism became popular with Greek ruling elites, and eventually with the Romans, who used its concept of a universal state to justify their empire. Many Stoic principles were later embraced by early Christian writers.

Epicureanism Epicurus (341–270 B.C.), an Athenian citizen, founded his philosophical school at around the same time as Zeno founded Stoicism. There were other similarities: both schools were empiricist and materialist (that is, they tended to trust the evidence of the senses), both sought peace of mind, and both inspired widespread followings. Epicurus, however, taught not in a public place but in a private garden. Whereas the Stoics encouraged political participation, the **Epicureans** counseled withdrawal from the rough-and-tumble of public life. "Calm" and "Live in hiding" are famous Epicurean (eh-pi-kyuh-REE-un) maxims.

Epicurus's materialism is based on the atomic theory of Democritus (see page 84). It envisions a thoroughly mechanistic universe in which the gods exist but play no active role in events. Individuals need fear neither fickle deities nor an unhappy afterlife because the soul is merely a combination of atoms that ceases to exist after death. The purpose of life was the avoidance of pain and the pursuit of pleasure. The latter was called hedonism (from *hedone*, Greek for "pleasure"), but not, as the word has come to mean today, indulgence in food, drink, or sex. Instead, Epicureans meant intellectual pleasure. Friendship and fraternity were Epicurean ideals—the private analogs, as it were, of Stoic brotherhood.

The Epicureans raised eyebrows and sometimes ire, occasionally suffering persecution by the state. They were accused of atheism and sensuality; to this day, *epicurean* connotes a fondness for luxury and pleasure. Classical Greek philosophy defined virtue as the highest good. The Epicurean emphasis on pleasure, even spiritual pleasure, seemed perverse to some. Yet Epicureanism was simple, sure of itself, and practical, and it offered both friendship and a sense of community. It became a popular philosophy, especially among the wealthy.

Online Study Center **Improve Your Grade**
Primary Source: A Materialist Ethic: The Principal Doctrines of Epicureanism

Skepticism Skepticism (SKEP-tih-sizm) was founded by Pyrrho of Elis (ca. 360–270 B.C.), a Greek who traveled with Alexander to India. Like Stoics and Epicureans, Skeptics sought peace of mind. They rejected those thinkers' conclusions, however, on the grounds that they were dogmatic—that is, based not on positive proof but merely on opinion (*doxa*). Considering the senses unreliable, Skeptics rejected the commonsense approach of Stoics and Epicureans. They preferred to suspend judgment on the great philosophical questions (hence our term *skepticism* for a doubting state of mind). Whoever was able to do so could accept the customs of the community, avoid politics, and thereby obtain peace of mind.

THE MYSTERY RELIGIONS

The name "mystery religion" comes from the Greek word for "secret." A mystery religion initiated worshipers into secret teachings. Long a feature of Greek religion, the **mystery religions**—there were several different ones—grew very popular in Hellenistic times. Their rise is a sign of the decline of the traditional Greek religion of the Olympian gods.

The old Greek gods came under attack on every front in the Hellenistic era. The newly divinized kings stole their spotlight, while philosophers criticized the Olympians as primitive and immoral. Scholarship got into the act as well. Around 300 B.C. Euhemerus of Messene wrote that Zeus and others were not gods but merely great kings of the past who were rewarded with deification, much as a Hellenistic monarch might be.

The Olympians retained their temples, but the rituals seemed hollow and antiquarian. What was to replace them? Of the several new religious movements that marked the age, three stand out: the divinization of kings, the cult of Tyche (Fortune), and the mystery religions.

Under the Ptolemies and Seleucids, ruler-worship became standard procedure. Some no doubt considered it just a patriotic formality while others prayed to the god-king or god-queen to intercede for them in heaven. Meanwhile, the old Greek city-states, especially democracies, bristled. "To transfer to men the honor due to the gods," the Athenian playwright Philippides (active ca. 300 B.C.) wrote, "is to dissolve the democracy."

He might have said as much about the Hellenistic cult of Tyche (TOO-kay) (Fortune or Luck), often worshiped as a goddess, sometimes as the protector of a particular city. The most famous example was the Tyche of Antioch, personified as a statue of a woman wearing the battlements of the city on her head as a kind of crown—a very popular statue, to judge by the many copies found around the Hellenistic world.

The mystery religions offered relief similar to that of the philosophical schools: ethical guidance, comfort, release from worries, reassurance about death, and

Epicureans Adherents of the Athenian philosopher Epicurus, they emphasized the avoidance of pain and the pursuit of intellectual pleasure.

mystery religions Popular Hellenistic cults featuring the initiation of worshipers into secret doctrines, they replaced the traditional Greek religion of the Olympian gods.

A Cretan Dream Interpreter in Egypt
A painted stele (ca. 200 B.C.) advertises the services of a Greek in Memphis near the Temple of Serapis, a Greco-Egyptian god. The inscription and pediment are Greek, while the pilasters, women, and sacred bull (facing an altar) are Egyptian.
(Egyptian Museum, Cairo)

a sense of unity. Consider the cult of Demeter at Eleusis, a town just outside the city of Athens. Demeter was the goddess of fertility. Her daughter, Persephone, supposedly spent half the year in the underworld, among the dead, but came back to earth each spring, which symbolized the promise of a blessed afterlife. The precise details of the ritual remain unknown to this day. What is clear is that they included fasting, ritual bathing in the sea, a procession, and a torch-lit ceremony in the great hall at Eleusis.

Various new mystery religions from outside Greece became more popular, particularly the Hellenized Egyptian cults of Serapis and of Isis. Created under Ptolemy I, Serapis (SEH-ruh-pis) was meant to combine Osiris, the Egyptian god of the afterlife, with Apis, the god of the Nile flood. Serapis also suggested Pluto, the Greek god of the underworld. Hence it is an early example of the common Hellenistic practice of religious syncretism, or fusion. Despite its roots, Serapis-worship had little appeal to native Egyptians, but the god became popular in the Greek world as the patron of healing and sailing.

Another traditional Egyptian deity, Osiris's wife, Isis (EYE-sis), also became a popular Greek and, later, Roman goddess. Called the Goddess of Ten Thousand Names, Isis was said to symbolize all the female deities of antiquity. Hers was a cult of the afterlife and of the suffering but tender and loving mother; she was particularly popular among women. Thus, under Ptolemaic sponsorship, ancient Egyptian cults were recast and spread throughout the Greek-speaking world, circulating such notions as the suffering mother, the Last Judgment, and blessed eternal life after death. Early Christianity was much influenced by such Greco-Egyptian religious notions, but it was more directly the product of debate and ferment within Hellenistic Judaism.

HELLENISTIC JUDAISM

Few consequences of Alexander's conquests had so lasting an impact as the mixing of Greeks and Jews. Even before Alexander took Judea from the Persians in 332 B.C., the two peoples were in occasional contact, but in the Hellenistic era, their fates became intertwined. The Greeks governed Judea and then lost it to a Jewish independence movement. Meanwhile, millions of Jews settled in Egypt, Syria, Anatolia, and Greece.

Changed by its contact with Greek culture, Hellenistic Judaism placed a greater emphasis on salvation, martyrdom, and individual study and prayer. Jewish responses to Greek culture varied: they ranged from admiration to resistance to outreach—that is, the desire to convert Greeks to Judaism.

Hellenistic Judea was governed first by the Ptolemies until 200 B.C., then by the Seleucids, until the establishment of an independent Jewish state in 142 B.C., which came under Roman suzerainty in 63 B.C. The Greeks were not absentee rulers. Rather, they established a large number of Greek colonies in and around Judea, especially under the Seleucids. Many Jews, especially wealthy ones, adopted some degree of Greek culture. Some Hellenizers gave up Jewish customs altogether for the Greek gymnasium, theater, and political institutions. With the help of the Seleucid king Antiochus IV Epiphanes (r. 175–163 B.C.), Jewish Hellenizers in 175 B.C. had Jerusalem proclaimed a Greek polis, renamed Antioch, like many a Seleucid city; they even built a gymnasium at the foot of the Temple Mount. In 167 B.C. they went further by outlawing Sabbath observance, prohibiting circumcision, and rededicating the Temple to Olympian Zeus.

The traditionalists, however, resisted. Aided by the political ineptitude of their opponents, who raised taxes, they rallied the Jewish masses into opposition. Soon a guerrilla revolt began in the countryside, led by the Hasmonean family, also known as the **Maccabees,** whose successes are celebrated today by Jews during the religious holiday of Hanukkah. The guerrilla movement developed into a disciplined armed uprising, which forced the Seleucids to tolerate an independent state under the Hasmonean dynasty.

During the struggle over Hellenism, new elements of lasting significance became part of Judaism. First, the Jews developed a literature of spiritual resistance to the foreigner. This literature was apocalyptic—that is, it claimed to reveal dramatic, heretofore secret truths. Drawing on both biblical and Mesopotamian traditions, Jewish apocalyptic writing predicted a future cataclysm, when a royal redeemer would evict the foreigner and establish a new kingdom of Israel. The redeemer was often identified with another notion that first became popular in this era: the Messiah (literally, "anointed one"), someone anointed with oil signifying his election as king, a descendant of King David, who would save Israel. Another new aspect of Hellenistic Judaism was martyrdom, the notion of the holy sacrifice

Maccabees Traditionalist Jews led by the Hasmonean family, who in 167 B.C. revolted against Hellenizing laws and influences.

Bronze Coin with Menorah
This issue of Mattathias Antigone (r. 40–37 B.C.), the last Hasmonean king, is an early example of the use of the seven-branched candelabrum as the symbol of the Jewish people. A similar candelabrum was used in the Temple of Jerusalem. *(Erich Lessing/Art Resource, NY)*

of one's life for a religious cause. There was also a growing belief in a final Judgment Day and resurrection, when God would raise the meritorious dead to live again on earth in their own bodies.

Hellenistic Judaism was diverse. Various sects each proposed its own version of Judaism. Among these sects were the Sadducees (SAJ-oo-seez) ("righteous ones"), a wealthy establishment group for whom the rituals of the Temple in Jerusalem were the heart of Judaism. Their opponents, the Pharisees (FAIR-ih-seez) ("those who separated themselves"), insisted on the validity of the oral tradition of interpretation alongside the written law of the Hebrew Bible and the Temple rituals. The Pharisees proposed a kind of democratization of Judaism, emphasizing study and prayer in small groups. A third group was the Essenes (EH-seenz), generally identified with the Qumran (koom-RAHN) community in the Judean desert (see page 173). Hellenizers wanted to bring Jewish teachings to non-Jews, or Gentiles ("the nations").

Most Jews of the Hellenistic era lived outside Judea. The Diaspora had spread into (among other places) Syria, Anatolia, the Greek mainland, and Egypt, where a strong Jewish presence during the Persian period grew even stronger, particularly in Alexandria. Jews served the Ptolemies as soldiers, generals, bureaucrats, and tax collectors. They also prospered in private enterprise. Hostility to Jews by some Greeks and Egyptians spawned the first anti-Semitic literature. Sporadic violence at times broke into riots and persecution. Yet there was also considerable admiration among Greek intellectuals for what they saw as Jewish virtue and antiquity.

Greek was the common tongue of Diaspora Jews. Between around 300 and 100 B.C. in Alexandria the Hebrew Bible was translated into Greek. Known as the Septuagint, or Seventy, from the number of translators who, legend has it, labored on the project, this text made the Bible accessible to a Jewish community increasingly unable to understand Hebrew or Aramaic. In later centuries the Septuagint became the Old Testament of Greek-speaking Christians.

Foreign conversions and immigration into the Diaspora began to change the meaning of the word *Jew*. The word came to mean less "inhabitant of Judea" than "practitioner of Judaism."

═══════ S E C T I O N   S U M M A R Y ═══════

- Philosophy changed its emphasis from politics to ethics and won a wide following in the Greek-speaking elite.

- Stoicism, austere and public-spirited, and Epicureanism, which called for withdrawal into private life, were the most popular Hellenistic philosophies.

- The traditional Olympian religion of Greece declined while so-called mystery religions, which offered secret teachings, grew popular.

- While some Jews adopted the Greek customs of their Seleucid rulers, traditionalists revolted and re-established an independent Jewish state in Palestine.

- Most Jews in the Hellenistic era lived outside Palestine, in the Diaspora, where they had frequent contacts with other peoples.

CHAPTER SUMMARY

Online Study Center **ACE the Test**

How did Macedon under Philip and Alexander conquer both the Greek city-states and the Persian Empire?

What new states emerged as a result of Alexander's conquests and how did they integrate Greek settlers with native peoples?

How did Greek civilization spread during the Hellenistic era, and what were the main trends in literature, science, and art?

What new philosophies and religions emerged in the Hellenistic period?

As king, Philip built a state and an army that allowed Macedon to conquer the Greek city-states and prepared to invade the Persian Empire. Upon Philip's assassination his son Alexander replaced him and led an army of invasion. Although outnumbered and outspent by Persia, the Macedonians won because of their army. As Alexander's empire stretched into India, he became despotic and he planned a fusion of Greeks and Persians. His conquests laid the foundation of the Hellenistic age.

After fifty years of war following Alexander's death, several new states emerged: the most important were Macedonia under the Antigonid dynasty, Egypt under the Ptolemies, and western Asia under the Seleucids. Hellenistic Greek kingdoms were founded in lands as far away as Afghanistan, Pakistan, and India, and they lasted for centuries. Greek and Macedonian colonists to the Ptolemaic and Seleucid kingdoms dominated the army and administration but there was some room for natives. But few natives adopted Greek ways and native culture thrived in these multi-ethnic empires. New cities such as Alexandria, Antioch, and Pergamum were flourishing centers of commerce and culture.

Under royal patronage the Museum (a research institute) and Library were founded in Alexandria and became a focus of Hellenistic literature and science.

Hellenistic writers turned away from civic life and heroic themes toward private life and ordinary events. Hellenistic science flourished and there were great achievements in mathematics, astronomy, and medicine. Hellenistic women made small gains in status and power compared to earlier Greek women.

New beliefs emerged as faith in the Olympian gods declined. Ethics replaced politics as the focus of philosophy. The two most popular new philosophical schools were Stoicism and Epicureanism, the first austere and public-spirited, the second emphasizing withdrawal into private life. So-called mystery religions, which offered secret teachings, drew a wide public. Greeks and Jews came into increasing contact, both in the Diaspora and in Palestine, where Ptolemaic and Seleucid kings ruled in turn. Jews were divided into various schools of thought, with Hellenizers and traditionalists representing the two poles of opinion.

LOOKING AHEAD

The interaction between Greeks and Jews would become a lasting theme of Western civilization. It grew enormously in importance after the Hellenistic kingdoms were conquered by Rome. Under the Romans, whom we examine in Chapters 5 through 7, Hellenism and Judaism would be combined in a new and powerful form: Christianity.

KEY TERMS

Macedon (p. 94)

Philip II (p. 94)

Alexander the Great (p. 95)

Hellenism (p. 100)

Ptolemies (p. 100)

Seleucids (p. 100)

Antigonids (p. 102)

Alexandria (p. 103)

Antioch (p. 104)

Stoics (p. 114)

Epicureans (p. 115)

mystery religions (p. 115)

Maccabees (p. 117)

Online Study Center
Improve Your Grade Flashcards

SUGGESTED READING

Bosworth, A. B. *The Legacy of Alexander: Politics, Warfare, and Propaganda Under the Successors.* 2001. A study of the emergence of the Hellenistic kingdoms in the thirty years after Alexander's death.

Bowman, Alan K. *Egypt After the Pharaohs.* 1986. An excellent and highly readable introduction to the social history of the Ptolemaic and later periods.

Cartledge, Paul. *Alexander the Great: The Search for a New Past.* 2004. A crisp and concise introduction.

Cohen, Shaye. *From the Maccabees to the Mishnah.* 1987. An excellent introduction by a distinguished scholar of Second Temple Judaism.

Grant, Michael. *From Alexander to Cleopatra: The Hellenistic World.* 1982. A lively and readable introduction; at its best on cultural history.

Green, P. *Alexander to Actium: An Essay in the Historical Evolution of the Hellenistic Age.* 1989. A collection of elegant essays synthesizing scholarship on a wide variety of topics in political, cultural, and social history.

Long, A. A. *Hellenistic Philosophy: Stoics, Epicureans, Sceptics.* 2d ed. 1986. A concise critical analysis of the main ideas and methods of thought of the major Hellenistic philosophers.

Walbank, F. W. *Hellenistic World.* Rev. ed. 2006. A sound and up-to-date introduction.

Wood, Michael. *In the Footsteps of Alexander the Great: A Journey from Greece to Asia.* 2001. An engaging story that retraces Alexander's path today while it narrates his history; magnificent color photos of seldom-seen sites.

NOTES

1. Isocrates, "Panegyricus," trans. H. I. Marrou, in *A History of Education in Antiquity,* trans. George Lamb (New York: Mentor Books/New American Library, 1956), p. 130.

2. Romila Thapar, *Aśoka and the Decline of the Mauryas* (Oxford: Oxford University Press, 1961), p. 256.

3. Quoted in Charles Rowan Beye, *Ancient Greek Literature and Society,* 2d ed. (Ithaca, N.Y.: Cornell University Press, 1987), p. 265.

5

ROME, FROM REPUBLIC TO EMPIRE

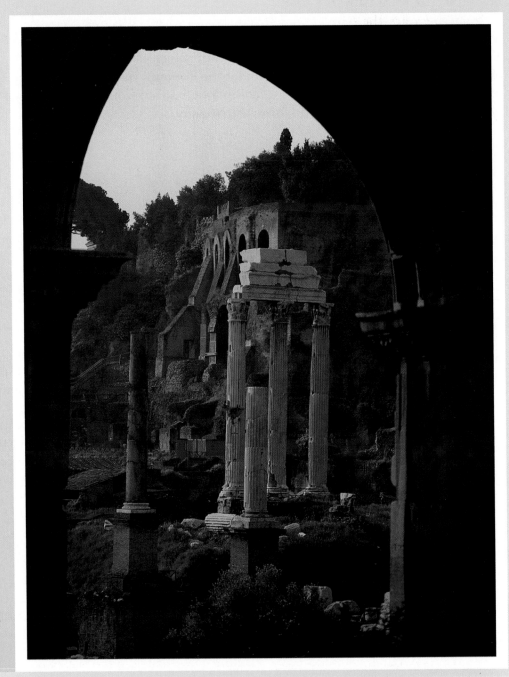

The Forum, Rome
(Michael Yamshita/Woodfin Camp &
Associates)

ere is the Roman Forum. We are standing in the heart of the ancient city, under the arch of the emperor Septimius Severus, looking south toward two columns that once held statues of great citizens. Beyond them are the Sacred Way, Rome's oldest street, and the three elegant columns of the Temple of Castor and Pollux. In the background, beyond a market and vaulted warehouse, is the Palatine Hill. The photograph takes us from an arch celebrating military triumph to ruins evoking citizenship and piety, to a reminder of the everyday needs of the masses of Rome, and finally to a historic hill. On this hill shepherds founded the city of Rome, and on this hill, centuries later, emperors lived. We see, in short, the civic center of the city destined to give the Western world many of its fundamental ideas about government and empire. It is arguably the single most important public space in the history of the world.

The ancient Romans were a practical people. Virgil (70–19 B.C.), for example, the greatest Roman poet (see page 157), celebrates not his countrymen's artistry or cultivation but rather their pragmatic accomplishments:

> For other peoples will, I do not doubt,
> still cast their bronze to breathe with softer features,
> or draw out of the marble living lines,
> plead causes better, trace the ways of heaven
> with wands and tell the rising constellations;
> but yours will be the rulership of nations,
> remember, Romans, these will be your arts:
> to teach the ways of peace to those you conquer,
> to spare defeated peoples, tame the proud.[1]

The Romans turned an Italian city-state into one of the largest empires in history, including all the countries of the Mediterranean as well as large parts of western Asia and of northern and central Europe. By holding this empire for centuries and by promoting prosperity in every corner, Rome planted in what would become Britain, France, Germany, and Spain (among other places) the seeds of the advanced civilizations of the Mediterranean.

Rome is no less important for its influence on the Western civic tradition. Much of the modern vocabulary of politics, from *president* to *inauguration*

CHAPTER OUTLINE

BEFORE THE REPUBLIC, 753–509 B.C.

THE EARLY AND MIDDLE REPUBLIC AT HOME, CA. 509–133 B.C.

THE EARLY AND MIDDLE REPUBLIC ABROAD, CA. 509–133 B.C.

THE LATE REPUBLIC AND ITS COLLAPSE, 133–31 B.C.

KEY TERMS

Latin	legion
Etruscans	Punic Wars
res publica	Cato the Censor
senate	Gracchi
paterfamilias	Caesar
triumph	Cicero

Online Study Center

This icon will direct you to interactive map and primary source activities on the website **college.hmco.com/pic/noble5e**

to *forum,* can be traced back to Rome. After an early period of monarchy, Rome was for centuries a republic (Latin, *res publica,* literally "public thing") before becoming essentially a monarchy again under the Caesars. The Roman Republic mixed popular power with government controlled by wealthy landowners. The government was divided into three branches, which created a system of checks and balances that tended toward consensus. The result was efficiency and, for centuries, stability.

Roman politicians sought to control ordinary citizens but in some ways were more flexible than Greek democrats. Unlike Greece, Rome extended its citizenship to a large population, first throughout Italy and then across its entire empire. The modern nation-state with its mass citizenship owes much to Rome. Indeed, although Rome was not democratic, modern democracy—that is, popular government with a large population, whose officials are elected by the people—has roots in the Roman Republic as well as in the Greek city-state.

Fueled by fear, ambition, and greed, Roman expansion generated its own momentum. Rome's arrogance matched its success: in consolidating power over huge territories, the Romans committed atrocities, enslaved whole peoples, and destroyed cities with little provocation. Ironically, military success slowly undermined both Rome's political stability at home and the socioeconomic basis of its army. Meanwhile, the Romans showed great open-mindedness in borrowing from other societies, in particular from the Greeks, to whom the Republic owed great cultural debts. Also fascinating is the shrewdness and generosity with which the Romans shared their citizenship with the elites whom they had conquered, thereby winning their loyalty and strengthening Rome's grip on their territories.

Historians conventionally divide the Republic into three periods: Early (509–287 B.C.), Middle (287–133 B.C.), and Late (133–31 B.C.). This chapter begins with the origins of the city of Rome in the early first millennium B.C. and then traces the Republic from its foundation to its imperial conquests to its collapse under their weight. Success spoiled Rome. The unintended consequences of conquest on Rome's society, politics, and culture led to a revolution that, in the century beginning in 133 B.C., saw the Republic's downfall.

FOCUS QUESTIONS

What was early Rome like and how was it shaped by relations with its neighbors?

How was the Roman Republic governed, and how did that government shape the Western political tradition?

How did Rome conquer an empire?

How did the unintended consequences of conquest on Rome lead to a revolution that destroyed the Republic?

BEFORE THE REPUBLIC, 753–509 B.C.

What was early Rome like and how was it shaped by relations with its neighbors?

The ancient Romans believed that their city was founded on April 21, 753 B.C., by Romulus, a descendant of refugees from the Trojan War. Although the name "Romulus" supplies a convenient etymology for "Rome," little stock can be placed in this story. Nevertheless, archaeology shows that by the eighth century B.C. Rome was already on its way to being a city and it had a king. Archaeologists have recently discovered a palace in the Forum from this era. They have also found traces of sanctuaries and a defensive wall. Nearby, a simple village of farmers and shepherds—a collection of huts—stood on the Palatine Hill, one of the seven hills on which Rome would cluster and the place where tradition puts the settlement of 753 (see inset, Map 5.2, on page 135). But the first settlers on the hills of Rome came even earlier, around 1000 B.C., as pottery and graves show.

Archaeological evidence raises some basic questions: What were Rome's origins, and how did it grow? Are seeds of Roman greatness visible in its early history? By examining the data of archaeology and of those elements in ancient historiography that seem to be based on accurate tradition, we can answer these questions, at least in outline.

THE FIRST ROMANS AND THEIR NEIGHBORS

Italy is a long peninsula, shaped roughly like a boot, extending about 750 miles from the Alps into the Mediterranean (see **MAP 5.1**). In the far north, the high Alps provide a barrier to the rest of Europe. To the east, the Adriatic Sea separates Italy from modern Slovenia and Croatia; to the west, the Tyrrhenian Sea faces the large islands of Sardinia and Corsica (and the smaller but iron-rich island of Elba) and, beyond, the coasts of France and Spain. Off the "toe" of the Italian boot, and separated from the mainland by a narrow, 3-mile strait of water, is the large island of Sicily, rich farm country in ancient times. Sicily is only 90 miles from North Africa. In short, Italy is centrally located in the Mediterranean. It was both a target for conquerors and a springboard for conquest.

Italy contained some of the ancient Mediterranean's most fertile and metal-rich land. From the watershed of the Po and Adige Rivers in the north, the agriculturally rich plains of Etruria (modern Tuscany), Latium (the region of Rome), and Campania (the region of Naples) unfold southward down Italy's west coast. Although the Apennine (AP-puh-nine) mountains run north-south along most of the Italian peninsula, they are low compared with the Alps and contain many passes, permitting the movement of armies.

A sensational recent archaeological discovery opens a window into second-millennium B.C. Italy. Poggiomarino is a prehistoric village consisting of houses that were built on oak pilings and separated by canals. The village, located on a river near Naples, was inhabited from around the 1500s B.C. to around 700 B.C. A masterpiece of prehistoric engineering, the village covered at least 7 acres and was a center of bronze production.

In the first millennium B.C., Italy was a hodgepodge of peoples and languages. They included the Etruscans in the north, Greek colonists in southern Italy and in Sicily, and such mountain peoples as the Sabines and the Samnites. The Samnites spoke Oscan, an Indo-European language, as did the Campanians, who lived around Naples, and the Lucanians, who lived in south-central Italy. Both the Samnites and the Lucanians were warlike peoples who conquered their neighbors before

753–509 B.C.	Monarchy (traditional dates)
509–287 B.C.	Early Republic
449 B.C.	Law of the Twelve Tables
338 B.C.	Latin League dissolved; Roman citizenship extended
289 B.C.	First Roman coinage (traditional date)
287–133 B.C.	Middle Republic
264–146 B.C.	Punic Wars
240 B.C.	First play produced at Rome
197 B.C.	Rome defeats Macedonian phalanx
146 B.C.	Rome destroys Carthage and Corinth
133–31 B.C.	Late Republic
133–121 B.C.	The Gracchi
107–78 B.C.	Marius and Sulla
73–71 B.C.	Spartacus's revolt
66–62 B.C.	Pompey's eastern campaigns
63 B.C.	Consulship of Cicero
58–51 B.C.	Caesar conquers Gaul
44 B.C.	Caesar assassinated
31 B.C.	Antony defeated at Actium; Octavian in power

finally being conquered by Rome. (See the feature "The Visual Record: From Poseidonia to Paestum.")

Latium (LAY-shum) was home to a number of small Latin-speaking towns, one of them Rome. In the fifth century B.C. another important people arrived on the Italian scene: Celts (called Gauls by the Romans), large numbers of whom crossed the Alps and settled in northern Italy after roughly 500 B.C. Most of these various peoples spoke Indo-European languages, of which Latin, the language of the Romans (as well as other peoples of Latium), was one.

Rome's location in Italy was central and protected. Rome is located in Latium, which is about halfway down the Italian peninsula. Located 15 miles inland on the Tiber (TY-ber), the largest river on Italy's west coast, Rome had access to the sea. A midstream island makes Rome the first crossing place upstream from the Tiber's mouth, which offered the Romans freedom of movement north and south. Yet strategically, Rome

Latin Indo-European language of ancient Rome and its empire, from which today's Romance languages developed.

MAP 5.1 Early Italy and Region of City of Rome

Early Italy comprised a variety of terrain and peoples. Rome is located in the central Italian region of Latium. The Alps separate Italy from northern Europe. The Apennine mountain range runs almost the entire length of the Italian peninsula. Much of the rest of Italy is fertile plain.

Etruscan Tomb Painting
This wall painting from Tarquinia shows a married aristocratic couple at a banquet. The style of the figures is derived from Greek art, but the depiction of husband and wife dining on the same couch is characteristically Etruscan.
(National Museum, Tarquinia/Scala/ Art Resource, NY)

was protected. It was far enough from the sea to be safe from raiders and pirates. And its seven hills offered a natural defense—from nature as well as humans, because the Tiber often flooded its banks.

In the eighth century B.C. Archaic Rome (as the pre-Republican period is called) began to change from a large village into a city. By the sixth century B.C., Rome had streets, walls, drains, temples, and a racetrack. What caused the transformation? Perhaps the key factor was contact with Magna Graecia (MAG-nuh GREE-shuh), the Greek colonies to the south (see Map 5.1). Established in the eighth and seventh centuries B.C., the colonies transported westward the sophisticated urban civilization of the eastern Mediterranean.

More controversial is the impact on early Rome of its neighbors to the north, the **Etruscans** (ee-TRUS-kunz). The twelve Etruscan city-states were organized in a loose confederation centered in Etruria (ee-TROO-ree-uh). They grew rich from the mining of iron, copper, and silver, from piracy, from trade, and from a network of influential Etruscan emigrants throughout central Italy, probably including Rome's last three kings (traditionally dated 616–509 B.C.).

The Etruscans were brilliant, wealthy, and warlike. We know less about them than we would like, from their language, which is only partly understood, to their origins, which probably lay in Italy but possibly in Anatolia. Etruscan power extended to many places in central, northern, and even southern Italy. Many scholars argue that the Etruscans conquered pre-Republican Rome, but the evidence does not support that theory. Rather, an Etruscan nobleman, Lucius Tarquinius Priscus, migrated to Rome and was eventually elected king. Under him and his son (or perhaps grandson), Lucius Tarquinius Superbus, who was Rome's last king, Etruscan culture left an impact on Rome. For example, the Tarquins sponsored several building projects in Rome, including the great Temple of Jupiter on the Capitoline Hill in the center of Rome. But scholars disagree as to whether the Etruscan impact on Roman culture was superficial or deep.

At least we can be sure that the Etruscans were great artists and architects and very religious. They believed that it was possible to learn the will of the gods by interpreting the sight and sound of lightning and thunder and by carefully examining the internal organs, especially the liver, of sacrificial animals. Etruscan elite

Etruscans Inhabitants of twelve loosely confederated city-states north of Rome; they were conquered by the Romans by the early third century B.C.

From Poseidonia to Paestum

Between them, the elegant Greek painting and the rough Roman bronze statue shown here sum up the history of the ancient city of Paestum. Paestum is located in southern Italy about 200 miles south of Rome. It was a port and commercial center in a rich farming region on the Gulf of Salerno. Founded as the Greek colony of Poseidonia around 600 B.C., Paestum ended up as a thriving Roman city after being conquered by the Romans in 273 B.C. In between (410–273 B.C.), Paestum was overrun and ruled by the Oscan-speaking Lucanian warriors of southern Italy. Somehow, no matter who ruled it or what it was called, Paestum managed to flourish. Its remains present a picture of the wealth, high civilization, and ethnic diversity of first-millennium B.C. Italy.

Look first at the painting from Greek-era Poseidonia of the man reclining on a couch. He wears a wreath and is holding a lyre in his right hand. He is one of ten men, in a series of paintings, shown participating in a *sumposion,* or "wine party," a typical gathering of aristocratic Greek culture. (Ironically, we get our word *symposium,* or "academic meeting," from this ancient, alcoholic merrymaking.) His manicured beard and trim physique identify him as a member of the leisure class.

A superb example of ancient painting, it was discovered on the outskirts of Paestum in 1968 and dates to 480/470 B.C. It is part of one of five tomb paintings from the Tomb of the Diver, named after the painting, on the lid of the tomb, of a young man in the act of diving, perhaps a symbol of the journey into the underworld.

The artistic style, the clothing, and the sumposion are all Greek. Yet the practice of painting a tomb and the use of diving as a symbol of death are Etruscan in origin. Thus the paintings demonstrate the cultural mix of Greek Italy.

This sums up the experience of Poseidonia well, because the city grew rich as a commercial center between the Etruscans and the Greeks farther south. Poseidonia's Greekness is underlined by its excellent Doric temples; the ruins of these are among the best such ruins in the world today. Also of note is the Greek-style rectangular public space, with its central agora, three broad avenues, and thirty-two cross streets, as well as the strong walls.

Under the Lucanian conquerors, Poseidonia continued the traditions of tomb painting and cultural interchange. Many Lucanian tomb paintings from the town survive, and they illustrate a lively mix of Greek and Italic styles.

A Guest Holding a Lyre
(painting from Tomb
of the Diver, Paestum)
(Scala/Art Resource, NY)

After Poseidonia was conquered by Rome in 273 B.C., it became known as Paestum and acquired the status of a Latin colony. As soldiers and sailors, the citizens of Paestum defended Roman interests in southern Italy. In return, and because they were Latin colonists, they enjoyed the privileges of free trade with Rome and intermarriage with Romans, as well as the more theoretical possibility of becoming Roman citizens by moving to Rome (but only after leaving a son in the colony). The citizens consisted of around five thousand Roman and Latin settlers as well as the local elite. Many non-elite inhabitants of Paestum no doubt lost land to the settlers.

Meanwhile, both the landscape and the politics of the city were transformed. The agora of Poseidonia became the forum of Paestum, on whose sides were built Roman-style buildings, including a council hall and a temple of Jupiter (like the temple on Rome's Capitoline Hill). Eventually Paestum would acquire an amphitheater and Roman baths.

Paestum also acquired a copy of a famous Roman work of art, the bronze statue of Marsyas, which is reproduced here. This statue dates to the mid-third century B.C. It was cast in imitation of a well-known statue of Marsyas in Rome and erected at the center of Paestum on the west side of the forum.

For the Romans, Marsyas symbolized liberty. He was a character from Greek mythology and had been adopted by the prominent plebeian family of Marcius Rutilus to symbolize the victory of the plebeians in their struggle with the patricians.

The statue's right hand would have been raised in a gesture of authority. His calves are ringed by metal bands, like the legs of a slave, except that the chains of slavery have been broken off. For the citizens of Paestum, the statue celebrated their identification with Rome, their liberation from Lucanian rule, their privileged status as Latin colonists, and perhaps their freedom from economic need as landholders in a fertile territory.

The statue of Marsyas is considered today to be one of the most important works of the new culture of an Italy dominated by Rome. But it is many other things as well: It symbolizes the combined plebeian-patrician elite of Rome and its success in extending Roman power throughout the peninsula. It demonstrates the continued impor-

Marsyas (bronze statue, Paestum)
(Scala/Art Resource, NY)

tance of Greek culture, since Marsyas was a Greek character, but it also shows the flexibility with which the Roman elite adapted Greek symbols for its own purposes. And it reminds us of the willingness of the Romans to trample on local customs and impose Roman culture throughout Italy.

QUESTIONS

1. How does the history of Paestum illustrate the ethnic diversity of first-millennium B.C. Italy?

2. What light on the life of a Greek colony is shed by the Tomb of the Diver?

3. What does the statue of Marsyas symbolize about Roman rule in Italy?

Online Study Center
Improve Your Grade Visual Record Activities

women had high status compared with their Greek or Roman counterparts. Etruscan women kept their own names, and Etruscan children bore the names of both parents. In addition, Etruscan elite women were permitted to attend athletic contests in spite of the presence of naked male athletes.

THE ROMAN MONARCHY

Tradition says that Rome was ruled by seven kings before the foundation of the Republic. Although the number of kings may be a later invention, their existence is undoubted. In addition to traces of the monarchy in Republican institutions, there is archaeological proof: a form of the Latin word *rex* ("king"), for example, has been found inscribed on a Roman monument from the early sixth century B.C. The king's power, called *imperium* (from *imperare*, "to command"), was very great, embracing religious, military, and judicial affairs.

The king was advised by a council of elders, called the "fathers" (*patres* in Latin) or the "senate" (*senatus*, from *senex*, "old man"). In theory, the senate was primarily an advisory body, but in practice it was very powerful. Senators were the heads of the most important families in Rome, so the king rejected their advice at his peril. Romans spoke of the senate's *auctoritas*, a quasi-religious prestige.

Most senators were patricians (puh-TRIH-shunz), as early Rome's hereditary aristocracy was known. The rest of the people, the bulk of Roman society, were called plebeians (pleh-BEE-unz). Plebeians were free; most were ordinary people, though some were wealthy. Patricians monopolized the senate and priesthoods, and they did not intermarry with plebeians.

The whole people, probably both patricians and plebeians, met in an assembly organized in thirty local units, or *curiae*, hence the name *curiate assembly*. Although the assembly's numbers were large, its powers were limited. Before becoming law, resolutions of the assembly required approval by the senate.

Early Rome was a class-based society, but it was open to foreigners. Among others, Etruscans, Sabines, and Latins—as the inhabitants of other Latin-speaking towns are called—came to settle in Rome. Foreigners at first had low status, but they gained equality around 550 B.C., for pragmatic purposes. Rome needed soldiers to fight its wars; in order to expand the body of loyal infantrymen, the immigrants were granted citizenship—a reform traditionally associated with King Servius Tullius (578–535 B.C.).

Servius probably introduced to Rome the hoplite phalanx (see page 61), with immigrants included in its ranks. The changes in the army contributed to the process that, within several generations of Servius's reform, took Rome from monarchy to republic.

━━━━ S E C T I O N　 S U M M A R Y ━━━━

- Rome was first settled as a village around 1000 B.C. and added a palace and sanctuaries in the 700s B.C.

- Rome borrowed much from the more advanced culture of the Greek colonies in southern Italy and Sicily.

- The twelve Etruscan city-states, north of Rome, were rich, powerful, and sophisticated.

- Rome's last three kings were probably Etruscan immigrants who added Etruscan elements to Roman culture.

- Early Rome was a class-based society with a monarchy and a sharp division between patricians (aristocrats) and plebeians (commoners).

THE EARLY AND MIDDLE REPUBLIC AT HOME, CA. 509–133 B.C.

How was the Roman Republic governed, and how did that government shape the Western political tradition?

Tradition says that the Roman Republic was established in 509 B.C., when the kings were overthrown. Nowadays, scholars envision a long process rather than a single, dramatic upheaval. In either case, the Republic differed from the monarchy in two basic ways. First, the Republic stood for liberty, which for the Romans meant both freedom from the arbitrary power of a king and freedom to participate in

public affairs. Second, the Republic was a commonwealth, in Latin, **res publica** (rays POO-blee-kuh), literally "public thing," as opposed to *res privata*, "private thing," as the Romans characterized monarchy. As a kingdom Rome belonged to the royal family, but as a

> **res publica**　Latin for "public thing," it was the Romans' concept of their republic, which uniquely influenced Western political institutions.

republic it belonged to the Roman people. In theory, the Roman people were sovereign—that is, the people ruled the state.

But which people? This is a key question because the Romans did *not* embrace another principle that might seem to follow from liberty: equality. Rather, they believed in order, balance, and competition, all of which are central themes of Roman Republican history. Roman society and culture, moreover, were conservative. Once the young Republic had its new values in place, it tried to maintain those values over the centuries with little change. Nor did the Republic give up entirely on the old values of the monarchy. Rather, it continued some of those values.

We know relatively little about the Early Republic (509–287 B.C.) but enough to know that it witnessed centuries of social and political conflict. The Middle Republic (287–133 B.C.) was a shorter and better-documented period of relative consensus at home and massive expansion abroad. Social and political conflict broke out again with a vengeance in the Late Republic (133–31 B.C.), ultimately rendering the Republic a deathblow.

POLITICAL INSTITUTIONS

The best and most even-handed ancient analyst of Roman politics is the historian Polybius (po-LIH-bee-us) (ca. 200–118 B.C.). A Greek and former hostage who lived in Rome, Polybius observed his adopted city with an outsider's careful eye. Polybius argued that in the Middle Republic of his day, Rome was a "mixed constitution," balancing the power of the masses with the authority of the elite. The result was a strong and stable state.

Polybius divides Roman political institutions into three branches: executive, deliberative, and legislative. The American founders adopted a similar division, but they combined the legislative and deliberative functions and added a judicial branch. In Rome the executive branch also administered justice. Rome's executive branch was made up of magistrates—that is, public officials; the deliberative branch consisted of the Roman senate; and the legislative branch was composed of four different assemblies of the people.

Executive power lay in the hands of Rome's powerful magistrates. They were elected and not chosen by lottery, as in Greek democracy. Election required campaigning, which in turn took money and connections. Magistracies were time-consuming jobs but offered no salary, unlike in Greek democracy. Thus only a wealthy few could afford to hold public office in Rome.

Eager for strong magistrates but afraid that power corrupts, Romans imposed the principles of *collegiality* and *annuality* on their officials. Every magistrate had one or more colleagues and held office for only one year. The chief magistrates were eventually called con-

suls, of which there were two. Each consul had the power to veto the other's actions. Like the former king, each consul had *imperium,* the power to issue commands and order punishments, including execution.

From about 500 B.C. to about 300 B.C., other public offices were created to help the consuls as administration grew more complex. In addition, the Romans elected two censors, older men chosen once every few years for eighteen-month terms. At first their job was to supervise the census, the military register of citizens that recorded each man's property class. Later the censors became, as it were, supervisors of public morals, since they could punish "bad" citizens.

The Republic's government adapted flexibly to trying circumstances. In times of emergency, for example, the Republic turned power over to a single magistrate. The dictator, as he was called, made binding decisions, but he held office for only six months.

The Roman **senate** guided and advised the magistrates. During most of the Republic, the senate consisted of three hundred men, all former magistrates and each of whom served for life. Senators possessed great authority. They supervised public expenditures and were for all practical purposes in charge of foreign policy.

Only the assemblies of the people could make laws. There were four assemblies: the curiate assembly, the centuriate assembly, the council of the plebs, and the tribal assembly. Roman assemblies combined democratic and nondemocratic features. On the one hand, all decisions were made by majority vote, and only after speeches or campaigning. Assembly meetings were often preceded by public meetings, typically in the Forum, which featured lively debate. Women, free noncitizens, and even slaves could attend. On the other hand, voting took place by groups, and those groups were unrepresentative. Furthermore, in contrast to Greece, assembly participants stood rather than sat down and received no salary for attendance.

Although the curiate assembly of the monarchy survived, in the Republic it had a largely ceremonial role. The centuriate assembly held real power: it elected magistrates, voted on laws and treaties, accepted declarations of war and peace, and acted as a court in cases of treason, homicide, and appeals of the magistrates' decisions. But this assembly was dominated by wealthy men, especially the equestrians, or cavalrymen. The poorest men, known as *proletarii* ("breeders"), often did not have even the chance to vote.

The two other assemblies were the council of the plebs and the tribal assembly. The tribal assembly eventually replaced the plebs and, in fact, became Rome's main legislative body in the third century B.C.,

senate   In the ancient Roman Republic and Empire, the powerful council of elders that advised the monarchs.

A Clear Sign of Power

The lictor, or official, depicted in this bronze statuette (ca. first century A.D.) accompanied Roman magistrates, who had *imperium*, the power to issue punishments resulting in execution. That power is visible in the fasces—an ax in a bundle of wooden rods bound with straps—that he holds. *(Courtesy of the Trustees of the British Museum)*

outstripping the centuriate assembly in making laws. To understand the evolution and workings of the tribal assembly, we turn now to the class conflicts in Rome during the fifth through third centuries B.C.

CONFLICT OF THE ORDERS, 494–287 B.C.

Social and political conflict between the patricians and plebeians severely tested the Roman state in the fifth century. There were only 136 patrician families in 509 B.C., but they dominated the Early Republic. The plebs, in contrast, comprised masses of peasants and a tiny number of men who, though wealthy, were not patricians. Plebeian artisans, traders, and shopkeepers made up only a small part of the population. The various plebeian groups each wanted to break patrician power. Wealthy plebeians wanted access to high office, from which they had been largely excluded. Ordinary plebeians demanded relief from debt, redistribution of land, and codification and publication of the law. For a century and a half, the two groups of plebeians worked together, writing an important chapter in the history of political resistance.

Debt and hunger loomed large in the Early Republic. If a free man could not repay a loan, he had to work off what he owed, often for the rest of his life. Plebeians wanted this harsh system abolished. The average farm was too small to feed a family, so most peasants depended on public land for farming and grazing. Time and again throughout Republican history, however, public land was taken by the wealthy, who denied access to the poor. The only plebeian hope was to change the system.

The story of the plebs in the fifth century B.C. is one of solidarity. They organized themselves as a kind of state within the state, complete with their own assembly (the council of the plebs) and officials (the tribunes of the plebs). The decisions of the council of the plebs, called *plebiscita* (from which *plebiscite* comes), were binding only on the plebs; they did not receive the full force of law for over two hundred years. Yet the plebs did not retreat. On several occasions during the Early Republic, they resorted to secession: the plebs as a whole left the city, often for the Aventine Hill, where they stayed until their grievances were addressed (see inset, Map 5.2).

The ten tribunes (TRIB-yoonz), elected annually by the plebs, were the people's champions. A tribune's house stood open to any plebeian who needed him, and he could not leave the city limits. Inside the city of Rome, a tribune also had the right to veto any act of the magistrates, assembly, or senate that harmed plebeians. In return, the plebs swore to treat the tribunes as sacrosanct and to lynch anyone who harmed them.

But the patricians struck back. They controlled important priesthoods and had many supporters in the military. Furthermore, the new tribal assembly, created around the same time as the council of the plebs, used a system of representation that heavily favored landowners such as patricians. The tribal assembly elected lower magistrates and, like the centuriate assembly, voted on laws and acted as a court of appeals.

Still, the plebeians pressed onward and forced concessions from the patricians, until finally the patricians retreated. They decided to neutralize the poor by meeting the main demands of the plebeian elite. The outcome was a new nobility that combined patricians and plebeians. The patricians had decided to compromise to keep most of their privileges. The personnel changed, but the elite maintained power in Rome.

The specific events in the patrician-plebeian conflict follow two lines of development: concessions to wealthy plebeians and concessions to poor ones. A key moment came in 449 B.C. with publication of the law code known as the "Twelve Tables," eventually, if not at first, on twelve bronze tablets in the Forum. By modern standards, the code was tough and primitive, but its very existence was a plebeian victory because published law was accessible and dependable. Unfortunately, the complex legal procedure remained a secret of the priests for another 150 years, which meant that no poor man could go to court without the help of a rich patron.

Continued plebeian pressure slowly yielded other gains through the fourth century B.C. Around 445 B.C. the patricians accepted patrician-plebeian intermarriage, but it took nearly another eighty years, until 367 B.C., until they agreed to plebeian consuls. That same year saw a debt-relief law, and further debt relief came in 326 B.C.

Finally, in 287 B.C., the patrician and plebeian orders were formally merged, and a law called the "lex Hortensia" made decisions of the council of the plebs and the tribal assembly binding on the whole community, including patricians. Rome's new, combined patrician-plebeian elite was based on wealth, not heredity. Most Romans were non-elite, but at least they had won something: debt relief, access to the published laws, increased power for their assembly, and, most important, protection from arbitrary power.

THE ROMAN HOUSEHOLD

Roman government was once thought to be nothing more than the maneuvering of a few powerful families. Today a more balanced picture of Rome's constitution prevails. Yet there remains no doubt that elite Roman families wielded great power.

The Latin word *familia* is broader in meaning than the English word *family*. Better translated as "household," it connotes slaves, animals, and property, as well as the members of a nuclear family and their ancestors or descendants. The familia was the basic unit of Roman society and a model of political authority. In theory,

though not always in practice, the Roman household was an authoritarian institution governed by a male; thus the familia is an example of patriarchy.

The legal head of the familia was the ***paterfamilias*** (pah-ter-fah-MIL-ee-us)—the oldest living male, usually the father. According to Roman law, the paterfamilias had supreme power within the household. Although he was supposed to call a council of senior male relatives to consult on major decisions, he was not required to follow their advice. He had the right to sell family members into slavery and the rarely used power to kill an errant wife or child. A son, no matter how old, was always legally subject to the authority of a living paterfamilias.

Roman respect for the paterfamilias stemmed from Roman esteem for ancestors, who were more important than in Greek culture. All patricians and some plebeians belonged to a *gens* (plural, *gentes*), a kinship group that traced its ancestry back to a purported common ancestor. All Roman males had a personal and a family name, and patricians and elite plebeians also had a third (middle) name, indicating their gens—for example, Gaius Julius Caesar, whose personal name "Gaius" was followed by the gens name "Julius" and the familia name "Caesar."

In theory, the paterfamilias was the focus of power in the household, but practice was more complex. The sources are full of fathers who showed affection, love, and even indulgence toward their children. Moreover, Roman women usually married in their late teens and men in their late twenties. Given the low life expectancies, it was common for a man of 25 to have already buried his father. Many, perhaps even most, adult males were independent of a paterfamilias.

Unlike men, Roman women never became legally independent, even on the death of a paterfamilias. Instead of receiving a personal name, a daughter was called by the name of her father's gens. For example, Gaius Julius Caesar's daughter was called Julia; if Caesar had had a second daughter, she would have been Julia Secunda ("Julia the Second"). Although fathers were expected to support all male children, they had to support only the first of their daughters. In other words, they were free to "expose" additional daughters—that is, leave them in the open to die or, as was perhaps more likely, to be adopted or raised as a slave. A father also arranged a daughter's marriage and provided her with a dowry. In theory, again, the customs suggest a most severe relationship, but the evidence shows considerable father-daughter affection, including married daughters who sought advice or aid from their fathers.

Most women in early Rome married *cum manu* (kum MAN-oo) (literally, "with hand")—that is, they were "handed over" to their husbands, who became

paterfamilias   Oldest living male in an ancient Roman family, who had supreme legal power within the household.

Shrine of a Wealthy Household
This painting from Pompeii shows the spirit of the paterfamilias in a toga, which is wrapped around his head in keeping with the Roman procedures of sacrifice. He is flanked by the spirits of departed ancestors. A snake symbolizes fertility. *(Alinari/Art Resource, NY)*

their new paterfamilias. Even so, Roman wives and mothers had more prestige and freedom than their counterparts in Classical Greece. Legends of early Rome mention some who were peacemakers, negotiators, or catalysts of quarrels among men. Roman women regularly shared meals and social activities with their parents and were expected to take an interest in their husbands' political lives.

PATRONS AND CLIENTS

Patron (derived from *pater,* "father") means "defender" or "protector." *Client* means "dependent." Just as the Roman family was hierarchical, so Roman society consisted of pyramidal patron-client networks. Most patrons were in turn clients of someone more powerful; only a very few men stood at the top of the pyramid. To the Romans, justice meant not that patron and client treated each other as equals but rather that they showed each other respect and fulfilled mutual obligations.

Various paths led to the status of client. A peasant in need of help on his farm might ask a wealthy neighbor to become his patron. A manumitted slave became the client of his former owner. A conquered foe became the client of the victorious general. The status of client or patron was hereditary.

Patron and client might help each other in various ways. A patron might provide a client with food or with property for a dowry. He might settle disputes or provide legal assistance. In return, a client owed his patron respect and service. He escorted his patron in public on important occasions—possession of a large clientele signified prestige and power. If his patron sought political office, the client voted for him and urged others to do so.

Cloaked in an elaborate language of goodwill, the patron-client relationship was considered a matter of *fides* (FEE-days) ("good faith" or "trustworthiness"). Romans spoke not of a client submitting to a patron's power but rather of a client "commending himself" to the patron's fides. A patron spoke not of his clients but of his "friends," especially if they were men of standing or substance.

A patron was supposed to put his clients before his kin by marriage; only blood or adoptive relations were to take precedence. According to the Twelve Tables, a patron who defrauded his client was accursed and subject to death with impunity.

Patronage played an important role in Roman domestic politics. A wealthy patron expected his humble clients to vote as he wished, but he abused them at his peril. If a man's clients grew discontented, they might find a new patron. Patronage was more straightforward in foreign affairs. Experience as patrons schooled Roman leaders in treating the peoples they conquered as clients, often as personal clients. Moreover, the Roman state sometimes took foreign countries into its collective fides—much as a patron did a client—thus allowing Rome to extend its influence without the constraints of a formal alliance.

RELIGION AND WORLDVIEW

If we knew nothing about early Roman religion, we could deduce much about it from the familia and patronage. We could expect to find an emphasis on powerful fathers and binding agreements, and both are indeed present. The task of a Roman priest, whether an official of the state or an individual paterfamilias, was to establish what the Romans called the "peace of the gods." Roman cults aimed at obtaining the gods' agreement to human requests, at "binding" the gods—the Latin term for which is *religio*.

The earliest Roman religion was animistic—that is, it centered on the spirits that, the Romans believed, haunted the household and the fields and forests and determined the weather. The Lares, or spirits of departed ancestors, guarded the house, and the Penates watched over stored grain. The spirit of the hearth was Vesta, of the door Janus, of the rain and sun Jupiter (later identified with the Greek sky-god and the father-god Zeus), and of the crops and vegetation Mars (later identified with the Greek war-god Ares). The Romans believed that these spirits needed to be appeased—hence the contractual nature of their prayers and offerings. Over the years, as a result of Greek influence, anthropomorphism (that is, the worship of humanlike gods and goddesses) replaced Roman animism.

Roman state religion grew out of house religion. Vesta, the hearth-goddess, became goddess of the civic hearth; Janus, the door-god, became god of the city's gates; Jupiter became the general overseer of the gods; and Mars became the god of war. When trade and conquest brought the Romans into contact with foreign religions, the Romans tended to absorb them. The senate screened and sometimes rejected new gods, but by and large Roman polytheism was tolerant and inclusive.

The Republic sponsored numerous priestly committees, or colleges, to secure the peace of the gods. Originally restricted to patricians, most of the highest priesthoods were opened to plebeians by law in 300 B.C. Although some priesthoods were full-time jobs, most left the officeholder free to pursue a parallel career as a magistrate or a senator. The two most important priestly colleges were the augurs (AW-gers), who were in charge of foretelling the future from omens and other signs, and the pontiffs, who exercised a general supervision of Roman religion. The chief pontiff, the *pontifex maximus* (PON-tih-fex MAX-ih-mus), was the head of the state clergy. He was chosen by election. The pontiffs alone controlled the interpretation of the law until the fourth century B.C. The Romans allowed priests to interpret the law on the theory that an offense against humans was also an offense against the gods.

The system provided for only two colleges of priestesses: those of Ceres, goddess of fertility and death, and those of the Vestal Virgins. The six Vestals tended the civic hearth and made sure that its fire never went out. They served, as it were, as wives of the whole community, as guardians of the civil household. The Vestals were the only Roman women not under the authority of a paterfamilias. Chosen between the ages of 6 and 10 by the pontifex maximus, they had to remain virgins for thirty years or face death.

Roman ideology promoted simple and austere farmers' virtues—discipline, hard work, frugality, temperance, and the avoidance of public displays of affection even between spouses. Such virtues underlined the difference between the Republic and the kings, with their luxury and sophistication. At the same time, these virtues papered over class distinctions between rich and poor and so promoted stability.

Other Roman ideals included the supreme virtue of the household, *pietas*—devotion and loyalty to the familia, the gods, and the state. Household duties and gender obligations were defined clearly. Women were to be modest, upright, and practical. Men were to project *gravitas* ("weight" or "seriousness"), never lightness or levity. A serious man would display self-control and constancy, the ability to persevere against difficult odds. The masculine ideal was *virtus* (literally, "manliness"), which indicated excellence in war and government.

Roman men who attained virtus considered themselves entitled to the reward of *dignitas,* meaning not only public esteem but the tangible possession of a dignified position and official rank—in short, public office. The ultimate test of virtus, however, was in battle. Rome's wars supplied ample occasion to display it.

━━━━━ S E C T I O N   S U M M A R Y ━━━━━

- Republican government consisted of three branches: executive, deliberative, and legislative.

- The magistrates, the senate, and the assemblies were Rome's three main political institutions.

- The Conflict of the Orders led to debt relief for the poor and a combined patrician-plebeian nobility for the rich.

- The Roman household, headed by the *paterfamilias,* was a model of political authority.

- Roman society was made up of networks of patrons and clients.

- Romans idealized *pietas,* that is, loyalty to household, the gods, and the Republic.

THE EARLY AND MIDDLE REPUBLIC ABROAD, CA. 509–133 B.C.

How did Rome conquer an empire?

At the beginning of the Republic (ca. 509 B.C.), Roman territory comprised about 500 square miles. By 338 B.C. Rome controlled the 2,000 square miles of Latium and was moving north into Etruria and south into Samnite country. Three-quarters of a century later, in 265 B.C., Rome controlled all of the Italian peninsula south of an imaginary line from Pisae (modern Pisa) to Ariminum (modern Rimini), an area of about 50,000 square miles (see **MAP 5.2**). By 146 B.C. Roman provinces included Sicily, Cisalpine Gaul (northernmost Italy), Sardinia, Corsica, and Spain (divided into two provinces). Once-great Carthage was the Roman province of Africa (roughly, modern Tunisia), and once-mighty Macedon was the province of Macedonia, whose governor was also effectively in charge of Greece. The Seleucid kingdom was free but fatally weakened. Rome was the supreme power between Gibraltar and the Levant. It was the greatest empire of the ancient West. How and why had Rome, from its humble beginnings as a local power, reached this breathtaking height?

REPUBLICAN EXPANSION: THE CONQUEST OF ITALY, CA. 509–265 B.C.

Romans maintain that they conquered an empire without ever committing an act of aggression. When war was declared, a special college of priests informed the gods that Rome was merely retaliating for foreign injury. True, the Romans were frequently attacked by others, but often only after provocative behavior by Rome had left its rivals little choice.

Why Rome Fought   Rome's early conquests reveal many of its lasting motives for expansion. No doubt lust for conquest played a part, as did fear and hatred of outsiders, but self-control and shrewdness were stronger Roman characteristics. Greed, particularly land-hunger, was a perennial theme. Sometimes a domestic political motive was at work, for foreign adventure was a convenient way of deflecting plebeian energies. Perhaps the most significant factors, however, were the personal ambitions of a warrior elite and the presence of conflict in early Italy.

Victory in battle promised both prestige and booty and the political success that might follow. Military achievement brought unique acclaim. For example, certain victorious generals were allowed to celebrate a triumph; no such ceremony rewarded the feats of peacemakers or distinguished judges or other public benefactors. The triumphant general rode a chariot through the city to the Temple of Jupiter on the Capitoline Hill. He was accompanied by his troops, by the spoils of victory including famous captives, and by the magistrates and senators.

The harsh reality of Italian politics also ruled against pacifism. Without the willingness to fight, Rome could never have maintained its freedom. Yet what began as a pragmatic response to present dangers hardened into a habit of meeting even remote threats with force. In the fourth century B.C., having gained control of Latium, Rome considered the Samnites of central and southern Italy to be a potential threat. In the third century B.C., once Rome controlled Italy, it felt threatened by Carthage. After Carthage, the threat of Macedon was squelched, and after Macedon, Seleucid Syria, and so on.

Though flexible and far-reaching, Roman diplomacy sometimes ended up in war. Rome made formal alliances with some states, granting protection in return for obedience and troops or ships when needed by Rome. Short of a formal commitment, however, Rome might accept a state "into its fides"—that is, treat the state as a client. The result was only a moral, and not a legal, commitment, which sometimes sufficed to frighten any would-be aggressor from harassing Rome's new friend. If not, Rome had to go into battle to prove its trustworthiness as a patron.

How Rome Fought   Military success requires tenacity, discipline, and flexibility—all qualities that Rome cultivated. Roman organizational ability and love of order made the Roman military camp a much more regular and systematic place than anything seen since Assyrian days. Beginning in the fourth century B.C., Rome began to reward its soldiers with regular pay; this and the distribution of conquered land improved morale. Two other points are even more significant: the willingness to utilize foreign military technology and the combination of generosity and firmness with which Rome treated its allies.

Borrowed from the Greeks in the sixth century B.C., the hoplite phalanx suited Rome on the relatively level ground of Latium but fared poorly in the rugged

triumph   Elaborate procession through the streets of ancient Rome to salute a general's victory over a foreign army.

MAP 5.2 Roman Italy, ca. 265 B.C.

Rome controlled a patchwork of conquered territory, colonies, and allied states in Italy, held together by a network of treaties and of roads. The city of Rome (*inset*) was built on seven hills beside the Tiber River.

ALPS

Extent of Roman Italy by 218 B.C.

Aquileia

Verona

Adige

Cremona

Placentia

Po

Genua (Genoa)

CISALPINE GAUL

Bononia (Bologna)

Ariminum (Rimini)

Pisae (Pisa)

Arno

Florentia (Florence)

Fanum Fortunae

Ancona

Ligurian Sea

Arretium

UMBRIA

PICENUM

Castrum Truentinum

ILLYRIA

Pòpulonia

ETRURIA

Castrum Novum

Elba

Saturnia

Tiber

Reate

Adriatic Sea

Corsica

Aleria

Veii

Rome

Corfinium

SAMNIUM

Appian Way

LATIUM

Arpinum

APULIA

Barium

Tarracina

Beneventum

CAMPANIA

Venusia

Appian Way

Capua

Misenum

Neapolis (Naples)

LUCANIA

Tarentum

CALABRIA

Brundisium

Paestum

Gulf of Tarentum

Sardinia

Tyrrhenian Sea

Thurii

Neapolis

Carales

Croton

BRUTTIUM

Mediterranean Sea

Messana

Locri

Rhegium

Lilybaeum

Sicily

Utica

Cape Bon

Syracuse

Hippo Regius

Carthage

NORTH AFRICA

Malta

Rome

FIELD OF MARS

QUIRINAL HILL

VIMINAL HILL

Tiber

CAPITOLINE MT.

Senate House

ESQUILINE MT.

Forum

Regia

Tiber Island

Temple of Jupiter

PALATINE MT.

Hills of Rome

CAELIAN MT.

Circus Maximus

AVENTINE MT.

Servian Wall

Legend:

- Roman territory (full citizens)
- Roman territory (citizens without suffrage)
- Roman allies
- Latin colonies
- Carthaginian possessions
- ■ Greek cities
- — Major roads by 100 B.C.

0   500   1000 M.

0   1500   3000 Ft.

0   50   100 Km.

0   50   100 Mi.

The Appian Way

Named for the censor Appius Claudius Caecus, who proposed its construction, Rome's first great road was built in 312 B.C. during the Samnite Wars. It originally ran 132 miles from Rome to Capua and was extended an additional 234 miles, probably by 244 B.C., to Brundisium, on Italy's southern Adriatic coast. *(F. H. C. Birch/Sonia Halliday Photographs)*

Apennines against the Samnites. Following a major defeat in 321 B.C., the Romans adopted with great success the Samnites' equipment and tactics.

Unlike the phalanx, which overpowered the enemy by fighting as one thickly massed unit, a Roman **legion** was flexible and adaptable. Legions were drawn up into three lines, thirty maniples ("handfuls"), and sixty centuries (literally "hundreds," although the number of men per century varied); each century was commanded by a centurion. A legion marched in a checkerboard pattern, leaving gaps in the lines. In battle each line closed its gaps as it attacked in turn. Unlike hoplites, who engaged the enemy at short range, legionnaires first threw their javelins at long range. Then, having broken the enemy's order, they charged and fought with sword and shield. The semi-independence of the maniples, each with its own commander and banner, created a more maneuverable army than that of the phalanx and one better suited for mountain fighting. When Rome's legions beat the Macedonian phalanx decisively in 197 B.C., military history entered a new era.

legion   Ancient Roman battle formation in which many semi-independent groups broke their enemies' order with javelins at long range, then charged with sword and shield.

The Latin League and Beyond Rome was the leading power among the Latins, whom it led in an alliance known as the Latin League. Rome was first among equals, but the citizens of even the humblest Latin state had reciprocal rights of intermarriage and commerce with Romans and the right to become a citizen of another state by migrating there. Under Roman leadership the Latin League successfully defended Latium's borders against a series of enemies during the fourth and fifth centuries B.C. But eventually Rome had to confront a bitter two-year-long Latin revolt (340–338 B.C.).

The year 338 B.C. marked a turning point. Defeated peoples in the ancient world were often executed, deported, or enslaved. Victorious against the Latins, Rome, by contrast, pursued generosity. The Latin League was dissolved. Some of its member states were annexed, and their inhabitants became Roman citizens; others retained independence and alliance with Rome though no longer with one another. The non-Latin allies of the former rebels were also annexed by Rome, but they received the unique halfway status of "citizenship without suffrage." They shared the burdens of Roman citizenship but also all the rights except the vote; they also retained the right of local self-government. The settlement of 338 B.C. broke new ground by making it possible for Rome and its former allies and enemies to live together on the basis of relative equality.

The settlement also set a precedent for future Roman expansion. As Rome conquered Italy, a number of privileged Italian cities (called *municipia*) received the status of citizenship without suffrage. Others remained independent but were tied to Rome by perpetual alliance. Romans often annexed a portion of the land of these states.

If municipia were the carrots of Roman imperialism, the stick was a network of military roads and colonies crisscrossing Italy, allowing Rome to keep an eye on potential rebels. Roman roads allowed the swift movement of troops and linked the growing network of colonies. Colonies were established in strategically vital areas. The inhabitants, Roman and Latin, owed military service to Rome.

In later years, Italians would complain about treatment by Rome, but compared with inhabitants of Roman provinces outside Italy, they had a privileged status. Romans too would complain about allied demands for equality, but Rome received from its allies a huge pool of military manpower. The allies staffed the Roman armies that conquered the Samnites, Etruscans, and Gauls, all of whom came into the Roman orbit by the early third century B.C. Manpower abundance won Rome's war (280–276 B.C.) against the Greek general Pyrrhus (PIR-us) of Epirus (319–272 B.C.), an adventurer who intervened in southern Italy. Although Pyrrhus won battle after battle, he was unable to match Roman willingness to sustain thousands of casualties time and again. Pyrrhus's seeming victories, therefore, turned out to be defeats, which sent him home to Greece disappointed and left us with the expression "Pyrrhic victory."

As for Rome, by 265 B.C. it emerged as the ruler of all of Italy south of the Pisae-Ariminum line (see Map 5.2). One might say that Rome unified Italy, although Italy was less a unity than a patchwork of Roman territory and colonies and of diverse cities, states, and peoples each allied to Rome by separate treaties.

ROME VERSUS CARTHAGE: THE PUNIC WARS, 264–146 B.C.

The conquest of Italy made Rome one of two great powers in the central Mediterranean. The other was Carthage (CAR-thidge). Founded around 750 B.C. by Phoenicians from Tyre, Carthage controlled an empire in North Africa, Sicily, Corsica, Sardinia, Malta, the Balearic Islands, and southern Spain. (The adjective *Phoenician* is *Punicus* in Latin, hence the term *Punic* [PYOO-nik] for *Carthaginian*.) Like Rome, Carthage was guided by a wealthy elite, but it was mercantile in character rather than agrarian. Rome was a land power, Carthage a sea power. Rome had virtually no navy. Carthage commanded a great war fleet, and its merchant ships dominated the western Mediterranean and played a major role in the east.

Carthage was an economic powerhouse. The Carthaginians exploited the mineral-rich mines of Spain. They were the first Mediterranean people to organize large-scale plantations of slaves for the production of single crops. Even though the Romans zealously wiped out most of Carthaginian elite culture, they did make sure to preserve one Carthaginian classic: a multivolume work on agriculture by Mago. Translated from Punic into Latin by order of the senate, Mago's treatise had an enormous impact on Roman landowners, who, with the importation of massive numbers of slaves, adopted the plantation system in Italy (see pages 139–141).

Carthage boasted brilliant generals, especially in the Barca family, whose most famous member was Hannibal (HAN-uh-bull) (247–183 B.C.). Carthage might have been a handicapper's favorite at the outbreak of its long wars with Rome in 264 B.C., yet the end result was disaster for Carthage. A combination of Carthaginian weaknesses and Roman strengths accounts for the outcome.

Unlike Rome, Carthage did not have a citizen army. The commanders were Carthaginian, but most of the soldiers were mercenaries and of questionable loyalty.

Carthaginian Craftsmanship
These pendants of male heads are made of colored glass and come from Carthage. The Phoenicians and their colonists excelled in glasswork as a medium for the production of luxury goods. *(Erich Lessing/Art Resource, NY)*

Unlike Rome, which treated its Italian allies well, Carthage showed contempt for its troops, who repaid the favor by revolting whenever they had the chance. Carthage fielded large armies but not as large as Rome's.

At the start of the **Punic Wars,** Rome had no navy or commanders to match the Barca family, but it proved adaptable, tenacious, and ruthless. To win the First Punic War (264–241 B.C.), for example, Rome not only built a navy but outlasted the enemy in a long and bloody conflict. After initially granting a mild peace treaty, Rome took advantage of later Carthaginian weakness to seize Sardinia and Corsica and to demand an additional indemnity.

Forced to give in to Rome's demands, Carthage decided to build a new and bigger empire in Spain, beginning in 237 B.C., under Barca family leadership. Hannibal's father, the general Hamilcar Barca (d. 229 B.C.), had gone undefeated in the First Punic War and is said to have raised his son to seek a rematch. With Spain's rich deposits of silver and copper in its hands, Carthage once again posed a credible threat to Rome. In the mid-220s B.C., an ever watchful Rome challenged Carthaginian power in Spain through a Roman client there. The new Carthaginian commander, 27-year-old Hannibal Barca, was not to be cowed, however, and the Second Punic War ensued (218–201 B.C.).

Carthage was willing to risk war because Hannibal promised a quick, cheap, and easy victory. Because Carthage no longer had a fleet, the Romans felt secure in Italy; Hannibal surprised them by marching overland to Italy, making a dangerous passage across the Alps. A tactical genius, Hannibal reckoned that with his superior generalship, he could defeat the Romans in battle and cause them enormous casualties, and he was right. Hannibal's forces dominated the battlefield. Among his victories was the Battle of Cannae in Apulia (southeastern Italy), where, in 216 B.C., Carthage gave Rome the bloodiest defeat in its history, killing perhaps thirty thousand Romans.

But huge casualties alone could not bring Rome to its knees. Nor did all of Rome's allies revolt, as Hannibal had hoped. Most stood by Rome, which had treated them relatively well in the past and which now threatened rebels with reprisals. After Cannae, Rome's leadership followed a cautious strategy of harassment, delay, refusal to fight, and attrition. Hannibal was stymied by an enemy who lost battles but refused to surrender. In addition, Hannibal did not have the power to take the city of Rome.

In the meantime, Rome had bought valuable time to regroup. A new military star emerged: Publius Cornelius Scipio (SIP-ee-o) (236–183 B.C.), a Roman who finally understood Hannibal's tactics and matched them. First Scipio conquered Carthage's Spanish dominions, and then he forced Hannibal back to North Africa for a final battle in 202 B.C. near Zama (in modern Tunisia). Scipio won the battle and gained the surname Africanus ("the African"). As for Hannibal, he played a prominent role in Carthaginian politics for about a decade, until Rome forced him into exile in

Punic Wars (264–146 B.C.) Three wars during which the Roman Empire eventually destroyed Carthage.

Syria. In about 183 B.C., after taking part in the Seleucids' unsuccessful war against Rome, he committed suicide rather than face extradition to Rome.

The peace settlement of 201 B.C. stripped Carthage of its empire. Yet soon its economy rebounded, reviving old Roman fears of Carthage's political ambitions. In the Third Punic War (149–146 B.C.), Rome mounted a three-year siege under the leadership of Scipio Aemilianus (185–129 B.C.), finally destroying the city of Carthage in 146 B.C. Approximately a century later, Carthage was resurrected as a Roman colony and became one of the empire's greatest cities. In the meantime, it was left desolate, its people killed or enslaved.

Online Study Center **Improve Your Grade**
Primary Source: Cato the Elder: "Carthage Must Be Destroyed"

Rome emerged from the Punic Wars as the greatest power in the Mediterranean. It had acquired new provinces in Sicily, Sardinia, Corsica, Spain, and North Africa (where Carthage's former territory was annexed as the province of Africa). The road to further conquest seemed to lead in all directions.

VICTORIES IN THE HELLENISTIC EAST, CA. 200–133 B.C.

Most countries would have savored peace after an ordeal such as the Punic Wars, but Rome immediately leaped into a long conflict in Greece and Anatolia. Its aims were to weaken the power of Macedon, which it feared might threaten Rome one day, especially since the Macedonian king Philip V (r. 221–179 B.C.) had made an alliance with Hannibal after Cannae. Rome won a relatively quick and easy victory when in 197 B.C. the legions crushed the Macedonian phalanx at Cynoscephalae in central Greece (see **MAP 5.3**).

Rome had hoped to impose a patron-client relationship on Greece and Macedon, thereby avoiding having to sustain a permanent military presence, but that hope failed. The independent-minded Greeks chafed at Roman domination. Several years of miscommunication and intrigue followed, only to lead to renewed wars. First the Seleucids, under the ambitious king Antiochus III (r. 223–187 B.C.), challenged Rome for hegemony on the Greek peninsula. It was in this war that Hannibal took a small, doomed part. Roman forces made short work of the enemy. Driven out not only from Greece but from Anatolia as well, the Seleucids in effect recognized Roman supremacy in the Mediterranean (188 B.C.).

Then came another two rounds of war that pitted Rome against Macedon and various Greek states (171–167 and 150–146 B.C.). Victorious in both wars, Rome deprived the Greeks and Macedonians of their independence. Wherever democracy had survived in Greece, it was replaced with oligarchy. In 146 B.C. Rome destroyed Corinth, one of Greece's wealthiest cities, as a warning against further rebellion. Greece then suffered Roman neglect and taxation for nearly two hundred years.

By annexing Carthage, Macedon, and Greece in the mid-second century B.C., Rome created a dynamic for expansion around the entire Mediterranean. Before the century was over, southern Gaul was annexed, and Rome had gained a foothold in Asia. The kingdom of Pergamum (northwestern Anatolia) had supported Rome throughout Rome's wars in the east. When Attalus III of Pergamum died without an heir in 133 B.C., he surrendered his kingdom to the Roman people, who made it into a province of Asia.

Two great Hellenistic states remained independent: the Seleucid kingdom, that is, Syria, and Ptolemaic Egypt. Roman ambassadors and generals frequently interfered in their affairs, however, and no one was surprised when, in the first century B.C., they too were annexed by Rome.

THE SOCIOECONOMIC CONSEQUENCES OF EXPANSION

Expansion led to enormous and unintended changes in Rome's society, economy, and culture. Already wealthy, the Roman elite now came into fabulous riches. Huge profits awaited the generals, patrons, diplomats, magistrates, tax collectors, and businessmen who followed Rome's armies. In Italy most profits were in the form of land; in the provinces wealth was found not only in land but also in slaves, booty, and graft. One of the worst grafters, Gaius Verres, governor of Sicily from 73 to 71 B.C., was prosecuted by Cicero (see page 149), then beginning his oratorical career, for allegedly extorting tens of thousands of pounds of silver from his province. But even Cicero skimmed off several thousand pounds of silver as governor of the province of Cilicia (southern Anatolia) from 51 to 50 B.C.

The first Roman coinage, traditionally dated to 289 B.C., facilitated commercial transactions. Previously, the Romans had made do with barter, uncoined bronze, and cast bronze bars, but now they imitated the workmanship and style of Greek coins. Equally prominent in the homes of wealthy Romans were Greek metalwork, jewelry, art objects, and other luxury goods. Conservatives bemoaned the decline of traditional Roman austerity, but they fought a hopeless rear-guard action.

Ordinary Romans needed no reminder of the virtues of austerity, for they did not share in the elite's profit from Roman expansion. Indeed, a century of intensive warfare—from the outbreak of the Punic Wars in 264 B.C. to the destruction of Carthage and Corinth in

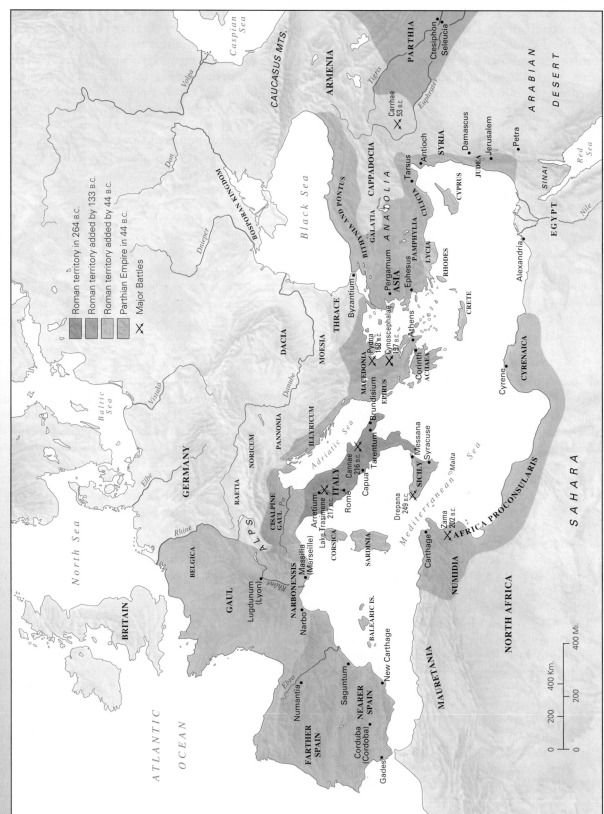

MAP 5.3 Roman Expansion, 264–44 B.C.
Wars against Carthage, the major Greco-Macedonian powers, Gauls, Germans, North Africans, and other peoples brought Rome an empire on three continents.

Online Study Center **Improve Your Grade**
Interactive Map: Roman Expansion During the Republic

Roman territory in 264 B.C.
Roman territory added by 133 B.C.
Roman territory added by 44 B.C.
Parthian Empire in 44 B.C.
X Major Battles

ATLANTIC OCEAN
North Sea
Baltic Sea
BRITAIN
GERMANY
BELGICA
GAUL
Lugdunum (Lyon)
NARBONENSIS
Narbo
Massilia (Marseille)
ALPS
CISALPINE GAUL
Arretium
Lake Trasimene 217 B.C.
Rome
Capua
ITALY
Cannae 216 B.C.
Tarentum
Brundisium
CORSICA
SARDINIA
BALEARIC IS.
New Carthage
Saguntum
Numantia
NEARER SPAIN
Corduba (Corduba)
FARTHER SPAIN
Gades
Ebro
Rhine
Rhone
RAETIA
NORICUM
PANNONIA
ILLYRICUM
Adriatic Sea
Po
Drepana 249 B.C.
SICILY
Messana
Syracuse
Malta
Zama 202 B.C.
Carthage
NUMIDIA
MAURETANIA
NORTH AFRICA
AFRICA PROCONSULARIS
SAHARA
Mediterranean Sea
MACEDONIA
Pydna 168 B.C.
EPIRUS
Cynoscephalae 197 B.C.
Corinth
Athens
ACHAEA
CRETE
CYRENAICA
Cyrene
THRACE
MOESIA
DACIA
Byzantium
BITHYNIA AND PONTUS
Black Sea
Pergamum
Ephesus
ASIA
GALATIA
CAPPADOCIA
ANATOLIA
PAMPHYLIA
LYCIA
CILICIA
RHODES
CYPRUS
Tarsus
Antioch
SYRIA
Damascus
Jerusalem
JUDEA
Petra
EGYPT
Alexandria
SINAI
Nile
Red Sea
ARABIAN DESERT
CAUCASUS MTS.
ARMENIA
PARTHIA
Ctesiphon
Seleucia
Carrhae 53 B.C.
Tigris
Euphrates
Caspian Sea
Volga
Don
Dnieper
Vistula
Elbe
Danube
BOSPORAN KINGDOM

0   200   400 Km.
0   200   400 Mi.

146 B.C.—strained the lot of the Roman people to the breaking point. Hannibal's invasion left much of the farmland of southern Italy devastated and Italian manpower considerably reduced. Yet most people might have rebounded from these problems within a generation or two, if they had not faced other serious troubles.

Conscription had become the norm. The average term of military service between ages 17 and 46 was six years; the maximum term was twenty years. Because experienced legionnaires were at a premium, commanders were loath to release them from service. But the longer a man was away in the army, the harder it was for his wife and children to keep the family farm running. With help from a patron, they might be able to make do, though most patrons in fact added to the problem through the introduction to Italy of large-scale agricultural entrepreneurship. Those who sought wealth monopolized Italian farmland, imported huge numbers of slaves, and brought ruin on the free peasantry of Italy.

The last two centuries B.C. witnessed the transformation of Roman rural society from one of independent farmers to one in which slave labor played a major role. By the end of the first century B.C., Italy's slave population was estimated at two million, about a third of the peninsula's total. Prisoners of war and conquered civilians provided a ready supply of slaves. Most worked in agriculture or mining, and their treatment was often abominable; the fewer house slaves were usually better off.

Wealthy Romans wanted to invest in large landed estates, or *latifundia* (lat-uh-FUN-dee-uh), worked by slaves. These estates were either mixed farms (most often devoted to cultivating vines, olives, and grain) or ranches (establishments where animals were raised for meat, milk, and wool). One devotee of the latter was the prominent conservative Marcus Porcius Cato (KAY-toe) (234–149 B.C.), known as **Cato the Censor**. Cato argued that there were only three ways to get rich: "pasturage, pasturage, and pasturage." All a would-be entrepreneur needed was land, which Rome had conquered a huge amount of in Italy. Called public land, Rome's new territory belonged to the Roman people, but an individual was legally entitled to claim about 320 acres as his own. Many entrepreneurs flouted the law, however, and grabbed much more than their fair share of public land. In addition, they often forced families of absent soldiers off private land, either by debt foreclosure or by outright violence. Sometimes families would leave the land for the city, but usually they stayed as tenants.

Before about 170 B.C., poor Romans were sometimes able to find land in colonies. By 170 B.C., however, Rome had established all the colonies in Italy that its security demanded, so this avenue of escape from poverty was closed. A displaced farmer who wanted to compete in the labor market would have found it difficult to underbid cheap slave labor. In any case, Roman ideology frowned on wage labor by citizens. Nor was it practical for a poor farmer to sue a wealthy patron who seized his land, because a plaintiff himself had to bring the accused into court.

The situation of the Italian peasantry was becoming increasingly miserable by the mid-second century B.C. As one modern scholar has put it, "In conquering what they were pleased to call the world, the Romans ruined a great part of the Italian people."[2]

THE IMPACT OF GREECE ON ROME AND ITS EMPIRE

Rome learned much from its new encounters with foreign peoples—and from none more than the Greeks. Wealthy Romans cultivated interests in Greek art, literature, rhetoric, and speculative thought; poor and rich alike enjoyed Greek drama. Before the mid-third century B.C. Roman literature was virtually nonexistent. An oral tradition of songs, ballads, and funeral oratory kept alive the deeds of the famous, for writing was generally restricted to commercial and government records and inscriptions. In short, the Romans conquered Italy without writing about it.

Contact with the Greek cities brought changes. Large numbers of Roman soldiers in Magna Graecia (southern Italy and Sicily) were introduced to comedy, tragedy, mimes, and sophisticated song lyrics, and many developed a permanent taste for them. It is no accident that the first production of a drama at Rome took place in 240 B.C., the year after the end of the First Punic War. Afterward, the annual production of such dramas became standard procedure.

No one could accuse the Romans of rushing headlong into a new age, however. The authorities continued to have their doubts about theater, which seemed excessively emotional and probably corrupt. They did not allow the building of a permanent theater in Rome until 55 B.C., insisting that the wealthiest city in the Mediterranean make do with makeshift wooden structures. Nor did the Roman elite readily become playwrights or poets. The first gentleman poet in Rome, Lucilius (180–102 B.C.), did not arrive until the second century B.C., and he was a Latin, not a Roman. His predecessors, the founders of Latin literature, were all of low social status; little of their work survives.

The two great early Latin playwrights are Titus Maccius Plautus (ca. 254–184 B.C.) and Publius Terentius Afer, today known as Terence (ca. 195–159 B.C.). Both of them wrote comedies on the model of the great Greek comic playwright Menander (see pages 107–108). Plautus was an Umbrian and a poor man who

Cato the Censor   Name given to Marcus Porcius Cato, a Roman general and statesman. He was the first Roman historian to write in Latin.

learned his Latin in Rome; Terence was a North African slave, educated and freed in Rome. Twenty-one plays by Plautus and six by Terence survive. Plautus's plays are generally earthy slapstick farces. They are invariably set in Greece, not Rome, in part out of escapism (many were written during the Second Punic War), in part out of the censorial demands of the Roman authorities. They nonetheless reveal much about Roman society. Terence's plays are more subtle than Plautus's, indicating the growing sophistication of Roman theatergoers.

Latin prose developed more slowly than did poetry and drama. The first histories by Romans, composed after the Second Punic War, were written in Greek, for Latin lacked the vocabulary or the audience for history. Cato the Censor was the first historian of Rome to write in Latin. His *Origines,* of which we have only remnants, recounted Roman history from the origin of the city to about 150 B.C. The earliest surviving Latin prose work is Cato's *On Agriculture.*

In the traditional education of a Roman aristocrat, parents and close family friends played the primary role. Although this practice continued, wealthy Romans in

the second century B.C. began acquiring Greek slaves to educate their sons in the Greek language and Greek literature. Soon Greek freedmen began setting up schools offering the same subjects. Before long, similar Latin grammar schools also opened.

One of the forms of Greek literature that appealed most to the practical-minded Romans was rhetoric. Roman orators studied Greek models, and many would say that they eventually outdid the Greeks. Cato was the first Roman to publish his speeches, and he also wrote a book on rhetoric. Both gave impetus to the spread of sophisticated rhetoric in Rome.

Scipio Aemilianus, conqueror of Carthage in 146 B.C., had a distinguished political and military career. He was also patron of a group of prominent statesmen and soldiers who shared his love of Hellenism. Among the writers whom they supported were the playwright Terence, the poet Lucilius, the historian Polybius, and the Stoic philosopher Panaetius (ca. 185–109 B.C.). The Stoic emphases on duty, wisdom, and world brotherhood appealed both to Rome's traditional ideology and to its more recent acquisition of empire. Yet not all Romans shared Scipio's admiration of Greek culture; Cato, for example, was famously ambivalent.

Cornelia, Scipio Aemilianus's mother-in-law, was an educated lover of Hellenism who wrote letters that existed several hundred years later as examples of elegant Latin prose. Her villa in the resort of Misenum on the Bay of Naples was well known for the distinguished guests whom she received there. When her husband, an outstanding statesman and general, died, Cornelia chose to remain a widow. One of the men who tried to change her mind was no less a figure than the king of Egypt. The widow spent her time managing her own estate and supervising the education of her two sons, the future tribunes Tiberius and Gaius Gracchus.

Although Cornelia's privileges were extraordinary, she is nonetheless a reminder of the opportunities that imperial expansion offered to wealthy Roman women. Marriage practices are one example of change. Few women were married *cum manu* anymore—that is, handed over by their fathers to their husbands. A woman's father or nearest male relative, not her husband, was most likely to be her paterfamilias, which meant that a husband's control over his wife's dowry was limited. The result was more freedom, at least for wealthy women.

Cornelia is also a reminder of the fundamental conservatism of Roman society. Although we know the years of birth and death of numerous elite Roman males of the second century B.C., we do not know Cornelia's. Nor did her literary interests entail any neglect of home and family. Cornelia bore twelve children, though only three of them lived to adulthood (such was the reality of infant mortality even for the wealthiest Romans).

Luxurious Earrings

A wealthy Roman woman might have been proud to wear these refined and expensive gold earrings, produced in a Greek city of southern Italy in the second century B.C. Only 2 inches long, each earring shows a dove standing on a small, garland-trimmed base.

(Pair of earrings with pendant doves, Greek, Hellenistic period, 150–100 B.C.; Gold, garnet, and glass paste; L. 5.2 cm. Courtesy of the Museum of Fine Arts, Boston, Harriet Otis Cruft Fund, 68.5a.b)

══════════ S E C T I O N   S U M M A R Y ══════════

- The flexible infantry formation known as the legion was the key to Roman success in battle.

- Rome consolidated its control of Italy by wisely treating its allies with a mixture of firmness and generosity, including the extension of Roman citizenship.

- The strength of Rome's alliance led to success in the Punic Wars with Carthage and then drew Rome into conquering all the Hellenistic Greek states.

- Military expansion brought fabulous riches to the Roman elite, brought misery to the peasants of Italy, and established a slave system of two million people.

- Conquest of and contact with Greek civilization led to the rise of Latin literature.

THE LATE REPUBLIC AND ITS COLLAPSE, 133–31 B.C.

How did the unintended consequences of conquest on Rome lead to a revolution that destroyed the Republic?

A citizen of the Roman Republic in the mid-second century B.C. might have looked forward to a long and happy future for his country, unaware that the Republic—after 350 years of expansion—was about to begin a century of domestic and foreign unrest that would bring down the whole system. Why and how did the Republic collapse? More than a century of warfare weighed heavily on the ordinary people of Italy—the Romans and allied peasants whose farms were ruined while they were off fighting. The Roman elite was bitterly divided over what to do about the problems of the peasants. One group wanted to redistribute land on behalf of the poor; another group had no sympathy for them.

By the Late Republic the city of Rome was crowded and populous: scholars estimate the number of inhabitants to have reached one million by the end of the first century B.C. The government had to take charge of the grain supply. But elite politicians exploited the issue for partisan purposes. Once before, during the struggle between the patrician and plebeian orders in the Early Republic, the elite had been similarly divided and had resolved its differences through compromise (see page 131). The Late Republic, however, was an age of individualism, sophistication, and cynicism. Ambitious nobles were no longer willing to subordinate themselves to the community. It was not long before competing armies of land-hungry peasants, thwarted from above, were marching across Italy.

THE GRACCHI

Many Romans fretted over the military dimension of the agrarian crisis. In modern societies, draftees are often the poorest people. In Rome, military service was a prestigious activity, so a property qualification was imposed and the poor were not drafted. As fewer and fewer potential soldiers could afford to own property, however, during the second century it became necessary to reduce the property qualification several times. By 150 B.C. a conscript had to own property worth only 400 denarii—roughly a small house, a garden, and some personal belongings. If the peasantry continued its decline, Rome would either have to drop the property qualification for the military altogether or stop fielding armies. Clearly, something had to be done.

Into the breach stepped Tiberius Sempronius Gracchus (GRAK-us) (d. 133 B.C.), one of the ten tribunes for the year 133 B.C. The son of Cornelia and a distinguished general and ambassador (whose name Tiberius shared), Tiberius belonged to the eminent **Gracchi** (GRAK-eye) family. He seemed an excellent spokesperson for a group of prominent senators who backed land reform. He proved, however, to be arrogant and overly ambitious. In pursuit of his goals, he deposed one of his fellow tribunes, Octavius, an opponent of reform, and thereby shocked and angered conservatives.

Tiberius's proposed law restored the roughly 320-acre limit to the amount of public land a person could own (plus an exception for a man with two sons, who was allowed to hold about 667 acres). A commission was to be set up to repossess excess land and redistribute it to the poor, in small lots that were to be inalienable—that is, the wealthy could not buy them back. The former landowners would be reimbursed for improvements they had made, such as buildings or plantings.

Gracchi   Led by Tiberius Sempronius Gracchus and later his brother Gaius, this ancient Roman faction challenged the conservative senate on behalf of the poor.

The proposal was moderate, but wealthy landowners repudiated it outright. Many senators suspected that Tiberius wanted to set himself up as a kind of superpatron, buoyed by peasant supporters. The senate was in fact more disturbed by Tiberius's methods than by the substance of his proposed law because those methods threatened the senate's power. In addition to deposing Octavius, Tiberius, when the bill became law, intervened in the senate's bailiwicks of foreign affairs and finances by earmarking tax receipts from the new province of Asia to finance land purchases. Finally, Tiberius broke with custom by running for a second consecutive term as tribune. While the tribal assembly prepared to vote on the new tribunes, some senators led a mob to the Forum and had Tiberius and three hundred of his followers clubbed to death.

This shocking event marked the first time in the Republic that a political debate was settled by bloodshed in Rome itself. The ancient sources agree that it was the beginning of a century of revolution. Tiberius's killers had not merely committed murder, but had attacked the traditional inviolability of the tribunes. Yet over the next century public violence grew as a weapon of politics in the Republic. The land commission went ahead with its work, even without Tiberius. His younger brother, Gaius (GUY-us) (d. 121 B.C.), ready to continue Tiberius's work, became tribune himself in 123 B.C. Gaius expanded Tiberius's coalition, adding to it supporters from the equestrian order and the urban populace, mainly composed of slaves and freedmen. He gave the plebs cheap grain at subsidized prices. The equestrians were wealthy, landed gentry, similar to senators in most respects except for their failure to have reached the senate; they yearned for political power. A small but important group of equestrians was engaged in commerce and tax collection in the provinces. The senate regulated their activities through the so-called extortion courts, which tried corruption cases. Gaius staffed those courts with equestrians. Alluding to the new equestrian power, Gaius remarked, "I have left a sword in the ribs of the senate."

Gaius's ultimate aims are unclear, but one thing is certain: he posed a dangerous threat to the senate's power. He sponsored an extension of his brother's agrarian law, new colonies, public works, and relief for poor soldiers. Eventually Gaius ran aground on a plan to include the Italian allies as beneficiaries of agrarian reform—a farsighted notion but one unpopular with the Roman people, who were jealous of their privileges. Gaius was denied a third term as tribune in 121 B.C. (he had won a second the previous year). Soon his supporters engaged in violent scuffling with their opponents. The senate responded to his action by passing a declaration of public emergency, empowering the magistrates to use any means necessary to protect the state.

One of the consuls had Gaius and 250 of his followers killed. Another 3,000 Gracchans were executed soon thereafter. Within a few years the Gracchan land commission was abolished. It is estimated that approximately 75,000 citizens had been given land. The law, however, was amended to permit the resale of redistributed land, and with the wealthy poised to buy land back, the settlers' future was uncertain. The senatorial oligarchy was back in control.

Or so it seemed. In fact, Roman politics had become an unstable brew. In time, it became clear that the Gracchi had divided the political community into two loose groupings. On one side were the *optimates* (op-tee-MAH-tayz) ("the best people"; singular, *optimas*), conservatives who asserted the rule of the senate against popular tribunes and the maintenance of the estates of the wealthy in spite of the agrarian crisis. On the other side were the *populares* (pah-poo-LAH-rayz) ("men of the people"; singular, *popularis*), who challenged the rule of the senate in the name of relief of the poor. The populares were not democrats. Like the optimates, they were Roman nobles who believed in hierarchy, but they advocated the redistribution of wealth and power as a way of restoring stability and strengthening the military.

MARIUS AND SULLA

By 100 B.C. Rome's agrarian crisis had become a full-scale military crisis, too. Roman armies under senatorial commanders fared poorly, both in Numidia (modern Algeria) and in southern Gaul against Germanic invaders (see Map 5.3). The situation was saved by an outsider to established privilege, an equestrian named Gaius Marius (157–86 B.C.), the first member of his family to be elected consul, for 107 B.C. This "new man" proved to be a military reformer and a popularis. Marius made several moves to streamline and strengthen the Roman army: Camp followers were reduced in number, and individual soldiers were made to carry their own equipment. To meet the Germans, who attacked in overwhelming waves, maniples—the tactical subunits of a legion—were reorganized and combined into larger units called cohorts, rendering the army firmer and more cohesive. Most important, Marius abandoned altogether the property qualification for the military. As a result, Roman soldiers were no longer peasants doing part-time military service but rather landless men making a profession of the military.

Politically they became a force to be reckoned with. As an indispensable general, Marius demanded and won six elections to the consulship, unconstitutional though that was. Furthermore, after winning the wars in North Africa and Gaul, Marius championed his soldiers. In 100 B.C. he asked that land be distributed to them. The senate refused, but its victory was temporary. The poor recognized that only military leaders such as Marius desired to meet their need for land. As a result, ordinary Romans, who were all now eligible for the army, transferred their loyalty from the senate to their commander.

The Republic was weak, and it became weaker still as a result of two new wars. First, its Italian allies rose against Rome in a bloody and bitter struggle from 91 to 89 B.C. known as the "Social War"—that is, war with the *socii* ("allies"). The allies fought hard, and Rome, in order to prevail, had to concede to them what they had demanded at the outset: full Roman citizenship. The war wrought devastation in the countryside, further destabilizing the Republic. The other conflict of this period pitted Rome against Mithridates (120–63 B.C.), a rebellious king in northern Anatolia. Mithridates conquered Roman territory in western Anatolia and slaughtered the numerous Italian businessmen and tax collectors there. Once again a military man rose to save the day for Rome: Marius's rival and former lieutenant, Lucius Cornelius Sulla Felix (ca. 138–78 B.C.), consul for the year 88 B.C., patrician and optimas.

Yet Marius was jealous, and his troops and Sulla's fought over the issue of the command against Mithridates. Sulla's forces won the first round by marching on Rome, but after they departed for the east, Marius's men retook the city and settled scores. Victorious over Mithridates, Sulla returned to Italy in 83 B.C. and engaged in all-out civil war. Sulla defeated Marius's men in battle (minus Marius himself, who had died in 86), then sealed his victory with proscription. He had posted the names of his political opponents, as many as two thousand men. Their land was confiscated, their sons disenfranchised, and they were executed. Sulla settled his veterans, about eighty thousand men, on land in Italy from which he had expelled entire communities that had opposed him.

Having assumed the long-dormant office of dictator—but without a time limit on his tenure—Sulla attempted to restore the senatorial rule of pre-Gracchan days. To this end, he greatly weakened the tribunate and strengthened the senate, whose size he doubled, from about three hundred to about six hundred members.

The most long-lasting of Sulla's measures was his reform of the courts. He abolished trials before popular assemblies and equestrian-staffed courts. Criminal cases were now heard before one of seven standing courts, whose juries were composed of senators. Although later Roman criminal law evolved considerably, it was founded on Sulla's actions. Generally only wealthy people had access to the standing courts; alleged crimes involving ordinary people were heard before lesser magistrates.

Sulla retired in 79 B.C. and died a year later. His hope of restoring law and order under the senate died with him. Within ten years the old powers of the tribunes had been restored. Discontent smoldered among the men whose land Sulla had confiscated. Equally serious, many senators, aspiring to what Sulla had done and not to what he had said, pursued personal power, not the collective interests of the senate.

POMPEY AND CAESAR

New would-be Mariuses or Sullas now arose. The dominant leader of the seventies and sixties B.C. was the optimas Pompey the Great (106–48 B.C.), a brilliant general and a supporter of Sulla. Young Pompey (POM-pee) went from command to command: he put down an agrarian rebellion in Italy and a rebellion in Spain, cleared the Mediterranean of pirates, defeated Mithridates again, and added rich conquests to the empire in Anatolia, Syria, Phoenicia, and Palestine. In the fifties B.C. the tide began turning in favor of **Gaius Julius Caesar** (100–44 B.C.), an even more gifted general and politician—indeed, perhaps one of history's greatest. A popularis, Caesar (SEE-zer) had family connections to Marius and his supporters. Caesar's career depended on his dazzling oratory, his boldness, and his sheer talent at war and politics. Caesar conquered Gaul, gained a foothold in Britain, and laid the foundations of Roman rule in Egypt (see Map 5.3).

While the elite of the Late Republic struggled to maintain order and secure power, ordinary people struggled for survival itself. Violence had become a way of life in rural Italy. Many once-prosperous farmers, dispossessed peasants, and runaway slaves ended up as robbers or bandits. It was also an era of slave revolts, the most serious of which lasted from 73 to 71 B.C. under the leadership of Spartacus, a Thracian slave who had been a gladiator. An able commander, Spartacus beat nine separate Roman armies in two years before finally suffering defeat. (See the box "The Written Record: Spartacus's Slave Revolt.") At the same time, Rome also faced major wars in Spain and Anatolia.

Roman women were sometimes pawns, sometimes partners in the political careers of Pompey and Caesar. In 80 B.C., for example, Pompey divorced his first wife to advance his career by marrying Aemilia, Sulla's stepdaughter. Aemilia was not only married at the time but pregnant by her first husband. Soon after her divorce and remarriage, she died in childbirth. Caesar took many mistresses, among whom was the queen of Egypt, Cleopatra (see pages 112–113). Caesar had a penchant for certain Egyptian institutions, such as the Egyptian calendar, and he toyed with becoming a monarch himself, an inclination that Cleopatra perhaps encouraged.

Gaius Julius Caesar Roman general gifted at war and politics, he was named dictator in 49 B.C. and was later assassinated by the members of the senate in 44 B.C.

Bust of Julius Caesar
This marble sculpture accurately conveys the conqueror's firmness of expression and perhaps his intelligence—but not his looks, since Caesar was bald.   *(Vatican Museums/Scala/Art Resource, NY)*

Another of Caesar's mistresses was Servilia, stepsister of Marcus Porcius Cato (Cato the Younger, 95–46 B.C.), great-grandson of the famous censor (see page 141). She was also the mother of Brutus, the man who would eventually help murder Caesar.

Pompey was an optimas, Caesar a popularis, but the two of them agreed that they, not the senate or the assemblies, should dominate Rome. Each man's ambition was more important to him than any political principles. In 60 B.C. they entered into a pact with a third ambitious noble, Marcus Licinius Crassus (d. 53 B.C.). Known today as the "First Triumvirate," this coalition amounted to a conspiracy to run the state. Their individual ambitions rebuffed by the senate, each man had an agenda that could be achieved by pooling resources in the triumvirate: for Pompey, ratification of his acts in the east and land for his veterans; for Caesar, who became consul for 59 B.C., a long period of command in Gaul and a free hand in his behavior there; for Crassus, a rebate for the tax collectors of Roman Asia, whom he championed, and eventually a command in Syria to make war on Parthia (the new Persian Empire).

Having achieved its goal, the triumvirate did not long survive, but its very existence shows how little the Republic now meant. Crassus died in an inglorious defeat at Carrhae in Syria in 53 B.C., tarnished further by the Parthians' successful capture of Roman legionary standards (see Map 5.3). Frightened by Caesar's stunning victories in Gaul, Pompey returned to the senatorial fold, now led by Cato the Younger. Cato and his supporters stood for the traditional rule of the senatorial oligarchy. In 49 B.C. they ordered Caesar to give up his command in Gaul, but instead Caesar marched on Italy with his army. Italy's northern boundary was marked by a tiny stream called the Rubicon; when Caesar defiantly crossed it, he declared, "The die is cast." Indeed it was, for civil war. Caesar swept to victory against the senate's army, led by Pompey, at Pharsalus in Greece in 48 B.C. Pompey fled but was assassinated. The complete destruction of the senate's forces took until 45 B.C.

The years of civil war took Caesar from Spain to Anatolia. During the fighting he showed the qualities that made him great: he was fast, tough, smart, adaptable, and a risk-taker. He was a diplomat, too, offering mercy to any of his enemies who joined him. A talented writer, Caesar published two books about his military campaigns—*On the Gallic War* and *On the Civil War*—the latter appearing after his death. These works glorified Caesar's conquests and defended his decision to wage civil war. (See the box "The Global Record: Caesar on the Gauls.")

Back in Rome, Caesar sponsored a huge number of reforms. His political goal was to elevate Italians and others at the expense of old Roman families. To achieve this, Caesar conferred Roman citizenship liberally, on all of Cisalpine Gaul (northernmost Italy) as well as on certain provincial towns. He enlarged the senate from six hundred to nine hundred, adding his supporters, including some Gauls, to the membership. Caesar sponsored social and economic reforms, too, including reducing debt and founding the first colonies outside Italy, where veterans and poor citizens were settled. He undertook a grand public building program in the city of Rome. Caesar's most long-lasting act was to introduce the calendar of 365¼ days, on January 1, 45 B.C. Derived from the calendar of Egypt, it is known as the Julian calendar.

Caesar did not hide his contempt for Republican constitutional formalities. By accepting a dictatorship

SPARTACUS'S SLAVE REVOLT

Spartacus's revolt was the third and most famous of three great slave rebellions that rocked Italy and Sicily between 135 and 71 B.C. The revolt itself was not a success; all of the slaves were either imprisoned or killed. But Spartacus terrified the Roman elite and became a powerful symbol of the struggle for freedom to all who were oppressed. This account, by the ancient writer Appian, illustrates his fight.

At about this same time, at the city of Capua in Italy, gladiators were being trained to fight in spectacles. Spartacus, a Thracian whom the Romans had imprisoned and then sold to be trained as a gladiator, had once fought as a soldier for the Roman army. He persuaded about seventy of the enslaved men to risk a break for freedom rather than to allow themselves to be put on display for the entertainment of others. Using force to overcome their guards, the men made their escape. The fugitives armed themselves with wooden clubs and daggers that they seized from travelers on the roads nearby, and then rushed to take refuge on Mount Vesuvius. Many fugitive slaves and even some free men from the surrounding countryside came to this place to join Spartacus. They began to stage bandit raids on nearby settlements. Spartacus had his fellow gladiators Oenomaus and Crixus as his two subordinate commanders. Since Spartacus divided the profits of his raiding into equal shares, he soon attracted a very large number of followers. . . .

[Spartacus wins victories in southern and northern Italy.] With the 120,000 men under his command, he began a march on Rome. So that traveling would be as light as possible, he torched all unnecessary supplies, killed all prisoners of war, and slaughtered all pack animals. Many deserters from the Roman army came to him, but he accepted none of them. The consuls made a stand against him in a place in the land of Picenum. Another great armed struggle took place here and the Romans were defeated again. Spartacus changed his mind about an attack on Rome. He decided that he was not ready for an all-out battle and that his whole army was not yet properly armed for regular warfare. Moreover, so far no city had come over to his side, but only slaves, deserters, and the flotsam and jetsam of humanity. . . .

[After many successes and some defeats, Spartacus is forced into a final battle with a Roman army led by Crassus.] Since so many tens of thousands of desperate men were involved, the result was a protracted battle of epic proportions. Spartacus took a spear wound in his thigh. Collapsing on one knee, he held his shield up in front of him and fought off those who were attacking him, until he and the large number of men around him were finally surrounded and cut down. The rest of his army was thrown into disarray and confusion and was slaughtered in large numbers. The killing was on such a scale that it was not possible to count the dead. The Romans lost about a thousand men. The body of Spartacus was never found. When the survivors among Spartacus's men, who were still a large number, fled from the battle, they went up into the mountains, where they were pursued by Crassus's forces. Splitting themselves into four groups, they continued to fight until all of them had perished—all, that is, except six thousand of them, who were taken prisoner and crucified along the whole length of the highway that ran from Capua to Rome.

QUESTIONS

1. Why do you think Spartacus attracted so many followers?

2. Why do you think Spartacus was able to defeat the Romans time and again? Why do you think he finally failed?

3. What evidence does the passage offer to show that Spartacus and his men were brave and determined?

Source: Copyright © 2001 by Bedford/St. Martin's, from *Spartacus and the Slave Wars* by Brent D. Shaw, translator and editor. Reprinted with permission of Bedford/St. Martin's.

for life he offended the old guard; by flirting with the title of king he infuriated them. With one eye toward avenging Crassus and another toward equaling the achievements of Alexander the Great, Caesar made preparations for a war against Parthia, but in vain. His career ended abruptly on March 15, 44 B.C. (the Ides of March by the Roman calendar), when sixty senators stabbed him to death. The assassination took place in the portico attached to the Theater of Pompey, in front of a statue of Pompey himself, where the senate was meeting that day. It had been eighty-nine years since the murder of Tiberius Gracchus.

Online Study Center **Improve Your Grade**
  Primary Source: A Man of Unlimited Ambition: Julius Caesar

CAESAR ON THE GAULS

Julius Caesar (ca. 100–44 B.C.) advertised his achievements in conquering Gaul (58–51 B.C.) in his Commentaries on the Gallic War. *The book focuses on battles and negotiations, but here Caesar discusses the society of the Gauls (also known as Celts). He depicts the inhabitants as superstitious and warlike.*

In the whole of Gaul two types of men are counted as being of worth and distinction. The ordinary people are considered almost as slaves: they dare do nothing on their own account and are not called to counsels. When the majority are oppressed by debt or heavy tribute, or harmed by powerful men, they swear themselves away into slavery to the aristocracy, who then have the same rights over them as masters do over their slaves. Of the two types of men of distinction, however, the first is made up of the druids (priests), and the other of the knights.

The druids are involved in matters of religion. They manage public and private sacrifices and interpret religious customs and ceremonies. Young men flock to them in large numbers to gain instruction, and they hold the druids in great esteem. For they decide almost all disputes, both public and private: if some crime has been committed, if there has been murder done, if there is a dispute over an inheritance or over territory, they decide the issue and settle the rewards and penalties. If any individual or group of people does not abide by their decision, the druids ban them from sacrifices. This is their most severe punishment. Those who are banned in this way are counted among the wicked and criminal: everyone shuns them and avoids approaching or talking to them, so as not to suffer any harm from contact with them. . . .

Druids are not accustomed to take part in war, nor do they pay taxes like the rest of the people. . . . The principal doctrine they attempt to impart is that souls do not die but after death cross from one person to another. Because the fear of death is thereby set aside, they consider this a strong inducement to physical courage. Besides this, they debate many subjects and teach them to their young men—for example, the stars and their movements, the size of the universe and the earth, the nature of things, and the strength and power of the immortal gods.

The second class is that composed of the knights. When necessity arises and some war flares up—which before Caesar's arrival used to happen almost every year, so that they were either on the offensive themselves or fending off attacks—they are all involved in the campaign. Each man has as many retainers and dependents about him as is appropriate to his status in terms of his birth and resources. This is the sole form of power and influence they know.

The whole of the Gallic nation is much given to religious practices. For this reason those who are afflicted with serious illnesses and those who are involved in battles and danger either offer human sacrifice or vow that they will do so, and employ the druids to manage these sacrifices. For they believe that unless one human life is offered for another, the power and presence of the immortal gods cannot be propitiated.

QUESTIONS

1. According to Caesar, who were the druids, and what did they do? How did they help the Gauls succeed as warriors? How did the druids differ from the knights?

2. What was the status of ordinary people in Gaul?

3. What do you think Caesar and his readers thought of the Gauls' practice of human sacrifice?

Source: Julius Caesar, *Seven Commentaries on the Gallic War with an Eighth Commentary by Aulus Hirtius,* trans. Carolyn Hammond, pp. 126–128. Copyright © 1996 Oxford University Press. Reprinted by permission of Oxford University Press.

The assassins called themselves Liberators, believing that they were freeing themselves from tyranny just as the founders of the Republic had done centuries before. Indeed, one of the chief conspirators, Marcus Junius Brutus (ca. 85–42 B.C.), claimed descent from Lucius Junius Brutus, traditional leader of the revolt against the Tarquins that was thought to have established the Republic. Like his co-conspirator Gaius Longinus Cassius (d. 42 B.C.), Brutus had been a magistrate, military officer, and provincial administrator.

The assassination of Caesar threw Rome back into turmoil. Civil war followed for the next thirteen years, first between the Liberators and Caesar's partisans and then between the two leading Caesarians. The final struggle pitted Mark Antony (Marcus Antonius, ca. 83–30 B.C.), Caesar's chief lieutenant and the man who inherited his love affair with Cleopatra, against Octavian (Gaius Julius Caesar Octavianus, 63 B.C.–A.D. 14), Caesar's grandnephew and adopted son and heir to Caesar's name and his huge fortune. At first it looked as if Antony had the upper hand because Octavian was young and inexperienced, was not a general, and was cursed with poor health. Octavian was, however, a man of unusual cunning and prudence. His forces defeated Antony and Cleopatra at the naval battle of Actium (off northwestern Greece) in 31 B.C.; their suicides followed shortly. The Roman world held its breath to see how Octavian would govern it.

THE WORLD OF CICERO

Marcus Tullius **Cicero** (106–43 B.C.) is one of the best-known figures of all antiquity. Like Marius, he was a wealthy equestrian from the central Italian town of Arpinum who, as consul (in 63 B.C.), became a "new man." Cicero (SIS-er-o) was an optimas and defender of the senate, though ready for compromise with the equestrians, from whose ranks he himself had arisen. He made his name by successfully leading the opposition to Lucius Sergius Catilina, a down-and-out patrician who organized a debtors' revolt in Etruria; the army smashed the rebellion.

Cicero was intelligent, ambitious, and talented. As a young man he studied philosophy and oratory in Greece. As a result, he produced elevated and serious writings. Never as original as Plato or Aristotle, Cicero nonetheless was crucial in making the Latin language a vessel for the heritage of Greek thought. A prolific writer, Cicero produced over a hundred orations, of which about sixty survive; several treatises on oratory; philosophical writings on politics, ethics, epistemology (the study of the nature of knowledge), and theology; poetry, of which little survives; and numerous letters. After his death in 43 B.C., his immense correspondence was published, with little censored. The letters and speeches provide a vivid, detailed, and sometimes damning picture of politics.

Politics, Society, and Law   Politics in the Late Republic was loud and boisterous. The elite prided itself on free speech and open debate. In senate deliberations, court cases, and public meetings in the Forum that preceded assembly votes, oratory—sometimes great oratory—was common. Few orators in history, though, have matched Cicero's ability to lead and mislead an audience by playing on its feelings. He knew every rhetorical trick and precisely when each was appropriate.

Because of increased freedom and greater educational opportunities, during the Late Republic it was possible for elite women as well as men to study oratory. Private tutors were common among the aristocracy, and girls often received lessons alongside their brothers. Girls sometimes also profited from a father's expertise. A particularly dramatic case is that of Hortensia, daughter of Quintus Hortensius Hortalus (114–50 B.C.), a famous orator and rival of Cicero. An excellent speaker

Cicero   Philosopher, writer, and statesman who was Rome's greatest orator.

herself, Hortensia defied tradition by arguing successfully in the Roman Forum in 42 B.C. against a proposed war tax on wealthy women.

Ordinary people lacked the education and freedom to express themselves in the manner of a woman like Hortensia, but a less civilized means of expression was open to them: the political gang. Brawls and violence between the rival groups of Clodius, a supporter of Caesar, and Milo, a supporter of the senate, became increasingly common in the fifties B.C. As dictator, Caesar abolished the gangs.

Cicero's works provide evidence of a crucial development in the practice of Roman law. Often unheralded, what Cicero's contemporaries did was invent the notion of the legal expert, a person devoted to explaining and interpreting the law. Roman law needed interpretation because it was complex and intricate. Much of it was the work not of legislators but of magistrates, who issued annual statements setting forth how their courts would work. The result was unsystematic and sometimes contradictory and cried out for someone to make sense of it. Enter the jurisconsults, legal interpreters who emerged in the third and second centuries B.C. At first they had no special standing, but in the first century B.C. they became true jurists; their interpretations began to be considered authoritative. No earlier Mediterranean society had a professional class of legal experts, but no earlier society had faced issues as complicated and turbulent, or had grown to three million citizens, as the Roman Republic did in the mid-first century B.C. The Western tradition of legal science has its roots in Rome.

A New Elite?   Rome's political system, unlike its legal system, did not adapt flexibly to changing circumstances. The disenfranchised of the Late Republic had reasonable goals: land for those who had fought for their country and admission to the senate of a wider group. Yet the old elite resisted both. Cicero's solution was to build on Sulla's reforms by uniting the senatorial and equestrian orders and by widening the Roman ruling class to include the elite of all Italy. The expanded ruling class could close ranks and establish *otium cum dignitate*, "peace with respect for rank." Cicero's proposed new order was distinctly hierarchical.

In the turbulent times of the Late Republic, the Roman elite often turned to the Hellenistic philosophers. The poet Lucretius (loo-CREE-shus) (ca. 94–55 B.C.) describes the Epicurean ideal of withdrawal into the contemplative life in a long didactic epic called *On the Nature of Things*. Most elite Romans, however, including Cicero, preferred the activist philosophy of Stoicism (see page 114). Cicero put forth a generous view of human brotherhood. He argued that all people share a spark of divinity and are protected by natural law. Consequently, all persons have value and importance and should treat others generously. Such ideas would be influential in the new Roman Empire when, under the leadership of Augustus, fair treatment of provincials was a major theme. For Cicero, however, these ideas existed more as theory than as practice.

Cicero did not hide his lack of sympathy for his fellow citizens who were poor. In one speech he castigated "artisans and shopkeepers and all that kind of scum"; in a letter he complained about "the wretched half-starved populace, which attends mass meetings and sucks the blood of the treasury." Cicero also made his disdain for democracy clear: "The greatest number," he said, "should not have the greatest power."

Elitist as Cicero's views were, they were by no means extremist. Cassius, Brutus, and the other Liberators had little interest in even Cicero's limited compromises. Their stubbornness proved to be their downfall, for dispossessed peasants and ambitious equestrians transferred their loyalties to Julius Caesar and, later, to Augustus. One of Caesar's supporters, Sallust (86–ca. 34 B.C.), wrote biting and bitter works of history that indicted the greed and corruption of the optimates, whom he blamed for the decline of the Republic. In any case, peace was not restored, for the generation of Liberators was wiped out in renewed civil war, and a new generation emerged, weary for peace.

SECTION SUMMARY

- After the Gracchi brothers' failed attempts at reform, the Roman poor threw their support to new patrons, military leaders who raised private armies to win land for their followers and glory for themselves.

- The general Marius turned Rome's citizen soldiers into professionals, and then fought a civil war against another general, Sulla.

- The next generation of Roman politics was divided into factions led by Pompey and Caesar, leading to another civil war.

- Caesar reformed Rome as dictator for life before being assassinated.

- The great orator Cicero symbolizes the rough-and-tumble of civilian politics in the Late Republic.

CHAPTER SUMMARY

Online Study Center **ACE the Test**

What was early Rome like and how was it shaped by relations with its neighbors?

How was the Roman Republic governed, and how did that government shape the Western political tradition?

How did Rome conquer an empire?

How did the unintended consequences of conquest on Rome lead to a revolution that destroyed the Republic?

Rome was destined to provide Western civilization with many basic notions about government and empire, but Rome sprang from humble origins. A central Italian village at first, Rome was urbanized after contact with more sophisticated neighbors, especially Greeks and Etruscans. Rome became a monarchy and then a republic.

In the Early and Middle Republic, Rome was a mixed constitution. It combined popular power with control by an oligarchy. Government was shared by the magistrates, the senate, and the assemblies. The so-called Conflict of the Orders brought debt relief for the poor and a combined patrician-plebeian nobility for the rich. Roman society was composed of a network of households tied in patron-client relationships. The ingrained hierarchy of the Roman social and cultural system helped keep politics stable.

The elite channeled popular energies into protecting the young Republic from its numerous rivals in central Italy. Greed and ambition, as well as fear, were powerful motives of Rome's military expansion. Rome conquered most of Italy by 265 B.C., then fought the bloody Punic Wars against Carthage (264–202, 148–146 B.C.) and conquered all the Hellenistic Greek states (201–30 B.C.).

Rome consolidated its control of Italy by wisely treating its allies with a mixture of firmness and generosity. By extending Roman citizenship, Rome gave them a stake in continued Roman hegemony. Having defeated all opponents near and far, Rome seemed to have won absolute security by the mid-second century B.C. Yet its strength was deceptive. Contact with Greek culture liberated the Romans from ruder, peasant ways but also loosened previous restraints. A huge influx of slaves made acquisition of large estates profitable, at the expense of Italy's peasant farmers. The result was a growing and dangerous social instability with military and political ramifications. After the Gracchis' failed reform attempts, the poor threw their support to new patrons, military leaders who raised private armies to win land for their followers and glory for themselves. First Marius and Sulla, then Caesar and Pompey, led Roman armies against each other in civil war.

LOOKING AHEAD

By the first century B.C., the Republic had collapsed under the weight of political maneuvering, judicial murders, gang warfare, and civil war. The time was right for the last of the private commanders—Octavian—to re-create the Roman state under his leadership as Augustus, first of the emperors. In the next chapter we examine the world that he remade.

KEY TERMS

Latin (p. 123)

Etruscans (p. 125)

res publica (p. 128)

senate (p. 129)

paterfamilias (p. 131)

triumph (p. 134)

legion (p. 136)

Punic Wars (p. 138)

Cato the Censor (p. 141)

Gracchi (p. 143)

Caesar (p. 145)

Cicero (p. 149)

Online Study Center
Improve Your Grade Flashcards

SUGGESTED READING

Barker, H., and T. Rasmussen. *The Etruscans.* 1997. Excellent historical introduction and guidebook, written with gusto.

Beard, Mary, and Michael Crawford. *Rome in the Late Republic: Problems and Interpretations.* 2d ed. 1999. An unusual and innovative approach to the subject, emphasizing sociocultural and institutional analysis more than narrative.

Cornell, T. J. *The Beginnings of Rome: Italy and Rome from the Bronze Age to the Punic Wars (c. 1000–264 B.C.).* 1995. A readable and ambitious survey combining archaeological and literary evidence, often in support of iconoclastic conclusions.

Cornell, T. J., and J. Matthews. *Atlas of the Roman World.* 1982. A readable introduction to Roman history written by two scholars; the maps and photos are beautiful.

Crawford, Michael. *The Roman Republic.* 2d ed. 1993. The best short introduction; sophisticated, lively, and concise.

Dixon, Suzanne. *The Roman Family.* 1992. A good historical study in complexity; strongly aware of the difference between the myth and reality of the Roman family and nicely written.

Goldsworthy, Adrian. *The Complete Roman Army.* 2003. An excellent introduction to the organization that won an empire.

Lendon, J. E. *Soldiers and Ghosts: A History of Battle in Classical Antiquity.* 2005. Fascinating and provocative analysis of the culture of Greek and Roman warfare.

Talbert, Richard A. *Barrington Atlas of the Greek and Roman World.* 2000. The most thorough, detailed, and scholarly atlas of this subject ever attempted.

Ward, A. M., F. M. Heichelheim, and C. A. Yeo. *A History of the Roman People.* 4th ed. 2002. The best introductory textbook; scholarly and readable.

NOTES

1. *The Aeneid of Virgil,* trans. Allen Mandelbaum (Berkeley: University of California Press, 1971), pp. 160–161.

2. P. A. Brunt, *Social Conflicts in the Roman Republic* (New York: Norton, 1971), p. 17.

IMPERIAL ROME,
31 B.C.–A.D. 284

Ara Pacis (detail), Rome
(Scala/Art Resource, NY)

The imperial family of Rome walks in stately procession to a sacrifice: Livia, wife of Augustus, first of the emperors; his daughter, Julia; Julia's husband, Agrippa; and various cousins and in-laws and their children. They are formally dressed in togas and gowns, heads wreathed. The men and women gaze seriously; the boys and girls have impish looks, betraying thoughts of mischief as they hold their parents' hands. They are all carved in stone, one of several sculptured reliefs decorating the walls of a public monument in Rome. Dedicated on Livia's birthday in 9 B.C., the monument shown here illustrates the propaganda themes of the new regime, among them the happy family as a symbol of peace after generations of civil war. The senate, which had commissioned the monument, called it the *Ara Pacis Augustae,* or "Altar of Augustan Peace."

Having made peace was no idle boast on Augustus's part. Not only did he end the Roman revolution, but he began a period of two hundred years of prosperity and stability in the Roman Empire. Augustus took advantage of Rome's war-weariness to create a new government out of the ruins of the Republic. Like the builders of the Early Republic's constitution, Augustus displayed the Roman genius for compromise. He had superb political instincts. Although he retained the final say, he shared a degree of power with the senate. He made financial sacrifices to feed the urban poor and distribute farms to landless peasants. He ended Rome's seemingly limitless expansion and stabilized the borders of the empire. He began to raise the provinces to a status of equality with Italy.

The *pax Romana* (PAHKS ro-MAHN-uh) ("Roman peace"), at its height between A.D. 96 and 180, was an era of enlightened emperors, thriving cities, intellectual vitality, and artistic and architectural achievement in an empire of 50 million to 100 million people. Yet it was also an era of slavery. More positively, the Roman peace was a period of heightened spirituality. In the peaceful and diverse empire, ideas traveled from people to people, and the religious beliefs of an obscure sect from western Asia began to spread around the Mediterranean and into northern Europe. The new religion was Christianity.

After 180 Rome slowly passed into a grim period marked in turn by bad emperors, civil war, inflation, plague, invasion, and defeat. After reaching a nadir around 235 to 253, Rome's fortunes began to improve under a series of reforming emperors who would forge a stronger and vastly different empire.

CHAPTER OUTLINE

AUGUSTUS AND THE PRINCIPATE, 31 B.C.–A.D. 68

THE ROMAN PEACE AND ITS COLLAPSE, A.D. 69–284

EARLY CHRISTIANITY

KEY TERMS

Augustus	Tacitus
Principate	third-century crisis
Virgil	Jesus of Nazareth
Livia	rabbinic Judaism
Julio-Claudians	Paul of Tarsus
pax Romana	Christianity
Flavians	

Online Study Center

This icon will direct you to interactive map and primary source activities on the website **college.hmco.com/ pic/noble5e**

F O C U S   Q U E S T I O N S

How did Augustus establish a new imperial government to replace the Roman Republic? Why was he so successful?

What was life like in the era of the Roman peace?

Why did peace end during the third century A.D.?

What were the origins of Christianity, and how did it fare among the other religions of the Roman world?

AUGUSTUS AND THE PRINCIPATE, 31 B.C.–A.D. 68

How did Augustus establish a new imperial government to replace the Roman Republic? Why was he so successful?

In 31 B.C. Gaius Julius Caesar Octavianus (63 B.C.–A.D. 14), or Octavian, as Augustus was then known, stood at the top of the Roman world. His forces had defeated those of Mark Antony and Cleopatra at the Battle of Actium in northwestern Greece, whereupon his two chief enemies committed suicide. Few could have predicted the vision and statesmanship that Octavian now displayed. He spent the next forty-five years healing the wounds of a century of revolution. He did nothing less than lay the foundations of the prosperous two centuries enjoyed by the empire under the Roman peace (see MAP 6.1).

THE POLITICAL SETTLEMENT

Octavian was both an astute politician and a lucky one. He was lucky in the length and violence of the civil wars. After Actium, most of his enemies were dead, so establishing the one-man rule that he claimed was necessary to restore stability was relatively easy. He was also lucky to live to be nearly 80—he had plenty of time to consolidate his rule. He was a cagey man and a sharp judge of others. Octavian learned the lesson of Caesar's greatest mistake. He understood that the Roman elite, however weakened, was still strong enough to oppose a ruler who flaunted monarchical power. To avoid a second Ides of March, therefore, Octavian was infinitely diplomatic.

Rather than call himself dictator, Octavian took the title of *princeps* (PRIN-keps) ("first citizen"), an old title of respect in the senate. From *princeps* comes Principate (PRIN-sih-pate), a term often used to describe the constitutional monarchy of the "Early Empire," the

name that historians have given to the period from 31 B.C. to A.D. 192. Four years after Actium, in 27 B.C., the senate granted Octavian the honorific title *augustus*, symbolizing the augmentation, or increase, of his authority. He was also known as *Caesar* and *divi filius* ("son of a god"), which tied him to Julius Caesar. Another name, *imperator* ("commander" and, later, "emperor"), recalled the military might that Augustus (as we shall henceforth call him) could call on if needed.

In 27 B.C. Augustus proclaimed "the transfer of the state to the free disposal of the senate and the people"— that is, the restoration of the Republic. Remembering similar claims by Sulla and Julius Caesar, few Romans were likely to believe this, and few would have wanted the Republic restored in any case. They no doubt appreciated their ruler's tact, however.

Two strokes of genius marked the new regime. First, Augustus held power without monopolizing public offices. He held the civil authority of the tribunate without being a tribune and the military authority of provincial generals without holding a specific command. Generalships remained open to ambitious Romans as long as they accepted Augustus's power. Second, the new government divided the provinces between Augustus and the senate. To check any new would-be Caesar, Augustus kept for himself the frontier provinces, with the main concentration of armies, as well as grain-rich Egypt (which had been annexed as a Roman province after Actium). The local commanders were loyal equestrians who owed their success to Augustus. Most of the other provinces continued to be ruled as before by senators serving as governors.

Augustus wanted advice without dissent. He used the senate, or rather a committee of senators and magistrates, as a sounding board; the group evolved into a permanent advisory body. Ordinary senate meetings, however, what with informers and secret agents, lost

Augustus   Honorific title of Gaius Julius Caesar Octavianus, his forty-five-year rule laid the foundations of two hundred years of prosperous Roman peace.

Principate   The constitutional monarchy of the Early Roman Empire, from 31 B.C. to A.D. 192.

their old freedom of speech. The popular assemblies fared even worse, as their powers were limited and eventually transferred to the senate. Nor would unruly crowds be tolerated. Augustus established the city of Rome's first police force and also stationed there his own personal guard. Called the praetorians (pre-TOR-ee-unz), or Praetorian Guard, the name used for a Roman general's bodyguard, the guard would play a crucial role in future imperial politics.

More important for the public good, Augustus established the first civil service, consisting of a series of prefectures—or departments—supervising, for example, the city watch, the grain supply, the water supply, the building of roads and bridges, tax collection, and the provisioning of the armies. Equestrians and freedmen were prominent in these prefectures and in provincial government, so they enthusiastically supported the Principate.

Although one may speak loosely of "imperial bureaucracy," neither Augustus nor his successors ever established a tight administrative grip on their far-flung empire. As in all ancient empires, Roman government tended to be decentralized and limited. In an age in which few public officials received a salary, bribes were winked at.

THE ECONOMIC AND SOCIAL SETTLEMENT

The old Roman ruling class made its peace with Augustus, but some never forgave him for ending their ancient privileges. The conservative historian Tacitus (TASS-ih-tus) (ca. A.D. 55–117) looked back wistfully to the Late Republic as a golden era of freedom, eloquence, and "the old sound morality." Even Tacitus, however, was forced to admit that most people in the Roman world welcomed and admired the Principate. The reason is simple: Augustus and his successors brought peace and prosperity after a century of disasters under the Late Republic. The Augustan period enjoyed affluence, especially in Italy; the other provinces caught up with Italy by the second century A.D. Agriculture flourished with the end of civil war. Italian industries became leaders in exports. Italian glass bowls and windowpanes, iron arms and tools, fancy silver eating utensils and candlesticks, and bronze statues and pots circulated from Britain to central Asia.

The city of Rome's urban poor, many of them freedmen, enjoyed a more efficient system of free grain distribution under Augustus and a large increase in games and public entertainment—the imperial policy of "bread and circuses" designed to content the masses. Augustus also set up a major public works program, which provided jobs for the poor. He prided himself on having found Rome "a city of brick" and having left it "a city of marble."

31 B.C.	Octavian defeats Antony and Cleopatra at Actium
27 B.C.	Augustus establishes Principate
14 B.C.–A.D. 68	Julio-Claudian dynasty
19 B.C.	Death of Virgil
ca. A.D. 27–30	Ministry of Jesus
ca. 67	Death of Paul of Tarsus
69–96	Flavian dynasty
70	Temple in Jerusalem destroyed
79	Eruption of Vesuvius
96–180	The "Five Good Emperors"
ca. 117	Death of Tacitus
193–235	Severan dynasty
ca. 200	Mishnah and New Testament each completed
212	Almost all free inhabitants of empire awarded Roman citizenship
235–284	Period of military anarchy

The perennial problem of the Late Republic had been land-hunger, which drove peasants into the arms of ambitious generals. Augustus kept his troops happy by compensating 300,000 loyal veterans with land, money, or both, often in new overseas colonies. At first he paid out these rewards from his own private sources; after A.D. 6, he made the rich pay via new taxes. The result kept the peace, but many nonsoldiers in Italy remained poor, as of course did the huge number of slaves.

As for the renegade commanders who had bedeviled the Late Republic, Augustus cut their potential power base by reducing the size of the army, gradually cutting the number of legions from over sixty to twenty-eight. The total size of the army, including light infantry and cavalry, was about 300,000. This reduction lightened Rome's tax burden but left Augustus with little room to expand the empire. In A.D. 9 Rome lost three legions to a native revolt against Rome's plan to extend its rule in Germany as far east as the Elbe River. Short of manpower, Augustus had to accept the Rhine River as Rome's new German frontier (see Map 6.1).

Imperial defense remained a major issue. Strong Roman armies were a necessity along the hostile European frontier. On the friendlier border in western Asia and northern Africa, Augustus and his immediate successors

MAP 6.1   The Roman World in the Early Empire

Many modern cities are built on the sites of Roman foundations, evidence of the immense extent of the Roman Empire at its height.

Roman Empire by death of Augustus, A.D. 14

Roman territory added by death of Hadrian, A.D. 138

Parthian territory conquered by Trajan, then lost, A.D. 114–117

Parthian Empire

X   Major battles

PARTHIA

ARMENIA

ASSYRIA

MESOPOTAMIA

Caspian Sea

Tigris

Volga

Ctesiphon
Seleucia

CAUCASUS MTS.

CAPPADOCIA

SYRIA

Palmyra

Damascus

Antioch

Tarsus

Jerusalem

Petra

ARABIA

JUDEA

CYPRUS

Red Sea

ARABIAN DESERT

Nile

EGYPT

BAHRIYA OASIS

Alexandria

BITHYNIA AND PONTUS

GALATIA

ANATOLIA

Pergamum

ASIA

PAMPHYLIA

LYCIA

Ephesus

RHODES

CRETE

Black Sea

Dnieper

Don

BOSPORAN KINGDOM

THRACE

Byzantium

Thessalonica

MACEDONIA

Athens

Corinth

ACHAEA

Cyrene

CYRENAICA

DACIA

MOESIA

EPIRUS

Brundisium

Actium
31 B.C.

X

Aquincum
(Budapest)

Danube

PANNONIA

Singidunum
(Belgrade)

DALMATIA

Adriatic Sea

Syracuse

SICILY

Malta

Mediterranean Sea

Leptis Magna

Baltic Sea

Elbe

Vindobona
(Vienna)

NORICUM

RAETIA

Moguntiacum
(Mainz)

GERMANY

Colonia Claudia Agrippinensis
(Cologne)

LOWER
GERMANY

BELGICA

UPPER
GERMANY

Rhine

A L P S

Mediolanum
(Milan)

CISALPINE
GAUL

Po

Arretium

ITALY

Rome

Mt. Vesuvius

Pompeii

Ostia

North Sea

Hadrian's Wall
A.D. 122

Eburacum
(York)

Camulodunum
(Colchester)

Londinium
(London)

BRITAIN

Lutetia Parisiorum
(Paris)

LUGDUNENSIS

GAUL

AQUITANIA

Lugdunum
(Lyon)

NARBONENSIS

Nemausus
(Nîmes)

Massilia
(Marseille)

Narbo

Rhône

CORSICA

SARDINIA

BALEARIC IS.

Tarraco

TARRACONENSIS

Ebro

Burdigala
(Bordeaux)

ATLANTIC OCEAN

LUSITANIA

Emerita Augusta
(Mérida)

SPAIN

Corduba
(Córdoba)

BAETICA

Carthage

AFRICA PROCONSULARIS

NUMIDIA

MAURETANIA

NORTH AFRICA

SAHARA

0   200   400 Mi.

0   200   400 Km.

set up client kingdoms, such as Judea and Armenia, to protect Roman territory. As for Parthia, Augustus compromised. He won no new territory but did achieve the symbolic victory of a return of the legionary standards lost by Crassus at Carrhae in 53 B.C.

To promote his ideology of renewal, Augustus sponsored social legislation embodying the old Republican virtues. He passed a series of laws encouraging marriage and childbearing and discouraging promiscuity and adultery. Such legislation was so flagrantly disobeyed that in 2 B.C. Augustus felt compelled to make an example of his own daughter, Julia (39 B.C.–A.D. 14), his only child, whose adulteries were the talk of Rome. As punishment she was banished to a barren islet.

Augustus's era marks the beginning of the classical period of Roman jurisprudence, during which the professionalism that had begun to mark Roman law in the Late Republic became a permanent fact. It was probably Augustus who established the practice, followed by later emperors, of granting a few distinguished jurists the exclusive right to issue legal opinions "on behalf of the princeps." He ensured, therefore, that experts guided the administration of justice. The first law school was opened in Rome under Augustus. Roman jurists, many of them provincials, adapted Roman law to the practices of the provinces. Although various provincial legal systems remained in use, the international system of Roman law was also used widely in the provinces.

In religion, too, Augustus was a legislator and reformer. He restored once-neglected cults and temples in order to appear as Rome's savior. He would probably have approved when, after his death, he was deified, just as Julius Caesar had been. Even while he was still alive, Augustus was worshiped in the provinces as a god—in both the East, where the cult of Roma and Augustus grew in popularity, and the West, where centers of emperor-worship were established at the sites of Lyon and Cologne (see Map 6.1). The imperial cult, an important part of state propaganda until the empire became Christian in the fourth century A.D., was well underway.

Deification, whether formal or informal, was a heady brew, but Augustus deserved it more than most. He not only ended the Late Republican era of civil wars but established the Roman Empire on a completely new footing. Republican freedom was gone, but the emperor and bureaucrats brought stability. The peace of the Augustan Principate would last, with few interruptions, for two hundred years. Few people in history have created order so successfully.

THE CULTURE OF THE AUGUSTAN AGE

Like *Periclean,* the adjective *Augustan* (aw-GUS-tin) has come to signify an era of literary and artistic flowering. In both periods strong elements of classicism shaped the arts—that is, an attempt to project fundamental, heroic, and idealized values, the values that the self-confident rulers of each epoch wished to promote. Both prose and poetry flourished in Augustus's empire. The emperor and his close adviser Maecenas (d. 8 B.C.) were patrons of a number of important poets, chief among them Virgil (70–19 B.C.) and Horace (65–8 B.C.). The historian Livy (59 B.C.–A.D. 17), who wrote his history of Rome from the founding of the city to 9 B.C. under Augustus, also elicited the princeps's interest in his work. All three men contributed in their writings to the Augustan renewal and rededication of Rome.

In many ways **Virgil** (VER-jill) speaks for his contemporaries. In the *Eclogues*—poems that, following an Alexandrian model (see page 109), have rustic settings—Virgil describes the miseries of the civil wars and the blessings of peace under Augustus. "A god created this peace for us; for he will always be a god to me," one character says. In the Fourth Eclogue, Virgil speaks of the birth of a child to usher in a restored Golden Age. At the Council of Nicaea in A.D. 325 (see page 188) and later, this poem was given a Christian interpretation. In the *Georgics,* Virgil describes the glories of Italian agriculture, which, thanks to Augustus, could be practiced peacefully again.

Virgil's masterpiece is an epic poem, the *Aeneid* (ee-NEE-id), "the story of Aeneas," the legendary Trojan founder of Rome, or at least of the Latin town from which Rome's founders eventually came. Legend also makes Aeneas the ancestor of Augustus. Thus the *Aeneid* indirectly celebrates Augustus, often considered Rome's second founder. The poem explores the pain and burden as well as the glory of empire.

If Virgil's work has the grandeur of marble, Horace's poems—*Odes, Epodes, Satires, Epistles,* and *Ars Poetica (Art of Poetry)*—are more like finely cut gems. They tend to be polished, complex, and detached. Like Virgil, Horace explores the themes of war and peace and praises Augustus. "With Caesar [Augustus] holding the lands, I shall fear neither turmoil nor violent death," declares one of the *Odes.* Both Horace and Virgil successfully adapted Greek models and, in the process, created something new. Few writers have had a greater influence on the later Western literary tradition.

Only 35 of the original 142 books of Livy's ambitious history have survived. Livy (LIV-ee) is both a master storyteller and a superb ironist. His anecdotes of Roman history are vivid and told in a grand rhetorical style. Livy is our major source for the Roman monarchy and Early Republic, although his account of early Rome is long on myth and short on fact. Nevertheless, Livy is not merely an entertaining stylist but a profound thinker on the meaning of history. He embroiders the facts and engages in frank, subjective

Virgil   Roman poet whose works, including the *Aeneid,* contributed to the Augustan renewal.

Mosaic of the Doves
This exquisite mosaic shows a number of doves drinking from or positioned around a gilded bronze basin on a marble pedestal. Derived from a Hellenistic work from Pergamum, this mosaic comes from a wealthy house in Pompeii.
(Scala/Art Resource, NY)

judgments intended to inspire both patriotism and reflection on the ironies of history.

Another patron of writers in Augustus's circle was Messalla, himself an orator as well as a statesman. Love poetry was his special interest. Among the poets Messalla supported were Ovid, best known for works on love and mythology; Tibullus, an elegist; and his ward, Sulpicia. Although little survives of Sulpicia's work, more of her work exists than of any other Roman woman. She describes her passion for one Cerinthus: "a worthy man . . . at last a love . . . of such a kind that my shame, Gossip, would be greater if I kept it covered than if I laid it bare."[1]

Augustus and his entourage were also great patrons of the arts and of architecture, which they considered propaganda tools. They sponsored many major building projects throughout the empire, especially in Rome, which gained temples, a new Forum of Augustus, the Theater of Marcellus, the Baths of Agrippa, the Pantheon, and the Mausoleum of Augustus.

The Julio-Claudians

Augustus and his successors presented the imperial household to the world as the ideal family, the very model of social order. Behind the walls of the palace, however, dwelt a troubled reality.

Augustus had only one child, Julia, from his first marriage, which ended in divorce. In 38 b.c. Augustus took as his second wife **Livia** (58 b.c.–a.d. 29), who divorced her husband to marry Augustus even though she was pregnant with their second son. Livia (LIV-ee-uh) did not bear Augustus children. Seeking a male successor, Augustus used Julia as a pawn in a game of dynastic marriage, divorce, and remarriage, but to no avail. Julia's first two husbands both predeceased her, as did two sons, each of whom Augustus had adopted. (In Rome it was common for a man without a birth son to adopt a son.) In the end, Augustus was forced to choose as successor, and adopt, a man he disliked, Tiberius (ty-BEER-ee-us) (42 b.c.–a.d. 37), Livia's elder son.

Livia was among the most powerful women in Roman history. One of Augustus's main advisers, she developed a reputation for intrigue, aimed, so gossip had it, at securing the succession for Tiberius. Livia's enemies accused her of poisoning many people, including Julia's husbands and sons; her own grandson, Germanicus (a brilliant general whose popularity threatened Tiberius's); and even Augustus himself, who died in bed after a short illness in a.d. 14.

From a.d. 14 to 68, Rome was ruled by other emperors from Augustus's family. The dynasty, known

Livia Wife of Augustus, she was suspected of poisoning several family members, including Augustus himself.

as the **Julio-Claudians**, consisted of Augustus's stepson Tiberius, great-grandson Caligula, grandnephew Claudius, and great-great-grandson Nero. For many elite Romans, this era was one of decadence, scandal, and oppression of the old nobility. Ordinary people, however, generally enjoyed the benefits of stable, effective, and peaceful government.

The reign of Tiberius (r. 14–37) was later remembered by the elite for its treason trials and murders. The senate complained as it steadily lost power to the princeps. The Roman masses grumbled because Tiberius cut back on games and building projects. But despite his shortcomings, Tiberius was a skilled and prudent administrator. He wisely drew back from war on the borders, reduced taxes and spending, and promoted honesty among provincial governors.

His successor, his nephew Gaius (r. 37–41), nicknamed Caligula (ca-LIG-yoo-luh) ("Baby Boots," after the boots he had worn as a little boy in his father's army camp), humiliated the senate. It was bad enough that he tried to have himself declared a living god. On top of that, he appointed his favorite horse not only high priest of a new cult in his honor but also a member of the senate. Caligula raised taxes and accused people of treason in order to confiscate property. He wanted to have his statue erected in the Temple at Jerusalem, and he would have done so, but he was assassinated first, the victim of a high-level conspiracy. After his death the senate debated restoring the Republic, but it was not to be.

Caligula's uncle, Claudius, was named emperor by the Praetorian Guard, which forced the senate to support him. Physically handicapped, Claudius (r. 41–54) was often the butt of jokes, but he was a man of substance: a historian, politician, and priest and someone fully versed in the cunning ways of his family. An activist emperor, he expanded the imperial offices with their powerful freedmen; oversaw the construction of an artificial harbor at Rome's silt-clogged port of Ostia; and conquered Britain, where Roman arms had not intervened since Julius Caesar's forays in 55 to 54 B.C.

Claudius's death may have been the result of poisoning by his wife, who was also his niece, Agrippina (a-grip-PIE-nuh) the Younger (15–59); in any case, her son by a previous marriage, Nero, became emperor (r. 54–68). Nero's scandalous behavior rivaled Caligula's, and his treason trials outdid Tiberius's. After a great fire destroyed half of Rome in 64, Nero mounted a big rebuilding program and was accused of having started the fire just so that he could become famous as a builder. He found a scapegoat for the fire in the members of a small religious sect, the Christians, whom he persecuted. Ordinary Romans supported Nero because he gave them good government. He was unpopular

with the senators and, more serious, with the army, because he failed to pay all his troops promptly. Confronted with a major revolt in 68, Nero committed suicide. (See the box "The Written Record: Nero and His Mother.")

The next year, 69, witnessed Rome's first civil war in about a century. Three men claimed the imperial

Agrippina the Younger
This statue shows the mother of the emperor Nero praying. It is carved in basanite, a stone whose use is typical of the imperial Roman taste for art objects in exotic materials.
(Courtesy, Mondadori Electa S.P.A.)

Julio-Claudians Dynasty of Roman emperors founded by Augustus and ruling from A.D. 14 to 68.

NERO AND HIS MOTHER

Tacitus, a member of the senatorial elite of the Early Empire, offered a scathing view of the emperors. His Annals *portray the emperor Nero as a pawn and his mother Agrippina as domineering and power mad. After marrying the emperor Claudius, she schemed to have both him and his son Britannicus murdered so that Nero could have the throne. Nero became emperor, but eventually he turned on her.*

Everyone longed for the mother's domination to end. But no one believed that her son's hatred would go as far as murder. . . .

Finally, however, he [Nero] concluded that wherever Agrippina was she was intolerable. He decided to kill her. His only doubt was whether to employ poison, or the dagger, or violence of some other kind. Poison was the first choice. But a death at the emperor's table would not look fortuitous after [Nero's stepbrother] Britannicus had died there. . . .

However, a scheme was put forward by Anicetus, an ex-slave who commanded the fleet at Misenum. In Nero's boyhood Anicetus had been his tutor; he and Agrippina hated each other. A ship could be made, he now said, with a section which would come loose at sea and hurl Agrippina into the water without warning. Nothing is so productive of surprises as the sea, remarked Anicetus; if a shipwreck did away with her, who could be so unreasonable as to blame a human agency instead of wind and water? Besides, when she was dead the emperor could allot her a temple and altars and the other public tokens of filial duty. . . .

[But Agrippina survives the shipwreck, so Nero sends Anicetus and his men to kill her on land.] "If you have come to visit me," she said, "you can report that I am better. But if you are assassins, I know my son is not responsible. He did not order his mother's death." The murderers closed round her bed. First the captain hit her on the head with a truncheon. Then as the lieutenant was drawing his sword to finish her off, she cried out: "Strike here!"—pointing to her womb. Blow after blow fell, and she died. . . .

This was the end which Agrippina had anticipated for years. The prospect had not daunted her. When she asked astrologers about Nero, they had answered that he would become emperor but kill his mother. Her reply was, "Let him kill me—provided he becomes emperor!"

QUESTIONS

1. What are the signs of corruption and wickedness at Nero's court?

2. Who is the more sympathetic character, Nero or Agrippina? Why?

3. How did imperial Rome display both science and superstition?

Source: Tacitus. *The Annals of Imperial Rome.* Translated with an introduction by Michael Grant. Revised edition. Baltimore: Penguin, 1971, pp. 313–317. Reproduced by permission of Penguin Books Ltd.

purple after Nero. A fourth, Vespasian (ves-PAY-zhun) (Titus Flavius Vespasianus, r. 69–79), commander of the army quelling a revolt in the province of Judea, was able to make his claim stick. Peace was restored, but not the rule of Augustus's family. Vespasian founded a new dynasty, the Flavians (r. 69–96), which was followed in turn by the Nervo-Trajanic (r. 96–138) and Antonine (r. 138–192) dynasties. The ultimate tribute to Augustus may be that his regime was stable enough to survive the extinction of his family.

SECTION SUMMARY

- Augustus, Rome's first emperor, shared a degree of power with the senate while keeping the armies firmly under his control.

- Augustus gave Rome its first civil service and first police force; he gave Italy prosperity; he began to raise the status of the provinces.

- Augustus reduced military spending and compromised with Rome's enemies in order to stabilize the frontiers.

- The poets Virgil and Horace and the historian Livy are among the great writers of the flourishing culture of Augustan Rome.

- Although they included such scandalous figures as Nero, the Julio-Claudian emperors (A.D. 14–68) delivered peaceful and effective government.

THE ROMAN PEACE AND ITS COLLAPSE, A.D. 69–284

What was life like in the era of the Roman peace? Why did peace end during the third century A.D.?

Much about Rome in the second century A.D. appears attractive today. Within the multi-ethnic empire, opportunities for inhabitants to become part of the elite were increasing. The central government was on its way to granting Roman citizenship to nearly every free person in the empire, a process completed in the year 212. The emperors emphasized sharing prosperity and spreading it through the provinces. Italy was no longer the tyrant of the Mediterranean, but merely first among equals. To be sure, rebellions were crushed, but few people rebelled. This period, known as the **pax Romana,** or "Roman peace," seems particularly golden in contrast with what followed: the disastrous and disordered third century A.D., in which the empire came close to collapse but survived because of a radical and rigid transformation.

THE FLAVIANS AND THE "GOOD EMPERORS"

The **Flavian** dynasty of Vespasian (r. 69–79) and his sons Titus (r. 79–81) and Domitian (r. 81–96) provided good government, and their successors built on their achievements. Unlike the Julio-Claudians, Vespasian hailed not from the old Roman nobility but from an Italian propertied family. A man of rough-and-ready character, Vespasian is supposed to have replied when Titus complained that a new latrine tax was beneath the dignity of the Roman government, "Son, money has no smell." Unlike his father and brother, Domitian reverted to frequent treason trials and persecution of the aristocracy, which earned him assassination in 96, although the empire as a whole enjoyed peace and sound administration under his reign.

The so-called Five Good Emperors are Nerva (r. 96–98), Trajan (r. 98–117), Hadrian (r. 117–138), and the first two Antonines, Antoninus Pius (r. 138–161) and Marcus Aurelius (r. 161–180). They are in several ways examples of the principle of merit. Trajan, a Roman citizen born in Spain, was Rome's first emperor from outside Italy. Hadrian and Marcus Aurelius also came from Spain, and Antoninus Pius from Gaul. Each

of the Five Good Emperors except Marcus Aurelius adopted the most competent person, rather than the closest blood relative, as his son and successor, thus elevating duty over sentiment. Marcus Aurelius, a deeply committed Stoic, gave full vent to his sense of duty in his *Meditations,* which he wrote in Greek while living in a tent on the Danube frontier, where he fought long and hard against German raids. Antoninus was surnamed "Pius" (Dutiful) because he was devoted to his country, the gods, and his adoptive father, Hadrian.

The Five Good Emperors made humaneness and generosity the themes of their reigns. Trajan, for example, founded a program of financial aid for the poor children of Italy. They also went to great lengths to care for the provinces. These emperors not only commonly received petitions from cities, associations, and individuals in far-off provinces but answered them. Yet humaneness does not mean softness. Hadrian, for instance, ordered a revolt in Judea (132–135) suppressed with great brutality.

Like the Julio-Claudians, the Five Good Emperors advertised their wives to the world as exemplars of traditional modesty, self-effacement, and domesticity. In fact, they were often worldly, educated, and influential. Trajan's wife, Plotina, for example (d. 121 or 123), acted as patron of the Epicurean school at Athens, whose philosophy she claimed to follow. She advised her husband on provincial administration as well as dynastic matchmaking. Hadrian's wife, Sabina, traveled in her husband's entourage to Egypt (130), where her aristocratic Greek friend, Julia Balbilla, commemorated the trip by writing Greek poetry, which she had inscribed alongside other tourists' writings on the leg of one of two statues of Amenhotep III at Thebes, referred to in classical times as the "colossi of Memnon."

A darker side of the second-century empire was the problem of border defense. Augustus and the Julio-Claudians had established client kingdoms where possible, to avoid the expense and political dangers of raising armies. The emperors of the day tended to be more aggressive on the borders than their predecessors. They moved from client kingdoms to a new border policy of stationary frontier defense. Expensive fortification systems of walls, watchtowers, and trenches were built along the perimeter of the empire's border and manned with guards. A prominent example is Hadrian's Wall, which separated Roman Britain from the enemy

pax Romana   Latin for "Roman peace," the term refers to the period of peace and prosperity in the Roman Empire from A.D. 69 to 180.

Flavians   Dynasty of the Roman emperors Vespasian, Titus, and Domitian, whose rule was a time of relative peace and good government.

tribes to the north. Stretching 80 miles, the wall required fifteen thousand defense troops.

The most ambitious frontier policy was that of Trajan, who crossed the Danube to carve out the new province of Dacia (modern Romania) and who used an excuse to invade Parthian Mesopotamia. He won battles as far away as the Persian Gulf, but he lost the war. As soon as his army left, Mesopotamia rose in revolt, followed by Germany. Trajan's reign marked the empire's greatest geographic extent, but Trajan had overextended Rome's resources. When he died, his successor, Hadrian, had to abandon Trajan's province of Mesopotamia (see Map 6.1).

PROSPERITY AND ROMANIZATION IN THE PROVINCES

Compared with a modern economy, the Roman economy was underdeveloped. Most people worked in agriculture, employed primitive technology, and lived at a subsistence level. Even so, the Roman Empire experienced modest economic growth during the first two centuries A.D. The chief beneficiaries were the wealthy few, but ordinary people shared in the economic expansion as well. In addition to stability and peace, several other factors encouraged economic development. The western provinces witnessed the opening of new lands to agriculture, where improved techniques were applied. The growth of cities increased agricultural demand. Changes in Roman law aided commerce by making it easier to employ middlemen in business transactions. Travel and communications were relatively easy and inexpensive.

Prosperity   Trade boomed, as a recent archaeological discovery in the Italian city of Pisa (PEE-zuh) recalls. Nineteen Hellenistic and Roman ships were found at the site of the ancient harbor beginning in 1999. Several are merchant ships, both coastal freighters and small harbor craft. One of the ships was filled with amphoras (storage jars), still stacked in neat rows and filled with wine and sand. Both of those goods come from the region of the Bay of Naples, whose sand was used for concrete that could set underwater. The finds, which seem to date from the mid-second century A.D., offer a vivid picture of trade up and down the west coast of Italy. When the cargo was unloaded at Pisa, the ships probably picked up the local grain and marble, which was shipped in turn to Rome.

Rome was an economic magnet, but so, to a lesser extent, were all cities, and the second century A.D. was a great age of city life. New cities were founded far from the Mediterranean. They began as veterans' colonies, market towns, and even army camps, and some grew into cities of permanent importance in European history: Cologne (Colonia Claudia Agrippinensis), Paris

Double Portrait, Pompeii
This wall painting from a house joined to a bakery depicts a married couple, possibly the wealthy baker P. Paquius Proculus and his wife. The portraiture is realistic. The couple carry symbols of education: she holds wax tablets and a stylus (pen), while he grasps a sealed scroll.   *(Scala/Art Resource, NY)*

(Lutetia Parisiorum), Lyon (Lugdunum), London (Londinium), Mérida (Emerita Augusta), Vienna (Vindobona), and Budapest (Aquincum).

Whether old or new, cities attracted large elite populations. The Principate was not a domain of country gentry but one in which ambitious people wanted to live in great cities, in emulation of the greatest city of the empire, Rome, which was by Augustus's day a city of perhaps a million people. In cities men competed for positions as magistrates, in imitation of the two consuls, or for seats on the local town council, often called a *curia* (KYOO-ree-uh), like the senate in Rome. Town councilors were called *decurions* (day-KYOO-ree-uns) and known collectively as the *curial order*. Decurions played one-upmanship in sponsoring public buildings in the Roman style—one man endowing a new forum, another a triumphal arch, a third a library, a fourth an amphitheater, and so on. From Ephesus in Anatolia to Colchester in Britain, from Mainz in Germany to Leptis Magna in Libya, a Roman could find familiar government institutions, architecture, and street plans. At Zeugma on the Euphrates River, for example, a city of seventy thousand people, aristocrats on Rome's eastern frontier lived in Italian-style villas decorated with classical frescoes and mosaics and adorned with bronze statues of the Greco-Roman gods.

Unlike men, women did not usually hold magistracies, but wealthy women of the empire could and did lavish money on public benefactions. Women endowed temples and synagogues, amphitheaters and monumental gateways, games and ceremonies. They were rewarded with wreaths, front-row seats, statues, priesthoods, and inscriptions honoring them as "most distinguished lady," "patron," and even "father of the city," to cite an extraordinary case from Roman Egypt.

Romanization   The buildings were visible examples of Romanization, although the Romans did not use the term. If they had, it would have had a limited meaning because the emperors neither would nor could impose a lockstep cultural uniformity on their subjects. The empire was too big and ancient technology too primitive for that. The total population of the empire consisted of between 50 million and 100 million people, most of whom lived in the countryside. The small and largely urbanized Roman administration had little direct contact with most people. So, for example, only a minority of the inhabitants of the empire spoke Latin; in the East, Greek was the more common language of administration. Millions of people spoke neither Greek nor Latin. Celtic, Germanic, Punic, Berber, Coptic, Aramaic, and Syriac were other common languages in Roman domains. In short, the empire lacked the unity of a modern nation-state.

What, then, besides buildings and language might Romanization entail? One index has already been suggested: the participation of provincials in the central government, even as emperor. By around A.D. 200, for example, about 15 percent of the known Roman equestrians and senators came from North Africa. By this time the senate was no longer dominated by Italians but was representative of the empire as a whole.

Participation in government implies another index of Romanization—the extension of Roman citizenship outside Italy to magistrates, decurions, or even whole cities. Citizens took Roman names reflecting the emperor or promagistrate who had enfranchised them. Thus the provinces were full of Julii, Claudii, and Flavii, among others.

The spread of Roman customs is another measure of Romanization. For example, the gladiatorial shows that Romans loved became popular from Antioch to England. These combats advertised both Roman culture and Roman brutality. (See the feature "The Visual Record: Gladiators.")

By the same token, native customs might be adopted by Romans. Consider the case of Egypt, where, in the late 1990s, archaeologists discovered a vast Roman-era cemetery about 230 miles southwest of Cairo, in the Bahriya Oasis, Roman Egypt's wine country. The population was Romanized here. Yet the cemetery, with its dozens of gilded mummies from the first and second centuries A.D., shows the persistence of the mummification processes of the pharaohs.

Another ambiguous symbol of Romanization is found in A.D. 212. In a law known as the *Constitutio Antoniana*, the emperor Caracalla (r. 211–217) rendered nearly all of the free inhabitants of the empire Roman citizens. On the one hand, the law is a historical landmark. Near-universal Roman citizenship was a kind of halfway point between ancient empire and modern mass democracy. On the other hand, the *Constitutio Antoniana* was something of a gimmick. It was probably less an instrument of unification than of taxation, for citizens had a heavier tax burden than noncitizens.

The Roman army, by contrast, did promote Romanization. In antiquity as today, military service offered education and social mobility. Only citizens could join the legions; non-Romans served as auxiliaries. They received Roman citizenship after completing their regular term of service, twenty-five years, and with good reason: a Syrian or Gallic peasant, for example, who served in the Roman military would experience a way of life with old and deep roots in central Italy.

Non-Italians had, and took, the opportunity to rise high in the army or government. This was all to Rome's credit. Yet as Italians became a minority in the Roman army, and as ever larger numbers of frontier peoples were recruited, it became conceivable that someday the army might abandon its loyalty to Rome.

Gladiators

Historians and novelists write about them, filmmakers portray them, revolutionaries salute them, and a few years ago television athletes claimed to be American updates of them. They are gladiators, literally men who carried a *gladius,* or sword. They fought to the death as entertainment, and they enraptured the Roman Empire.

Gladiators took part in so-called games or combat before large crowds. Armed with various specialized weapons, they fought each other and sometimes wild animals. Some unfortunates were thrust into fights with no weapons at all. The audience, seated in rank order, ranged from slaves to senators to the emperor himself. There was nothing tame about what they had come to see. Consider the word *arena,* referring to the site of the games. It literally means "sand," which is what covered the floor—and soaked up the blood.

Our fascination with the gladiator is nothing compared to the Romans'. Everybody in Rome talked about gladiators. At Pompeii, graffiti celebrated a star of the arena whom "all the girls sigh for." Jokes poked fun at gladiators, philosophers pondered their meaning, and literature is full of references to them.

Gladiatorial images decorated art around the empire, from mosaics to household lamps. Look at this mosaic from a Roman villa in Germany, one of several mosaic panels on the floor of the building's entrance hall, depicting scenes from the arena. The illustration shows a *retiarius,* or net-and-trident bearer, fighting a better-armed *secutor,* literally "pursuer," under the watchful eyes of a *lanista,* or trainer. As was typical, the retiarius wears no armor except for a shoulder piece protecting his left side. To defend himself against the dagger wielded by the secutor (in the mosaic, hidden behind the shield), the retiarius had to be fit enough to be able to keep moving. The difference between various types of gladiators would have been as obvious to a Roman as the difference between a catcher and a pitcher is to a baseball fan today.

As for the amphitheaters where gladiatorial combats took place, they were as common in Italy and the Roman Empire as skyscrapers are in a modern city. Look, for example, at this photograph of the amphitheater in the city of El Djem in modern Tunisia (the Roman province of Africa). Built of high-quality local stone in the third century A.D., the structure was meant to have sixty-four arches,

but it was never completed. The openings in the floor permitted animals to be released into the arena. A large amphitheater like this one held at least thirty thousand spectators, and the largest amphitheater of all, the Flavian Amphitheater—or Colosseum—at Rome, seated around fifty thousand. Amphitheaters were less common in the east, but the fans there also were loyal, so the games went on—in theaters.

Most gladiators were condemned criminals, prisoners of war, or slaves bought for the purpose. The most famous slave gladiator was Spartacus, a Thracian. Along with seventy-seven other gladiators in the Italian city of Capua, Spartacus instigated a slave rebellion that attracted thousands and shook Italy for two years (73–71 B.C.).

Yet some gladiators were free men who volunteered for a limited term of service. Once even the emperor Commodus (r. 180–192) served, to the disgust of other Roman nobles, who found the arena fascinating but low-class. The gladiator was part warrior, part athlete, part showman, and part butcher. Yet there was something of the pagan priest in the gladiator, too, for his was a solemn profession. Every gladiator took an oath to endure being burned, bound, beaten, and killed by the sword. They began each combat by greeting the official in charge (in Rome, the emperor) in this way: "We who are about to die salute you."

Students of the Romans find it hard to believe that they adored such a murderous sport, in which dozens and occasionally hundreds of men might die in a single day, to the roar of the crowds. Yet perhaps the arena makes us uncomfortable not so much because it is foreign but because it is familiar. Although we no longer flock to games in which men kill each other, we do go in droves to blood sports such as boxing, and we pack hockey rinks to watch men regularly give each other concussions. Modern people no longer kill animals in the arena for sport, but we hunt, fish, go on big-game safaris, watch cockfights, and, in Spain, kill bulls and occasionally get killed by them.

Besides, perhaps our discomfort reflects our instinctive understanding of the symbolism of the arena. The games were brutal, but so was the empire. Rome had brought peace to three continents, but it had done so by brandishing a sword, and it kept the peace by its readiness to fight. The arena kept Romans tough and warlike, or so an intellec-

Roman Amphitheater, El Djem, Tunisia
(Adina Tovy/Robert Harding World Imagery)

Gladiator Mosaic, Nennig, Germany
(Bildarchiv Preussischer Kulturbesitz)

tual could argue, as does Pliny the Younger, who describes gladiatorial games:

> [The games] inspired a glory in wounds and a contempt of death, since the love of praise and desire for victory could be seen, even in the bodies of slaves and criminals. (*Panegyric* 33)

Arguably the arena also contributed to public order. This was no small achievement, since the imperial army could not police a population of 50 million to 100 million, and few places had even the elementary police force that the city of Rome did. The violence that bloodied the amphitheater stepped into the breach by reminding criminals— or those defined as criminals—what punishment awaited them. Rob or kill, and you might end up in the arena. Refuse to worship the emperor, and you might be fed to the lions, as Christians were from time to time. Rebel against Rome, and you might find yourself on a chain gang building a new am-

phitheater, as tradition says thirty thousand prisoners of the First Jewish Revolt (A.D. 66–70) did. The result was the Colosseum.*

Occasionally pagan as well as Christian writers condemned gladiatorial games. Seneca the Younger (ca. 4 B.C.–A.D. 65), for example, criticized them for inciting greed, aggression, and cruelty. Yet so popular was Rome's theater of power that gladiators and their games were not abolished until around A.D. 400.

QUESTIONS

1. What does the scene on the mosaic show, and what does it indicate about the Roman public's interest in gladiators?

2. What were the main features of the amphitheater at El Djem?

3. How might gladiatorial games have contributed to public order in the Roman Empire?

---

*The preceding two paragraphs lean heavily on the fine discussion in Colin Wells, *The Roman Empire*, 2d ed. (Cambridge, Mass.: Harvard University Press, 1995), pp. 248–255.

Online Study Center
Improve Your Grade Visual Record Activities

ROMAN LAW ON CLASS AND MARRIAGE

Roman law is one of the ancient world's most influential and enduring legacies. Logical, practical, orderly, and—within the limits of a society of slaves and masters—relatively fair, Roman law has influenced the legal systems of most Western countries and many non-Western countries. The law governing Roman citizens was called *ius civile,* or "civil law." Originally this term covered a very broad range of legal matters, but in the empire its meaning was narrowed to private matters. Criminal law became a separate category.

The law helped Rome administer its empire. Roman law was not universal, and noncitizens continued to use their own laws for local matters, but the governors used Roman law to run their provinces, so local elites had to become familiar with it. Like so many Roman customs, the law was both hierarchical and flexible. Let us consider two areas in which the law affected daily life: class and marriage.

The law reflected Roman society's ingrained social inequality. Traditional special classes such as senators and equestrians survived, to be joined by the new distinction between citizens and noncitizens. Another important division cut across the citizen-alien distinction, that between *honestiores* (in general, the curial order) and *humiliores* (everyone else). Privileges previously inherent in citizenship, such as exemption from flogging by officials, now tended to be based on this new distinction, enshrined in private and criminal law.

The most basic legal distinction was that between free and slave—and the empire contained millions of slaves. A third category, ex-slaves or freedmen, also became increasingly important. Freedmen technically owed service to their former masters, who became their patrons, and most freedmen were humble. A few, however, grew rich in commerce or wielded enough power in imperial administration to lord it over even Roman aristocrats. The result was strong elite hostility toward freedmen, which is often reflected in Roman literature. Witness the stereotype of the vulgar freedman, embodied in Trimalchio in the *Satyricon* (suh-TEER-uh-con), a novel by Petronius (first century A.D.). Trimalchio had more estates than he could remember and so much money that his wife counted it by the bushel-load.

As regards marriage, Roman family law was strict and severe in principle. In practice, however, it often proved pragmatic and even humane. Consider three cases: elite marriages, slave marriages, and soldiers' marriages.

As in the Late Republic, so in the Early Empire most Roman women married without legally becoming members of their husbands' families—or their children's. This gave women a degree of freedom from their husbands, but it left elite women, who owned property, with a problem: technically that property was controlled by their fathers or brothers. Yet society recognized a woman's wish to leave her property to her children, and imperial law increasingly made it possible for her to do so—although the conservative Romans waited until the sixth century A.D. before abolishing completely the rights of greedy uncles. Another case is a mother's right to have a say in her children's choice of marriage partner. This maternal prerogative became accepted social practice even though Roman law gave women no such right.

Roman slaves married and had children, but they had to do so in the face of both legal and practical obstacles. Roman law gave slaves no right to marry, and it made slave children the property of the owner of the slave mother. Owners could and did break up slave families by sale. Even if a slave was freed, the law expressed far more concern with the continuing obligations of freedmen to their former masters than with the rights of slave families. Yet during the Early Empire cracks appeared in the wall of law that allowed slave families to slip through.

For example, although the law insisted that a slave be age 30 before being freed, it made an exception for an owner who wished to free a female slave younger than 30 in order to marry her. To take another example, the law conceded that slave children owed devotion and loyalty (*pietas*) to their slave parents.

Career soldiers from at least the time of Augustus on could not marry, probably on the grounds of military discipline. Yet many soldiers cohabited anyhow, often with noncitizen women in the areas where they served, and frequently children were the result. Not until the reign of Septimius Severus (SEH-ver-us) (r. 193–211) were soldiers permitted to marry formally, and then only after twenty-five years of service. Yet not only had commanders permitted cohabitation for two centuries, but the law also made concessions now and then. For example, the Flavians gave soldiers a degree of freedom to make wills, which could allow them to leave property to illegitimate children. Various emperors gave groups of soldiers the privilege, on discharge, to legalize a marriage with a noncitizen, which ordinary Romans were not permitted to do.[2]

THE CULTURE OF THE ROMAN PEACE

In Latin poetry the century or so after the death of Augustus is often referred to as the "Silver Age," a term sometimes applied to prose as well. The implication is that this period, though productive, fell short of the golden Augustan era. It might be fairer to say that the self-confidence of the Augustan writers did not last. As the permanence of monarchy became clear, many in the elite looked back to the Republic with nostalgia and bitterness. Silver Age writing often takes refuge in satire or rhetorical flourish. Writing under Trajan, for example, the historian **Tacitus** poured scorn on the Julio-Claudians and Flavians. Other Silver Age writers indulged in flattery and obsequiousness toward the emperor.

The Silver Age was an era of interest in antiquities and in compiling handbooks and encyclopedias; it was also an era of self-consciousness and literary criticism. In the first two centuries A.D., Roman writers came from an ever greater diversity of backgrounds and wrote for an ever wider audience, as prosperity and educational opportunities increased. Consider Lucian (ca. A.D. 115–185), an essayist and satirist. A native of Syria who probably spoke Aramaic before learning Greek, he served as an administrator in Roman Egypt.

Many writers of the era pursued public careers, which offered access to patronage. Tacitus, for instance, rose as high as proconsul of the province of Asia. Prominent literary families emerged, such as that of Pliny (PLIH-nee) the Elder (A.D. 23–79), an encyclopedic author on natural science, geography, history, and art; and his nephew, Pliny the Younger (ca. A.D. 62–ca. 113), an orator and letter writer. The most notable literary family is that of Seneca the Elder (ca. 55 B.C.–A.D. 40), a historian and scholar of rhetoric; his son, Seneca the Younger (ca. 4 B.C.–A.D. 65); and Seneca the Younger's nephew, the epic poet Lucan (A.D. 39–65).

Born in Cordoba, Spain, the younger Seneca moved at an early age to Rome, where he became a successful lawyer and wealthy investor. He was banished in A.D. 41 for alleged adultery with a sister of Caligula. Recalled in 49, he was tutor to the young Nero. When Nero became emperor in 54, Seneca became one of his chief advisers and helped bring good government to the empire. Seneca eventually fell out of favor, however, and was forced first into retirement and then, in A.D. 65, into suicide. He had been the major literary figure of his age, a jack-of-all-trades: playwright, essayist, pamphleteer, student of science, and noted Stoic philosopher.

A literary career was safer under the Five Good Emperors. Consider Tacitus and his contemporary, the poet Juvenal (JOO-veh-nal) (ca. A.D. 55–130). Juvenal's *Satires* are bitter and brilliant poems offering social commentary. He laments the past, when poverty and war had supposedly kept Romans chaste and virtuous. Amid "the woes of long peace," luxury and foreign ways had corrupted Rome, in his opinion. Critics often blame society's troubles on marginal groups. Juvenal, for example, launches harsh attacks on women and foreigners. Tacitus, too, is sometimes scornful of women. Yet if he is biased on matters of gender, Tacitus is far from ethnocentric. Few historians have expressed graver doubts about the value of their country's alleged success. For example, Tacitus highlighted the simple virtues of the Germanic tribes, so different from the sophisticated decadence of contemporary Rome. Nostalgia for the Republic pervades his two greatest works, *The Histories,* which covers the civil wars of A.D. 69, and *The Annals* (only parts of which survive), chronicling the emperors from Tiberius through Nero. A masterpiece of irony and pithiness, Tacitus's style makes an unforgettable impression on the reader.

Plutarch (PLOO-tark) (ca. A.D. 50–120), whose *Parallel Lives of Noble Greeks and Romans* later captured the imagination of Shakespeare, is probably the best-known pagan Greek writer of the first two centuries A.D. Like Livy, Plutarch emphasizes the moral and political lessons of history. A careful scholar, Plutarch found his true calling in rhetorical craftsmanship—polished speeches and carefully chosen anecdotes. As in Rome, rhetoric was the basis of much of Greek literary culture in this period.

Another star of Greek culture at this time was the physician Galen of Pergamum (A.D. 129–?199). In his many writings, Galen (GAY-len) was to medicine what Aristotle had been to philosophy: a brilliant systematizer and an original thinker. He excelled in anatomy and physiology and proved that the arteries as well as the veins carry blood. He was destined to have a dominant influence on European medicine in the Middle Ages.

THE CRISIS OF THE THIRD CENTURY, A.D. 235–284

Leaving the relative calm of the second century A.D. behind, the third-century Roman Empire descended into an ever widening spiral of crisis. Barbarian invasions, domestic economic woes, plague, assassinations, brigandage, urban decline—the list of Rome's problems is dramatic. The empire went "from a kingdom of gold to one of iron and rust," as Dio Cassius put it, summing up Roman history after the death of Marcus Aurelius in 180, when the seeds of the **third-century crisis** were sown.

Stability first began to slip away during the reign of the last of the Antonines, Marcus Aurelius's birth son, Commodus (KOM-uh-dus) (r. 180–192), a man with Nero's taste for decadence and penchant for terrorizing the senatorial elite. His predictable assassination led to civil war, after which Septimius Severus, commander of the Danube armies, emerged as the unchallenged emperor (r. 193–211). He founded the Severan dynasty, which survived until 235.

Severan reformers attempted to re-establish the empire on a firmer footing, but they only brought the day of crisis nearer. The main theme of Septimius's

Tacitus   Roman historian of the "Silver Age," his greatest works were *The Histories* and *The Annals.*

third-century crisis   Period from A.D. 235 to 284, when the Roman Empire suffered barbarian invasions, domestic economic problems, plague, assassinations, and urban decline.

Hadrian's Wall

Built in A.D. 122–126, this extensive structure protected Roman England from raids by the tribes of Scotland. It represents the strategy of stationary frontier defense.

(Roy Rainford/Robert Harding World Imagery)

reign was the transfer of power—from the senate to the army and from Italy to the provinces. To extend the Roman frontier in North Africa and western Asia, Septimius expanded the army and improved the pay and conditions of service. These measures might have been necessary, but Septimius went too far by indulging in war with Parthia (197–199)—unnecessary war, because the crumbling Parthian kingdom was too weak to threaten Rome. What the war did accomplish, however, was to inspire the enemy's rejuvenation under a new Eastern dynasty, the Sassanids (SASS-uh-nids).

The Sassanid Persians spearheaded increased pressure on Rome's frontiers. The Sassanids overran Rome's eastern provinces and captured the emperor Valerian himself in 260. (See the box "The Global Record: Syria Between Rome and Persia.") The caravan city of Palmyra (in Syria) took advantage of Rome's weakness to establish independence; its most famous leader was the queen Zenobia. Meanwhile, two Germanic tribes, the Franks and the Goths, hammered the empire from the northwest and northeast.

Fending off invasions at opposite fronts stretched Rome to the breaking point. To pay for defense, the em-

perors devalued the currency, but the result was massive inflation. As if this were not bad enough, a plague broke out in Egypt at midcentury and raged through the empire for fifteen years, compounding Rome's military manpower problems.

Assassinations and civil wars shook the stability of the government. Between 235—when the last Severan emperor, Severus Alexander, was murdered—and 284, twenty men were emperor, however briefly in some cases. Civilians suffered in the resulting disorder.

Yet the empire rebounded, which is a tribute to Roman resilience as well as a sign of the disunity and lack of staying power among the empire's enemies. Recovery began during the reign of Gallienus (r. 253–268), who ended the Frankish threat and nearly polished off the Goths. By 275 Aurelian (r. 270–275) had defeated the Goths and reconquered the eastern provinces, including Palmyra. Gallienus excluded senators from high military commands and replaced them with professionals. Moreover, he began a new, more modest policy of border defense. The Romans now conceded much of the frontier to the enemy and shifted to a defensive mode: fortified cities near the frontier served as bases

SYRIA BETWEEN ROME AND PERSIA

Rome and Persia fought three great battles in western Asia in A.D. 244, 252, and 260, all resounding victories for Persia under King Shapur I (r. ca. 241–272). In the first selection Shapur celebrates his success in an inscription carved in rock near Persepolis. The second selection provides a Greek view of what Syria's inhabitants endured when Shapur "burned, ruined and pillaged" in A.D. 252. It comes from the Thirteenth Sibylline Oracle, a verse commentary on contemporary events, purporting to be ancient prophecy.

The Persian Inscription

I, the Mazda worshipping lord Shapur, king of kings of Iran and non-Iran, whose lineage is from the Gods. . . .

When at first we had become established in the empire, Gordian Caesar raised in all of the Roman Empire a force from the Goth and German realms and marched on Babylonia against the Empire of Iran and against us. On the border of Babylonia at Misikhe, a great "frontal" battle occurred. Gordian Caesar was killed and the Roman force was destroyed. And the Romans made Philip Caesar. Then Philip Caesar came to us for terms, and to ransom their lives, gave us 500,000 denars, and became tributary to us. . . .

And Caesar lied again and did wrong to Armenia. Then we attacked the Roman Empire and annihilated at Barbalissos a Roman force of 60,000 and Syria and the environs of Syria we burned, ruined and pillaged all. In this one campaign we conquered of the Roman Empire fortresses and towns . . . a total of 37 towns with surroundings.

In the third campaign when we attacked Carrhae and Urhai [Edessa] and were besieging Carrhae and Edessa Valerian Caesar marched against us. He had with him a force of 70,000. . . .

And beyond Carrhae and Edessa we had a great battle with Valerian Caesar. We made prisoner ourselves with our own hands Valerian Caesar and the others, chiefs of that army, the praetorian prefect, senators; we made all prisoners and deported them to Persis.

And Syria, Cilicia and Cappadocia we burned, ruined and pillaged. . . .

And men of the Roman Empire, of non-Iranians, we deported. We settled them in the Empire of Iran. . . .

We searched out for conquest many other lands, and we acquired fame for heroism, which we have not engraved here, except for the preceding. We ordered it written so that whoever comes after us may know this fame, heroism, and power of us.

The Sibylline Oracle

. . . the evil Persians . . .

. . . the Persians, arrogant men . . .

. . . the arrow-shooting Persians . . . Now for you, wretched Syria, I have lately been piteously lamenting; a blow will befall you from the arrow-shooting men, terrible, which you never thought would come to you. The fugitive of Rome will come, waving a great spear; crossing the Euphrates with many myriads, he will burn you, he will dispose all things evilly. Alas, Antioch, they will never call you a city when you have fallen under the spear in your folly; he will leave you entirely ruined and naked, houseless, uninhabited; anyone seeing you will suddenly break out weeping. . . .

Alas . . . they will leave ruin as far as the borders of Asia, stripping the cities, taking the statues of all and razing the temples down to the all-nourishing earth.

QUESTIONS

1. According to Shapur's inscription, what were Rome's misdeeds toward Persia? According to the *Sibylline Oracle,* what were Persia's misdeeds toward Rome?

2. How did Persia retaliate, according to Shapur's inscription and according to the *Sibylline Oracle?* How and why do the two accounts differ?

3. Which account do you find more convincing? Why?

Source: Inscription: Richard N. Frye, trans., *History of Ancient Iran* (Munich: C. H. Beck's che Verlagsbuchhandlung, 1984), pp. 371–372. Reprinted by permission of Richard N. Frye. Oracle: D. S. Potter, trans., *Prophecy and History in the Crisis of the Roman Empire* (Oxford: Clarendon Press, 1990), p. 175.

---

from which to prevent deeper enemy penetration into Roman territory. They also concentrated mobile armies at strategic points in the rear, moving them where needed.

Gallienus's reforms pointed the way to imperial reorganization, but they remained to be completed by the two great reforming emperors at the end of the third century and the beginning of the fourth: Diocletian (r. 284–305) and Constantine (r. 306–337), subjects of the next chapter. When their work was done, the new Roman Empire of Late Antiquity might have been barely recognizable to a citizen of the Principate.

S E C T I O N   S U M M A R Y

- The Flavian dynasty (A.D. 69–96) and the so-called Five Good Emperors (96–180) brought Rome a long era of stability and good government.

- A modest prosperity, an upturn in trade, and a flourishing city life all characterized the Roman Empire of the first two centuries A.D.

- Most of the empire's 50–100 million inhabitants lived in the countryside and had little contact with Rome, but the urban elite often adopted Roman ways.

- Pragmatic, orderly, and relatively fair, Roman law is one of antiquity's great legacies.

- The historian Tacitus, the poet Juvenal, the essayist and scholar Plutarch, and the man of letters and philosophy Seneca the Younger are among the great writers of Rome's so-called Silver Age.

- Invasions, plague, inflation, crime, and political assassination were among the many woes that made the third century A.D. a period of crisis for the Roman Empire.

EARLY CHRISTIANITY

What were the origins of Christianity, and how did it fare among the other religions of the Roman world?

Increasing contact between Rome and its western provinces served to plant Roman cities, Roman law, and the Latin language (or its derivatives) in western Europe. As Rome in turn owed much to other Mediterranean peoples, it may be said that the Roman Empire was a vessel that transported ancient Mediterranean civilization to northern and western Europe. No feature of that civilization was to have a greater historical impact than the religion born in Tiberius's reign: Christianity.

Christianity began in the provincial backwater of Palestine among the Jews, whose language, Aramaic, was understood by few in Rome. It immediately spread to speakers of the two main languages of the empire, Greek and Latin, and the new movement addressed the common spiritual needs of the Roman world. By the reign of Diocletian, Christians had grown from Jesus's twelve original followers to perhaps millions, despite government persecution (see Map 6.2 on page 173). In the fourth century A.D., Christianity unexpectedly became the official religion of the entire Roman Empire, replacing polytheism—one of the most momentous changes in Mediterranean history. We turn to that change in the next chapter; here we consider the career of Jesus and the early spread of the Christian Gospel (literally, "Good Tidings"). But first, to set the stage, we look at other religions of the Roman Empire.

MYSTERY RELIGIONS

The Romans were polytheists. They did not try to impose a single, unified religion on the empire. Instead, Romans were usually willing to admit new gods to their pantheon, as long as their worshipers took part in the patriotic emperor cult. Roman conservatism, moreover, engendered respect for other peoples' traditional faiths. Although Roman authorities had tried occasionally to expel these faiths from the city itself, the spread of new religions during the first three centuries A.D. proved irresistible. Besides Christianity and Judaism, the most important religions were Greek mystery cults, the cults of Isis and Mithras, and Manichaeism. These religions displayed a tendency toward syncretism, often borrowing rites, doctrines, and symbols from one another.

Greek mystery cults included the cults of Dionysus, the god of wine, and of Demeter, the goddess of grain, who was worshiped at annual ceremonies at Eleusis, a town outside Athens. The "mystery" consisted of secret rites revealed only to initiates. In the case of Demeter, the rites apparently had something to do with the promise of eternal life.

The cult of Isis derived from the ancient Egyptians' worship of Isis (see page 116), her brother and husband, Osiris, and their son, Horus. Like the cult of Demeter, its central theme was eternal life, through the promise of resurrection achieved by moral behavior in this life. Isis, the "Goddess of Ten Thousand Names," was portrayed as a loving mother, and elements of Isis were later syncretized in the cult of the Virgin Mary. Her followers were known to march in colorful, and at times terrifying, parades through Roman streets, flagellating themselves as a sign of penitence.

Online Study Center **Improve Your Grade**
Primary Source: Mystery Revealed: The Promise of Rebirth of the Goddess Isis

Although men joined in the worship of Isis, the cult appealed particularly to women. The goddess's popularity crossed class lines; devotees ranged from slaves to one Julia Felix, whose estate at Pompeii included a garden shrine to Isis and Egyptian statuettes. By contrast, the worship of Mithras (MYTH-rus) was dominated by men, and especially by soldiers. Mithras, a heroic Persian god of light and truth, also promised eternal life. His worshipers believed that Mithras had captured and killed a sacred bull whose blood and body were the source of life. Accordingly, Mithraism focused on bull sacrifice carried out in a vaulted, cavelike temple called a *Mithraeum*. Initiates were baptized with bull blood and participated in various other rituals, among them a sacramental meal. Their moral code advised imitating the life of their hero.

Manichaeism (MAN-ih-kee-izm) also originated in Persia, but later, in the third century A.D. Its founder, the Persian priest Mani, was martyred by conservative religious authorities. Manichaeism attempted to be the

Mithraeum

This sculpted relief comes from an underground sanctuary along the Rhine frontier. It shows the hero-god Mithras sacrificing a bull, the central symbol of Mithraism. Actual bull sacrifices were carried out in temples known as Mithraea. *(Private Collection)*

true synthesis of the religious beliefs of the period, recognizing not only Jesus but also Zoroaster and Buddha as prophets. The main tenet of Manichaeism was philosophical dualism, which emphasized the universal struggle between good (Light) and evil (Darkness). According to believers, the world had been corrupted by Darkness, but eventually the Light would return. In the meantime, good Manichaeans were to attempt to lead pure lives. Manichaeism was a powerful religious force for two centuries, and its believers were spread as far as India. The great theologian Augustine even flirted with it before becoming a Christian.

A new philosophy that developed in the same intellectual world as these Roman religions was Neo-Platonism (nee-oh-PLAY-ton-ism), which was founded by Plotinus (ploh-TIE-nus) (A.D. 209–270). Using the works of Plato as a starting point, Plotinus developed a philosophy in which the individual could first seek inner unity and then achieve oneness with the supreme unity of what Plotinus called the One or the Good. By this he meant an intangible and impersonal force that is the source of all values. Like the mystery cults, Plotinus's philosophy was difficult to understand, but it promised a kind of salvation. Neo-Platonism was destined to have a great influence on Western thought.

JESUS OF NAZARETH

Christianity begins with **Jesus of Nazareth.** For all its historical importance, Jesus's life is poorly documented. The main source of information about it is the New Testament books of Matthew, Mark, Luke, and John. Jesus left no writings of his own. Early Christians, however, wrote a great deal. Between the second and fourth centuries A.D., Christians settled on a holy book consisting of both the Hebrew Bible, called the "Old Testament" by Christians, and a collection of writings about Jesus and his followers, called the "New Testament." The account of the Gospel according to Mark, probably the earliest Gospel, was most likely written about forty years after Jesus's crucifixion; several of the letters written by Paul of Tarsus (see page 175) date from the 40s A.D.; and the earliest non-Christian sources are later in date and are scanty. In 2002 some archaeologists thought that they had found new documentation of Jesus in the form of an ancient burial box supposed to have held the bones of Jesus's brother, James. But the box has been judged a fake by most experts.

No personality has generated as much discussion among Western scholars as has Jesus. Many would distinguish the Jesus of theology, the object of faith, from the Jesus of history, the figure who really lived in first-century Palestine. Recent work argues that the historical Jesus must be understood within the Judaism of his day. He was a product of the popular culture of the Palestinian countryside, a culture that was peasant and oral. Much of what the Gospels have to say about Jesus, some argue, must be rejected as later invention. These are controversial points, but many scholars would agree with one thing: we must be careful to avoid anachronism. By A.D. 200 two new religions had emerged: Orthodox Christianity and **rabbinic Judaism.** The proponents of both religions claimed to be the rightful heirs of the biblical covenant. They engendered new perspectives that have colored the way Christians and Jews envisage the past before 200. The following account of Jesus seeks a middle ground among today's schools of interpretation.

The Jewish Background   Jesus was born a Jew. A speaker of Aramaic, he may also have known at least some Greek, widely spoken by both Jews and non-Jews in the several Hellenized cities of Palestine. To his followers, Jesus was Christ—"the anointed one" (from the Greek *Christos*), the man anointed with oil and thus marked as the king of Israel. They considered him the Messiah (from the Hebrew for "anointed one"), foretold in the Hebrew Bible, who would redeem the children of Israel and initiate the kingdom of heaven. The dynamism and popularity of his teachings led to a clash with Jewish and Roman authorities in Jerusalem, the capital city of Judea, and to his crucifixion. His mission began, however, in a corner of the Jewish world, in the northern region of Galilee (GAL-uh-lee), where he lived in the town of Nazareth (NAZ-uh-reth) (see inset, **MAP 6.2**).

Jesus was probably born not long before the death in 4 B.C. of Herod, the Roman-installed client-king of Judea. (The date of A.D. 1 for Jesus's birth, a mistaken calculation of Late Antiquity, does not accord with the data of the New Testament.) At around age 30, Jesus was baptized by the mysterious preacher John the Baptist. Soon afterward Herod Antipas, the Romans' client-king of Galilee, ordered the execution of John. John had preached that God's kingdom was about to arrive—a time of universal perfection and an end of misery. In preparation, sinful humankind needed to repent. Just how much influence John had on Jesus is a matter of debate, as is the question of John's relationship to the religious community of the Essenes. Debate may be appropriate, for Judaism in the first century A.D. was in a state of creative disagreement. This era en-

Jesus of Nazareth   Founder of Christianity. To his followers, he was Christ, "the anointed one," foretold in the Hebrew Bible as the redeemer of Israel who would initiate the kingdom of heaven.

rabbinic Judaism   Main form of Judaism, which emerged during the first century A.D. under the leadership of the rabbis. It clarified Jewish practice, elevated the oral law to equal authority with the written Torah, and enabled Judaism to evolve flexibly.

MAP 6.2   The Expansion of Christianity to A.D. 200

After its origin in Palestine, early Christianity found its main centers in the Greek-speaking cities of the Roman East. Missionaries such as Paul also brought the new faith to the Latin-speaking West, as well as to Ethiopia and Mesopotamia.

dorsed no one normative Judaism but rather a variety of Judaisms.

The Essenes lived apart from society in pursuit of a new covenant with God. The community at Qumran in the Judean desert, whose history is documented in the Dead Sea Scrolls, ancient texts discovered in 1947, was probably Essene. The tenets of Qumran included frugality, sharing, participating in a sacred communal meal, and avoiding oath-taking. Adherents anticipated the coming of the Messiah and an end of days in which God would punish the wicked. Although Essene doctrine has much in common with early Christianity, early Christians did not withdraw from the world as the Essenes did but instead faced it.

Jesus's Teaching   There are both similarities and differences between Jesus's teaching and contemporary

doctrines of Palestinian Judaism. The most popular group among Palestinian Jews, the Pharisees, focused on the spiritual needs of ordinary folk (see page 117). The Pharisees believed that law was central to Judaism but argued that it could be interpreted flexibly, in light of the oral tradition that had grown up alongside the written text of the Hebrew Bible. The Pharisees emphasized charity toward the poor and spoke in parables—vivid allegories that made their teaching accessible.

Jesus argued similarly. Like the Pharisees, he strongly criticized the pillar of the Jewish establishment, the Sadducees, the priests and wealthy men who saw the Temple at Jerusalem and its rites as the heart of Judaism. Also like the Pharisees, Jesus rejected the growing movement of the Zealots (ZELL-ots), advocates of revolt against Roman rule, although there were Zealots among his followers. Yet Jesus was neither a

The Good Shepherd
This ceiling painting comes from a Christian catacomb in Rome dating before A.D. 284. The pastoral image, common in the early church, recalls Christ's ministry. It symbolizes both his beneficence and his sacrifice, as well as his closeness to ordinary people.
(Scala/Art Resource, NY)

Pharisee nor an Essene. His teaching went further than the Pharisees' in rejecting the need to follow the letter of biblical law. Inward purity became the key principle, as reflected in Jesus's statement to his disciples (that is, his close followers): "Whoever does not accept the kingdom of God like a child will never enter it" (Mark 10:15). Only an adult could become expert in biblical law, but it is probably easier for a child than for an adult to attain spiritual innocence.

Jesus argued that the kingdom of God, which John the Baptist had said was coming soon, was actually already beginning to arrive. Moreover, Jesus said that he himself, acting through the direct order of God, could forgive sins. He emphasized the notion of God as a loving and forgiving father. He often spoke in parables and announced himself through miracles, particularly faith healing. He welcomed marginalized groups, including prostitutes and lepers.

Jesus's teaching is typified in the Sermon on the Mount, addressed to his many followers in Galilee. He praised the poor and the humble and scorned the pursuit of wealth instead of righteousness. He called for generosity and forgiveness, recalling the traditional Jewish golden rule—to treat others as one would like to

be treated. He said that prayer, fasting, and acts of charity should be conducted in private, not in public, in order to emphasize purity of motive. He called on his followers to endure persecution in order to spread his teachings: "You are light for all the world," he told them.

Online Study Center **Improve Your Grade**
Primary Source: The Gospel According to Matthew:
The Sermon on the Mount

Jesus spoke with conviction and persuasiveness—with "authority," as his followers said. In Galilee they greeted him as king. For some this was a purely spiritual designation; others planned an overthrow of Roman rule, although Jesus rejected that course of action. In any case, his teachings won him hostility from some Pharisees, who considered his claim to be able to forgive sins blasphemous, and from Sadducees stung by his criticisms. Neither group accepted Jesus as the Messiah. It should be emphasized, nevertheless, that most of Jesus's followers were Jewish.

Jesus in Jerusalem   Jesus challenged central authority by going to Jerusalem and teaching and healing in the Temple under the eyes of the priests whom he criticized. Nor did he confine his opposition to words: he drove merchants and moneychangers away from the Temple precincts by overturning their tables and perhaps even threatening them with a whip. Jesus attracted large crowds of followers, at least some of whom were armed. Sadducee authorities feared trouble, and so did the overlords of Judea, the Romans. The governor, Pilate (Pontius Pilatus), had already endured vehement Jewish objections to the display in Jerusalem of an imperial medallion and of an inscription that seems to have asserted Augustus's divinity. Pilate had no need of further uproar. Temple police and Roman soldiers were called on to arrest Jesus quietly.

Jesus's subsequent trial and execution have always been controversial. The New Testament emphasizes the role of the Jewish leadership and the Jerusalem mob in Jesus's death. Written after the First Jewish Revolt (A.D. 66–70), however, the Gospels may reflect anti-Jewish sentiment in the empire. Crucifixion, the method used to execute Jesus, was a Roman penalty (the traditional Jewish method was stoning), and Jesus was executed by Romans, not Jews. Jesus probably appeared in informal and hurried proceedings before both the Jewish Council and Pilate. He suffered slow death by crucifixion on Golgotha (Calvary) Hill, just outside the city. It was a spring Friday, on the eve of the Passover festival, around A.D. 30.

PAUL OF TARSUS

According to the Gospel writers, Jesus died on a Friday and rose from the dead on Sunday, an event commemorated by Christians at Easter. He is said to have then spent forty days on earth, cheering and commissioning his disciples in Galilee and working miracles, before finally ascending to heaven. Heartened, the disciples returned to Jerusalem and spread Jesus's teachings.

The Apostles   Jesus's followers preached in synagogues, private households, and even the Temple, and to speakers of Greek as well as of Aramaic. Their movement spread in the 30s and 40s A.D. throughout Palestine and into Syria. In Jerusalem Christians were known as Nazarenes—that is, followers of Jesus of Nazareth; it was at Antioch that they were first called "men of Christ" (*christianoi*).

The leaders of the movement were known as apostles, from the Greek *apostolos,* "one who is sent" and who enjoys the authority of the sender. The apostles believed that Jesus had sent them and given them authority. The apostles included Jesus's twelve original followers, or disciples. The most prominent disciple was Peter, a Galilean fisherman whom Jesus endowed with particular authority. After the crucifixion, Peter became a miracle-worker and leading apostle. According to a reliable tradition, he went to Rome, whose church he headed and where he died as a martyr in A.D. 64.

Paul's Faith   It was not clear at first that Christians would form a new religion separate from Judaism. Although the Sadducees and Jewish civil officials were hostile, Christians found much support among the Pharisees. Some Christians, however, contemplated a radical break; among them no one was more important than **Paul of Tarsus** (d. A.D. 67?). Only Jesus himself played a greater role than Paul in the foundation of Christianity. A remarkable figure, Paul embodied three different and interlocking worlds. Born with the name of Saul, he was a Jew of the Diaspora from the southern Anatolian city of Tarsus. A learned Pharisee, Paul was a native speaker of Aramaic and knew Hebrew and Greek. His father was one of the few Jews to attain Roman citizenship, a privilege that Paul inherited. Paul's heritage speaks volumes about the variety of the Roman peace, and his religious odyssey speaks volumes more (see Map 6.2).

At first Paul joined in the persecution of the Christians, whom he considered blasphemous. Around A.D. 36, however, he claimed to see a blinding light on the road to Damascus, a vision of Jesus that convinced him to change from persecutor to believer. It was a complete turnaround, a *conversio* ("conversion"), to use the Latin word that would grow so important in years to come. Saul changed his name to Paul and became a Christian.

He also changed what being a Christian meant. The key to Paul's faith was not so much Jesus's life, although that was a model for Christian ethics, as it was Jesus's death and resurrection. Jesus's fate, Paul wrote, offered all humanity the hope of resurrection, redemption, and salvation. Paul retained his belief in Jewish morality and ethics but not in the rules of Jewish law. Following the law, no matter how carefully, would not lead to salvation; only faith in Jesus as Messiah would.

Such doctrines bespoke a break with Judaism, as did Paul's attitudes toward converts. Hellenistic Judaism had long reached out to Gentiles. Some became Jews. Others, scattered throughout the cities of the Roman Empire, were known as "God-fearers"—that is, they accepted the moral teachings of Judaism but refrained from following strict dietary laws, circumcision, and other Jewish rituals. Seneca the Younger, writing in the 60s, complains about the spread of Judaism: "The customs of this accursed race have gained such influence that they are now received throughout the world."[3]

The Jerusalem church baptized converts and considered them Jews, but Paul considered them not Jews but

Paul of Tarsus   Christian apostle and saint, under whom Christianity began its complete separation from Judaism.

converts in Christ. For Pauline Christians, circumcision, dietary laws, and strict observance of the Sabbath were irrelevant. From the late forties to the early sixties A.D., Paul tirelessly undertook missionary journeys through the cities of the Roman East and to Rome itself. He aimed to convert Gentiles, and so he did, but many of his followers were Hellenized Jews and "God-fearers."

Judaism Paul started Christianity on the road to complete separation from Judaism. Events over the next century widened the division. First, while Pauline churches prospered, departing ever more from Jewish customs, the Jerusalem church was decimated. Jewish authorities persecuted its leaders, and after Rome's suppression of the First Jewish Revolt and destruction of the Jerusalem Temple in A.D. 70, the rank and file of Palestinian Jews rallied to the Pharisees. Second, Jews and Christians competing for converts emphasized their respective differences. Third, although many Jews made their peace with Rome in A.D. 70, enough Jewish-Roman hostility remained to lead to uprisings in the Diaspora in 115 and to the Second Jewish Revolt in 132 to 135. Both were suppressed mercilessly by Rome, and Judaism became ever more stigmatized among Gentiles.

Bereft of the Temple at Jerusalem, Judaism nonetheless continued to prosper as a religion. Indeed, Jewish missionary activities continued, although they did not keep pace with the number of converts gained by Christianity. More striking is the emergence of the rabbis (the religious leaders of the Pharisees) as the mentors of Judaism. Popular among Jews, the rabbis also attracted the Romans because most rabbis opposed revolt. After both A.D. 70 and 135, the Romans made the rabbis responsible for Jewish self-government in Palestine. The rabbis left their mark on history, however, not in administration but in an intellectual movement. Continuing in the tradition of the Pharisees, the rabbis amplified the oral law—that is, they wrote interpretations of the Hebrew Bible that clarified the practice of Judaism. They developed the notion of the "dual Torah," elevating the oral law to equal authority with the written law of the Hebrew Bible. The notion legitimized the rabbis' enterprise, which made it possible for Judaism to evolve flexibly. The basic text of rabbinic Judaism is the Mishnah (MISH-nuh) (ca. A.D. 200), a study of Jewish law. In rabbinic Judaism lies the basis of the medieval and modern forms of the Jewish religion.[4]

EXPANSION, DIVERGENCE, AND PERSECUTION

Although Jesus's mission was mainly in the countryside, early Christianity quickly became primarily an urban movement. Through missionary activity and word of mouth, the religion slowly spread. It was concentrated in the Greek-speaking East, but by the second century A.D. Christian communities dotted North Africa and Gaul and, beyond Roman boundaries, appeared in Parthian Iraq and in Ethiopia (see Map 6.2).

By around A.D. 200, an orthodox (Greek for "right-thinking") **Christianity** had emerged. Rooted in Judaism, it was nonetheless a distinct and separate religion that found most of its supporters among Gentiles. A simple "rule of faith," emphasizing the belief in one God and the mission of his son, Jesus, as savior, united Christians from one end of the empire to the other. Christianity attracted both rich and poor, male and female; its primary appeal was to ordinary, moderately prosperous city folk. Believers could take comfort from the prospect of salvation in the next world and in a caring community in the here and now. Christians emphasized charity and help for the needy, qualities all too often absent in Greco-Roman society. A Christian writer justly described a pagan's amazed comment on Christian behavior: "Look how they love each other." Most early Christians expected Christ's return—and the inauguration of the heavenly kingdom—to be imminent.

Early churches were simple and relatively informal congregations that gathered for regular meetings. The liturgy, or service, consisted of readings from the Scriptures (the Old and New Testaments), teaching, praying, and singing hymns. Baptism was used to initiate converts. The Lord's Supper, a communal meal in memory of Jesus, was a major ritual. The most important parts of the meal were the breaking and distribution of bread at the beginning and the passing of a cup of wine at the end; these recalled the body and blood of Christ. As organizational structures emerged (see pages 188–189), churches in different cities were in frequent contact with one another, discussing common concerns and coordinating doctrine and practice.

Just as Jewish women were not rabbis, so early Christian women did not hold the priesthood. Jewish women, however, did hold office in the synagogue, and Christian women likewise served as deaconesses. Both endowed buildings and institutions. For example, consider the Italian Jewish woman Caelia Paterna, an officeholder honored by her congregation as "mother of the synagogue of the people of Brescia." Or the two Christian deaconesses, both slaves, whom Pliny the Younger tortured during his governorship of the Anatolian province of Bithynia (buh-THIN-ee-uh) in about A.D. 110 in an attempt to extract information about the worrisome new cult. Deaconesses played an active part in church charities and counseling and now and then preached sermons.

Christianity Sect originally rooted in Judaism that emerged as a fully separate religion by around A.D. 200. It emphasized belief in one God and the mission of his son, Jesus of Nazareth, as savior.

As Christianity spread, its troubles with the authorities deepened. For one thing, Christians met in small groups, a kind of assembly that conservative Romans had long suspected as a potential source of sedition. More troubling, however, was Christians' refusal to make sacrifices to the emperor. The Romans expected all subjects to make such sacrifices as a sign of patriotism. The only exception was the Jews, who were permitted to forgo the imperial cult because their ancestral religion prohibited them from worshiping idols. The Christians, however, were a new group, and the Romans distrusted novelty.

As a result, the emperors considered Christianity at best a nuisance and at worst a threat. Christians were tested from time to time by being asked to sacrifice to the emperor; those who failed to do so might be executed, sometimes in the arena. More often, however, the Romans tacitly tolerated Christians as long as they kept their religion private. Christians could not proselytize in public places, put up inscriptions or monuments, or build churches. Christianity thus spread under severe restrictions, but spread it did, particularly in the cities of the East. The willingness of martyrs to die for the faith made a strong impression on potential converts. Although the number of Christians in the empire is not known, it is clear that by the late third century they were a significant and growing minority.

SECTION SUMMARY

- The cult of Demeter, the cult of Isis, Mithraism, and Manichaeism are among the mystery religions that spread in the Roman Empire during the first three centuries A.D.

- Jesus was born a Jew and was hailed by his followers as the Messiah or redeemer foretold in the Hebrew Bible.

- Jesus's teachings emphasized purity of soul, humility, charity, and the endurance of persecution to spread the word.

- Paul of Tarsus played an enormous role in spreading faith in Jesus outside the Jewish world, but Christianity took a long time to separate from its Jewish roots.

- By around A.D. 200 Orthodox Christianity had emerged as a systematic set of beliefs and a fully distinct religion from Judaism.

- The Roman peace provided the conditions for the spread of Christianity.

CHAPTER SUMMARY

Online Study Center **ACE the Test**

How did Augustus establish a new imperial government to replace the Roman Republic? Why was he so successful?

What was life like in the era of the Roman peace? Why did peace end during the third century A.D.?

What were the origins of Christianity, and how did it fare among the other religions of the Roman world?

The Roman Republic collapsed under the weight of political maneuvering, judicial murders, gang skirmishes, and civil war. A shrewd and sickly outsider, Octavian, confounded expectations by creating a new empire that would enjoy two centuries of stability; as Augustus, he served as its first emperor. Augustus reconciled the senatorial class by sharing a degree of power, but he guaranteed peace by keeping most of the armies in his own hands. He wisely reduced military spending and compromised with Rome's enemies to stabilize the frontiers. He solved the problem of rebellious soldiers by raising taxes to provide farms for veterans. Perhaps most important, he began a new policy toward the provinces, which were slowly raised to equality with Italy. In short, Augustus initiated the prosperous Roman peace. Under imperial patronage, culture flourished in the Augustan Age, including such writers as Virgil, Horace, and Livy. Augustus's successors, the Julio-Claudian emperors, included scandalous figures like Nero, but nevertheless they delivered peaceful and effective government.

The Flavian dynasty (A.D. 69–96) and the so-called Five Good Emperors (96–180) brought Rome a long era of stability and good government. In the provinces, the Roman peace made possible an era of architectural and literary flowering. It was a prosperous era but not for everyone, as slavery remained widespread. Rome was a multi-ethnic empire whose inhabitants increasingly mixed with one another and exchanged ideas. Latin literature flourished in its so-called Silver Age, and so did

the practical and relatively fair-minded system that was Roman law, one of antiquity's greatest legacies. The Roman peace did not last forever: invasions, plague, inflation, crime, and political assassination were among the many woes that made the third century A.D. a period of crisis for the Roman Empire.

The cult of Demeter, the cult of Isis, Mithraism, and Manichaeism are among the mystery religions that spread in the Roman Empire during the first three centuries A.D. But the most important religion of the empire turned out to be Christianity, which began with Jesus of Nazareth. Born a Jew and hailed by his followers as the Messiah, Jesus taught humility, charity, and endurance of persecution to spread the word. The most important early Christian was Paul of Tarsus, who spread faith of Jesus outside the Jewish world. By around A.D. 200 Christianity had emerged as a systematic and fully distinct religion from Judaism.

LOOKING AHEAD

To survive the crisis of the third century, it was necessary for Rome to maintain a bigger army supported by higher taxes collected by a larger bureaucracy—requirements that would shake the social, political, and cultural foundations of the empire. The most momentous consequence was the emergence of Christianity as Rome's official religion, as Chapter 7 discusses.

KEY TERMS

Augustus (p. 154)

Principate (p. 154)

Virgil (p. 157)

Livia (p. 158)

Julio-Claudians (p. 159)

pax Romana (p. 161)

Flavians (p. 161)

Tacitus (p. 167)

third-century crisis (p. 167)

Jesus of Nazareth (p. 172)

rabbinic Judaism (p. 172)

Paul of Tarsus (p. 175)

Christianity (p. 176)

Online Study Center
Improve Your Grade Flashcards

SUGGESTED READING

Adkins, Leslie, and Roy A. Adkins. *Handbook to Life in Ancient Rome*. 1998. An excellent reference book, arranged thematically, by two archaeologists.

Earl, D. C. *The Age of Augustus*. 1968. A beautifully illustrated introduction to government, society, and religion.

Fantham, Elaine, Helene Peet Foley, Natalie Boymel Kampen, Sarah B. Pomeroy, and H. A. Shapiro.

Women in the Classical World: Image and Text. 1994. Chapters 10–13 provide an excellent introduction to the social and cultural history of women in the Roman Empire.

Meier, John P. *A Marginal Jew: Rethinking the Historical Jesus*. 3 vols. 1991–2001. An excellent and thorough introduction that combines superb scholarship with readability.

Meijer, Fik. *The Gladiators, History's Most Dangerous Sport.* 2005. A good introduction by a leading scholar.

Panetta, Marisa Ranieri. *Pompeii: The History, Life, and Art of the Buried City.* 2004. Gorgeous photos and an expert text make this an alluring introduction to antiquity's greatest dead city.

Ramage, Nancy H., and Andrew Ramage. *Roman Art.* 3d ed. 2004. An excellent introductory text, especially good on the Roman Empire.

Wells, Colin. *The Roman Empire.* 2d ed. 1995. A sweeping, lively, and thoughtful overview of the subject from 44 B.C. to A.D. 235.

NOTES

1. Mary R. Lefkowitz and Maureen B. Fant, trans., *Women's Life in Greece & Rome: A Source Book in Translation,* 2d ed. (Baltimore: Johns Hopkins University Press, 1992), p. 9.

2. This discussion of marriage and law owes much to Susanne Dixon, *The Roman Family* (Baltimore: Johns Hopkins University Press, 1992), pp. 36–60.

3. Seneca, *De Superstitione,* trans. Menachem Stern, in *Greek and Latin Authors on Jews and Judaism,* vol. 1 (Jerusalem: Israel Academy of Sciences and Humanities, 1976), p. 431.

4. On these points, see Lawrence H. Schiffman, *From Text to Tradition: A History of Second Temple and Rabbinic Judaism* (Hoboken, N.J.: Ktav Publishing House, 1991), pp. 1–16.

THE WORLD OF LATE ANTIQUITY, 284–CA. 600

Santa Maria Maggiore
Santa Maria Maggiore (or Saint Mary Major) looks today much as it did when it was built. It was Rome's first church dedicated to Mary, the mother of Jesus.
(Erich Lessing/Art Resource, NY)

The magnificent church of Santa Maria Maggiore in Rome was dedicated by Pope Sixtus III in 432. This building encapsulates many of the themes we shall encounter in this chapter. How is it that a pope, a Christian bishop, had the power and resources to construct such a building in the empire's capital? For centuries only emperors had built on such a scale. In architectural form the building is a basilica, the traditional name for the rectangular halls that served the Romans well for public business. Now the Christian church was adapting an old Roman form to its own purposes. Moreover, the beautiful mosaics and frescoes reveal ways in which the church was adapting Roman crafts and artistic motifs to its needs. In 410 Rome was sacked by barbarians and yet, within twenty years, the city's resources had rebounded sufficiently to make a building like this possible. In other words, this building itself testifies to the profound processes of continuity and change that are the hallmarks of Late Antiquity.

The reigns of Diocletian (284–305) and Constantine (306–337) inaugurated a period that scholars now label "Late Antiquity." For many years educated people, often taking their lead from the elegant and influential *Decline and Fall of the Roman Empire* by the British historian Edward Gibbon (1737–1794), believed that, beset by insurmountable problems, the Roman Empire "fell" in the fifth century. With that fall, such a view insisted, the glories of classical civilization gave way to the gloom of the "Dark Ages." Today, on the contrary, specialists in the period from roughly 300 to 600 see vigor and achievement. They emphasize continuity and coherence over calamity and collapse. No one denies that the Roman world of 600 was different from the Roman world of 300. But recent scholarship stresses how the Romans themselves created a stable framework for change. No catastrophic time, place, or event marked the "fall of Rome."

From the time of its founding, the Roman Empire had suffered from various structural problems. In particular, the Roman world was vast geographically and diverse in its human and material resources. Changes were inevitable in such a world. This chapter identifies the most important changes that took place while the Roman Empire was evolving into its medieval European, Byzantine, and Muslim successors.

CHAPTER OUTLINE

REBUILDING THE ROMAN EMPIRE, 284–395

THE CATHOLIC CHURCH AND THE ROMAN EMPIRE, 313–604

THE RISE OF GERMANIC KINGDOMS IN THE WEST, CA. 370–530

THE ROMAN EMPIRE IN THE EAST, 395–565

SOCIETY AND CULTURE IN LATE ANTIQUITY

KEY TERMS

tetrarchy	monasticism
Edict of Milan	Visigoths
heresy	Justinian
Arianism	Hagia Sophia
Council of Nicaea	Vulgate Bible
papacy	Augustine of Hippo

Online Study Center

This icon will direct you to interactive map and primary source activities on the website **college.hmco.com/ pic/noble5e**

What were the most important reforms of Diocletian, Constantine, and their successors, and what roles did those reforms play in saving and transforming the empire?

How and why did a Roman and Catholic Church emerge in Late Antiquity?

Who were the "barbarians," and what kinds of relations did Romans and barbarians have in Late Antiquity?

What challenges did the eastern empire face and what were some of its major contributions?

How did women and men, elites and ordinary people, urban dwellers and farmers experience continuity and change in Late Antiquity?

REBUILDING THE ROMAN EMPIRE, 284–395

What were the most important reforms of Diocletian, Constantine, and their successors, and what roles did those reforms play in saving and transforming the empire?

The third-century Roman Empire had lurched from crisis to crisis. Decisive action was needed if Rome was to survive. The chronic civil wars had to be brought to an end. The army needed to be reformed and expanded to meet new threats on the frontiers. And the economy had to be stabilized to bring in the revenue the government needed for administrative and military reforms. Rome was fortunate in raising up two rulers, Diocletian (dy-oh-KLEE-shun) and Constantine, with more than fifty years of rule between them, who understood the empire's problems and legislated energetically to address them. Although these rulers thought of themselves as traditional Romans, they actually initiated a far-reaching transformation of the Roman Empire.

THE REFORMS OF DIOCLETIAN (R. 284–305)

The son of a poor Dalmatian farmer, Diocletian rose through the ranks of the army until he attained a key position in the emperor's elite guards. When the emperor was murdered, the soldiers elevated Diocletian to the imperial office.

In about 293 Diocletian devised a regime that historians call the **tetrarchy** (see **MAP 7.1**). Diocletian intended the tetrarchy (teh-TRAR-kee), "government by four," to address the empire's political instability and huge size, as well as to promote experienced men and

provide an orderly succession to the imperial office. First Diocletian decided to divide the empire into eastern and western halves and then selected an imperial colleague for himself. Ruling from Nicomedia and retaining the position of senior emperor, he took charge of the wealthy and militarily threatened eastern half of the empire. Diocletian and his colleague each selected a subordinate official who would eventually succeed to the imperial office. The advantage of the tetrarchy was that it yielded four men of imperial rank who could lead armies and make decisions in political and administrative matters.

Historians call the regime instituted by Augustus in 31 B.C. the "Principate" (see pages 154–155) because the emperor pretended to be the "first citizen" and heir of the Republican magistrates, even though his real power depended on control of the army. By contrast, Diocletian abandoned all pretense of being a magistrate. Scholars call his regime the "Dominate," from the Latin *Dominus,* meaning "lord and master." Diocletian adopted Eastern, especially Persian, habits, such as wearing a gilded cloak and a jeweled diadem, sprinkling gold dust in his hair, sitting on an elevated throne, rarely appearing in public, and requiring those who approached to prostrate themselves before him. Diocletian succeeded in enhancing the prestige of the imperial office but did so at the price of making the emperor more remote from his subjects.

Given its size and problems, the Roman Empire was dramatically *under*governed. The empire had some fifty provinces, which varied greatly in size, population, wealth, strategic importance, and degree of Romanization, but the imperial administration was made up

tetrarchy Government ruled by four leaders. It was established about 293 by Emperor Diocletian to address the Roman Empire's political instability, huge size, and complexity.

largely of aristocratic amateurs and numbered only a few hundred men when Diocletian ascended the throne. Rome had traditionally asked for relatively little from its empire—primarily taxes, military recruits, and loyalty. Local authorities generally did the tax collecting and military recruiting, with little interference from imperial agents.

Diocletian increased the number of officials and doubled the number of provinces by dividing old, large provinces into smaller ones. He then organized groups of provinces into thirteen dioceses and joined the dioceses into four prefectures. Diocletian subordinated each prefecture to a tetrarch and equipped each prefecture with a force of military, legal, financial, and secretarial officials headed by a praetorian prefect. By 350 the number of officers from the provincial to the prefectorial level had risen from a few hundred to thirty-five or forty thousand. Diocletian wished to fill the bureaucracy with trained administrators instead of with wealthy senators and equestrians, who viewed gov-

284–337	Reforms of Diocletian and Constantine
300–400	Origins and spread of Christian monasticism
324–360	Foundation and development of Constantinople
325–553	First five ecumenical councils of the Christian church
350s–ca. 600	Age of the Church Fathers
370s–530s	Beginnings of the Germanic kingdoms inside the Roman Empire
379–395	Reign of Theodosius I, last emperor of a united empire
408–450	Reign of Theodosius II; consolidation of eastern Roman Empire
410	Visigoths sack Rome
412–418	Visigoths settle in Gaul
429	Vandals begin conquest of North Africa
440–604	Development of the Roman papacy
450–600	Anglo-Saxons settle in Britain
476	Last Roman emperor in the West deposed
481–511	Clovis founds Frankish kingdom
493	Beginning of Ostrogothic kingdom in Italy
527–565	Reign of Justinian I

Tetrarchy

Ideal and reality are both evident in this sculpture of the tetrarchy. The rulers, depicted equal in size, embrace one another but also bare their weapons—to one another and to the world. *(Scala/Art Resource, NY)*

ernment service as a means of enriching themselves and advancing the interests of their families.

Diocletian also attended to Rome's military problems. His major initiative was an attempt to double the size of the army from about 300,000 to 600,000 men, although the final total ended up being only around 450,000. Diocletian also built new forts along the frontiers and improved the roads that supplied frontier defenders. He began the systematic incorporation of barbarians into the army, a step that led to a blurring of the distinction between Romans and barbarians. Military service had long been attractive to people in the empire because it provided Roman citizenship as well as a secure income. After 212 almost every free man in the empire enjoyed automatic citizenship. As a result, mainly noncitizen barbarians living along the frontiers, whose only hope of citizenship was military service, found the army attractive. For a while the army tended to Romanize the barbarians, but as the proportion of barbarian soldiers and officers grew, the culture and ethos of the army began to change.

ARMENIA

Caspian Sea

Tigris

Volga

Don

Dnieper

ARABIAN DESERT

Euphrates

Antioch • SYRIA • Damascus

JUDEA

Petra •

Jerusalem

CAPPADOCIA

Red Sea

Prefecture of Gaul
Prefecture of Italy
Prefecture of Illyricum
Prefecture of the East

CYPRUS

Tarsus •

CILICIA

EGYPT

Nile

CRIMEA

Black Sea

Nicomedia • PHRYGIA
LYDIA
Pergamum • Smyrna • ASIA

RHODES

Alexandria •

Byzantium •

CRETE

THRACE

Athens •

MOESIA

DACIA

MACEDONIA

Corinth •

LIBYA

Cyrene •

Line of division
between east
and west

Mediterranean Sea

PANNONIA

DALMATIA

Adriatic Sea

Brundisium •

GERMANY

NORICUM

RAETIA

Danube

Ravenna •

Po

Tiber Rome •

CISALPINE
GAUL

SICILY

Syracuse •

SAHARA

Elbe

Rhine

North Sea

CORSICA

SARDINIA

Massilia •

NARBONENSIS

Carthage •

NUMIDIA

GAUL

Lyon •

Rhône

BALEARIC IS.

NORTH AFRICA

BRITAIN

400 Mi.

400 Km.

200

200

0

0

Ebro

MAURETANIA

NEARER
SPAIN

*ATLANTIC
OCEAN*

FARTHER
SPAIN

Diocletian's reforms were expensive and required a predictable income. Thus Diocletian attempted to regularize the tax system in the empire. The government conducted a census to identify all taxpayers and assessed the productive value of land. To address the mounting inflation of the third century, Diocletian issued in 302 the Edict of Maximum Prices, which froze the costs of goods. Since senators successfully defended their long-standing exemptions from taxes and the taxation of business ventures remained low, virtually the whole cost of the Roman system continued to fall on agriculture, in particular on small farmers. Diocletian's reform of the tax structure brought in more revenue, but it also caused hardships. A rising tax burden threatened those who were most vulnerable. And with more officials handling vastly greater sums of money, corruption ran rampant. Most people never saw the emperor, but they saw too much of his tax-gouging local minions.

The rationale behind Diocletian's reforms is easy to understand; their results were less easy to anticipate. The actions were costly in three unintended respects: moral, social, and economic. The emperors had always been military dictators, but Diocletian removed all pretense that they served at the behest of the Roman people. His frankness may have enhanced the aura of the imperial office, but it also loosened the ties between the ruler and his subjects. By reducing the official duties of the senatorial order, Diocletian alienated an influential group of about two thousand leading citizens. The enlarged imperial administration necessarily impinged on the autonomy of cities and their local leaders, for three centuries the key components of the imperial system. Finally, the expanded administration and army cost dearly in real cash. That cash had to be extracted from an empire that was in serious economic distress.

THE REFORMS OF CONSTANTINE (R. 306–337)

Diocletian's careful plans for the imperial succession collapsed almost immediately after his voluntary retirement in 305. When Diocletian's Western colleague (Constantius I) died in 306, his troops reverted to the hereditary principle and declared his son, Constantine, emperor. From 306 to 313 as many as six men claimed to be emperor somewhere in the empire. From 313 to 324 Constantine shared rule with one man, and from 324 to 337 he ruled alone over a reunited empire, although he made his sons subordinates in various parts of the empire. This compromise between the hereditary and tetrarchal systems persisted for the next two centuries.

Constantine had entered the imperial court as a young man in 293, when his father was made co-emperor, and he later served with his father in Britain and Gaul. He knew the system well and maintained the administrative structure that Diocletian had introduced. Constantine continued the eastward shift of power by creating a second imperial capital in the East. In 324 he selected an old Greek city, Byzantium (bizz-AN-tee-um), and renamed it after himself, "Constantine's polis" or Constantinople (modern Istanbul). Byzantium's location, more than its size, wealth, or fame, recommended it. The city straddled military roads between the eastern and western halves of the empire, overlooked crucial trade lanes to and from the Black Sea region, and was well sited to respond to threats along both the Balkan and the eastern frontiers (see Map 7.1).

In financial affairs, too, Constantine's work echoed his predecessor's. He issued a new gold *solidus,* the principal money of account in the Roman Empire. This coin promoted monetary stability in the Mediterranean world for nearly a thousand years. Unfortunately, both a stable currency and Diocletian's price controls braked but could not stop the headlong rush of inflation.

In military affairs, Constantine believed that Rome's frontiers stretched too far to be held securely by garrisons, so he expanded the use of mobile field armies. These armies, recruited largely (as under Diocletian) from barbarians living along or beyond the frontiers, were stationed well inside the borderlands so that they could be mobilized and moved quickly to any threatened point. They were given their own command structures, under officers whom the Romans called "Masters of the Soldiers." The praetorian prefects were deprived of their military responsibilities and became exclusively civilian officials. The separation of civilian and military command made sense administratively and politically because it meant that no individual could combine the command of an army with the authority of a government post.

Whereas Diocletian will always be remembered for launching the last persecution of Christianity (303–305), Constantine legalized the new faith. Each man's motivation has evoked scholarly controversy. Diocletian was a Roman of conventional piety, who seems to have been convinced that the presence of Christian soldiers in his army offended the ancestral gods and denied victory to

MAP 7.1   Diocletian's Division of the Roman Empire, 286
Diocletian divided the empire into eastern and western halves; each half was divided into two prefectures. Thus four regions, rulers, and bureaucratic administrations replaced the ineffective rule of one man.

Online Study Center **Improve Your Grade**
Interactive Map: The Roman World Divided

Chi-Rho

the Roman troops. Constantine's mother, Helena, was a devout Christian, and there were Christians in his father's court circle. In 312, while marching toward Rome to fight one of his rivals, Constantine believed that he saw in the sky a cross accompanied by the words "In this sign you shall conquer." Persuaded, Constantine put a chi-rho (from the first two letters of *Christos,* "Christ" in Greek) monogram on his soldiers' uniforms. He defeated his foe at the Milvian Bridge near Rome, and, certain that Christ had assured his victory, he and his Eastern colleague issued the **Edict of Milan** in 313, granting Christianity full legal status in the empire.

Online Study Center **Improve Your Grade**
Primary Source: Religious Toleration for All:
The Edict of Milan

Diocletian's persecution had been harsh and systematic. He ordered churches to be closed and the Scriptures seized, arrested members of the clergy, and required all citizens to make a public act of sacrifice in a temple. Constantine did far more than merely stop the persecution or legalize Christianity. He granted the church tax immunities, exempted the clergy from military and civic obligations, and provided money to replace books and buildings that had been destroyed in the persecution. He and his mother sponsored the construction of impressive churches, such as Saint Peter's in Rome and the Church of the Holy Sepulcher over the traditional site of Christ's tomb in Jerusalem.

Scholars have long debated the strategic and political wisdom of Constantine's arrangements. Moving experienced troops away from the frontiers may have invited rather than deterred attacks. Recruiting barbarians into the field armies and leaving frontier defenses to barbarian auxiliaries may have created divided loyalties and conflicts of interest. Most Roman provincials had not lived near soldiers. Now the soldiers and the veterans of the field armies became daily companions. One certain result of the reforms of Diocletian and Constantine was the militarization of Roman society— the transformation of the Roman Empire into a vast armed camp. The financial resources of that empire were now largely devoted to maintaining an expensive military establishment that was socially diverse and potentially politically volatile. Christians were still a minority of the population in Constantine's lifetime, so

his legalization and patronage of the new faith may have been visionary but certainly offended the elites of his day.

Diocletian and Constantine responded with imagination to the third-century crisis. They created a new kind of rulership and a new type of imperial regime. Constantine erected a statue of himself in Rome that was more than 30 feet high; its head alone was about 8 feet tall. This statue is an indicator of the late antique imperial ideology. Constantine's size in stone serves to emphasize a distance that the viewer cannot articulate but cannot help feeling. The huge statue does not so much depict Constantine as proclaim emperorship. The majesty of Constantine and his long, productive reign, in conjunction with Diocletian's success and longevity, stands in stark contrast to the troubles of the third century. But we may ask, as contemporaries did, whether order was purchased at too high a price in terms of personal freedom.

THE FOURTH-CENTURY EMPIRE: A FRAGILE STABILITY

Diocletian and Constantine considered themselves to be Roman traditionalists, but their wide-ranging reforms had actually introduced deep changes in the Roman system. When Constantine died in 337, the Roman Empire was more peaceful and stable than it had been throughout the crisis-ridden third century. But Rome's rulers were now more despotic; Rome's government was bigger, more intrusive, and more expensive; and Rome's military was larger and increasingly barbarian in composition. The open question in 337 was whether Rome would revert to the chaos of the third century or continue along the path marked out by the reforms of Diocletian and Constantine.

Succession to the imperial office remained a troubling issue despite the introduction of the tetrarchy. Constantine had employed a combination of the tetrarchal and dynastic systems. He had three subordinates, all of them his sons. They did not base their activities in the four prefectures, and they succeeded him jointly when he died. Constantine's sons had no heirs of their own, and when the last of them died in 361, the army turned to Julian (331–363), Constantine's nephew. Julian was a great leader and a man who looked out for his troops. Nevertheless, people were trying to find a legitimate heir to Constantine, not merely a general who would reward the army.

Julian ruled for only two years before he was killed fighting in Mesopotamia. Because Julian had no heirs, the army controlled the succession. The choice fell on Valentinian (r. 364–375) and his brother, Valens (r. 364–378). Valentinian ruled in the west, his brother in the east. Valentinian established a dynasty that ruled the Roman world for ninety-one years (364–455). In 378,

Edict of Milan   Issued jointly by Constantine and his colleague Licinius, it granted freedom of worship to all and restored properties seized from the Christian church during Diocletian's persecution.

when Valens was killed in battle, Valentinian's sons sent their brother-in-law, Theodosius (thee-oh-DOE-zhus) I (r. 379–395), who had risen through the military ranks in Spain, to the east to restore order.

Until his own death in 395 Theodosius was the most powerful man in the Roman world and, after his last brother-in-law died in 392, sole ruler. He enjoyed the confidence of the people and the army—the former because he was exceptionally competent and honest and the latter because he was an old military man and a superb general. He divided the empire between his two sons without dynastic or military challenge. His branch of the family lived on until the deaths of Theodosius II in the East in 450 and Valentinian III in the West in 455. Later rulers of the dynasty sometimes ruled alone, sometimes with chosen colleagues or subordinates. Dynastic and tetrarchal systems were thus blended effectively.

Following the reforms of Diocletian and Constantine, the army was supposed to protect the empire, not play a role in Roman politics. Events proved otherwise. In the 340s the Romans faced a renewed threat in the east from Persia, where an ambitious king sought to revive the glories of his ancestors. The Romans did not take this Persian threat lightly, for they knew that in the Persians they faced an old and formidable foe. In the west, Rome faced one serious challenge from the Visigoths (discussed later in this chapter). These military provocations inevitably enhanced the role of the army in public life and elevated military concerns over civilian ones. The presence of new threats contributed to the army's prominence in selecting emperors.

The fourth century did not witness the kind of intensive and sustained administrative reforms that characterized the reigns of Diocletian and Constantine. But emperors did introduce many modest measures, some of which had outcomes very different from those intended by their implementers. One example may stand for many.

During the reign of Valentinian I, a soldier raised to the imperial office by the army, the emperor wanted to make military careers more attractive and soldiers' lives more comfortable. To achieve these ends, Valentinian proposed providing soldiers with plots of land and seed grain. He aimed to supplement soldiers' pay, to tie them more securely to a particular region, and to make them more loyal to him. This creative idea complemented earlier military reforms.

Nonetheless, Valentinian's program angered the senators, who were still rich and influential. They agitated against the reform because, they said, the emperor was spending too much time worrying about the army, and he was depriving them of lands they desired. The senators also complained that the new program was expensive, and they were absolutely right. To pay for land and seed, Valentinian had to raise taxes.

Higher taxes were especially unpopular in the cities, where the burden of collecting them fell on the *decurions,* the main local officials who composed the town councils. From the time of Valentinian in the late fourth century, evidence points to a steady decline in loyalty to Rome among these provincial urban elites. Part of Rome's success under the Principate had been directly tied to the regime's ability to win over local elites all over the empire. Now a military reform whose rationale was clear and defensible actually provoked suspicion and disloyalty among senators and decurions.

In the late fourth century, the empire may have numbered 50 million to 60 million inhabitants. Of these, not more than 5 million to 10 million lived in towns. Because Roman government was based on towns, the actual capacity of the Roman administration to keep track of, tax, coerce, and Romanize the population as a whole was limited. Nevertheless, as the Roman Empire became an increasingly militarized state, its towns were being dominated by central authorities as never before, and its rural population was being pressed hard by tax policies necessitated by larger civil and military structures. The reforms of Diocletian and Constantine continued to provide the framework within which these changes took place.

When Theodosius died in 395, the Roman world still seemed reasonably secure. The families of Constantine and Valentinian had produced effective rulers. Scattered threats clouded the frontiers, but for the moment conditions appeared stable. Programs of institutional and economic reform continued apace, generally along the lines marked out by Diocletian and Constantine.

SECTION SUMMARY

- Diocletian and Constantine enhanced the prestige of the imperial office but made it more remote and despotic.

- Diocletian and Constantine expanded and redeployed the army but turned the empire into an armed camp.

- Diocletian and Constantine increased taxes and stabilized the currency.

- Diocletian and Constantine expanded the government and made it more effective yet also more intrusive.

- Diocletian persecuted but Constantine legalized Christianity.

THE CATHOLIC CHURCH AND THE ROMAN EMPIRE, 313–604

How and why did a Roman and Catholic Church emerge in Late Antiquity?

While Rome's rulers were trying to stabilize the state during the fourth century, the empire was experiencing a dynamic process of religious change. The formerly small and persecuted communities of Christians were achieving majority status in the Roman world. The Christianization of the empire's population (see Map 7.2), first in towns and then in the countryside, and the emergence of the Catholic Church as a hierarchical, institutional structure were two of the greatest transformations of the ancient world. Many Christians, now able to practice their faith in public, discovered that they had sharp disagreements with one another on fundamental points of doctrine. Attempts to resolve those controversies entangled the church with the Roman authorities and strengthened the bishops of Rome. Moreover, numerous Christians—monks and nuns—sought a life of perfection away from the bustle of the world.

EMPERORS, BISHOPS, AND HERETICS

Constantine discovered that his support of the church drew him into heated disputes over doctrine and **heresy.** *Heresy* comes from a Greek word meaning "to choose." Heretics are persons who choose teachings or practices that religious or state authorities deem wrong. The two greatest and most difficult heresies of Late Antiquity involved the central doctrines of Christianity: the deity of Jesus Christ himself and the relationship between his divine and human natures.

Christian belief holds that there is one God who exists as three distinct but equal persons: Father, Son, and Holy Spirit. But around 320 a priest of Alexandria, Arius (AIR-ee-us) (ca. 250–336), began teaching that Jesus was the "first born of all creation." Christians had long been stung by the charge that their monotheism was a sham, that they really worshiped three gods. **Arianism,** as the faith of Arius and his followers is called, preserved monotheism by making Jesus slightly subordinate to the Father. Arianism won many adherents.

Constantine was scandalized by disagreements over Christian teachings and distressed by riotous quarrels among competing Christian factions. He dealt with religious controversies by summoning individual theologians to guide him and by assembling church councils to debate controversies and reach solutions. In 325 at Nicaea (Ny-SEE-uh), near Constantinople (see **MAP 7.2**), the emperor convened a council of two or three hundred bishops, the largest council by far that had met up to that date. The **Council of Nicaea** condemned Arius and his teachings. The bishops issued a creed, or statement of beliefs, which maintained that Christ was "one in being with the Father," co-equal and co-eternal.

Religious unity remained elusive, however. The Council of Nicaea's attempt to eliminate Arianism was unsuccessful in the short term. Constantius II (r. 337–361), Constantine's son and successor in the eastern half of the empire, was an avowed Arian, as were some later emperors. For more than forty years, Rome's rulers occasionally embraced a faith that had been declared heretical. It was during this time that the Visigothic priest Ulfilas entered the empire, was converted to Arian Christianity, and returned to spread this faith among his people. Arian Christianity spread widely among the barbarian peoples living along the empire's frontiers. By the time those people began to enter the empire in significant numbers (see page 194), catholic Christianity, universal (for that is what *catholicos* means) Christianity proclaimed by councils and emperors, had triumphed over Arianism, leaving the barbarians as heretics.

One emperor—Constantine's nephew Julian, called "the Apostate" by his Christian opponents—made a last-ditch attempt to restore paganism during his short reign (361–363). He did not resort to persecution but forbade Christians to hold most government or military positions or to teach in any school. Although Christianity had been legalized only in 313, by the 360s it was too well entrenched to be barred from the public sphere, and Julian's pagan revival died with him.

In the fifth century Monophysitism emerged as a result of bitter quarrels between Christian thinkers in Alexandria and Antioch. Theologians were struggling to find a way to talk about the divine and human natures in Christ. Some emphasized one nature, some the other.

heresy   An opinion that goes against religious or political doctrine and beliefs.

Arianism   A term for the teaching of Arius and the beliefs of his followers. They believed that Jesus Christ, as "the first born of all creation," was later than the Father and their teachings challenged the doctrine of the Trinity.

Council of Nicaea   The first "ecumenical" or "all-the-world council." Several more ecumenical councils would meet in Late Antiquity to deal with major heresies.

MAP 7.2   The Spread of Christianity to A.D. 600

From its beginnings in Palestine (see Map 6.2 on page 173), Christianity, while still illegal, spread mainly in heavily urbanized regions. After Constantine legalized Christianity, the faith spread into every corner of the Roman world.

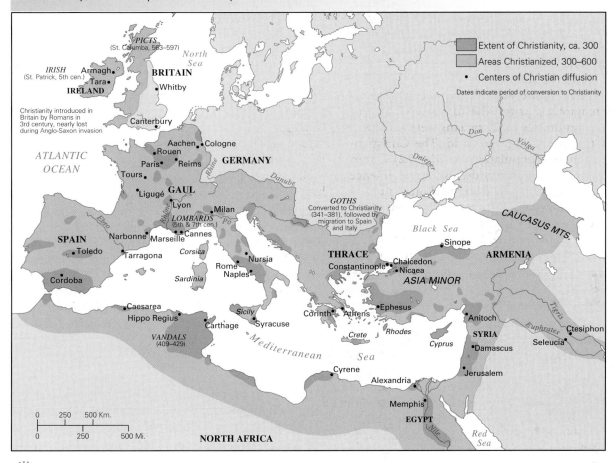

Online Study Center   **Improve Your Grade**   Interactive Map: The Expansion of Christianity to 600

In 451 an emperor called a new council at Chalcedon (KAL-see-dun) to deal with the issue of Monophysitism. Like his predecessors, the emperor sought unity, and he was willing to let the theologians define the doctrines. At Chalcedon the theologians condemned the Monophysites and pronounced that Jesus Christ was true God and true man—that he had two authentic natures. By 451 the Roman world had a large Catholic majority that derived its teachings from Nicaea and Chalcedon and many heretical minorities who themselves believed that the Catholics were the heretics.

THE INSTITUTIONAL DEVELOPMENT OF THE CATHOLIC CHURCH, CA. 300–600

The earliest Christian communities were urban and had three kinds of officials, whose customary titles in English are *bishop, priest,* and *deacon.* Deacons were responsible for charitable works and for arranging meetings.

Bishops and priests presided at celebrations—most prominently the Eucharist (or Holy Communion, as it came to be called)—preached, and taught. Distinctions between bishops and priests developed over time. Depending on their relative size, towns would have many independent Christian groups, each headed by a priest. By about 200, as a sign of unity and authority, the eldest priest came to be called "overseer," the literal meaning of *bishop.* As more people converted, as the church acquired property, and as doctrinal quarrels began to cause divisions among the faithful, bishops began to be influential local officials. By the late fourth century, the bishops in the major cities of the empire were called *metropolitan bishops,* or sometimes *archbishops,* and they had responsibility for territories often called *dioceses.* In essence, the church was adapting to its own purposes the administrative geography of the Roman Empire—another sign of change and continuity in Late Antiquity. (See the box "The Global Record: Christianity Arrives in Nubia.")

CHRISTIANITY ARRIVES IN NUBIA

In the early fifth century a Constantinopolitan lawyer, Socrates Scholasticus (389–450), wrote an Ecclesiastical History, *drawing upon many earlier sources. In the following passage he recounts the introduction of Christianity into "India," by which he means Nubia, or what is basically today Ethiopia. This document presents the first evidence for Christianity in Africa.*

A certain philosopher, Meropius, was determined to acquaint himself with the country of the Indians. Having taken with him therefore two youths to whom he was related . . . Meropius reached the country by ship; . . . he touched at a certain place which had a safe harbor, for the purpose of procuring some necessaries. It so happened that a little before that time the treaty between the Romans and Indians had been violated. The Indians, therefore, having seized the philosopher and those who sailed with him, killed them all except his two youthful kinsmen; but sparing them from compassion for their tender age, they sent them as a gift to the king of the Indians. He, pleased with the personal appearance of the youths, made one of them, whose name was Edesius, cup-bearer at his table; the other, named Frumentius, he entrusted with the care of the royal records. The king dying soon after, left them free, the government devolving on his wife and infant son. Now the queen seeing her son thus left in his minority, begged the young men to undertake the charge of him, until he should become of adult age. The youths accepted the task, and entered on the administration of the kingdom. Frumentius controlled all things and made it a task to enquire whether among the Roman merchants trafficking with that country, there were any Christians to be found: and having discovered some, he informed them who he was, and exhorted them to select and occupy some appropriate places for the celebration of Christian worship. In the course of a little while he built a house of prayer; and having instructed some of the Indians in the principles of Christianity, they fitted them for participation in the worship. On the young king's reaching maturity, Frumentius and his associates resigned to him the administration of public affairs . . . and sought permission to return to their own country. Both the king and his mother entreated them to remain; but being desirous of revisiting their native place, they could not be prevailed on, and consequently departed. Edesius for his part hastened to Tyre to see his parents and kindred; but Frumentius arriving at Alexandria, reported the affair to Athanasius, who had recently been made bishop, and acquainted him with his wanderings and the hopes Indians had of receiving Christianity. He also begged him to send a bishop and clergy there, and by no means to neglect those who might thus be brought to salvation. Athanasius . . . requested Frumentius himself to accept the bishopric, declaring that he could appoint no one more suitable than he was. Accordingly this was done; Frumentius invested with episcopal authority, returned to India and became there a preacher of the Gospel, built several churches, and aided by divine grace, he performed various miracles, healing with the souls also the bodily diseases of many.

QUESTIONS

1. By what routes would a person be likely to sail to Nubia, and how would Frumentius have traveled from Nubia to Alexandria?

2. What impressions does this text give you of the knowledge possessed by Romans of the peoples outside the empire?

3. Do Frumentius and Edesius remind you of Moses?

4. What techniques did Frumentius use to institute Christianity in Nubia?

Source: Socrates Scholasticus, *The Ecclesiastical History,* Book 1, chapter 19, in Philip Schaff and Henry Wace, eds., *A Select Library of Nicene and Post-Nicene Fathers of the Christian Church,* Second Series, Volume 2 (1890; repr. Grand Rapids, Mich.: Eerdmans Publishing Co., 1978).

The Emergence of the Roman Papacy From its earliest days the Christian community had espoused the doctrine of *apostolic succession.* In other words, just as Jesus had charged his apostles with continuing his earthly ministry, that ministry was passed on to succeeding generations of Christian bishops and priests through the ceremony of ordination. When one or more bishops laid their hands on the head of a new priest or bishop, they were continuing an unbroken line of clerics that reached back through the apostles to Jesus himself. The bishops of Rome coupled this general notion of apostolic succession with a particular emphasis on the original primacy of Peter, in tradition the leader of the apostles and the first bishop of Rome. The theory of "Petrine Primacy" was based on Matthew's Gospel (16:16–18), where Jesus founded his church on

Peter, "the Rock," and conferred upon him the keys to the kingdom of heaven. The theory held that just as Peter had been the leader of the apostles, so the successors to Peter, the bishops of Rome, continued to be the leaders of the church as a whole. By the late fourth century the bishop of Rome was usually addressed as *papa*, or "pope" in English. The steadily growing importance of bishops everywhere was a marked feature of the age, and the growing authority of the bishop of Rome within the church is the most striking organizational process of the fourth and fifth centuries.

Christians in the Roman world frequently disagreed on matters of jurisdiction and theology. Attempts to resolve these controversies strengthened the ecumenical council as a regular organ of church government, increased the power of the **papacy,** and drew emperors more deeply into the public life of the church. In a series of laws issued between 378 and 381, Theodosius virtually outlawed the pagan cults, thereby making Christianity and Judaism the only legal religions, and required all Christians to believe as the bishop of Rome did, in the hope of imposing religious unity on battling groups of Christians. Unity under Roman leadership was essential, Theodosius said, because Peter had transmitted the unblemished faith directly to Rome and Peter's successors had preserved it there. The bishops of Rome took an ambivalent view of Theodosius's actions. On the one hand, they were glad to have the emperor's support. On the other hand, they did not wish for their authority or teaching to rest on imperial decrees. Theodosius's decree reflects the growing power of the bishop of Rome and demonstrates the degree to which the state and the church were becoming intertwined. The decree itself failed to achieve the unity Theodosius desired. Accordingly, in 381 he summoned another ecumenical council in Constantinople. This council again condemned Arianism, which thereafter declined in significance within the empire, although it remained vigorous among the barbarian peoples living along Rome's frontiers.

Ever since Nicaea, councils, with active participation by the emperors, had settled major disagreements in the church. Pope Leo I (r. 440–461) began to assert papal prerogatives. He had sent representatives to the Council of Chalcedon bearing his doctrinal formulation. Leo insisted that, as the bishop of Rome, he had full authority to make decisions in doctrinal controversies. The emperor skillfully steered Leo's "Tome" to acceptance by the council, but to appease many Eastern bishops, who felt that too much authority was being claimed by the pope, the emperor also encouraged the council to assert that the bishop of Constantinople (or

papacy   The name for the institution ruled by the bishop of Rome who was considered to be the successor of Saint Peter and, gradually, the leader of the Christian church as a whole.

patriarch, as he was often called) was second in eminence and power to the bishop of Rome. Leo, the greatest exponent of "Petrine Primacy" though not its originator, objected strenuously to the Council of Chalcedon's procedures. He disliked the prominent role of the emperor, complained that Eastern bishops had no right to challenge his doctrinal authority, and particularly opposed the elevation of Constantinople's status. Indeed, Leo said, Rome's position derived from its Petrine succession and not from imperial or conciliar decrees.

A generation later Pope Gelasius I (r. 492–496) sent a sharply worded letter to the emperor Anastasius (r. 491–518), who had intervened in a quarrel between the Catholics and the still-numerous Monophysites. Gelasius protested the emperor's intervention. He told the emperor that the world was governed by the "power" of kings and by the "authority" of priests. Ordinarily, the pope said, the jurisdictions of kings and priests are distinct. In a controversy between them, however, priestly authority must have precedence, because priests are concerned with the salvation of immortal souls, whereas kings rule only mortal bodies. Gelasius was telling the emperor to stay out of theology, but he was implying much more. His opposition of the words *power*—meaning mere police power, the application of brute force—and *authority*—legitimacy, superior right—was of great importance. Gelasius elevated the church, with the pope at its head, above the whole secular regime, with the emperor at its head. Despite his lofty claims, Gelasius had no means of coercing emperors. Moreover, many clergy in the eastern Mediterranean refused to accept the idea that the pope had supreme authority in either doctrine or church government.

Online Study Center **Improve Your Grade**
Primary Source: Church and State: Spiritual Authority Trumps Temporal Authority

The pontificate of Pope Gregory I "the Great" (r. 590–604) exemplifies the position of the papacy as Late Antiquity drew to a close. Gregory was the scion of an old senatorial family. He had risen through several important positions in the Roman administration but then decided to abandon public life, sell off his family's property, and pursue a life of spiritual retreat. Soon, however, the Roman people elected him pope. His reputation for holiness was important to his election, but so too were his impeccable social credentials and wide political connections. Rome was threatened by the Lombards (a barbarian group that had entered Italy in the 560s), the local economy was in a shambles, and relations with the imperial government had been strained. Gregory did not wish to be elected pope, but given his conventional Roman sense of duty and obligation, he had little choice but to accept the office. Immediately he undertook dangerous diplomatic measures to ward off the Lombard threat. He also tried hard to improve relations with the emperor. And he put the local economy on reasonably sound footing. He reorganized the vast estates of the church to place their products and revenues at the disposal of the Romans. In the absence of effective imperial administration in and around Rome, Gregory also began to attend to urban services and amenities, such as streets, aqueducts, and baths.

By 600, then, the bishop of Rome—the pope—viewed himself as the head of a universal, or catholic, church. Many members of the clergy disputed that view. Some simply disagreed with specific papal teachings. Others claimed that Jesus had given his authority equally to all the apostles and not uniquely to Peter and thus to Peter's successors. Emperors, too, rejected papal overreaching. After all, they had always claimed for themselves authority in all aspects of their subjects' lives, religious affairs included. By 600, however, there were no longer emperors in the West, and the Eastern rulers had few means of controlling the bishops of Rome. For their part, the bishops of Rome were gradually focusing their efforts on the western regions of the old Roman world.

The Role of the Elite The rise of the pope in the church as a whole was paralleled by the rise of bishops throughout the empire. By the last years of the fourth century, various ranking members of the social elite were everywhere entering the clergy and rising to its highest offices. This capture of the elite was the final, decisive factor in the triumph of Christianity.

The clergy was an outlet for the talents and ambitions of the elite. For some time senators had been excluded from military offices and reduced in civilian influence, and decurions were growing dissatisfied with public service. The *episcopal* office (that is, the office of bishop) was desirable to prominent men for many reasons. It was prestigious. Bishops wore distinctive clothing when officiating and were addressed by special titles—traditional Roman marks of respect. They had opportunities to control patronage in the way that prominent Romans always had done. They could intervene on behalf of individuals at the imperial court. They controlled vast wealth, as the generosity of pious Christians put more resources at their disposal. Communities elected their own bishops, and by the middle of the fifth century the dominant person in most towns was the bishop, not a civilian official. The bishops, however, were the same persons, from the same families, who had once dominated local society through civic service. The overall effect of these social changes was dramatic in the long run, but it happened very gradually.

The change from a secular to an ecclesiastical elite in Roman cities even led to alterations of the topography of the cities themselves. The elite usually financed local building projects, such as temples, basilicas, forums, and amphitheaters. Such benefactions declined sharply during the third century because of the uncertainty of the times. The fourth century at first saw little building on private initiative, but then came the construction of Christian cathedrals (a bishop's church, from *cathedra,* the chair or seat of the bishop's authority), episcopal residences, baptisteries, and local parish churches. Such buildings as a rule were not placed in the old city centers, which had associations with the pagan past. Instead, they were placed on the edges of populated districts. In the future these Christian centers served as poles around which ancient towns were reconfigured. The Roman elites built to show pride in their cities and to promote themselves. This did not change in Late Antiquity, but this time the elites were bishops or rich Christians, and the buildings were religious—look again at Santa Maria Maggiore on page 180.

THE RISE OF CHRISTIAN MONASTICISM

For some men and women the call of the Gospel was radical. They yearned to escape the world and everything that might come between them and God. To do so, many of them embraced a new way of life—**monasticism.** Christian monks and nuns developed a theology and an institution that were among the most creative and long-lived achievements of Late Antiquity.

The practice of rigorous self-denial (*askesis*) was common to several religious and philosophical sects in antiquity—for example, the Pythagoreans and the Stoics—and was well known among the Jews in the time of Christ, as the Essenes show (see page 172). Ascetics believed that if they could conquer the desires of the body, they could commune with the supernatural beings who were greater and purer than humans encumbered by lust for food, drink, knowledge, sex, and adventure. Sometimes ascetic practices were adopted by tightly knit groups, sometimes by heroic solitaries.

The founder of Christian monasticism was a young Egyptian layman, named Anthony (d. 356). At age 19 Anthony gave away all his possessions and took up in the Egyptian desert a life of prayer and renunciation. His spiritual quest became famous, and many disciples flocked to him. Finally he decided to organize these seekers into a very loose community. His followers remained in solitude except for worship and meals. Anthony's form of monasticism is called *eremitic,* from the Greek *heremos,* or "desert," hence the word *hermit.*

Pachomius (pack-OH-mee-us) (290–346) created a more communal form of monastic life. A former Roman soldier, he was baptized a Christian in 313 and

monasticism A way of life involving the renunciation of worldly pleasures and the embrace of a life of prayer and solitude. Monasticism arose in fourth-century Egypt and spread all over the Roman world.

retired to the Egyptian desert, where he studied with a hermit. Eventually Pachomius founded a community of ascetics, which before long had grown to thousands of members. Perhaps because of his military background, or because his religious instincts favored order and unity, Pachomius wrote the first Rule, or code for daily living, for a monastic community. He organized most aspects of his community by designing a common life based on routines of private prayer, group worship, and work. By the time of his death, Pachomius led nine male and two female communities. Pachomius's pattern of monasticism is called *cenobitic* (sen-oh-BIT-ik), from the Greek for "common life." People living this common life were called *monks,* and the place where they lived was called a *monastery.* The head of the community was designated the *abbot,* a word meaning "father." In later times the term *abbess,* meaning "mother," was coined for the woman who led a female community, and a community of nuns came to be called a *convent.*

Monasticism spread from Egypt by means of texts such as the *Life of Anthony* (a late antique "bestseller"), collections of the wise sayings of famous desert abbots, and books written by persons who went to Egypt seeking a more perfect life—among whom were several prominent women. One attraction of monasticism among the devout was that it seemed to be a purer form of Christian life, uncorrupted by the wealth, power, and controversy of the hierarchical church. Many pious women embraced monasticism at least partly because they could not be ordained priests. Positions in monasteries, including that of abbess, provided responsible roles for talented women. Monasticism gave women a chance to choose a kind of family life different from the one available in households dominated by fathers and husbands.

Eremitic monasticism was prominent in Palestine and Syria and eventually throughout the Greek-speaking world. Eastern monasticism produced a great legislator in Basil (330–379), whose Rule was the most influential in the Orthodox Church (see page 207). Generally these monks assembled only for weekly worship and otherwise ate, prayed, and worked alone.

Eremitic monasticism arrived in the West in the person of Martin of Tours (336–397). Like Pachomius, Martin was a pagan Roman soldier who, after his military service, embraced both Christianity and asceticism. Even though he was elected bishop of Tours, Martin kept to his rigid life of denial. Martin's form of monasticism influenced many in the western regions of the Roman world but set especially deep roots in Ireland. There the whole organization of the church was based on monasteries. At Kildare the abbess Brigid (d. 523) had more authority than the local bishop.

In the West cenobitic monasticism became the dominant pattern. Benedict of Nursia (480–545) abandoned his legal studies and a potential government career to pursue a life of solitary prayer in a mountain cave east of Rome. Benedict's piety attracted a crowd of followers, and in about 520 he established a monastery at Monte Cassino, 80 miles south of Rome. The Rule he drafted for his new community is marked by shrewd insights into the human personality. It emphasizes the bond of mutual love among the monks and obedience to the abbot. The Rule assigns the abbot wide powers but exhorts him to exercise them gently. The Rule allows monks a reasonable diet and decent, though modest, clothing. Although providing for discipline and punishment, the Rule prefers loving correction. In later centuries Benedict's Rule dominated monastic life.

Eremitic or cenobitic, East or West, monasticism was a conscious alternative and an explicit challenge to the civic world of classical antiquity. Monks and nuns did not seek to give their lives meaning by serving the state or urban communities. They went into remote places to serve God and one another. They sought not to acquire but to abandon. Spiritual wisdom was more important to them than secular learning, and they yearned for acknowledgment of their holiness, not recognition of their social status. Still, monasticism was sometimes controversial. Whereas many people admired and emulated these holy men and women, others disputed their claims to elite spiritual status.

At the dawn of Late Antiquity the church was persecuted and struggling. By the end of the period the church was rich and powerful, its leaders were prominent and prestigious, and in the monasteries, at least, its spiritual fervor was deep. This change was gradual but fundamental.

SECTION SUMMARY

- Imperial legislation and church councils imposed a universal, a catholic, form of Christianity.

- The church developed a hierarchy of officers over which the bishops of Rome gradually achieved preeminence.

- Christians disagreed strongly on basic teachings such as the Trinity (God is Father, Son, and Holy Spirit) and the divine and human natures of Jesus Christ.

- Some men and women rejected the values of the late antique world and embraced the monastic life of prayer and renunciation, achieving in the process a new kind of status: holiness.

THE RISE OF GERMANIC KINGDOMS IN THE WEST, CA. 370–530

Who were the "barbarians," and what kinds of relations did Romans and barbarians have in Late Antiquity?

The years from the 370s to the 530s were decisive in the history of the Roman Empire in the West. When this period opened, the dynasty of Valentinian was firmly in control. When it closed, the western provinces of the empire had become a number of Germanic kingdoms, most of which maintained some formal relationship with the eastern Roman Empire. Roman encounters with the barbarians took many different forms, ranging from violent conflict to peaceful accommodation. The key point to understand is that although the barbarians supplanted Roman rule in the West, they did so slowly and often with Roman permission and assistance.

INVASIONS AND MIGRATIONS

Few images of the ancient world are more fixed in the popular imagination than the overrunning of the Roman Empire by hordes of barbarians who ushered in a dark age. The Romans inherited the word *barbarian* from the Greeks, who had divided the world between those who spoke Greek and those who did not. Barbarians were literally babblers, foreigners who spoke an unknown language. After the Romans granted citizenship to virtually everyone in the empire in 212, they adopted a Greek-style differentiation between Romans and barbarians. Technically the latter were merely foreigners, but in practice Romans thought barbarians inferior to themselves.

Online Study Center **Improve Your Grade**
Primary Source: A Comparison of Roman and Barbarian Behavior: Rome Loses!

Individual groups of barbarians did invade the empire in various places at different times, but there was never a single, coordinated barbarian invasion of the Roman world that had well-formulated objectives. The Romans and barbarians did not face one another as declared enemies. Indeed, peaceful encounters outnumbered violent confrontations in the history of Romano-barbarian relations. The Romans had long traded with the barbarian peoples, carried out complicated diplomacy with them, and recruited them into their armies. Barbarian veterans were settled in most provinces of the empire.

If we cannot label one grand movement as "the barbarian invasions," we must also avoid the idea that the barbarians were naturally nomadic and migratory.

Holding this view would tempt us to see the entry of the barbarians into the empire as one stage in a long process of human movement. Archaeological evidence collected to date makes it clear that the barbarians were settled agriculturists. They lived in villages, farmed the surrounding country, and raised livestock. If barbarians moved from one place to another, their movement must be explained with reference to specific developments and cannot be attributed to migratory habits.

Who were the barbarians? Linguists classify them as belonging to the Germanic branches of the Indo-European family of languages. The Germanic peoples can be differentiated from the Celts and Slavs with whom they shared much of central and eastern Europe, but apart from some minor linguistic variations, it is difficult to distinguish one Germanic group from another. What are we to make of the profusion of names offered to us by our sources: Franks, Saxons, Vandals, Visigoths, Ostrogoths, Lombards, Burgundians? The Romans referred to the Germanic peoples as tribes, but that does not mean that they were actually groups of related people. Every Germanic "tribe" was a confederation, and these confederations formed, dissolved, and re-formed many times. For example, the **Visigoths** who crossed the Danube in 376 included Visigoths proper and more than a half dozen other peoples. The confederations were formed either by powerful leaders who coerced less powerful people to join them or by groups of villages that banded together to protect themselves from aggressive neighbors. As a tribe was forming, its constituent peoples would intermarry and adopt the language, law, and lifestyle of the dominant group.

INCORPORATING THE BARBARIANS

The transformation of the western Roman Empire began as a result of an unexpected set of events involving the Huns, nomadic warriors from the central Asian steppes. (See the box "The Written Record: Two Views of the Huns.") After plundering the frontiers of Persia and China for centuries, they turned west in search of booty and tribute. In 374 or 375 they fell on the Ostrogoths, who lived near the Black Sea, and frightened the

Visigoths   A "West" Germanic people who coalesced along the Danube frontier in the fourth century, allied with the Romans, eventually entered the empire, sacked Rome in 410, and finally established a kingdom in Gaul.

THE WRITTEN RECORD

TWO VIEWS OF THE HUNS

The dread and disgust inspired by the Huns is well captured in the first passage, from the Roman historian Ammianus Marcellinus. The second passage, from a surviving fragment of the history of Priscus, shows the Huns in quite a different light. Only rarely can we contrast two different views, and these documents permit us to do so.

(a)

From the moment of their birth they make deep gashes in their children's cheeks, so that when in due course hair appears its growth is checked by the wrinkled scars; as they grow older this gives them the unlovely appearance of beardless eunuchs. They have squat bodies, strong limbs, and thick necks, and are so prodigiously ugly and bent that they might be two-legged animals. Their shape, however disagreeable, is human. They have no use for seasoned food, but live on the roots of wild plants and the half-raw flesh of any animal, which they warm a little by placing it between their thighs and the backs of their horses. They have no buildings to shelter them. They wear garments of linen or of the skins of field-mice stitched together. Once they have put their necks into some dingy shirt they never take it off or change it until it rots and falls to pieces. They have round caps of fur on their heads, and protect their hairy legs with goatskins. They are ill-fitted to fight on foot, and remain glued to their horses, hardy but ugly beasts, on which they sometimes sit like women to perform their everyday business and they even bow forward over their beasts' narrow necks to enjoy a deep and dreamy sleep.

(b)

[The Roman ambassadors] came upon a very large village in which the dwelling of Attila was said to be more notable than those elsewhere. It had been fitted together with highly polished timbers and encircled with a wooden palisade, conceived not for safety but for beauty. Next to the king's dwelling that of Onegisus [chief minister to Attila] was outstanding, and it also had a circuit of timbers but was not embellished with towers in the same way as Attila's. Not far from the enclosure was a large bath. . . . Maidens came to meet Attila as he entered this village, advancing before him in rows under fine white linen cloths stretched out to such a length that under each cloth, which was held up by the hands of the women along either side, seven or even more girls walked. There were many such formations of women under the linen cloths, and they sang Scythian songs. When he [Attila] came near the house of Onegisus, the wife of Onegisus came out with a host of servants, some bearing dainties and others wine, greeted him and asked him to partake of the food which she had brought for him with friendly hospitality. To gratify the wife of his intimate friend, he ate sitting on his horse, the barbarians accompanying him having raised the silver platter up to him. Having also tasted the wine, he went on to the palace, which was higher than the other houses and situated on a high place.

QUESTIONS

1. How do these two accounts differ in tone, emphasis, and details?

2. Leaving aside the question of whether these accounts are true, what impressions do you think they would have made on the Romans? What impressions were they intended to make?

3. How do the public rituals of the Huns compare with those of the Romans?

Sources: Excerpt (a): Ammianus Marcellinus, *The Later Roman Empire* (A.D. 354–378), 31.2, ed. and trans. Walter Hamilton (Harmondsworth, U.K.: Penguin, 1986), pp. 411–412. Excerpt (b): Priscus, Fragment 8, in C. D. Gordon, *The Age of Attila: Fifth-Century Byzantium and the Barbarians* (Ann Arbor: University of Michigan Press, 1961), pp. 84–85.

Visigoths, who requested permission to cross the Danube and enter the empire.

Recent years had been difficult for the empire. Julian had fallen in battle with the Persians in 363, and dynastic quarrels were disturbing the West. The Romans thus delayed responding to the Visigoth request. Fearful of the Huns, the Visigoths crossed the Danube on their own and then asked if they might settle in the Balkans. Reluctantly, Valens (VAY-lenz) (r. 364–378) agreed but postponed permanent arrangements. While the central government considered how to deal with the Visigoths, local authorities sold them food at exorbitant prices and even traded dog meat for Gothic children, who were then enslaved. When the Visigoths revolted, Valens foolishly marched north to meet them with a small force. The Visigoths defeated his army and killed him at Adrianople in 378.

The history of the Visigoths thus presents an instructive example of Romano-Germanic relations. They had served as auxiliary troops entrusted with defending a stretch of the Danube frontier for a long time when they requested permission to enter the empire in 376. They did not cross the border as part of a massive invasion but because they were sorely threatened. In 382 Theodosius, whom we have met several times already, marched east to pacify the situation. He agreed to grant the Visigoths what they had been demanding: land to settle on and a Roman military title—that is, official status—for their king. A spokesman for Theodosius explained the emperor's motives: "Which is better: To fill Thrace with corpses or with farmers? To fill it with graves or with people? To travel through wilderness or cultivated land? To count those who have perished or those who are ploughing?" For decades barbarians had been settling inside the Roman frontiers, and they had served loyally in the army. Beginning in the fourth century, most high military officers in the Roman world were barbarians. The only peculiarity about the Visigoths' situation was that never before had the Romans admitted a whole people.

For about thirty years the Visigoths struggled to improve the terms of their settlements in the Balkans. Alaric (AL-uh-rik), the Visigothic king after 395, grew tired of unfulfilled promises and forced matters by attacking Italy. In 410 the Visigoths sacked Rome. The taking of the city for the first time in eight hundred years shocked the entire Roman world and has loomed large for centuries in people's ideas about the "fall" of the Roman Empire. Actually it was a ploy by Alaric to improve the terms of his already official status. Alaric died in 410, and his brother led the Visigoths north into southern Gaul. For good measure the new Visigothic king captured the Western emperor's sister, Galla Placidia, and forced her to marry him. However objectionable this act must seem, the Visigoths viewed it as a further demonstration of their loyalty to Rome and their determination to effect a satisfactory new treaty.

In 418 the Roman government gave in. A treaty permitted the Visigoths to settle in southern Gaul, with Toulouse as their base of operations. They were assigned the task of protecting the area from marauding bands of brigands. In return for their service, the Visigoths were given land allotments and a portion of Roman tax receipts as pay.

The Visigoths' treaty with Rome made theirs the first Germanic kingdom on Roman soil. From 418 to 451 the Visigoths served Rome loyally and earned the respect of the Gallo-Roman aristocrats among whom they ruled. Between 466 and 484 the Visigothic kingdom in Gaul reached its high point and continued to receive official recognition from Roman rulers. Southern Gaul, one of Rome's oldest provinces, gradually passed from the hands of the Roman bureaucracy and the local nobility into the control of the Visigoths. Nevertheless, from Constantine's first treaty with the Visigoths through the continuing recognition by the Romans

of Visigothic kings, it was Roman policy more than Visigothic policy that determined the accommodation of this first Germanic kingdom within the framework of the western Roman Empire.

While they were dealing with the Visigoths, the Roman authorities realized that the Huns, who had settled in the Danube basin after driving the Visigoths into the empire, were a serious menace. They raided the Balkans, preyed on trade routes that crossed the region, and demanded tribute from the Eastern emperor. In 434 the fearsome warrior Attila murdered his brother and became sole ruler of the Huns. In return for a huge imperial subsidy, he agreed to cease raiding the Balkans. At the same time, a Roman general in Gaul concluded an alliance with the Huns in an attempt to use them to check the expansion of the Burgundians, an allied people who lived in the central Rhineland.

Together Attila and the Romans routed the Burgundians, but Attila realized the weakness of the Roman position in the West. He attacked Gaul in 451 and was stopped only by a combined effort of Romans, Visigoths, Burgundians, and Franks. Attila turned to Italy in 452, even approaching Rome, where Pope Leo I, not the emperor, convinced or bribed him to withdraw. Attila died in 454, and before another year was out, the short-lived Hunnic kingdom, largely Attila's personal creation, had vanished.

MORE KINGDOMS: THE END OF DIRECT ROMAN RULE IN THE WEST

To meet threats in Gaul and elsewhere, the Romans had begun pulling troops out of Britain in the fourth century and abandoned the island to its own defense in 410. Thereafter, raiding parties from Scotland and Ireland, as well as seaborne attackers—called "Saxons" by contemporaries because some of them came from Saxony in northern Germany—ravaged Britain. The British continually appealed to the military authorities in Gaul for aid, but to no avail. Between 450 and 600 much of southern and eastern Britain was taken over by diverse peoples whom we call the "Anglo-Saxons." The newcomers jostled for position with the Celtic Britons, who were increasingly confined to the north and west of the island. Amid these struggles was born the legend of King Arthur, a Briton who defended his people and led them to victory. Gradually several small kingdoms emerged. Although Britain retained contacts with Gaul, the island had virtually no Roman political or institutional inheritance.

Valentinian III (r. 425–455) was born in 419 and became emperor of the West as a 6-year-old. Even when he came of age, his court was weakened by factional strife, and his regime was dominated by military men. After Valentinian, the western empire saw a succession of nonentities, the last of whom was deposed by a Germanic

MAP 7.3   The Germanic Kingdoms, ca. 530

By 530 the western provinces of the Roman Empire (compare Map 6.1 on page 156) had evolved into Germanic kingdoms. Just as Roman provincial boundaries had changed numerous times, the existence and extent of Germanic kingdoms were also impermanent.

Online Study Center   Improve Your Grade   Interactive Map: The Germanic Kingdoms, ca. 530

general in 476. Ruling in Italy, he simply sent the imperial regalia to Constantinople and declared that the West no longer needed an emperor. This is all that happened in 476, the traditional date for the "fall" of the Roman Empire.

After the vast coalition defeated the Huns in Gaul in 451, the remaining Roman authorities in the Paris region discovered that the Visigoths were expanding north of the Loire River into central Gaul. To check this advance, the Roman commander in Paris forged an alliance with the Franks. The Franks, long Roman allies, had been expanding their settlements from the mouth of the Rhine southward across modern Holland and Belgium since the third century.

The fortunes of the Frankish kingdom, indeed of all of Gaul, rested with Clovis. He became king of one group of Franks in 481 and spent the years until his death in 511 subjecting all the other bands of Franks to his rule. He gained the allegiance of the Frankish people by leading them to constant military victories that brought territorial gains, plunder, and tribute. The greatest of Clovis's successes came in 507, when he defeated the Visigoths and drove them over the Pyrenees into Spain.

Clovis was popular, not only with the Franks but also with the Gallo-Roman population, for three reasons. First, Clovis and the Romans had common enemies: Germanic peoples still living beyond the Rhine and pirates who raided the coast of Gaul. Second, whereas most of the Germanic peoples were Arian Christians, the majority of the Franks passed directly from paganism to Catholicism. Thus Clovis and the Gallo-Romans had a shared faith that permitted Clovis to portray his war against the Visigoths as a kind of crusade against heresy. Third, Clovis eagerly sought from Constantinople formal recognition and titles, appeared publicly in the dress of a Roman official, and practiced such imperial rituals as distributing gold coins while riding through crowds. The Frankish kingdom under Clovis's family—called "Merovingian," from the name of one of his semilegendary ancestors—became the most successful of all the Germanic realms.

Several early Germanic kingdoms were short-lived. The Burgundian kingdom, which had once prompted the Romans to ally with the Huns, was swallowed up by the Franks in the 530s. The Vandals, who crossed the Rhine in 406 and headed for Spain, crossed to North Africa in 429 (see **MAP 7.3**). They were ardent Arians, who persecuted the Catholic population. They refused imperial offers of a treaty on terms similar to those accepted by other Germanic peoples. And they constantly plundered the islands of the western Mediterranean and the Italian coast, even sacking Rome in 455. Roman forces from Constantinople eliminated the Vandals in 534.

Amalasuntha, Daughter of Theodoric

This ivory plaque (ca. 530) depicts Amalasuntha in the way that Roman consuls and emperors had long been depicted on their assumption of office. Since the late fifth century empresses had been depicted this way, too. Amalasuntha projects an image of legitimacy. *(Kunsthistorisches Museum, Vienna)*

The Ostrogoths, allies who had been living in Pannonia since the 370s as subjects of the Huns, began to pose a threat to the eastern empire after Attila's death. In 493 the emperor decided to send them to Italy to recover that area for the imperial government. The government at Constantinople was familiar with the Ostrogoths' king, Theodoric, because he had been a hostage there for several years. The emperor also wished to remove the Ostrogoths from the Danube basin. Sending Theodoric to Italy seemed like a way to solve two problems simultaneously.

Theodoric conquered Italy quickly and set up his capital in Ravenna, the swamp-surrounded and virtually impregnable city that had sheltered the imperial administration for much of the fifth century. Through the force of his personality, and by a series of marriage alliances, Theodoric became the dominant ruler in western Europe. In Italy he promoted peace, stability, and good government. Still, Theodoric had two strikes against him. First, he and his people were Arians. Second, although the population of Italy was accustomed to having an imperial court dominated by barbarians and to having Germanic military men in Gaul as the real powers in the state, they had never been directly ruled by a barbarian, and some of them could not accept Theodoric. By the 520s Theodoric grew increasingly suspicious and dictatorial.

When Theodoric died, his daughter Amalasuntha (498–535) served as regent for her son Athalaric from 526 to 534 and then briefly served as queen. A contemporary said that she was beautiful and well educated. Clearly she favored the Romans in Italy and promoted cultural fusion. For this she evoked the keen hatred of the staunch Goths, who deposed and then murdered her. Her death was Justinian's pretext to launch the Gothic Wars (535–554), which put an end to the Ostrogothic kingdom.

By the 530s the western Roman Empire had vanished, the conclusion of a process initiated by the entry of the Visigoths into the Balkans in 376. Of all the peoples who had contested for a share of Rome's legacy, only the Franks in Gaul, the Visigoths in Spain, and the Anglo-Saxons in Britain had created durable political entities. Most of the two prefectures with their several dozen provinces had turned into a small number of kingdoms (see Map 7.3).

Why did the Roman government perish in the West? Beginning with Diocletian, Rome's best rulers were resident in and concerned mainly about the East. The Visigoths and other peoples were settled in their own kingdoms on Roman soil instead of being enrolled in and dispersed among Roman army units. Also during Diocletian's rule, the army was increasingly Germanized, and Germanic military men gained high offices in the state. Those leaders often dominated imperial courts and negotiated the series of treaties that submitted former provinces to barbarian peoples. Provincial elites had long been accustomed to having prominent Germans in their midst. The new situation was not unusual to them. Churchmen readily embraced the Catholic Franks and tolerated Arians, such as the Visigoths, when they promoted peace and good government without abusing the Catholic population.

OLD AND NEW IN THE WEST

The Germanic kingdoms had a great deal in common with one another and very much resembled the late Roman Empire, which had been their common tutor. Each realm was led by a king who usually appeared in two distinct guises. To his people, the king was the military leader. The essential bond of unity among each Germanic people was loyalty to the leader, who repaid his followers in booty, tribute, land, legal protection, and military security. To the Romans, the king appeared as an ally and magistrate. Almost all Germanic kings bore Roman titles such as *consul* or *patrician,* and in these officially conferred titles resided the authority necessary to govern Roman populations. The kings also succeeded to a long line of Germanic Masters of the Soldiers, the title of the highest military officers in a prefecture. Each monarchy was led by a dynasty—for example, the Merovingians among the Franks—that

was pre-eminent in wealth and possessed a sacral aura not unlike that of the Roman emperors.

The most common local officials were counts, a combined civilian-military position that made its first appearance in the fifth century. Initially a direct representative of the emperor, a count had financial, judicial, and military responsibilities. Local notables, usually great landowners, initially resented counts but gradually aspired to the office. Kings were careful to promote important locals, both Romans and their own people, to the office of count.

Local administration remained based in cities and towns. Taxes continued to be paid to royal governments throughout the sixth century. Provincial populations did not find this policy odd or unjust. Their taxes had always gone primarily to pay for the Roman military establishment, and the monarchies were the heirs of that establishment. Latin persisted as the language of administration. Until the end of Late Antiquity, notaries continued to draw up wills, records of land transactions, and legal documents of all kinds. Law codes issued by the Germanic kingdoms were largely adaptations of Roman provincial law. In other words, the legal conditions under which most people lived stayed pretty much the same. In sum, people's daily lives changed surprisingly little as a result of the replacement of Roman provinces by Germanic kingdoms.

=========== S E C T I O N   S U M M A R Y ===========

- The Romans had long-standing relations with the Germanic barbarians living beyond their frontiers.

- The barbarian "tribes" were actually loose confederations of peoples, which achieved coherence only in kingdoms inside the empire.

- The Visigoths' change from allies, to enemies, and back to allies of the Romans is an instructive example of Romano-barbarian relations.

- The barbarian kingdoms retained many public and private aspects of Roman life.

THE ROMAN EMPIRE IN THE EAST, 395–565

What challenges did the eastern empire face and what were some of its major contributions?

The creation of the tetrarchy at the end of the third century had separated the eastern and western halves of the Roman Empire administratively. In theory, there was only one empire, ruled by one senior emperor, but in practice the Eastern and Western courts followed different policies in many areas, notably in their relations with the Germanic peoples. Fundamental cultural differences also distinguished East from West. The East was more populous, more heavily urbanized, and more prosperous. The eastern Mediterranean was Greek in culture and livelier intellectually

than the West. From Diocletian in the third century to Justinian in the sixth, the eastern Roman Empire evolved slowly along the path marked out by its first great reformers. Moreover, the eastern empire survived as the western empire was being parceled out into kingdoms.

CONSTANTINOPLE AND ITS RULERS

Constantius II (r. 337–361), Constantine's son and his successor in the East, began making Constantinople a truly imperial city. He gave "New Rome" its own senate and urban magistrates, placing the city on an equal constitutional footing with Rome. Constantinople did not have an ancient aristocracy, so Constantius had to create a senatorial order. This he did by recruiting some Romans and promoting prominent and cultivated persons from cities in the eastern half of the empire, thereby forging bonds between the capital and its hinterland. Constantius and his successors also built palaces, public buildings, and churches to give the city a truly imperial character (see **MAP 7.4**).

With the exception of the founder, the ablest members of the dynasty of Valentinian ruled in the East. The greatest of these was Theodosius II (r. 408–450), who enjoyed the longest imperial reign in Roman history. Through skillful diplomacy and the occasional application of force, he managed to keep the eastern empire free of serious Germanic incursions and the Persians at bay in Mesopotamia. To protect his capital on the landward side, he built massive walls, whose ruins are impressive even today. He promoted learning in the city and both added and beautified important buildings. Theodosius and his family made the new capital a real intellectual center.

Born in 401, Theodosius ascended the throne as a child. Throughout his life the two greatest influences on him were his sister, Pulcheria (399–453), and his

MAP 7.4 Constantinople in Late Antiquity

Protected by the sea, the Golden Horn, and its massive landward walls, Constantine's new city was an impregnable fortress for a thousand years. Note how the city was equipped with palaces, forums, wide thoroughfares, and other urban amenities.

(*Source:* The Cambridge Illustrated History of THE MIDDLE AGES, *edited by Robert Fossier, translated by Janet Sondheimer. Copyright © 1989. Used by permission of Cambridge University Press.*)

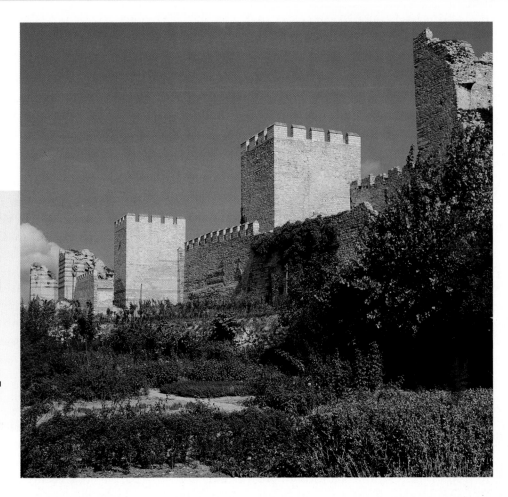

Theodosian Walls
By 413 Theodosius II had erected a massive set of walls, extending more than four miles, to protect Constantinople on the landward side. The wall system consisted of a double set of walls with brick facings and rubble-filled interiors. The main walls (shown here) were about 35 feet high with towers about every 240 feet.
(Sonia Halliday Photographs)

wife, Athenais-Eudoxia (ca. 400–460). Theodosius's moderate religious policy owed much to his wife, while his deep personal piety seems attributable to his sister. Pulcheria achieved the appointment and dismissal of imperial officers, guided foreign policy, and patronized scholars and churchmen. Only rarely do surviving sources permit us to observe the activities of imperial women. The cases of Pulcheria and Eudoxia hint at how much we do not know.

Theodosius's greatest achievement was his law code of 438. The most comprehensive collection of Roman law yet produced, this code brought together all Roman laws issued since Constantine and arranged them in systematic fashion. The principal Germanic kingdoms were established just after the Theodosian code was issued. From this text, and from the Roman institutional structures that employed it, the barbarians were taught the rule of law and regulations for the conduct of daily affairs.

THE EMPEROR JUSTINIAN (R. 527–565)

After Theodosius II died in 450, the eastern empire endured seventy-seven years of rule by military men who lacked the culture, vision, or administrative capacity of their predecessors. But they preserved the empire and kept its government functioning. It was from these rough soldiers that **Justinian** emerged to become the greatest ruler of Late Antiquity, one of the greatest of all Rome's emperors. (See the feature "The Visual Record: The Ravenna Mosaics.")

Justinian was born in an Illyrian village (Croatia, today), entered the army, and secured high office under his illiterate uncle Justin, who had likewise risen from the peasantry to the imperial office (r. 518–527). Despite growing up in rural military camps, Justinian showed a wide range of interests and abilities. He surrounded himself with remarkable people and gave them considerable latitude. In 525 he flouted convention by marrying the actress Theodora (ca. 497–548). A woman of intelligence, imagination, and great courage, Theodora was one of Justinian's key advisers. Contemporaries believed that she guided the emperor's religious policy. She certainly spent lavishly on charitable activities, not least on homes for former prostitutes. Justinian also identified and promoted such previously obscure figures as the gifted general Belisarius (bel-uh-SAR-ee-us), the administrative genius John the

Justinian   Emperor of the eastern empire, he is best known for his law code and for overseeing the construction of the Church of Hagia Sophia.

The Ravenna Mosaics

Propaganda. The word has unsavory connotations. It suggests that someone is trying to convince someone else to do or to believe what is wrong. Actually the word means only "things to be propagated," a message to be gotten out. The message itself may be good or bad, true or false.

When we think of propaganda, we must consider both the message and the medium in which it is conveyed. In antiquity, governments had several means of getting their messages out. Almost all the means were public, visible, striking.

Mosaics are among the most spectacular art forms of Late Antiquity, and in the churches of Ravenna they attained the summit of their propagandistic power. A mosaic is a picture formed by the intricate arrangement of thousands of tiny bits (called *tesserae*) of glass, stone, or metal. An artist created a rough sketch of the intended picture and then laid out the tesserae to conform to the sketch. Next the artist applied wet plaster to a small section of the surface, usually a wall or a floor, that was to receive the picture and then embedded that section's tesserae into the plaster. This process was repeated until the mosaic was completed. The result was a durable art form of great beauty and visual interest. In the picture on the opposite page, you can see the tesserae and even some of the sparkle produced by the effect of sunlight and candlelight reflecting off the mosaic.

Mosaics were sometimes placed in private homes by the very wealthy, but more often they were put in conspicuous public places. Churches commonly received them in Late Antiquity. As more of society became Christian, aristocrats in particular were happy to spend lavishly to adorn their places of worship with beautiful decorations. Masses of people saw those decorations, reflected on who had financed them, and pondered the meaning of the images themselves.

The greatest patron of all was the emperor. By putting up any work of art, the emperor proclaimed his power and influence. His reach was vast even if he never left Constantinople. Nothing shows this better than the Ravenna mosaics erected by Justinian.

Let us recall the situation. The Arian Ostrogoths had taken over Italy in 493. Ruling from Ravenna, they claimed to be imperial allies and representatives. Down to 535 there were strains between Ravenna and Constantinople, and in that year Justinian launched the twenty-year-long Gothic Wars. During and after the wars, churches were erected as symbols of the imperial restoration.

The mosaic pictured here is located on the left-hand side of the sanctuary, above and behind the altar, in the Church of San Vitale in Ravenna. Its central figure is the emperor Justinian. Immediately opposite it is another mosaic focusing on the empress Theodora. San Vitale was a monument to the defeat of the Arian Goths. Any worshiper who raised his or her eyes from the altar saw immediately both Justinian and Theodora. These images made a powerful statement in a city that had been ruled by a Gothic king for thirty-three years. Justinian was leaving no doubt about who was in charge. Consider, too, the prominence accorded to Theodora. Justinian really did view her as a partner in his rule.

That the emperor and empress were in charge is indicated in several distinct ways. They are slightly larger and are standing in front of their attendants. They are not quite like the other humans shown in the mosaic. They wear crowns and rich purple—that is to say, imperial—garments. They present gifts: he a gold paten holding the eucharistic bread and she a golden chalice containing the eucharistic wine. Thus the emperor and empress are represented as the donors of the church and as the guarantors of authentic worship.

Justinian tried throughout his reign to promote *homonoia* ("concord"). He tried to reconcile many political and religious factions. Notice the figure to Justinian's left (your right), over whose bald head you can read MAXIMIANUS. This man was the archbishop of Ravenna, a close ally of the emperor and the person responsible both for eradicating Arianism and for reconciling Arians. His prominent position next to the emperor, and the fact that he alone is named, assured everyone of the correct doctrinal position. And in case anyone needed a further reminder, Maximianus holds in his hand the cross of Christ: there would be no more Arian subordination of the second person of the Trinity to the first.

We may note one more piece of propaganda. Look at the man standing to the left of Justinian and slightly behind him—between Justinian and Maximianus. This is Julianus Argentarius, a wealthy layman who was in all things the emperor's agent

Justinian and His Courtiers, Sanctuary Mosaic, San Vitale, Ravenna   *(Scala/Art Resource, NY)*

in Ravenna. He helped to finance and oversaw the construction of not only San Vitale but also several other churches in Ravenna. His presence signifies *homonoia,* the traditional concord between the emperor and the elite throughout the empire. Relations between the court and the Italian elite had been very strained under the Ostrogoths. Julianus's presence signaled that all was well once again. Vanity played a role, too. Julianus paid for the art, so he had himself included in it.

The Church of San Vitale was itself a propaganda statement. Theodoric was buried in a grand octagonal tomb. Justinian's builders chose an octagonal form for San Vitale. This church is also a sepulcher—a shrine for the remains of Saint Vitalis, an early Ravenna Christian who was martyred for the true faith.

In a world without the modern mass media, the media of antiquity served well to broadcast messages to people who understood their real and symbolic language. Recall the image on a Hellenistic coin (page 112). Look again at the statue of the tetrarchs (page 183). Cassiodorus once said that Rome was "a forest of statues." Every one of them was a propaganda statement.

QUESTIONS

1. Mosaics are public and visible. They convey messages. What images or monuments can you think of that convey messages?

2. How many propaganda "messages" can you find in this picture?

3. What do you think of Justinian as a propagandist?

Online Study Center
Improve Your Grade Visual Record Activities

Cappadocian, and the greatest legal mind of the age, Tribonian (tree-BONE-ee-un). He entrusted two mathematicians, Anthemius (an-THEE-mee-us) of Tralles and Isidore of Miletus, with the task of designing the Church of Hagia Sophia (AYE-yuh so-FEE-yuh), which remains his principal monument.

Almost immediately on assuming the throne, Justinian put John the Cappadocian to work reforming an administration that had been little altered in two centuries despite vast changes in the scope of the empire. John worked particularly to secure tighter control of provincial administrators, to ensure a steady flow of tax revenue, and to eliminate official corruption. Tribonian and a commission were assigned the task of producing the first comprehensive collection of Roman law since that of Theodosius II in 438. Between 529 and 533 Justinian's code was issued in three parts. The *Code* was a systematically organized collection of all imperial legislation. The *Digest* was a collection of the writings of the classical Roman jurists, the legal philosophers of the Early Empire. The *Institutes* was a textbook for law students. Justinian's code, based on the idea that law should "give everyone his due," is the most influential legal collection in human history. It summarizes a thousand years of legal work, remained valid in the eastern empire until 1453, and has subsequently influenced almost every legal system in the modern world.

Not long after undertaking his legal and administrative reforms, Justinian launched an ambitious attempt to reunite the empire by reconquering its lost western provinces. Belisarius retook Africa from the Vandals and Italy from the Ostrogoths. Justinian also landed an army in Spain in an unsuccessful attempt to wrest Iberia from the Visigoths.

Justinian's ability to sustain major campaigns in the West was limited by the need to ward off constant threats in the East. The empire faced new enemies—Bulgars and Slavs—in the Balkans and a resurgent old foe—the Persians—in Mesopotamia. Costly treaties and humiliating subsidies bought a string of cease-fires but no definitive settlements in these areas. The emperor's campaigns were so expensive that his administrative reforms wound up looking like contrivances to make more money for the emperor to waste. In 532 violent mobs coursed through the streets of Constantinople demanding the dismissal of John the Cappadocian and other imperial agents. Justinian almost fled, but Theodora persuaded him to put down the riot. In 542 the Mediterranean world was visited by the most devastating plague in centuries, one more blow to the empire.

Justinian's religious policy also met with sharp opposition. A genuinely pious man, Justinian legislated frequently on behalf of the church and, along with Theodora, practiced generous charitable benefactions. Still, by both personal conviction and a sense of official duty, Justinian desired religious unity. Justinian was mildly Monophysite, and his wife was enthusiastically so. Justinian tried again and again to find a compromise that would bring all parties together. His church council of 553 assembled amid high hopes, but his proposed doctrinal compromises alienated the clergy in Syria, Egypt, and Rome.

To create a monument equal to his lofty vision of the empire, Justinian sought out Anthemius and Isidore. He charged the two great mathematicians to design a church that would represent the place where heaven and earth touched. Regular meetings in this place of the emperor, the patriarch, and the people gave repeated symbolic confirmation of the proper ordering of the state. There is no evidence that Justinian dictated the form of his church—the Church of Hagia Sophia—but the fact that he did not turn to any of the city's regular builders suggests that he was not looking for a traditional basilica. Tradition says that when Justinian first saw his new church he said "Solomon, I have outdone thee."

Hagia Sophia was the largest Christian church until the construction of Saint Peter's in Rome (1503–1614). The building begins with a square just over 100 feet on a side, 70 feet above which are four great arches. Two of the arches are solid and form the nave walls of the church; the other two give way to semicircular continuations of the nave. Above the main square is a dome that seems to float on the blaze of light that pours through its windows. The inside is a riot of color, achieved by marble fittings in almost every imaginable hue and by the mysterious play of light and shadow. The effect of the whole is disorienting. The space in most basilicas is ordered, controlled, elegant. The space in Hagia Sophia is horizontal and vertical, straight and curved, square and round. The inside is by turns dark and light, purple and green, red and blue. It is indeed as if one has entered a realm that is anchored to this world but gives access to another.

It is appropriate that in assessing his church, Justinian should have looked backward to Solomon, the Hebrew king who built Jerusalem's Temple. In almost all respects Justinian was a traditional, backward-looking ruler. His concern for the administrative minutiae of his empire would have made perfect sense to Diocletian. His combination of military and diplomatic initiatives would have been appreciated by Theodosius I, whose namesake, Theodosius II, would have admired Justinian's legal code. In his religious policies, especially his quest for unity, Justinian drew from a deep well of imperial precedent. Even in his attempt to restore direct rule in Rome's former western provinces, Justinian showed himself a traditionalist.

Hagia Sophia Constructed during the reign of the emperor Justinian, this church in Constantinople was the largest Christian church until the construction of Saint Peter's in the sixteenth century.

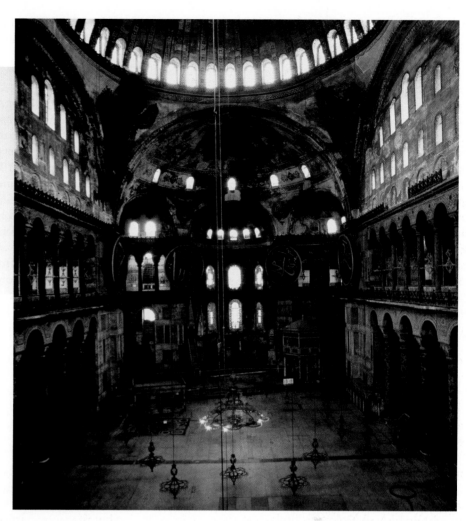

Hagia Sophia
Interior view of Hagia Sophia, the church of "Holy Wisdom," built by Justinian between 527 and 532. The church combines traditional Roman features and stunning new elements. When Constantinople fell to the Turks in 1453, this church became a mosque, an Islamic house of worship. In the early twentieth century, it became a museum. *(Werner Forman/Art Resource, NY)*

═══════════ S E C T I O N   S U M M A R Y ═══════════

- As the western empire was disappearing, the eastern empire experienced two centuries of capable, enlightened leadership.

- Constantinople was developed into a magnificent capital city.

- East Roman rulers continued to reform the administration and tax system.

- Both Theodosius II and Justinian made important contributions to the development of Roman law.

SOCIETY AND CULTURE IN LATE ANTIQUITY

How did women and men, elites and ordinary people, urban dwellers and farmers experience continuity and change in Late Antiquity?

During these centuries of the ascendancy of the eastern Roman Empire, and the splintering of the western, the daily lives of men and women of every social class changed relatively little in terms of power relationships and economic opportunities. Nevertheless, provincial elites, members of the clergy, and barbarians gained unprecedented influence.

Ordinary farmers, the overwhelming majority of the population, experienced changes in their legal status but not in their material well-being. Secular intellectual life lost most of its vitality, but a vibrant Christian culture flourished in the writings of the Church Fathers. Christianity added yet another element to the diversity that always characterized the Roman world.

SOCIAL HIERARCHIES AND REALITIES

Roman society had long been hierarchical, and from Republican times Rome had been governed by a hereditary class. Although the members of this class affected a style of life that set them apart, they were never a closed caste. First, they did not reproduce themselves very effectively. About two-thirds of the Roman aristocracy was replaced every century—a typical pattern in premodern societies. This turnover created significant opportunities for social mobility. Second, just as the empire had been born in a social transformation that brought the Italian aristocracy into the Roman governing class, so Late Antiquity was characterized by a transformation that brought provincial elites and barbarians into the framework of power. Paradoxically, social change was always masked as social continuity, because when new men reached the top, they tried to embrace the culture and values of those whom they had replaced.

Three ideals guided the lives of elite men: *otium*, *amicitia*, and *officium*. *Otium*, "leisure," meant that the only life worth living was one of withdrawal in which the finer things in life—literature especially—could be cultivated. *Amicitia*, "friendship," implied several things. It could mean the kinds of literary contacts that the thousands of surviving letters from Late Antiquity reveal. Friendship also could mean patronage. The doorstep of every noble household was crowded every morning with hangers-on who awaited their patron's small offerings and any commands as to how they might do his will. *Officium*, "duty," was the sense of civic obligation that Roman rulers communicated to the provincial upper classes.

Aristocrats governed in both public and private ways, which are almost impossible to differentiate. Though gradually excluded from key military and administrative posts, nobles did not lose their influence. They used their wealth to win or reward followers, bribe officials, and buy verdicts. In towns decurions controlled local market privileges, building trades, police forces, fire brigades, and charitable associations. Their public and private means of persuasion and intimidation were immense. In the West, in the growing absence of an imperial administration, Roman public power did not so much "decline and fall" as find itself privatized and localized. Patronage and clientage in Roman society had a benevolent dimension, but they also revealed the raw realities of power.

In Roman society power was everything, and those who lacked power were considered "poor," regardless of their financial status. On this reckoning, much of the urban population was poor because they lacked access to the official means of coercion and security that the notables enjoyed. Merchants, artisans, teachers, and others were always vulnerable because their social, political, or economic positions could change at a moment's notice. They lacked the influence to protect themselves.

Most citizens of the late antique world can be classed as farmers, but this categorization is misleading because it lumps together the greatest landowners and the poorest peasants. Late Antiquity saw a trend in the countryside that continued into the Middle Ages: freedom and slavery declined simultaneously. Many small, independent farmers, probably people who had long been the clients of local grandees, handed over their possessions—*commended* them is the technical term—and received back the use of them in return for annual rents in money or in kind. They became *coloni*, "tenants." Their patrons promised to protect them from lawsuits and from severe economic hardship. More and more, these coloni were bound to their places of residence and forced to perform services or pay fees that marked their status as less than fully free. At the same time, many landlords who could no longer afford to house, feed, and equip slaves gave them their freedom and elevated them to the status of coloni. Probably the day-to-day lives of the great mass of the rural population and their position at the bottom of the social hierarchy changed very little.

Women's lives are not as well known to us as men's. "Nature produced women for this very purpose," says a Roman legal text, "that they might bear children and this is their greatest desire." Ancient philosophy held that women were intellectually inferior to men, science said they were physically weaker, and law maintained that they were naturally dependent. In the Roman world women could not enter professions, and they had limited rights in legal matters. Christianity offered women opposing models. There was Eve, the eternal temptress through whom sin had fallen on humanity, and then there was Mary, the virginal mother of God. The Bible also presented readers with powerful, active women, such as Deborah and Ruth, and loyal, steadfast ones, such as Jesus's female disciples. Amid this varied popular and learned opinion, we can still detect some possibilities for independent and influential activity on the part of women.

Girls usually did not choose their marriage partners. Betrothals could take place as early as age 7 and lawful marriages at 12. Most marriages took place when the girl was around 16; husbands were several years older. A daughter could reject her father's choice only if the intended man was unworthy in status and behavior. Women could inherit property from their fathers and retained some control over their marital dowries. Divorce was possible but only in restricted cases. A divorced woman who had lost the financial security provided by her husband and father was at a distinct disadvantage legally and economically unless she had great wealth.

Christianity brought some interesting changes in marriage practices. Since the new faith prized virginity and celibacy, women now had the option of declining marriage. The church at Antioch supported three thousand virgins and widows. Christian writers tried to attract women to the celibate life by emphasizing that housework was drudgery. Christianity required both men and women to be faithful in marriage, whereas Roman custom had permitted men, but not women, to have lovers, prostitutes, and concubines. Christianity increased the number of days when men and women had to abstain from sex. Ancient cultures often prohibited sexual intercourse during menstruation and pregnancy, but Christianity added Sundays and many feast days as forbidden times. Further, Christianity disapproved of divorce, which may have accorded women greater financial and social security, although at the cost of staying with abusive or unloved husbands.

Traditionally women were not permitted to teach in the ancient world, although we do hear of women teachers such as Hypatia of Alexandria (355–415), renowned for her knowledge of philosophy and mathematics. Until at least the sixth century the Christian church had deaconesses who had important responsibilities in the instruction of women and girls. Medical knowledge was often the preserve of women, particularly in areas such as childbirth, sexual problems, and "female complaints."

Christianity also affected daily life. Churchmen were concerned that women not be seen as sex objects. They told women to clothe their flesh, veil their hair, and use jewelry and cosmetics in moderation. Pious women no longer used public baths and latrines. Male or female, Christians thought and lived in distinctive new ways. All Christians were sinners, and so all were equal in God's eyes and equally in need of God's grace. Neither birth, wealth, nor status was supposed to matter in this democracy of sin. Theological equality did not, however, translate into social equality.

The church also introduced some new status distinctions. Holiness became a badge of honor, and holy men and women became Late Antiquity's greatest celebrities. After their death they were venerated as saints. Sanctuaries were dedicated to them, and people made pilgrimages to their tombs to pray and seek healing from physical and spiritual ailments. Miracle stories became popular. Thus in some ways Christianity produced a society the likes of which the ancient world had never known, a society in which the living and the dead jockeyed for a place in a hierarchy that was at once earthly and celestial. But in other ways Christianity reoriented traditional Roman patron-client relations so that client sinners in this world were linked to sanctified patrons in heaven.

THE QUEST FOR A CATHOLIC TRADITION

By the middle of the fifth century the Nicene Creed, first spelled out in 325, had taken definitive shape; it is still recited regularly in many Christian churches. With the Council of Nicaea we see the first clear evidence that people were striving for a *catholic*, a universal, form of Christianity. Strictly speaking, catholic Christianity would be the one form professed by all believers. A fifth-century writer said that the catholic faith was the one believed "everywhere, all the time, by everyone." It is no accident that the Catholic Church grew up in a Roman world steeped in ideas of universality. The most deeply held tenet of Roman ideology was that Rome's mission was to civilize the world and bend it to Roman ways. As we have seen, however, it proved impossible to attain or impose a single set of beliefs.

One intriguing development in Late Antiquity is the emergence of several Christian communities claiming fidelity to a universal, or catholic, tradition. The Latin Christian church in the West clung tightly to the doctrinal formulations of Nicaea and Chalcedon and took its bearings from Latin church writers. In the eastern Mediterranean writers tended to use the word *Orthodox*, which means "right believing" but also carries clear implications of catholicism, or "universality." The Orthodox Church centered primarily on the emperors and patriarchs, used Greek, and followed Greek Christian writers. The Coptic Church in Egypt was Monophysite, followed the teachings of the patriarchs of Alexandria, and used the Coptic language. The Jacobite Church, a mildly Monophysite, Syriac-speaking group, was originally strong in Syria, from which it spread to Mesopotamia and beyond. Each of these churches produced a literature, an art, and a way of life that marked its members as a distinct community. These traditions did not reflect the emergence of something new in Late Antiquity so much as a Christian reinterpretation of very old cultures and ideals. Each of these traditions exists today.

Christianity drew much from the pagan and Jewish environments within which it grew, but its fundamental inspiration was the collection of writings called in modern times the Bible. In antiquity this material was called *ta hagia biblia* or *sacra biblia*, meaning "the holy books." It was understood to be a collection of sacred writings, and the individual items in that collection had different meanings. From the second century, Christian writers began trying to define a canon, a definitive list of genuine Old and New Testament scriptures. It was widely recognized that without an official, standardized set of Christian writings, there could be no uniformity of Christian belief. This process of determining authentic Scripture was not completed until the middle of the fifth century.

Sarcophagus of Junius Bassus

Junius Bassus, prefect of Rome, died in 359 and was laid to rest in this splendid sarcophagus (from the Greek "body eater"). Three points are important: First, as members of the Roman elite became Christian, they could afford to employ the finest craftsmen. Second, as Christianity became legal, it could search for artistic expression. Third, these Old and New Testament scenes proclaim Christ's divinity but, in an age of intense theological quarrels, glide over his humanity. Compare Santa Maria Maggiore on page 180.

(Hirmer Verlag München)

While the search was underway for an authoritative list of books, it was also necessary to try to get uniform versions of the books that were being pronounced canonical. The Greek East used the Greek version of the Old Testament and the Greek New Testament. But that version was unsuitable in the West, where Latin was the principal tongue. Late in the fourth century Pope Damasus (DAM-uh-sus) commissioned Jerome (331–420), a man who had renounced his wealth for a life of monasticism and scholarship, to prepare a Latin version based on a new translation of the Hebrew Scriptures and Greek New Testament. Jerome's version was called the **Vulgate Bible** because it was the Bible for the "people" (*vulgus*), who knew Latin.

The development of a scriptural canon paralleled the elaboration of a creedal statement that would set down precisely what Christians believed. As we have seen, the Councils of Nicaea and Constantinople defined the nature of the Trinity, and Chalcedon formulated the relationship between the human and divine natures of Christ. There were also debates about the nature of the priesthood, the structure and authority of the church, and the problem of human free will. Practical questions came up, too. How could Christians fulfill the moral demands of their faith while living in a world whose values were often at odds with church teachings?

Answers to these kinds of questions were provided by a group of Greek and Latin writers who are called the "Church Fathers" and whose era is called "patristic" (from *patres*, the Latin word for "fathers"). In versatility and sheer output they have few rivals at any time. Their intellectual breadth was matched by their elegant style and trenchant reasoning.

Many Christian writers addressed the problems of moral living in the world. In his treatise *On Duties*, Ambrose of Milan (339–397) attempted to Christianize the public ethos that Cicero had spelled out many years before in his book of the same name. Cicero talked of citizens' obligations to one another and to the law and the need for those in power to be above reproach in the conduct of their personal lives. Ambrose reinterpreted these obligations as duties that Christians owed to one another because of their common worship of God.

Pope Gregory I wrote *The Pastoral Rule* to reformulate Cicero's and Ambrose's ideas in ways that made them relevant to society's Christian leaders, the clergy. John Chrysostom (KRIH-sus-tum) (347–407), a patriarch of Constantinople and one of the most popular and gifted preachers of Late Antiquity (his name means "golden tongued"), bitterly castigated the immorality of the imperial court and aristocracy: by setting a bad example, they endangered the souls of their subjects.

Boethius (bow-EE-thee-us) (480–524) illustrates contemporary themes well. Descended from one of Rome's oldest families, he held high offices but eventually earned the enmity of Theodoric the Ostrogoth, who imprisoned and executed him. He was a prolific writer, whose Latin translations of Greek philosophical texts bequeathed those writings to the Middle Ages. In his most famous book, *The Consolation of Philosophy*, written while he was in prison, Boethius describes how the soul could rise through philosophy to a knowledge of God. Once again we see the classical and the Christian blended in a new synthesis.

Vulgate Bible   Prepared by Jerome in the late fourth century, it was a Latin translation of the Hebrew Scriptures (Old Testament) and the Greek New Testament.

SAINT AUGUSTINE AND THE CHRISTIAN TRADITION

The most influential Christian thinker after Saint Paul was **Augustine of Hippo** (354–430). Augustine was born in North Africa to a pagan father and a Christian mother. His family was of modest means, but at great sacrifice they arranged for him to receive the best education available. He embarked on a career as a professor of rhetoric. Once he had established himself, he moved on to Rome and then to Milan, which in the fourth century was the unofficial Western capital. Augustine fell under the spell of Ambrose and embraced the Christianity that his mother, Monica, had been urging on him throughout his life. Later Augustine chronicled his quest for truth and spiritual fulfillment in his *Confessions,* a classic of Western literature. In 395 Augustine became a bishop and until his death served the North African community at Hippo, and the wider Christian world, with a torrent of writings.

Not a systematic thinker, Augustine never set out to provide a comprehensive exposition of the whole of Christian doctrine. Instead, he responded to problems as they arose. Crucial among these were the relationship between God and humans, the nature of the church, and the overall plan of God's creation.

In the early fifth century some people believed that they could achieve salvation by the unaided operation of their own will. Augustine responded that although God did indeed endow humankind with free will, Adam and Eve had abused their will to rebel against God. Ever since that first act of rebellion, a taint, called by theologians "original sin," predisposed all humans to continual rebellion, or sin, against God. Only divine grace can overcome sin, and only by calling on God can people receive grace. Here was a decisive break with the classical idea of humanity as good in itself and capable of self-improvement, perhaps even perfection, in this world. According to Augustine, all people are sinners, in need of God's redemption.

Some North African heretics taught that sacraments celebrated by unworthy priests are invalid. Augustine believed that the validity of the church's sacraments—those ritual celebrations that are considered to be channels for the communication of grace, of God's special aid and comfort to the faithful—does not depend on the personal merit of the minister. A priest or a bishop acts in God's place and through divine grace. Therefore, faith in God is paramount. The church is thus a community of acknowledged sinners led by the clergy in a quest for eternal salvation. To Augustine, God alone is perfect. Clergy, rulers, and churches are all human institutions, all more or less good in particular circumstances.

Augustine of Hippo   North African bishop and influential Christian thinker, he authored the *Confessions* and *The City of God.*

To many adherents of the traditional Roman religion, the sack of Rome by the Visigoths in 410 was repayment for Rome's abandonment of its traditional gods. To refute them, Augustine wrote the most brilliant and difficult of all his works, *The City of God.* This book is a theology of history. Augustine sees time not as cyclical—the traditional classical view—but as linear. Since the creation of the world, a plan has been in operation—God's plan—and that plan will govern all human activity until the end of time. History is the struggle between those who call on divine grace, who are redeemed, who are citizens of the City of God, and those who keep to the ways of the world, who persist in sin, who live in the earthly city. One may observe the unfolding of the divine plan by seeing how much of the earthly city has been redeemed at any given time.

Even though the Roman Empire was officially Christian, Augustine refused to identify his City of God with it. Nor would he say that the church and the City of God were identical. What he did say was that the sack of Rome was a great irrelevance because many kingdoms and empires had come and gone and would continue to do so, but only the kingdom of God was eternal and, in the long run, important. To a Roman people whose most cherished belief held that the world would last exactly as long as Rome's dominion, Augustine's dismissal of Rome's destiny sounded the death knell of the classical worldview.

Augustine also addressed the problem of education. He regarded salvation as the goal of life but realized that people have to carry on with their ordinary occupations. He also knew that almost the entire educational establishment was pagan in design and content. Education was confined mainly to the elite, who sought schooling partly to orient themselves within their cultural tradition and partly to gain employment, often in the imperial or urban service. This education had three mainstays. Latin or Greek grammar—rarely both—was the first. Augustine, for instance, knew little Greek, and by the sixth century few people in the East knew Latin. The second mainstay of education was rhetoric, once the art of public speaking but now, increasingly, literary criticism. The third was dialectic, or the art of right reasoning. In Late Antiquity public schools were fast disappearing as the need for them slipped away. But the church still needed educated persons, so it provided schools in cathedrals and monasteries.

In a treatise entitled *On Christian Doctrine,* Augustine expressed some ideas about education that proved influential for a millennium. He argued that everything a person needs to know to achieve salvation is contained in the Bible. But the Bible, written in learned language, is full of difficult images and allusions. How is an ordinary person to learn what he or she needs to know in order to master this great book of life? Only by getting some schooling, and that education would inevitably be in the classical languages and literatures. To express his attitude toward that schooling, Augustine used the image of "spoiling the Egyptians," borrowed from the account of the Hebrews' Exodus from Egypt, when they took with them whatever they could use. Augustine's attitude toward classical learning was that it was useful only to the extent that it equipped individuals to read the Bible, to understand it, and to seek salvation. Classical culture had no intrinsic merit. It might give pleasure, but it was equally likely to be a distraction or a temptation to immorality.

The Italian writer Cassiodorus (ca. 485–580) gave this Augustinian interpretation of the classical heritage its definitive statement in his treatise *On Divine and Human Readings.* After the fall of the Ostrogothic kingdom, whose king Theodoric he had served loyally, Cassiodorus (cass-ee-oh-DOR-us) retired and set up a school of Christian studies. His treatise served as a kind of annotated bibliography and curriculum of the major writings on school subjects, such as grammar, rhetoric, and dialectic, and on biblical commentary. For centuries, schools organized on Augustine's and Cassiodorus's model did an estimable job of preparing the clergy to carry out their functions.

SECTION SUMMARY

- Despite dramatic political changes, Late Antiquity witnessed relatively little social or economic change.

- Christianity did, however, introduce many changes in morals and values.

- Late Antiquity presents us with the paradox of multiple "Catholic" traditions, that is, different Christian groups who believed that their tradition was universal.

- In the Latin and Greek churches, a catholic tradition was built upon a canon of sacred writings, a creed, and the writings of the Church Fathers.

- The greatest intellectual of Late Antiquity was Saint Augustine, who wrote on theology, history, and education.

CHAPTER SUMMARY

Online Study Center **ACE the Test**

What were the most important reforms of Diocletian, Constantine, and their successors, and what roles did those reforms play in saving and transforming the empire?

How and why did a Roman and Catholic Church emerge in Late Antiquity?

Who were the "barbarians," and what kinds of relations did Romans and barbarians have in Late Antiquity?

What challenges did the eastern empire face and what were some of its major contributions?

How did women and men, elites and ordinary people, urban dwellers and farmers experience continuity and change in Late Antiquity?

When the late antique period opened, Rome's vast and diverse empire was beset with innumerable political, military, and economic problems. The classical culture that had evolved over centuries in the Mediterranean world seemed to have lost much of its vigor and appeal. But energetic rulers such as Diocletian and Constantine undertook half a century of intense military, economic, and administrative reform. On religious issues, the rulers differed—Diocletian persecuted Christians while Constantine legalized the new faith. Their reforms put the empire on firm footing while simultaneously changing forever the basic nature of the Roman state.

The fourth century was a period of religious change for the empire. Church officials attempted to resolve disagreements over Christian teachings with ecumenical councils, but religious unity was never fully achieved. Further attempts to resolve controversies strengthened the power of the bishops and created the new role of the papacy. As the power of the pope increased, so too did the role of the elite. However, some men and women yearned to escape the trappings of the world and turned toward a new way of life—monasticism.

In 300 barbarians were a worrisome threat along the northern frontiers of the empire. By 600 barbarians had created, from Britain to Spain, a succession of kingdoms, the most successful of which owed great debts to Rome. The barbarians did not appear suddenly in Late Antiquity. Rome knew these people and had traded, fought, and allied with them for centuries. The barbarians did not come to destroy Rome but to join it, to benefit from it, to learn its ways. The creation of the barbarian kingdoms was in many ways one of Rome's most creative political acts.

In the eastern empire, Constantinople rose to become a truly imperial city under the emperors Theodo-sius and Justinian. Justinian's code, which collected and organized Roman law, is the most influential legal collection in history. Equally impressive was the construction of a new Christian church, the Hagia Sophia. Yet despite these achievements, Justinian had to deal with new enemies, expensive military campaigns, and a devastating plague.

While these centuries were a period of great political and religious change, the daily lives of men and women stayed remarkably unchanged. Society was hierarchical and most of the population was categorized as poor. Christianity brought some changes to social practices, such as marriage and relationships between men and women. Believers strived for a universal, or catholic, form of Christianity and this led to the development of a scriptural canon. New writings on Christianity, from Saint Augustine and others, also helped to shape beliefs.

LOOKING AHEAD

Late Antiquity was not a period of "decline and fall" so much as a period of dynamic change, evolution, and transformation. We may ask: What happened next? In fact, the Roman Empire gave birth to three new cultures and traditions: the Germanic West, the Byzantine East, and the Islamic world. In the next chapter we turn to those traditions as we move into what is customarily called "the Middle Ages."

KEY TERMS

tetrarchy (p. 182)
Edict of Milan (p. 186)
heresy (p. 188)
Arianism (p. 188)
Council of Nicaea (p. 188)

papacy (p. 191)
monasticism (p. 192)
Visigoths (p. 194)
Justinian (p. 201)
Hagia Sophia (p. 204)

Vulgate Bible (p. 208)
Augustine of Hippo (p. 209)

Online Study Center
Improve Your Grade Flashcards

SUGGESTED READING

Bowersock, G. W., P. Brown, and O. Grabar, eds. *Late Antiquity: A Guide to the Post-Classical World.* 1999. Though basically an encyclopedia, this masterful volume contains long entries on all the major topics and up-to-date essays on big themes.

Brown, Peter. *The World of Late Antiquity.* 1971. A sprightly and beautifully illustrated interpretation of cultural crosscurrents by the most gifted interpreter of Late Antiquity.

Clark, Gillian. *Women in Late Antiquity: Pagan and Christian Lifestyles.* 1993. A first-ever attempt to capture the lives of late antique women in all respects.

Heather, Peter. *The Fall of the Roman Empire.* 2005. A comprehensive and beautifully written treatment of Rome's transformation that challenges much current thinking.

Markus, Robert. *The End of Ancient Christianity.* 1990. This stimulating and eloquent book explores the changing meanings of sacred and secular in the period from 400 to 600.

Noble, Thomas F. X. *From Roman Provinces to Medieval Kingdoms.* 2006. A collection of important and accessible essays with a comprehensive introduction treating central issues in the history of the barbarians and their relations with Rome.

8

EARLY MEDIEVAL CIVILIZATIONS, 600–900

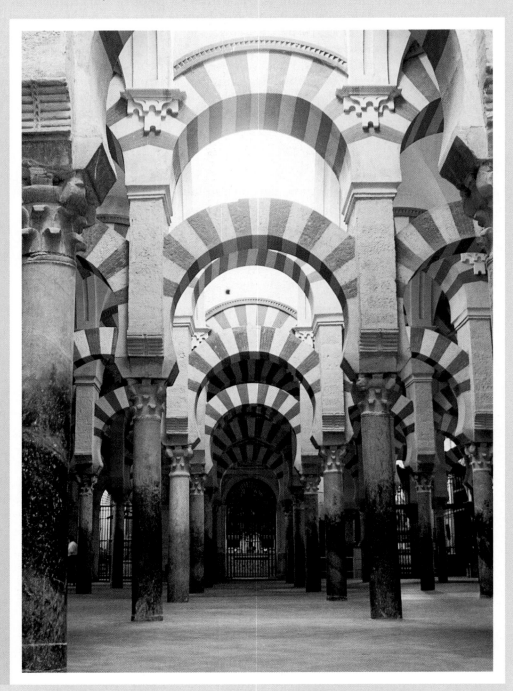

The Great Mosque of Cordoba
(Christopher Rennie/Robert Harding World Imagery)

The Great Mosque of Cordoba, erected by Abd ar-Rahman in 786–787, at first glance appears much like a late antique building: elegant columns, arches arranged in arcades, rectangular space. But this is a *mosque,* an Islamic house of worship, and it was built in Spain, one of Rome's oldest provinces. We saw in Chapter 7 that Spain had fallen to the Visigoths in the sixth century and that Justinian had been unable to reconquer the region. Between 711 and 716 an army of Arabs and North African tribesmen overwhelmed Spain and inaugurated seven centuries of Islamic rule on the Iberian Peninsula. A time traveler transported to the Mediterranean world of 600 would almost certainly have predicted only two heirs to Rome: the eastern empire and the kingdoms of the barbarian West. It is extremely unlikely that our intrepid wanderer would have foreseen one of the most dramatic developments in the history of Western civilization: the rise of the Arabs and their Islamic faith.

In this chapter three areas and histories engage our attention: the Islamic East, the Byzantine Empire, and the Latin West. For each, the seventh century was an era of dramatic change, the eighth century a period of reform and consolidation, and the ninth century a time of upheaval. A new imperial tradition developed in all three areas. Muslims, Orthodox Christians, and Catholics all believed themselves to be chosen by God, and their rulers defined themselves as God's earthly agents. In all three realms the interaction of local traditions and the Roman past produced new forms of central government that would prove influential for centuries. Commercial ties began to transform the Mediterranean world into a community of peoples who needed to balance mutual interests with bitter rivalries.

The Great Mosque serves as a remarkable reminder of how much changed—and how much remained the same—in the early Middle Ages. Arches and arcades graced classical architecture for more than a millennium. But Cordoba's arches are horseshoe shaped, a minor innovation. The arches incorporate alternating bands of red and cream-colored stone. These shapes and colors may be local traditions, an imitation of the Roman aqueduct at Mérida, Byzantine imports, or Syrian characteristics. The building is basilican in shape. In a basilica the space is oriented to the area where officials presided—to an altar when the basilica is a church. In a mosque the space is

CHAPTER OUTLINE

THE ISLAMIC EAST

THE BYZANTINE EMPIRE

CATHOLIC KINGDOMS IN THE WEST

THE CAROLINGIAN EMPIRE

EARLY MEDIEVAL ECONOMIES AND SOCIETIES

KEY TERMS

Muhammad	Orthodox
Five Pillars	Charlemagne
Quran	vassals
caliphate	Carolingian
Papal States	Renaissance
iconoclasm	manor

Online Study Center

This icon will direct you to interactive map and primary source activities on the website **college.hmco.com/pic/noble5e**

oriented to the *qibla* wall—the wall facing Mecca, the birthplace of Muhammad and Islam. The elements of the Great Mosque were old, but the overall effect was new.

The period from 600 to 900 is commonly called the "early Middle Ages." What does this term mean? In the seventeenth century a Dutch scholar wrote of the *Medii Aevi*, the "Middle Times" that lay between antiquity and the dawning modern world. The name stuck. As a label for the post-Roman world, "Middle Ages" (whose adjectival form is "medieval") has become traditional. The fact that we no longer talk of an abrupt and catastrophic "fall" of the Roman Empire means that we no longer use the word *medieval* in negative ways.

FOCUS QUESTIONS

What were the most important factors in the rise of the Arab peoples and the Islamic faith?

Why did a distinctive civilization that can be called "Byzantine" emerge?

What strengths and weaknesses were exhibited by the small states that survived Rome's collapse in the West?

What were the greatest achievements of the Carolingians and why were they so successful?

What were the chief similarities and differences among the early medieval civilizations?

THE ISLAMIC EAST

What were the most important factors in the rise of the Arab peoples and the Islamic faith?

Ancient writers took little notice of the Arabs, who inhabited much of the area from the Arabian peninsula to the Euphrates River. Around 600 the prophet **Muhammad** (570–632) appeared among them preaching a faith old in its basic elements but new in its formulation. With unprecedented spiritual and military fervor, converts to that new faith conquered territories from Spain to the frontiers of China. Slowly, they built an imperial system with a coherent government and ideology. At the same time, cultural elites began forging a new civilization out of the ethnic, religious, and historical diversity of that vast realm.

ARABIA BEFORE MUHAMMAD

The Arab world in 600 was large and turbulent. Long dominated by the Roman and Persian Empires, the region had no stable, large-scale political entities. People belonged to close-knit clans, or extended families, that in varying associations formed tribes. In theory, tribes were groups of people tracing descent from a known ancestor; in reality—and in this, Arab and Germanic peoples were alike—tribes were complex groups of relatives, allies, and political or economic clients.

Muhammad   Prophet and founder of Islam. He began receiving revelations to preach about Allah in around 610. Before his death he had converted most of Arabia.

The Arab East was also economically intricate and fragile. Bedouins (Arabs who were nomadic pastoralists) provided for their own needs from their herds of sheep and goats, from small-scale trading in towns, and from regular raids on one another and on caravans. Some farmers worked the land, but in many areas soils were too poor and rain was too infrequent to support agriculture. Cities supported traders who carried luxury goods, such as spices, incense, and perfumes, from the Indian Ocean region and southern Arabia along caravan routes to the cities of the eastern Mediterranean. These traders formed the economic and political elite of Arabia, and they led the tribes. Mecca, dominated by the powerful tribe of the Quraysh (KOOR-aysh), was the foremost city of Arabia, but competition among cities and tribes was fierce.

A solution to the competition among tribes and towns for control of trade routes was the institution of *harams* (HAR-ahms), or sanctuaries—places where contending parties could settle disputes peacefully. Mecca was one of the chief harams in Arabia, and its founding was attributed to the Israelite patriarch Abraham and one of his sons, Ishmael. The focus of the sanctuary was the black stone shrine known as the Kaaba (KAH-bah), founded by Abraham, according to Arab tradition. For centuries people from all over Arabia had made pilgrimages to Mecca, to the Kaaba, supposedly following Abraham's example.

The region's ethnic and religious composition was complicated, too. The Roman world was overwhelmingly Christian, although there were many kinds of Christians. The Persian realm was officially Zoroastrian, but it had Jewish, Christian, Manichaean, and Buddhist minorities. The Arabs themselves were generally pagans, but Arabia had Jewish and Christian minorities.

THE PROPHET AND HIS FAITH

Muhammad was born in 570 to a respectable though not wealthy or powerful clan of the Quraysh tribe. His father died before he was born, his mother shortly afterward, leaving Muhammad under the care of his grandparents and an uncle. Like many young Meccans, he entered the caravan trade. By the time he was 20, Muhammad had such a reputation for competence and moral uprightness that he became financial adviser to a wealthy Quraysh widow, Khadija (KAH-dee-ah) (555–619). Though older than Muhammad, she became his wife in 595, and they had a loving marriage until her death.

From his youth Muhammad was a man of spiritual insight. In 610 he received the first of many revelations that commanded him to teach all people a new faith that called for an unquestioned belief in one god, Allah, and a deep commitment to social justice for believers. Muhammad began teaching in Mecca, but he converted few people outside his own circle; his wife was his first convert. Some Meccans were envious of Muhammad. Others feared that his new faith and new god might call into question the legitimacy of the shrines in Mecca and jeopardize the traditional pilgrimages to the Kaaba and the trade that accompanied them. By 619 Muhammad's well-connected wife and uncle were dead, and his position was precarious.

At this juncture citizens from Medina, a smaller trading community wracked by dissension among pagan Arabs, Jews, and followers of Muhammad, asked Muhammad to establish a haram there. In the summer of 622 small groups of Muhammad's disciples made their way to Medina, and in September Muhammad joined them. His journey from Mecca to Medina, the *hijra* (HEEZH-rah), marks the beginning of a new era, symbolized to this day in the Arab world by a calendar that dates "In the year of the Hijra."

Although Muhammad was fully in control in Medina, Mecca remained the focus of his attention. In addition to his sentimental attachment to Mecca, its political and economic importance were critical to his emerging desire to convert all of Arabia. His followers began attacking Meccan caravans and battled with the Meccans several times in the 620s. In 630 Muhammad and many of his followers returned to Mecca in triumph. Muhammad left the Quraysh in control, and he retained the Kaaba as a focus of piety. After making lo-

cal arrangements, he returned to Medina and set about winning over the bedouins of the Arabian desert. By the time Muhammad died in 632, he had converted most of Arabia (see **MAP 8.1**).

To what exactly had Muhammad and his followers converted? At the most basic level, people were asked to surrender completely to Allah, the one true God—that is, they were asked to make *al-Islam,* "the surrender." Those who surrendered became *Muslims* and joined the *umma muslima* (OO-mah MOOSE-lee-mah), a completely new kind of community in which membership depended only on belief in Allah and acceptance of Muhammad as Allah's prophet. No longer were one's duties confined to a particular clan, tribe, or town. All members of the umma were understood to have personal and communal responsibility for all other members. Because of the experience of the hijra, Islam was a religion of exile, of separation from the ordinary world, and of reliance on God.

570–632	Life of Muhammad
597	Pope Gregory I sends missionaries to England
610–641	Reign of Heraclius in Byzantium
622	Hijra
632–733	Muslim conquests
661–750	Umayyad caliphate
664	Council of Whitby
711–716	Muslim conquest of Spain
726–787, 815–842	Byzantine iconoclasm
750	Founding of Abbasid caliphate
751	Lombard conquest of Ravenna
755–756	Foundation of Papal States
755–774	Frankish conquest of Lombards
757–796	Reign of Offa of Mercia
768–814	Reign of Charlemagne
780s–860s	Carolingian Renaissance
786–809	Reign of Harun al-Rashid
800	Imperial coronation of Charlemagne
843	Treaty of Verdun creates three Frankish kingdoms
867–886	Reign of Basil I

MAP 8.1   Arab Conquests to 733

This map vividly illustrates the spectacular gains by the Arabs in the time of Muhammad, under the first caliphs, and under the Umayyads. Later slow, steady gains in Africa, central Asia, and India expanded the empire even farther. Muslim conquest did not at first mean widespread conversion to Islam; Egypt, for example, was not majority Muslim before the tenth century.

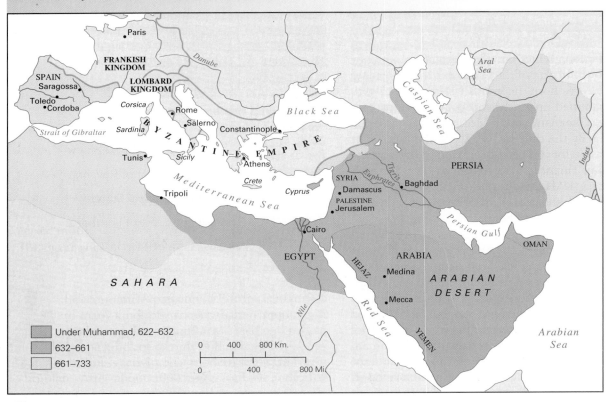

Online Study Center   Improve Your Grade Interactive Map: The Expansion of Islam

The basic teachings of Islam are traditionally described as **Five Pillars:** (1) the profession of faith, "There is no God but Allah and Muhammad is His Prophet"; (2) individual prayer five times daily, plus group prayer at noon on Friday in a *mosque,* a Muslim house of prayer; (3) the sunup-to-sundown fast for one month per year; (4) the donation of generous alms to the poor; and (5) a pilgrimage to Mecca at least once in a person's lifetime. These pillars are still the central requirements of Islam.

In the early decades the pillars sustained a faith that stressed strict monotheism and practices that affirmed Islam and built up a sense of community. At certain times of the day all Muslims everywhere bowed in prayer, with their heads facing toward Mecca. Everyone paid alms, creating thereby a feeling of solidarity among all members of the umma. Mecca itself and the experience of pilgrimage were central to all Muslims.

Originally there was no elaborate theology, intricate doctrinal mysteries, creed, or clergy. Men called *imams* led the Friday prayers in the mosque and usually offered sermons that applied Muslim teaching to the issues of the day, but Islam involved no ordained priesthood as in Judaism or Christianity and no hierarchy as in the Christian churches.

Muhammad communicated God's teaching to his followers, always insisting that he was transmitting a direct, verbal revelation and not offering his own interpretations. That revelation came in the form of "recitations" that make up the **Quran** (koo-RAHN), the Scriptures of Islam. Not long after Muhammad's death his closest followers arranged the recitations into 114 *Suras,* or chapters. The Quran contains legal and wisdom literature like the Hebrew Scriptures and moral teaching like the Christian New Testament. It also prescribes regulations for diet and for personal conduct.

Five Pillars   The basic beliefs and practices of Islam.

Quran   Containing Allah's revelations to Muhammad, it constitutes the scriptures of Islam.

THE WRITTEN RECORD

THE MESSAGE OF THE QURAN

The Quran consists of 114 Suras, literally the "steps" (we might say chapters) by which one rises to knowledge of Allah. The earliest versions of the Quran were equipped with a running commentary. The first four extracts here illustrate the simplicity and elegance of Muslim prayer and the absolute transcendence of Allah. The last two extracts demonstrate the profound sense of religious continuity that marked Muhammad's teaching.

Sura 1

In the name of Allah, Most Gracious, Most Merciful. / Praise be to Allah, the Cherisher and Sustainer of worlds; / Most Gracious, Most Merciful. / Master of the Day of Judgment. / Thee do we worship and Thine aid we seek. Show us the straight way, the way of those on whom Thou hast bestowed Thy grace, Thou whose portion is not wrath, and who do not go astray.

Sura 4.171

O People of the Book! Commit no excesses in your religion, nor say of Allah anything but truth. Christ Jesus the son of Mary was a messenger of Allah . . . so believe in Allah and in His messengers. Say not "Trinity" . . . for Allah is One God. Glory be to Him for He is exalted above having a son. To Him belong all things in the heavens and on earth.

Sura 3.84

Say ye: We believe in Allah, and the revelation given to us, and to Abraham, Ismail, Isaac, Jacob and the descendants (children of Jacob), and that given to Moses and to Jesus and that given to all prophets from their Lord, but we make no difference between one and another of them, and we bow to Allah.

Sura 2.87

We gave Moses the book and followed him up with a succession of messengers; We gave Jesus the son of Mary clear signs and strengthened him with the Holy Spirit.

Sura 48

If the People of the Book rely upon Abraham, let them study his history. His posterity included both Israel and Ismail. Abraham was a righteous man of Allah, a Muslim, and so were his children. Abraham and Ismail built the Kaaba as the house of Allah and purified it, to be a centre of worship for all the world: For Allah is the God of all peoples.

Sura 56

God's truth is continuous, and His prophets from Adam, through Noah and Abraham, down to the last of the prophets, Muhammad, form one brotherhood. Of Imran father of Moses and Aaron sprang a woman, who devoted her unborn offspring to Allah. That child was Mary the mother of Jesus. Her cousin was the wife of the priest Zakariya, who took charge of Mary. To Zakariya, in his old age, was born a son Yahya, amid prodigies: Yahya was the herald of Jesus the son of Mary and was known as John the Baptist.

QUESTIONS

1. What can you discern from these suras about the similarities and differences among Islam, Christianity, and Judaism?

2. Who are the "people of the book"? Why do you think they matter?

3. How is Allah portrayed in these suras?

Source: The Meaning of the Holy Qur'an, new edition with revised translation, commentary, and newly compiled comprehensive index by Abdullah Yusuf Ali (Beltsville, Md.: Amana Publications, 1988), pp. 14, 40, 51, 55–56, 134–135.

For example, the Quran forbids alcohol and gambling, censures luxury and ostentation, and imposes strict sexual restraints on both men and women. (See the box "The Written Record: The Message of the Quran.")

Initially the Quran was interpreted rather freely within the umma, doubtless because there was no clergy to impose a uniform interpretation. After the Prophet's death, some people felt the need for an authoritative teaching—as early Christians had felt the need for a canon of Christian scripture and teaching—and their efforts resulted in the collections called the *sunna,* which means roughly "good practice"—that is, the words and customs of Muhammad himself. Crucial in the development of the sunna were the *hadith,* the "sayings" of the Prophet, the comments he sometimes made about how God's revelation was to be understood and applied. Extant compilations of the sunna date from the ninth century, and scholars are not sure what portion of them derives authentically from the age of the Prophet.

THE ARAB CONQUESTS

Muhammad's death brought a crisis. Who or what was to succeed him? In 632 the Meccan elite chose Abu Bakr as *caliph* (KAY-lif), or "successor to the Prophet." Abu Bakr was elderly, an early convert to Islam, and a former secretary to Muhammad. He and his three successors down to 661 (Umar, Uthman, and Ali) were all Meccans, relatives of the Prophet by marriage, and early converts. Islamic tradition calls them the "Rightly Guided Caliphs."

Abu Bakr left his successor, Umar, a united Arabia (see Map 8.1), no small feat in that fractious world. Umar began the lightning conquests by the Arabs of much of the Roman and Persian Empires. He initiated the policy of granting choice positions in the expanding **caliphate,** the Arab empire, to old converts and of ranking them according to precedence in conversion. As the old elite divided up the new provinces of the caliphate, some of them became *emirs* (governors), and others became lower administrators. Arab administrators then collected from all conquered people personal taxes and land taxes. Converts to Islam paid only land taxes. Arab settlers paid no taxes and received salaries from the taxes paid by others.

Umar was murdered by a slave in 644, leaving his successor, Uthman, a huge empire to administer. A great centralizer, Uthman chose emirs, regulated the finances of the provinces, and authorized the preparation of the definitive text of the Quran. In attempting to preserve the advantages of the old Meccan elite, Uthman alienated many people, particularly in Egypt, Syria, and Iraq, who had benefited from conquest and who guarded jealously their newfound local wealth and power. Uthman was murdered in 656 and replaced by Ali, Muhammad's son-in-law, whose goal was to create a truly Islamic government by emphasizing the religious side of the caliph's office as the leader of the umma. Ali was in turn killed by a disillusioned follower in 661. Years later some Muslims looked back to Ali as the true model for the caliph. These Muslims formed the *Shi'a,* the "Party of Ali."

When Ali was killed, the caliphate passed to Mu'-awiya (MOO-ah-wee-uh), a Meccan who was the governor of Syria and commander of the finest army in the Arab world. That army ensured Mu'awiya's position. From 661 to 750 the Umayyads (OO-my-ahdz), as Mu'-awiya's family is called, built many of the caliphate's institutions.

The Umayyads instituted greater centralization. This involved the introduction of a unified coinage, the Arabization of the administration (granting all key positions to Arabs), and taking tight control of provincial government and taxation. The Umayyads moved the capital of the caliphate to Damascus in their own power base of Syria, more centrally located than the old towns of Mecca and Medina and closer to the militarily active zones in eastern Iran and along the Byzantine frontier in Syria. In addition, the Umayyads presided over the final territorial expansion of the caliphate (see Map 8.1). To the west, the caliph's forces took North Africa and Spain and conducted raids deep into Gaul. In the east, though stymied by unsuccessful sieges against Constantinople, campaigns moved the frontier against the Byzantine Empire into the mountains of southern Anatolia and, farther east, established nominal authority as far as the Indus River valley.

Rome's empire expanded for 350 years, but the caliphate reached its zenith in scarcely 100. How can we account for the astonishingly rapid creation of such a vast empire? External factors were important. Byzantium and Persia had financially and militarily weakened themselves in a series of wars that ended just as the caliphate of Umar commenced. Moreover, the Byzantine and Persian states were exceedingly diverse, and the Arab armies dismantled them piecemeal. Both old empires, but especially the Byzantine, had deep religious divisions. Coptic Egypt and Jacobite Syria, for example, willingly yielded to the Arabs, who demanded taxes and submission but otherwise left them alone. The Byzantines and Persians tended to depend on static frontier garrisons and large armies that could not be quickly mobilized and moved long distances. The Arabs rarely risked great pitched battles. They preferred a gradually expanding military frontier gained by numerous lightning strikes.

Internal factors were more significant, however. For centuries, raiding and plundering had been a way of life in Arabia, but because Islam forbade Muslims from raiding other Muslims, a new outlet for traditional violence was needed. The Prophet himself had believed firmly in the need to expand the faith, and his successors shared that belief. Muslim ideology divided the world into the "House of Islam" and the "House of War." In the House of Islam the justice of Allah reigned supreme. In the House of War *jihad,* or holy war, was the rule. Christians and Jews, as fellow "Peoples of the Book"—sharers in a scriptural tradition reaching back to Abraham—were spared the choice of conversion or death, but "infidels" were expected to submit and convert. The Arab conquests were carefully planned and directed to channel violence out of Arabia, to populate much of western Asia with loyal Muslims, and to reward members of the umma.

caliphate The name for the territory conquered by Muhammad's successors and for the governmental regime they established.

Dome of the Rock
This magnificent mosque in Jerusalem (built in 691–692) is the third-holiest shrine of Islam—after the Kaaba in Mecca and the Prophet's mosque in Medina. Muslims believe that Muhammad ascended to heaven from this spot. *(Michael Holford)*

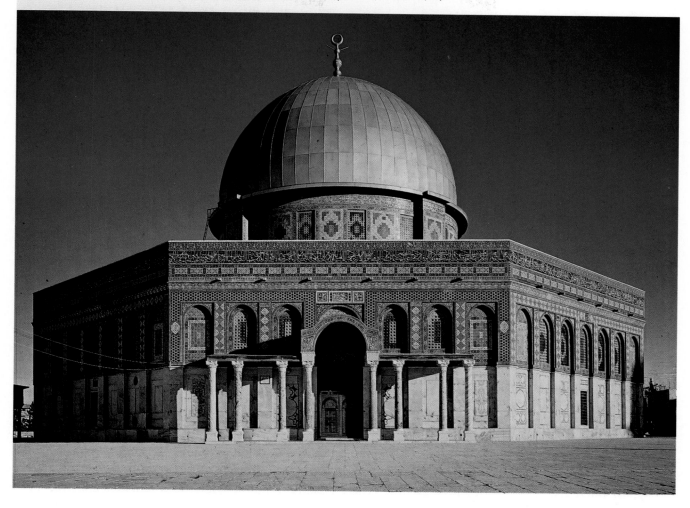

THE ABBASID REVOLUTION

Despite their military and administrative successes, the Umayyads were not popular. Many people resented their bureaucratic centralization. Such resentment was acute in areas heavily populated by recent converts, who had always disliked the old Arabian elites, and in frontier provinces, where Arab immigrants along with local converts desired autonomy. The secular nature of Umayyad rule also offended those pious Muslims who expected a high standard of personal morality from their rulers. The opposition came to a head in a series of rebellions that culminated in the naming of a rival caliph, Abu'l Abbas, in 749. In 750 he defeated his Umayyad opponent.

The Abbasids (uh-BASS-idz) reigned until the thirteenth century. Initially, especially in the caliphate of Harun al-Rashid (hah-ROON al-rah-SHEED) (r. 786–809), they brought the Islamic world its first golden

age. Harun's reign was marked by political stability, economic prosperity, and cultural achievements. Abbasid successes are attributable to political acumen and ideological restructuring.

With their frontier origins, the Abbasids were sympathetic to the caliphate's provincial populations. Thus they created a more international regime. Non-Arabs and recent converts felt toward Islam, the Prophet, and the Prophet's family a loyalty that they would not grant to the old Arabian potentates who had led and initially benefited from the Arab conquests. The Abbasid polity was based on the idea of the fundamental equality of all believers, old or new, Arab or not.

Members of the Abbasid family received some key government posts, as did Iranians and other non-Arabs. Most important, however, local persons got more choice positions than Meccan or Syrian aristocrats. The capital of the caliphate was moved from

Syria to Iraq, but to avoid favoring any existing group or region, the Abbasids built a new city, Baghdad, which they called "the navel of the universe." By addressing regional and ethnic sensitivities in an effective way, they were able to maintain, even extend, the centralized state of the Umayyad period.

The daily business of governing was usually in the hands of the *wazir*, who headed the administration, advised the caliph, and often exercised a powerful formative influence on the caliph's children and heirs. The first caliphs chose administrators from loyal Arabs and from experienced Christian subjects. Under the Umayyads the regime was Arabized. Then under Harun al-Rashid the government became international, professional, and hereditary. The chief agency of government was the treasury, which had separate branches dealing with Muslim alms, land and poll taxes paid by subjects, and land taxes paid by converts. Alone among early medieval governments, the caliphate could draw up annual budgets. Alongside the treasury in exerting power was a prestigious group of palace servants. They did not hold major offices, but their informal influence on the caliph and his family was great. The army was another prominent body within the state.

The central government had several links to the provinces. In addition to controlling the army and provincial governorships, the caliph employed a network of regular envoys and spies. The court, especially under the Abbasids, drew able young men from all over into the service of the caliph and created hopes among provincial elites that they, too, might be chosen. In every district and city there were judges, or *qadi* (KAH-dee), to oversee the application of Islamic law. Qadi were under the authority of the caliph.

The death of Harun in 809 sparked a century of problems. Intense family rivalries touched both the succession to the caliphate and the possession of key provincial positions. The bureaucracy became an increasingly influential pressure group, and the palace servants began to foment intrigues. The army became more and more a professional body comprising non-Arabs, especially Turks, hired from the frontiers and beyond because Arabs, enjoying their salaries, declined to serve. The parallel with the Germanization of the late Roman army is striking. The army, the bureaucracy, and the courtiers all had different and conflicting interests and did not hesitate to press their own advantages. Religious divisions persisted, even intensified. Many felt that the Abbasids had not gone far enough in erecting a truly Islamic regime, but some felt that the caliphs had gone too far in claiming both the political and religious authority of the Prophet. Whole regions took advantage of Abbasid leniency in granting local autonomy and began to fall away. After the early tenth century the Abbasid caliphs had little effective power.

THE EMERGENCE OF ISLAMIC CULTURE

Two currents are apparent in the culture of the Islamic East: One is the elaboration of religious thought; the other is the assimilation of multiple cultural heritages. Both were influenced by the spread of Islam that mixed Greek, North African, Iranian, Turkish, and even Hindu elements into a culture already rich with Arab, Christian, and Jewish ingredients.

Muslims assembled for prayer in mosques, the often beautiful buildings usually modeled on the original mosque in Medina. The worshipers—with men and women in separate areas—arrayed themselves in parallel rows and were led in prayer by an imam. In time the imams started offering interpretations of the Quran, and collections of these interpretations began to circulate. Similarly, Muslim judges began to issue opinions on how the Quran and sunna might be applied to the daily lives of believers. Teachers in mosque schools also were influential. Together these authority figures, collectively the *ulama*, developed a body of religious thought. Lacking elaborate theology and creeds, Islamic religious thought pertains to practice and allegiance more than ideas. The point is less to *know* Islam than to *live* it.

The late ninth and early tenth centuries saw the emergence of a religious split in the Islamic world that persists to this day. The opposing groups are Shi'ite and Sunni Muslims. Shi'ites believe that caliphs should be chosen only according to strict standards of moral and spiritual worthiness. Further, they insist that the only way to ensure such worthiness is to choose caliphs from the line of Ali, the fifth caliph, husband of Muhammad's daughter Fatima and, in 661, a victim of assassination. Moreover, they believe that the whole ulama should measure up to Shi'ite standards. Sunni Muslims, always the vast majority, proclaim that only they adhere to the sunna, the "good practice" of Muhammad himself. Sunnis accept the legitimacy of the whole line of Umayyad and Abbasid caliphs and the teachings of the ulama.

In 832 an Abbasid caliph endowed the "House of Wisdom," an academy for scholars in Baghdad (compare Charlemagne's palace school; see pages 236–237), and from this point on Muslim scholars had the leisure and wherewithal to begin tackling the corpus of Greek thought, especially the scientific writers. The earliest Arab scholars sought mainly to master the learning of the past. Greek, Persian, and Indian works were collected and translated, manuscripts were copied, and libraries were built. Muslims showed little interest in the *literary* heritage of antiquity, the ancient legacy that was so important and controversial to Christian scholars.

So we may ask: Was the Islamic caliphate part of the West or not? Was it brother, or cousin, to the emerging Byzantine and Latin worlds? From the vantage point of 900, the answer we might give to those questions—"largely Western"—differs from the answer we might give today—"largely Eastern." In later chapters we will see how the Islamic world became less Western and more Eastern.

━━━━━━━━━ S E C T I O N   S U M M A R Y ━━━━━━━━━

- Muhammad was a great teacher who emphasized *al-Islam,* surrender to Allah.

- The Islamic faith may be summarized in the "Five Pillars."

- Internal and external factors contributed to the lightning conquests of Islam in the century after Muhammad's death.

- Islamic culture was rooted in the religious teachings of the *ulama* and in the scholarship of those who tackled Greek and Persian learning.

THE BYZANTINE EMPIRE

Why did a distinctive civilization that can be called "Byzantine" emerge?

The century after Justinian's death in 565 was difficult for the eastern Roman Empire. Attacks by Persians, Bulgars, and Muslims; riots and rebellions; plagues and famines; and some weak rulers put the empire in a perilous position. Two fundamental changes transformed the eastern Roman Empire into a new civilization that we call "Byzantine," from "Byzantium," the ancient Greek name for the capital city, Constantinople. In external affairs the empire experienced a sharp geographic contraction until it stabilized into the shape it would hold into the thirteenth century. In internal affairs the empire changed both its basic administrative structures and its cultural orientation.

SHIFTING FRONTIERS

In 600 the empire still laid claim, along the southern and eastern shores of the Mediterranean, to most of the lands that Rome had ruled for centuries. But in the East the empire had been suffering recurrent losses to Persia. In 610 Heraclius (her-ACK-lee-us), a gifted ruler, ascended the throne. Between 622 and 629 Heraclius campaigned brilliantly and recovered almost everything that had been lost. But he faced a cruel irony. When the Arab expansion began, Heraclius's empire was militarily and financially exhausted. As the seventh century wore on, Arabs captured Syria, Palestine, and Mesopotamia and began a centuries-long push into Anatolia. Eventually they even threatened the capital, Constantinople.

In the Balkans Heraclius and his successors fought constant battles, with mixed results. They checked the advance of the Slavic peoples, who had been expanding southward for some years. The Slavic advance was partly generated by social and political forces among the Slavs themselves and partly a result of pressure from the Avars and Bulgars. These peoples, who were related to the Huns, had begun penetrating into the Danube basin in the late sixth century. The empire tried hard, with varying success, to check their forward march.

Where the West was concerned, Heraclius and his successors were powerless to stop the Arab advance in North Africa and Spain. In Italy imperial control was confined to a few outposts around Rome, Ravenna, and Sicily. Generally Italy was too far away and strategically insignificant to attract much attention from the imperial government.

By around 700 the empire was assuming the basic geographic shape it would hold for centuries. In contrast to the vast lands once ruled by Rome, the empire was now confined to the eastern Balkans and western Anatolia. Then in 717 Leo III became emperor in a moment of acute crisis. Arab armies had seized much of Anatolia and had laid siege to Constantinople. The city would surely have fallen had it not been for the "Greek fire" that made it impossible for the attacking navy to operate beneath the seaward walls (see Map 7.4 on page 200). Leo repulsed the attack and then ruled successfully until 741. He was followed by his able and charismatic son, Constantine V (r. 741–775). Constantine held the line in Anatolia and enjoyed decades of military success along the Balkan frontier.

In Italy alone Byzantine (BIZZ-un-teen) policy was unsuccessful. When Justinian reconquered Italy from the Ostrogoths (see page 198), his armies devastated the region and left it poor and weak. Into the gap stepped

Greek Fire

Invented in the seventh century by Callimachus, a Syrian engineer, Greek fire was a mixture formed from petroleum, sulfur, saltpeter, and lime that ignited on contact with water. It was first used to repel the Muslim siege of Constantinople in 678.

(Institut Amatller d'Art Hispanic)

the Lombards, who gradually built a kingdom in the north of Italy—Lombardy still bears their name—and set up a series of duchies in the center and south of Italy. The Byzantines prudently dedicated their resources to holding their Balkan and Anatolian frontiers, but this strategy left their subjects in Italy clamoring for aid. Eventually the popes put themselves at the head of a movement in Italy that turned to the Franks for protection. In 755 and 756 the Frankish king marched to Italy, defeated the Lombards, and donated the territories he seized from them to the pope. On the one hand, this inaugurated the **Papal States,** the ever changing set of lands in Italy whose current remnant is Vatican City. On the other hand, this military encounter put an end to effective Byzantine control in Italy, except for the areas around Naples and Sicily. In 827 Muslims seized Sicily, and in the ensuing decades they subjected southern Italy to continuous raids and occasional conquests.

Constantine V's promising son, Leo IV (r. 775–780), survived him only briefly. He left a 6-year-old heir, Constantine VI, and a remarkable widow, Irene (ca. 752–803), as regent for her son. Irene was a skilled politician, but under her the army grew restive because she preferred to make treaties, sometimes on unfavorable terms, than to send troops into the field. She did not trust the military's loyalty. Moreover, Irene had to contend with a foolish son who spent his time trysting with ladies of the court rather than attending to his official duties. In 797 Irene had him blinded, ironically in the very palace chamber where she had given birth to him. This was not a barbaric act in the Byzantine way of thinking. By mutilating Constantine VI, she merely rendered him unfit to rule: Roman ideology held that only a physically perfect person could reign; the alternative would have been to murder him. In any case, Irene's credibility sank to nothing, and in 802 she was deposed by a wily old soldier, Nicephorus (nye-SEFF-for-us) (r. 802–811).

Whether in some ideal situation Nicephorus might have been successful is impossible to say. His problems came from two fearsome foes. In Anatolia he faced the redoubtable and aggressive Harun al-Rashid, and in the Balkans he contended with the clever Bulgarian Khan Krum (r. ca. 803–814). Nicephorus got a break when Harun died in 809, but he fell in battle with Krum, who gruesomely made a drinking cup out of his skull.

For two generations Byzantium suffered through short reigns, usurpations, political unrest, and military reverses. In 867 a rough soldier, Basil I (r. 867–886),

Papal States   The lands in central Italy ruled by the popes, initially with Frankish help, from the eighth century to 1870.

seized the throne and, like Heraclius and Leo III before him, reversed the fortunes of the state. He established a new dynasty, the "Macedonian," and for the first time in years won important military victories. Faced as they were by worthy foes in both Anatolia and the Balkans, the Byzantines, the heirs of the Romans, might have vanished from history. But capable leaders emerged just often enough, especially in the eighth century, to preserve a state that, even in a vastly reduced shape, carried the Roman legacy into the future.

NEW FORMS OF GOVERNMENT

Even as its territory was shrinking, Byzantium undertook military and administrative reforms, revised its laws, and refocused its culture, particularly its religious practices. In the early Middle Ages a distinctive "Byzantium" emerged in place of Rome.

Leo and Constantine are reminiscent of Diocletian and Constantine, or of Justinian. They energetically brought to completion military reforms that had been pursued intermittently since the late sixth century. These reforms amounted to a major administrative change. For centuries Rome had recruited, trained, and paid professional troops out of tax revenues; they even used tax revenues to settle barbarian soldiers in their midst. Leo and Constantine put the finishing touches on a new "theme" system.

Men from frontier regions were now recruited and settled on farms in military districts called *themes*. All themes, whether land-based army ones or sea-based naval ones, were under the command of a leader who was simultaneously the civil and military chief of his theme. The farmer-soldiers did not pay taxes on their farms but discharged their obligation to the state by personal service. Some standing troops were retained, mainly around the capital, but henceforth the thematic armies (see **MAP 8.2**) formed the backbone of the Roman system.

The new system was less of a drain on the state treasury than the old one. Lower tax revenues were needed, and, correspondingly, so were fewer bureaucrats to collect the money. The empire was smaller than in the past and needed a different kind of army: smaller squadrons concentrated near the threatened frontier regions in Anatolia and the Balkans rather than large armies that were expensive to maintain and cumbersome to transport over long distances.

There were other reforms, too. Leo issued the *Ecloga* (ECK-low-guh), the first major revision and updating of Roman law since Justinian's. Issuing a law code was a matter of pride and a clear representation of power and authority. But the *Ecloga* was "a selection of laws," an abridgment whose purpose was to provide a simplified code adapted to the empire's new circumstances.

Leo and Constantine also instituted far-reaching reforms in imperial administration, which had changed little in centuries. Roman bureaucracy had consisted of a few large departments headed by officials with immense responsibilities and power. The revised Byzantine system was characterized by a profusion of departments under officers who had little real power or sway. The emperor neutralized the bureaucrats by drawing them from all social classes, paying them well, and giving them pompous titles and lots of public recognition, all the while dividing their responsibilities, curbing their influence, and making them dependent on himself. The Byzantine government was never a breeding ground for factional squabbles as in the caliphate.

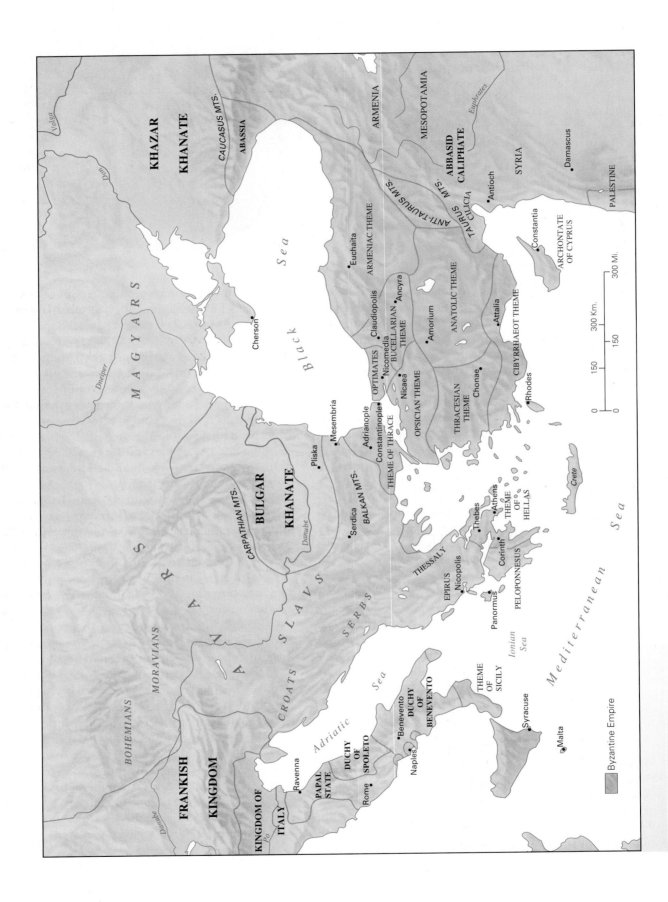

KHAZAR
KHANATE

CAUCASUS MTS.

ABASSIA

ARMENIA

MESOPOTAMIA

Euphrates

ABBASID
CALIPHATE

SYRIA

Damascus

PALESTINE

ANTI-TAURUS MTS.

TAURUS MTS.

CILICIA

Antioch

Constantia

ARCHONTATE
OF CYPRUS

Volga

Dneiper

Danube

MAGYARS

Euchaita

ARMENIAC THEME

Cherson

Claudiopolis

Ancyra

BUCELLARIAN
THEME

Amorium

ANATOLIC THEME

Attalia

CIBYRRHAEOT THEME

Black Sea

OPTIMATES

Nicomedia

Nicaea

OPSICIAN THEME

THRACESIAN
THEME

Chonae

Rhodes

300 Mi.

300 Km.

150

150

150

0

0

Mesembria

Pliska

Adrianople

Constantinople

THEME OF THRACE

BULGAR
KHANATE

Serdica

BALKAN MTS.

Danube

CARPATHIAN MTS.

MORAVIANS

BOHEMIANS

FRANKISH
KINGDOM

Po

KINGDOM OF

ITALY

Ravenna

PAPAL
STATE

Rome

DUCHY
OF
SPOLETO

Benevento

DUCHY
OF
BENEVENTO

Naples

THEME
OF
SICILY

Panormus

Syracuse

Malta

THESSALY

EPIRUS

Nicopolis

Thebes

Athens

THEME
OF
HELLAS

Corinth

PELOPONNESUS

Ionian Sea

Mediterranean Sea

Crete

Adriatic Sea

CROATS

SERBS

SLAVS

A V A R S

Danube

Byzantine Empire

THE BIRTH OF BYZANTINE CULTURE

Byzantine culture came to be increasingly defined by the church. The massive Arab conquests that stripped Byzantium of so much territory also removed the ancient patriarchates of Alexandria, Jerusalem, and Antioch from effective contact with Constantinople. Often in the past the empire had been disturbed by severe theological quarrels generated by the differing views held in the several patriarchates. These disputes had been disruptive, but they had also prompted a great deal of learned religious writing. Now, deprived of this stimulus, Byzantium turned inward.

Inside the smaller Byzantine Empire, monasticism gradually assumed a more prominent place in religious life. So many members of elite families sought to become monks that some emperors actually tried to limit entry into the religious life. Byzantine monks tended to be deeply learned, intensely critical of the patriarchs of Constantinople—whom they regarded as worldly and political—and opposed to imperial interference in the church.

In 726 Emperor Leo III embarked on a bold new religious policy: **iconoclasm.** For centuries a beautiful and inspiring religious art had been emerging that troubled the emperor. Leo, a man of simple but fervent piety, believed that the presence of religious images, called "icons," in churches and public places was offensive to God. Moreover, Leo was convinced that the military disasters suffered by the empire in recent years were attributable to divine displeasure at the violation of Moses' prohibition of "graven images." Accordingly, he and his son banned religious images. They and some of their more enthusiastic followers even destroyed a few of them. Hence they were called "iconoclasts," which means "image breakers." Iconoclasm was officially proclaimed by a church council in 754, repudiated by another council in 787, proclaimed again in 815, and then definitively rejected in 843.

Online Study Center **Improve Your Grade**
Primary Source: Defending Icons: A Rebuttal to Iconoclasm

Although it might seem like an odd and local dispute, iconoclasm had several important consequences in its own time and reveals important aspects of emerging Byzantium to the modern observer. Iconoclasm was categorically rejected as heretical by the popes. This difference drove a sharp wedge between Eastern and Western Catholics. The debates over iconoclasm finally sharpened Byzantine thinking on the role and function of art in religious life. To this day the icon plays a more prominent role in religious devotion in the East than in the West. (See the feature "The Visual Record: Icons.") Moreover, the battle over iconoclasm evoked some of the most sophisticated Greek religious writing since Late Antiquity. Writers produced learned treatises in defense of religious art that drew on Greek patristic writing (see page 208) and on ancient Greek philosophy in ways that sharply differentiated Byzantine and Western religious thought.

As the Byzantines turned more and more deeply into their own traditions, they exposed other differences between themselves and the West. Some of these were important, such as the dispute over the so-called *filioque*. In the East people taught and believed that the Holy Spirit proceeded "from the Father." In the West people said that the Holy Spirit proceeded "from the Father *and from the Son*" (*filioque* in Latin). Greek monks shaved the front of their heads, whereas Western monks shaved a circlet on the top. The Greek church used leavened (with yeast) bread in worship, whereas the Western church used unleavened bread. Taken together these differences amounted to a sharpening of the divide between Christian groups whom we may now label **"Orthodox"** and "Roman Catholic." Neither group wished to see a division in the Christian world, but physical separation and independent cultural evolution were producing two different traditions based, paradoxically, on a single late antique Christianity.

With its new geographic shape, institutional structure, and its Orthodox faith, Byzantium was at once something old and something new. In official Byzantine ideology, the Roman Empire had always been one and inseparable. It is interesting to ask how familiar Augustus Caesar would have found the empire of Constantine V. With its indebtedness to classical and Christian traditions, there can be no question that Byzantium was a part of the West. But in its comparatively modest

MAP 8.2   The Byzantine Empire in the Eighth and Ninth Centuries

After suffering tremendous territorial losses to the barbarians and Arabs, the Byzantine Empire transformed its military, institutional, and cultural structures to create a regime that lasted until it was conquered by Crusaders in 1204. This map shows the Byzantium's major institutional innovation.

Online Study Center **Improve Your Grade**
Interactive Map: The Byzantine Empire in the Eighth Century

iconoclasm   Literally means "image breaking"; it describes the rejection or destruction of religious pictures called "icons."

Orthodox   The Christian faith of Byzantium. It is known for its use of Greek, inclusion of icons in worship, and adherence to the Greek Church Fathers.

Icons

The word *icon* comes from the Greek *eikōn*, which means "image." Scholarly conventions, however, tend to use the term to signify a particular kind of religious image that emerged in Late Antiquity and became prominent in Byzantium. Although large frescoes or mosaics can be called icons, the word is typically restricted to panel paintings painted with *encaustic* (en-COST-ik). This is a technique that involves mixing pigment with beeswax and then heating the painted surface to fuse the painting to the surface.

Icons portrayed saints, the Virgin Mary, and sometimes Jesus Christ. They were believed to be genuinely holy, to capture in some mysterious way the holiness of the person whom they represented. Icons may have arisen from funeral portraits, or they may have been miniature versions of much larger images on the walls of churches. One of the earlier examples of icons relates to Saint Symeon Stylites (STILL-ee-tays) (ca. 390–459). Symeon was a recluse who lived for many years on top of a pillar in the Syrian desert. After his death, his reputation for holiness drew many people to worship at his tomb. Soon people began to take away pictures of Symeon. We hear that in far-off Rome shopkeepers affixed icons of Symeon to the doorposts outside their shops to ward off evil.

Eventually Byzantine armies carried icons into battle and hung them over the walls of Constantinople to repel enemy attacks. Some churches became famous for their icons. Individuals possessed icons, too, and carried them around in sacks or installed them in their houses. People touched, kissed, or caressed icons to invoke the power of the person who was at once portrayed and spiritually present in the icon. Icons were believed to ward off demons, to heal illnesses, to overcome complications in pregnancy, and to secure victory in lawsuits—among many other uses to which they were put.

Pictured here is an icon of Saint Peter from the monastery of Saint Catherine in Sinai. It is one of the oldest surviving icons, believed to date back to the sixth century. Let us note some of its formal characteristics. Peter is depicted frontally and the background is indistinct, as if Peter is removed from earthly time and space. Peter is represented holding keys, which symbolize the keys to the kingdom of heaven mentioned by Christ. Notice that Peter's eyes look out hauntingly, taking in everything, yet are not focused on anything in particular. This feature, too, gives the icon a sense of timelessness, and of holiness. The style of this icon is very similar to that of a consular diptych. When the emperor named two men consuls each year, they often had portraits done. In such a portrait, one consul was front and center while medallions above or beside him depicted the other consul, the emperor, and the empress. In this icon, Peter is likewise shown with three medallions: Christ in the center, Mary on the viewer's right, and Saint John the Evangelist on the viewer's left. One can see right away how ancient artistic motifs were being adapted to new purposes in Christian art.

Icon of Saint Peter from Saint Catherine's, Mount Sinai
(Alexandria-Michigan-Princeton Archaeological Expedition to Mount Sinai/Roger Wood/Corbis)

In the eighth century, Byzantium's emperors initiated a policy of iconoclasm; literally, "icon-breaking." Many icons were destroyed, some were simply removed from view, while still others were whitewashed. The emperors believed that icons violated the biblical prohibition of "graven images" (Exodus 20:4). They felt that God had forsaken the empire because of idolatry and that only by removing the offending pictures could divine favor be won again. The monastery of Saint Catherine, where the icon of Saint Peter was, and still is, was so remote that iconoclasm did not touch it (see Map 2.2, top, on page 43). Eventually iconoclasm came to an end and icons were restored to their honored position in Byzantium and later in all the lands religiously influenced by the Byzantines. For an example of a Russian Orthodox icon, see the Virgin of Vladimir in Chapter 9 (page 275).

Iconoclasm was a particularly bitter episode in Byzantine history. There were polemical writings on all sides. Byzantine artists also commented on the controversy. In this image from the early-ninth-century Khludov Psalter—a psalter is a book containing the psalms—you can see two pictures. One is of a crucifixion. It is placed opposite verse 22 in Psalms 68 (modern 69): "They gave me also gall for my food and vinegar for my thirst." Note the soldier on Jesus's left (the viewer's right) who is holding up a sponge soaked in vinegar. But note too the soldier on Jesus's right (the viewer's left). This is the figure, later named Longinus, who pierced Jesus's side with a spear. Now look at the lower image. Depicted here is a man whitewashing an icon of Christ. The message is clear, and powerful. Just as Longinus had tortured Jesus, so too do the iconoclasts.

We learned in Chapter 7 (see "The Visual Record: The Ravenna Mosaics" on pages 202–203) that art could serve propaganda purposes. The Ravenna mosaics were large and public. Some icons were also large and public, but many more were small and private. And the picture from the

Khludov Psalter (Courtesy, State Historical Museum, Moscow [Khludov Psalter, cod.Gr. 129 d])

Khludov Psalter is tiny and very private, very intimate. But it conveys well the depth of anger provoked by iconoclasm, by an attack on Byzantium's revered icons.

QUESTIONS

1. What kinds of ideas enter your mind when you hear words like icon, or iconic?

2. How does the icon of Saint Peter compare with the diptych-like representation of Amalasuntha on page 198?

3. How well do the images from the Khludov Psalter convey their message?

Online Study Center
Improve Your Grade Visual Record Activities

size, its constantly threatened frontiers, and its Orthodox traditions, Byzantium was going to have a somewhat different future than the portions of the West situated inside Rome's former western provinces. It is worth noting, too, that as was the case in the Muslim world, the seventh and ninth centuries were acutely tumultuous in Byzantium, whereas the eighth was marked by consolidation and achievement.

=================== S E C T I O N   S U M M A R Y ===================

- The Byzantine Empire faced hard challenges from Persians and then Muslims in the east; from Slavs, Avars, and Bulgars in the Balkans; and from Lombards in Italy.

- The "theme" system was a comprehensive and effective revision of the empire's traditional governmental structure.

- Byzantine culture was based on the Greek language, the Greek Church Fathers, Orthodox religious traditions, and distinctive local practices.

CATHOLIC KINGDOMS IN THE WEST

What strengths and weaknesses were exhibited by the small states that survived Rome's collapse in the West?

In the Latin West the seventh century also was marked by challenges, the eighth century by innovation and accomplishment, and the ninth century by new threats and in some areas near collapse. The social and political heritages of both the Germanic and the Roman past interacted with Christianity and the church to produce the third early medieval civilization: Catholic Europe. Crucial to these developments were the evangelization of the countryside, the growth of an ecclesiastical hierarchy, the shift of papal interests away from the Mediterranean world toward western Europe, and the evolving relationship between royal governments and the Catholic Church.

THE STRUGGLES OF VISIGOTHIC SPAIN

After their defeat at Clovis's hands in 507, the Visigoths were never able to re-establish dynastic continuity. As a result, Spain witnessed rebellions and usurpations more frequently than any other area in the West. In addition to internal struggles, Spain faced external threats from the Franks, the Ostrogoths in Italy, the Byzantines, and finally the Muslims.

The accomplishments of the Visigothic king Leovigild (r. 568–586) seem remarkable given the state of Spain on his accession. He nearly unified the country, and he established a capital (Toledo) and a seat of government—which the Visigoths had been lacking since they lost Toulouse in 507. Leovigild (lee-OH-vuh-gild) was a good general and a charismatic leader who understood the value of enhancing the royal office. He

wore royal vestments, sat on a throne, and issued coins with his own image and name. Leovigild's greatest problem was the Arianism of the Visigothic minority in the midst of the Catholic population. An Arian himself, he tried hard to convert Catholics to Arianism but failed. In 589, under King Reccared (r. 586–601), the Visigoths officially embraced Roman Catholicism.

The conversion of the Visigoths permitted close cooperation between the church and the monarchy and placed the resources of the church at the disposal of the king as he attempted to unite and govern the country. The career of Archbishop Isidore of Seville (560–636) is a prime indicator of those resources. He came from an old Hispano-Roman family, received a fine education, and wrote histories, biblical commentaries, and a learned encyclopedia. By the mid-seventh century, economic prosperity, a high degree of assimilation between Goths and Hispano-Romans, and a brilliant culture marked the high point of Visigothic Spain. The succession problem, however, was never overcome, and a stable central government was beyond reach.

In 711 Muslims from North Africa invaded Spain. Within five years Berbers (native North Africans and recent converts to Islam who were led by Arabs) completed the conquest of much of the Iberian Peninsula, except for the northwest. In 716 the caliph at Damascus introduced an emir who ruled from Cordoba. The emirate of Cordoba struggled to make good its authority over all of Spain but failed to do so. Christians in the rugged mountains of the northwest—the region called

Asturias (ahs-TOUR-ee-ahs)—could not be dislodged, and the Muslims' part of Spain—known as al-Andalus (al-AHN-dah-loose)—was plagued by the same divisions as the Islamic East: Arab factions against other Arab factions, Arabs against non-Arab Muslims, and Muslims against non-Muslims. Secure in mountainous Asturias (see Map 8.3 on page 233), Christian kings built a capital at Oviedo and, in the ninth century, launched attacks against al-Andalus. For six hundred years this conflict between Christians and Muslims was the chief dynamic of Spanish history.

ITALY AND THE PAPAL STATES

In 600 the Italian political scene was crowded. Several Germanic groups, several Byzantine outposts, and the popes were all contending for power. By the late eighth century the Franks dominated northern Italy, the popes had created a state in the center, and the Byzantines clung to Naples and Sicily, much of which they lost to Muslims in the ninth century.

As we have seen, the Lombards conquered most of the Italian peninsula after the Gothic Wars. Neither numerous nor united, the Lombards were also Arians. Although the Lombard kings converted to Catholicism by 680, formed a strong government, and issued a sophisticated law code, they always faced a dilemma. The kings had not systematically organized the conquest of Italy. From their capital at Pavia they dominated the Po Valley, but other Lombards settled elsewhere and created independent duchies. Kings were weakened because they did not control the duchies and because between Lombardy and the duchies lay Rome and Ravenna, which were nominally Byzantine.

The strongest Lombard king of the eighth century, Aistulf (ICE-tulf) (r. 749–757), decided to risk the consequences of attacking Ravenna and Rome. He conquered the former but caused the pope to turn to Pippin III, the king of the Franks, for aid and protection. Pippin came to Italy, defeated Aistulf, and forced him to give to the pope all the lands he had taken from Rome and Ravenna. A few years later Aistulf's successor reopened hostilities in central Italy. In 774 Charlemagne, Pippin's son and successor, defeated the Lombards, deposed their king, and took the Lombard crown for himself (see page 232).

The Franks guaranteed to the popes undisputed possession of a substantial territory in central Italy. This first Papal State was the culmination of three processes. First, as Roman imperial power declined in Late Antiquity, bishops often became the effective leaders of their towns. This position brought them power and prestige but also burdens. The popes found themselves responsible for Rome's food and water supply, the upkeep of its public buildings, and local charitable services. To pay for these functions, the popes began to organize the efficient bureaucratic administration of the patrimonies, the lands of the Roman church.

Second, the popes took the lead in protecting many people in central Italy, whether they lived on the patrimonies or not, thus preserving their purses from Byzantine taxes and their souls from the heresy of iconoclasm. This effort, too, forged bonds between the popes and the Italians.

Third, eighth-century Rome spawned a justification for papal temporal rule. According to the *Donation of Constantine,* a document written in Rome (probably in the 760s), when Constantine departed Rome for the East in the 320s, he allegedly gave to the pope the authority to rule Rome and the whole West. In reality, no pope ever made such grandiose claims, and no concrete claims were ever based on the *Donation.* But the existence of the document signals a crucial progression from protection to direct rule. From the beginning, however, the Papal States were vulnerable and required a protector.

THE FATE OF THE BRITISH ISLES

Britain was less thoroughly Romanized, more quickly abandoned by the Romans, and more deeply influenced by Germanic peoples than any other locality in the West. Around 600 the small Anglo-Saxon kingdoms created in the sixth century took the first steps toward converting to Christianity, transforming Britain into England, and joining England inseparably to the European world (see Map 8.3). And another history was unfolding in the British Isles, that of the Celtic peoples in the north and west of Britain itself and in Ireland. The Celts—Britain's inhabitants before the Romans invaded in the first century—were related to peoples who lived in a broad band from Anatolia to Ireland and Spain. The Anglo-Saxons confined the British Celts to the western regions of Cornwall and Wales and to the northern area of Scotland. Ireland, seemingly beyond reach, had almost no Roman or Anglo-Saxon imprint.

The Conversion of the British Isles   The period between 600 and 900 saw only the faint beginnings of consolidation in the Celtic realms, where the development of the Catholic Church preceded large-scale political organization. Each Celtic region produced an elaborate mythology connected with heroic missionaries who supposedly brought the Christian faith in Late Antiquity. The best-known stories swirl around Ireland's Saint Patrick (390?–461?). The son of a Roman official in the north of Britain, Patrick was captured by pirates, enslaved in Ireland, freed, and eventually made a priest; he then returned to Ireland as a missionary. From his base at Armagh (ARR-mah), Ireland's first bishopric, Patrick and his successors spread Christianity, and a vigorous monasticism, throughout the island. Historical, too, is the Irish aristocrat Columba (521–597), who, after his family lost a great battle, migrated in 563 to the isle of Iona off the coast of Scotland. From his monastery on Iona, Columba and his successors began the evangelization of the native Picts in Scotland.

Two issues proved crucial in the Christianization of what became England: the conversion to Christianity and the development of an ecclesiastical hierarchy. In 597 Pope Gregory I sent a small band of missionaries under a Roman monk named Augustine (d. 604) to King Aethelbert of Kent, whose Christian

Lindisfarne Gospels: Opening Page of the Gospel According to Matthew

In the last years of the seventh century in the north of England, scribes and painters produced this exquisite book, which combines the artistic styles of the Mediterranean and Celtic worlds. *(British Library)*

wife, Bertha, had prepared the ground for the newcomers. From their base of operations at Canterbury in southeastern England, Augustine and his successors had limited success spreading Christianity, but a new field of influence was opened to them when Aethelbert's daughter married a king of Northumbria and took missionaries to her new home. Monks from Iona, as noted, were already introducing Christianity into central and lowland Scotland. When later Northumbrian kings turned to Iona for missionaries and bishops, Roman and Celtic Christianity came face-to-face in Northumbria.

The Christianity brought from Ireland did not differ in fundamental ways from the Roman Christianity imported at Canterbury. Indeed, the Irish were Roman Catholics. But Ireland had been isolated from the centers of Christian life since Late Antiquity, and its church had developed a number of distinctive local customs. For example, the two traditions used different calendars and thus celebrated Easter—the commemoration of the resurrection of Jesus Christ and the central celebration of the Christian year—on different days. In 664 a Northumbrian king called a church council at the monastery of Whitby, whose abbess was the former royal princess Hilda (614–680), a champion of Celtic customs. At Whitby, Roman and Irish representatives debated their positions. The king, choosing the universal over the particular, decided for Rome.

In 668 the pope sent to England a new archbishop of Canterbury, Theodore (r. 668–690). He was a Syrian monk who had traveled widely in the East, lived for a time in Rome, gained great experience in church administration, and acquired a reputation for both learning and discretion. The church in England was in an administrative shambles. Working tirelessly, Theodore built up a typical Roman ecclesiastical structure, introduced authoritative Roman canon law for the church, and promoted Christian education. Theodore laid the foundations for a unified English church that contributed to the eventual political unification of England.

Ecclesiastical peace led to the flourishing of monastic life. Monasteries played two important roles in this period. First, they led the way in bringing Christianity to ordinary people. Despite early gains among kings and nobles, Christianity had barely begun to penetrate the countryside. Second, monks maintained international connections, ranging from Ireland to Rome, that attached England to the major intellectual currents of the day and enabled the English to make their own contributions.

After Theodore's school at Canterbury, the most important early center of learning was in Northumbria. There English, Irish, Frankish, and Roman currents flowed together in the monasteries of Lindisfarne, Wearmouth, and Jarrow and in the cathedral school of York. British schools produced some of the most beautiful illuminated manuscripts—books whose texts are adorned with gorgeous paintings—of the early Middle Ages.

The greatest product of this intellectual tradition was Bede (673–735). When he was 7, his parents placed him in the monastery at Wearmouth. He soon transferred to neighboring Jarrow and spent the rest of his life there. Bede was a teacher of genius, an erudite scholar, and a superb Latin stylist. His *Ecclesiastical History of the English People,* the most important source for English history from the fifth century to the eighth, did much to identify the Anglo-Saxons as a single English people. His biblical commentaries remained influential all over Europe for centuries. His studies of temporal reckoning popularized the use of A.D. dating, which replaced a bewildering array of local systems.

The Emergence of England Among the most successful Anglo-Saxon kingdoms were Wessex, Northumbria, and Mercia. Each had a reasonably large population and territory and opportunities for expansion. Wessex, for example, spread south and west into Devon, Cornwall, and Wales; Northumbria, which stretched along the North Sea coast, spread west to the Irish Sea and north into lowland Scotland (see Map 8.3). These kingdoms had ambitious rulers whose wars provided booty, land, and glory for old followers and new

recruits. English kings quickly adopted symbolic aspects of rule to legitimize their authority and enhance their prestige. Archaeologists have found fine scepters and coins bearing early kings' names. The kings of Northumbria presided in a magnificent wooden hall, and their movements were preceded and announced by banners.

The career of King Offa of Mercia (MUR-sha) (r. 757–796) shows the trends in early Britain. His ancestors were pagans, but he was a patron of the church, convener of councils, and recipient of papal envoys. He dominated all of Britain and was the first to call himself "King of the English." He issued a law code, reformed Mercia's institutions, and signed England's first international trade agreement—with Charlemagne.

After Offa's death, Viking raiders (see page 239) destroyed whatever unity had been achieved. For two generations local rulers struggled just to survive, and in 865 a Viking army launched a conquest of the whole country. In 871 Alfred the Great (r. 871–899) ascended the throne of Wessex, won a series of military victories, rallied the English, and began the slow reconquest of northern and eastern England from the Vikings. Alfred promoted intellectual recovery, church reform, and political stability. After half a century of chaos, Alfred revived the centralizing and unifying work of his eighth-century predecessors and laid the foundations for the English state of the tenth and eleventh centuries.

═══════════ S E C T I O N   S U M M A R Y ═══════════

- Visigothic Spain suffered from religious, political, and military disunity.

- Italy developed three stable regions: a Lombard and then Frankish north; a papal center; and a Byzantine and then Muslim south.

- In the British Isles the conversion to Catholic Christianity and the development of ecclesiastical

organization were forces for unity and cultural achievement.

- In the British Isles, political development in the Celtic regions was slow, but England began emerging as a more and more coherent political entity.

THE CAROLINGIAN EMPIRE

What were the greatest achievements of the Carolingians and why were they so successful?

Clovis and the Franks created the most effective of the early Germanic kingdoms. During the seventh century that kingdom, too, experienced difficulties but did not disappear. Just as Roman aristocrats had borne the ancient heritage into the Middle Ages, so now a Frankish family, called "Carolingian" from

the name of its greatest member, Charlemagne, assembled the talent and resources of the Frankish realm in a new way. Charlemagne reformed his government and church, patronized learning, and resurrected the western empire. Early medieval civilization reached its culmination in the work of Charlemagne and his dynasty.

THE RISE OF THE CAROLINGIAN FAMILY, 600–768

When Clovis died in 511, he divided his realm among his sons, and thereafter several kingdoms coexisted. The Merovingian royal families feuded constantly, sought to expand at one another's expense, and drew local aristocracies into their battles. Trade and intellectual life declined, and some regions that had been conquered in the sixth century slipped away.

Nevertheless, the *idea* of a single kingdom of the Franks persisted. Kings and aristocrats in the small kingdoms competed for leadership of the realm as a whole. The flourishing culture of late antique Gaul was largely gone, but a creative Christian monastic culture was growing up in all parts of the Frankish kingdom. Monks began accomplishing the difficult task of converting the countryside to Christianity. The seventh century, in other words, was a time when the late antique regime was slowly changing into the medieval regime.

Central to this development was the rise to prominence of the Carolingians. The family appeared in history just after 600 and thereafter monopolized the office of mayor of the palace (sort of a prime minister) to the king in Austrasia (the easternmost kingdom; see **MAP 8.3**). The Carolingians were the boldest and wealthiest family in Austrasia (aw-STRAY-zhuh), perhaps in the Frankish world. Within two generations they unified the Frankish realm and increased their own power.

The Carolingians used several methods to accomplish their ends. They formed alliances with powerful noble families in many regions. They waged war against the enemies of the Franks to restore the territorial integrity of the kingdom. Charles Martel (d. 741), Charlemagne's grandfather, led the Frankish forces that put an end to Arab raiding in Gaul, defeating a large force near Poitiers in 733. With booty from their wars, tribute from conquered peoples, spoils taken from recalcitrant opponents, and even lands seized from the church, the Carolingians attracted and rewarded more and more followers until no one was a match for them. The Carolingians also allied themselves very early with leading churchmen, both episcopal and monastic. They aided missionaries in the work of converting central Germany, thereby expanding Frankish influence in that area.

For years the Carolingians were content with the office of mayor of the palace. Then in 749 Pippin III (son of Charles Martel) decided to send envoys to the pope to ask whether it was right that the person who had all the power in the land of the Franks was not the king. The pope responded that this situation ran counter to the divine plan. Accordingly, in 751 the last Merovingian king was deposed, and Pippin was elected in his place (r. 751–768). Pippin had prepared his usurpation very carefully with his Frankish supporters, but he appealed to the pope to make it appear that he had become king with divine approval and not by crude seizure. Hard-pressed by the Lombards in Italy, the pope probably gave Pippin the answer he wanted primarily to enlist him as an ally. Three years later the pope visited the Frankish kingdom, where he crowned and anointed Pippin and his sons, including Charlemagne. (The practice of anointing the head of a ruler with holy oil, which renders the recipient sacred, dates back to the kings of Israel. The head and hands of Catholic bishops also were anointed. The anointing of rulers and churchmen persisted throughout the Middle Ages and into the modern world.) The pope also forbade the Franks ever to choose a king from a family other than the Carolingians and received from their new favorites a promise of aid in Italy.

THE EMPIRE OF CHARLEMAGNE, 768–814

Charlemagne (Carolus Magnus, "Charles the Great" in Latin) was a huge man, and his stature has grown in European history and legend. Like all great leaders, Charlemagne (r. 768–814) was complex. He spoke and read Frankish, Latin, and some Greek but never learned to write. He promoted Christian morality but perpetrated unspeakable brutalities on his enemies and enjoyed several concubines. Many battles were fought in his name, but he rarely accompanied his armies and fought no campaigns that are remembered for strategic brilliance. Determination and organization were the hallmarks of his forty-six-year reign.

Online Study Center **Improve Your Grade**
Primary Source: The Life of Charlemagne: The Emperor Himself

It took until the mid-780s for Charlemagne to assess and understand his world (see Map 8.3). His first major achievement was the articulation of a new ruling

Charlemagne The greatest ruler of the early Middle Ages and a major figure in European lore and legend.

MAP 8.3 The Carolingian World
The territory over which Charlemagne exerted direct or indirect control was vast. The areas beyond the Rhine and Danube, never part of the Roman Empire, became under the Carolingians a permanent part of Western civilization. The Treaty of Verdun (see inset), signed by Charlemagne's grandsons in 843, was the first and most important of many divisions of the Carolingian Empire that eventually led to the emergence of France and Germany.

Online Study Center **Improve Your Grade**
Interactive Map: The Carolingian World

TREATY OF VERDUN, 843

KINGDOM OF LOUIS THE GERMAN

TRIBUTARY PEOPLES

Aachen

Paris •Verdun

Strasbourg

KINGDOM OF CHARLES THE BALD

KINGDOM OF LOTHAIR

PAPAL STATES

Rome•

0   200   400 Km.

0   200   400 Mi.

Asturias Kingdom

Frankish Kingdom, 768

Areas conquered by Charlemagne

Tributary peoples

Byzantine territories

0   150   300 Km.

0   150   300 Mi.

Iona   SCOTLAND

Armagh•

IRELAND Dublin•

Jarrow•

NORTHUMBRIA

York•

DANISH MARCH

MERCIA

WALES

EAST ANGLIA

ESSEX

CORNWALL WESSEX

DEVON   SUSSEX

Canterbury• KENT

•Utrecht

SAXONY 804

FLANDERS

Aachen•

AUSTRASIA

•Fulda

TRIBUTARY

•Rouen

Echternach•

•Mainz

BRITTANY

Rhine

•Paris

NEUSTRIA •Orléans

ALEMANNIA

BAVARIA 788

SLAVIC

Danube

•Tours

•Poitiers

BURGUNDY

Lyon•

PEOPLES

AQUITAINE

•Bordeaux

Milan• VENETIA

Venice•

ISTRIA

Pavia•

GASCONY

Oviedo•

ASTURIAS Roncesvalles•

Aniane•

LOMBARDY Ravenna•

DALMATIA

Ebro

Marseille• •Lérins

PAPAL STATES

DUCHY OF SPOLETO

SPANISH MARCH 811

UMAYYAD SPAIN

CORSICA

Spoleto•

Rome•

DUCHY OF BENEVENTO

Barcelona•

Monte Cassino•

Salerno•

Toledo•

SARDINIA

•Cordoba

BALEARIC IS.

BYZANTINE EMPIRE

SICILY

ideology in the Latin West. In capitularies (kuh-PITCH-u-lar-eez)—royal executive orders—of 789, Charlemagne required all males to swear an oath of allegiance to him, and he compared himself to a biblical king in his responsibility to admonish, to teach, and to set an example for his people. He referred to the people of his realm as a "New Israel," a new chosen people. Interestingly, this chosen people was not exclusively Frankish. No distinctions were to be made among Franks or Bavarians or Saxons. Everyone was to be equal in allegiance to the king and in membership in a sort of Augustinian City of God.

Einhard (ca. 770–840), Charlemagne's friend and biographer, reports that Augustine's *City of God* (see page 209) was the king's favorite book. The king understood it to mean that two opposing domains contended for power on earth: a City of God consisting of all right-thinking Christians—the "New Israel"—and a City of Man consisting of pagans, heretics, and infidels. This idea is similar to the Islamic umma (see page 215). To Charlemagne and his advisers, it was obvious that as God was the sole legitimate ruler in heaven, Charlemagne was the sole legitimate and divinely appointed ruler on earth.

Modern readers may think that Charlemagne had crossed a boundary between church and state. It is crucial to understand that to Charlemagne, as to his Muslim and Byzantine contemporaries, no such boundary existed. Church (or religion) and state were complementary attributes of a polity whose end was personal salvation, not military security or personal fulfillment. Charlemagne's ideological legacy was twofold. On the one hand, it created possibilities for bitter struggles later in the Middle Ages between secular rulers and ecclesiastical powers about the leadership of Christian society. On the other hand, it made it hard to define the state and its essential purposes in other than religious terms.

The most disputed event in the reign of Charlemagne was his imperial coronation in Rome on Christmas Day in 800. It is important to separate how this event happened from what it meant to the participants. In April 799 some disgruntled papal bureaucrats and their supporters attacked Pope Leo III (r. 795–816) in an attempt to depose him. Leo was saved by an ally of Charlemagne and then traveled all the way to Saxony, where the king was camped with his army. Charlemagne agreed to restore the pope to Rome and, as his ally and protector, to investigate those who had attacked him. No real offenses could be proved against the pope, who appeared publicly in Rome to swear that he had done nothing wrong. Everything was handled to avoid any hint that the pope had been put on trial. When Charlemagne went to Saint Peter's Basilica on Christmas, he prayed before the main altar. As he rose from prayer, Pope Leo placed a crown on his head, and the assembled Romans acclaimed him as emperor.

Debate over this coronation arises from a remark of Einhard, who said that if Charlemagne had known what was going to happen, he would not have gone to church that day, even though it was Christmas. Einhard's point was not that Charlemagne did not wish to be emperor. For at least fifteen years, prominent people at the Carolingian court had been addressing Charlemagne in imperial terms in letters, treatises, and poems. Moreover, some were saying that because of Irene's usurpation (see page 222), the imperial throne was vacant—implying that a woman could not truly rule. What Einhard did mean was that Charlemagne saw himself as a Frankish and Christian emperor, not as a *Roman* emperor. The imperial office dignified his position as leader of the Frankish "Israel." Charlemagne did not wish to be beholden to the pope or to the Romans.

Charlemagne's policies did not change after his coronation. He continued his program of legal and ecclesiastical reform and put the finishing touches on some military and diplomatic campaigns. In 806 he divided his empire among his three legitimate sons. Two of them died, so in 813 he made Louis his sole heir and successor. Charlemagne outlived most of the friends and companions of his youth and middle age. He outlived four wives and many of his children. Old and alone, ill and lame, he died in early 814.

Charlemagne's legacy was great. He brought together the lands that would become France, Germany, the Low Countries, and northern Italy and endowed them with a common ideology, government, and culture. He provided a model that Europeans would look back to for centuries as a kind of golden age. His vast supra-regional and supra-ethnic entity, gradually called "Christendom," drew deeply on the universalizing ideals of its Roman, Christian, and Jewish antecedents but was, nevertheless, original. With its Roman, Germanic, and Christian foundations, the Carolingian Empire represented the final stage in the evolution of the Roman Empire in the West. (See the box "The Global Record: 'Persian' Visitors to the Court of Charlemagne.")

CAROLINGIAN GOVERNMENT

Charlemagne accomplished much through the sheer force of his personality and his boundless energy. But he also reformed and created institutional structures. These helped him to carry out his tasks, guaranteed a measure of permanence to his reforms, and created government patterns that lasted in many parts of Europe until the twelfth century.

The king (or emperor—the offices differed little in practical importance) was the heart of the system. In theory, the king ruled by God's grace and did not have to answer for his conduct to any person. In reality, the king necessarily sought consensus through a variety of

"PERSIAN" VISITORS TO THE COURT OF CHARLEMAGNE

In the 880s a monk named Notker wrote the Deeds of Charles the Great. *The work is not a continuous historical narrative but instead a lengthy series of anecdotes, including this one about some "Persian" (probably, in fact, Arab) envoys to Charlemagne. The story is fanciful but revealing of attitudes prevalent in the West. In reading, one has to work through the flattery and exaggeration.*

Envoys of the Persians were sent to him. They arrived in the last week of Lent. They were announced to the emperor but he put off seeing them until the eve of Easter. On the special feast that incomparable man was decked out incomparably and he ordered the people from the race that had once seemed terrible to all the world to be introduced. To them the most excellent Charles seemed amazing before all others, as if they had never seen a king or an emperor. He received them kindly and bestowed on them this gift: As if they were one of his children they had permission to go wherever they wished, look over anything whatsoever, and ask about or investigate anything. They jumped excitedly at the chance to be near him, to look upon him, to admire him; they valued this more than the riches of the East. They climbed up to the balcony that ran around the basilica and looked down on the clergy and soldiers but coming back again and again to the emperor they were unable to keep from laughing on account of their immense joy and they clapped their hands, saying "Before we have only seen men of clay but now we have seen men of gold."

At dawn Charles, unable to tolerate idleness or leisure, prepared to go hunting in the forest for bison or wild oxen, and to take along the Persian envoys. When they saw those huge animals they were struck with terror and turned in flight. But the hero Charles was unperturbed and sat on his bold horse as he approached one of them, drew his sword, and tried to cut right through its neck. But his blow was in vain. The monstrous beast tore through the boot and legwrap of the king and grazed his leg with the tip of his horn, rendering him a little slower than he was before. Angered by this slight wound, the beast fled safe and sound into a valley made tough by trees and rocks. Just about everyone in the service of the lord wanted to take off their leggings but he stopped them.

The Persians also brought the emperor an elephant, monkeys, balsam, nard, and various ointments, spices, perfumes, and different medicines to such an extent that the East seemed emptied and the West, filled. When they had begun to become extremely familiar with the emperor, one day they were a little sillier than usual, heated up with strong white-beer, and they spoke these words in jest to Charles, who was always armed with seriousness and sobriety: "Your power, O Emperor, is very great but much less than the report of your power that is spread in the eastern kingdoms." On hearing this, Charles concealed his great indignation and asked them with a smile "Why do you speak so, my sons? Or why do things seem so to you?" So they went back to the beginning and told him everything that had happened to them in these lands across the sea saying "We Persians, or Medes, and Armenians, Indians, Parthians, Elamites, and all the peoples of the East, fear you much more than our own ruler Harun. What should we say about the Macedonians or Achaeans? Nowadays they fear the pressure of your greatness more than they do the waves of the Ionian Sea. The peoples of all the islands through which we passed on our journey were as ready and determined in your service as if they had been raised in your palace and honored with huge favors."

QUESTIONS

1. How likely do you think it is that "Persian" visitors would have been so dazzled by Charlemagne?

2. Reading between the lines, so to speak, what does this document tell you about Frankish attitudes toward Arabs?

3. What aspects of this story seem most credible to you?

Source: Notker Balbulus, *Gesta Karoli,* 2.8, ed. Reinhold Rau (Darmstadt: Wissenschaftliche Buchgesellschaft, 1975), pp. 386–390. Translated by Thomas F. X. Noble.

means. The king controlled vast lands, which gave him great wealth of his own and also the means to reward loyal followers. By controlling appointments to key positions, the king required men to come to him for power, wealth, and prestige.

The Eastern contemporaries of the Carolingians relied on large numbers of carefully trained, paid civil servants. In contrast, the Carolingians employed a limited number of men who were tied to them by bonds of familial and personal allegiance. The Carolingian court included several ceremonial officers and a domestic staff, all desirable positions. For example, the constable, an officer in charge of transporting the royal entourage, was usually a great aristocrat; the real work of the office was carried out by underlings. The treasurer was the keeper of the king's bedchamber, where the royal treasure chest was kept. Several chaplains, whose primary duty was to see to the spiritual needs of the court, kept official records. The queen controlled the domestic staff and the stewards who managed the royal estates.

Local government was mainly entrusted to counts. About six hundred counts, and several times that number of minor officials, managed the empire. As in Merovingian times, the counts were administrative, judicial, and military officials. Most came from prominent families, and the office increased the wealth and importance of its holders. Counts had to promulgate and enforce royal orders and preside in regular sessions of local courts. They got one-third of the fines, so the zealous pursuit of justice was in their interest.

The royal court and the localities were linked in several ways. Under Charlemagne and his successors it became usual for all major officers, whether secular (counts and their subordinates) or ecclesiastical (bishops and abbots), to be **vassals** of the king. Vassals solemnly pledged loyalty and service to the king. Vassalage drew on both Roman and Germanic customs. Patron-client ties had always been socially and politically important among the Romans, and the allegiance of warriors to a chief was a key Germanic bond. But by connecting personal loyalty with public office, Charlemagne created something essentially new. Only a few thousand men, a tiny fraction of the total population, were vassals at any time. They constituted the political and social elite.

Another connection between the king and his local agents was the assembly that met in various places once or twice a year. In theory, all free men could attend these gatherings, which sometimes had separate secular and ecclesiastical sessions, to advise the king on matters of great importance, such as war and peace or legal reforms. In practice, only the vassals had the means or the interest to ensure their presence. Most of the great Carolingian reforms were formulated in these assemblies by cooperation between the king and his most important subjects. The assemblies served to defuse dissension, but the king also brought his power to bear locally by traveling widely. The monarchy possessed estates all over the heartlands of the kingdom, and the royal entourage often moved from one place to another. Monasteries and cathedrals provided hospitality to the king. As the royal party traveled about the realm, they were able to check on local conditions and to compel local officials to comply with royal wishes.

In 788 Charlemagne began to build a palace at Aachen (AH-ken), and in the last twenty years of his life he usually resided there (see Map 8.3). The later Carolingian rulers all tended to have fixed residences, as did the Byzantines and the Abbasids. In adopting fixed residences and elaborate court rituals, the Carolingians may have been returning to Roman precedents or copying their contemporaries to appear as sophisticated as they. Elegant courts and intricate rituals project an aura of grandeur that enhances people's respect for their rulers. It is no accident that a key innovation of Charlemagne's reign coincided with his permanent residence in Aachen. In the late 780s he began to send out pairs of roving inspectors, or *missi dominici* (MISS-ee doe-MEE-nee-kee), envoys of the lord king. Their function was to see that royal orders were being observed, that counts were dispensing justice honestly, and that persons of power were not oppressing the powerless.

THE CAROLINGIAN RENAISSANCE

Charlemagne's reforms culminated in a revival of learning that scholars have named the **Carolingian Renaissance** (*renaissance* is French for "rebirth"). Charlemagne's fundamental ideas are revealed by the constant use in contemporary sources of words such as *rebirth, renewal, reform,* and *restoration.* Charlemagne, his advisers, and his successors looked back for inspiration to Christian and papal Rome, to Saint Peter and Constantine, and to the Church Fathers. To them the rebirth of Western society as a "New Israel" was equivalent to the theological rebirth of an individual in baptism. The Carolingians were the driving force behind intellectual growth in their era.

To accomplish his objectives, Charlemagne required every cathedral and monastery to establish a school. To set up and run those schools, he summoned to his court many of the most able and influential intellectual figures of the day, among them Franks, such as his biographer Einhard, grammar teachers from Italy, and Visigothic theologians from the Spanish border. His most famous recruit was the Anglo-Saxon Alcuin (AL-kwin) (735–804), the most learned man of his day and the heir of Bede and of the brilliant culture of Northumbria.

Much of the work of Alcuin and his associates was devoted to producing textbooks and to teaching elementary knowledge. Charlemagne was convinced that people needed to be taught the basic truths of Christianity if he were to accomplish his task of leading them to salvation. A massive effort was thus undertaken to copy manuscripts of the Bible and the writings of the Latin Church Fathers. These books, the essential resources for the whole program, needed to be

---

vassals Generally high-status men who pledged personal loyalty to a lord in return for public offices and material benefits.

Carolingian Renaissance Major revival of learning, combined with reform of religious and political institutions, that occurred under Charlemagne and his successors.

Ivory Cover of the Lorsch Gospels
In 810 the monks at Lorsch produced a Gospel book and probably its covers, too. This cover (front or back? scholars are not sure) is now in London. It depicts an enthroned Mary with Jesus on her lap, flanked by Zacharias and his son, John the Baptist. The ivory carving is of such exquisite quality that scholars long refused to believe that this was not a late antique work. *(V&A Images/Victoria and Albert Museum)*

disseminated as widely as possible. The process of copying was facilitated by a new script, Caroline minuscule.

It is significant that Charlemagne could attract Alcuin from York, the most renowned school in the West, to head his palace school, just then forming. Alcuin recognized that Charlemagne could place more resources at his disposal than anyone else and had the will to do so. Alcuin also saw the long-term benefits that would come from his work. Alcuin's pupils spread out in the next generation to create a network of schools that went right on multiplying across the ninth century. That is a powerful legacy. And Alcuin did more than just teach. He wrote learned works and poetry and was for twenty years Charlemagne's most trusted adviser.

With his plan, personnel, and schools in place, Charlemagne took many concrete steps. He secured from Rome a copy of the authoritative canon law of the church. Charlemagne also got from the pope a *sacramentary,* a service book for worship in cathedral churches. Charlemagne sought an authoritative copy of the *Rule of St. Benedict,* and after study and commentary, this Rule was imposed on all monasteries in the kingdom.

Secular reforms mirrored religious ones. Orders regularized the management of all royal estates. Charlemagne attempted to update local law codes and to make them as uniform as possible. Not since Rome had governments possessed either the interest in or the means to promote such centralization. It is striking that in the eighth century the caliphate, the Byzantine Empire, and the Carolingian Empire were engaged in similar centralizing activities.

Versatility was a hallmark of Carolingian learning. Various scholars excelled at poetry, history, and biography. Biblical studies and theology attracted a lot of attention. One figure who personifies the Carolingian Renaissance is the Visigoth Theodulf (ca. 760–821). He came to court in about 790 and served thereafter as a missus, royal adviser, abbot of several monasteries, and bishop of Orléans. He issued important legislation for his diocese. He was the foremost Old Testament expert of his day and the only one who knew Hebrew. He wrote the official Frankish response to Byzantine iconoclasm. He also composed theological treatises, many letters, and dozens of poems. At Germigny (JHER-mee-nee) he designed a church that is a masterpiece of early Carolingian architecture.

Carolingian art is a crowning glory of the age. Several distinct currents inspired and informed Carolingian art. Most prominent were the animal and geometric decorative motifs of Irish and Anglo-Saxon art; the elegance, formality, and sense of composition of classical art; basic elements of style from Byzantine painting; actual scenes from papal Rome; and the mysteries of Christian theology. Every element was borrowed, but the finished product was new.

Architecture shows the same trends. Charlemagne's palace complex at Aachen has parallels in imperial Constantinople, papal Rome, and Ostrogothic Ravenna. Workers and building materials were fetched from all over the empire. From 768 to 855, 27 cathedrals were built along with 417 monasteries and 100 royal residences. For basic buildings the Carolingians adapted the basilica. The classical basilica was a horizontal building, but the Carolingians, by altering the western end and façade (the "westworks"), added the dimension of verticality. In Romanesque and Gothic architecture this innovation would have a long career (see pages 306–309).

THE FRAGMENTATION OF CHARLEMAGNE'S EMPIRE, 814–887

The Carolingian Empire did not outlive the ninth century. Rome's empire lasted much longer, as did Byzantium's and Islam's. All of these realms were fatally weakened by similar problems, but those problems arose more quickly and acutely in the Carolingian world than elsewhere. By the end of the ninth century small political entities had replaced the unified Carolingian Empire.

Size and ethnic complexity contributed to the disintegration of the empire. The empire included many small regions—Saxony, Bavaria, Brittany, and Lombardy, for example—that had their own resident elites, linguistic traditions, and distinctive cultures, which had existed before the Carolingians came on the scene and persist to this day. The Merovingian and Carolingian periods were basically a unifying intrusion into a history characterized by regional diversity. The Carolingians made heroic efforts to build a common culture and to forge bonds of unity, but the obstacles were insuperable.

Another key issue in the breakup of the Carolingian Empire was political and dynastic. The Carolingians regularly tried to create subkingdoms for all their legitimate sons while preserving the imperial title for one of them. This was a creative attempt to concede limited autonomy to particular regions by means of local kingships—for instance, in Bavaria, Italy, and Aquitaine—while preserving the "Augustinian" unity of the empire as a whole. Unfortunately, younger sons rarely yielded to their older brothers, and the bonds of loyalty among cousins, nephews, and grandchildren grew weak. Frequent divisions of the empire, or of segments of it, placed local nobilities in the difficult position of changing their allegiance frequently and of jeopardizing their offices and landholdings.

New Political Divisions In the Treaty of Verdun in 843 (see inset, Map 8.3) the three grandsons of Charlemagne—Charles the Bald, Louis the German, and Lothair—divided the empire into three realms: the West Frankish, the East Frankish, and the Middle Kingdoms. After fierce battles among the brothers, each appointed forty members to a study commission that traversed the empire to identify royal properties, fortifications, monasteries, and cathedrals so that an equitable division of these valuable resources could be made. Each brother needed adequate resources to solidify his rule and to attract or hold followers. The lines drawn on the map at Verdun did not last even for a generation.

Slowly large West Frankish and East Frankish Kingdoms emerged, swallowing the Middle Kingdom, and created a framework for the future France and Germany. But they had to compete with many smaller entities. Some of these—in Italy, the Rhineland, and southern France—were old and distinctive regions that recaptured their former independence. Others were essentially new creations, born in the absence of firm Carolingian control. Newcomers also appeared on the scene, most prominently Scandinavian and Slavic principalities.

Before the ninth century, Scandinavia had known only small-scale political units under local chieftains and their trusted followers. Economic and political pressure from the Carolingians gradually began to push both Denmark and Norway in the direction of greater political consolidation. A single Danish monarchy has a continuous history from the late ninth century, and Norway's monarchy dates from the early tenth.

To the east of the Carolingian Empire lay a vast swath of Slavic lands. The Carolingians fought, allied, and traded with these peoples for decades. Charlemagne destroyed the Avar khanate in the Danube basin in campaigns between 788 and 804. By the middle of the ninth century the princes of Great Moravia dominated the region and played a complicated diplomatic game between the East Frankish rulers and the Byzantine emperors. To the east of the Moravians, the Bulgarians profited from the Avar and then the Carolingian collapse to expand their kingdom. For two centuries the Bulgarians dominated the northern Balkans and threatened Byzantium.

The most durable consequence of this political restructuring along the eastern frontier of the Frankish world was religious. In 863, on an invitation from Moravia and in hopes of countering the Franks, the Byzantine emperor sent the missionaries Cyril (826–869) and Methodius (805–884) into eastern Europe. The emperor hoped to erect an Orthodox union of his own realm, the southern Slavs, and the newly converted Bulgarians. Likewise he was seeking a diplomatic bulwark between the Bulgarians in the East and the Franks in the West. Unfortunately for Byzantium, Cyril and Methodius agreed with the pope to introduce Roman Catholic Christianity in return for the pope's permission to use the Slavonic language in worship. Cyril and Methodius were formidable linguists who created a religious literature in "Church Slavonic" that went far toward creating a new cultural realm in central Europe.

Ninth-Century Invasions Finally a new wave of attacks and invasions contributed decisively to the fragmentation of the Carolingian Empire. In the middle decades of the ninth century, Muslims, Vikings, and Magyars wreaked havoc on the Franks.

Based in North Africa and the islands of the western Mediterranean, Muslims attacked Italy and southern France. The Byzantines lost Sicily to raiders from North Africa in 827 and found themselves seriously challenged in southern Italy. In the 840s Muslims raided the city of Rome. These same brigands preyed on trade in the western Mediterranean and even set up camps in the Alps to rob traders passing back and forth over the mountains.

"From the fury of the Northmen, O Lord, deliver us," was a plaintive cry heard often in ninth-century Europe. Those Northmen were Vikings, mainly Danes and Norwegians, seeking booty, glory, and political opportunity. Most Viking bands were formed by leaders who had lost out in the dawning institutional consolidation of the northern world. Some were opportunists who sought to profit from the weakness of Carolingian, Anglo-Saxon, and Irish rule. In the mid-ninth century, Vikings began settling and initiated their own state-building activities in Ireland, England, northwestern France ("Normandy"—the region of the Northmen), and Rus (early "Russia").

Magyars, relatives of the Huns and Avars who had preceded them into eastern Europe, were accomplished horsemen whose lightning raids, beginning in 889, hit Italy, Germany, and even France. East Frankish Carolingians tried to use the Magyars as mercenaries against the troublesome Moravians. In the end, the Magyars destroyed the incipient Moravian state and raided with impunity.

All of these attacks were unpredictable and caused local regions to fall back on their own resources rather than look to the central government. Commerce was disrupted everywhere. Schools, based in ecclesiastical institutions, suffered severe decline. The raids represented a thousand pinpricks, not a single deadly sword stroke. Yet their collective effect amounted to despair and disruption on a massive scale.

Even though the Carolingian Empire itself disintegrated, the idea of Europe as "Christendom," as a single political-cultural entity, persisted. The Latin Christian culture promoted by Carolingian schools and rulers set the tone for intellectual life until the twelfth century. Likewise, Carolingian governing structures were inherited and adapted by all of the successor states that emerged in the ninth and tenth centuries. In these respects the Carolingian experience paralleled the Roman, and the Islamic and Byzantine, too. A potent, centralizing regime disappeared but left a profound imprint on its heirs. For hundreds of years Western civilization would be played out inside the lands that had been Charlemagne's empire and between those lands and their Byzantine and Muslim neighbors.

SECTION SUMMARY

- The Carolingian family rose steadily to power, first as mayors of the palace, then as kings, and finally as emperors.

- Charlemagne instituted far-reaching governmental innovations and reforms intended to make his power effective and to unify the lands under his rule.

- Carolingian rulers launched a cultural revival, called the Carolingian Renaissance, that aimed to master and then communicate basic Christian teachings.

- The Carolingian Empire broke down because of geographic diversity, political disunity, and new waves of invasion.

EARLY MEDIEVAL ECONOMIES AND SOCIETIES

What were the chief similarities and differences among the early medieval civilizations?

The economic and social history of the early Middle Ages provides additional evidence of the similarities among the three early medieval civilizations, while also revealing differences. Overall the world remained rural, society was hierarchical, and women were excluded from public power. Although broad political frameworks changed, the lives of most people changed rather little.

TRADE AND COMMERCE

In the simplest terms, trade is a mechanism for exchanging goods from one person or group to another. There are many such exchange mechanisms. The Roman government, for example, moved large amounts of goods from the center of the empire to the frontiers to supply its armies. Roman, Byzantine, and Islamic governments raised taxes in one place, bought goods in another, and then consumed their purchases someplace else. Tribute and plunder were also effective exchange mechanisms, as were diplomatic gifts: a caliph, for example, sent Charlemagne an elephant.

The most common exchanges were intensely local, but several major trading networks operated during the early Middle Ages. In the East, Mesopotamia was linked by rivers to the Persian Gulf, East Africa, and southern Asia; by land and sea to Byzantium; and by land and rivers to the Black Sea region, Slavic Europe, and the Baltic. Byzantines traded mainly by sea. The whole Mediterranean was open to them, and from the Black Sea they received the products of the Danube basin. The Muslim world was fundamentally a land empire that had relatively poor roads and primitive wheeled vehicles, so transport considerations were cru-

Oseberg Ship
Discovered in 1880, the Oseberg ship was buried in Norway in (probably) the tenth century. The ship may have belonged to a king and contained the remains of Queen Asa. It is 70 feet long and 16 feet wide. Its crew would have been thirty to forty men.
(University Museum of National Antiquities, Oslo)

cial: a caravan of some five hundred camels could move only one-fourth to one-half the cargo of a normal Byzantine ship.

The West had many trade routes. The Rhône-Saône river system carried goods, as did the land routes through the Alpine passes. The North and Baltic Seas were the hubs of a network that linked the British Isles, the whole of the Frankish north (by means of its rivers), the Rhineland, Slavic Europe, Byzantium, and the Muslim world. The Danube was also a major highway. The major trade networks intersected at many points. Despite religious and ideological differences, Rome's three heirs regularly traded with one another. Recent research has documented hundreds of east-west and north-south contacts across the early medieval period.

Food and other bulk goods never traveled very far because the cost was prohibitive. Most towns were supplied with foodstuffs by their immediate hinterlands, so the goods that traveled long distances were portable and valuable. Cotton and raw silk were transported to the Mediterranean, where they were made into cloth in, respectively, Egypt and Byzantium. Paper and pottery were transported around the caliphate. Asian spices and perfumes were avidly sought everywhere. The Byzantines traded in silk cloth, fine ivories, delicate products of the gold- and silversmiths' art, slaves, and naval stores. Byzantium, with its large fleet, usually controlled the Black and Mediterranean Seas. Reduced in prosperity, the empire could no longer dictate trade terms to subject peoples and competed badly with the Muslims. Trade in the West was partly in high-value luxury goods but mainly in ordinary items such as plain pottery, raw wool, wool cloth, millstones, weapons, and slaves.

TOWN AND COUNTRYSIDE

To think of the ancient world is to think of cities, but to think of the medieval world is to envision forests and fields. Actually 80 to 90 percent of people in antiquity lived in rural settings, and in the early Middle Ages the percentage was not much higher. What changed was the place occupied by towns in the totality of human life. Fewer government functions were based in towns, cultural life was less bound to the urban environment, and trade in luxuries, which depended on towns, declined.

Towns in the West lost Roman governmental significance but often survived as focal points of royal or, more often, ecclesiastical administration. A cathedral church required a large corps of administrators. Western towns were everywhere attracting *burgs*, new settlements of merchants, just outside their centers. Because Vikings frequently raided these burgs, their existence was precarious. Few Western towns were impressive in size or population. Rome may have numbered a million people in the time of Augustus, but only about thirty thousand lived there in 800. Paris had perhaps twenty

thousand inhabitants at that time. These were the largest cities by far in Catholic Europe.

In the Byzantine East, apart from Constantinople, the empire had a more rural aspect after the Muslims took control of the heavily urbanized regions of Syria, Egypt, and parts of Anatolia in the seventh century. The weakening of the caliphate in the second half of the ninth century was a spur to renewed urban growth in the Byzantine Empire. In provincial cities population growth and urban reconstruction depended heavily on military conditions: cities threatened by Arabs or Bulgarians declined.

The Arabs were great city-builders. Baghdad—four times larger in area than Constantinople, with a million residents to the latter's 400,000—was created from scratch. The most magnificent city in the West was Cordoba, the capital of Muslim Spain. Its population may have reached 400,000, and its Great Mosque, begun in 786, held 5,500 worshipers, more than any Latin church except Saint Peter's. The city had 900 baths, 1,600 mosques (Rome had about 200 churches), 60,000 mansions, and perhaps 100,000 shops. Its libraries held thousands of books, while the largest Carolingian book collections numbered a few hundred.

Agriculture nevertheless remained the most important element in the economy and in the daily lives of most people in all three realms. Farming meant primarily the production of cereal grains, which provided diet staples such as bread, porridge, and beer. Regions tended to specialize in the crops that grew most abundantly in local circumstances. For example, olives and grapes were common in the Mediterranean area, whereas cereals predominated around the Black Sea and in central Gaul. Animal husbandry was always a major part of the rural regime. English sheep provided wool and meat. In Frankish and Byzantine regions pigs, which were cheap to raise, supplied meat, but for religious reasons pork was almost absent in the Muslim East—Islam adopted the Jewish prohibition against it.

A key development in the Frankish West was the appearance of a bipartite estate, sometimes called a **manor.** On a bipartite estate, one part of the land was set aside as a reserve (or *demesne* [duh-MEEN]), and the rest was divided into tenancies. The reserve, consuming from one-quarter to one-half of the total territory of the estate, was exploited directly for the benefit of the landlord. The tenancies were generally worked by the peasants for their own support. The bipartite estate provided the aristocrats with a livelihood while freeing them for military and government service.

Estates were run in different ways. A landlord might hire laborers to farm his reserve, paying them with money exacted as fees from his tenants. Or he

manor   A common term for an agricultural estate that typically had its lands divided between the manor's lord and dependent peasants.

might require the tenants to work a certain number of days per week or weeks per year in his fields. The produce of the estate might be gathered into barns and consumed locally or hauled to local markets. The reserve might be a separate part of the estate, a proportion of common fields, or a percentage of the harvest. The tenants might have individual farms or work in common fields. Although the manor is one of the most familiar aspects of European life throughout the Middle Ages, large estates with dependent tenants also were evolving in the Byzantine and Islamic worlds.

SOCIAL PATTERNS

Most of the surviving medieval records were written by elite members of society and reveal little about the middle and lower orders of society. Nevertheless, certain similarities are evident in the social structures of all levels in all three societies. The elites tended to be large landholders, to control dependent populations, and to have access to government offices. There were regional differences, too. Scholars ranked higher in Byzantium and the caliphate than in the West; churchmen, especially bishops, were powerful in Christian societies but had no counterparts in Muslim ones. Literature, surely reflecting social realities, portrays the cultivated Muslim gentleman in the Abbasid period. This social type, marked by learning, good manners, and a taste for finery, does not appear in Byzantium or in the West until the twelfth century.

The middling classes show some disparities among the regions. Merchants, for example, often rose through the social ranks to become great aristocrats in Muslim society. Islamic society often evinced great mobility because of its restless, expanding nature and because Islamic ideology rejected distinctions in the umma. In Byzantium traditional Roman prejudices against merchants and moneymaking activities persisted. Thus rich merchants whose wealth gave them private influence frequently lacked public power and recognition. In the West merchants were neither numerous nor powerful in the Carolingian period. In some towns, moreover, commerce was in the hands of Jews, always outsiders in a militantly Christian society.

Merchants were not the only people occupying the middle rungs of the social ladder. All three societies, in fact, possessed both central elites and provincial elites. Service at the Carolingian, Byzantine, or Abbasid court counted for more than service in a provincial outpost. It was one thing to be abbot of a great monastery and quite a different thing to preside over a poor, tiny house. The thematic generals in Byzantium were lofty personages; their subordinates held inferior positions. The vassals of a Carolingian king formed a real aristocracy, but vassals' vassals were of decidedly lower rank.

Degrees of freedom and local economic and political conditions shaped the lives of peasants. In all three societies some farmers were personally free and owed no cash or labor services to anyone but the central government. In areas such as Abbasid Iraq ordinary free farmers led a comfortable life. In the Frankish world most peasants existed outside the dawning manorial system. They were free, and if they lived in areas of good land and political security, such as the Paris basin, their lives most likely were congenial. Byzantine peasants, though free, often lived in areas of military danger, and in some parts of the Balkans they eked out a living from poor soils. Highly taxed and perpetually endangered, they may have viewed their freedom as small compensation for their economic and personal insecurity. All peasants were alike in their subjection to political forces over which they had no control.

At the bottom of the social scale everywhere were slaves. Christianity did not object to slavery in general but forbade the enslavement of Christians. Islam likewise prohibited Muslims from enslaving other Muslims. Slaves, therefore, tended to be most common in pagan societies—Scandinavia, for example—or in frontier regions where neighboring pagans could be captured and sold. There were more slaves in the Muslim world than in Byzantium, which had, in turn, more than the West.

THE EXPERIENCES OF WOMEN

Women were bound to the same social hierarchies as men. Predictably enough, women had few formal, public roles to play. Their influence, however great, tended to function in the private sphere, rarely revealed to us by sources that stem from the public realm of powerful men. Aristocratic women had opportunities and power that were denied ordinary women. Irene ruled at Byzantium as empress. Frankish and Anglo-Saxon queens were formidable figures in their realms. Carolingian queens managed the landed patrimony of the dynasty—dozens of huge estates with tens of thousands of dependents. The combination of a lack of evidence and the rigorous exclusion of women from public life in the Islamic world means that virtually no Muslim women emerge as distinct personalities in the early Middle Ages.

The conversion of England to Christianity was fostered by women. Most convents had aristocratic abbesses who presided over complex enterprises and often schools. In the Frankish world aristocratic women secured some learning, and one, Dhuoda, wrote in 841 a manual of advice for her son that conveys biblical and patristic teachings as well as practical wisdom. The Frankish convent at Chelles was a renowned center for the copying of manuscripts. Some Anglo-Saxon nuns owned ships and invested in commercial activities to support their convents. Almost all aspects of the cloth industry were in women's hands.

One example of the problems in the evidence concerning women relates to church roles. Women could not hold priestly office, and although deaconesses served at Hagia Sophia in the sixth century, they disappeared soon after and had long before vanished in the West. Religious power could come from personal sanctity as well as holding office. One study of some 2,200 saints from the early Middle Ages finds only about 300 females. It was hard for women to gain recognition as saints. And if a woman became a saint, her holiness was inevitably described either as "manly"—an extreme ascetic was praised for having the strength and courage of a man—or as beautiful, virginal, and domestic—in other words, with female stereotypes.

The domestic sphere is another difficult realm to enter. The Quran permitted a man to have up to four wives if he could care for them and would treat them equitably. A Muslim woman, however, was given her dowry outright, and multiple marriages may have meant that relatively more Muslim women could gain a measure of security. In Byzantium and the West, families rarely arranged marriages for more than one or two daughters. Others remained single or entered convents. Women at all social levels tended to pass from the tutelage of their fathers to that of their husbands. In antiquity a suitor usually paid a fee, or "bride price," to his prospective wife's father and then endowed his wife with a "morning gift," money or possessions of her own. Gradually this practice changed to a system whereby a bride's father paid a dowry to her future husband. Thus a wife who was cast aside could be left impoverished, for in most places the law did not permit her to inherit land if she had brothers. Females were such valuable property in the marriage market that rape was an offense not against a girl but against her father. A man could divorce, even kill, his wife for adultery, witchcraft, or grave robbing and then marry again. A woman could usually gain a divorce only for adultery, and she could not remarry. For the vast majority of women, daily life was hedged about with legal limitations and personal indignities.

SECTION SUMMARY

- The early Middle Ages witnessed the elaboration of several major trading networks that made ordinary and luxury goods available over long distances.

- Cities continued to play important roles in the life of the Islamic and Byzantine worlds but played comparatively little role in western Europe.

- Arab, Byzantine, and European societies were elitist and hierarchical. Merchants were less important in Europe than elsewhere. Agriculture was dominant everywhere.

- Women played important political, social, and economic roles in all societies, but women's lives were hedged with restrictions.

CHAPTER SUMMARY

Online Study Center **ACE the Test**

What were the most important factors in the rise of the Arab peoples and the Islamic faith?

Why did a distinctive civilization that can be called "Byzantine" emerge?

What strengths and weaknesses were exhibited by the small states that survived Rome's collapse in the West?

What were the greatest achievements of the Carolingians and why were they so successful?

What were the chief similarities and differences among the early medieval civilizations?

We have traced three parallel histories in the development of early medieval civilizations: that of the Arabs and Islam; that of the Byzantines; and that of Catholic Europe and the Carolingians. Muhammad was a great teacher who emphasized *al-Islam*, surrender to Allah. He taught a faith that may be summarized in the "Five Pillars" of Islam. Both internal and external factors contributed to the lightning conquests of Islam in the century after Muhammad's death, spreading Islam and Arab rule from Spain to the frontiers of China. Islamic culture was rooted in the religious teachings of the *ulama* and in the scholarship of those who tackled Greek and Persian learning.

The Byzantine Empire faced hard challenges from Persians and then Muslims in the east, from Slavs, Avars, and Bulgars in the Balkans, and from Lombards in Italy. The Byzantine Empire in the early Middle Ages was much smaller than the Roman Empire that preceded it. The "theme" system was a comprehensive and effective revision of the empire's traditional governmental structure. A distinctive Byzantine culture was based on the Greek language, the Greek Church Fathers, Orthodox religious traditions, and distinctive local practices.

Visigothic Spain suffered from religious, political, and military disunity while Italy developed three stable regions: a Lombard and then Frankish north; a papal center; and a Byzantine and then Muslim south. In the British Isles the conversion to Catholic Christianity and the development of ecclesiastical organization were forces for unity and cultural achievement. In the British Isles, political development in the Celtic regions was slow, but England began emerging as a more and more coherent political entity under ambitious and effective kings.

The Carolingian family rose steadily to power, first as mayors of the palace, then as kings, and finally as emperors. The greatest Carolingian, Charlemagne, instituted far-reaching governmental innovations and reforms intended to make his power effective and to unify the lands under his rule. Carolingian rulers launched a cultural revival, called the Carolingian Renaissance, that aimed to master and then communicate basic Christian teachings. The Carolingian Empire broke down because of geographic diversity, political disunity, and new waves of invasion.

The early Middle Ages witnessed the elaboration of several major trading networks that made ordinary and luxury goods available over long distances. Cities continued to play important roles in the life of the Islamic and Byzantine worlds but played comparatively little role in western Europe except as ecclesiastical centers. Arab, Byzantine, and European societies were elitist and hierarchical. Merchants were less important in Europe than elsewhere. Agriculture was dominant everywhere. Women played important political, social, and economic roles in all societies, but women's lives were hedged by legal limitations, social conventions, and religious restrictions.

LOOKING AHEAD

Late Antiquity was dynamic and turbulent but productive, too: It "produced" three kindred cultures. The ninth century was also dynamic and turbulent. In the next chapter we will see what became of the Islamic, Byzantine, and European worlds between about 900 and 1300, a period of great energy and achievement.

KEY TERMS

Muhammad (p. 214)

Five Pillars (p. 216)

Quran (p. 216)

caliphate (p. 218)

Papal States (p. 222)

iconoclasm (p. 225)

Orthodox (p. 225)

Charlemagne (p. 232)

vassals (p. 236)

Carolingian Renaissance (p. 236)

manor (p. 241)

Online Study Center
Improve Your Grade Flashcards

SUGGESTED READING

Barbero, Alessandro. *Charlemagne: Father of a Continent.* 2004. A comprehensive and engaging book that emphasizes culture and material life.

Berkey, Jonathan P. *The Formation of Islam: Religion and Society in the Near East, 600–1800.* 2003. Compact yet comprehensive and readable; equipped with fine "Suggestions for Further Reading," this book is now the place to start on the Islamic world.

Brown, Peter. *The Rise of Western Christendom.* 2d ed. 2003. A verbal feast, now fully documented, this book presents a stimulating assessment of the place of Christianity in the rise of Western culture.

Denny, Frederick M. *An Introduction to Islam.* 2d ed. 1994. By far the most accessible, readable account of the Islamic faith; the book covers all periods but is helpful for the early centuries.

Herrin, Judith. *Women in Purple: Rulers of Medieval Byzantium.* 2003. A series of biographical and analytical portraits of Byzantium's empresses.

McCormick, Michael. *Origins of the European Economy: Communications and Commerce, AD 300–900.* 2001. A stupendous achievement, this richly detailed book is *the* starting point for an understanding of the early medieval commercial economy.

Smith, Julia M. H. *After Rome: A New Cultural History.* 2005. A brilliant, thematically organized treatment of the early Middle Ages, destined to become a classic.

Smith, Julia M. H., and Leslie Brubaker, eds. *Gender in the Early Medieval World: East and West, 30–900.* 2004. A collection of excellent, accessible essays by specialists that is true to its title.

Whittow, Mark. *The Making of Orthodox Byzantium, 600–1025.* 1996. Lively, readable, controversial, and engaging, this book challenges standard views.

9

THE EXPANSION OF EUROPE IN THE HIGH MIDDLE AGES, 900–1300

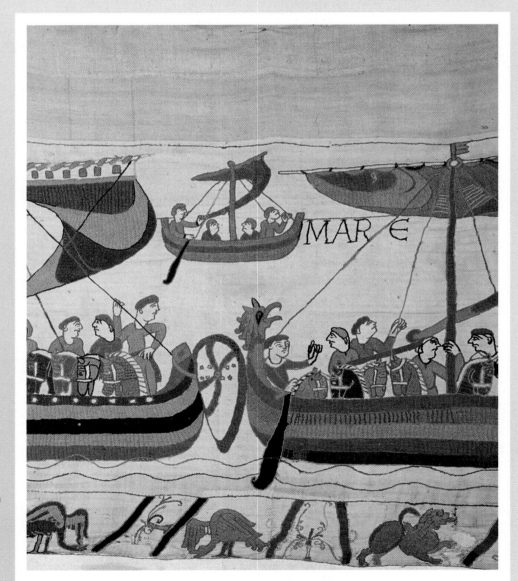

Bayeux Tapestry
The tapestry (ca. 1077) depicts the fleet of William the Conqueror of Normandy sailing to England in 1066. *(Michael Holford)*

The picture to the left represents one small section of the Bayeux Tapestry, a narrative account—in words and illustrations—of the conquest of England in 1066 by Duke William of Normandy. This scene is an apt introduction to the central theme of this chapter: expansion.

This section of the 230-foot-long tapestry depicts William setting sail for England. William had already gained greater authority in the duchy of Normandy than any duke before him. Now he was about to press his claim to the throne of England. He gathered soldiers from all over western France and boldly crossed the English Channel. Leaving nothing to chance, he transported horses, too, as you can see in the picture.

One group of Normans conquered England, while another seized control of southern Italy. Still other Normans played a decisive role in the period's most prominent manifestation of expansion: the Crusades. Meanwhile, certain Scandinavians settled Iceland and Greenland to the west, while others founded the first state on Russian soil. Spanish Christians pushed back the Muslims in Iberia. From the Baltic to the Balkans, Slavic rulers founded new states and pressed hard against their neighbors. German rulers crossed the Alps into Italy, French kings reached the Pyrenees, and English monarchs pushed into Wales, Scotland, and Ireland. Seldom has Europe's political geography expanded so dramatically as during the High Middle Ages.

Between 900 and 1300 Europe's population began one of its longest periods of sustained growth. People brought more land under cultivation, introduced new crops, and made agriculture more efficient. Villages, towns, and cities grew in number and size. Trade expanded in every material and in every direction.

Europe witnessed the re-emergence of centralizing monarchies in France, England, and Spain. Some new realms, such as Denmark and Hungary, built strong central governments. And an explosion of new states occurred along the frontiers of the old Carolingian Empire.

The "West" began taking on a more *western European* character. The Crusades complicated relations between Christian Europeans and Muslims, and both the Crusades and increasing religious differences alienated western Europe from Byzantium, and Roman Catholics from Orthodox believers. The center of Western civilization became more and more anchored to northwestern Europe. And that same western Europe was expanding to influence

CHAPTER OUTLINE

ECONOMIC EXPANSION

THE HEIRS OF THE CAROLINGIAN EMPIRE: GERMANY, ITALY, AND FRANCE

THE BRITISH ISLES

THE GROWTH OF NEW STATES

THE CRUSADES

KEY TERMS

guilds

lay investiture

communes

Papal Monarchy

feudal revolution

Magna Carta

parliaments

Reconquista

Crusades

Online Study Center

This icon will direct you to interactive map and primary source activities on the website **college.hmco.com/ pic/noble5e**

lands in Scandinavia and the Slavic world that had played no role at all in the West's classical, Mediterranean phase. The High Middle Ages repeatedly posed the question: Where is the West?

FOCUS QUESTIONS

In how many different realms of life do you see signs of growth and innovation, of expansion?

What did Germany, Italy, and France owe to the Carolingian past? How alike and different were these areas by 1300?

What were the chief dynamics in the development of medieval Britain?

How did new states emerge in Spain, Scandinavia, and the Slavic world, and how do those states compare with their western neighbors?

What basic factors contributed to the rise, persistence, and eventual decline of the crusading movement?

ECONOMIC EXPANSION

In how many different realms of life do you see signs of growth and innovation, of expansion?

The economic expansion of Europe is manifest in many kinds of evidence that are more often qualitative than quantitative. Medieval people did not keep the kinds of records of births, deaths, population, or business activity that modern states routinely accumulate. After about 1000 every available indicator points to a growing population and an expanding scale and sophistication of economic activity.

THE GROWING POPULATION

The population of Europe began rising slowly in the Carolingian period and may have doubled between 1000 and 1200. Available evidence suggests that the total population of western Europe grew from around 30 million in 1000 to 55 million or 60 million in 1200. In the thirteenth century population growth gradually slowed.

In a few regions where family size can be estimated, fertile marriages were producing on the average 3.5 children in the tenth century and from 6 to 7 in the twelfth. People were also living longer than their forebears. Studies of aristocrats, high clergy, and soldiers show that a surprising 40 percent of them were over 40 years old. Male life expectancy was surely longer than female because of the dangers of childbirth, always the great killer of women in the premodern world. The general trend is clear: more babies being born, more infants living into adulthood, more adults living longer.

Everywhere in Europe new land was brought into cultivation. More than half of the French documents relating to land in the twelfth century show new land being brought under the plow. Thousands of acres of forest were cut down. Marshes were reclaimed from the sea. Some 380,000 acres were drained along the western coast of France and probably twice that amount in both Flanders and England. This activity is inexplicable without assuming a growing number of mouths to feed.

Agriculture benefited from a warmer and drier climate through this whole period. Not a single vegetable blight was recorded. Food was more abundant and more nutritious. Animals were increasingly reared for their meat, and higher meat consumption meant more protein in the diet. Beans and other legumes, also rich in protein, were more widely cultivated. People of every class and region were almost certainly eating better and living longer and healthier lives.

TECHNOLOGICAL GAINS

The eleventh century was a decisive period in the spread of new technologies in Europe. Innovations occurred in agriculture, transportation, mining, and manufacturing. Agricultural changes came first as a rising population created an increased demand for food that could be met only by new practices. By the late twelfth century an acre of farmland in a fertile region was probably yielding a crop three to four times larger than in the Carolingian era. Given the combination of more land under cultivation and more yield per acre, the overall gains in the food supply were enormous.

The increases can be accounted for in several ways. Horses were more frequently used as draft animals. They were more expensive to acquire than oxen but no more costly to feed, and they did, in a day, a third or half again as much work. For much less "fuel" horses could haul loads farther and faster than oxen. Thus fewer people could, with horses, cultivate more land than their predecessors managed with oxen. In addition, they could cultivate the land more frequently and increase yields because more seed would fall on more finely plowed soil. The dissemination of the horse collar made possible the expanded use of horses—older forms of harnesses suitable for the low-slung, broad-shouldered ox would have choked a horse.

Plows, too, were improved. The light wooden scratch plow used by the Romans was satisfactory for the thin soils of the Mediterranean region but barely disturbed the heavy soils of northern Europe. The invention of a heavy wheeled plow with an iron coulter (or plowshare) and a moldboard was a real breakthrough. The iron plowshare cut deep furrows, and then the moldboard turned and aerated the soil. This heavy plow allowed farmers to exploit good soils more fully without exhausting the ground too rapidly. This plow seems to have been introduced into Carolingian Europe from the Slavic world, but it was not widely adopted before the eleventh century.

Wider adoption of nitrogen-fixing crops, such as peas and some kinds of beans, retarded soil exhaustion and also put more protein in the diet. Leaving land fallow was another means of avoiding soil exhaustion. In the early Middle Ages this meant setting aside about half of the arable land every year (the two-field system) or working the land intensively for a few years and then moving on. By the twelfth century three-field schemes of crop rotation were common.

Under the three-field system, two-thirds of the arable land saw nearly constant use. The amount of an estate under cultivation rose from 50 to 67 percent. Crop rotation brought other benefits as well. Horses ate oats, but (except in a few places such as Scotland) medieval people generally did not. If farmers wished to use horses, they had to dedicate some of their land to growing oats. A three-field rotation allowed some flexibility. Finally the alternation of winter crops (wheat and rye), spring crops (oats, barley, and legumes), and fallow ensured against a single season of unusually harsh weather.

Surplus produce was intended mainly for the growing towns. To supply that market, improvements in transportation were necessary. Kings often passed laws to secure the safety of highways, and popes three times (in 1097, 1132, and 1179) threatened highwaymen—robbers who preyed on travelers—with excommunication. Landlords required their dependents to maintain

roads and bridges. Many stone bridges were constructed in France between 1130 and 1170 because wooden bridges were so vulnerable to fire. Indeed, fire destroyed the bridge at Angers (in western France) five times between 1032 and 1167.

Transport improved not only because of safer roads but also thanks to better vehicles. The old two-wheeled cart, drawn by oxen, began giving way to the sturdy four-wheeled, horse-drawn wagon. Because greater quantities of foodstuffs could be moved farther and faster, urban communities could be supplied from larger areas. This was a crucial factor in enabling cities to grow and in providing urban residents with a predictable and diverse range of foods.

Seaborne trade expanded, too. The stern rudder, better sails, the compass (in use by 1180), and better navigational charts facilitated sea travel, as did the growing use of larger ships. An Italian fleet sailed to Flanders in 1277, and within a few years the old overland trade routes, and with them the Champagne fairs, began a decline that was not reversed until the invention of the railroad in the nineteenth century.

At any time of year, travel was difficult and costly. Few dared to venture across the Alps in the winter, and the northern seas, especially the passage around Denmark, were treacherous in cold weather. Even in the relatively calm Mediterranean, the Venetians refused to send out their trading fleet between November and March. Overland trade was impeded by snow, rain, mud, and highwaymen, who would rob travelers on the road. Governments tried to restrain robbers, but no one could change the weather.

There were notable improvements in both the quarrying of stone and the mining of metals. Mines were not deep because people lacked the means to keep the shafts and galleries free of water. Still, the exploitation of surface and near-surface veins of ore—principally iron but also tin and silver—intensified, to supply the increased demand for plowshares, tools, weapons, construction fittings, and coins. Stone quarrying, the most common form of mining in the Middle Ages, benefited directly from more efficient stone saws and indirectly from improvements in transport. Better techniques in stonecutting, construction, and conveyance help to explain, for example, the increase in the number of England's stone religious buildings from sixty to nearly five hundred in the century after 1050.

Heavy Wheeled Plow

The improved plow, the horse collar, and the cooperative labors of many peasants in preparing the fields led to an agricultural boom in the European countryside.   *(Bibliothèque nationale de France)*

FORMS OF ENTERPRISE

Agricultural specialization became common. People began to cultivate intensively those crops that were best suited to local conditions. The area around Toulouse, for example, concentrated on herbs from which blue and yellow dyes were made. The central regions of France focused on cereal grains, while the Bordeaux and Burgundy regions emphasized the grapes that produced wine. Northern Germany specialized in cattle raising; northern England favored sheep.

Agricultural specialization helps to explain the growth in trade everywhere (see **MAP 9.1**). For certain commodities local trade continued to flourish. Italian wines and olive oil, for example, were not produced for far-off markets; they tended to move from countryside to town within a region. The same was true of French or English grains. However, French wines were much prized throughout Europe, especially in England, and certain products, such as English wool and Flemish cloth, were carried far and wide. Salt fish from the Baltic found its way all over the continent. Lumber was routinely traded across the Mediterranean to the wood-poor Muslim world. Spain was a source of warhorses. Southern Europe supplied the northern demand for spices, oranges, raisins, figs, almonds, and other exotic foodstuffs. Caen, in Normandy, sent shiploads of its beautifully colored and textured stone to England for the construction of churches and monasteries. Rising population, higher productivity, and greater prosperity added up to a larger volume of goods moving farther and more frequently.

The lumber industry reveals many facets of medieval economic activity. Before the twelfth century wood was the main building material, and even later it yielded to stone mainly for the church and aristocracy. But wood could be used for more than construction. For example, the Venetian shipyards needed about twenty oaks, twenty towering pines, and fifty or so beeches to make a ship. In the early twelfth century the Venetians were making about ten vessels a year, twice the number they had been building two centuries earlier. Whether for ships or for homes, the demand for wood grew steadily.

Wood exemplifies the expansion and interconnectedness of the medieval economy and society. Forests were essential to daily life, providing the wood for houses, fences, and fuel in villages and towns. Animals, especially pigs, were grazed at the edges of the forest to permit as much land as possible to be dedicated to food crops. Wild animals were hunted in the forest. For aristocrats hunting was as much for sport as for food. For poorer rural people, however, wild game made up a significant part of the regular diet. The forest was also a plentiful source of fruits, nuts, and honey. Thus the decision to cut down a stand of trees was a serious one.

TABLE 9.1

Population Increases in Italian Cities, 1200–1300

City	1200	1300	Percentage Increase
Florence	15,000	96,000	+640%
Siena	19,000	52,000	+274%
Pisa	20,000	38,000	+190%

Source: Adapted from Malcolm Barber, *The Two Cities: Medieval Europe, 1050–1320* (London: Routledge, 1992), p. 270.

THE ROLES OF CITIES AND TOWNS

All over Europe towns grew impressively in size and importance. **TABLE 9.1** shows the growth of three Italian cities. Such growth also occurred in cities in Flanders, such as Bruges and Ghent, and in Paris, London, and other cities that were becoming national capitals. Ghent expanded its city walls five times between 1160 and 1300, a sure sign of growth even in the absence of population figures. Similar forces were operating in the countryside. In 1100 about 11 fortified villages surrounded Florence, but by 1200 the city was ringed by 205 such villages.

For the first time since Late Antiquity, cities were becoming centers for many activities. Governments, which required larger staffs of trained personnel, settled in towns. The towns of Italy and Flanders, though not national capitals, ruled over extensive hinterlands. Schools and eventually universities (see pages 301–303) were urban institutions. Mercantile, industrial, and legal organizations were located in towns. Ecclesiastical organization was always urban based. Towns began to compete with royal and aristocratic courts as literary centers, and cathedrals, the great buildings of the age, were exclusively urban.

Towns were focal points in commercial networks. The basic trade routes and networks had existed since Carolingian times, but a novelty of the twelfth century was the emergence of the Champagne fairs as a meeting point for the commerce of north and south. Since the early Middle Ages a few locations hosted permanent fairs, and many places sponsored occasional fairs. By the middle of the twelfth century, however, the spices, silks, and dyes of the Mediterranean, the wool of England, the furs and linens of Germany, and the leather products of Spain began to be sold in a series of six fairs held in the Champagne region of France from spring to autumn.

One distinctive urban phenomenon was the rise of **guilds.** In 1200, for example, Paris had one guild of

guilds Voluntary associations of people who shared common crafts or trades.

merchants and four or five craft or trade associations. By 1270 the city had 101 craft or trade guilds, and by 1292 the number had risen to 130.

The guilds had many functions. Their main purpose was economic: to regulate standards of production, to fix prices, and to control membership in their respective trades. But as towns grew larger and more impersonal, these associations of people engaged in similar occupations fostered a sense of belonging, a feeling of community. Members tended to live in the same areas and to worship together in a parish church. Growing wealth in general, coupled with fierce local pride, produced building competitions whose results are still visible in the huge neighborhood churches that survive in most European towns. The guilds indulged in elaborate festivals and celebrations, which sometimes turned into drunken debauches despite being held to honor saints. The guilds were also mutual assurance societies. That is, they assisted colleagues who fell on hard times, saw to the funeral expenses of members, and provided for widows and orphans.

The guilds had a damaging impact on women. As more economic activity came under the umbrella of the guild structures, women were more systematically excluded from guild membership. Usually women could become guild members only as wives or widows. They could not open economic enterprises of their own, although they were workers in many trades. Despite a growing, diversifying economy, women were increasingly denied opportunities, although later centuries would find women establishing their own guilds.

CHANGING ECONOMIC ATTITUDES

As medieval society generated more wealth and populations concentrated in cities, people who were relatively well-off became more conscious of those who were less fortunate. Moralists began to argue that the poor were a special gift of God to the rich, who could redeem their own souls by generous charitable benefactions.

Most towns established schemes of poor relief. But the numbers of poor people grew so rapidly, particularly in large towns, that helping seemed hopeless, and some gave up trying. Hospitals, for example, began to refuse abandoned babies for fear that they would be deluged with them.

Efforts to alleviate the condition of the poor constituted one ethical concern of medieval thinkers, but two issues attracted even more attention. First, theologians and lawyers alike discussed the "just price," the price at which goods should be bought and sold. Christian teaching had long held that it was immoral to hoard food during a famine or knowingly to sell a damaged item. But what was the correct price in ordinary circumstances? A theological view, often dismissed as unrealistic, held that items could be sold for only the cost of the materials in them and the labor absolutely necessary to produce them. A commercial view, often dismissed as immoral, insisted that a fair price was whatever the market would bear, regardless of costs or consequences. A working consensus held that a just price was one arrived at by bargaining between free and knowledgeable parties.

The other ethical issue concerned usury, the lending of money at interest. Christian writers were always hostile to commercial enterprise, and they had plenty of biblical warrant for their view. Psalm 15 warned that no one can be blameless "who lends his money at usury." Luke's Gospel admonished Christians to "give without expecting to be repaid in full." Luke actually forbade the profit that makes most commercial enterprises possible. In the twelfth century churchmen began to be much more assiduous in their condemnations of usury, a practice that had been winked at for centuries.

Prohibitions against usury in twelfth-century Europe (a society in full economic expansion) produced some remarkably inventive ways to get around the prohibitions. One person might agree to sell another person an item at a certain price and then buy it back on a fixed date at a higher price. Exchange rates between currencies could be manipulated to mask usurious transactions. Gradually thinkers began to defend usury on the grounds that a person who lent money incurred a risk and deserved to be compensated for that risk.

Investment demands credit, and credit requires some payback for the lender. Even in the face of deep hostility, credit mechanisms spread in thirteenth-century Europe. They were held up to minute scrutiny by theologians and popular preachers and were found to be evidence of man's sinfulness, acquisitiveness, greed. But all these practices persisted, fueled by the expansion of the European economy, and began putting individual profit alongside community interest at the heart of social and economic thought.

═══════ S E C T I O N   S U M M A R Y ═══════

- Europe's population grew dramatically until the late 1200s owing to better diets and more plentiful foods.

- Technological gains came with wider use of horses, improved plows, and more productive farming techniques.

- Many regions began to specialize in growing or manufacturing products, and this local specialization prompted larger-scale trade.

- Towns came to play a larger role in almost all aspects of economic and social life.

- Economic growth widened the gap between rich and poor and induced theologians to write about the just price and usury.

THE HEIRS OF THE CAROLINGIAN EMPIRE: GERMANY, ITALY, AND FRANCE

What did Germany, Italy, and France owe to the Carolingian past? How alike and different were these areas by 1300?

The scope of political and institutional life expanded everywhere between 900 and 1300. In 900 the Carolingian Empire was collapsing. By 1300 France had emerged as a large, stable kingdom, and Italy had turned into several reasonably coherent regional entities. One might have predicted these post-Carolingian outcomes from the pre-Carolingian experience of these two areas. The most surprising political development within the old Carolingian lands, indeed within Europe as a whole, was Germany's rise to a premier position in the tenth century and then its long, slow decline. The states that evolved out of the Carolingian Empire faced common challenges: the achievement of territorial integrity; the growing responsibility of the central government; complicated political relations among kings, aristocrats, and churchmen; and the elaboration of new ideas about the state and its responsibilities.

GERMANY AND THE EMPIRE, 911–1272

From the ninth century to the present, no state in Europe has been less stable territorially and politically than Germany and the German Empire. An investigation of two questions in particular will help us comprehend German history after the Carolingians. First, what role did dynastic and territorial instability play in German history? Second, how did German rulers regulate relations with the leaders of the church?

Germany's Land and Rulers The Treaty of Verdun (see page 238) created something essentially new in 843: an East Frankish kingdom. Frankish rulers had long claimed authority over some of the lands that eventually became Germany, but before 843 no unified kingdom had ever existed in the territories east of the Rhine River (see **MAP 9.2**). The lands had no tradition of common or unified rule. There was no single "German" people; Saxons thought of themselves as Saxon, for example, not as German. Roman culture had barely penetrated into German lands, and Christian culture was recent and fragile. "Germany" had—has—no natural frontiers. Germany was, finally, the most thoroughly rural area of the Carolingian world.

After the last East Frankish Carolingian died in 911, the dukes, or leaders, of Germany's major regions chose one of their number as king. In 919 they did so again, their choice this time falling on Duke Henry of Saxony. Henry and his successors ruled capably until 1024, when Henry II died without an heir. This time the German dukes turned to a distantly related family, the Salians. The Salian family died out in the middle of the twelfth century and was replaced by the Staufer, who ruled until 1250. Then, after twenty-two years without a recognized ruler, the Germans elected a member of the Habsburg family. This record of frequent dynastic change might be contrasted with the situation in France (see pages 262–266), where one family reigned from 987 to 1328. Our task now is to see how this dynastic instability affected the course of German history.

Who were these dukes, and why were they so influential? German romantic tradition regarded them as the heroic leaders of distinct ethnic communities, the so-called Tribal Duchies. In fact, the dukes were the descendants of local rulers introduced by the Carolin-

MAP 9.2   Germany and Its Duchies, ca. 1000–1200
The chief political dynamic in Germany was a contest for power between the kings and the dukes. The duchies emerged in the ninth and tenth centuries and outlived one dynasty of kings after another.

gians. They were wealthy and powerful; they contested with kings for control of the bishops and abbots in their duchies; and sometimes they managed to make vassals out of the lower ranks of the aristocracy in their territories, effectively denying kings connections with these people. In sum, the dukes were extremely jealous of their independence.

At the beginning of Saxon rule, Germany comprised five duchies: Saxony, Franconia, Lorraine, Swabia, and Bavaria. When the Saxons came to power, they concentrated on using both force and strategic alliances to attempt to control one or more of these duchies. Hoping to win new territories and distract troublesome aristocrats, the Saxons began Germany's centuries-long drive

to the east, into Slavic Europe. In 955 Otto I gained power and prestige when he led a combined German force to victory against the Magyars at Lechfeld.

The Saxons also tried to control the church, especially bishops and abbots, to gain the allegiance of powerful and articulate allies. In 962 Otto I, who had begun expanding into Italy in 952, was crowned emperor in Rome by the pope. Why did he seek to revive the Carolingian imperial office? The imperial title conferred two benefits on the German kings: it gave them immense prestige and power that owed nothing to the dukes, and it raised the possibility of securing huge material resources in Italy, where, as emperors, they did not have to share power the way they did in Germany.

Rulers of Medieval Germany

Saxons

Henry I (919–936)
Otto I (936–973)
Otto II (973–983)
Otto III (983–1002)
Henry II (1002–1024)

Salians

Conrad II (1024–1039)
Henry III (1039–1056)
Henry IV (1056–1106)
Henry V (1106–1125)

Staufer

Conrad III (1138–1152)
Frederick Barbarossa (1152–1190)
Henry VI (1190–1197)
Frederick II (1212–1250)

The marriage of Otto II to a Byzantine princess was a sign of Germany's growing stature. Their son, Otto III, sponsored a brilliant court, patronizing writers and painters. When he died in 1002, Germany was the preeminent land in Europe.

The eleventh century and early twelfth century brought dramatic changes to Germany. The Salians, distant relatives of the Saxons, mounted the throne in 1024, opening opportunities for political disruption. When the second Salian ruler, Henry III, died in 1056, he left behind a 6-year-old heir and a decade of civil war. Military expansion virtually ceased, and powerful aristocrats struggled with one another and with their kings. Chief among these aristocrats were the dukes, who had chafed under Saxon and Salian efforts to control them.

When Henry IV came of age in 1066, he faced opposition on all sides, controlled no duchies, was not yet emperor, and had lost much of his father's control of the church. When he tried to make church appointments in the traditional way, he encountered the fierce opposition of the newly reformed papacy in the person of Pope Gregory VII (r. 1073–1085). Gregory was brilliant, proud, and inflexible—and determined to bend Henry to his will. Their battles inaugurated the so-called investiture controversy, which lingered on until 1122, when both of the original foes were long dead.

Meanwhile, in the middle of the twelfth century, the Salian dynasty died out. With the accession of Frederick Barbarossa ("Red Beard") in 1152, a new family,

the Staufer, consolidated its hold on the German throne. Frederick, whose base was in Swabia, patiently worked to get the other dukes to recognize his overlordship, even though he was powerless to demand payments or services from them. His plan was slowly to build up the idea that the king was the highest lord in the land (a plan that his French and English contemporaries used effectively). In 1158 Frederick summoned representatives of the major Italian cities to demand full recognition of his regalian, or ruler's, rights. These included military service; control of roads, ports, and waterways; administration of tolls, mints, fines, vacant fiefs, and confiscated properties; appointment of magistrates; construction of palaces; and control of mines, fisheries, and saltworks. Frederick's attempts to control northern Italy resulted in the creation of the Lombard League, a union of Italian cities that inflicted a humiliating defeat on German forces at Legnano (len-YAN-oh) in 1176.

Frederick also struggled for more than twenty years to get the popes to recognize his claim to the imperial office, which he viewed as a source of prestige and as a legitimation of his right to rule Italy. When he spoke of his "Holy Roman Empire," he meant that his power came, on the one hand, from God himself and, on the other hand, from the Romans via Charlemagne. Theory did not match reality, however, and the papacy was able to thwart virtually all his political initiatives. The handsome, energetic, and athletic Frederick accomplished much, and he might have done more had he not drowned in Anatolia in 1190 while on his way to the Third Crusade.

In 1197 Germany's heir was an infant, Frederick II (r. 1212–1250), who had been born in Sicily. His mother, Constance, had no standing in Germany and little influence in Italy. Accordingly, she placed her son under the tutelage of Pope Innocent III (r. 1198–1216). By the time Frederick came of age, he so despaired of governing Germany that he conceded the "Statute in Favor of the Princes," which lodged royal power in ducal hands in return for a vague acknowledgment of his overlordship. Frederick concentrated his own efforts in Italy. Although he made good progress, he faced constant opposition from the popes, who were unwilling to trade a German ruler with interests in Italy for an essentially Italian ruler with interests in Germany. When Frederick II died in 1250, effective central authority in both Germany and Italy collapsed. After twenty-two years of contested rule, the German dukes turned to Rudolf of Habsburg, whose descendants remained influential in German politics until the early twentieth century. Neither the Habsburgs nor any subsequent German emperors restored the position held by the Saxons.

An understanding of Germany's fate requires that we return to the first question with which we began

Henry IV, Duchess Matilda of Tuscany, and Abbot Hugh of Cluny
The embattled Henry IV here implores Matilda, a tremendously wealthy landowner and ally of Pope Gregory VII, to intercede with the pope. The powerful abbot of Cluny looks over the scene protectively. Written documents do not portray women's power as vividly as this image does. *(Vatican Library, Rome)*

this discussion. One wonders: Might a long-lived dynasty have made a difference? Germany was not without great rulers: Otto I, Otto III, Frederick Barbarossa, and even Frederick II were the equals of any contemporary ruler. But repeated changes of ruling family in the context of a fragile political regime provided repeated opportunities for fragmentation. The German monarchy had a very limited territorial base and, compared with these kings' Carolingian predecessors and their French and English contemporaries, they possessed unimpressive government institutions. The kings themselves were dukes, and as such their areas of truly effective control were usually limited to one duchy. The Saxons were based in the north, the Salians in the center, and the Staufer in the south. Thus continuity of rule was constantly threatened by huge dynastic, institutional, and geographical challenges.

Was the Italian venture a mistake? Germany's involvement with Italy and the imperial title has occasioned no end of controversy. To some, royal involvement in Italy signals a failure to deal imaginatively with Germany itself. To others, the quest for prestige, power, and money in Italy was actually a creative solution to the monarchy's relative impotence in Germany. The dramatic German defeat at Legnano is representative of the ongoing challenges and provocations to German authority.

The Investiture Controversy   Now we must try to answer the second question with which we started this discussion of Germany: How did Germany's rulers regulate their relations with the church? The key issue is the investiture controversy. In the middle of the eleventh century a group of ardent church reformers, who were committed to improving the moral and intellectual caliber of the clergy all over Europe, targeted the chief impediment to reform: the control of church appointments by laymen—or **lay investiture,** as they called it. Gregory VII prohibited lay investiture. This brought the reformers into direct conflict with the Salians, who, like their predecessors back to Charlemagne, believed that they reigned supreme in the "City of God." These German rulers stood, in their own view,

lay investiture   A term for the appointment ("investiture") of members of the clergy by laymen.

THE ISSUES IN THE INVESTITURE CONTROVERSY

These two documents illustrate the range of issues involved in the conflict between the emperor Henry IV and Pope Gregory VII. The first excerpt is from a long letter written by Henry in 1076. The second is a decree issued by Gregory in 1078.

Henry Denounces the Pope

Henry, king not by usurpation but by the holy ordination of God, to Hildebrand, not now pope but false monk:

Such greeting as this you have merited through your disturbances, for there is no rank in the church on which you have brought, not honor but disgrace, not blessing but curse. To mention only a few notable cases, you have dared to assail the holy rulers of the church, archbishops, bishops, and priests, and you have trodden them underfoot like slaves ignorant of what their master is doing; . . . you have regarded them as knowing nothing, yourself as knowing all things. . . .

We have endured all this in our anxiety to save the honor of the apostolic see, but you have mistaken our humility for fear and have ventured to attack the royal power conferred on us by God, and threatened to divest us of it. As if we had received our kingdom from you! As if the kingdom and empire were in your hands, not God's! For our Lord Jesus Christ did call us to the kingdom. . . . You have assailed me who, though unworthy of anointing, have nevertheless been anointed to the kingdom and who, according to the traditions of the holy fathers, are subject to the judgment of God alone. . . . The true pope Peter exclaims "Fear God, honor the king." But you, who do not fear God, dishonor me, His appointed one. . . .

You, therefore, damned by this curse and by the judgment of all our bishops and ourselves, come down and relinquish the apostolic chair which you have usurped. I, Henry, king by the grace of God, together with all our bishops, say to you: "Come down, come down, to be damned throughout all eternity."

Gregory Strikes Back

Inasmuch as we have learned that, contrary to the ordinances of the holy fathers, the investiture of churches is, in many places, performed by lay persons, and that from this cause many disturbances arise in the church by which the Christian religion is degraded, we decree that no one of the clergy shall receive the investiture of a bishopric, abbey, or church from the hand of an emperor, or king, or of any lay person, male or female. If anyone shall presume to do so, let him know that such investiture is void by apostolic authority, and that he himself shall lie under excommunication until fitting satisfaction shall have been made.

QUESTIONS

1. On what foundations does Henry IV challenge Gregory VII?

2. How does Gregory see the issues?

3. What aspects of medieval thought and politics made this quarrel possible?

Source: Slightly adapted from James Harvey Robinson, *Readings in European History*, vol. 1 (Boston: Ginn, 1904), pp. 279–281, 275.

nearest to God in a great hierarchy; the clergy occupied the rungs beneath them in human society. Thus the king was God's specially chosen agent on earth, and the higher clergy were the king's natural helpers in governing the realm. To the reformers, the proper organization of society was just the opposite: the clergy, with the pope at its head, stood nearest to God, with secular monarchs subordinate to the church.

When these reformers challenged royal supremacy on ideological grounds, the particular quarrel over the appointment of churchmen mushroomed into a general struggle for leadership in Christian society. In Germany the struggle between Henry IV and Gregory VII became a pretext for ducal and aristocratic opposition to the king. Even though the kings could not control the dukes, they had sometimes wrested the naming of bishops from them. Meanwhile, Henry expended time and resources in Italy trying in vain to control Rome and the pope. (See the box "The Written Record: The Issues in the Investiture Controversy.")

The Concordat of Worms (VORM) concluded in 1122 between Henry V (r. 1106–1125) and Pope Calixtus II (r. 1119–1124) brought the investiture controversy to an end. The decree stipulated that episcopal (bishopric) elections should be free and conducted according to church law. Only after a man had been duly elected bishop could a king, or emperor, invest him with the symbols and offices of secular authority. The

MAP 9.3   The Communal Movement in Italy
Beginning in the late eleventh century, many towns in northern Italy, some in the central regions, and a very few in the south erected communal forms of government. This distribution reflects the relative wealth of north and south and the power of the popes in the center. North of the Alps only Flanders and northern France experienced comparable communal movements.

Concordat was a blow to the German political system as it had existed for centuries. When Otto III died in 1002, Germany was powerful and confident. When Henry V died in 1125, Germany was weak, disunited, and searching for new bases of authority.

With its promise, undoubted achievements, and yet ultimate failure, Germany is the political mystery of medieval Europe. In turning now to other regions of Europe, we will continue to explore the roles dynasty, geography, institutions, and ideology played there.

THE VARYING FORTUNES OF ITALY

The history of Italy has always been played out in three regions: north, central, and south. The Carolingians and the Germans after them laid a heavy hand on northern Italy. In the center of the peninsula the Papal States was the key player. Outsiders always dominated the south, but their identities changed often.

The Communal Movement   As we have seen, German attempts to impose their authority on northern Italy met with limited success. One key obstacle to German rule was the communal movement (see **MAP 9.3**), the most dynamic element on the Italian scene. Two conditions help to explain the rise of **communes.** The first relates to economic expansion. In the early eleventh century Italian towns began to rid the Mediterranean of Muslim pirates. By 1100 Italian merchants could trade anywhere in the Mediterranean world with confidence.

The second contributing factor relates to political developments in Italian towns. The Carolingians governed towns through resident counts, and German emperors tried to maintain this system. The powers of the counts tended to be weak, however, so the Germans also relied on bishops, who were, in Italy as in Germany, key props to the system of imperial rule. But

communes   Self-governing Italian towns.

bishops and counts were not alone in holding urban power. Since the late tenth century both bishops and counts had been granting fiefs to local men in order to strengthen their own authority and to procure defenses for the towns. Gradually these men, whose lands made them wealthy in the expanding economy, moved into the towns and, in turn, gave fiefs to other men in the countryside. These lords were wealthy and jealous of their power.

Communes were sworn associations of the local nobility—these landed lords—and their vassals. Commune members swore to uphold one another's rights and called themselves the *popolo*, or "people," although the people as a whole had nothing to do with the early communes. A commune accorded a high degree of participation to its members in choosing leaders and in coming together in an assembly that voted on matters of common concern. The leaders of the early communes were usually called *consuls*—a deliberate attempt to evoke the Roman past. Usually elected for a single year, the consuls varied in number from four to twenty in different cities. The consuls proposed matters to an assembly for ratification. By the 1140s every significant city in northern and central Italy had a commune.

The communes did not necessarily originate as attempts to make cities independent. Frequently, however, as communal governments became more established and confident, that is what they did. One by one, cities either refused to recognize papal or imperial overlordship or else renegotiated the terms under which they would acknowledge the rule of their historic masters. The working out of this ongoing relationship was a major development in the history of the Italian cities in the twelfth century.

Although each Italian commune constituted an entity unto itself, a fairly coherent evolution is evident. By the late twelfth century the consular communes were still governed by oligarchies of men whose wealth and power came from land, trade, and industry. Guild interests, however, gained in prominence at the expense of the landed groups among whom the communal movement had arisen, and ordinary workers began to clamor for participation. The communes were becoming increasingly volatile and violent.

One solution to this potential crisis was the introduction of the *podestà* (poe-des-TAH), a sort of city manager chosen by the local oligarchy. The podestà often came from the outside, served for a set period (usually six months or a year), and underwent a careful scrutiny at the conclusion of his term. He was expected to be competent not only at ordinary administration but also at military leadership, so that he could police the city as well as defend it. He brought with him a group of seasoned officials as subordinates. Normally he could not be a property owner in the town, marry

into local society, or dine privately with any citizen. By the middle of the thirteenth century some podestàs were becoming virtual professional administrators. One man, for example, was elected sixteen times in nine cities over a period of thirty-four years, four times in Bologna alone.

The Italian commune was a radical political experiment. Everywhere else in medieval Europe power was thought to radiate downward—from God, the clergy, the emperor, the king. In a commune power radiated upward from the popolo to its leaders. For several centuries the Italian city was arguably the most creative institution in the Western world.

Although some communes emerged in central Italy—even, briefly, in Rome in the 1140s—the key power in this region was the papacy, and the main political entity was the Papal States. In the political turmoil of the tenth and eleventh centuries, the papacy lost a great deal of territory. Throughout the twelfth and thirteenth centuries, therefore, a basic objective of papal policy was to recover lost lands and rights. This quest to restore the territorial basis for papal power and income helps explain why the popes so resolutely opposed German imperial influence in Italy.

The Papal Monarchy The most striking development pertaining to the papacy is the expansion of its institutions. Gradually there emerged what historians have long called the **Papal Monarchy**. This term is meant to characterize a church whose power was increasingly centralized in the hands of the popes. In Rome the pope presided over the *curia*, the papal court. The College of Cardinals, potentially fifty-three in number, formed a kind of senate for the church. They elected the popes (by majority after 1059 and by a two-thirds majority after 1179), served as key advisers, headed the growing financial and judicial branches of the papal government, and often served as legates. Legates were papal envoys, some of whom were sent to particular people or places provisionally, to communicate a message or to conduct an investigation, and some of whom were more like resident ambassadors who represented the pope on a continuing basis. Lateran Councils met often and gathered the clergy from all over Europe to legislate for the church as a whole. The hierarchical structure of the church became more visible as ecclesiastical business tended to accumulate in Rome.

High medieval popes also reserved to themselves certain jurisdictional and coercive prerogatives. Popes could excommunicate persons—that is, exclude them from the sacraments of the church and the community of Christians. This was a form of social death in that

Papal Monarchy   A term meant to signify the enlarged and centralized papal government beginning in the twelfth century.

Gregory VII (1073–1085)

Urban II (1088–1099)

Innocent III (1198–1216)

Boniface VIII (1294–1303)

excommunicated persons could not eat, converse, or socialize with others. Popes could lay a territory under interdict. This decree forbade all religious services except baptisms and burials and was designed to bring maximum pressure to bear on a particular individual. Finally, popes could invoke the inquisition. Despite horror stories about the inquisition, this was a judicial mechanism fully rooted in Roman law and widely used in the medieval West. Basically, an inquisition involved churchmen taking sworn testimony in an attempt to discover heresy.

Institutions were important, but personalities mattered, too. Innocent III, for example, was the most powerful man ever to hold the papal office. He came from a minor Italian noble family, received early training in theology and law, and entered the papal administration while in his twenties. His entire life was dedicated to promoting the legal prerogatives of the papacy and the moral improvement of Christian society. As a young man Innocent wrote *On the Contempt of the World,* in which he expressed his hope for a life of peace and contemplation. As an older man he hurled legal thunderbolts at the greatest public figures of the day.

The Fate of Southern Italy   From the ninth century on, the region south of Rome was contested among Byzantines, North African Muslims, and local potentates. In 1026 Norman pilgrims bound for the Holy Land landed in southern Italy, where local people invited them to enlist in the fight against the Muslims. By the 1040s the original Normans had been joined by many more who were seeking land and adventure. Initially opposed to the Normans, the papacy later allied with their leader as a counterweight against the Germans.

From his capital at Palermo, Roger II, also known as "Roger the Great" (r. 1130–1154), ruled a complex state that blended Byzantine, Lombard, and Norman structures. In Italy, as in England (see page 268), the Normans showed a genius for adaptation. Perched advantageously at the juncture of the Latin, Greek, and Arab worlds, the Norman court was more advanced in finance and bureaucratic administration than any of its European contemporaries. No one forgot for a moment, however, that the Normans were primarily great warriors. A chronicler said of the Normans, "They delight in arms and horses."

Once the popes had defeated Frederick II, they decided to look for more pliant allies in the south. They invited a succession of French and Spanish princes to assume the Crown, thus touching off long-standing rivalries in the area. A profusion of outsiders always dominated southern Italy.

Coronation of Roger II in Sicily, 1130
Roger's coronation by Jesus Christ makes a powerful ideological statement: he owes his office to no earthly power. The cultural crosscurrents of Sicily are visible: Roger is depicted more like a Byzantine emperor than a Western king. The inscriptions above his head ("Rogerios Rex") and next to Christ's are in Greek, not Latin. Beside Christ's head are the customary Greek abbreviations **IC** (the first and last letters of **I**esu**S**) and **XP,** for **ChR**istos. (The original surely contains the full XP symbol.)
(Scala/Art Resource, NY)

CAPETIAN FRANCE, 987–1314

When the Treaty of Verdun created the West Frankish Kingdom in 843, no one knew what the future of France might be. Referring to France's tremendous diversity, the twentieth-century French leader Charles de Gaulle once quipped, "It is impossible to govern a country with 325 kinds of cheese." During the late ninth century and much of the tenth, the area suffered cruelly from constant waves of Viking attacks and from repeated failures of the Carolingian family to produce adult heirs to the throne. Chroniclers often quoted the lament of King Solomon: "Woe to thee, O land, whose king is a child." At the end of the tenth century, however, the Carolingians were replaced by the Capetians (kuh-PEE-shunz), the family of Hugh Capet (r. 987–996). The Capetians ruled France for more than three hundred years—an impressive achievement in light of the repeated failure of German dynasties. The first key issue we must pursue pertains to the power and prestige of the monarchy. Then, bearing in mind de Gaulle's joke, we explore how a large but very complex group of territories was assembled into a kingdom. Finally we look at the nature of government in medieval France and the principles on which that government rested.

Capetian Prestige From the very beginning the Capetian kings of France sought to preserve the royal office, increase its prestige, and consolidate its political base. Hugh Capet inaugurated the tradition of crowning his son as his successor during his own lifetime. This meant that when the old king died, a new king was already in place and the nobility could not easily meddle in the succession. Robert II (r. 996–1031) displayed the "royal touch," a ceremony in which the king was believed to be able to cure people of scrofula (a common respiratory ailment) by touching them. No French nobleman, no matter how powerful, ever laid claim to such miraculous powers. Capetian kings capitalized on their control of the old, rich, prestigious, and centrally located city of Paris. The kings promoted the shrine of Saint Denis, the legendary first bishop of Paris, as a kind of "national" shrine for France. Louis VII (r. 1137–1180) began to make elegant tours of the country to put himself, his office, and his sparkling entourage on display. In Louis IX (r. 1226–1270) the Capetian family actually produced a saint of the Catholic Church—Saint Louis.

Building the Capetian Kingdom The Capetians were heirs of the dukes of Paris. This meant that initially they controlled no more than Paris and its immediate region. They contested for control of this region with a number of ambitious and aggressive families, finally ground them down, and made the Île-de-

France one of the best-governed regions in all of France. (See the feature "The Visual Record: The Medieval Castle.") The kings also controlled about two dozen bishoprics and some fifty monasteries in northern France. This power base gave the kings unrivaled opportunities to extend their influence and, in turn, to build up a cadre of loyal and articulate supporters. Although French kings provoked a few battles with the papacy, France experienced no investiture controversy.

France's territorial expansion was tightly connected to military success. The background to French military success is complicated. In the late eleventh and early twelfth centuries one family of French magnates, the counts of Anjou (see **MAP 9.4**), acquired control over a good deal of western France by marriage, diplomacy, and intimidation. Then Geoffrey of Anjou (ahn-JHOU) married the heiress of the duchy of Normandy, whose father, William the Conqueror, we will meet later. A bit later Geoffrey's son and heir married Duchess Eleanor of Aquitaine, the recently divorced wife of Louis VII of France. In 1154 Henry of Anjou, as a result of incredibly complicated political and matrimonial alliances, became King Henry II of England, but he still retained control of about 60 percent of France.

For several generations the kings of France hammered away at this Angevin (AN-juh-vin) empire. Henry of Anjou's four sons were viciously jealous of one another, and the French kings exploited their rivalries to weaken Angevin authority in western and southwestern France. When one of Henry's sons, King John of England, absconded with the fiancée of a vassal of King Philip II (r. 1180–1223), the king of France, Philip summoned John to court to answer for his conduct. John's refusal to appear led to war in 1202. By 1204 Philip had won a resounding victory and control over a substantial portion of western France. The English and French kings came to blows over their competing claims to French territory several more times in the thirteenth century. Each time the French won, including a major victory over an allied English and German army at Bouvines (BOO-veen) in 1214.

Southeastern France was gained by wars of a different kind. In the last decades of the twelfth century sev-

---

The Capetian Kings of France

Hugh Capet (987–996)	Philip II (1180–1223)
Robert II (996–1031)	Louis VIII (1223–1226)
Henry I (1031–1060)	Louis IX (1226–1270)
Philip I (1060–1108)	Philip III (1270–1285)
Louis VI (1108–1137)	Philip IV (1285–1314)
Louis VII (1137–1180)	

MAP 9.4 **French Territorial Principalities, ca. 1200**
As the Carolingian West Frankish Kingdom (see Map 8.3 on page 233) broke down and feudal bonds proliferated, many territories arose under counts and dukes. Their struggles to impose control locally and to fight off royal supervision animated French history.

eral cities in the southeast became hotbeds of the Albigensian (al-buh-JEN-see-un) heresy—an important religious movement (see page 292). Some Catholic locals and many churchmen urged the kings to undertake military action against the heretics. The French kings were prudent and bided their time until they had the resources to deal with this turbulent region. Under Louis VIII (r. 1223–1226) and Louis IX the French

monarchy finally extended its authority to France's Mediterranean coast.

Strategies of Capetian Government The chief political dynamic in France was the contest for power between the kings and the territorial princes (see Map 9.4). At stake was the monarchy's ability to introduce effective rule into the lands won in all those battles. Who were the

The Medieval Castle

Storybook castles, in the manner of Disneyland, figure prominently in almost everyone's idea of the Middle Ages. The reality was different. Medieval castles were generally small, stark, and uncomfortable, not beautiful and romantic.

Castles represent a stage in the history of both dwellings and fortifications. Initially, castles were private, residential, and military. A consideration of these three elements will place the castle in historical context and illustrate what historians learn from the impressive ruins that dot the landscape of Europe and the crusader states.

The first medieval castles were constructed in the tenth century. The French word *château* (from the Latin *castellum*) means "great house," signifying the castle's residential purpose. Powerful aristocrats erected castles not just as their principal dwellings but also as a base for securing and extending their social and political influence. From his castle a lord could dominate the surrounding region. The castle also sheltered the lord's immediate dependents temporarily in the event of an attack and his military retainers more or less permanently.

A few castles were built exclusively for military purposes. In 1110 Crusaders captured a strategic plateau rising 2,000 feet above the main road from inner Syria to the Mediterranean. Between 1142 and 1205 Crusaders continually expanded the fortifications of the castle pictured here, the "Krak des Chevaliers" (from Syriac *karka*, meaning "fortress," and the Old French word for "horsemen"). This castle fell to Muslim attackers in 1271. The techniques of fortification developed in the crusader East influenced castle building in Europe.

The medieval city of Murviedro, Spain, takes its name from the Latin *mures veteres* (old walls). In 1871 the city was given back its ancient name, Sagunt. The hilltop above ancient Saguntum (attacked by Hannibal, thus affronting the Romans and providing a pretext for the Second Punic War between Rome and Carthage; see page 138) reveals fortifications from the prehistoric, Carthaginian, Roman, Visigothic, and Muslim periods. The most spectacular visible remains date from the Muslim period, between 900 and 1098, when El Cid captured the site.

Castles took many forms. From 900 to 1200 the "motte and bailey" castle was the most common. A lord commanded his dependents to dig a circular ditch and heap the dirt into a mound (the motte). The ditch, together with a wooden palisade—a fencelike wall—was the bailey. A wooden tower was often built atop the mound. Some castles included an elaborate series of mounds, ditches, and wooden walls, but usually these structures were quite simple.

As siege techniques improved (catapults could hurl projectiles weighing 600 pounds), the wooden building of the bailey began to be replaced by stone. By 1150 or 1200, stone towers (*donjons*, from the Latin *dominium* for "lordship") were only the inner portion—the "keep"—of a more complicated structure of walls, towers, and gates. It was not unusual for walls to be 75 or 100 feet high. Because of the growing power of bombarding engines, castle walls often had to be made thicker. Towers built at 40- or 50-foot intervals projected beyond the walls so that defenders armed with bows and arrows could fire at attackers along the length of a castle wall. Look at the spacing of the towers in the castles pictured here. At Krak des Chevaliers we see one of the earliest examples of a double ring of walls. Two walls made it more difficult for attackers to take the keep and permitted defenders to battle invaders from inside both the inner and the outer walls.

To allow people to enter and leave, castles had gate towers, usually with two gates, one on the outside and one on the inside. Intricate systems of winches, cranks, and counterweights regulated the raising and lowering of the gates. Speedy operation was essential. Some castles had small "sallyports" from which soldiers could make a rapid dash to attack a besieging enemy.

When possible, lords sited their castles on the edges of cliffs, because fewer sides were open to assault and a garrison of modest size could defend the remaining walls. Krak sits on an impressive natural site. The fortress of Murviedro, perched on a hilltop, commands the surrounding territory. Rulers and conquerors from Roman to modern times have exploited this dominating site. To walls and natural defenses were sometimes added ditches.

Much can be learned from the number of castles in a particular area. The presence of numerous small castles across the countryside suggests an extreme decentralization of power in that place and time. Remains of several hundred castles have been found in France alone; and England in 1100 boasted a castle every 10 miles. Conversely, areas with only a few large, strategically sited castles were likely sub-

Krak des Chevaliers,
Syria, ca. 1200
*(Michael Jenner/Robert
Harding World Imagery)*

Muslim Fortress of
Murviedro, Valencia,
Spain, Eleventh Century
(Institut Amatller d'Art Hispanic)

ject to greater central control. Careful mapping of the known locations of castles can tell historians a great deal about the structure of social and political relationships.

Castles both contributed and responded to developments in military technology, such as more powerful catapults. Stone castles proliferated as Europe grew wealthier and as quarrying technology improved. Castles grew larger as monarchies rather than private individuals built them. Like cathedrals, massive state-funded castles tended to be built by professionals rather than by local laborers.

Both fortifications and magnificent dwellings have existed in Western civilization for millennia. From about 900 to 1200 the castle met the needs of a politically dominant warrior-aristocracy for a private residence with military significance. In later centuries, the castle, as a château, retained its private and residential nature but lost much of its military character to garrisoned fortresses in the service of kings and princes.

QUESTIONS

1. Who built castles and why did they build them?

2. What were the essential characteristics of a castle?

3. How does a castle differ from a residence?

Online Study Center
Improve Your Grade Visual Record Activities

territorial princes? They were locally powerful magnates, rather like the German dukes, most of whose ancestors had been officials appointed by the Carolingians. But whereas Germany comprised five major duchies, France had a dozen or more territorial principalities. In the tumultuous circumstances of the tenth and eleventh centuries some individuals and families had been remarkably successful in building castles, reducing the local population to subjection, and gathering into their own hands the powers that the Carolingian kings had once exercised in their localities.

Ironically, the territorial princes also faced localized rivalries for power and influence. Countless individuals built castles, brutally subjected local peasants, and became lords. Sometimes these individuals were the vassals of the territorial princes—say, the dukes of Normandy or the counts of Anjou—and sometimes they had vassals of their own. In the Carolingian world the number of vassals was small, their fidelity reasonably solid, and their services reliable. By 1100 the number of vassals was immense, their fidelity was constantly shifting, and they tended to provide only local military service. Scholars call this shift from effective Carolingian government to myriad local lordships a **feudal revolution.**

For the kings of France to re-create central government, they had to overcome the disruptive tendencies of this revolution and then consolidate institutions. Under Louis VI and Louis VII some of the most powerful men in the realm visited court and swore allegiance to the Crown. Under Philip II and Louis IX the Capetians gradually turned this ceremonial obedience into effective subjection, just as Frederick Barbarossa had tried but failed to do in Germany.

In the twelfth and thirteenth centuries the Capetians followed a few basic policies to increase their ability to govern. They circumvented the local lords as much as possible. When they won military victories, the kings did not dole out the seized lands to lords as new fiefs but instead kept them in their own hands, or in the hands of family members. What is more, the kings introduced into these lands local officials, called bailiffs or provosts, who were of modest social background,

had no personal ties to their assigned regions, often had some schooling in law, and were intensely loyal to the kings. By the time of Louis IX, officials called *enqueteurs* (on-KEH-tur) were sent around the country to inspect the work of bailiffs and provosts. Such roles had been unheard-of since the Carolingian *missi dominici* (see page 236). Louis also began to issue *ordonnances,* what we might call executive orders, that were binding on all the land under the king's control. These precepts are reminiscent of Carolingian capitularies (see page 234).

If in 1000 France was a land of innumerable tiny lordships, then by 1300 it was the best-governed kingdom in Europe. Indicative of France's position is the outcome of two battles between King Philip IV (r. 1285–1314) and Pope Boniface VIII (r. 1294–1303). First Philip attempted to tax the French clergy, and then he sought to bring a bishop before his court. Boniface angrily objected to Philip's intervention in ecclesiastical affairs. But things had changed drastically since the fateful confrontation between Henry IV and Gregory VII. Boniface had to back down.

The Welsh humorist Walter Map (1140–1209) provides this assessment of France in his day:

> The emperor of Byzantium and the king of Sicily may boast about their gold and silken cloth, but they have no men who can do more than talk, men incapable of war. The Roman emperor or, as they say, the emperor of the Germans, has men apt in arms and warlike horses, but no gold, silk or any other wealth. . . . The king of England lacks nothing and possesses everything, men, horses, gold, silk, jewels, fruits and wild beasts. And we in France have nothing except bread, wine and joy.[1]

Walter comically underestimates the resources of the French. In 1300 theirs was the largest, richest, and best-governed kingdom in Europe. French culture and language were increasingly dominant. Considering France's situation in 900, and compared with Germany's in 1300, these were impressive achievements.

SECTION SUMMARY

- German political development was impeded by short-lived dynasties, territorial complexity, and battles with the papacy.

- Italy experienced the communal movement in the north, the consolidation of the Papal States and Papal Monarchy in the center, and the continued fragmentation of the south, where foreigners ruled.

- France had a prestigious and long-lived royal dynasty, patient territorial expansion, and a slowly, steadily centralizing government.

feudal revolution   A term that refers to the proliferation of lord-vassal bonds as key elements of governmental and social control.

THE BRITISH ISLES

What were the chief dynamics in the development of medieval Britain?

n the British Isles expansion had three dimensions: the tremendous growth of the English government, England's relentless push into the Celtic world, and the emergence of states in the Celtic world. England, about the size of Alabama, is smaller than France or Germany and more homogeneous in population, culture, and language than either of them, or than Italy. Building effective governance in England was, therefore, a somewhat easier task than it was elsewhere. Nevertheless, England faced some acute dynastic, military, and political crises. Moreover, England shared an island with two Celtic neighbors, Wales and Scotland, whose inhabitants were close kin to the people of England's neighboring island, Ireland (see **MAP 9.5**). For better or worse, the fates of the English and Celtic inhabitants of the British Isles are inseparable.

VIKING AND NORMAN INVASIONS IN ENGLAND

Alfred (r. 871–899; see page 231) rallied the English against the Vikings, and his descendants ruled England for more than a century. They gradually rolled back the frontier of the "Danelaw," the areas of eastern and northern England controlled by Viking settlers (mainly Danes, hence the name). Alfred and his successors built strong central institutions. All free men in the realm owed allegiance to the king and could in principle be called to the militia, or *fyrd* (FEERD). The great men of the realm attended meetings of the royal council, or *witan* (WHIT-un), which was partly a court of law and partly a deliberative, consultative body. The king could issue writs—executive orders rather like Carolingian capitularies. The Danegeld—literally "money for the

MAP 9.5   Northern and Eastern Europe, ca. 1200

Apart from Germany, the core states of Europe emerged inside the former Roman frontiers or right alongside them. After 900 an arc of new states emerged, from the Celtic realms and Iceland in the west, to Scandinavia in the north, to the western, southern, and eastern Slavs in eastern Europe.

Danes"—was originally collected solely in times of danger and then slowly transformed into a regular tax. All of England was divided into shires, and each shire had a royally appointed officer, the *shire-reeve* (or sheriff).

Late in the tenth century English leadership failed in the face of a severe threat from a new generation of Vikings. The powerful king of Denmark, Swein Forkbeard, conquered England in 1014, but survived his conquest by only two years. His son Cnut then ruled from 1016 to 1035, at which point power passed to Cnut's sons.

Cnut did not match the stereotype of the wild and woolly barbarian. He was simultaneously king of Denmark and England, and for a time of Norway, too. He wed his daughter to Emperor Henry III and himself to Emma, the widow of the last English king. He was cultured, Christian, and an acquaintance of the pope.

When Cnut's sons died in 1042 without heirs, the English nobles called over from Normandy Edward, called "the Confessor," the son of the last English king. Edward, who was unusually pious, had taken a vow of chastity. Because he was not going to have an heir, claimants to the English throne began jockeying for position. Edward seems to have promised his throne to William, the duke of Normandy. Most of the English nobles preferred Harold of Wessex, one of their number. In Norway Harald (who became known as Hardrada, or "Hard-Ruler") prepared to make a claim as Cnut's rightful heir.

When Edward died, the English elected Harold, and immediately he learned that Hardrada had invaded. He marched to meet the Norse challenger and won an impressive victory, only to learn that William had meanwhile landed in the south. Foolishly Harold rushed south to meet William, without resting or reinforcing his troops. At Hastings William defeated Harold, and England was his for the taking.

Amid these frequent changes in rulers one thing remained constant: the smooth functioning of the Anglo-Saxon state. It is no surprise that neither Cnut nor William, known as "the Conqueror" (r. 1066–1089), desired to dismantle or replace the old English institutions. But William had won England by conquest, and he did introduce some changes. He turned most of the estates in England into fiefs and distributed them among some 180 of his most loyal followers. Each of these vassals held his fief in return for a fixed quota of soldiers for the royal army. To raise the approximately five thousand soldiers required by William, each of his vassals had to create vassals of his own. The technical name for this process of vassals creating vassals is *subinfeudation*. In 1087 William exacted the Salisbury Oath, which established the principle of liege homage (LEEGE AHM-idge), according to which the king was the final lord of all vassals. To avoid creating territorial

principalities on the French model, William scattered his vassals' holdings around the kingdom. Finally, to learn as much as he could about his new kingdom, and about the fiefs he had assigned to his followers, William conducted a massive survey of England that resulted in 1086 in the *Domesday Book,* named for the Day of Judgment, against which there was no appeal. No comparable survey of any state was accomplished until the American census of 1790.

Online Study Center **Improve Your Grade**
Primary Source: William the Conqueror and Domesday Book: A Contemporary Description

THE DEVELOPMENT OF ENGLISH LAW AND GOVERNMENT

William was succeeded by two of his sons in turn, William II (r. 1089–1100) and Henry I (r. 1100–1135). Henry's only son drowned in a shipwreck, and the English nobles would accept neither his daughter Matilda as their queen nor her husband, Geoffrey of Anjou, as their king. Owing to William's conquest and settlement, most of the English elite were in fact Normans, and the Normans and Angevins were old foes. Consequently, the English turned in 1135 to a French prince, Stephen of Blois, who was a grandson of William the Conqueror through a daughter. Stephen I died childless in 1154 and bequeathed his kingdom to Henry of Anjou, the son of Geoffrey and Matilda, who ruled as Henry II (r. 1154–1189).

Henry was as much a French prince as an English king. From his father, mother, and wife (Eleanor of Aquitaine; see page 262), he had inherited a large part of France and was much preoccupied with his continental realm. He constantly battled his four sons for control of these vast French holdings. Two of these sons eventually became king. Richard I, also known as "Richard the Lionhearted" (r. 1189–1199), was a dashing prince who spent only ten months in England, preferring to pass his time on crusade or campaigning in

---

Important Kings of England

Alfred (871–899)	William II (1089–1100)
Ethelred II (978–1016)	Henry I (1100–1135)
Cnut (1016–1035)	Stephen I (1135–1154)
Edward the Confessor (1042–1066)	Henry II (1154–1189)
	Richard I (1189–1199)
Harold of Wessex (1066)	John (1199–1216)
William I (the Conqueror) (1066–1089)	Henry III (1216–1272)
	Edward I (1272–1307)

France. John (r. 1199–1216) was defeated by France's Philip II, inducing contemporaries to mock him as "John Lackland" and "John Softsword."

On the surface it looks as though dynastic turmoil and military adventures make up the central themes of England's history. But just as Viking and Norman rulers built on the solid foundations of the Anglo-Saxon state, so the Anglo-Normans and Angevins retained and expanded those very foundations. They refined the financial machinery of the English government, the Exchequer, named for the checkerboard table on which the accounts were reckoned. They vastly improved the judicial institutions. Henry I began to send itinerant justices around the realm. He brought the royal court, with its swift, fair, and competent justice, within the reach of most people, and he made royal justice more attractive than the justice available in local lords' courts. This expansion of the work of the royal courts led to the emergence of a common law in England—a law common to all people, courts, and cases.

Henry II used the sworn inquest to learn about his realm. He conducted an inquest of knights' service to find out what service vassals owed to which people. He conducted an inquest of sheriffs to learn how the sheriffs were performing their jobs and replaced those found shirking their responsibilities. This action is the context for the Robin Hood stories about the cruel sheriff of Nottingham and the kind king who looks out for the people. Finally the Anglo-Norman and Angevin kings employed in their government "men raised from the dust," as one aristocratic contemporary contemptuously called them. These were men from the middling ranks of society, perhaps with some training in law, who were loyal to the king and advanced his interests against the aristocrats, who were intensely jealous of their own rights and privileges.

England's relations with the church fell somewhere between Germany's and France's in both intensity and outcome. Anglo-Saxon kings generally enjoyed cordial relations with the church on a traditional Carolingian model. William the Conqueror controlled the church with an iron hand but introduced reforms and reformers who were acceptable to Rome. Archbishop Anselm of Canterbury and Henry I had a quarrel that lasted several years, but they finally mended their differences in a settlement that anticipated the terms of the Concordat of Worms. Henry II was always anxious to extend the influence of his courts. In 1164 he decided that "criminous clerks," or members of the clergy who had committed a crime, should be judged in royal courts. The archbishop of Canterbury, Thomas Becket (ca. 1118–1170), protested that clerics could be tried only in church courts. Although the two sides came to a reconciliation, a band of overly zealous knights mur-

Swift and Certain Justice
This picture from about 1130 depicts some of the forty-four thieves hung by Sheriff Ralph Basset in 1124. As a common law spread throughout England, criminals were more likely to be caught and punished. (*The Pierpont Morgan Library, New York/Art Resource, NY*)

dered Becket, believing that they were doing the king's bidding. In fact, the crime so outraged the church and the public that Henry had to back down on criminous clerks and give up some authority to Rome. Despite these religious quarrels, however, England experienced no investiture controversy.

John's conflict with the church resulted in far more dramatic changes for England. The loss of Normandy had been costly in terms of prestige and resources. In difficult circumstances John got into a row with Pope Innocent III because he refused to admit to England the pope's candidate for archbishop of Canterbury. John had already had minor scrapes with ecclesiastical officials because of his exploitation of the church's revenues. Eventually he submitted because Innocent had laid England under interdict and John needed the pope's support for his planned war against Philip II of France. True to his nickname "Softsword," John lost at Bouvines (see page 262) and thus ended his quarrel with Rome.

With John's inglorious defeat and shameful capitulation, the barons of England had had enough. These barons (a general name for the upper ranks of English society) were increasingly upset that an expanding royal government limited their influence. In 1215 a large group of disgruntled barons forced King John to sign the **Magna Carta,** or "Great Charter" (so called because it was written on an unusually large sheet of parchment). This document required the king to respect the rights of feudal lords, not abuse his judicial powers, and consult his "natural" advisers—that is, the barons.

Online Study Center **Improve Your Grade**
Primary Source: The Making of the Magna Carta

John tried to wiggle out of the Magna Carta, but he died in 1216, leaving only a minor heir, and the barons exacted many concessions from the regency government. When Henry III came of age in 1234, he struggled to win a limited application of the Magna Carta. The barons, on the contrary, wanted a voice in devising royal policy, especially military policy, in light of recent defeats. They also wished to have some say in naming the king's closest advisers and in controlling the work of the king's agents, especially judges. This tension between king and barons led to several meetings of the royal court, often called **parliaments,** a French word meaning, roughly, "talking together." (The genuine ancestors of England's historic Parliament met in 1265 and 1295.) Initially these meetings had no fixed rights or procedures, no set group of attendees, and no defined role. The kings viewed them as clever political devices to win support for royal policies. The barons viewed them as opportunities to play a real role in a government that had been marginalizing them. In retrospect we can see that the English were groping to find a way to build consultation into their system.

The reign of Edward I (1272–1307) sums up the achievements of England's rulers in the High Middle Ages. Like his predecessors, Edward instituted sworn inquests to ascertain his rights and resources. He issued numerous statutes, laws that bear comparison with Louis IX's *ordonnances* (see page 266)—which earned him the nickname "the English Justinian." He worked skillfully with the newly emerging Parliament. And like other English rulers before him, Edward balanced political and military accomplishments, bravely fighting for years on the Welsh and Scottish frontiers.

Magna Carta   1215 English document that sets limits on the power of the king.

parliaments   Initially expanded meetings of the royal court intended to secure consensus for royal policies.

THE CELTIC REALMS

When the Romans appeared on the scene, Celtic peoples could be found in virtually every region from Ireland to Anatolia. Most Celts were absorbed by more numerous and powerful Germanic and Slavic peoples. It was in the British Isles that the most durable and distinctive Celtic regions evolved into Ireland, Wales, and Scotland. Two essential dynamics characterized each of these regions. First, tiny political entities gradually turned into larger kingdoms. Second, relations between England and the Celtic realms were everywhere decisive in the historical development of the latter (see Map 9.5).

In each of the Celtic realms the movement toward greater unity was opened by the efforts of powerful, ambitious leaders to subjugate numerous well-entrenched local potentates, many of whom had expanded their power during the period of Viking invasions. In Ireland Brian Boru (r. 976–1014) became the first ruler to exercise real authority over most of the island. In Wales Rhodri the Great (d. 898) and Howell the Good (d. 950) were the first rulers to gain at least nominal authority over the whole of the land. Although disunity is a continuous theme of Scottish history, the centuries after the reign of Kenneth MacAlpin (843–858) reveal the slow creation of a national tradition.

The course of development in the Celtic lands was disrupted by the English in the eleventh and especially the twelfth centuries. The Norman Conquest of England brought adventurers to the frontiers of Wales and Scotland. Sometimes these continental knights advanced with the support of William the Conqueror and his sons, but more often they looked to wild frontier regions for opportunities to escape tight control. In Wales some Normans allied with various local princes who resented the growing power of the Welsh kings. Henceforth, the actual power of Welsh rulers varied greatly, and English kings usually claimed some authority over the region. Scottish kings managed to enlist a good many Norman knights into their service, but this recruitment effort angered the English kings and spurred them to greater intervention. Civil disturbances in Ireland induced King Rory O'Connor (r. 1156–1186) to turn to King Henry II of England for mercenaries to help him establish his power. But by 1171 Henry had invaded Ireland himself and inaugurated the complicated English involvement that persists to this day.

Edward I of England intervened repeatedly in the Celtic world. In 1277 he invaded Wales with the intention of totally subduing the Welsh. He built immense castles, whose ruins are still impressive today. Edward also made his son the Prince of Wales—still the title of the heir to the British throne. Between 1100 and 1260

Howell the Good

This picture of Howell, from a manuscript of his laws, depicts him wearing a crown, holding a scepter, and sitting on a tufted throne that looks like a palace. These are key symbols of rule.
(The National Library of Wales)

England and Scotland went to war four times, and Edward resolved to put an end to this struggle by annexing Scotland. The Scots, however, rallied to the standard of Robert Bruce (r. 1306–1329), a dashing knight who was, ironically, of Norman extraction. Robert managed to free Scotland for centuries.

===== S E C T I O N   S U M M A R Y =====

- England's kings survived several changes of dynasty (compare Germany) without making fundamental changes in English society or government.

- English kings built on Anglo-Saxon precedents to secure revenues, extend the work of the royal courts, and limit the power of the barons.

- English kings brought constant pressure to bear on the Celtic realms that surrounded England, in the process retarding political development in these regions and involving themselves in dangerous and costly ventures.

THE GROWTH OF NEW STATES

How did new states emerge in Spain, Scandinavia, and the Slavic world, and how do those states compare with their western neighbors?

The proliferation of new states constitutes one of the most remarkable examples of expansion in high medieval Europe. In Spain Christian rulers waged a steady war of reconquest against the Islamic caliphate of Cordoba that led to the emergence of the kingdoms of Portugal, Castile, and Aragon. In Scandinavia mighty leaders built durable kingdoms in Denmark, Norway, and Sweden. Local rulers created a band of new Slavic states running from the Baltic to the Balkans. To the east of those Slavic realms, around the city of Kiev, the Scandinavian Rus founded the first state on Russian soil. Between 900 and 1300 the geographic range of Europe's political entities more than doubled.

MAP 9.6 The Christian Reconquista of Muslim Spain

From slow beginnings in the ninth century to the epochal Battle of Las Navas de Tolosa (1212), the Christians in Spain pushed back the Muslim frontier and built durable states behind it. *(Source: David Nicholas, The Evolution of the Medieval World, Pearson Education Limited. Copyright © 1992 The Longman Group UK. Reprinted by permission of Pearson Education Limited.)*

Reconquered:
- Before 914
- 914–1080
- 1080–1130
- 1130–1210
- 1210–1250
- 1250–1480
- After 1480
- ✕ Major battles
- Kingdoms, mid-twelfth century

Online Study Center **Improve Your Grade** Interactive Map: The Christian Reconquista of Muslim Spain

RECONQUISTA AND KINGDOM BUILDING IN SPAIN

Historians perceive two driving forces in the rich and colorful history of medieval Spain. One is the bloody experience of several centuries of war along an expanding frontier. The other is the constant interplay within the Iberian Peninsula of three vibrant cultures: Christian, Jewish, and Muslim. We describe the first of these forces in this chapter and the second in the next.

The emirate of Cordoba (see pages 228–229) began breaking up after 1002, and the weakness of the tiny successor realms afforded an unprecedented opportunity to the Christians living in the north of the peninsula. King Sancho I (r. 1000–1035) of Navarre launched an offensive against the Muslims. This war, carried on intermittently until the fifteenth century,

came to be called the **Reconquista** (ray-con-KEE-stuh), the "Reconquest."

Before Sancho died, he divided his realm among his sons; thus the kingdoms of Aragon and Castile arose alongside Navarre. Castile really advanced the Reconquista. In 1085 its forces captured the Muslim stronghold and old Visigothic capital of Toledo, an important moral and strategic victory. Now the Reconquista began moving on three fronts (see **MAP 9.6**). In the east the emerging kingdom of Aragon-Catalonia advanced along the Mediterranean coast. In the center León-Castile pressed hard against al-Andalus. In the west the nascent kingdom of Portugal became a factor in Iberian politics. Christian successes, and the reconquest of Toledo, led the retreating Muslims to summon

Reconquista The name for the centuries-long battle of Christians against Muslims in Spain.

Alfonso the Wise
The Spanish king Alfonso X, depicted here in a thirteenth-century manuscript from Spain, is judging his Muslim and Christian subjects. Alfonso's reputation for impartiality was important in his culturally diverse realm. *(Biblioteca Nacional, Madrid)*

aid in the 1150s from militant North African Muslims. The Christian advance temporarily stopped.

In the early thirteenth century Pope Innocent III stirred up crusading zeal and lent encouragement to clerics and nobles in Spain who wished to reopen hostilities against the Muslims. In 1212 a combined Castilian-Aragonese army won a decisive victory at Las Navas de Tolosa, south of Toledo. The victory of Las Navas de Tolosa was a great turning point in Spanish history. The outcome of the Reconquista, which did not conclude until the fifteenth century, was never again in doubt.

Twelfth-century Spanish kings, especially in Castile, imposed hereditary rule and exacted oaths of allegiance from their free subjects. The kings tried to force powerful nobles to become their vassals. They were more successful on the military frontier than back in their homelands because in the war zones nobles could be assigned new fiefs carved out of recent conquests. Kings profited from the Reconquista to enhance their status and power.

In the thirteenth century Spain produced kings of genius, especially Alfonso X (r. 1252–1284) of Castile. These rulers were pious men, genuinely inspired by the ideal of the Crusades (discussed later in this chapter) and zealous in the promotion of the church. They also were hardheaded rulers. Aragon-Catalonia became the greatest naval power of the western Mediterranean and a formidable economic power. Military victories brought as well a flow of booty and a supply of lands to reward the nobles who spent their energy on the frontier rather than on attacking the king. These kings built strong central governments. Increasingly they used professional officers in key government posts and dispatched roving officials from the court to check on local rulers. Alfonso issued a major law book for the whole of Castile. These laws were based on Roman law and emphasized royal power. The Cortes, a representative assembly made up primarily of urban notables,

began forging an alliance between the king and the towns. Iberia was not united in the thirteenth century, but it had evolved into four coherent blocks: a small and impotent Muslim region in Valencia and Granada, and three vibrant kingdoms centered on Portugal, Castile, and Aragon.

SCANDINAVIA

Europe's expanding map saw new states in Scandinavia, the Roman name for the lands that became Denmark, Norway, and Sweden. Although the faint beginnings of political consolidation in Denmark can be traced to the Carolingian period, actual development of the states of Scandinavia dates from the tenth and eleventh centuries. Overseas expansion played one key role in northern political development. Another was the slow achievement of political unity by kings who had to overcome powerful local interests (see Map 9.5).

The sea, not the land, is the great fact of Scandinavian history. Norway has more than 1,000 miles of coastline, and no point in Denmark is more than 35 miles from the sea. Scandinavia did not offer opportunities for large, land-based kingdoms or empires, but the sea provided Scandinavians with a wide scope for activities.

More than any other people of the north, the Vikings capitalized on the sea as a highway. Vikings were raiders, of course, but also settlers. Much of northeastern England, the Danelaw, was settled by Northmen. In 911 Norwegians settled what became Normandy in northern

France. Between 870 and 930 many Norwegians and some Danes settled Iceland and a little later established bases in Greenland. In 862 a Swedish force, accustomed to raiding and trading along the rivers of what would become Russia, established a base at Novgorod. Raiders, traders, and settlers, the Scandinavians fostered the expansion of Europe.

Because the sea made exit from Scandinavia so easy, and because the whole region had absolutely no tradition of unified government, kings had a hard time establishing their power. Essentially kings were war leaders with loyal bands of followers. Territorial states were thus built up as powerful leaders persuaded or forced more and more men to join them. Denmark's was the first of the northern monarchies to emerge in the early tenth century. Norway's monarchy arose a little later in the tenth century, but for much of the eleventh century Norway was under Danish control. As the Danes fell more and more under German influence in the eleventh century, Norway managed to break free. Sweden's monarchy was the last to emerge in the northern world; it was not fully stable until the twelfth century, but by 1300 it had become the most powerful.

Christianity came rather late to Scandinavia, with the first missionaries entering the region in the ninth century and widespread conversion ensuing in the eleventh. Norway's King Olaf (r. 1016–1028), affectionately remembered as Saint Olaf, was the first northern king who actively promoted Christianization. Scandinavian kings viewed the church as a useful adjunct to their power. They cooperated in creating bishoprics on the assumption that members of the high clergy would be educated, talented allies in the process of building central governments. Ironically, the church was a stabilizing force in Scandinavia during the very years when the investiture controversy wreaked havoc in Germany.

THE SLAVIC WORLD

In eastern Europe, between the Elbe and Dnieper (NEEper) Rivers, lived numerous peoples customarily called Slavs. Partly because of language differences and partly because of the areas in which these people settled, scholars divide them into western, southern, and eastern Slavs. These peoples were never conquered by the Romans, assimilated few influences from the classical world, and received Christianity later than western Europe. Still, as states began emerging in eastern Europe, they exhibited many of the same problems that older and more westerly states had encountered: shifting frontiers, clashes between ambitious rulers and powerful nobles, and outside military and cultural influences (see Map 9.5).

The first western Slavic state was Great Moravia, created in the 830s by capable dukes while the Carolingian Empire was experiencing civil wars. As we saw earlier (see page 239), the Moravian leaders invited the missionaries Cyril and Methodius to their realm, thereby beginning the establishment of Christianity in eastern Europe. Moravia's early promise was cut short in 906 by the Magyars. Also in the late ninth century the Přemysl (PURR-em-ih-sill) dynasty forged a kingdom in Bohemia that lasted through the Middle Ages, although for long periods it was under German domination.

The greatest of the western Slavic states was Poland. In the 960s and 970s Duke Mieszko (mee-ESH-koe) (d. 992) unified a substantial territory and received Christianity from Rome. The first action created the Polish state, and the second anchored Poland firmly within the orbit of the Latin West. Mieszko's descendants, the Piast dynasty of kings, ruled until the kingdom was divided in 1138. For more than two centuries Polish development was retarded as weak rulers contested for power with local magnates, who themselves were successfully subordinating both peasants and men of middling status.

The creation of a Hungarian state played a decisive role in dividing the western and southern Slavs. The Magyars were disruptive raiders from the 880s until their defeat by Otto I in 955. After that disaster the Magyars concentrated on building a state within the Danube basin, the home base from which they had launched their raids. The Magyars blended with the local Slavs. King (later Saint) Stephen (r. 997–1038), who received Christianity from Rome, was the real founder of Hungary. Like Poland, Hungary was attached to the Latin West. Stephen's family, the Arpads, ruled in Hungary for centuries. They built ruling centers at Buda and Esztergom, created an impressive territorial organization, and promoted the growth of the church. They also expanded in almost every direction.

The southern Slavs built a band of states that extended across the Balkans. The first, reaching back to the seventh century, was Bulgaria. The Bulgars were a Turkic people who first led and then merged into the local Slavic population. The first Bulgarian state lasted until the early eleventh century, when the Byzantines, who had suffered many defeats at Bulgarian hands, destroyed it. By the late twelfth century, when Byzantium itself had weakened, a new Bulgarian state emerged, but its rulers never had the firm control that their predecessors had wielded. Under Khan Boris (r. 852–879) Bulgaria made the momentous decision to accept Orthodox Christianity from Constantinople instead of Roman Catholicism, despite the pope's best efforts.

To the west of Bulgaria lay Serbia, a region dominated until the fourteenth century by Bulgaria and Byzantium. Perhaps because of constant outside threats, Serbia made little progress toward internal unity. The region accepted Orthodox Christianity. To the west of Serbia lay Croatia, a land formed when two originally independent areas, Dalmatia on the Adriatic coast and Croatia itself, were joined together in the early tenth century. Through much of the tenth and eleventh centuries, Croatia managed to preserve itself and evade the clutches of Hungary, Byzantium, and Venice. By 1107, however, Croatia was incorporated by Hungary as a more or less autonomous region. Croatia, owing to Italian and Hungarian influences, became Roman Catholic.

The creation of the major eastern Slavic state is shrouded in mystery and legend. It seems that in 862 a Swedish Viking named Rurik and his followers, called Varangians, established or seized a trading camp at Novgorod. A few years later Oleg (r. 879–912) took over Kiev and made it his base of operations. Thus was founded Kievan Rus, a state that, like Hungary and Bulgaria, began with an outside, elite leadership over a local Slavic majority.

Kiev was ruled by grand dukes who pursued four basic policies. They created a vast trading network that linked Germany, Scandinavia, Byzantium, and the caliphate. They shared power with regional nobles who built up several important towns of their own. They received Orthodox Christianity from Constantinople in 988. And, finally, they struggled to defend Kiev, indeed Rus territory as a whole, from wave after wave of invaders from the eastern steppes.

Kievan Rus was destroyed by the Mongols. These were a loose coalition of pastoral nomads from Mongolia (lands lying east of the Caspian Sea and north of China) and Turkic soldiers. The charismatic leader Jenghiz Khan (1154–1227) turned the Mongols into an invincible fighting force. He and his successors built an empire stretching from China to eastern Europe. In 1221 the Mongols began their attacks on Rus, and in 1240 Kiev fell.

Jenghiz Khan's empire was divided into several khanates on his death, with Rus dominated by the Golden Horde, so called because of the splendid golden tent from which they ruled. The Mongols accorded subject people considerable autonomy, but they demanded heavy taxes and occasionally carried out brutal raids to remind everyone who was in control. Through their domination of trade, the Mongols weakened the urbanization and commerce built up by Kievan Rus. Throughout the West, people were alarmed by the Mongol onslaught. (See the box "The Global Record: The Mongol Khan Writes to the Pope.")

When Charlemagne was crowned emperor in 800, only Bulgaria existed as a state in the vast lands of east-

Virgin of Vladimir
The holiest icon of Russia, once the miraculous protector of the city of Vladimir and later of Moscow, this image was painted in Constantinople in 1131. Rus, and later Russian, icons tended to follow Byzantine traditions very closely. *(Scala/Art Resource, NY)*

ern Europe. But the overriding trends of the era inexorably swept into that region. Three centuries later those lands were home to several small states and also to some impressively large and successful ones. The Slavic world was thoroughly pagan in 800 and largely Christian by 1200. State building and Christianization in eastern Europe represent two significant examples of European expansion in the High Middle Ages.

SECTION SUMMARY

- The Reconquista motivated Spanish kings to military victories and political consolidation.

- Although Scandinavian Vikings were influential and disruptive, large-scale states began to emerge in Denmark, Norway, and Sweden.

- Slavic states emerged from resolute local action (Poland, Bohemia) or from a fusion of elite outsider and dependent local populations (Hungary, Bulgaria, Rus).

- Christianity expanded everywhere, sometimes Roman Catholic (Spain, Scandinavia, Poland, Hungary) and sometimes Orthodox (Bulgaria, Rus).

THE MONGOL KHAN WRITES TO THE POPE

Alarmed, like many of his contemporaries, by the Mongol onslaught, Pope Innocent IV (r. 1243–1254) sent missionaries to try to convert the Mongol khan Guyuk to Christianity. Large groups of Mongols had only recently converted to Christianity. Innocent not only did not get the answer he was hoping for, but he must have been shocked by Guyuk's haughty reply in 1246.

We, by the power of the eternal heaven, Khan of the great Ulus [compare the Islamic umma; see page 215], Our Command: This is a version sent to the great pope that he may know and understand in the Muslim [actually, Persian] tongue, what has been written. If he reaches you with his own report, You, who are the great pope, together with all the princes, come in person to serve us. You have also said that supplication and prayer have been offered by you, that I might find a good entry into baptism. This prayer of yours I have not understood. Other words which you have sent me: "I am surprised that you have seized all the lands of the Magyar [i.e., Hungarians] and the Christians. Tell us what their fault is." These words of yours I have also not understood. The eternal God has slain and annihilated these lands and peoples, because they have neither adhered to Chingis [Jenghiz] Khan, nor to the Khagan, both of whom have been sent to make known God's command, nor to the command of God. Like your words, they also were impudent, they were proud and they slew our messengers. How could anybody seize or kill by his own power contrary to the command of God?

Though you likewise say that I should become a trembling Nestorian [probably the only form of Christianity well known to the Mongols] Christian, worship God, and be an ascetic, how do you know whom God absolves, in truth to whom He shows mercy? How do you know that such words as you speak are with God's sanction? From the rising of the sun to its setting, all the lands have been made subject to me. Who could do this contrary to the command of God?

Now you should say with a sincere heart: "I will submit and serve you." You yourself, at the head of all the princes, come at once to serve and wait upon us! At that time I shall recognize your submission.

If you do not observe God's command, and if you ignore my command, I shall know you as my enemy. Likewise, I shall understand you. If you do otherwise, God knows what I know.

QUESTIONS

1. How does Guyuk try to convince Innocent that he and he alone has God's favor?

2. Do you think that Guyuk was, literally or figuratively, diplomatic?

3. Suppose that we had Innocent's response to Guyuk (we do not). What might he have said in reply?

Source: Christopher Dawson, *Mission to Asia*, pp. 85–86, copyright © 1980, published by Sheed & Ward.

THE CRUSADES

What basic factors contributed to the rise, persistence, and eventual decline of the crusading movement?

In 1096 an army of Christian knights who called themselves pilgrims left Europe to liberate the Holy Land from the Muslim "infidel." (This was the first of many **Crusades,** so called because the warriors were *crucesignati*, "signed by the cross.") By the late eleventh century Europe was a fortress that had marshaled its resources for an attack on the world around it. Europe's expanding population, economic dynamism, political consolidation, and buoyant optimism made possible not only the First Crusade but also many more over two centuries.

Crusades   Armed pilgrimages intended to recover the Holy Land from the "infidel."

THE BACKGROUND: EAST AND WEST

With the accession in 867 of the Macedonian dynasty in the person of Basil I, the Byzantine Empire experienced a period of vigorous, successful rule that lasted until 1025. Although the Macedonians fostered striking cultural achievements, carried out significant administrative reforms, and established the kind of tight control of the church that had been so elusive in the iconoclastic era (see page 225), they were primarily great soldiers. Along the Balkan frontier the Macedonian rulers kept both the Bulgarians and Kievan Rus at bay while also neutralizing many smaller Slavic principalities. In the West the Macedonians maintained an effective diplomacy with Venice that permitted lucrative commercial opportunities in the Adriatic. In the East the Macedonian rulers profited from the gradual dissolution of the Abbasid caliphate by expanding their frontier in Anatolia.

By contrast, throughout the ninth and tenth centuries the ability of the caliphs in Baghdad to control their vast empire declined precipitously. Egypt and North Africa escaped Baghdad's control almost completely, and religious strife between Sunni and Shi'ite Muslims further destabilized the Islamic state.

After Basil II's death in 1025, Byzantium suffered a long period of short reigns and abrupt changes in policy. In the capital factional squabbling swirled around the imperial court, and in the person of Patriarch Michael Cerularius (r. 1043–1058) the church sought to break out from two centuries of domination. When in 1054 Cerularius and Pope Leo IX (r. 1049–1054) quarreled so bitterly over ecclesiastical customs that they excommunicated each other, the traditionally cooperative papal-Byzantine religious diplomacy gave way to a deep schism between the Catholic and Orthodox Churches that still exists. Religious tensions were complicated when the staunchly anti-Byzantine Normans began creating their kingdom in southern Italy.

It was in these divisive circumstances that the Seljuk Turks appeared on the eastern frontier of Anatolia. Bands of Turks, peoples from central Asia, had been serving the caliphs as mercenaries since the ninth century. With new leaders at their head, and with both the caliphate and the empire distracted, the Turks broke into Anatolia with a vengeance. In 1071 at Manzikert a skirmish between Byzantine and Turkish soldiers turned into a rout in which Byzantium lost an army, an emperor, and the Macedonian reputation for military prowess.

Ever since the emergence of the Turkish threat in the early eleventh century, the Byzantines had been seeking mercenary help. The imperial defeat at Manzikert made their search more urgent and led to appeals to the West. Some troops were rounded up but not enough, so in 1095 Emperor Alexius Comnenus (r. 1081–1118) sent envoys to ask Pope Urban II (r. 1088–1099) to plead for mercenary help against the Turks.

To most people in western Europe, the Turkish threat to Byzantium mattered little. What *did* alarm Westerners was Turkish attacks on pilgrims to Jerusalem. The popes saw in the plight of the Byzantines and of Western pilgrims some opportunities to manifest their leadership of the church. The papacy also wanted very much to heal the Roman-Orthodox rift. The popes, therefore, placed a high value on aiding the Byzantines.

Moreover, a crusade was perfectly consonant with the ethos of the knights of western Europe. Knights were born and trained to fight. The literature of the age glorified war and warriors. But churchmen had for some years been advancing an ideal of Christian knighthood that stressed fighting God's enemies. In the late tenth century there arose, first in France and then in many other places, peace movements called the "Peace of God" or the "Truce of God." These movements sought to prevent war in certain seasons, such as around Christmas and Easter, and on certain days of the week, chiefly Sunday. Peace movements also attempted to outlaw fighting near churches, protect noncombatants, and soften the treatment of enemies and captives. Together the movements induced knights to fight non-Christians outside Europe. Along with religious zeal, a quest for fame and fortune motivated many young men whose political prospects at home were limited.

THE "PILGRIMAGE" TO JERUSALEM

Pope Urban II received Alexius's envoys in 1095 and then left Italy for France. He was actually a fugitive because Henry IV controlled Rome. In November at Clermont, Urban delivered a rousing speech to a vast Christian assembly. He ignored the Eastern emperor's appeal for aid and instead promised salvation to soldiers who would enlist in a great struggle to free the Holy Land. The crowd acclaimed his words with a shout of "God wills it!"

Online Study Center **Improve Your Grade**
Primary Source: Call for Crusade: Urban II at the Council of Clermont

By 1096 four large armies, which eventually swelled to perhaps a hundred thousand men—mostly French knights, with a smattering of troops from other parts of Europe—assembled under the leadership of the pope's legate. The forces were to rendezvous at Constantinople, where they seem to have expected a cordial imperial welcome and all necessary assistance. Alexius, however, took a rather different view, for several reasons. First, a ragtag band of ordinary people preceding the Crusaders had torn through the Balkans like a plague of locusts. Second, the crusading armies themselves sorely taxed the imperial authorities, who spent a lot of time and money arranging their passage from the frontier of Hungary to the gates of Constantinople. Finally, Alexius wanted mercenaries to fend off Turks in Anatolia, not armed pilgrims intent on liberating Palestine (see **MAP 9.7**).

After receiving nominal promises of loyalty and the return or donation of any lands captured, Alexius moved the Crusaders into Anatolia. Almost immediately the Latin army defeated a Turkish force, thus earning a valuable, though short-lived, reputation for invincibility. The troops then entered Syria and laid siege to Antioch, which did not fall until 1098. At this point rivalries among the Crusaders came into the open. One force went to the frontier of Armenia and carved out a principality.

MAP 9.7 **The Crusades**

The long-standing Western interest in the Holy Land is vividly illustrated by the Crusades. Note the numerous routes taken, lands traversed, destinations attained, and points of cultural encounter.

Online Study Center **Improve Your Grade** Interactive Map: The Crusades

One of the ubiquitous Normans kept Antioch for himself. The main army pressed on to Jerusalem and, after a short but fierce siege, conquered it in July 1099. A Muslim historian describes the scene:

> In the Masjid [Mosque] al-Aqsa the Franks slaughtered more than 70,000 people, among them a large number of Imams and Muslim scholars, devout and ascetic men who had left their homelands to live lives of pious seclusion in the Holy Place. The Franks stripped the Dome of the Rock [the Mosque of Umar, near the al-Aqsa mosque, pictured on page 219] of more than forty silver candelabra, each of them weighing 3,600 drams [almost 40 pounds], and a great silver lamp weighing forty-four Syrian pounds, as well as a hundred and fifty smaller candelabra and more than twenty gold ones, and a great deal more booty.[2]

Godfrey of Bouillon, leader of the troops that had "liberated" Jerusalem, was named "Advocate of the Holy Sepulcher" and became ruler of the Christians in the East. He lived only a short time, however, and was replaced by his brother, Baldwin, as king of Jerusalem in 1100.

Judged on its own terms, the First Crusade was a success. The Holy Land was retaken from the infidel, and the pilgrim routes were passable once more. Entirely uncertain, however, were the prospects of the crusader states, the future course of Western relations with Byzantium, and the reaction of the Islamic world once it recovered from its initial shock.

THE LATER CRUSADES

Crusading was intended to protect the Holy Land and keep open the pilgrim routes to Jerusalem. The creation of the small crusader states in the hostile environment of Syria and Palestine made continued crusading almost inevitable. In 1144 the tiny crusader state at Edessa on the Armenian frontier fell to a Muslim army. Although the news saddened Europeans, it took immense efforts by the papacy and other religious leaders to launch another crusade. Finally Conrad III of Germany and Louis VII of France agreed to lead it, but because neither would willingly submit to the other's authority, the Second Crusade accomplished little. Its one achievement was an accident. In 1147 an army of English, French, and Flemish soldiers who were proceeding to the Holy Land by sea put in on the Iberian coast and captured Lisbon. This opened a new front in the Reconquista and laid the foundations for the later kingdom of Portugal (see Map 9.7).

The papacy called for the Third Crusade when Saladin (sah-lah-DEEN) (1138–1193), a powerful local leader typical of the disintegrating Abbasid caliphate, recaptured Jerusalem in 1187. It is a measure of the force of the crusading ideal that the greatest crowned heads of the day—Frederick Barbarossa, Philip II, and Richard the Lionhearted—answered the call. It must be said, however, that only Frederick did so enthusiastically. Frederick died en route in 1190, while Philip returned home in 1191 and Richard in 1192. Because neither Richard nor Philip would stay in Palestine to fight Saladin, this crusade merely won access to Jerusalem for pilgrims.

Disappointed with the results of the Third Crusade, Innocent III began calling for another crusade immediately on his election in 1198. Popular preachers summoned an army, once again largely French, and the pope and the Fourth Crusade's military leaders engaged the Venetians to construct a fleet of war and transport ships. In less than eighteen months they produced 50 galleys and 450 transports, a tribute to the awesome capabilities of the Venetian shipyards.

Ships, however, were expensive, and the Venetians drove hard bargains. When too few Crusaders and too little money appeared, the Venetians suggested that the Crusaders could discharge some of their debt by recapturing from the Hungarians the formerly Venetian port of Zara on the Dalmatian coast. This idea outraged the pope, but he could do little about it. Then into the camp of the Crusaders came a pretender to the Byzantine throne, who promised that if the Crusaders would help him to claim his patrimony, he would contribute to the cost of the Crusade. The Venetians urged the indebted Crusaders to accept this offer, and, to the horror of Innocent III, the Fourth Crusade turned to Constantinople.

Once in Constantinople the Crusaders learned that their new ally had few friends in the Byzantine capital, but the venture hardly collapsed. The Venetians saw an opportunity to expand business opportunities in the East, and the soldiers welcomed a chance to plunder the Mediterranean's greatest city and to avenge what they regarded as a century of Byzantine perfidy. Thus the Fourth Crusade captured not Jerusalem but Constantinople. Until 1261, the Eastern and Western churches were reunited under papal leadership, and substantial tracts of the Balkans fell to Western knights under a "Latin emperor" of Constantinople.

In later decades popes began to take a more active role in planning crusades. No pope wanted to lose control of a crusade as Innocent had done, and all popes saw that the liberation of Jerusalem required a solid base of operations in the eastern Mediterranean. Egypt was the objective of the Fifth (1218–1221) and Sixth (1248–1250) Crusades. Despite a few victories, the Crusaders could not win a secure base. No further crusades to the East were organized in the thirteenth century. In 1291 Acre, the last Crusader stronghold, fell, and the original crusading era ended.

During the crusading period the Holy Land was not the sole object of Crusaders' attentions. In about 1140 the pope preached a crusade against the Normans in southern Italy, and several popes in the thirteenth century, fearful of imperial encroachment, preached crusades against the Staufer dynasty in Italy. In 1147 the papacy authorized a crusade in the Baltic that opened nearly four centuries of German expansion into the pagan Slavic lands to the east of Saxony. In 1208 Innocent III proclaimed a crusade against the Albigensians in southwestern France.

THE AFTERMATH OF THE CRUSADES

Why did the Crusades end? There are several reasons. By the late thirteenth century more violence was being directed inward against heretics and political foes of the papacy than outward against the alleged enemies of Christendom itself. As rulers became more sophisticated and controlled more territory, they had less interest in the intangible benefits of crusading, such as prestige. Whereas the cities of Italy once needed to open up Mediterranean ports, now they wished to secure comparative advantage over one another. The Christian ideals of poverty, charity, and service were incompatible with warfare. Literary images provide another insight into the decline of the Crusades. After 1300 we are less likely to read about a Christian knight fighting honorably for God and king than about a gentleman of manners seeking the favor of a fair lady.

Crusading was brutal. Soldiers and their clerical companions spent years away from their homes and families, endured scorching Mediterranean heat, and suffered shortages of food and basic supplies. The vulnerable crusader states never received enough settlers to be viable communities, and consequently intermarriage with locals was common and gradually produced a hybrid culture that was neither European nor Middle Eastern. Warfare was constant on all sides. When Crusaders conquered a town, they executed many locals. When Muslims recaptured a town, they did the same. The tremendous enthusiasm evident in 1095 could not be sustained over two centuries.

An examination of the crusading movement as a whole reveals more losses than gains. The Crusades exported many violent men from Europe, but it is not clear that Europe became a less violent place. As might be expected, the Crusades devastated relations between Christian Europe and the Muslim world. The Fourth Crusade mortally wounded Byzantium and worsened the already tense standoff between the Catholic and Orthodox Churches. Crusading zeal was directed deliberately against heretics and coincidentally against Jews. The Jewish populations of several towns were massacred on the eve of the First and Second Crusades. The Crusades did not create anti-Semitism, but they aggravated it. Some women, particularly in France, from which the majority of all Crusaders came, may have enjoyed momentary benefits in terms of control of land, wealth, and people while their husbands were away. But the long-term trend in feudal society was disadvantageous to women, and the Crusades did not change that. Finally, the Crusades may have done as much to disrupt Mediterranean trade as to promote it. Italian urban rivalries took the place of Latin-Muslim-Byzantine ones. That a single new product, the apricot, entered Europe in the crusading era seems small reward for such a huge effort.

SECTION SUMMARY

- Weakness and disunity in the Byzantine Empire and the caliphate were important background factors in the Crusades.

- Heightened religious zeal in western Europe along with growing papal leadership were also significant background factors.

- Mixed motives stood behind the initial Crusades: The Byzantines wanted mercenaries to fight in Anatolia, the popes wanted to extend their authority and free the Holy Land, urban Italians sought commercial opportunities, and western knights sought both worldly glory and eternal reward.

- The momentum of the early crusading movement could not be sustained over a long time, and the Holy Land was not definitively liberated.

CHAPTER SUMMARY

Online Study Center **ACE the Test**

In how many different realms of life do you see signs of growth and innovation, of expansion?

What did Germany, Italy, and France owe to the Carolingian past? How alike and different were these areas by 1300?

What were the chief dynamics in the development of medieval Britain?

How did new states emerge in Spain, Scandinavia, and the Slavic world, and how do those states compare with their western neighbors?

What basic factors contributed to the rise, persistence, and eventual decline of the crusading movement?

Between 900 and 1300 Western civilization expanded as never before in human, material, geographical, and political terms. Europe's population grew dramatically until the late 1200s owing to better diets and more plentiful foods. Technological gains came with wider use of horses, improved plows, and more productive farming techniques. Many regions began to specialize in the products that they grew or made, and this local specialization prompted larger-scale trade. Towns came to play a larger role in almost all aspects of economic and social life. Economic growth widened the gap between rich and poor and induced theologians to write about the just price and usury.

German political development was impeded by short-lived dynasties, territorial complexity, and battles with the papacy. From being Europe's greatest state in the tenth century, Germany declined into weakness in the thirteenth. Italy experienced the communal movement in the north, the consolidation of the Papal States and Papal Monarchy in the center, and the continued fragmentation of the south, where foreigners ruled. Differences among these three zones are characteristic of Italian history. France had a prestigious and long-lived royal dynasty, patient territorial expansion, and a slowly, steadily centralizing government. By 1300 France was the most powerful state in Europe.

England's kings survived several changes of dynasty (compare Germany) without having to make fundamental changes in English society or government. English kings built on Anglo-Saxon precedents to secure revenues, extend the work of the royal courts, and limit the power of the barons.

English kings brought constant pressure to bear on the Celtic realms that surrounded England, in the process retarding political development in these regions and involving themselves in dangerous and costly ventures. By 1300 England was a unified and well-governed kingdom.

The growth of new states is an impressive achievement of the High Middle Ages. The Reconquista motivated Spanish kings to military victories and political consolidation. Although Scandinavian Vikings were influential and disruptive, large-scale states began to emerge in Denmark, Norway, and Sweden. Slavic states emerged from resolute local action (Poland, Bohemia) or from a fusion of elite outsider and dependent local populations (Hungary, Bulgaria, Rus). Christianity expanded everywhere, sometimes Roman Catholic (Spain, Scandinavia, Poland, Hungary) and sometimes Orthodox (Bulgaria, Rus). The "West" was a lot bigger in 1300 than it had been in 900.

The Crusades represent a key sign of western Europe's expansion. Weakness and disunity in the Byzantine Empire and the caliphate were important background factors in the Crusades. Heightened religious zeal in western Europe along with growing papal leadership were also significant background factors. Mixed motives stood behind the initial Crusades: the Byzantines wanted mercenaries to fight in Anatolia, the popes wanted to extend their authority and free the Holy Land, urban Italians sought commercial opportunities, and western knights sought both worldly glory and eternal reward. The momentum of the early crusading movement could not be sustained over a long time, and the Holy Land was not definitively liberated.

LOOKING AHEAD

Granted that the preceding account of western Europe's expansion is persuasive, one might still ask: What about all the things the Middle Ages are famous for? What about Gothic cathedrals, Dante, and Thomas Aquinas? In the next chapter we will look at Europe's *cultural* expansion.

KEY TERMS

 Online Study Center **Improve Your Grade** Flashcards

guilds (p. 251)

lay investiture (p. 257)

communes (p. 259)

Papal Monarchy (p. 260)

feudal revolution (p. 266)

Magna Carta (p. 270)

parliaments (p. 270)

Reconquista (p. 272)

Crusades (p. 276)

SUGGESTED READING

Bartlett, Robert. *The Making of Europe: Conquest, Colonization and Cultural Change, 950–1350*. 1993. An engaging account of the expansion and "Europeanization" of Europe.

Bisson, Thomas, ed. *Cultures of Power: Lordship, Status, and Process in Twelfth-Century Europe*. 1995. The thirteen sparkling essays in this book cover much of Europe and attempt to explain how power was actually wielded in a society in which states were just emerging.

Bloch, Marc. *Feudal Society*. Translated by L. A. Manyon. 2 vols. 1964. This best-known book by one of this century's greatest historians seeks to explain the total history of the post-Carolingian world in terms of the ideals and practices of feudalism.

Jordan, William Chester. *Europe in the High Middle Ages*. 2002. Comprehensive and absorbing, this is the best available survey, and by a master historian, too.

Moore, Robert I. *The First European Revolution*. 2000. A distinguished historian offers the first comprehensive, synthetic treatment of the High Middle Ages in fifty years. Stimulating and readable.

Reynolds, Susan. *Fiefs and Vassals*. 1994. Brilliant, controversial, and difficult, this massive book challenges many long-standing ideas about feudalism.

Riley-Smith, Jonathan, ed. *The Oxford Illustrated History of the Crusades*. 2002. A set of essays with lavish illustrations that explores almost every aspect of the Crusades and the world that produced them.

NOTES

1. Walter Map, *De nugis curialum*, 5.5, in John H. Mundy, *Europe in the High Middle Ages* (London: Longman, 1973), p. 387.

2. Slightly adapted from the *Gesta Francorum*, trans. August C. Krey, in *The First Crusade* (Princeton, N.J.: Princeton University Press, 1921), p. 257.

MEDIEVAL CIVILIZATION AT ITS HEIGHT, 900–1300

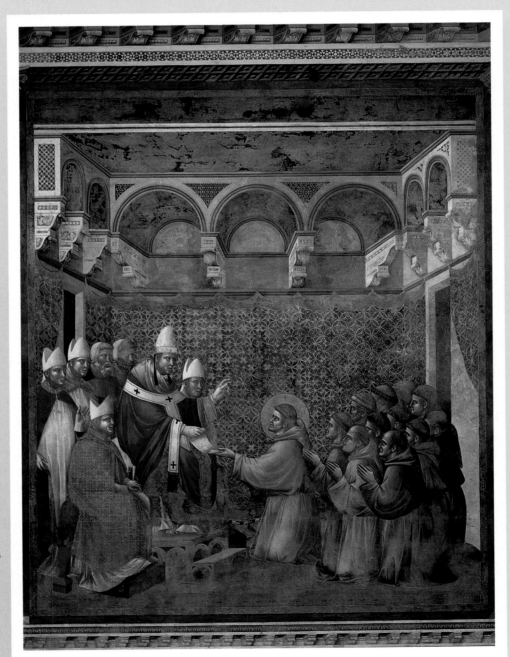

The Confirmation of the Rule of Saint Francis, 1223
Pope Honorius III confirms the revised version of Francis's Rule.
(Scala/Art Resource, NY)

This painting by the renowned artist Giotto di Bondone depicts Pope Honorius III confirming the Rule of Saint Francis in 1223. Saint Francis kneels humbly before the pope, along with several of his Franciscan followers. Note the simplicity of their dress, especially as compared against the regal clothing worn by the pope and his bishops. The plain brown robes are recognized as the traditional clothing of Franciscans, who lived according to the scriptural ideals of poverty, preaching, and service. Unlike monastic orders who withdrew from the world, the Franciscans pledged themselves to working among Europe's outcasts—the poor, the sick, and the old.

The Franciscans, and similar orders such as the Dominicans, led one of the most powerful religious movements of the Middle Ages. Yet they were just one part of the religious climate of the period. Several social and religious movements, including heretical movements and religious communities of women, also emerged during the twelfth and thirteen centuries.

We know about Saint Francis and others from many Latin documents, but also from ones written in Italian. The culture of the High Middle Ages saw Latin cede some space to the *vernacular* languages. Religious themes were still foremost in writings of all kinds, but adventures, romances, and other works dedicated to secular themes were gaining in prominence. Intellectual life was broadened by encounters with long-lost Greek texts and with the writings of Jewish and Muslim scholars. Franciscans would also become professors in Europe's emerging universities. Universities owed much to earlier cathedral and monastic schools but were new institutions—one of medieval Europe's greatest, and most durable, inventions.

The previous chapter concentrated on the economic foundations of society and on the ways in which people organized themselves politically. This chapter begins by introducing the increasingly complex social structures within which people lived and then turns to a study of what those people thought, said, and built.

CHAPTER OUTLINE

THE TRADITIONAL ORDERS OF SOCIETY

SOCIAL AND RELIGIOUS MOVEMENTS, CA. 1100–1300

LATIN CULTURE: FROM SCHOOLS TO UNIVERSITIES

THE VERNACULAR ACHIEVEMENT

KEY TERMS

Cluny
Francis of Assisi
Dominic de Guzman
canon law
Bernard of Clairvaux
Hildegard of Bingen
Thomas Aquinas
summa
chivalry
Romanesque
Gothic

Online Study Center

This icon will direct you to interactive map and primary source activities on the website **college.hmco.com/pic/noble5e**

FOCUS QUESTIONS

Into what principal social groups were the people of high medieval Europe organized?

Why did some spiritual movements result in heresy, while others ended in new religious orders?

What signs do you find of an expanding intellectual climate in high medieval Europe?

What were the hallmarks of vernacular culture?

THE TRADITIONAL ORDERS OF SOCIETY

Into what principal social groups were the people of high medieval Europe organized?

A new and distinctly medieval social order had evolved by 900. Alfred the Great (r. 871–899) of England once said that a kingdom needed "men of prayer, men of war, and men of work." In the tenth century two French bishops wrote lengthy works exploring this same theme. This threefold division reveals the way the elite looked at the world. It provided neat places for the clergy, warrior-aristocrats, and peasants. The clergy and the nobility agreed that they were superior to the "workers," but fierce controversies raged over whether ultimate leadership in society belonged to the "prayers" or the "fighters."

By the time this three-part view of society was fully established in the West, it had begun to fit social realities less well. It excluded townspeople, who were becoming ever more important. Town residents worked for a living, of course, but only farmers were considered "workers." Alfred and the bishops did not speak about women, and they consciously excluded minorities, chiefly Jews. To form a full picture of Europe's increasingly intricate social relations, we begin with contemporary theoretical pronouncements and then look for the people whom the theoreticians neglected.

THOSE WHO PRAY: THE CLERGY

As the church promoted its own vision of the three-part ordering of society, it assigned primacy to the prayers—its own leaders. Within the clergy, however, sharp disagreements arose over whether the leading prayers were the monks in the monasteries or the bishops in their cathedrals. Whereas in the Carolingian world the clergy served occasionally as an avenue of upward social mobility for talented outsiders, in the High Middle Ages church offices were usually reserved for the younger sons of the nobility. The church was always hierarchical in organization and outlook, so the increasingly aristocratic character of the church's leadership tended to reinforce those old tendencies.

In the aftermath of the Carolingian collapse, a great spiritual reform swept Europe. It began in 910 when Duke William of Aquitaine founded the monastery of **Cluny** (CLUE-nee) in Burgundy on land that he donated (see Map 9.4 on page 263). At a time when powerful local families dominated almost all monasteries, Cluny was a rarity because it was free of all lay and episcopal control and because it was under the direct authority of the pope. Cluny's abbots were among the greatest European statesmen of their day and became influential advisers to popes, French kings, German emperors, and aristocratic families.

In the tradition of the Carolingian monastic reforms, Cluny placed great emphasis on liturgical prayer. The monks spent long hours in solemn devotions and did little manual work. Because Cluniac prayer was thought to be especially effective, nobles all over Europe donated land to Cluny and placed local monasteries under Cluniac control. Many independent monasteries also appealed to Cluny for spiritual reform. By the twelfth century hundreds of monasteries had joined in a Cluniac order. Individual houses were under the authority of the abbot of Cluny, and their priors had to attend an annual assembly. Although the majority of houses reformed by Cluny were male, many convents of nuns also adopted Cluniac practices.

Cluny promoted two powerful ideas. One was that the role of the church was to pray for the world, not to be implicated deeply in it. The other was that freedom from lay control was essential if churches were to concentrate on their spiritual tasks.

The same spiritual forces that motivated the Cluniacs inspired Bishop Adalbero of Metz in 933 to promote the restoration of Benedictine practices in the dilapidated Lorraine monastery of Gorze (GORTZ-eh). Customs at Gorze resembled those at Cluny, and they

Cluny   A monastery in France that became a model for religious reform.

spread widely in Lorraine, Germany, and England. The Gorze reform was well received by kings and nobles; its aim was not so much to withdraw from the world as to improve it. Monks from the Gorze and Cluniac traditions bitterly condemned clerical immorality and inappropriate lay interference in the church. They preached against clerical marriage and simony, the buying and selling of church offices.

Reformers in the more ascetic eremitic tradition (see pages 192–193) desired more profound changes. They criticized the monastery at Cluny, saying that it had become too opulent and successful, and the monastery at Gorze because it seemed too immersed in worldly affairs. A desire to build new communities according to their vision of the apostolic church, featuring a life of poverty, self-denial, and seclusion, captivated the ascetics. Thus the eleventh and early twelfth centuries saw a proliferation of both male and female experiments in eremitic monasticism. Other Europeans believed that the apostolic calling demanded not only an austere regimen of personal renunciation but also an active life of Christian ministry. Cathedral clergy, called canons, in particular, adapted the Rule of Saint Augustine so that they could live a communal life and also carry out priestly duties.

The greatest critics of the Cluniac tradition, and the real monastic elite of the early twelfth century, were the Cistercians. In 1098 Abbot Robert left his Burgundian monastery of Molesme (MOE-lem) because he believed it had abandoned the strict teachings of Saint Benedict. He founded a new monastery at Cîteaux (SEE-toe) in Burgundy. This house was to follow the Benedictine Rule literally and to refuse all secular entanglements: lands, rents, and servile dependents. So rigorous and poor was the community that it struggled until a charismatic young Burgundian nobleman named Bernard (1090–1153) joined in 1112. Three years later Bernard left to found a daughter house at Clairvaux (KLARE-voe), where he remained abbot for the rest of his life. Through his writing, preaching, and personal example, Bernard dominated the religious life of Europe in his lifetime. By the end of the twelfth century there were about five hundred Cistercian (from the Latin for *Cîteaux*) monasteries in Europe, and Bernard's own Clairvaux had seven hundred monks. Initially the Cistercians wished to be an order of adult men. They successfully avoided admitting young boys, but by 1200 they had authorized about one hundred convents of Cistercian nuns.

And it was not just the Cistercians and the traditional Benedictines who attracted women. The twelfth century saw many new communities of women from England to eastern Europe. The age's growing prosperity and population contributed both potential nuns and healthy endowments, but the key factor was that women were responding to the spiritual forces of the age in the same way men were.

ca. 900	*Beowulf*
910	Foundation of Cluny
940–1003	Gerbert of Aurillac
960–1028	Fulbert of Chartres
d. 970	Roswitha of Gandersheim
1000–1088	Berengar of Tours
ca. 1033–1109	Anselm of Canterbury
ca. 1050–1150	Maturation of the Romanesque
1079–1142	Peter Abelard
1090–1153	Bernard of Clairvaux
1098	Foundation of Cîteaux
1098–1179	Hildegard of Bingen
ca. 1100	*Song of Roland*
1135–1183	Chrétien de Troyes
1170–1221	Dominic de Guzman
ca. 1177–1213	Mary of Oignies
1181–1226	Francis of Assisi
1184	Waldensians declared heretics
1194–1253	Clare of Assisi
1208	Albigensian Crusade launched
1210–1280	Mechtild of Magdeburg
1225–1274	Thomas Aquinas
1265–1321	Dante Alighieri

With the monastic clergy gaining so much in prestige and visibility, the episcopal clergy countered with its own view of society. Surely, the bishops agreed, spiritual, moral, and intellectual improvement were desirable. Likewise, it was time to end the grossest examples of lay interference in the church. But precisely because so many bishops came from great families and were so well connected, they were less inclined to be rigid about the line of demarcation between lay and clerical responsibilities. In Germany, for example, the king's chapel recruited young noblemen to train them as clerics and to inculcate in them the policies and ethos of the court. Many of these chaplains were appointed to bishoprics and then advanced the king's interests in their new ecclesiastical areas of authority. They were often men of spiritual depth and resented what they regarded as monastic carping about their worldliness. By the middle of the twelfth century bishops, and finally popes, had

Reconstruction of Cluny

A view of the monastic complex at Cluny in the early twelfth century. Note the basilica (the largest church in Europe until the sixteenth century), the cloister (to the left, actually south, of the basilica, with its dormitory in the foreground and refectory opposite the basilica), and the workshops. *(Based on a drawing from* Cluny des Églises et la Maison du Chef d'Ordre, *by R. J. Conant. Courtesy, Medieval Academy of America)*

imposed on the church a view that monks belonged in their monasteries and that bishops should lead society.

It was always the special responsibility of the clergy to look after the moral order of society. In the turbulent world of gentlemen warriors, the church had its own ideas about what a perfect "fighter" should do. The English bishop and scholar John of Salisbury (d. 1180), reflecting on knighthood in the twelfth century, concluded that it existed "to protect the church, to attack infidelity, to reverence the priesthood, to protect the poor, to keep the peace, to shed one's blood and, if necessary, to lay down one's life for one's brethren."

Turning large numbers of violent young men into servants of the church was a tall order for the clergy, and they had only limited success. One strategy that worked was the creation of military orders. The Palestine-based Knights of St. John, or Hospitallers, and Knights of the Temple, or Templars, are the major examples, but others existed in Spain and Germany. The Hospitallers started near Jerusalem as a foundation under Benedictine auspices dedicated to charitable works and care of the sick. They evolved into a monastic order using a version of the Rule of Saint Benedict and devoted themselves to the defense of pilgrims to the Holy Land. The Templars were men living under religious rule and sworn to protect the small states created by the Crusaders (see pages 278–280). These military orders measured up very well to the clergy's idea of what a perfect knight should be.

The clergy could also regulate disputes in society. For example, when a community was divided by a dif-

ficult conflict that demanded resolution, it might turn to the *ordeal*—a judicial procedure that sought divine judgment by subjecting the accused to a physically painful or dangerous test. An accused person might walk a certain distance carrying hot iron or plunge a hand into a boiling cauldron to pluck out a pebble. The resulting wounds would be bandaged for a set time and then examined. If they were healing, the person was considered innocent; if festering, guilty. The clergy officiated at ordeals until the papacy forbade their participation in 1215.

Clergymen were also the conservators of the shrines where people gained special access to the holiness of the saints. The clergy wrote and preached about the miracles of the saints, and stories circulated through the church about relics, or artifacts associated with these martyrs. The shrines where relics were preserved attracted pilgrims seeking healing from illness, injury, or misfortune. The clergy thus played unique roles in forming and nurturing communities in the world and in interceding for this world with God in the next.

THOSE WHO FIGHT: THE NOBILITY

In recent years scholars have spilled a sea of ink trying to define the medieval nobility. The matter is important because even though the nobility constituted only a small minority of the total population, nobles were and expected to be the ruling class. To appreciate their crucial role, we need to consider the shape of the nobility and the nobles' lifestyle and ethos.

In English the word *noble* can be either an adjective or a noun. More commonly, it is an adjective, as in a "noble sentiment" or a "noble deed." Before the twelfth century the Latin *nobilis* was almost exclusively an adjective. The word pertained to certain desirable personal qualities. Then, gradually, the word became a noun and pertained to a certain kind of person.

What kind of person? In the ideal case a noble was a well-born, cultivated, office-holding soldier. In the earlier Middle Ages many men held offices without necessarily being considered noble. Virtually all free men were expected to be soldiers, but few of them ranked as nobles. It was in the century or so following the feudal revolution (see page 266) that these distinct elements were fused into a single social order.

In a world in which lords were everywhere extending their power, military prowess became more valuable. At the same time the need for horses and for more expensive arms and armor made it almost impossible for ordinary freemen to be soldiers. Likewise, ambitious lords who wished to expand their influence, and who were often, in an expanding economy, more prosperous than their forebears, were looking for ways to use their resources to gain followers. These trends came together as lords granted to their followers either military gear or lands, which would generate the income necessary to obtain arms and horses. We call those followers "vassals" and the lands they obtained "fiefs." Vassalage became a widespread institution all over Europe, and fief-holding became a normal accompaniment to vassalage. By contrast, in the Carolingian world vassalage was unusual and rarely connected with fief-holding.

Vassals and fiefs bring to mind the concept of *feudalism* or the term *feudal system*. As we saw in Chapter 9, England, France, and, to a lesser degree, Germany and Italy were in some respects feudal realms. That is, lords, right up to the king, secured some personal and political services from vassals in return for material rewards, often landed estates called fiefs. Today historians are reluctant to use the term *feudal system* because across Europe and through many centuries, there was nothing systematic about how services were obtained or discharged.

Online Study Center **Improve Your Grade**
Primary Source: The Feudal Contract: Mutual Duties of Vassals and Lords

Contemporary sources often call vassals "knights." Knights rarely boasted high birth or venerable ancestry. Nor were they initially officeholders appointed by kings or emperors. Moreover, they were not wealthy and could not sustain the kind of lavish lifestyle that one might expect from nobles. Across the eleventh and twelfth centuries knights saw their status change, in part because they mimicked the behavior of the nobles, who themselves accepted the necessity of military ability.

All over Europe, especially where royal power was ineffective, both knights and nobles secured tighter control of peasant labor. This process provided knights and nobles with the money to build castles and to acquire fine possessions. As governments expanded their competence, these nobles and knights often held high offices, or if they did not, they pressured kings to concede such offices to them. Lords also tended to gather their lands into coherent blocks and to name themselves after the castles they built on their lands. Families also began to produce genealogies tracing their ancestry to relatives in the distant past, and to kings if at all possible. At the same time families began to practice primogeniture—that is, reserving their lands, castles, and titles to the *primus genitus*, or "firstborn" son.

This allotment of the choicest inheritances to a shrinking group turned loose a large number of younger sons. Many of them entered the clergy, a tendency that helps to explain the rising aristocratic character of the church. It should be emphasized right away, however, that this was not a punishment. Sons were not "dumped" on the church. Clerical careers were prestigious and relatively comfortable. But more numerous than clerics were the young men who were without an estate and who lacked the means to secure a bride and to form a family of their own. These men traipsed about Europe looking for fame and fortune, or failing that, a lord to serve. Many of these "young" men were 30 or 40 years old. They were called young because they had not yet established themselves.

By 1200 the nobility was a group identified by the profession of arms, the holding of office, a consciousness of family traditions, and an elevated lifestyle. A specific ethos—chivalry—belonged to the nobility. Today chivalry is often thought of as either an elaborate code of conduct regulating relations between the sexes or the value system behind the literary image of dashing knights in shining armor saving damsels in distress from fire-breathing dragons. Actually its very name derives from *cheval*, French for "horse," the classic conveyance of a knight. Chivalry began as the code of conduct for mounted warriors.

Chivalry highly esteemed certain masculine, militant qualities. Military prowess was the greatest of chivalric virtues. A knight who was not a great warrior was useless. Literature of the time exalts the knight who slays fearsome beasts or the hero who single-handedly overwhelms impossible numbers of the enemy. Open-handed generosity was another key virtue. The truly noble person engaged in sumptuous display to manifest his power, to show concern for his dependents, and to enlarge his entourage. Medieval literature is full of rich banquets and stunning presents. In Anglo-Saxon England the king was called "the giver of rings." Knights were obsessed with their honor, their reputations. They sought glory, the better to win a lord or a bride or, if a lord already, to attract followers.

Chivalry also involved loyalty, the glue that held feudal society together. But we must take into account statements such as the following by a twelfth-century English historian, William of Malmesbury: "They [knights] are faithful to their lords, but swift to break faith. A breath of ill fortune and they are plotting treachery, a bag of money and their mind is changed." Knights, especially the "young," were loyal to their lords when they could be, but fundamentally they were loyal to themselves.

What role was left to noblewomen in a world of chivalry and lordship? By the late eleventh century three developments adversely affected the position of aristocratic women. First, the elaboration of the chivalric ethos defined most key social and political roles as military and "manly" and thereby excluded women. By the middle of the twelfth century it was rare for a woman to hold a castle and unheard-of for one to ride to arms. Second, the consolidation of lineages by aristocratic families accompanied a moral campaign by the church to promote monogamous, unbreakable marriages. This situation subordinated women's freedom in the marriage market to the dynastic and patrimonial demands of great families. Third, the spread of lordship, with its intricate network of personal and proprietary relationships based on military service, tended to deprive women of independent rights over land.

But every rule has its exceptions. As noble families married off fewer of their daughters to noblemen, "extra" daughters accounted in part for the dramatic increase in the number and size of convents. Convents of aristocratic nuns were places where women could be highly educated and almost entirely in control of their own affairs. Matilda, daughter of the German empress Adelaide, was abbess of Quedlinburg, mistress of vast estates in northern Germany, and a dominant figure in German politics. But knights looking for brides would often marry the younger daughters of noblemen, because if they could establish a household, any children born of that marriage could lay claim to the noble lineage of their maternal grandfathers.

Less predictably, Gaita, wife of a Norman prince in Italy, fought in helmet and armor alongside her husband, as did Duchess Agnes of Burgundy. And let us reflect on the career of Adela of Blois (ca. 1067–1137). She was the daughter of William the Conqueror, the wife of a powerful French count, and the mother of King Stephen I of England (see page 268). In addition to regularly accompanying her husband as he administered his county, Adela founded monasteries, promoted religious reform, hosted Pope Paschal II, helped to reconcile her brother Henry I with the archbishop of Canterbury (thus averting an English investiture controversy), issued formal legal judgments, held fairs, and skillfully negotiated the aristocratic politics of western France after her husband's death. Adela is unusual because we know so much about her. In other words, noblewomen in high medieval society may often have led interesting, active lives, but there are few surviving records to document this.

THOSE WHO WORK: THE PEASANTS

The peasants were the "workers" in the three-part model. An extremely diverse segment of society, "peasants" ranged from slaves to free persons of some means. Except in frontier zones, where victims were available and religious scruples diminished, slaves declined dramatically in numbers during the tenth and eleventh centuries (as illustrated by the shift in meaning of the classical Latin *servus* from "slave" to "serf"). Serfs, persons bound to the soil, constituted the majority of the peasants, although their legal and social statuses differed considerably from place to place. In the twelfth century serfdom was disappearing in France even as its terms were hardening in central and eastern Europe. Serfdom was a mixture of economic, legal, and personal statuses. The serf could be flogged in public, could be set upon by dogs, was excluded from many judicial proceedings, required approval to contract a marriage, and was denied the right to bear arms.

The tenth and eleventh centuries were decisive in the reshaping of rural society. As lordships of all kinds and sizes formed in the countryside, they drew communities of people. Castles were critical. Powerful men generally sited their castles in close proximity to wood, water, and iron. Sometimes a monastery, rural church, or graveyard also attracted a castle or else grew up near one and helped to anchor a site. (See the feature "The Visual Record: The Medieval Castle" on pages 264–265 in Chapter 9.) People from a fairly wide area settled in the vicinity of the castle. Many, originally free, commended themselves to the local lord by handing over their properties and receiving them back in return for rents or personal services. Other people fell into dependent status through military or economic misfortune. What eventually emerged was the manor, an institution best described as a powerful lord controlling the lives of an often large number of dependents. He required payments and services from them and regulated their ordinary disputes. His control was simultaneously public and private.

A minor castellan, or lord of a castle, might control only a small manor and would probably be the vassal of a great lord. A powerful landed lord, on the other hand, would generally control many manors and would often give some of them to retainers as fiefs. In other words, the reorganization of the countryside affected the nobility and the peasantry and created parallel sets of vertical bonds of association: feudal lords and vassals entered into political bonds; lords and peasants entered into economic bonds.

The structure of individual manors, and the dues owed by peasants, varied tremendously across Europe. Certain trends were fairly consistent, however. As the economy expanded, as trade brought more and different products into Europe, and as a more consciously aristocratic lifestyle spread, the nobility began to want disposable cash. Thus in many places corvées (KOR-vay) (labor services) were commuted into cash payments. Peasants were required to pay rent from their own holdings instead of working on the lord's lands. But lords still needed provisions, so they sometimes split peasant payments into cash and kind. Old forms of service could be wholly retained, involving many days per year of work on the lord's demesne, the portion of the manor the lord reserved for his own benefit. In such cases the lord could still extract money from his peasants by requiring them to use his mill and oven and then charging them gristing and kilning fees.

The trend everywhere, however, was for labor services to diminish. In one region in northern France, twelfth-century peasants owed only three corvées of two days each per year for harvesting and haymaking. Elsewhere, peasants might still be required to haul crops to market or to keep roads, bridges, and buildings in repair. On many estates where the menfolk had been largely freed from corvées, the women might still have to work in the lord's house washing laundry, sewing, plucking fowl, cooking, minding dogs, and tending to other household chores.

In the expanding economy of the eleventh and twelfth centuries, the peasants grew more prosperous, and their lords constantly sought new ways to extract the fruits of that prosperity. Peasants thus began to band together to demand that "customs" be observed. These customs were more or less formal agreements spelling out the terms under which work and fees would be arranged. In general life improved for the peasants in terms of both legal status and living conditions.

The European village was a key product of the tenth and eleventh centuries. People who originally gathered together around a castle for security and livelihood began to form a durable human community. Their church and graveyard helped to reinforce the community by tying together the living and the dead and by giving the village a sense of memory and continuity. Peasants generally worked only 250 to 270 days per year, so they had a good deal of time for festivals and celebrations. Births, baptisms, betrothals, and deaths provided opportunities for the community to come together and affirm its mutual ties. Market days and sessions of the lord's court also assembled the village. Villagers needed to cooperate in many of the operations of daily life. They shared tools, plow teams, and wagons. They performed their corvées together. The peasants experienced much less social differentiation than the nobility, and so less tension.

The status of women in peasant society tended to be, in legal theory and in daily reality, the same as that of men at a time when the status of aristocratic women was fragile. Marriage contracts from northern Italy show that brides often entered marriages with a complement of valuable tools. This suggests that peasant women retained some control over their own personal property and also reminds us that the huge gains in rural productivity were almost certainly attributable in part to the work and ingenuity of women.

THOSE LEFT OUT: TOWNSPEOPLE AND JEWS

The three-part model excluded two important groups of people. The first neglected group consisted of the increasingly numerous citizens of Europe's growing towns. Obviously people in towns worked, but the prejudices of the aristocracy were rural, so the only "workers" deemed necessary to the smooth functioning of the social order were farmers. In the second group were Europe's principal religious minority, the Jews. Jews could be found almost everywhere, although they constituted only about 1 percent of the population as a whole and, outside of Rome and parts of Spain, formed no single community numbering more than 1,500 to 2,000.

The central factor in the growth of towns was the rise in the productivity and profitability of medieval agriculture. For the first time in history a regular and substantial farm surplus could support an urban population that did not produce its own food. Increased local exchange, coupled with the relentless growth of a money economy, meant there were fortunes to be made and cash to be spent. Some of that cash was spent on luxury and exotic products that increasingly became the objects of far-flung commercial networks. A good part of the cash was spent by rural nobles, who earned it from rents, booty, and the profits of the private exercise of public power. When those nobles moved into towns, they created opportunities for merchants, craftsmen, day laborers, domestic servants, and professional people such as notaries and lawyers. This was particularly true in Europe's most heavily urbanized regions: Flanders, southern France, and northern Italy. The key point is that the growth of the medieval city and of its human community began in the medieval countryside.

Town society was hierarchical, but its structures were new, ill-defined, and flexible. Rich men built up bands of followers who supported them in urban politics, protected their neighborhoods, and occasionally raided the houses of their enemies in the next neighborhood. Relatives, friends, neighbors, people from a common rural district, or those engaged in similar trades tended to worship together in particular churches, observe certain festivals, and look after one another's families.

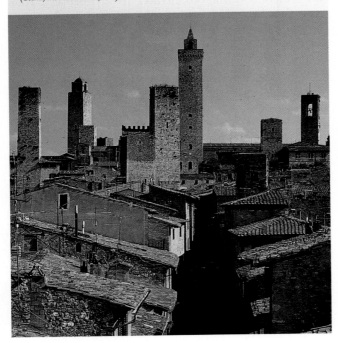

San Gimignano

The towers of this Tuscan city reveal the concentrated and competitive nature of power in the Italian communes. Most of these towers date from around 1300.

(Scala/Art Resource, NY)

In the rapidly changing world of the tenth and eleventh centuries, towns provided numerous opportunities for women. In urban industries such as cloth-making, tanning, laundering, and brewing, women sometimes managed and even owned enterprises. Apart, perhaps, from finance and the law, distinctions between male and female roles were not as sharp in towns as in rural areas.

If urban men and all women stood in an ambiguous relationship to the ideals of the male, rural, aristocratic elite, we can hardly imagine what it must have been like for Jews. Jewish communities had existed in most European towns since antiquity. Then, because the Byzantine and Islamic worlds vacillated between persecution and toleration, many Jews migrated to western Europe, with the largest numbers settling in northern France and the German Rhineland. The Jewish community in England formed only around 1100. Paris had northern Europe's largest Jewish community, perhaps two thousand people in the twelfth century. Many cities had Jewish populations numbering two hundred to three hundred, but groups of forty to fifty were common. Although some Jews in Italy, Spain, and Germany owned farms and vineyards, most Jews settled in cities, where they could live and worship in community with other Jews. Urban clusters also provided strength in numbers for people who could at any moment fall victim to persecution and whose power was not based on landholding.

Three of the most important developments in high medieval Europe were disastrous for Jews. First, the growth of the European economy, with its attendant urban and commercial expansion, brought countless Christians into the practice of trade, an occupation dominated by Jews since Late Antiquity. As Jews were excluded from commercial opportunities, they were more and more confined to moneylending. Jews had been moneylenders before the economic surge of the High Middle Ages, but the expanding economy made financial operations more widespread than ever before. Given that, as we saw in Chapter 9, Christian moralists considered handling money to be the Devil's work, the visibility of Jews as moneylenders brought them much criticism, although they were never alone in this practice.

The second phenomenon that adversely affected Jews was the reform of the church. With so much attention being paid to the proper Christian life and the correct organization of the church, it was inevitable that more attention would be directed to the one prominent group in Western society that was not Christian.

Third, the Crusades unleashed vicious attacks on Jews. As crusading armies headed east in 1096, they visited unspeakable massacres on the Jewish communities of several German towns. This awful process was repeated on the eve of the Second Crusade in 1146–1147 and again just before the third in 1189. Popular frenzy identified the Jews as Christ-killers and equated them with Muslims as the enemies of Christianity. In fact, and despite grotesque and groundless stories about Jews kidnapping and ritually killing Christian children, Jews everywhere wished to live in peace with their Christian neighbors and to be left alone to observe their distinctive religious, dietary, and social customs.

The Jews were not without sympathetic champions, however. From the time of Gregory I (r. 590–604), the papacy urged peaceful coexistence and prayers for Jewish conversion. In the twelfth and thirteenth centuries popes forcefully reminded Christians that while converting Jews was highly desirable, Jews were to be tolerated and left in peace. The Carolingians protected the Jews, and some kings in succeeding centuries repeated or even expanded upon Carolingian legislation. Spanish Jews were taken under royal protection in reconquered areas in 1053, and Henry IV took German Jews under his protection in 1084. In England and France Jews enjoyed royal protection until the late twelfth century. Jews frequently served as royal advisers in Spain and were often entrusted with sensitive diplomatic missions elsewhere.

Despite such policies, Jews were vulnerable to attack at almost any time from people who simply disliked them or who owed them money. In 1181 Philip II of France, always on the lookout for income, had his henchmen arrest Jews and confiscate their possessions. In 1182 he expelled them from the royal demesne. Across the thirteenth century French kings accorded the Jews less and less protection and often abused them financially. In 1306 Philip IV expelled the Jews from France after confiscating their goods. In England the story is much the same. The ever-needy Henry II laid crushing taxes on the Jews in 1171. In 1189 in London and in 1190 in York, massive riots stirred by false ru-

mors raged against the Jewish populations. In 1290 Edward I seized Jewish possessions and expelled Jews from the country. Royal protection of German Jews was reasonably effective until the death of Frederick II in 1250, after which time local princes often repudiated debts to Jewish lenders and appropriated Jewish property.

Online Study Center **Improve Your Grade**
Primary Source: Philip Augustus Expels French Jews

═══════════════ S E C T I O N   S U M M A R Y ═══════════════

- Among the elite, society was divided into "those who pray," "those who fight," and "those who work."

- Constant waves of monastic reform modeled good spiritual behavior.

- Warrior-nobles were the governing class, marked by chivalry, their distinctive ethos.

- Peasants did much of the "work" in medieval society and generally found their lives improving.

- Townspeople enjoyed expanding opportunities but always suffered under the prejudices of landholding elites.

- In religious life, urban occupations, and rural pursuits, women experienced some improvements in their conditions of life.

- The condition of Europe's Jews grew progressively dangerous.

SOCIAL AND RELIGIOUS MOVEMENTS, CA. 1100–1300

Why did some spiritual movements result in heresy, while others ended in new religious orders?

Twelfth- and thirteenth-century Europe witnessed several social movements unlike any that had occurred before. Spurred by increasingly intrusive governments, economic dislocation, and spiritual turmoil, they involved large numbers of people; cut across lines of gender, wealth, status, and occupation; and appeared in many places. Most of these movements had cohesive beliefs, even ideologies, and well-determined goals. They are the first large-scale social movements in European history.

HERETICS AND DISSIDENTS

The canon lawyer Gratian (see page 297) defined *heresy* as a situation in which "each man chooses for himself the teaching he believes to be the better one"—that is, he ignores official doctrines. For Gratian and his like-minded contemporaries, faith was not an individual matter. Unity of belief was crucial in a catholic ("universal") Christian Europe. In the twelfth century, the church reacted ever more strictly to challenges to its teachings or to its exclusive right to teach. The effort by the church to define its law, theology, and bureaucratic

procedures with greater precision drew lines more sharply than ever before between what was and was not acceptable.

Heretics did not see themselves as secessionists from the true church. Quite the contrary, they saw themselves as its only representatives. Church teachings always encountered a degree of popular skepticism. Not everyone believed, for example, that Jesus was born of a virgin or that he was true God and true man. But such doubts had not previously led to mass defections. Before the middle of the twelfth century, challenges to the church came from men—as far as we can tell the ringleaders were all men—who saw themselves as inspired reformers.

Tanchelm (TANK-elm) of Antwerp preached between 1100 and 1115 in the Netherlands. He scandalized the mainstream by calling churches brothels and clerics whores. He rejected the sacraments and the payment of tithes. Although Tanchelm was radical and pugnacious, his ideas constituted a fairly coherent program of criticism. Like many others, he was concerned about the immorality and wealth of the church. But Tanchelm and his followers went even further. The heretic distributed his nail and hair clippings as relics of a sort, and in a bizarre public ceremony he "married" a statue of the Virgin Mary. Across the twelfth century church orthodoxy was challenged by others whose influence seems to have been local. What is interesting is how numerous, and similar, they all were.

Coherent movements of much larger proportions emerged later in the century. In 1173 Waldo, a rich merchant of Lyon, decided to sell all his property, give the proceeds to the poor, and embrace a life of poverty and preaching. Waldo was motivated by the same quest for the apostolic life that had animated the eremitic movement of the eleventh century. But there was a difference: he was a layman. Waldo attracted many followers (known as Waldensians), and in 1179 Pope Alexander III (r. 1159–1181) scrutinized him closely, found his beliefs to be essentially correct, and approved his vow of poverty. But the pope commanded Waldo to preach only when invited to do so by bishops. The bishops, jealous about their own power, extended no such invitations.

Waldo and his "Poor Men of Lyon" went right on preaching and in 1184 were formally declared heretics. Until this point it was not their ideas so much as their appropriation of a clerical duty, preaching, that had set the church against them. From this time on, however, the Waldensians became more radical in their attacks. In about 1204 one group of Waldensians was reconciled to the Catholic Church, but the majority, who had spread all over southern France and Italy, into Germany, and as far away as Poland, remained estranged. Waldensian communities exist to this day.

The most serious of the popular heretical movements was Catharism (from the Greek *katharos,* meaning "pure"). Because there were numerous Cathars near the southern French town of Albi, the whole movement is sometimes called "Albigensian." In fact, Cathars could be found all over Europe, although they did cluster in northern Italy and southern France. Cathars were the religious descendants of Mani (see page 171), a third-century Persian who taught an extreme dualism that featured polarities in almost all things: good-evil, love-hate, flesh-spirit. Extreme Cathars abstained from flesh in all ways: they were vegetarians and renounced sexual intercourse so as not to produce offspring— that is, more flesh. Probably radiating from Bulgaria, Cathar ideas had spread widely in the West by the 1140s. Catharism attracted many converts when Nicetas, the Cathar bishop of Constantinople, visited northern Italy and southern France between 1166 and 1176. People of every station joined the new church, which, in its own view, was the only true church.

The Catholic Church sent isolated preachers against the Cathars, but with little success. In 1198 and 1203, Pope Innocent III organized systematic preaching tours

in southern France, but these, too, lacked solid results, and in 1208 the pope's legate was murdered by a supporter of the count of Toulouse, who was sympathetic to the Cathars. The killing led to the launching of the Albigensian Crusade, a loosely structured military action that lasted into the 1260s. Although the crusade itself was largely over by the 1220s, violence against Albigensians sputtered for decades: a massacre in 1244 and inquisitorial campaigns in 1246 and again in 1256 to 1257. Isolated resisters struggled on into the fourteenth century.

Albigensians denounced the clergy of their day as rich and corrupt. These teachings attracted urban dwellers who resented the wealth and pretensions of the clergy—the same people who followed Waldo. Nobles may have been drawn to the movement because it gave them opportunities to take possession of extensive tracts of church lands, something the investiture controversy had denied them. In addition, embracing Catharism may have been a way for nobles to resist the increasing encroachment of the government of far-off Paris. The Albigensians also attracted many women. Unlike the Catholic Church, which denied clerical, preaching, and teaching offices to women, the heretical sects tended to permit women to hold leading roles.

The Albigensians, like the Waldensians, were driven by the same spiritual zeal and desire for ecclesiastical reform that moved many of their contemporaries. They differed from other would-be reformers in that they did not seek to reform the Catholic Church from within but departed from it or insisted that they alone represented it. Thus these heretical movements marked the first serious challenge to the ideology of a uniformly "catholic" Christendom since Late Antiquity.

REFORM FROM WITHIN: THE MENDICANT ORDERS

Traditional monastic orders continued to win adherents, but their interpretation of the apostolic life meant ascetic withdrawal from the world, not pastoral work and preaching. Laymen who wished both to embrace poverty and to preach fell under the suspicion of the ecclesiastical authorities. Early in the thirteenth century a new movement arose, the mendicants (literally, beggars). Mendicants were men who aimed to preach, to be poor, and to create formal but noncloistered religious orders. Though similar to the heretics in many ways, they submitted willingly to ecclesiastical authority.

The mendicant phenomenon began when **Francis of Assisi** (1181–1226), the son of a rich Italian merchant, decided to renounce the wealth and status that

Francis of Assisi An Italian layman who renounced his wealth and founded a religious order dedicated to charitable works.

were his birthright. He carried out his renunciation in a most public display before the bishop of Assisi (uh-SEE-zee) in 1206. Francis had gradually grown tired of a life of ease and luxury, but he also experienced a blinding moment of spiritual insight when, by chance, his eyes fell on the passage in the Scriptures in which Christ commanded the rich young ruler, "Go, sell all you have, and follow me." Francis stripped himself naked so that "naked he might follow the naked Christ."

For a few years Francis wandered about Italy begging for his meager sustenance, repairing churches, caring for the sick, and preaching repentance to all who would listen. By 1210 he had attracted many followers, and together they set out to see Innocent III to win approval. After considering the matter for a while, Innocent decided to approve the new order of friars (that is "brothers," from the Latin *fratres*) as long as they would accept monastic tonsure—a ritual haircut signifying submission—profess obedience to the pope, and swear obedience to Francis. The pope was genuinely won over by Francis himself, but he also sensed that by permitting the formation of the Franciscan order, he could create a legitimate and controllable repository for the explosive spiritual forces of the age.

Francis prepared a simple Rule based on his understanding of the scriptural ideals of poverty, preaching, and service. Alarmed by the vagueness of the first Rule and by the extraordinary influx of new members, the papal curia in 1223 prevailed on Francis to submit a revision that stressed order, a hierarchy of officials, and a novitiate—a regularized period of training for new members. Somewhat disappointed by this regulated formality, Francis withdrew more and more from the world and lived reclusively in the hills near Assisi.

After Francis died, the issues of property, power, education, and ordination provoked deep controversies within his order. Usually called "Franciscan," Francis's order is technically the "Friars Minor." The movement had begun among laymen, but over time more Franciscan brothers became ordained priests. Franciscans established schools in most great cities, and by the middle of the thirteenth century some of Europe's greatest intellects were Franciscans. This prominence, like the sacramental power of ordination, was a kind of wealth that Francis had wished to avoid. The real issue of wealth, however, turned on the possession of property. Francis had aimed for both personal and corporate poverty. In the 1230s papal legislation had alleviated strict poverty by permitting the order to acquire property to support its work. Nevertheless, the issue of property continued to spark controversy among the Franciscans.

Of the nine or ten mendicant orders that developed, the other major one was the Dominican, a prod-uct of very different experiences than the Franciscan. Its founder, **Dominic de Guzman** (1170–1221), was the son of a Spanish nobleman. He became a priest and later a cathedral canon. While traveling, he saw first-hand the Albigensian heresy in southern France, and in 1206 he went to Rome to seek permission to preach against the heretics. The Albigensian Crusade began in 1208, but Dominic's methods were those of persuasion, not coercion.

Albigensian criticisms of the ignorance, indifference, and personal failings of the clergy could never be applied to Dominic and his fellow preachers. Dominic and his followers were supported enthusiastically by the bishop of Toulouse, who saw how useful these zealous preachers of unblemished lives could be. In 1215 Dominic, with his bishop's assistance, attempted to form a new order, but by that time Rome had forbidden the creation of new orders for fear of heresy or uncontrollable diversity. Thus Dominic's "Order of Preachers" (the proper name for the "Dominicans") adopted the Rule of Saint Augustine, which many communities of cathedral canons had been using since the eleventh century.

In 1217 Dominic presided at the first general meeting of the order. The Dominicans decided to disperse, some going to Paris, some (including Dominic) to Rome, some to other cities in Europe. Henceforth the order saw its mission as serving the whole church. Dominican schools were set up all over Europe, and the order acquired a reputation for learning and scholarship. The Dominicans were voluntarily poor, but the order was never rent by a controversy over property as the Franciscans were. Dominic's was a vision of personal, not corporate, poverty. Likewise, as a preaching order, the Dominicans had to be learned and ordained. Franciscan misgivings on these issues did not touch them.

Both the Franciscan and Dominican orders reflected a widespread desire to emulate the apostolic life of the early church by poverty and preaching. Both submitted to legitimate authority. Francis's religious vision of charity and service was the product of a heartfelt need for repentance and renewal. This concern for the soul often caused Franciscans to serve as missionaries. Dominic set out to save the church from its enemies. He desired preachers who were sufficiently learned that they could combat the errors of heretics. Both men saw the need for exemplary lives. Francis was a more charismatic figure than Dominic, and his apostolate to the urban poor was more compelling. By 1300 Franciscan houses outnumbered Dominican by 3 to 1. The mendicants were the greatest spiritual force in high medieval Europe.

Dominic de Guzman   A Spanish nobleman who preached against Albigensian heretics and founded a religious order dedicated to preaching.

COMMUNITIES OF WOMEN

The religious forces that attracted men drew women as well. Traditional orders, however, tended to be hostile toward women. Cluniacs and Cistercians struggled to keep women out of their ranks. The wandering preachers of the twelfth century, without exception, acquired women as followers, but the usual results were either segregation of the women in cloisters or condemnation of the whole movement.

In 1212 Francis attracted the aristocrat Clare of Assisi (1194–1253), who was fleeing from an arranged marriage. She wanted to live the friars' life of poverty and preaching, and Francis wanted to assist her. Aware that the sight of women begging or preaching would be shocking, in 1215 he gave Clare and his other female followers their own rule. Clare became abbess of the first community of the "Poor Clares." Though cloistered and forbidden to preach, the Clares lived lives of exemplary austerity and attracted many adherents.

Beguines (BAY-geenz) were communities of women who lived together, devoted themselves to charitable works, but did not take vows as nuns. The Beguine movement grew from the work in Nivelles, near Liège (lee-EZHE), of Mary of Oignies (ca. 1177–1213). She was drawn to the ideals of voluntary poverty and service to others. So strong was the pull that she renounced her marriage, gave away all her goods, worked for a while in a leper colony, and thought of preaching against the Cathars. Instead, she formed a community.

Groups of Beguines appeared all over the Low Countries, western Germany, and northern France.

The Parting of Mary from the Apostles

Duccio di Buoninsegna lived from the middle of the thirteenth century to 1318 or 1319. He did his finest work in Siena, including a huge altarpiece, one of whose panels depicts the touching scene of Mary taking leave of the apostles just before her death. Note the clever way Duccio has arranged the figures and how he balances Saint Paul, standing in the doorway, with Mary, reclining on the bed. *(Scala/Art Resource, NY)*

This was the first exclusively women's movement in the history of Christianity. Beguines sometimes vowed poverty and sometimes did not. They sometimes cloistered themselves into communities and sometimes taught and served the poor and outcast. They neither challenged the officials and teachings of the church nor demanded a right to preach. As laywomen, they did not give rise to scandal as noncloistered nuns would have. They were content to have power over their own lives and communities but not seek a voice in the wider world around them.

Thirteenth-century Europe knew more female than male mystics, and female mysticism tended to focus on Jesus, especially on His presence in the Eucharist. This is the first religious devotion that can be shown to have been more common to women than to men. Most of the mystics were either nuns or Beguines. As the clergy was defining its own prerogatives more tightly, and excluding women more absolutely from the exercise of formal public power, female communities provided a different locus for women's activity.

Women who spent their lives in community with other women reveal, in their writings, none of the sense of moral and intellectual inferiority that was routinely attributed to women by men and often by women themselves. Women who were in direct spiritual communion with God acquired, as teachers, mediators, and counselors in their communities, power that they simply could not have had outside those settings.

=========== S E C T I O N S U M M A R Y ===========

- Some men and women who opposed the wealth and immorality of some clerics, and who wished to preach and teach, veered off into heresy.

- The Mendicants—Franciscans and Dominicans, chiefly—led holy lives, worked among the poor or preached against heretics, and always had the approval of the papacy.

- Several religious movements were especially popular among women and constituted the first women's movements in the history of Christianity.

LATIN CULTURE: FROM SCHOOLS TO UNIVERSITIES

What signs do you find of an expanding intellectual climate in high medieval Europe?

As in the late antique and Carolingian periods, courts and churches were the greatest patrons of artists and authors. But in this age of expansion the number and geographic spread of such patrons increased dramatically. By 1150 the church comprised 50 percent more bishoprics and about three times as many monasteries as it had in 900. In 1300 monarchies reigned in many places—Scandinavia and the Slavic world, for example—where none had existed in 900 (see **MAP 10.1**). In addition to an increase in the sheer amount of cultural activity, the years between 900 and 1300 also witnessed innovations. Logic replaced grammar at the heart of the school curriculum. Latin letters remained ascendant, but literature in many vernacular (native) languages began to appear in quantity and quality. Romanesque art and architecture were fresh and original interpretations of their Carolingian ancestors. Europe's incipient urbanization produced the first stirrings of a distinctively urban culture. In one of those cities, Paris, a new kind of academic institution emerged—the university—which was arguably the period's greatest legacy to the modern world.

THE CAROLINGIAN LEGACY

Cultural life depends on both creative geniuses and generous patrons. Political dislocation and constant attacks in the ninth and tenth centuries initially deprived schools and masters of the Carolingian patronage that they had enjoyed for a century or more. The Carolingians left firm enough foundations in a few centers for intellectual life to continue, but the scale of activity between 900 and 1050 was smaller than before. Three examples serve to capture the spirit of the age that set the stage for the High Middle Ages.

Gerbert of Aurillac (DJAIR-bear of OR-ee-ak) (940–1003) was the most distinguished intellect of his age. He left his home in Aquitaine to study in Spain and Italy before settling in Reims, in northern France, where he was a teacher and then briefly a bishop. He attracted the attention of the emperor Otto III and spent some time at the German court, earning appointments as abbot of Bobbio, bishop of Ravenna, and, finally, pope. Gerbert followed Carolingian tradition in being a collector of manuscripts and critic of texts, but he

Major battles

Boundary of the Holy Roman Empire

MAP 10.1   Europe, ca. 1230

By the early thirteenth century the European states that would exist into modern times were clearly visible, although each would continue to undergo changes. To gain a sense of the evolution of Europe, compare this map with Maps 6.1, 7.3, and 8.3.

Online Study Center **Improve Your Grade**
Interactive Map: Europe, ca. 1230

departed from older traditions in his interest in mathematics and in his study of logic—the formal rules of reasoning that, in the Western tradition, trace back over many thinkers to Aristotle (see page 86).

Fulbert of Chartres (FULL-bear of SHART), Gerbert's finest pupil, elevated the cathedral school of Chartres to the paramount place in academic Europe. Fulbert (960–1028) wrote letters in elegant Latin and composed fine poems. He carried on his master's literary interests more than his scientific ones, and well into the twelfth century Chartres remained a major center of literary studies.

Another figure of interest is the aristocratic German nun Roswitha of Gandersheim (d. 970). She wrote poems on saints and martyrs, as well as a story about a priest who sold his soul to the Devil. In her mature years, Roswitha wrote Latin plays in rhymed verse based on the Roman writer Terence. In these plays she refashioned tales from Roman and biblical history to convey moral truths.

THE STUDY OF LAW

Law was a field of major innovation. The increasing sophistication of urban life demanded a better understanding of law. The growing responsibilities of the church called for orderly rules, and the church's frequent quarrels with secular rulers demanded careful delineations of rights and responsibilities. Governments issued more laws and regulations than at any time since antiquity.

In about 1012 Burchard, the bishop of Worms, produced a collection of **canon law** that was influential for more than a century and heightened reformers' awareness of the law of the church. By midcentury scholars studying canon law in Italy and France helped to promote the papal view of reform. In Bologna, Irnerius (d. ca. 1130), a transplanted German and protégé of Emperor Henry V, began teaching Roman law from the law code of Justinian (see pages 201–204). This legal

canon law   The law of the church (as distinguished from civil law). It is based on papal decrees and the rulings of church councils.

work culminated in the publication in 1140 of the *Decretum* of the Bolognese monk Gratian (GRAY-shun). The most comprehensive and systematic book of canon law yet written, Gratian's work remained authoritative for centuries.

Throughout the twelfth century canon lawyers studied and wrote commentaries on Gratian's *Decretum*. These legists are called "decretists." Gratian had systematically collected earlier papal *decretals* (official pronouncements), but popes continued to issue them. Several collections of these new decretals were prepared in the thirteenth century, and the scholars who studied these later decrees are called "decretalists." The church thus produced a vast corpus of law and legal commentary.

Law was by no means confined to the church. England was precocious in creating a common law, a single law applied uniformly in its courts. But English law was based on the careful accumulation of legal decisions—or precedents—and not on the routine application of the provisions of a law code. There were many law codes elsewhere. Alfonso X of Castile issued the *Siete Partidas*, a comprehensive law code largely reliant on Roman law. Prince Iaroslav (d. 1054) is reputed to have issued the first version of the laws of Kievan Rus. Iaroslav's laws were written in Old Russian, but they drew heavily on the laws and legal traditions of neighboring peoples. Byzantine law was revised under the Macedonian dynasty.

GREEK, ARAB, AND JEWISH CONTRIBUTIONS

Norman and German settlement in southern Italy and Sicily, the Reconquista in Spain, the Crusades, and the creation of Italian communities in many Mediterranean cities brought European thinkers face-to-face with the intellectual traditions of Classical Greece, Islam, and medieval Judaism. Between 1100 and 1270 almost the whole corpus of Aristotle's writings, virtually unknown in the West for a millennium, became available. Arab commentaries on Aristotle, as well as Jewish philosophical and theological works, began to circulate. The presence of all these texts and currents of thought was decisive in expanding the range and raising the level of Western thought.

Prior to about 1100 only a few of Aristotle's writings, primarily some of his early writings on logic, had been available in the West. Gradually scholars recovered Aristotle's full treatment of logic, then his scientific writings, and finally his studies of ethics and politics. Aristotle's books posed a number of problems for Christian scholars. If knowledge is a good thing and good things are gifts of God, how did a pagan get so smart? Is it possible that faith is unnecessary to knowledge? What relationship exists between faith and

Muslim Scholars in a Garden

From a thirteenth-century Iraqi manuscript, this picture shows literary men in a pleasure garden. Beasts are driving a water wheel to refresh them, and a lute player accompanies their poetry with music.

(Bibliothèque nationale de France)

reason? Aristotle taught that the universe is eternal and mechanistic. His thought left no room for creation or for the continuing role of a Creator. For Christian thinkers Aristotle asked questions that demanded answers: Were the Scriptures true? Did God create the world as Genesis said? Did God continue to intervene in this world?

Between 750 and 900, mainly in Iran, a group of Arabic-speaking Christians began translating into Arabic the Greek texts of Aristotle as well as the more than fifteen thousand pages of commentary on Aristotle that had been produced between about A.D. 100 and 600. This flood of material inspired generations of Arab scholars to tackle the thought of the man often called simply "the Philosopher."

Two major Arab thinkers were particularly influenced by the vast Aristotelian corpus. Ibn-Sina (980–1037), called Avicenna (ah-vih-SENN-uh) in the West, was drawn to the fundamental problem of how to understand the relationship between objects that exist in the world and the knowledge of those objects that is formed and held in the human mind. (See the box "The Global Record: The Making of an Arab Scholar.")

Ibn Rushd (1126–1198), called Averroes (uh-VERR-oh-eese), wrote no fewer than thirty-eight commentaries on the works of Aristotle, and at least fifteen of these were translated into Latin in the thirteenth century. Among many contributions, Averroes particularly tried to clarify the relationship between truths acquired through the exercise of reason and truths that depend on divine revelation. Although his exact meaning remains controversial, his contemporaries and many later scholars understood him to teach the "double truth": Truths about the natural world are more or less accessible to everyone depending on a person's intellectual ability. Revealed truths, however, are available only to the most enlightened.

Spain and northern France were both important centers of Jewish thought. In Spain some Jewish thinkers also grappled with Aristotle. Solomon ibn Gebirol (1021–1070), called Avicebron, wrote *The Fountain of Life,* a treatise that attempted to reconcile Aristotle with the Jewish faith by finding a role for God in communicating knowledge to every human mind. The greatest of all medieval Jewish thinkers, Moses ben Maimon (1135–1204), called Maimonides (my-MON-uh-deez),

THE MAKING OF AN ARAB SCHOLAR

These excerpts from the engaging life of Avicenna (980–1037) reveal not only his remarkable intellectual attainments but also his ongoing encounter with Greek thought. Avicenna was deeply influenced by Aristotle, and, in turn, his writings influenced Jewish and Christian writers who were also coming to grips with the greatest of Greek philosophers. His writings on medicine were authoritative until the seventeenth century.

My father was from Balkh and moved from there to Bukhārā [now Turkmenistan] . . . where I was given teachers of the Quran and polite letters [literature, especially poetry]. By the time I was ten years old I had mastered the Quran and so much of polite letters as to provoke wonderment. My father decided to send me to a certain grocer who knew Indian arithmetic so that I could learn it from him. Then Abu Abdallah al-Natili, who claimed to be a philosopher, came to Bukhārā. My father lodged him in our house in the hope that I would learn something from him. Before he came I was studying jurisprudence . . . and I was one of the best pupils. Then, under the guidance of al-Natili, I began to study the *Isagogue* [a commentary on some of Aristotle's works]. Thus I learned from him the broad principles of logic, but he knew nothing of the subtleties. Then I began to read books and study commentaries on my own until I mastered logic. I also read the geometry of Euclid. Then I passed on to the *Almagest* [Ptolemy's second-century astronomical treatise]. Eventually I busied myself with the study of the [treatises] and other commentaries on physics and metaphysics [subjects treated at great length by Aristotle and by Avicenna's Arab predecessors, especially al-Farabi], and the doors of knowledge opened before me. Then I took up medicine and began to read books written on this subject. Medicine is not one of the difficult sciences, and in a very short time I undoubtedly excelled in it, so that physicians of merit studied under me. At the same time I carried on debates and controversies in jurisprudence. At this point I was sixteen years old.

I resumed the study of logic and all parts of philosophy. During this time I never slept a whole night through and I did nothing but study all day long. Whenever I was puzzled by a problem . . . I would go to the mosque, pray, and ask the Creator of All to reveal to me that which was hidden from me and to make easy for me that which was difficult. Then at night I would return home, put a lamp in front of me, and set to work reading and writing.

I returned to the study of divine science. I read the book called *Metaphysics* [by Aristotle], but could not understand it, the aim of its author remaining obscure for me. I read the book forty times, until I knew it by heart, but I still could not understand its meaning or its purpose. Then one afternoon I happened to be in the market of the booksellers, and a crier was holding a volume in his hand and shouting the price. I bought it and found that it was Abu'l Nasr al-Farabi's book explaining the meaning of the *Metaphysics*. I returned to my house and made haste to read it. Immediately the purposes of this book became clear to me because I already knew it by heart. I was very happy at this, and the next day I gave much alms to the poor in thanksgiving to Almighty God.

In my neighborhood there lived a man who asked me to write him an encyclopedic work on all the sciences. I compiled the *Majmū* for him and named it after him. In it I dealt with all sciences other than mathematics. I was then twenty-one years old.

QUESTIONS

1. In what academic subjects was Avicenna particularly interested?

2. In what ways was Avicenna's education like and unlike that received by students in Europe?

3. How did faith and reason play complementary roles in Avicenna's education?

Source: Bernard Lewis, ed., *Islam: From the Prophet Muhammad to the Capture of Constantinople*, vol. 2 (New York: Harper and Row, 1974), pp. 177–181.

wrote *A Guide for the Perplexed*. The perplexed he had in mind were those who had trouble reconciling the seemingly opposed claims of reason and faith. Maimonides taught a doctrine very close to Averroes's double truth.

Solomon ben Isaac (1040–1105), called Rashi, was educated in Jewish schools in the Rhineland and then set up his own school in Troyes (TWAH). He became the most learned biblical and Talmudic scholar of his time, indeed one of the wisest ever. The Talmud was a detailed and erudite commentary on the scriptural studies of the ancient rabbis. It existed in two collections made in the fifth century, one in Palestine and one in Babylon. Later in the twelfth century Rashi's grandsons carried on his work and earned great fame on their own. Christian scholars who wished to know the exact meaning of passages in the Bible sometimes consulted them.

From Persia to Spain to France, then, countless thinkers were engaged in serious reflection on the mechanics of knowing, the nature of reality, the relationship between reason and faith, and the meaning and significance of revelation. In the years just around 1100 Latin Christian scholars began to encounter this torrent of thought and writing.

THE DEVELOPMENT OF WESTERN THEOLOGY

Carolingian schools had focused on grammar—that is, on the basic foundations of language. Gradually logic supplanted grammar at the center of both intellectual interests and school curricula. Problems inside Europe initiated this shift, but soon the external influences we just described increased its scope. Eventually the wider application of logic produced a new intellectual style and also evoked bitter criticisms.

Berengar (ca. 1000–1088), master of the school of Tours, wrote a treatise that denied Christ's presence in the Eucharist—the Communion bread and wine received by Catholics and Orthodox Christians in the celebration of the mass. This position was heretical. Ordinarily churchmen would have refuted Berengar simply by quoting various passages from the Scriptures or from the writings of the Church Fathers, along with conciliar pronouncements about the consecrated elements. The evidence, however, was ambiguous. Berengar's claim was finally proved false, at least to the satisfaction of his opponents, by Lanfranc, archbishop of Canterbury during the reign of William the Conqueror. Lanfranc used Aristotelian logical argumentation to dispose of Berengar's heretical arguments.

Anselm (ca. 1033–1109), Lanfranc's successor as archbishop of Canterbury, developed an ingenious logical proof for the existence of God. The French theologian and philosopher Peter Abelard (1079–1142) used logic to reconcile apparent contradictions in the Scriptures and in the writings of the Church Fathers. We must not suppose that Anselm and Abelard were skeptics. Anselm's motto was "Faith seeking understanding." For him logic was the servant of divine truth. He would have agreed completely with Abelard's assessment that "faith has no merit with God when it is not the testimony of divine truth that leads us to it, but the evidence of human reason."

For conservatives such as **Bernard of Clairvaux** (see page 285) and **Hildegard of Bingen** (1098–1179), however, faith and immediate divine inspiration were

primary. To them logical approaches to divine truth were the height of arrogance. Hildegard—well educated, musically gifted, and knowledgeable in medical matters—was perhaps the most profound psychological thinker of her age. More than anyone before her, Hildegard opened up for discussion the feminine aspects of divinity. She, like Bernard, believed that God was to be found deep within the human spirit, not in books full of academic wrangling.

The future lay with Anselm and Abelard, however. Anselm was the most gifted Christian thinker since Augustine. He wrote distinguished works on logic, and his theological treatise *Why God Became Man* (ca. 1100) served for three hundred years as the definitive philosophical and theological explanation of the incarnation of Christ, the central mystery of the Christian faith.

Peter Abelard was a more colorful figure. He argued rudely and violently with all his teachers, though in the end he was probably more intelligent than any of them. He rose to a keener understanding of Aristotle than anyone in centuries, and he developed a sharper sense of both the power and the limitations of language than anyone since the Greeks. He concerned himself with ethics, too, and was one of the first writers to see intention as more important than simple action.

Abelard seduced and then secretly married Heloise, one of his pupils and the daughter of an influential Paris churchman. Heloise's relatives castrated Abelard for his refusal to live openly with his wife. Abelard then arranged for Heloise to enter a convent, and he joined a monastic community, where he continued writing and teaching. The two carried on a voluminous correspondence that reveals Heloise as a first-rate philosophical thinker and one of her age's most knowledgeable connoisseurs of Classical literature. Some of Abelard's more imaginative ideas earned him formal ecclesiastical condemnations in 1121 and 1140. He popularized the schools of Paris, however, and attracted to them promising scholars from all over Europe.

Abelard and several of his contemporaries engaged in one of the first widespread intellectual debates in Western history, the quarrel over "universals." *Universal* is the philosophical name for a concept that applies to more than one seemingly related object. The dispute over universals went to the heart of people's understanding of reality, their sense of the limitations of human reason, and their awareness of problems of language.

To illustrate: May we agree that you are reading a book right now? May we further agree that the book you are reading is not identical to any other book on your bookshelf? And may we go one step further and agree that no book on your bookshelf is exactly like any other book on that shelf? So, why do we call all of these objects books? "Book" is here the universal that we are trying to understand.

Bernard of Clairvaux A church reformer, adviser to rulers, and conservative intellectual who opposed the wide application of logic.

Hildegard of Bingen A German Benedictine abbess and prolific author.

A medieval "realist," whose thought may be traced back to Plato, would say that there is a concept, let us call it "bookness," that exists in our minds before we ever encounter any particular object that we label a book. Just as no book is ever identical to any other, so too no specific book is a perfect representation of that concept "bookness." The concept is fully real, and all representations of it in the world are mere hints, suggestions of a more perfect reality.

A medieval "nominalist," on the contrary, would say that "book" is merely a name (*nomen* in Latin, whence nominalism) that we apply to objects that we deem to bear sufficient similarity to one another that they can be adequately captured by one name. But only each particular book is fully real.

Problems aplenty surround the quarrel over universals: Is reality purely an intellectual proposition, or is reality a quality of existence in the world? How does the mind acquire knowledge of the universal? How does the mind know to which objects to apply the universal? What specific differences exist between objects to which the same name is applied?

With the emergence of the problem of universals, we enter fully into a new intellectual approach that has long been called "Scholasticism." This word has come to have many different meanings, but at the most basic level it describes a movement that attempted to show that Christian theology is inherently rational, that faith and reason need not be contradictory or antithetical. Scholasticism also implies a certain systematization of thought. Gratian's attempt to organize all of canon law rationally and systematically was a Scholastic exercise. Twelfth-century biblical scholars tried to produce a single, systematic commentary on the Bible. In 1160 Peter Lombard produced the *Four Books of Sentences,* a comprehensive treatment of all of Christian theology.

Thomas Aquinas (1225–1274) was the greatest of the Scholastics, the most sensitive to Greek and Arab thought, and the most prolific medieval philosopher. A Dominican friar, Thomas was educated at Naples, Cologne, and Paris. Apart from brief service at the papal court, he spent the years after 1252 teaching and writing in Paris. His two most famous works are the *Summa Contra Gentiles* and the *Summa Theologiae.* A *summa* is an encyclopedic compendium of carefully arrayed knowledge on a particular subject. One might think of Gratian's and Peter Lombard's works as precursors to the great summas of the thirteenth century. Thomas's first summa addresses natural truth—that is, the kinds of things that any person can know through the operation of reason. His second summa is a summation of the revealed truths of the Christian faith.

Thomas Aquinas A Dominican theologian and the greatest of the Scholastics.

summa A compendium of knowledge within a particular field.

Online Study Center **Improve Your Grade**
Primary Source: Summa Theologiae: On Dispensing the Eucharist

Thomas's works are distinctive for two reasons. First, no one before him had so rigorously followed the dialectical method of reasoning through a whole field of knowledge, not just a particular problem. For thousands of pages Thomas poses a question, suggests answers, confronts the answers with objections, refutes the objections, and then draws a conclusion. Then he repeats the process. Second, Thomas carefully distinguishes between two kinds of truths. On the one hand are *natural truths,* truths (even theological ones) that anyone can know (or so Thomas thought)—for example, that God exists. On the other hand are *revealed truths,* truths that can be known (if not understood) only through faith in God's revelation—for example, the Trinity or the incarnation of Christ. Thomas maintains that natural and revealed truths simply cannot contradict one another because God is ultimately the source of both. If a natural truth—for example, Aristotle's contention that the world is eternal—appears to contradict a revealed truth, the natural truth is wrong. Thomas was accused by some contemporaries of applying reason too widely, and after his death some of his ideas were condemned by the church. But he actually steered a middle path between intellectual extremes. In this respect Thomas was like Maimonides and Averroes.

THE UNIVERSITY

In the early decades of the twelfth century students gathered wherever famous teachers might be found. Such teachers—figures like Peter Abelard—clustered in a few centers, and the students congregated there as well. The last decades of the twelfth century saw a swarm of masters and students in Paris. Like members of secular guilds (see page 251), the masters organized. The University of Paris was the result of their efforts. By 1300 universities had formed elsewhere in France, as well as in Italy, England, and western Germany.

Several forces drove masters to organize. They wanted to negotiate with the bishop's chancellor, the traditional head of all schools in an episcopal city. They wanted to regulate the curriculum that students followed and to prescribe the requirements for entry into their own ranks. They also desired to set the fees to be charged for instruction. By 1209 the bishop of Paris, the pope, and the king of France had granted formal recognition to the university.

In Bologna the university developed a little differently. Here the students came primarily to study law, after already acquiring a basic education. These law students were usually older and more affluent than students elsewhere, and foreign to Bologna. Consequently,

THE WRITTEN RECORD

WOMEN AND MEDICINE IN TWELFTH-CENTURY SALERNO

Late in the twelfth century an anonymous author compiled three lengthy medical texts into one that came to be called the "Trotula." The second of these treatises, "On the Cures of Women," was almost certainly written by a woman named Trota. For centuries scholars argued that a woman could not have written the widely disseminated Trotula because women could neither study nor teach in the Salerno schools. Absolutely nothing is known about Trota herself, but her text presents an intriguing question: How was she able to acquire vast learning in the Greek, Arab, and Persian medical traditions? Perhaps Trota "practiced" medicine. Whatever the case, most of her text involves either physical appearance or problems connected with menstruation and childbirth. Trota's treatise put her ahead of her time, but just maybe there were other women like her, concealed by ignorance and prejudice.

There are some women who, when they come to their time of menstruation, have either no or very few menses. For these, we proceed thus. Take root of the red willow with which large wine jars are tied and clean them well of the exterior bark, and, having pulverized them, mix them with wine or water and cook them, and in the morning give them in a potion when it has become lukewarm.

To those giving birth with difficulty we give aid in this manner. We should prepare a bath and we put the woman in it, and after she leaves let there be a fumigation of spikenard and similar aromatic substances. For strengthening and for opening the birth canal, let there be sternutatives [substances that induce sneezing] of white hellebore well ground into a powder. For just as Copho [a twelfth-century Salerno medical teacher] says, the organs are shaken and the uterus ruptures and thus the fetus is brought out and comes out.

For making the face red, take root of red and white bryony and clean it and chop it finely and dry it. Afterward, powder it and mix it with rose water, and with cotton or a very fine cloth we anoint the face and it induces redness. For the woman having a naturally white complexion, we make a red color if she lacks redness, so that with a kind of fake or cloaked whiteness a red color will appear as if it were natural.

For freckles of the face which appear by accident, take root of bistort and reduce it to powder, and cuttlefish bones and frankincense, and from all these things make a powder. And mix with a little water and smear it, rubbing, on the (face) in the morning . . . until you have removed the freckles.

An ointment for whitening the face. Take two ounces of the very best white lead, let them be ground; afterward let them be sifted through a cloth, and that which remains in the cloth, let it be thrown out. Let it be mixed in with rainwater and let it cook until the consumption of the water, which can be recognized when we see it almost completely dried out. Then let it be cooled. And when it is dried out and cooled, let rose water be added, and again boil it until it becomes hard and thick, so that from it very small pills can be formed. And when you wish to be anointed, take one pill and liquefy it in the hand with water and then rub it well on the face, so that the face will be dried. Then let it be washed with pure water, and this will last for eight days.

QUESTIONS

1. Does it make sense that a medical treatise by a woman would emphasize issues of particular concern to women?

2. Why do you suppose that scholars long refused to believe that a woman could have written this book?

3. Do you detect in Trota's writing evidence of experimental, empirical science?

Source: Monica H. Green, ed. and trans., *The Trotula: A Medieval Compendium of Women's Medicine* (Philadelphia: University of Pennsylvania Press, 2001), pp. 117–119, 139, 141, 163. Reprinted by permission of the University of Pennsylvania Press.

---

in Bologna the university arose from a guild of students who united to set standards in fees and studies and to protect themselves against unscrupulous masters.

Universities were known for certain specializations: Paris for arts and theology, Bologna for law, Salerno in Italy and Montpellier in France for medicine, Oxford for mathematical and scientific subjects. Still, the basic course of study was similar. At Paris a young scholar came to the city, found lodgings where he could, and attempted to find a master who would guide him through the arts curriculum. These boys might be in their early teens or several years older, depending on their earlier education and financial resources. The arts course, which was the prerequisite to all higher faculties, usually lasted from four to six years. The bachelor's degree was a license to teach, but a bachelor who wished to teach in a university needed to go on for a master's degree. The master's degree required at least eight years of study (including the baccalaureate years), which culminated in a public oral examination. Some masters went on to become doctors in theology, law, or medicine. A doctorate required ten to fifteen years of study. Medieval academicians were immensely learned.

Student life was difficult. In many ways students were always foreigners. Although their presence in a town enhanced its prestige, townspeople exploited them by charging exorbitant prices for food and rent. Students' own behavior was not always above reproach. There was surely some truth in the frequently lodged charge that students were noisy, quarrelsome, given to drinking, and excessively fond of prostitutes. England's Oxford and Cambridge were unique in always providing residential colleges for students; Paris got one later, and the mendicants often established houses of study. Typically, though, students were on their own.

Students had to work very hard. The arts curriculum demanded a thorough acquaintance with all the famous texts of grammar, logic, and rhetoric. Higher studies added more Aristotle, particularly his philosophical writings. In theology the students had to master the Scriptures, the principal biblical commentaries from patristic times to the present, and the *Four Books of Sentences.* In medicine the ancient writings of Galen and Hippocrates were supplemented by Arab texts as well as by observation and experimentation.

The basic method of teaching provides yet another definition of Scholasticism—that is, the method of studying in the schools. The teacher started by reciting a short piece of a set text, carried on with the presentation and discussion of many authoritative commentaries on that text, and concluded with his own explanations. The teacher then presented another passage of the set text and repeated the whole process. This education focused on standard books and accepted opinions and required students to remember large amounts of material. The curriculum nevertheless produced thinkers of prodigious originality.

In principle, universities were open to free men, but in practice they were restricted to those who had the means to attend them. Women were not accepted at universities, either as students or as teachers. It was generally thought, by men, that learning made women insubordinate. Lacking the required education, women were denied entry into the learned professions of theology, law, and medicine, despite the fact that many rural and some urban medical practitioners were women. Nevertheless, women commonly possessed and transmitted knowledge of both folk remedies and scientific medicine. Trota of Salerno, who probably lived in the twelfth century, wrote a knowledgeable treatise, *On the Care of Women.* (See the box "The Written Record: Women and Medicine in Twelfth-Century Salerno.") Documents from medieval Naples record the names of twenty-four women surgeons between 1273 and 1410. How these women were educated is utterly unknown.

===== S E C T I O N   S U M M A R Y =====

- Latin studies in literature, law, theology, and philosophy remained important.

- Europe's expansion brought scholars into increasing contact with ancient Greek, Jewish, and Arab thought.

- The increasing prominence of logic drove theology and philosophy to the center of the curriculum and led to the production of majestic summas.

- Formed as guilds of either masters or students, universities were among the most original and durable medieval achievements.

THE VERNACULAR ACHIEVEMENT

What were the hallmarks of vernacular culture?

A major achievement of high medieval civilization, from Iceland to Kievan Rus, was the appearance of rich literatures in native tongues. Vernacular, from the Latin *vernaculus,* meaning "home-born" or "domestic," is the name for the languages other than Latin—say, English or French. Although Latin remained the language of the clerical elite, writers of vernacular prose and poetry produced some of the greatest works in Western literature.

LITERATURES AND LANGUAGES

The number of people who could speak, read, or write Latin was always a minority in western Europe, just as native Greek-speakers were a minority in Byzantium. As Latin, beginning in Late Antiquity, slowly evolved into the Romance (from Roman) languages, people who used what eventually became French, Italian, and Spanish had some advantages over the people in Celtic,

Germanic, or Slavic lands, where the languages bore no obvious relationship to Latin. Persons who spoke Old French in their towns and villages would have had an easier time learning Latin than people who spoke Irish or Polish. Nevertheless, vernacular literatures began to appear at roughly the same time all over Europe, between about 800 and 1000.

Of course, many writers continued to use Latin for several centuries. University scholars continued to compose their learned treatises in the ancient tongue, but now often in a style that was less ornate than before. Most law books and public documents were still in Latin, but in a "vulgar" Latin that was reasonably close to the vernacular in areas where Romance languages were spoken. Technical manuals—on farming and animal husbandry, on warfare and armaments, or on law and government—were prepared in Latin, too, but again in a style that was far more accessible than that of their ancient models. Popular literature—poetry, history and biography, and romance and adventure—was still often written in Latin. Some of this material was serious, but some breathed a light and carefree spirit. The anonymous German known as the Archpoet (d. 1165) wrote poems about drinking and womanizing. These lines are typical of his work:

> *In the public house to die*
> *Is my resolution;*
> *Let wine to my lips be nigh*
> *At life's dissolution:*
> *That will make the angels cry,*
> *With glad elocution*
> *"Grant this drunkard, God on high,*
> *Grace and Absolution!"*[1]

No less insouciant were the authors of biting satires such as the anonymous *The Gospel According to the Silver Marks*, which parodies the wealth and greed of the papal curia. But after 1200 this fresh spirit was largely confined to writings in the vernacular. For after that year Latin was rarely used as the language for serious, original literary compositions.

The literary masterpieces of the High Middle Ages are almost entirely written in vernacular languages. The epic poem *Beowulf* is the first classic of English literature. We do not know who wrote it or when it was written. Scholars formerly assigned it to the eighth century, but they now usually place it later, in the ninth or possibly the tenth century. The story focuses on three great battles fought by the hero, Beowulf. The first two are against the monster Grendel and Grendel's mother, who have been harrying the kingdom of an old ally of Beowulf's family; the third is against a dragon. *Beowulf* is a poem of adventure and heroism, of loyalty and treachery. It treats lordship, friendship, and kinship. Themes of good and evil resound throughout. The poem is barely Christian but nevertheless deeply moral.

It speaks, in a mature, vigorous, and moving language, to and for the heart of a warrior society.

Beowulf is the best-known Anglo-Saxon work but by no means the only one. Several volumes of elegiac and lyric poetry, mostly on religious themes, also survive. And Anglo-Saxon writers produced chronicles, legal materials and charters, and at least one large collection of homilies.

Some fragments of poetry in Old French survive from the ninth century, but the great *chansons de geste* ("songs of deeds," or celebrations of the great) appeared in the eleventh century. Undoubtedly they were transmitted orally for a long time before they were written down. The best is the *Song of Roland*, written around 1100. In 778 as Charlemagne's army was returning from Spain, Basques raided the baggage train and killed Count Roland. By 1100 this obscure event, long kept alive in oral traditions, had been transformed into a heroic struggle between Charlemagne and his retinue and an army of countless thousands of "paynim," who are crude caricatures of Muslims.

Like *Beowulf*, the *Song of Roland* is a story about loyalty and treachery, bravery in the face of insuperable odds, and the kindness and generosity of leaders. Both take us into a man's chivalric world, where females are all but absent. The two works do not show us personal hopes, fears, or motivations. What pours forth is the communal ethos and the dominant values of the elite, male social group. Although *Beowulf* is lightly clothed in Christianity, the *Song of Roland* is thickly vested in the faith.

The heroic epic tradition that *Beowulf* and the *Song of Roland* represent did not disappear as the Middle Ages unfolded, but literary energies were applied in new directions. Southern France, in the middle and late twelfth century, added something new to Western literature: the love lyrics of the troubadours. This poetry, composed by both men and women, profoundly influenced an age and created the literary movement that has long been called "courtly love." **Chivalry** was initially a code for men interacting with other men. In the world of courtly love, chivalry became an elaborate set of rules governing relations between men and women.

Courtly love had several sources. The classical poet Ovid (43 B.C.–A.D. 17?), who wrote *The Art of Love*, a manual of seduction, was one. Another was the lyrical poetry of Muslim Spain. Ironically, feudal values such as loyalty and service played a critical role as men became, in effect, love vassals. Platonic ideas made some contribution, too, particularly the notion that any love in this world could be only a pale imitation of real love. The courtly poets sang of *fin' amours*, a pure love in contrast

chivalry Beginning as the dominant ethos of the warrior-nobility, it changed into rules governing relations between men and women.

to the mere lust of the masses. A lover cherished an unattainable lady. He would do anything for the merest display of pleasure or gratitude on her part, as we see in these lines from Bernart de Ventadorn, court poet of the counts of Toulouse in the late twelfth century:

> *Down there, around Ventadorn, all my friends*
> *have lost me, because my lady does not love me;*
> *and so, it is right that I never go back there again,*
> *because always she is wild and morose with me.*
> *Now here is why the face she shows me is gloomy*
>   *and full of anger:*
> *because my pleasure is in loving her and I have*
>   *settled down to it.*
> *She is resentful and complains for no other reason.*[2]

Male troubadours placed women on pedestals and, in ballads, worshiped them from afar. Women troubadours took a different line. Women's poems were more realistic, human, and emotionally satisfying. Castellozza (KAHS-teh-lohtz-eh) (b. ca. 1200), the southern French wife of a Crusader, idealized not at all when she wrote these lines:

> *Friend, if you had shown consideration,*
> *meekness, candor and humanity,*
> *I'd have loved you without hesitation,*
> *but you were mean and sly and villainous.*

And she did not assign the active role exclusively to the man:

> *Handsome friend, as a lover true*
> *I loved you, for you pleased me,*
> *But now I see I was a fool,*
> *for I've barely seen you since.*[3]

Count William IX of Poitou (1071–1127) was among the first of the troubadours, and his daughter, Eleanor of Aquitaine, brought the conventions of this poetry and point of view to the French and Angevin courts. She and her daughters were the greatest literary patrons of the late twelfth century. The wives of kings and nobles who were frequently away from home maintained stunning courts and cultivated vernacular literature.

The courtly literature of northern France owed much to the troubadour tradition of the south but broke new ground in both forms and content. The romance and the lay were the chief new forms. Both drew on Classical literature, the heroic Germanic past, and the Arthurian legends of the Celtic world to create stories of love and adventure. The romance usually develops a complex narrative involving several major characters over a long time. The lay is brief and focuses on a single incident. The most famous twelfth-century writer of romance was Chrétien de Troyes (1135–1183), the court writer of Marie of Champagne, the daughter of Eleanor of Aquitaine. The greatest writer of lays was Marie de France, who wrote at the Angevin court in the 1170s.

The romances and lays explore the contradictions and tensions in a variety of human relationships. Loyalty and honor make frequent appearances. Lancelot, a paragon of knightly virtue, desperately loves his lord Arthur's wife, Guinevere. What is he to do? How can he be loyal to his lord, to his love, and to himself? What will he do when a single course of action brings both honor and dishonor? In the epics speeches are made to swords, to horses, or sometimes to no one in particular; the points being made are universalized. In the romances credible human beings struggle to resolve powerful and conflicting emotional and moral dilemmas.

Slavic literatures began with the missionaries Cyril and Methodius (see page 239), who developed both a language, Church Slavonic, and a script, Glagolitic. The Glagolitic script was modified into the Cyrillic, which was adopted by all the Slavic peoples who embraced Orthodoxy and remains in use today. The earliest writing in the Slavic languages was religious: biblical translations, saints' lives, and selections from the Church Fathers. Historical writings and imaginative literature, such as the *Tale of Igor*, made their appearance in Kievan Rus in the twelfth century. The latter work, a semilegendary account of Prince Igor and his many battles, is reminiscent of the *chansons de geste*.

The Scandinavians who settled Iceland produced a diverse literature. They created law books, detailed accounts of their settlements, and a mighty saga tradition. *Saga* means "things said," and it is almost certainly the case that the greatest sagas were oral tales long before they were written down between about 1150 and 1350. Sagas fall into two categories: Historical sagas blend fact and fiction to praise the deeds of the great heroes of the Viking age. Family sagas mix history and myth to relate the stories of the great families who settled Iceland.

France led the way in the production of vernacular literature, but French models did not inspire slavish imitation. This is seen most clearly in the work of the master of all vernacular writers, Dante Alighieri (DAHN-tay ah-lih-GYAIR-ee). Dante (1265–1321) began as a poet in *la dolce stil nuova*, "the sweet new style," which came from France and captivated Italians. But he moved beyond it in many ways. Dante was a man of extraordinarily wide learning and reading. He served Florence in public capacities and became an exile amid political strife. He wrote a long treatise in defense of the empire—or, really, against the secular rule of the church. But he is best known for one of the masterpieces of world literature, *The Divine Comedy*.

The secret of the *Comedy*'s success is not easy to grasp. It is a long and difficult poem, but it is also humorous, instructive, and moving. In an exquisitely beautiful Italian, Dante took the most advanced theology and philosophy of his time, the richest poetic traditions, a huge hoard of stories, many contemporary events, and a lot of common sense and wove them into an allegorical presentation of the journey of the whole human race and of the individual lives of all people.

Accompanied by the Roman poet Virgil (see page 157), Dante travels through Hell and Purgatory, commenting along the way on the condition of the people he meets. Then, because Virgil is a pagan and only Dante's true love can accompany Dante into Paradise, Beatrice, the love of Dante's youth, joins him for a visit to Heaven. The poet's central metaphor is love; the love he feels for Beatrice symbolizes the love God feels for the world. Dante canvasses humanity from the pits of Hell, which he reserved for traitors, to the summit of Paradise, where a man inspired by pure love might, despite his sinfulness, dare to look into the face of God.

Although the romances and lays were by no means the exclusive preserve of the elite, very little is known about popular literature. Two exceptions are the mystery play and women's devotional writing. Mystery plays made their first appearance in the eleventh century. The liturgy of the church, which formally re-enacted the life of Christ, was confined to the clergy. But this limitation did not prevent troupes of actors from staging, on church porches or village greens, scenes from the life of Christ in simple, direct language. By the twelfth and thirteenth centuries guilds in many towns sponsored the production of plays commemorating the Christian mysteries. Such plays served as both a form of popular entertainment and a device for teaching elementary Christian ideas. The female religious movements of the age gave rise to prose and verse works in various vernaculars. Mechtild of Magdeburg (1210–1280), a German Beguine, wrote *The Flowering Light of Divinity,* a mystical, allegorical account of the marriage between God and a spiritual woman. The vernaculars opened avenues of expression to women, who were normally denied Latin learning.

INNOVATIONS IN ARCHITECTURE

Romanesque, "in the Roman style," is a term that was coined in the nineteenth century to characterize the architecture and, to a lesser extent, the painting of the period between the waning of Carolingian art and the full emergence of **Gothic** art in the late twelfth century. Today scholars view the Romanesque style as a transition between Carolingian and Gothic.

Romanesque The name assigned to architecture "in the Roman style" that dominated the period from about 900 to 1150.

Gothic The name assigned to the architecture that emerged in twelfth-century France, spread all over Europe, and dominated construction until the fifteenth century.

At several places in Ottonian Germany, a return of political stability led to the construction of churches. Ducal dynasties and women of the imperial family were among the most generous patrons. Pride in their Carolingian inheritance and their new imperial dignity led the Germans to a distinctive architectural style marked by very thick walls, alternating piers and columns in the nave, and galleries. As this architectural style spread all over Europe in the eleventh century, it produced true Romanesque, a style that differed from Roman and Carolingian styles mainly in the greater internal height and space made possible by vaulting (see **FIGURE 10.1**). To the rectangular elegance of the classical basilica and the height of the Carolingian westworks (see page 238), Romanesque builders added a refined verticality.

Among the distinctive features of Romanesque churches were their wall paintings and frescoes, sculpture, reliquaries, pulpits, and baptisteries—in short, their exuberant decoration and ornament. Europe's growing wealth and sophistication, and the pride of the church's aristocratic patrons, are very much in evidence. Especially in the south of France, the façades of Romanesque churches provided space for sculpture. The tympanum above the doors, a space seen by all who entered, was a favored location. Large-scale sculpture made a comeback after its almost total absence in the early Middle Ages.

It is surely no coincidence that Gothic art and architecture emerged just as the West was absorbing the rediscovery of Euclid's mathematical writings and applying the intensely ordered logic of Aristotle to every-

FIGURE 10.1 The Structure of Romanesque Architecture
The basic structural element of Romanesque architecture was the barrel vault, which, when two were joined at right angles, formed a groin vault. These vaults produced great height and strength but gave buildings a massive, fortresslike appearance. *(Source: Anne Shaver-Crandell, The Middle Ages. Copyright © 1982 Cambridge University Press. Reprinted with permission of Cambridge University Press.)*

Barrel vault   Groin vault

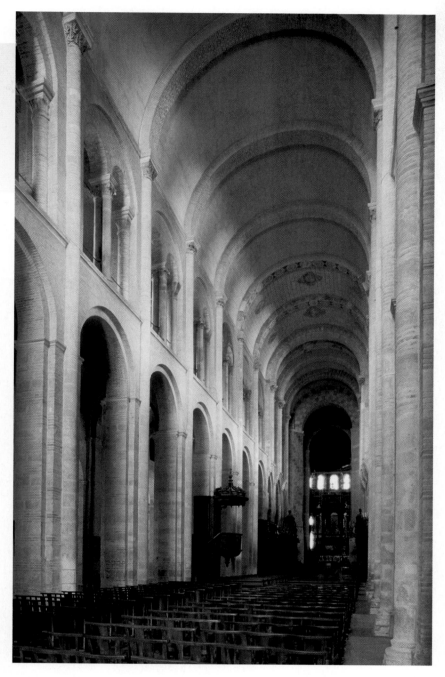

Romanesque Interior, Saint Sernin, Toulouse
The interior space of Saint Sernin is elegant, high, and well-ordered. But its typical Romanesque effect—from "barrel" vaulting—is that of a tunnel. Massive piers support the gallery and roofing above. *(Éditions Gaud)*

thing from legal problems to theological mysteries. One of the most familiar images of the Middle Ages is the inspiringly beautiful Gothic cathedral. It is thus ironic that the word *Gothic* first appeared in the sixteenth century as a term of derision for what was then regarded as an outmoded style so ugly that only the horrible conquerors of Rome, the Goths, could have been responsible for it. The name stuck, but today it simply identifies a period in European architecture, sculpture, and painting that began in the middle of the twelfth century and that in some places lasted until the early sixteenth century.

Gothic is a French invention. It was Abbot Suger (SOO-jhay) (1085–1151) of Saint-Denis, a monastery outside Paris, who, in rebuilding his basilica beginning in 1135, consciously sought a new style. He desired to achieve effects of lightness, almost weightlessness, in the stonework of his church and to admit large amounts of light to create a dazzling and mysterious aura on the inside. The Bible often uses images of light to refer to God, and Suger wished to give expression to those images in the house of God for which he was responsible.

Suger produced something startlingly original by combining a number of elements that had long been in use—three in particular: A *pointed arch* is more elegant than a round one; it also permits the joining of two arches of identical height but different widths, which, in turn, permits complex shapes and sizes (see **FIGURE 10.2**). The *ribbed vault* is lighter and more graceful than the barrel and groin vaults characteristic of Romanesque architecture; it also exerts less stress and facilitates experimentation with shapes. Finally, *point*

support—basically, the support of structural elements at only certain points—permits the replacement of heavy, stress-bearing walls with curtains of stained glass. The points of support might be massive internal piers or intricate skeletal frameworks, called *buttresses,* on the outside of the church.

These three elements—pointed arch, ribbed vault, and point support—produce a building that is characterized by verticality and translucency. Everything seems to spring upward, and stone surfaces appear so frequently punctured by light as almost to disappear altogether. The desired, and achieved, effect is one of harmony, order, and mathematical precision.

FIGURE 10.2   The Structure of Gothic Architecture

The adoption of pointed arches, an import from the Islamic world, let Gothic builders join structures of identical height but different widths (something that barrel and groin vaulting could not do; see Figure 10.1 on page 306). The resulting structures were high, light, airy, and visually interesting.   *(Source: Anne Shaver-Crandell, The Middle Ages. Copyright © 1982 Cambridge University Press. Reprinted with permission of Cambridge University Press.)*

Gothic Interior, Chartres Cathedral

Looking down the early-thirteenth-century nave of Chartres Cathedral provides an opportunity to visualize each of the major building components of Gothic architecture: pointed arch, ribbed vault, point support. The desired verticality is evident.

(Éditions Gaud)

The Gothic style soon spread in central and northern France. The Cathedral of Notre-Dame of Paris was built beginning in the 1150s. Gothic churches could be huge. The interior of Notre-Dame, for example, is 493 feet long and 107 feet high. To avoid a sense of sheer mass, Gothic builders used triple or quadruple elevations inside the buildings and took advantage of point support to pierce the walls at frequent intervals with stained glass windows. Exterior surfaces were broken up with windows, sculptures, colonnades, and towers. No opportunity was missed to create visual interest and complexity. (See the feature "The Visual Record: Stained Glass.")

The thirteenth century was the most mature period for French Gothic architecture and also the time when Gothic spread most widely throughout Europe. Its popularity may be attributed to the superiority of French masons and stonecutters and also to the tremendous prestige of French culture. By 1300 distinctive Gothic traditions shaped the urban landscape in almost all parts of Europe from Iceland to Poland.

SECTION SUMMARY

- Vernacular literature spread quickly and widely in high medieval Europe.

- Vernacular literature produced *chansons de geste*, romances, lays, sagas, and poetry.

- The High Middle Ages saw the full flowering of Romanesque architecture and then its eclipse by the Gothic style.

CHAPTER SUMMARY

Online Study Center **ACE the Test**

Into what principal social groups were the people of high medieval Europe organized?

Why did some spiritual movements result in heresy, while others ended in new religious orders?

What signs do you find of an expanding intellectual climate in high medieval Europe?

What were the hallmarks of vernacular culture?

Comparisons between the Europe of 900 and the Europe of 1300 are instructive both as reminders of what had happened and as suggestions of what was to come. In 900 Carolingian Europe was being attacked on every side. By 1300 Europe was vastly larger than in Carolingian times; not only was its geography greater, but it also had expanded in economic, political, military, and cultural terms.

At least among the elite, society was divided into "those who pray," "those who fight," and "those who work." Constant waves of monastic reform modeled good spiritual behavior, and monks thought of themselves as society's natural leaders. Bishops embraced reform, too, but as they were often nobles, their views were more flexible than those held by monks. They also saw themselves as leaders. Warrior-nobles *were* the governing class, marked by chivalry, their distinctive ethos that emphasized prowess, courage, loyalty, and generosity. Peasants did much of the "work" in medieval society and generally found the conditions of their lives improving. Townspeople enjoyed expanding opportunities but always suffered under the prejudices of landholding elites. In religious life, urban occupations, and rural pursuits, women experienced some improvements in their conditions of life but always faced legal and social prejudices. The condition of Europe's Jews grew progressively dangerous.

The High Middle Ages saw the birth of powerful religious movements. Some men and women who opposed the wealth and immorality of some clerics, and who wished to preach and teach, veered off into heresy. The Mendicants—Franciscans and Dominicans, chiefly—led holy and blameless lives, worked among the poor or

(continued on page 312)

Stained Glass

To walk into one of Europe's great churches is to enter a realm of mystery and beauty produced by the play of light—the brilliant light of the morning sun, the softer glow of the evening sun, the muted tones of a cloudy day—on thousands of square feet of colored glass. This mystery and beauty were created intentionally in Europe in the High Middle Ages. But the magnificent surviving medieval windows are not important solely for their beauty. Their images provide unique and crucial insights into religious and secular life.

Pictured here are two thirteenth-century cathedral windows. The one from Canterbury depicts that city's great bishop and martyr, Thomas Becket. A large window at Chartres depicts Saint Lubin, a sixth-century bishop of the city who was the patron saint of the town's inn and tavern keepers, and Noah, according to the Bible the first planter of grapevines. Here, in a window donated by the vintners guild, we see barrels of wine being hauled to market.

Many of Canterbury's windows represent aspects of the life of the murdered archbishop. The one pictured here shows Thomas as a bishop, not as a martyr. He is wearing a miter, the traditional headgear of a bishop. He also wears a *pallium*, a white wool band sent to a new archbishop by the pope. Becket's vestments are green, the most common liturgical color of the religious year (others were white, purple, and red). This window, then, would have served to remind people of their beloved bishop as he was in life, not martyrdom.

In Chartres wine was important to the church because of its use in mass, and it was also a staple of the local economy. Accordingly, the vintners are portrayed in twenty-three of this window's forty-one panels. By comparison, most guilds are depicted only once in the windows they donated. These windows remind us, as they reminded contemporaries, of how these magnificent buildings fitted into the daily life of their communities. Religious devotions and secular preoccupations blended in one spot.

Glass is made by heating silica, found naturally in sand, flint, and quartz, to a very high temperature and then fusing the molten silicate with a borate or phosphate often obtained from ashes produced by burning natural substances. Colored glass was made by adding metal oxides to the molten mixture. Iron oxide produced red, copper oxide produced green, and cobalt produced blue. Such glass, called "pot glass," tended to be opaque, obviously unsuitable

Canterbury, Thirteenth-Century Window: Thomas Becket *(Sonia Halliday Photographs)*

for windows. To achieve greater translucency, glassmakers made "flashed glass" by fusing at low temperatures a layer of colored liquid to the surface of a panel of clear glass. Although fine glass vessels were made in a number of places, notably in Venice and the Rhineland, the large sheets of colored glass used for church windows were commonly manufactured in Lorraine and Normandy.

To make a stained glass window, a master glazier first drew a cartoon—a sort of rough draft—on a flat board, or perhaps on a piece of parchment. He then cut pieces of colored glass into various irregular shapes according to his design. To produce facial features, folds in garments, or other details, the glazier painted the inner sides of the colored glass pieces with dark-colored paints and

Chartres, Thirteenth-Century Window: Story of
Saint Lubin   (© Clive Hicks)

then fired them at low temperatures to produce an enamel-like effect. You can see this patina on Thomas's face. Once the glazier had all his pieces cut and placed, he joined them together by means of lead strips that were H shaped. If you look closely, you can see the pieces of glass, lead stripping, and painted details in the images on these pages. The whole picture was then fitted into a metal frame and mounted in a window opening.

Documents first mention the use of glass in church windows in the sixth century. The oldest surviving fragments of stained glass date from the ninth century, and the oldest complete windows from around 1100. With large Romanesque churches, and even more with the huge Gothic churches, came opportunities to use more and more glass. First the greater height of Romanesque buildings meant that tall windows could be placed high up in the nave walls. Then the structural innovations of Gothic architecture that removed stress, and hence stone, from the walls permitted them to become vast expanses of glass. Chartres Cathedral has 176 windows. Many high medieval churches had windows more than 50 feet high.

So far we have looked at *how* medieval Europeans created stained glass and incorporated it into their greatest churches. But *why* did they undertake such time-consuming and costly decoration? Suger, the scholarly twelfth-century abbot of Saint-Denis outside Paris who rebuilt his basilica in the Gothic style, spoke of the spiritual force of his new glass windows:

When . . . the loveliness of the many-colored gems has called me away from external cares . . . then it seems to me that I see myself dwelling in some strange region of the universe which neither exists entirely in the slime of the earth nor entirely in the purity of heaven; and that, by the grace of God, I can be transported from this inferior to that higher world.[*]

In the Greek philosophers, the Bible, and the Church Fathers, light always represents one way of imagining the unimaginable reality of God. For Suger and his contemporaries the luminous effect of stained glass suggested the very presence of God.

Earthquakes, fires, and wars have destroyed most of the glass that was installed in the Middle Ages. Today's visitor to Europe views more or less valid nineteenth-century reconstructions, except at Canterbury in England and Chartres in France, where almost all of the original glass survives. Usually medieval churches were laid out on an east-west axis. The western façade was normally pierced by tall "lancet" windows and by a single "rose" window. These windows typically portrayed scenes from the life of Christ and/or the Virgin Mary. The northern aisle windows usually contained Old Testament scenes, the southern windows New Testament scenes.

Stained glass played a key role, alongside sculpture, preaching, and churchyard dramas, in communicating the faith to ordinary people. Seldom has a teaching tool been so beautiful. Scholars also speak of stained glass as "painting with glass." Indeed, the art form most like stained glass is painting, especially the painting of illuminations on the pages of manuscripts.

QUESTIONS

1. How was stained glass made and assembled into windows?

2. What kinds of subjects were depicted on stained glass windows?

3. Who was the audience for stained glass windows?

---

[*]Suger, *De rebus in administratione sua gestis*, ed. E. Panofsky, 2d ed. (Princeton, N.J.: Princeton University Press, 1979), pp. 63–65.

Online Study Center
  Improve Your Grade Visual Record Activities

preached against heretics, and always had the approval of the papacy. Several religious movements were especially popular among women and constituted the first exclusively women's movements in the history of Christianity.

Latin studies in literature, law, theology, and philosophy remained important. Europe's expansion brought scholars into increasing contact with ancient Greek, Jewish, and Arab thought, which spurred new research and opened new questions. The increasing prominence of logic drove theology and philosophy to the center of the curriculum and led to the production of majestic summas, compendiums of knowledge in various fields. Formed as guilds of either masters or students, universities were among the most original and durable medieval achievements.

Vernacular literature, literature in "native" languages, spread quickly and widely in high medieval Europe, achieving visibility and prominence everywhere. Vernacular literature was written in many genres: *chansons de geste*, romances, lays, sagas, and poetry. The High Middle Ages saw the full flowering of Romanesque architecture and then its eclipse by Gothic. Magnificent cathedrals are testimony to the prosperity and pride of high medieval Europe.

LOOKING AHEAD

What would follow this dynamic, expanding world of the High Middle Ages? Ironically, the next two centuries would witness both crisis—famine, pestilence, war—and the amazing achievements of the Renaissance.

KEY TERMS

Cluny (p. 284)

Francis of Assisi (p. 292)

Dominic de Guzman (p. 293)

canon law (p. 297)

Bernard of Clairvaux (p. 300)

Hildegard of Bingen (p. 300)

Thomas Aquinas (p. 301)

summa (p. 301)

chivalry (p. 304)

Romanesque (p. 306)

Gothic (p. 306)

Online Study Center
Improve Your Grade Flashcards

SUGGESTED READING

Bony, Jean. *French Gothic Architecture of the Twelfth and Thirteenth Centuries.* 1983. Huge, clearly presented, and magnificently illustrated, this is a browser's book as well as a sustained essay by a master of his subject.

Bouchard, Constance B. *Strong of Body, Brave and Noble: Chivalry and Society in Medieval France.* 1998. A superb summation of the social and cultural history of the medieval aristocracy.

Colish, Marcia. *Medieval Foundations of the Western Intellectual Tradition.* 1997. The first original and comprehensive history of medieval thought in a generation.

Jaeger, C. Stephen. *Ennobling Love: In Search of a Lost Sensibility.* 1999. A beautiful and moving interpretation of the love literature of the High Middle Ages and of its philosophical and theological dimensions.

Kenny, Anthony. *Medieval Philosophy.* 2005. A concise and readable presentation of the key themes and thinkers, Arab, Jew, and Catholic.

Lambert, Malcolm. *Medieval Heresy: Popular Movements from the Gregorian Reform to the Reformation.* 3d ed.

2002. Brilliant and readable, this book is the best history of medieval heresy ever written and one of the best books on medieval religion generally.

Rubenstein, Richard. *Aristotle's Children: How Christians, Muslims, and Jews Rediscovered Ancient Wisdom and Illuminated the Middle Ages.* 2003. Beautifully written for a nonspecialist audience, this book traces the influence of Aristotle from antiquity to the late Middle Ages.

Southern, R. W. *Scholastic Humanism and the Unification of Europe.* 1995. A truly brilliant overview of twelfth-century culture by its greatest twentieth-century student.

NOTES

1. John Addington Symonds, *Wine, Women and Song: Medieval Latin Students' Songs* (reprint, New York: Cooper Square, 1966), p. 69.

2. Frederick Goldin, *Lyrics of the Troubadours and Trouvères: An Anthology and a History* (New York: Doubleday, 1973), p. 135.

3. Meg Bogin, *The Women Troubadours* (New York: Norton, 1976), p. 69.

11

CRISIS AND RECOVERY IN LATE MEDIEVAL EUROPE, 1300–1500

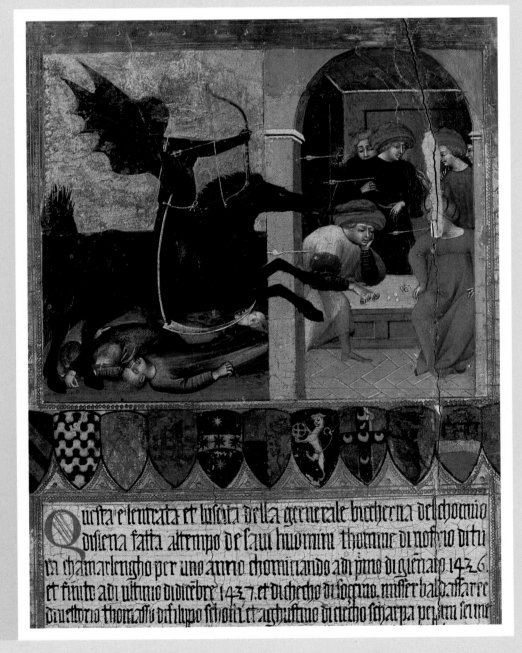

A Time of Judgment
On this cover for a fifteenth-century government account book, symbols of death—arrows, a scythe, and a horse—carry the angel of death from place to place. *(Bildarchiv Preussischer Kulturbesitz/Art Resource, NY)*

I n the fourteenth century, Europeans sang an old Franciscan hymn, "Day of Wrath, Day of Burning." Its verses described the fear and disorder that would accompany the end of the world and God's judgment of the saved and the damned. That hymn could well have been in the mind of the painter of the facing illustration. When countless Europeans, such as these poor souls beneath the winged angel of death, fell victim to epidemic disease, many people thought they knew why. The illustrator seems to believe it was God's judgment against sinners, including these gamblers sickened by the angel's plague-tipped arrows. The flood, fire, and pestilence that ravaged late medieval Europe were thought to be premonitions of the breakdown of the world and a time of judgment.

The late Middle Ages (ca. 1300–1500) are often described as a period of continued crisis and decline that put an end to the growth and expansion of the previous three centuries. In truth, however, the years of crisis in the fourteenth and early fifteenth centuries gave way to a dramatic economic, social, and political recovery in the fifteenth century. The cultural and intellectual changes that accompanied the crisis and recovery are the focus of Chapter 12, "The Renaissance."

Military, political, religious, economic, and social crises burdened Europe in the fourteenth and early fifteenth centuries. Between 1337 and 1453 France and England fought a war that touched most of the states of western Europe. The Hundred Years' War, as it has come to be known, was fought primarily over English claims to traditionally French lands. Problems were not confined to England and France. Aristocrats in many parts of Europe challenged the hereditary rights of their rulers. In the towns of Germany and Italy patrician classes moved to reduce the influence of artisans and laborers in government, instituting oligarchies or even aristocratic lordships in place of more democratic governments.

Questions of power and representation also affected the Christian church as ecclesiastical claims to authority came under attack. Secular governments challenged church jurisdictions. Disputed papal elections led to the so-called Great Schism, a split between rival centers of control in Rome and Avignon (a city in what is now the south of France). In the aftermath of

CHAPTER OUTLINE

THE CRISIS OF THE WESTERN CHRISTIAN CHURCH

WAR AND THE STRUGGLE OVER POLITICAL POWER, 1300–1450

CRISIS IN ECONOMY AND SOCIETY

THE CONSOLIDATION OF POLITICAL POWER, 1450–1500

KEY TERMS

Babylonian Captivity of the Papacy

Great Schism

conciliarists

Jan Hus

Council of Constance

Hundred Years' War

Joan of Arc

Black Death

Hanseatic League

Spanish Inquisition

Golden Bull

Online Study Center
This icon will direct you to interactive map and primary source activities on the website **college.hmco.com/pic/noble5e**

the crisis, the papacy was forced to redefine its place in both the religious life and the political life of Europe.

A series of economic and demographic shocks worsened these political and religious difficulties. Part of the problem was structural: the population of Europe had grown too large to be supported by the resources available. Famine and the return of the plague in 1348 sent the economy into long-term decline. In almost every aspect of political, religious, and social life, then, the fourteenth and early fifteenth centuries marked a pause in the growth and consolidation that had characterized the earlier medieval period.

Yet out of the crises a number of significant changes emerged. By 1500 the European population and economy were again expanding. England and France emerged strengthened by military and political conflicts. And the consolidation of the Spanish kingdoms, the Ottoman Empire, and the states of eastern Europe altered the political and social makeup of Europe. None of the transformations could have been predicted in 1300 as Europe entered a religious, political, and social whirlwind.

FOCUS QUESTIONS

How did the Great Schism change the church and the papacy?

What forces limited the political power of rulers in England, France, and Italy?

How were economic and social structures changed by plague and economic crisis?

How did the political makeup of Europe in 1500 differ from that in 1300?

THE CRISIS OF THE WESTERN CHRISTIAN CHURCH

How did the Great Schism change the church and the papacy?

Early in the fourteenth century the king of France attempted to kidnap the pope. His act initiated a series of crises that challenged traditional ideas about church government and the role of the church in the various countries of Europe. First the popes and their entourages abandoned their traditional residences in central Italy and moved to Avignon, an imperial enclave in the south of modern France. Then, in the wake of a disputed election, two and later three rivals claimed the papal throne. Simultaneously, the church hierarchy faced challenges from radical reformers who wished to change it. At various times all the European powers became entangled in the problems of the church. In the wake of the crisis, the papacy realized that it needed a stronger, independent base. Papal recovery in the fifteenth century was predicated on political autonomy in central Italy.

THE BABYLONIAN CAPTIVITY, 1309–1377

The Christian church was in turmoil as a result of an attack on Pope Boniface VIII (r. 1294–1303) by King Philip IV (r. 1285–1314) of France. The king attempted to kidnap Boniface, intending to try him for heresy because of the pope's challenges to the king's authority within his own kingdom. The outstanding issues revolved around the powers of the pope and the responsibilities of the clergy to political leaders. It was, in fact, largely because of tensions with the northern kingdoms that the French archbishop of Bordeaux (bor-DOE) was elected Pope Clement V (r. 1305–1314). Clement chose to remain north of the Alps in order to seek an end to warfare between France and England and to protect, to the extent possible, the wealthy religious order of the Knights of the Temple, or Templars (see page 286), which Philip was in the process of suppressing. Clement also hoped to prevent the king from carrying through his threatened posthumous heresy trial of Boniface. After the death of Boniface it was clear that the governments of Europe had no intention of recognizing papal political authority as absolute.

Clement's pontificate marked the beginning of the so-called Babylonian Captivity, a period from 1309 to 1378 when popes resided almost continuously outside of Italy. In 1309 Clement moved the papal court to Avignon, on the Rhône River in a region that was still part of the Holy Roman Empire—the name that by the fourteenth century was given to the medieval empire whose origin reached back to Charlemagne. His successor, Pope John XXII (r. 1316–1334), set the tone for the brilliant papal court. To celebrate the marriage of his grandniece in 1324, for example, he ordered a wedding feast during which the numerous guests consumed 4,012 loaves of bread, 8¾ oxen, 55¼ sheep, 8 pigs, 4 boars, and vast quantities of fish, capons, chickens, partridges, rabbits, ducks, and chickens. The feast was topped off with 300 pounds of cheese, 3,000 eggs, and assorted fruits. The guests washed down this feast with about 450 liters of wine. It was the sort of celebration worthy of royalty or aristocrats. John's expenditures set the tone for the Avignonese papacy.

The papacy and its new residence in Avignon became a major religious, diplomatic, and commercial center. The size of the court changed as dramatically as its venue: although the thirteenth-century papal administration required only two hundred or so officials, the bureaucracy in Avignon grew to about six hundred. It was not just the pope's immediate circle that expanded the population of Avignon. Artists, writers, lawyers, and merchants from across Europe were drawn to the new center of administration and hub of patronage. Papal administrators intervened actively in local ecclesiastical affairs, and the pope's revenues from annates (generally a portion of the first year's revenues from an ecclesiastical office granted by papal letter), court fees, and provisioning charges continued to grow.

Not everyone approved of this situation. It was the Italian poet and philosopher Francesco Petrarch (1304–1374) who first referred to the Avignon move as a **Babylonian Captivity of the Papacy.** Recalling the account in the Hebrew Bible of the exile of the Israelites and New Testament images of Babylon as the center of sin and immorality, he complained of

> [an] unholy Babylon, Hell on Earth, a sink of iniquity, the cesspool of the world. There is neither faith, nor charity, nor religion, nor fear of God, nor shame, nor truth, nor holiness, albeit the residence . . . of the supreme pontiff should have made it a shrine and the very stronghold of religion.[1]

Two of the most vigorous critics were Saint Catherine of Siena (1347–1380) and Saint Bridget of Sweden (1303–1373). They were part of a remarkable flowering of religious feeling among women. Unlike others, they left their homes and neighborhoods and led the call for religious reform and a return of the papacy to Rome.

THE GREAT SCHISM, 1378–1417

In 1377 Pope Gregory XI (r. 1370–1378) bowed to critics' pressure and did return to Rome. He was shocked by what he found: churches and palaces in ruin and the

Babylonian Captivity of the Papacy Term used to describe the period from 1309 to 1378 when popes resided outside of Italy, relating the pontificate's move to the period when the tribes of Israel lived in exile.

Year	Event
1303	Pope Boniface VIII attacked at Anagni and dies
1305	Election of Pope Clement V
1309	Clement V moves papal court to Avignon; beginning of Babylonian Captivity
1337	Beginning of Hundred Years' War between England and France
1348–1351	Black Death
1356	German emperor issues Golden Bull
1378	Great Schism
1381	English Rising
1397	Union of Kalmar unites Denmark, Norway, and Sweden
1410	Battle of Tannenberg
1414–1418	Council of Constance
1415	Battle of Agincourt
1420	Treaty of Troyes
1431	Execution of Joan of Arc
1438	Pragmatic Sanction of Bourges
1453	End of the Hundred Years' War Ottoman Turks conquer Constantinople
1469	Marriage of Ferdinand and Isabella unites kingdoms of Aragon and Castile
1480	Ivan III ends Tatar overlordship of Moscow
1485	Tudor dynasty established in England
1492	Spanish conquest of Granada Jews expelled from Spanish lands Columbus commissioned to discover new lands
1494	Charles VIII invades Italy

city violent and dangerous. By the end of 1377 he had resolved to retreat to Avignon, but he died before he could flee Rome. In a tumultuous election during which the Roman populace entered the Vatican Palace and threatened to break into the conclave itself, the cardinals finally elected a compromise candidate acceptable to both the French cardinals and the Roman mob. Urban VI (r. 1378–1389) may have been electable, but he was also violent, intemperate, and eager to reduce the privileges of the clerical hierarchy. In response, the French cardinals questioned the legitimacy of the election, which they came to believe had been

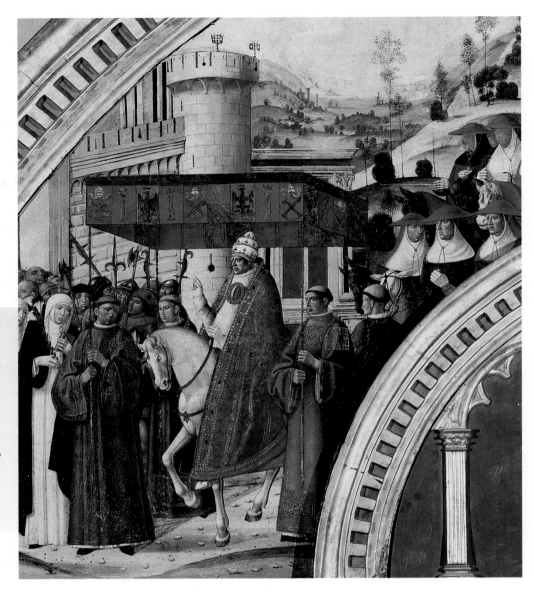

Gregory XI Returns to Rome This highly stylized painting conveys the hopes of European Christians when Gregory XI returned from Avignon in 1377. Saint Catherine of Siena, who had pleaded for the pope's return, is seen in the foreground. *(Scala/Art Resource, NY)*

conducted under duress. Within months they deposed Urban and elected in his place a French cardinal who took the name Clement VII (r. 1378–1394). Urban responded by denouncing the cardinals and continuing to rule in Rome. The church now had two popes.

After some hesitation Western Christians divided into two camps, initiating the **Great Schism** (SKIZ-em), a period of almost forty years during which no one knew for sure who was the true pope. This was a deadly serious issue for all. The true pope had the right to appoint church officials, decide important moral and legal issues, and allow or forbid taxation of the clergy by the state. Each side found ready supporters among the states of Europe; however, support for one pope or the other often had more to do with political rivalries than with religious convictions.

Great Schism The period from 1378 to 1417 when there were two and eventually three claimants to the papal throne.

Online Study Center **Improve Your Grade**
Primary Source: The Downfall of the Church: Condemnation of the Papacy During the Great Schism

The crisis gave impetus to new discussions about church government: Should the pope be considered the sole head of the church? Debates within the church followed lines of thought already expressed in the towns and kingdoms of Europe. Representative bodies—the English Parliament, the French Estates General, the Swedish Riksdag (RIX-dog)—already claimed the right to act for the realm, and in the city-states of Italy ultimate authority was thought to reside in the body of citizens. Canon lawyers and theologians similarly argued that authority resided in the whole church, which had the right and duty to come together in council to correct and reform the church hierarchy. Even the most conservative of these conciliarists agreed that the "universal church" had the right to respond in periods of heresy or schism. More radical conciliarists argued that the pope as bishop of Rome was merely the first among equals in the church hierarchy and that he, like any other bishop, could be corrected by a gathering of his peers—that is, by an ecumenical council.

The rival popes resisted international pressure to end the schism. In exasperation the cardinals, the main ecclesiastical supporters of the rival popes, called a general council in Pisa, which deposed both popes and elected a new one. Since the council lacked the power to force the rivals to accept deposition, the result was that three men now claimed to be the rightful successor of Saint Peter. Conciliarists, by themselves, could not mend the split in the church.

Resolution finally came when the Holy Roman emperor Sigismund (r. 1411–1437) forced the diplomatically isolated third papal claimant, John XXIII (r. 1410–1415), to call a general council of the church. The council, which met from 1414 to 1418 in the German imperial city of Constance, could never have succeeded without Sigismund's support. At one point he forced the council to remain in session even after Pope John had fled the city in an attempt to end deliberations.

HERESY AND THE COUNCIL OF CONSTANCE, 1414–1418

Sigismund hoped that a council could help him heal deep religious and civil divisions in Bohemia, the most important part of his family's traditional lands (see Map 11.3). Far from healing religious division, however, the actions of the council exacerbated tensions in central Europe and created a climate of religious distrust that poisoned relations for more than a century. Bohemia and its capital, Prague, were Czech-speaking. But Prague was also the seat of the Luxemburg dynasty of German emperors and the site of the first university in German or Slavic lands. Religious and theological questions quickly became entangled with the competing claims of Czech and German factions. The preaching and teaching of the Czech reformer **Jan Hus** (ca. 1370–1415) were at the center of the debate. As preacher in the Bethlehem Chapel in Prague from 1402 and eventually as rector of the university, Hus was the natural spokesman for the non-German townspeople in Prague and the Czech faction at the university. His

criticisms of the church hierarchy, which in Prague was primarily German, fanned into flames the smoldering embers of Czech national feeling. It was Sigismund's hope that a council might clarify the orthodoxy of Hus's teachings and heal the rift within the church of Bohemia.

The council's response to the theological crisis was based on the church's experience with heresy over the previous forty years, primarily the teachings of John Wyclif (1329–1384). In the 1370s Wyclif, an Oxford theologian and parish priest, began to criticize in increasingly angry terms the state of the clergy and the abuses of the church hierarchy. By 1387 his ideas had been declared heretical and his followers were hunted out. Wyclif believed that the church could be at once a divine institution and an earthly gathering of individuals. Thus, in his opinion, individual Christians need not unquestioningly obey the pronouncements of the church hierarchy. Final authority lay only in the Scriptures, insisted Wyclif, who sponsored the first translations of the Bible into English. He gathered about himself followers called "Lollards," who emphasized Bible reading and popular piety; some even supported public preaching by women. According to one disciple, "Every true man and woman being in charity is a priest."[2]

Wyclif's influence continued on the Continent, especially in the circle of Jan Hus and the Czech reformers. By 1403 the German majority in the university had condemned Hus's teaching as Wycliffite, thus initiating almost a decade of struggle between Czechs and Germans, Hussites and Catholics. This was the impasse that Sigismund hoped the **Council of Constance** could settle. Accordingly, he offered a suspicious Hus a safe conduct pass to attend the council. The council, however, revoked the pledge of safe conduct and ordered Hus to recant his beliefs. He refused. The council condemned him as a heretic and burned him at the stake on July 6, 1415.

Far from ending Sigismund's problems with the Bohemians, the actions of the council provided the Czechs with a martyr and hero. The execution of Hus provoked a firestorm of revolution in Prague. Czech forces roundly defeated an imperial army sent in to restore order. The Hussite movement gathered strength and spread throughout Bohemia. Moderate Hussites continued Hus's campaign against clerical abuses and claimed the right to receive both the bread and the wine during the sacrament of Communion. Radical Hussites argued that the true church was the community of spiritual men and women; they had no use for ecclesiastical hierarchy of any

conciliarists People who argued that the pope was merely "the first among equals" and that therefore a council of church leaders could correct or discipline a pope.

Jan Hus Czech reformer who attacked clerical privileges and advocated church reform. He was executed as a heretic at the Council of Constance in 1415.

Council of Constance General council of the church convened by the Holy Roman emperor to deal with schism and church reform. It elected Pope Martin V to end the Great Schism.

kind. The German emperors were unable to defeat a united Hussite movement. In 1433 a new church council and moderate Hussites negotiated an agreement that allowed the Hussites to continue some of their practices, including receiving both bread and wine at Communion, while returning to the church. Radical Hussites refused the compromise, and the war dragged on until 1436. Bohemia remained a center of religious dissent, and the memory of Hus's execution at a church council would have a chilling effect on discussions of church reform during the Reformation in the sixteenth century.

THE REUNION AND REFORM OF THE PAPACY, 1415–1513

To most of the delegates at the Council of Constance, the reunion and reform of the papacy were more important than the issue of heresy. And as we will see, attempts to deal with reform and reunion seemed in the eyes of the popes to threaten the political independence and the moral leadership of the papacy itself. This too would remain a problem well into the sixteenth century.

After initially agreeing to abdicate if his rivals did the same, John changed his mind and fled from Constance. Sigismund recaptured him and returned him to the council, where he was deposed. Pope Gregory XII (r. 1406–1415), the Roman pope, realizing he had lost all his support, resigned—after himself calling the council, as a rightful pope should do. Benedict III (r. 1394–1417), the pope in Avignon, refused to resign and he also was deposed. Finally, in 1417, the council elected a Roman nobleman as Pope Martin V (r. 1417–1431).

The council justified its actions in what was perhaps its most important decree, *Haec sancta synodus* ("This sacred synod"): "This sacred synod of Constance . . . declares . . . that it has its power immediately from Christ, and that all men, of every rank and position, including even the pope himself are bound to obey it in those matters that pertain to the faith."[3] Popes could no longer expect to remain unchallenged if they made claims of absolute dominion, and ecclesiastical rights and jurisdictions increasingly were matters for negotiation.

Critics agreed that the pope no longer behaved like the "Servant of the Servants of Christ" but instead acted like the "Lord of Lords." Cardinals claimed to represent the church at large as counterweights to papal abuse, but as the nobility of the church, they and other members of the hierarchy required the income from multiple offices to maintain their presence at the papal court. Both the cardinals and the popes viewed any reforms to the present system as potential threats

to their ability to function. The council, however, recognized the need for further reforms. A second reform council met at Basel from 1431 to 1449, but with modest results. The council again tried to reduce papal power, but this time it received little support from European governments.

Because of the continuing conciliarist threat, the papacy needed the support of the secular rulers of Europe. Thus the papacy was forced to accept compromises on the issues of reform, on ecclesiastical jurisdictions and immunities, and on papal revenues. Various governments argued that it was they, and not the pope, who should be responsible for ecclesiastical institutions and jurisdictions within their territories.

Lay rulers focused on several issues. They wanted church officials in their territories to belong to local families. They wanted ecclesiastical institutions to be subject to local laws and administration. And by the 1470s it was clear that they wanted to have local prelates named as cardinal-protectors. These were not churchmen who could serve the church administration in Rome; rather they functioned as mediators between local governments and the papacy. The most famous of these new political cardinals was Thomas Wolsey of England (ca. 1470–1530), who was an important supporter of King Henry VII and chancellor of England under Henry VIII.

The reunited papacy had to accept claims it would have staunchly opposed a century earlier. One of the most important of these was the Pragmatic Sanction of Bourges of 1438. The papacy was unable to protest when the French clergy, at the urging of the king, abolished papal rights to annates, limited appeals to the papal court, and reduced papal rights to appoint clergy within France without the approval of the local clergy or the Crown. Similar concessions diminished church authority throughout Europe. Perhaps the most momentous was a bull (official papal document) issued in 1478 by Pope Sixtus IV (r. 1471–1484) that allowed Ferdinand and Isabella of Aragon and Castile to institute a church court, the Spanish Inquisition, under their own auspices (see page 346).

With reduced revenues from legal fees, annates, and appointments, the popes of the fifteenth century were forced to derive more and more of their revenue and influence from the Papal States. By 1430 the Papal States accounted for about half of the annual income of the papacy. Papal interests increasingly centered on protecting the papacy's influence as a secular ruler of a large territory in central Italy. Further, it saw political independence as essential to its continued moral leadership. Thus the papacy had to deal with many of the same jurisdictional, diplomatic, and military challenges that faced other medieval governments.

═══════════════════════════ S E C T I O N   S U M M A R Y ═══════════════════════════

- A political crisis forced the papacy to abandon central Italy and move to the south of France.

- A disputed papal election left two claimants—one French, the other Italian—and no clear way to resolve the issue.

- The religious beliefs of John Wyclif and Jan Hus challenged the basis of papal authority.

- In addition to resolving the disputed election, conciliarists claimed authority to correct and reform the papacy.

- By 1450, the papacy was reunited but weakened in relation to the European kingdoms.

WAR AND THE STRUGGLE OVER POLITICAL POWER, 1300–1450

What forces limited the political power of rulers in England, France, and Italy?

A lawyer who served King Philip IV of France (r. 1285–1314) observed that "everything within the limits of his kingdom belongs to the lord king, especially protection, high justice and dominion."[4] Royal officials in England and France generally believed that "liberties"—that is, individual rights to local jurisdictions—originated with the king. These ideas were the result of several centuries of centralization of political power in royal hands. At almost the same time, however, an English noble challenged royal claims on his lands, saying, "Here, my lords, is my warrant," as he brandished a rusty long sword. "My ancestors came with William the Bastard [that is, William the Conqueror, in 1066] and conquered their lands with the sword, and by the sword I will defend them against anyone who tries to usurp them."[5] The views of the royal lawyer and the feisty earl exemplify the central tension over power in the late Middle Ages. The struggle over political power was played out in the context of the **Hundred Years' War,** which affected not just England and France but also most of western Europe, especially Italy as mercenary soldiers traveled south during temporary lulls in the fighting. In England and France the crisis led to strengthened monarchies. In Italy, however, local and regional entities that exercised many of those liberties the old Englishman wanted to protect with his sword.

THE HUNDRED YEARS' WAR, 1337–1453

In the twelfth and thirteenth centuries centralization of royal power in England and France had proceeded almost without interruption. In the fourteenth century

Hundred Years' War   Series of conflicts, 1337–1453, fought over English claims within the French monarchy. It ended with the nearly complete expulsion of the English from French lands.

matters changed in both countries. Questions of the nature of royal power, common responsibility, and hereditary rights to rule challenged the power of the English and French monarchs. In both countries, competition began largely over dynastic issues, but by the mid-fifteenth century, resolution of the wars led to governments with a more distinctly national tone to them.

England   In England fears arising from the growing power of the English crown and the weakness of a gullible king brought issues to a head during the reign of Edward II (r. 1307–1327). By the early fourteenth century, resident justices of the peace (JPs) were replacing the expensive and inefficient system of traveling justices. In theory, the JPs were royal officials doing the king's bidding, but this was often not the case in reality. These unpaid local officials were modestly well-to-do gentry who were often clients of local magnates. When the king was not vigilant, justices were prone to use their offices to carry out local vendettas and feuds and to protect the interests of the wealthy and powerful.

The barons, the titled lords of England, were interested in controlling more than just local justices. Fearing that Edward II would continue many of the centralizing policies of his father, the barons passed reform ordinances in 1311 limiting the king's right to wage war, leave the realm, grant lands or castles, or appoint chief justices and chancellors without the approval of Parliament, which they dominated. Special taxes or subsidies were to be paid to the public Exchequer rather than into the king's private treasury. Some of these ordinances were later voided, but the tradition of parliamentary consent remained a key principle of English constitutional history.

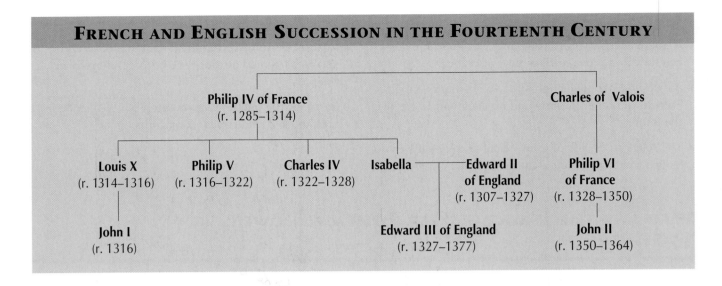

FRENCH AND ENGLISH SUCCESSION IN THE FOURTEENTH CENTURY

The baronial influence grew because Edward II was a weak and naive king, easily influenced by court favorites. After a humiliating defeat at the hands of the Scots at the Battle of Bannockburn (1314), his position steadily deteriorated until he was deposed in 1327 by a coalition of barons led by his wife, Queen Isabella. After a short regency, their son, Edward III (r. 1327–1377), assumed the throne. He was a cautious king, ever aware of the violence and rebelliousness of the baronage.

France   French kings seemed significantly more powerful in the early fourteenth century. A complex succession crisis, however, made clear the limits of French kingship. In 1328 the direct Capetian line, which had sired the kings of France since the election of Hugh Capet in 987, finally died out. The last Capetians did produce daughters, but by the fourteenth century many argued that according to custom the French crown should pass through the male line only. Thus the French nobility selected as king Philip of Valois (Philip VI; r. 1328–1350), a cousin of the last king through the male line (Charles IV; r. 1322–1328). He was chosen in preference to the daughters of the last Capetian kings and, more significantly, in preference to King Edward III of England, whose mother, Isabella, was the daughter of King Philip IV (r. 1285–1314).

Controversy over succession was just one of the disputes between the French and English. An even longer-standing issue was the status of lands within France that belonged to the English kings. In 1340, climaxing a century of tensions over English possessions in France, Edward III of England formally claimed the title "King of France," and the Hundred Years' War was on.

The war was marked by quick English raids and only occasional pitched battles. With a population of about 16 million, France was far richer and more populous than England. On at least one occasion the French managed to field an army of over 50,000; the English mustered only 32,000 at most. These armies were easily the largest ever assembled by a medieval European kingdom. In almost every engagement the English were outnumbered. Their strategy, therefore, was to avoid pitched battles except on the most advantageous terms. Edward III engaged in extremely destructive raids, hoping to lure the French into ill-considered attacks. The English stole what they could, destroyed what they could not steal, and captured enemy knights to hold for ransom.

Stages of the War   The war can be divided into four stages. The first stage (1337–1360) was characterized by a rapid series of English assaults and victories. The few pitched battles, including Crécy (1346) and Poitiers (1356), show how Edward's strategy worked (see **MAP 11.1**). In these cases the English gathered their forces in careful defensive positions and took advantage of an individualistic French chivalric ethos according to which, in the words of one knight, "who does the most is worth the most." The key to the English defensive position was the use of longbowmen and cannon. Arrows from the longbow had more penetrating power than a bolt from a crossbow, and the longbow could be fired much more rapidly. Gunpowder probably arrived in the West from China in the late thirteenth century. By 1300 Europeans had forged cannon for use in siege warfare and to protect defensive positions. Although there is a debate over how effective they were, when used in combination with the longbow, they effectively disrupted and scattered advancing troops.

In the second stage of the war (1360–1396), French forces responded more cautiously to the English tactics and slowly regained much of the territory they had lost. But during this stage, the disruptions and expenses of war placed a huge burden on both French and English society. In the confusion and unrest following the

MAP 11.1   England and France in the Hundred Years' War

The succession of maps depicts both why hit-and-run tactics worked for the English early in the war and why the English were ultimately unable to defeat the French and take control of all of France.

ENGLAND

Southampton

Calais

FLANDERS

PONTHIEU

English Channel

NORMANDY

Paris

CHAMPAGNE

Seine

BRITTANY

MAINE

ANJOU

Loire

HOLY
ROMAN
EMPIRE

TOURAINE

BURGUNDY

POITOU

AUVERGNE

AQUITAINE

Bordeaux

Garonne

DAUPHINÉ

Rhône

Saint-Sardos

GASCONY

LANGUEDOC

Toulouse

SPAIN

**1337
(before the Battle of Crécy)**

- English holdings
- French holdings
- Extent of English holdings after Treaty of Paris, 1259

*Mediterranean
Sea*

0   100 Km.

0   100 Mi.

ENGLAND

Calais

FLANDERS

Crécy
1346

English Channel

Rouen

NORMANDY

Paris

CHAMPAGNE

Seine

BRITTANY

MAINE

ANJOU

Loire

HOLY
ROMAN
EMPIRE

TOURAINE

Poitiers
1356

BURGUNDY

POITOU

AUVERGNE

AQUITAINE

Bordeaux

Garonne

DAUPHINÉ

Rhône

GASCONY

LANGUEDOC

Toulouse

SPAIN

**1360
(after the Battle of Poitiers)**

- English holdings
- French holdings
- ✕ Major battles

*Mediterranean
Sea*

0   100 Km.

0   100 Mi.

ENGLAND

Calais

FLANDERS

HOLY
ROMAN
EMPIRE

Agincourt
1415

English Channel

Rouen

Reims

NORMANDY

Paris

CHAMPAGNE

Seine

Domrémy

BRITTANY

MAINE

ANJOU

Orléans

Loire

Bourges

DUCHY OF
BURGUNDY

COUNTY OF
BURGUNDY

TOURAINE

POITOU

AUVERGNE

AQUITAINE

Bordeaux

Garonne

DAUPHINÉ

Rhône

GASCONY

LANGUEDOC

Toulouse

SPAIN

**ca. 1429
(after the siege of Orléans)**

- English holdings
- French holdings
- Burgundian lands allied with England to 1435
- ✕ Major battle

*Mediterranean
Sea*

0   100 Km.

0   100 Mi.

ENGLAND

Calais

FLANDERS

BRABANT

LUXEMBOURG

English Channel

HOLY
ROMAN
EMPIRE

NORMANDY

Paris

CHAMPAGNE

Seine

BRITTANY

MAINE

ANJOU

Loire

DUCHY OF
BURGUNDY

COUNTY OF
BURGUNDY

TOURAINE

POITOU

AQUITAINE

AUVERGNE

Bordeaux

Castillon-sur-Dordogne
1453

Garonne

DAUPHINÉ

Rhône

GASCONY

LANGUEDOC

Toulouse

SPAIN

**1453
(end of war)**

- English holdings
- French holdings
- Burgundian lands reconciled with France after 1435
- ✕ Last battle

*Mediterranean
Sea*

0   100 Km.

0   100 Mi.

The Battle at Agincourt
The English victory at Agincourt marked the high point of English influence in France. Once again English archers defeated a larger, mounted force.
(The Granger Collection, New York)

French disaster at Poitiers in 1356, Étienne Marcel, provost (director) of the merchants of Paris, mobilized a protest movement designed to reduce royal and aristocratic power. This revolution seemed too radical to conservative townspeople in the provinces, and Marcel's only allies were bands of rebellious countrymen roaming the region around Paris. These rebels, and eventually Marcel himself, were isolated and then defeated by aristocratic armies.

England was soon rocked by unrest as well. The Rising of 1381 is often called the Peasants' Revolt, despite the fact that townsfolk as well as peasants participated. Already England seethed with unrest as a result of the plague (see pages 329–330) and landlord claims for traditional dues. But the final straw was a poll tax levied to pay for the war. Commoners responded with violent protests. The heart of the uprising was a revolt by rural peasants and artisans in the southeast, primarily in Kent and Essex. Popular armies led by Wat Tyler (d. 1381) converged on London in June 1381. Tyler was murdered during a dramatic meeting with Richard II outside London, and a reaction against the rebels quickly ensued.

The rest of Richard's reign was anything but tranquil. Recognizing the dangers of noble influence, Richard tried to insulate himself from the peers of the realm by choosing advisers from the lesser nobility and the middle classes as well as from the peerage. The re-

sult was increasing tensions with the peers and charges that Richard's rule was tyrannical. Simmering discontent boiled over, and leaders of the peers captured Richard and forced him to abdicate in 1399. Parliament then elected as king Henry IV (r. 1399–1413), the first ruler from the House of Lancaster. Richard died in prison under mysterious circumstances in 1400.

A fateful shift occurred in the third stage of the war (1396–1422). King Charles VI (r. 1380–1422) of France suffered bouts of insanity throughout his long reign, which made effective French government almost impossible. The English king Henry V (r. 1413–1422) renewed his family's claim to the French throne. At Agincourt in 1415 the English (led by Henry himself) again enticed a larger French army into attacking an English position fortified by longbows and cannon. By the terms of the Treaty of Troyes (1420), Charles VI's son (the future Charles VII) was declared illegitimate and disinherited; Henry married Catherine, the daughter of Charles VI, and he was declared the legitimate heir to the French throne. A final English victory seemed assured, but both Charles VI and Henry V died in 1422, leaving Henry's infant son, Henry VI (r. 1422–1461), to inherit both thrones.

The kings' deaths ushered in the final stage of the Hundred Years' War (1422–1453), the French reconquest. In 1428 military and political power seemed firmly in the hands of the English and the great aristo-

THE INQUISITION OF JOAN OF ARC

An important question at the trial of Joan of Arc was whether her acts had any authoritative value: Did the voices she heard originate with God or the Devil? The judges wanted to demonstrate to their own satisfaction that Joan was one of "the sowers of deceitful inventions" of which the Gospels warned. They fully expected that external signs could reveal hidden truths. The following memorandum is a summation of the commission's case against the maid.

You said that your king received a sign by which he knew you were sent from God, that it was St. Michael, in the company of a host of angels. . . . You have said that you are certain of future and contingent events that you recognized men you had never seen, through the voices of St. Catherine and St. Margaret. . . . Regarding this article, the clergy find superstition, divination, . . . and vain boasting.

You said that you wore and still wear man's dress at God's command and to His good pleasure, for you had instruction from God to wear this dress, and so you put on a short tunic, jerkin, and hose with many points. You even wear your hair cut above the ears, without keeping about you anything to denote your sex, save what nature has given you. . . . The clergy declare that you blaspheme against God, despising Him and His sacraments, that you transgress divine law, Holy Scripture and the canons of the Church, . . . that you are given to idolatry and worship of yourself and your clothes, according to the customs of the heathen.

You have declared that you know well that God loves certain living persons better than you, and that you learned this by revelation from St. Catherine and St. Margaret; also that those saints speak French, not English, as they are not on the side of the English. And since you knew that your voices were for your king, you began to dislike the Burgundians. . . . Such

matters the clergy pronounce to be a rash and presumptuous assertion, a superstitious divination, a blasphemy uttered against St. Catherine and St. Margaret, and a transgression of the commandment to love our neighbors. . . .

You declared that to those whom you call St. Michael, St. Catherine and St. Margaret, you did reverence, bending the knee . . . vowing them your virginity . . . now touching these matters, the clergy affirm. . . . You are an idolatress, an invoker of demons, an apostate from the faith, a maker of rash statements, a swearer of an unlawful oath.

And you have said . . . that you know that all the deeds of which you have been accused in your trial were wrought according to the command of God and that it was impossible for you to do otherwise. . . . Wherefore the clergy declare you to be schismatic, an unbeliever in the unity and authority of the Church, apostate and obstinately erring from the faith. . . . [The inquisitor admonished her,] "You have believed in apparitions lightly, instead of turning to God in devout prayer to grant you certainty; and you have not consulted prelates or learned ecclesiastics to enlighten yourself: although, considering your condition and the simplicity of your knowledge, you ought to have done so."

QUESTIONS

1. What are the signs that indicated to the judges that Joan was a heretic?

2. Why do the judges believe that Joan's "voices" are false?

Source: W. P. Barrett, trans., *The Trial of Jeanne d'Arc* (New York: Gotham House, 1932), pp. 331–338.

---

crats. Yet in a stunning series of events the French were able to reverse the situation.

Joan of Arc In 1429, with the aid of the mysterious **Joan of Arc** (d. 1431), the French king, Charles VII, was able to raise the English siege of Orléans (or-lay-OHN) and begin the reconquest of the north of France. Joan was the daughter of prosperous peasants from an area of Burgundy that had suffered under the English and their Burgundian allies. Her "voices" told her to go to the king and assist him in driving out the English. Like

many late medieval mystics, she reported regular visions of divine revelation. Even politically or militarily important female leaders depended initially on religious charisma. One of the tests that supported Joan's claim to divine direction was her identification of Charles, who had disguised himself among his courtiers. Dressed as a man, she was Charles's most famed and feared military leader. With Joan's aid, the king was crowned in the cathedral at Reims, the traditional site of French coronations. Joan was captured during an audacious attack on Paris itself and eventually fell into English hands. Because of her "unnatural dress" and her claim to divine guidance, she was condemned and burned as a heretic in 1431. (See the box "The Written Record: The Inquisition of Joan of Arc.") A heretic only

Joan of Arc Charismatic peasant who heard voices telling her to assist the French crown in its war against England. She was captured and eventually executed as a heretic.

to the English and their supporters, Joan almost instantly became a symbol of French resistance. Pope Calixtus III reversed the condemnation in 1456, and Joan was canonized in 1920. The heretic became Saint Joan, patron of France.

Online Study Center **Improve Your Grade**
Primary Source: The Trial of Joan of Arc

Despite Joan's capture, the French advance continued. By 1450 the English had lost all their major centers except Calais (Ca-lay). In 1453 the French armies captured the fortress of Castillon-sur-Dordogne (kasti-YON sir dor-DON-ya) in what was to be the last battle of the war (see Map 11.1). There was no treaty, only a cessation of hostilities.

The war touched almost every aspect of life in western Europe: political, religious, economic, and social. It ranged beyond the borders of France as Scotland, Castile, Aragon, and German principalities were at various times drawn into the struggle. French and English support for rival popes prevented early settlement of the Great Schism in the papacy (see pages 317–319). Further, the war caused a general rise in the level of violence in society. As Henry V casually observed, "War without fire is as bland as sausages without mustard."[6] And because of the highly profitable lightning raids, this war was never bland. During periods of truce many soldiers simply ranged through France, pillaging small towns and ravaging the countryside. Others went in search of work as mercenaries, especially in Germany, Poland, and Italy. Truces in France did not necessarily mean peace in Europe.

ITALY

Compared with France and England, fourteenth- and fifteenth-century Italy was a land of cities. In northern Europe a town of over 20,000 or 30,000 people was unusual; only Paris and London boasted more than 100,000 people in the fourteenth century. Yet at one time or another in the late Middle Ages, Milan, Venice, Florence, and Naples all had populations near or exceeding 100,000, and countless other Italian towns boasted populations of well over 30,000. Unlike northern European states with their kings or emperors, however, the Italian peninsula lacked a unifying force. The centers of power were in Italy's flourishing cities. Political life revolved around the twin issues of who should dominate city governments and how cities could learn to coexist peacefully.

City-States By the late thirteenth century, political power in most Italian towns was divided among three major groups. First was the old urban nobility that could trace its wealth back to grants of property and rights from kings, emperors, and bishops in the tenth and eleventh centuries. Second was the merchant families who had grown wealthy in the twelfth and thirteenth centuries as Italians led the European economic expansion into the Mediterranean. Third, challenging these entrenched urban groups were the modest artisans and merchants who had organized trade, neighborhood, or militia groups and referred to themselves as the *popolo,* or "people." Townspeople gathered together in factions based on wealth, family, profession, neighborhood, and even systems of clientage that reached back into the villages from which many of them had come. "War and hatred have so multiplied among the Italians," observed one Florentine, "that in every town there is a division and enmity between two parties of citizens."

Riven with factions, townspeople often would turn control of their government over to a *signor* (sin-YOUR), a "lord" or "tyrant," often a local noble with a private army. Once firmly in power, the tyrant often allowed the government to continue to function as it had, requiring only that he control all major political appointments. The process might appear democratic, but it represented a profound shift in power. The transformation was clear in Mantua, where, according to one chronicler, "[Pinamonte Bonacolsi (d. 1293)] usurped the lordship of his city and expelled his fellow-citizens and occupied their property. . . . He was feared like the devil."[7] In the case of Milan, the noble Viscontis (vis-KON-tees) used support from the emperor Henry VII (r. 1308–1313) to drive their opponents out of the city. Eventually granted Milan and its territories as a duchy, the Viscontis, and later their Sforza successors, made marriage alliances with the French crown and created a splendid court culture. In a series of wars between the 1370s and 1450s, the dukes of Milan expanded their political control throughout most of Lombardy, Liguria, and, temporarily, Tuscany. The Viscontis maintained control of the city and much of the region of Lombardy until the last scion of the family died in 1447.

The Republics The great republics of Venice and Florence escaped domination by signori, but only by undertaking significant constitutional change. In both republics political life had been disrupted by the arrival of immigrants and by the demands of recently enriched merchants and speculators for a voice in government. In 1297, reacting to increased competition for influence, the Venetian government enacted a reform that would come to be known as the "Closing of the Grand Council." The act enlarged to about eleven hundred the number of families eligible for public office, but its eventual effect was to freeze out subsequent arrivals from ever rising to elite status. The Venetian patriciate became a closed urban nobility. Political, factional, and economic tensions were hidden beneath a veneer of serenity as Venetians developed a myth of public-spirited patricians who governed in the interests of all the people, leaving others free to enrich themselves in trade and manufacture.

In Florence the arguments over citizenship and the right of civic participation disrupted public life. Violent wealthy families, immigrants, and artisans of modest background were cut off from civic participation. A series of reforms culminating in the Ordinances of Justice of 1293 to 1295 restricted political participation in Florence to members in good standing of certain merchant and artisan guilds. Members of violence-prone families were defined as *Magnate* (literally, "the powerful") and disqualified from holding public office. In spite of the reforms, political power remained concentrated in the hands of the great families, whose wealth was based primarily on banking and mercantile investments. These families used their political influence and economic power to dominate Florentine life.

There were short-lived attempts to reform the system and extend the rights of political participation to include the more modest artisans and laborers. The most dramatic was in 1378 when the Ciompi (CHOMP-ee), unskilled workers in Florence's woolen industry, led a popular revolution hoping to expand participation in government and limit the authority of the guild masters over semiskilled artisans and day laborers. They created new guilds to represent the laborers who had no voice in government. Barely six weeks after the Ciompi insurrection, however, wealthy conservatives began a reaction suppressing, exiling, or executing the leaders of the movement and eventually suppressing the new guilds. Political and economic power was now even more firmly in the grip of influential patricians.

Following a crisis in 1434 brought on by war and high taxes, virtual control of Florentine politics fell into the hands of Cosimo de' Medici (day-MAY-di-chi), the wealthiest banker in the city. From 1434 to 1494, Cosimo; his son, Piero; his grandson, Lorenzo; and Lorenzo's son dominated the government in Florence. Although the Medicis were always careful to pay homage to Florentine republican traditions, their control was virtually as complete as that of the lords of towns such as Ferrara and Milan.

Indeed, by the middle of the fifteenth century little differentiated the republics—Florence and Venice—from cities such as Milan and Mantua, where lords held sway. Although Florentines maintained that they intervened to protect Florentine and Tuscan "liberty" when the Viscontis of Milan threatened Tuscany and central

The Journey of the Magi
The story of the journey of the Magi to Bethlehem to find the baby Jesus seemed a perfect image of the power and wisdom of rulers. This painting (a detail) of the Magi was commissioned for the private chapel of Cosimo de' Medici, the de facto ruler of Florence. *(Palazzo Medici Riccardi, Florence/Scala/Art Resource, NY)*

Italy, their interests went beyond simple defense. Relations among the great cities of Milan, Venice, Florence, Rome, and Naples were stabilized by the Peace of Lodi and the creation of the Italian League in 1454. In response to endemic warfare in Italy and the looming threat of the Ottoman Turks in the eastern Mediterranean (see pages 340–343), the five powers agreed to the creation of spheres of influence that would prevent any one of them from expanding at the expense of the others.

The Italian Wars The limits of these territorial states became clear when King Charles VIII of France invaded Italy in 1494 to assert his hereditary claim to the kingdom of Naples. The French invasion touched off a devastating series of wars called the Habsburg-Valois Wars (1496–1559). French claims were challenged by the Habsburg emperors and also by the Spanish, who themselves made claims on southern Italy and much of Lombardy. The cost of prolonged warfare kept almost all governments in a state of crisis. Unrest brought on by the invasion even allowed Pope Alexander VI (r. 1492–1503) to attempt to create a state for his son, Cesare Borgia (BOR-zheh) (1475–1507), in central Italy.

In Florence the wars destroyed the old Medici-dominated regime and brought in a new republican government. Anti-Medici efforts were initially led by the popular Dominican preacher Girolamo Savonarola (1452–1498). In the constitutional debates after 1494,

Savonarola argued that true political reform required a sweeping purge of the evils of society. Gangs of youth flocked to his cause, attacking prostitutes and homosexuals. Many of his followers held "bonfires of vanities," burning wigs, silks, and other luxuries. In 1498, when his followers had lost influence in the government, Savonarola was arrested, tortured, and executed.

In spite of republican reforms, new fortresses, and a citizen militia, the Florentine government was unable to defend itself from papal and imperial armies. In 1512 the Habsburg emperor restored Medici control of Florence. The Medicis later became dukes and then grand dukes of Tuscany. The grand duchy of Tuscany remained an independent, integrated, and well-governed state until the French Revolution of 1789. Venice also managed to maintain its republican form of government and its territorial state until the French Revolution, but like the grand dukes of Tuscany, the governors of Venice were no longer able to act independently of the larger European powers.

The Habsburg-Valois Wars ended with the Treaty of Cateau-Cambrésis (kah-toe kam-bray-SEE) in 1559, which left the Spanish kings in control of Milan, Naples, Sardinia, and Sicily. Thus the Spanish dominated Italy, but without the centralizing control typical of England and France. Venice, Tuscany, the Papal States, and even lesser republics and principalities retained significant influence, as Italy remained a land of regional governments.

═══════ S E C T I O N S U M M A R Y ═══════

- The Hundred Years' War was fought over English dynastic claims within the French kingdom.

- The costs of war contributed to social and political unrest in both countries.

- As a result of the war, the English lost all their significant possessions within the French kingdom.

- Italy was a land of populous, independent cities and regional states.

- By the fifteenth century, most Italian governments were dominated by merchant oligarchies or by lords.

CRISIS IN ECONOMY AND SOCIETY

How were economic and social structures changed by plague and economic crisis?

After nearly three centuries of dramatic growth, Europe in 1300 was seriously overpopulated, with estimates ranging from about 80 million to as high as 100 million. In some parts of Europe, population would not be this dense again until the late eighteenth century. Opportunities dwindled because of overpopulation, famine, war, and

epidemic, which also brought changes in trade and commerce. As the population began to decline, this trend, along with deflation and transformed patterns of consumption, affected agriculture, which was still the foundation of the European economy. Recovery from all these crises altered the structure and dynamics of families, the organization of work, and the culture in many parts of Europe. As a result of the crises, there had been a relative shift in economic and demographic vitality from Italy to England, France, and central Europe.

FAMINE AND DECLINING BIRTHS

People in many parts of Europe were living on the edge of disaster in 1300. Given the low level of agricultural technology and the limited amount of land available for cultivation, it became increasingly difficult for the towns and countryside to feed and support the growing population. The nature of the problem varied from place to place.

Growing numbers of people competed for land to farm and for jobs. Farm sizes declined throughout Europe as parents tended to divide their land among their children. Rents for farmland increased as landlords found that they could play one land-hungry farmer against another. Competition for jobs kept urban wages low, and when taxes were added to high rents and low wages, many peasants and artisans found it difficult to marry and raise families. Thus, because of reduced opportunities brought on by overpopulation, poor townspeople and peasants tended to marry late and have smaller families.

More dramatic than this crisis of births were the deadly famines that occurred in years of bad harvests. The great famine of 1315 to 1322 marks a turning point in the economic history of Europe. Wet and cold weather repeatedly ruined crops in much of northern Europe. Food stocks were quickly exhausted, and mass starvation followed. People died so quickly, English chroniclers reported, that survivors could not keep up with the burials. At Ypres, in Flanders, 2,800 people (about 10 percent of the population) died in just six months. And shortages continued. Seven other severe famines were reported in the south of France or Italy during the fourteenth century.

If Europe's problem had merely been one of famine brought on by overpopulation, rapid recovery should have been possible. But the difficulties of overpopulation were exacerbated by war and plague. As noted previously, the devastation of cities and the countryside was a common tactic in the Hundred Years' War. It was also typical of the local wars in parts of Spain, Germany, and especially Italy. The destruction of trees and vineyards and the theft of livestock made it difficult for rural populations to survive. Then, in 1348, the **Black Death** or "the great Mortality" as contemporaries called it, struck Europe.

Black Death   An epidemic, possibly of bubonic plague, that wiped out one-third or more of Europe's population between 1348 and 1351. It initiated almost three centuries of epidemics.

THE BLACK DEATH

Today there is no consensus as to what caused the Black Death. In the early twentieth century, after the bacillus that causes bubonic plague was identified by French and Japanese physicians in Hong Kong, it was assumed that bubonic plague was the cause. Subsequently, there have been controversial claims that DNA fragments of bubonic plague have been found in mass graves. Yet bubonic plague usually travels slowly and infects a relatively small portion of a given population. By contrast, the Black Death seemed to race across Europe, wiping out entire families and infecting whole cities. Because of this evidence, some historical epidemiologists have speculated that the cause may actually have been anthrax or even a "hemorrhagic plague" similar to the Ebola virus.

The Spread of the Disease   Although the historical identification of the Black Death remains controversial, contemporaries had little doubt about where the disease came from. Genoese traders, they believed, contracted the plague in Caffa, on the Black Sea coast. Infected sailors carried the disease south into Egypt and west into Sicily, then on to Genoa and Venice. From there it followed established trade routes first into central Italy; later to the south of France, the Low Countries, and England; and finally, through the North and Baltic Seas, into Germany and the Slavic lands to the east (see **MAP 11.2**).

Mortality rates varied, but generally 60 percent or more of those infected died. In the initial infestation of 1348 to 1351, 25 to 35 percent of Europe's population may have died. In some of Europe's larger cities the death rate may have been as high as 60 percent. In Florence, for example, the population probably declined from about 90,000 to about 50,000 or even less. And the nearby town of Siena likely fared even worse, with the town and its suburbs losing 55 percent of their people. The shock and disruption were immense. Governments in some towns simply ceased to function at the height of the epidemic. Chroniclers reported that no one could be found to care for the sick or bury the dead. Although abandonment of the sick was probably more a fear than a reality, the epidemic nonetheless significantly disrupted daily life.

Online Study Center   **Improve Your Grade**
Primary Source: The Plague Hits Florence

Just as areas were rebounding from the initial outbreak of the plague, it returned between 1360 and 1363, and then for three centuries thereafter almost no generation could avoid it. It has been calculated that in central Italy, where the best records are available, the plague returned on average every eleven years between

MAP 11.2   The Progress of the Black Death

The Black Death did not advance evenly across Europe; rather, as is clear from the dates at which it struck various regions, it followed the main lines of trade and communication.

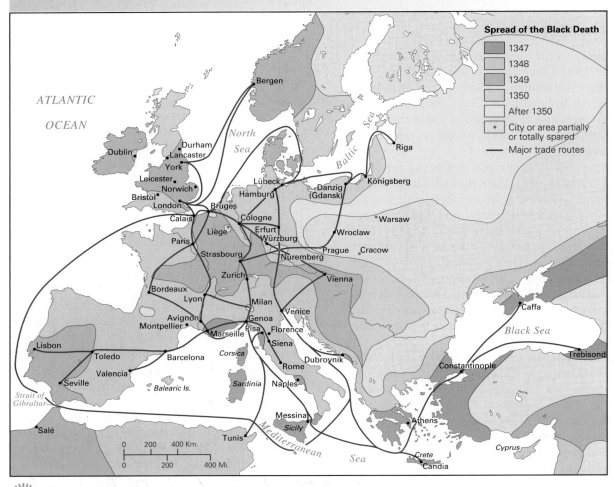

Online Study Center   **Improve Your Grade**   Interactive Map: The Progress of the Black Death

1350 and 1400. Less is known about the plague in Muslim lands and in the eastern Mediterranean, but the situation seems to have been similar to the European experience. Because the plague tended to carry off the young, the almost generational return of the disease accounts for the depressed population levels found in many parts of Europe until the late fifteenth century and in western Asia until the late seventeenth or eighteenth century.

Lacking an understanding of either contagion or infection, fourteenth-century doctors depended on traditional theories inherited from the Greeks, especially the work of Galen (GAY-len), to treat the plague. In Galenic medicine good health depended on the proper balance of bodily and environmental forces; it could be upset by corrupt air, the movement of planets, and even violent shifts in emotions. Yet in the fifteenth and six-

teenth centuries, as the rhythms of the infestations became clearer, towns and, later, territorial governments perceived the contagious nature of the disease. Officials instituted increasingly effective quarantines and embargoes to restrict the movement of goods and people from areas where the plague was raging. Some argue that this innovative effort at public health regulation probably explains the disappearance of the plague from western Europe by the early eighteenth century.

Social and Cultural Responses   Alongside medical theory, however, another class of explanations developed. Taking a lead from miracle stories in which Jesus linked illness and sin, many Christians considered the Black Death a signal of the Last Judgment, or at least a sign of the severe judgment of God on a sinful world. Given that view, a traditional, and logical, religious response was to urge various moral reforms and penitential acts, such as charitable gifts, special prayers, and holy processions. (See the feature "The Visual Record: A Painting of the Plague.") Many Muslim theologians also concluded that "the plague is part of Allah's punishment." Women were often thought to be a source of moral pollution and hence one of the causes of God's wrath. In Muslim Egypt, women were ordered off the streets; in Christian Europe prostitutes were driven out of towns.

A movement of penitents called "flagellants" arose in Hungary and spread quickly into Germany and across France and the Low Countries. In an imitation of Christ's life and sufferings, they sought to atone in their own bodies for the sins of the world. Following an ancient Christian tradition, they ritually beat (flagellated) themselves between the shoulders with metal-tipped whips. Through their processions and sufferings, these pilgrims hoped to bring about a moral and religious transformation of society. The arrival of flagellants was often an occasion for an end of feuds and political violence within a community. But their arrival just as often was an occasion for political and even religious unrest. Authorities recognized the flagellants and the leaders of the religious riots as dangerous and drove them from towns.

In a quest for a purer, truly Christian society, the flagellants brought suspicion on all those who were not Christian or who were otherwise suspect. Some parts of Europe witnessed murderous attacks on outsiders, especially lepers and Jews, who were suspected of spreading the contagion in an attempt to bring down Latin Christendom. These attacks probably have more to do with tensions and fears already existing in parts of Europe than with the provocations of the flagellants. Like many other anti-Semitic myths, the rumors of wells poisoned by lepers and Jews seemed to arise in the south of France and spread in their most virulent forms to German towns along the Rhine. In Strasbourg attacks on Jews preceded the arrival of the plague. Except in a few districts, officials opposed attacks on Jews, lepers, and heretics. Doctors and churchmen often observed that Jews were unlikely culprits, since the plague claimed Jewish as well as Christian victims. Despite

Saint Roch Cured by an Angel
Saint Roch is often shown with an exposed plague bubo. The image offered Christians comfort since he was cured because of his faith and charity. It offers modern historians evidence that bubonic plague was responsible for at least some of the mortality.
(Courtesy, Bayerisches Nationalmuseum)

A Painting of the Plague

Writers who survived the coming of pestilential disease in 1348 described a world of terror in which things seemed changed forever. Look at this painting, *St. Sebastian Interceding for the Plague-Stricken,* created by the Flemish artist Josse Lieferinxe between 1497 and 1499. One dying man seems to be falling terrified to the ground, while a female bystander in the background screams in alarm. Images of Christ, Saint Sebastian (pierced by arrows), a devil, and a priest seem to indicate that something terrifying and undreamed-of is happening. But what exactly was the terror, and what had changed?

The art of the later Middle Ages is an extremely valuable source for understanding social and religious values. As you look at *St. Sebastian Interceding for the Plague-Stricken,* the first step is to understand what men and women in the fourteenth and fifteenth centuries thought about death. After 1400 European Christians often depicted the universality of death in paintings showing the Dance of Death. The motif varies, but typically Death grasps the hands of men and women, rich and poor, noble and peasant, and leads them away. Deathbed scenes were another popular motif. In the late Middle Ages most people believed that at death the good and evil acts committed by an individual were tallied in the Book of Life and the person was either granted eternal life, first in Purgatory and then Paradise, or consigned to eternal suffering in Hell. Judgment scenes often depict the Virgin Mary or another saint pleading before God or contending with the Devil or demons over the souls of the dying.

It was essential for people to prepare for a good death. Individuals studied the *artes moriendi,* or "arts of dying." A lingering, painful illness was often interpreted as an opportunity for penitential suffering that would benefit the soul. At the point of death, the dying person could confess and receive absolution for sins and the last sacraments of the church. From that moment on, he or she needed to maintain a calm faith, free from fear. Salvation and eternal life depended on avoiding further sin, especially the questioning of God's forgiveness and mercy. Death was a public event. Clergy, family, religious societies, even neighbors helped the dying person to avoid losing faith at the end. The person might pray, "Virgin Mary, Mother of God, I have placed my hope in you. Free my soul from care, and from Hell, and bitter death."[*]

The concept of a good death is critical to understanding the European response to the plague. To be sure, individuals rarely look forward to death, then or now. Numerous writers and chroniclers lamented the suddenness of death and the lack of priests to hear confessions. Individuals who were healthy in the morning might be dead by nightfall. The suddenness, the lack of time to prepare for a good death, heightened the dread that accompanied the onset of the illness.

Medieval Christians turned to saints to represent them before God at the point of death and to stop the onslaught of the plague. Three patron saints were especially popular. The Virgin Mary was often shown using her cloak to shelter towns and individuals from arrows carrying pestilence. Saint Roch, himself a victim of the plague, was thought to intercede and protect those who prayed in his name. And Saint Sebastian, an early Christian who as part of his elaborate martyrdom survived being shot with arrows (later understood as symbols of death caused by the plague), was thought to be an especially effective patron during epidemics. In times of plague, people went on pilgrimages to local shrines dedicated to these or local saints, carried images of the saints in processions, and built churches and chapels in honor of the saints in thanks for deliverance from the plague.

With these issues in mind, what do we see in Lieferinxe's painting? The painting portrays an outbreak of the plague. We note first the body of the dead person, carefully shrouded. Ideally the dead, like the corpse here, were taken to a church by friends and relatives and given a Christian burial. This was an important part of the ritual meant to ease the suffering of the soul in Purgatory. But chroniclers often reported that so many died, and died so quickly, that no one could be found to bury them properly. In many towns the dead were gathered on carts and hauled to gaping common graves outside the towns. We can see one such cart leaving the castle in the background. In a series of images, then, Lieferinxe shows what mattered most

---

[*]Quoted in Philippe Ariès, *The Hour of Our Death* (New York: Knopf, 1981), p. 108.

Lieferinxe: St. Sebastian Interceding for the Plague-Stricken

(Collection of The Walters Art Museum. Photo © The Walters Art Museum, Baltimore)

to people. In the foreground is the shrouded body attended by a priest and other clerics bearing a cross. This person experienced a good death. In contrast, the man who has fallen behind the body is suffering a bad death, one that caught him unaware. He is the object of the concern and grief of those near him. In the sky just above the castle walls, a white-robed angel and a horned, ax-wielding demon contend over the souls of the dead and dying. At the top of the painting Christ listens to the prayers of Saint Sebastian. The painting thus portrays the impact and horror of plague and also the way Christians were expected to respond to it.

Returning to our original question, we can conclude that the terror of epidemic plague was not entirely like a modern panic. Medieval people saw the Black Death, its ghastly devastation, and its only possible solution or meaning in terms of traditional religious values: the true terror was to be caught unaware.

QUESTIONS

1. What is a good death?

2. What responses to epidemic diseases can you find in this image?

3. Which parts of the image illustrate panic and which do not?

Online Study Center

Improve Your Grade Visual Record Activities

official rejection of popular rumors and fears, from the mid-fourteenth century, life became more difficult for the Jews of Christian Europe.

It was a commonplace among contemporary chroniclers that "so many did die that everyone thought it was the end of the world." Yet it was the very young, the elderly, and the poor—those least likely to pay taxes, own shops, or produce children—who were the most common victims. And even in towns such as Florence, where mortality rates were extraordinarily high, recovery from the initial epidemic was rapid. Government offices were closed at most for only a few weeks; markets reopened as soon as the death rate began to decline; and within two years tax receipts were back at preplague levels. Yet plague, fear of plague, and social and economic disruption caused by epidemic disease became a regular feature of European life. Thus famine, warfare, plague, and population decline fueled the economic and social transformations of the late Middle Ages.

TRADE AND AGRICULTURE

In the aftermath of plague, the economy of Europe changed in a number of profound ways. Disruptions brought on by population decline were accompanied by changes in the basic structure of economic life. In particular, Italy's domination of the European economy was challenged by the growth of trade and manufacturing in many other parts of Europe. Further, by 1500 the relative power of Italian bankers declined as they came to face competition from equally astute northern bankers.

Italian and Northern Merchants   Discussions of the economy must begin with Italy because it was the key point of contact between Europe and the international economy. In 1300 Italian merchants sold woolens produced in Flanders and Italy to Arab traders in North Africa, who sold them along the African coast and as far south as the Niger Delta. The Italians used the gold that they collected in payment to buy spices and raw materials in Byzantium, Egypt, and even China. They resold these highly prized goods in the cities and at regional fairs of northern Europe. Italian traders also sold spices, silks, and other luxuries throughout Europe, from England to Poland.

Because of their expertise in moving bullion and goods and their ready sources of capital, Italian merchants, such as the Ricciardis of Lucca who flourished in England, were ideal bankers and financial advisers to the popes and European rulers, who appreciated sources of ready capital. In time of war rulers tended to trade the rights to various revenues to Italian bankers, who had cash at hand. Merchants from Cremona,

Genoa, Florence, and Siena forged commercial agreements with the kings of France, Aragon, and Castile, and with the papacy.

The most powerful bank in fifteenth-century Europe was the Medici bank of Florence. Founded in 1397 by Giovanni de' Medici (1360–1429), the bank grew quickly because of its role as papal banker. Medici agents transferred papal revenues from all parts of Europe to Rome and managed papal alum mines, which provided an essential mineral to the growing cloth industry. Cosimo de' Medici (1389–1464), Giovanni's son and successor, transformed the enterprise into a series of bilateral partnerships with easily controlled junior partners in other parts of Europe. In this way he avoided the problem of supervision and control that plagued other banks, whose partners were equal and free to speculate and invest as they wished.

The dramatic career of the Frenchman Jacques Coeur (1395?–1456) demonstrates that by the mid-fifteenth century, Italian merchants were not the only Europeans who understood international trade. After making a fortune trading in southern France, Coeur managed the French royal mint and became the financial adviser of King Charles VII (r. 1422–1461). He put the French monarchy back on a solid financial footing after the Hundred Years' War, becoming in the process the wealthiest individual in France. Not surprisingly, his wealth and influence earned him jealous enemies, who tried to bring him down with outrageous claims: he was accused of murdering the king's mistress, trading with Muslims, and stealing royal funds. In 1451 his property was confiscated, and he was jailed for a short time. He later led a papal expedition against the Turks in the Aegean, where he died.

New Trading Patterns   By 1500 Italians faced increased competition from local merchants throughout Europe. From as early as the late thirteenth century, trade along the North and Baltic Seas in northern Europe was dominated by the **Hanseatic League,** an association of over a hundred trading cities centered on the German city of Lübeck. By the late fourteenth and early fifteenth centuries, the Hansa towns controlled grain shipments from eastern Europe to England and Scandinavia. The league's domination waned in the second half of the fifteenth century, however, as Dutch, English, and even southern German merchants gained shares of the wool, grain, and fur trades. Towns in the eastern Baltic found that their interests no longer coincided with those of the towns in western Germany that made up the Hanseatic League. Wroclaw (VROT-swav) (in modern Poland) signaled the nature of the change

Hanseatic League   An association of over a hundred German trading towns, which dominated trade in the North Sea and Baltic Sea regions during the fourteenth and fifteenth centuries.

when it resigned from the league in 1474 to expand trade connections with the southern German towns.

In contrast to the Hanseatic League of towns, merchants in southern Germany adopted Italian techniques of trade, manufacture, and finance to expand their influence throughout central Europe. German merchants regularly bought spices in the markets of Venice and distributed them in central and eastern Europe. By the fifteenth century the townspeople of southern Germany also produced linen and cotton cloth, which found ready markets in central and eastern Europe.

The Fugger (FOO-ger) family of Augsburg in southern Germany, the most prosperous of the German commercial families, exemplifies the variety of activities undertaken by south German merchants. Hans Fugger (1348–1409) moved to Augsburg from a nearby village in the 1360s and quickly established himself as a weaver and wool merchant. By the 1470s Hans's grandson, Jacob Fugger (1459–1525), was a dominant figure in the spice trade and also participated in a number of unusually large loans to a succession of German princes. The Fuggers became leaders in the Tyrolean silver-mining industry, which expanded dramatically in the late fifteenth century. And in the early sixteenth cen-tury they handled all transfers of money from Germany to the papacy. Jacob Fugger's wealth increased fourfold between 1470 and 1500. The Fuggers were indispensable allies of the German emperors. Jacob himself ensured the election of Charles V as Holy Roman emperor in 1519, making a series of loans that allowed Charles to buy the influence that he needed to win election.

The Rural Economy   As wealthy as the great merchants were, in most parts of Europe prosperity was still tied to agriculture and the production of food grains. In northern and western Europe foodstuffs were produced on the manorial estates of great churchmen and nobles. These estates were worked by a combination of farmers paying rents, serfs who owed a variety of labor services, and day laborers who were hired during planting and harvesting. In the face of a decimated population, landlords and employers found themselves competing for the reduced number of laborers who had survived the plague. In 1351 the English crown issued the Statute of Laborers, which pegged wages and the prices of commodities at preplague levels. According to the statute, regulation was necessary because laborers "withdrew themselves from serving great men and others unless they have living [in food] and wages double

Street Life in Medieval Towns
In a world dependent on natural lighting, shops were entirely open to the street. It made social and economic life much more public than it is in the modern world.
(Bibliothèque nationale de France)

or treble of what they were [before the plague]." This statute and similar ones passed in other parts of Europe were dead letters. So long as population levels remained low, landowners were unable to keep wages low and rents high.

Cloth manufacture, not agriculture, was the part of the European economy that changed most dramatically in the late Middle Ages. First in Flanders, then later in England, Germany, and the rest of Europe, production shifted from urban workshops to the countryside. Industries in rural areas tended to be free of controls on quality or techniques. Rural production, whether in Flanders, England, or Lombardy, became the most dynamic part of the industry.

Rural cloth production, especially in southwestern Germany and parts of England, was organized through the putting-out system. Merchants who owned the raw wool contracted with various artisans in the city, suburbs, or countryside—wherever the work could be done most cheaply—to process the wool into cloth. Rural manufacture was least expensive because it could be done as occasional or part-time labor by farmers, or by their wives or children, during slack times of the day or season. Because production was likely to be finished in the countryside (beyond guild supervision), the merchant was free to move the cloth to wherever it could be sold most easily and profitably; guild masters had no control over price or quality.

Two other developments also changed the woolen trade of the fifteenth century: the rise of Spain as an exporter of unprocessed wool and the emergence of England, long recognized as a source of prime wool, as a significant producer of finished cloth. Spain was an ideal region for the pasturing of livestock. By the fifteenth century highly prized Spanish wool from merino sheep was regularly exported to Italy, Flanders, and England. By 1500 over three million sheep grazed in Castile alone, and revenues from duties on wool formed the backbone of royal finance.

In England, in contrast, economic transformation was tied to cloth production. During the fifteenth century England reduced its export of its high-quality raw wool and began instead to export its own finished cloth. In 1350 the English exported just over 5,000 bolts of cloth. By the 1470s exports had risen to 63,000 bolts, and they doubled again by the 1520s. The growth of cloth exports contributed enormously to the expansion of London. During the fourteenth and fifteenth centuries English commerce became increasingly controlled by London merchant-adventurers. Soon after 1500 over 80 percent of the cloth for export passed through the hands of the Londoners. This development, coupled with the rise of London as a center of administration and consumption, laid the foundation for the economic and demographic growth that would make London the largest and most prosperous city in western Europe by the eighteenth century.

Patterns of Economic Life The new structures of agriculture, manufacture, and trade in the fifteenth century challenged customs and institutions by admitting new entrepreneurs into the marketplace. But Europe was still a conservative society in which social and political influence was more prized than economic wealth. Patricians in many European towns acted to dampen competition and preserve traditional values. Great banking families such as the Medicis of Florence tended to avoid competition and concentrations of capital. They did not try to drive their competitors out of business because the leaders of rival banks were their political and social peers. In northern Europe, governments in towns such as Leiden restricted the concentration of resources in the hands of the town's leading cloth merchants. Their aim was to ensure full employment for the town's laborers, political power for the guild masters, and social stability in the town.

Full employment was not just for men. Although men had controlled the guilds and most crafts in the thirteenth and early fourteenth centuries, women's guilds existed in several European cities, including Paris and Cologne. In Italy some women could be found among the more prosperous crafts. Women often practiced their trades in the context of the family. In Cologne, for instance, women produced the linen yarn and silk cloths that their husbands sold throughout Europe. Speaking of the silkmakers of Cologne, a report noted that "the women are much more knowledgeable about the trade than are the men." Unlike southern Europe, where women had no public roles, some northern towns apparently allowed women's guilds to protect their members' activities as artisans and even peddlers. Because they often worked before marriage, townswomen in northern Europe tended to marry at a later age than did women in Italy. Many women earned their own marriage dowries. Since they had their own sources of income and often managed the shop of a deceased husband, women could be surprisingly independent. They were consequently under less pressure to remarry at the death of a spouse. Although their economic circumstances varied considerably, up to a quarter of the households in northern towns such as Bern and Zurich were headed by women. Many of them were widows, but many others, perhaps a third, were women who had never married.

If plague and population decline created new opportunities for women, the fifteenth century brought new restrictions to women's lives. In England brewing ale had been a highly profitable part-time activity that women often combined with the running of a house-

Women at Work
Although guild records tend to ignore the contributions of women, many women worked in their husbands' shops. In this miniature a woman is selling jewelry. Widows often managed the shops they inherited. *(Bibliothèque nationale de France)*

hold. Ale was usually produced in small batches for household use, and whatever went unconsumed would be sold. The introduction of beer changed matters. Because hops were added as a preservative during brewing, beer was easier to produce, store, and transport in large batches. Beer brewing became a lucrative full-time trade, reducing the demand for the alewife's product and providing work for men as brewers. At the same time the rights of women to work in urban crafts and industries were reduced. Wealthy fathers became less inclined to allow wives and daughters to work outside the home. Guilds banned the use of female laborers in many trades and severely limited the rights of widows to supervise their spouses' shops. For reasons that are not entirely clear, journeymen—employees of guild masters who themselves hoped to become masters—objected to working alongside women. These complaints may have come from workers who realized that their status as employees was permanent instead of a temporary stage before promotion to master. By the early sixteenth century journeymen in Germany considered it "dishonorable" for a woman, even the master's wife or daughter, to work in a shop.

Despite the narrowing of economic opportunities for women, the overall economic prospects of peasants and laborers improved. Lower rents and increased wages in the wake of the plague meant a higher standard of living for small farmers and laborers. Before the plague struck in 1348, most poor Europeans had subsisted on bread or grain-based gruel, consuming meat, fish, and cheese only a few times a week. A well-off peasant in England had lived on a daily ration of about two pounds of bread and a cup or two of oatmeal porridge washed down with three or four pints of ale. Poorer peasants generally drank water except on very special occasions. After the plague laborers were more prosperous. Adults in parts of Germany may have consumed nearly a liter of wine, a third of a pound of meat, and a pound or more of bread each day. Elsewhere people could substitute an equivalent portion of beer, ale, or cider for the wine. Hard times for landlords were good times for peasants and day laborers.

Landlords in England responded to the shortage of labor by converting their lands to grazing in order to produce wool for the growing textile market. In parts of Italy landlords invested in canals, irrigation, and new crops in order to increase profits. In eastern Germany and Poland landlords were able to take advantage of political and social unrest to force tenants into semi-free servile status. This so-called second serfdom created an impoverished work force whose primary economic activity was in the lord's fields, establishing commercial grain farming. Increasingly in the second half of the century grains cultivated in Poland and Prussia found their way to markets in England and the Low Countries. Europe east of the Elbe River became a major producer of grain, but at a heavy social cost.

The loss of perhaps a third of the urban population to the plague had serious consequences in the towns of Europe. Because of lower birthrates and higher death rates, late medieval towns needed a constant influx of immigrants to expand or even to maintain their populations. These immigrants did not find life in the cities easy, however. Citizenship in most towns was restricted to masters in the most important guilds, and local governments were in their hands, if not under their thumbs. In many towns citizens constructed a system of taxation that worked to their own economic advantage and fell heavily on artisans and peasants living in territories controlled by the towns. Unskilled laborers and members of craft guilds depended for their economic well-being on personal relationships with powerful citizens who controlled the government and the markets. Peace and order in towns and in the countryside required a delicate balance of the interests of the well-to-do and the more humble. When that balance was shattered by war, plague, and economic depression, the result was often a popular revolt, such as the Ciompi insurrection of 1378 in Florence and the Rising of 1381 in England.

━━━━━━━━ SECTION SUMMARY ━━━━━━━━

- The Black Death may have killed one-third or more of Europe's population.

- In response to the epidemics many groups attacked outsiders, lepers, and Jews.

- Italy's medieval bankers and merchants dominated trade between Europe, North Africa, and the eastern Mediterranean.

- By the late fifteenth century, north European merchants challenged Italian economic leadership.

- Cloth production, arranged by a putting-out system, was Europe's most important industry.

- By the end of the fifteenth century, women found it increasingly difficult to maintain a significant role in Europe's craft industries.

THE CONSOLIDATION OF POLITICAL POWER, 1450–1500

How did the political makeup of Europe in 1500 differ from that in 1300?

By 1500 it seemed that the French royal lawyer's claim that all within the kingdom belonged to the king was finally accepted. With the exception of Italy and Germany, strong central governments recovered from the crises of war and civil unrest that wracked the fourteenth and fifteenth centuries. The Hundred Years' War and the resulting disorganization in France and England seemed to strike at the heart of the monarchies. But through the foundation of standing armies and the careful consolidation of power in the royal court, both countries seemed stronger and more able to defend themselves in the second half of the century. And as the Italians learned in the wars following the French invasion of 1494, small regional powers were no match for the mighty monarchies.

FRANCE, ENGLAND, AND SCANDINAVIA

In France recovery from a century of war was based on a consolidation of the monarchy's power. A key to French military successes had been the creation of a paid professional army, which replaced the feudal host and mercenary companies of the fourteenth century. Charles VII created Europe's first standing army, a cavalry of about eight thousand nobles under the direct control of royal commanders. Charles also expanded his judicial claims. He and his son, Louis XI (r. 1461–1483), created new provincial *parlements*, or law courts, at Toulouse, Grenoble, Bordeaux, and Dijon. They also required that local laws and customs be registered and approved by the parlements.

A second key to maintaining royal influence was the rise of the French court as a political and financial center. Through careful appointments and judicious offers of annuities and honors, Charles VII and Louis XI drew the nobility to the royal court and made the nobles dependent on it. "The court," complained a frustrated noble, "is an assembly of people who, under the pretense of acting for the good of all, come together to diddle each other; for there's scarcely anyone who isn't engaged in buying and selling and exchanging . . . and sometimes for their money we sell them our . . . humanity."[8] One of Louis XI's advisers noted that Charles VII never had revenues greater than 18,000 francs in a single year but that Louis collected 4.7 million. By 1500 France had fully recovered from the crisis of war and was once again a strong and influential state.

The fate of the English monarchy was quite different. Henry VI (r. 1422–1461) turned out to be weak-willed, immature, and prone to bouts of insanity—inherited, perhaps, from his French grandfather, Charles VI (see page 324). The infirmity of Henry VI and the loss of virtually all French territories in 1453 led to factional battles known as the Wars of the Roses—the red rose symbolized Henry's House of Lancaster, the white the rival House of York. Edward of York eventually deposed Henry and claimed the Crown for himself as Edward IV (r. 1461–1483). He faced little opposition because few alternatives existed. English public life was again thrown into confusion, however, at Edward's death. The late king's brother, Richard, duke of Gloucester, claimed the protectorship over the 13-year-old king, Edward V (r. April–June 1483), and his younger brother. Richard seized the boys, who were placed in the Tower of London and never seen again. He proclaimed himself king and was crowned Richard III (r. 1483–1485). He withstood early challenges to his authority but in 1485 was killed in the Battle of Bosworth Field, near Coventry, by Henry Tudor, a leader of the Lancastrian faction. Henry married Elizabeth, the surviving child of Edward IV. Symbolically at least, the struggle between the rival claimants to the Crown appeared over.

Henry VII (r. 1485–1509), like Edward IV who preceded him, recognized the importance of avoiding war and taxation. Just as the French kings did, Henry created a patronage network of local officials to secure allies for his dynasty. Royal power, however, was not based on a transformation of the institutions of government. Following Edward's example, Henry controlled local affairs through the traditional system of royal patronage. He also imitated Edward in emphasizing the dignity of the royal office. Though careful with his funds, he was willing to buy jewels and clothing if they added to the brilliance of his court. As one courtier summed up his reign, "His hospitality was splendidly generous. . . . He knew well how to maintain his majesty and all which pertains to kingship." Henry solidified ties with Scotland and Spain by marrying his daughter, Margaret Tudor, to James IV of Scotland and his sons, Arthur and (after Arthur's death) Henry, to Catherine of Aragon, daughter of the Spanish rulers Ferdinand and Isabella.

The English monarchy of the late fifteenth century departed little from previous governments. The success of Henry VII was based on several factors: the absence of powerful opponents; lower taxation thanks to twenty-five years of peace; and the desire, shared by ruler and ruled alike, for an orderly realm built on the assured succession of a single dynasty.

In the fourteenth and fifteenth centuries the Scandinavian kingdoms of Denmark, Sweden, and Norway lay open to economic and political influences from Germany. German merchants traded throughout the area and completely controlled access to the important port of Bergen in Norway. German nobles sought to influence northern political life, especially in Denmark. The Scandinavian aristocracy, however, especially in Denmark, remained wary of German interests. Alert to outside pressures, Scandinavian elites tended to marry among themselves and forge alliances against the Germans.

Public authority varied greatly across Scandinavia. In Norway, Denmark, and Sweden the power of the king was always mediated by the influence of the council, made up of the country's leading landowners. Power was based on ownership or control of lands and rents. All the Scandinavian countries were home to a significant class of free peasants, and they were traditionally represented in the Riksdag in Sweden and the Storting in Norway, popular assemblies that had the right to elect kings, authorize taxes, and make laws. Scandinavians spoke similar Germanic languages and were linked by close social and economic ties. Thus it is not surprising that the crowns of the three kingdoms were joined during periods of crisis. In 1397 the dowager queen Margaret of Denmark was able to unite the Scandinavian crowns by the Union of Kalmar, which would nominally endure until 1523.

EASTERN EUROPE AND RUSSIA

Two phenomena had an especially profound effect on the governments of eastern Europe. One was the emergence of a newly important ruling dynasty. The other was the decline of Mongol, or Tatar, influence in the region. Since the thirteenth century much of eastern Europe had been forced to acknowledge Tatar dominion and pay annual tribute. Now the Tatar subjugation was challenged and finally ended.

As in much of Europe, political power was segmented and based on personal relationships between family members, communities, clients, and friends. Life in the East was further complicated by the mix of languages, cultures, and religions. Native Catholic and Orthodox populations were further diversified in the fourteenth century by the arrival of Muslims in the Balkans and Ashkenazi Jews throughout most of the region. Escaping growing persecution in western Europe, the Ashkenazim migrated to Poland, Lithuania, and Ruthenian lands (parts of modern Russia), where they lived under their own leaders and followed their own laws.

Poland and Lithuania   This mix of cultures and religions played a role in the growth of new states. Under the pretext of converting their pagan neighbors to Christianity, the mostly German Teutonic knights sought to expand eastward against the kingdom of Poland and the Lithuanian state. They were thwarted, however, by a profound dynastic shift. In 1386 Grand Duke Jagiello (yahg-YELL-loh) of Lithuania, who reigned from 1377 to 1434, converted to Catholic Christianity and married Hedwig, the daughter and heir of King Louis of Poland (r. 1370–1382). The resulting dynastic union created a state with a population of perhaps six million that reached from the Baltic nearly to the Black Sea. Polish-Lithuanian power slowed and finally halted the German advance to the east. Most serious for the Teutonic knights was their defeat in 1410 at Tannenberg, in Prussia, by a Polish-Lithuanian army led by Jagiello's cousin, Prince Vytautus of Lithuania. The Polish-Lithuanian union was only dynastic. The descendants of Jagiello, called Jagiellonians, had no hereditary right to rule Poland, and the Lithuanians opposed any Polish administrative influence in their lands. Yet because of Jagiellonian power, the Poles continued to select them as kings. At various times Jagiellonians also sat on the thrones of Bohemia and Hungary.

Poland and Lithuania remained more closely tied to western Europe than to the Russian East. They tended to be Catholic rather than Orthodox Christians. They wrote in a Roman rather than a Cyrillic script. And their political institutions resembled those of western Europe. Polish nobles managed to win a number of important concessions, the most significant being freedom from arbitrary arrest and confinement. This civil right was secured in Poland well before the more famous English right of habeas corpus. It was during this period, and under the influence of the Polish kings, that Cracow emerged as the economic and cultural center of Poland. Cracow University was founded in 1364 in response to the foundation of Prague University by the emperor Charles IV in 1348. After the dynastic union of Poland and Lithuania, Polish language and culture increasingly influenced the Lithuanian nobility. This union laid the foundation for the great Polish-Lithuanian commonwealth of the early modern period.

The Rise of Moscow   Lithuania had never been conquered by the Tatars, and its expansion contributed to the decline of Tatar power. The rise of Moscow, however, owed much to the continuing Tatar domination. Since the Mongol invasions in the thirteenth century, various towns and principalities of Kievan Rus had been part of a Tatar sphere of influence. This primarily meant homage and payment of an annual tribute.

A key to the emergence of Moscow occurred when Ivan I (r. 1328–1341), Prince of Moscow, was named Grand Prince and collector of tribute from the other Russian princes. Not for nothing was he called "the Moneybag." It was during this same period that the head of the Russian Orthodox Church was persuaded to make his home in Moscow. And in 1367 the princes began to rebuild the Kremlin walls in stone.

The decisive change for Moscow, however, was the reign of Ivan III (r. 1462–1505). By 1478 Ivan III, called "Ivan the Great," had seized the famed trading center of Novgorod. Two years later he was powerful enough to renounce Mongol overlordship and refuse further payments of tribute. After his marriage to an émigré Byzantine princess living in Rome, Ivan began to call himself "Tsar" (Russian for "Caesar"), implying that in the wake of the Muslim conquest of Constantinople, Moscow had become the new Rome.

THE OTTOMAN EMPIRE

The most profound political and cultural transformation of the late Middle Ages took place in the Balkans with the conquest of Constantinople (1453) and the emergence of the Ottoman Turks as a major European power (see **MAP 11.3**). They solidified a fragmented and unstable area and from their base spread their influence throughout the Mediterranean and Europe.

The eastern Mediterranean region was a politically tumultuous area in the fourteenth century, when the Ottoman Turks were first invited into the Balkans by the hard-pressed Byzantine emperor. In the 1420s as the Turks and the Hungarians fought for influence in Serbia, the Serbian king moved easily from alliance with one to alliance with the other. Elites often retained their political and economic influence by changing religion. The Christian aristocracy of late-fifteenth-century Bosnia, for example, was welcomed into Islam and instantly created a cohesive elite fighting force for the Turks. Conversely, as Turkish power in Albania grew, one noble, George Castriota (d. 1467), known by his Turkish name Skanderbeg, reconverted to Christianity and became a leading figure in the resistance to the

MAP 11.3   Turkey and Eastern Europe

With the conquest of Constantinople, Syria, and Palestine, the Ottoman Turks controlled the eastern Mediterranean and dominated Europe below the Danube River. The Holy Roman emperors, rulers of Italy, and kings of Spain had to be concerned about potential invasions by land or by sea.

1490
- Ottoman Empire
- Ottoman vassals
- Venetian lands
- Genoese lands
- Land of the Hospitallers
- ✕ Major battles

Online Study Center **Improve Your Grade** Interactive Map: Turkey and Eastern Europe

Turks. Only after his death were the Turks able to integrate Albania into their empire.

An Ottoman victory over a Christian crusading army at Varna, on the Black Sea coast, in 1444 changed the dynamics and virtually sealed the fate of Constantinople. It was only a matter of time before the Turks took the city. When Mehmed (MEH-met) II (r. 1451–1481) finally turned his attention to Constantinople in 1453, the siege of the city lasted only fifty-three days. The destruction of the last vestiges of the Roman imperial tradition that reached back to the emperor Augustus sent shock waves through Christian Europe and brought forth calls for new crusades to liberate the East from the evils of Islam. It also stirred anti-Christian feelings among the Turks. The rise of the Ottoman Turks transformed eastern Europe and led to a profound clash between Christian and Muslim civilizations.

After the fall of Constantinople the Turks worked to consolidate their new territories. Through alliance and conquest Ottoman hegemony extended through Syria and Palestine and by 1517 to Egypt. Even the Muslim powers of North Africa were nominally under Turkish control. In short order they expanded to the west and north, seizing Croatia, Bosnia, Dalmatia, Albania, eastern Hungary, Moldavia, Bulgaria, and Greece. Turkish strength was based on a number of factors. The first was the loyalty and efficiency of the sultan's crack troops, the Janissaries. These troops were young boys forcibly taken from the subject Christian populations, trained in the Turkish language and customs, and converted to Islam. Although they functioned as special protectors of the Christian community from which they were drawn, they were separated from it by their new faith. Because the Turkish population viewed them as outsiders, they were particularly loyal to the sultan.

The situation of the Janissaries underlines a secondary explanation for Ottoman strength: the unusually tolerant attitudes of Mehmed, who saw himself not only as the greatest of the *ghazi* (crusading warriors who were considered the "instruments of Allah") but also as emperor, heir to Byzantine and ancient imperial traditions. Immediately after the conquest of Constantinople he repopulated the city with Greeks, Armenians, Jews, and Muslims. Mehmed especially welcomed Sephardic Jews from Spain and Portugal to parts of his empire. Thessalonica (Salonika), for example, was sec-

ond only to Amsterdam as a Sephardic Jewish center until the community was destroyed in World War II. Religious groups in the cities lived in separate districts centered on a church or synagogue, and each religious community retained the right to select its own leaders. (See the box "The Global Record: A Disputation.") Mehmed made Constantinople the capital of the new Ottoman Empire. And by building mosques, hospitals, hostels, and bridges, he breathed new life into the city, which he referred to as Istanbul—that is, "the city." In the fifty years following the conquest, the population

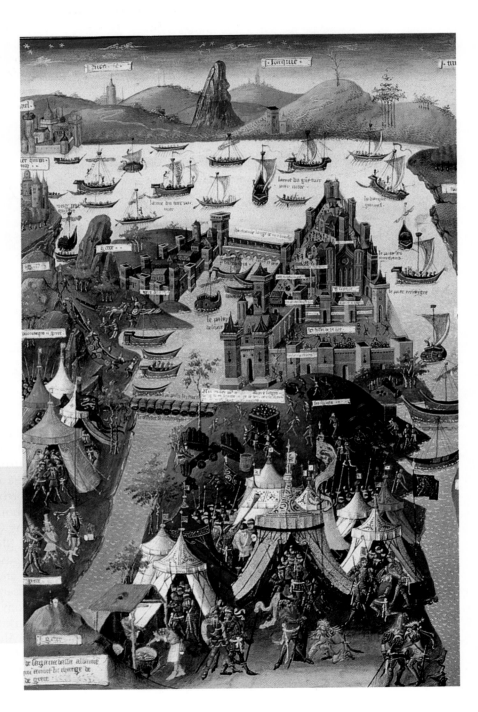

The Siege of Constantinople
The siege of Constantinople by the Turks required the attackers to isolate the city both by sea and by land. This miniature from the fifteenth century shows the Turkish camps, as well as the movements of Turkish boats, completing the isolation of the city. *(Bibliothèque nationale de France)*

A DISPUTATION

Konstantin Mihailovic, a Serb by birth, was captured by the Turks during the conquest of Constantinople in 1453. He later served with the Turks until he returned to the Christian forces in 1463. His description of a typical Turkish disputation, or debate, taking place in the presence of the sultan or another dignitary is an interesting example of how the Muslim, Jewish, and Christian peoples of the Balkans tried to understand one another.

The masters and scribes have among themselves this custom: they arrange their deliberations before the highest lord after the emperor. . . . And then they begin to argue one against the other, speaking mostly about the prophets. Some [of these Turkish scribes] recognize Our Lord Jesus Christ as a prophet, and others as an archprophet, alongside God the Creator of Heaven and earth. And also the Lord, from the time when the Mohammedan faith began, created eight hundred camels, like invisible spirits, which go around every night and gather evil *Busromane* [i.e., the Muslim, or the Chosen People of God] from our [Muslim] graves and carry them to *kaur* graves [the Kaury are "the Confused People," i.e., the Christians]; and then gather good kaury and carry them to our graves. And now the good kaury will stand with our Busroman council and the evil Busromane will stand with the kaur council on Judgment Day before God. For [a pious one] says . . . , "The Christians have a faith but have no works." Therefore Mohammed will lead the Busromane to Paradise and Jesus will order the Christians to hell. Moses will sorrow for the Jews that they have not been obedient to him. . . . He [one of the scribes] spoke in this way: "Elias and Enoch are both in body and soul in paradise; but before Judgment Day they must die. But Jesus both in body and in soul is in heaven. He is the only one who will not die a death but will be alive forever and ever. Mohammed both in body and soul was in heaven, but remained with us on earth." And then the masters began to dispute, one in one way and one in another, and there were many words among them. And having raised a cry one against another, they began to throw books at one another. [Then the official in charge of the disputation] . . . told them to cease this disputation and he ordered that food be brought them according to their custom and they gave them water to drink, since they do not drink wine. And then, having eaten their fill, they gave thanks to God, praying for the souls of the living and the dead and for those who fight against the kaury or Christians.

QUESTIONS

1. Like many people, the scribes in the debate are aware that good and evil behavior is not the special preserve of one people. How do they explain that individuals will be punished or rewarded for their deeds?

2. Christian theologians traditionally considered Muslims to be heretics who could not be saved. How do these debaters evaluate Christians?

Source: Konstantin Mihailovic, *Memoirs of a Janissary,* translated by Benjamin Stolz. Copyright © 1975. Reprinted by permission of Michigan Slavic Publications.

---

of the city grew an extraordinary 500 percent, from about 40,000 to over 200,000, making it the largest city in Europe, as it had been in Late Antiquity.

At a time when Christian Europe seemed less and less willing to tolerate non-Christian minorities, the Ottoman Empire's liberal attitude toward outsiders seemed striking. Muslims and non-Muslims belonged to the same trade associations and traveled throughout the empire. Mehmed had no qualms about making trade agreements with the Italian powers in an attempt to consolidate his control. And in Serbia, Bulgaria, Macedonia, and Albania he left in place previous social and political institutions, requiring only loyalty to his empire.

Mehmed had to tread carefully, though, because the Turks had a number of powerful enemies. Serious problems, for example, surfaced during the reign of Mehmed's son, Bayazid (r. 1481–1512). Following Turkish tradition, Mehmed had not chosen a successor but let his sons fight for control. Normally the successful claimant achieved the throne by doing away with his closest relatives. Bayazid's brother, Jem, however, fled into the protective custody of Christian powers, where he spent the rest of his life. In times of crisis kings and popes would threaten to foment rebellion in Ottoman lands by releasing him. Bayazid also had to worry about the Mamluk Turks, who controlled Egypt and Syria, and the new Safavid dynasty in Persia. Although both were Muslim, they were willing to join with various Christian states to reduce the power of the Ottomans. Only in the second decade of the sixteenth century, after Bayazid's son, Selim (r. 1512–1520), had defeated the Persians and the Mamluks, were the Ottomans finally safe from attack from the east or south.

THE UNION OF CROWNS IN SPAIN

While expanding across the Mediterranean, the Turks came in contact with the other new state of the fifteenth century, the newly unified kingdom of Spain. As in Poland-Lithuania, the Spanish monarchy was only a dynastic union. In 1469 Ferdinand, heir to the kingdom of Aragon and Catalonia, married Isabella, daughter of the king of Castile. Five years later Isabella became queen of Castile, and in 1479 Ferdinand took control of the kingdom of Aragon. This union of Crowns eventually would lead to the creation of a united Spain, but true integration was still a distant dream in 1469.

Castile and Aragon The permanence of the union was remarkable because the two kingdoms were so different. Castile was a much larger and more populous state. It had taken the lead in the Reconquista, the fight begun in the eleventh century to reclaim Iberia from Muslim rule. As a result, economic power within Castile was divided among the groups most responsible for the Reconquista: military orders and nobles. The military orders of Calatrava, Santiago, and Alcantara were militias formed by men who had taken a religious vow similar to that taken by a monk, with an added commitment to fight against the enemies of Christianity. In the course of the Reconquista, the military orders assumed control of vast districts. Lay nobles who aided in the Reconquista also held large tracts of land and proudly guarded their independence.

Castile's power stemmed from its agrarian wealth. During the Reconquista Castilians took control of large regions and turned them into ranges for grazing merino sheep, producers of the prized merino wool exported to the markets of Flanders and Italy (see page 336). To maximize the profits from wool production, the kings authorized the creation of the Mesta, a brotherhood of sheep producers. The pastoral economy grew to the point that by the early sixteenth century Castilians owned over three million sheep.

Economic power in Castile lay with the nobility, but political power rested with the monarch. Because the nobility was largely exempt from taxation, nobles ignored the Cortes (cor-TEZ), the popular assembly, which could do little more than approve royal demands. The towns of Castile were important only as fortresses and staging points for militias rather than as centers of trade and commerce.

The kingdom of Aragon was dramatically different. The center of the kingdom was Barcelona, an important trading center in the Mediterranean. In the fourteenth and fifteenth centuries the kings of Aragon concentrated their efforts on expanding their influence in the Mediterranean, especially south of France and Italy. By the middle of the fifteenth century the Aragonese empire included the kingdom of Naples, Sicily, the Balearic (ba-LEER-ik) Islands, and Sardinia.

The power of the Aragonese king, in sharp contrast to the Castilian monarchy, was limited because the Crown was not unified. The ruler was king in Aragon and Navarre but only count in Catalonia. Aragon, Catalonia, and Valencia each maintained its own Cortes. In each area the traditional nobility and the towns had a great deal more influence than did their counterparts in Castile. The power of the Cortes is clear in the coronation oath taken by the Aragonese nobility: "We who are as good as you and together are more powerful than you, make you our king and lord, provided that you observe our laws and liberties, and if not, not."[9] The distinction between Aragon and Castile could not be stronger.

Initially the union of the crowns of Aragon and Castile did little to unify the two monarchies. Nobles fought over disputed boundaries, and Castilian nobles felt exploited by Aragonese merchants. Trade duties and internal boundaries continued to be disputed. The two realms even lacked a treaty to allow for the extradition of criminals from one kingdom to the other. Castilians never accepted Ferdinand as more than their queen's consort. After the death of Isabella in 1504 he ruled in Castile only as regent for his infant grandson, Charles I (r. 1516–1556). "Spain" would not emerge in an institutional sense until the late sixteenth century.

Nonetheless, the reign of Isabella and Ferdinand marked a profound change in politics and society in the Iberian kingdoms and in Europe in general. Ferdinand and Isabella married their daughter Joanna to Philip of Habsburg in 1496 to draw the Holy Roman Empire into the Italian wars brought on by the French invasion (see page 328). The marriage of their daughter Catherine of Aragon to Prince Arthur of England in 1501 was designed to obtain yet another ally against the French. Those two marriages would have momentous consequences for European history in the sixteenth century.

1492: Muslims and Jews The reign of Ferdinand and Isabella is especially memorable because of the events of 1492. In January of that year a crusading army conquered Granada, the last Muslim stronghold in Iberia. In March Ferdinand and Isabella ordered the Jews of Castile and Aragon to convert or leave the kingdom within four months. In April Isabella issued her commission authorizing Christopher Columbus "to discover and acquire islands and mainland in the Ocean Sea" (see pages 395–397).

The conquest of Granada and the expulsion of the Jews represented a radical shift in the Spanish mentality. Until the beginning of the fifteenth century Spain maintained a level of religious tolerance unusual in Christendom. In the fourteenth century perhaps 2 percent of the population of Iberia was Jewish, and the Muslim population may have been as high as 50 percent. The various groups were inextricably mixed. The statutes of the Jewish community in Barcelona were written in Catalan, a Spanish dialect, rather than in Hebrew. *Maranos,* Jewish converts to Christianity, and *moriscos,* Muslim converts, mixed continuously with Christians and with members of their former religions. It was difficult at times to know which religion these converts, or *conversos,* actually practiced. One surprised northern visitor to Spain remarked that one noble's circle was filled with "Christians, Moors, and Jews and he lets them live in peace in their faith."

This tolerant mingling of Christians, Muslims, and Jews had periodically occasioned violence. All three communities, in fact, preferred clear boundaries between the groups. In 1391, however, a series of violent attacks had long-lasting and unfortunate effects on Iberian society. An attack on the Jews of Seville led to murders, forced conversions, and suppression of synagogues throughout Spain. In the wake of the assault, large portions of the urban Jewish population either converted to Christianity or moved into villages away from the large commercial cities. The Jewish population in Castile may have declined by a fourth. Although the anti-Jewish feelings were expressed in religious terms, the underlying cause was anger over the economic prominence of some Jewish or converso families. After 1391 anti-Jewish feeling increasingly became racial. As one rebel said, "The converso remains a Jew and therefore should be barred from public office."[10]

Hostility and suspicion toward Jews grew throughout the fifteenth century until Ferdinand and Isabella concluded that the only safe course was to order all Jews to accept baptism. Jews who would not convert would have to leave the kingdom within four months. The order was signed on March 31, 1492, and published in late April after an unsuccessful attempt by converso and Jewish leaders to dissuade the monarchs from implementing it.

Many Jews could not dispose of their possessions in the four months allowed and so chose to convert and remain. But it is estimated that about ten thousand Jews left Aragon and that even more left Castile. Many moved to Portugal and then to North Africa. Some went east to Istanbul or north to the Low Countries. A number of others moved to the colonies being established in the New World in the vain hope of avoiding the Inquisition, which was already underway when the expulsion order was issued (see below). In 1504 the expulsion order was extended to include all Muslims.

The economic and social costs of the expulsion were profound. Not every Muslim or Jew was wealthy and cultured, but the exiles did include many doctors, bankers, and merchants. Spanish culture, long open to

Alfonso de Espina's Fortress of Faith (1474)

The diatribe against heretics, Muslims, and Jews fanned religious tensions in Spain. In this image from the book, Jews, Muslims, heretics, and demons are depicted as related threats to Christianity. Blindfolded Jews (blind to Christian Truth), Muslim warriors, and the Devil himself are seen assaulting the fortress of faith.   *(© Topham/The Image Works)*

influences from Muslim and Jewish sources, became narrower and less willing to accept new ideas. After the expulsion a chasm of distrust opened between the "Old Christians" and the "New Christians"—that is, those newly converted. As early as the first decades of the fifteenth century, some religious orders had refused to accept "New Christians." They required that their members demonstrate *limpieza de sangre,* a purity of blood. By 1500 the same tests of blood purity became prerequisites for holding most religious and public offices. Thus by the end of the fifteenth century the Iberian kingdoms had created more powerful, unified governments, but at a terrible cost to the only portion of Christendom that had ever practiced religious tolerance.

Complaints that led to the expulsion arose from a variety of sources. The fact that many of the most important financiers and courtiers were Jews or conversos bred jealousies and tensions among the communities. All three religious communities favored distinct dress and identifying behaviors. Old Christians seemed concerned that many of the conversos might reconvert to Judaism, and the fear of reconversion, or "judaizing," led many to advocate the institution of the **Spanish Inquisition.**

Inquisitions were well known in many parts of Europe, but the Spanish Inquisition was unique because in 1478 Pope Sixtus IV placed the grand inquisitor under the direct control of the monarchs. Like most Christian rulers, Ferdinand and Isabella believed that uniform Christian orthodoxy was the only firm basis for a strong kingdom. Inquisitors attacked those aspects of converso tradition that seemed to make the conversos less than fully Christian. They were concerned that many conversos and maranos had converted falsely and were secretly continuing to follow Jewish or Muslim rituals—a fear that some recent scholars have argued was unfounded.

Because its administration, finances, and appointments were in Spanish, not papal, hands, the Spanish Inquisition quickly became an important instrument for the expansion of state power. Many inquisitors used their offices to attack wealthy or politically important converso families not just to drive them from public life but also to fill the royal treasury, which was where the estates of those judged guilty wound up. "This inquisition is as much to take the conversos' estates as to exalt the faith," concluded one despairing conversa woman.[11]

THE LIMITS OF CONSOLIDATION: GERMANY

The issue of central versus local control played a key role in German affairs as well. The Holy Roman Empire of the late Middle Ages was dramatically different from the empire of the early thirteenth century. Emperors generally were unable to claim lands and preside over jurisdictions outside Germany. And within Germany power shifted eastward. Imperial power had previously rested on lands and castles in southwestern Germany. These strongholds melted away as emperors willingly pawned and sold traditional crown lands in order to build up the holdings of their own families. Emperor Henry VII (r. 1308–1313) and his grandson, Charles IV

(r. 1347–1378), for example, liquidated imperial lands west of the Rhine in order to secure the House of Luxemburg's claims to the crown of Bohemia and other lands in the east. The Habsburgs in Austria, the Wittelsbachs in Bavaria, and a host of lesser families staked out power bases in separate parts of the empire. As a result, Germany unraveled into a loose collection of territories. And more seriously, the power of each emperor depended almost entirely on the wealth and power of his dynastic lands.

The power of regional authorities in the empire was further cemented by the so-called **Golden Bull** of 1356, the most important constitutional document of late medieval German history. In it Charles IV declared that henceforth the archbishops of Cologne, Mainz, and Trier, plus the secular rulers of Bohemia, the Rhenish Palatinate, Saxony, and Brandenburg, would be the seven electors responsible for the choice of a new emperor. He further established that the rulers of these seven principalities should have full jurisdictional rights within their territories. The Golden Bull acknowledged the power of regional princes, but it did nothing to solve the inherent weakness of an electoral monarchy. Between 1273 and 1519 Germany elected fourteen emperors from six different dynasties, and only once, in 1378, did a son follow his father. The contrast between Germany and the monarchies of Iberia, France, and England is striking. By 1350 Germany had no hereditary monarchy, no common legal system, no common coinage, and no representative assembly. Political power rested in the hands of the territorial princes.

Territorial integration was least effective in what is now Switzerland, where a league of towns, provincial knights, and peasant villages successfully resisted a territorial prince. The Swiss Confederation began modestly enough in 1291 as a voluntary association to promote regional peace. By 1410 the confederation had conquered most of the traditionally Habsburg lands in the Swiss areas. By the 1470s the Swiss had invented the myth of William Tell, the fearless woodsman who refused to bow his head to a Habsburg official, as a justification for their independent and anti-aristocratic traditions. Though still citizens of the Holy Roman Empire, the Swiss maintained an independence similar to that of the princes. Their expansion culminated with the Battle of Nancy in Lorraine in 1477, when the Swiss infantry defeated a Burgundian army and killed Charles the Bold, the duke of Burgundy. From then on "turning Swiss" was a common threat made by German towns and individuals who hoped to slow territorial centralization.

Spanish Inquisition A church court under monarchical control established in 1478 to look for "false Christians" among the newly converted Muslims and Jews.

Golden Bull Edict of Holy Roman Emperor Charles IV establishing the method of electing a new emperor. It acknowledged the political autonomy of Germany's seven regional princes.

SECTION SUMMARY

- By the end of the fifteenth century, both England and France had stronger, more centralized governments.

- By the fifteenth century a strong Polish-Lithuanian state had emerged to halt German expansion to the east.

- The rise of Moscow marked the end of Tatar domination in eastern Europe.

- Ottoman Turks established a strong empire that came to dominate the eastern Mediterranean and the Balkans.

- The union of the Aragonese and Castilian crowns created a Spanish monarchy intent on enforcing political unity and religious uniformity.

- In German lands, regional powers emerged to challenge and limit the power of the empire.

CHAPTER SUMMARY

Online Study Center **ACE the Test**

How did the Great Schism change the church and the papacy?

What forces limited the political power of rulers in England, France, and Italy?

How were economic and social structures changed by plague and economic crisis?

How did the political makeup of Europe in 1500 differ from that in 1300?

The Europe of 1500 was profoundly different from the Europe of two centuries earlier. The religious, political, and economic crises of the fourteenth and early fifteenth centuries seemed about to destroy the progress of the previous centuries. But the recovery of the second half of the fifteenth century was nearly as dramatic as the preceding disasters.

In the aftermath of schism and conciliar reform, the church also was transformed. Because of conciliar challenges to papal authority, popes had to deal much more carefully with the governments of Europe. They found themselves vulnerable to pressures from the other European powers. Recognizing that, in the end, popes could count on support only from those areas they controlled politically, the papacy became an Italian regional power.

The Hundred Years' War between England and France was a continuation of a long struggle between two royal houses. The English won dramatic battles, but they could not control the territory. As a result, by the end the English lost all their significant possessions in France. The result contributed to the eventual centralization and growth of royal power in the two kingdoms.

The economy had grown more complex in the wake of the epidemic disease and dramatic population decline. Changes included the relative decline of the Italian economy as new patterns of trade and banking and new manufacturing techniques spread throughout Europe. Commerce and manufacture were now more firmly rooted in northern Europe. Italian merchants and bankers faced stiff competition from local counterparts throughout Europe.

Recovery was equally dramatic for the governments of Europe. After the Hundred Years' War and challenges from aristocrats, townsmen, and peasants, governments grew stronger as kings, princes, and town patricians used royal courts and patronage to extend their control. Military advances in the fifteenth century, such as the institution of standing armies, gave the advantage to larger governments. This was as true in Hungary as it was in France. Yet recovery among the traditional Western powers was largely overshadowed by the emergence of the tsars in Moscow and the rise of the Ottoman and Spanish Empires. These three emergent powers upset the political and diplomatic balance in Europe and would dominate politics and diplomacy in the next century.

LOOKING AHEAD

In addition to their obvious political power, most of these states—from Spain to Scandinavia to the Ottoman Empire—became adept at using art, literature, and history to explain and magnify their courts and confirm their places in history and society. This was certainly true of the papacy, and over the course of the fifteenth century it became true of other governments as well. It is to the role of culture that we turn in the next chapter.

KEY TERMS

Babylonian Captivity of the Papacy (p. 317)

Great Schism (p. 318)

conciliarists (p. 319)

Jan Hus (p. 319)

Council of Constance (p. 319)

Hundred Years' War (p. 321)

Joan of Arc (p. 325)

Black Death (p. 329)

Hanseatic League (p. 334)

Spanish Inquisition (p. 346)

Golden Bull (p. 346)

Online Study Center
Improve Your Grade Flashcards

SUGGESTED READING

Bennett, J., and Froide, A., eds. *Singlewomen in the European Past.* 1999. The medieval essays in this collection are especially good on working women.

Duffy, E. *Saints & Sinners: A History of the Popes.* 1997. An excellent introduction to the papacy by a leading historian. The sections on the late Middle Ages are clear and balanced.

Dyer, C. *Making a Living in the Middle Ages: The People of Britain, 850–1520.* 2002. A masterful and accessible survey of the economic history of England that is especially good on rural life.

Goffman, D. *The Ottoman Empire and Early Modern Europe.* 2002. A general discussion of the growth of the Ottoman state emphasizing its close ties with Europe and its similarities to contemporary European societies.

Guenée, B. *States and Rulers in Later Medieval Europe.* Translated by Juliet Vale. 1985. The best general introduction to the nature of government in the late Middle Ages. It introduces recent trends in historical research.

Keen, M. H. *English Society in the Later Middle Ages, 1348–1500.* 1990. A general introduction to late medieval England that covers culture and religion as well as politics.

Naphy, W., and Spicer, A. *Plague: Black Death and Pestilence in Europe.* 2004. An excellent and engaging narrative of the Black Death and the successions of plague that followed. It discusses the social disruptions as well as the medical and governmental responses.

Nicholas, D. *The Transformation of Europe, 1300–1600.* 1999. A comprehensive survey of politics and society in Europe between 1300 and 1600; includes coverage of Scandinavia and the Slavic lands as well as northwestern Europe.

Oakley, Francis. *The Western Church in the Later Middle Ages.* 1979. The best general history of the church in the late Middle Ages. Oakley gives superior treatments of the Great Schism and conciliarism.

Warner, Marina. *Joan of Arc: The Image of Female Heroism.* 1981. An excellent and quite readable book that emphasizes the conflicting religious and political opinions about "the Maid."

NOTES

1. Quoted in Guillaume Mollat, *The Popes at Avignon, 1305–1378* (London: Thomas Nelson, 1963), p. 112.

2. Quoted in Mary Aston, *Lollards and Reformers: Images and Literacy in Late Medieval Religion* (Ronceverte, W.V.: Hambledon, 1984), p. 60.

3. Quoted in Francis Oakley, *The Western Church in the Later Middle Ages* (Ithaca, N.Y.: Cornell University Press, 1979), pp. 65–66.

4. Quoted in Charles T. Wood, *Joan of Arc and Richard III* (New York: Oxford University Press, 1988), pp. 56–57.

5. Quoted in Michael T. Clanchy, "Law, Government, and Society in Medieval England," *History* 59 (1974): 75.

6. A. Buchon, *Choix des Chroniques* (Paris, 1875), p. 565, as quoted in John Gillingham and J. C. Holt, eds., *War and Government in the Middle Ages* (Totowa, N.J.: Barnes & Noble, 1984), p. 85.

7. Salimbene de Adam, quoted in John Larner, *Italy in the Age of Dante and Petrarch, 1215–1380* (New York: Longman, 1980), p. 141.

8. Quoted in Peter Shervey Lewis, *Later Medieval France: The Polity* (New York: Macmillan, 1968), p. 15.

9. Quoted in Angus MacKay, *Spain in the Middle Ages: From Frontier to Empire, 1000–1500* (London: Macmillan, 1977), p. 105.

10. Quoted in Angus MacKay, "Popular Movements and Pogroms in Fifteenth-Century Spain," *Past & Present* 55 (1972): 52.

11. Haim Beinart, ed., *Records of the Trials of the Spanish Inquisition in Ciudad Real*, vol. 1, trans. Duane Osheim (Jerusalem: Israel Academy of Sciences and Humanities, 1974), p. 391.

12

THE RENAISSANCE

Raphael: School of Athens (detail) Raphael created this classical setting by using the technique of linear perspective. *(Scala/Art Resource, NY)*

The painting on the left, *School of Athens* by Raphael (1483–1520), was commissioned for the Stanze (STAN-zay), the papal apartments in the Vatican. At the center Plato and Aristotle advance through a churchlike hall, surrounded by the great thinkers and writers of the ancient world. But Raphael portrayed more than just ancient wisdom. The figure of Plato is, in fact, a portrait of Leonardo da Vinci. A brooding Michelangelo leans on a marble block in the foreground. In a companion painting on the opposite wall, Raphael depicted a gathering of the greatest scholars of Christendom. In this way he brought together Christian and classical, writers and artists, and captured the entire cultural reform plan of the Renaissance.

The revival these paintings celebrate was a response to the religious, social, economic, and political crises discussed in the previous chapter. Italians, and later Europeans generally, found themselves drawn to imitate Roman literature, ethics, and politics. The ideas of antiquity seemed to offer an opportunity to perfect the theological ideas about moral and political life current in the earlier Middle Ages. Further, Renaissance writers were convinced that all knowledge, pagan and Christian, ancient and modern, could be combined into a single, uniform view of the world.

Renaissance Italians wrote of themselves and their contemporaries as having "revived" arts, "rescued" painting, and "rediscovered" classical authors. They even coined the phrases "Dark Ages" and "Middle Ages" to describe the period that separated the Roman Empire from their own times. They believed that their society saw a new age, a rebirth of culture. And to this day we use the French word for "rebirth," *renaissance,* to describe the period of intense creativity and change that began in Italy in the fourteenth century and then extended to all of Europe.

This view comes to us primarily from the work of the nineteenth-century Swiss historian Jacob Burckhardt. In his book *The Civilization of the Renaissance in Italy* (1860) he argued that Italians were the first individuals to recognize the state as a moral structure free from the restraints of religious or philosophical traditions. Burckhardt believed that individuals too are entirely free. Their success or failure depends on personal qualities of creative brilliance rather than on family status, religion, or guild membership. Burckhardt thought he saw in Renaissance Italy the first signs of the romantic

CHAPTER OUTLINE

HUMANISM AND CULTURE IN ITALY, 1300–1500

PAINTING AND THE ARTS, 1250–1550

THE SPREAD OF THE RENAISSANCE, 1350–1536

THE RENAISSANCE AND COURT SOCIETY

KEY TERMS

Francesco Petrarch

Renaissance

humanism

civic humanism

On the Donation of Constantine

Niccolò Machiavelli

linear perspective

Leonardo da Vinci

Sistine Chapel

Johann Gutenberg

Thomas More

Desiderius Erasmus

Online Study Center

This icon will direct you to interactive map and primary source activities on the website **college.hmco.com/ pic/noble5e**

individualism and nationalism that characterized the modern world.

In fact, as brilliant as Renaissance writers and artists were, they do not represent a radical shift from the ideas or values of medieval culture. As we have seen, there were no "Dark Ages." Although the culture of Renaissance Europe was in many aspects new and innovative, it had close ties both to the ideas of the High Middle Ages and to traditional Christian values.

How, then, should we characterize the Renaissance in Europe? The Renaissance was an important cultural movement that aimed to reform and renew by imitating what the reformers believed were classical and early Christian traditions in art, education, religion, and political life. Italians, and then other Europeans, came to believe that the so-cial and moral values, as well as the literature, of classical Greece and Rome offered the best formula for changing their own society for the better. This enthusiasm for a past culture became the vehicle for changes in literature, education, and art that established cultural standards that were to hold for the next five hundred years.

FOCUS QUESTIONS

How did Italians use classical values to deal with cultural and political issues?

What was "new" about Renaissance art?

In what ways did humanism outside Italy differ from Italian humanism?

How did European rulers use Renaissance art and culture?

HUMANISM AND CULTURE IN ITALY, 1300–1500

How did Italians use classical values to deal with cultural and political issues?

Italians turned to models from classical antiquity in their attempts to deal with current issues of cultural, political, and educational reform. A group of scholars who came to be known as humanists began to argue the superiority of the literature, history, and politics of the past. As humanists discovered more about ancient culture, they were able to understand more clearly the historical context in which Roman and Greek writers and thinkers lived. And by the early sixteenth century their debates on learning, civic duty, and the classical legacy had led them to a new vision of the past and a new appreciation of the nature of politics.

THE EMERGENCE OF HUMANISM

Humanism initially held greater appeal in Italy than elsewhere in Europe because the culture in central and northern Italy was significantly more secular and more urban than the culture of much of the rest of Europe. Members of the clergy were less likely to dominate government and education in Italy. Quite the reverse: Boards dominated by laymen had built and were administering the great urban churches of Italy. Religious hospitals and charities were often reorganized and cen-tralized under government control. In 1300 four cities in Italy (Milan, Venice, Florence, and Naples) had populations of about 100,000, and countless others had populations of 20,000 or more. By contrast, London, which may have had a population of 100,000, was the only city in England with more than 40,000 inhabitants. Even the powerful Italian aristocracy tended to live at least part of the year in towns and conform to urban social and legal practices.

Differences between Italy and northern Europe are also apparent in the structure of local education. In northern Europe education was organized to provide clergy for local churches. In the towns of Italy education was much more likely to be supervised by town governments to provide training in accounting, arithmetic, and the composition of business letters. Public grammar masters taught these basics, and numerous private masters and individual tutors were prepared to teach all subjects. Giovanni Villani, a fourteenth-century merchant and historian, described Florence in 1338 as a city of about 100,000 people in which perhaps as many as 10,000 young girls and boys were completing elementary education and 1,000 were continuing their studies to prepare for careers in commerce. Compared with education in the towns of northern Europe, education in Villani's Florence seems broad-based and practical.

Logic and Scholastic philosophy (see page 301) dominated university education in northern Europe in the fourteenth and fifteenth centuries but had less influence in Italy, where education focused on the practical issues of town life rather than on theological speculation. Educated Italians of this period were interested in the *studia humanitatis*, which we now call humanism. By *humanism*, Italians meant rhetoric and literature—the arts of persuasion. Poetry, history, letter writing, and oratory based on standardized forms and aesthetic values consciously borrowed from ancient Greece and Rome were the center of intellectual life. In general, fourteenth-century Italians were suspicious of ideological or moral programs based on philosophical arguments or religious assumptions about human nature.

Italian towns were the focus of theorizing about towns as moral, religious, and political communities. Writers wanted to define the nature of the commune—the town government. Moralists often used "the common good" and "the good of the commune" as synonyms. By 1300 it was usual for towns to celebrate the feast days of their patron saints as major political as well as religious festivals. And town governments often supervised the construction and expansion of cathedrals, churches, and hospitals as signs of their wealth and prestige.

Literature of the early fourteenth century tended to emphasize the culture of towns. The most famous and most innovative work of the fourteenth century, *The Decameron* by Giovanni Boccaccio (1313–1375), pondered moral and ethical issues, but in the lively context of Italian town life. Boccaccio (bo-KAH-chi-o) hoped the colorful and irreverent descriptions of contemporary Italians, which make his *Decameron* a classic of European literature, would also lead individuals to understand both the essence of human nature and the folly of human desires. The plot involves a group of privileged young people who abandon friends and family during the plague of 1348 to go into the country. There, on successive days they mixed feasting, dancing, and song with one hundred tales of love, intrigue, and gaiety. With its mix of traditional and contemporary images, Boccaccio's book spawned numerous imitators in Italy and elsewhere. Many credit him with popularizing a new, secular spirit. But the point too often missed by Boccaccio's imitators was, as he himself said, that "to have compassion for those who suffer is a human quality which everyone should possess."

Like Boccaccio, the majority of educated Italians in the early fourteenth century were not particularly captivated by thoughts of ancient Rome. Italian historians chose to write the histories of their hometowns. Most,

CHRONOLOGY

including Giovanni Villani of Florence, were convinced that their towns could rival ancient Rome. Theirs was a practical world in which most intellectuals were men trained in notarial arts—the everyday skills of oratory, letter writing, and the recording of legal documents.

PETRARCH AND EARLY HUMANISM

The first Italians who looked back consciously to the literary and historical examples of ancient Rome were a group of northern Italian lawyers and notaries who imitated Roman authors. These practical men found Roman history and literature more stimulating and useful than medieval philosophy. Writers such as Albertino Mussato of Padua (1262–1329) adopted classical styles in their poetry and histories. Mussato used his play *The Ecerinis* (1315) to tell of the fall of Can Grande della Scala, the tyrannical ruler of Verona (d. 1329), and to warn his neighbors of the dangers of tyranny. From its earliest, the classical revival in Italy was tied to issues of moral and political reform.

This largely emotional fascination for the ancient world was transformed into a literary movement for reform by **Francesco Petrarch** (1304–1374), who popularized the idea of mixing classical moral and literary ideas with the concerns of the fourteenth century. Petrarch was the son of an exiled Florentine notary living at the papal court in Avignon. Repelled by the urban violence and wars he had experienced on his return to Italy, Petrarch was highly critical of his contemporaries: "I never liked this age," he once confessed. He criticized the papacy in Avignon, calling it the "Babylonian Captivity" (see pages 316–317); he supported an attempt to resurrect a republican government in Rome; and he believed that imitation of the actions, values, and culture of the ancient Romans was the only way to reform his sorry world.

Online Study Center **Improve Your Grade**
Primary Source: Letter to Posterity: Petrarch Writes His Autobiography

Petrarch believed that an age of darkness—he coined the expression "Dark Ages"—separated the Roman world from his own time and that the separation could be overcome only through a study and reconstruction of classical values: "Once the darkness has been broken, our descendants will perhaps be able to return to the pure, pristine radiance."[1] Petrarch's program, and in many respects the entire **Renaissance,** involved first of all a reconstruction of classical culture, then a careful study and imitation of the classical heritage, and finally a series of moral and cultural changes that went beyond the mere copying of ancient values and styles.

Petrarch labored throughout his life to reconstruct the history and literature of Rome. He learned to read and write classical Latin. While still in his twenties he discovered, reorganized, and annotated fragments of Livy's *Roman History,* an important source for the history of Republican Rome. His work on Livy was merely the first step. In the 1330s he discovered a number of classical works, including orations and letters by Cicero, the great philosopher, statesman, and opponent of Julius Caesar (see page 149). Cicero's letters to his friend Atticus were filled with gossip, questions about politics in Rome, and complaints about his forced withdrawal from public life. They create the portrait of

an individual who was much more complex than the austere philosopher of medieval legend.

Petrarch's **humanism** was not worldly or secular; he was and remained a committed Christian. He recognized the tension between the Christian present and pagan antiquity. He wrote a dialogue, *The Secret,* reflecting his own ambivalence. Did his devotion to reading and imitating classical authors involve a rejection of traditional Christian values? "My wishes fluctuate and my desires conflict, and in their struggle they tear me apart," he said.[2] Yet he prized the beauty and moral value of ancient learning. He wrote *The Lives of Illustrious Men,* biographies of men from antiquity whose thoughts and actions he deemed worthy of emulation. To spread humanistic values he issued collections of his poems written in Italian and his letters, written in classically inspired Latin. He believed that study and memorization of the writings of classical authors could lead to the internalization of the ideas and values expressed in those works, just as a honeybee drinks nectar to create honey. He argued that ancient moralists were superior to Scholastic philosophers, whose work ended with the determination of truth, or correct responses. "The true moral philosophers and useful teachers of the virtues," he concluded, "are those whose first and last intention is to make hearer and reader good, those who do not merely teach what virtue and vice are but sow into our hearts love of the best . . . and hatred of the worst."[3] (See the box "The Written Record: Petrarch Responds to His Critics.")

HUMANISTIC STUDIES

Petrarch's articulation of humanism inspired a broad-based transformation of Italian intellectual life that affected discussions of politics, education, literature, and philosophy. His style of historical and literary investigation of the past became the basis for a new appreciation of the present.

Petrarch's program of humanistic studies became especially popular with the wealthy oligarchy who dominated political life in Florence. The Florentine chancellor Coluccio Salutati (1331–1406) and a generation of young intellectuals who formed his circle evolved an ideology of **civic humanism.** Civic humanists wrote letters, orations, and histories praising their city's classical virtues and history. In the process they

---

Francesco Petrarch Influential poet, biographer, and humanist who strongly advocated imitation of the literary and moral values of the leading Greek and Roman writers.

Renaissance A word that has come to define any period of intense creativity. In this case it refers specifically to a cultural movement based on imitating classical culture.

humanism Western European literary and cultural movement, which emphasized the superiority of Greek and Roman literature and especially its values of personal and public morality.

civic humanism An ideology, popular with the political leaders of Florence, that emphasized Rome's classical republican virtues of duty and public service.

THE WRITTEN RECORD

PETRARCH RESPONDS TO HIS CRITICS

Many traditional philosophers and theologians criticized humanists as "pagans" because of their lack of interest in logic and theology and their love of non-Christian writers. In this letter defending humanistic studies Petrarch explains the value of Cicero's work to Christians.

[Cicero] points out the miraculously coherent structure and disposition of the body, sense and limbs, and finally reason and sedulous activity. . . . And all this he does merely to lead us to this conclusion: whatever we behold with our eyes or perceive with our intellect is made by God for the well-being of man and governed by divine providence and counsel. . . . [In response to his critics who argued for the superiority of philosophy he adds:] I have read all of Aristotle's moral books. Some of them I have also heard commented on. . . . Sometimes I have become more learned through them when I went home, but not better, not so good as I ought to be; and I often complained to myself, occasionally to others too, that by no facts was the promise fulfilled which the philosopher makes at the beginning of the first book of his *Ethics,* namely, that "we learn this part of philosophy not with the purpose of gaining knowledge but of becoming better." I see virtue, and all that is peculiar to vice as well as to virtue, egregiously defined and distinguished by him and treated with penetrating insight. When I learn all this, I know a little bit more than I knew before, but mind and will remain the same as they were, and I myself remain the same. . . . However, what is the use of knowing what virtue is if it is not loved when known? What is the use of knowing sin if it is not abhorred when it is

known? However, everyone who has become thoroughly familiar with our Latin authors knows that they stamp and drive deep into the heart the sharpest and most ardent stings of speech by which those who stick to the ground [are] lifted up to the highest thoughts and to honest desire. . . .

Cicero, read with a pious and modest attitude, . . . was profitable to everybody, so far as eloquence is concerned, to many others as regards living. This was especially true in [Saint] Augustine's case. . . . I confess, I admire Cicero as much or even more than all whoever wrote a line in any nation. . . . If to admire Cicero means to be a Ciceronian, I am a Ciceronian. I admire him so much that I wonder at people who do not admire him. . . . However, when we come to think or speak of religion, that is, of supreme truth and true happiness, and of eternal salvation, then I am certainly not a Ciceronian, or a Platonist, but a Christian. I even feel sure that Cicero himself would have been a Christian if he had been able to see Christ and to comprehend His doctrine.

QUESTIONS

1. Why is Cicero a valuable author to study?

2. Why does Petrarch believe Cicero is superior to Aristotle?

3. Does it seem that Petrarch sees any limits to the moral value of Cicero?

Source: Petrarch, "On His Own Ignorance and That of Many Others," in *The Renaissance Philosophy of Man,* ed. Ernst Cassirer, Paul Oskar Kristeller, and John H. Randall, pp. 86, 103, 104, 114, 115. Reprinted by permission of the publisher, The University of Chicago Press.

---

gave a practical and public meaning to the Petrarchan program. Civic humanists argued, as had Cicero, that there was a moral and ethical value intrinsic to public life. In a letter to a friend, Salutati wrote that public life is "something holy and holier than idleness in [religious] solitude." To another he added, "The active life you flee is to be followed both as an exercise in virtue and because of the necessity of brotherly love."[4]

More than Petrarch himself, civic humanists desired to create and inspire men of virtue who could take the lead in government and protect their fellow citizens from lawlessness and tyranny. In the early years of the fifteenth century civic humanists applauded Florence for remaining a republic of free citizens. Florence remained free of a lord, unlike Milan, whose government

was dominated by the Viscontis (see page 326). In his *Panegyric on the City of Florence* (ca. 1405) Leonardo Bruni (ca. 1370–1444) recalled the history of the Roman Republic and suggested that Florence could recreate the best qualities of the Roman state. To civic humanists, the study of Rome and its virtues was the key to the continued prosperity of Florence and similar Italian republics.

Educational Reform   One of Petrarch's most enthusiastic followers was Guarino of Verona (1374–1460), who became the leading advocate of educational reform in Renaissance Italy. After spending five years in Constantinople learning Greek and collecting classical manuscripts, he became the most successful teacher and

Women and Culture

This painting of Saint Barbara from the early fifteenth century shows a typical Flemish interior with a woman reading. It was not unusual for well-to-do women to read even if they could not write.

(Museo de Prado/Institut Amatller d'Art Hispanic)

translator of Greek literature in Italy. Greek studies had been advanced by Manuel Chrysoloras (1350–1415), who, after his arrival from Constantinople in 1397, taught Greek for three years in Florence. Chrysoloras was later joined by other Greek intellectuals, especially after the fall of Constantinople to the Turks in 1453. Guarino built on this interest in Greek culture.

Guarino emphasized careful study of grammar and memorization of large bodies of classical history and poetry. He was convinced that through a profound understanding of Greek and Latin literature and a careful imitation of the style of the great authors, a person could come to exhibit the moral and ethical values for which Cicero, Seneca, and Plutarch were justly famous. Although it is unclear whether Guarino's style of education produced such results, it did provide a thorough training in literature and oratory. In an age that admired the ability to speak and write persuasively, the new style of humanistic education pioneered by Guarino spread quickly throughout Europe. The elegy spoken at Guarino's funeral sums up Italian views of humanistic education as well as the contribution of Guarino himself: "No one was considered noble, as leading a blameless life, unless he had followed Guarino's courses."

Guarino's authority spread quickly. One of his early students, Vittorino da Feltre (1378–1446), was appointed tutor at the Gonzaga court of Mantua. Like Guarino, he emphasized close literary study and careful imitation of classical authors. But the school he founded, the Villa Giocosa (jo-KO-sa), was innovative because he advocated games and exercises as well as formal study. In addition, Vittorino required that bright young boys from poor families be included among the seventy affluent students normally resident in his school. Vittorino was so renowned that noblemen from across Italy sent their sons to be educated at the Villa Giocosa.

Women and Humanism Humanistic education had its limits, however. Leonardo Bruni of Florence once composed a curriculum for a young woman to follow. He emphasized literature and moral philosophy, but, he cautioned, there was no reason to study rhetoric: "For why should the subtleties of . . . rhetorical conundrums consume the powers of a woman, who never sees the forum? . . . The contests of the forum, like those of warfare and battle, are the sphere of men."[5] To what extent did women participate in the cultural and artistic movements of the fourteenth and fifteenth centuries? Was the position of women better than it had been previously? The current of misogyny—the assumption that women were intellectually and morally weaker than men—continued during the Renaissance, but it was not unopposed.

During the fifteenth century many women did learn to read and even to write. Religious women and wives of merchants read educational and spiritual literature. Some women needed to write in order to manage the economic and political interests of their families. Alessandra Macinghi-Strozzi (ma-CHIN-ghee STROT-zi) of Florence (1407–1471), for example, wrote numerous letters to her sons in exile describing her efforts to find spouses for her children and to influence the government to end their banishments.

Yet many men were suspicious of literate women. Just how suspicious is evident in the career of Isotta Nogarola of Verona (b. 1418), one of a number of fifteenth- and sixteenth-century Italian women whose literary abilities equaled those of male humanists. Isotta quickly became known as a gifted writer, but men's response to her work was mixed. One anonymous critic suggested that it was unnatural for a woman to have such scholarly interests and accused her of equally unnatural sexual interests. Guarino of Verona himself wrote warning her that if she was truly to be educated, she must put off female sensibilities and find "a man within the woman."[6]

The problem for humanistically educated women was that society provided no acceptable role for them. A noblewoman such as Isabella d'Este (duh-ES-tay) (see page 377), wife of the duke of Mantua, might gather humanists and painters around her at court, but it was not generally believed that women themselves could create literary works of true merit. When women tried, they were usually rebuffed and urged to reject the values of civic humanism and to hold instead to traditional Christian virtues of rejection of the world. In other words, a woman who had literary or cultural interests was expected to enter a convent. That was a friend's advice to Isotta Nogarola. It was wrong, he said, "that a virgin should consider marriage, or even think about that liberty of lascivious morals."[7] Throughout the fifteenth and early sixteenth centuries some women in Italy and elsewhere in Europe learned classical languages and philosophy, but they became rarer as time passed. The virtues of humanism were public virtues, and Europeans of the Renaissance remained uncomfortable with the idea that women might act directly and publicly.

THE TRANSFORMATION OF HUMANISM

The fascination with education based on ancient authorities was heightened by the discovery in 1416, in the Monastery of Saint Gall in Switzerland, of a complete manuscript of Quintilian's *Institutes of Oratory,* a first-century treatise on the proper education for a young Roman patrician. The document was found by Poggio Bracciolini (PO-joe bra-chi-o-LEE-nee) (1380–1459), who had been part of the humanist circle in Florence. The discovery was hardly accidental. Like Petrarch, the humanists of the fifteenth century scoured Europe for ancient texts to read and study. In searching out the knowledge of the past, these fifteenth-century humanists made a series of discoveries that changed their understanding of language, philosophy, and religion. Their desire to imitate led to a profound transformation of knowledge.

A Florentine antiquary, Niccolò Niccoli (1364–1437), coordinated and paid for much of this pursuit of "lost" manuscripts. A wealthy bachelor, Niccolò spent the fortune he had inherited from his father by acquiring ancient statuary, reliefs, and, most of all, books. When he died, his collection of more than eight hundred volumes of Latin and Greek texts became the foundation of the humanist library housed in the Monastery of San Marco in Florence. Niccolò had specified that all his books "should be accessible to everyone," and humanists from across Italy and the rest of Europe came to Florence to study his literary treasures. Niccolò's library prompted Pope Nicholas V (r. 1447–1455) to begin the collection that is now the Apostolic Library of the Vatican in Rome. The Vatican library became a lending library, serving the humanist community in Rome. Similar collections were assembled in Venice, Milan, and Urbino. The Greek and Latin sources preserved in these libraries allowed humanists to study classical languages in a way not possible before.

Lorenzo Valla and Historical Perspective

The career of Lorenzo Valla (1407–1457) illustrates the transformation that took place in the fifteenth century as humanism swept Europe. Valla was born near Rome and received a traditional humanistic education in Greek and Latin studies. He spent the rest of his life at universities and courts lecturing on philosophy and literature. Valla's studies had led him to understand that languages change with time—that they, too, have a life and a history. In 1440 he published a work called *On the Donation of Constantine,* which purported to record the gift by the emperor Constantine (r. 311–337) of jurisdiction over Rome and the western half of the empire to the pope when the imperial capital was moved to Constantinople (see page 185). In the High and late Middle Ages the papacy used the document to defend its right to political dominion in central Italy. The donation had long been criticized by legal theorists, who argued that Constantine had no right to make it. Valla went further and attacked the legitimacy of the document itself. Because of its language and form, he argued, it could not have been written at the time of Constantine:

On the Donation of Constantine   This work demonstrated that an important papal claim to political rule of central Italy was based on an eighth-century forgery.

Through his [the writer's] babbling, he reveals his most impudent forgery himself.... Where he deals with the gifts he says "a diadem ... made of pure gold and precious jewels." The ignoramus did not know that the diadem was [like a turban and] made of cloth, probably silk.... He thinks it had to be made of gold, since nowadays kings usually wear a circle of gold set with jewels.[8]

Valla was correct; the *Donation* was an eighth-century forgery.

Valla later turned his attention to the New Testament. Jerome (331–420) had put together the Vulgate edition of the Bible in an attempt to create a single accepted Latin version of the Hebrew Bible and the New Testament (see page 208). In 1444 Valla completed his *Annotations on the New Testament*. In this work he used his training in classical languages to correct Jerome's standard Latin text and to show numerous instances of mistranslations. His annotations on the New Testament were of critical importance to humanists outside Italy and were highly influential during the Protestant Reformation.

Renaissance Philosophy   The transformation of humanism exemplified by Valla was fully expected by some Florentines. They anticipated that literary studies would lead eventually to philosophy. In 1456 a young Florentine began studying Greek with just such a change in mind. Supported by the Medici rulers of Florence, Marsilio Ficino (1433–1499) began a daunting project: to translate the works of Plato into Latin and to interpret Plato in light of Christian doctrine and tradition.

Ficino believed that Platonism, like Christianity, demonstrated the dignity of humanity. He wrote that everything in creation was connected along a continuum ranging from the lowliest matter to the person of God. The human soul was located at the midpoint of this hierarchy and was a bridge between the material world and God. True wisdom, and especially experience of the divine, could be gained only through contemplation and love. According to Ficino, logic and scientific observation did not lead to true understanding. Humans, he observed, know logically only what they can define in human language; individuals can, however, love things, such as God, that they are not fully able to comprehend.

Ficino's belief in the dignity of man was shared by Giovanni Pico della Mirandola (mi-RAHN-do-la) (1463–1494), who proposed to debate with other philosophers nine hundred theses dealing with the nature of man, the origins of knowledge, and the uses of philosophy. Pico extended Ficino's idea of the hierarchy of being, arguing that humans surpassed even the angels in dignity. Angels held a fixed position in the hierarchy, just below God. In contrast, humans could move either up or down in the hierarchy, depending on the extent to which they embraced spiritual or worldly interests. Pico further believed that he had proved that all philosophies contain at least some truth. He was one of the first humanists to learn Hebrew and to argue that divine wisdom could be found in Jewish as well as Christian and pagan mystical literature. Along with others, he studied the Jewish Cabala, a collection of mystical and occult writings that humanists believed dated from the time of Moses. Pico's adoption of the Hebrew mystical writings was often controversial in the Jewish community as well as among Christians.

The Unity of Knowledge   Pico's ideas were shared by other humanists, who contended that an original, unified, divine illumination—a "Pristine Theology," they called it—preceded even Plato and Aristotle. These humanists found theological truth in what they believed was ancient Egyptian, Greek, and Jewish magic. Ficino himself popularized the *Corpus Hermeticum* (the Hermetic collection), an amalgam of magical texts of the first century A.D. that was mistakenly thought to be the work of an Egyptian magician, Hermes Trismegistos. Humanists assumed Hermes wrote during the age of Moses and Pythagoras. Like many mystical writings of the first and second centuries, Hermetic texts explained how the mind could influence and be influenced by the material and celestial worlds.

Along with exploring Hermetic magic, many humanists of the fifteenth and sixteenth centuries investigated astrology and alchemy. All three systems posit the existence of a direct, reciprocal connection between the cosmos and the natural world. In the late medieval and Renaissance world astrological and alchemical theories seemed reasonable. By the late fifteenth century many humanists assumed that personality was profoundly affected by the stars and that the heavens were not silent regarding human affairs. It was not by accident that for a century or more after 1500 astrologers were official or unofficial members of most European courts.

Interest in alchemy was equally widespread though more controversial. Alchemists believed that everything was made of a primary material and that therefore it was possible to transmute one substance into another. The most popular variation, and the one most exploited by hucksters and frauds, was the belief that base metals could be turned into gold. The hopes of most alchemists, however, were more profound. They were convinced that they could unlock the secrets of the entire cosmos. On a personal and religious as well as on a material level, practitioners hoped to make the impure pure. The interest in understanding and manipulating nature that lay at the heart of Hermetic magic, astrology, and alchemy was an important stimulus to scientific investigations and, ultimately, to the rise of modern scientific thought.

HUMANISM AND POLITICAL THOUGHT

The humanists' plan to rediscover classical sources meshed well with their political interests. "One can say," observed Leonardo Bruni, "that letters and the study of the Latin language went hand in hand with the condition of the Roman republic." Petrarch and the civic humanists believed that rulers, whether in a republic or a principality, should exhibit all the classical and Christian virtues of faith, hope, love, prudence, temperance, fortitude, and justice. A virtuous ruler would be loved as well as obeyed. The civic humanists viewed governments and laws as essentially unchanging and static. They believed that when change does occur, it most likely happens by chance—that is, because of fortune (the Roman goddess Fortuna). Humanists believed that the only protection against chance is true virtue, for the virtuous would never be dominated by fortune. Thus, beginning with Petrarch, humanists advised rulers to love their subjects, to be generous with their possessions, and to maintain the rule of law. Humanistic tracts of the fourteenth and fifteenth centuries were full of classical and Christian examples of virtuous actions by moral rulers.

The French invasions of Italy in 1494 (see page 328) and the warfare that followed called into question many of the humanists' assumptions about the lessons and virtues of classical civilization. Francesco Guicciardini (gwih-char-DI-nee) (1483–1540), a Florentine patrician who had served in papal armies, suggested that, contrary to humanistic hopes, history held no clear lessons. Unless the causes of separate events were identical down to the smallest detail, he said, the results could be radically different. An even more thorough critique was offered by Guicciardini's friend and fellow Florentine, **Niccolò Machiavelli** (1469–1527). In a series of writings Machiavelli developed what he believed was a new science of politics. He wrote *Discourses on Livy,* a treatise on military organization, a history of Florence, and even a Renaissance play titled *The Mandrake Root.* He is best remembered, however, for *The Prince* (1513), a small tract numbering fewer than a hundred pages.

Machiavelli felt that his contemporaries paid too little heed to the lessons to be learned from history. Thus in his discourses on Livy he comments on Roman government, the role of religion, and the nature of political virtue, emphasizing the sophisticated Roman analysis of political and military situations. A shortcoming more serious than ignorance of history, Machi-

avelli believed, was his contemporaries' ignorance of the true motivations for people's actions. His play *The Mandrake Root* is a comedy about the ruses used to seduce a young woman. In truth, however, none of the characters is fooled. All of them, from the wife to her husband, realize what is happening but use the seduction to their own advantage. In the play Machiavelli implicitly challenges the humanistic assumption that educated individuals will naturally choose virtue over vice. He explicitly criticizes these same assumptions in *The Prince.* Machiavelli holds the contrary view: that individuals are much more likely to respond to fear and that power rather than morality makes for good government.

Machiavelli's use of the Italian word *virtù* led him to be vilified as amoral. Machiavelli deliberately chose a word that meant both "manliness" or "ability" and "virtue as a moral quality." Earlier humanists had restricted *virtù* to the second meaning, using the word to refer to upright qualities such as prudence, generosity, and love. Machiavelli tried to show that in some situations these "virtues" could have violent, even evil, consequences. If, for example, a prince was so magnanimous in giving away his wealth that he was forced to raise taxes, his subjects might come to hate him. Conversely, a prince who, through cruelty to the enemies of his state, brought peace and stability to his subjects might be obeyed and perhaps even loved. A virtuous ruler must be mindful of the goals to be achieved—that is what Machiavelli really meant by the phrase often translated as "the ends justify the means."

Machiavelli expected his readers to be aware of the ambiguous nature of virtue—whether understood as ability or as morality. "One will discover," he concludes, "that something which appears to be a virtue, if pursued, will end in his destruction; while some other thing which seems to be a vice, if pursued, will result in his safety and his well-being."[9]

Like Guicciardini, Machiavelli rejected earlier humanistic assumptions that one needed merely to imitate the great leaders of the past. Governing is a process that requires different skills at different times, he warned: "The man who adapts his course of action to the nature of the times will succeed and, likewise, the man who sets his course of action out of tune with the times will come to grief."[10] The abilities that enable a prince to gain power may not be the abilities that will allow him to maintain it.

With the writings of Machiavelli humanistic ideas of intellectual, moral, and political reform came to maturation. Petrarch and the early humanists believed fully in the powers of classical wisdom to transform society. Machiavelli and his contemporaries admitted the importance of classical wisdom but also recognized the ambiguity of any simplistic application of classical learning to contemporary life.

Niccolò Machiavelli   A government functionary and political theorist in Florence whose most famous work, *The Prince,* emphasized that the successful ruler must anticipate and adapt to change.

=S E C T I O N   S U M M A R Y=

- The culture of Italy was more urban and less clerical than the rest of Europe.

- Francesco Petrarch popularized cultural movements that attempted to use Roman learning to change moral values and public behavior in Europe.

- Because women lacked a role in public life, their relationship to the humanistic movement was limited.

- By the end of the fifteenth century, humanists had developed a sense of historical change.

- Political crisis in Italy led Machiavelli to challenge the assumptions about morality and public life.

PAINTING AND THE ARTS, 1250–1550

What was "new" about Renaissance art?

Townspeople and artists in Renaissance Italy shared the humanists' perception of the importance of classical antiquity. Filippo Villani (d. 1405), a wealthy Florentine from an important business family, wrote that artists had recently "reawakened a lifeless and almost extinct art." In the middle of the fifteenth century the sculptor Lorenzo Ghiberti concluded that with the rise of Christianity "not only statues and paintings [were destroyed], but the books and commentaries and handbooks and rules on which men relied for their training." Italian writers and painters themselves believed that the recovery of past literary and artistic practices was essential if society was to recover from the "barbarism" that they believed characterized the recent past.

The Renaissance of the arts is traditionally divided into three periods. In the early Renaissance artists imitated nature; in the middle period they rediscovered

Giotto's Naturalism
Later painters praised the naturalistic emotion of Giotto's painting. In this detail from the Arena Chapel, Giotto portrays the kiss of Judas, one of the most dramatic moments in Christian history. *(Scala/Art Resource, NY)*

classical ideas of proportion; in the High Renaissance artists were "superior to nature but also to the artists of the ancient world," according to the artist and architect Giorgio Vasari (1511–1574), who wrote a famous history of the eminent artists of his day.

EARLY RENAISSANCE ART

The first stirrings of the new styles can be found in the late thirteenth century. The greatest innovator of that era was Giotto di Bondone of Florence (ca. 1266–1337). Although Giotto's background was modest, his fellow citizens, popes, and patrons throughout Italy quickly recognized his skill. He traveled as far south as Rome and as far north as Padua painting churches and chapels. According to later artists and commentators, Giotto broke with the prevailing stiff, highly symbolic style and introduced lifelike portrayals of living persons. He produced paintings of dramatic situations, showing events located in specific times and places. The frescoes of the Arena Chapel in Padua (1304–1314), for example, recount episodes in the life of Christ. In a series of scenes leading from Christ's birth to his crucifixion, Giotto situates his actors in towns and countryside in what appears to be actual space. Even Michelangelo, the master of the High Renaissance, studied Giotto's painting. Giotto was in such demand throughout Italy that his native Florence gave him a public appointment so that he would be required by law to remain in the city.

Early in the fifteenth century Florentine artists devised new ways to represent nature that surpassed even the innovations of Giotto. The revolutionary nature of these artistic developments is evident from the careers of Lorenzo Ghiberti (1378–1455), Filippo Brunelleschi (1377–1446), and Masaccio (1401–ca. 1428). Their sculpture, architecture, and painting began an ongoing series

The Doors of Paradise
Ghiberti worked on panels for the baptistery from 1401 to 1453. In his representations of scenes from the Old Testament he combined a love of ancient statuary with the new Florentine interest in linear perspective. *(Baptistery of San Giovanni, Florence/ Scala/Art Resource, NY)*

of experiments with the representation of space through **linear perspective.** Perspective is a system for representing three-dimensional objects on a two-dimensional plane. It is based on two observations: (1) as parallel lines recede into the distance, they seem to converge; and (2) a geometric relationship regulates the relative sizes of objects at various distances from the viewer. Painters of the Renaissance literally found themselves looking at their world from a new perspective.

In 1401 Ghiberti won a commission to design door panels for the baptistery of San Giovanni in Florence. He was to spend much of the rest of his life working on two sets of bronze doors on which were recorded the stories of the New Testament (the north doors) and the Old Testament (the east doors). Ghiberti used the new techniques of linear perspective to create a sense of space into which he placed his classically inspired figures. Later, in the sixteenth century, Michelangelo remarked that the east doors were worthy to be the "Doors of Paradise," and so they have been known ever since.

In the competition for the baptistery commission, Ghiberti had beaten the young Filippo Brunelleschi (broon-eh-LES-key), who, as a result, gave up sculpture for architecture and later left Florence to study in Rome. While in Rome he is said to have visited and measured surviving examples of classical architecture—the artistic equivalent of humanistic literary research. According to Vasari, he was capable of "visualizing Rome as it was before the fall." Brunelleschi's debt to Rome is evident in his masterpiece, Florence's foundling hospital. Built as a combination of hemispheres and cubes and resembling a Greek stoa or an arcaded Roman basilica, the long, low structure is an example of how profoundly different Renaissance architecture was from the towering Gothic of the Middle Ages. But his experience in Rome was also critical to his famous plan for constructing a dome over the Cathedral of Santa Maria del Fiore in Florence. The Florentines were replacing their old cathedral with a vast new one. But until Brunelleschi, no one had been able to design a dome to cover the 180-foot space created by the vast new nave. He designed mutually supporting internal and external domes that were stronger and lighter than a single dome would have been.

In the first decade of the fifteenth century, many commentators believed that painting would never be as innovative as either sculpture or architecture. They knew of no classical models that had survived for imitation. Yet the possibilities in painting became apparent in 1427 with the unveiling of Masaccio's *Trinity* in the Florentine Church of Santa Maria Novella. Masaccio (ma-SAH-cho) built on revolutionary experiments in linear perspective to create a painting in which a flat wall seems to become a recessed chapel. The space created is filled with the images of Christ crucified, the Father, and the Holy Spirit.

In the middle years of the fifteenth century, artists came to terms with the innovations of the earlier period. In the second half of the fifteenth century, however, artists such as the Florentine Sandro Botticelli (bot-ti-CHEL-ee) (1445–1510) added a profound understanding of classical symbolism to the technical innovations of Masaccio and Brunelleschi. Botticelli's famous *Primavera* (*Spring*, 1478), painted for a member of the Medici family, is filled with Neo-Platonic symbolism concerning truth, beauty, and the virtues of humanity.

HIGH RENAISSANCE ART

The high point in the development of Renaissance art came at the beginning of the sixteenth century. Artists in Venice learned perspective from the Florentines and added their own tradition of subtle coloring in oils. The works of Italian artists were admired well beyond the borders of Italy. Even Sultan Mehmed II of Constantinople valued Italian painters. (See the box "The Global Record: Gentile Bellini Travels to Meet the Turkish Sultan.") Italian painters, goldsmiths, and architects continued to work in the Ottoman Empire through the sixteenth century.

The work of two Florentines, **Leonardo da Vinci** (1452–1519) and Michelangelo Buonarroti (1475–1564), best exemplifies the sophisticated heights that art achieved early in the sixteenth century. Leonardo, the bastard son of a notary, was raised in the village of Vinci outside of Florence. Cut off from the humanistic milieu of the city, he desired above all else to prove that his artistry was the equal of his formally schooled social superiors. In his notebooks he confessed, "I am fully conscious that, not being a literary man, certain presumptuous persons will think they may reasonably blame me, alleging that I am not a man of letters."[11] But he defended his lack of classical education by arguing that all the best writing, like the best painting and invention, is based on the close observation of nature. Close observation and scientific analysis made Leonardo's work uniquely creative in all these fields. Leonardo is famous for his plans, sometimes prophetic, for bridges, fortresses, submarines, and airships. There seemed to be no branch of learning in which he was not interested. In painting he developed chiaroscuro, a technique for using light and dark in pictorial representation, and showed aerial perspective. He painted horizons as muted, shaded zones

---

linear perspective A revolutionary technique developed by early-fifteenth-century Florentine painters for representing three-dimensional objects on a two-dimensional plane.

Leonardo da Vinci A famous painter, engineer, and scientist who rejected arguments and ideas based on imitation of the ancients. Rather, he advocated careful study of the natural world.

GENTILE BELLINI TRAVELS TO MEET THE TURKISH SULTAN

Giovanni and Gentile Bellini were two of the leading Renaissance artists in Venice. Their fame spread throughout the Mediterranean and resulted in this unusual cultural meeting in 1479. A portrait of the emperor Mehmed II by Gentile now hangs in the National Gallery in London.

Some portraits having been taken to Turkey to the Grand Turk [the sultan] by an ambassador, that emperor was so struck with astonishment that, although the Mohammedan laws prohibit pictures, he accepted them with great goodwill, praising the work without end, and what is more, requesting that the master himself be sent to him. But the Senate, considering that Giovanni could ill support the hardships, resolved to send Gentile his brother, and he was conveyed safely in their galleys to Constantinople, where being presented to Mehmed [II], he was received with much kindness as an unusual visitor. He presented a beautiful picture to the prince, who admired it much, and could not persuade himself to believe that a mortal man had in him so much of the divinity as to be able to express the things of nature in such a lively manner. Gentile painted the Emperor Mehmed himself from life so well that it was considered a miracle, and the emperor, having seen many specimens of his art, asked Gentile if he had the courage to paint himself; and Gentile having answered "Yes," before many days were over he finished a lifelike portrait by means of a mirror, and brought it to the monarch, whose astonishment was so great that he would have it a divine spirit dwelt in him. And had not this art been forbidden by the law of the Turks, the emperor would never have let him go. But either from fear that people would murmur, or from some other cause, he sent for him one day, and having thanked him, and given him great praise, he bade him to ask whatever he would and it should be granted him without fail. Gentile modestly asked for nothing more than that he would graciously give him a letter of recommendation to the Senate and Lords of Venice. His request was granted in as fervent words as possible, and then, loaded with gifts and honors, and with the dignity of a cavalier, he was sent away. Among the other gifts was a chain of gold of two hundred and fifty crowns weight, worked in the Turkish manner. So, leaving Constantinople, he came safely to Venice, where he was received by his brother Giovanni and the whole city with joy, every one rejoicing in the honors which Mehmed had paid him. When the Doge and Lords [of Venice] saw the letters of the emperor, they ordered that a provision of two hundred crowns a year should be paid him all the rest of his life.

QUESTIONS

1. What seems to be the role of Renaissance art and artists in Venetian and Turkish diplomacy?

2. What does Bellini's trip to Constantinople suggest about relations between the Turks and Christians?

Source: Stories of the Italian Renaissance from Vasari, arranged and translated by E. L. Seeley (London and New York, 1908), pp. 135–137.

---

rather than with sharp lines. "I know," he said, "that the greater or less quantity of air that lies between the eye and the object makes the outlines of that object more or less distinct."[12] It was Leonardo's analytical observation that had the greatest influence on his contemporaries.

Michelangelo, however, was widely hailed as the capstone of Renaissance art. In the words of a contemporary, "He alone has triumphed over ancient artists, modern artists and over Nature itself." In his career we can follow the rise of Renaissance artists from the ranks of mere craftsmen to honored creators, courtiers who were the equals of the humanists—in fact, Michelangelo shared Petrarch's concern for reform and renewal in Italian society. We can also discern the synthesis of the artistic and intellectual transformations of the Renaissance with a profound religious sensitivity.

The importance of Michelangelo's contribution is obvious in two of his most important works: the statue *David* in Florence and his commissions in the **Sistine Chapel** of the Vatican in Rome. From his youth Michelangelo had studied and imitated antique sculpture, to the point that some of his creations were thought by many actually to be antiquities. He used his understanding of classical art in *David* (1501). Florentines recalled David's defeat of the giant Goliath, saving Israel from almost certain conquest by the Philistines. *David* thus became a symbol of the youthful Florentine republic struggling to maintain its freedom against great odds. As Vasari noted, "Just as David had protected his people and governed them

Sistine Chapel   The chapel at the Vatican Palace containing Michelangelo's magnificent paintings of the Creation and Last Judgment; it captures the cultural, religious, and ideological program of the papacy.

The Pietà
Michelangelo sculpted three versions of Mary holding the crucified Jesus. This late, unfinished work reveals Michelangelo's desire to show the suffering of Christ. *(Scala/Art Resource, NY)*

justly, so whoever ruled Florence should vigorously defend the city and govern it with justice."[13]

Michelangelo was a committed republican and Florentine, but he spent much of his life working in Rome on a series of papal commissions. In 1508 he was called by Pope Julius II (r. 1503–1513) to work on the ceiling of the Sistine Chapel. Michelangelo spent four years decorating the ceiling with hundreds of figures and with nine scenes from the Book of Genesis, including the famous *Creation of Adam*. In the late 1530s, at the request of Pope Clement VII (r. 1523–1534), he completed *The Last Judgment,* which covers the wall above the altar. In that painting the techniques of perspective and the conscious recognition of debts to classical culture recede into the background as the artist surrounds Christ in judgment with saints and sinners. In the hollow, hanging skin of flayed Saint Bartholomew we can detect a psychological self-portrait of an artist increasingly concerned with his own spiritual failings.

Online Study Center **Improve Your Grade**
Primary Source: Keeping Michelangelo Happy: "We Love You from the Heart"

Michelangelo's self-portrait reminds us that the intellectual content of the artist's work is one of its most enduring traits. He was a Platonist who believed that the form and beauty of a statue are contained, buried, in the stone itself. The artist's job is to peel away excess material and reveal the beauty within. As he noted in one of his poems, sculpting is a process not unlike religious salvation:

Just as by carving . . . we set
Into hard mountain rock
A living figure
Which grows most where the stone is most removed;
In like manner, some good works . . .
Are concealed by the excess of my very flesh.[14]

RENAISSANCE ART IN THE NORTH

In the early fifteenth century, while Brunelleschi and Masaccio were revolutionizing the ways in which Italian artists viewed their world, artists north of the Alps, especially in Flanders, were making equally striking advances in the ways they painted and sculpted. Artistic innovation in northern Europe began with changes tied closely to the world of northern courts; only later did artists take up the styles of the Italian Renaissance. Northerners took Italian Renaissance art and fit it to a new environment.

Northern art of the late fourteenth and fifteenth centuries changed in two significant ways. In sculpture, the long, austere, unbroken vertical lines typical of Gothic sculpture gave way to a much more complex and emotional style. In painting, Flemish artists moved from ornate, vividly colored paintings to experiments with ways to create a sense of depth. Artists strove to paint and sculpt works that more faithfully represented reality. The sculptures of Claus Sluter (1350–1406), carved for a family chapel of the Burgundian dukes at Champmol, captured a lifelike drama unlike the previous Gothic sculpture. Court painters such as Jan van Eyck (ca. 1390–1441), in miniatures, portraits, and altar paintings, also moved away from a highly formalized style to a careful representation of specific places. In van Eyck's portrait of the Italian banker and courtier

Giovanni Arnolfini and his bride, the image of the painter is reflected in a small mirror behind the couple, and above the mirror is written, "Jan van Eyck was here, 1434." Whereas Italians of the early fifteenth century tried to re-create space through linear perspective, the Flemish used aerial perspective, softening colors and tones to give the illusion of depth.

The influence of Renaissance styles in the north of Europe dates from the reign of the French king Francis I (r. 1515–1547), when Italian artists in significant numbers traveled north. Francis invited Italian artists to his court—most notably Leonardo da Vinci, who spent his last years in France. The most influential of the Italian-style creations in France was doubtless Francis's château Fontainebleau, whose decorations contained mythologies, histories, and allegories of the kind found in the Italian courts. Throughout the sixteenth century Italianate buildings and paintings sprang up throughout Europe.

Perhaps the most famous artist who traveled to Italy, learned Italian techniques, and then transformed them to suit the environment of northern Europe was Albrecht Dürer of Nuremberg (1471–1528). Son of a well-known goldsmith, Dürer became a painter and toured France and Flanders learning the techniques popular in northern Europe. Then in 1494 he left Nuremberg on the first of two trips to Italy, during which he sketched Italian landscapes and studied the work of Italian artists, especially in Venice. What he learned in Italy, combined with the friendship of some of Germany's leading humanists, formed the basis of Dürer's works, which blended northern humanistic interests with the Italian techniques of composition and linear perspective. Dürer worked in charcoal, watercolors, and paints, but

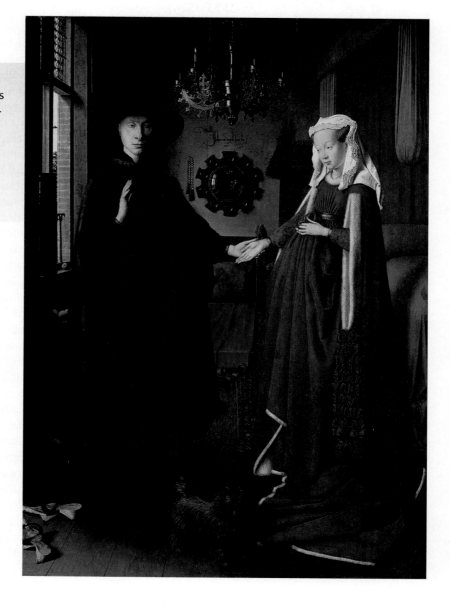

Van Eyck: The Arnolfini Wedding
Careful observation of people and places was typical of the new art of both northern and southern Europe. Van Eyck seems to have re-created this scene to the smallest detail. His own image appears in the mirror on the wall.
(Reproduced by courtesy of the Trustees, The National Gallery, London)

Portrait of a Black Man

Albrecht Dürer sketched this portrait in the early sixteenth century, most likely in a commercial center such as Venice or Nuremberg. By that time it was common to show one of the three Magi as black, but such depictions, unlike Dürer's drawing here, were rarely based on portrait studies.   *(Graphische Sammlung, Albertina, Vienna)*

ART AND PATRONAGE

The variety and vitality of art in the Renaissance depended in large measure on the economic prosperity of Europe's cities and towns. The patronage of artists and consumption of art created symbols and images through which individuals, especially in Italy, could reason about the most important issues of their communities. Italians willingly spent vast sums on art because of its ability to communicate social, political, and spiritual values.

Italy in the fourteenth and fifteenth centuries was unusually wealthy relative to the towns and principalities of northern Europe. Despite the population decline caused by plague and the accompanying economic dislocations, per person wealth in Italy remained quite high. Because of banking, international trade, and even service as mercenaries, Italians, and particularly Florentines, had money to spend on arts and luxuries. Thus the Italians of the Renaissance, whether as public or private patrons, could afford to use consumption of art as a form of competition for social and political status.

It was not just the elite who could afford art. Surprisingly modest families bought small religious paintings, painted storage chests, and decorative arts. Moralists advised families to buy small paintings of the Virgin Mary or the baby Jesus. Families also bought small paintings of saints considered special to their town or family. Wealthy and modest families alike bought brightly decorated terra-cotta pitchers, platters, and plates. Decorative arts were a critical social marker for families at all levels. (See the feature "The Visual Record: Renaissance Marriage Chests.") Thus the market for art steadily increased in the fourteenth and fifteenth centuries, as did the number of shops and studios in which artists could be trained.

Artists in the modern world are accustomed to standing outside society as critics of conventional ideas. In the late Middle Ages and Renaissance, artists were not alienated commentators. In 1300 most art was religious in subject, and public display was its purpose. Throughout Europe art fulfilled a devotional function. Painted crucifixes, altarpieces, and banners were often endowed as devotional or penitential objects. The Arena Chapel in Padua, with its frescoes by Giotto, was funded by a merchant anxious to pay for some of his sins.

In the late Middle Ages and Renaissance, numerous paintings and statues throughout Italy (and much of the rest of Europe) were revered for their miraculous powers. During plague, drought, and times of war people had recourse to the sacred power of the saints represented in these works of art. (See the feature "The Visual Record: A Painting of the Plague" in Chapter 11, pages 332–333.) The construction of the great churches of the period was often a community project that lasted

his influence was most widely spread through his numerous woodcuts covering classical and contemporary themes. His woodcut *Whore of Babylon,* prepared in the context of the debate over the reform of the church, is based on sketches of Venetian prostitutes completed during his first visit to Italy.

Numerous other artists and engravers traveled south to admire and learn from the great works of Italian artists. The engravings they produced and distributed back home made the southern innovations available to those who would never set foot in Italy. In fact, some now lost or destroyed creations are known only through the copies engraved by northern artists eager to absorb Italian techniques.

Men and Women Playing Cards
This fresco painted in the early fifteenth century in Milan is typical of the art used to decorate the homes of the wealthy. It depicts one of the pastimes of noble families.
(Scala/Art Resource, NY)

for decades, even centuries. The city council of Siena, for example, voted to rebuild its Gothic Cathedral of Saint Mary, saying that the Blessed Virgin "was, is and will be in the future the head of this city" and that through veneration of her "Siena may be protected from harm." Accordingly, although the subject of art was clearly and primarily religious, the message was bound up in civic values.

Art and the Commune   The first burst of artistic creativity in the fourteenth century was paid for by public institutions. Communal governments built and decorated city halls to house government functionaries and to promote civic pride. Most towns placed a remarkable emphasis on the beauty of the work. Civic of-

ficials often named special commissions to consult with a variety of artists and architects before approving building projects. Governments, with an eye to the appearance of public areas, legislated the width of streets, height limits, and even the styles of dwelling façades.

The series of paintings called the *Good Government of Siena* illustrates the use of art to communicate political ideas. Painted in the first half of the fourteenth century by Ambrogio Lorenzetti (ca. 1300–1348), *Good Government* combines allegorical representations of Wisdom and the cardinal virtues on one wall with realistic street scenes of a well-ordered Siena on an adjacent wall. Across from the scenes of good government are its opposite, graphic representations of murder, rape, and general injustice and mayhem. In this ambitious work, with its specific scenes and unmistakable tone, the government broadcast a clear political message in realistic brushstrokes. The popular preacher San Bernardino of Siena (1380–1444) reinforced the point of Lorenzetti's painting: "To see Peace depicted is a delight and so it is a shame to see War painted on the other wall." And Bernardino's sermon reminded listeners of the conclusions they should draw: "Oh my brothers and fathers, love and embrace each other . . . give your aid to this toil which I have undertaken so gladly, to bring about love and peace among you."[15]

Public art in Florence was often organized and supported by various guild organizations. Guild membership was a prerequisite for citizenship, so guildsmen set the tone in politics as well as in the commercial life of the city. Most major guilds commissioned sculpture for the Chapel of Or San Michele. This was a famous shrine in the grain market (its painting of the Virgin Mary was popularly thought to have wonderworking powers) and seat of the Guelf Party, the city's most powerful political organization. Guilds took responsibility for building and maintaining other structures in the city as well. Guildsmen took pride in creating a beautiful environment, but as the clothmakers' decision to supervise the baptistery shows and Ghiberti's doors, the work reflected not only on the city and its patron saint but also on the power and influence of the guild itself.

Individual Patrons The princes who ruled outside the republics of Italy often had similarly precise messages that they wished to communicate. Renaissance popes embarked on a quite specific ideological program in the late fifteenth century to assert their dual roles as spiritual leaders of Christendom and temporal lords of a central Italian state (see pages 378–379). Rulers such as the Este dukes of Ferrara and the Sforza dukes of Milan constructed castles within their cities or hunting lodges and villas in the countryside and adorned them with pictures of the hunt or murals of knights in combat—scenes that emphasized their noble virtues and their natural right to rule.

By the mid-fifteenth century patrons of artworks in Florence and most other regions of Italy were more and more likely to be wealthy individuals. Many of the patrons who commissioned and oversaw artists were women. Women paid for the construction of convents and chapels. In many cases their patronage can simply be understood as an extension of their families, but in many other cases it was not. One woman who had lived for years as a concubine of a merchant in Florence used her dead lover's bequest to commission a painting titled *Christ and the Adulteress*, making clear that even women in her situation could hope for God's mercy.

Republics, in which all families were in principle equal, initially distrusted the pride and ambition implied by elaborate city palaces and rural villas. By the middle of the fifteenth century, however, such reserve was found in none but the most conservative republics, such as Venice and Lucca. Palaces, gardens, and villas became the settings in which the wealthy could entertain their peers, receive clients, and debate the political issues of the day. The public rooms of these *palazzos* were decorated with portraits, gem collections, rare books, ceramics, and statuary. Many villas and palaces included private chapels. In the Medici palace in Florence, for example, the chapel is the setting for a painting of the Magi (the three wise men who came to worship the infant Jesus) in which the artist, Benozzo Gozzoli (1420–1498), used members of the Medici family as models for the portraits of the Magi and their entourage (see the painting on page 327). The Magi, known to be wise and virtuous rulers, were an apt symbol for the family that had come to dominate the city.

Artists at princely courts were expected to work for the glory of their lord. Often the genre of choice was the portrait. One of the most successful portraitists of the sixteenth century was Sofonisba Anguissola (1532–1625). Anguissola won renown as a prodigy because she was female and from a patrician family; one of her paintings was sent to Michelangelo, who forwarded it to the Medici in Florence. Since women would never be allowed to study anatomy, Anguissola concentrated her talents on portraits and detailed paintings of domestic life. Later she was called to the Spanish court, where the king, queen, and their daughter sat for her. She continued to paint after her marriage and return to Italy. Even in her nineties she welcomed painters from all parts of Europe to visit and discuss techniques of portraiture.

━━━━ S E C T I O N   S U M M A R Y ━━━━

- Renaissance painters were especially prized for their ability to depict particular events in realistic, natural-seeming settings.

- Beginning with Brunelleschi, artists consciously searched for ancient models for their work.

- Northern artists were keenly aware of Italian art, but they contributed a realism based on contrasts of dramatic colors.

- The work of Michelangelo shows the combination of artistic skill with humanistic moral and philosophical values.

THE SPREAD OF THE RENAISSANCE, 1350–1536

In what ways did humanism outside Italy differ from Italian humanism?

By 1500 the Renaissance had spread from Italy to the rest of Europe. Well beyond the borders of the old Roman Empire, in Prague and Cracow, for example, one could find a renewed interest in classical ideas about art and literature. As information about the past and its relevance to contemporary life spread, however, the message was transformed in several important ways. Outside Italy, Rome and its history played a much less pivotal role. Humanists elsewhere in the West were interested more in religious than in political reform, and they responded to a number of important local interests. Yet the Renaissance notion of renewal based on a deep understanding and imitation of the past remained at the center of the movement. The nature of the transformation will be clearer if we begin by considering the nature of vernacular literatures before the emergence of Renaissance humanism.

VERNACULAR LITERATURES

The humanistic movement was not simply a continuation of practical and literary movements. The extent of its innovation will be clearer if we look briefly at the vernacular literatures (that is, written in native languages, rather than Latin) of the fourteenth and fifteenth centuries.

As in Italy, fourteenth-century writers elsewhere were not immediately drawn to classical sources. Boccaccio's work, for example, influenced another vernacular writer, Geoffrey Chaucer (ca. 1343–1400), the son of a London burgher, who served as a diplomat, courtier, and member of Parliament. In addition to the pervasive French influence, Chaucer read and studied Boccaccio. Chaucer's most famous work, *The Canterbury Tales*, consists of stories told by a group of thirty pilgrims who left the London suburbs on a pilgrimage to the shrine of Saint Thomas Becket at Canterbury Cathedral. The narrators and the stories themselves describe a variety of moral and social types, creating an acute, sometimes comic, portrait of English life. The Wife of Bath is typical of Chaucer's pilgrims: "She was a worthy woman all her life, husbands at the churchdoor she had five." After describing her own marriages she observes that marriage is a proper way to achieve moral perfection, but it can be so only, she asserts, if the woman is master!

Online Study Center **Improve Your Grade**
Primary Source: Canterbury Tales: The Knight

Although Chaucer's characters present an ironic view of the good and evil that characterize society, Chaucer's contemporary, William Langland (ca. 1330–1400), took a decidedly more serious view of the ills of English life. Whereas Boccaccio and Chaucer all told realistic tales about life as it truly seemed to be, Langland used the traditional allegorical language (that is, symbolic language in which a place or person represents an idea) of medieval Europe. In *Piers Plowman* Langland writes of people caught between the "Valley of Death" and the "Tower of Truth." He describes the seven deadly sins that threaten all of society and follows with an exhortation to do better. Both Chaucer and Langland expected that their audiences would immediately recognize commonly held ideas and values.

Despite the persistence of old forms of literature, new vernacular styles arose, although they still dealt with traditional values and ideas. Throughout Europe many writers directly addressed their cares and concerns. Letters like those of the Paston family in England or Alessandra Macinghi-Strozzi in Italy described day-to-day affairs of business, politics, and family life. Letters dictated and sent by Saint Catherine of Siena and Angela of Foligno offered advice to the troubled. Small books of moral or spiritual writings were especially popular among women readers in the fourteenth and fifteenth centuries, among them *The Mirror for Simple Souls* by Marguerite of Porete (d. 1310). Though Marguerite was ultimately executed as a heretic, her work continued to circulate anonymously. Her frank descriptions of love, including God's love for humans, inspired many other writers in the fourteenth and fifteenth centuries. Less erotic but equally riveting was the memoir of Margery Kempe, an alewife from England, who left her husband and family, dressed in white (symbolic of virginity), and joined other pilgrims on trips to Spain, Italy, and Jerusalem.

One of the most unusual of the new vernacular writers was Christine de Pizan (1369–1430), the daughter of an Italian physician at the court of Charles V of France. When the deaths of her father and husband left her with responsibility for her children and little money, she turned to writing. From 1389 until her death, she lived and wrote at the French court. She is perhaps best known for *The Book of the City of the Ladies* (1405). In it she added her own voice to what is known as the *querelle des femmes*, the "argument over women." Christine wrote to counter the prevalent opinions of women as inherently inferior to men and incapable of

Renaissance Marriage Chests

The image here shows a marriage procession, including a servant carrying a large chest, or *cassone*. The picture is self-referential, since it was painted on the front of just such a cassone. We know that the painter of this image was Lo Scheggia (1406–1486), the younger brother of Masaccio, and that he was recording a popular story of a marriage between the Bardi and Buondelmonte families of Florence. Lo Scheggia's work exhibits many of the characteristics we associate with Renaissance style. But historians often want to evaluate more than just painting technique. Historians of material culture are interested in the objects themselves and in the meanings that contemporaries gave to the possession and exhibition of them. To understand this we need to know when and where cassoni were produced, why individuals prized them, and what the study of this image from a cassone can tell us about life in Renaissance Italy.

These highly practical chests were used by all but the poorest members of society. In houses that lacked closets, cabinets, and other kinds of storage space, everything was kept in wooden chests. Larger chests were used to store clothing, bedding, jewelry, and even weapons. Smaller chests were used for money, account books, and documents. Many of these chests had secret compartments where, for example, a businessman might keep his most sensitive papers. The most important chests made up the furnishings of the master of the house's bedroom. In a Renaissance palace the master's bedroom was also the room where he met with important allies and family members and conducted his most private business.

Cassoni took on new meaning between the late fourteenth and early sixteenth centuries. During that time it was common for a groom to commission a matched set of chests: one for himself and the second to hold the fine clothes and jewelry that were part of his wife's dowry. These chests were decorated inside and out with scenes from classical mythology, medieval romances, and other popular stories. Classical Roman figures such as Lucretia, who sacrificed her life to maintain her virtue, were common subjects. Some chests celebrated the virtues of chastity or fortitude—virtues thought to be essential in a proper wife. Thus cassoni came to represent the taste, wealth, and social status of the families involved.

With these thoughts in mind, let us look closely at Lo Scheggia's cassone painting. The first thing we should notice is the procession at the left of the picture. We see a man accompanying a woman dressed in black into a house. The two are followed by others leading a horse (a sign of nobility) and carrying bedclothes and the chest. The procession testifies to the very public completion of the marriage process, which often stretched over months, if not years. It began with an engagement, followed by a promise of marriage, then a symbolic ex-

Lo Scheggia: The Bardi-Buondelmonte Wedding *(Alberto Bruschi di Grassina Collection, Florence/Bridgeman Art Library International)*

change of rings and physical consummation of the marriage, usually at the bride's home. The marriage was finalized by a procession to the groom's home. This procession celebrated publicly the alliance between the two families, as well as their standing in the community. Everyone noted carefully what and how much was carried in the procession, which was an indication of the size of the bride's dowry. The decoration of the marriage chest(s) in some way reflected the families involved.

What does the cassone image by Lo Scheggia indicate? The bride is the key to the story. Typically a wealthy bride wore bright new clothes and jewelry, but this bride is dressed in black. The image tells a story not unlike that of Romeo and Juliet. The families of the bride and groom, Lionora de' Bardi and Ippolito Buondelmonte, had been enemies for generations. Despite this fact, the two were in love. We can read the tale of their love in three scenes from right to left. In the first scene on the right, Ippolito is caught in Lionora's house. He refuses to declare his love for her because he wants to protect her reputation. In the middle scene Lionora, dressed as a widow, interrupts Ippolito's trial and declares her love for him. By dressing as a widow, she symbolically declares that they have already made their wedding vows and are, in fact, married. The authorities accept her declaration, and in the final scene on the left, the marriage is made public. Ippolito leads Lionora in a marriage procession, complete with wedding chest, to their new home. According to tradition, their marriage ended the feud between the two families.

We do not know who commissioned this chest. Nonetheless, we can now step back and speculate a bit about what Florentines might have noticed when they viewed the procession in which this cassone was carried through the streets of Florence. The image of the wedding couple and the servants carrying expensive dowry items, as well as the chest itself, testifies to the importance of the families involved. In a community such as Florence, where certain families were at the center of politics and public life, this image no doubt reminded those watching the procession of the power of prominent families and the critical role of marriage alliances in maintaining civic peace.

QUESTIONS

1. Look carefully at the image. Can you identify what seems most significant in the procession of the bride and groom?

2. How would this particular image influence the meaning that observers might give to the procession of the bride and groom?

Online Study Center
Improve Your Grade Visual Record Activities

moral judgments. She argued that the problem was education: "If it were customary to send daughters to school like sons, and if they were then taught the natural sciences, they would learn as thoroughly and understand the subtleties of all the arts and sciences as well as sons." Christine described in her book an ideal city of ladies in which prudence, justice, and reason would protect women from ignorant male critics.

All these vernacular writings built on popular tales and sayings as well as on traditional moral and religious writings. Unlike the early humanists, the vernacular writers saw little need for new cultural and intellectual models.

THE IMPACT OF PRINTING

The spread of humanism beyond Italy was aided greatly by the invention of printing. In the fifteenth century the desire to own and to read complete texts of classical works was widespread, but the number of copies was severely limited. Manuscripts required time and money to hand-copy, collate, and check each new copy. Poggio Bracciolini's letters are filled with complaints about the time and expense of reproducing the classical manuscripts he had discovered. One copy he had commissioned was so inaccurate and illegible as to be nearly unusable. Traveling to repositories and libraries was often easier than creating a personal library. It was rarely possible for someone who read a manuscript once to obtain a complete copy to compare with other works.

The invention of printing with movable lead type changed things dramatically. Although block printing had long been known in China, it was only in the late fourteenth century that it became a popular way to produce playing cards and small woodcuts in Europe. In China an entire page would be carved on a single wooden block. **Johann Gutenberg** developed molds by which single letters or individual words could be cast in metal. Metal fonts could produce many more copies before they had to be recast. And further, they could be reused to print different pages. Between 180 and 200 copies of the so-called Gutenberg Bible were printed in 1452 and 1453. It was followed shortly by editions of the Psalms. By 1470 German printing techniques had spread to Italy, the Low Countries, France, and England. It has been estimated that by 1500 a thousand presses were operating in 265 towns (see **MAP 12.1**). The output of the early presses was extremely varied, ranging from small devotional books and other popular and profitable literature to complete editions

Johann Gutenberg German inventor of movable metal type. His innovations led to the publication of the first printed book in Europe, the Gutenberg Bible, in the 1450s.

of classical authors and their humanistic and theological texts. Printing allowed for a dramatic expansion of libraries. Early humanists had to strive to create a library of several hundred volumes. The Venetian printer Aldus Manutius (1450–1515) himself printed and distributed over 120,000 volumes!

Printing allowed for the creation of agreed-upon standard editions of works in law, theology, philosophy, and science. Scholars in different parts of the European world could feel fairly confident that they and their colleagues were analyzing identical texts. Similarly, producing accurate medical and herbal diagrams, maps, and even reproductions of art and architecture was easier. Multiple copies of texts also made possible the study of rare and esoteric literary, philosophical, and scientific works. An unexpected result of the print revolution was the rise of the printshop as a center of culture and communication. The printers Aldus Manutius in Venice and Johannes Froben (d. 1527) in Basel were humanists. Both invited humanists to work in their shops editing their texts and correcting the proofs before printing. Printshops became a natural gathering place for clerics and laymen. Thus they were natural sources of humanist ideas and later, in the sixteenth century, of Protestant religious programs.

HUMANISM OUTSIDE ITALY

As the influence of the humanist movement extended beyond Italy, the interests of the humanists changed. Although a strong religious strain infused Italian humanism, public life lay at the center of Italian programs of education and reform. Outside Italy, however, moral and religious reform formed the heart of the movement. Northern humanists wanted to renew Christian life and reinvigorate the church. Critics of the church complained that the clergy were wealthy and ignorant and that the laity were uneducated and superstitious. To amend those failings, northern humanists were involved in building educational institutions, in unearthing and publishing texts by Church Fathers, and in chronicling local customs and history. The works of the two best-known humanists, Thomas More and Desiderius Erasmus present a sharp critique of contemporary behavior and, in the case of Erasmus, a call to a new sense of piety. The religious views of Erasmus were so influential that northern humanism has generally come to be known as "Christian humanism."

Humanism and Universities The intellectual environment into which humanism spread from Italy had changed significantly since the thirteenth century. The universities of Paris and Oxford retained the status they had acquired earlier but found themselves

MAP 12.1 The Spread of Printing

Printing technology moved rapidly along major trade routes to the most populous and prosperous areas of Europe. The technology was rapidly adopted in peripheral areas as well as in highly literate centers such as the Low Countries, the Rhine Valley, and northern Italy.

Online Study Center **Improve Your Grade** Interactive Map: The Growth of Printing

competing with a host of new foundations. Like Paris, almost all had theological faculties dominated by Scholastically trained theologians. Nevertheless, the new foundations often had chairs of rhetoric, or "eloquence," which left considerable scope for those who advocated humanistic learning. These new universities, from Cracow (1367) to Uppsala in Sweden (1477), also reflected the increased national feeling in various regions of Europe. The earliest university in the lands of the German Empire, the Charles University in Prague (1348), was founded at the request of Emperor Charles

IV, whose court was in Prague. The foundation of a new university at Poszony (1465) by Johannes Vitéz was part of a cultural flowering of the Hungarian court at Buda. A supporter of King Matthias Corvinus, Vitéz corresponded with Italian humanists, collected manuscripts, and tried to recruit humanist teachers to come to Buda. The universities in Vienna (1365), Aix (1409), Louvain (1425), and numerous other cities owed their foundations to the pride and ambition of local leaders.

The humanists associated with the new universities were often educated in Italy, but they brought a new perspective to their work. Humanists in Sweden wrote histories of the Goths, celebrating the contributions of Germans to European culture. Polish humanists wrote similarly, in one case trying to define where in eastern Europe one could draw the line between Europe and Asia.

Humanists on faculties of law at French universities used humanistic techniques of historical and linguistic study. Italian-trained French lawyers introduced what came to be called the "Gallican style" of jurisprudence. Because legal ideas, like language, changed over time, they argued that Roman law had to be studied as a historically created system and not as an abstract and unchanging structure. Humanists like Guillaume Budé (1468–1540) moved from the study of law to considerations of Roman coinage, religion, and economic life in order to better understand the formation of Roman law. The desire to understand the law led other humanist-legists to add the study of society in ancient Gaul to their work on Rome, and then to examine the law of other societies as well.

Humanism and Religion   The new universities often became centers of linguistic studies. Humanistic interest in language inspired the foundation of "trilingual" colleges in Spain, France, and the Low Countries to foster serious study of Hebrew, Greek, and Latin. Like Italian humanists, other humanists believed that knowledge of languages would allow students to understand more clearly the truths of Christianity. Typical of this movement was the archbishop of Toledo, Francisco Jiménez de Cisneros (1436–1517), who founded the University of Alcalá in 1508 with chairs of Latin, Greek, and Hebrew. He began the publication of a vast new edition of the Bible, called the "Polyglot ('many tongued') Bible" (1522) because it had parallel columns in Latin, Greek, and, where appropriate, Hebrew. Unlike Valla, Jiménez intended his translations not to challenge the Vulgate but merely to clarify its meaning. The university and the Bible were part of an effort to complete the conversion of Muslims and Jews and to reform religious practices among the old Christians.

To these humanists, the discovery and publication of early Christian authors seemed critical to any reform within the church. Jacques Lefèvre d'Étaples (le-FEV-ra du-TAHP-le) (1455–1536) of France was one of the most famous and influential of these humanistic editors of early Christian texts. After 1500 he concentrated on editing the texts of the early Church Fathers. The true spirit of Christianity, he believed, would be most clear in the works and lives of those who had lived closest to the age of the apostles. Christian humanists inspired by Lefèvre became key players in the later Reformation movements in France. Lefèvre's faith in the value of classical languages was shared by John Colet (1467–

1519) of England, founder of St. Paul's School in London. He instituted a thorough program of teaching Latin and Greek aimed at creating scholars who would have access to the earliest Christian writings.

Tensions between the humanists and the advocates of Scholastic methods broke out over the cultural and linguistic studies that formed the heart of the humanist program. Taking to heart the humanistic belief that all philosophies and religions, not just Christianity, contained universal moral and spiritual truths, Johannes Reuchlin (RYE-klin) (1455–1522) of Württemberg embarked on a study of the Jewish Cabala. Johannes Pfefferkorn, a Dominican priest and recent convert from Judaism, attacked Reuchlin's use of Jewish traditions in the study of Christian theology. Sides were quickly drawn. The theological faculties of the German universities generally supported Pfefferkorn. The humanists supported Reuchlin. In his own defense Reuchlin issued *The Letters of Illustrious Men,* a volume of correspondence he had received in support of his position. This work gave rise to one of the great satires of the Renaissance, *The Letters of Obscure Men* (1516), written by anonymous authors and purporting to be letters from various narrow-minded Scholastics in defense of Pfefferkorn. Although the debate arose over the validity of Hebraic studies for Christian theology and not over humanistic ideas of reform or wisdom, it indicates the division between the humanists and much of the Scholastic community. Many people initially misunderstood the early controversies of the Protestant Reformation as a continuation of the conflicts between humanists and Scholastic theologians over the uses of Hebrew learning.

HUMANISTS AS CRITICS

The careers of two humanists in particular exemplify the strength—and the limits—of the humanistic movement outside Italy: **Sir Thomas More** (1478–1535) of London and **Desiderius Erasmus** (1466–1536) of Rotterdam. Their careers developed along very different paths. More was educated at St. Anthony's School in London and became a lawyer. He translated Lucan and wrote a humanistic history of Richard III while pursuing his public career. Erasmus, on the other hand, was born the illegitimate son of a priest in the Low Countries. Forced by relatives into a monastery, he disliked the conservative piety and authoritarian discipline of traditional monastic life. Once allowed out of the

Thomas More   Well-known humanist and chancellor of England under Henry VIII. His best-known work, *Utopia,* describes a fictional land of peace and harmony that has outlawed private property.

Desiderius Erasmus   Prominent Dutch humanist who is best known for his satire *The Praise of Folly.*

monastery to serve as an episcopal secretary, he never returned. He made his way as an author and editor.

Thomas More　More is most famous for his work *Utopia* (1516), the description of an ideal society located on the island of Utopia (literally, "nowhere") in the newly explored oceans. This powerful and contradictory work is written in two parts. Book I is a debate over the moral value of public service between Morus, a well-intentioned but practical politician, and Hythloday, a widely traveled idealist. Morus tries to make the bureaucrat's argument about working for change from within the system. Hythloday rejects the argument out of hand. Thomas More himself seems to have been unsure at that time about the virtues of public service. He was of two minds, and the debate between Morus and Hythloday reflects his indecision. As part of his critique of injustice and immoral governments in Europe, Hythloday describes in Book II the commonwealth of Utopia, in which there is no private property but strict equality of possessions, and, as a result, harmony, tolerance, and little or no violence.

Since the publication of *Utopia* debates have raged about whether More, or anyone, could ever really hope to live in such a society. Some scholars have questioned how seriously More took this work—he seems to have written the initial sections merely to amuse friends. Yet whatever More's intentions, Utopia's society of equality, cooperation, and acceptance continues to inspire social commentators.

Ironically, More, like his creation Morus, soon found himself trying to work for justice within precisely the sort of autocratic court that Hythloday criticized. Not long after the completion of *Utopia* More entered the service of King Henry VIII (r. 1509–1547), eventually serving as chancellor of England. As a staunch Catholic and royal official More never acted on utopian principles of peace and toleration. He was, in fact, responsible for the persecution of English Protestants in the years before the king's break with Rome (see pages 434–435). More's opposition to Henry's divorce and repudiation of papal authority, and his refusal to acknowledge Henry as the head of the English church, led him to resign his offices. He was eventually imprisoned and beheaded. More's writing was a stinging critique of political values. He implied that society could be reformed, yet in the period after 1521 his humanism and his vision of utopian justice and tolerance had no influence on his own public life.

Desiderius Erasmus　Unlike More, who was drawn to the power of king and pope, Erasmus always avoided working for authorities. Often called the "Prince of Humanists," he was easily the best-known humanist of the early sixteenth century. He lived and taught in France, England, Italy, and Switzerland. Of all the humanists it was Erasmus who most benefited from the printing revolution. The printer Aldus Manutius invited him to live and work in Venice, and he spent the last productive years of his life at Johannes Froben's press in Basel. He left the city only when Protestant reformers took control of the city government.

Over a long career Erasmus brought out repeated editions of works designed to educate Christians. His *Adages,* first published in 1500, was a collection of proverbs from Greek and Roman sources. The work was immensely popular, and Erasmus repeatedly issued expanded editions. He tried to present Greek and Roman wisdom that would illuminate everyday problems. *The Colloquies* was a collection of popular stories. Designed as primers for students, they presented moral lessons even as they taught good language. His ironic *The Praise of Folly* (1511) was dedicated to Thomas More. An oration by Folly in praise of folly, it is satire of a type unknown since antiquity. Folly's catalog of vices includes everyone from the ignoramus to the scholar. But more seriously Erasmus believed, as Saint Paul had said, that Christians must be "fools for Christ." In effect, human existence is folly. Erasmus's Folly first made an observation that Shakespeare would refine and make famous: "Now the whole life of mortal men, what is it but a sort of play in which . . . [each person] plays his own part until the director gives him his cue to leave the stage."[16]

Erasmus's greatest contributions to European intellectual life were his edition of and commentaries on the New Testament. His was a critical edition of the Greek text and a Latin translation independent of the fourth-century Latin Vulgate of Jerome. Unlike Jiménez, Erasmus corrected parts of the Vulgate. He rejected the authority of tradition, saying, "The sin of corruption is greater, and the need for careful revision by scholars is greater also, where the source of corruption was ignorance."[17] What was revolutionary in his edition was his commentary, which emphasized the literal and historical recounting of human experiences. Erasmus's Bible was the basis of later vernacular translations of Scripture during the Reformation.

Underlying Erasmus's scholarly output was what he called his "Philosophy of Christ." Erasmus was convinced that the true essence of Christianity was to be found in the life and actions of Christ. Reasonable, self-reliant, truly Christian people did not need superstitious rituals or magic. In his *Colloquies* he tells of a terrified priest who during a shipwreck promised everything to the Virgin Mary if only she would save him from drowning. But, Erasmus observed, it would have been more practical to start swimming!

Erasmus believed that a humanistic combination of classical and Christian wisdom could wipe away violence, superstition, and ignorance. Unlike More, Erasmus never abandoned the humanistic program. Yet his philosophy of Christ, based on faith in the goodness and educability of the individual, was swamped in the 1520s and 1530s by the sectarian claims of both Protestants and Catholics. Although Erasmus's New Testament was influential in the Reformation, his calls for reforms based on tolerance and reason were not.

════════════ S E C T I O N S U M M A R Y ════════════

- Vernacular literatures of northern Europe emphasized religious and moral themes drawn from daily life.

- The development of printing using movable type made books more widely available.

- Humanists in northern Europe were more closely linked to university life and less tied to ideas of Roman public life.

- Thomas More and Desiderius Erasmus used their humanistic learning to develop a sophisticated critique of contemporary life.

THE RENAISSANCE AND COURT SOCIETY

How did European rulers use Renaissance art and culture?

The educational reforms of the humanists and the innovations in the arts between 1300 and 1550 provided an opportunity for rulers and popes alike to use culture to define and celebrate their authority. Art, literature, and politics merged in the brilliant life of the Renaissance Italian courts, both secular and papal. To understand fully the Renaissance and its importance in the history of Europe, we need to examine the uses of culture by governments, specifically investigating the transformation of European ideas about service at court. We will take as a model the politics and cultural life at one noble court: the court of the Gonzaga family of Mantua. Then we will see how the Renaissance papacy melded the secular and religious aspects of art, culture, and politics in its glittering court in Rome. Finally, we will discuss the development of the idea of the Renaissance gentleman and courtier made famous by Baldassare Castiglione (ka-stil-ee-OH-nee), who was reared at the Gonzaga court.

THE ELABORATION OF THE COURT

The courts of northern Italy took an interest in the cultural and artistic innovations of the Renaissance. They recruited artists and humanists inspired by classical civilization, and they closely imitated many of the values and new styles that were developing in the courts of northern Europe, such as the court of Burgundy. Throughout Europe attendance at court became increasingly important to members of the nobility as a source of revenue and influence. Kings and the great territorial lords were equally interested in drawing people to their courts as a way to influence and control the noble and the powerful.

Rulers in most parts of Europe instituted monarchical orders of knighthood to reward allies and followers. The most famous in the English-speaking world was the Order of the Garter, founded in 1349 by King Edward III. The orders were but one of the innovations in the organization of the court during the fourteenth and fifteenth centuries. The numbers of cooks, servants, huntsmen, musicians, and artists employed at court jumped dramatically in the late Middle Ages. In this expansion the papal court was a model for the rest of Europe. The popes at Avignon in the fourteenth century already had households of nearly six hundred persons. If all the bureaucrats, merchants, local officials, and visitors who continually swarmed around the elaborate papal court were also counted, the number grew even larger.

Courts were becoming theaters built around a series of widely understood signs and images that the ruler could manipulate. Culture was meant to reflect the reputation of the ruler. On important political or personal occasions, rulers organized jousts or tournaments around themes drawn from mythology. The dukes of Milan indicated the relative status of courtiers by inviting them to participate in particular hunts or jousts. They similarly organized their courtiers during feasts or elaborate entries into the towns and cities of their realms.

The late fourteenth and fifteenth centuries were periods of growth in the political and bureaucratic power of European rulers. The increasingly elaborate and sumptuous courts were one of the tools that rulers used to create a unified culture and ideology. At the court of the Gonzagas in Mantua, one of the most widely known of the fifteenth-century courts, the manipulation of Renaissance culture for political purposes was most complete.

THE COURT OF MANTUA

The city of Mantua, with perhaps 25,000 inhabitants in 1500, was small compared with Milan or Venice—the two cities with which it was most commonly allied. Located in a rich farming region along the Po River, Mantua did not have a large merchant or manufacturing class. Most Mantuans were involved in agriculture and regional trade in foodstuffs. The town had been a typical medieval Italian city-state until its government was overthrown by the noble Bonacolsi family in the thirteenth century. The Bonacolsis in turn were ousted in a palace coup in 1328 by their former comrades, the Gonzagas, who ruled the city until 1627.

The Gonzagas faced problems typical of many of the ruling families in northern Italy. The state they were creating was relatively small, their right to rule was not very widely recognized, and their control over the area was weak. The first step for the Gonzagas was to construct fortresses and fortified towns that could withstand foreign enemies. The second step was to gain recognition of their right to rule. In 1329 they were named imperial vicars, or representatives in the region. Later, in 1432, they bought the title "marquis" from the emperor Sigismund for the relatively low price of £12,000—equivalent to a year's pay for their courtiers. By 1500 they had exchanged that title for the more prestigious "duke."

Presiding over a strategic area between the Milanese and Venetian states, the Gonzagas maintained themselves through astute diplomatic connections with other Italian and European courts and through service as well-paid mercenaries in the Italian wars of the fifteenth and sixteenth centuries. Marquis Lodovico (d. 1478) served the Venetians, the Milanese, the Florentines, and even the far-off Neapolitans. With considerable understatement, Lodovico concluded, "We have worn armor for a long time."

The family's reputation was enhanced by Gianfrancesco (jan-fran-CHES-ko) (d. 1444) and Lodovico, who brought the Renaissance and the new court style to Mantua. By 1500 as many as eight hundred or more nobles, cooks, maids, and horsemen may have gathered in the court. Critics called them idlers, "who have no other function but to cater to the tastes of the Duke." It was under the tutelage of the Gonzagas that Vittorino da Feltre created his educational experiment in Villa Giocosa, which drew noble pupils from throughout Italy. It would be hard to overestimate the value for the Gonzagas of a school that attracted sons of the dukes of Urbino, Ferrara, and Milan and of numerous lesser nobles. The family also called many artists to Mantua. Lodovico invited Antonio Pisano, called Pisanello (ca. 1415–1456), probably the most famous court artist of the fifteenth century. Pisanello created a series of frescoes on Arthurian themes for the Gonzaga palace. In these frescoes Lodovico is portrayed as a hero of King Arthur's Round Table.

The Gonzagas are best known for their patronage of art with classical themes. Leon Battista Alberti redesigned the façade of the Church of Sant'Andrea for the Gonzagas in the form of a Roman triumphal arch. The church, which long had been associated with the family, became a monument to the Gonzaga court just as the Arch of Constantine in Rome had celebrated imperial power a thousand years earlier. In the 1460s Lodovico summoned Andrea Mantegna (1441–1506) to his court. Trained in Padua and Venice, Mantegna was at that time the leading painter in northern Italy. His masterwork is the *Camera degli Sposi* (literally, "the room of the spouses"), completed in 1474. It features family portraits of Lodovico Gonzaga and his family framed in imitations of Roman imperial portrait medallions. One scene shows Lodovico welcoming his son, a newly appointed cardinal, back from Rome. Lodovico even included the portrait of the Holy Roman emperor who had never been to Mantua but was related to Lodovico's wife, Barbara of Brandenburg. As Mantegna finished the work, diplomats and rulers throughout Italy carefully monitored it—proof to all of the new status of the Gonzagas.

The Gonzaga court, like most others, was both public and private. On the one hand, finances for the city, appointments to public offices, and important political decisions were made by the men who dominated the court. On the other hand, as the prince's domestic setting, it was a place where women were expected to be seen and could exert their influence. Women were thus actively involved in creating the ideology of the court. Through the patronage of classical paintings, often with moral and political messages, wives of princes helped make the court better known and more widely accepted throughout Italy and Europe.

The arrival of Isabella d'Este (1494–1539) at court as the wife of Francesco Gonzaga marked the high point of the Renaissance in Mantua. Isabella had received a classical education at Ferrara and maintained an interest in art, architecture, and music all her life. As a patron of the arts, she knew what she wanted. Isabella was also an accomplished musician, playing a variety of string and keyboard instruments. She and others of the Gonzaga family recruited Flemish and Italian musicians to their court. By the end of the sixteenth century Mantua was one of the most important musical centers of Europe. One festival brought twelve thousand visitors to the city. Later it would be in Mantua that Claudio

Monteverdi (1567–1643) wrote works that established the genre of opera.

In the fourteenth century Petrarch had complained that however enjoyable feasting in Mantua might be, the place was dusty, plagued by mosquitoes, and overrun with frogs. By the end of the fifteenth century the Gonzagas had transformed their city and secured a prominent place for themselves on the Italian, and the European, stage.

THE RENAISSANCE PAPACY

The issues of power and how it is displayed had religious as well as secular dimensions. After its fourteenth- and fifteenth-century struggles over jurisdiction, the papacy found itself reduced in many respects to the status of an Italian Renaissance court. But popes still needed to defend their primacy within the church from conciliarists, who had argued that all Christians, including the pope, were bound to obey the commands of general councils. The ideological focus of the revived papacy was Rome.

The Transformation of Rome   The first step in the creation of a new Rome was taken by Pope Nicholas V (r. 1446–1455), a cleric who had spent many years in the cultural environment of Renaissance Florence. Hoping to restore Rome and its church to their former glory, Nicholas and his successors patronized the arts, established a lively court culture, and sponsored numerous building projects. Nicholas was an avid collector of ancient manuscripts that seemed to demonstrate the intellectual and religious primacy of Rome. He invited numerous artists and intellectuals to the papal court, including the Florentine architect and writer Leon Battista Alberti (1404–1472). Alberti based his treatise *On Architecture* (1452) on his research in topography and reading done in Rome. This was the most important work on architecture produced during the Renaissance. It was probably under Alberti's influence that Nicholas embarked on a series of ambitious urban renewal projects in Rome, which included bridges, roads, and a rebuilt Saint Peter's Basilica.

The transformation of Rome had an ideological purpose. As one orator proclaimed, "Illuminated by the

Giving of the Keys to Saint Peter
Pietro Perugino's painting of Saint Peter receiving from Christ the keys to "bind and loose" on earth and in heaven illustrates the basis of papal claims to authority within the Christian church. This is the central message of the decorative plan of the Sistine Chapel. *(Scala/Art Resource, NY)*

light of faith and Christian truth, [Rome] is destined to be the firmament of religion . . . , the secure haven for Christians."[18] Thus the papal response to critics was to note that Rome and its government were central to political and religious life in Christendom. By reviving the style and organization of classical antiquity, the church sought to link papal Rome to a magnificent imperial tradition reaching back to Augustus and even to Alexander the Great. To papal supporters only one authority could rule the church. Early tradition and the continuity of the city itself, they assumed, demonstrated papal primacy.

The Sistine Chapel   One particular monument in Rome captures most vividly the cultural, religious, and ideological program of the papacy: the Sistine Chapel in the Vatican Palace. The chapel is best known for the decoration of the ceiling by the Florentine artist Michelangelo (see pages 363–364) and for the striking images in his painting of the Last Judgment. The chapel, however, was commissioned by Pope Sixtus IV in 1475. It was to be an audience chamber in which an enthroned pope could meet the representatives of other states. In addition, it was expected that the college of cardinals would gather in the chapel for the election of new popes.

The decorations done before Michelangelo painted the ceiling reflect the intellectual and ideological values that Sixtus hoped to transmit to the ambassadors and churchmen who entered the chapel. Along the lower sidewalls are portraits of earlier popes, a feature typical of early Roman churches. More significant are two cycles of paintings of the lives of Moses and Christ, drawing parallels between them. To execute the scenes Sixtus called to Rome some of the greatest artists of the late fifteenth century: Sandro Botticelli, Domenico Ghirlandaio, Luca Signorelli, and Pietro Perugino. The works illustrate the continuity of the Old Testament and New Testament and emphasize the importance of obedience to the authority of God. The meaning is most obvious in Perugino's painting of Saint Peter receiving the keys to the Kingdom of Heaven from Christ. The allusion is to Matthew 16:18: "Thou art Peter and upon this rock I shall build my church." The keys are the symbol of the claim of the pope, as successor to Saint Peter, to have the power to bind and loose sinners and their punishments. Directly across from Perugino's painting is Botticelli's *The Judgment of Corah*, which portrays the story of the opponent who challenged the leadership of Moses and Aaron while the Israelites wandered in the wilderness. Corah and his supporters, according to Numbers 16:33, fell live into Hell. Various popes recalled the fate of Corah and the rebels. The pope was bound to oppose the council, Pope Eugenius argued, "to save the people entrusted to his care, lest together with those who hold the power of the council above that of the papacy they suffer a punishment even more dire than that which befell Corah."[19] The meaning of the painting and the entire chapel could not be clearer.

The effects of Renaissance revival were profound. Rome grew from a modest population of about 17,000 in 1400 to 35,000 in 1450. By 1517 the city had a population of over 85,000, five times its population at the end of the Great Schism. The papal program was a success. Rome was transformed from a provincial town to a major European capital, perhaps the most important artistic and cultural center of the sixteenth century. Visitors to the Sistine Chapel, like visitors to the papal city itself, were expected to leave with a profound sense of the antiquity of the papal office and of the continuity of papal exercise of religious authority. Because the building and decorating were being completed as the Protestant Reformation was beginning in Germany, some historians have criticized the expense of the political and cultural program undertaken by the Renaissance popes. But to contemporaries on the scene, the work was a logical and necessary attempt to strengthen the church's standing in Christendom.

CASTIGLIONE AND THE EUROPEAN GENTLEMAN

Renaissance ideas did not just spread in intellectual circles. They also were part of the transformation of the medieval knight into the early modern "gentleman." In 1528 Baldassare Castiglione (1478–1529) published *The Book of the Courtier*. The work, which describes the ideal behavior of a courtier, was based on Castiglione's own distinguished career serving in Italian courts. Set at the court of Urbino, the book chronicles a series of fictional discussions over the course of four nights in March 1507. Among the participants are the duchess of Urbino, Elizabeth Gonzaga; her lady-in-waiting; and a group of humanists, men of action, and courtiers. In four evenings members of the circle try to describe the perfect gentleman of court. In the process they debate the nature of nobility, humor, women, and love.

Castiglione describes, in many respects, a typical gathering at court, and the discourses reflect contemporary views of relations between men and women. The wives of princes were expected to be organizers of life at court but also paragons of domestic virtues. Thus in this book the women organize the discussion, and the men discuss. Although the women direct and influence the talk by jokes and short interventions, they cannot afford to dominate the debate: "[Women] must be more circumspect, and more careful not to give occasion for evil being said of them . . . for a woman has not so many ways of defending herself against false calumnies as a

Federigo da Montefeltro's Studiolo
The duchy of Urbino was a showpiece of Renaissance court life and was the eventual locale for Castiglione's *Book of the Courtier*. It owed much of its fame to Duke Federigo da Montefeltro. Federigo's study is decorated with an expensive inlaid wooden design. Its illusion of great space and the expense of its construction were meant to celebrate Federigo's wealth and power.
(Scala/Art Resource, NY)

man has."[20] Thus in debate, as in politics and diplomacy, the influence of women was most effective when it was indirect.

The topics of such discussions were not randomly chosen. Castiglione explains that he wished "to describe the form of courtiership most appropriate for a gentleman living at the courts of princes." Castiglione's popularity was based on his deliberate joining of humanistic ideas and traditional chivalric values. Although his topic is the court with all its trappings, he tells his readers that his models for the discussion were Latin and Greek dialogues, especially those of Cicero and Plato. As a Platonist he believed that all truly noble gentlemen have an inborn quality of "grace." It has to be brought out, however, just as Michelangelo freed his figures from stone. Castiglione held that all moral and courtly virtues exist in tension with their opposites: "no magnanimity without pusillanimity." With numerous examples of good and bad in the world, wisdom can be revealed only through careful imitation, for like the classical authors favored by humanists, Castiglione advises, "He who lacks wisdom and knowledge will have nothing to say or do."[21]

What struck Castiglione's readers most was his advice about behavior. Francesco Guicciardini of Florence once remarked, "When I was young, I used to scoff at knowing how to play, dance, and sing, and other such frivolities. . . . I have nevertheless seen from experience that these ornaments and accomplishments lend dignity and reputation even to men of good rank."[22] Guicciar-

dini's comment underlines the value that readers found in Castiglione's work. Grace may be inbred, but it must be brought to the attention of those who control the court. Courtiers should first of all study the military arts. They have to fight, but only on occasions when their prowess will be noticed. Castiglione adds practical advice about how to dress, talk, and participate in music and dancing: never leap about wildly when dancing as peasants might, but dance only with an air of dignity and decorum. Castiglione further urges the courtier to be careful in dress: the French are "overdressed"; the Italians too quickly adopt the most recent and colorful styles. Bowing to the political as well as social realities of Spanish domination of Italy, Castiglione advises black or dark colors, which "reflect the sobriety of the Spaniards, since external appearances often bear witness to what is within."

According to Castiglione, the courtier must take pains "to earn that universal regard which everyone covets." Too much imitation and obvious study, however, lead to affectation. Castiglione counsels courtiers to carry themselves with a certain diffidence or unstudied naturalness (*sprezzatura*) covering their artifice. Accomplished courtiers should exhibit "that graceful and nonchalant spontaneity (as it is often called) . . . so that those who are watching them imagine that they couldn't and wouldn't even know how to make a mistake." Thus Castiglione's courtier must walk a fine line between clearly imitated and apparently natural grace.

Castiglione's book was an immediate success and widely followed even by those who claimed to have rejected it. By 1561 it was available in Spanish, French, and English translations. The reasons are not difficult to guess. It was critical for the courtier "to win for himself the mind and favour of the prince," and even those who disliked music, dancing, and light conversation learned Castiglione's arts "to open the way to the favour of princes." Many of the courtly arts that Castiglione preached had been traditional for centuries. Yet Castiglione's humanistic explanations and emphasis on form, control, and fashion had never seemed so essential as they did to the cultured gentlemen of the courts of the Renaissance and early modern Europe.

SECTION SUMMARY

- Rulers found Renaissance art and culture to be convenient vehicles to explain or justify political power.

- The Gonzaga rulers of Mantua followed a conscious policy of recruiting famous artists to work at their court.

- The papacy used art and culture to explain and justify their predominance in Rome and the Christian church.

- Castiglione's dialogue on behavior at court became a European bestseller because of its explanation of how to succeed at court.

CHAPTER SUMMARY

Online Study Center **ACE the Test**

How did Italians use classical values to deal with cultural and political issues?

What was "new" about Renaissance art?

In what ways did humanism outside Italy differ from Italian humanism?

How did European rulers use Renaissance art and culture?

The Renaissance was a broad cultural movement that began in Italy in response to a series of crises in the early fourteenth century. It was a cultural and ideological movement based on the assumption that study and imitation of the past was the best method for reform and innovation in the future. The impulse for change arose from the belief, shared by thinkers from Petrarch to Machiavelli, that a great deal could be learned from study of the Roman past. This was the basis for humanistic innovations in language, history, and politics. Even revolutionary thinkers such as Lorenzo Valla and Niccolò Machiavelli began with the study of classical literature and history.

The same transformation is evident among the artists. Early in the fifteenth century Florentines who experimented with perspective were intent on recovering lost Roman knowledge, and Michelangelo was praised not only for mastering but also for surpassing Roman norms. Similar trends were evident in northern Europe where artists like Albrecht Dürer combined their understanding of Italian art with northern ideas.

Throughout Europe art was an important component of religious and political culture.

Humanistic studies outside of Italy were less tied to public life. Moral and spiritual issues were more important. Yet the same movement from imitation to transformation is evident. Erasmus and More valued humanistic learning from Italy, but in *The Praise of Folly* and *Utopia* the use of past ideas and models was neither simple nor direct. Both authors, however, shared with Italian humanists the idea that humanistic values could lead to a transformation of individuals and society as a whole.

The integration of art, literature, and public life was most evident in the ways that governments used art. The Gonzaga court and the papacy clearly recognized the value of artistic and literary works as vehicles for explaining and justifying power and influence. The beauty of Mantegna's painting and the power of Michelangelo's frescoes do not obscure their messages about power and authority.

LOOKING AHEAD

Innovation depended on the study of the past. As humanists came to know more fully the art and history of Greece and Rome, they recognized the extent to which classical culture represented only one source of legal, historical, or moral understanding. The European confidence in their own traditions would be tested in the sixteenth century, when they came face-to-face with a previously unknown world.

KEY TERMS

Francesco Petrarch (p. 354)

Renaissance (p. 354)

humanism (p. 354)

civic humanism (p. 354)

On the Donation of Constantine (p. 357)

Niccolò Machiavelli (p. 359)

linear perspective (p. 362)

Leonardo da Vinci (p. 362)

Sistine Chapel (p. 363)

Johann Gutenberg (p. 372)

Thomas More (p. 374)

Desiderius Erasmus (p. 374)

Online Study Center
Improve Your Grade Flashcards

SUGGESTED READING

Brown, A. *The Renaissance*. 2d ed. 1999. An excellent short introduction to Renaissance art and culture designed for those with little or no background in the field.

Burke, P. *The European Renaissance: Centres and Peripheries*. 1998. A broad account of Renaissance cultural movements in Europe.

———. *The Fortunes of the Courtier: The European Reception of Castiglione's Cortegiano*. 1995. A well-written survey of the influence of Castiglione's ideas.

Goldthwaite, R. *Wealth and the Demand for Art in Italy, 1300–1600*. 1993. A thoughtful essay about the social and economic influences on the creation and patronage of art.

Goodman, A., and A. Mackay, eds. *The Impact of Humanism*. 1990. A volume of basic surveys of the arrival of Italian humanistic ideas in the various lands of Europe.

Hale, John R. *The Civilization of Europe in the Renaissance*. 1994. A beautifully written survey of the culture of Europe in the fifteenth to seventeenth centuries.

King, M. L. *Women of the Renaissance*. 1991. A survey of the social, economic, and cultural experience of women during the Renaissance.

Nauert, C. G. *Humanism and the Culture of Renaissance Europe*. 1995. An excellent and accessible survey of Renaissance thought and learning.

Stinger, C. L. *The Renaissance in Rome*. 1985. An engaging survey of the vibrant cultural life at the papal court and in the city during the Renaissance.

Welch, E. S. *Art and Society in Italy, 1350–1500*. 1997. A well-written, well-illustrated discussion of the social context in which artists worked.

NOTES

1. Quoted in J. B. Trapp, ed., *Background to the English Renaissance* (London: Gray-Mills Publishing, 1974), p. 11.

2. Quoted in N. Mann, *Petrarch* (Oxford: Oxford University Press), p. 67.

3. Petrarch, "On His Own Ignorance and That of Many Others," in *The Renaissance Philosophy of Man*, ed. Ernst Cassirer, Paul Oskar Kristeller, and John H. Randall (Chicago: University of Chicago Press, 1948), p. 105.

4. Quoted in Benjamin G. Kohl and Ronald G. Witt, *The Earthly Republic* (Philadelphia: University of Pennsylvania Press, 1978), p. 11.

5. Quoted in M. L. King, *Women of the Renaissance* (Chicago: University of Chicago Press, 1991), p. 194.

6. Quoted ibid., p. 222.

7. Quoted ibid., p. 198.

8. K. R. Bartlett, *The Civilization of the Italian Renaissance* (Lexington, Mass.: D. C. Heath, 1992), p. 314.

9. Quoted in *The Portable Machiavelli*, ed. and trans. Peter Bondanella and Mark Musa (New York: Penguin, 1979), p. 128.

10. Quoted ibid., p. 160.

11. Quoted in *The Notebooks of Leonardo da Vinci,* ed. J. P. Richter, vol. 1 (New York: Dover, 1883 and 1970), p. 14.

12. Quoted ibid., p. 129.

13. Giorgio Vasari, *The Lives of the Artists,* trans. George Bull (Baltimore: Penguin, 1965), p. 338.

14. Julia Bondanella and Mark Musa, eds., *The Italian Renaissance Reader* (New York: Meridian Books, 1987), p. 377.

15. I. Origo, *The Merchant of Prato: Francesco di Marco Datini, 1335–1410* (New York: Knopf, 1957), pp. 155–156.

16. Quoted in A. Rabil, Jr., *Renaissance Humanism: Foundations, Forms, and Legacy,* vol. 2 (Philadelphia: University of Pennsylvania Press, 1988), p. 236.

17. Quoted ibid., p. 229.

18. Raffaele Brandolini, quoted in Charles L. Stinger, *The Renaissance in Rome* (Bloomington: Indiana University Press, 1985), p. 156.

19. Quoted in Leopold D. Ettlinger, *The Sistine Chapel Before Michelangelo* (Oxford: Oxford University Press, 1965), p. 105.

20. Quoted in R. M. San Juan, "The Court Lady's Dilemma: Isabella d'Este and Art Collecting in the Renaissance," *Oxford Art Journal* 14 (1991): 71.

21. Unless otherwise noted, quotes from Castiglione are from Baldassare Castiglione, *The Book of the Courtier,* trans. George Bull (Baltimore: Penguin, 1967).

22. Quoted in R. W. Hanning and D. Rosand, eds., *Castiglione: The Ideal and the Real in Renaissance Culture* (New Haven, Conn.: Yale University Press, 1983), p. 17.

13

EUROPEAN OVERSEAS
EXPANSION TO 1600

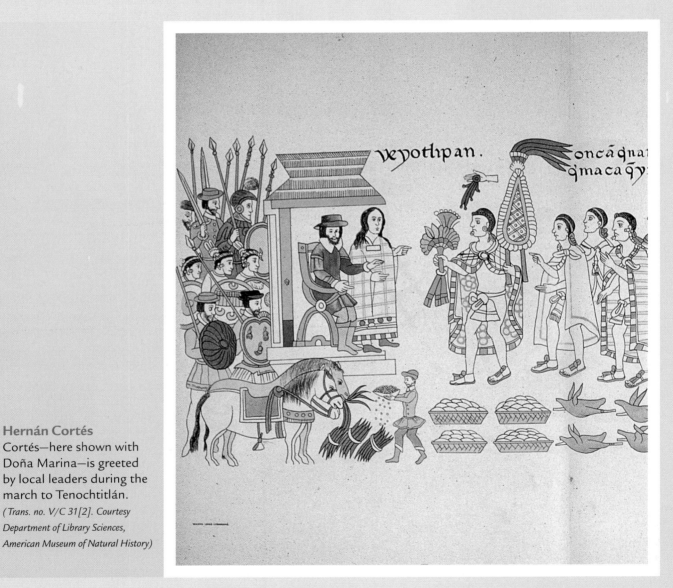

Hernán Cortés
Cortés—here shown with
Doña Marina—is greeted
by local leaders during the
march to Tenochtitlán.
*(Trans. no. V/C 31[2]. Courtesy
Department of Library Sciences,
American Museum of Natural History)*

ernán Cortés's march in 1519 through the Valley of Mexico toward Tenochtitlán (teh-NOCK-tit-lan), the Aztec capital, was recorded not only in Spaniards' journals but also by local witnesses. In the native portrayal shown here, an elegantly garbed Mexica leader brings food and supplies to Cortés (kor-TEZ). Behind the adventurer are his own Spanish soldiers and his native allies. Many native peoples saw the Spanish as their defenders against the Aztecs, their harsh, recently arrived overlords. The woman standing next to Cortés is Malintzin, who later adopted the Spanish name Doña Marina. She was an Aztec noblewoman traded by her stepfather to the Maya and eventually given to Cortés. As a translator and interpreter, she was an essential ally during the conquest of Mexico.

The image, with its baskets of bread, meats, and fodder, is part of a pictograph telling the story of Cortés in the Nahuatl (na-HWAT-luh) language of the Mexica peoples. The arrival of the Spanish began a cultural exchange between the Spanish and the peoples of the Americas that was more complex than even they initially imagined. The picture captures the contradictory aspects of European contact with Asia and the Americas. Europeans called it discovery, but they were entering sophisticated, fully functioning political and cultural worlds. Doña Marina's presence also reminds us of a more general truth—that without allies, pilots, and interpreters among the native peoples, Europeans would have been lost both in the New World and in the Old.

Cortés's meeting with the Mexica peoples was part of a program of European overseas expansion that began in the last decade of the fifteenth century and would eventually carry Europeans to every part of the world. It would change how Europeans thought of themselves and how they understood their own connections to the rest of the world. Their expansion unified the "Old World" continents of Asia, Africa, and Europe with a "New World"—the Americas and the islands of the Pacific. Accounts of contacts between the Old World and the New are influenced, perhaps more than any other episode of Western history, by the perspectives of the writers and the readers.

Those who focus on the transfer of European religion and culture view exploration and settlement as marking the creation of a new world with new

CHAPTER OUTLINE

THE EUROPEAN BACKGROUND, 1250–1492

PORTUGUESE VOYAGES OF EXPLORATION, 1350–1515

SPANISH VOYAGES OF EXPLORATION, 1492–1522

SPAIN'S COLONIAL EMPIRE, 1492–1600

THE COLUMBIAN EXCHANGE

KEY TERMS

Prince Henry "the Navigator"

Vasco da Gama

trading-post empire

Treaty of Tordesillas

Ferdinand Magellan

Aztecs

Inca

Hernán Cortés

Doña Marina

Council of the Indies

encomienda

Bartolomé de Las Casas

Columbian Exchange

Online Study Center

This icon will direct you to interactive map and primary source activities on the website **college.hmco.com/ pic/noble5e**

values. However, the descendants of the native peoples who greeted the newly arriving Europeans—the Amerindians and the Aborigines, Maori, and Polynesians of the Pacific islands—remind us that the outsiders invaded another world. Their arrival brought modern warfare and epidemic diseases that virtually destroyed indigenous cultures.

Spain sent its explorers west because the Portuguese already controlled the eastern routes to Asia around the African coast and because certain technological innovations made long open-sea voyages possible. Thus, as those who celebrate European expansion have said, the story includes national competition, the development of navigational techniques, and strategic choices.

Finally, the Europeans overthrew the great empires of the Aztecs and the Inca, but the transfer of European culture was never as complete as the Europeans thought or expected. As our image sug-gests, the language and customs of the conquered peoples, blanketed by European language and law, survived, though the lands colonized by the Europeans would never again be as they had been before their encounter with the Old World.

FOCUS QUESTIONS

What did Europeans know about the wider world in the Middle Ages?

How did the Portuguese exploit their new connection to the East?

Why did the Spanish choose to sail west in their attempt to find Asia?

How did the Spanish conquer and control the new world they entered?

What changes did European expansion bring to the Old World and the New?

THE EUROPEAN BACKGROUND, 1250–1492

What did Europeans know about the wider world in the Middle Ages?

By 1400 Europeans already had a long history of connections with Africa and Asia. They regularly traded with Arabs in North Africa, traveled through the Muslim lands on the eastern edge of the Mediterranean, and eventually reached India, China, and beyond. After 1400, however, Europeans developed the desire and the ability to travel overseas to distant lands in Africa and Asia. Three critical factors behind the exploratory voyages of the fifteenth and early sixteenth centuries were technology, curiosity and interest, and geographic knowledge. A series of technological innovations made sailing far out into the ocean less risky and more predictable than it had been. The writings of classical geographers, myths and traditional tales, and merchants' accounts of their travels fueled popular interest in the East and made ocean routes to the East seem safe and reasonable alternatives to overland travel.

EARLY EXPLORATION AND CULTURAL INTERACTIONS

Medieval Europeans knew there were lands to their west. Irish monks and Norse settlers traveled there. Indeed, by the late ninth century Norse sailors, primarily Norwegians, had constructed boats combining oars and sails with strong-keeled hulls, which they used to travel to Iceland, Greenland, and eventually Vinland—the coast of Labrador and Newfoundland. The Norse traveled in families. A woman named Gudridr gave birth to a son in North America before returning to Iceland and eventually going on a pilgrimage to Rome. Although the settlements in North America and Greenland ultimately failed, the Norse were followed by English, French, and Spanish fishermen who regularly visited the rich fishing grounds off North America.

Contacts Through Trade The Greeks and Romans had cultivated contacts with the civilizations of Asia and Africa, and despite the nation-building focus of the Middle Ages, interest in the lands beyond Christendom had never been lost. In the thirteenth and fourteenth centuries European economic and cultural contacts with these lands greatly increased. The rising volume of trade between Europe and North Africa brought with it information about the wealthy African kingdoms of the Niger Delta. The Mongols in the thirteenth century allowed European merchants and missionaries to travel along trade routes extending all the way to China, opening regions formerly closed to them by hostile Muslim governments.

Trade in the Mediterranean also kept Christians and Muslims, Europeans and North Africans, in close contact. Europeans sold textiles to Arab traders, who carried them across the Sahara to Timbuktu where they were sold for gold bullion to residents of the ancient African kingdoms of Ghana and Mali, located just above the Niger River. European chroniclers recorded the pilgrimage to Mecca of Mansa Musa, the fabulously wealthy fourteenth-century emperor of Mali. Italian merchants tried unsuccessfully to trade directly with these African kingdoms, but Arab merchants prevented any permanent contact.

Europeans enjoyed more successful trade connections farther east. The discovery in London of a brass shard inscribed with a Japanese character attests to the breadth of connections in the early fourteenth century. Since the Roman period the Mediterranean had been connected to Asia by the Silk Road, in reality a network of roads that carried people, ideas, and commerce. In the Middle Ages European access to the Silk Road had been restricted by local rulers. After the rise of the Mongols, Italian merchants regularly traveled east through Constantinople and on to India and China. By the fourteenth century they knew how long travel to China might take and the probable expenses along the way. European intellectuals also maintained an interest in the lands beyond Christendom. They had read the late classical and early medieval authors who described Africa, the Indies, and China.

Geographic Knowledge The work of the greatest of the classical geographers, Ptolemy (TOL-eh-mee) of Alexandria (ca. A.D. 127–145), was known only indirectly until the early fifteenth century, but medieval thinkers read avidly and speculated endlessly about the information contained in the works of authors from Late Antiquity. For instance, one author reported that snakes in Calabria, in isolated southern Italy, sucked milk from cows and that men in the right circumstances became wolves—the earliest mention of werewolves. By the twelfth century fictitious reports circulated widely in the West of a wealthy Christian country in the East or possibly in Africa. Chroniclers at that time talked of Prester John, who some thought was a wealthy and powerful descendant of the Magi, the wise men from the East who Scripture says visited the baby Jesus. The legend of the kingdom of Prester John probably reflects some knowledge of the Christian groups living near the shrine of Saint Thomas in India or the Christian kingdom of Ethiopia. In the fifteenth century European Christians looked to Prester John for aid against the rising Turkish empire.

Tales of geographic marvels are epitomized by *The Travels of Sir John Mandeville*, a book probably written in France but purporting to be the observations of a knight from St. Albans, just north of London. Mandeville says

ca. 1400	Portuguese reach Azores
1444	Prince Henry "the Navigator" discovers Cape Verde Islands
1487	Dias becomes first European to sail around Cape of Good Hope
1492	Columbus reaches New World
1494	Treaty of Tordesillas
1497	Da Gama sails to India around Cape of Good Hope
	Cabot sights Newfoundland
1501	Vespucci concludes Columbus discovered a new continent
1507	Waldseemüller issues the first map showing "America"
1510	Portuguese capture Goa
1513	Balboa becomes first European to see Pacific Ocean
1519–1522	Magellan's expedition sails around the world
1519–1523	Cortés conquers the Aztecs, destroys Tenochtitlán
1533	Pizarro conquers Cuzco, the Inca capital
1534	Cartier discovers St. Lawrence River
1542	Charles V issues "New Laws"
1545	Spanish discover Potosí silver mines

that he left England in 1322 or 1323 and traveled to Constantinople, Jerusalem, Egypt, India, China, Persia, and Turkey. Sir John describes the islands of wonders, inhabited by dog-headed humans, one-eyed giants, headless men, and hermaphrodites. Less fantastically, Mandeville reports that the world could be, and in fact had been, circumnavigated. He adds that the lands south of the equator, the Antipodes (an-TIP-o-deez), were habitable.

More reliable information became available in the thirteenth century, largely because of the arrival of the Mongols. Jenghiz Khan (JEN-gus KAHN) and his descendants created an empire that reached from eastern Hungary to China (see page 275). This *pax Mongolica,* or area of Mongol-enforced peace, was a region in which striking racial and cultural differences were tolerated. In the 1240s and 1250s a series of papal representatives traveled to the Mongol capital at Karakorum near Lake Baikal in Siberia. The letters of these papal ambassadors, who worked extensively to gain converts and allies for a crusade against the Turks, were widely read and greatly increased accurate knowledge about Asia. Other missionaries and diplomats journeyed to the Mongol court, and some continued farther east to India and China. By the early fourteenth century the church had established a bishop in Beijing.

Italian merchants followed closely on the heels of the churchmen and diplomats. The pax Mongolica offered the chance to trade directly in Asia and the adventure of visiting lands known only from travel literature. In 1262 Niccolo and Maffeo Polo embarked from Venice on their first trip to China. On a later journey they took Niccolo's son, Marco (1255–1324). In all they spent twenty-four years in China. Marco dictated an account of his travels to a Pisan as they both languished as prisoners of war in a Genoese jail in 1298. It is difficult to know how much of the text represents Marco's own observations and how much is chivalric invention by the Pisan. Some modern commentators have even speculated that Marco himself never traveled to China. His contemporaries, however, had no doubts. The book was an immediate success even among Venetians, who could have exposed any fraud. Christopher Columbus himself owned and extensively annotated a copy of Marco Polo's *Travels,* which combines a merchant's observations of ports, markets, and trade with an administrator's eye for people and organizations.

By 1300 a modest community of Italians had settled in China. By the late thirteenth and fourteenth centuries Italian traders were traveling directly to the East in search of Asian silks, spices, pearls, and ivory. They and other European merchants could consult the *Handbook for Merchants* (1340) compiled by the Florentine Francesco Pegalotti (pey-gah-LOW-tee), which described the best roads, the most hospitable stopping points, and the appropriate freight animals for a trip to the East. Fragmentary reports of Europeans in the Spice Islands (also known as the Moluccas), Japan, and India indicate that many Europeans other than merchants traveled simply for the adventure of visiting new lands.

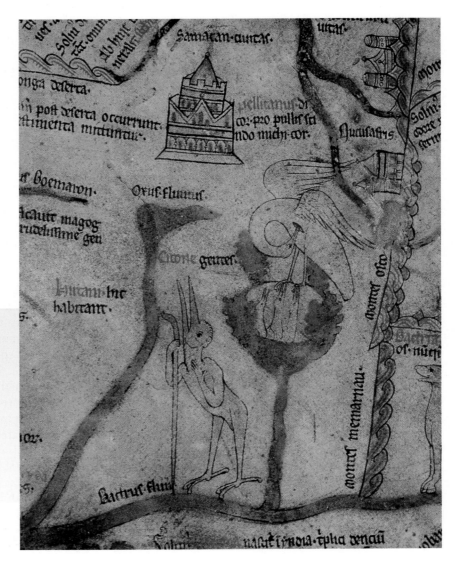

Hereford Mappa Mundi

Like other medieval illustrations of Eastern lands, this thirteenth-century map combines known fact with myth. The top section locates the city of Samarcand (modern-day Samarkand, Uzbekistan). At the bottom, next to a mythical bird-person, a pelican feeds its young with its own blood. *(The Dean and Chapter of Hereford and the Hereford Mappa Mundi Trust)*

NAVIGATIONAL INNOVATIONS

The invention of several navigational aids in the fourteenth and fifteenth centuries made sailing in open waters easier and more predictable. Especially important was the fly compass, consisting of a magnetic needle attached to a paper disk (or "fly"). The simple compass had been invented in China and was known in Europe by the late twelfth century, but because it was not initially marked off in degrees, it was only a rudimentary aid to navigation. By 1500 astrolabes and other devices enabling sailors to use the positions of the sun and stars to assist in navigation had also become available. An astrolabe allowed sailors to measure the altitude of the polestar in the sky and thereby calculate the latitude, or distance north or south of the equator, at which their ship was sailing. Still, until the general adoption of charts marked with degrees of latitude, most navigators sailed by relying on the compass, experience, and instinct.

The most common Mediterranean ship of the late Middle Ages was a galley powered by a combination of sails and oars. Such a vessel was able to travel quickly and easily along the coast, but it was ill-suited for sailing the open seas. Throughout the Mediterranean shipbuilders experimented with new designs, and during the fifteenth century the Portuguese and Spanish perfected the caravel and adapted the European full-rigged ships. Large, square sails efficiently caught the wind and propelled these ships forward, and smaller triangular sails (lateens) allowed them to tack diagonally across a headwind, virtually sailing into the wind.

By the 1490s the Portuguese and Spanish had developed the ships and techniques that would make long open-sea voyages possible. What remained was for Europeans, especially the Portuguese and Spanish, to conclude that such voyages were both necessary and profitable.

THE REVOLUTION IN GEOGRAPHY

Sea routes to Asia seemed more important by the end of the fourteenth century. With the conversion of the Mongols to Islam, the breakdown of Mongol unity, and the subsequent rise of the Ottoman Turks, the highly integrated and unusually open trade network fell apart. The caravan routes across southern Russia, Persia, and Afghanistan were abruptly closed to Europeans. Western merchants once again became dependent on Muslim middlemen.

The reports of travelers, however, continued to circulate long after the trade routes shut down, contributing to a veritable revolution in geographic knowledge in the decades before the Portuguese and Spanish voyages.

In 1375 Abraham Cresques (KRESK), a Jewish mathematician from the Mediterranean island of Majorca, produced what has come to be known as the *Catalan World Atlas*. He combined the traditional medieval *mappa mundi* (world map) with a Mediterranean *portolan*. The mappa mundi often followed the O-T form—that is, a circle divided into three parts representing Europe, Africa, and Asia, the lands of the descendants of Noah. Jerusalem—the heart of Christendom—was always at the center of the map. What the map lacked in accuracy, it made up in symbolism. The portolan, in contrast, was entirely practical. Sailors valued it because of its accurate outline of coasts, complete with sailing instructions and reasonable portrayals of ports, islands, and shallows along with general compass readings. The *Catalan World Atlas* largely holds to the portolan tradition but has more correct representations of the lands surrounding the Mediterranean.

In the fifteenth century, following Ptolemy's suggestions, mapmakers began to divide their maps into squares marking lines of longitude and latitude. This format made it possible to show with some precision the contours of various lands and the relationships between landmasses. Numerous maps of the world were produced in this period. The culmination of this cartography was a globe constructed for the city of Nuremberg in 1492, the very year Columbus set sail. From these increasingly accurate maps it has become possible to document the first exploration of the Azores, the Cape Verde Islands, and the western coast of Africa.

After his voyages Columbus observed that maps had been of no use to him. True enough. But without the accumulation of knowledge by travelers and the mingling of that knowledge with classical ideas about geography, it is doubtful whether Columbus or the Portuguese seaman Vasco da Gama would have undertaken—or could have found governments willing to support—the voyages that so dramatically changed the relations between Europe and the rest of the world.

=================== SECTION SUMMARY ===================

- Throughout the Middle Ages, Europe had indirect trade connections with Asia and Africa.

- In the fourteenth century Italian merchants traveled widely in central and eastern Asia.

- Technological advances in ship design and navigation made it possible to sail far into the Atlantic.

- Restrictions on land routes between Europe and Asia made sailing to Asia a practical economic venture.

PORTUGUESE VOYAGES OF EXPLORATION, 1350–1515

How did the Portuguese exploit their new connection to the East?

Portugal, a tiny country on the edge of Europe, for a short time led the European overseas expansion. Portuguese sailors were the first Europeans to perfect the complex techniques of using the winds and currents of the South Atlantic, especially along the western coast of Africa (see **MAP 13.1**). Portugal's experience reflects the range of options open to Europeans as they extended their influence into new areas. As the Portuguese moved down the African coast, and later as they tried to compete commercially

MAP 13.1 Winds and Currents

Winds and ocean currents move in giant clockwise and counterclockwise circles that limit the directions in which ships can sail efficiently. It was impossible, for example, for the explorers to sail directly south along the entire western coast of Africa.

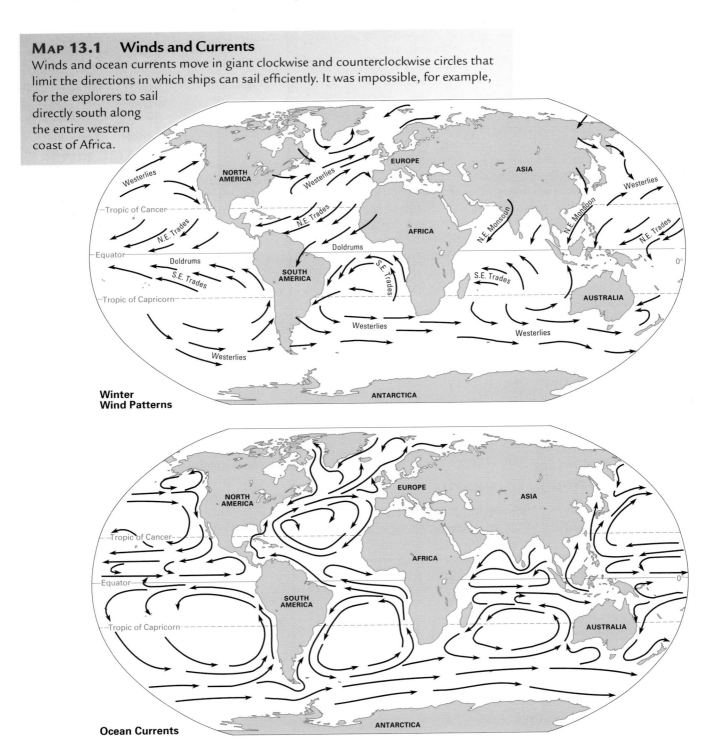

in Asia, they adapted traditional Mediterranean cultural and commercial attitudes to fit the new environment in which they found themselves. In some areas the Portuguese created networks of isolated naval and trading stations to control the movement of goods. In other areas they attempted to create substantial colonies, inhabited by Portuguese settlers. In still other areas they used slaves to produce commercial products for the international market. Spain and the other European states would use these same strategies in Asia and the New World as they expanded their economic and political interests overseas.

THE EARLY VOYAGES

Portugal, like other late medieval European states, hoped that exploration and expansion would lead to "gold and Christians." The search for Christians was accelerated in the fifteenth century by the growing power of the Ottoman Turks. Europeans increasingly desired an alliance with the mythical Christian kingdoms of the East to open a second front against the militant Turks. Further, rediscovering the "lost" Christians and the hope of reclaiming Jerusalem fed Christian expectations that they were living in the last days before Christ's return.

For the Portuguese, facing the Atlantic and insulated from a direct Turkish threat, the lure of gold was always mixed with their religious motives. The nearest source of gold was well known to late medieval Christians: the African kingdoms of the Niger Delta. The problem for European traders and their governments was that overland contacts with this wealthy region remained controlled by the Muslim merchants of North Africa. The Portuguese and Spanish hoped to break the monopoly by taking control of the North African coast or by means of a flanking movement along the western coast of Africa.

Actual exploration of the Atlantic had begun long before Europeans recognized the extent of the Turkish threat. By 1350 the Madeiras and the Canaries, groups of islands off the western coast of Africa, regularly were included on European maps. By about 1365 Portuguese, Spanish, and probably French sailors were visiting the Canary Islands. By 1400 the Azores (AY-zorz) a chain of islands one-third of the way across the Atlantic, were known and from early in the fifteenth century were routine ports of call for Portuguese ships (see **MAP 13.2**). These voyages were no mean feat, calling for sophisticated ocean sailing out of sight of land for weeks at a time.

In the second decade of the fifteenth century the Portuguese expansion began in earnest with the capture of the Muslim port of Ceuta (say-OO-tuh) on the coast of Morocco. From then on, the Portuguese moved steadily down the western coast of Africa. They were led by **Prince Henry "the Navigator"** (1394–1460), the younger son of King John I (r. 1385–1433). Legend has it that Prince Henry founded a school for the study of geography and navigation at Sagres, on the southwestern coast of Portugal. Whether he did or not, contemporaries agreed that Prince Henry was intent on reaching the "River of Gold"—that is, the Gold Coast of Africa and the Niger Delta. To accomplish this, he directed efforts to colonize the Canaries (which eventually were lost to the Spanish), the Azores, and Madeira, the largest of the Madeira Islands. He also sponsored a series of expeditions down the African coast, reaching Senegal and the Cape Verde Islands by 1444. The Portuguese quickly established trading stations in the region and soon were exporting gold and slaves to Lisbon.

The islands off the coast of Africa were uninhabited, except for the Canaries, which the Portuguese tried unsuccessfully to keep from the Spanish. Thus the Portuguese could not merely plant trading communities within a larger population, for the Azores and Madeira had no native population. As a result, by the early 1440s the Portuguese were bringing sheep, seed, and peasants to these hitherto unoccupied islands, and the Crown was granting extensive lordships to encourage reluctant nobles to relocate to the Azores. The islanders survived largely by exporting sheep and grain to Iberia.

A significant transformation occurred on Madeira in the 1440s, when the Portuguese introduced sugar cane to the island. Sugar production was capital- and labor-intensive. A great many workers were needed to cut the cane, and expensive mills and lengthy processing were required to extract and produce sugar. On Madeira most of the work was done by Portuguese peasants. But when the Portuguese extended sugar cultivation to the newly discovered and colonized Cape Verde Islands in the 1460s, they found that Portuguese peasants would not work voluntarily in the sultry equatorial climate. Soon the Portuguese introduced slave-based farming to maximize production and profits.

Slaves imported from the Black Sea areas had been used in agriculture since the introduction of sugar cultivation into the Mediterranean in the thirteenth century. The Portuguese had been trading in slaves along the western coast of Africa since the 1440s—the date from which black slaves appear in Lisbon. African slaves, along with slaves from northern and eastern Europe, could be found in Italy and throughout the Mediterranean in the fifteenth century, most often as domestics or laborers in small enterprises. Not since Roman times, however, had slave-based industries developed on the scale of the Portuguese sugar plantations.

Prince Henry "the Navigator"   The prince who directed Portuguese exploration and colonization along the west coast of Africa.

MAP 13.2 World Exploration, 1492–1535

The voyages of Columbus, da Gama, and Magellan charted the major sea-lanes that became essential for communication, trade, and warfare for the next three hundred years.

Online Study Center Improve Your Grade
Interactive Map: World Exploration, 1492–1535

Sugar production in the New World eventually would be modeled on a plantation system begun by the Portuguese on their island colonies in the Atlantic.

THE SEARCH FOR A SEA ROUTE TO ASIA

Until the middle of the fifteenth century the Niger Delta remained the focus of Portuguese interest. Only after securing control of the western coast of Africa did the Portuguese look seriously at sailing around Africa and discovering a sea route to Asia.

The fifteenth-century sailors who first tried to sail down the coast of Africa faced enormous difficulties. Water and wind currents tend to move in clockwise and counterclockwise circles against which it is difficult for a sail-powered ship to make progress (see Map 13.1). Winds near the equator generally blow from the east; farther north and south, the westerlies prevail. Some zones, in certain seasons, are pockets of stillness—called doldrums—with few breezes to propel ships. A navigator had to find winds and currents moving in the direction he wished to travel. Sailing directly from port to port was virtually impossible.

Knowledge of winds and currents allowed Bartholomeu Dias (1450?–1500) to explore the coast of southern Africa in 1487. He followed the traditional Portuguese routes until southeasterly winds forced him to sail south and west, almost to the Brazilian and Argentine coasts. Then he was able to ride the westerlies well past the southern tip of Africa, where he turned north. On his return he sighted what he called the "Cape of Storms," later renamed the "Cape of Good Hope" by the Portuguese king. Dias had perfected the techniques for searching out currents in the Southern Hemisphere and opened the way to India.

A decade after Dias's return from the Cape of Good Hope, **Vasco da Gama** (1460?–1524) set sail on a voyage that would take him to Calicut on the western coast of India (see Map 13.2). Using the information gathered from countless navigators, travelers, and even spies sent into East Africa, da Gama set sail in 1497 with four square-rigged, armed caravels and over 170 men. He had been provided with maps and reports that indicated what he might expect to find along the eastern coast of Africa. He also carried textiles and metal utensils, merchandise of the type usually traded along the western coast of Africa. This was a trading mission and in no sense a voyage of discovery.

Da Gama followed established routes beyond the Cape of Good Hope and into the Indian Ocean. He traveled up the coast until he reached Malindi in Mozambique, where he secured an Arab pilot who taught him

Vasco da Gama   Pioneering Portuguese trader whose voyage to East Africa and India began the four-hundred-year presence of the Portuguese in the Indian Ocean.

the route to Calicut. Although the goods the Portuguese traders presented were not appropriate for the sophisticated Asian market, da Gama did manage to collect a cargo of Indian spices, which he brought back to Portugal, arriving in 1499. From that pioneering voyage until the Portuguese lost their last colonies in the twentieth century (Goa, 1961; Mozambique, 1975), Portugal remained a presence in the Indian Ocean.

THE PORTUGUESE IN ASIA

Trade in the Indian Ocean was nominally controlled by Muslims, but in fact a mixture of ethnic and religious groups—including Muslims, Hindus, Chinese, Jains, and Nestorian Christians—participated in the movement of cottons, silks, and spices throughout the region. There were numerous small traders, as well as prosperous long-distance merchants with connections reaching into central Asia, Africa, and China.

Less than a century before Vasco da Gama's arrival, the Chinese seaman Zheng He (JUNG HUH) made a series of voyages into the Indian Ocean. In 1405 he led a huge armada of 317 ships and over 27,000 sailors on an expedition designed to expand the trade and political influence of Ming China. He would make six subsequent trips before a new emperor, intent on concentrating his resources on China's internal development, ended the ventures. With the retreat of the Chinese, trade returned to its previous patterns.

The hodgepodge of trade reflected the political situation. Vasco da Gama's arrival coincided with the rise of the Moguls, Muslim descendants of Jenghiz Khan. By 1530 they had gained control of most of northern India, and during the sixteenth century their influence increased in the south. The wealth and security of the Moguls depended on landed power. They generally left traders and trading ports to themselves. Throughout the sixteenth century the Moguls remained tolerant of India's religious, cultural, and economic diversity. Neither Muslim nor Hindu powers initially considered the Portuguese an unusual threat.

Asians may not have worried much about the Portuguese because at first there were so few of them. Vasco da Gama arrived with only three ships. And the subsequent fleet of Pedro Alvares Cabral carried only fifteen hundred men. In the 1630s, after more than a century of emigration, probably no more than ten thousand Portuguese were scattered from modern Indonesia to the east coast of Africa. In addition to government officials, Portuguese settlers were likely to be petty traders, local merchants, and poorly paid mercenaries.

The Portuguese faced a number of problems as they attempted to compete in Eastern markets. There were very few of them and the trade goods they brought with them had little value in sophisticated, highly developed Asian markets. In most cases they bought spices, textiles,

Portuguese in India
This watercolor by a Portuguese traveler shows the varied peoples and customs and the great wealth to be found in India. Europeans were fascinated by all that seemed different from their own world. *(Biblioteca Casanatense, Rome. Photo: Humberto Nicoletti Serra)*

and dyes with gold and silver brought from mines in central Europe and the New World. In response to this difficult situation, they created a seaborne **trading-post empire**—an empire based on control of trade rather than on colonization. It was, in fact, a model that fit well with their crusading experience in North Africa and their desire to push back Muslim control.

Portugal's commercial empire in the East was based on fortified, strategically placed naval bases. As early as Vasco da Gama's second expedition in 1502, the Portuguese bombarded Calicut and defeated an Arab fleet off the coast of India. This encounter set the stage for Portugal's most important imperial strategist, Alfonso d'Albuquerque (1453–1515), governor-general of Portuguese colonies in India. He convinced the monarchy that the key to dominance in the region was the creation of fortified naval bases commanding the Bay of Bengal and thereby controlling access to the coveted Spice Islands. (See the box "The Written Record: Albuquerque Defends the Portuguese Empire.") By 1600 the

Portuguese had built a network of naval bases that reached from Mozambique and Mombasa on the east coast of Africa to Goa on the west coast of India and the island of Macao off southeastern China (see Map 13.2).

The Portuguese established a royal trading firm, the Casa da India, to manage the booming market in cinnamon, ginger, cloves, mace, and a variety of peppers. Although their control was far from total, the Portuguese did become significant exporters of spices to Europe. More significant was the creation of the Portuguese Estado da India, or India office, to oversee Portuguese naval forces, administer ports, and regulate maritime trade. Under the Portuguese system all merchants were expected to acquire export licenses and to ship products through Portuguese ports. Asians often found it more convenient to cooperate than to resist, and most agreed to pay for export licenses and trade through Portuguese ports. They even found it expedient to ship in European-style vessels and to use Portuguese as the language of commerce.

═══════════ S E C T I O N   S U M M A R Y ═══════════

- The Portuguese were especially interested in trade with the West African kingdoms along the Gold Coast.

- The Portuguese developed complex navigational techniques that allowed them to sail around the tip of Africa and into the Indian Ocean.

- Before the arrival of the Portuguese, the Muslim Mogul Empire left seaborne trade under the control of various ethnic and religious groups.

- The Portuguese established a trading-post empire that allowed them to dominate trade in the Indian Ocean.

trading-post empire A system developed by the Portuguese to allow them to use fortified naval bases to dominate commerce in the Indian Ocean.

ALBUQUERQUE DEFENDS THE PORTUGUESE EMPIRE

In this letter of 1512 to the king of Portugal, Alfonso d'Albuquerque, the governor-general of Portugal's colonies in India, informs the king of conditions in the East, explains his strategy, and defends himself against his critics.

The first time the Muslims entered Goa, we killed one of their captains. They were greatly grieved by the [Portuguese] capture of Goa and there is great fear of Your Highness among them. You must reduce the power of [the Muslim] rulers, take their coastal territories from them and build good fortresses in their principal places. Otherwise you will not be able to set India on the right path and you will always have to have a large body of troops there to keep it pacified. Any alliance which you may agree with one or other Indian king or lord must be secured, Sire, because otherwise you may be certain that, the moment your back is turned, they will at once become your enemies.

What I am describing has now become quite usual among them. In India there is not the same punctiliousness as in Portugal about keeping truth, friendship and trust, for nobody here has any of these qualities. Therefore, Sire, put your faith in good fortresses and order them to be built; gain control over India in time and do not place any confidence in the friendship of the kings and lords of this region because you did not arrive here with a just cause to gain domination of their trade with blandishments

and peace treaties. Do not let anybody in Portugal make you think that this is a very hard thing to achieve and that, once achieved, it will place you under great obligation. I tell you this, Sire, because I am still in India and I would like people to sell their property and take part in this enterprise that is so much to your advantage, so great, so lucrative and so valuable. . . .

In a place where there is merchandise to be had and the Muslim traders will not let us have precious stones or spices by fair dealing, and we want to take these foods by force, then we must fight the Muslims for them. If, on the other hand, they see us with a large body of troops, they do us honor, and no thought of deceit or trickery enters their heads. They exchange their goods for ours without fighting and they will abandon the delusion that they will expel us from India.

QUESTIONS

1. Why does Albuquerque believe that fortresses are essential to a Portuguese presence in India?

2. What Portuguese reaction does Albuquerque fear?

Source: T. F. Earle and J. Villiers, eds., *Albuquerque: Caesar of the East*, p. 109. Copyright © 1990 by Aris and Phillips. Reprinted by permission of the publisher.

SPANISH VOYAGES OF EXPLORATION, 1492–1522

Why did the Spanish choose to sail west in their attempt to find Asia?

Spanish overseas expansion seems a logical continuation of the centuries-long Reconquista (see pages 272–273). In 1492, just before Columbus set sail, Castile was finally able to conquer the last Muslim kingdom of Granada and unify all of Iberia, with the exception of Portugal, under a single monarchy. Initially, in 1479, the Spanish kingdoms had agreed to leave the exploration and colonization of the African coast to the Portuguese, yet they watched nervously as the Portuguese expanded their African contacts. Portuguese successes led Castilians to concentrate their efforts on what came to be called the "Enterprise of the Indies"—that is, the conquest and settlement of Central and South America.

The sailing and exploring necessary to compete with the Portuguese produced critical information about ocean winds and currents and facilitated later voyages. They also established the basic approaches that the Spanish would follow in their exploration, conquest, and colonization of the lands where they dropped anchor.

THE ROLE OF COLUMBUS

The story of the enterprise begins with Christopher Columbus (1451–1506), a brilliant seaman, courtier, and self-promoter who has become a symbol of European expansion. Columbus, however, was not a bold pioneer who fearlessly did what no others could conceive of doing. He benefited from long-standing interests in the world beyond European shores.

Columbus was born into a modest family in Genoa and spent his early years in travel and in the service of the Castilian and Portuguese crowns. His vision seems to have been thoroughly traditional and medieval. He knew the medieval geographic speculations inherited from Arab and ultimately Classical Greek sources. Medieval seafarers did not fear a flat earth; rather, the concern was whether a ship could cover the vast distances necessary to sail west to Asia. Studying information in *Imago Mundi* (*Image of the World,* 1410), by the French philosopher Pierre d'Ailly (die-YEE) (1350–1420), Columbus convinced himself that the distance between Europe and Asia was much less than it actually is. D'Ailly's estimate put the east coast of Asia within easy reach of the western edge of Europe. "This sea is navigable in a few days if the wind is favorable," d'Ailly concluded.

D'Ailly's theories seemed to be confirmed by the work of the Florentine mathematician Paolo Toscanelli. Columbus knew of Toscanelli's calculations and even revised them downward. From his own study he concluded that the distance from the west coast of Europe to the east coast of Asia was about 5,000 miles, instead of the actual 12,000. Columbus's reading of traditional sources put Japan in the approximate location of the Virgin Islands. (It is not surprising that Columbus remained convinced that the Bahamas were islands just off the coast of Asia.) When Amerindians told him of Cuba, he concluded that it "must be Japan according to the indications that these people give of its size and wealth."[1]

On the basis of first-century descriptions Columbus assured Spanish authorities that King Solomon's mines were only a short distance west of his newly discovered islands. In addition to finding the gold of Solomon, Columbus expected that by sailing farther west he could fulfill a series of medieval prophecies that would lead to the conversion of the whole world to Christianity. This conversion, he believed, would shortly precede the Second Coming of Christ. In Columbus's own view, then, his voyages were epochal not because they were ushering in a newer, more empirical world but because they signaled the fulfillment of history.

Columbus's enthusiasm for the venture was only partially shared by the Spanish monarchs, Ferdinand and Isabella. Vasco da Gama had been well supplied with a flotilla of large ships and a crew of over 170 men, but Columbus sailed in 1492 with three small vessels and a crew of 90. Da Gama carried extra supplies and materials for trade and letters for the rulers he knew he would meet. Columbus had nothing similar in his sea chest. His commission did authorize him as "Admiral of Spain" to take possession of all he should find, but royal expectations do not seem to have been great.

Yet on October 12, about ten days later than he had expected, Columbus reached landfall on what he assumed were small islands in the Japanese chain. He had actually landed in the Bahamas. Because Columbus announced to the world that he had arrived in the Indies, the indigenous peoples have since been called "Indians" and the islands are called the "West Indies."

Columbus reported to the Spanish monarchs that the inhabitants on the islands were friendly and open to the new arrivals. He described a primitive, naked people eager, he believed, to learn of Christianity and European ways. Indeed, the Tainos, or Arawaks, whom he had misidentified, did live simple, uncomplicated lives. The islands easily produced sweet potatoes, maize, beans, and squash, which along with fish provided an abundant diet. Initially these people shared their food and knowledge with the newcomers, who they seem to have thought were sky-visitors.

The Spanish, for their part, praised the Tainos. The visitors generally believed that they had discovered a compliant, virtuous people who, if converted, would be exemplars of Christian virtues to Europeans. Columbus himself observed:

> They are very gentle and do not know what evil is; nor do they kill others, nor steal; and they are without weapons. They say very quickly any prayer that we tell them to say, and they make the sign of the cross, †. So your Highnesses ought to resolve to make them Christians.[2]

The Spanish authorities changed their opinion quickly. The settlers Columbus left at his fortress set an unfortunate example. They seized food stocks, kidnapped women, and embarked on a frenzied search for gold. Those who did not kill one another were killed by enraged Tainos.

During succeeding voyages, Columbus struggled to make his discoveries the financial windfall he had promised the monarchs. He was utterly unable to administer this vast new land. He quickly lost control of the colonists and was forced to allow the vicious exploitation of the island population. He and other Spanish settlers claimed larger and larger portions of the land and required the Indians to work it. Islands that easily supported a population of perhaps a million natives could not support those indigenous peoples and the Spanish newcomers and still provide exports to Spain. Scholars have estimated that the native population of the islands may have fallen to little more than thirty thousand by 1520, largely because of diseases (see pages 408–409). By the middle of the sixteenth century the native population had virtually disappeared.

Columbus remained convinced that he would find vast fortunes just over the horizon. But he found neither the great quantities of gold he promised nor a sea passage to Asia. With the islands in revolt and his explorations seemingly going nowhere, the Spanish monarchs stripped Columbus of his titles and commands. Once he was returned to Spain in chains. Even after his final transatlantic trip, he continued to insist that he had finally found either the Ganges (GAN-jeez) River of India or one of the rivers that according to the Hebrew Bible flow out of the earthly paradise. Although Columbus died in 1506 rich and honored for his discoveries, he never did gain all the power and wealth he had expected. He remained frustrated and embittered by the Crown's refusal to support one more voyage, during which he expected to find the mainland of Asia.

In 1501, after sailing along the coast of Brazil, the Florentine geographer Amerigo Vespucci (1451-1512) drew the obvious conclusion from the information collected by Columbus's explorations. He argued that Columbus had discovered a new continent unknown to the classical world. These claims were accepted by the German mapmaker Martin Waldseemüller (vald-SAY-mill-er), who in 1507 honored Amerigo's claim by publishing the first map showing "America."

COLUMBUS'S SUCCESSORS

Columbus's explorations set off a debate over which nations had the right to be involved in trade and expansion. Portuguese claims were based on a papal bull of 1481, issued by Pope Sixtus IV (r. 1471-1484), that granted Portugal rights to all lands south of the Canaries and west of Africa. After Columbus's return, the Spaniards lobbied one of Sixtus's successors, Alexander VI (r. 1492-1503), whose family, the Borgias, was from the kingdom of Aragon. In a series of bulls Pope Alexander allowed the Spanish to claim all lands lying 400 miles or more west of the Azores. Finally, in the **Treaty of Tordesillas** (tor-day-SEE-yas) (1494), Spain and Portugal agreed that the line of demarcation between their two areas should be drawn 1,480 miles west of the Azores. The treaty was signed just six years before Pedro Alvares Cabral (1467-1520) discovered the coast of Brazil. Thus the Spanish unwittingly granted the Portuguese rights to Brazil.

Adventurers and explorers worried little about the legal niceties of exploration. Even as Columbus lay dying in 1506, others, some without royal permission, sailed up and down the eastern coasts of North and South America. Amerigo Vespucci traveled on Spanish vessels as far as Argentina, while Spanish explorers sailed among the islands of the Caribbean and along the coast of the Yucatán Peninsula. Vasco Nuñez de Balboa (1475-1519) crossed the Isthmus of Panama in 1513 and found the Pacific Ocean exactly where the natives living in the region said it would be.

Ferdinand Magellan   The most important of the explorations that Columbus inspired was the voyage undertaken by **Ferdinand Magellan** in 1519 (see Map 13.2). Although his motives are unclear, Magellan (1480?-1521) may have planned to complete Columbus's dream of sailing to the Indies. By the 1510s mariners and others understood that the Americas were a new and hitherto unknown land, but they did not know what lay beyond them or what distance separated the Americas from the Spice Islands of Asia. After sailing along the well-known coastal regions of South America, Magellan continued south, charting currents and looking for a passage into the Pacific. Late in 1520 he beat his way through the dangerous straits (now the Strait of Magellan) separating Tierra del Fuego (ti-AIR-ah del foo-WAY-go) from the mainland. These turbulent waters marked the boundary of the Atlantic and Pacific Oceans. It took almost four months to travel from the straits to the Philippines. The crew suffered greatly from scurvy and a shortage of water and at times had to eat the rats aboard ship to survive. One crew member reported, "We ate biscuit, which was no longer biscuit, but powder of biscuit swarming with worms, for they had eaten the good."[3] Nevertheless, Magellan managed to reach the Philippines by March 1521. A month later he was killed by natives.

Spanish survivors in two remaining ships continued west, reaching the Moluccas, or Spice Islands, where they traded merchandise that they had carried along for a small cargo of cloves. A single surviving ship continued around Africa and back to Spain, landing with a crew of 15 at Cádiz in September 1522, after a voyage of three years and the loss of four ships and 245 men. Magellan completed and confirmed the knowledge of wind and ocean currents that European sailors had been accumulating. One of his sailors wrote of him, "More accurately than any man in the world did he understand sea charts and navigation."[4] The way was now open for the vast expansion of Europeans and European culture into all parts of the world.

English and French Explorers   Spanish adventurers were not the only ones to follow in Columbus's wake. The French and the English concentrated their explorations farther north. Building on a tradition of fishing off the coast of Newfoundland, English sailors

---

Treaty of Tordesillas   A treaty negotiated between Spain and Portugal dividing the newly explored lands in the New World and the Old. All New World lands except Brazil were given to the Spanish.

Ferdinand Magellan   The Spanish explorer who established the routes by which ships could sail around the world.

under the command of John Cabot (1450?–1499?) sighted Newfoundland in 1497, and later voyages explored the coast as far south as New England. Cabot initiated an intense period of English venturing that would lead to an unsuccessful attempt to found a colony on Roanoke Island in 1587 and eventually to a permanent settlement at Jamestown in 1607. French expeditions followed Cabot to the north. In 1534 Jacques Cartier (kar-ti-YAY) (1491–1557) received a royal commission to look for a northern passage to the East. He was the first European to sail up the St. Lawrence River and began the process of exploration and trading that would lead to a permanent presence in Canada beginning in the early seventeenth century. But British and French settlements in the New World came later. The sixteenth century belonged to the Spanish.

═══════════ S E C T I O N   S U M M A R Y ═══════════

- Columbus was a brilliant seaman whose exploration was based on geographic knowledge accumulated in the previous centuries.

- The frenzied Spanish search for wealth destroyed the economies of the island peoples.

- Magellan's voyage around the world completed the geographic knowledge necessary for commerce connecting Europe, Asia, and the New World.

- It was only with the writings of Amerigo Vespucci that most Europeans accepted the idea that Columbus had sailed to a previously unknown continent.

SPAIN'S COLONIAL EMPIRE, 1492–1600

How did the Spanish conquer and control the new world they entered?

Spanish penetration of the New World was a far cry from the model of the Portuguese in Asia. The Spaniards established no complex network of trade and commerce, and no strong states opposed their interests. A trading-post empire could not have worked in the New World. To succeed, the Spaniards needed to colonize and reorganize the lands they had found.

Between 1492 and 1600 almost 200,000 Spaniards immigrated to the New World. "New Spain," as they called these newly claimed lands, was neither the old society transported across the ocean nor an Amerindian society with a thin veneer of Spanish and European culture. To understand the history of New Spain it is essential to grasp what it replaced, and how: the Spaniards overthrew two major civilizations and created new institutions in the wake of conquest. The whole story is not conquest and extermination—many of the Spanish attempted to secure fair treatment for the indigenous peoples who were now part of the Spanish Empire.

THE AMERICAS BEFORE THE EUROPEAN INVASION

The Spaniards and later their European peers entered a world vastly different from their own. It was a world formed by two momentous events—one geological, the other anthropological. The first was the creation of the continents of North and South America. The Americas, along with Africa and the Eurasian landmass, were once part of a single supercontinent. The breakup of this supercontinent left the Americas, Africa, and Eurasia free to evolve in dramatically different ways. The continental breakup occurred millions of years ago, long before the appearance of human beings and many other forms of mammalian life.

The second momentous event was the peopling of the Americas. Some migrants may have come over the seas. Most, though, arrived thanks to a temporary rejoining of the Americas to the Eurasian landmass by land and ice bridges that allowed Asians to cross over what is now the Bering Strait to the Americas in the period between 40,000 and 15,000 B.C. Their timing had a great impact. They arrived in the Americas long before the beginnings of the Neolithic agricultural revolution, which involved the domestication of numerous plants and animals. The agricultural revolution in the Americas occurred around 3000 B.C., perhaps six thousand years after similar developments in the Old World. The peoples of the Americas created complex societies, but those societies lacked large domesticated meat or pack animals (the llama was the largest), iron, other hard metals, and the wheel.

Nonetheless, by the time of Columbus's arrival, relatively populous societies were living throughout North and South America. Population estimates for the two continents range from 30 million to 100 million—the lower figure is probably more accurate. North America saw the development of complex Mound Builder societies in the East and along the Mississippi River and pueblo societies in the deserts of the American Southwest. In Central and South America there may have

Tenochtitlán

The Aztec capital was built on an island. Its central temples and markets were connected to the rest of the city and the suburbs on the lakeshore by numerous canals. The city and its surrounding market gardens seemed to the Spanish to be floating on water. *(The Newberry Library, Chicago)*

been 350 tribal or clan groups concentrated around fifteen or more cultural centers. But the greatest powers in the Amerindian world were the **Aztecs** in central and coastal Mexico and the **Inca** in the mountains of Peru.

The Aztecs When the collection of tribes now known as the "Aztec" (or Mexica) peoples appeared in central Mexico in the early fourteenth century, they found an already flourishing civilization concentrated around the cities and towns dotting the Valley of Mexico. The Aztecs conquered and united the many Nahuatl-speaking groups living in the valley, forming a confederation centered in Tenochtitlán, a city of perhaps 200,000 people built on an island in Lake Texcoco (see **MAP 13.3**). In early-sixteenth-century Europe only Lon-

don, Constantinople, and Naples would have been as large as the Aztec capital. It literally rose out of the water of Lake Texcoco. Only Venice could have equaled the sight. The whole valley supported an unusually high population of about a million. Using canals along the edge of the lake and other canals in Tenochtitlán itself, merchants easily moved food, textiles, gold and silver ornaments, jewels, and ceremonial feathered capes into the city markets. Spaniards later estimated that fifty thousand or more people shopped in the city on market days.

Religion was integral to the Aztecs' understanding of their empire. They believed that the world was finite and that they lived in the last of five empires. It was only regular human sacrifice to Huitzilopochtli (wheat-zeel-oh-POSHT-lee) that allowed the world to continue: the hearts of victims were necessary to sustain their god, to ensure that the sun would rise each morning. Thus life for the Aztecs required a relentless parade of death.

Aztecs People who dominated the Valley of Mexico from the fourteenth to the sixteenth centuries and whose empire was destroyed by Cortés.

Inca A mountain empire that flourished in Peru. It was conquered for Spain by Pizzaro.

MAP 13.3   Mexico and Central America

The Valley of Mexico was a populous region of scattered towns, most of which were part of the Aztec Empire. As Cortés marched inland from Vera Cruz toward the valley, he passed through lands that for generations had been in an almost constant state of war with the Aztecs.

Tenochtitlán was the center of an imperial culture based on tribute. Towns and villages under Aztec control owed ongoing allotments of food and precious metals to the Aztecs. To emphasize that Aztec power and dominance were complete, the Aztecs not only collected vast quantities of maize, beans, squash, and textiles but demanded payment in everything down to centipedes and snakes. The most chilling tribute, however, was in humans for sacrifice. When the wars of expansion that had provided prisoners came to an end, the Aztecs and their neighbors fought "flower wars"—highly ritualized battles to provide prisoners to be sacrificed. Five thousand victims were sacrificed at the coronation of Moctezuma II (r. 1502–1520) in 1502. Even more, reportedly twenty thousand, were sacrificed at the dedication of the great temple of Huitzilopochtli in Tenochtitlán.

Aztec society maintained a perpetual state of war with the peoples beyond the mountains that ringed the Valley of Mexico—especially the people along the Caribbean coast. Given this constant state of war, plus the heavy burdens in tribute placed on the nearby sub-

ject cities, it is no wonder that the Aztecs were obsessed by the contingencies of life. At the end of each calendar cycle of fifty-two years, all fires in the empire were extinguished until fire-priests ascertained that the world would continue. And the Aztec world did continue until August 1523 (see page 403).

The Inca   The other great Amerindian empire of the fifteenth century, the empire of the Inca, was also of recent origin. During the fifteenth century the Inca formed efficient armies and expanded their control beyond the central highlands of Peru. Fifteen thousand miles of roads and a sophisticated administrative system allowed the Inca to create a state that extended from modern-day Ecuador to Chile (see **MAP 13.4**). As they expanded, they demanded political control and tribute but seem to have been tolerant of local traditions and language. The Inca perfected systems of irrigation and bridge-building initiated by earlier inhabitants of the region. The empire, centered on the city of Cuzco high in the mountains of Peru, was able to sustain a population that

MAP 13.4   The Inca Empire

The Inca Empire was accessible from Spanish strongholds in Mexico only by sea. Spanish exploration and domination brought the destruction of Inca mountain citadels and the transfer of administrative power to the new Spanish city of Lima on the coast.

Inca Empire in 1532

Network of Inca roads

0   600   1200 Km.

0   600   1200 Mi.

Online Study Center **Improve Your Grade**
Interactive Map: The Inca Empire

may have reached 10 million by the end of the fifteenth century.

Human sacrifice, though not unknown to the Inca people, was not an essential part of their religious life. Their state was unsettled, however, by increasingly harsh tax exactions. Under the Inca system the title Sapa Inca, or "Emperor," was inherited by the eldest son of the ruler's principal wife. The ruler's wealth, however, was retained by the rest of his family, who maintained the court as if the ruler still lived. Thus each new ruler needed money to finance the creation of an entirely new court, and taxes were not only high but continuously climbing.

Both great Amerindian empires, despite their brilliance, rested on uneasy conquests. Subject groups would be willing allies for any invader.

THE SPANISH CONQUESTS

Hernán Cortés (1485–1546) was ambitious to make something of himself in the New World. Of a poor but aristocratic background from the Extremadura region of southwestern Spain, he had gone to the West Indies in 1504 to seek his fortune in the service of the governor of Cuba. The governor gave him a commission to lead an expeditionary force to investigate reports of a wealthy and prosperous mainland Indian civilization. From the beginning Spanish authorities seem to have distrusted Cortés's aims. In fact, he departed hastily from Cuba to evade formal notification that the governor had revoked his commission because of insubordination.

Cortés landed in Mexico at the site of the city he would name Vera Cruz ("True Cross") early in 1519 with a tiny command of five hundred men, sixteen horses, eleven ships, and a few pieces of artillery. Aided by a devastating outbreak of smallpox and Amerindian peoples happy to shake off Aztec control, Cortés and his troops managed to destroy the network of city-states dominated by the Aztecs of Tenochtitlán in two years and lay claim to the Valley of Mexico for the king of Spain. The manner in which Cortés explained and justified his mission can serve as a model against which to measure the adventures of other sixteenth-century Europeans in the Americas.

Online Study Center **Improve Your Grade**
Primary Source: Cortés on the Aztecs: Two Letters to Charles V

The Conquest of Mexico   Cortés, like Machiavelli (see page 359), believed in the power of truly able leaders (men of *virtù*) to overcome chance through bold acts. Even so, an attempt to capture a city of 200,000 with an army of 500 appears more foolhardy than bold. Cortés seems to have attempted it simply because he found himself with very little choice. With his commission revoked by the governor of Cuba, Cortés arrived on the mainland as a rebel against both the governor of Cuba and the king of Spain. He burned his ships in Vera Cruz harbor, making clear to all his men that there was no turning back. Much of what he did and said concerning the great Aztec Empire was an attempt to justify his initial act of insubordination and win back royal support. He quickly found allies among native groups who, for their own reasons, wished to see the Aztec Empire destroyed. The allied forces moved toward Tenochtitlán.

Cortés was greatly aided by fortune in the form of Malintzin, a Mexica woman who after her conversion

Hernán Cortés   The Spanish commander who conquered the Aztec Empire with a tiny force of Spaniards reinforced by numerous Indian allies.

to Christianity called herself **Doña Marina** (ca. 1501–1550). Malintzin was Cortés's interpreter and, later, his mistress. Without her, one of Cortés's followers recalled, "we could not have understood the language of New Spain and Mexico." Her story illustrates many of the complex interactions at play in sixteenth-century Mexico. Born a noble Aztec, she was sold by her stepfather and mother, ending up in the hands of the Maya. They gave her, along with twenty other women, to Cortés. Knowing both the Maya and Mexica languages, and quickly learning Spanish, she was the one person who could mediate between Spaniard and native. After bearing Cortés a son, she finished her life in Spain as the wife of a Spanish gentleman. Like many of the natives who felt no affection for the Aztecs of Tenochtitlán, she did not find it difficult to aid the Spaniards.

Despite the help of Malintzin and Spaniards who had previously lived with the natives, the meeting of Aztecs and Spaniards demonstrated the breadth of the chasm separating the Old World and the New. At first the Aztec king Moctezuma was unconcerned about the coming of the Spaniards. Later he seems to have attempted to buy them off. And finally he and his successors fought desperately to drive them out of Tenochtitlán. The Aztecs' indecision was caused in large part by the fact that in neither words nor gestures did the two groups speak the same language. Hearing that the Spaniards were on the march, Moctezuma sent ambassadors bearing gold, silver, and other costly gifts, which they presented in a most humble fashion to the Spaniards. To a modern ear the gifts sound like (and have often been interpreted to be) desperate attempts to buy off the invaders. To Cortés, or any European or Asian resident of the Old World, such gifts were a sign of submission. But to Moctezuma and most Amerindians the giving of gifts with great humility by otherwise powerful and proud people could be a show of status, power, and wealth. Seen in that light, Moctezuma's lavish gifts and apparent humility were probably meant to demonstrate the superiority of his civilization, and Cortés's acceptance of the gifts indicated to the Aztecs, at least, a recognition of Spanish inferior status.

Spaniards later claimed that Moctezuma was confounded by the sudden appearance of these peoples from the East. Cortés himself reported to the king of

Spain that when he first met Moctezuma, the Aztec leader said, "We have always held that those who descended from [the god Quetzalcoatl (ket-zahl-coh-AH-tal)] would come and conquer this land and take us as his vassals." Later Spaniards explained that the Aztecs believed that Quetzalcoatl, the serpent-god symbolically conquered by Huitzilopochtli, had traveled to the east, promising one day to return and reclaim his lands, thus ending Aztec rule. The Spaniards believed that Moctezuma's ambivalence toward them was rooted in his belief in that myth.

Neither story holds up in light of the evidence. There is no surviving contemporary source for Moctezuma's supposed confession, and the myth of the return of Quetzalcoatl was first recorded in Spanish, not Mexica, sources long after the conquest. In truth, neither Cortés nor historians can satisfactorily explain in Western terms Moctezuma's initial response to the Spaniards. Cortés took the Aztec leader captive in 1521 and began what would be a two-year battle to take control of the capital and its empire. Although weakened by the arrival of smallpox and other virulent Old World diseases, the Aztecs continued to fight even as more and more of the subject peoples joined the Spanish besiegers. The Spaniards cut off food and water to Tenochtitlán, but still the Aztecs fought.

Doña Marina   An enslaved Mexica noblewoman who served as translator and guide for Cortés.

Different understandings of the rules of war, different traditions of diplomacy, and different cultures prevented the Aztecs and Cortés from reaching any understanding. Warfare in pre-conquest America was highly ritualized. Armies captured enemies either to enslave them or to sacrifice them in one of the temples. The Spaniards, to Aztec eyes, killed indiscriminately and needlessly on the battlefield. Cortés later complained of the Aztecs' refusal to negotiate: "We showed them more signs of peace than have ever been shown to a vanquished people." It was a conflict that neither side could resolve in any other way; thus, by August 1523 Cortés and his allies had destroyed completely the garden city of Tenochtitlán.

Later Conquests Cortés's recurring insubordination was an unfortunate model. His own lieutenants later rebelled against his control and attempted to create their own governments as they searched for riches and El Dorado, a mythical city of gold. Later adventurers marched throughout the North American Southwest and Central and South America following rumors of hidden riches. Using private armies and torturing native peoples, veterans of Cortés's army and newly arrived speculators hoped to find wealth that would allow them to live like nobles on their return to Spain. Like Cortés, they claimed to be acting for the monarchy and the church, but in fact they expected that success would justify their most vicious acts.

Francisco Pizarro (1470–1541) was the most successful of the private adventurers. Poor and illegitimate at birth, he arrived in the Americas ambitious for riches and power. After serving in Balboa's army, participating in several slaving expeditions, and helping to found Panama City, Pizarro was prosperous but still not wealthy. Rumors of Inca wealth filtered through to Central America. Pizarro and two partners resolved in 1530 to lead an expedition down the west coast of South America in search of the Inca capital. Benefiting from disorganization caused by a smallpox epidemic and ensuing civil war, Pizarro was able to find local sympathizers.

Like Cortés, he used numerous Indian allies in his most important battles. Aided by Amerindians eager to throw off Inca domination, he captured and executed the Sapa Inca and conquered the capital of Cuzco by 1533. He later built a new capital on the coast at Lima (see Map 13.4), from which he worked to extend his control over all of the old Inca Empire. Pizarro and his Spanish partners seized vast amounts of gold and silver from the Inca. The Spanish eventually found silver mines at Potosí (po-to-SEE), which would be a critical source of revenue for the Spanish monarchy. Resistance to Spanish rule continued into the 1570s, when the last of the independent Inca strongholds was finally destroyed.

COLONIAL ORGANIZATION

The Spanish crown needed to create a colonial government that could control the actions of its headstrong adventurers and create an orderly economy. Although the Spaniards proclaimed that they would "give to those strange lands the form of our own [land]," the resulting political and economic organization of the new Spanish possessions was a curious mixture of old and new.

The head of the administration was the monarchy. As early as the reigns of Ferdinand and Isabella, Spanish monarchs had tried to curb the excesses of the explorers and conquerors who traveled in their name. Isabella initially opposed the enslavement of Amerindians and any slave trade in the new lands. Further, the monarchs promoted a broad-based debate about the rights of Amerindians and the nature of religious conversion. It was royal policy that native rights, even the right not to become Christian, were to be protected. Mexicans had to accept missionaries, but they did not have to convert. Royal control, however, was limited by the sheer distance between the court and the new provinces. On average it took the Spanish fleet two years to complete a round-trip voyage. It could easily take two years for a royal response to a question to arrive at its destination. Things moved so slowly that as one viceroy ruefully noted, "If death came from Madrid, we should all live to a very old age." Given the difficulties of communication, the powers of local administrators had to be very broad.

By 1535 Spanish colonial administration was firmly established in the form it would retain for the next two hundred years. The king created the **Council of the Indies,** located at court, eventually in Madrid, which saw to all legal and administrative issues pertaining to the new possessions. The new territories themselves were eventually divided into the viceroyalty of New Spain (primarily Central America and part of Venezuela) and the viceroyalty of Peru.

In Spain, Castilian conquerors completely dominated newly won lands, but in New Spain royal administrators created Indian municipalities, or districts, in which Spaniards had no formal right to live or work. Government in these municipalities remained largely in the hands of pre-conquest native elites. Throughout the sixteenth century, official documents in these communities continued to be written in Nahuatl, the Aztec language. These native communities were, however, fragile. Colonists and local administrators often interfered in the hope of gaining control. (See the box "The Global Record: An Inca Nobleman Defends His Civilization.")

Council of the Indies An administrative body established in 1524 to oversee commerce and administration in Spain's colonial possessions.

AN INCA NOBLEMAN DEFENDS HIS CIVILIZATION

Felipe Guaman Poma was born into a noble Inca family with a long history of service first to the Inca kings and later to the Spanish administrators. Although Guaman Poma became a Christian and adapted to Spanish rule, he appealed to the king of Spain in 1613 to intervene on behalf of the Indian peoples. In this section he describes the evils he has seen and suggests how the king could remedy them.

The aforementioned priests . . . do not act like the blessed priests of Saint Peter. . . . Rather, they give themselves over to greed for silver, clothing, and things of the world. . . . [They] ask for Indians to carry to market their wine, peppers, coca, and maize. Some have Indians bring mountain wine and coca down from the high plains to the hot lowlands. Being highland people, they die from fever and chills. . . . [They] have thread spun and woven, oppressing the widows and unmarried women, making them work without pay. . . . And in this [dealing with the priests] the Indian women become notorious whores. . . . [They] clamor to involve themselves too much in judicial matters. . . . As a result they enter into disputes and initiate petitions and are bad examples for the pueblo [i.e., village]. . . . They treat them so imperiously and thereby destroy the Indians of this kingdom.

The ancient [Andean] priests . . . acted devoutly and gave good example, as with the virgins and nuns of the temples. And so the rest [of the Indians] submitted to their justice and law. They were Christians in everything but their idolatry.

Because of such damage and so many complaints lodged against them, these fathers and pastors should be appointed on an interim basis—for a year at a time if he is good; and if he is not, may he not remain a single day. He should be at least fifty years old because a child's or a young man's follies are not good. . . . They should be proven and tested for academic preparation as well as for humility, charity, love and fear of God and justice, and for knowledge of the Quechua [or] Aymara languages of the Indians, needed to reach them, confess them, and preach the Gospel and sermons [to them].

They should be examined by the reverend fathers . . . who are great scholars and preachers in the world. Those [who pass the examinations] should be sent to Your Lordship and to the head viceroy for appointment as interim pastors, posting a guaranteed bond. With this they will lose their arrogance; they will obey your lordship.

In the time of the conquest of a province there was only one priest in charge of instruction; . . . he demanded no silver and only enough to eat. Thus these first ones were exemplary saints. They . . . did not pretend to be a bishop or a magistrate. Thus [the people] converted to God giving themselves over to peace and to the royal Crown.

QUESTIONS

1. What are the complaints about the behavior of Christian priests? What do these complaints imply about the place of a priest in a village?

2. What role does Guaman Poma expect priests to play in a village?

3. What are the benefits Guaman Poma expects villagers to receive from Spanish administrators?

Source: Kenneth Mills and William B. Taylor, eds., *Colonial Latin America: A Documentary History.* Copyright 2002 by Scholarly Resources, Inc. Reprinted by permission of Scholarly Resources, Inc.

THE COLONIAL ECONOMY

The problem that most plagued the government was the conquerors' desire for laborers to work on the lands and in the mines that they had seized. From Columbus's first visit the Spanish adopted a system of forced labor developed in Spain. A colonist called an *encomendero* (en-co-men-DARE-o) was offered a grant, or *encomienda* (en-co-mi-EN-da), of a certain number of people or tribes who were required to work under his direction. The Spanish government expected that the encomendero was to be a protector of the conquered peoples, someone who would Christianize and civilize them. In theory, Indians who voluntarily agreed to listen to missionaries or to convert to Christianity could not be put under the control of an encomendero. If they refused, however, the Spaniards believed they had the right of conquest. In many areas encomenderos allowed life to continue as it had, simply collecting traditional payments that the pre-conquest elites had claimed. In other cases, where the subject peoples were forced into mining districts, the conditions were brutal. The treatment of native peoples was "more unjust and cruel," one reformer concluded, "than Pharaoh's oppression of the Jews."

The pressures exerted by the encomenderos were worsened by the precipitous fall in the indigenous population. Old World diseases such as smallpox and measles swept through peoples with no previous exposure to

encomienda A royal protectorship granted with the obligation to protect and Christianize the people. Instead natives became virtual slaves.

them (see pages 408–409). In central Mexico, where we know most about population changes, the pre-conquest population was at least 10 million to 12 million and may have been twice that. By the mid-sixteenth century, the native population may have declined to just over 6 million, and it probably plunged to less than 1 million early in the seventeenth century before beginning to grow again.

A large population was essential to the Spanish and the Portuguese. The Caribbean islands and Brazil were ideal for the production of sugar—a commercial crop in great demand throughout Europe. At first plantations and mines were worked by Amerindians, but when their numbers shrank, the Spanish and Portuguese imported large numbers of slaves from Africa.

Africans had participated in the initial stages of the conquest. (See the feature "The Visual Record: The Mulattos of Esmeraldas.") Some had lived in Spain and become Christian; indeed, Amerindians called them "black whitemen." Most Africans, however, were enslaved laborers. African slaves were in Cuba by 1518; they labored in the mines of Honduras by the 1540s. After the 1560s the Portuguese began mass importations of African slaves into Brazil to work on the sugar plantations. It has been estimated that 62,500 slaves were brought into Spanish America and 50,000 into Brazil during the sixteenth century. By 1810, when the movement to abolish the slave trade began to gather momentum, almost 10 million Africans had been involuntarily transported to the New World to work the fields and mines on which the colonial economy depended.

The conquerors had hoped to find vast quantities of wealth that they could take back to the Old World. In the viceroyalty of Mexico the search for El Dorado remained largely unsuccessful. The discovery in 1545 of the silver mines at Potosí in Peru, however, fulfilled the Spaniards' wildest dreams. Between 1550 and 1650 the Spanish probably sent back to Spain 181 tons of gold and 16,000 tons of silver, one-fifth of which was paid directly into the royal treasury.

The tonnage of precious metals was so great that the French scholar Jean Bodin (bo-DAN) (see page 484) held this infusion of wealth responsible for the rampant inflation that disrupted the European economy in the late sixteenth century. Although Bodin overestimated the European-wide effect of the precious metals on prices, the flood of silver and gold did have a significant impact on the Continent. The treasure represents one-quarter of the income of King Philip II of Spain in the 1560s and made him the richest monarch in Europe. The New World bonanza funded Spanish opposition to the Protestant Reformation and Spain's attempts to influence the politics of most of its neighbors. And the Spanish coins, the *reales* (re-AL-es) and *reales a ocho* (re-AL-es a O-cho) (the "pieces of eight" prized by English pirates), became the common coin of European traders and even Muslim and Hindu traders in the Indian Ocean. In a world with limited commercial credit, the Spanish treasure was critical for a truly integrated system of world trade.

THE DEBATE OVER INDIAN RIGHTS

To most conquerors the ruthless pursuit of wealth and power needs little justification, but the more thoughtful among the Spaniards were uneasy. "Tell me," demanded Friar Antonio Montesinos (mon-teh-SEE-nos) in 1511, "by what right or justice do you hold these Indians in such cruel and horrible slavery? By what right do you wage such detestable wars on these people who lived idly and peacefully in their own lands?"[5]

Initially the conquerors claimed the right to wage a just war of conquest if Amerindians refused to allow missionaries to live and work among them. Later, on the basis of reports of human sacrifice and cannibalism written by Columbus and other early explorers, Europeans concluded that the inhabitants of the New World rejected basic natural laws. Juan Gines de Sepulveda (HWAN HE-nays de se-PUL-ve-da), chaplain of King Charles I of Spain, argued in 1544 that the idolatry and cannibalism of the Indians made them, in Aristotle's terms, natural slaves—"barbarous and inhuman peoples abhorring all civil life, customs and virtue." People lacking "civil life" and "virtue" clearly could not be allowed self-government. Other writers commented that nakedness and cannibalism were both signs of the lack of "civility" among the Amerindians. Sepulveda implied that Indians were merely "humanlike," not necessarily human.

Franciscan and Dominican missionaries were especially vocal opponents of views such as Sepulveda's. Missionaries initially argued that Indians were innocents and ideal subjects for conversion to the simple piety of Christ and his first apostles. In their eyes Indians were like children who could be converted and led by example and, where necessary, by stern discipline. The simple faith of the newly Christian native peoples was to be an example, the missionaries believed, for the lax believers of old Europe. These mendicants saw themselves as advocates for Indians; they desired to protect the natives from the depredations of the Spanish conquerors and the corruptions of European civilization.

The most eloquent defender of Indian rights was **Bartolomé de Las Casas** (1474–1566), a former encomendero who became a Dominican missionary and eventually bishop of Chiapas in southern Mexico. Las Casas passionately condemned the violence and brutality of the Spanish conquests. In a famous debate with

Bartolomé de Las Casas   A former encomendero and the first bishop of Chiapas who passionately defended Indian rights and urged the passage of laws abolishing Indian slavery.

THE VISUAL RECORD

The Mulattos of Esmeraldas

This painting, which is entitled *Los Mulatos de Esmeraldas*, is the earliest known signed colonial portrait, dating back to 1599. It was commissioned by Juan del Barrio de Sepúlveda, judge of the Audiencia of Quito. He sent it to the Spanish king in Madrid, where the painting still resides. The artist who painted this very European-styled painting was an Amerindian named Andrés Sánchez Galque who had trained with a Spanish Dominican. The resulting work is a striking mix of native and Spanish cultures and leads a historian to ask, "What does this image suggest about colonial Latin America?"

It demonstrates first of all how quickly even isolated areas became integrated into a complex international culture. In the center of the painting stands Don Francisco de Arobe, the head of one of two important Afro-Indian clans that dominated the region since the middle of the sixteenth century. He is flanked by his two sons, Don Petro (on his right) and Don Domingo (on his left). Don Francisco is of mixed ancestry—his father was African, his mother an enslaved Nicaraguan. The parents had escaped into the wild region of Esmer-

aldas, an isolated coastal area northwest of Quito (see Map 13.2). It was an area that the Spanish imagined was filled with gold and perhaps, as its name seemed to imply, emeralds. It was also an area that various missionaries and private adventurers attempted to control in the name of the Crown. They were convinced that had they subdued Esmeraldas, their reward would have been treasure and political power.

In the half-century before this portrait was painted, the mulatto groups had variously negotiated with, helped, and avoided the Spanish. Clan leaders regularly promised to become Christian, to give food to the explorers, and to help in the search for gold and other treasures. Throughout the sixteenth century they regularly and successfully resisted incorporation into the empire. The leader of one clan had offered allegiance to the Spanish if they would name him governor "over your subjects and vassals and natives." And so it is no doubt significant that the Spanish named Don Francisco governor. It was, in fact, his peaceful submission to the Audiencia that occasioned this surprising work. All this makes the portrait fascinating, but

The Mulattos of Esmeraldas   *(Institut Amatller d'Art Hispanic)*

ambiguous. Are the three, as some have suggested, "trophies, stuffed and mounted on a wall of blue" or perhaps crafty diplomats who preferred "Renaissance dissimulation to . . . rebellion?"*

The three figures have struck a pose typical in Renaissance portraits. Don Francisco looks directly at the viewer, while his sons look only at him. The three are wearing Spanish cloaks and ruffled collars over what is probably a South American poncho, but the design of the material suggests it is European or Asian in origin. What is most striking is the gold jewelry—earrings and noseplugs. These very likely were scavenged from burial mounds left in the region by earlier native peoples. Spanish visitors to Esmeraldas often commented on the gold jewelry of the mulattos. The mulatto clans often used promises of gold to mesmerize the adventurers who came. The three also are wearing shell necklaces—a tradition among coastal peoples reaching back perhaps a millennium. And finally, they are carrying spears, probably a combination of local wood and imported steel tips.

But how to interpret the image? The first thing a historian must do is acknowledge that we cannot know for sure the thoughts of the painter, the patron, or the three who posed. But we can line up the visual evidence that might lead us to a tentative conclusion. First, notice the interesting mix of dress. The three men doubtless would not have worn so many layers of clothing at home, along the steamy seacoast. Are the Spanish additions indications that Don Barrio, the judge of the Audiencia in Quito, dressed them to look more subdued, Spanish, and civilized? All three are addressed as "don," an honorific title that indicates both Christian conversion and elevated social status. But if that is the case, why are there no crosses, no signs of deference? They still wear their coastal shells and their gold jewelry taken from sites still unknown to the Spanish. Their hats are in their hands, perhaps a sign of respect or submission, but their eyes are not downcast or submissive. Don Francisco looks directly at the viewer and all three hold their spears. They may now be Spanish subjects, but Don Francisco does have the look of a governor.

In the end, it may be that Don Francisco and Judge Barrio would not have agreed on what the painting signified. But the ambiguity of the portrait does demonstrate to subsequent historians the extent to which understanding the Spanish role in Latin America requires more than simply ideas of conquest, domination, or rebellion. Identities may have been transformed, but persons like Don Francisco seem to be more than just obedient subjects.

QUESTIONS

1. Look at the portrait and try to identify those items that seem native or Spanish.
2. Can you find indications of either submission or independence in the portraits?

Online Study Center
Improve Your Grade Visual Record Activities

---

*The first conclusion is from Kenneth Mills and William B. Taylor, eds., *Colonial Latin America: A Documentary History* (Wilmington, Del.: SR Books, 2002), p. 160; the second from Kris Lane, *Quito, 1599* (Albuquerque: University of New Mexico Press, 2002), p. 33.

Sepulveda, Las Casas rejected the "humanlike" argument. "All races of the world are men," he declared. All are evolving along a historical continuum. It was wrong, he added, to dismiss any culture or society as outside or beyond natural law. Like all other peoples, Indians had reason. That being the case, even the most brutal could be civilized and Christianized, but by conversion, not coercion. In the view of Las Casas, the argument for natural slavery was indefensible.

Online Study Center **Improve Your Grade**
Primary Source: A Dominican Voice in the Wilderness:
Preaching Against Tyranny in Hispaniola

King Charles accepted Las Casas's criticisms of the colonial administration. In 1542 he issued "New Laws" aimed at ending the virtual independence of the most adventurous encomenderos. He further abolished Indian slavery and greatly restricted the transfer of encomiendas. We should have no illusion, however, that these measures reflected a modern acceptance of cultural pluralism. The very mendicants who protected the Indians assumed that Westernization and Christianization would quickly follow mercy. When it did not, as during revolts in the 1560s, the mendicants themselves sometimes reacted with a puzzled sense of anger, frustration, and betrayal.

SECTION SUMMARY

- Before the arrival of the Spanish, the Aztecs and Inca were large empires that dominated surrounding tribes and clans.

- Cortés found ready allies among the peoples dominated by the two empires.

- The conquest of Mexico set off a Spanish expansion barely under the control of the Crown.

- The Crown eventually attempted to protect Amerindians by restricting encomiendas, outlawing Indian slavery, and forming Indian-controlled communities.

THE COLUMBIAN EXCHANGE

What changes did European expansion bring to the Old World and the New?

The conquerors, adventurers, and traders who completed the expansion begun by the voyages of Christopher Columbus and Vasco da Gama profoundly altered the Old World and the New. A system of world trade had been in place before 1492, but now, as the Spanish proclaimed, Europe and especially Spain were at the center of economic and political life. As the Spanish and other Europeans moved throughout the world, they carried with them religions, ideas, people, plants, animals, and diseases—forever uniting the Old World and the New. This blending of cultures is known as the **Columbian Exchange.**

DISEASE

Columbus and those who followed him brought not only people to the New World but also numerous Old World diseases. "Virgin-soil" epidemics—that is, epidemics of previously unknown diseases—are invariably

fierce. Although the New World may have passed syphilis to Spain, from which it quickly spread throughout the Old World, diseases transferred from the Old World to the New were much more virulent than syphilis. Smallpox spread from Cuba to Mexico as early as 1519. It was soon followed by diphtheria, measles, trachoma, whooping cough, chickenpox, bubonic plague, malaria, typhoid fever, cholera, yellow fever, scarlet fever, amoebic dysentery, influenza, and some varieties of tuberculosis. Disease served as the silent ally of the conquerors. At critical points during the conquest of Tenochtitlán, smallpox was raging in the Aztec population. The disease later moved along traditional trade networks. An epidemic shortly before Pizarro's expedition to Peru carried off the Sapa Inca and may have contributed to the unrest and civil war that worked to the advantage of the invaders.

Lacking sources, historians cannot trace accurately the movement of epidemic diseases or their effects on New World populations, yet many archaeologists and historians remain convinced that Old World diseases moved north from Mexico and ravaged and disrupted Amerindian populations in eastern North America long before the arrival of European immigrants. In

Columbian Exchange A term used to describe the blending of cultures between the Old World and the New. Columbus and others who followed brought plants, animals, and diseases that transformed North and South America.

Images of the New World

A mix of fact and fiction characterized many early images of the New World. The text below this illustration claims that these natives share everything, even wives; that they are cannibals; and that they have no government. The woodcut seems to justify Spanish domination. *(Spencer Collection, New York Public Library/Art Resource, NY)*

Dye figur anzaigt vns das voick vnd insel die gefunden ist durch den chnstenlichen künig zü Portigal oder von feinen vnderthonen. Die leüt sind also nacket hübsch braun wolgestalt von leib ir heübeer. halß aens schäm füß. frawen vnd mann ain wenig mit federn bedeckt. Auch haben die mann in iren angesichten vnd brust vil edel gestain. Es hat auch nyemann nichzs finder sind alle ding gemain. Vnnd die mann habendt weyber welche in gefallen es sey mütter. schwester oder freündt. darinn haben sy kain vnderschayd. Sy streyten auch mit einander. Sy essen auch ainander selbs die erschlagen werden vnd hencken das selbig fleisch in den rauch. Sy werden alt hundert vnd fünffzig iar. Vnd haben kain regiment.

most of the New World 90 percent or more of the native population was destroyed by wave after wave of previously unknown afflictions. Explorers and colonists did not enter an empty land but rather an *emptied* one.

It was at least partially because of disease that both the Spanish and the Portuguese needed to import large numbers of African slaves to work their plantations and mines. With the settlement of southeastern North America, commercial agriculture was extended to include the production of tobacco and later cotton. As a result of the needs of plantation economies and the labor shortages caused by epidemics, African slaves were brought in by the thousands, then hundreds of thousands. In the Caribbean and along the coasts of Central and South America, the Africans created an African Caribbean or African American culture that amalgamated African, European, and American civilizations.

PLANTS AND ANIMALS

It became increasingly clear to the Spaniards that the New World had been completely isolated from the Old. The impact of Old World peoples on native populations was immediately evident to all parties. But scholars have recently argued that the importation of plants and animals had an even more profound effect than the arrival of Europeans. The changes that began in 1492 created "Neo-Europes" in what are now Canada, the United States, Mexico, Argentina, Australia, and New Zealand. The flora and fauna of the Old World, accustomed to a relatively harsh, competitive environment, found ideal conditions in the new lands. Like the rabbits that overran the Canary Islands and eventually Australia, Old World plants and animals multiplied, driving out many New World species.

Gardening in Spanish Mexico
This closed Spanish-style garden is a mix of the old and the new. Workers use both a Spanish hoe and an indigenous spade to cultivate new plants introduced by the Spanish.
(Biblioteca Nacional, Madrid/Institut Amatller d'Art Hispanic)

The most important meat and dairy animals in the New World today—cattle, sheep, goats, and pigs—are imports from the Old World. Sailors initially brought pigs or goats aboard ship because they were easily transportable sources of protein. When let loose on the Caribbean islands, they quickly took over. The spread of horses through what is now Mexico, Brazil, Argentina, the United States, and Canada was equally dramatic. To the list of domesticated animals can be added donkeys, dogs, cats, and chickens. The changes these animals brought were profound. Cattle, pigs, and chickens quickly became staples of the New World diet. Horses enabled Amerindians and Europeans to travel across and settle the vast plains of both North and South America.

The flora of the New World was equally changed. Even contemporaries noted how Old World plants flourished in the New. By 1555 European clover was widely distributed in Mexico—Aztecs called it "Castilian grass." Other Old World grasses, as well as weeds such as dandelions, quickly followed. Domesticated plants, including apples, peaches, and artichokes, spread rapidly and naturally in the hospitable new environment. The Old World also provided new and widely grown small grains such as oats, barley, and wheat. Early in the twentieth century it was estimated that only one-quarter of the grasses found on the broad prairies of the Argentine pampas were native before the arrival of Columbus.

The exchange went both ways. Crops from the New World also had an effect on the Old. By the seventeenth century maize (or American corn), potatoes, sweet potatoes, and many varieties of beans had significantly altered the diets of Europe and Asia. New crops supported the dramatic population growth that invigorated Italy, Ireland, and Scandinavia. With the addition of the tomato in the nineteenth century, much of the modern European diet became dependent on New World foods. The new plants and new animals, as well as the social and political changes initiated by the Europeans, pulled the Old World and the New more closely together.

CULTURE

One reason for the accommodation between the Old World and the New was that the Europeans and Amerindians tended to interpret conquest and cultural transformation in the same way. The peoples living in the Valley of Mexico believed that their conquest was fated by the gods and that their new masters would bring in new gods. The Spaniards' beliefs were strikingly similar, based on the revelation of divine will and the omnipotence of the Christian God. Cortés, by whitewashing former Aztec temples and converting native priests into white-clad Christian priests, was in a way fulfilling the Aztecs' expectations about the nature of conquest.

Acculturation was also facilitated by the Spanish tendency to place churches and shrines at the sites of former Aztec temples. The shrine of the Virgin of Guadalupe (gwa-da-LOO-peh) (on the northern edge of modern Mexico City), for example, was located on the site of the temple of the goddess Tonantzin (to-NAN-tzin), an Aztec fertility-goddess of childbirth and midwives. The shrine of Guadalupe is a perfect example of the complex mixture of cultures. The shrine initially appealed to *creoles*—people of mixed Spanish and Mexican descent. In the seventeenth century and after, it came to symbolize the connection of poor Mexicans to Christianity and was a religious rallying point for resisting state injustices.

The colonists tended to view their domination of the New World as a divine vindication of their own culture and civilization. During the sixteenth century they set about remaking the world they had found. In the century after the conquest of Mexico, Spaniards founded 190 new cities in the Americas. Lima, Bogota, and many others were proudly modeled on and compared with the cities of Spain. In 1573 King Philip II (r. 1556–1598) established ordinances requiring all new cities to be laid out on a uniform grid with a main plaza, market, and religious center. The new cities became hubs of social and political life in the colonies. In these cities religious orders founded colleges for basic education much like the universities they had organized in the Old World. In the aftermath of conquest there were schools to teach Spanish, the liberal arts, and trades to the Amerindian population. By midcentury, however, the urban colleges were primarily for the mestizo and Spanish populations. In 1551, a century before English colonists founded Harvard University in Massachusetts, the Crown authorized the first universities in the New World. The universities in Mexico City and Lima mirrored the great Spanish university in

Salamanca, teaching law and theology to the colonial elites. Colonists attempted to re-create in all essentials the society of Spain.

The experience of the Spanish and Portuguese in the sixteenth century seemed confirmed by the later experiences of the French and English in the seventeenth century. In seventeenth-century New England the English Puritan John Winthrop concluded, "For the natives, they are nearly all dead of smallpox, so as the Lord hath cleared our title to what we possess."[6] A seventeenth-century French observer came to a similar conclusion: "Touching these savages, there is a thing that I cannot omit to remark to you, it is that it appears visibly that God wishes that they yield their place to new peoples."[7] Political philosophers believed that in the absence of evidence that the indigenous peoples were improving the land, the rights to that land passed to those who would make the best use of it. Thus colonists believed that they had divine and legal sanction to take and to remake these new lands in a European image.

SECTION SUMMARY

- Old World diseases introduced into the New World destroyed perhaps 90 percent of the indigenous population.

- Thousands of enslaved Africans were brought to the New World to replace the lost population.

- Old World plants and animals transformed the economy of the New World.

- The cult of the Virgin of Guadalupe shows how religious practices of the Old World were influenced by New World religious practices.

CHAPTER SUMMARY

 Online Study Center **ACE the Test**

What did Europeans know about the wider world in the Middle Ages?

How did the Portuguese exploit their new connection to the East?

Why did the Spanish choose to sail west in their attempt to find Asia?

How did the Spanish conquer and control the new world they entered?

What changes did European expansion bring to the Old World and the New?

As we have seen, there was never a time when Europeans were unaware of or unconcerned about the outside world. In addition to traditional geographical knowledge reaching back to the classical world, Europeans had valuable trade contacts via Muslim traders with both Africa and Asia. Further,

in the thirteenth century, Italian merchants and adventurers began making regular trips through central Asia to China and even to Japan.

Yet the expansion begun by the Portuguese along the coast of Africa and then on to India began a fateful transformation of European economic, political, and cultural influence. The Portuguese voyages were almost never adventures of discovery. By rumor and careful reading, explorers had ideas about what they would find. Nonetheless, they were faced with challenges that led them to adapt their Mediterranean and European ways of organization. The Portuguese developed a trading-post system to control trade in Asia.

Portuguese control of the African coast seemed to foreclose Spanish connections to Asian markets. Yet based on a misunderstanding of classical texts, Columbus convinced the Spanish that the shortest route to Asia involved sailing west. Although Columbus never acknowledged it, by early in the sixteenth century, the Spanish knew that he had found a world unknown to the Old World.

In the wake of savage conquest and exploitation by adventurers, the Spanish developed a system of law and administration that transformed the world they had found. In the New World, even as the Spanish conquered peoples and changed their languages, governments, and religions, many aspects of Amerindian culture survived in the local Indian municipalities.

The meeting of the Old World and the New brought unexpected changes to both. The old empires of the Americas were replaced by a Spanish colonial government. They brought with them foods, livestock, religion, and traditional European culture. They also brought diseases that decimated populations and transformed economies.

Modern historians considering decolonization, economic revolutions in many parts of Asia, and multiculturalism have been changing their thinking about European expansion in the fifteenth century. They have made us very aware of what was lost during the violent and tragic conquests that were part of European expansion. It is impossible to say whether the economic and technical benefits of the amalgamation of the Old World and the New outweigh the costs. Even those who celebrate the transformation of the New World would probably agree with the conclusions of a Native American in the Pacific Northwest: "I am not sorry the missionaries came. But I wish they had known how to let their news change people's lives from the inside, without imposing their culture over our ways."[8]

LOOKING AHEAD

The economic, political, and cultural changes brought about by the conquest created a hybrid culture. But it was a hybrid based on a belief in the superiority of a particular vision of Christian society. That vision of a Christian society was to be hotly contested in the sixteenth century. The inability to understand and tolerate this debate was to be a key to the strife created by the other great event of the sixteenth century—the movement to reform church and society.

KEY TERMS

Prince Henry "the Navigator" (p. 391)

Vasco da Gama (p. 393)

trading-post empire (p. 394)

Treaty of Tordesillas (p. 397)

Ferdinand Magellan (p. 397)

Aztecs (p. 399)

Inca (p. 399)

Hernán Cortés (p. 401)

Doña Marina (p. 402)

Council of the Indies (p. 403)

encomienda (p. 404)

Bartolomé de Las Casas (p. 405)

Columbian Exchange (p. 408)

Online Study Center
Improve Your Grade Flashcards

SUGGESTED READING

Burkholder, Mark A., and Lyman L. Johnson. *Colonial Latin America*. 5th ed. 2003. A thorough introduction to the conquest and colonization of Central and South America by the Spanish and Portuguese.

Clendinnen, Inga. *Aztecs: An Interpretation*. 1991. A dramatic, beautifully written essay on the Aztecs that shows how daily life, religion, and imperialism were linked.

Crosby, A. W. *Ecological Imperialism: The Biological Expansion of Europe, 900–1900.* 1986. A discussion of how migrating peoples carried plants, animals, and diseases; includes excellent maps and illustrations.

Curtin, P. *The Tropical Atlantic in the Age of the Slave Trade.* 1991. An introductory pamphlet that is an excellent first work for students interested in the history of slavery and the movement of peoples from Africa to the New World.

Friedman, John Block, and Kristen Mossler Figg, eds. *Trade, Travel, and Exploration in the Middle Ages.* 2000. This encyclopedia includes discussions of the earliest stage of European expansion, especially contacts with Asia.

Lane, Kris. *Quito, 1599.* 2002. An engaging collection of studies showing the variety of experiences that made up colonial life in the New World.

Mills, Kenneth, and William B. Taylor, eds. *Colonial Latin America: A Documentary History.* 1998. This engaging collection of primary documents and short essays also includes unique discussions of contemporary maps and drawings.

Phillips, J. R. S. *The Medieval Expansion of Europe.* 1988. The best survey of European interest in and knowledge of the world beyond Christendom; especially good on European travelers to the East in the thirteenth century.

Phillips, William D., Jr., and Carla Rahn Phillips. *The Worlds of Christopher Columbus.* 1992. Though written for a popular audience, this is an excellent survey of Columbus and his voyages and an up-to-date summary of recent work on Columbus, maritime technology, and Spanish colonial interests.

Subrahmanyam, S. *The Portuguese Empire in Asia, 1500–1700: A Political and Economic History.* 1993. A thoughtful introduction to Portuguese expansion by a renowned Indian economic historian.

NOTES

1. Quoted in William D. Phillips, Jr., and Carla Rahn Phillips, *The Worlds of Christopher Columbus* (Cambridge: Cambridge University Press, 1992), p. 163.

2. Quoted ibid., p. 166.

3. Quoted in J. H. Parry, ed., *The European Reconnaissance: Selected Documents* (New York: Harper & Row, 1968), p. 242.

4. Quoted in Alfred W. Crosby, *Ecological Imperialism: The Biological Expansion of Europe, 900–1900* (Cambridge: Cambridge University Press, 1986), p. 125.

5. Quoted in Mark A. Burkholder and Lyman L. Johnson, *Colonial Latin America* (Oxford: Oxford University Press, 1990), p. 29.

6. Quoted in Crosby, p. 208.

7. Quoted ibid., p. 215.

8. Quoted in Maria Parker Pascua, "Ozette: A Makah Village in 1491," *National Geographic* (October 1991), p. 53.

14

THE AGE OF THE
REFORMATION

El Greco: The Burial of the Count de Orgaz
This traditional chapel painting shows the close connection between the earthly and celestial realms in traditional Catholic Christianity. *(Institut Amatller d'Art Hispanic)*

l Greco's *The Burial of the Count de Orgaz* encapsulates the hopes and contradictions of the age of the Reformation. El Greco ("the Greek") first learned to paint on the island of Crete, then studied and worked in Venice and Rome before settling in Spain. This painting expresses the medieval Christian understanding of a good death. We see a saintly knight surrounded by clergy and witnesses as his soul (in the form of a cloud-wrapped body) is commended to Christ. But El Greco (1541–1614) painted during a period of social, political, and religious turmoil, when medieval assumptions about the unity of the Christian world and the nature of salvation were being challenged by religious reformers and their political supporters.

If we look more closely at the painting, we can see what El Greco and Roman Catholic Christians wished to emphasize. The two figures holding the count's body are Saint Stephen, the first Christian martyr, and Saint Augustine, perhaps the most important of the early Church Fathers. They represent the continuity of the Christian tradition. But just as important is the heavenly hierarchy of saints and angels reaching from the count upward to Christ. At the very top are Saint John and Saint Mary, who are interceding with Christ for the count's soul. The hierarchy of saints and intercessors so vividly painted by El Greco represents one of the clearest differences between the two contending visions of Christian life and society. Most reformers rejected the idea that salvation depended on the intervention of others, no matter how saintly. Salvation was a simpler process. The hierarchy of saints and angels depicted by El Greco seemed unnecessary.

The crisis of the Reformation began with a challenge to the religious authority of the papacy. Debates over the power and status of the church that raged during this period, however, did not occur in a political vacuum. Support for the old church was an issue of state that profoundly affected the exercise of political authority in the Holy Roman Empire. In England and Scandinavia, in contrast, monarchs viewed the church as a threat to strong royal government, and reformers soon found themselves with royal patrons. Elsewhere, especially in eastern Europe, no strong central governments existed

CHAPTER OUTLINE

THE REFORMATION MOVEMENTS, CA. 1517–1545

THE EMPIRE OF CHARLES V (R. 1519–1556)

THE ENGLISH REFORMATION, 1520–1603

FRANCE, SCANDINAVIA, AND EASTERN EUROPE, 1523–1560

THE LATE REFORMATION, CA. 1545–1600

KEY TERMS

Martin Luther

justification by faith

sola scriptura

Charles V

Huldrych Zwingli

John Calvin

Anabaptists

Augsburg Confession

Henry VIII

Act of Supremacy

Society of Jesus

Ignatius Loyola

Index of Prohibited Books

Council of Trent

Online Study Center

This icon will direct you to interactive map and primary source activities on the website **college.hmco.com/pic/noble5e**

to enforce religious unity, and so a variety of Christian traditions coexisted.

By the second half of the sixteenth century political and religious leaders concentrated their energies on a process of theological definition and institutionalization that led to the formation of the major Christian religious denominations we know today. They created Roman Catholic, Anglican, Reformed (Calvinist), and Lutheran churches as clearly defined confessions, with formally prescribed religious beliefs and practices.

An important aspect of the reform movement was the emphasis on individual belief and religious participation. Far from freeing the individual, however, the Christian churches of the late sixteenth century all emphasized correct doctrine and orderliness in personal behavior. Although early Protestants rejected a system that they accused of oppressing the individual, the institutions that replaced the old church developed their own traditions of control. The increased moral discipline advocated by churches accompanied and even fostered the expansion of state power that would characterize the late sixteenth and seventeenth centuries.

FOCUS QUESTIONS

Why did the reformers feel it was necessary to establish entirely new churches outside the Roman Catholic Church?

What political factors limited Charles V's ability to respond to the religious crisis?

Why did the English monarchs take the lead in efforts to reform the English church?

How did ideas of church reform influence social and political developments in the rest of Europe?

How did Catholic and Protestant Christians differ from each other by the end of the Reformation?

THE REFORMATION MOVEMENTS, CA. 1517–1545

Why did the reformers feel it was necessary to establish entirely new churches outside the Roman Catholic Church?

In 1517 **Martin Luther,** a little-known professor of theology in eastern Germany, launched a protest against practices in the late medieval church. Luther's criticisms struck a responsive chord with many of his contemporaries and led to calls for reform across much of Europe. All the reformers, even the most radical, shared with Luther a sense that the essential sacramental and priestly powers claimed by the late medieval church were illegitimate. These reformers initially had no intention of forming a new church; they simply wanted to return Christianity to what they believed was its earlier, purer form. Although their various protests resulted in the creation of separate and well-defined religious traditions, the differences among the reformers became clear only in the second half of the sixteenth century. Thus it is appropriate to speak of "Reformation movements" rather than a unified Protestant Reformation.

We call the men and women who joined these new churches "Protestants," but the reformers tended to think of themselves as "evangelical reformed Christians." The word *evangelical* derived from *evangel* (literally, "good news"), the New Testament Gospel. They were evangelical in the sense that they believed that authority derived from the Word of God, the Bible. They were reformed Christians because their aim was to restore Christianity to the form they believed it exhibited in the first centuries of its existence.

THE LATE MEDIEVAL CONTEXT

Although reformers claimed religious life was in crisis before the Reformation, medieval Christianity was, in fact, flourishing. Questions of an individual's salvation and personal relationship to God and to the Christian community remained at the heart of religious practice and theological speculation. Nominalist theologians,

Martin Luther German theologian and religious reformer who began the Protestant Reformation in 1517 by questioning and finally discarding Catholic teaching about penance and salvation.

the leading thinkers of the late Middle Ages, rejected the key assumption of previous Scholastics—that moral life was circumscribed by universal ideas and generally applicable rules. In the words of William of Ockham (ca. 1285–1347), "No universal reality exists outside the mind." Truth was to be found in daily experience or in revealed Scripture, not in complex logical systems. At the heart is Ockham's method—known as "Ockham's razor"—the observation that what can be explained simply "is vainly explained by assuming more."

Nominalist theologians dismissed ponderous systems of logic, but they held on to the traditional rituals and beliefs that united the Christian community. They believed in a holy covenant in which God would save those Christians who, by means of the church's sacraments and through penitential and charitable acts, were partners in their own salvation. Foremost among the penitential acts was the feeding of "Christ's Poor," especially on important feast days. The pious constructed and supported hospices for travelers and hospitals for the sick. Christians went on pilgrimages to shrines such as the tomb of Saint Thomas Becket in Canterbury or the Church of Saint James of Compostela in Spain. They also endowed chapels, called chantry chapels, to pray for their own souls. To moralists work itself was in some sense a penitential and ennobling act.

Popular Religion The most common religious practice of the late Middle Ages was participation in religious brotherhoods. Urban brotherhoods were usually organized around a craft guild or neighborhood; rural brotherhoods were more likely to include an entire village or parish. Members vowed to attend monthly meetings, to participate in processions on feast days, and to maintain peaceful and charitable relations with fellow members.

The most typical religious feast was that of *Corpus Christi* (the "Body of Christ"). The feast celebrated and venerated the sacrament of the mass and the ritual by which the bread offered to the laity became the actual body of Christ. Corpus Christi was popular with the church hierarchy because it emphasized the role of the priest in the central ritual of Christianity. The laity, however, equated Corpus Christi with the body of citizens who made up the civic community. Thus religious identity seemed to be at the very heart of social identity.

Kingdoms, provinces, and towns all venerated patron saints who, believers thought, offered protection from natural as well as political disasters. There were royal saints such as Edward of England, Louis of France, and Olaf of Norway. Festivals in their honor were major events in towns or kingdoms. The most revered saint in the late Middle Ages was the Virgin Mary, the mother of Jesus. The most popular new pilgrimage shrines in the north of Europe were dedicated to the Virgin. It was she, townspeople believed, who

1513–1517	Fifth Lateran Council meets to consider reform of the Catholic Church
1517	Luther makes public his "Ninety-five Theses"
1518	Zwingli is appointed people's priest of Zurich
1520	Pope Leo X condemns Luther's teachings
1521	Luther appears at the Diet of Worms
1524–1525	Peasant revolts in Germany
1527	Imperial troops sack Rome
1530	Melanchthon composes the Augsburg Confession summarizing Lutheran belief
1534	Calvin flees Paris
	Loyola founds the Society of Jesus
1535	Anabaptist community of Münster is destroyed
1536	Calvin arrives in Geneva and publishes *Institutes of the Christian Religion*
1545–1563	Council of Trent meets to reform Catholic Church
1555	Emperor Charles V accepts the Peace of Augsburg
1559	Parliament passes Elizabethan Act of Supremacy and Act of Uniformity

protected them from invasion, plague, and natural disasters. In such a society it was impossible to distinguish between religion and society, church and state.

Women and Religion Women played a prominent role in late medieval religious life. Holy women who claimed any sort of moral standing often did so because of visions or prophetic gifts such as knowledge of future events or discernment of the status of souls in Purgatory. Reputations for sanctity provided a profound moral authority. The Italian Blessed Angela of Foligno (fo-LIN-yo) (ca. 1248–1309) had several visions and became the object of a large circle of devoted followers. She was typical of a number of late medieval religious women who on the death of a spouse turned to religion. They tended to gather "families" around them, people whom they described as their spiritual "fathers" or "children." They offered moral counsel and boldly warned businessmen and politicians of the dangers of lying and sharp dealings. "Oh my sons, fathers, and brothers," counseled Angela, "see that you love one another . . . [and] likewise unto all people."[1]

In the late Middle Ages religious houses for women probably outnumbered those for men. For unmarried or unmarriageable (because of poverty or disabilities) daughters, convents provided an economical, safe, and controlled environment. Moralists denounced the dumping of women in convents: "They give [unmarriageable daughters] to a convent, as if they were the scum and vomit of the world," Saint Bernardino of Siena (1380–1444) concluded. The general public, however, believed that well-run communities of religious women promoted the spiritual and physical health of the general community. In a society in which women were not allowed to control their own property and, except among the nobility, lacked a visible role in political and intellectual life, a religious vocation may have had a compelling appeal. At the least it permitted women to define their own religious and social relationships. Well-to-do or aristocratic parents also appreciated the fact that the traditional gift that accompanied a daughter entering a religious house was much smaller than a dowry.

Some women declined to join convents, which required vows of chastity and obedience to a Rule and close male supervision. They could be found among the many pilgrims who visited local shrines, the great churches of Rome, or even the holy city of Jerusalem. Many other women chose to live as anchoresses, or recluses, in closed cells beside churches and hospitals or in rooms in private homes. Men and women traveled from all parts of England seeking the counsel of the Blessed Julian of Norwich (d. after 1413), who lived in a tiny cell built into the wall of a parish church.

The most controversial group of religious women were the Beguines, who lived in communities without taking formal vows and often with minimal connections to the local church hierarchy. By the early fifteenth century Beguines were suspect because clerics believed that these independent women rejected traditional religious cloistering and the moral leadership of male clergy; consequently, it was thought, they were particularly susceptible to heresy. Critics maintained that unsupervised Beguines held to what was called the "Heresy

Crowning with Thorns
Late medieval Christians meditated on Christ's sufferings and preferred images like this one that shows a tortured Christ living in their own time. *(Courtesy, Augustiner Chorherrenstift, Herzogenburg. Photo: Fotostudio Wurst Erich)*

of the Free Spirit," a belief that one who had achieved spiritual perfection was no longer capable of sin. Fantastic rumors of sexual orgies, spread by fearful clerical opponents, quickly brought suspect women before local church authorities. Although some Beguines may have held such a belief in spiritual perfection, the majority certainly did not. Even so, they were feared by an ecclesiastical hierarchy that distrusted independence.

A more conservative movement for renewal in the church was the Brothers and Sisters of the Common Life, founded by the Dutchman Geert Groote (HIRT HROW-ta) (1340–1384). A popular preacher and reformer, Groote gathered male and female followers into quasi-monastic communities at Deventer in the Low Countries. Eventually a community of Augustinian canons was added at Windesheim. Brothers and Sisters of the Common Life supported themselves as book copyists and teachers in small religious schools. Members of these communities followed a strict, conservative spirituality that has come to be known as the *devotio moderna,* or "modern devotion." Although they called themselves "modern," their piety was traditional. Their ideas are encapsulated in *The Imitation of Christ,* a popular work of traditional monastic spirituality written by Thomas à Kempis (ca. 1380–1471), a canon of Windesheim. They advocated the contrary ideals of fourteenth-century religious life: broader participation by the laity and strict control by clerical authorities.

Religious life in the late medieval period was broadly based and vigorous. Theologians, laypeople, and popular preachers could take heart that they were furthering their own salvation and that of their neighbors. Thus the Reformation of the sixteenth century involved more than simple moral reform.

MARTIN LUTHER AND THE NEW THEOLOGY

Martin Luther (1483–1546) eventually challenged many of the assumptions of late medieval Christians. He seemed to burst onto the scene in 1517, when he objected to the way in which papal indulgences—that is, the remission of penalties owed for sins—were being bought and sold in the archbishopric of Magdeburg. Luther's father, a miner from the small town of Mansfeld, had hoped that his son would take a degree in law and become a wealthy and prestigious lawyer. Luther chose instead to enter a monastery and eventually become a priest.

Justification by Faith   Luther recalled having been troubled throughout his life by a sense of his own sinfulness and unworthiness. According to late medieval theology, the life of a Christian was a continuing cycle of sin, confession, contrition, and penance, and the only way to achieve salvation was to have confessed all one's sins and at least begun a cycle of penance at the time of one's death. Christians lived in fear of dying suddenly, unconfessed. The purchase of indulgences, membership in penitential brotherhoods, ritualized charity, and veneration of popular saints were seen as ways to acquire merit in the eyes of God.

Luther came to believe that the church's requirement that believers achieve salvation by means of confession, contrition, and penance made too great a demand on the faithful. Instead, Luther said, citing the New Testament, salvation (or justification) was God's gift to the faithful. Luther's belief is known as **justification by faith.** Acts of charity were important products resulting from God's love, but in Luther's opinion, they were not necessary for salvation. Late in his life Luther explained how he came by these ideas:

> Though I lived as a monk without reproach, I felt that I was a sinner before God with an extremely disturbed conscience. I could not believe that he was placated by my [acts of penance]. I did not love, yes, I hated the righteous God who punishes sinners. At last, by the mercy of God, I gave context to the words, namely, "In it the righteousness of God is revealed, as it is written, 'He who through faith is righteous shall live.'" There I began to understand that the righteous lives by a gift of God, namely by faith. Here I felt that I was altogether born again and had entered paradise itself through open gates.[2]

Although Luther recalled a sudden, dramatic revelation, it now seems clear that his insight developed slowly over the course of his academic career and during his defense of his teachings. Nonetheless, his recollection conveys a sense of the novelty of his theology and suggests why his attack on the late medieval church proved to be so much more devastating than the complaints of earlier critics.

Others had complained of impious priests, an unresponsive bureaucracy, and a church too much involved in matters of government, but the theology that Luther developed struck at the doctrinal foundations of the church itself. Luther separated justification from acts of sanctification—from the good works or charity expected of all Christians. In Luther's theology the acts of piety so typical of the medieval church were quite unnecessary for salvation because Christ's sacrifice had brought justification once and for all. Justification came entirely from God and was independent of human works. Luther argued that the Christian was at the same time sinner and saved, so the penitential cycle and careful preparation for a "good death" were, in his opinion, superfluous.

justification by faith   Luther's doctrine that Christians can be saved only by grace, a free gift of God and independent of any penitential or charitable acts.

Luther also attacked the place of the priesthood in the sacramental life of the church and, by extension, the power and authority a church might claim in public life. The church taught that, through the actions of ordained priests, Christ was really present in the bread and wine of the sacrament of Holy Communion. Luther agreed that the sacrament transformed the bread and wine into the body and blood of Christ, but he denied that priests had a role in the transformation. Priests, in Luther's view, were not mediators between God and individual Christians. John Wyclif and Jan Hus (see page 319) had argued against the spiritual authority of unworthy priests. Luther, however, challenged the role of all clergy, and of the institutional church itself, in the attainment of salvation. Thus he argued for a "priesthood of all believers."

Controversy over Indulgences

In the years before 1517 Luther's views on salvation and his reservations about the traditional ways of teaching theology attracted little interest outside his own university. Matters changed, however, when he questioned the sale of indulgences. Indulgences were often granted as rewards for pilgrimages or for noteworthy acts of charity or sacrifice. The papacy frequently authorized the sale of indulgences to pay various expenses. Unscrupulous priests often left the impression that purchase of an indulgence freed a soul from Purgatory. After getting no response to his initial complaints, Luther made his "Ninety-five Theses" public. He probably posted his document on the door of the Wittenberg Castle church, the usual way to announce topics for theological debates. His text created a firestorm when it was quickly translated and printed throughout German-speaking lands. His charges against the sale of indulgences encapsulated German feelings about unworthy priests and economic abuses by the clergy. Luther was acclaimed as the spokesman of the German people.

Online Study Center **Improve Your Grade**
Primary Source: Instruction for Selling Indulgences

In a debate with a papal representative in Leipzig in 1519, Luther was forced to admit that in some of his positions he agreed with the Czech reformer Jan Hus, who had been burned at the stake as a heretic in 1415. In the Leipzig debate and in hearings the following year, Luther responded to his critics and tried to explain more fully the nature of the changes he advocated. Three tracts were especially important. In *Address to the Christian Nobility of the German Nation* Luther urged the princes to reject papal claims of temporal and spiritual authority. (See the box "The Written Record: Martin Luther's Address to the Christian Nobility of the German Nation.") In *On the Babylonian Captivity of the Church*

he argued for the principle of *sola scriptura*—that is, church authority had to be based on biblical teachings. In *On Christian Freedom* he explained clearly his understanding of salvation: "A Christian has all he needs in faith and needs no works to justify him." Luther was speaking of spiritual freedom from unnecessary ritual, not social or political freedom. This distinction would later be crucial to Luther's opposition to political and economic protests by peasants and artisans.

In 1520 Pope Leo X (r. 1513–1521) condemned Luther's teachings and gave him sixty days to recant. Luther refused to do so and publicly burned the papal letter. In 1521 Emperor **Charles V** called an imperial diet, or parliament, at Worms to deal with the religious crisis. Charles demanded that Luther submit to papal authority. Luther, however, explained that religious decisions must be based on personal experience and conscience, as both were informed by a study of Scripture:

> Unless I am convicted by the testimony of Scripture or by clear reason, for I do not trust either in the Pope or in councils alone, since it is well known that they have often erred and contradicted themselves, I cannot and will not retract anything, for it is neither safe nor right to go against conscience.[3]

Luther's confession was a dramatic rejection of church authority. It became a statement of personal conscience when a later editor added the famous "Here I stand. I can do no other, may God help me."

The emperor and his allies stayed firmly in the papal camp (see **MAP 14.1**), and the excommunicated Luther was placed under an imperial ban—that is, declared an outlaw. As Luther left the Diet of Worms, friendly princes took him to Wartburg Castle in Saxony, where they could protect him. During a year of isolation at Wartburg, Luther used Erasmus's edition of the Greek New Testament as the basis of a translation of the New Testament into German, which became an influential literary as well as religious work.

THE REFORMATION OF THE COMMUNITIES

Luther challenged the authority of the clerical hierarchy and called on laypeople to take responsibility for their own salvation. His ideas spread rapidly in the towns and countryside of Germany because he and his followers took advantage of the new technology of

sola scriptura   Luther's doctrine that all religious doctrines and authority had to be based on biblical teachings.

Charles V   Holy Roman emperor and King Charles I of Spain. His empire included Spain, Italy, the Low Countries, Germany, and the New World.

MARTIN LUTHER'S ADDRESS TO THE CHRISTIAN NOBILITY OF THE GERMAN NATION

Luther wrote this tract to the rulers of Germany to explain the nature of his conflict with the church over ecclesiastical authority. In this excerpt he outlines his disagreements with the system of clerical status and immunities that had grown throughout the Middle Ages.

The Romanists have very cleverly built three walls around themselves. In the first place, when pressed by the temporal power, they have made decrees and declared that the temporal power had no jurisdiction over them, but that on the contrary, the spiritual power is above the temporal. In the second place, when the attempt is made to reprove them with the Scriptures, they raise the objection that only the Pope may interpret the Scriptures. In the third place if threatened with a council, their story is that no one may summon a council but the Pope.

Let us begin by attacking the first wall. It is pure invention that the Pope, bishops, priests, and monks are called the spiritual estate while princes, lords, craftsmen, and peasants are the temporal estate. This is indeed a piece of deceit and hypocrisy: all Christians are truly of the spiritual estate. The Pope or bishop anoints, shaves heads, ordains, consecrates, and prescribes garb different from that of the laity, but he can never make a man into a Christian or into a spiritual man by so doing. He might well make a man into a hypocrite or a humbug and a blockhead, but never a Christian or a spiritual man. Therefore a priest in Christendom is nothing else but an office-

holder. As long as he holds his office, he takes precedence; where he is deposed, he is a peasant or a townsman like anybody else.

The second wall is still more loosely built and less substantial. The Romanists want to be the only masters of Holy Scripture, although they never learn a thing from the Bible their life long. Besides, if we are all priests, and all have one faith, one gospel, one sacrament, why should we not also have the power to test and judge what is right or wrong in matters of faith?

The third wall falls of itself, when the first two are down. When the Pope acts contrary to the Scriptures, it is our duty to stand by the Scriptures and to reprove him and to constrain him, according to the word of Christ. The Romanists have no basis in Scripture for their claim that the Pope alone has the right to call or to confirm a council. This is just their own ruling, and it is only valid so long as it is not harmful to Christendom or contrary to the laws of God.

QUESTIONS

1. What are the ideas that Luther claims the papacy uses to protect itself from criticism?

2. Under what conditions does Luther allow that church authorities may make rules?

Source: Martin Luther, "Three Treatises," in *The American Edition of Luther's Works* (Philadelphia: Fortress Press, 1970), pp. 10–22. Copyright © 1943 Muhlenberg Press. Used by permission of Augsburg Fortress.

---

printing. (See the feature "The Visual Record: A Reformation Woodcut.") Perhaps 300,000 copies of his early tracts were published in the first years of the protest. Luther's claim that the Scriptures must be the basis of all life and his appeal to the judgment of the laity made sense to the men and women in towns and villages, where councils of local people were accustomed to making decisions based on ideas of the common good. It is also true that townspeople and villagers saw religious and civic life as being inextricably interconnected. For them the notion of a religiously neutral act was unthinkable.

The impact of Luther's ideas quickly became evident. If the active intercession of the clergy was not necessary for the salvation of individuals, then, according to Luther's followers, there was no reason for the clergy to remain unmarried and celibate, nor for men and

women to cloister themselves in monasteries and convents. Also, maintained Luther's partisans, the laity's participation in the sacrament of the Eucharist need not be restricted. Thus the priest must distribute wine to the congregants along with the bread. With the spread of Luther's ideas came the end of a very visual part of clerical power. Because Luther's followers believed that penitential acts were not prerequisites for salvation, they tended to set aside the veneration of saints and give up pilgrimages to the shrines and holy places all over Europe.

Many historians have referred to the spread of these reform ideas as the "Reformation of the Common Man." In Strasbourg, Nuremberg, Zurich, and other towns ideas about the primacy of the Bible and attacks on clerical privilege were spread by "people's priests." These individuals were hired by the town

MAP 14.1   Reform in Germany, 1517–1555
The pattern of religious reform in Germany was complex. Although some territorial princes, such as the dukes of Bavaria, rejected reform, most free towns, particularly those in the southwest, adopted it.

government to preach and teach, and to care for the souls in the community. Many of the most famous reformers initially gained a following through preaching. The message seems to have spread especially quickly among artisan and mercantile groups, which put pressure on town governments to press for reform. Agitation was often riotous. One resident of Augsburg exposed himself during a church service to protest what he believed was an evil and idolatrous service. Women on both sides of the reform stepped out of traditional ideas about male and female roles. For instance, a "common man" was understood to be the sturdy bulwark of the sacred community, but a "common woman" was a prostitute. Even women tended to accept these stereotypes. Nonetheless, aristocratic women such as Margaret of Angoulême (ohn-goo-LEM) in France (see page 439) supported and protected reformers. Other women wrote tracts advocating reform or defending the old order, and still others used shovels and rakes to defend religious values.

The process of reform in Zurich is instructive. In 1519 the people's priest of Zurich was **Huldrych Zwingli** (SVING-lee) (1484–1531), son of a rural official from a nearby village. After a university education he became a typical late medieval country priest, right down to his publicly acknowledged mistress. Yet after experiences as a military chaplain and an acquaintance with the humanist writings of Erasmus, Zwingli began to preach strongly biblical sermons. In 1522 he defended a group of laymen who protested by breaking the required Lenten fast. Later in the same year he requested episcopal permission to marry. Early in 1523 he led a group of reformers in a public debate over the nature of the church. The city council declared in favor of the reformers, and Zurich became in effect a Protestant city.

Huldrych Zwingli   Town preacher of Zurich and leading reformer in Switzerland and southwest Germany. He emphasized the role of the godly community in the process of individual salvation.

Unlike Luther, Zwingli believed that reform should be a communal movement—that town governments should take the lead in bringing reform to the community. Zwingli explained that the moral regeneration of individuals was an essential part of God's salvation. In the years following 1523 the reformers restructured church services, abolishing the mass. They also removed religious images from churches and suppressed monastic institutions. Zwingli further disagreed with Luther about the nature of the sacrament of Holy Communion. Whereas Luther, like Catholic theologians, accepted that Christ was truly present in the bread and wine, Zwingli argued that Christ's presence was merely spiritual—that the bread and wine only signified Christ. This disagreement created within the reform movement a division that made a common response to papal or imperial pressure difficult.

The reform message spread from towns into the countryside, but often with effects that the reformers did not expect or desire. Luther thought his message was a spiritual and theological one. Many peasants and modest artisans, however, believed that Luther's message of biblical freedom carried material as well as theological meaning.

In many parts of Germany villagers and peasants found themselves under increasing pressure from landlords and territorial princes. Taking advantage of changed economic and political conditions, these lords were intent on regaining claims to ancient manorial rights, on suppressing peasant claims to use common lands, and on imposing new taxes and tithes. Like townspeople, peasants saw religious and material life as closely connected. They argued that new tithes and taxes not only upset tradition but violated the Word of God. Using Luther's argument that authority should be based on the Scriptures, peasants from the district of Zurich, for example, petitioned the town council in 1523 and 1524, claiming that they should not be required to pay tithes on their produce because there was no biblical justification for doing so. Townsmen rejected the peasants' demand, noting that although the Bible did not stipulate such payments, it also did not forbid them. Accordingly, the peasants should make them "out of love"—that is, because they were traditional.

Demands that landlords and magistrates give up human ordinances and follow "Godly Law" soon turned violent. Peasants, miners, and villagers in 1524 and 1525 participated in a series of uprisings that began on the borderlands between Switzerland and Germany and spread throughout southwestern Germany, upper Austria, and even northern Italy. Bands of peasants and villagers, perhaps a total of 300,000 in the empire, revolted against their seigneurial lords or even their territorial overlords.

Luther initially counseled landlords and princes to redress the just grievances. As reports of riots and increased violence continued to reach Wittenberg, however, Luther condemned the rebels as "mad dogs" and urged that they be suppressed. Territorial princes and large cities quickly raised armies to meet the threat. The peasants were defeated and destroyed in a series of battles in April 1525. When it became clear that the reformers were unwilling to follow the implications of their own theology, villagers and peasants lost interest in the progress of the reform. As a townsman of Zurich commented, "Many came to a great hatred of the preachers, where before they would have bitten off their feet for the Gospel."[4]

JOHN CALVIN AND THE REFORMED TRADITION

The revolts of 1524 and 1525 demonstrated the mixed messages traveling under the rubric "true" or "biblical" religion. In the 1530s the theological arguments of the reformers began to take on a greater clarity, mostly because of the Franco-Swiss reformer **John Calvin** (1509–1564). Calvin had a humanistic education in Paris and became a lawyer before coming under the influence of reform-minded thinkers in France. In 1534 he fled from Paris as royal pressures against reformers increased. He arrived in Geneva in 1536, where he would remain, except for a short exile, until the end of his life.

Because of Geneva's central location and the power of Calvin's theology, it quickly came to rival Wittenberg as a source of Protestant thought. Reformed preachers moved easily from Geneva to France, Scotland, England, and the Low Countries, carrying with them Calvin's ideas about salvation and the godly. Until the end of his life Calvin was a magnet drawing people interested in reform.

The heart of Calvin's appeal lay in his formal theological writings. In 1536 he published the first of many editions of the *Institutes of the Christian Religion*, which was to become the summa of Reformed theology. In it Calvin laid out a doctrine of the absolute power of God and the complete depravity and powerlessness of humanity.

Like Luther, Calvin viewed salvation as a mysterious gift from God. Yet Calvin differed from Luther in a crucial aspect. Salvation was by grace, but it was part of a progressive sanctification. This was a critical difference, for Luther did not believe that human behavior could be transformed. We are, he said, "simultaneously justified and sinners." By contrast, Calvin believed that there could be no salvation "if we do not also live a holy life." Thus the religious behavior of the individual and the community was an essential gift of justification. As

John Calvin   A Franco-Swiss theologian whose *Institutes of the Christian Religion* was the key text of Reformed theology. He stressed the absolute power of God.

THE VISUAL RECORD

A Reformation Woodcut

Erhard Schön's 1533 woodcut "There Is No Greater Treasure Here on Earth Than an Obedient Wife Who Desires Honor" and other broadsheets like it informed and amused Europeans of all walks of life in the late fifteenth and sixteenth centuries. Schön's image of a henpecked husband and his wife followed by others would have been instantly recognizable to most people. Accompanying texts clarified the message implied in the woodcut itself. But how may we, centuries later, "read" this message? How does the modern historian analyze Schön's broadsheet to investigate popular ideas about social roles, religion, and politics? What do this and similar broadsheets tell us about popular responses to the social and religious tumults of the sixteenth century?

Look at the simple and clear lines of the woodcut. They give a clue about the popularity of broadsheets. They were cheap and easy to produce and were printed on inexpensive paper. Artists would sketch an image that an artisan would later carve onto a block. A printer could produce a thousand or more copies from a single block. Even famous artists such as Albrecht Dürer (see pages 365–366) sold highly profitable prints on religious, political, and cultural themes.

Almost anyone could afford broadsheets. Laborers and modest merchants decorated their houses with pictures on popular themes. In the middle of the fifteenth century, before the Reformation, most images were of saints. It was widely believed, for example, that anyone who looked at an image of Saint Christopher would not die on that day.

During the political and religious unrest of the sixteenth century, artists increasingly produced images that referred to the debates over religion. Schön himself made his living in Nuremberg producing and selling woodcuts. He and other artists in the city were closely tuned to the attitudes of the local population. One popular image was titled "The Roman Clergy's Procession into Hell."

Schön's "Obedient Wife" reflects a fear shared by both Protestants and Catholics: the rebellious nature of women. Evidence suggests that women in the late fifteenth and sixteenth centuries may have been marrying at a later age and thus were likely to be more independent-minded than their younger

sisters. The ranks of single women were swollen by widows and by former nuns who had left convents and liberated themselves from male supervision. Thus it was not difficult for men in the sixteenth century to spot women who seemed dangerously free from male control.

Let us turn again to the woodcut, to see what worried villagers and townspeople and how Schön depicted their fears. Notice the henpecked husband. He is harnessed to a cart carrying laundry. Both the harness and the laundry were popular images associated with women's duties. During popular festivals German villagers often harnessed unmarried women to a plow to signify that they were shirking their duty by not marrying and raising children. Doing the laundry was popularly thought to be the first household chore that a powerful wife would force on her weak-kneed husband. Countless other images show women, whip in hand, supervising foolish husbands as they pound diapers with a laundry flail. "Woe is me," says the poor man, all this because "I took a wife." As if the message were not clear enough, look at what the woman carries in her left hand: his purse, his sword, and his pants. (The question "Who wears the pants in the family?" was as familiar then as it is now.) But the woman responds that he is in this position not because of marriage but because he has been carousing: "If you will not work to support me, then you must wash, spin, and draw the cart."*

The figures following the cart are commenting on the situation. The young journeyman is asking the maiden at his side, "What do you say about this?" She responds coyly, "I have no desire for such power." The woman dressed as a fool counsels the young man never to marry and thus to avoid anxiety and suffering. But an old man, identified as "the wise man," closes the procession and ends the debate. "Do not listen to this foolish woman," he counsels. "God determines how your life together will be, so stay with her in love and suffering and always be patient."

---

*Keith Moxey, *Peasants, Warriors and Wives: Popular Imagery in the Reformation* (Chicago: University of Chicago Press, 1989), pp. 108–109; includes a translation of portions of the text in the broadsheet.

"There Is No Greater Treasure Here on Earth Than an Obedient Wife Who Desires Honor,"
Erhard Schön   *(Schlossmuseum, Gotha)*

If we think about this woodcut's images and text, we can understand the contrary hopes and fears in sixteenth-century Germany. Like the young woman, the Christian wife was expected to eschew power either inside or outside the home. Martin Luther concluded that "the husband is the head of the wife even as Christ is head of the Church. Therefore as the Church is subject to Christ, so let wives be subject to their husbands in everything" (Ephesians 5:23–24). Authority was to be in the hands of husbands and fathers. But if the good wife was required to avoid power, the good husband was expected to follow Luther's precepts for the Christian family. As the wise old man observes, the husband must be a loving and forgiving master.

Schön's woodcut and others similar to it should remind you of the "argument over women" discussed in Chapter 12 (see page 369). The words of the wise man and the young maid bring to mind Christine de Pizan's *Book of the City of the Ladies* when they urge love and understanding, but their

hopefulness is undercut by the power and immediacy of the image. As the broadsheet clearly demonstrates, suspicion of women characterized even the most simple literature of Reformation Europe.

QUESTIONS

1. What conclusion might a viewer draw about women from thinking about the three women pictured in this woodcut?

2. How does the image of the godly marriage differ in this woodcut and the picture of the holy household (page 445)?

Online Study Center
Improve Your Grade Visual Record Activities

a result, Calvin believed that it was the church's duty to promote moral progress. Public officials were to be "vicars of God." They had the power to lead and correct both the faithful and the unregenerate sinners who lived in Christian communities. In his years in Geneva Calvin tried to create a "Christian Commonwealth," but Geneva was far from a theocracy. Calvin's initial attempts to create a Christian community by requiring public confession and allowing church leaders to discipline sinners were rejected by Geneva's city council, which exiled Calvin in 1538.

On his return in 1541 he sought to institute church reforms modeled on those he had observed in the Protestant city of Strasbourg. Calvin's Reformed church hierarchy was made up of four offices: preachers, teachers, deacons, and elders. Preachers and teachers saw to the care and education of the faithful. Deacons, as in the early church, were charged with attending to the material needs of the congregation. Elders—the true leaders of the Genevan church—were selected from the patriciate who dominated the civil government of the city. Thus it makes as much sense to speak of a church governed by the town as a town dominated by the church. The elders actively intervened in education, charity, and attempts to regulate prostitution. Consistories, or church courts, made up of preachers and community elders who enforced moral and religious values, became one of the most important characteristics of Reformed (Calvinist) communities.

Most reformers accepted a commonplace medieval idea that since salvation depended on God's gift of grace, God in effect "predestined" some people to be saved. They differed on whether this meant that God predestined others to damnation. Luther argued that

Iconoclasm

Calvinists believed that Christians had to live in communities in which "true religion" was practiced. Iconoclasts (image smashers) cleansed churches of all paintings and statuary that might lead people back to the worship of idols—that is, the medieval cult of saints. This illustration shows just how organized iconoclasm really was.
(The Fotomas Index, U.K.)

Christians could never know why some people were saved and others were not. Calvin, however, believed that God's power was such that "eternal life is foreordained for some, eternal damnation for others."

Calvin suggested that the elect, those predestined for salvation, would benefit from "signs of divine benevolence," an idea that would have a profound impact on the Calvinist understanding of the relationship of wealth to spiritual life. Calvin believed that good works and a well-ordered society were the result of God's grace. By the seventeenth century many followers of Calvin in Europe's commercial centers believed that the elect had a duty to work in the secular world and that wealth accumulated in business was a sign of God's favor. It was an idea nicely adapted to the increasingly wealthy society of early modern Europe.

Online Study Center   **Improve Your Grade**
Primary Source: Institutes: Calvin on Predestination and the Elect

That connection between salvation and material life, however, lay in the future. The aspect of election that most interested Calvin was the creation by the elect of a truly Christian community. To accomplish this, Reformed churches—that is, those that took their lead from Zwingli and Calvin—purged themselves of any manifestation of "superstition." Like Zwinglians, they rejected the idea that Christ was really present in the sacrament of Holy Communion. They rejected the role of saints. They removed from their churches and destroyed paintings and statuary that they believed were indications of idolatry.

Reformed churchmen reacted promptly and harshly to events that seemed to threaten either church or state. The most famous episode involved the capture, trial, and execution of Michael Servetus (1511–1553), a Spanish physician and radical theologian who rejected traditional doctrines such as the Trinity and specifically criticized many of Calvin's teachings in the *Institutes*. After corresponding with Servetus for a time, Calvin remarked that if Servetus were in Geneva, "I would not suffer him to get out alive." After living in various parts of Europe, Servetus eventually did come anonymously to Geneva. He was recognized and arrested. Calvin was as good as his word. After a public debate and trial Servetus was burned at the stake for blaspheming the Trinity and the Christian religion. Calvin's condemnation of Servetus was all too typical of Christians in the sixteenth century. Lutherans, Calvinists, and Catholics all believed that protection of true religion required harsh measures against the ignorant, the immoral, and the unorthodox. All too few would have agreed with the humanist reformer Sebastian Castellio that "To burn a heretic is not to defend a doctrine, but to burn a man."[5]

THE RADICAL REFORM OF THE ANABAPTISTS

Michael Servetus was but one of a number who felt Luther, Zwingli, and Calvin had not gone far enough. Called **Anabaptists** (or "rebaptizers" because of their rejection of infant baptism) or simply "radicals," they tended to take biblical commands more literally than the mainline reformers. They represented a broad social movement dominated by peasants and modest townspeople. They were more interested in behavior and community standards than in learned theological arguments. They believed that only adults should be baptized, and then only after confession of sin. They believed that Christians should live apart in communities of the truly redeemed. Thus they refused to take civil oaths or hold public office, for to do so would be to compromise with "the Abomination," that is, unreformed civil society.

Online Study Center   **Improve Your Grade**
Primary Source: An Anabaptist Martyr Takes the Stand: Michael Sattler Condemned to Death

The earliest of the radicals allied themselves with the rebels of 1524 and 1525. Thomas Müntzer (1490–1525) was an influential preacher who believed in divine revelation through visions and dreams. His visions told him that the poor were the true elect and that the end of the world was at hand. An active participant in the uprisings of 1525, Müntzer called on the elect to drive out the ungodly. After the defeat of the rebels, he was captured and executed by the German princes.

Other radicals, such as the revolutionaries who took control of the northern German city of Münster, rejected infant baptism, adopted polygamy, and proclaimed a new "Kingdom of Righteousness." The reformers of Münster instituted the new kingdom in the city by rebaptizing those who joined their cause and expelling those who opposed them. They abolished private property rights and instituted new laws concerning morality and behavior. Leadership in the city eventually passed to a tailor, Jan of Leiden (d. 1535), who proclaimed himself the new messiah and lord of the world. The Anabaptists were opposed by the prince-bishop of Münster, the political and religious lord of the city. After a sixteen-month siege, the bishop and his allies recaptured the city in 1535. Besieging forces massacred men, women, and children. Jan of Leiden was captured and executed by mutilation with red-hot tongs.

The Münster revolutionaries were a sign that Anabaptist critics of civil society had to walk a careful

Anabaptists   Radical reformers in Germany and Switzerland who emphasized that baptism should only be of adults and that Christians should separate themselves into communities of the "truly redeemed."

line. Groups like the Swiss Brethren remained suspicious of civil society even as they limited the more radical enthusiasts. With the destruction of the Münster revolutionaries in 1535, the Anabaptist movement turned inward. Under leaders such as Menno Simons (1495–1561), who founded the Mennonites, and Jakob Hutter (d. 1536), who founded the Hutterian Brethren, or Hutterites, they rejected their predecessors' violent attempts to establish truly holy cities. To varying degrees they also rejected connections with civil society, military service, and even civil courts. They did, however, believe that their own communities were exclusively of the elect. They tended to close themselves off from outsiders and enforce a strict discipline over their members. The elders of these communities were empowered to excommunicate or "shun" those who violated the groups' precepts. Anabaptist communities have proved unusually durable. Hutterite and Mennonite communities continue to exist in western Europe, North America, and parts of the former Soviet Union.

Like Luther, all of the early reformers appealed to the authority of the Bible in their attacks on church tradition. Yet in the villages and towns of Germany and Switzerland, many radicals were prepared to move far beyond the positions Luther had advocated. When they did so, Luther found himself in the odd position of appealing for vigorous action by the very imperial authorities whose previous inaction had allowed his own protest to survive.

SECTION SUMMARY

- Women played an important role in popular religious observance in the Middle Ages.

- Luther's religious ideas challenged the late medieval church's understanding of sin and salvation rather than immoral behavior.

- The key to Luther's theology was his emphasis on the role of grace and biblical authority.

- Calvin's religious reforms centered on the role of the Reformed community in enforcing religious discipline.

- Radical reformers and Anabaptists formed small, tightly controlled communities suspicious of the outside world.

THE EMPIRE OF CHARLES V (R. 1519–1556)

What political factors limited Charles V's ability to respond to the religious crisis?

uther believed that secular authorities should be neutral in religious matters. In his eyes the success of the early Reformation was simply God's will:

> I simply taught, preached and wrote God's Word; otherwise I did nothing. And while I slept or drank Wittenberg beer with my friends, the Word so greatly weakened the Papacy that no prince or emperor ever inflicted such losses on it.[6]

Luther's belief in the Word of God was absolute, yet he must have known, even as he drank his beer, that the Holy Roman emperor could have crushed the reform movements if he had been able to enforce imperial decrees. But attempts to resolve religious conflict became entangled with attempts to hold together the family lands of the Habsburg emperor. And political rivalries among the various German princes made a uniform policy impossible. The eventual religious settlement required a constitutional compromise that preserved the virtual autonomy of the great princes of Germany. Charles had dreamed of using his imperial office to restore and maintain the political and religious unity of Europe. The realities of sixteenth-century Europe, however, made nobles afraid of the emperor even when he tried to preserve the unity of the church.

IMPERIAL CHALLENGES

Emperor Charles V (r. 1519–1556) was the beneficiary of a series of marriages that, in the words of his courtiers, seemed to re-create the empire of Charlemagne (see Map 15.1 on page 454). From his father, Philip of Habsburg, he inherited claims to Austria, the imperial crown, and Burgundian lands that included the Low Countries and the county of Burgundy. Through his mother, Joanna, the daughter of Ferdinand and Isabella of Spain, Charles became heir to the kingdoms of Castile, Aragon, Sicily, Naples, and Spanish America. During

THE HABSBURG SUCCESSION, 1493–1556

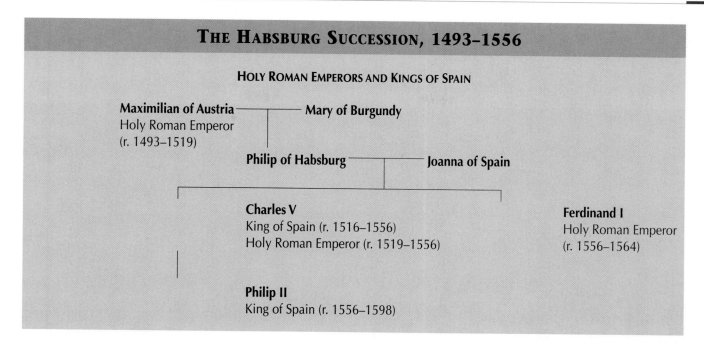

HOLY ROMAN EMPERORS AND KINGS OF SPAIN

Maximilian of Austria ——— **Mary of Burgundy**
Holy Roman Emperor
(r. 1493–1519)

Philip of Habsburg ——— **Joanna of Spain**

Charles V
King of Spain (r. 1516–1556)
Holy Roman Emperor (r. 1519–1556)

Ferdinand I
Holy Roman Emperor
(r. 1556–1564)

Philip II
King of Spain (r. 1556–1598)

the Italian wars of the early sixteenth century Charles's holdings in Italy expanded to include the duchy of Milan and most of the rest of Lombardy. By 1506 he was duke in the Burgundian lands, in 1516 he became king of Aragon and Castile, and in 1519 he was elected Holy Roman emperor. Every government in Europe had to deal with one part or another of Charles's empire. His chancellor enthused, "[God] has set you on the way towards a world monarchy, towards the gathering of all Christendom under a single shepherd."

Charles seems to have sincerely desired such a world monarchy, but he faced challenges in each of the areas under his control. In Castile, for example, grandees, townspeople, and peasants felt they had grounds for complaint. They objected that taxes were too heavy and that Charles disregarded the Cortes and his natural advisers, the old nobility. But most of all they complained that too many of his officials were foreigners whom he had brought with him from his home in Flanders. Protests festered in the towns and villages of Castile and finally broke out into a revolt called the *Comunero* (townsmen's or citizens') movement. Between 1517 and 1522, when religious reform was making dramatic advances in Germany, many of the most important towns of Spain were in open rebellion against the Crown. Charles's forces eventually took control of the situation, and by 1522 he had crushed the Comuneros. But in the critical years between 1522 and 1530 he was careful to spend much of his time in his Spanish kingdoms.

Charles's claims in Italy, as well as in the Pyrenees and the Low Countries, brought him into direct conflict with the Valois kings of France. In the critical 1520s the Habsburgs and the Valois fought a series of wars (see page 328). Charles dramatically defeated the French at Pavia in northern Italy in 1525, sacked and occupied Rome in 1527, and became the virtual arbiter of Italian politics. The volatile situation in Italy made for cynical alliances. In the course of the struggle the Catholic Francis I of France, whose title was "the Most Christian King," found it to his advantage to ally himself with Charles's most serious opponents, the Protestants and the Turks. Francis demonstrated the truth of Machiavelli's dictum that private virtues play a small role in political and diplomatic life. The Habsburg-Valois Wars dragged on until, in exhaustion, the French king Henry II (r. 1547–1559) and the Spanish king Philip II (r. 1556–1598) signed the Treaty of Cateau-Cambrésis in 1559 (see page 328).

Charles was not the only ruler to claim the title "emperor" and a tradition of authority reaching back to the Roman Empire. After the conquest of Constantinople in 1453, the sultan of the Ottoman Turks began to refer to himself as "the Emperor." After consolidating control of Constantinople and the Balkans, Turkish armies under the command of the emperor Suleiman (r. 1520–1566), known as "the Magnificent," resumed their expansion to the north and west. After capturing Belgrade, Turkish forces soundly defeated a Hungarian army at the Battle of Mohács in 1526. Charles appealed for unity within Christendom against the threat. Even Martin Luther agreed that Christians should unite during invasion.

Suleiman's army besieged Vienna in 1529 before being forced to retreat. The Turks also deployed a navy in the Mediterranean and, with French encouragement,

The Capture of Belgrade, 1521

During the sixteenth century Ottoman Turks dominated the Balkans militarily and were a significant force in European diplomacy. They were masters of coordinated attacks combining artillery and infantry. *(Österreichische Nationalbibliothek)*

began a series of raids along the coasts of Italy and Spain. The Turkish fleet remained a threat throughout the sixteenth century. The reign of Suleiman marked the permanent entry of Turkey into the European military and diplomatic system. Turkish pressure was yet another reason Charles was unable to deal with German Protestants in a direct and uncompromising way. (See the box "The Global Record: Duels Among Europeans and Turks.")

GERMAN POLITICS

The political configuration of Germany had an ongoing influence on the course of religious reform. In 1500 Germany was much less centralized than France or England. The emperor's claims in most areas amounted to the right to collect modest taxes on households and individuals, a court of high justice, and the authority to proclaim imperial truces. Yet the empire lacked a unified legal system, and the emperor himself had only one vote on the imperial council. In many respects political centralization and innovation were characteristics of individual territories, not of the empire as a

whole. The power of the emperor depended on his relations with the towns and princes of Germany.

In the first years after Luther issued his "Ninety-five Theses," he was defended by the elector Frederick of Saxony, who held a key vote in Charles's quest for election as Holy Roman emperor. As long as Frederick protected Luther, imperial officials had to proceed against the reformer with caution. When Luther was outlawed by the imperial Diet of Worms in 1521, Frederick and many other princes and towns refused to enforce the edict against him and his followers unless their own grievances against the emperor and their complaints about the church were taken up at the same time. At the Diet of Speyer in 1526, delegates passed a resolution empowering princes and towns to settle religious matters in their territories as they saw it. In effect, this resolution legitimated the reform in territories where authorities chose to follow the new teachings and presaged the final religious settlement in Germany.

German princes took advantage of the emperor's relative powerlessness and made choices reflecting a complex of religious, political, and diplomatic issues. Electoral Saxony and ducal Saxony, the two parts of the

DUELS AMONG EUROPEANS AND TURKS

Augier Ghislain De Busbecq (1522–1592), a Flemish diplomat in the service of Ferdinand I of Austria (who became Emperor Ferdinand I after the abdication of Charles V), was twice sent to Constantinople as ambassador. Understanding the Turks and their interests was critical for the Germans as attacks by the Turks in eastern Europe prevented the empire from either suppressing the German Protestants or pressing German claims against the French. The following selection is part of a letter written from Constantinople in 1560. In it Busbecq discusses violence among the Turks. He contrasts Turkish political and individual control with the Europeans' desire for a violent defense of personal honor. Duels were an increasing problem in sixteenth-century Europe.

The mention I made a while ago of matters in the confines of Hungary, gives me occasion to tell you, what the Turks think of duels, which among Christians are accounted a singular badge of personal valor. There was one Arstambey, a sanjack [district official], who lived on the frontier of Hungary, who was very much famed as a robust person [Arsta signifies a lion in Turkish]. He was an expert with the bow; no man brandished his sword with more strength; none was more terrible to his enemy. Not far from his district there also dwelt one Ulybey, also a sanjack, who was jealous of the same praise. And this jealousy (initiated perhaps by other occasions) at length occasioned hatred and many bloody combats between them. It happened thus, Ulybey was called to Constantinople, upon what occasion I know not. When he arrived there, the Pashas [governors] had asked many questions of him in the Divan [court] concerning other matters. At last they demanded how it was that he and Arstambey came to fall out. To put his own cause in the best light, he said that once Arstambey had laid an ambush and wounded him treacherously. Which he said Arstambey need not have done, if he would have shown himself worthy of the name he bears because Ulybey often challenged him to fight hand to hand and never refused to meet him on the field. The Pashas, taking great offense, replied, "How dare you challenge a fellow soldier to a duel? What? Was there no Christian to fight with? Do both of you eat your emperor's bread? And yet, you attempt to take one another's life? What precedent did you have for this? Don't you know that whichever of you had died, the emperor would have lost a subject?" Whereupon, by their command, he was carried off to prison where he lay pining for many months. And at last, with difficulty, he was released, but with the loss of his reputation.

It is quite different among us Christians. Our people will draw their swords many times against each other before they ever come in sight of a public enemy, and unfortunately, they count it a brave and honorable thing to do. What should one do in such a case? Vice has usurped the seat of virtue and that which is worthy of punishment is counted noble and glorious.

QUESTIONS

1. How did Turkish officials understand the significance of private violence?

2. What most distinguishes the Turkish empire from Christendom?

Source: The Four Epistles of A.G. Busbequius Concerning His Embassy to Turkey (London: J. Taylor & J. Wyat, 1694), pp. 196–198.

---

province of Saxony, split over the issue of reform. Electoral Saxony, Luther's homeland, was Lutheran. Ducal Saxony was strongly Catholic. Especially in the autonomous towns many decisions about religion were often made with one eye on the choices made by neighbors and competitors.

Some rulers acted in ways that were even more consciously cynical and self-serving. The grand master of the religious order of the Teutonic Knights, Albrecht von Hohenzollern (1490–1568), who controlled the duchy of Prussia, renounced his monastic vows. Then, at the urging of Luther and other reformers, he secularized the order's estates (that is, he transferred them from church to private ownership), which then became East Prussia, hereditary lands of the Hohenzollern family. In other territories rulers managed to claim the properties of suppressed religious orders. Even when, as in the case of Count Philip of Hesse (1504–1567), much of the revenue from secularization was used to create hospitals and an organized system of charity, the reforming prince was still enriched.

Some rulers found their personal reservations about Luther reinforced by their fears of popular unrest. Luther's call for decisions based on personal conscience seemed to the dukes of Bavaria, for example, to repudiate princely authority and even to provoke anarchy. In the confused and fluid situation of the 1520s and 1530s, imperial interests were never the primary issue.

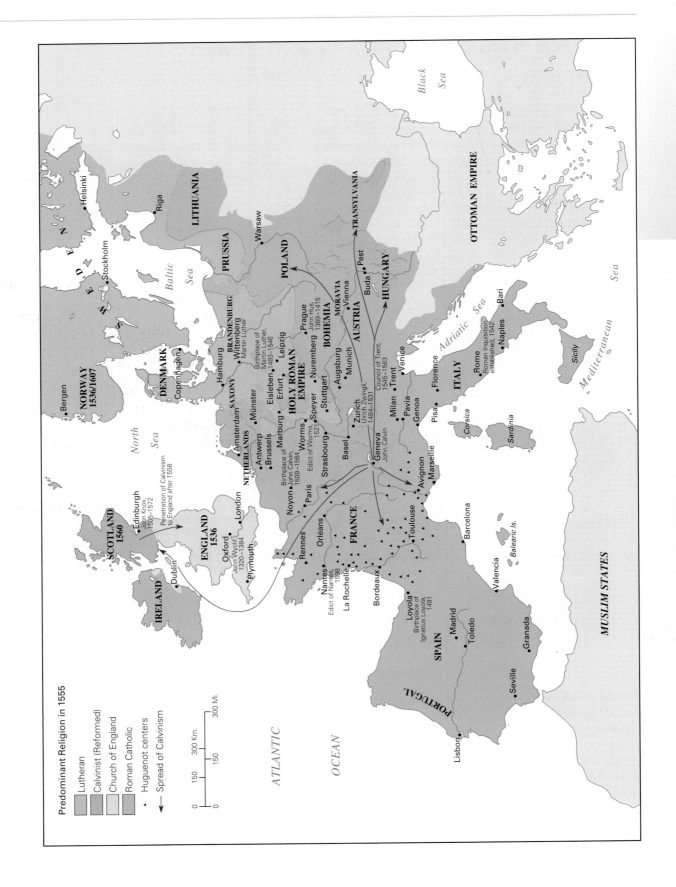

Predominant Religion in 1555

- Lutheran
- Calvinist (Reformed)
- Church of England
- Roman Catholic
- ◄ Huguenot centers
- → Spread of Calvinism

0   150   300 Km.

0   150   300 Mi.

ATLANTIC

OCEAN

North
Sea

IRELAND
Dublin

SCOTLAND
1560
Edinburgh
John Knox,
1505–1572

ENGLAND 1536
Oxford
John Wyclif,
1320–1384
London
Plymouth

Penetration of Calvinism
to England after 1558

NORWAY
1536/1607
Bergen

S W E D E N
Stockholm
Helsinki
Riga

Baltic
Sea

LITHUANIA

PRUSSIA
Warsaw

POLAND

DENMARK
Copenhagen
Hamburg

BRANDENBURG
Wittenberg
Martin Luther

SAXONY
Birthplace of
Martin Luther,
Eisleben 1483–1546
Erfurt
Leipzig

NETHERLANDS
Amsterdam
Münster
Antwerp
Brussels
Marburg

HOLY ROMAN
EMPIRE
Nuremberg
Speyer
Worms
Edict of Worms,
1521
Strasbourg
Birthplace of
John Calvin,
1509–1564
Noyon
Paris

Prague
John Hus,
1369–1415
BOHEMIA
MORAVIA
Vienna
AUSTRIA

Stuttgart
Augsburg
Munich

Basel
Zurich
Ulrich Zwingli,
1484–1531
Geneva
John Calvin

BUDA Pest
HUNGARY

TRANSYLVANIA

OTTOMAN EMPIRE

Black
Sea

Council of Trent,
1545–1563
Milan Trent
Pavia Venice
Genoa
Pisa Florence

Adriatic
Sea

Corsica

Sardinia

ITALY
Rome
Roman Inquisition
established, 1542

Bari
Naples

Sicily

Mediterranean
Sea

MUSLIM STATES

FRANCE
Rennes
Orléans
Toulouse
Marseille
Avignon

Nantes
Edict of Nantes,
1598
La Rochelle
Bordeaux

Barcelona

Balearic Is.

Valencia

Loyola
Birthplace of
Ignatius Loyola,
1491

SPAIN
Madrid
Toledo
Granada
Seville

PORTUGAL
Lisbon

THE RELIGIOUS SETTLEMENT

With the fading of the Turkish threat on Vienna in 1529, Charles V renewed his pressure on the German principalities at a meeting of the imperial diet at Augsburg in 1530. It was for this diet that Philipp Melanchthon (1497–1560), Luther's closest adviser, prepared the **Augsburg Confession,** which would become the basic statement of the Lutheran faith. Melanchthon hoped that the document would form the basis of compromise with Catholic powers, but that possibility was rejected out of hand by the imperial party. Charles aimed to affirm his strength in Germany by forcing the princes to end the reform movement and enforce bans on Luther's teachings.

The Protestant princes responded by forming the League of Schmalkalden. At first the founders of the league claimed that they were interested in protecting Lutheran preaching, but the league quickly developed as a center of opposition to imperial influence in general. Eventually Charles and a group of allied princes managed to defeat the league at the Battle of Mühlberg in 1547. The emperor was unable to continue pressure on the Protestants, however, because he had depended on the support of some Protestant princes in his battles with the league. As a result, even after military defeat, the Protestant princes were able to maintain religious autonomy. In the religious Peace of Augsburg of 1555, the emperor formally acknowledged the principle that sovereign princes could choose the religion to be practiced in their territories—*cuius regio, eius religio* ("whose territory, his religion"). There were limits, however: leaders had only two choices—remain under papal authority or adopt the Augsburg Confession outlined by Melanchthon. Reformed churches associated with Zwingli or Calvin were not legally recognized (see **MAP 14.2**).

Shortly after the settlement, Charles abdicated his Spanish and imperial titles. Exhausted by years of political and religious struggle, he ceded the imperial crown to his brother, Ferdinand (r. 1556–1564). He transferred his possessions in the Low Countries, Spain, Italy, and the New World to his son, Philip II (r. 1556–1598). Charles had believed his courtiers when they had compared his empire to that of the ancient Romans. He had accepted that his duty as emperor was to unite Christendom under one law and one church. But in no part of his empire did he ever command the authority that would have allowed him to unite his lands politically, let alone to re-establish religious unity. Following his abdication Charles retired to a monastery in Spain, where he died in 1558.

━━━━━━━ S E C T I O N   S U M M A R Y ━━━━━━━

- Charles V united under his personal rule Germany, the Low Countries, Spain, most of Italy, and Latin America.

- Political control in the area of Charles's empire was just weak enough that Charles was never able to act effectively against Luther and his allies.

- Throughout the sixteenth century the Ottoman Turks were a major threat to the western European powers.

- The religious Peace of Augsburg (1555) recognized the political and religious autonomy of the independent princes and towns.

THE ENGLISH REFORMATION, 1520–1603

Why did the English monarchs take the lead in efforts to reform the English church?

The Reformation in England is often called a monarchical Reformation. In contrast with Germany, where reform occurred in spite of imperial opposition, in England the Crown instituted the reform. As in Germany, however, institutional change in the church followed from both secular issues and reform ideas. In England an initially hostile monarch began to tolerate reform when he perceived the papacy as an unbiblical, tyrannical force blocking essential state policy. Although reformers were active in England, their success depended entirely on royal support. And by the middle of the sixteenth century, it was

Augsburg Confession Document written by Philipp Melanchthon that became the most widely accepted statement of the Lutheran faith.

royal interest in compromise that brought a settlement that left England a curious hybrid of reformed and traditional religious practices.

HENRY VIII AND THE MONARCHICAL REFORMATION

England was closely tied to Germany. Since the twelfth century large numbers of German merchants had lived and traded in England, and Cologne was home to a considerable English community. Anglo-German connections became especially significant during the Reformation. Reformers from Wittenberg and other Protestant towns had contact with English merchants from London who traded and traveled on the Continent. One reformer, William Tyndale (ca. 1494–1536), served as a bridge between the Continent and England. He had a humanistic education in classical languages and began working on a translation of the Bible in the 1520s. Forced by the church hierarchy to flee London, he visited Luther in Wittenberg before settling in Antwerp, where he completed his English New Testament. By 1526 copies of his translation and his religious tracts flooded England. By the 1520s Lutheran influence was noticeable in London and Cambridge. There is still debate about just how strong this early influence was. To some extent the ground may have been prepared for the reformers by the few surviving Lollards (see page 319), who tended to be literate and were an ideal market for Tyndale's English Bible and his numerous reformist tracts. But religious brotherhoods, lay piety, and traditional forms of penance remained an important part of religious life. If reform was to succeed, it required support from the king.

Henry VIII (r. 1509–1547) began his reign as a popular and powerful king. Handsome, athletic, and artistic, he seemed to be the ideal ruler. Henry took an interest in theology and humanistic culture. At first he was quite hostile to Luther's reform ideas. He wrote *Defense of the Seven Sacraments,* which earned him the title "Defender of the Faith" from a grateful Pope Leo X. Throughout his life Henry remained suspicious of many Protestant ideas, but he led the initial phase of the break with the papacy because of his political problems with the highly orthodox Holy Roman emperor Charles V. The first phase of the English Reformation was thus monarchical.

Henry VII had initiated closer relations with Spain when he married his eldest son, Arthur, Prince of Wales, to Ferdinand of Aragon's daughter, Catherine. After Arthur's death the future Henry VIII was married to his brother's widow in 1509. **Henry VIII** later tried to further the Anglo-imperial alliance when he arranged a treaty by which the emperor Charles V, who was Catherine of Aragon's nephew, agreed to marry Henry's daughter, Mary Tudor. But by the late 1520s the Anglo-imperial alliance fell apart when Charles, responding to Spanish pressures, renounced the proposed marriage and instead married a Portuguese princess.

Divorce Henry's relations with Charles were further hampered by what the English called "the King's Great Matter"—that is, his determination to divorce Catherine. Recalling the unrest of the Wars of the Roses (see page 339), Henry believed that he needed a son to ensure that the Tudors could maintain control of the English crown. By 1527 Henry and Catherine had a daughter, Mary, but no living sons. Henry became convinced that he remained without a male heir because, by biblical standards, he had committed incest by marrying his brother's widow. As Leviticus 20:21 says, "If a man takes his brother's wife, it is impurity; they shall remain childless." Henry desired an annulment. Unfortunately for him, Leo X's successor, Pope Clement VII (r. 1523–1534), was a virtual prisoner of imperial troops who had recently sacked Rome and taken control of most of Italy. As long as Charles supported Catherine of Aragon and his forces occupied Rome, a papal annulment was out of the question.

The king's advisers quickly divided into two camps. Sir Thomas More, humanist writer (see page 375), royal chancellor and staunch Catholic, urged the king to continue his policy of negotiation with the papacy and his efforts to destroy the growing Protestant party. Until his resignation in 1532, More led royal authorities in a vigorous campaign against the dissemination of the newly translated Tyndale Bible and against the spread of Protestant ideas. More was opposed and eventually ousted by a radical party of Protestants led by Thomas Cranmer (1489–1556) and Thomas Cromwell (1485?–1540), who saw in the king's desire for a divorce an effective wedge to pry Henry out of the papal camp. Cromwell, who eventually replaced More as chancellor, advised the king that the marriage problem could be solved by the English clergy without papal interference.

Monarchical Reformation Between 1532 and 1535 Henry and Parliament took a number of steps that effectively left the king in control of the church in England. Early in 1533 Cranmer was named archbishop of Canterbury. Later that year Parliament ruled that appeals of cases concerning wills, marriages, and ecclesiastical grants had to be heard in England. In May an English court annulled the king's marriage to Catherine. Four months later Henry's new queen, Anne Boleyn, gave birth to a daughter, Elizabeth.

Henry VIII King of England who broke with the church over the issue of his divorce. In the end Henry claimed that as king he was the head of the Church in England.

Reform of the Old Church
This woodcut shows the Protestant understanding of the reforms of Edward VI, the removal of Catholic paraphernalia, and Edward's patronage of the Bible and Holy Communion. *(Courtesy, Brown University Library)*

After the split began, the king started to seize church properties. Parliamentary action culminated in the passage of the **Act of Supremacy** in 1534, which declared the king to be "the Protector and only Supreme Head of the Church and the Clergy of England." Henry meant to enforce his control by requiring a public oath supporting the act. Sir Thomas More refused to take the oath and was arrested, tried, and executed for treason. In some respects Parliament had acted as an instrument of reform, in the manner of the German and Swiss town councils that moderated debates over church reform. In England, however, Parliament and perhaps a majority of the laity perceived this reform primarily as a political issue.

Cromwell and Cranmer had hoped to use "the King's Great Matter" as a way to begin a Lutheran-style reform of the church. But, though separated from the papal party, Henry remained suspicious of religious change. He complained of radicals who "do wrest and interpret and so untruly allege [novel understandings of Scripture] to subvert and overturn as well the sacraments of Holy Church as the power and authority of princes and magistrates." Between 1534 and Henry's death in 1547, neither the Protestant nor the Catholic party was able to gain the upper hand at court or at Canterbury. Substantive changes in the English church would be made by Henry's children.

REFORM AND COUNTER-REFORM UNDER EDWARD AND MARY

Prince Edward, Henry's only surviving son in 1547, was born to Henry's third wife, Jane Seymour. He was only 10 years old when his father died. By chance Edward Seymour, who was Prince Edward's uncle, and the Protestant faction were in favor at the time of Henry's death. Seymour was named duke of Somerset and Lord Protector of the young King Edward VI (r. 1547–1553). Under Somerset the Protestants were able to make significant

Act of Supremacy   Act of the English Parliament during the Protestant Reformation that finalized the break with the Catholic Church by declaring the king to be head of the Church of England. Henry VIII required a public oath supporting the act, which Sir Thomas More refused to take; More was then executed for treason.

changes in religious life in England. Edward completed the "dissolution of the monasteries"—the process of confiscating properties belonging to chapels and shrines—that his father had begun. In an act of great symbolic meaning, priests were legally allowed to marry; many had already done so. Finally, Archbishop Cranmer introduced the first edition of the English *Book of Common Prayer* in 1549. The publication updated some late medieval English prayers and combined them with liturgical and theological ideas taken from Luther, Zwingli, and Calvin. In its beautifully expressive English, it provided the laity with a primer on how to combine English religious traditions with reform theology. Later, continental Protestants were named to teach theology at Oxford and Cambridge. If Edward had not died of tuberculosis in 1553, England's reform would have looked very much like the movement in Switzerland and southern Germany.

Protestant reformers attempted to prevent Mary Tudor (r. 1553–1558), Henry's Catholic daughter, from claiming the throne, but Mary and the Catholic party quickly took control of the court and the church. Mary immediately declared previous reform decrees to be void. Cardinal Reginald Pole (1500–1558), who had advocated reform within the Catholic Church, became the center of the Catholic restoration party in Mary's England. Pole rooted out Protestants within the church. More than eight hundred gentlemen, clerics, and students fled England for Protestant havens on the Continent. Some officials, including Cranmer, chose to remain and paid with their lives. In all, three hundred Protestants, mostly artisans and laborers, were tried and executed by church courts, earning the queen her nickname, "Bloody Mary."

The policies of the queen brought about an abrupt change in official policy. Many parishes quickly and easily returned to traditional Roman religious practices. Statues were removed from hiding and restored to places of honor in churches and chapels. In many others there was an uneasy amalgam of traditional and reformed. Although conclusive evidence is lacking, the queen's initial successes may indicate that the Reformation was not broadly supported by the people. In fact, a Catholic reform led by Mary might have succeeded had the queen not died after little more than six years on the throne. At her death the final settlement of the reform in England was far from certain.

THE ELIZABETHAN SETTLEMENT

Queen Elizabeth (r. 1558–1603), daughter of Anne Boleyn, succeeded to the throne at the death of her half sister. The reign of Elizabeth was one of the most enigmatic and successful of English history. At home she managed to gain control of the various political and re-

ligious factions in the country, and abroad she exploited the rivalries of a variety of international powers to her own advantage. She seems to have clearly recognized the necessity of striking a balance between opposing forces.

Her first pressing task was to effect a religious settlement. Early in her reign she twice left church services at the elevation of the bread by the priest. Since in Catholic thought it was this action of the priest that made Christ present in the bread, she was indicating symbolically her opposition to a purely Catholic understanding of the sacraments. In the next few years she continued to work for the restoration of many features of her father's and her half brother's reforms. In 1559 the new Act of Supremacy and an Act of Uniformity reinstituted royal control of the English church

The Queen in Parliament
This image was meant to show the willingness of Parliament to support the queen, a key element of the Elizabethan Settlement. *(Bibliothèque nationale de France)*

and re-established uniform liturgical and doctrinal standards. A revised version of Cranmer's *Book of Common Prayer* was brought back, and final changes were made in the liturgy.

Protestants had hoped for a complete victory, but the "Elizabethan Settlement" was considerably less than that. Although figures are lacking, it is likely that a large portion of the English population did not support a return to Henry's and Edward's reforms. After making clear her significant differences with Rome, Elizabeth confounded her most fervent Protestant supporters by offering a number of concessions to Anglo-Catholics. She remained celibate, and she ordered the Anglican clergy to do the same—although she could do little to prevent clerical marriage. More important, she and her closest advisers allowed a great variety of customs and practices favored by Anglo-Catholics. These matters, the queen's supporters argued, were not essential to salvation, and thus individuals could be allowed to choose. Many of the prayers in the *Book of Common Prayer*, for example, seemed "papist" to the most radical

Protestants. Similarly, many of the traditional clerical vestments and altar furnishings remained unchanged. Elizabeth probably knew that the Protestants had no alternative but to support her and thus felt free to win back the support of the Anglo-Catholics.

Toward the end of Elizabeth's reign Richard Hooker (1554-1600) published his *Laws of Ecclesiastical Polity*, which provides an excellent description of the Anglican (English) Church born of the Elizabethan Settlement. England, Hooker maintains, had its own way of handling religious affairs. Theologically it represented a middle ground between the traditions cultivated by the Roman church and the more radically biblical religion favored by the Lutherans of Germany and the Calvinists of Switzerland. The Church of England moderated Luther's and Calvin's absolute reliance on Scriptures with history and tradition. In areas where tradition was strong, processions and other pre-Reformation traditions continued to animate village life. In other areas more austere reformed practices were likely to predominate.

━━━━━━━━ S E C T I O N　　S U M M A R Y ━━━━━━━━

- England's Reformation was monarchical because it was shaped and directed by the cultural and political needs and attitudes of the monarchs.

- Cranmer's *Book of Common Prayer* organized and introduced into England the ideas of the continental Reformation.

- Queen Mary might have succeeded in restoring much of traditional church practice had she not died after just a short reign.

- The Elizabethan Settlement represented a middle way combining elements of both Protestant and Catholic beliefs.

FRANCE, SCANDINAVIA, AND EASTERN EUROPE, 1523-1560

How did ideas of church reform influence social and political developments in the rest of Europe?

In England and in the empire of Charles V, the success of the new religious reforms depended greatly on the political situation. It would be naive to conclude, as Luther claimed, that "the Word did everything." Yet this complex religious reform movement cannot be reduced to the politics of kings and princes. The issues will be clearer if we survey politics and reform in the rest of Europe, noting whether and to what extent the new ideas took root. In France, for example, the widespread, popular support of the old religion limited the options of the country's political leaders. Similarly, in northern Europe religious reform was an issue of both popular feeling and royal politics.

FRANCE

Luther's work, and later the ideas of the urban reformers of southwestern Germany and Switzerland, passed quickly into France. Geneva is in a French-speaking area close to the French border. It, like Strasbourg, was easy for French Protestants to reach. Perhaps because of France's proximity to the Calvinists in French-speaking Switzerland or because of the clarity and power of Calvin's *Institutes*, French Protestants, known as Huguenots, were tied more closely to the Calvinists of Geneva than to the Lutherans of Germany.

It is difficult, however, to know how many French Christians were Protestants. At the height of the Reformation's popularity Protestants probably represented no more than 10 percent of the total population of France. It has been estimated that Protestant congregations numbered about 2,100 in the 1560s—in a country that had perhaps 32,000 traditional parishes. Protestants seem to have comprised a diverse mix that included two of the three most important noble families at court: the Bourbon and Montmorency families. Clerics interested in moral reform and artisans who worked at new trades, such as the printing industry, also made up a significant portion of the converts. Perhaps reflecting the numerous printers and merchants in their numbers, Protestants tended to be of higher than average

literacy. The Protestant population was spread throughout the country. Protestants were particularly well represented in towns and probably constituted a majority in the southern and western towns of La Rochelle, Montpellier, and Nîmes. Paris was the one part of the realm in which they had little influence, and their absence in the capital may have been their undoing.

The conservative theologians of the Sorbonne in Paris were some of Luther's earliest opponents. They complained that many masters at the University of Paris were "Lutheran." As early as 1523 Parisian authorities seized and burned books said to be by Luther. But as in Germany, there was no clear understanding of who or what a Lutheran was. The Sorbonne theologians were also suspicious of a number of

The Great Cauldron

In dramatic images, this French woodcut shows the Protestant expectation that the Bible carried down by the Holy Spirit will overturn the whole cauldron of false images and errors that supported the old church. *(Bibliothèque nationale de France)*

"pre-reformers," including the humanistic editor Jacques Lefèvre d'Étaples (1455–1536; see page 374), who late in life had come to an understanding of justification quite like Luther's. Others were clerics intent on religious reform within the traditional structures. Unlike Luther and the French Protestants, these pre-reformers did not challenge the priests' relationship to the sacraments. They were interested in the piety and behavior of churchmen. They never challenged the role of the clergy in salvation. King Francis's own sister, Margaret of Angoulême (1492–1549), gathered a group of religious persons, including several reformers, at her court. But Margaret herself urged that theology be left to scholars; she believed that the laity should stick to simple pieties. Like Margaret, most French Christians had no clear sense that Protestant teachings required a complete break with medieval Christian traditions.

Like previous French kings, Francis I (r. 1515–1547) hoped to extend royal jurisdictions in France and make France an international power. Engaged in the seemingly intractable wars with the Habsburgs, Francis generally ignored religious questions. In 1525 he was taken captive in the wake of a military disaster at Pavia in Lombardy. He was held prisoner for nearly a year, during which time conservatives at the Sorbonne and in Paris moved actively against suspected Protestants. Francis was not initially opposed to what seemed to be moral reform within the church. His own view was that the king's duty was to preserve order and prevent scandal, and at first carrying out that duty meant protecting reformers whom the conservative militants persecuted. The king feared disorder more than he feared religious reform.

On October 18, 1534, however, Francis's attitude changed when he and all Paris awoke to find the city littered with anti-Catholic placards containing, in the words of the writers, "true articles on the horrible, great and insufferable abuses of the Papal Mass." The response of the Parisians was outrage. They attacked foreigners, especially those who by dress or speech seemed "Lutheran"—that is, German or Flemish. Several months later Francis led a religious procession through Paris in honor of the Blessed Sacrament. The "Affair of the Placards" changed Francis's ideas about the sources of disorder. Opposition to traditional religious practices became more difficult and more dangerous. John Calvin himself was forced to leave Paris, and eventually France, because he feared persecution. Between 1534 and 1560 some ten thousand Protestants fled France, many joining Calvin in Geneva.

By the middle of the sixteenth century it was clear that neither Protestant nor Catholic factions would be able to control religious and political life in France. Francis I died in 1547, and the stage was set for a series of destructive factional struggles over religion and political power that would continue for the rest of the century (see Chapter 15).

SCANDINAVIA

All of Scandinavia became Lutheran. Initial influences drifted north from Germany, carried by Hanseatic merchants and students who had studied at the universities of northern Germany. Yet the reform in Sweden and Denmark even more than in England was monarchical. In both Scandinavian kingdoms the kings began with an attack on the temporal rights and properties of the church. Changes in liturgy and practice came later as reformers gained royal protection.

Since 1397 all Scandinavia had been united in theory in the Union of Kalmar (see page 339). But early in the sixteenth century the last pretenses of unity were shattered. Christian I of Denmark (r. 1513–1523) invaded Sweden and captured Stockholm, the capital. So great was his brutality that within a few years Gustav Vasa, a leading noble, was able to secure the loyalty of most of the Swedes and in 1523 was elected king of Sweden. Gustav's motto was "All power is of God." Like Henry VIII of England, Gustav (r. 1523–1560) moved carefully in an attempt to retain the loyalty of as many groups as possible. Although he never formally adopted a national confession of faith, the Swedish church and state gradually took on a more Lutheran character. In an effort to secure royal finances, the Riksdag, or parliament, passed the Vasteras Ordinances, which secularized ecclesiastical lands and authorized the preaching of the "Pure Word of God." Olaus Petri (1493–1552), Sweden's principal reform preacher, was installed by royal order in the Cathedral of Stockholm.

In Denmark the reformers also moved cautiously. Frederick I (r. 1523–1533) and his son, Christian III (r. 1534–1559), continued the policy of secularization and control that Christian I had initiated. Danish kings seemed interested in reform as a diplomatic means of attack on the Roman church. It seems that in Denmark the old religion simply suffered from a sort of royal indifference. The kings tended to support reformers as a way to attack the political power of the bishops. The Danes finally accepted the Augsburg Confession, which was becoming the most widely accepted exposition of Lutheran belief, in 1538. The transformation of practice proceeded slowly over the next decades.

In the frontier regions of Scandinavia—Finland, Iceland, and Norway—the reform was undertaken as a matter of royal policy. Initially only a handful of local reformers introduced and proselytized the new theology and practice. In many regions resistance to the Reformation continued for several generations. One valley hidden in the mountains of western Norway continued to follow the old religion for three centuries after its contacts with Rome had been severed.

EASTERN EUROPE

In some respects there was less opposition to the expansion of Protestantism in eastern Europe. The result was the creation of a unique religious culture. The church hierarchy was not in a position to enforce orthodoxy. Some Christian rulers were indifferent to religious debates, as were the Muslim Ottoman Turks, who controlled much of eastern Hungary and what is now Romania. Other rulers whose societies already contained Orthodox and Catholic Christians, as well as Muslims and Jews, offered toleration because they could ill afford to alienate any portion of their subject populations.

Protestant ideas initially passed through the German communities of Poland and the trading towns along the Baltic coast. But in the 1540s Calvinist ideas spread quickly among the Polish nobles, especially those at the royal court. Given the power and influence of some of the noble families, Catholics were unable to suppress the various secret Calvinist congregations. During the first half of the sixteenth century Protestantism became so well established in Poland that it could not be rooted out. Throughout the sixteenth century Protestantism remained one of the rallying points for those Polish nobles opposed to the expansion of royal power.

Much was the same in Hungary and Transylvania. Among German colonists, Magyars, and ethnic Romanians, many individuals were interested first in Luther's message and later in Calvin's revisions of the Reformed theology. The situation was exacerbated after the Turkish victory at Mohács in 1526, which destroyed the traditional political and religious elite of Hungary. Because no one could hope to enforce uniformity, some cities adopted a moderate Lutheran theology, and others followed a Calvinist confession. In 1568 the Estates (representative assemblies) of Transylvania had decreed that four religions were to be tolerated—Catholic, Lutheran, Reformed (Calvinist), and Unitarian. Further, when various radical groups migrated from the west in search of toleration, they were able to create their own communities in Slavic and Magyar areas.

The Reformation was to have virtually no influence farther to the east, in Russia. The Orthodox Church in Russia was much more firmly under government control than was the church in the West. The Russian church followed the traditions of the Greek church, and Western arguments over justification made little sense in Orthodox churches. Given the historic suspicion of the Orthodox churches toward Rome, the Russians were more tolerant of contacts with the Protestants of northern Europe, but there would be no theological innovation or reform in sixteenth-century Russia.

========== SECTION SUMMARY ==========

- Widespread support for traditional religious practices in France limited the spread of reformed ideas.

- Francis I tolerated religious dissent until it seemed that religious strife might lead to civil unrest.

- In Scandinavia religious change was fostered by monarchs who wished to reduce the influence of the church in public life.

- Religious toleration was much more common in eastern Europe, where many rulers declined to support one religious movement over another.

THE LATE REFORMATION, CA. 1545–1600

How did Catholic and Protestant Christians differ from each other by the end of the Reformation?

In the first half of the sixteenth century Catholics applied the term *Lutheran* to anyone who was anticlerical. As Francesco Guicciardini (1483–1540), a papal governor in central Italy, remarked:

> I know of no one who loathes the ambition, the avarice, and the sensuality of the clergy more than I. . . . In spite of all this, the positions I have held under several popes have forced me, for my own good, to further their interests. Were it not

for that, I should have loved Martin Luther as much as myself—not so that I might be free of the laws based on Christian religion as it is generally interpreted and understood; but to see this bunch of rascals get their just deserts, that is, to be without vices or without authority.[7]

Guicciardini's remarks catch both the frustration many Christians felt toward the traditional church and the very real confusion over just what it was that

Luther had said. In parts of Germany by the late 1520s and across Europe by the 1550s, political and religious leaders attempted to explain to the people just what *Lutheran, Reformed (Calvinist),* and *Catholic* had come to mean. It was only in the second half of the sixteenth century that these terms came to have any clarity. After the middle of the sixteenth century it was true that along with theological and political changes, the Reformation represented a broad cultural movement.

The profound changes that began in the sixteenth century continued into the seventeenth. People began to sort out what it meant to belong to one church instead of to another. Central governments supported religious authorities who desired religious uniformity and control over individual Christians. In all parts of Europe, religious behavior changed. Both Protestants and Catholics became more concerned with the personal rather than the communal aspects of Christianity. After the sixteenth century the nature of Christianity and its place in public life, whether in Protestant or in Catholic countries, differed profoundly from Christianity in the Middle Ages.

CATHOLIC REFORM, 1512–1600

Historians commonly speak of both a movement for traditional reform and renewal within the Catholic Church, and a "Counter-Reformation," which was a direct response to and rejection of the theological positions championed by the Protestants. It is certainly true that one can categorize certain acts as clearly challenging the Protestants. However, to do so is to miss the point that the energetic actions of the Roman Catholic Church during the sixteenth century both affirmed traditional teachings and created new institutions better fitted to the early modern world.

The idea of purer, earlier church practices to which the "modern" church should return had been a commonplace for cen-

turies. The great ecumenical Council of Constance early in the fifteenth century had called for "reform in head and members" (see pages 319–320). In 1512, five years before Luther made his public protests, Pope Julius II (r. 1503–1513) convened another ecumenical council, the Fifth Lateran Council (1513–1517), which was expected to look into the problems of nonresident clergy, multiple benefices, and a host of other issues. This tradition of moral reform was especially strong in Spain, Portugal, and Italy, lands whose political rulers were either indifferent or opposed to Protestant reforms.

The desire for reform along traditional lines was deeply felt within the Catholic Church. In the wake of the sack of Rome by imperial troops in 1527, one Roman cardinal, Bishop Gian Matteo Giberti (ji-BARE-ti) of Verona (1495–1543), returned to his diocese and began a thoroughgoing reform. He conducted visitations of the churches and other religious institutions in

A Marian Shrine
Shrines, such as this one in Regensburg dedicated to the Virgin Mary, remained important centers of Catholic piety. As we see here, shrines drew large crowds made up of individuals and religious groups who came in search of spiritual and physical healing. *(Foto Marburg/Art Resource, NY)*

Verona, preached tirelessly, worked hard to raise the educational level of his clergy, and required that priests live within their parishes. Giberti believed that morally rigorous traditional reform and renewal could counter the malaise he perceived. Other reforming bishops could be found throughout Catholic Europe.

The Role of Music and Mysticism

New religious foundations sprang up to renew the church. The Spanish mystic Teresa of Avila (1515–1582) reflected the thinking of many when she lamented, "No wonder the Church is as it is, when the religious live as they do." Members of the new orders set out to change the church through example. The Florentine Filippo Neri (1515–1595) founded the Oratorian order, so named because of the monks' habit of leading the laity in prayer services. Filippo was joined in his work by Giovanni Palestrina (ca. 1525–1594), who composed music for the modest but moving prayer gatherings in Rome. Palestrina's music combined medieval plainchants with newer styles of polyphony, creating complex harmonies without obscuring the words and meaning of the text. The popularity of the Oratorians and their services can be measured in part by the fact that oratories, small chapels modeled on those favored by Filippo, remain to this day important centers of the musical life in the city of Rome.

The Catholic reform of the sixteenth century, however, was better known for its mystical theology than for its music. In Italy and France, but especially in Spain, a profusion of reformers chose to reform the church through austere prayer and contemplative devotions. Teresa of Avila, who belonged to a wealthy converso family (see pages 344–345), led a movement to reform the lax practices within the religious houses of Spain. Famed for her rigorous religious life, her trances, and her raptures, Teresa animated a movement to reform the order of Carmelite nuns in Spain. Because of her writings about her mystical experiences she was named a "Doctor of the Church," a title reserved for the greatest of the church's theologians.

Jesuits

The most important of the new religious orders was the **Society of Jesus**, or Jesuits, founded in 1534 by **Ignatius Loyola** (1491–1556). A conservative Spanish nobleman, Loyola was wounded and nearly killed in battle. During a long and painful rehabilitation he continuously read accounts of the lives of the saints. After recovering he went on a pilgrimage and experienced a profound conversion.

Loyola initially meant to organize a missionary order directed at converting the Muslims. The structure of his order reflected his military experience. It had a well-defined chain of command leading to the general of the order and then to the pope. To educate and discipline the members, Loyola composed *Spiritual Exercises*, emphasizing the importance of obedience. He encouraged his followers to understand their own attitudes, beliefs, and even lives as less important than the papacy and the Roman church. If the church commands it, he concluded, "I will believe that the white object I see is black." He prohibited Jesuits from holding any ecclesiastical office that might compromise their autonomy. After papal approval of the order in 1540, the Jesuits directed their activities primarily to education in Catholic areas and reconversion of Protestants.

Throughout Europe Jesuits gained fame for their work as educators of the laity and as spiritual advisers to the political leaders of Catholic Europe. In the late sixteenth and early seventeenth centuries they were responsible for a number of famous conversions, including that of Christina (1626–1689), the Lutheran queen of Sweden, who abdicated her throne in 1654 and spent the rest of her life in Rome. Jesuits were especially successful in bringing many parts of the Holy Roman Empire back into communion with the papacy. They have rightly been called the vanguard of the Catholic reform movement.

Orthodox Beliefs and the Council of Trent

Catholic reformers were convinced that one of the reasons for the success of the Protestants was that faithful Christians had no clear guide to orthodox teachings. The first Catholic response to the reformers was to try to separate ideas they held to be correct from those they held to be incorrect. Successive popes made public lists of books and ideas that they considered to be in error. The lists were combined into the *Index of Prohibited Books* in 1559. The climate of suspicion was such that the works of humanists such as Erasmus were prohibited alongside the works of Protestants such as Martin Luther. In times of religious tensions, the *Index* could be vigorously enforced. In Italy, for example, no editions of the Holy Bible in Italian translation were published in the late sixteenth and seventeenth centuries. In general, however, it did little to inhibit the circulation of books and ideas. It was finally suppressed in 1966.

Council of Trent

During the first half of the sixteenth century Catholics joined Protestants in calls for an ecumenical council that all believed would solve the

---

Society of Jesus (Jesuits)   Religious group founded in 1534 by Ignatius Loyola; they were famed for their role in the Catholic Counter-Reformation.

Ignatius Loyola   A Spanish nobleman and founder of the Society of Jesus. Loyola's order vowed absolute authority to the papacy.

Index of Prohibited Books   A list of books banned by the Roman Catholic Church because of moral or doctrinal error. It was thought that this would inhibit the spread of Protestant ideas.

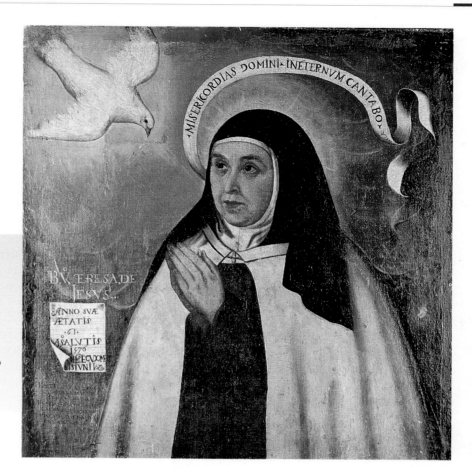

A Mystical Reformer
Saint Teresa of Avila came from a
converso family. She believed that
renewal within the Christian church
would come through mysticism,
prayer, and a return to traditional
religious practices. She founded a
reformed Carmelite order of nuns to
further religious renewal in Spain.
(Institut Amatller d'Art Hispanic)

problems dogging the Christian church. But in the unsettled political and diplomatic atmosphere that lasted
into the 1540s, it was impossible to find any agreement
about where or when a universal council should meet.
Finally, in 1545, at a time when the hostilities between
the Valois and Habsburgs had cooled, Pope Paul III
(r. 1534–1549) was able to convene an ecumenical council in the city of Trent, a German imperial city located
on the Italian side of the Alps.

It is difficult to overemphasize the importance of
the **Council of Trent.** It marked and defined Roman
Catholicism for the next four hundred years. Reformers
within the Catholic Church hoped that it would be
possible to create a broadly based reform party within
the church and that the council would define theological
positions acceptable to the Protestants, making reunion
possible. Unfortunately for the reformers, conservatives
quickly took over the papal-controlled council.

The Council of Trent sat in three sessions between
1545 and 1563. The initial debates were clearly meant
to mark the boundaries between Protestant heresy and
the orthodox positions of the Catholic Church. In response to the Protestant emphasis on the Scriptures,
the council said that the church always recognized the
validity of traditional teaching and understanding.
Delegates rejected the humanists' work on the text of
the Bible, declaring that the Latin Vulgate edition compiled by Jerome in the late fourth century was the
authorized text. In response to the widely held Protestant belief that salvation came through faith alone,
the council declared that good works were not merely
the outcome of faith but prerequisites to salvation. The
council rejected Protestant positions on the sacraments, the giving of wine to the laity during Holy Communion, the marriage of clergy, and the granting of
indulgences.

Protestant critics often point to these positions as
evidence that the work of the council was merely negative. To do so, however, is to ignore the many ways in
which the decrees of the council were an essential part
of the creation of the Roman Catholic Church that
would function for the next four centuries. The delegates at Trent generally felt that the real cause behind
the Protestant movement was the lack of leadership
and supervision within the church. Many of the acts of
the council dealt with that issue.

Council of Trent   An ecumenical council of the
Roman Catholic Church called to both respond to
the Protestant challenge and institute reforms in the
Catholic Church. Its decrees established the basic tenets
of Roman Catholicism for the next four hundred years.

First, the council affirmed apostolic succession—the idea that the authority of a bishop is transmitted through a succession of bishops, ultimately leading back through the popes to Saint Peter. Thus the council underlined the ultimate authority of the pope in administrative as well as theological matters. The council ordered that local bishops should reside in their dioceses; that they should establish seminaries to see to the education of parish clergy; and that, through regular visitation and supervision, they should make certain that the laity participated in the sacramental life of the church. In the final sessions of the council the nature of the Roman Catholic Church was summed up in the Creed of Pius IV, which like the Lutheran Augsburg Confession expressed the basic position of the church.

CONFESSIONALIZATION

The labors of the Jesuits and the deliberations of the Council of Trent at midcentury proved that reconciliation between the Protestant reformers and the Catholic Church was not possible. Signs of the separation include the flight of several important Protestant religious leaders from Italy in the late 1540s and the wholesale migration of Protestant communities from Modena, Lucca, and other Italian towns to France, England, and Switzerland. These actions signify the beginnings of the theological, political, and social separation of "Protestant" and "Catholic" in European society. Further, the states of Europe saw themselves as the enforcers of religious uniformity within their territories. It is from this time forward that denominational differences become clearer.

The theological separation was marked in a number of concrete and symbolic ways. Churches in which both bread and wine were distributed to the laity during the sacrament of Holy Communion passed from Catholic to Protestant. Churches in which the altar was moved forward to face the congregation but the statuary was retained were likely to be Lutheran. Churches in which statues were destroyed and all other forms of art were removed were likely to be Reformed (Calvinist), for Calvin had advised that "only those things are to be sculpted or painted which the eye is capable of seeing; let not God's majesty, which is far above the perception of the eyes, be debased through unseemly representations."[8] Even matters such as singing differentiated the churches. Although the Calvinist tradition tended to believe that music, like art, drew the Christian away from consideration of the Word, Luther believed that "next to the Word of God, music deserves the highest praise." Lutherans emphasized congregational singing and the use of music within the worship service. Countless pastors in the sixteenth and seventeenth centuries followed Luther in composing hymns and even theoretical tracts on music. This tradition would reach its zenith in the church music of Johann Sebastian Bach (1685–1750), most of whose choral works were composed to be part of the normal worship service.

Music had played an important role in Catholic services since well before the Reformation. It was really architecture that distinguished Catholic churches from Protestant churches in the late sixteenth and seventeenth centuries. In Rome the great religious orders built new churches in the baroque style (see page 484). Baroque artists and architects absorbed all the classical lessons of the Renaissance and then went beyond them, sometimes deliberately violating them. Baroque art celebrates the supernatural, the ways in which God is not bound by the laws of nature. Whereas Renaissance art was meant to depict nature, baroque paintings and sculpture seem to defy gravity. The work celebrates the supernatural power and splendor of the papacy. This drama and power are clear in the construction of the Jesuit Church of the Gesù (jeh-SUE) in Rome and even more so in Gianlorenzo Bernini's (1598–1680) throne of Saint Peter, made for Saint Peter's Basilica in the Vatican. The construction of baroque churches, first in Spain and Italy but especially in the Catholic parts of Germany, created yet another boundary between an austere Protestantism and a visual and mystical Catholicism.

THE REGULATION OF RELIGIOUS LIFE

Because of the continuing religious confusion and political disorder brought on by the reforms, churchmen, like state officials, were intent on maintaining religious order within their territories by requiring what they understood to be the practice of true Christianity. In an ironic twist, both Protestant and Catholic authorities followed much the same program. In both camps regulation of religion became a governmental concern. Religious regulation and state power grew at the same time. This true religion was much less a public and communal religion than medieval Christianity had been. Medieval Christians had worried greatly about public sins that complicated life in a community. In the age of confessionalization, theologians—both Protestant and Catholic—became preoccupied with the moral status and interior life of individuals. Sexual sins and gluttony now seemed more dangerous than economic sins such as avarice and usury. Even penance was understood less as a "restitution" that would reintegrate the individual into the Christian community than as a process of coming to true contrition for one's sins.

The changed attitude toward penance made the sense of Christian community less important and left individuals isolated and more subject to the influence of the church and secular authorities. In all parts of Europe officials were consumed with the control and supervision of the laity.

All of the major religious groups in the late sixteenth century emphasized education, right doctrine, and social control. In Catholic areas it was hoped that a renewed emphasis on private confession by the laity would lead to a proper understanding of doctrine. During this period Charles Borromeo, archbishop of Milan (1538–1584), introduced the private confessional box, which isolated priest and penitent from the prying ears of the community. This allowed confessors the time and opportunity to instruct individual consciences with care. As early as the 1520s some Lutheran princes had begun visitations to ensure that the laity understood basic doctrine.

Churchmen in both Protestant and Catholic areas used catechisms—handbooks containing instruction for the laity. The first and most famous was by Luther himself. Luther's *Small Catechism* includes the Lord's Prayer, Ten Commandments, and Apostles' Creed, along with simple, clear explanations of what they mean. More than Catholic rulers, Protestant rulers used church courts to enforce discipline within the community. Churchmen began to criticize semireligious popular celebrations such as May Day, harvest feasts, and the Feast of Fools, whose origins lay in popular myths and practices that preceded Christianity. Such observances were now scorned for encouraging superstition and mocking the social and political order with, for example, parodies of ignorant clergy and foolish magistrates.

Religious authorities were also concerned by what seemed to be out-of-control mysticism and dangerous religious practices, especially among women. The impact of the Reformation on the status of women has often been debated. The Protestant position is that the Reformation freed women from the cloistered control of traditional convents. Further, the Protestant attack on state-controlled prostitution reduced one of the basest forms of exploitation. To the realists who argued that young, unmarried men would always need sexual outlets, Luther replied that one cannot merely substitute

The Holy Household

One of the most popular ideas among Protestants was that true religion should be taught and preserved in the Christian family, presided over by the father. The detail in this painting shows not only the interior of a Flemish home but also the role of the father and the symbolic importance of meals eaten together. *(The Shakespeare Birthplace Trust)*

one evil practice for another. Critics of the Reformation counter that a convent was one of very few organizations that a woman could administer and direct. Women who took religious vows, Catholics point out, could engage in intellectual and religious pursuits similar to those enjoyed by men. The destruction of religious houses for women, Catholics argue, destroyed one of the few alternatives that women had to life in an authoritarian, patriarchal society.

In fact, in the late sixteenth and early seventeenth centuries both Protestant and Catholic authorities viewed with suspicion any signs of religious independence by women. In the first years of the Reformation some women did leave convents, eager to participate in the reform of the church. Early in the 1520s some women wrote tracts concerning the morality of the clergy. And for a time women served as deacons in some Reformed (Calvinist) churches. Yet like the female witches discussed in Chapter 15, these religious women seemed somehow dangerous. Lutheran and Calvinist theologians argued that a woman's religious vocation should be in the Christian care and education of her family. And even the most famous of the sixteenth- and seventeenth-century female Catholic mystics were greeted with distrust and some hostility. Religious women in Catholic convents were required to subordinate their mysticism to the guidance they received from male spiritual advisers. Calvinist theologians exhibited similar suspicions toward the theological and spiritual insights of Protestant women. For the laity in general and for women in particular, the late Reformation brought increased control by religious authorities.

SECTION SUMMARY

- Catholic reform emphasizing moral reform and renewed piety had begun before Luther's protests.

- The Council of Trent defined Catholic doctrine for the next four hundred years.

- During the second half of the sixteenth century, Protestant and Catholic churches became more clearly differentiated by architecture and ritual.

- Both traditions emphasized personal discipline and self-control, which became an important part of the early modern state.

CHAPTER SUMMARY

Online Study Center **ACE the Test**

Why did the reformers feel it was necessary to establish entirely new churches outside the Roman Catholic Church?

What political factors limited Charles V's ability to respond to the religious crisis?

Why did the English monarchs take the lead in efforts to reform the English church?

How did ideas of church reform influence social and political developments in the rest of Europe?

How did Catholic and Protestant Christians differ from each other by the end of the Reformation?

During the age of the Reformation Europe experienced a number of profound shocks. The medieval assumption of a unified Christendom in the West was shattered. No longer could Europeans assume that at heart they held similar views of the world and the place of individuals in it. Charles V had begun his reign with hopes for one law, one faith, and one empire. He ended it by dividing his empire and retiring to a monastery.

The Protestant challenge did not simply attack the institutional structure or the moral lapses as previous heretical movements had done. The early Protestant reformers rejected the penitential system that was at the heart of the medieval church. Peasants and artisans argued that Luther's message of Christian freedom liberated them from both economic and spiritual oppression. Both Protestant and peasant claimed all authority must rest on Holy Scripture. They rejected the traditions of the late Middle Ages.

Emperor Charles V was opposed to Luther and wanted to maintain the unity of the church and of his empire. But he faced almost continuous problems in one part or another of his empire. Both the French and the Turks did all they could to reduce his power. Consequently, even after years of struggle he was forced in the religious Peace of Augsburg to accept the principle that the towns and regional principalities had the right to accept either traditional Catholic worship or the new Lutheran reform.

In England, on the other hand, the monarchy was powerful enough that Henry VIII was able to shift religious debate and declare himself the head of the Church in England. But Henry's children were alternately Protestant, Catholic, and Protestant again. The result in England was a church that maintained certain aspects of traditional Catholic Christianity even as it allowed a married clergy and accepted other Protestant reforms.

Monarchies and republics throughout Europe came to view religious institutions and religious choices as matters of state. In Scandinavia, monarchs seemed to have favored the Lutherans as a way to weaken the power of the Catholic clergy. While in France, Francis I was willing to allow some Protestant protests until it seemed that religious unrest threatened public order. At that point he began to suppress Protestant worship, acknowledging the fact that France had largely remained Catholic. Much of the rest of eastern Europe followed no clear pattern. When faced with theological challenges and cries for moral reform, governments reacted in ways that offered religious change and bolstered the claims of secular authorities.

By the second half of the sixteenth century, Protestants and Catholics had largely adopted patterns that made clear which religion was favored. Calvinist churches were spare; Catholic churches, ornate; and Lutheran churches, filled with varieties of music.

As a part of their reform movements, both Protestant and Catholic governments redoubled their efforts to regulate religion and moral life. In Catholic countries the church hierarchy extended its control over the religious life of the laity. Thus both Reformation and Counter-Reformation brought about a significant strengthening of religious and secular authorities.

LOOKING AHEAD

Ironically, the reforms that Luther and other Protestants advocated on the basis of individual study and conscience led to new confessional beliefs and a conviction that right religion was a matter of state interest. Religious power, which to some extent had been a matter of personal conscience and local community, became an issue to be decided by the aggressive states of Europe. Thus enforcing the right religion was one aspect of the growth of government power in the late sixteenth and seventeenth centuries. Powerful government control is a topic we turn to next.

KEY TERMS

Martin Luther (p. 416)

justification by faith (p. 419)

sola scriptura (p. 420)

Charles V (p. 420)

Huldrych Zwingli (p. 422)

John Calvin (p. 423)

Anabaptists (p. 427)

Augsburg Confession (p. 433)

Henry VIII (p. 434)

Act of Supremacy (p. 435)

Society of Jesus (p. 442)

Ignatius Loyola (p. 442)

Index of Prohibited Books (p. 442)

Council of Trent (p. 443)

Online Study Center
Improve Your Grade Flashcards

SUGGESTED READING

Bennedict, Philip. *Christ's Churches Purely Reformed: A Social History of Calvinism.* 2002. A magisterial survey of the Reformed (Calvinist) tradition that emphasizes the dynamics of religious communities.

Bireley, Robert. *The Refashioning of Catholicism: A Reassessment of the Counter Reformation.* 1999. A well-written survey that places the Roman Catholic Church in the context of political, social, and religious developments between 1450 and 1600.

Dickens, Arthur G. *The English Reformation.* 1991. First published in 1964, this is a classic, clear discussion of English religion, emphasizing the popular enthusiasm for reform, which Dickens believes was connected to the earlier Lollard movements.

Haigh, Christopher, ed. *The English Reformation Revised.* 1987. A collection of essays criticizing Dickens's thesis on the popular basis of reform in England; the introduction is especially useful for following what is still an important debate over reform.

Hillerbrand, Hans J., ed. *The Oxford Encyclopedia of the Reformation.* 1996. An essential source on almost all topics of sixteenth-century history; the entries are accessible and up-to-date.

McCulloch, Dairmaid. *The Reformation: A History.* 2003. A lively, up-to-date account of the Reformation with an especially good summary of the social and cultural impact of religious reform.

McGrath, Alister E. *A Life of John Calvin: A Study in the Shaping of Western Culture.* 1990. An excellent biography emphasizing the definitive role of Calvin's religious thought.

Oberman, Heiko. *Luther: Man Between God and the Devil.* 1989. A brilliant, beautifully written essay connecting Luther to prevailing late medieval ideas about sin, death, and the Devil.

Oberman, Heiko, Thomas Brady, and James Tracy, eds. *Handbook of European History, 1400–1600: Late Middle Ages, Renaissance, and Reformation.* 1994–1995. A collection of excellent introductory studies of political, religious, and social life.

Pettegree, Andrew, ed. *The Reformation World.* 2000. A demanding but very comprehensive survey of the most recent work on the Reformation.

NOTES

1. *The Book of Divine Consolation of the Blessed Angela of Foligno,* trans. Mary G. Steegmann (New York: Cooper Square Publishers, 1966), p. 260.

2. Martin Luther, *Works,* vol. 34 (Philadelphia: Muhlenberg Press, 1960), pp. 336–337.

3. Quoted in Steven Ozment, *The Age of Reform, 1250–1550* (New Haven, Conn.: Yale University Press, 1980), p. 245.

4. Quoted in Robert W. Scribner, *The German Reformation* (London: Macmillan, 1986), p. 32.

5. Quoted in Carter Lindberg, *The European Reformations* (New York: Blackwell Publishers, 1996), p. 269.

6. Quoted in Euan Cameron, *The European Reformation* (Oxford: Clarendon Press, 1991), pp. 106–107.

7. Francesco Guicciardini, *Maxims and Reflections (Ricordi),* trans. Mario Domandi (Philadelphia: University of Pennsylvania Press, 1965), p. 48.

8. Quoted in Lindberg, p. 375.

15

EUROPE IN THE AGE OF RELIGIOUS WARS, 1560–1648

The Saint Bartholomew's Day Massacre
(Musée Cantonal des Beaux-Arts, Lausanne)

Three well-dressed gentlemen stand over a mutilated body; one of them holds up the severed head. Elsewhere sword-wielding men engage in indiscriminate slaughter, even of babies. Corpses are piled up in the background. This painting memorializes the grisly events of August 24, 1572. A band of Catholic noblemen accompanied by the personal guard of the king of France had hunted down a hundred Protestant nobles, asleep in their lodgings in and around the royal palace, and murdered them in cold blood. The king and his counselors had planned the murders as a preemptive political strike because they feared that other Protestant nobles were gathering an army outside Paris. But the calculated attack became a general massacre when ordinary Parisians, overwhelmingly Catholic and believing they were acting in the king's name, turned on their neighbors. About three thousand Protestants were slain in Paris over the next three days.

This massacre came to be called the Saint Bartholomew's Day Massacre for the Catholic saint on whose feast day it fell. Though particularly horrible in its scope, the slaughter was not unusual in the deadly combination of religious and political antagonisms it reflected. Religious conflicts were by definition intractable political conflicts since virtually every religious group felt that all others were heretics who could not be tolerated and must be eliminated. Rulers of all faiths looked to divine authority and religious institutions to uphold their power.

In the decades after 1560 existing political tensions contributed to instability and violence, especially when newly reinforced by religious differences. Royal governments continued to consolidate authority, but resistance to royal power by provinces, nobles, or towns accustomed to independence now might have a religious sanction. Warfare over these issues had consumed the Holy Roman Empire in the first half of the sixteenth century. The conflict had now spilled over into France and the Netherlands and threatened to erupt in England. In the early seventeenth century the Holy Roman Empire once again was wracked by a war simultaneously religious and political in origin. Regardless of its roots, warfare itself had become more destructive than ever before thanks to innovations in military technology and

CHAPTER OUTLINE

IMPERIAL SPAIN AND THE LIMITS OF ROYAL POWER

RELIGIOUS AND POLITICAL CONFLICT IN FRANCE AND ENGLAND

RELIGIOUS AND POLITICAL CONFLICT IN CENTRAL AND EASTERN EUROPE

ECONOMIC CHANGE AND SOCIAL TENSIONS

WRITING, DRAMA, AND ART IN AN AGE OF UPHEAVAL

KEY TERMS

Philip II	Thirty Years' War
Armada	Peace of Westphalia
Huguenots	Ivan IV, "the Terrible"
Edict of Nantes	price revolution
Elizabeth I	gentry
Puritans	baroque

Online Study Center
This icon will direct you to interactive map and primary source activities on the website **college.hmco.com/ pic/noble5e**

campaign tactics. Tensions everywhere were also worsened by economic changes, especially soaring prices and grinding unemployment. The political and religious struggles of the era took place against a background of increasing want, and economic distress was often expressed in both political and religious terms.

A period of tension, even extraordinary violence, in political and social life, the era of the late sixteenth and early seventeenth centuries was also distinguished by great creativity in some areas of cultural and intellectual life. The plays of Shakespeare, for example, mirrored the passions but also reflected on the dilemmas of the day and helped to analyze Europeans' circumstances with a new degree of sophistication.

FOCUS QUESTIONS

What circumstances permitted Spain's ambitious policies and to what degree were they successful?

What conditions led to civil war in France? How did religious and political conflict develop differently in England?

Why did war erupt again within the Holy Roman Empire and what was the significance of the conflict?

What caused the economic stresses of these decades and how did ordinary people cope with them?

In what ways do the literature and art of this period reflect the political, social, and religious conflicts of the age?

IMPERIAL SPAIN AND THE LIMITS OF ROYAL POWER

What circumstances permitted Spain's ambitious policies and to what degree were they successful?

To contemporary observers, no political fact of the late sixteenth century was more obvious than the ascendancy of Spain. **Philip II** (r. 1556–1598) ruled Spanish conquests in the New World as well as wealthy territories in Europe, including the Netherlands and parts of Italy. Yet imperial Spain did not escape the political, social, and religious turmoil of the era. Explosive combinations of religious dissent and political disaffection led to revolt against Spain in the Netherlands. This conflict revealed the endemic tensions of sixteenth-century political life: nobles, towns, and provinces trying to safeguard remnants of medieval autonomy against efforts at greater centralization—with the added complications of economic strain and religious division. The revolt also demonstrated the material limits of royal power, since even with treasure from the American conquests pouring in, Philip could at times barely afford to keep armies in the field. As American silver dwindled in the seventeenth century, Philip's successors faced severe financial and political strains even in their Spanish domains.

THE REVOLT OF THE NETHERLANDS

Philip's power stemmed in part from the far-flung territories he inherited from his father, the Habsburg king of Spain and Holy Roman emperor Charles V: Spain, the Low Countries (the Netherlands), the duchy of Milan, the kingdom of Naples, the conquered lands in the Americas, and the Philippine Islands in Asia. (Control of Charles's Austrian lands had passed to his brother, Ferdinand, Philip's uncle; see **MAP 15.1**.) Treasure fleets bearing precious metals from the New World began to reach Spain regularly during Philip's reign. Spain was now the engine powering a trading economy unlike any that had existed in Europe before. To supply its colonies Spain needed timber and other shipbuilding materials from the hinterlands of the Baltic Sea. Grain from the Baltic fed the urban populations of Spain (where wool was the principal cash crop) and the Netherlands, while the Netherlands, in turn, was a source of finished goods, such as cloth. The major exchange point for all of these goods was the city of Antwerp in the Netherlands, the leading trading center of all of Europe by 1550.

Philip II King of Spain (r. 1556–1598), son of Charles V who ruled Spain at the height of its influence.

The Netherlands were the jewel among Philip's European possessions. These seventeen provinces (constituting mostly the modern nations of Belgium and the Netherlands) had been centers of trade and manufacture since the twelfth century. In the fourteenth and fifteenth centuries they had enjoyed political importance and a period of cultural innovation under the control of the dukes of Burgundy. Like his father, Philip was, technically, the ruler of each province separately—that is, he was count of Flanders, duke of Brabant, and so forth. (See Map 15.2.) By the time Philip inherited the provinces from his father, a sort of federal system of government had evolved to accommodate the various centers of power. Each province had an assembly (Estates) in which representatives of leading nobility and towns authorized taxation, but each also acknowledged a central administration in Brussels that represented Philip. Heading the council of state in Brussels was a governor-general, Philip's half sister, Margaret of Parma.

Background to the Revolt Philip's clumsy efforts to adjust this distribution of power in his favor pushed his subjects in the Netherlands into revolt. Though conscientious to a fault, Philip was a rigid, unimaginative man. Born and raised in Spain, he had little real familiarity with the densely populated, linguistically diverse Netherlands, and he never visited there after 1559. Early in Philip's reign, tensions in the Netherlands arose over taxation and Spanish insistence on maintaining tight control. Bad harvests and disruptions of trade caused by wars in the Baltic region in the 1560s depressed the Netherlands' economy and made it difficult for the provinces to pay the taxes Spain demanded. When the Peace of Cateau-Cambrésis (kah-toe kam-bray-SEE) of 1559 brought an end to the long struggle between the Habsburgs and the Valois (val-WAH) kings of France, the people of the Netherlands had reason to hope for lower taxes and reduced levels of Spanish control, yet neither was forthcoming. Indeed, Philip named to the council of state in Brussels officials who were Spaniards themselves or had close ties to the Spanish court, bypassing local nobles who had fought for Philip and his father before 1559 and who expected positions of influence in his government.

Philip only added to the economic and political discontent by unleashing an invigorated repression of heresy. Unlike his father, Philip directed the hunt for heretics not just at lower-class dissenters but also at well-to-do Calvinists—followers of the French Protestant religious reformer John Calvin—whose numbers were considerable. Punishment for heresy now included confiscation of family property along with execution of the individual. By 1565 municipal councils in the Netherlands were routinely refusing to enforce Philip's religious policies, believing that urban prosper-

ity—as well as their personal security—depended on restraint in the prosecution of heresy. Leading nobles also stopped enforcing the policies on their estates.

Encouraged by greater tolerance, Protestants by 1566 had begun to hold open-air meetings and attract new converts in many towns. In a series of actions called the "iconoclastic fury," Calvinist townsfolk around the provinces stripped Catholic churches of the relics and statues they believed idolatrous. At the same time, reflecting the economic strain of these years, some townsfolk rioted to protest the price of bread. One prominent nobleman warned Philip, "All trade has come

Lands ruled by the Spanish Habsburgs

Lands ruled by the Austrian Habsburgs

Boundary of the Holy Roman Empire

Spanish military corridor ("Spanish Road")

X Major battles

POLAND - LITHUANIA

Dniester

Danube

Vistula

Elbe

Baltic Sea

Constantinople

Lepanto X

Sea

Malta

HOLY ROMAN EMPIRE

Vienna

Augsburg

Danube

Rhine

Venice

PAPAL STATES

Rome

Naples

THE NETHERLANDS

Milan

MILAN

Genoa

Florence

Mediterranean

Tunis

North Sea

Antwerp

Gravelines X

ENGLAND

London

Paris

FRANCE

Loire

Algiers

400 Mi.

400 Km.

200

200

0

0

ATLANTIC OCEAN

NAVARRE

ARAGON

Ebro

SPAIN

Madrid

CASTILE

Granada

GRANADA

PORTUGAL

(1580)

Lisbon

Tagus

A F R I C A

MAP 15.1   The Spanish Habsburgs and Europe, ca. 1556

Philip II's control of territories in northern Italy permitted the overland access of Spanish troops to the Netherlands and heightened the Spanish threat to France. Lands bordering the western Mediterranean made the sea a natural sphere of Spanish influence as well. Habsburg lands in central Europe were controlled after 1556 by Charles V's brother Ferdinand and his descendants.

general revolt that would secure freedom of worship. Margaret of Parma quelled the uprisings by rallying city governments and loyal nobles, now fearful for their own property and power. But by then, far away in Spain, a decision had been made to send in the Spanish duke of Alba with an army of ten thousand men.

Alba arrived in August 1567 and, to bolster his own shaky standing at the Spanish court, acted more like a conqueror than a peacemaker. He billeted troops in friendly cities, established new courts to try rebels, arrested thousands of people, executed about a thousand rebels (including Catholics as well as prominent Protestants), and imposed heavy new taxes to support his army. Thus Alba repeated every mistake of Spanish policy that had triggered rebellion in the first place.

Margaret of Parma resigned in disgust and left the Netherlands. Protestants from rebellious towns escaped into exile, where they were joined by nobles who had been declared traitors for resisting Alba's extreme policies. The most important of these was William of Nassau (NAS-saw), prince of Orange (1533–1584), whose lands outside the Netherlands, in France and the Holy

to a standstill, so that there are 100,000 men begging for their bread who used to earn it . . . which is [important] since poverty can force people to do things which otherwise they would never think of doing."[1]

The Provinces Revolt   In early 1567 armed bands of Calvinist insurgents seized two towns in the southern Netherlands by force of arms in hopes of stirring a

The City of Antwerp

Antwerp, in the southern Netherlands, was the point of sale for Portuguese spices brought around Africa from India; the selling and transshipping center for Baltic goods, including timber, fur, and grain; and the source for manufactured goods such as cloth.   *(Musées royaux des Beaux-Arts de Belgique)*

Roman Empire, lay beyond Spanish reach and so could be used to finance continued warfare against Spain. A significant community with military capability began to grow in exile.

In 1572 ships of exiled Calvinist privateers known as the "Sea Beggars" began preying on Spanish shipping and coastal fortresses from bases in the northern provinces. These provinces, increasingly Calvinist, became the center of opposition to the Spanish, who concentrated their efforts against rebellion in the wealthier southern provinces. Occasionally the French and English lent aid to the rebels.

The war in the Netherlands was a showcase for the new and costly technology of warfare in this period. Many towns were (or came to be, as a consequence of the revolt) equipped with "bastions," newly designed walled defenses that could resist artillery fire; such cities could not be taken by storm. Where bastions had been built, military campaigns consisted of grueling sieges, skirmishes in surrounding areas for control of supplies, and occasional pitched battles between besiegers and forces attempting to break the siege. Vast numbers of men were required both for effective besieging forces and for garrisoning the many fortresses that controlled the countryside and defended access to major towns.

In an attempt to supply the Netherlands with seasoned veterans and materiel from Spain and Spanish territories in Italy, the Spanish developed the "Spanish Road," an innovative string of supply depots where provisions could be gathered in advance of troops marching to the Netherlands (see Map 15.1). Maintaining its large armies, however, taxed Spain's resources to the breaking point. Even with American silver at hand, Philip could at times barely afford to keep armies in the field. Inevitably, large numbers of troops also exhausted the countryside, and both soldiers and civilians suffered great privations. On occasion Spanish troops reacted violently to difficult conditions and to delayed pay (American treasure dwindled badly between 1572 and 1578). In 1576 Spanish troops sacked the hitherto loyal city of Antwerp and massacred about eight thousand people. This event was bitterly remembered afterward as the "Spanish Fury." The massacre prompted leaders in the southern provinces to raise their own armies to protect themselves against the Spanish. Late in 1576 they concluded an alliance with William of Orange and the northern rebels.

Formation of the United Provinces

The alliance between northern and southern provinces did not last. The provinces and their inhabitants were increasingly divided by religion, and their differences were skillfully exploited by Philip's new commander, Margaret of Parma's son Alexander Farnese (far-NAY-zee), duke of Parma. With silver from America filling the king's coffers again, Parma wooed the Catholic elites of the southern provinces back into loyalty to Philip, in return for promises to respect their provincial liberties and safeguard their property from troops.

In 1579 the northern provinces united in a defensive alliance, the Union of Utrecht (OO-trekt), against the increasingly unified south. Parma's forces could not surmount the natural barrier of the Meuse and Rhine Rivers that bisect the Low Countries (see **MAP 15.2**). Nor could he meet the increasing costs of siege warfare in waterlogged terrain, particularly as Spain diverted money to conflicts with England in 1588 and France after 1589. In 1609 a truce was finally concluded between Spain and the northern provinces. This truce did not formally recognize the "United Provinces" as an independent entity, though in fact they were. The modern nations of Belgium (the Spanish provinces) and the Netherlands are the distant result of this truce.

The independent United Provinces (usually called, simply, the Netherlands) was a fragile state, an accident of warfare at first. But commercial prosperity began to

MAP 15.2   The Netherlands, 1559–1609

The seventeen provinces of the Netherlands were strikingly diverse politically, economically, and culturally.

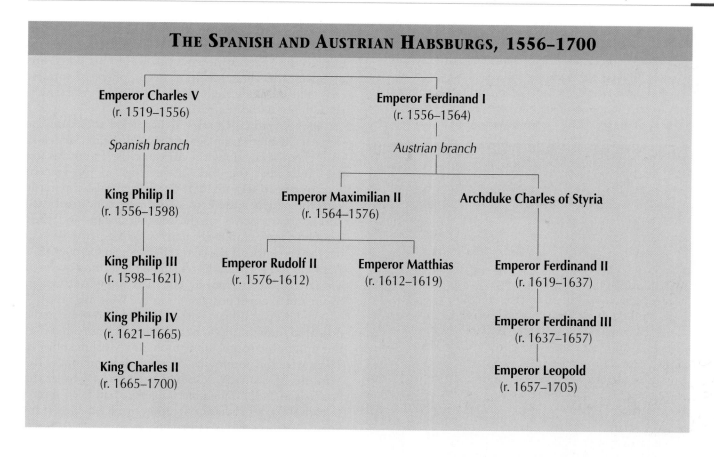

The Spanish and Austrian Habsburgs, 1556–1700

Emperor Charles V
(r. 1519–1556)

Spanish branch

Emperor Ferdinand I
(r. 1556–1564)

Austrian branch

King Philip II
(r. 1556–1598)

Emperor Maximilian II
(r. 1564–1576)

Archduke Charles of Styria

King Philip III
(r. 1598–1621)

Emperor Rudolf II
(r. 1576–1612)

Emperor Matthias
(r. 1612–1619)

Emperor Ferdinand II
(r. 1619–1637)

King Philip IV
(r. 1621–1665)

Emperor Ferdinand III
(r. 1637–1657)

King Charles II
(r. 1665–1700)

Emperor Leopold
(r. 1657–1705)

emerge as its greatest strength. Much of the economic activity of Antwerp had shifted north to Amsterdam in the province of Holland because of fighting in the south and a naval blockade of Antwerp by rebel ships. Philip's policies had created a new enemy nation and had enriched it at his expense.

The Failure of the Invincible Armada

The revolt of the Netherlands lured Spain into wider strategic involvement, particularly against England. Spain and England had a common foe in France and common economic interests, and Philip had married Mary Tudor, the Catholic queen of England (r. 1553–1558). Even after Mary's death and the accession of her Protestant half sister, Queen Elizabeth (r. 1558–1603), Spanish-English relations remained cordial. Relations started to sour, however, when Elizabeth began tolerating the use of English ports by the rebel Sea Beggars and authorizing attacks by English privateers on Spanish treasure fleets. In response Spain supported Catholic resistance to Elizabeth within England, including plots to replace her on the throne with her Catholic cousin, Mary, Queen of Scots. Greater Spanish success in the Netherlands, raids by the Spanish and English on each other's shipping, and Elizabeth's execution of Mary in 1587 prompted Philip to order an

invasion of England. A fleet (*armada*) of Spanish warships sailed in 1588.

"The enterprise of England," as the plan was called in Spain, represented an astounding logistical effort. The **Armada** was supposed to clear the English Channel of English ships in order to permit an invading force—troops under Parma in the Netherlands—to cross on barges. The sheer number of ships required for the undertaking—about 130—meant that some, inevitably, were slower supply ships, or vessels designed for the more protected waters of the Mediterranean. The English also had the advantage in arms, since they had better long-range artillery and better-trained gunners.

When the Armada entered the Channel on July 29, the English harassed the Spanish with artillery from a distance without sustaining much damage themselves. Parma could not get his men readied on their barges quickly enough once the fleet's presence in the Channel had been confirmed by messenger, nor could the fleet protect itself while waiting offshore. On the night of August 7 the English launched eight fire ships—burning vessels set adrift to deliver arson—into the anchored Spanish fleet. At dawn on the next day, they attacked

Armada   Massive fleet of Spanish warships sent against England by Philip II but defeated by the English navy and bad weather in 1588. The tactics used by the English helped set the future course of naval warfare.

Philip II in 1583
Dressed in the austere black in fashion at the Spanish court, Philip holds a rosary and wears the Order of the Golden Fleece, an order of knighthood, around his neck. At age 56 Philip had outlived four wives and most of his children. *(Museo del Prado, Madrid)*

the weakened fleet off Gravelines (grahv-LEEN), sank many ships, and dispersed what remained.

The Battle at Gravelines was the first major artillery battle by sailing ships and helped set the future course of naval warfare. It was a disaster for Philip's hopes and for thousands of sailors and soldiers in Spanish pay. Many of the surviving ships sank in bad weather or were forced into hostile harbors as the Armada sailed for home around the northern tip of the British Isles. Less than half of Philip's great fleet made it back to Spain.

SUCCESSES AT HOME AND AROUND THE MEDITERRANEAN

Despite his bountiful overseas empire and his preoccupation with the Netherlands, many of Philip's interests still centered on the Mediterranean. Spain and the kingdom of Naples had exchanged trade for centuries.

Newer ties had been forged with the duchy of Milan and the city-state of Genoa, whose bankers were financiers to the Spanish monarchy. It was in his kingdoms of Spain and their Mediterranean sphere of interest that Philip made his power felt more effectively, though not without effort.

Philip's father, Charles V, had tried to secure the western Mediterranean against the Ottoman Turks and their client states along the African coast, but it was under Philip that the Turkish challenge in the western Mediterranean receded. The Spanish allied temporarily with the papacy and Venice—both were concerned with Turkish naval power in the Mediterranean—and their combined navies inflicted a massive defeat on the Turkish navy at Lepanto, off the coast of Greece, in October 1571 (see Map 15.1). The Turks remained the leading power in the eastern Mediterranean, but their ability to threaten Spain and Spanish possessions in the West was over.

To Philip and his advisers, the Turks represented a potential internal threat as well, since it was feared that they might incite rebellion among his Muslim subjects. These were the nominally Christian descendants of the Muslims of Granada, who had been conquered by the Spanish in 1492. Called *moriscos,* they had been forced to convert to Christianity in 1504 or be expelled from Spain. Yet no serious effort had been made to teach them Christian beliefs in their own language (Arabic), and they had not been assimilated into Spanish society. Philip inaugurated a new wave of persecution and provoked a massive rebellion by the moriscos that began on Christmas Day in 1568. The revolt took two years to suppress. After it was crushed, the moriscos of Granada were forcibly exiled and dispersed farther north in Spain.

Philip's power in each of his Spanish kingdoms was limited by the traditional privileges of towns, nobility, and clergy. In Aragon, for example, he could raise revenues only by appealing to local assemblies, the Cortes (core-TEZ). Philip made significant inroads into Aragonese independence by the end of his reign, however. Noble feuds and peasant rebellions in Aragon during the 1580s provided a pretext for sending in veteran troops from the Netherlands campaigns to establish firmer royal control. Philip was successful in the long run in Aragon, as he had not been in the Netherlands, because he used adequate force but tempered it afterward with constitutional changes that were cleverly moderate. He cemented the peace by appearing in Aragon in person, in the words of a contemporary, "like a rainbow at the end of a storm."[2]

In Castile, the arid kingdom in the center of the Iberian Peninsula, the king was able to levy taxes with greater ease but only because of concessions that gave nobles undisputed authority over their peasants. Philip established his permanent capital, Madrid, and his principal residence, the Escorial, there. The Spanish

The Battle of Lepanto
On October 7, 1571, vessels of the Holy League (Spain, Venice, and the papacy) defeated the Ottoman fleet off the coast of Greece. Lepanto was the last great battle between galleys—the oared warships that had dominated Mediterranean waters since ancient times.   *(Courtesy, National Maritime Museum)*

Empire became more and more Castilian as the reign progressed, with royal advisers and counselors increasingly drawn only from the Castilian elite. Yet the rural economy of Castile was stunted by the dual oppression of landholders and royal tax collectors.

Philip also invaded and annexed Portugal in 1580, temporarily unifying the Iberian Peninsula. The annexation was ensured by armed force but had been preceded by careful negotiation to guarantee that Philip's claim to the throne—through his mother—would find some support within the country. When Philip died in 1598, he was old and ill, a man for whom daily life had become a painful burden. His Armada had been crushed; the Netherlands had slipped through his fingers. Yet he had learned from his mistakes and had been more successful, by his own standards, in other regions that he ruled.

SPAIN IN DECLINE, 1600–1648

Spain steadily lost ground economically and strategically after the turn of the century. Imports of silver declined. The American mines were exhausted, and the natives forced to work in them were decimated by European diseases and brutal treatment. Spain's economic health was further threatened by the very success of its colonies: local industries in the Americas began to produce goods formerly obtained from Spain. The increasing presence of English, French, and Dutch shipping in the Americas provided colonists with rival sources for the goods they needed. Often these competitors could offer their goods more cheaply than the Spanish, for Spanish productivity was low and prices were high because of the inflationary effects of the influx of precious metals.

Spain renewed hostilities with the United Provinces in 1621, after the truce of 1609 had expired. Philip IV (r. 1621–1665) also aided his Habsburg cousins in the Thirty Years' War in the Holy Roman Empire (see page 472). Squeezed for troops and revenue for these commitments, other Spanish territories revolted. The uprisings reflected both economic distress and unresolved issues of regional autonomy. Castile bore the brunt of the financial support of the state. The chief minister to Philip IV, Gaspar de Guzmán, Count Olivares (oh-lih-VAR-ez) (1587–1645), was an energetic Castilian aristocrat determined to distribute the burdens of government more equitably among the various regions of Spain. His policies provoked rebellions in Catalonia and Portugal.

In Catalonia, a province of the kingdom of Aragon, the revolt began as a popular uprising against the billeting of troops. At one point Catalan leaders invited French troops to defend them and solemnly transferred their loyalty to the French king in the hope that he would respect their autonomy. Spain resumed control only in 1652, after years of military struggle and promises to respect Catalan liberties.

In Portugal a war of independence began in 1640, also launched by popular revolt. The Spanish government tried to restore order with troops under the command of a leading Portuguese prince, John, duke of Braganza. The duke, however, was the nearest living relative to the last king of Portugal, and he seized this opportunity to claim the crown of Portugal for himself. Although war dragged on until 1668, the Portuguese under John IV (r. 1640–1656) succeeded in winning independence from Spain.

As a result of these uprisings, Count Olivares resigned in disgrace in 1643. In 1647 upheaval would shake Spain's Italian possessions of Sicily and Naples. By midcentury Spain had lost its position as the preeminent state in Europe.

════════ S E C T I O N   S U M M A R Y ════════

- Spain was the most powerful state in Europe in the second half of the sixteenth century because it controlled territory in Italy and in the Netherlands as well as colonies in the Americas.

- The prosperous Netherlands revolted against Spanish control for political, economic, and religious reasons.

- The invention of new kinds of fortifications increased the cost and destructiveness of the war.

- The northern provinces within the Netherlands, called the United Provinces, won independence from Spanish control by 1609.

- Spain attempted, but failed, to invade England with the Armada.

- The Spanish state weakened economically and politically in the seventeenth century as its income from colonies declined.

RELIGIOUS AND POLITICAL CONFLICT IN FRANCE AND ENGLAND

What conditions led to civil war in France? How did religious and political conflict develop differently in England?

In the second half of the sixteenth century France was convulsed by civil war that had both religious and political causes. Although a temporary resolution was achieved by 1598, the kingdom was still divided by religion and by military and political challenges to royal authority. England, in contrast, was spared political and religious upheaval in the second half of the century, in part because of the talents and long life of its ruler, Elizabeth I. But in the seventeenth century constitutional and religious dissent began to reinforce each other in new ways and dramatically threatened royal power.

THE FRENCH RELIGIOUS WARS, 1562–1598

Civil war wracked France from 1562 until 1598. As in the Netherlands, the conflicts in France had religious and political origins and international ramifications. The French monarch, like Philip, was unable to monopolize military power. In 1559 the king of France, Henry II (r. 1547–1559), had concluded the Peace of Cateau-Cambrésis with Philip II, ending the Habsburg-Valois Wars, but had died in July of that year from wounds suffered at a tournament held to celebrate the new treaty. His death was a political disaster. Great noble families vied for influence over his 15-year-old son, Francis II (r. 1559–1560). The queen mother, Catherine de' Medici (day MAY-di-chi) (1519–1589), worked carefully and intelligently to balance the nobles' interests. She gained greater authority when, in late 1560, the sickly Francis died and was succeeded by his brother, Charles IX—a 10-year-old for whom Catherine was officially the regent. But keeping the conflicts among the great courtiers from boiling over into civil war proved impossible.

Background to Civil War   In France, as elsewhere, noble conflict invariably had a violent component. Noblemen carried swords and daggers and were accompanied by armed entourages. Although they relied on patronage and army commands from the Crown, the Crown depended on their services. Provincial land-

Massacre at Vassy

This contemporary engraving by two Protestant artists depicts the Duke of Guise (*center left*) and his men coldly butchering Huguenot worshipers at Vassy. In a Catholic version of the event, the Protestants were killed by gunfire after pelting Guise's men with rocks when they tried to disperse the worshipers. *(HIP/Art Resource, NY)*

holdings, together with the royal offices they enjoyed, afforded enough resources to support private warfare, and the nobles assumed the right to wage it.

In addition, religious tension was rising throughout France. Henry II had welcomed the 1559 treaty in part because he wanted to turn his attention to "heresy." Public preaching by and secret meetings of Protestants (known as **Huguenots** in France) were causing unrest in towns. At court members of leading noble families—including the Bourbons, who were princes of royal blood—had converted to Protestantism and worshiped openly in their rooms in the palace. In 1561 Catherine convened a national religious council, known as the Colloquy of Poissy (pwa-SEE), to reconcile the two faiths. When it failed, she chose provisional religious toleration as the only practical course and issued a limited edict of toleration of Huguenots (HEW-guh-nots) in the name of the king in January 1562.

The edict led only to further unrest. Ignoring its restrictions, Protestants armed themselves, while townspeople of both faiths insulted and attacked one another at worship sites and religious festivals. In March 1562 the armed retainers of a Catholic duke killed a few dozen Protestants gathered in worship at Vassy (vah-SEE), near one of the duke's estates. The killing, in bringing the military power of the nobility to bear on the broader problem of religious division, sparked the first of six civil wars.

Decades of Civil War In some ways the initial conflict in 1562 was decisive. The Protestant army lost the principal pitched battle of the war in December of that year. This defeat checked the growth of the Protestant movement by reducing the appeal of the movement to nobles. The peace edict granted in 1563 curtailed the reach of the Huguenot movement; the limited rights granted to Protestants in the Crown's edict made it difficult for Protestants in towns—where

Huguenots French Protestants, followers of the teachings of John Calvin.

the vast majority of them lived—to worship. But if the Protestants were not powerful enough to win, neither were they weak enough to be decisively beaten.

The turning point most obvious to contemporaries came a decade later. The Protestant faction was still represented at court by the Bourbon princes and by the very able and influential nobleman Gaspard de Coligny (gas-PAR duh koh-leen-YEE), related to the Bourbons by marriage. Coligny was pressing the king for a war against Spain in order to aid Protestant rebels in the Netherlands. Opposed to entanglement in another war against Spain and alarmed by rumors of Huguenot armies massing outside Paris, Charles IX (r. 1560–1574) and his mother authorized royal guards to murder Coligny and other Protestant leaders on August 24, 1572—Saint Bartholomew's Day. Coligny's murder touched off a massacre of Protestants throughout Paris and, once news from Paris had spread, throughout the kingdom.

The Saint Bartholomew's Day Massacre revealed the degree to which religious differences had strained the fabric of community life. Neighbor murdered neighbor in an effort to rid the community of heretical pollution; bodies of the dead, including Coligny's, were mutilated. Gathered in the south of France, the remaining Huguenot forces vowed "never [to] trust those who have so often and so treacherously broken faith and the public peace."[3] Huguenot writers published tracts arguing that royal power was by nature limited and that rebellion was justified against tyrants who overstepped their legitimate authority.

Further war produced the inevitable truces and limited toleration, but many Catholics also renounced reconciliation. Some noblemen formed a Catholic league to fight in place of the weakened monarchy. Charles's brother, Henry III (r. 1574–1589), was another king of limited abilities. Middle-aged, Henry had no children. The heir to his throne was the Protestant Henry of Navarre, and the assumption of the throne by a Protestant was unimaginable to the zealous Catholic faction at court and to many ordinary Catholics. By the end of Henry III's reign, the king had almost no royal authority left to wield. He was forced to cooperate with first one of the warring parties and then another. In December 1588 he resorted to murdering two courtiers who led the ultra-Catholic faction; in turn he was murdered by a priest in early 1589.

Henry of Navarre, the Bourbon prince who became Henry IV (r. 1589–1610), had to fight for his throne. He faced Catholic armies now subsidized by Philip II of Spain, an extremist Catholic city government in Paris, and subjects who were tired of war but mainly Catholic, and he could count on only meager support from Protestants abroad. Given these obstacles, the politically astute Henry agreed to convert to Catholicism.

Henry IV and Fragile Peace   After Henry's conversion in 1593, the wars continued for a time, but after thirty years of civil strife many of Henry's subjects believed that only rallying to the monarchy could save France from chaos. Nobles grew increasingly disposed, for both psychological and practical reasons, to cooperate with the Crown. Service to a successful king could be a source of glory, and Henry was personally esteemed because he was a talented general and brave, gregarious, and charming. The nobility forced the citizens of Paris and other cities to accept Henry's authority. The civil war period thus proved to be an important phase in the incremental accommodation of the nobility to the power of the state.

In April 1598 Henry granted toleration for the Huguenot minority in a royal edict proclaimed in the city of Nantes (NAHNT). The **Edict of Nantes** was primarily a repetition of provisions from the most generous edicts that had ended the various civil wars. Nobles were allowed to practice the Protestant faith on their estates; townspeople were granted more limited rights to worship in selected towns in each region. Protestants were also guaranteed rights of self-defense—specifically, the right to maintain garrisons in about two hundred towns. About half of these garrisons would be paid for by the Crown.

Online Study Center   **Improve Your Grade**
Primary Source: Henry IV's Edict of Nantes Grants Limited Toleration to the Huguenots

The problem was that the Edict of Nantes, like any royal edict, could be revoked by the king at any time. Moreover, the provision allowing Protestants to keep garrisoned towns reflected concessions to Protestant aristocrats, who could support their followers by paid garrison duty. It also reflected the assumption that living peacefully amid religious diversity might prove to be impossible. Thus, although Henry IV ended the French religious wars, he had not solved the problem of religious and political division within France.

THE CONSOLIDATION OF ROYAL AUTHORITY IN FRANCE, 1598–1643

During Henry IV's reign, France recovered from the long years of civil war. Population and productivity began to grow; the Crown encouraged internal improvements to facilitate commerce. Henry's chief minister, Maximilien de Béthune (bay-TOON), duke of Sully (soo-LEE) (1560–1641), increased royal revenue by nibbling away at traditional local self-government and control of taxation. He succeeded in creating a budget

Edict of Nantes   1598 edict of Henry IV granting France's Protestants (Huguenots) the right to practice their faith and maintain defensive garrisons.

THE FRENCH SUCCESSION, 1515–1715

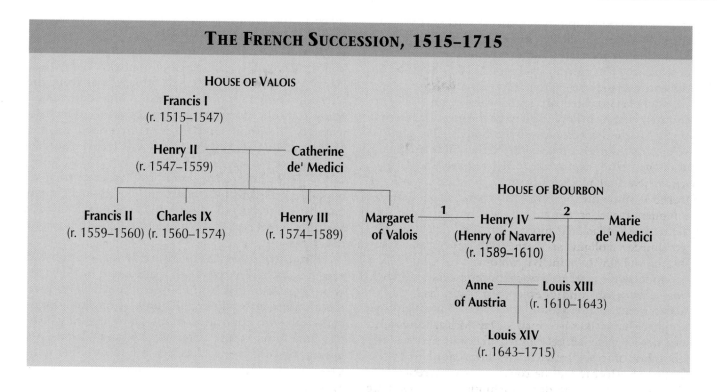

HOUSE OF VALOIS

Francis I
(r. 1515–1547)

Henry II —————— **Catherine**
(r. 1547–1559)   **de' Medici**

HOUSE OF BOURBON

Francis II   **Charles IX**   **Henry III**   **Margaret** — 1 — **Henry IV** — 2 — **Marie**
(r. 1559–1560) (r. 1560–1574) (r. 1574–1589) **of Valois**   **(Henry of Navarre)**   **de' Medici**
                                                                  (r. 1589–1610)

Anne ———— **Louis XIII**
of Austria   (r. 1610–1643)

Louis XIV
(r. 1643–1715)

surplus and in extending mechanisms of centralized government.

Yet Henry's regime was stable only in comparison with the preceding years of civil war. The power of the great nobility had not been definitively broken. Moreover, the king had agreed to a provision, known as the *paulette* (named for the functionary who first administered it), that allowed royal officeholders not merely to own their offices but also to pass on those offices to their heirs in return for the payment of an annual fee. Primarily a device to raise revenue after decades of civil war, the paulette also helped cement the loyalty of royal bureaucrats at a critical time, particularly that of the royal judges of the supreme law court, the Parlement of Paris, who had recently agreed to register the Edict of Nantes only under duress. However, the paulette made royal officeholders largely immune from royal control since their posts were now in effect property, like the landed property of the traditional nobility.

In 1610 a fanatical Catholic assassinated Henry IV. Henry's death brought his 9-year-old son, Louis XIII (r. 1610–1643), to the throne with Louis's mother, Marie de' Medici, serving as regent. Marie was disgraced when her unpopular leading minister—resented for monopolizing patronage—was assassinated with Louis's approval in 1617.

Four years later Louis faced a major rebellion by his Huguenot subjects in southwestern France. Huguenots felt that Louis's recent marriage to a Spanish princess and other ominous policies meant that royal support for toleration was wavering. A group of Huguenot nobles initiated fighting as a show of force against the king. The wars persisted, on and off, for eight years, as the French royal troops, like the Spanish in the Netherlands, had difficulty breaching the defenses of even small fortress towns. The main Huguenot stronghold was the well-fortified port city of La Rochelle, which had grown wealthy from European and overseas trade. Not until the king took the city, after a siege lasting more than a year and costing thousands of lives, did the Protestants accept a peace on royal terms.

The Peace of Alais (ah-LAY) (1629) reaffirmed the policy of religious toleration but rescinded the Protestants' military and political privileges. It was a political triumph for the Crown because it deprived French Protestants of the means for further rebellion while reinforcing their dependence on the Crown for religious toleration. Most of the remaining great noble leaders began to convert to Catholicism.

The Peace of Alais was also a personal triumph for the king's leading minister, who crafted the treaty and who had directed the bloody siege that made it possible. Armand-Jean du Plessis (1585–1642), Cardinal Richelieu (RISH-el-yiuh), came from a provincial noble family and rose in the service of the queen mother. He was admired and feared for his skill in the political game of seeking and bestowing patronage—a crucial skill in an age when elites received offices and honors through carefully cultivated relationships at court. His control of many lucrative church posts gave him the resources to build up a large network of clients. He and the king—whose sensitive temperament Richelieu handled adeptly—formed a lasting partnership that had a decisive impact not only on French policy but also on the entire shape of the French state.

Richelieu favored an aggressive foreign policy to counter what he believed still to be the greatest external threat to the French crown: the Spanish Habsburgs. When war resumed between the Netherlands and Spain after their truce expired in 1621 (see page 472), Richelieu sent troops to attack Spanish possessions in Italy. In the 1630s, with the king's full confidence, he superintended large-scale fighting against Spain in the Netherlands itself, as well as in Italy, and he began subsidizing Swedish and German Protestant armies fighting the Habsburgs in Germany.

Richelieu's policies were opposed by many French people, who saw taxes double, then triple, in just a few years. Many courtiers and provincial elites favored keeping the peace with Spain, a fellow Catholic state, and objected to alliances with German Protestants. They were alarmed by the increasing taxes and by the famine, disease, and, above all, the revolts that accompanied the peasants' distress. Their own status was also directly threatened by Richelieu's monopoly of royal patronage and by his creation of new offices, which diluted and undermined their power. In 1632, for example, Richelieu created the office of *intendant*. Intendants had wide powers for defense and administration in the provinces that overrode the established bureaucracy.

By 1640 Richelieu's ambitious foreign policy seemed to be bearing fruit. The French had won territory along their northern and eastern borders by their successes against Habsburg forces. But when Richelieu and Louis XIII died within five months of each other, in December 1642 and May 1643, Richelieu's legacy was tested. Louis XIII was succeeded by his 5-year-old son, and the warrior-nobility, as well as royal bureaucrats, would waste little time before challenging the Crown's new authority.

PRECARIOUS STABILITY IN ENGLAND: THE REIGN OF ELIZABETH I, 1558–1603

England experienced no civil wars during the second half of the sixteenth century, but religious dissent challenged the stability of the monarchy. In **Elizabeth I** (r. 1558–1603), England—in stark contrast to France—possessed an able and long-lived ruler. Elizabeth was well educated in the humanistic tradition and was already an adroit politician at the age of 25, when she ac-

ceded to the throne at the death of her Catholic half sister, Mary Tudor (r. 1553–1558).

Elizabeth faced the urgent problem of reaching a policy of consensus in religious matters. Her father, Henry VIII (r. 1509–1547), had broken away from the Catholic Church for political reasons but had retained many Catholic doctrines and practices. A Calvinist-inspired Protestantism had been prescribed for the Church of England by the advisers of Henry's successor, Elizabeth's young half brother, Edward VI (r. 1547–1553). True Catholicism, such as Mary had tried to reimpose, was out of the question. The Roman church had never recognized Henry VIII's self-made divorce and thus regarded Elizabeth as a bastard with no right to the throne.

Elizabeth adopted a cleverly moderate solution and used force, where necessary, to maintain it. In 1559 Parliament passed a new Act of Supremacy, which restored the monarch as head of the Church of England. Elizabeth dealt with opposition to the act by arresting bishops and lords whose votes would have blocked its passage by Parliament. Elizabeth and most of her ministers, all moderate realists, were willing to accept some flexibility in personal belief. For example, the official prayer book in use in Edward's day was revised to include elements of both traditional and radical interpretations of Communion. But church liturgy, clerical vestments, and, above all, the hierarchical structure of the clergy closely resembled Catholic practices. The Act of Uniformity required all worship to be conducted according to the new prayer book. Although uniformity was required in worship, Elizabeth was careful, in her words, not to "shine beacons into her subjects' souls."

Catholicism continued to be practiced, especially by otherwise loyal nobility and gentry in the north of England, who worshiped privately on their estates. But priests returning from exile beginning in the 1570s, most newly imbued with the proselytizing zeal of the Counter-Reformation (the Catholic response to the Protestant Reformation), practiced it more visibly and were zealously prosecuted for their boldness. In the last twenty years of Elizabeth's reign, approximately 180 Catholics were executed for treason, two-thirds of them priests. (By 1585 being a Catholic priest in itself was a crime.)

In the long run, the greater threat to the English crown came from the most radical Protestants in the realm, known (by their enemies initially) as **Puritans**. Puritanism was a broad movement for reform of church practice along familiar Protestant lines: an emphasis on Bible reading, preaching, and private scrutiny

Elizabeth I Able and long-lived ruler who firmly established Protestantism in England and defended the nation against the Spanish Armada, but who bequeathed financial, religious, and political problems to her successors.

Puritans Radical Protestants in late-sixteenth- and seventeenth-century England who became a majority in Parliament during the reign of Charles I and led opposition to the king.

of conscience; a de-emphasis on institutional ritual and clerical authority. Most Puritans had accepted Elizabeth's religious compromise for practical reasons but grew increasingly alienated by her insistence on clerical authority and her refusal to change any elements of the original religious settlement. A significant Presbyterian underground movement began to form among them. Presbyterians wanted to dismantle the episcopacy—the hierarchy of priests and bishops—and to govern the church instead with councils, called "presbyteries," that included lay members of the congregation. Laws were passed late in the queen's reign to enable the Crown to prosecute more easily, and even to force into exile, anyone who attended "nonconformist" (non-Anglican) services.

The greatest challenge Elizabeth faced from Puritans came in Parliament, where they were well represented by many literate gentry. Parliament met only when called by the monarch. In theory members could merely voice opinions and complaints; they could not initiate legislation and prescribe policy. However, only Parliament could vote taxes. Further, since it had in effect helped constitute royal authority by means of the two Acts of Supremacy, Parliament's merely advisory role had been expanded by the monarchy itself. During Elizabeth's reign, Puritans capitalized on Parliament's enlarged scope, using meetings to press for further religious reform. In 1586 they went so far as to introduce

bills calling for an end to the episcopacy and the Anglican prayer book. Elizabeth had to resort to imprisoning one Puritan leader to end debate on the issue and on Parliament's right to address it.

Also during Elizabeth's reign, efforts at English expansion in the New World began, in the form of unsuccessful attempts at colonization and successful raids on Spanish possessions. However, the main focus of her foreign policy remained Europe itself. Elizabeth, like all her forebears, felt her interests tightly linked to the independence of the Netherlands, whose towns were a major outlet for English wool. Philip II's aggressive policy in the Netherlands increasingly alarmed her, especially in view of France's weakness. She began to send small sums of money to the rebels and allowed their ships access to southern English ports, from which they could raid Spanish-held towns on the Netherlands' coast. In 1585, in the wake of the duke of Parma's successes against the rebellions, she committed troops to help the rebels.

Her decision was a reaction not only to the threat of a single continental power dominating the Netherlands but also to the threat of Catholicism. From 1579 to 1583 the Spanish had helped the Irish fight English domination and were involved in several plots to replace Elizabeth with her Catholic cousin, Mary, Queen of Scots. These threats occurred as the return of Catholic exiles to England peaked. The victory over the Spanish

Elizabeth I: The Armada Portrait
Both serene and resolute, Elizabeth is flanked by "before" and "after" glimpses of the Spanish fleet; her hand rests on the globe in a gesture of dominion that also memorializes the circumnavigation of the globe by her famous captain, Sir Francis Drake, some years before. *(By kind permission of Marquess of Tavistock and Trustees of Bedford Estate)*

Armada in 1588 was quite rightly celebrated, for it ended any Catholic threat to Elizabeth's rule.

The success against the Armada has tended to overshadow other aspects of Elizabeth's foreign policy, particularly with regard to Ireland. Since the twelfth century an Anglo-Irish state dominated by great princely families had been loosely supervised from England, but most of Ireland remained under the control of Gaelic chieftains. Just as Charles V and Philip II attempted to tighten their governing mechanisms in the Netherlands, so did Henry VIII's minister, Thomas Cromwell, streamline control of outlying areas such as Wales and Anglo-Ireland. Cromwell proposed that the whole of Ireland be brought under English control partly by the established mechanism of feudal ties: the Irish chieftains were to pay homage as vassals to the king of England.

Under Elizabeth this legalistic approach gave way to virtual conquest. Elizabeth's governor, Sir Henry Sidney, appointed in 1565, inaugurated a policy whereby Gaelic lords, by means of various technicalities, could be entirely dispossessed of their lands. Any Englishman capable of raising a private force could help enforce these dispossessions and settle his conquered lands as he saw fit. This policy provoked stiff Irish resistance, which was viewed as rebellion and provided the rationale for further military action, more confiscations of lands, and more new English settlers. Eventually the Irish, with Spanish assistance, mounted a major rebellion, consciously Catholic and aimed against the "heretic" queen. The rebellion gave the English an excuse for brutal suppression and massive transfers of lands to English control. The political domination of the Irish was complete with the defeat, in 1601, of the Gaelic chieftain Hugh O'Neill, lord of Tyrone, who had controlled most of the northern quarter of the island. Although the English were unable to impose Protestantism on the conquered Irish, to Elizabeth and her English subjects the conquests in Ireland seemed as significant as the victory over the Spanish Armada.

The English enjoyed relative peace at home during Elizabeth's reign. However, her reign ended on a note of strain. The foreign involvements, particularly in Ireland, had been very expensive. Taxation granted by Parliament more than doubled during her reign, and local taxes further burdened the people. Price inflation related to government spending, social problems caused by returned unemployed soldiers, and a series of bad harvests heightened popular resentment against taxation. Despite her achievements, therefore, Elizabeth passed two problems on to her successors: unresolved religious tensions and financial instability. Elizabeth's successors would also find in Parliament an increasing focus of opposition to their policies.

RISING TENSIONS IN ENGLAND, 1603–1642

In 1603 Queen Elizabeth died, and James VI of Scotland, the Protestant son of Mary, Queen of Scots, ascended to the English throne as James I (r. 1603–1625). Religious tensions between Anglicans and Puritans were briefly quieted under James because of a plot, in 1605, by Catholic dissenters. The Gunpowder Plot, as it was called, was a conspiracy to blow up the palace housing both king and Parliament at Westminster. Protestants of all stripes again focused on their common enemy, Catholics—but only temporarily. Political and religious tensions rose under James and, especially, under James's son, Charles.

James I Financial problems, some of which were inherited from Elizabeth, were James's most pressing concern. Court life became more elaborate and an increasing drain on the monarchy's resources. James's extravagance was partly to blame for his financial problems, but so were pressures for patronage from courtiers. Added to the debts left from the Irish conflicts and wars with Spain were new military expenses as James helped defend the claims of his daughter and her husband, a German prince, to rule Bohemia (see page 472).

To raise revenue without Parliament's consent, James relied on sources of income that the Crown had enjoyed since medieval times: customs duties, wardship (the right to manage and liberally borrow from the estates of minor nobles), and the sale of monopolies, which conveyed the right to be sole agent for a particular kind of goods. To rebuild his treasury James increased the number of monopolies for sale and even created a new noble title—baronet—which he sold to socially ambitious commoners.

The monopolies were widely resented. Merchants objected to the arbitrary restriction of production and trade; common people found that they could no longer afford certain ordinary commodities, such as soap. Resentments among the nobility were sharpened, and general criticism of the court escalated, as James indulged in extreme favoritism of certain courtiers, including the corrupt George Villiers (VIL-yerz) (1592–1628), duke of Buckingham, who served as the king's first minister.

When James summoned Parliament to ask for funds in 1621, Parliament used the occasion to protest court corruption and the king's financial measures. The members revived the medieval procedure of impeachment and removed two royal ministers from office. In 1624, still faced with expensive commitments to Protestants abroad and in failing health, James again called Parliament, which voted new taxes but also openly debated the wisdom of the king's foreign policy.

thus leader of the Church of England. He tried to impose changes in worship, spread Arminian ideas, and censor opposing views. He also challenged the redistribution of church property, which had occurred in the Reformation of the sixteenth century, and thereby alienated the gentry on economic as well as religious grounds.

Charles's style of rule worsened religious, political, and economic tensions. Cold and intensely private, he did not inspire confidence or have the charm or the political skills to disarm his opponents. His court was ruled by formal protocol, and access to the king was highly restricted—a serious problem in an age when proximity to the monarch was a guarantee of political power.

Revenue and religion dominated debate in the Parliament of 1628–1629, which Charles had called, once again, to get funds for his foreign wars. In 1628 Parliament presented the king with a document called the Petition of Right, which protested his financial policies as well as arbitrary imprisonment. (Seventeen members of Parliament had been imprisoned for refusing loans to the Crown.) Though couched conservatively as a restatement of customary practice, the petition in fact claimed a tradition of expanded parliamentary participation in government. Charles dissolved Parliament in March 1629, having decided that the money he might extract was not worth the risk.

For eleven years Charles ruled without Parliament. When he was forced by necessity to summon it again in 1640, the kingdom was in crisis. Royal finances were in desperate straits, even though Charles had pressed collection of revenues far beyond traditional bounds. In 1634, for example, he had revived annual collection of "ship money"—a medieval tax raised in coastal regions to help support the navy during war. England, however, was not at war at that time, and the tax was levied not only on seaports but on inland areas, too.

Charles I Tensions between Crown and Parliament increased under James's son, Charles I (r. 1625–1649). One reason was the growing financial strain of foreign policy as well as the policies themselves. Charles declared war on Spain and supported the Huguenot rebels in France. Many wealthy merchants opposed this aggressive foreign policy because it disrupted trade. In 1626 Parliament was dissolved without granting any monies, in order to stifle its objections to royal policies. Instead, Charles levied a forced loan and did not hesitate to imprison gentry who refused to lend their money to the government.

Above all, Charles's religious policies were a source of controversy. Charles was personally inclined toward "high church" practices: an emphasis on ceremony and sacrament reminiscent of Catholic ritual. He also was a believer in Arminianism, a school of thought that rejected the Calvinist notion that God's grace cannot be earned, and hence emphasized the importance of the sacraments and the authority of the clergy. Charles's attempt to fashion the Church of England into an instrument that would reflect and justify royal claims to power put him on a collision course with gentry and aristocrats who leaned toward Puritanism.

Charles's views were supported by William Laud (1573–1645), archbishop of Canterbury from 1633 and

1640: The Kingdom in Crisis The immediate crisis in 1640—and the reason for Charles's desperate need for money—was a rebellion in Scotland. Like Philip II in the Netherlands, Charles tried to rule in Scotland through a small council of men who did not represent the local elite. Worse, he also tried to force his "high church" practices on the Scots. The Scottish church had been more dramatically reshaped during the Reformation and now was largely Presbyterian in structure. The result of Charles's policies was riots and rebellion. Unable to suppress the revolt in a first campaign in 1639, Charles was forced to summon Parliament to obtain funds to raise a more effective army.

But the Parliament that assembled in the spring of 1640 provided no help. Instead, members questioned the war with the Scots and other royal policies. Charles's political skills were far too limited for him to re-establish a workable relationship with Parliament under the circumstances. Charles dissolved this body, which is now known as the "Short Parliament," after just three weeks. Even more stinging than Charles's dissolution of the Parliament was the lack of respect he had shown the members: a number of them were harassed or arrested. Mistrust fomented by the eleven years in which Charles had ruled without Parliament thus increased.

Another humiliating and decisive defeat at the hands of the Scots later in 1640 made summoning another Parliament imperative. Members of the "Long Parliament" (it sat from 1640 to 1653) took full advantage of the king's predicament. Charles was forced to agree not to dissolve or adjourn Parliament without the members' consent and to summon Parliament at least every three years. Parliament abolished many of his unorthodox and traditional sources of revenue and impeached and removed from office his leading ministers, including Archbishop Laud. The royal commander deemed responsible for the Scottish fiasco, Thomas Wentworth, earl of Strafford, was executed without trial in May 1641.

The execution of Strafford shocked many aristocrats in the House of Lords (the upper house of Parliament), as well as some moderate members of the House of Commons. Meanwhile, Parliament began debating the perennially thorny religious question. A bare majority of members favored abolition of Anglican bishops as a first step in thoroughgoing religious reform. Working people in London, kept updated on the issues by the regular publication of parliamentary debates, demonstrated in support of that majority. Moderate members of Parliament, in contrast, favored checking the king's power but not upsetting the Elizabethan religious compromise.

An event that unified public and parliamentary opinion at a crucial time—a revolt against English rule in Ireland in October 1641—temporarily eclipsed these divisions. The broad consensus of anti-Catholicism once again became the temporary driving force in politics, but it did not diminish suspicion of the king. Fearing that Charles would use Irish soldiers against his English subjects, Parliament demanded that it have control of the army to put down the rebellion. In November the Puritan majority introduced a document known as the "Grand Remonstrance," an appeal to the people and a long catalog of parliamentary grievances against the king. It was passed by a narrow margin, further setting public opinion in London against Charles. The king's remaining support in Parliament eroded in January 1642 when he attempted to arrest five leading members on charges of treason. The five escaped, and the stage was set for wider violence. The king withdrew from London, unsure he could defend himself there, and began to raise an army. In mid-1642 the kingdom stood at the brink of civil war.

Online Study Center **Improve Your Grade**
Primary Source: Charles I Authorizes Sunday Recreations

═══════ S E C T I O N   S U M M A R Y ═══════

- France suffered through more than thirty years of civil war after 1562, caused by religious conflict, weak rulers, and powerful nobility.

- The French religious wars ended in the 1590s when war-weary elites rallied behind the talented king Henry IV; Henry decreed religious toleration in the Edict of Nantes.

- After Henry, religious and political conflict broke out again, but the king's minister Cardinal Richelieu successfully reinforced royal authority.

- Elizabeth I of England weathered religious and political tensions at home and challenges from abroad during her long reign.

- James I and Charles I struggled with limited financial resources, unpopular policies, and religious division.

- Parliamentary resistance to Charles's authority and policies led England to a political crisis in 1640.

RELIGIOUS AND POLITICAL CONFLICT IN CENTRAL AND EASTERN EUROPE

Why did war erupt again within the Holy Roman Empire and what was the significance of the conflict?

The Holy Roman Empire enjoyed a period of comparative quiet after the Peace of Augsburg halted religious and political wars in 1555. The 1555 agreement, which permitted rulers of the various states within the empire to impose either Catholicism or Lutheranism in their lands, proved to be a workable solution, for a time, to the problem of religious division. By the early seventeenth century, however, fresh causes of instability brought about renewed fighting. One factor was the rise of Calvinism, for which no provision had been necessary in 1555. Especially destabilizing was the drive by the Austrian Habsburgs to reverse the successes of Protestantism both in their own lands and in the empire at large and to solidify their control of their diverse personal territories. The result was a devastating conflict known as the **Thirty Years' War** (1618–1648).

Like conflicts elsewhere in Europe, the Thirty Years' War reflects religious tensions, regionalism versus centralizing forces, and dynastic and strategic rivalries between rulers. The war was particularly destructive because of the size of the armies and the degree to which army commanders evaded control by the states for which they fought. As a result of the war, the empire was eclipsed as a political unit by the regional powers that composed it. Meanwhile, a Polish state resembling the Habsburg territories in its regional diversity remained the dominant state in northeastern Europe. But it would soon face challenges, particularly from a powerful new state being crafted in Russia.

FRAGILE PEACE IN THE HOLY ROMAN EMPIRE, 1556–1618

The Austrian Habsburgs ruled over a diverse group of territories in the Holy Roman Empire, as well as northwestern Hungary (see **MAP 15.3**). On his abdication in 1556, Emperor Charles V granted Habsburg lands in central Europe to his brother, Ferdinand (see the chart on page 457), who had long been the actual ruler there in Charles's stead. On Charles's death in 1558, Ferdinand was duly crowned emperor.

Thirty Years' War   Destructive war (1618–1648) involving most European countries but fought in Germany, resulting from religious tensions, regionalism versus centralizing forces, and dynastic and strategic rivalries between rulers.

Though largely contiguous, Ferdinand's territories comprised independent duchies and kingdoms, each with its own institutional structure, and included speakers of Italian, German, and Czech, plus a few other languages. The non-German lands of Bohemia (the core of the modern Czech Republic) and Hungary had been distinct kingdoms since the High Middle Ages. Both states bestowed their crowns by election and had chosen Ferdinand, the first Habsburg to rule them, in separate elections in the 1520s and 1530s. Most of Hungary was now under Ottoman domination, but Bohemia, with its rich capital, Prague, was a wealthy center of population and culture.

Unlike the Netherlands, these linguistically and culturally diverse lands were still governed by highly decentralized institutions. Moreover, unlike their Spanish cousins, the Austrian Habsburgs made no attempt to impose religious uniformity in the late sixteenth century. Ferdinand was firmly Catholic but tolerant of reform efforts within the church. Both he and his son, Maximilian II (r. 1564–1576), believed that an eventual reunion of the Catholic and Protestant faiths might be possible. During his reign Maximilian worked to keep religious peace in the empire as a whole and granted limited rights of worship to Protestant subjects within his ancestral lands (separate territories more or less equivalent to modern Austria in extent). Catholicism and many strands of Protestantism flourished side by side in Maximilian's domains, above all in Hungary and, especially, Bohemia, which had experienced its own religious reform movement under Jan Hus in the fifteenth century.

Maximilian's son, Rudolf II (r. 1576–1612), shared the religious style of his father and grandfather. He was an energetic patron of the arts and humanist education and sponsored the work of scientists. Yet Rudolf was a weak leader politically and was challenged by his brother and ambitious cousins for control both of Habsburg lands and of the empire itself. Meanwhile, the resurgence of Catholicism in the wake of the Council of Trent (1545–1563) had begun to shift the religious balance. Members of the Jesuit order arrived in Habsburg lands in the reign of Maximilian. Tough-minded and well trained, they established Catholic schools and became confessors and preachers to the upper classes. Self-confident Catholicism emerged as one form of cultural identity among the German-speaking ruling

MAP 15.3   Europe During the Thirty Years' War, 1618–1648

The Thirty Years' War was fought largely within the borders of the Holy Roman Empire. It was the result of conflicts within the empire as well as the meddling of neighbors for their own strategic advantages.

Legend:
- Austrian Habsburg lands
- Spanish Habsburg lands
- Other German states
- Swedish lands by 1648
- Ottoman Empire and Tributary States
- ——— Boundary of Holy Roman Empire

0   150   300 Km.
0   150   300 Mi.

Online Study Center   Improve Your Grade   Interactive Map: Europe During the Thirty Years' War, 1618–1648 classes, and thus as a religious impetus to further political consolidation of all the Habsburg territories.

Resurgent Catholicism was evident, too, in the empire as a whole, where certain princes were confident they might now eliminate Protestantism, as their ancestors had failed to do. In the face of this challenge, certain Protestant princes formed a defensive pact known as the Evangelical Union in 1608. In response Catholic princes formed an alliance, the Holy League, the next year. A major war between the two alliances over a disputed territory was narrowly averted the following year. Like the English under Elizabeth, Habsburg subjects and peoples in the empire had enjoyed a period of calm in political and religious matters. Now, as in England, the stage was set for conflict of both kinds.

The Thirty Years' War, 1618–1648

The Thirty Years' War was touched off in 1618 by a revolt against Habsburg rule in the kingdom of Bohemia. Bohemia was populous and prosperous; Rudolf II had made its bustling capital, Prague, his imperial capital. Its powerful and diverse Protestant community had wrested formal recognition of its right to worship from Rudolf and his younger brother, Matthias (r. 1612–1619).

Background to War Matthias was quickly succeeded by his cousin Ferdinand II (r. 1619–1637), who was the ideal Counter-Reformation prince and unlikely to honor these agreements. Educated by the Jesuits,

Ferdinand sincerely believed that reimposing Catholicism was his Christian duty; he once stated that he would "sooner beg than rule over heretics."[4] He had virtually eliminated Protestantism, by persuasion as well as by compulsion, in the small duchy in southern Austria he had governed before assuming the throne.

Ferdinand would not tolerate the political independence of nobles and towns in Bohemia or the religious pluralism that independence defended. As Philip II had done in the Netherlands, Ferdinand appointed a regency council to govern in his name. That council enforced unpopular policies: the right to build new Protestant churches was denied, Bohemian crown lands were given to the Catholic Church, and non-Catholics were barred from serving in government.

On May 23, 1618, delegates to a Protestant assembly that had unsuccessfully petitioned Ferdinand to end his violations of earlier guarantees marched to the palace in Prague where the royal officials met. After a confrontation over their demands, the delegates "tried" the officials on the spot for treason and, literally, threw them out of the palace window. The incident became known as the "Defenestration of Prague" (from the Latin *fenestra*, or "window"). (The officials' lives were saved only because they fell into a pile of refuse in the moat.) The rebels proceeded to set up their own government.

This upstart Bohemian government officially deposed Ferdinand and elected a new Protestant king in 1619: Frederick, elector of the Palatinate and a Calvinist prince. His election had implications for the Holy

The Defenestration of Prague

This contemporary print memorializes the events of May 23, 1618. Bohemian Protestants "tried" two imperial officials for violating agreements that safeguarded their religious liberties. The two officials and their secretary were thrown out of the windows of Prague castle. *(Corbis)*

Roman Empire as a whole because his role as leader of the territories in west-central Germany called the Lower and Upper Palatinate conveyed the right to be one of the seven electors who chose the emperor.

Emboldened by these events, Protestant subjects in other Habsburg lands asked for guarantees of freedom of worship similar to those enjoyed by Protestants in Bohemia. Other princes saw their chance to make political gains. For example, rival claimants to Habsburg rule in Hungary took up arms against Ferdinand.

The Conflict Widens The revolt in Bohemia set off a wider war because foreign rulers also felt their interests to be involved. The English king, James I, supported Frederick because Frederick was married to his daughter. Spain's supply routes north from Italy to the Netherlands passed next to Frederick's lands in western Germany. France's first interest was its rivalry with Spain; thus France kept its eye on the border principalities that were strategically important to Spain. In addition, France desired to keep Protestant as well as Catholic princes within the empire strong enough to thwart Austrian Habsburg ambitions. Thus, from the outset, the war was a conflict not only over the Habsburgs' power in their own lands but also over the balance of religious and political power in the empire and in Europe (see Map 15.3).

Ferdinand secured aid from the Catholic duke of Bavaria and from his cousin, King Philip III (r. 1598–1621) of Spain, by promising them Frederick's lands in the Palatinate. By the fall of 1620 a Catholic army was closing in on Bohemia. On November 8, on a hillside near Prague, the Catholic force faced a Bohemian army that had received little aid from its Protestant allies. The Battle of White Mountain was a complete Catholic victory.

Despite the rout, fighting did not cease but instead became more widespread. The truce between Spain and the Netherlands, established in 1609, expired in 1621, and the nearby Lower Palatinate, now in Spanish hands, offered a staging point for Spanish forces and thus threatened the peace in that corner of the empire. Claiming to be a Protestant champion, the Protestant king of Denmark, Christian IV (r. 1588–1648), who was also duke of Holstein in northern Germany, sought to conquer additional German territory. His goals were to gain greater control over profitable German Baltic seaports and to defend himself against any Catholic attempt to seize northern German territory. Christian received little help from fellow Protestants, however. The Dutch were busy with Spain, the English were wary of fighting after Frederick's defeat, and Denmark's regional rivals, the Swedes, were uninterested in furthering Danish ambitions in the Baltic.

The confusing blend of politics and religion that motivated the Protestant rulers was also evident on the Catholic side. When imperial forces defeated Christian's armies in 1626, Catholic princes became alarmed at the possibility of greater imperial power in northern Germany. Led by the duke of Bavaria, they arranged a truce that resulted in Denmark's withdrawal from the fighting on relatively generous terms. At the same time, Protestants outside Bohemia saw the potential consequences of imperial victory and took up arms. As his armies defeated Christian, Ferdinand issued new edicts that in effect voided the religious settlement in place since 1555. His victorious armies brutally enforced his edicts wherever they passed.

Intervention of Sweden and France The Danish king's rival, Gustav Adolf, king of Sweden (r. 1611–1632), now assumed the role of Protestant leader. An innovative military leader, Gustav Adolf hoped to gain territory along the Baltic seacoast, but personal aggrandizement also was one of his goals. His campaigns were capped by a victory over an imperial army at Breitenfeld, in Saxony, in 1631. After he was killed in battle in 1632, however, the tide turned in favor of Ferdinand's forces. A decisive imperial victory over a combined Swedish and German Protestant army at Nördlingen (NERD-ling-un) in 1634 led to the Peace of Prague (1635), a general peace treaty favorable to Catholics.

The Peace of Prague brought only a temporary peace, however, because Ferdinand died shortly thereafter and French involvement increased now that other anti-Habsburg forces had been eclipsed. France tried to seize imperial territory along its own eastern border and generously subsidized continued fighting within the empire by channeling monies to Protestant princes and mercenaries there. The fighting dragged on. By the end of the Thirty Years' War order had disintegrated so completely in the wake of the marauding armies that both staunchly Catholic rulers and firmly Protestant ones allied with religious enemies to safeguard their states.

A comprehensive peace treaty became possible when France withdrew its sponsorship of the fighting in order to concentrate on its conflict with Spain. The French wanted only a workable balance of power in the empire, which was achieved once they and their allies convincingly defeated imperial forces in 1645. More urgent to the French was the continued rivalry with the Spanish Habsburgs for control of territory along France's eastern and northern borders and in Italy. A defeat by France in the Spanish Netherlands in 1643 had convinced Spain to concentrate on that rivalry, too, and fighting between them continued separately until 1659. Negotiations for peace had begun in 1643 among war-weary states of the empire and resulted in a group of agreements known as the **Peace of Westphalia** (west-FAIL-yuh) in 1648.

Peace of Westphalia Treaty that ended the Thirty Years' War in 1648. The principalities within the Holy Roman Empire were recognized as virtually autonomous, severely weakening the power of the emperor.

THE PEACE OF WESTPHALIA

The Peace of Westphalia, which ended fighting in the empire, was one of the most important outcomes of the war. The various treaties composing the peace effectively put an end to religious war in the empire. Calvinism was recognized as a tolerated religion. The requirement that all subjects must follow their ruler's faith was retained, but some leeway was allowed for those who now found themselves under new rulers.

In political matters the treaties reflected some of the recent successes of the Swedes by granting them territory on the Baltic coast. France gained the important towns of Metz, Toul, and Verdun on its eastern border. Spain formally recognized the independence of the Netherlands.

The most important political outcome of the peace was a new balance of power in the empire. Most of the major Catholic and Protestant rulers extended their territories at the expense of smaller principalities and cities. The son of Frederick, Protestant king of Bohemia, received back the smaller of the two Palatine territories that his father had held. The Upper Palatinate—as well as the right to be a new elector of the emperor—was given to the powerful duke of Bavaria. The principalities within the empire were acknowledged, in the peace, to be virtually autonomous, both from the emperor and from one another. In addition, the constitution of the empire was changed to make it very difficult for one prince or a group of princes to disrupt the peace in their own interests. As a result, the agreements at Westphalia were the beginning of one hundred years of peace within the Holy Roman Empire.

Another outcome was that the Habsburgs, though weakened as emperors, were strengthened as rulers of their own hereditary lands on the eastern fringes of the empire. Except in Hungary, Protestantism—and its contrary political baggage—had been eliminated early in the wars, and the peace did not alter these circumstances. The Habsburgs moved their capital back to Vienna from Prague, and the government of their hereditary lands gained in importance as administration of the empire waned.

THE EFFECTS OF THE WAR

The Thirty Years' War ruined the economy and decimated the population in many parts of the empire and had long-term political consequences for the empire as a whole. One reason for the war's devastation was a novel application of firepower to warfare that increased both the size of armies and their deadly force in

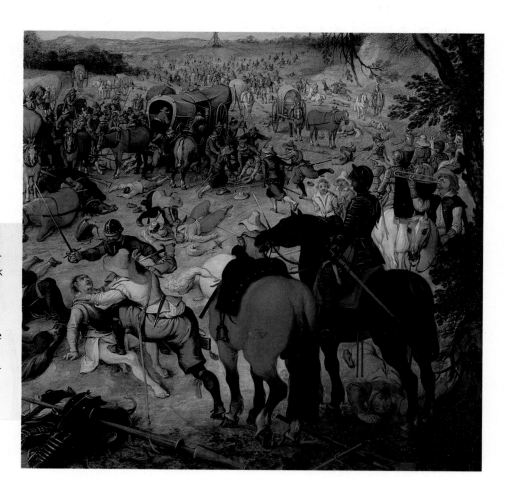

The Horrors of War
This painting by a seventeenth-century artist depicts an attack on a supply convoy by opposing troops. Control of supplies to feed and equip the increasing numbers of troops was one of the most important aspects of warfare. *(Staatsgalerie Aschaffenburg [Schloss], Bayerische Staatsgemäldesammlungen/Godwin Alfen-ARTOTHEK)*

battle. This was the use of volley fire, the arrangement of foot soldiers in parallel lines so that one line of men could fire while another reloaded. This tactic, pioneered in the Netherlands around the turn of the century, was further refined by Gustav Adolf of Sweden. Gustav Adolf amassed large numbers of troops and increased the rate of fire so that a virtually continuous barrage was maintained. He also used maneuverable field artillery to protect the massed infantry from cavalry charges.

Following Gustav Adolf's lead, armies of all the major states adopted these new offensive tactics. But defensive expertise—as in holding fortresses—also remained important, and pitched battles, such as at Nördlingen in 1634, still tended to be part of sieges. The costs in resources and human life of this kind of warfare reached unheard-of dimensions. Popular printed literature and court drama both condemned the horrors of the war.

Where fighting had been concentrated, as in parts of Saxony, between one-third and one-half of the inhabitants of rural villages and major towns may have disappeared. Many starved, were caught in the fighting, or were killed by marauding soldiers. The most notorious atrocity occurred in the aftermath of the siege of Magdeburg (MAHG-duh-boorg) in 1631. After the city surrendered to besieging Catholic forces, long-deprived soldiers ate and drank themselves into a frenzy, raped and killed indiscriminately, and set fires that destroyed the town. Some victims of war migrated to other regions in search of peaceful conditions and work. Some joined the armies in order to survive. Others formed armed bands to fight off the soldiers or to steal back enough goods to live on.

Compounding these effects of war were the actions of armies hired by enterprising mercenary generals for whom loyalty to the princes who paid them took a back seat to personal advancement. They contracted to provide, supply, and lead troops and thus were more willing than the princes would have been to allow troops to live "economically" on plunder. European states thus had managed to field large armies but had not yet evolved the mechanisms fully to fund, and thus control, them.

STABILITY AND DYNAMISM IN EASTERN EUROPE

On the southern frontier of Austrian Habsburg lands, the empire of the Ottoman Turks continued to control southeastern Europe in the late sixteenth and early seventeenth centuries. The Ottoman state had reached the practical limits of its expansion with the conquests of Suleiman I (r. 1520–1566), known to Europeans as "the Magnificent." Sporadic fighting between the Ottomans and the Habsburgs continued in Hungary, which the Ottomans largely controlled, but the fighting there was secondary to the Ottomans' rivalry with the Safavid rulers of Persia. The Ottomans succeeded in extending their territory eastward into modern Iraq, Azerbaijan, and Georgia at Safavid expense. Despite the Ottomans' many commitments and a succession of weak rulers, their presence in southeastern Europe remained secure, partly because they respected the cultural and religious diversity of their Christian subjects. Aristocratic and regional independence were factors, too: Christian princes, particularly in the Hungarian borderlands, found distant Turkish overlords more palatable than closer Habsburg ones. The naval defeat at Lepanto in 1571 (see page 458) had been a setback for the Ottomans, but they quickly rebuilt their fleet and re-established supremacy in the eastern Mediterranean.

Russia Ottoman power was a constant presence in European affairs, but a more dynamic state in the late sixteenth century was the newly proclaimed empire in Russia (see **MAP 15.4**). Through the late Middle Ages Muscovite princes had accumulated land and authority as they vied for pre-eminence with other principalities after the decline of Kievan Rus (modern Ukraine). Ivan III (r. 1462–1505) absorbed neighboring Russian principalities and ended Moscow's subservience to Mongol overlords. He then took the title of "Tsar," Russian for "Caesar." In 1547 his grandson, **Ivan IV** (r. 1533–1584), was officially proclaimed "Tsar of All the Russias" and became the first ruler to routinely use the title. For Russians this title placed Ivan IV in higher esteem than the neighboring Polish-Lithuanian and Swedish kings.

Ivan's use of the title reflects his imperial intentions, as he continued Moscow's push south, into lands that were once part of Kievan Rus, and east, against the Tatar states of Astrakhan, Kazan, and Sibir (Siberia). Within his expanding empire Ivan ruled as an autocrat. The practice of gathering tribute money for Mongol overlords had concentrated many resources in the hands of Muscovite princes. Ivan was able to bypass noble participation and intensify the centralization of government by creating ranks of officials loyal only to him. Part of his authority stemmed from his personality. He was willing, perhaps because of mental imbalance, to use ruthless methods—including torture and the murder of thousands of subjects—to enforce his will.

Ivan came to be called "the Terrible," from a Russian word meaning "awe-inspiring." Although a period of disputed succession to the throne known as the

Ivan IV, "the Terrible" First Russian ruler routinely to use the title "tsar" (Russian for "Caesar"), he presided over the expansion and centralization of the Russian state from 1533 to 1584.

MAP 15.4 Two Empires in Eastern Europe, ca. 1600
Poland-Lithuania dominated the Baltic coast and its productive hinterland in the sixteenth century, but it would face increasing challenges for control of its eastern territories by the expanding Russian state.

Legend:
- Duchy of Lithuania
- Kingdom of Poland
- Principality of Moscow in 1300
- Acquisition by Ivan III's accession (1462)
- Acquisitions under Ivan III (1462–1505)
- Acquisitions by death of Ivan the Terrible (1584)
- Ottoman Empire
- ✕ Major battles

"Time of Troubles" followed Ivan's death in 1584, the foundations of the large and cohesive state he had built survived until a new dynasty of rulers was established in the seventeenth century.

Poland-Lithuania Checking Russian expansion to the west was the commonwealth of Poland-Lithuania, a large, multi-ethnic state at the height of its power (see Map 15.4). The duchy of Lithuania had conquered the territories known as Ruthenia (comprising most of modern Belarus and Ukraine) in the fourteenth century. Then in 1386 a marriage had brought the duchy of Lithuania and the kingdom of Poland under a joint ruler. Like the union of Castile and Aragon in Spain, the union of Poland and Lithuania was initially only dynastic. But two hundred years later, in 1569, they were brought under a single set of institutions by the Treaty of Lublin. Even so, the two states retained distinct traditions. Poles spoke Polish, a Slavic language, and were primarily Catholic, although there were also large minorities of Protestants, Orthodox Christians, and Jews in Poland. Lithuanians, whose language was only distantly related to the Slavic languages, were mostly Catholic as well, although Orthodox Christianity predominated among the Ruthenians, who spoke a Slavic language related to both Russian and Polish. Poland-Lithuania was unusual among European states in that religious toleration was a long-standing practice and was even enshrined in law in 1573.

Valuable resources such as grain, timber, and other naval stores passed through Polish-controlled ports on the Baltic Sea on their way to western Europe. Poland itself also became an increasingly important source of grain for Spanish, French, and English cities. Russia and Sweden, however, challenged Polish control of the lucrative Baltic coast. Polish forces were able to defeat efforts by Ivan the Terrible to control Livonia (modern Latvia), with its important port of Riga (REE-guh), and briefly placed a Polish claimant on the Russian throne during the Time of Troubles. They were not as successful against the Swedes, who, under the expansionist Gustav Adolf, took Riga and the Baltic coast to its north in 1621 (as part of the same drive for Baltic territory that lay behind his involvement in the Thirty Years' War). The Turks also were a constant threat to Poland-Lithuania on its southern border.

In addition to the foreign challenges it faced by virtue of its geography, Poland-Lithuania had internal weaknesses. It was a republic of the nobility, with a weak elected king at its head. (The elective crown was a tradition that had developed over centuries when the throne had been contested by rival claimants from within Poland or from other states.) The great nobles, whose fortunes increased with the grain trade, ran the affairs of state through the national parliament, the Sejm (SAME), as well as local assemblies and various lifelong offices. They drastically limited the ability of the Crown to tax and to grant new titles of nobility, as was the practice throughout Europe. These limitations meant that the king could not reward and reinforce the loyalty of wealthy gentry or the small numbers of urban elites so that they might be a counterweight to noble power. Limited funds also meant that the Polish crown would be hard put to defend its vast territories later in the seventeenth century.

======== S E C T I O N   S U M M A R Y ========

- The Holy Roman Empire was relatively peaceful until destabilized by the spread of Calvinism and the ambition of the Austrian Habsburgs to extend their political and religious control within the empire.

- The Thirty Years' War started in Bohemia (modern Czech Republic) when local leaders challenged Habsburg policies.

- The Bohemian revolt led to a wider war because many rulers, inside and outside Germany, had a stake in the balance of religious and political power there.

- Large armies of mercenaries caused widespread devastation in certain areas of Germany.

- The Peace of Westphalia established a new balance of power between states within the Holy Roman Empire, but the empire itself declined as a political entity.

- The large and diverse state of Poland-Lithuania was the major power in eastern Europe but would soon be challenged by the expanding Russia.

ECONOMIC CHANGE AND SOCIAL TENSIONS

What caused the economic stresses of these decades and how did ordinary people cope with them?

Religious strife disrupted the everyday lives of whole communities as well as individuals in the late sixteenth and early seventeenth centuries. Wars were devastating to many areas of western Europe and contributed to especially severe economic decline in parts of the Low Countries (the Netherlands), France, and the Holy Roman Empire. But other factors, most notably a steady rise in prices, also played a role in the dramatic economic and social changes of the century after 1550. A series of economic changes altered power relations in cities, in the countryside, and in the relationship of both to central governments. Ordinary people managed their economic difficulties in a variety of ways: they sought new sources of work; they protested against burdensome taxes; sometimes they found scapegoats for their distress among their neighbors.

ECONOMIC TRANSFORMATION AND THE NEW ELITES

The most obvious economic change was an unrelenting rise in prices, which resulted in the concentration of wealth in fewer and fewer hands. Sixteenth-century observers attributed rising prices to the inflationary effects of the influx of precious metals from Spanish territories in the New World. Historians now believe that European causes may also have helped trigger this **price revolution.** Steady population growth caused a relative shortage of goods, particularly food, and the result was higher prices. Both the amount and the effect of price changes were highly localized, depending on factors such as the structure of local economies and the success of harvests. Between 1550 and 1600, however, the price of grain may have risen between 50 and 100 percent, and sometimes more, in cities throughout Europe—including eastern Europe, the breadbasket for growing urban areas to the west. Wages did not keep pace with prices; historians estimate that wages lost between one-tenth and one-fourth of their value by the end of the century.

These economic changes affected wealthy elites as well as common people. During this period monarchs were making new accommodations with the hereditary aristocracy—with the Crown usually emerging stronger, if only through concessions to aristocrats' economic interests. Underlying this new symbiosis of monarchy and traditional warrior-nobles were the effects of the widespread economic changes. Conditions in the countryside, where there were fewer resources to feed more mouths, grew less favorable. But at the same time, more capital became available to wealthy urban or landholding families to invest in the countryside, by buying land outright on which to live like **gentry** or by making loans to desperate peasants. This capital came from profits from expanded production and trade and was also an effect of the scarcity of land as population and prices rose. Enterprising landholders raised rents

on farming and grazing land wherever they could, or they converted land to the production of wool, grain, and other cash crops destined for distant markets.

As a result, a stratum of wealthy, educated, and socially ambitious "new gentry," as these families were called in England, began growing and solidifying. Many of the men of these families were royal office-holders. Where the practice existed, many bought titles outright or were granted nobility as a benefit of their offices. They often lent money to royal governments. The monumental expense of wars made becoming a lender to government, as well as to individuals, an attractive way to live off personal capital.

No one would have confused this up-and-coming gentry with warrior-aristocrats from old families, but the social distinctions between them are less important (to us) than what they had in common: legal privilege, the security of landownership, a cooperative relationship with the monarchy. Monarchs deliberately favored the new gentry as counterweights to independent aristocrats.

City governments also changed character. Town councils became dominated by small numbers of privileged families, now more likely to live from landed wealth than from trade or manufacture as they formerly had. By the beginning of the seventeenth century traditional guild control of government had been eliminated in many places. Towns became more closely tied to royal interests by means of the mutual interests of Crown and town elites. The long medieval tradition of towns serving as independent corporate bodies had come to an end.

ECONOMIC CHANGE AND THE COMMON PEOPLE

The growth of markets around Europe and in Spanish possessions overseas, as well as population growth within Europe, had a marked effect on patterns of production and the lives of artisans and laborers. Production of cloth on a large scale for export, for example, now required huge amounts of capital—much more than a typical guild craftsman could amass. Cloth production was increasingly controlled by new investor-producers with enormous resources and access to distant markets. These entrepreneurs bought up large amounts of wool and hired it out to be cleaned, spun into thread, and woven into cloth by wage laborers in urban workshops or by pieceworkers in their homes. Thousands of women and men in the countryside around urban centers helped to support themselves and their families in this way.

The new entrepreneurs had sufficient capital entirely to bypass guild production. In towns guilds still regulated most trades but could not accommodate the numbers of artisans who sought to join them. Fewer and fewer apprentices and journeymen could expect to

price revolution Steady rise in prices in the sixteenth and seventeenth centuries, resulting from population growth and the importation of precious metals from Spain's New World territories.

gentry Class of wealthy, educated, and socially ambitious families in western Europe, especially England, whose political and economic power was greatly enhanced during the sixteenth century.

become master artisans. The masters began to treat apprentices virtually as wage laborers, at times letting them go during slow periods. The household mode of production, in which apprentices and journeymen had worked and lived side by side with the master's family, also began to break down, with profound economic, social, and political consequences.

One of the first reflections of the dire circumstances faced by artisans was an attempt to reduce competition at the expense of the artisans' own mothers, sisters, daughters, and sons. Increasingly, widows were forbidden to continue practicing their husbands' enterprises, though they headed from 10 to 15 percent of households in many trades. Women had traditionally learned and practiced many trades but rarely followed the formal progress from apprenticeship to master status. A woman usually combined work of this kind with household production, with selling her products and those of her husband, and with bearing and nursing children. Outright exclusion of women from guild organization appeared as early as the thirteenth century but now began regularly to appear in guild statutes. In addition, town governments tried to restrict women's participation in work such as selling in markets, which they had long dominated. Even midwives had to defend their practices, even though as part of housewifery women were expected to know about herbal remedies and practical medicine. Working women thus began to have difficulty supporting themselves if single or widowed and difficulty supporting their children. In the changing position of such women we can see the distress of the entire stratum of society that they represent.

Wealth in the countryside was also becoming more stratified. Population growth caused many peasant farms to be subdivided for numerous children, creating tiny plots that could not support the families who lived on them. Countless peasants lost what lands they had to wealthy investors—many of them newly wealthy gentry—who lent them money for renting more land or for purchasing seed and tools, and then reclaimed the land when the peasants failed to repay. Other peasants were simply unable to rent land as rents rose. To survive, some sought work as day laborers on the land of rich landlords or more prosperous farmers. But with the shrinking opportunities for farming, this option became less feasible. Many found their way to cities, where they swelled the ranks of the poor. Others, like some of their urban counterparts, coped by becoming part of the newly expanding network of cloth production, combining spinning and weaving with subsistence farming. However, one bad harvest might send them out on the roads begging or odd-jobbing; many did not long survive such a life.

In eastern Europe peasants faced other dilemmas, for their lands had a different relationship to the wider European economy. The more densely urbanized western Europe, whose wealth controlled the patterns of trade, sought bulk goods, particularly grain, from eastern Germany, Poland, and Lithuania. Thus there was an economic incentive for landowners in eastern Europe to bind peasants to the land just as the desire of their rulers for greater cooperation had granted the landlords more power. Serfdom now spread in eastern Europe, while precisely the opposite condition—a more mobile labor force—grew in the West.

COPING WITH POVERTY AND VIOLENCE

The common people of Europe did not submit passively to either the economic difficulties or the religious and political crises of their day. Whatever their religion, common people took the initiative in attacking members of other faiths to rid their communities of them. Heretics were considered to be spiritual pollution that might provoke God's wrath, and ordinary citizens believed that it was up to them to eliminate heretics if the state failed to do so. Common people, as well as elites and governments, were thus responsible for the violence that sometimes occurred in the name of religion.

Ordinary people fought in wars not only from conviction but also from the need for self-defense and from economic choice. It was ordinary people who defended the walls of towns, dug siege works, and manned artillery batteries. Although nobles remained military leaders, armies consisted mostly of infantry made up of common people, not mounted knights. Women were part of armies, too. Much of the day-to-day work of finding food and firewood, cleaning guns, and endlessly repairing inadequate clothing was done by women looking after their husbands and lovers among the troops.

Many men joined the armies and navies of their rulers because, given the alternatives, the military seemed a reasonable way of life. Landless farm hands, day laborers, and out-of-work artisans found the prospect of employment in the army attractive enough to outweigh the dangers of military life. Desertion was common; nothing more than the rumor that a soldier's home village was threatened might prompt a man to abandon his post. Battle-hardened troops could threaten their commanders not only with desertion but with mutiny. A mutiny of Spanish soldiers in 1574 was a well-organized affair, for example, somewhat like a strike. Occasionally mutinies were brutally suppressed; more often they were successful and troops received some of their back wages.

Townspeople and country people participated in riots and rebellions to protest their circumstances when the situation was particularly dire or when other means of action had failed. The devastation of religious war led to both peasant rebellions and urban uprisings.

Former soldiers, prosperous farmers, or even noble landlords whose economic fortunes were tied to peasant profits might lead rural revolts. Urban protests could begin spontaneously when new grievances worsened existing problems. In 1585 food riots in Naples were provoked not simply by a shortage of grain but also by a government decision to raise the price of bread during the shortage. Rebels sometimes seized property—for example, they might distribute looted bread among themselves—and occasionally killed officials. Their protests rarely generated lasting political change and were usually brutally quashed.

Governments at all levels tried to cope with the increasing problem of poverty by changing the administration and scale of poor relief. In both Catholic and Protestant Europe caring for the poor became more institutionalized and systematic, and more removed from religious impulses. In the second half of the sixteenth century, governments established public almshouses and poorhouses to dispense food or to care for orphans or the destitute in towns throughout Catholic and Protestant Europe. Initially these institutions reflected an optimistic vision of an ideal Christian community attentive to material want. But by 1600 the charitable distribution of food was accompanied by attempts to distinguish "deserving" from "undeserving" poor, by an insistence that the poor work for their ration of food, and even by an effort to compel the poor to live in almshouses and poorhouses.

These efforts were not uniformly successful. Begging was outlawed by Catholic and Protestant city governments alike, but never thoroughly suppressed. Catholic religious orders and parishes often resisted efforts at regulating their charitable work—even when they were imposed by Catholic governments. Nonetheless, the trend was clear. From viewing poverty as a fact of life and as an occasional lesson in Christian humility, European elites were beginning to see it as a social problem. And they saw the poor as people in need of control and institutional discipline.

THE HUNT FOR WITCHES

Between approximately 1550 and 1650 Europe saw a dramatic increase in the persecution of women and men for witchcraft. Approximately one hundred thousand people were tried and about sixty thousand executed. The surge in witch-hunting was closely linked to communities' religious concerns and also to the social tensions that resulted from economic difficulties.

Certain types of witchcraft had long existed in Europe. So-called black magic of various kinds—one peasant casting a spell on another peasant's cow—had been common since the Middle Ages. What now made the practice seem particularly menacing, especially to elites, were theories linking black magic to Devil worship.

Catholic leaders and legal scholars began to advance such theories in the fifteenth century, and by the late sixteenth century both Catholic and Protestant elites viewed a witch not only as someone who might cast harmful spells but also as a heretic.

The impetus for most individual accusations of witchcraft came from within the communities where the "witch" lived—that is, from common people. Usually targeted were solitary or unpopular people whose difficult relationships with fellow villagers made them seem likely sources of evil. Often such a person had practiced black magic (or had been suspected of doing

Publicizing Witch Trials
Printed pamphlets, such as this one describing the execution of three women in Essex, England, spread the news of local "outbreaks" of witchcraft. One of the women, Joan Prentis, is also depicted surrounded by her animal familiars. The ferret in Joan's lap, the pamphlet relates, was the Devil himself in animal form. *(Lambeth Palace Library)*

A CITY OFFICIAL WORRIES ABOUT WITCH-HUNTING

In this letter written to a friend in 1629, the chancellor to the prince-bishop of the German city of Würzburg describes the witch-hunt in his community.

As to the affair of the witches, which Your Grace thinks brought to an end before this, it has started up afresh, and no words can do justice to it. Ah, the woe and misery of it—there are still four hundred in the city, high and low, of every rank and sex, nay, even clerics, so strongly accused that they may be arrested at any hour. It is true that, of the people of my Gracious Prince here, some out of all the offices and faculties must be executed: clerics, elected councilors and doctors, city officials, court assessors several of whom Your Grace knows. There are law students to be arrested. The Prince-Bishop has over forty students who are soon to be pastors; among them thirteen or fourteen are said to be witches. A few days ago a Dean was arrested; two others who were summoned have fled.

The notary of our Church consistory, a very learned man, was yesterday arrested and put to the torture. In a word, a third part of the city is surely involved. The richest, most attractive, most prominent of the clergy are already executed. A week ago a maiden of nineteen was executed, of whom it is everywhere said that she was the fairest in the whole city, and was held by everybody a girl of singular modesty and purity. She will be followed by seven or eight others of the best and most attractive persons. . . . And thus many are put to death for renouncing God and being at the witch-dances, against whom nobody has ever else spoken a word.

To conclude this wretched matter, there are children of three or four years, to the number of three hundred, who are said to have had intercourse with the Devil. I have seen put to death children of seven, promising students of ten, twelve, fourteen and fifteen. Of the nobles—but I cannot and must not write more of this misery. There are persons of yet higher rank, whom you know, and would marvel to hear of, nay, would scarcely believe it; let justice be done. . . .

P.S. Though there are many wonderful and terrible things happening it is beyond doubt that, at a place called the Fraw-Rengberg, the Devil in person, with eight thousand of his followers, held an assembly and celebrated mass before them all, administering to his audience (that is, the witches) turnip-rinds and pairings in place of the Holy Eucharist. There took place not only foul but most horrible and hideous blasphemies, whereof I shudder to write. It is also true that they all vowed not to be enrolled in the Book of Life, but all agreed to be inscribed by a notary who is well known to me and my colleagues. We hope, too, that the book in which they are enrolled will yet be found, and there is no little search being made for it.

QUESTIONS

1. Which townspeople are victims of the witch-hunt?
2. Does the document reveal why the hunt is continuing? Who is in charge?
3. What is the author's attitude toward the events he describes? Does the chancellor believe that witchcraft exists?

Source: Alan C. Kors and Edward Peters, eds., *Witchcraft in Europe, 1100–1700: A Documentary History* (Philadelphia: University of Pennsylvania, 1972), pp. 251–252. Reprinted by permission of the University of Pennsylvania Press.

so) for years, and the villagers took action only when faced with a community crisis, such as an epidemic.

The majority of accused witches were women. Lacking legal, social, and political resources, women may have been more likely than men to use black magic for self-protection or advancement. Women's work often made them vulnerable to charges of witchcraft since families' food supplies and routine medicines passed through women's hands. The deaths of young children or of domestic animals, such as a milk cow, were among the most common triggers for witchcraft accusation. The increase in poverty during the late sixteenth and early seventeenth centuries made poor women frequent targets of witch-hunts. It was easier to find such a woman menacing—and to accuse her of wrongdoing—than to feel guilty because of her evident need.

Both Christian dogma and humanistic writing portrayed women as morally weaker than men and thus more susceptible to the Devil's enticements. Writings on witchcraft described Devil worship in sexual terms, and the prosecution of witches had a voyeuristic, sexual dimension. The bodies of accused witches were searched for the "Devil's mark"—a blemish thought to be Satan's imprint. In some regions women accounted for 80 percent of those prosecuted and executed. A dynamic of gender stereotyping was not always at work, however; in other regions prosecutions were more evenly divided between men and women, and occasionally men made up the majority of those accused.

Because they were often prompted by village disasters or tragedies, individual accusations of witchcraft increased in these decades in response to the crises that beset many communities. In addition, isolated accusations often started localized frenzies of active hunting for other witches. Dozens of "witches" might be identified and executed before the whirlwind subsided. These more widespread hunts were driven in part by the anxieties of local elites about disorder and heresy and were facilitated by contemporary legal procedures that they applied. These procedures permitted lax rules of evidence and the use of torture to extract confessions. Torture or the threat of torture led most of those accused of witchcraft to "confess" and to name accomplices or other "witches." In this way a single initial accusation could lead to dozens of prosecutions. In regions where procedures for appealing convictions and sentences were fragile or nonexistent, witch-hunts could expand with alarming speed. Aggressive hunts were common, for example, in the small principalities and imperial cities of the Holy Roman Empire, which were largely independent of higher political authority. (See the box "The Written Record: A City Official Worries About Witch-Hunting.")

The widespread witch-hunts virtually ended by the late seventeenth century, in part because the intellectual energies of elites shifted from religious to scientific thought. The practice of witchcraft continued among common folk, although accusations of one neighbor by another never again reached the level of these crisis-ridden decades.

SECTION SUMMARY

- A price revolution caused a decline in the value of wages in the sixteenth century.

- Elites, particularly new gentry families, could grow rich by controlling increasingly scarce and valuable land.

- Economic hardship led common people to seek jobs in cities, join armies, and protest taxation.

- Persecutions for witchcraft dramatically increased between 1550 and 1650, reflecting both common people's search for scapegoats for their hard lives and elites' anxiety about controlling common people's religion.

WRITING, DRAMA, AND ART IN AN AGE OF UPHEAVAL

In what ways do the literature and art of this period reflect the political, social, and religious conflicts of the age?

Both imaginative literature and speculative writing, such as political theory, bear the stamp of their times. In the late sixteenth and early seventeenth centuries, political speculation often concerned questions of the legitimacy of rulers and of the relationship of political power to divine authority—urgent problems in an age when religious division threatened the very foundations of states. Authors and rulers alike often relied on still-prevalent oral modes of communication to convey their ideas. Indeed, some of the greatest literature and some of the most effective political statements of the period were presented as drama and not conveyed in print. Nevertheless, literacy continued to spread and led to greater opportunities for knowledge and reflection. The medium of print became increasingly important to political life. In the visual arts, the dramatic impulse was wedded to religious purposes to create works that conveyed both power and emotion.

LITERACY AND LITERATURE

Traditional oral culture changed slowly under the impact of the spread of printing, education, and literacy. Works of literature from the late sixteenth and early seventeenth centuries incorporate material from traditional folktales, consciously reflecting the coexistence of oral and literate culture. In *Don Quixote* (key-HO-tay), by Spain's Miguel de Cervantes (sair-VAHN-tayz) (1547–1616), the title character and his companion, Sancho Panza, have a long discussion about oral and literate traditions. The squire Panza speaks in the style that was customary in oral culture—a rather round-about and repetitive style, which enabled the speaker and listener to remember what was said. Much of the richness of *Don Quixote* is due to the interweaving of prose styles and topical concerns from throughout Cervantes' culture—from the oral world of peasants to the refined world of court life. Yet the perspective that enabled Cervantes to accomplish this rich portrayal came from his own highly developed literacy and the awareness of language that literacy made possible.

Online Study Center **Improve Your Grade**
Primary Source: Don Quixote, a Deranged Knight-Errant as Symbol for a Decadent Spain

The spread of education and literacy in the late sixteenth century had a dramatic impact on attitudes toward literature and on literature itself. The value of education—particularly of the continuing humanist recovery of ancient wisdom—was reflected in much of the literature of the period. Writers found in humanistic education a vision of what it meant to be cultivated and disciplined men of the world. This vision provided the beginnings of a new self-image for members of the warrior class.

It is customary to regard the French author Michel de Montaigne (1533–1592) as the epitome of the reflective—and, more important, the *self*-reflective—gentleman. Montaigne (mon-TEN-yuh) was a judge in the parlement (law court) of Bordeaux. In 1570 he resigned from the court and retired to his small château, where he wrote his *Essais* (from which we derive the word *essays*), a collection of short reflections that were revolutionary in both form and content. Montaigne invented writing in the form of a sketch, an "attempt" (the literal meaning of *essai*) that enabled him to combine self-reflection with formal analysis.

Montaigne's reflections range from the destructiveness of the French civil wars to the consequences of European exploration of the New World. Toward all of these events and circumstances, Montaigne was able to achieve an analytic detachment remarkable for his day. For example, he noted an irony in Europeans, labeling New World peoples "savages," given Europeans' seemingly endless and wanton violence against those "savages" and one another. (See the box "The Global Record: Montaigne Discusses Barbarity in the New World and the Old.") Owing to the spread of printing and literacy, Montaigne had a virtually unparalleled opportunity to reflect on the world through reading the wide variety of printed texts available to him. For the first time it was possible for a leisured lay reader to consider and compare different events, values, and cultures.

Montaigne's essays also reveal a distancing from himself. This distancing was another result of literacy—not simply the ability to read and write but the capacity to enjoy long periods of solitude and reflection in the company of other solitary, book-bound voices. Montaigne's works mark the beginning of what we know as the "invention" of private life, in which an individual is known more by internal character and personality traits than by social role and past behavior.

LITERATURE, SOCIETY, AND POLITICS

The works of the great English poet and playwright William Shakespeare (1564–1616) are still compelling to us because of the profundity of the questions he asked about love, honor, and political legitimacy, but he asked these questions in terms appropriate to his own day. One of his favorite themes—evident in *Hamlet* and *Macbeth*—is the legitimacy of rulers. He was at his most skilled, perhaps, when exploring the contradictions in values between the growing commercial world he saw around him and the older, seemingly more stable world of feudal society. Subtle political commentary distinguishes Shakespeare's later plays, written near and shortly after the death of Queen Elizabeth in 1603, when political and economic problems were becoming increasingly visible and troublesome. Shakespeare explored not only the duties of rulers but also the rights of their subjects. In *Coriolanus* he portrays commoners as poor but neither ignorant nor wretched; they are in fact fully rational and capable of analyzing their situation—perhaps more capable, Shakespeare hints, than their ruler is. The play is safely set in ancient Rome, but the social and political tensions it depicts clearly applied to the Elizabethan present.

Shakespeare, Cervantes, and other writers of their day were also representatives of what were starting to be self-consciously distinct national literatures. The spread of humanism added a historical dimension to their awareness of their own languages and to their distinct subject matter: each one's own society and its past. This kind of self-consciousness is evident in Shakespeare's historical plays, such as *Henry V* and *Richard II*. In *Richard II* he depicts the kingdom in terms that reflect the Elizabethan sense of England as a separate and self-contained nation:

> *This royal throne of kings, this scept'red isle,*
> *This earth of majesty, this seat of Mars,*
> *This other Eden, demi-paradise,*
> *This fortress built by Nature for herself*
> *Against infection and the hand of war,*
> *This happy breed of men, this little world,*
> *This precious stone set in the silver sea . . .*
> *This blessed plot, this earth, this realm, this*
> *   England . . .*
> *(Richard II, act 2, sc. 1, lines 40–50)*[5]

MONTAIGNE DISCUSSES BARBARITY IN THE NEW WORLD AND THE OLD

In one of his most famous essays, the French jurist and essayist Michel de Montaigne (1533–1592) ironically compares the customs of Native Americans with the customs of his own society. Information about Native Americans came from published reports of European voyages and from news of individual Native Americans who had journeyed (usually forcibly) to Europe. Europeans' encounters with peoples in the New World gave Montaigne a vantage point from which to criticize his own society.

They have their wars with [other] nations, to which they go quite naked, with no other arms than bows or wooden spears. . . . It is astonishing that firmness they show in their combats, which never end but in slaughter and bloodshed; for, as to routs and terror, they know nothing of either.

Each man brings back as his trophy the head of the enemy he has killed. . . . After they have treated their prisoner well for a long time with all the hospitality they can think of . . . they kill him with their swords. This done, they roast him and eat him in common and send some pieces to their absent friends.

I am not sorry that we notice the barbarous horror of such acts, but am heartily sorry that . . . we should be so blind to our own. I think there is more barbarity . . . in tearing by tortures and the rack a body still full of feeling, in roasting a man bit by bit, having him bitten and mangled by dogs (as we have not only read but seen within fresh memory . . .

among neighbors and fellow citizens, and what is worse, on the pretext of piety and religion).

Three of these men (were brought to France) . . . and [someone] wanted to know what they had found most amazing. . . . They said that in the first place they thought it very strange that so many grown men, bearded, strong and armed who were around the king . . . should submit to obey a child [the young French king] . . . Second (they have a way in their language of speaking of men as halves of one another), they had noticed that there were among us men full and gorged with all sorts of good things, and that their other halves were beggars at their doors, emaciated with hunger and poverty; and they thought it strange that these needy halves could endure such injustice.

QUESTIONS

1. What practices in the two cultures is Montaigne commenting on in this excerpt?

2. In what ways does he find Native American culture admirable by comparison to his own? What aspects of his own culture is he criticizing?

3. How are contemporary events and conditions in France reflected in Montaigne's remarks?

Source: Donald M. Frame, trans., *The Complete Essays of Montaigne* (Stanford, Calif.: Stanford University Press, 1948), pp. 153, 155–159. Reprinted by permission of the publisher.

THE GREAT AGE OF THEATER

Shakespeare's extraordinary career was possible because his life coincided with the rise of professional theater. In the capitals of England and Spain professional theaters first opened in the 1570s. Some drama was produced at court or in aristocratic households, but most public theaters drew large and very mixed audiences, including the poorest city dwellers. Playwrights, including Shakespeare, often wrote in teams under great pressure to keep acting companies supplied with material. The best-known dramatist in Spain, Lope de Vega (LOW-pah day VAY-guh) (1562–1635), wrote more than fifteen hundred works on a wide range of topics. Although religious themes remained popular in Spanish theater, as an echo of medieval drama, most plays in England and Spain treated secular subjects and, as in *Coriolanus,* safely disguised political commentary.

Over time theater became increasingly restricted to aristocratic circles. In England Puritan criticism of the "immorality" of public performance drove actors and playwrights to seek royal patronage. The first professional theater to open in Paris, in 1629, as political and religious turmoil quieted, quickly became dependent on Cardinal Richelieu's patronage. Inevitably, as court patronage grew in importance, the wide range of subjects treated in plays began to narrow to those of aristocratic concern, such as family honor and martial glory. These themes are depicted in the works of the Spaniard Pedro Calderón (kall-day-ROHN) (1600–1681), who wrote for his enthusiastic patron, Philip IV, and of the Frenchman Pierre Corneille (kore-NAY) (1606–1684), whose great tragedy of aristocratic life, *Le Cid,* was one of the early successes of the seventeenth-century French theater.

Drama's significance as an art form is reflected in its impact on the development of music: the opera, which weds drama to music, was invented in Italy in the early seventeenth century. The first great work in this genre is generally acknowledged to be *Orfeo* (*Orpheus*, 1607) by Claudio Monteverdi (mon-tay-VAIR-dee) (1567–1643). Opera, like drama, reflected the influence of humanism in its secular themes and in its emulation of Greek drama, which had used both words and music. The practice of music itself changed under the dramatic impulse. Monteverdi was the first master of a new musical style known as "monody," which emphasizes the progression of chords. Monodic music is inherently dramatic, creating a sense of forward movement, expectation, and resolution.

DRAMA, ART, AND POLITICAL THOUGHT

Whether produced on a public stage or at court or in a less formal setting, drama was a favored method of communication in this era because people responded to and made extensive use of the spoken word. Dramatic gesture and storytelling to get a message across were commonplace and were important components of politics.

What we might call "street drama" was an ordinary occurrence. When great noble-governors entered major towns, such as when Margaret of Parma entered Brussels, a solemn yet ostentatious formal "entry" was often staged. The dignitary would ride through the main gate, usually beneath a canopy made of luxurious cloth. The event might include staged dramas in the town's streets, with costumed townspeople acting out brief symbolic scenes, such as of the story of David and Goliath, and it might end with an elaborate banquet. A remnant of these proceedings survives today in the ceremony by which distinguished visitors are given "the keys to the city," which, in the sixteenth century, really were functional.

Royalty made deliberate and careful use of dramatic ceremony. Royal entries into towns took on an added weight, as did royal funerals and other such occasions. These dramas reinforced political and constitutional assumptions in the minds of witnesses and participants. Thus over time we can see changes in the representations of royal power. In France, for example, the ritual entry of the king into Paris had originally stressed the participation of the leading guilds, judges, and administrators, symbolizing their active role in governing the city and the kingdom. But in the last half of the sixteenth century the procession began to glorify the king alone. Speculation about and celebration of power, as well as dramatic emotion, also occurred in the visual arts—most notably in painting and architecture, in the style now known as **baroque.** Baroque (ba-ROKE) style was a new kind of visual language that could project power and grandeur and simultaneously engage viewers' senses. (See the feature "The Visual Record: Baroque Art.")

The very fact that rulers experimented self-consciously with self-representation suggests that issues pertaining to the nature and extent of royal power were profoundly important and far from settled. Queen Elizabeth I had the particular burden of assuming the throne in a period of great instability. Hence she paid a great deal of attention to the image of herself that she conveyed in words and authorized to be fashioned in painting. Elizabeth styled herself variously as mother to her people and as a warrior-queen (drawing on ancient myths of Amazon women). She made artful use of the image of her virginity to buttress each of these images—as the wholly devoted, self-sacrificing mother (which, of course, had religious tradition behind it) or as an androgynous ruler, woman but doing the bodily work of man.

More formal speculation about constitutional matters also resulted from the tumult of the sixteenth and seventeenth centuries. As we have seen, the Protestant faction in France advanced an elaborate argument for the limitation of royal power. Alternative theories enhancing royal authority were offered, principally in support of the Catholic position though also simply to buttress the beleaguered monarchy itself. The most famous of these appeared in *The Six Books of the Republic* (1576), by the legal scholar Jean Bodin (bo-DAHN) (1530–1596). Bodin was a Catholic but offered a fundamentally secular perspective on the purposes and source of power within a state. His special contribution was a vision of a truly sovereign monarch. Bodin offered a theoretical understanding that is essential to states today and is the ground on which people can claim rights and protection from the state—namely, that there is a final sovereign authority. For Bodin that authority was the king. He recognized that in practice royal power was constrained by limitations, but he was intrigued more by the theoretical grounding for royal authority than by its practical application.

Contract theory devised by French Protestants to legitimize resistance to the monarchy had to be abandoned when Henry IV granted toleration to the Huguenots in 1598. In England theoretical justification of resistance to Charles I was initially limited to invoking tradition and precedent. Contract theory, as well as other sweeping claims regarding subjects' rights, would be more fully developed later in the century.

baroque Style of European art and architecture popular from the late sixteenth to early eighteenth centuries. Baroque art modified Renaissance techniques, adding dynamism and emotional energy, which resulted in works that were both impressively grand and emotionally engaging.

An Image of Royalty

This dramatic painting of Charles I on horseback was one of several likenesses of the king painted by the baroque artist Anthony Van Dyck. This painting was originally hung at the end of a long gallery in one of the royal palaces, next to similarly triumphal images of Roman emperors.   *(The Royal Collection © 2003, Her Majesty Queen Elizabeth II)*

Bodin's theory of sovereignty, however, was immediately echoed in other theoretical works, most notably that of Hugo Grotius (GROW-shus) (1583–1645). A Dutch jurist and diplomat, Grotius developed the first principles of modern international law. He accepted the existence of sovereign states that owed no loyalty to higher authority (such as the papacy) and thus needed new principles to govern their interactions. His major work, *De Jure Belli ac Pacis* (*On the Law of War and Peace*, 1625), was written in response to the turmoil of the Thirty Years' War. Grotius argued that relations between states could be based on respect for treaties voluntarily reached between them. In perhaps his boldest move he argued that war must be justified, and he developed criteria to distinguish just wars from unjust ones.

SECTION SUMMARY

- Literacy and access to printed books enabled new levels of self-consciousness and self-reflection, as in the work of Montaigne.

- The rise of professional theater began in the 1570s; drama was a favored means of communication by writers as well as political leaders.

- Shakespeare and other writers and artists reflected on many of the current concerns about legitimate authority, religion, and human life in this period.

- Baroque art appealed to viewers' emotions but also expressed power and grandeur.

- Political theorist Bodin developed the notion of sovereign authority within the state.

Baroque Art

If today you were to walk through the cathedral in the Belgian city of Antwerp and notice this painting, titled *The Raising of the Cross*, it might not strike you as remarkable. The crucifixion of Jesus is a frequent subject of religious painting, after all. But let us look at the image more carefully. First of all, this is a portrayal not of Jesus on the cross but rather of the *raising* of the cross. In other words, it captures a moment of action, not its aftermath. The frame of the painting is filled with action as well. The figures on the left and at the center support the cross and push it up. At the bottom right we see figures straining at ropes as they pull the cross upright. Our eye is drawn to the movement in the painting partly by the use of light, which floods the figure of Jesus. We also note the unexpected diagonal position of the crucified figure, and we survey the image in order to make sense of it.

This is a dynamic painting, and simultaneously an emotionally engaging one. We encounter Jesus not as a static, perhaps already dying, figure on the cross, but at the very moment of his crucifixion. There is also a striking similarity between the figure of Jesus and those of the men who are working hard to accomplish his crucifixion: they are all men, whose muscled bodies are more alike than not. The human pathos of the moment is brought to life.

The image you see before you is one of three panels in a triptych, or three-paneled altarpiece. The left-hand panel depicts Saint John, the Virgin Mary, and others witnessing Jesus's crucifixion. The panel on the right shows a Roman officer watching over his soldiers as they crucify two thieves. Whereas most triptychs of the period contained three unrelated images, here the panels combine to form a single story of the crucifixion.

This altarpiece was executed in 1610 by the influential painter Peter Paul Rubens (1577–1640), a native of Antwerp, in the southern Netherlands. Rubens was one of the great masters of what came to be called the baroque style. Baroque techniques were pioneered in the late sixteenth century in Italy, first in church design, and spread slowly, with many regional variations, especially throughout Catholic Europe, during the seventeenth century. The origin of the term *baroque* has been debated; it may have come from the Portuguese *barroco*, used to describe irregularly shaped pearls. The term as applied to the arts was initially derogatory, denoting distortion, illogic, and irregularity. Baroque painting was distinguished by the dramatic use of color and shading and by the dynamic energy of figures. Baroque artists based their work on Renaissance achievements in representing the human form in a convincing three-dimensional space. But with the strong use of light, movement, and more robust and realistic human figures, these artists enhanced the drama and emotional impact of what they depicted.

Like baroque artists, baroque architects modified the precision, symmetry, and orderliness of Renaissance architecture to produce a sense of greater dynamism in space. Baroque churches, for example, were impressively grand and monumental yet emotionally engaging at the same time. Façades and interiors were both massive and, through the clever use of architectural and decorative components, suggestive of movement. A good example of this is the work of Gianlorenzo Bernini (bare-NEE-nee) (1598–1680), who designed the portico outside Saint Peter's Basilica in Rome, as well as the highly ornate bronze canopy over the altar inside the basilica. Dramatic illusion in the interior of buildings—such as painting a chapel ceiling with figures receding as if ascending to heaven—was a common device in baroque architecture. One of the primary purposes of baroque architecture and art was to create simultaneously a display of power and an invitation to sensory experience. Baroque art encouraged piety that was not only emotionally involved, and thus satisfying, but also awe-inspired. In this way it reflected the aims of the Counter-Reformation church, whose leaders were among its most important patrons.

Peter Paul Rubens's early training in Italy shaped him as an artist and established his secondary career as a diplomat. Throughout his life he undertook diplomatic missions for the Habsburg viceroys in the Spanish Netherlands, gaining artistic commissions wherever he went. Rubens's subject matter varied widely, including church design and decoration, portraiture, and landscape painting, reflecting the fact that baroque art also had important secular applications. Indeed, magnificent baroque palaces symbolized the wealth and power of the elites (see the photos on pages 498 and 507).

Rulers began to employ artists as portrait painters, such as Rubens's pupil Anthony Van Dyck (1599–1641), whose painting of Charles I of England appears on page 485. Because portraits have become so common, we cannot fully appreciate how arresting this image would have been in its day. Like Rubens's *Raising of the Cross,* Van Dyck's image of Charles was an innovative rendering of familiar elements. The image of a ruler on horseback was well known, but it had never been exploited as fully by English monarchs as it had been by rulers on the Continent. This large portrait of the king was designed to be hung at the end of a long palace corridor so that, from a distance, a courtier would have the illusion of actually seeing the king riding proudly through a triumphal arch.* Compare this portrait with the much more stilted one of Elizabeth I on page 465. It is striking how effective the technical and stylistic innovations of baroque art and architecture were in expressing secular as well as spiritual power.

QUESTIONS

1. How does baroque art involve the viewer by appealing to senses and emotions?

2. Why was baroque painting effective for conveying political messages, as in Van Dyck's portrait of Charles I?

---

*This discussion draws on the work of Roy Strong, *Van Dyck: Charles I on Horseback* (New York: Viking, 1972), pp. 20–25.

Online Study Center

Improve Your Grade Visual Record Activities

CHAPTER SUMMARY

What circumstances permitted Spain's ambitious policies and to what degree were they successful?

What conditions led to civil war in France? How did religious and political conflict develop differently in England?

Why did war erupt again within the Holy Roman Empire and what was the significance of the conflict?

What caused the economic stresses of these decades and how did ordinary people cope with them?

In what ways do the literature and art of this period reflect the political, social, and religious conflicts of the age?

The late sixteenth and early seventeenth centuries were an era of intense struggle over political and religious authority. Rulers everywhere, through a variety of means, tried to buttress and expand their power. They were resisted by traditional centers of power, such as independent-minded nobles and wealthy townspeople. But they were also resisted by the novel challenge of religious dissent, which empowered even common people both to claim a greater right to question authority and to risk more in their attempts to oppose it.

The most powerful monarch of the day, the king of Spain, could not defeat a religious and political rebellion in the prosperous Netherlands, even with the resources of treasure from the New World. France was torn apart by decades of civil war before the Crown was able to impose a workable peace and reassert royal authority. In England, political and religiously inspired challenges to royal authority were contained by Elizabeth I but not as effectively addressed by her successors. Meanwhile, the various states of the Holy Roman Empire were engulfed in a thirty-year war that also had political and religious roots, and which became one of the most bitter and complex conflicts of the period.

War itself became more destructive owing to new technologies and increasing resources devoted to it.

Ordinary people also coped with the price revolution, which caused their wages to lose value and many to lose their land. The difficult economic circumstances of these decades meant that working people, desperate for a secure livelihood, rioted or took up arms out of economic as well as religious concerns.

Yet however grim the circumstances people faced, the technology of print and the spread of literacy helped spur speculative and creative works by providing the means for reflection and the audiences to receive and appreciate it. Ironically, the increased importance and grandeur of court life, though a cause of political strain, resulted in a new wave of patronage for art, literature, and drama. Other works, such as Shakespeare's plays, both reflect and reflect on the conflicts in the society of the day. Baroque art expressed both the religious passions of the era and the claims to authority by rulers.

LOOKING AHEAD

In some areas of Europe, such as the Holy Roman Empire, the religious and political struggles reached some resolution. In other areas, such as England, decades of bloody conflict still lay ahead.

KEY TERMS

Philip II (p. 452)

Armada (p. 457)

Huguenots (p. 461)

Edict of Nantes (p. 462)

Elizabeth I (p. 464)

Puritans (p. 464)

Thirty Years' War (p. 469)

Peace of Westphalia (p. 472)

Ivan IV, "the Terrible" (p. 474)

price revolution (p. 477)

gentry (p. 477)

baroque (p. 484)

Online Study Center
Improve Your Grade Flashcards

SUGGESTED READING

Berenger, Jean. *A History of the Habsburg Empire, 1273–1700,* trans. C. A. Simpson. 1990. A detailed treatment of Habsburg rule in the Holy Roman Empire and in their own principalities. Considers economic and cultural changes as well as political ones.

Bonney, Richard. *The European Dynastic States, 1494–1660.* 1991. A rich survey of the period that is solid on eastern as well as western Europe. Written from an English point of view, it does not consider England as part of Europe.

Eagleton, Terry. *William Shakespeare.* 1986. A brief and highly readable interpretation of Shakespeare that emphasizes the tensions in the plays caused by language and by ideas from the new world of bourgeois commercial life.

Edwards, Philip. *The Making of the Modern English State.* 2001. A readable survey of political and religious developments in England that incorporates much new scholarship.

Holt, Mack P. *The French Wars of Religion, 1562–1629.* 1995. An up-to-date synthesis that evaluates social and political context while not slighting the importance of religion.

Lynch, John. *Spain, 1516–1598: From Nation-State to World Empire.* 1991. A survey covering the reign of Philip II by a leading scholar of Spanish history.

Parker, Geoffrey. *The Dutch Revolt.* 2d ed. 1985. The best survey of the revolt available in English.

Parker, Geoffrey. *The Military Revolution.* 1988; and Black, Jeremy. *A Military Revolution?* 1991. Two works that disagree about the nature and extent of the changes in military practices and their significance for military, political, and social history. Black tries to refute claims of a dramatic military "revolution."

Wiesner, Merry. *Women and Gender in Early Modern Europe.* 1993. Discusses all aspects of women's experience, including their working lives.

NOTES

1. Geoffrey Parker, *The Dutch Revolt* (London: Penguin, 1985), p. 288, n. 5.

2. Quoted in A. W. Lovett, *Early Habsburg Spain, 1517–1598* (Oxford: Oxford University Press, 1986), p. 212.

3. Quoted in R. J. Knecht, *The French Wars of Religion, 1559–1598* (London: Longman, 1989), p. 109.

4. Quoted in Jean Berenger, *A History of the Habsburg Empire, 1273–1700,* trans. C. A. Simpson (London and New York: Longman, 1990), p. 239.

5. *The Riverside Shakespeare,* ed. G. Blakemore Evans, 2d ed. (Boston: Houghton Mifflin, 1997), p. 855. Copyright © 1997 by Houghton Mifflin Company. Reprinted by permission of the publisher.

16

EUROPE IN THE AGE OF LOUIS XIV, CA. 1640–1715

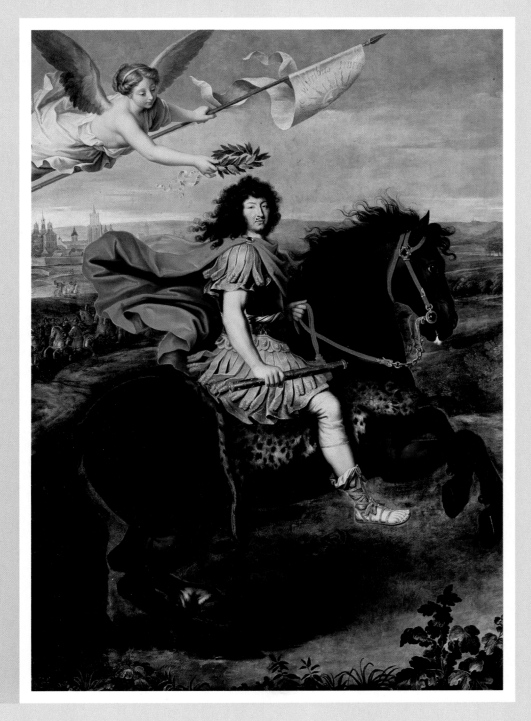

Louis XIV in Roman Armor

(Scala/Art Resource, NY)

The portrait of King Louis XIV of France as a triumphant warrior, to the left, was one of hundreds of such images of the king that decorated his palace at Versailles and other sites around his kingdom—where they made his subjects aware of his presence, regardless of whether he was in residence. In this painting, the contemporary artist Charles Le Brun depicts Louis as a Roman warrior, and his power is represented by a mixture of other symbols—Christian and pagan, ancient and contemporary. An angel crowns him with a victor's laurel wreath and carries a banner bearing the image of the sun. In his hand Louis holds a marshal's baton—a symbol of military command—covered with the royal emblem of the fleur-de-lys (flur-duh-LEE). In the background, behind the "Roman" troops following Louis, is an idealized city.

These trappings symbolized the significant expansion of royal power during Louis's reign. He faced down the challenges of warrior-nobles, suppressed religious dissent, and tapped the nation's wealth to wage a series of wars of conquest. A period of cultural brilliance early in his reign and the spectacle of an elaborate court life crowned his achievements. In his prime, his regime was supported by a consensus of elites; such harmony was made possible by the lack of institutional brakes on royal authority. However, as his attention to symbolism suggests, Louis's power was not unchallenged. By the end of the Sun King's reign the glow was fading: France was struggling under economic distress brought on by the many wars fought for his glory and had missed opportunities for commercial success abroad. Elites throughout France who had once accepted, even welcomed, his rule became trenchant critics, and common people outright rebels.

In England, by contrast, the Crown faced successful rebellion by subjects claiming religious authority and political legitimacy for their causes. Resistance to the expansion of royal authority, led by Parliament, resulted in the execution of the king and the establishment of a short-lived republic, the Commonwealth. Although the monarchy was restored, the civil war had long-term consequences for royal power in England. After the Thirty Years' War, vigorous rulers in central and eastern Europe undertook a program of territorial expansion and state building that led to the dominance in the region of Austria, Brandenburg-Prussia, and Russia. The power of these states

CHAPTER OUTLINE

FRANCE IN THE AGE OF ABSOLUTISM

THE ENGLISH CIVIL WAR AND ITS AFTERMATH

NEW POWERS IN CENTRAL AND EASTERN EUROPE

THE EXPANSION OF OVERSEAS TRADE AND SETTLEMENT

KEY TERMS

absolutism

Louis XIV

mercantilism

Parliament

Oliver Cromwell

Glorious Revolution

Treaty of Carlowitz

Brandenburg-Prussia

Cossacks

Peter the Great

Dutch East India Company

plantation system

Online Study Center

This icon will direct you to interactive map and primary source activities on the website **college.hmco.com/pic/noble5e**

derived, in part, from the economic relationship of their lands to the wider European economy. In all the major states of continental Europe, princely governments were able to monopolize military power for the first time, in return for economic and political concessions to noble landholders.

The seventeenth century also witnessed a dynamic phase of European expansion overseas, following on the successes of the Portuguese and the Spanish in the fifteenth and sixteenth centuries. The Dutch created the most successful trading empire. Eager migrants settled in the Americas in ever increasing numbers, while forced migrants—enslaved Africans—were transported by the thousands to work on the profitable plantations of European colonizers. Aristocrats, merchants, and peasants back in Europe jockeyed to take advantage

of—or to mitigate the effects of—the local political and economic impact of Europe's expansion.

FOCUS QUESTIONS

How did Louis XIV successfully expand royal power in France and what were some of the achievements of his reign?

What were the long-term consequences of the English civil war?

Which states began to dominate central and eastern Europe and why were they successful?

How and why did Europe's overseas trade and colonization expand in the seventeenth century and what effects did this expansion have on Europe itself?

FRANCE IN THE AGE OF ABSOLUTISM

How did Louis XIV successfully expand royal power in France and what were some of the achievements of his reign?

Absolutism is a term often used to describe the extraordinary concentration of power in royal hands achieved by the kings of France, most notably **Louis XIV** (r. 1643–1715), in the seventeenth century. Louis continued the expansion of state power begun by his father's minister, Cardinal Richelieu (see page 463). The extension of royal power, under Louis as well as his predecessor, was accelerated by his desire to sustain an expensive and aggressive foreign policy. The policy itself was partly traditional—fighting the perpetual enemy, the Habsburgs, and seeking military glory—and partly new—expanding the borders of France. Louis XIV's successes in these undertakings made him both envied and emulated by other rulers: the French court became a model of culture and refinement. But increased royal authority was not accepted

without protest: common French people as well as elites dug in their heels over the cost of Louis's policies to them.

THE LAST CHALLENGE TO ABSOLUTISM: THE FRONDE, 1648–1653

When Louis came to the throne in 1643 he was only five years old, leaving his mother, Anne of Austria (1601–1666), to act as his regent. Together with her chief minister and personal friend, Cardinal Jules Mazarin (mah-zah-RAHN) (1602–1661), she defended Louis against opposition from royal bureaucrats and the traditional nobility as well as the common people.

Revolts against the concentration of power in royal hands and against the exorbitant taxation that had prevailed under Louis's father began immediately. In one province a group of armed peasants cornered the intendant and forced him to agree to lower taxes; elsewhere provincial parlements tried to abolish special ranks of officials, especially the intendants, created by Richelieu. In 1648, after several more years of foreign war and the financial expedients to sustain it, the most

absolutism Extraordinary concentration of power and symbolic authority in royal hands, achieved particularly by the king of France (Louis XIV) in the seventeenth century.

Louis XIV Longest-reigning ruler in European history, he imposed "absolute" rule in France and his reign witnessed a great flowering of French culture.

serious revolt began, led by the Parlement (par-luh-MAWNH) of Paris and the other sovereign law courts in the capital.

The source of the Parlement's leverage over the monarchy was its traditional right to register laws and edicts, which amounted to judicial review. Now the Parlement, as a guardian of royal authority, attempted to extend this power by debating and even initiating government policy. The sovereign courts sitting together drew up a reform program abolishing most of the machinery of government established under Richelieu and calling for consent to future taxation. The citizens of Paris rose to defend the courts when royal troops were sent against them in October.

Mazarin was forced to accept the proposed reform of government, at least in theory. He also had to avert challenges by great nobles for control of the young king's council. Civil war waxed and waned around France from 1648 to 1653. The main combatants were conventionally ambitious great nobles, but reform-minded urban professionals, such as lawyers and judges, often made common cause with them, to benefit from their military power. Meanwhile, middling nobles in the region around Paris began to devise a thoroughgoing reform program and to prepare for a meeting of the Estates General—a representative assembly—to enact it.

These revolts begun in 1648 were derided with the name "Fronde," which was a popular children's game. However, the Fronde (FRAWND) was not child's play; it constituted a serious challenge to the legacy of royal government as it had developed under Richelieu. It ended without a noteworthy impact on the growth of royal power for several reasons. First, Mazarin methodically regained control of the kingdom through armed force and artful concessions to individual aristocrats, who were always eager to trade their loyalty for the fruits of royal service. Meanwhile, the Parlement of Paris, as well as many citizens of the capital, welcomed a return to royal authority when civil war caused starvation as well as political unrest.

Moreover, the Parlement of Paris was a law court, not a representative assembly. Its legitimacy derived from its role as upholder of royal law, and it could not, over time, challenge the king on the pretext of upholding royal tradition in his name. Parlementaires tended to see the Estates General as a rival institution and helped quash the proposed meeting of representatives. Above all, they wanted to avert reforms such as the abolition of the paulette, a fee guaranteeing the hereditary right to royal office (see page 463).

Unlike in England, there was in France no single institutional focus for resistance to royal power. A strong-willed and able ruler, as Louis XIV proved to be, could obstruct or override challenges to royal power, particularly when he satisfied the ambitions of aristocrats and

1602	Dutch East India Company formed
1607	Jamestown colony founded in Virginia
1608	Champlain founds Quebec City
1613	Michael becomes first Romanov tsar in Russia
1620	Pilgrims settle at Plymouth (Massachusetts)
1642–1648	Civil war in England
1643	Louis XIV becomes king of France
1648–1653	Fronde revolts in France
1649	Execution of Charles I
1649–1660	English Commonwealth
1659	Peace of the Pyrenees
1660	Monarchy restored in England
1661	Louis XIV assumes full control of government
1672–1678	Dutch War
1682	Peter the Great becomes tsar of Russia
1685	Edict of Nantes revoked
1688	Glorious Revolution
1699	Treaty of Carlowitz
1700–1721	Great Northern War
1701–1714	War of the Spanish Succession
1713	Peace of Utrecht
1715	Death of Louis XIV

those bureaucrats who profited from the expansion of royal power. Moreover, the young Louis had been traumatized by the uprisings of the Fronde and grew up determined never to allow another such challenge to his absolute sovereignty.

FRANCE UNDER LOUIS XIV, 1661–1715

Louis XIV fully assumed control of government at Mazarin's death in 1661. It was a propitious moment. The Peace of the Pyrenees in 1659 had ended in France's favor the wars with Spain that had dragged on since the end of the Thirty Years' War. As part of the peace agreement, Louis married a Spanish princess, Maria Theresa. In the first ten years of his active reign Louis achieved a degree of control over the mechanisms of government unparalleled in the history of monarchy in France or anywhere else in Europe. Louis was extremely vigorous and proved a diligent king. He put in hours a day at a desk while sustaining the ceremonial life of the court, with its elaborate hunts, balls, and other public events.

Government Reforms   Louis did not invent any new bureaucratic devices but rather used existing ranks of officials in new ways that increased government efficiency and further centralized control. He radically reduced the number of men in his High Council, the advisory body closest to the king, to include only three or four great ministers of state affairs. This intimate group, with Louis's active participation, handled all policymaking. The ministers of state, war, and finance were chosen exclusively from non-noble men of bourgeois background whose training and experience fitted them for such positions. Jean-Baptiste Colbert (coal-BEAR) (1619–1683), perhaps the greatest of them, served as minister of finance and supervised most domestic policy from 1665 until his death. He was from a merchant family and had served for years under Mazarin.

Several dozen other officials, picked from the ranks of up-and-coming lawyers and administrators, drew up laws and regulations and passed them to the intendants for execution at the provincial level. Sometimes these officials at the center were sent to the provinces on short-term supervisory missions. The effect of this system was to bypass many entrenched provincial bureaucrats, particularly those known as tax farmers. Tax farmers were freelance businessmen who bid for the right to collect taxes in a region in return for a negotiated fee they paid to the Crown. The Crown, in short, did not control its own tax revenues. The money Louis's regime saved by the more efficient collection of taxes (revenues almost doubled in some areas) enabled the government to streamline the bureaucracy: dozens of the offices created over the years to bring cash in were bought back by the Crown from their owners.

The system still relied on the bonds of patronage and personal service—political bonds borrowed from aristocratic life. Officials rose through the ranks by means of service to the great, and family connection and personal loyalty still were essential. Of the seventeen different men who were part of Louis XIV's High Council during his reign, five were members of the Colbert family, for example. In the provinces important local families vied for minor posts, which at least provided prestige and some income.

Economic Development   Further benefits of centralized administration can be seen in some of the achievements in the early years of Louis's regime. Colbert actively encouraged France's economic development. He reduced the internal tolls and customs barriers,

which were relics of medieval decentralization—for example, the right of a landholder to charge a toll on all boats along a river under his control. He encouraged industry with state subsidies and protective tariffs. He set up state-sponsored trading companies—the two most important being the East India Company and the West India Company, established in 1664.

Mercantilism is the term historians use to describe the theory behind Colbert's efforts. This economic theory stressed self-sufficiency in manufactured goods, tight control of trade to foster the domestic economy, and the absolute value of bullion. Both capital for development—in the form of hard currency, known as bullion—and the amount of world trade were presumed to be limited in quantity. Therefore, state intervention in the form of protectionist policies was believed necessary to guarantee a favorable balance of payments.

This static model of national wealth did not wholly fit the facts of growing international trade in the seventeenth century. Nevertheless, mercantilist philosophy was helpful to France. France became self-sufficient in the all-important production of woolen cloth, and French industry expanded notably in other sectors. Colbert's greatest success was the systematic expansion of the navy and merchant marine. By 1677 the navy had increased almost sixfold, to 144 ships. By the end of Louis XIV's reign the French navy was virtually the equal of the English navy.

Colbert and the other ministers began to develop the kind of planned government policymaking that we now take for granted. Partly by means of their itinerant supervisory officials, they tried to formulate and execute policy based on carefully collected information. How many men of military age were available? How abundant was this year's harvest? Answers to such questions enabled not only the formulation of economic policy but also the deliberate management of production and services to achieve certain goals—above all, the recruitment and supply of the king's vast armies.

Religious Life   Beginning in 1673 Louis tried to bring the religious life of the realm more fully under royal control, claiming for himself—with mixed success—some of the church revenues and powers of ecclesiastical appointment that still remained to the pope. Partly to bolster his position with the pope, he also began to attack the Huguenot community in France. First he offered financial inducements for conversion to Catholicism. Then he took more drastic steps, such

mercantilism   Economic policy pursued by western European states in the seventeenth and eighteenth centuries that stressed self-sufficiency in manufactured goods, tight government control of trade, and the absolute value of bullion.

as destroying Protestant churches and quartering troops in Huguenots' homes to force them to convert. In 1685 he declared that France would no longer abide any Protestant community, and he revoked the Edict of Nantes. A hundred thousand Protestant subjects—including some six hundred army and navy officers—refused even nominal conversion to Catholicism and chose to emigrate.

Meanwhile, Louis faced resistance to his claims against the pope from within the ranks of French clergy. These churchmen represented a movement within French Catholicism known as Jansenism, after Cornelius Jansen, a professor of theology whose writings were its inspiration. Jansenists practiced an austere style of Catholic religiosity that, in its notions about human will and sinfulness, was akin to some Protestant doctrine. Louis was suspicious of Jansenism because its adherents included many of his political enemies, particularly among families of parlement officials. Louis was wary of any threat to either the institutional or symbolic unity of his regime, such as Protestants and Jansenists represented. At the end of Louis's long reign another pope obligingly declared many Jansenist doctrines to be heretical as part of a compromise agreement with Louis on matters of church governance and finance. Louis's efforts to exert greater control over the church had brought him modest practical gains, but at the price of weakening the religious basis of his authority in the eyes of many sincere Catholics.

By modern standards the power of the Crown was still greatly limited. The "divine right" of kingship, a notion formulated by Louis's chief apologist, Bishop Jacques Bossuet (BOS-soo-way) (1627–1704), did not mean unlimited power to rule; rather it meant that hereditary monarchy was the divinely ordained form of government, best suited to human needs. *Absolutism* was not ironfisted control of the realm but rather the successful focusing of energy, loyalties, and symbolic authority in the Crown. The government functioned well in the opening decades of Louis's reign because his role as the focal point of power and loyalty was both logical, after the preceding years of unrest, and skillfully exploited. Much of the glue holding together the absolutist state lay in informal mechanisms such as patronage and court life, as well as in the traditional hunt for military glory—all of which Louis amply supplied.

THE LIFE OF THE COURT

An observer comparing the lives of prominent noble families in the mid-sixteenth and mid-seventeenth centuries would have noticed striking differences. By the second half of the seventeenth century, most sovereigns or territorial princes had the power to crush re-

volts, and the heirs of the feudal nobility had to accommodate themselves to the increased power of the Crown. The nobility relinquished its former independence but retained economic and social supremacy and, as a consequence, considerable political clout. Nobles also developed new ways to symbolize their privilege by means of cultural refinement. This process was particularly dramatic in France as a strong Crown won out over a proud nobility.

One sign of Louis's success in marshaling the loyalty of the aristocracy was the brilliant court life that his regime sustained. No longer able to wield independent political power, aristocrats lived at court whenever they could. There they competed for patronage and prestige—for commands in the royal army and for honorific positions at court itself. A favored courtier might, for example, participate in the elaborate daily *lever* (arising) of the king; he might be allowed to hand the king his shirt—a demeaning task, yet a coveted one for the attention by the king that it implied and guaranteed. Courtiers now defended their honor with private duels, not warfare, and more routinely relied on elegant ceremonial, precise etiquette, and clever conversation to demarcate their political and social distinctiveness. (See the feature "The Visual Record: Table Manners.")

As literacy became more widespread and the power of educated bureaucrats of even humble origin became more obvious, nobles from the traditional aristocracy began increasingly to use reading and writing as a means to think critically about their behavior—in the case of men, to re-imagine themselves as gentlemen rather than warriors. Noblewomen and noblemen alike began to reflect on their new roles in letters, memoirs, and the first novels. A prominent theme of these works is the increasing necessity for a truly private life of affection and trust, with which to counterbalance the public façade necessary to an aspiring courtier. The most influential early French novel was *The Princess of Cleves* by Marie-Madeleine Pioche de la Vergne (1634–1693), best known by her title, Madame de Lafayette. Mme. de Lafayette's novel treats the particular difficulties faced by aristocratic women who, without military careers to bring glory and provide distraction, were more vulnerable than men to gossip and slander at court and more trapped by their arranged marriages.

Louis XIV's court is usually associated with the palace he built at Versailles (vare-SIGH), southwest of Paris. Some of the greatest talent of the day worked on the design and construction of Versailles from 1670 through the 1680s. It became a masterpiece of luxurious but restrained baroque style—a model for royal and aristocratic palaces throughout Europe for the next one hundred years.

Before Louis's court in his later years withdrew to Versailles, it traveled among the king's several châteaux

Table Manners

If you were to sit down in a fancy restaurant, order a juicy steak, and then eat it with your bare hands, other diners would undoubtedly stare, shocked by your bad manners. It has not always been the case that table manners meant very much—were able to signal social status, for example. It was not always the case that table manners existed at all in the sense that we know them. How did they evolve? How did they come to have the importance that they do? And why should historians pay any attention to them?

Imagine that you have been invited to dinner at a noble estate in the year 1500. As you sit down, you notice that there are no knives, forks, and spoons at your place, and no napkins either. A servant (a young girl from a neighboring village) sets a roast of meat in front of you and your fellow diners. The lords and ladies on either side of you hack off pieces of meat with the knives that they always carry with them, and then they eat the meat with their fingers. Hunks of bread on the table in front of them catch the dripping juices.

One hundred fifty years later, in 1650, dinner is a much more "civilized" meal. Notice the well-to-do women dining in this engraving by the French artist Abraham Bosse (1602–1676). The table setting, with tablecloths, napkins, plates, and silverware, is recognizable to us. The lady at the extreme right holds up her fork and napkin in a somewhat forced and obvious gesture. These diners have the utensils that we take for granted, but the artist does not take them for granted: they are intended to be noticed by Bosse's elite audience.

In the seventeenth century aristocrats and gentry signaled their political and social privilege with behavior that distinguished them from the lower

Table Manners of the Upper Class in the Seventeenth Century   *(Courtesy of the Trustees of the British Museum)*

classes in ways their more powerful ancestors had found unnecessary. Historians have called this the invention of civility. As we have seen, proper courtesy to one's superiors at court was considered essential. It marked the fact that rituals of honor and deference were increasingly taking the place of armed conflict as the routine behavior of the upper classes. Also essential, however, were certain standards of physical privacy and delicacy. Something as seemingly trivial as the use of a fork became charged with symbolic significance. As the actual power of the aristocrats was circumscribed by the state, they found new expressions of status. Since the sixteenth century new kinds of manners had been touted in handbooks, reflecting changes that already had occurred at Italian courts. During the seventeenth century these practices became more widespread and opened up a gulf between upper- and lower-class behavior.

Some of the new behaviors concerned bodily privacy and discretion. A nobleman now used a handkerchief instead of his fingers or coat sleeve, and he did not urinate in public. The new "rules" about eating are particularly interesting. Why did eating with a fork seem refined and desirable to aristocrats trying to buttress their own self-images? As any 3-year-old knows, eating with a fork is remarkably inefficient.

Using a fork kept you at a distance—literal and symbolic—from the animal you were eating. Napkins wiped away all trace of bloody juices from your lips. Interestingly, as diners began to use utensils, other eating arrangements changed in parallel ways. Sideboards had been in use for a long time, but pieces of meat were now discreetly carved on the sideboard and presented to diners in individual portions. The carcass was brought to the sideboard cut into roasts instead of unmistakably whole, and it was often decorated—as it is today—to further disguise it.

The new aristocrat was increasingly separated from the world of brute physical force, both in daily life and on the battlefield. In warfare brute force was no longer adequate. Training, discipline,

and tactical knowledge were more important and heightened the significance of rank, which separated officers from the vast numbers of common soldiers. Aristocrats now lived in a privileged world where violence—except for an occasional duel—was no longer a fact of life. Their new behavior codes signaled their new invulnerability to others. Above all, they worked to transform a loss—of the independence that had gone hand in hand with a more violent life—into a gain: a privileged immunity to violence.

Specific manners became important, then, because they were symbols of power. The symbolic distance between the powerful and the humble was reinforced by other changes in habits and behavior. A sixteenth-century warrior customarily traveled on horseback and often went from place to place within a city on foot, attended by his retinue. A seventeenth-century aristocrat was more likely to travel in a horse-drawn carriage. The presence of special commodities from abroad—such as sugar—in the seventeenth century created further possibilities for signaling status.

It is interesting to note that other personal habits still diverged dramatically from what we would consider acceptable today. Notice the large, stately bed in the same room as the dining table in Bosse's engraving. Interior space was still undifferentiated by our standards, and it was common for eating, talking, sleeping, and estate management all to go on in a single room. The grand bed is in the picture because, like the fork, it is a mark of status. Like virtually everything else, what is "proper" varies with historical circumstance.

QUESTIONS

1. Why did elites become interested in table manners in the seventeenth century?
2. How did manners function as effective symbols of power?

Online Study Center
Improve Your Grade Visual Record Activities

Versailles Palace, The Hall of Mirrors

This ornate gallery, more than 75 yards long, connects the two wings of the palace. Seventeen huge windows and opposing walled mirrors flood the gallery with light. In addition to these dramatic effects, the designers included many thematic details, such as miniature fleur-de-lys entwined with suns to symbolize the union of France and Louis, in the gilded work near the ceiling. *(Réunion des musées nationaux/Art Resource, NY)*

around the kingdom, and in this itinerant period of the reign, court life was actually at its most creative and productive. These early years of Louis's personal reign were the heyday of French drama. The comedian Jean-Baptiste Poquelin, known as Molière (mole-YARE) (1622–1673), impressed the young Louis with his productions in the late 1650s and was rewarded with the use of a theater in the main royal palace in Paris. Like Shakespeare earlier in the century, Molière explored the social and political tensions of his day. He satirized the pretensions of the aristocracy, the social climbing of the bourgeoisie, and the self-righteous piety of clerics. Some of his plays were banned from performance, but most were not only tolerated but extremely popular with the elite audiences they mocked. Their popularity is testimony to the confidence of Louis's regime in its early days.

Also popular at court were the tragedies of Jean Racine (rah-SEEN) (1639–1699), who was to the French

theater what Shakespeare was to the English: the master of poetic language. His plays, which treat familiar classical stories, focus on the emotional and psychological lives of the characters and often stress the unpredictable, usually unhappy, role of fate, even among royalty. The pessimism in Racine foreshadowed the less successful second half of Louis's reign.

THE BURDENS OF WAR AND THE LIMITS OF POWER

Wars initiated by Louis XIV dominated the attention of most European states in the second half of the seventeenth century. Louis's wars sprang from traditional causes: the importance of the glory and dynastic aggrandizement of the king and the preoccupation of the aristocracy with military life. But if Louis's wars were spurred by familiar concerns about territorial and economic advantage, they were far more demanding on state resources than any previous wars.

In France and elsewhere the size of armies grew markedly. And with the countryside still smarting from the rampaging armies of the Thirty Years' War, so did the need for greater management of troops. Louis XIV's victories in the second half of the seventeenth century are partly traceable to his regime's attention to the bureaucratic tasks of recruitment, training, and supply, which together constituted another phase of the "military revolution." The new offensive tactics developed during the Thirty Years' War (see page 474) changed the character of armies in ways that demanded more resources for training. A higher proportion of soldiers became gunners, and their effectiveness lay in how well they operated as a unit. Armies began to train seriously off the field of battle because drill and discipline were vital to success. France was the first to provide its soldiers with uniforms, which boosted morale and improved discipline. The numbers of men on the battlefield in-

creased somewhat as training increased the effectiveness of large numbers of infantry, but the total numbers of men in arms supported by the state at any time increased dramatically once the organization to support them was in place. Late in the century France kept more than 300,000 men in arms when at war (which was most of the time).

Louis's first war, in 1667, reflects the continuing French preoccupation with Spanish power on French frontiers. Louis invoked rather dubious dynastic claims to demand from Spain lands in the Spanish Netherlands and the large independent county on France's eastern border called the Franche-Comté (FRAWNSH–con-TAY) (see **MAP 16.1**). After a brief conflict, the French obtained only some towns in the Spanish Netherlands. Louis had already begun to negotiate with the Austrian Habsburgs over the eventual division of Spanish Habsburg lands, for it seemed likely that the Spanish king, Charles II (r. 1665–1700), would die without an heir. So, for the moment, Louis was content with modest

MAP 16.1   Territorial Gains of Louis XIV, 1667–1715
Louis's wars, though enormously expensive for France, produced only modest gains of territory along France's eastern and northern frontiers.

gains at Spain's expense, confident that he would get much more in the future.

The Dutch War Louis's focus then shifted to a new enemy, the Dutch. The Dutch had been allied with France since the beginning of their existence as provinces in rebellion against Spain. The French now turned against the Dutch for reasons that reflect the growth of the international trading economy: Dutch dominance of seaborne trade. The French at first tried to offset the Dutch advantage in trade with tariff barriers against Dutch goods. But confidence in the French army led Louis's generals to urge action against the vulnerable Dutch lands. "It is impossible that his Majesty should tolerate any longer the insolence and arrogance of that nation," rationalized the usually pragmatic Colbert in 1670.[1]

The Dutch War began in 1672, with Louis personally leading one of the largest armies ever fielded in Europe—perhaps 120,000 men. At the same time, the Dutch were challenged at sea by England. The English had fought the Dutch over trade in the 1650s; now Louis secretly sent the English king, Charles II, a pension to secure an alliance against the Dutch.

At first the French were spectacularly successful against the tiny Dutch army. However, the Dutch opened dikes and flooded the countryside, and what had begun as a rout became a soggy stalemate. Moreover, the Dutch were beating combined English and French forces at sea and were gathering allies who felt threatened by Louis's aggression. The French soon faced German and Austrian forces along their frontier, and by 1674 the English had joined the alliance against France as well.

Nonetheless, the French managed to hold their own, and the negotiated peace in 1678 gave the illusion of a French victory. Not only had the French met the challenge of an enemy coalition, but Spain ceded them further border areas in the Spanish Netherlands as well as control of the Franche-Comté.

Ensconced at Versailles since 1682, Louis seemed to be at the height of his powers. Yet the Dutch War had in fact cost him more than he had gained. Meeting the alliance against him had meant fielding ever increasing numbers of men. Internal reforms in government and finance ended under the pressure of paying for war, and old financial habits of borrowing money and selling privileges were revived. Other government obligations, such as encouraging overseas trade, were neglected. Colbert's death in 1683 dramatically symbolized the end of an era of innovation in the French regime.

The Nine Years' War Louis's unforgiving Dutch opponent, William of Orange, king of England from 1689 to 1702, renewed and stirred up anti-French alliances. The war, now known as the Nine Years' War, or

King William's War, was touched off late in 1688 by French aggression—an invasion of Germany to claim an inheritance there. In his ongoing dispute with the pope, Louis seized the papal territory of Avignon (ah-veen-YOHN) in southern France. Boldest of all, he helped the exiled Catholic claimant to the English crown mount an invasion to reclaim his throne.

A widespread war began with all the major powers—Spain, the Netherlands, England, Austria, the major German states—ranged against France. The French also carried the fighting abroad by seizing English territory in Canada. As with the Dutch War, the Nine Years' War was costly and, on most fronts, inconclusive. This time, though, there was no illusion of victory for Louis. In the Treaty of Ryswick (1697) Louis gave up most of the territories in Germany, the Spanish Netherlands, and northern Spain that he managed to occupy by war's end. Avignon went back to the pope, and Louis relinquished his contentious claim to papal revenues. The terrible burden of war taxes combined with crop failures in 1693 and 1694 caused widespread starvation in the countryside. French courtiers began to criticize Louis openly.

The War of the Spanish Succession The final major war of Louis's reign, called the War of the Spanish Succession, broke out in 1701. In some ways it was a straightforward dynastic clash between France and its perennial nemesis, the Habsburgs. Both Louis and Habsburg Holy Roman emperor Leopold I (r. 1657–1705) hoped to claim for their heirs the throne of Spain, left open at the death in 1700 of the last Spanish Habsburg, Charles II. Leopold represented the Austrian branch of the Habsburg family (see page 457), but Charles II bequeathed the throne to Louis's grandson, Philip of Anjou, by reason of Louis's marriage to the Spanish princess Maria Theresa. Philip quickly proceeded to enter Spain and claim his new kingdom. War was made inevitable when Louis renounced one of the conditions of Charles's will: Philip's accession to the throne of Spain, Louis insisted, did not preclude his becoming king of France as well. This declaration was an act of sheer belligerence, for Philip was only third in line for the French throne. The Dutch and English responded to the prospect of so great a disruption of the balance of power in Europe by joining the emperor in a formal Great Alliance in 1701. The Dutch and English also wanted to defend their colonial interests since the French had already begun to profit from new trading opportunities with the Spanish colonies.

Again the French fought a major war on several fronts on land and at sea. Again the people of France felt the cost in crushing taxes worsened by harvest failures. Major revolts inside France forced Louis to divert troops from the war. For a time it seemed that the French would be soundly defeated, but they were saved by the superior organization of their forces and by dynastic accident: unexpected deaths in the Habsburg family meant that the Austrian claimant to the Spanish throne suddenly was poised to inherit rule of Austria and the empire as well. The English, more afraid of a revival of unified Habsburg control of Spain and Austria than of French domination of Spain, quickly called for peace negotiations.

The Peace of Utrecht in 1713 resolved long-standing political conflicts and helped to set the agenda of European politics for the eighteenth century. Philip of Anjou was recognized as Philip V, the first Bourbon king of Spain, but on the condition that the Spanish and French crowns would never be worn by the same monarch. To maintain the balance of power against French interests, the Spanish Netherlands and Spanish territories in Italy were ceded by a second treaty in 1714 to Austria, which for many decades would be France's major continental

rival. The Peace of Utrecht also marked the beginning of England's dominance of overseas trade and colonization. The French gave to England lands in Canada and the Caribbean and renounced any privileged relationship with Spanish colonies. England was allowed to control the highly profitable slave trade with Spanish colonies.

Louis XIV had added small amounts of strategically valuable territory along France's eastern border (see Map 16.1), and a Bourbon ruled in Spain. But the costs in human life and resources were great for the slim results achieved. Moreover, the army and navy had swallowed up capital that might have fueled investment and trade; strategic opportunities overseas were lost, never to be regained. Louis's government had been innovative in its early years but remained constrained by traditional ways of imagining the interest of the state.

SECTION SUMMARY

- The Fronde were revolts against royal power early in Louis XIV's reign.

- Louis successfully rebuilt royal power using control of taxation, a reformed bureaucracy, and traditional political bonds such as aristocratic patronage.

- The power Louis wielded has been labeled "absolutism" because there were no formal institutional limits on his authority.

- Court life in Louis's reign sponsored artistic creativity and encouraged a new emphasis on cultural refinement in the aristocracy.

- Louis started a series of costly wars from which the French state gained little.

THE ENGLISH CIVIL WAR AND ITS AFTERMATH

What were the long-term consequences of the English civil war?

In England, unlike in France, a representative institution—**Parliament**—became an effective, permanent brake on royal authority. The process by which Parliament gained a secure role in governing the kingdom was neither easy nor peaceful, however. As we saw in Chapter 15, conflicts between the English crown and its subjects, culminating in the Crown-Parliament conflict, concerned control over taxation and the direction of religious reform. Beginning in 1642 England was beset by civil war between royal and parliamentary forces. The king was eventually defeated and executed, and for a time the monarchy was abolished altogether. It was restored in 1660, but Parliament retained a crucial role in governing the kingdom—a role that was

confirmed when, in 1688, it again deposed a monarch whose fiscal and religious policies became unacceptable to its members.

Online Study Center **Improve Your Grade**
Primary Source: Parliament Chastises Charles I: The Grand Remonstrance

CIVIL WAR, 1642–1649

Fighting broke out between the armies of Charles I and parliamentary armies in the late summer of 1642. The Long Parliament (see page 468) continued to represent a broad coalition of critics and opponents of the monarchy, ranging from aristocrats concerned primarily with abuses of royal prerogative to radical Puritans eager for thorough religious reform and determined to

Parliament   English legislative institution, which used control over monies to bargain with the Crown over foreign and domestic policies, leading to civil war and the deposition of Charles I.

defeat the king. Fighting was halfhearted initially, and the tide of war at first favored Charles.

In 1643, however, the scope of the war broadened. Charles made peace with Irish rebels and brought Irish troops to England to bolster his armies. Parliament in turn sought military aid from the Scots in exchange for promises that Presbyterianism would become the religion of England. Meanwhile, **Oliver Cromwell** (1599–1658), a Puritan member of the Long Parliament and a cavalry officer, helped reorganize parliamentary forces. The eleven-hundred-man cavalry trained by Cromwell and known as the "Ironsides," supported by parliamentary and Scottish infantry, defeated the king's troops at Marston Moor in July 1644. The victory made Cromwell famous.

Shortly afterward Parliament further improved its forces and created the New Model Army, rigorously trained like Cromwell's Ironsides. Sitting members of Parliament were barred from commanding troops; hence upper-class control of the army was reduced. This army played a decisive role not only in the war but also in the political settlement that followed the fighting.

The New Model Army won a convincing victory over royal forces at Naseby in 1645. In the spring of 1646 Charles surrendered to a Scottish army in the north. In January 1647 Parliament paid the Scots for their services in the war and took the king into custody. In the negotiations that followed, Charles tried to play his opponents off against one another, and, as he had hoped, divisions among them widened.

Most members of Parliament were Presbyterians, Puritan gentry who favored a strongly unified and state-controlled church along Calvinist lines. They wanted peace with the king in return for acceptance of the new church structure and parliamentary control of standing militias for a specified period. They did not favor expanding the right to vote to ordinary people or other dramatic constitutional or legal change. These men were increasingly alarmed by the rise of sectarian differences and the actual religious freedom that many ordinary people were claiming for themselves. With the weakening of royal authority and the disruption of civil war, censorship was relaxed, and public preaching by ordinary men and even women who felt divinely inspired was becoming commonplace.

Above all, Presbyterian gentry in Parliament feared more radical groups in the army and in London who had supported them up to this point but who favored more sweeping political and religious change. Most officers of the New Model Army, such as Cromwell, were Independents, Puritans who favored a decentralized church, a degree of religious toleration, and a wider sharing of political power among men of property, not just among the very wealthy gentry. In London a well-organized artisans' movement known as the "Levellers" went even further; Levellers favored universal manhood suffrage, law reform, better access to education, and decentralized churches—in short, the separation of political power from wealth and virtual freedom of religion. Many of the rank and file of the army were deeply influenced by Leveller ideas.

In May 1647 the majority in Parliament voted to offer terms to the king and to disband the New Model Army—without first paying most of the soldiers' back wages. This move provoked the first direct intervention by the army in politics. Representatives of the soldiers were chosen to present grievances to Parliament; when this failed, the army seized the king and, in August, occupied Westminster, Parliament's meeting place. Independent and Leveller elements in the army debated the direction of possible reform to be imposed on Parliament. One Leveller participant argued for universal manhood suffrage: "every man that is to live under a government ought first by his own consent to put himself under that government; and I do think that the poorest man in England is not at all bound . . . to that government that he hath not had a voice to put himself under."[2]

In November, however, their common enemy Charles escaped from his captors and raised a new army among his erstwhile enemies, the Scots, who were also alarmed by the growing radicalism in England. Civil war began again early in 1648. Although it ended quickly with a victory by Cromwell and the New Model Army in August, the renewed war further hardened political divisions and enhanced the power of the army. The king was widely blamed for the renewed bloodshed, and the army did not trust him to keep any agreement he might now sign. When Parliament, still dominated by Presbyterians, once again voted to negotiate with the king, army troops under Colonel Thomas Pride prevented members who favored Presbyterianism or negotiating with the king from attending sessions. The "Rump" Parliament that remained after "Pride's Purge" voted to try the king. A hasty trial ensued, and, on January 30, 1649, Charles I was executed for "treason, tyranny and bloodshed" against his people.

THE INTERREGNUM, 1649–1660

A Commonwealth—a republic—was declared. Executive power resided in a council of state. The House of Lords having been abolished, legislative power resided in the one-chamber Rump Parliament. Declaring a republic proved far easier than running one, however. The execution of the king shocked most English and Scots and alienated many elites from the new regime. The legitimacy of the Commonwealth government would always be in question.

Oliver Cromwell English Puritan general during the English civil war who governed as Lord Protector during the interregnum from 1653 to 1658.

The tasks of making and implementing policy were hindered by the narrow political base on which the government now rested. Excluded were the majority of the reformist gentry who had been purged from Parliament. Also excluded were the more radical Levellers; Leveller leaders in London were arrested when they published tracts critical of the new government. Within a few years many disillusioned Levellers would join a new religious movement called the Society of Friends, or Quakers, which espoused complete religious autonomy. Quakers declined all oaths or service to the state, and they refused to acknowledge social rank.

Above all, the new government was vulnerable to the power of the army, which had created it. In 1649 and 1650 Cromwell led expeditions to Ireland and Scotland, partly for sheer revenge and partly to put down resistance to Commonwealth authority. In Ireland Cromwell's forces acted with shameful ruthlessness. English control there was strengthened by more dispossession of Irish landholders, which also served to pay off the army's wages. Meanwhile, Parliament could not agree on systematic reforms, particularly the one reform Independents in the army insisted on: more broadly based elections for a new Parliament. Fresh from his victories, Cromwell led his armies to London and dissolved Parliament in the spring of 1652.

In 1653 a cadre of army officers drew up the "Instrument of Government," England's first and only written constitution. It provided for an executive, the Lord Protector, and a Parliament to be based on somewhat wider male suffrage. Cromwell was the natural choice for Lord Protector, and whatever success the government of the Protectorate had was due largely to him.

Cromwell was an extremely able leader who was not averse to compromise. Although he had used force against Parliament in 1648, he had worked hard to reconcile the Rump Parliament and the army before marching on London in 1652. He believed in a state church, but, unlike his Presbyterian opponents, one that allowed for local control, including choice of minister, by individual congregations. He also believed in toleration for other Protestant sects, as well as for Catholics and Jews, as long as no one disturbed the peace.

As Lord Protector, Cromwell oversaw impressive reforms in law that testify to his belief in the limits of governing authority. For example, contrary to the practice of his day, he opposed capital punishment for petty crimes. The government of the Protectorate, however, accomplished little given Parliament's internal divisions and opposition to Cromwell's initiatives. The population at large still harbored royalist sympathizers; after a royalist uprising in 1655, Cromwell divided England into military districts and vested governing authority in army generals.

Popular Preaching in England
Many women took advantage of the collapse of royal authority to preach in public—a radical activity for women at the time. This print satirizes the Quakers, a religious movement that attracted many women. *(Mary Evans Picture Library)*

In the end the Protectorate could not survive the strains over policy and the challenges to its legitimacy. When Cromwell died of a sudden illness in September 1658, the Protectorate did not long survive him. In February 1660 the decisive action of one army general enabled all the surviving members of the Long Parliament to rejoin the Rump. The Parliament summarily dissolved itself and called for new elections. The newly elected Parliament recalled Charles II, son of Charles I, from exile abroad and restored the monarchy. The chaos and radicalism of the late civil war and "interregnum"—the period between reigns, as the years from 1649 to 1660 came to be called—now spawned a conservative reaction.

Online Study Center **Improve Your Grade**
Primary Source: An Anonymous Pamphlet Urges Restoration of the Stuart Dynasty

THE RESTORATION, 1660–1685

Charles II (r. 1660–1685) claimed his throne at the age of 30. He had learned from his years of uncertain exile and from the fate of his father. He did not seek retribution but rather offered a general pardon to all but a few rebels (mostly those who had signed his father's death warrant), and he suggested to Parliament a relatively tolerant religious settlement that would include Anglicans as well as Presbyterians. He was far more politically adept than his father and far more willing to compromise.

That the re-established royal government was not more tolerant than it turned out to be was not Charles's doing but Parliament's. During the 1660s, the "Cavalier" Parliament, named for royalists in the civil war, passed harsh laws aimed at religious dissenters. Anglican orthodoxy was reimposed, including the re-establishment of bishops and the Anglican *Book of Common Prayer*. All officeholders and clergy were required to swear oaths of obedience to the king and to the established church. As a result, hundreds were forced out of office and pulpits. Holding nonconformist religious services became illegal, and Parliament passed a "five-mile" act to prevent dissenting ministers from traveling near their former congregations. Property laws were tightened and the criminal codes made more severe.

The king's behavior in turn began to mimic prerevolutionary royalist positions. Charles II began to flirt with Catholicism, and his brother and heir, James, openly converted. Charles promulgated a declaration of tolerance that would have included Catholics as well as nonconformist Protestants, but Parliament would not accept it. Anti-Catholic feeling still united all Protestants. In 1678 Charles's secret treaties with the French became known (see page 500), and rumors of a Catholic plot to murder Charles and reimpose Catholicism became widespread. No evidence of any plot was ever unearthed, although thirty-five people were executed for alleged participation. Parliament focused its attention on anti-Catholicism, passing the Test Act, which barred all but Anglicans from public office. As a result, the Catholic James was forced to resign as Lord High Admiral.

When Parliament moved to exclude James from succession to the throne, Charles dissolved it. A subsequent Parliament, worried by the specter of a new civil war, backed down. But the legacy of the civil war was a potent one. First, despite the harsh laws, to silence all dissent was not possible. After two decades of religious pluralism and broadly based political activity, it was impossible to reimpose conformity; well-established communities of various sects and self-confidence bred vigorous resistance. The clearest reflection of the legacy of events was the power of Parliament. Though reluctant to press too far, Parliament had tried to assert its policies against the desires of the king.

Nevertheless, by the end of his reign Charles was financially independent of Parliament, thanks to increased revenue from overseas trade and secret subsidies from France, his recent ally against Dutch trading rivals. This financial independence and firm political tactics enabled Charles to regain, and retain, a great deal of power. If he had been followed by an able successor, Parliament might have lost a good measure of its confidence and independence. But his brother James's reign and its aftermath further enhanced Parliament's power.

THE GLORIOUS REVOLUTION, 1688

When James II (r. 1685–1689) succeeded Charles, Parliament's royalist leanings were at first evident. James was granted customs duties for life and was also given funds to suppress a rebellion by one of Charles's illegitimate sons. James did not try to impose Catholicism on England as some had feared, but he did try to achieve toleration for Catholics in two declarations of indulgence in 1687 and 1688. However admirable his goal—toleration—he had essentially changed the law of the realm without Parliament's consent and further undermined his position with heavy-handed tactics. When several leading Anglican bishops refused to read the declarations from their pulpits, he had them imprisoned and tried for seditious libel. However, a sympathetic jury acquitted them.

James also failed because of the coincidence of other events. In 1685, at the outset of James's reign, Louis XIV of France had revoked the Edict of Nantes. The possibility that subjects and monarchs in France and, by extension, elsewhere could be of different faiths seemed increasingly unlikely. Popular fears of James's Catholicism were thus heightened early in his reign, and his later declarations of tolerance, though benefiting Protestant dissenters, were viewed with suspicion. In 1688 not only were the Anglican bishops acquitted but the king's second wife, who was Catholic, gave birth to a son. The birth raised the specter of a Catholic succession.

In June 1688, to put pressure on James, leading members of Parliament invited William of Orange, husband of James's Protestant daughter, Mary, to come to England. William mounted an invasion that became a rout when James refused to defend his throne. James simply abandoned England and went to France. William called Parliament, which declared James to have abdicated and offered the throne jointly to William and Mary. With French support James eventually invaded Ireland in 1690—bound for Westminster—but was defeated by William at the Battle of Boyne that year.

THE WRITTEN RECORD

THE ENGLISH BILL OF RIGHTS

After King William and Queen Mary accepted the throne, they signed this Bill of Rights presented to them by Parliament in 1689. They therefore accepted not only the limits of royal power enshrined in the document but also the fact that Parliament could legislate how the monarchy was to function.

Whereas the Lords Spiritual and Temporal and Commons assembled at Westminster, lawfully, fully and freely representing all the estates of the people of this realm, did upon the thirteenth of February . . . present unto their Majesties, then called and known by the names and style of William and Mary, prince and princess of Orange, being present in their proper persons, a certain declaration in writing made by the said Lords and Commons in the words following, viz.:

Whereas the late King James the Second, by the assistance of diverse evil counselors, judges and ministers employed by him, did endeavor to subvert and extirpate the Protestant religion and the laws and liberties of this kingdom;

By assuming and exercising a power of dispensing with and suspending of laws and the execution of laws without consent of Parliament; . . .

By levying money for and to the use of the Crown by pretense of prerogative for other time and in other manner than the same was granted by Parliament;

By raising and keeping a standing army within this kingdom in time of peace without consent of Parliament, and quartering soldiers contrary to law;

By causing several good subjects being Protestants to be disarmed at the same time when papists were both armed and employed contrary to law;

By violating the freedom of election of members to serve in Parliament;

By prosecutions in the Court of King's Bench for matters and causes cognizable only in Parliament, and by diverse other arbitrary and illegal courses; . . .

And excessive bail hath been required of persons committed in criminal cases to elude the benefit of the laws made for the liberty of the subjects;

And excessive fines have been imposed;

And illegal and cruel punishments inflicted; . . .

All which are utterly and directly contrary to the known laws and statutes and freedom of this realm;

And whereas the said late King James the Second having abdicated the government and the throne being thereby vacant, his Highness the prince of Orange (whom it hath pleased Almighty God to make the glorious instrument of delivering this kingdom from popery and arbitrary power) did . . . cause letters to be written to the Lords Spiritual and Temporal being Protestants, and other letters to the several counties, cities, universities, boroughs and cinque ports, for the choosing of such persons to represent them as were of right to be sent to Parliament. . . .

And thereupon the said Lords Spiritual and Temporal and Commons, pursuant to their respective letters and elections, being now assembled in a full and free representative of this nation, taking into their most serious consideration the best means for attaining the ends aforesaid, do in the first place (as their ancestors in like case have usually done) for the vindicating and asserting their ancient rights and liberties declare;

That the pretended power of suspending of laws or the execution of laws by regal authority without consent of Parliament is illegal;

That the pretended power of dispensing with laws or the execution of laws by regal authority, as it hath been assumed and exercised of late, is illegal; . . .

That levying money for or to the use of the Crown by pretense of prerogative, without grant of Parliament, for longer time, or in other manner than the same is or shall be granted, is illegal;

That it is the right of the Subjects to petition the king, and all commitments and prosecutions for such petitioning are illegal;

That the raising or keeping a standing army within the kingdom in time of peace, unless it be with consent of Parliament, is against law;

That the subjects which are Protestants may have arms for their defense suitable to their conditions and as allowed by law;

That election of members of Parliament ought to be free;

That the freedom of speech and debates or proceedings in Parliament ought not to be impeached or questioned in any court or place out of Parliament;

That excessive bail ought not to be required, nor excessive fines imposed nor cruel and unusual punishments inflicted; . . .

And that for redress of all grievances, and for the amending, strengthening and preserving of the laws, Parliaments ought to be held frequently.

QUESTIONS

1. How, specifically, does this document limit royal power?
2. What rights were the creators of this document most concerned to protect, in your view?
3. Would any of the rights protected here have been useful to common English people?

Source: The Statutes: Revised Edition, vol. 1 (London: Eyre and Spottiswoode, 1871), pp. 10–12.

The substitution of William (r. 1689–1702) and Mary (r. 1689–1694) for James, known as the **Glorious Revolution,** was engineered by Parliament and confirmed its power. Parliament presented the new sovereigns with a Declaration of Rights upon their accession and, later that year, with a Bill of Rights that defended freedom of speech, called for frequent Parliaments, and required subsequent monarchs to be Protestant (see "The Written Record: The English Bill of Rights"). The effectiveness of these documents was reinforced by Parliament's power of the purse. Parliament's role in the political process was ensured by William's interests in

funding his ambitious military efforts, particularly the Netherlands' ongoing wars with France.

The issues that had faced the English since the beginning of the century were common to all European states: religious division and elite power, fiscal strains and resistance to taxation. Yet the cataclysmic events in England—the interregnum, the Commonwealth, the Restoration, the Glorious Revolution—had set it apart from other states. Consequently, the incremental assumption of authority by a well-established institution, Parliament, made challenge of the English monarchy more legitimate and more effective.

=========== S E C T I O N   S U M M A R Y ===========

- In England, unlike in France, a representative institution controlled taxation and could effectively challenge royal policies.

- A civil war between Charles I and parliamentary forces ended with the defeat and execution of the king in 1649.

- Several groups, including wealthy gentry and ordinary townspeople, had allied to support Parliament, but they did not agree on a program of political and religious reform.

- The government of the interregnum did not last after the death of the Lord Protector, Oliver Cromwell,

because too few of the original supporters of Parliament believed it legitimate or approved of its policies.

- The Crown was restored under Charles II but began to conflict again with Parliament over political and religious policy under his successor James II.

- The role of Parliament in English government was confirmed when William and Mary accepted the Crown under conditions stated in the Bill of Rights.

NEW POWERS IN CENTRAL AND EASTERN EUROPE

Which states began to dominate central and eastern Europe and why were they successful?

By the end of the seventeenth century three states dominated central and eastern Europe: Austria, Brandenburg-Prussia, and Russia. After the Thirty Years' War the Habsburgs' dominance in the splintering empire waned, and they focused on expanding and consolidating their power in their hereditary possessions, centered in what became modern Austria. Brandenburg-Prussia, in northeastern Germany, emerged from obscurity to rival the Habsburg state. The rulers of Brandenburg-Prussia had gained lands in the Peace of Westphalia, and astute management trans-

formed their relatively small and scattered holdings into one of the most powerful states in Europe. Russia's new stature in eastern Europe resulted in part from the weakness of its greatest rival, Poland, and the determination of one leader, Peter the Great, to assume a major role in European affairs. Sweden controlled valuable Baltic territory through much of the century but eventually was also eclipsed by Russia as a force in the region.

The internal political development of these states was dramatically shaped by their relationship to the wider European economy: they were sources of grain and raw materials for the more densely urbanized West. The development of and the competition among states in central and eastern Europe were closely linked to developments in western Europe.

Glorious Revolution Bloodless English revolution in 1688 in which Parliament replaced the Catholic King James II with William (of Orange) and his wife, Mary (James's Protestant daughter), and imposed on the new rulers a Bill of Rights that confirmed Parliament's power.

THE CONSOLIDATION OF AUSTRIA

The Thirty Years' War (see pages 471–474) weakened the Habsburgs as emperors but strengthened them in their own lands. The main Habsburg lands in 1648 were a collection of principalities comprising modern Austria, the kingdom of Hungary (largely in Turkish hands), and the kingdom of Bohemia (see Map 16.2). In 1714 Austria acquired the Spanish Netherlands, which were renamed the Austrian Netherlands. Although language and ethnic differences prevented an absolutist state along French lines, Leopold I (r. 1657–1705) instituted political and institutional changes that enabled the Habsburg state to become one of the most powerful in Europe through the eighteenth century.

Much of the coherence that already existed in Leopold's lands had been achieved by his predecessors in the wake of the Thirty Years' War. The lands of rebels in Bohemia had been confiscated and redistributed among loyal, mostly Austrian, families. In return for political and military support for the emperor, these families were given the right to exploit their newly acquired land and the peasants who worked it. The desire to recover population and productivity after the destruction of the Thirty Years' War gave landlords further incentive to curtail peasants' autonomy, particularly in devastated Bohemia. Austrian landlords throughout the Habsburg domains provided grain and timber for the export market and foodstuffs for the Austrian armies, while elite families provided the army with officers. This political-economic arrangement provoked numerous serious peasant revolts, but the peasants were not able to force changes in a system that suited both the elites and the central authority.

Although Leopold had lost much influence within the empire itself, an imperial government made up of various councils, a war ministry, financial officials, and the like still functioned in his capital, Vienna. Leopold worked to extricate the government of his own lands from the apparatus of imperial institutions, which were staffed largely by Germans more loyal to imperial than to Habsburg interests.

In addition, Leopold used the Catholic Church as an institutional and ideological support for the Habsburg state. Leopold's personal ambition was to re-establish devout Catholicism throughout his territories. Acceptance of Catholicism became the litmus test of loyalty to the Habsburg regime, and Protestantism vanished among elites. Leopold encouraged the work of Jesuit teachers and members of other Catholic orders. These

Baroque Splendor in Austria

The Belvedere Palace (whose name means "beautiful view") was built near Vienna as the summer residence of the great aristocratic general Prince Eugene of Savoy, who had successfully led Habsburg armies against the Turks and had reaped many rewards from Leopold and his successors. The palace shares many features in common with Louis XIV's palace of Versailles. *(Erich Lessing/Art Resource, NY)*

men and women helped staff his government and administered religious life down to the most local levels.

Leopold's most dramatic success, as a Habsburg and a religious leader, was his reconquest of the kingdom of Hungary from the Ottoman Empire. Since the mid-sixteenth century the Habsburgs had controlled only a narrow strip of the kingdom. Preoccupied with countering Louis XIV's aggression, Leopold did not himself choose to begin a reconquest. His centralizing policies, however, alienated nobles and townspeople in the portion of Hungary he did control, as did his repression of Protestantism, which had flourished in Hungary. Hungarian nobles began a revolt, aided by the Turks, aiming for a reunited Hungary under Ottoman protection.

The Habsburgs emerged victorious in part because they received help from the Venetians, the Russians, and especially the Poles, whose lands in Ukraine were threatened by the Turks. The Turks overreached their supply lines to besiege Vienna in 1683. When the siege failed, Habsburg armies slowly pressed east and south, recovering Buda, the capital of Hungary, in 1686 and Belgrade (modern Serbia) in 1688. The Danube basin lay once again in Christian hands. The **Treaty of Carlowitz** ended the fighting in 1699, after the first conference where European allies jointly dictated terms to a weakening Ottoman Empire. Austria's allies had also gained at the Ottomans' expense: the Poles recovered the threatened Ukraine, and the Russians gained a vital foothold on the Black Sea.

Leopold gave land in the reclaimed lands to Austrian officers who he believed were loyal to him. The traditions of Hungarian separatism, however, were strong, and Hungary's great aristocrats—whether they had defended the Habsburgs against Turkish encroachment or guarded the frontier for Turkish overlords—retained their independence. The peasantry, as elsewhere, suffered a decline in status as a result of the Crown's efforts to ensure the loyalty of elites. In the long run Hungarian independence weakened the Habsburg state, but in the short run Leopold's victory over the Turks and the recovery of Hungary itself were momentous events, confirming the Habsburgs as the pre-eminent power in central Europe.

THE RISE OF BRANDENBURG-PRUSSIA

Three German states, in addition to Austria, gained territory and stature after the Thirty Years' War: Bavaria, Saxony, and **Brandenburg-Prussia.** By the end of the

seventeenth century the strongest was Brandenburg-Prussia, a conglomeration of small territories held, by dynastic accident, by the Hohenzollern family. The two principal territories were electoral Brandenburg, in northeastern Germany, with its capital, Berlin, and the duchy of Prussia, a fief of the Polish crown along the Baltic coast east of Poland proper (see **MAP 16.2**). In addition, the Hohenzollerns ruled a handful of small principalities near the Netherlands. The manipulation of resources and power that enabled these unpromising lands to become a powerful state was primarily the work of Frederick William, known as "the Great Elector" (r. 1640–1688).

Frederick William used the occasion of a war to effect a permanent change in the structure of government. He took advantage of a war between Poland and its rivals, Sweden and Russia (described in the next section), to win independence for the duchy of Prussia from Polish overlordship. When his involvement in the war ended in 1657, he kept intact the general war commissariat, a combined civilian and military body that had efficiently directed the war effort, bypassing traditional councils and representative bodies. He also used the standing army to force the payment of high taxes. Most significantly, he established a positive relationship with the Junkers (YUNG-kurz), hereditary landholders, which ensured him both revenue and loyalty. He agreed to allow the Junkers virtually total control of their own lands in return for their agreement to support his government—in short, they surrendered their accustomed political independence in exchange for greater economic and social power over the peasants who worked their lands.

Peasants and townspeople were taxed, but nobles were not. The freedom to control their estates led many nobles to invest in profitable agriculture for the export market. The peasants were serfs who received no benefits from the increased productivity of the land. Frederick William further enhanced his state's power by sponsoring state industries. These industries did not have to fear competition from urban producers because the towns had been frozen out of the political process and saddled with heavy taxes. Though an oppressive place for many Germans, Brandenburg-Prussia attracted many skilled refugees, such as Huguenot artisans fleeing Louis XIV's France.

Bavaria and Saxony, in contrast to Brandenburg-Prussia, had vibrant towns, largely free peasantries, and weaker aristocracies but were relative nonentities in international affairs. Power on the European stage depended on military force. Such power, whether in a large state like France or in a small one like Brandenburg-Prussia, usually came at the expense of the people.

Treaty of Carlowitz Treaty imposed by the European allies on the Ottoman Empire by which the Austrians, Venetians, Russians, and Poles gained territory at the Turks' expense.

Brandenburg-Prussia Group of German territories ruled by the Hohenzollern family that became one of Europe's most powerful states in the seventeenth century.

MAP 16.2 New Powers in Central and Eastern Europe, to 1725

The balance of power in central and eastern Europe shifted with the strengthening of Austria, the rise of Brandenburg-Prussia, and the expansion of Russia at the expense of Poland and Sweden.

Legend:
- Prussian territory in 1640
- Prussian acquisitions in 1688
- Russian territory in 1693
- Seized by Peter the Great from Sweden, 1694–1725
- Austrian territory by 1699
- Ottoman Empire in 1699
- Boundary of the Holy Roman Empire

COMPETITION AROUND THE BALTIC

The rivers and port cities of the Baltic coast were conduits for the growing trade between the Baltic hinterland and the rest of Europe. In 1600 a large portion of the Baltic hinterland lay under the control of Poland-Lithuania, a vast and diverse state at the height of its power, but one that would prove an exception to the pattern of expanding royal power in the seventeenth century. Wars in the middle of the century were extremely destructive in regard not only to lives and property but also, unlike in neighboring Prussia, to the coherence of the state as well.

The Decline of Poland Internal strains began to mount in Poland-Lithuania in the late sixteenth century. The spread of the Counter-Reformation, encouraged by the Crown, created tensions with both Protestant and Orthodox subjects in the diverse kingdom. The greatest source of political instability was the power of landholding nobles, whose fortunes grew as Poland became the granary of western Europe. Impoverished peasants were bound to the land, and lesser gentry, particularly in the Ruthenian lands of Lithuania, were shut out of political power by Polish aristocrats. In Ukraine, communities of **Cossacks,** nomadic farmer-warriors, grew as Polish and Lithuanian peasants fled harsh conditions to join them. The Cossacks had long been tolerated because they served as a military buffer against the Ottoman Turks to the south, but now Polish landlords wanted to reincorporate the Cossacks into the profitable political-economic system they controlled.

In 1648 the Polish crown faced revolt and invasion that it could not fully counter. The Cossacks led a major uprising, which included Ukrainian gentry as well as peasants. The Cossacks held their own against the Polish armies. Meanwhile, the Crown's efforts to reach a peace agreement were blocked by the noble landlords against whom the revolt had been directed. In 1654 the Cossacks tried to assure their autonomy by transferring their allegiance to Moscow. They became part of a Russian invasion of Poland-Lithuania that by the next year had engulfed much of the eastern half of the dual state. At the same time, Poland's perennial rival, Sweden, seized central Poland in a military campaign marked by extreme brutality. Many Polish and Lithuanian aristocrats continued to act like independent warlords and cooperated with the invaders to preserve their own local power.

Operating with slim resources, Polish royal armies eventually managed to recover much territory—most important, the western half of Ukraine (see Map 16.2). But the invasions and subsequent fighting were disastrous. These wars were afterward referred to as "the deluge," and with good reason. The population of Poland declined by as much as 40 percent, and vital urban economies were in ruins. The Catholic identity of the Polish heartland had been a rallying point for resistance to the Protestant Swedes and the Orthodox Russians, but the religious tolerance that had distinguished the Polish kingdom and had been mandated in its constitution was now abandoned. In addition, much of its recovery of Lithuanian territory was only nominal.

The elective Polish crown passed in 1674 to the military hero Jan Sobieski (so-BYESS-key) (r. 1674–1696),

known as "Vanquisher of the Turks" for his role in raising the siege of Vienna in 1683. Given Poland's internal weakness, however, Sobieski's victories in the long run helped the Ottomans' other foes—Austria and Russia—more than they helped the Poles. Moreover, though a brilliant tactician, he was a master of an increasingly outmoded form of warfare that was almost wholly reliant on cavalry. He was unable to force reforms that would have led to increased royal revenue and a more up-to-date royal army. After his death Poland would be vulnerable to the political ambitions of its more powerful neighbors. The next elected king, Augustus II of Saxony (r. 1697–1704, 1709–1733), dragged Poland back into war, from which Russia would emerge the clear winner in the power struggle in eastern Europe.

The Rise of Swedish Power The Swedes, meanwhile, had successfully vied with the Poles and other competitors for control of the lucrative Baltic coast. Swedish efforts to control Baltic territory began in the sixteenth century, first to counter the power of its perennial rival, Denmark, in the western Baltic. It then competed with Poland to control Livonia (modern Latvia), whose principal city, Riga, was an important trading center for products such as grain, timber, and fur from both Lithuania and Russia. By 1617, under Gustav Adolf, the Swedes gained the lands to the north surrounding the Gulf of Finland (the most direct outlet for Russian goods), and in 1621 they displaced the Poles in Livonia itself. Swedish intervention in the Thirty Years' War came when imperial successes against Denmark both threatened the Baltic coast and created an opportunity to strike at Sweden's old enemy. The Treaty of Westphalia (1648) confirmed Sweden's earlier gains and added control of further coastal territory, mostly at Denmark's expense.

The port cities held by Sweden were profitable but simply served to pay for the costly wars necessary to seize and defend them. Indeed, Sweden's efforts to hold Baltic territory were driven by dynastic and strategic needs as much as economic objectives. The ruling dynasty struggled against Denmark's control of western Baltic territory in order to safeguard its independence from the Danes, who had ruled the combined kingdoms until 1523. Similarly, competition with Poland for the eastern Baltic was part of a dynastic struggle after 1592. Sigismund Vasa, son of the king of Sweden, had been elected king of Poland in 1587 but also inherited the Swedish throne in 1592. Other members of the Vasa family fought him successfully to regain rule over Sweden and extricate Swedish interests from Poland's continental preoccupations. Although Sigismund ruled Poland until his death in 1632, a Vasa uncle replaced him on the Swedish throne in 1604.

The one permanent gain that Sweden realized from its aggression against Poland in the 1650s was the

---

Cossacks Russian term meaning "free men" originally applied to people of central Asian origin in the hinterland of the Black Sea. After 1500, many peasants escaping serfdom in Poland-Lithuania and Russia fled and became "Cossacks."

renunciation of the Polish Vasa line to any claim to the Swedish crown. Owing to its earlier gains, Sweden reigned supreme on the Baltic coast until the end of the century, when it was supplanted by the powerful Russian state.

RUSSIA UNDER PETER THE GREAT

The Russian state expanded dramatically through the sixteenth century under Ivan IV and weathered the period of disputed succession known as the "Time of Troubles" (see pages 474–475). The foundations of the large and cohesive state laid by Ivan enabled Michael Romanov (ROH-man-off) to rebuild autocratic government with ease after being chosen tsar in 1613.

The Romanovs were an eminent aristocratic family related to Ivan's. Michael (r. 1613–1645) was selected to rule by an assembly of aristocrats, gentry, and commoners who were more alarmed at the civil wars and recent Polish incursions than at the prospect of a return to strong tsarist rule. Michael was succeeded by his son, Alexis (r. 1645–1676), who presided over the extension of Russian control to eastern Ukraine in 1654 following the wars in Poland and developed an interest in cultivating relationships with the West.

Shifting the balance of power in eastern Europe and the Baltic in Russia's favor was also the work of Alexis's son, Peter I (r. 1682–1725), "the Great." **Peter the Great** accomplished this by military successes against his enemies and by forcibly reorienting Russian government and society toward involvement with the rest of Europe.

Peter was almost literally larger than life. Nearly 7 feet tall, he towered over most of his contemporaries and had physical and mental energy to match his size. He set himself to learning trades and studied soldiering by rising through the ranks of the military like a common soldier. He traveled abroad to learn as much as he could about western European economies and governments. He wanted the revenue, manufacturing output, technology and trade, and, above all, up-to-date army and navy that other rulers enjoyed. In short Peter sought for Russia a more evolved state system because of the strength it would give him.

Immediately on his accession to power, Peter initiated a bold series of changes in Russian society. His travels had taught him that European monarchs coexisted with a privileged but educated aristocracy and that a brilliant court life symbolized and reinforced their authority. So he set out to refashion Russian society in what amounted to an enforced cultural revolution. He provoked a direct confrontation with Russia's traditional aristocracy over everything from education

to matters of dress. He elevated numerous new families to the ranks of gentry and created an official ranking system for the nobility to encourage and reward service to his government.

Online Study Center   **Improve Your Grade**
Primary Source: Peter the Great Imposes Western Styles on the Russians

Peter's effort to reorient his nation culturally, economically, and politically toward Europe was most apparent in the construction of the city of St. Petersburg on the Gulf of Finland, which provided access to the Baltic Sea (see Map 16.2). In stark contrast to Moscow, dominated by the medieval fortress of the Kremlin and churches in the traditional Russian style, St. Petersburg was a modern European city with wide avenues and palaces designed for a sophisticated court life.

Although Peter was highly intelligent, practical, and determined to create a more productive and better governed society, he was also cruel and authoritarian.

Peter the Great
This portrait by a Dutch artist captures the tsar's "westernizing" mission by showing Peter in military dress according to European fashions of the day.
(Rijksmuseum-Stichting, Amsterdam)

Peter the Great   Energetic and tyrannical Russian tsar who forcibly westernized Russian state and society and made Russia into a great power.

Peasants already were bearing the brunt of taxation, but their tax burden worsened when they were assessed arbitrarily by head and not by output of the land. The building of St. Petersburg cost staggering sums in both money and workers' lives. Peter's entire reform system was carried out tyrannically; resistance was brutally suppressed. Victims of Peter's oppression included his son, Alexis, who died after torture while awaiting execution for questioning his father's policies.

Peter faced elite as well as populist rebellions against the exactions and the cultural changes of his regime. The most serious challenge was the revolt in 1707 of the Cossacks in the Don River region against the regime's tightened controls. A major reason for the high cost of Peter's government to the Russian people was his ambition for territorial gain—hence his emphasis on an improved, and costly, army and navy. Working side by side with workers and technicians, many of whom he had recruited while abroad, Peter created the Russian navy from scratch. At first ships were built in the south to contest Turkish control of the Black Sea. Later they were built in the north to secure and defend the Baltic. Peter also modernized the Russian army by employing tactics, training, and discipline he had observed in the West. He introduced military conscription and munitions plants. By 1709 Russia was able to manufacture most of the up-to-date firearms its army needed.

Russia waged war virtually throughout Peter's reign. Initially with some success, he struck at the Ottomans and their client state in the Crimea. Later phases of these conflicts brought reverses, however. Peter was spectacularly successful against his northern competitor, Sweden, for control of the weakened Polish state and the Baltic Sea. The conflicts between Sweden and Russia, known as the Great Northern War, raged from 1700 to 1709 and, in a less intense phase, lasted until 1721. By the Treaty of Nystadt in 1721, Russia gained its present-day territory in the Gulf of Finland near St. Petersburg, plus Livonia and Estonia. These acquisitions gave Russia a secure window on the Baltic and, in combination with its gains of Lithuanian territory earlier in the century, made Russia the preeminent Baltic power, at Sweden's and Poland's expense.

================ S E C T I O N   S U M M A R Y ================

- After the Thirty Years' War Austria, Brandenburg-Prussia, and Russia became the dominant states in central and eastern Europe.

- Central and eastern Europe provided raw materials for the wider European economy, which enhanced elites' power over peasants, increased revenues to states, and caused wars between states over these resources.

- The Austrian Habsburgs consolidated their power in their territories within the Holy Roman Empire and reconquered Hungary from the Ottoman Turks.

- Although composed of a collection of small principalities, Brandenburg-Prussia became a powerful state.

- Poland-Lithuania declined in the seventeenth century because the elective monarchy could not defend itself against independent aristocrats, rebellious Cossacks, or powerful neighboring states.

- Russia was forcibly modernized by Peter the Great and became the most powerful state in eastern Europe under his reign, eclipsing Sweden in control of Baltic territories.

THE EXPANSION OF OVERSEAS TRADE AND SETTLEMENT

How and why did Europe's overseas trade and colonization expand in the seventeenth century and what effects did this expansion have on Europe itself?

y the beginning of the seventeenth century competition from the Dutch, French, and English was disrupting the Spanish and Portuguese trading empires in Asia and the New World. During the seventeenth century European trade and colonization expanded and changed dramatically. The Dutch not only became masters of the spice trade but broadened the market to include many other commodities. In the Americas a new trading system linking Europe, Africa, and the New World came into being with the expansion of tobacco and, later, sugar production. French and English colonists began settling in

North America in increasing numbers. By the end of the century trading and colonial outposts around the world figured regularly as bargaining chips in disagreements between European states. More important, overseas trade had a crucial impact on life within Europe: on patterns of production and consumption, on social stratification, and on the distribution of wealth.

THE GROWTH OF TRADING EMPIRES: THE SUCCESS OF THE DUTCH

By the end of the sixteenth century the Dutch and the English were making incursions into the Portuguese-controlled spice trade with areas of India, Ceylon, and the East Indies. Spain had annexed Portugal in 1580, but the drain on Spain's resources from its wars with the Dutch and French prevented Spain from adequately defending its enlarged trading empire in Asia. The Dutch and, to a lesser degree, the English rapidly

supplanted Portuguese control of this lucrative trade (see **MAP 16.3**).

The Dutch were particularly well placed to be successful competitors in overseas trade. They already dominated seaborne trade within Europe, including the most important long-distance trade, which linked Spain and Portugal—with their wine and salt, as well as spices, hides, and gold from abroad—with the Baltic seacoast, where these products were sold for grain and timber produced in Germany, Poland-Lithuania, and Scandinavia. The geographic position of the Netherlands and the fact that the Dutch consumed more Baltic grain than any other area, because of their large urban population, help to explain their dominance of this trade. In addition, the Dutch had improved the design of their merchant ships to maximize their profits. By 1600 they were building the *fluitschip* (flyship) to transport cargo economically; it was a vessel with a long, flat hull, simple rigging, and cheap construction.

MAP 16.3 Dutch Commerce in the Seventeenth Century

The Dutch supplanted Portuguese control of trade with Asia and dominated seaborne trade within Europe.

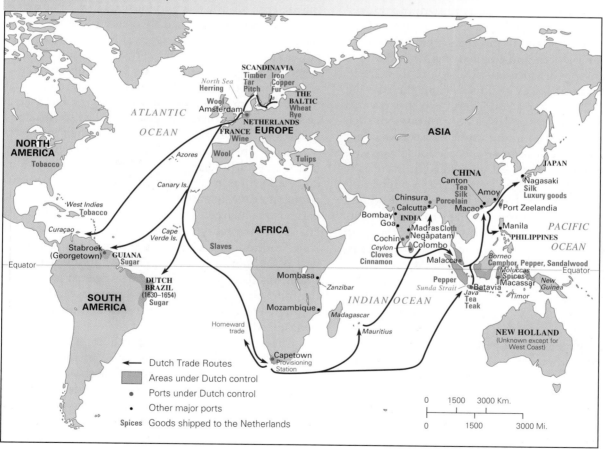

The Dutch were successful in Asia because of institutional as well as technological innovations. In 1602 the **Dutch East India Company** was formed. The company combined government management of trade, typical of the period, with both public and private investment. In the past groups of investors had funded single voyages or small numbers of ships on a one-time basis. The formation of the Dutch East India Company created a permanent pool of capital to sustain trade. After 1612 investments in the company were negotiable as stock. These greater assets allowed proprietors to spread the risks and delays of longer voyages among larger numbers of investors. In addition, more money was available for warehouses, docks, and ships. The English East India Company, founded in 1607, also supported trade, but more modestly. It had one-tenth the capital of the Dutch company and did not use the same system of permanent capital held as stock by investors until 1657. The Bank of Amsterdam, founded in 1609, became the depository for the bullion that flowed into the Netherlands with the flood of trade. The bank established currency exchange rates and issued paper money and instruments of credit to facilitate commerce.

A dramatic expansion of trade with Asia resulted from the Dutch innovations, so much so that by 1650 the European market for spices was glutted, and traders' profits had begun to fall. To control the supply of spices, the Dutch seized some of the areas where they were produced. The Dutch and English further responded to the oversupply of spices by diversifying their trade. The proportion of spices in cargoes from the East fell from about 70 percent at midcentury to just over 20 percent by the century's end. New consumer goods such as tea, coffee, and silk and cotton fabrics took their place. The demand of ordinary people for inexpensive yet serviceable Indian cottons grew steadily. Eventually the Dutch and the English, alert for fresh opportunities in the East, entered the local carrying trade among Asian states. Doing so enabled them to make profits even without purchasing goods, and it slowed the drain of hard currency from Europe—currency in increasingly short supply as silver mines in the Americas were depleted.

THE "GOLDEN AGE" OF THE NETHERLANDS

The prosperity occasioned by the Netherlands' "mother trade" within Europe and its burgeoning overseas commerce helped foster social and political conditions unique among European states. The concentration of trade and shipping sustained a healthy merchant oligarchy and also an extensive and prosperous artisanal

sector. Disparities of wealth were smaller here than anywhere else in Europe. The shipbuilding and fishing trades, among others, supported large numbers of workers with a high standard of living for the age.

The Netherlands appeared to contemporaries to be an astonishing exception to the normal structures of politics. Political decentralization in the Netherlands persisted. The Estates General (representative assembly) for the Netherlands as a whole had no independent powers of taxation. Each of the seven provinces retained considerable autonomy. Wealthy merchants in the Estates of the province of Holland, in fact, constituted the government for the entire nation for long periods because of Holland's economic dominance. The head of government was the executive secretary, known as the pensionary, of Holland's Estates.

Holland's only competition in the running of affairs came from the House of Orange, aristocratic leaders of the revolt against Spain (see pages 455–457). They exercised what control they had by means of the office of *stadtholder* (STAHT-hole-der)—a kind of military governorship—to which they were elected in individual provinces. Their principal interest was the traditional one of military glory and self-promotion. Therein lay a portion of their influence, for they continued to lead the defense of the Netherlands against Spanish attempts at reconquest until the Peace of Westphalia in 1648 and against French aggression after 1672. Their power also came from their status as the only counterweight within the Netherlands to the dominance of Amsterdam's (in Holland) mercantile interests. Small towns dependent on land-based trade or rural areas dominated by farmers and gentry looked to the stadtholders of the Orange family to defend their interests.

As elsewhere, religion was a source of political conflict. The stadtholders and the leading families of Holland, known as regents, vied for control of the state church. Regents of Holland generally favored a less rigid and austere form of Calvinism than did the stadtholders. Their view reflected the needs of the diverse urban communities of Holland, where thousands of Jews, as well as Catholics and various Protestants, lived. Foreign policy was also disputed: Hollanders desired peace in order to foster seaborne commerce, whereas stadtholders willingly engaged in warfare for landed territory and dynastic advantage.

These differences notwithstanding, Dutch commercial dominance involved the Netherlands in costly wars throughout the second half of the century. Between 1657 and 1660 the Dutch defended Denmark against Swedish ambitions in order to safeguard the sealanes and port cities of the Baltic. More costly conflicts arose because of rivalry with the more powerful England and France. Under Cromwell the English attempted to close their ports to the Dutch carrying trade. In 1672 the English under Charles II allied with the French, assum-

Dutch East India Company Commercially innovative Dutch company formed in 1602 that combined government management of trade with both public and private investment.

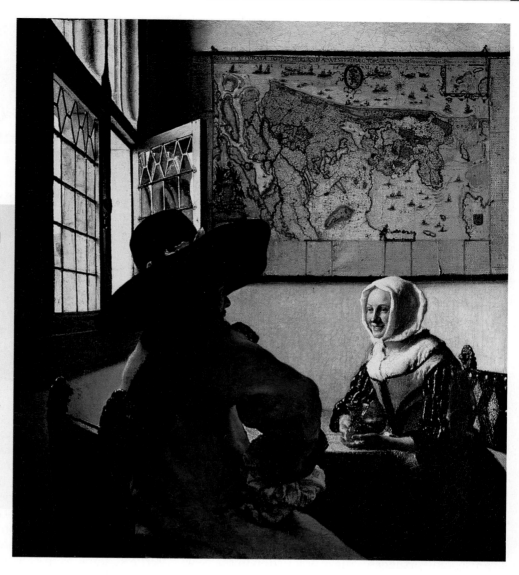

Vermeer: The Soldier and the Laughing Girl
This is an early work by one of the great artists of the Dutch "Golden Age." Dutch art was distinguished by its treatment of common, rather than heroic, subjects. The masterful use of light and perspective in paintings such as this one would not be equaled until the invention of photography. Notice the careful rendering of the map on the wall. *(Copyright The Frick Collection, New York)*

ing that together they could destroy Dutch power and perhaps even divide the Netherlands' territory between them. The Dutch navy, rebuilt since Cromwell's challenge, soon forced England out of the alliance.

Owing largely to the land war with France, the Estates in Holland lost control of policy to William of Nassau (d. 1702), prince of Orange after 1672. William drew the Netherlands into his family's long-standing close relationship with England. Like other members of his family before him, William had married into the English royal family: his wife was Mary, daughter of James II.

Ironically, after William and Mary assumed the English throne, Dutch commerce suffered more in alliance with England than in its previous rivalry. William used Dutch resources for the land war against Louis XIV and reserved for the English navy the fight at sea. By the end of the century Dutch maritime strength was being eclipsed by English sea power.

THE GROWTH OF ATLANTIC COMMERCE

In the seventeenth century the Dutch, the English, and the French joined the Spanish as colonial and commercial powers in the Americas. The Spanish colonial empire, in theory a trading system closed to outsiders, was in fact vulnerable to incursion by other European traders. Spanish treasure fleets were themselves a glittering attraction. In 1628, for example, a Dutch captain seized the entire fleet. But by then Spain's goals and those of its competitors had begun to shift. The limits of an economy based on the extraction, rather than the production, of wealth became clear with the declining output of the Spanish silver mines during the 1620s. In response, the Spanish and their Dutch, French, and English competitors expanded the production of cash crops: tobacco, dyestuffs, and, above all, sugar.

The European demand for tobacco and sugar, both addictive substances, grew steadily in the seventeenth

Sugar Manufacture in Caribbean Colonies
Production of sugar required large capital outlays, in part because the raw cane had to be processed quickly, on-site, to avoid spoilage. This scene depicts enslaved workers operating a small sugar mill on the island of Barbados in the seventeenth century. In the background a press crushes the cane; in the foreground the juice from the cane is boiled down until sugar begins to crystallize.
(Mary Evans Picture Library)

century. The **plantation system**—the use of forced labor to produce cash crops on vast tracts of land—had been developed on Mediterranean islands in the Middle Ages by European entrepreneurs, using slaves procured in Black Sea ports by Venetian and Genoese traders. Sugar production by this system had been established on Atlantic islands, such as the Cape Verde Islands, using African labor, and then in the Americas by the Spanish and Portuguese. Sugar production in the New World grew from about 20,000 tons a year in 1600 to about 200,000 tons by 1770.

In the 1620s, while the Dutch were exploiting Portuguese weakness in the Eastern spice trade, they were also seizing sugar regions in Brazil and replacing the Portuguese in slaving ports in Africa. The Portuguese were able to retake most of their Brazilian territory in the 1650s. But the Dutch, because they monopolized the carrying trade, were able to become the official supplier of slaves to Spanish plantations in the New World and the chief supplier of slaves as well as other goods to most other regions. (See the box "The Global Record: Journal of a Dutch Slave Ship.") The Dutch were able to make handsome profits dealing in human cargo until the end of the seventeenth century, when they were supplanted by the British.

The Dutch introduced sugar cultivation to the French and English after learning it themselves in Brazil.

plantation system Agricultural system, first developed by the Portuguese, in which forced labor produced cash crops on large estates owned by absentee landlords.

Sugar plantations began to supplant tobacco cultivation, as well as subsistence farming, on the Caribbean islands the English and French controlled. Beginning in the late sixteenth century English and French seamen had seized island territories to serve as provisioning stations and staging points for raids against or commerce with Spanish colonies. Some island outposts had expanded into colonies and attracted European settlers—some, as in North America, coming as indentured servants—to work the land. Sugar cultivation, though potentially more profitable than tobacco, demanded huge outlays of capital and continual supplies of unskilled labor, and it drastically transformed the settlements' characters. Large plantations owned by wealthy, often absentee landlords and dependent on slave labor replaced smaller-scale independent farming. The most profitable sugar colonies were, for the French, the islands of Martinique and Guadeloupe and, for the English, Barbados and Jamaica.

EARLY COLONIES IN NORTH AMERICA

Aware of the overwhelming Spanish territorial advantage in the New World, and yet still hoping for treasures such as the Spanish had found, the English, French, and Dutch were also eager to explore and settle North America. From the early sixteenth century on, French, Dutch, English, and Portuguese seamen had fished and traded off Newfoundland. By 1630 small French and Scottish settlements in Acadia (near modern Nova Scotia) and on

JOURNAL OF A DUTCH SLAVE SHIP

These excerpts from a journal kept by the captain of the Dutch ship St. Jan *record a 1659 slave-trading voyage that began in Africa and ended on Curaçao, a Dutch island colony in the Caribbean.*

The 8th [of March]. We arrived with our ship on Saturday before Arda [in modern Benin] to take on board the surgeon's mate, and tamarinds as refreshment for the slaves. We set sail the next day to continue our voyage to Rio Reael.

The 22nd [of May]. We weighed anchor again and sailed out of the Rio Reael. . . . We acquired there in trade two hundred and nineteen slaves, men and women, boys as well as girls; and we set our course for [islands in the Gulf of Biafra] in order to seek food for the slaves, because nothing was to be had in Rio Reael.

The 26th ditto. On Monday we arrived [on the islands]. We spent seven days there looking but barely obtained enough for the slaves' daily consumption; therefore we decided to sail [up a nearby river] to see whether any food could be found there.

The 29th [of June]. On Sunday we decided to continue our voyage because there was also little food [up the river mouth] for the slaves because of the heavy rain which we had daily and because many slaves were suffering from dysentery caused by the bad food supplied to us at [St. George del Mina, a Dutch fort established to serve the slave trade]. . . .

The 11th [of August]. We lay sixteen days at Cape Lopez [modern Gabon] in order to take on water and firewood. Among the water barrels some forty were taken apart to be repaired because our cooper died . . . [and] we had no one who could repair them.

The 24th [of September]. On Friday we arrived at the island of Tobago [in the Caribbean] where we took on water and also bought some bread for our crew because for three weeks they have had no rations.

The 1st of November. We lost our ship on the reef [east of Curaçao] and our crew fled in the boat immediately. There was no chance to save the slaves because we had to abandon the ship on account of heavy surf.

The 4th ditto. We arrived with the boat at . . . Curaçao. The [governor] dispatched two sloops to retrieve the slaves from the shipwreck. One of the sloops was taken by a pirate together with eighty-four slaves.

QUESTIONS

1. Note the dates in the captain's journal. How much time was devoted to trade and provisioning in Africa? How much time to the transatlantic journey?

2. Note the details the captain includes. What do these details reveal about how the voyage was planned? For whom is he recording these details, and why?

3. A companion document reveals that 110 of the 219 captive men, women, and children died during the voyage across the Atlantic. What happened to the captives who survived the journey?

Source: Charles T. Gehring and J. A. Schiltkamp, eds., *New Netherlands Documents,* vol. 17 (Interlaken, N.Y.: Heart of the Lakes Publishing, 1987), pp. 128–131. Used by permission from the *New Netherlands Project,* The New York State Library.

the St. Lawrence River and English settlements in Newfoundland were established to systematically exploit the timber, fish, and fur of the North Atlantic coasts.

English Settlements   In England rising unemployment and religious discontent created a large pool of potential colonists, some of whom were initially attracted to the Caribbean. The first of the English settlements to endure in what was to become the United States was established at Jamestown, named for James I, in Virginia in 1607. ("Virginia," named for Elizabeth I, the "Virgin Queen," was an extremely vague designation for the Atlantic coast of North America and its hinterland.)

The Crown encouraged colonization, but a private company similar to those that financed long-distance trade was established to organize the enterprise. The directors of the Virginia Company were London businessmen. Investors and would-be colonists purchased shares. Shareholders among the colonists could participate in a colonial assembly, although the governor appointed by the company was the final authority.

The colonists arrived in Virginia with ambitious and optimistic instructions. They were to open mines, establish profitable agriculture, and search for sea routes to Asia. But at first they struggled merely to survive in the unfamiliar environment. "Though there be fish in the seas . . . and beasts in the woods . . . they are so wild and we so weak and ignorant, we cannot trouble them much," wrote Captain John Smith from Virginia to the directors in London.[3] The indigenous peoples in

Virginia, unlike those in Spanish-held territories, were not organized in urbanized, rigidly hierarchical societies that, after conquest, could provide the invaders with a labor force. Indeed, much of the local native population was quickly wiped out by European diseases. The introduction of tobacco as a cash crop a few years later saved the colonists economically—although the Virginia Company had already gone bankrupt and the Crown had assumed control of the colony. With the cultivation of tobacco, the Virginia colony, like the Caribbean islands, became dependent on forced, eventually slave, labor.

Among the Virginia colonists were impoverished men and women who came as servants indentured to those who had paid their passage—that is, they were bound by contract to pay off their debts by several years of labor. Colonies established to the north, in what was called "New England," also drew people from the margins of English society. Early settlers there were religious dissidents. The first to arrive were the Pilgrims, who arrived at Plymouth (modern Massachusetts) in 1620. They were a community of religious Separatists who had originally immigrated to the Netherlands from England for freedom of conscience.

Following the Pilgrims came Puritans escaping escalating persecution under Charles I. The first, in 1629, settled under the auspices of another royally chartered company, the Massachusetts Bay Company. Among their number were many prosperous Puritan merchants and landholders. Independence from investors in London allowed them an unprecedented degree of self-government once the Massachusetts Bay colony was established.

Nevertheless, the colonies in North America were disappointments to England because they generated much less wealth than expected. Shipping timber back to Europe proved too expensive, although New England forests did supply some of the Caribbean colonists' needs. The fur trade became less lucrative as English settlement pushed the Native Americans, who did most of the trapping, west and as French trappers to the north encroached on the trade. Certain colonists profited enormously from the tobacco economy, but the mother country did so only moderately because the demand in Europe for tobacco never grew as quickly as the demand for sugar. The English settlements did continue to attract more migrants than other colonizers' outposts. By 1640 Massachusetts had some fourteen thousand European inhabitants. Through most of the next century the growth of colonial populations in North America would result in an English advantage over the French in control of New World territory.

French Settlements The French began their settlement of North America at the same time as the English, in the same push to compensate for their

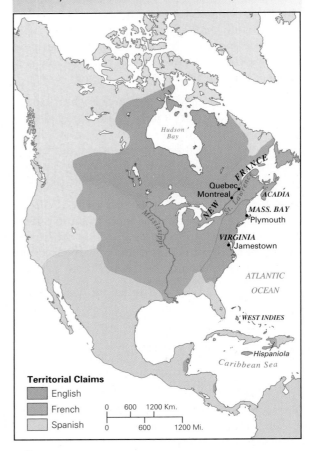

MAP 16.4 The English and French in North America, ca. 1700

By 1700 a veritable ring of French-claimed territory encircled the coastal colonies of England. English-claimed areas, however, were more densely settled and more economically viable.

Territorial Claims
- English
- French
- Spanish

Online Study Center **Improve Your Grade**
Interactive Map: English and French in
North America, ca. 1700

mutual weakness vis-à-vis the Spanish (see **MAP 16.4**). The French efforts, however, had very different results, owing partly to the sites of their settlements but mostly to the relationship between the mother country and the colonies. The French hold on territory was always tenuous because of the scant number of colonists who could be lured from home. There seems to have been less economic impetus for colonization from France than from England. And after the French crown took over the colonies, any religious impetus evaporated, for only Catholics were allowed to settle in New France. Moreover, control by the Crown forced a traditional hierarchical political organization on the French colonies. A royal governor directed the colony, and large tracts of land were set aside for privileged investors. Thus North

America offered little to tempt French people of modest means who were seeking a better life.

The first successful French colony was established in Acadia in 1605. This settlement was an exception among the French efforts because it was founded by Huguenots, not by Catholics. A few years later the explorer Samuel de Champlain (1567?–1635) navigated the St. Lawrence River and founded Quebec City (1608). He convinced the royal government, emerging from its preoccupations with religious wars at home, to promote the development of the colony. French explorers went on to establish Montreal, farther inland on the St. Lawrence (1642), and to explore the Great Lakes and the Mississippi River basin (see Map 16.4).

Such investment as the French crown was able to attract went into profitable trade, mainly in furs, and not into the difficult business of colonization. French trappers and traders who ventured into wilderness areas were renowned for their hardiness and adaptability, but they did not bring their families and establish settled, European-style towns. Quebec remained more of a trading station, dependent on shipments of food from France, than a growing urban community. Added to the commercial dimension of New France was the church's interest: much of the energy of French colonization was expended by men and women of religious orders—the "Black Robes"—bringing their zeal to new frontiers. By the middle of the seventeenth century all of New France had only about three thousand European inhabitants.

The seeming weakness of the French colonial effort in North America was not much noticed at the time. French and English fishermen, trappers, and traders competed intensely, and the French often reaped the greater share of profits, owing to their closer ties with Native American trading systems. Outright battles occasionally erupted between English and French settlements. But for both England and France the major profits and strategic interests in the New World lay to the south, in the Caribbean. The Dutch experience reveals the degree to which North America, for all colonial powers, was of secondary importance to the plantation profits farther south. In 1624 the Dutch founded a trading center, New Amsterdam, at the site of modern-day New York City. Fifty years later they relinquished New Amsterdam—the cornerstone of their northern enterprise—to the English in return for recognition of the Dutch claims to sugar-producing Guiana (modern Suriname) in South America.

Consequently, by far the largest group of migrants to European-held territories in the Americas were forced migrants: African men and women sold into slavery and transported across the Atlantic to work the plantations established by Europeans. A conservative estimate is that approximately 1.35 million Africans were forcibly transported as slave labor to the New World during the seventeenth century.

THE IMPACT OF TRADE AND WARFARE WITHIN EUROPE

Within Europe the economic impact of overseas trade was profound. Merchants and investors in a few of Europe's largest cities reaped great profits. Mediterranean ports such as Venice, once the heart of European trade, did not share in the bonanza from the new trade with Asia or the Americas. Atlantic ports such as Seville, through which most Spanish commerce with the New World flowed, and, above all, Amsterdam began to flourish. The population of Amsterdam increased from about 30,000 to 200,000 in the course of the seventeenth century.

All capital cities, however, not just seaports, grew substantially during the 1600s. Increasing numbers of government functionaries, courtiers and their hangers-on, and people involved in trade lived and worked in capital cities. These cities also grew indirectly from the demand such people generated for services and products, ranging from fashionable clothing to exotic foodstuffs. For the first time cities employed vast numbers of country people. Perhaps as much as one-fifth of the population of England passed through London at one time or another, creating the mobile, volatile community so active in the English civil war and its aftermath.

The economy became more productive and flexible as it expanded, but social stratification intensified. Patterns of consumption in cities reflected the economic gulfs between residents. Most people could not afford to buy imported pepper or sugar. Poverty increased in cities, even in vibrant Amsterdam, because cities attracted people fleeing rural unemployment with few skills and fewer resources. As growing central governments heaped tax burdens on peasants, many rural people were caught in a cycle of debt; the only escape was to abandon farming and flock to cities.

Peasant rebellions occurred throughout the century as a result of depressed economic conditions and the heavy taxation that accompanied expanded royal power and extensive warfare. Some small-scale revolts involved direct action, such as seizing the tax collector's grain or stopping the movement of grain to the great cities. Urban demand often caused severe food shortages in rural areas in western Europe, despite the booming trade in grain with eastern Europe via the Baltic.

The typical peasant revolt in western Europe during the seventeenth century, however, was directed against escalating taxation. Tax rebellions often formed spontaneously, perhaps as tax officials passed through a village, but they were not mere chaotic gatherings of rabble. Country folk were accustomed to defending themselves as communities—against brigands and marauding soldiers, for example. Local gentry or prosperous farmers who ordinarily fulfilled the function of local constable led such revolts from time to time, convinced that they represented the legitimate interests of the community against rapacious officials higher up. The scale of peasant violence meant that thousands of troops sometimes had to be diverted from a state's foreign wars. As a matter of routine, soldiers accompanied tax officials and enforced collection all over Europe. Thus, as the ambitions of rulers grew, so too did the resistance of ordinary people to the exactions of the state.

SECTION SUMMARY

- The Dutch innovations in ship design and forms of investment helped them dominate overseas trade.

- The wealth from trade supported a higher standard of living, wider political participation, and more religious tolerance in the Netherlands than elsewhere in Europe.

- The Dutch, the English, and the French expanded their trade and colonization in the Americas following Spain and Portugal's earlier successes.

- Most European profits from trade and settlement in the Americas came from plantation agriculture, using slave labor, established on Caribbean islands.

- Overseas trade, together with more centralized governments, resulted in the spectacular growth of coastal and capital cities, wider divisions between rich and poor, and increased peasant rebellions.

CHAPTER SUMMARY

Online Study Center **ACE the Test**

How did Louis XIV successfully expand royal power in France and what were some of the achievements of his reign?

What were the long-term consequences of the English civil war?

Which states began to dominate central and eastern Europe and why were they successful?

How and why did Europe's overseas trade and colonization expand in the seventeenth century and what effects did this expansion have on Europe itself?

Following the most powerful monarchy in Europe, France, most states had moved from internal division—with independent provinces and aristocrats going their own way—to greater coherence. In France, Louis XIV successfully weathered an early revolt that aimed to check royal power. Louis's brand of government, which has been labeled "absolutism," arose from successful use of traditional political mechanisms such as patronage, plus the defeat of any institutional brakes on his authority. Court life in Louis's reign sponsored artistic creativity and encouraged a new emphasis on cultural refinement in the aristocracy. In the military realm, however, Louis started a series of costly wars from which the French state gained little.

In England, a civil war over the very issue of parliamentary participation in government led to the temporary abolition of the monarchy itself. The Crown was restored under Charles II, but conflicts arose again over political and religious policy under his successor James

II. The year 1688 marked the "Glorious Revolution" in which Parliament helped bring William and Mary to the throne. Parliament's power was ensured by the Declaration of Rights and Bill of Rights, which have lasting significance today.

States troubled by religious and political turmoil or on the political margins early in the century had evolved into secure and dynamic centers of power: the Netherlands, the Habsburg domains, Brandenburg-Prussia, and Russia. This stability was both cause and consequence of rulers' desires to make war on an ever larger scale. The Austrian Habsburgs reconquered Hungary from the Ottoman Turks while the power of Poland-Lithuania declined in the seventeenth century because it was unable to defend itself against independent aristocrats, rebellious Cossacks, or powerful neighboring states. Russia was forcibly modernized by Peter the Great and became the most powerful state in eastern Europe, eclipsing Sweden in control of Baltic territories. By the end of the century only those states able to field massive armies were competitive on the European stage. The Netherlands, a stark exception to the pattern of centralized royal control, began more closely to resemble other states under the pressure of warfare by century's end.

At the beginning of the century, overseas trade and colonization had been the near monopoly of Spain and Portugal. At the end of the century the English, French, and Dutch had supplanted them in controlling trade with Asia and were reaping many profits in the Americas, especially from the extension of plantation agricul-

ture. The Dutch were a successful trading empire because of their innovations in ship design and forms of investment. With their wealth from trade, they supported a higher standard of living, wider political participation, and more religious tolerance. Beneath all these developments lay subtle but significant economic, social, and cultural shifts. One effect of the increased wealth generated by overseas trade and the increased power of governments to tax their subjects was a widening gulf between rich and poor. New styles of behavior and patterns of consumption highlighted differences between social classes.

LOOKING AHEAD

Long-term effects of overseas voyages on Old World attitudes, as well as fundamental changes in worldviews that were paving the way for modern science, would have a revolutionary impact on Europeans and their cultures.

KEY TERMS

 Online Study Center **Improve Your Grade** Flashcards

absolutism (p. 492)	**Oliver Cromwell** (p. 502)	**Cossacks** (p. 510)
Louis XIV (p. 492)	**Glorious Revolution** (p. 506)	**Peter the Great** (p. 511)
mercantilism (p. 494)	**Treaty of Carlowitz** (p. 508)	**Dutch East India Company** (p. 514)
Parliament (p. 501)	**Brandenburg-Prussia** (p. 508)	**plantation system** (p. 516)

SUGGESTED READING

Collins, James B. *The State in Early Modern France.* 1995. An up-to-date synthesis by one of the leading scholars of French absolutism.

Howard, Michael. *War in European History.* 1976. A general study of warfare emphasizing the relationship between war making and state development.

Ingrao, Charles. *The Habsburg Monarchy, 1618–1815.* 1994. A treatment of the Austrian Habsburgs that stresses the distinctiveness of the Habsburg state.

Kishlansky, Mark. *A Monarchy Transformed.* 1996. The most recent full scholarly treatment of political events in England.

Musgrave, Peter. *The Early Modern European Economy.* 1999. A recent survey of the scholarship on the expanding European economy.

Oakley, Stewart P. *War and Peace in the Baltic, 1560–1790.* 1992. An excellent survey of the Baltic region in the early modern period.

Pennington, D. H. *Europe in the Seventeenth Century.* 2d ed. 1989. A general history of the century.

Riasanovsky, Nicolas V. *A History of Russia.* 6th ed. 2000. A reliable and readable survey of Russian history

from medieval times; includes an extensive bibliography of major works available in English.

Schama, Simon. *The Embarrassment of Riches: An Interpretation of Dutch Culture in the Golden Age.* 1997. An innovative study of Dutch culture that explores the social and psychological tensions created by its growing wealth in the seventeenth century.

Wolf, Eric R. *Europe and the People Without History.* 1982. A survey of European contact with and conquest of peoples after 1400; includes extensive treatments of non-European societies and detailed explanations of the economic and political interests of the Europeans.

NOTES

1. Quoted in D. H. Pennington, *Europe in the Seventeenth Century,* 2d ed. (London: Longman, 1989), p. 508.

2. G. E. Aylmer, ed., *The Levellers in the English Revolution* (Ithaca, N.Y.: Cornell University Press, 1975), pp. 100–101.

3. Philip A. Barbour, ed., *The Complete Works of Captain John Smith (1580–1631),* vol. 2 (Chapel Hill: University of North Carolina Press, 1986), p. 189.

A REVOLUTION IN WORLDVIEW

The year is 1649. Queen Christina of
Sweden welcomes us with her gaze and
her gesture to witness a science lesson
at her court. Her illustrious instructor,
the French philosopher René Descartes, clutches a
compass and points to an astronomical drawing.
The young queen, 23 years old at the time, was already well known as a patron of artists and scholars. Christina had invited Descartes to her court
because of his achievements in physics and philosophy. This painting depicts the fact that during
Christina's lifetime, new theories in the field of astronomy revolutionized the sciences and required
new definitions of matter to explain them. Descartes earned fame both for his novel theories
about matter and for his systematic approach to
the application of human reason to understanding the universe. This painting celebrates both
Descartes's work and Christina's sponsorship of it.

The revolution within the sciences had been
initiated in the sixteenth century by the astronomical calculations and hypotheses of Nicholas
Copernicus, who posited that the earth moves around the sun. The work of
the Italian mathematician and astronomer Galileo Galilei, as well as others,
added evidence to support this hypothesis. Their work overturned principles of physics and philosophy that had held sway since ancient times. Later
generations of scientists and philosophers, beginning with Descartes, labored to construct new principles to explain the way the physical universe
behaves. The readiness of scientists, their patrons, and educated laypeople
to push Copernicus's hypothesis to these conclusions came from several
sources: their exposure to the intellectual innovations of Renaissance
thought, the intellectual challenges and material opportunities represented
by the discovery of the New World, and the challenge to authority embodied in the Reformation. Also, the new science offered prestige and technological advances to the rulers, such as Christina, who sponsored it.

By the end of the seventeenth century a vision of an infinite but orderly
cosmos appealing to human reason had, among educated Europeans,
largely replaced the medieval vision of a closed universe centered on the
earth and suffused with Christian purpose. Religion became an increasingly subordinate ally of science as confidence in an open-ended, experimental approach to knowledge came to be as strongly held as religious
conviction. It is because of this larger shift in worldview, not simply because

CHAPTER OUTLINE

THE REVOLUTION IN ASTRONOMY, 1543–1632

THE SCIENTIFIC REVOLUTION EXPANDS, CA. 1600–1700

THE NEW SCIENCE IN CONTEXT: SOCIETY, POLITICS, AND RELIGION

KEY TERMS

Nicholas Copernicus

heliocentric theory

Johannes Kepler

Galileo Galilei

Francis Bacon

empirical method

René Descartes

Isaac Newton

laws of motion

mechanistic
    worldview

Thomas Hobbes

John Locke

Online Study Center

This icon will direct you to
interactive map and primary
source activities on the
website **college.hmco.com/
pic/noble5e**

of particular scientific discoveries, that the seventeenth century may be labeled the era of the Scientific Revolution.

Because religious significance had been attached to previous explanations and religious authority defended them, the new astronomy automatically led to an enduring debate about the compatibility of science and religion. But the revolution in worldview was not confined to astronomy or even to science generally. As philosophers gained confidence in human reason and the intelligibility of the world, they turned to new speculation about human affairs. They began to challenge traditional justifications for the hierarchical nature of society and the sanctity of authority just as energetically as Copernicus and his followers had overthrown old views about the cosmos.

FOCUS QUESTIONS

How did the Copernican theory challenge traditional views of the universe?

How and why did new theories about astronomy lead to a broader Scientific Revolution?

How did the new scientific worldview lead people to challenge traditional notions of society, the state, and religion?

THE REVOLUTION IN ASTRONOMY, 1543–1632

How did the Copernican theory challenge traditional views of the universe?

The origins of the seventeenth-century revolution in worldview lie, for the most part, in developments in astronomy. Because of astronomy's role in the explanations of the world and human life that had been devised by ancient and medieval scientists and philosophers, any advances in astronomy were bound to have widespread intellectual repercussions. By the early part of the seventeenth century fundamental astronomical beliefs had been successfully challenged. The consequence was the undermining of both the material (physics) and the philosophical (metaphysics) explanations of the world that had been standing for centuries.

THE INHERITED WORLDVIEW

Ancient and medieval astronomy accepted the perspective on the universe that unaided human senses support—namely, that the earth is fixed at the center of the universe and the celestial bodies rotate around it. The regular movements of heavenly bodies and the obvious importance of the sun for life on earth made astronomy a vital undertaking for both scientific and religious purposes in many ancient societies. Astronomers in ancient Greece carefully observed the heavens and learned to calculate and to predict the seemingly circular motion of the stars and the sun about the earth. The orbits of the planets were more difficult to explain, for the planets

seemed to travel both east and west across the sky at various times and with no regularity that could be mathematically understood. Indeed, the very word *planet* comes from a Greek word meaning "wanderer."

We now know that all the planets simultaneously orbit the sun at different speeds in paths that are at different distances from the sun. The relative positions of the planets constantly change; sometimes other planets are "ahead" of the earth and sometimes "behind." In the second century A.D. the Greek astronomer Ptolemy (TAHL-eh-mee) attempted to explain the planets' occasional "backward" motion by attributing it to "epicycles"—small circular orbits within the larger orbit. Ptolemy's mathematical explanations of the imagined epicycles were extremely complex, but neither Ptolemy nor medieval mathematicians and astronomers were ever able fully to account for planetary motion.

Ancient physics, most notably the work of the Greek philosopher Aristotle (384–322 B.C.), explained the fact that some objects (such as cannonballs) fall to earth but others (stars and planets) seem weightless relative to earth because of their composition: different kinds of matter have different inherent tendencies and properties. In this view all earthbound matter (like cannonballs) falls because it is naturally attracted to earth—heaviness being a property of earthbound things.

In the Christian era the Aristotelian explanation of the universe was infused with Christian meaning and purpose. The heavens were said to be made of different, pure matter because they were the abode of the angels. Both the earth and the humans who inhabited it were changeable and corruptible. Yet God had given human beings a unique and special place in the universe, which was thought to be a closed world with the stationary earth at the center. Revolving around the earth in circular orbits were the sun, moon, stars, and planets. The motion of all lesser bodies was caused by the rotation of all the stars together in the vast crystal-like sphere in which they were embedded.

A few ancient astronomers theorized that the earth moved about the sun. Some medieval philosophers also adopted this heliocentric thesis (*helios* is the Greek word for "sun"), but it remained a minority view because it seemed to contradict both common sense and observed data. The sun and stars *appeared* to move around the earth with great regularity. Moreover, how could objects fall to earth if the earth was moving beneath them? Also, astronomers detected no difference in angles from which observers on earth viewed the stars at different times. Such differences would exist, they thought, if the earth changed positions by moving around the sun. It was inconceivable that the universe could be so large and the stars so distant that the earth's movement would produce no measurable change in the earth's position with respect to the stars.

Several conditions of intellectual life in the sixteenth century encouraged new work in astronomy and led to the revision of the earth-centered worldview. The most important was the work of Renaissance humanists in recovering and interpreting ancient texts. Now able to work with new Greek versions of Ptolemy, mathematicians and astronomers noted that his explanations for the motion of the planets were imperfect and not simply inadequately transmitted, as they had long believed. Also, the discovery of the New World dramatically undercut the assumption that ancient knowledge was superior. The existence of the Americas specifically undermined Ptolemy's authority once again, for it disproved many of the assertions in his *Geography*, which had just been recovered in Europe the previous century.

The desire to explain heavenly movements better was still loaded with religious significance in the sixteenth century and was heightened by the immediate need for reform of the Julian calendar (named for Julius Caesar). Ancient observations of the movement of the sun, though remarkably accurate, could not measure the precise length of the solar year. By the sixteenth century the cumulative error of this calendar had resulted in a change of ten days: the spring equinox fell on March 11 instead of March 21. An accurate and uniform system of dating was necessary for all rulers and their tax collectors and record keepers. And because the calculation of the date of Easter was at stake, a reliable calendar was the particular project of the church.

CHRONOLOGY

1543	Copernicus, *De Revolutionibus Orbium Caelestium* Vesalius, *On the Fabric of the Human Body*
1576	Construction of Brahe's observatory begins
1603	Accadèmia dei Lincei founded in Rome
1609	Kepler's third law of motion
1610	Galileo, *The Starry Messenger*
1620	Bacon, *Novum Organum*
1628	Harvey, *On the Motion of the Heart*
1632	Galileo, *Dialogue on the Two Chief Systems of the World*
1633	Galileo condemned and sentenced to house arrest
1637	Descartes, *Discourse on Method*
1651	Hobbes, *Leviathan*
1660	Boyle, *New Experiments Physico-Mechanical* Royal Society of London founded
1666	Académie Royale des Sciences founded in France
1686	Fontenelle, *Conversations on the Plurality of Worlds*
1687	Newton, *Principia (Mathematical Principles of Natural Philosophy)*
1690	Locke, *Two Treatises of Government* and *Essay on Human Understanding*
1702	Bayle, *Historical and Critical Dictionary*

Impetus for new and better astronomical observations and calculations arose from other features of the intellectual and political landscape as well. Increasingly, as the century went on, princely courts became important sources of patronage for and sites of scientific activity. Rulers eager to buttress their own power by symbolically linking it to dominion over nature sponsored investigations of the world, as Ferdinand and Isabella had so successfully done, and displayed the marvels of nature at their courts. Sponsoring scientific inquiry also yielded practical benefits: better mapping of the ruler's domains and better technology for mining, gunnery, and navigation.

Finally, schools of thought fashionable at the time, encouraged by the humanists' critique of received tradition, hinted at the possibilities of alternative physical and metaphysical systems. The ancient doctrine of Hermeticism (named for the mythical originator of the ideas, Hermes Trismegistos), revived since the Renaissance, claimed that matter is universally imbued with divine (or magical) spirit. Drawing on Hermeticism was Paracelsianism, named for the Swiss physician Philippus von Hohenheim (1493–1541), who called himself

The Traditional Universe
In this print from around 1600, heavenly bodies are depicted orbiting the earth in perfectly circular paths. Notice the horse-drawn chariot near the top of the image, which represents the Greek god of the sun circling the earth. *(Bettmann/Corbis)*

Paracelsus (literally "beyond Celsus," an acclaimed Roman physician whose works had just been recovered). Paracelsus (pair-uh-SEL-sus) scoffed at the notion that ancient authorities were the final word on the workings of nature. "He who is born in imagination," he wrote, "discovers the latent forces of nature."[1] Paracelsus offered an alternative to accepted medical theory, put forth by the physician Galen (ca. 131–201), the premier medical authority of antiquity, now as revered as Aristotle. Galen (GAY-len) believed that an imbalance of bodily "humors" caused illness. Paracelsus substituted a theory of chemical imbalance that was a forerunner of modern understandings of pathology. He was wildly popular wherever he taught because of the success of his treatments of illness and his willingness to lecture openly to laymen.

Neo-Platonism, another school of thought, had a more systematic and far-reaching impact. Neo-Platonism was a revival, primarily in Italian humanist circles, of certain aspects of Plato's thought. It contributed directly to innovation in science because it emphasized the abstract nature of true knowledge and thus encouraged mathematical investigation. This provided a spur to astronomical studies, which, since ancient times, had been concerned more with mathematical analysis of heavenly movements than with physical explanations for them. Also, like Hermeticism and Paracelsianism,

Neo-Platonism had a mystical dimension that fostered creative speculation about the nature of matter and the organization of the universe. Neo-Platonists were particularly fascinated by the sun as a symbol of the one divine mind or soul at the heart of all creation.

THE CHALLENGE BY COPERNICUS

Nicholas Copernicus (1473–1543), son of a German merchant family in Poland, pursued wide-ranging university studies in philosophy, law, astronomy, mathematics, and medicine—first in Cracow in Poland and then in Bologna and Padua in Italy. In Italy he was exposed to Neo-Platonic ideas. Copernicus (kuh-PURR-nih-kus) took a degree in canon (church) law in 1503 and became a cathedral canon (a member of the cathedral staff) in the city of Frauenburg (modern Poland), where he pursued his own interests in astronomy while carrying out administrative duties. When the pope asked Copernicus to assist with the reform of the Julian calendar, he replied that reform of the calendar required reform in astronomy. His major work, *De Revolutionibus Orbium Caelestium* (*On the Revolution of Heavenly Bodies*, 1543), was dedicated to the pope in the hopes that it would help with the task of calendar reform—as indeed

Nicholas Copernicus   Polish astronomer who initiated the Scientific Revolution by proposing that the earth and other planets orbit the sun.

it did. The Gregorian calendar, issued in 1582 during the pontificate of Gregory XIII (r. 1572–1585), was based on Copernicus's calculations.

Copernicus postulated that the earth and all the other planets orbit the sun. He did not assert that the earth does in fact move around the sun but offered the heliocentric system as a mathematical construct, useful for predicting the movements of planets, stars, and the sun. However, he walked a thin line between making claims for a mathematical construct on the one hand and physical reality on the other. Scholars now believe that Copernicus was himself persuaded that the **heliocentric theory** was correct. He had searched in ancient sources for thinkers who believed the earth moved. Other astronomers familiar with his work and reputation urged him to publish the results of his calculations. But not until 1542, twelve years after finishing the work, did he send *De Revolutionibus* to be published. He received a copy just before his death the next year.

By affirming the earth's movement around the sun while also salvaging features of the old system, Copernicus faced burdens of explanation not faced by Ptolemy. For example, Copernicus still assumed that the planets traveled in circular orbits, so he was forced to retain some epicycles in his schema to account for the circular motion. In general, however, the Copernican account of planetary motion was simpler than the Ptolemaic account. It appealed to other astronomers of the age because it was useful and because it highlighted the harmony of heavenly motion, which remained a fundamental physical and metaphysical principle. Inaccessible except to other astronomers, Copernicus's work only slowly led to conceptual revolution, as scientists worked with his calculations and assembled other evidence to support the heliocentric theory.

The most important reason that fundamental conceptual change followed Copernican theory so gradually was that Copernicus did not resolve the physical problems his ideas raised. If Copernicus were right, the earth would have to be made of the same material as other planets. How, then, would Copernicus explain the motion of objects on earth—the fact that they fall to earth—if it was not in their nature to fall toward the heavy, stationary earth? In Copernicus's system, the movement of the earth caused the *apparent* motion of the stars. But if the stars did not rotate in their crystalline sphere, what made all other heavenly bodies move?

Copernicus was not as troubled by these questions as we might expect him to be. Since ancient times, mathematical astronomy—the science of measuring and predicting the movements of heavenly bodies—had been far more important than, and had proceeded independently of, physical explanations of observed motion.

Nevertheless, as Copernicus's own efforts to support his hypothesis reveal, his theories directly contradicted many of the supposed laws of motion. The usefulness of his theories to other astronomers meant that the contradictions between mathematical and physical models for the universe would have to be resolved. Copernicus himself might be best understood as the last Ptolemaic astronomer, working within inherited questions and with known tools. His work itself did not constitute a revolution, but it did initiate one.

THE FIRST COPERNICAN ASTRONOMERS

In the first generation of astronomers after the publication of *De Revolutionibus* in 1543 we can see the effects of Copernicus's work. His impressive computations rapidly won converts among fellow astronomers. Several particularly gifted astronomers continued to develop the Copernican system. Thus, by the second quarter of the seventeenth century, they and many others accepted the heliocentric theory as a reality and not just as a useful mathematical fiction. The three most important astronomers to build on Copernican assumptions, and on the work of one another, were the Dane Tycho Brahe (1546–1601), the German Johannes Kepler (1571–1630), and the Italian Galileo Galilei (1564–1642).

Tycho Brahe   Like generations of observers before him, Tycho Brahe (BRAH) had been stirred by the majesty of the regular movements of heavenly bodies. After witnessing a partial eclipse of the sun, he abandoned a career in government befitting his noble status and became an astronomer. Brahe was the first truly post-Ptolemaic astronomer because he was the first to improve on the data that the ancients and all subsequent astronomers had used. Ironically, no theory of planetary motion could have reconciled the data that Copernicus had used: they were simply too inaccurate, based as they were on naked-eye observations, even when errors of translation and copying, accumulated over centuries, had been corrected.

In 1576 the king of Denmark showered Brahe with properties and pensions enabling him to build an observatory, Uraniborg, on an island near Copenhagen. At Uraniborg Brahe improved on ancient observations with large and very finely calibrated instruments that permitted precise measurements of celestial movements by the naked eye. His attention to precision and frequency of observation produced results that were twice as accurate as any previous data had been.

As a result of his observations, Brahe agreed with Copernicus that the various planets did rotate around the sun, not around the earth. He still could not be persuaded that the earth itself moved, for none of his data supported such a notion. Brahe's lasting and crucial

heliocentric theory   Means "sun-centered." Theory of Nicholas Copernicus that the earth and other planets orbit the sun.

Tycho Brahe's Observatory
Brahe gathered the best talent, including German instrument makers and Italian architects, to build his state-of-the-art observatory near Copenhagen. Brahe named the complex Uraniborg, for Urania, the muse of astronomy.
(The Fotomas Index/The Bridgeman Art Library)

contribution was his astronomical data. They would become obsolete as soon as data from telescopic observations were accumulated about a century later. But in the meantime they were used by **Johannes Kepler** to further develop Copernicus's model and arrive at a more accurate heliocentric theory.

Johannes Kepler   Kepler was young enough to be exposed to Copernican ideas from the outset of his training, and he quickly recognized in Brahe's data the means of resolving the problems in Copernican analysis. Though trained in his native Germany, Kepler went to Prague, where Brahe spent the last years of his life at the court of the Holy Roman emperor after a quarrel with the Danish king. There Kepler became something of an apprentice to Brahe. After Brahe's death in 1601, Kepler kept his mentor's records of astronomical observations and continued to work at the imperial court as Rudolf II's court mathematician.

Kepler's contribution to the new astronomy, like that of Copernicus, was fundamentally mathematical. In it we can see the stamp of the Neo-Platonic conviction about the purity of mathematical explanation. Kepler spent ten years working to apply Brahe's data to the most intricate of all the celestial movements—the

motion of the planet Mars—as a key to explaining all planetary motion. Mars is close to the earth, but its orbital path is farther from the sun. This combination produces very puzzling and dramatic variations in the apparent movement of Mars to an earthly observer.

The result of Kepler's work was laws of planetary motion that, in the main, are still in use. First, Kepler eliminated the need for epicycles by correctly asserting that planets follow elliptical and not circular orbits. Elliptical orbits could account, both mathematically and visually, for the motion of the planets when combined with Kepler's second law, which describes the *rate* of a planet's motion around its orbital path. Kepler noted that the speed of a planet in its orbit slows proportionally as the planet's distance from the sun increases. A third law demonstrates that the distance of each planet from the sun and the time it takes each planet to orbit the sun are in a constant ratio.

Kepler's work was a breakthrough because it mathematically confirmed the Copernican heliocentric hypothesis. In so doing, the work directly challenged the ancient worldview, in which heavenly bodies constantly moved in circular orbits around a stationary earth. Hence Kepler's laws invited speculation about the properties and movements of heavenly and terrestrial bodies alike. A new physics would be required to explain the novel motion that Kepler had posited. Kepler himself, in Neo-Platonic fashion, attributed planetary motion to

Johannes Kepler   German astronomer who developed three laws of planetary motion, known as Kepler's laws, which mathematically confirmed the Copernican heliocentric theory.

the sun: "[The sun] is a fountain of light, rich in fruitful heat, most fair, limpid and pure . . . called king of the planets for his motion, heart of the world for his power. . . . Who would hesitate to confer the votes of the celestial motions on him who has been administering all other movements and changes by the benefit of the light which is entirely his possession?"[2]

GALILEO AND THE TRIUMPH OF COPERNICANISM

Galileo Galilei holds a pre-eminent position in the development of astronomy because, first, he provided compelling new evidence to support Copernican theory and, second, he contributed to the development of a new physics—or, more precisely, mechanics—that could account for the movements of bodies in new terms. In short he began to close the gap between the new astronomy and new explanations for the behavior of matter. Just as important, his efforts to publicize his findings and his condemnation by the church spurred popular debate about Copernican ideas in literate society and helped to determine the course science would take.

Galileo's career also illustrates, in dramatic fashion, the dependence of scientists on and their vulnerability to patronage relationships. Born to a minor Florentine noble family, Galileo began studying medicine at the nearby University of Pisa at the age of 17 but became intrigued by problems of mechanics and mathematics. He began studying those disciplines at Pisa under the tutelage of a Florentine court mathematician and became a lecturer in mathematics there in 1589, at age 25, after publishing promising work in mechanics. Three years later, well-connected fellow mathematicians helped him secure a more lucrative and prestigious professorship at the University of Padua, where Copernicus had once studied. Galileo skillfully cultivated the learned Venetian aristocrats (Venice ruled Padua at this time) who controlled academic appointments and secured renewals and salary raises over the next eighteen years.

During his years at Pisa and Padua, Galileo pursued his revolutionary work in mechanics, although he did not publish the results of his experiments until much later. Galileo's principal contribution to mechanics lay in his working out of an early theory of inertia. As a result of a number of experiments with falling bodies (balls rolling on carefully constructed inclines—not free-falling objects that, according to myth, he dropped from the Leaning Tower of Pisa), Galileo ventured a new view of what is "natural" to objects. Galileo's view was that uniform motion is as natural as a state of rest. In the ancient and medieval universe, all

Galileo Galilei Italian physicist and astronomer who provided evidence supporting the heliocentric theory and helped develop the science of mechanics.

motion needed a cause, and all motion could be explained in terms of purpose. "I hold," Galileo countered, "that there exists nothing in external bodies . . . but size, shape, quantity and motion."[3] Galileo retained the old assumption that motion was somehow naturally circular. Nevertheless, his theory was a crucial step in explaining motion according to new principles and in fashioning a worldview that accepted a mechanical universe devoid of metaphysical purpose.

The results of this work were, for the most part, not published until the end of his life. In the meantime, Galileo became famous for his astronomical observations, which he began in 1609 and which he parlayed into a position back at the Florentine court. Early that year Galileo learned of the invention of a primitive telescope (which could magnify distant objects only three times) and quickly improved on it to make the first astronomically useful instrument. In *Sidereus Nuncius (The Starry Messenger,* 1610) he described his scrutiny of the heavens with his telescope in lay language. He documented sighting previously undetectable stars, as well as moons orbiting the planet Jupiter. In another blow to ancient descriptions of the universe, he noted craters and other "imperfections" on the surface of the moon. Three years later he published his solar observations in *Letters on Sunspots.* Sunspots are regions of relatively cool gaseous material that appear as dark spots on the sun's surface. For Galileo sunspots and craters on the moon proved that the heavens are not perfect and changeless but rather are like the supposedly "corrupt" and changeable earth. His telescopic observations also provided further support for Copernican heliocentrism. Indeed, Galileo's own acceptance of Copernicanism can be dated to this point because magnification revealed that each heavenly body rotates on its axis: sunspots, for example, can be tracked across the visible surface of the sun as the sun rotates.

Online Study Center **Improve Your Grade**
Primary Source: Galileo Discovers the Moons of Jupiter

Galileo had already been approached by various Italian princes and in turn sought to woo their support with gifts of some of his earlier inventions, such as a military compass. He aimed his *Starry Messenger* at the Medici dukes of Florence, naming Jupiter's moons the "Medicean Stars" and publishing the work to coincide with the accession of the young Cosimo II, whom he had tutored as a youth. In 1610 he returned in triumph to his native Tuscany as court philosopher to the grand duke. Soon, however, his own fame and the increasing acceptance of Copernicanism, especially vindicated by his work on sunspots, aroused opposition. In 1615 Galileo was denounced to the Inquisition by a Florentine friar. (See the box "The Written Record: Galileo

GALILEO ASSERTS SCIENCE AND RELIGION ARE COMPATIBLE

After Galileo Galilei's work on sunspots was released, many learned followers grew anxious about the implications of the new science. In the letter excerpted here, published in 1615 and widely circulated, Galileo reassures the mother of Cosimo II, the dowager grand duchess of Tuscany, that the new science does not contradict Christianity. The Catholic Church would eventually condemn Galileo for his beliefs, arguing that it was wrong to contradict established knowledge about the heavens. Although the church's actions constrained the development of science in some (predominantly Catholic) regions, throughout Europe investigators continued to find ways to make the new science fully compatible with their faiths.

Some years ago, as Your Serene Highness well knows, I discovered in the heavens many things that had not been seen there before our own age. The novelty of these things, as well as some consequences which followed from them . . . stirred up against me no small number of professors—as if I had placed these things in the sky with my own hands in order to upset nature and overturn the sciences. . . . [These professors] go about invoking the Bible, which they would have minister to their deceitful purposes. Contrary to the sense of the Bible and the intention of the holy Fathers, if I am not mistaken, they would extend such authorities until even in purely physical matters—where faith is not involved—they would have us altogether abandon reason and the evidence of our own senses in favor of some biblical passage, though under the surface meaning of its words this passage may contain a different sense. . . .

I think that in discussions of physical problems we ought to begin not from the authority of scriptural passages, but from sense experience and necessary demonstrations. . . . I should judge that the authority of the Bible was designed to persuade men of those articles and propositions which, surpassing all human reasoning, could not be made credible by science, or by any means other than through the very mouth of the Holy Spirit. . . .

But I do not feel obliged to believe that the same God who has endowed us with senses, reason and intellect has intended to forgo their use and by some other means to give us knowledge which we can attain by them. He would not require us to deny sense and reason in physical matters which are set before our eyes and minds by direct experience or necessary demonstrations. This must be especially true in those sciences of which but the faintest trace . . . is to be found in the Bible. Of astronomy, for instance, so little is found that none of the planets except Venus are so much as mentioned. . . .

Now, if the Holy Spirit has purposely neglected to teach us propositions of this sort as irrelevant to the highest goal (that is, to our salvation), how can anyone affirm that it is obligatory to take sides on them, and that one belief is required by faith, while another side is erroneous? . . . I would assert here something that was heard from [a respected cleric]: . . . "the intention of the Holy Ghost is to teach us how to go to heaven, not how heaven goes." . . . [And] in St. Augustine we read: "If anyone shall set the authority of Holy Writ against clear and manifest reason, . . . he opposes to the truth not the meaning of the Bible, which is beyond his comprehension, but rather his own interpretation. . . ."

Moreover, we are unable to affirm that all interpreters of the Bible speak with divine inspiration, for if that were so there would exist no differences between them about the sense of a given passage. Hence [it would be wise] not to permit anyone to usurp scriptural texts and force them in some way to maintain any physical conclusion to be true, when at some future time the senses . . . may show the contrary. Who indeed will set bounds to human ingenuity? Who will assert that everything in the universe capable of being perceived is already discovered and known?

QUESTIONS

1. How does Galileo justify pursuing scientific investigation against certain claims of faith?

2. Do you think that Galileo's arguments would have been reassuring to the grand duchess? Why or why not?

3. Why might the arguments have further angered those church officials already hostile toward Galileo's work?

Source: Discoveries and Opinions of Galileo, by Galileo Galilei, translated by Stillman Drake, copyright © 1957 by Stillman Drake. Used by permission of Doubleday, a division of Random House, Inc.

Asserts Science and Religion Are Compatible.") After an investigation, the geokinetic theory (that the earth moves) was declared heretical, but Galileo himself was not condemned. He could continue to use Copernican theory, but only as a theory. Indeed, a number of the most fervent practitioners of the new science continued to be clergymen who followed Galileo's work with interest. A new pope, elected in 1623, was a Tuscan aristocrat and an old friend of Galileo. Galileo dedicated his work on comets, *The Assayer* (1624), to Urban VIII in honor of his election.

Now in his 60s, Galileo began to work on a book that summarized his life's work—*Dialogue on the Two Chief Systems of the World* (1632), structured as a conversation among three characters debating the merits of Copernican theory. Given the work's sensitive subject matter, Galileo obtained explicit permission from the pope to write it and cleared some portions with censors before publication. The work was the most important single source in its day for the popularization of Copernican theory, but it led to renewed concerns in Rome. Galileo had clearly overstepped the bounds of dis-cussing Copernicanism in theory only and appeared to advocate it. Simplicio, the character representing the old worldview, was, as his name suggests, an example of ignorance, not wisdom.

Moreover, the larger political context affecting Galileo's patrons and friends had changed. The pope was being threatened by the Spanish and Austrian Habsburgs for his tepid support in the Thirty Years' War, in which Catholic forces were now losing to Protestant armies, and he could no longer be indulgent with his friend. (The pope tended to favor French foreign policy as a counterweight to the enormous power of the Habsburgs.) Galileo was forced to stand trial for heresy in Rome in 1633. When, in a kind of plea-bargain arrangement, he pled guilty to a lesser charge of inadvertently advocating Copernicanism, Pope Urban intervened to insist on a weightier penalty. Galileo's book was banned, he was forced to formally renounce his "error," and he was sentenced to house arrest. Galileo lived confined and guarded, continuing his investigations of mechanics, until his death eight years later.

SECTION SUMMARY

- The Scientific Revolution began in 1543 with the publication of Copernicus's mathematical calculations supporting the heliocentric theory.

- Tycho Brahe and Johannes Kepler confirmed Copernicus's hypothesis with new data and more thorough mathematical explanations of the motions of planets.

- Galileo's observations with his telescope provided new evidence to support Copernican theory; his experiments in mechanics contributed to new explanations for the behavior of matter.

- Galileo's advocacy of Copernicanism led to his condemnation by the church.

THE SCIENTIFIC REVOLUTION EXPANDS, CA. 1600–1700

How and why did new theories about astronomy lead to a broader Scientific Revolution?

Galileo's work found such a willing audience in part because Galileo, like Kepler and Brahe, was not working alone. Dozens of other scientists were examining old problems from the fresh perspective offered by the breakthroughs in astronomy. Some analyzed the nature of matter, now that it appeared that all matter in the universe was somehow the same despite its varying appearances. Many of these thinkers addressed the metaphysical issues that their investigations inevitably raised. They began the complex intellectual and psychological journey toward a new worldview, one that accepted the existence of an infinitely large universe of undifferentiated matter with no obvious place in it for humans.

THE USES OF THE NEW SCIENCE

No less a man than **Francis Bacon** (1561–1626), lord chancellor of England during the reign of James I, wrote a utopian essay extolling the benefits of science for a peaceful society and for human happiness. In *New Atlantis,* published one year after his death, Bacon argued that science would produce "things of use and practice for man's life."[4] In *New Atlantis* and *Novum Organum* (1620) Bacon reveals his faith in science by advocating patient, systematic observation and experimentation to

Francis Bacon   England's lord chancellor during the reign of James I and author of influential works encouraging the empirical scientific method and inductive reasoning.

accumulate knowledge about the world. He argues that the proper method of investigation "derives axioms from . . . particulars, rising by gradual and unbroken ascent, so that it arrives at the most general axioms of all. This is the true way but untried."[5]

Bacon himself did not undertake experiments, although his widely read works were influential in encouraging both the **empirical method** (relying on observation and experimentation) and inductive reasoning (deriving general principles from particular facts). Indeed, Bacon was a visionary. Given the early date of his writings, it might seem difficult to account for his enthusiasm and confidence. In fact, Bacon's writings reflect the widespread interest and confidence in science within his elite milieu, an interest actively encouraged by the state. In another of his writings he argues that a successful state should concentrate on effective "rule in religion *and nature,* as well as civil administration."[6]

Online Study Center **Improve Your Grade**
Primary Source: Francis Bacon Rejects Superstition and Extols the Virtue of Science

Bacon's pronouncements reflect the fact that an interest in exploring nature's secrets and exercising "dominion over nature" had become an indispensable part of princely rule. Princely courts were the main sources of financial support for science and the primary sites of scientific work during Bacon's lifetime. Part of the impetus for this development had come from the civic humanism of the Italian Renaissance, which had celebrated the state and service to it and had provided models both for educated rulers and for cultivated courtiers. Attention to science and to its benefits for the state also reflect the scope, and pragmatism, of princely resources and ambitions: the desire of rulers for technical expertise in armaments, fortification, construction, navigation, and mapmaking. (See the feature "The Visual Record: Modern Maps.")

The promise of the New World and the drive for overseas trade and exploration especially encouraged princely support of scientific investigation. A renowned patron of geographic investigation, from mapmaking to navigation, was Henry, prince of Wales (d. 1612), eldest son of James I. Prince Henry patronized technical experts such as experienced gunners and seamen, as well as those with broader and more theoretical expertise. One geographer at his court worked on the vital problem of calculating longitude, sketched the moon after reading and emulating Galileo's work with the telescope, and, in the spirit of empiricism often associated with Bacon, compiled information about the new territory Virginia, including the first dictionary of any Native American language.

Science was an ideological as well as a practical tool for power. Most courts housed collections of marvels, specimens of exotic plants and animals, and mechanical contrivances. These demonstrated the ruler's interest in investigation of the world—in other words, his or her status as an educated individual. These collections and the work of court experts also enhanced the ruler's reputation as a patron and person of power. Galileo was playing off such expectations when he named his newly discovered moons of Jupiter "Medicean Stars." Like all patronage relationships, the status was shared by both partners; indeed, the attention of a patron was a guarantee of the researcher's scientific credibility.

By the beginning of the seventeenth century, private salons and academies where investigators might meet on their own were another significant milieu of scientific investigation. These, too, had their roots in the humanist culture of Italy, where circles of scholars without university affiliations had formed. Though also dependent on private resources, these associations were an important alternative to princely patronage, since a ruler's funds might wax and wane according to his or her other commitments. Private organizations could avoid the stark distinctions of rank that were inevitable at courts yet mimicked courts in the blend of scholars and educated courtiers they embraced. This more collegial but still privileged environment also fostered a sense of legitimacy for the science pursued there: legitimacy came from the recognition of fellow members and, in many cases, from publication of work by the society itself.

The earliest academy dedicated to scientific study was the *Accadèmia Segreta* (Secret Academy) founded in Naples in the 1540s. The members pursued experiments together in order, in the words of one member, "to make a true anatomy of the things and operations of nature itself."[7] During the remainder of the sixteenth century and on into the seventeenth, such academies sprang up in many cities. The most celebrated was the *Accadèmia dei Lincei* (ack-uh-DAY-mee-uh day-ee lin-CHAY-ee), founded in Rome by an aristocrat in 1603. Its most famous member, Galileo, joined in 1611. The name "Lincei," from *lynx,* was chosen because of the legendary keen sight of that animal, an appropriate mascot for "searchers of secrets."

Galileo's notoriety and the importance of his discoveries forced all such learned societies to take a stand for or against Copernicanism. Throughout the seventeenth century, specific investigation of natural phenomena would continue in increasingly sophisticated institutional settings. The flowering of scientific thought in the

empirical method Philosophical view developed by Bacon and Locke, which holds that all knowledge is based on observation and experimentation and that general principles should be derived from particular facts.

A Collection of Naturalia

Collections of exotic specimens, such as this display in Naples, symbolized the ruler's authority by suggesting his or her power over nature. *(From Ferrante Imperato, Dell' Historia Naturale [Naples, 1599]. By permission of the Houghton Library, Harvard University)*

seventeenth century occurred because of the specific innovations in astronomy and the general spread of scientific investigation that had been achieved by the end of Bacon's life.

SCIENTIFIC THOUGHT IN FRANCE

Philosophers, mathematicians, and educated elites engaged in lively debate and practical investigation throughout Europe in the first half of the seventeenth century. In France the great questions about cosmic order were being posed, ironically, at a time of political disorder. The years following the religious wars saw the murder of Henry IV, another regency, and further civil war in the 1620s (see pages 462–463). In this environment questions about order in the universe and the possibilities of human knowledge took on particular

urgency. It is not surprising that a Frenchman, **René Descartes** (1596–1650), created the first fully articulated alternative worldview.

Descartes and a New Worldview Descartes (day-KART) developed and refined his thinking in dialogue with a circle of other French thinkers. His work became more influential among philosophers and laypeople than the work of some of his equally talented contemporaries because of its thoroughness and rigor, grounded in Descartes's mathematical expertise, and because of his graceful, readable French. His system was fully presented in his *Discours de la méthode* (*Discourse on*

René Descartes French philosopher and mathematician who emphasized skepticism and deductive reasoning in his most influential treatise, *Discourse on Method*. He offered the first alternative physical explanation of matter after the Copernican revolution.

Modern Maps

Modern mapping was developed during the Scientific Revolution. Like most of the changes associated with the Scientific Revolution, changes in mapping were the result of several influences: innovations in Renaissance art, knowledge gleaned from voyages of exploration, the impact of new astronomical discoveries, the interest and support of princely patrons, and the spread of new ideas by means of print. All of these factors enabled Europeans of this era to have a literally new view of their world. Yet, as in the work of Copernicus, developments in mapping also depended on the continued use of data accumulated in previous centuries. In the examples shown here, we can see how dramatic was the progress in mapmaking over the course of the sixteenth and seventeenth centuries.

Consider the brightly colored map of western Europe and North Africa reproduced here. It is a reproduction from a 1584 atlas of printed sea charts made by a Dutchman, Lucas Waghenauer. To our eye, the map may look decorative, even quaint. Sailing ships and sea monsters, not drawn to scale, populate the oceans. Most of the major states, such as England and France, are adorned with a crest identifying their ruling dynasties.

Because some of its features appear decorative to us, we may not realize the considerable innovation that the map represented in its day. First, it is an example of the revolutionary method of depicting space achieved in the Renaissance. The discovery of linear perspective by Renaissance artists enabled them to create the illusion of three-dimensional space in their paintings and to likewise depict territory, on a map, as imagined from the perspective of a distanced observer. In addition, the landforms appear in relatively accurate relationship to one another because mapmakers, following the newly recovered *Geography* by Ptolemy, used increasingly accurate projections of the globe to represent landforms on a two-dimensional map.*

The projection used for this map was particularly useful because compass bearings could be represented as straight lines. The many straight lines that crisscross this map are called "rhumb" lines; they represent compass headings that could be used to navigate between two points. Compass bearings between points on coastlines appeared on hand-drawn medieval sea charts (after the invention of the compass in about 1250). So this sixteenth-century map combines medieval knowledge with new knowledge of geography and of how to depict landforms accurately. In addition, the information in this map was all the more useful because it was published, along with many other sea charts, in book form.

Now let us look at the apparently simpler map of the coastline of France, made about one hundred years later, in 1693. We immediately note that virtually all the decorative elements are gone. There are no sea monsters and no ships to sail the abundant seas. The map is a line drawing; it is not even colored. The simplified style of the map by itself testifies to further progress in mapmaking, and

Europe and North Africa, 1584   *(The Art Archive)*

*This discussion of the evolution of mapmaking and of these examples draws on the work of Norman J. W. Thrower, *Maps and Civilization* (Chicago: University of Chicago Press, 1996), chaps. 5 and 6.

to the ability of users to absorb information from maps. To make sense of this map, the viewer would need to be familiar with the representation of France from other maps since, for example, the land borders are not sketched in.

Indeed, the map conveys abundant information, all of which reflects scientific advancement over the intervening 100 years. The figure of a compass marks the Paris meridian, advertising that the site of the city has been precisely determined by means of its longitude. A horizontal line marks its latitude. More accurate calculation of longitude had been made possible by the work of Johannes Kepler and Galileo Galilei, whose mapping of heavenly bodies provided known points in the night sky from which to calculate the longitude of the observer's position on earth. Calculation of latitude had always been easier, since it involved only determining the angle of the sun above the horizon, but it also became more precise by use of better instrumentation in the seventeenth century. (Note: Above and to the right of the compass symbol are modern circular and oval stamps identifying the archive where the map is housed; these marks would not have appeared when the map was originally published.)

After 1650, French cartographers, among others, systematically collected astronomical observations from around the world so they could map all known lands more precisely. In addition to claiming the correct coordinates for Paris, this map also dramatically corrects earlier maps of the coastline of France. The map superimposes a corrected view (the darker line) of the coastline over an older rendering (the fainter line, mostly outside of the darker line). Thus, this map not only provides information but also boldly demonstrates the progress of mapmaking itself.

The legend of the map calls attention to this progress. It reads, "Map of France, corrected by order of the King by the observations of Messieurs of the Academy of Sciences." The map thus also documented royal patronage of scientific work. It is interesting, however, that the king is mentioned discreetly, in what is coming to be a standardized label on the map. The information in the map stands alone, without royal crests or decorations, because the public that viewed the map by now accepted and expected updated knowledge about the world.

QUESTIONS

1. What different types of information does the first map supply? Identify as many as you can.

2. What would have appeared most impressive about the second map, to a contemporary?

Online Study Center

Improve Your Grade Visual Record Activities

Method, 1637). Descartes described some of his intellectual crises in his later work, *Meditations* (1641).

Descartes accepted Galileo's conclusion that the heavens and the earth are made of the same elements. In his theorizing about the composition of matter he drew on ancient atomic models that previously had not been generally accepted. His theory that all matter is made up of identical bits, which he named "corpuscles," is a forerunner of modern atomic and quantum theories. Descartes believed that all the different appearances and behaviors of matter (for example, why stone is always hard and water is always wet) could be explained solely by the size, shape, and motion of these "corpuscles." Descartes's was an extremely mechanistic explanation of the universe. It nevertheless permitted new, more specific observations and hypotheses and greater understanding of inertia. For example, because he re-imagined the universe as being filled with "corpuscles" free to move in any direction, "natural" motion no longer seemed either circular (Galileo's idea) or toward the center of the earth (Aristotle's idea). The new understanding of motion would be crucial to Isaac Newton's formulations later in the century.

In his various works Descartes depicts and then firmly resolves the crisis of confidence that the new discoveries about the universe had produced. The collapse of the old explanations about the world made Descartes and other investigators doubt not only what they knew but also their capacity to know anything at all. Their physical senses—which denied that the earth moved, for example—had been proved untrustworthy. Descartes's solution was to re-envision the human rational capacity, the mind, as completely distinct from the world—that is, as distinct from the human body—and the unreliable perceptions it offers the senses. In a leap of faith Descartes presumed that he could count on the fact that God would not have given humans a mind if that mind consistently misled them. For Descartes, God became the guarantor of human reasoning capacity, and humans were distinguished by that capacity. This is the significance of his famous claim "I think, therefore I am."

Descartes thus achieved a resolution of the terrifying doubt about the world—a resolution that exalted the role of the human knower. The Cartesian universe was one of mechanical motion, not purpose or mystical meaning, and the Cartesian human being was preeminently a mind that could apprehend that universe. In what came to be known as "Cartesian dualism," Descartes proposed that the human mind is detached from the world and yet at the same time can objectively analyze the world.

Descartes's ambitious view of human reason emphasizes deductive reasoning (a process of reasoning in which the conclusion follows necessarily from the stated premises), a natural consequence of his philosophical rejection of sense data. The limits of deductive reasoning for scientific investigation would be realized and much of Cartesian physics supplanted by the end of the century. Nevertheless, Descartes's assumption about the objectivity of the observer would become an enduring part of scientific practice. In Descartes's day the most radical aspect of his thought was the reduction of God to the role of guarantor of knowledge. Many fellow scientists and interested laypeople were fearful of Descartes's system because it seemed to encourage "atheism." In fact, a profound faith in God was necessary for Descartes's creativity in imagining his new world system—but the system did work without God.

Although Descartes would have been surprised and offended by charges of atheism, he knew that his work would antagonize the church. He moved to the Netherlands to study in 1628, and his *Discourse* was first published there. He had lived in the Netherlands and in Germany earlier in his life; fearful of the tense atmosphere during the renewed war against French Protestants, he now left France virtually for good. Unlike Galileo, Descartes enjoyed personal wealth that enabled him to travel widely, work in solitude, and sample the intellectual environment of courts and universities without depending on powerful patrons. Long residence in the Netherlands led him to advocate religious toleration late in his life. In 1649, at the urging of an influential friend with contacts at the Swedish court, Descartes accepted the invitation of Queen Christina to visit there. Christina was an eager but demanding patron, who required Descartes to lecture on scientific topics at 5:00 a.m. each day. The long hours of work and harsh winter weather took their toll on his health, and Descartes died of pneumonia after only a few months in Sweden.

Pascal and the Limits of Scientific Knowledge

A contemporary of Descartes, fellow Frenchman Blaise Pascal (1623–1662), drew attention in his writings and in his life to the limits of scientific knowledge. The son of a royal official, Pascal (pahss-KAHL) was perhaps the most brilliant mind of his generation. A mathematician like Descartes, he stressed the importance of mathematical representations of phenomena, built one of the first calculating machines, and invented probability theory. He also carried out experiments to investigate air pressure, the behavior of liquids, and the existence of vacuums.

Pascal's career alternated between periods of intense scientific work and religious retreat. Today he is well known for his writings justifying the austere Catholicism known as Jansenism (see page 495) and for his explorations of the human soul and psyche. His *Pensées* (*Thoughts,* 1657) consists of the published fragments of his defense of Christian faith, which remained unfinished at the time of his death. Pascal's appeal for generations after him may lie in his attention to matters of faith and of feeling. His most famous statement, "The heart has its reasons which reason knows not," can be read as a declaration of the limits of the Cartesian worldview.

SCIENCE AND REVOLUTION IN ENGLAND

The new science had adherents and practitioners throughout Europe by 1650. Dutch scientists in the commercial milieu of the Netherlands, for example, had the freedom to pursue practical and experimental interests. The Dutch investigator Christiaan Huygens (HI-ghenz) (1629–1695) worked on a great variety of problems, including air pressure and optics. In 1657 he invented and patented the pendulum clock, the first device to measure accurately small units of time, essential for a variety of measurements.

England proved a unique environment for the development of science in the middle of the century. In a society torn by civil war, differing positions on science became part and parcel of disputes over Puritanism, church hierarchy, and royal power. Scientific investigation and speculation were spurred by the urgency of religious and political agendas. Scientific, along with political and religious, debate was generally encouraged by the collapse of censorship beginning in the 1640s.

During the 1640s natural philosophers with Puritan leanings were encouraged in their investigations by dreams that science, of the practical Baconian sort, could be the means by which the perfection of life on earth could be brought about and the end of history—the reign of the saints preceding the return of Christ—could be accelerated. Their concerns ranged from improved production of gunpowder (for the armies fighting against Charles I) to surveying and mapmaking. Perhaps the best-known member of this group was Robert Boyle (1627–1691). In his career we can trace the evolution of English science through the second half of the seventeenth century.

Boyle and his colleagues were theoretically eclectic, drawing on Cartesian mechanics and even Paracelsian chemical theories. They attacked the English university system, still under the sway of Aristotelianism, and proposed widespread reform of education. They were forced to moderate many of their positions, however, as the English civil wars proceeded. Radical groups such as the Levellers used Hermeticism and the related Paracelsianism as part of their political and religious tenets. The Levellers and other radical groups drew on the Hermetic notion that matter is imbued with divine spirit; they believed that each person was capable of divine knowledge and a godly life without the coercive hierarchy of church and royal officials.

Boyle and his colleagues responded to these challenges. They gained institutional power, accepting posi-

tions at Oxford and Cambridge. They formed the core of the Royal Society of London, which they persuaded Charles II to recognize and charter on his accession to the throne in the Restoration of 1660. They worked out a theoretical position that combined the orderliness of mechanism, a continued divine presence in the world, and a Baconian emphasis on scientific progress. This unwieldy set of notions was attractive to the educated elite of their day, who embraced the certainties of science but also clung to certain authoritarian aspects of the old Christian worldview.

Their most creative contribution, both to their own cause and to the advancement of science, was their emphasis on and refinement of experimental philosophy and practice. In 1660 Boyle published *New Experiments Physico-Mechanical*. The work describes the results of his experiments with an air pump he had designed, and it lays out general rules for experimental procedure. Descartes had accounted for motion by postulating that "corpuscles" of matter interact, thereby eliminating the possibility of a vacuum in nature. Recent experiments on air pressure suggested otherwise, however, and Boyle tried to confirm their findings with his air pump.

Boyle's efforts to demonstrate that a vacuum could exist—by evacuating a sealed chamber with his pump— were not successes by modern standards because his experiments could not readily be duplicated. Boyle tied the validity of experimental results to the agreement of witnesses to the experiment—a problematic solution, for only investigators sympathetic to his hypothesis and convinced of his credibility usually witnessed the results. In response to a Cambridge scholar who criticized his interpretation of one of his experiments, Boyle replied that he could not understand his critic's objections, "the experiment having been tried both before our whole society [the Royal Society of London], and very critically, by its royal founder, his majesty himself."[8] Rather than debate differing interpretations, Boyle thus appealed to the authority and prestige of the participants. In English science of the mid-seventeenth century, therefore, we have a further example of the fact that new truths, new procedures for determining truth, and new criteria for practitioners were all being established simultaneously.

THE ACHIEVEMENT OF ISAAC NEWTON

The Copernican revolution reached its high point with the work of the Englishman **Isaac Newton** (1643–1727), born one year almost to the day after Galileo

Isaac Newton   English physicist, mathematician, and natural philosopher. His mathematical computation of the laws of gravity and planetary motion, which he combined with a fully developed theory of inertia, completed the explanation for motion initiated by Nicholas Copernicus.

died. Newton completed the new explanation for motion in the heavens and on earth that Copernicus's work had initiated and that Kepler, Galileo, and others had sought.

After a difficult childhood and an indifferent education, Newton entered Cambridge University as a student in 1661. Copernicanism and Cartesianism were being hotly debated, though not yet officially studied. Newton made use of Descartes's work in mathematics to develop his skill on his own, and by 1669 he had invented calculus. (He did not publish his work at the time, and another mathematician, Gottfried von Leibniz [LIBE-nits], later independently developed calculus and vied with Newton for credit.)

Newton was elected to a fellowship at Cambridge in 1667 and was made a professor of mathematics in 1669 at the recommendation of a retiring professor with whom he had shared his work on calculus. With less demanding teaching assignments, he was able to devote much of the next decade to work on optics—an important area of study for testing Descartes's corpuscular theory of matter.

In the 1680s Newton experienced a period of self-imposed isolation from other scientists after a particularly heated exchange with one colleague, provoked by Newton's difficult temperament. During this decade he returned to the study of alternative theories about matter. As a student at Cambridge he had been strongly influenced by the work of a group of Neo-Platonists who were critical of Cartesian dualism. This controversial theory posited God as a cause of all matter and motion but removed God, or any other unknown or unknowable force, as an explanation for the behavior of matter. The Neo-Platonists' concerns were both religious and scientific. As Newton says in some of his early writing while a student, "However we cast about we find almost no other reason for atheism than this [Cartesian] notion of bodies having . . . a complete, absolute and independent reality."[10]

Newton now read treatises in alchemy and Hermetic tracts and began to imagine explanations for the behavior of matter (such as for bits of cloth fluttered from a distance by static electricity) that Cartesian corpuscular theory could not readily explain. Precisely what the forces were that caused such behavior he was not sure, but his eclectic mind and his religious convictions enabled him to accept their existence.

It was this leap that allowed him to propose the existence of gravity—a mysterious force that accounts for the movements of heavenly bodies in the vacuum of space. Others had speculated about the existence of gravity; indeed, the concept of inertia as so far elaborated by Galileo, Descartes, and others suggested the need for the concept of gravity. Otherwise, if a planet were "pushed" (say, in Kepler's view, by the "motive force" of the sun), it would continue along that course forever unless "pulled back" by something else.

Newton's extraordinary contribution to a new mechanistic understanding of the universe was the mathematical computation of the laws of gravity and planetary motion, which he combined with a fully developed concept of inertia. In 1687 Newton published *Philosophia Naturalis Principia Mathematica* (*Mathematical Principles of Natural Philosophy;* usually called *Principia*). In this mathematical treatise—so intricate that it was baffling to laypeople, even those able to read Latin—Newton laid out his **laws of motion** and expressed them as mathematical theorems that can be used to test future observations of moving bodies. Then he demonstrated that these laws also apply to the solar system, confirming the data already gathered about the

laws of motion   The laws of gravity, planetary motion, and inertia first laid out in the seventeenth century by Isaac Newton.

planets and even predicting the existence of an as yet unseen planet. His supreme achievement was his law of gravitation, with which he could predict the discovery of the invisible planet. This law states that every body, indeed every bit of matter, in the universe exerts over every other body an attractive force proportional to the product of their masses and inversely proportional to the square of the distance between them. Newton not only accounted for motion but definitively united heaven and earth in a single scheme and created a convincing picture of an orderly nature.

Neither Newton nor anyone else claimed that his theorems resolved all questions about motion and matter. Exactly what gravity is and how it operates were not clear, as they still are not. Newton's laws of motion are taught today because they still adequately account for most problems of motion. The fact that so fundamental a principle as gravity remains unexplained in no way diminishes Newton's achievement but is clear evidence of the nature of scientific understanding: science provides explanatory schemas that account for many—but not all—observed phenomena. No schema explains everything, and each schema contains open doorways that lead both to further discoveries and to blind alleys. Newton, for example, assumed that the forces that accounted for gravity would mysteriously work on metals so that, as alchemists predicted, they might "quickly pass into gold."[11]

After the publication of *Principia* Newton was more of a celebrated public figure than a practicing scientist. He helped lead resistance to James II's Catholicizing policies in the university, and he became the familiar of many other leading minds of his day, such as John Locke (see page 546). Newton became the president of the Royal Academy of Sciences in 1703 and was knighted in 1705, the first scientist to be so distinguished. By the end of his life universities in England were dominated by men who acclaimed and built on his work. The transformation of the institutional structure of science in England was complete.

DEVELOPMENTS IN CHEMISTRY, BIOLOGY, AND MEDICINE

The innovations in astronomy that led to the new mechanistic view of the behavior of matter did not automatically spill over to other branches of science. In astronomy innovation came after the ancient and medieval inheritance had been fully assimilated and its errors disclosed. Other branches of science followed their own paths, though all were strongly influenced by the **mechanistic worldview.**

mechanistic worldview Seventeenth-century philosophical view that saw the world as a machine that functions in strict obedience to physical laws, without purpose or will.

In chemistry the mechanistic assumption that all matter was composed of small, equivalent parts was crucial to understanding the properties and behaviors of compounds (combinations of elements). But knowledge of these small units of matter was not yet detailed enough to be of much use in advancing chemistry conceptually. Nevertheless, the flawed conceptual schema did not hold back all chemical discovery and development. Lack of understanding of gases, and of the specific elements in their makeup, for example, did not prevent the development and improvement of gunpowder. Indeed, unlike the innovations in astronomy, eventual conceptual innovation in chemistry and biology owed a great deal to the results of plodding experiment and the slow accumulation of data.

A conceptual leap forward was made in biology in the sixteenth and seventeenth centuries. Because biological knowledge was mostly a byproduct of the practice of medicine, biological studies remained very practical and experimental. The recent discovery of *On Anatomical Procedures*, a treatise by the ancient physician Galen, encouraged dissection and other practical research. Andreas Vesalius (1514–1564), in particular, made important advances by following Galen's exhortation to anatomical research. Born in Brussels, Vesalius (vuh-SAY-lee-us) studied at the nearby University of Louvain and then at Padua, where he was appointed professor of surgery. He ended his career as physician to Emperor Charles V and his son, Philip II of Spain. In his teaching at Padua Vesalius acted on the newly recovered Galenic teachings by doing dissections himself rather than giving the work to technicians. In 1543 he published versions of his lectures as an illustrated compendium of anatomy, *De Humani Corporis Fabrica (On the Fabric of the Human Body)*.

The results of his dissections of human corpses, revealed in this work, demonstrated a number of errors in Galen's knowledge of human anatomy, much of which had been derived from dissection of animals. Neither Vesalius nor his immediate successors, however, questioned overall Galenic theory about the functioning of the human body, any more than Copernicus had utterly rejected Aristotelian physics.

The slow movement from new observation to changed explanation is clearly illustrated in the career of the Englishman William Harvey (1578–1657). Much like Vesalius, Harvey was educated first in his own land and then at Padua, where he benefited from the tradition of anatomical research. He also had a career as a practicing physician in London and at the courts of James I and Charles I.

Harvey postulated the circulation of the blood—postulated rather than discovered, because owing to the technology of the day, he could not observe the tiny capillaries where the movement of arterial blood into the veins occurs. After conducting vivisectional experiments

Vesalius on Human Anatomy
The meticulous illustrations in Vesalius's work helped ensure its success. The medium of print was essential for accurate reproduction of scientific drawings. Note also the way the human body, in this drawing of musculature, is depicted as dominating the landscape.
(Courtesy, Dover Publications)

on animals that revealed the actual functioning of the heart and lungs, he reasoned that circulation must occur. He carefully described his experiments and his conclusions in *Exercitatio Anatomica de Motu Cordis et Sanguinis in Animalibus* (1628), usually shortened to *De Motu Cordis* (*On the Motion of the Heart*).

Harvey's work challenged Galenic anatomy and, like Copernicus's discoveries, created new burdens of explanation. According to Galenic theory, the heart and lungs helped each other to function. The heart sent nourishment to the lungs through the pulmonary artery, and the lungs provided raw material for the "vital spirit," which the heart gave to the blood to sustain life. The lungs also helped the heart sustain its "heat." This heat was understood to be an innate property of organs, just as "heaviness," in traditional physics, had been considered an innate property of earthbound objects.

From his observations Harvey came to think of the heart in terms consonant with the new mechanistic notions about nature: as a pump to circulate the blood. But he adjusted, rather than abandoned, Galenic theories concerning "heat" and "vital spirit." The lungs had been thought to "ventilate" the heart by providing air to maintain "heat," just as a bellows aerates a fire. In light of his discovery of the pulmonary transit (that all of the blood is pumped through the lungs and back through the heart), Harvey suggested instead that the lungs carried out some of these functions for the blood, helping it to concoct the "vital spirit." Only in this sense did he think of the heart as a machine, circulating this life-giving material throughout the body.

Harvey's explanation of bodily functions in light of his new knowledge did not constitute a rupture with Galenic tradition. But by the end of his life Harvey's own adjustments of Galenic theory were suggesting new conceptual possibilities. His work inspired additional research in physiology, chemistry, and physics. Robert Boyle's efforts to understand vacuums can be traced in part to questions Harvey raised about the function of the lungs and the properties of air.

SECTION SUMMARY

- Interest in the new science spread in the seventeenth century as many scholars accepted Copernican theory and as rulers realized the possible advantages of scientific advances.

- René Descartes built on the work of Galileo to formulate a new theory about the nature of matter.

- Descartes believed that humans could understand nature by using reason, not by trusting sensory data.

- English scientists such as Robert Boyle began to use experimental methods.

- Isaac Newton developed new laws of motion, still in use today, that explain the behavior of matter on earth and in space with a single set of mathematical principles.

- Advances in the life sciences included new anatomical discoveries by Andreas Vesalius and work by William Harvey on the circulation of the blood.

THE NEW SCIENCE IN CONTEXT: SOCIETY, POLITICS, AND RELIGION

How did the new scientific worldview lead people to challenge traditional notions of society, the state, and religion?

Scientists wrestled with questions about God and human capacity every bit as intently as they attempted to find new explanations for the behavior of matter and the motion of the heavens. Eventually the profound implications of the new scientific worldview would affect thought and behavior throughout society. Once people no longer thought of the universe in hierarchical terms, they could question the hierarchical organization of society. Once people questioned the authority of traditional knowledge about the universe, the way was clear for them to begin to question traditional views of the state, the social order, and even the divine order. Such profound changes of perspective took hold very gradually, however. The advances in science did lead to revolutionary cultural change, but until the end of the seventeenth century traditional institutions and ideologies limited its extent.

THE BEGINNINGS OF SCIENTIFIC PROFESSIONALISM

Institutions both old and new supported the new science developing in the sixteenth and seventeenth centuries. Some universities were the setting for scientific breakthroughs, but court patronage, a well-established institution, also sponsored scientific activity. The development of the Accadèmia dei Lincei, to which Galileo belonged, and of other academies was a step toward modern professional societies of scholars, although these new organizations depended on patronage.

In England and France, royally sponsored scientific societies were founded in the third quarter of the century. The Royal Society of London, inaugurated in 1660, received royal recognition but no money and remained an informal institution sponsoring amateur scientific interests as well as specialized independent research. The Académie Royale des Sciences in France, established in 1666 by Jean-Baptiste Colbert, Louis XIV's minister of finance (see page 494), sponsored research and supported chosen scientists with pensions. These associations were extensions to science of traditional kinds of royal recognition and patronage. Thus the French Académie was well funded but tightly controlled by the government of Louis XIV, and the Royal Society of London received little of Charles II's scarce resources or precious political capital. Like the earlier academies, these royally sponsored societies published

their fellows' work; in England the *Philosophical Transactions of the Royal Society* began in 1665.

The practice of seventeenth-century science took place in so many diverse institutions—academies, universities, royal courts—that neither *science* nor *scientist* was rigorously defined. Science as a discipline was not yet detached from broad metaphysical questions. Boyle, Newton, Pascal, and Descartes all concerned themselves with questions of religion, and all thought of themselves not as scientists but, like their medieval forebears, as natural philosophers. These natural philosophers were still members of an elite who met in aristocratic salons to discuss literature, politics, or science with equal ease and interest. Nevertheless, the beginnings of a narrowing of the practice of science to a tightly defined, truly professional community are evident in these institutions.

The importance of court life and patronage to the new science had at first enabled women to be actively involved. Women ran important salons in France; aristocratic women everywhere were indispensable sources of patronage for scientists; and women themselves were scientists, combining, as did men, science with other pursuits. Noblewomen and daughters of gentry families had access to education in their homes, and a number of such women were active scientists—astronomers, mathematicians, and botanists. The astronomer Maria Cunitz (KOO-nits) (1610–1664), from Silesia (a Habsburg-controlled province, now in modern Poland), learned six languages with the encouragement of her father, who was a medical doctor. Later she published a useful simplification of some of Kepler's mathematical calculations. Women from artisanal families might also receive useful training at home. Such was the case of the German entomologist Maria Sibylla Merian (1647–1717). Merian learned the techniques of illustration in the workshop of her father, an artist in Frankfurt. She later used her artistic training and her refined powers of observation to study and record the features and behaviors of insects and plants in the New World.

Margaret Cavendish, duchess of Newcastle (1623–1673), wrote several major philosophical works, including *Grounds of Natural Philosophy* (1668). She was a Cartesian but was influenced by Neo-Platonism. She believed matter to have "intelligence" and thus disagreed with Descartes's views on matter, but she criticized fellow English philosophers on the grounds that, like Descartes, she distrusted sensory knowledge as a guide to philosophy.

Women were routinely accepted as members of Italian academies, but they were excluded from formal membership in the academies in London and Paris, although they could use the academies' facilities and received prizes from the societies for their work. One reason that women were barred was that the amount of available patronage was limited, and coveted positions automatically went to men. Moreover, the hierarchical distinction signified by gender made the exclusion of women a useful way to define the academies as special and privileged.

Margaret Cavendish was aware of the degree to which her participation in scientific life depended on informal networks and on the resources available to her because of her aristocratic status. Women scientists from more modest backgrounds, without Cavendish's resources, had to fight for the right to employment as public institutions gained importance as settings for the pursuit of science. The German astronomer Maria Winkelman (VINK-el-mahn) (1670–1720), for example, tried to succeed her late husband in an official position in the Berlin Academy of Sciences in 1710, after working as his unofficial partner during his tenure as astronomer to the academy. The academy withheld an

Astronomers Elisabetha and Johannes Hevelius
The Heveliuses were one of many collaborating couples among the scientists of the seventeenth century. Women were usually denied pensions and support for their research when they worked alone, however. *(From Hevelius,* Machinae coelestis. *By permission of the Houghton Library, Harvard University)*

Fig. M.

official position from Winkelman after her husband's death, however, despite her experience and accomplishments (she had discovered a new comet, for example, in 1702). The secretary of the academy stated: "That she be kept on in an official capacity to work on the calendar or to continue with observations simply will not do. Already during her husband's lifetime the society was burdened with ridicule because its calendar was prepared by a woman. If she were now to be kept on in such a capacity, mouths would gape even wider."[12]

Winkelman worked in private observatories but was able to return to the Berlin Academy only as the unofficial assistant to her own son, whose training she herself had supervised. As the new science gained in prestige, women scientists often found themselves marginalized.

THE NEW SCIENCE, THE STATE, AND THE CHURCH

The new natural philosophy had implications for traditional notions about the state. The new worldview that all matter, whether in the heavens or on earth, was identical and answerable to discernible natural laws gradually undermined political systems resting on a belief in the inherent inequality of persons and on royal prerogative. By the middle of the eighteenth century a fully formed alternative political philosophy would argue for more "rational" government in keeping with the rational, natural order of things. But the change came slowly, and while it was coming, traditional rulers found much to admire and utilize in the new science.

Technological possibilities of the new science were very attractive to governments. Experiments with vacuum pumps had important applications in the mining industry, for example. Governments also sponsored pure, and not only applied, scientific research. A French naval expedition to Cayenne, in French Guiana, led to refinements of the pendulum clock but had as its main purpose progressive observations of the sun to permit the calculation of the earth's distance from the sun. Members of the elite saw the opportunity not only for practical advances but also for prestige and, most important, confirmation of the orderliness of nature. It is hard to overestimate the psychological impact and intellectual power of this fundamental tenet of the new science—namely, that nature is an inanimate machine that reflects God's design not through its purposes but simply by its orderliness. Thus, in the short run, the new science supported a vision of order that was very pleasing even to a monarch of absolutist pretensions such as Louis XIV.

As we have seen, scientists themselves flourished in close relationships with princes and actively sought their patronage for its many benefits. Christiaan Huy-

gens left the Netherlands to accept the patronage of Louis XIV, producing in France some of his most important work in optics and mechanics. Huygens had learned from his father, secretary to the princes of Orange in the Netherlands, that a princely court not only offered steady support but also opened doors to other royal academies and salons. Huygens published some of his early research through the Royal Society in London, thanks to contacts his father had established. When Galileo left his position at Padua for the Medici court in Florence, he wrote to a friend, "It is not possible to receive a salary from a Republic [Venice] . . . without serving the public, because to get something from the public one must satisfy it and not just one particular person; . . . no one can exempt me from the burden while leaving me the income; and in sum I cannot hope for such a benefit from anyone but an absolute prince."[13]

Scientists and scientific thought also remained closely tied to religion in both practical and institutional ways during the seventeenth century. Both religion and the Catholic Church as an institution were involved with scientific advancement from the time of Copernicus. Copernicus himself was a cleric, as were many philosophers and scientists after him. This is not surprising, for most research in the sciences to this point had occurred within universities sponsored and staffed by members of religious orders, who had the education, time, and resources necessary for scientific investigation. Some of Descartes's closest collaborators were clerics, as were certain of Galileo's aristocratic patrons and his own protégés. Moreover, religious and metaphysical concerns were central to the work of virtually every scientist. The entire Cartesian process of reasoning about the world, for example, was grounded in Descartes's certainty about God. Copernicus, Kepler, Newton, and others perceived God's purpose in the mathematical regularity of nature.

The notion that religion was the opponent of science in this era is a result of Galileo's trial, and represents a distortion even of that event. It is true that the new astronomy and mechanics challenged traditional interpretations of Scripture, as well as the fundamentals of physics and metaphysics that were taught in universities. Thus, in its sponsorship of universities, the church was literally invested in the old view, even though individual clerics investigated and taught Copernican ideas. The rigid response of the church hierarchy to Galileo is partially explained by the aftermath of the Protestant Reformation, which, in the minds of many churchmen—including Galileo's accusers and some of his judges—had demonstrated the need for a firm response to any challenge to the church's authority. Galileo seemed particularly threatening because he was well known, wrote for a wide audience,

Science and Royal Power

This painting memorializes the founding of the French Académie des Sciences and the building of the royal observatory in Paris. Louis himself is at the center of the painting, reflecting the symbolic importance of royal power in the sponsorship of science. *(Château de Versailles/Laurie Platt Winfrey, Inc.)*

and, like the Protestants, presumed to interpret the Scriptures. Galileo may well have escaped punishment entirely had it not been for the political predicament faced by the pope coincident with his trial, however.

The condemnation of Galileo shocked many clerics, including the three who had voted for leniency at his trial. Clerics who were also scientists continued to study and teach the new science where and when they could. Copernicanism was taught by Catholic missionaries abroad. (See the box "The Global Record: Jesuits and Astronomy in China.") To be sure, Galileo's trial did have a chilling effect on scientific investigation in most Catholic regions of Europe. Investigators could and did continue their research, but many could publish results only by smuggling manuscripts to Prot-

estant lands. Many of the most important empirical and theoretical innovations in science occurred in Protestant regions after the middle of the seventeenth century.

Protestant leaders, however, were also not initially receptive to Copernican ideas because they defied scriptural authority as well as common sense. In 1549 one of Martin Luther's associates wrote: "The eyes are witnesses that the heavens revolve in the space of twenty-four hours. But certain men, either from love of novelty or to make a display of ingenuity, have concluded that the earth moves. . . . Now it is want of honesty and decency to assert such notions publicly and the example is pernicious. It is part of a good mind to accept the truth as revealed by God and to acquiesce in it."[14]

THE GLOBAL RECORD

JESUITS AND ASTRONOMY IN CHINA

The Italian Matteo Ricci (1552–1610) was one of the first Jesuit missionaries to establish himself at the imperial court in China. Ricci's willingness to learn the Chinese language and his own scientific knowledge was crucial to his acceptance at the Chinese court. Jesuit missionaries who followed Ricci in the seventeenth century found their scientific expertise equally valued, and several openly taught Copernican theory in the East. Chinese interest in European knowledge was itself new. In previous centuries Europeans had eagerly borrowed from China, including knowledge of papermaking and printing.

The Chinese have not only made considerable progress in moral philosophy but in astronomy and in many branches of mathematics as well. At one time they were quite proficient in arithmetic and geometry, but in the study and teaching of these branches of learning they labored with more or less confusion. They divide the heavens into constellations in a manner somewhat different from that which we employ. Their count of the stars outnumbers the calculations of our astronomers by fully four hundred, because they include in it many of the fainter stars which are not always visible. And yet with all this, the Chinese astronomers take no pains whatever to reduce the phenomena of celestial bodies to the discipline of mathematics. Much of their time is spent in determining the moment of eclipses and the mass of the planets and the stars, but here, too, their deductions are spoiled by innumerable errors. Finally they center their whole attention on that phase of astronomy which our scientists term astrology, which may be accounted for by the fact that they believe that everything happening on this terrestrial globe of ours depends upon the stars.

Some knowledge of the science of mathematics was given to the Chinese by the Saracens [Mongols], who penetrated into their country from the West, but very little of this knowledge was based upon definite mathematical proofs. What the Saracens left them, for the most part, consisted of certain tables of rules by which the Chinese regulated their calendar and to which they reduced their calculations of planets and the movements of the heavenly bodies in general. The founder of the family which at present regulates the study of astrology prohibited anyone from indulging in the study of this science unless he were chosen for it by hereditary right. The prohibition was founded upon fear, lest he who should acquire a knowledge of the stars might become capable of disrupting the order of the empire and seek an opportunity to do so.

QUESTIONS

1. In what ways is Ricci both appreciative and critical of Chinese science?

2. What do Ricci's comments about Chinese science reveal about his own assumptions concerning astronomy and mathematics and how to study them appropriately?

Source: Louis J. Gallagher, trans., *China in the Sixteenth Century: The Journals of Matthew Ricci: 1583–1610* (New York: Random House, 1953), pp. 30–31. Copyright 1942, 1953 and renewed 1970 by Louis J. Gallagher, S.J. Used by permission of Random House, Inc.

Protestant thinkers were also as troubled as Catholics by the metaphysical dilemmas that the new theories seemed to raise. In 1611, one year after Galileo's *Starry Messenger* appeared, the English poet John Donne (1573–1631) reflected on the confusion that now reigned in human affairs, with the heavenly hierarchy dismantled:

[The] new Philosophy calls all in doubt,
The Element of fire is quite put out;
The Sun is lost, and th'earth, and no man's wit
Can well direct him where to look for it.
. . . .
'Tis all in pieces, all coherence gone;
All just supply, and all Relation:
Prince, Subject, Father, Son, are things forgot,

For every man alone thinks he hath got
To be a Phoenix, and that then can be
None of that kinde, of which he is, but he.[15]

The challenge of accounting in religious terms for the ideas of Copernicus and Descartes became more urgent for Protestants as the ideas acquired an anti-Catholic status after the trial of Galileo in 1633 and as they became common scientific currency by about 1640. A religious certainty about divine force that could account for the motion of bodies in a vacuum enabled Newton to develop his theories on motion and gravity. In short, religion did not merely remain in the scientists' panoply of explanations; it remained a fundamental building block of scientific thought and central to most scientists' lives, whether they were Catholic or Protestant.

THE NEW SCIENCE AND POLITICAL THOUGHT AT THE END OF THE SEVENTEENTH CENTURY

Traditional institutions and ideologies checked the potential effects of the new science for a time, but by the middle of the seventeenth century political theory was beginning to reflect the impact of the mechanistic worldview. Political philosophers began to doubt that either the world or human society was an organic whole in which each part was distinguished in nature and function from the rest. Thomas Hobbes, John Locke, and others recast the bonds that link citizens to one another and to their rulers.

Thomas Hobbes Because of the political turmoil in England, **Thomas Hobbes** (1588–1679) spent much of his productive life on the Continent. After the beginnings of the parliamentary rebellion he joined a group of royalist émigrés in France. He met Galileo and lived for extended periods in Paris, in contact with the circle of French thinkers that included Descartes. Like Descartes, he theorized about the nature and behavior of matter and published a treatise on his views in 1655.

Online Study Center **Improve Your Grade**
Primary Source: Hobbes Describes the Natural State of War

Hobbes is best known today for *Leviathan* (1651), his treatise on political philosophy. *Leviathan* applies to the world of human beings Hobbes's mostly Cartesian view of nature as composed of "self-motivated," atom-like structures. Hobbes viewed people as mechanistically as he viewed the rest of nature. In his view, people are made up of appetites of various sorts—the same kind of innate forces that drive all matter. The ideal political system, he concluded, is one in which a strong sovereign controls the disorder that inevitably arises from the clash of people's desires. Unlike medieval philosophers, Hobbes did not draw analogies between the state and the human body (the king as head, judges and magistrates as arms, and so forth). Instead, he compared the state to a machine that "ran" by means of laws and was kept in good working order by a skilled technician—the ruler.

Hobbes's pessimism about human behavior and his insistence on the need for restraint imposed from above reflect, as does the work of Descartes, a concern for order in the wake of political turmoil. This concern was one reason he was welcomed into the community of French philosophers, who were naturally comfortable with royalty as a powerful guarantor of order. But Hobbes's work, like theirs, was a radical departure because it envisioned citizens as potentially equal and constrained neither by morality nor by natural obedience to authority.

John Locke Another Englishman, **John Locke** (1632–1704), offered an entirely different vision of natural equality among people and, consequently, of social order. Locke's major works, *Essay on Human Understanding* (1690) and *Two Treatises of Government* (1690), reflect the experimentalism of Robert Boyle, the systematizing rationality of Descartes, and other strands of the new scientific thought. In his *Essay* Locke provides a view of human knowledge more pragmatic and utilitarian than the rigorous mathematical model of certainty used by many other philosophers. He argues that human knowledge is largely the product of experience. He agrees with Descartes that reason orders and explains human experience, but unlike Descartes, he doubts that human reason has unlimited potential to comprehend the universe. Locke, however, offered a more optimistic vision of the possible uses of reason. Whereas Descartes was interested in mentally ordering and understanding the world, Locke was interested in actually functioning *in* the world.

Locke's treatises on government reflect his notion of knowledge based on experience, as well as his particular experiences as a member of elite circles following the Restoration in England. Trained in medicine, he served as personal physician and general political assistant to one of the members of Parliament most opposed to Charles II's pretensions to absolutist government. When James II acceded to the throne in 1685, Locke remained in the Netherlands, where he had fled to avoid prosecution for treason. He became an adviser to William of Orange and returned to England with William and Mary in 1688. Locke's view of the principles of good government came to reflect the pro-parliamentary stance of his political milieu.

Unlike Hobbes, Locke argued that people are capable of self-restraint and mutual respect in their pursuit of self-interest. The state arises, he believed, from a contract that individuals freely enter into to protect themselves, their property, and their happiness from possible aggression by others. They can invest the executive and legislative authority to carry out this protection in monarchy or any other governing institution, though Locke believed that the English Parliament was

Thomas Hobbes English philosopher who argued in *Leviathan* that people are made up of mechanistic appetites and so need a strong ruler to govern them. However, he also envisioned citizens as potentially equal and constrained neither by morality nor by natural obedience to authority.

John Locke English philosopher who asserted that the state arises from a contract that individuals freely endorse. Therefore, because sovereignty resides with the people, rebellion against abuse of power is justified—a revolutionary vision of a political society based on human rights.

the best available model. Because sovereignty resides with the people who enter into the contract, rebellion against the abuse of power is justified. At the core of Locke's schema is thus a revolutionary vision of political society based on human rights.

Locke's experience as an English gentleman is apparent in his emphasis on private property, which he considered a fundamental human right. Nature, he believed, cannot benefit humankind unless it is worked by human hands, as on a farm, for example. Private ownership of property guarantees its productivity and entitles the owner to participate in Locke's imagined contract. Indeed, Locke's political vision is unequivocal, and unbending, on the nature of property. Locke even found a justification for slavery. He also did not consider women to be independent beings in the same way as men. The family, he felt, is a separate domain from the state, not bound by the same contractual obligations.

Locke and many other seventeenth-century thinkers were unable to imagine a new physical or political reality without invoking a notion of gender as a "natural" principle of order and hierarchy. Margaret Cavendish, among others, disputed the validity of such arbitrary distinctions in capacities and rights between men and women; nevertheless, men frequently used them. Locke's use of gender as an arbitrary organizing principle gave his bold new vision of rights for certain men a claim to being "natural." The use of gender-specific vocabulary to describe nature itself had the effect of making the new objective attitude toward the world seem "natural." Works by seventeenth-century scientists are filled with references to nature as a woman who must be "conquered," "subdued," or "penetrated."

Traditional gender distinctions limited and reinforced most facets of political thought, but in other areas the fact of uncertainty and the need for tolerance were embraced. In another of Locke's influential works, the impassioned *Letter on Toleration* (1689), he argues that religious belief is fundamentally private and that only the most basic Christian principles need be accepted by everyone. Others went further than Locke by entirely removing traditional religion as necessary to morality and public order. Fostering this climate of religious skepticism were religious pluralism in England and the self-defeating religious intolerance of Louis XIV's persecution of Protestants.

Pierre Bayle   Pierre Bayle (1647–1706), a Frenchman of Protestant origins, argued that morality can be wholly detached from traditional religion. Indeed, Bayle concluded, one need not be a Christian at all to be a moral being. Bayle cited as an example of morality the philosopher Baruch Spinoza (1632–1677), a Dutch Jew who had been cast out of his local synagogue for supposed atheism. Even so, Spinoza believed the state to have a moral purpose and human happiness to have spiritual roots.

Bayle's skepticism toward traditional knowledge was more wide-ranging than his views on religion. His best-known work, *Dictionnaire historique et critique* (*Historical and Critical Dictionary,* 1702), was a compendium of observations about and criticisms of virtually every thinker whose works were known at the time, including such recent and lionized figures as Descartes and Newton. Bayle was the first systematic skeptic, and he relentlessly exposed errors and shortcomings in all received knowledge. His works were very popular with elite lay readers.

Bayle's countryman Bernard de Fontenelle (fon-tuh-NEL) (1657–1757), secretary to the Académie des Sciences from 1699 to 1741, was the greatest popularizer of the new science of his time. His *Entretiens sur la Pluralités des Mondes* (*Conversations on the Plurality of Worlds,* 1686) was, as the title implies, an informally presented description of the infinite universe of matter. A great success, it went through numerous editions and translations. As secretary to the Académie, Fontenelle continued his work as popularizer by publishing descriptions of the work of the Académie's scientists. At his death (at age 99) in 1757, it was said that "the Philosophic spirit, today so much in evidence, owes its beginnings to Monsieur de Fontenelle."[16]

SECTION SUMMARY

- New institutions, such as academies, supported scientific work and were forerunners of modern scientific associations.

- European rulers were eager to sponsor scientific work both for its practical benefits and for its symbolic importance for their power.

- Scientific work remained closely tied to religion in both intellectual and institutional ways.

- Political thought in the seventeenth century, as represented by Locke and Bayle, began to reflect the new science's confidence in human reason.

- Women scientists were disadvantaged by the institutional settings for the new science and by the way notions about gender were used in the new science and political philosophy.

CHAPTER SUMMARY

Online Study Center **ACE the Test**

How did the Copernican theory challenge traditional views of the universe?

How and why did new theories about astronomy lead to a broader Scientific Revolution?

How did the new scientific worldview lead people to challenge traditional notions of society, the state, and religion?

The Scientific Revolution began with developments in astronomy. Because of astronomy's role in explanations of the world and human life that prevailed in the Middle Ages, changes in astronomical theory were bound to have widespread effects on other knowledge and beliefs. Copernicus's heliocentric theory led to wider scientific and philosophical innovation also because of the context in which it was received. Recent recoveries of new ancient texts in the Renaissance and the discovery of previously unknown lands in the New World made it possible to imagine challenging ancient scientific authority. The interest of princes in both the prestige and the practical use of science helped support the work of scientists. Other scientists, following Copernicus, built on his theories, culminating in the work of Galileo, who supported Copernican theory with additional data and widely published his findings.

The Frenchman Descartes was the first to fashion a systematic explanation for the operations of nature to replace the medieval view. The political and intellectual climate in England, meanwhile, encouraged the development of experimental science and inductive reasoning. Isaac Newton provided new theories to explain the behavior of matter and expressed them in mathematical terms that could apply to either the earth or the cosmos. With his work traditional astronomy and physics were overturned, replaced by a vision of a universe of matter that behaves not according to a higher purpose but rather as a machine.

New institutions in the form of private as well as officially sponsored scientific societies rose up to support scientists' work. These societies were particularly important before the new science became accepted in universities, although they excluded some practitioners of the new science, particularly women. Rulers made use of the new science for the practical results it offered despite the ideological challenges it presented to their power. The relationship of religion to the new science was equally complex and contrary. Some religious leaders scorned the new science; most scientists, whether Catholic or Protestant, worked to accommodate both the new science and their religious beliefs. Indeed, religious faith—in the case of Newton, for example—was a spur to innovation. By the end of the seventeenth century, the hierarchical Christian worldview grounded in the old science was being challenged on many fronts, most notably in the work of the political philosophers Hobbes and Locke, who both challenged traditional justifications for royal authority. Locke's work was particularly important for the future because he argued that governments can exist only with the consent of the governed.

LOOKING AHEAD

Fontenelle is a fitting figure with whom to end a discussion of the Scientific Revolution because he represents, and worked to accomplish, the transference of the new natural philosophy into political and social philosophy—a movement we know as the "Enlightenment." A fully articulated secular worldview would be the product of the Enlightenment in the next century.

KEY TERMS

Nicholas Copernicus (p. 526)

heliocentric theory (p. 527)

Johannes Kepler (p. 528)

Galileo Galilei (p. 529)

Francis Bacon (p. 531)

empirical method (p. 532)

René Descartes (p. 533)

Isaac Newton (p. 537)

laws of motion (p. 538)

mechanistic worldview (p. 539)

Thomas Hobbes (p. 546)

John Locke (p. 546)

Online Study Center
Improve Your Grade Flashcards

SUGGESTED READING

Biagioli, Mario. *Galileo, Courtier.* 1993. A study that stresses the power of patronage relations to shape scientific process.

Dear, Peter. *Revolutionizing the Sciences: European Knowledge and Its Ambitions, 1500–1700.* 2001. An excellent general overview of the era of the Scientific Revolution.

Kuhn, Thomas. *The Copernican Revolution.* 1985. A classic treatment of the revolution in astronomy that lucidly explains the Aristotelian worldview; to understand the Copernican revolution, start here.

Schiebinger, Londa. *The Mind Has No Sex?* 1989. An examination of the participation of women in the practice of science and an explanation of how science began to reflect the exclusion of women in its values and objects of study—above all, in its claims about scientific "facts" about women themselves.

Shapin, Steven, and Simon Schaffer. *Leviathan and the Air-Pump.* 1985. One of the most important studies of seventeenth-century science; traces the conflict between Cartesian science, as represented by Hobbes, and experimental science, in the work of Boyle; shows the relationship of Hobbes and Boyle to their respective contexts and the widespread philosophical implications of each school of thought.

Westfall, Richard S. *Never at Rest: A Biography of Isaac Newton.* 1993. A biography by one of the best-known historians of science.

NOTES

1. Quoted in *Encyclopaedia Britannica,* 15th ed., vol. 9, p. 35.

2. Quoted in Thomas S. Kuhn, *The Copernican Revolution* (Cambridge, Mass.: Harvard University Press, 1985), p. 131.

3. Quoted in Margaret C. Jacob, *The Cultural Meaning of the Scientific Revolution* (Philadelphia: Temple University Press, 1988), p. 18.

4. Quoted ibid., p. 33.

5. Quoted in Alan G. R. Smith, *Science and Society in the Sixteenth and Seventeenth Centuries* (New York: Science History Publications, 1972), p. 72.

6. Quoted in Jacob, p. 32 (emphasis added).

7. Quoted in Bruce T. Moran, ed., *Patronage and Institutions: Science, Technology and Medicine at the European Court* (Rochester, N.Y.: Boyden Press, 1991), p. 43.

8. Quoted in Steven Shapin, *A Social History of Truth* (Chicago: University of Chicago Press, 1994), p. 298.

9. Quoted in Smith, p. 130.

10. Quoted in Jacob, p. 89.

11. Quoted ibid., p. 25.

12. Quoted in Londa Schiebinger, *The Mind Has No Sex?* (Cambridge, Mass.: Harvard University Press, 1989), p. 92.

13. Quoted in Richard S. Westfall, "Science and Patronage," *ISIS* 76 (1985): 16.

14. Quoted in Kuhn, p. 191.

15. *Complete Poetry and Selected Prose of John Donne,* ed. John Hayward (Bloomsbury, England: Nonesuch Press, 1929), p. 365, quoted in Kuhn, p. 194.

16. Quoted in Paul Edwards, ed., *The Encyclopedia of Philosophy,* vol. 3 (New York: Macmillan, 1967), p. 209.

EUROPE ON THE THRESHOLD
OF MODERNITY, CA. 1715–1789

**Café Society in the
Eighteenth Century**
(G. Dagli Orti/The Art Archive)

rinks are set before these gentlemen on their table, but something tells us this is more than just a social gathering. The men are absorbed in intense conversation. One man raises his hand, perhaps to emphasize his point, while another listens with a skeptical smirk. Several others eagerly follow their conversation. Other animated discussions go on at nearby tables. The setting depicted here was altogether new in the eighteenth century, when this picture was made, and a caption that originally accompanied the illustration speaks to its importance: "Establishment of the new philosophy: our cradle was the café."

Cafés were one of the new settings in which literate elites could discuss the "new philosophy"—what we now call Enlightenment philosophy—and could explore its implications for social and political life. Men gathered in clubs and cafés; women directed private gatherings known as salons. Both men and women read more widely than ever before.

The Enlightenment was the extension into political and social thought of the intellectual revolution that had already occurred in the physical sciences. Hence it constituted a revolution in political philosophy, but it was also much more. The era witnessed the emergence of an informed body of public opinion, critical of the prevailing political system. The relationship between governments and the governed had begun to change: subjects of monarchs were becoming citizens of nations.

The notion that human beings, using their rational faculties, could not only understand nature but might also transform their societies was appealing to rulers as well, in part for the traditional reason—strengthening state power. Frederick the Great of Prussia, Catherine the Great of Russia, and other monarchs self-consciously tried to use Enlightenment precepts to guide their efforts at governing. They had mixed success because powerful interests opposed their efforts at reform and because, ultimately, their own hereditary and autocratic power was incompatible with Enlightenment perspectives.

Profound changes in economic and social life accompanied this revolution in intellectual and political spheres. The increasing economic and strategic importance of overseas colonies made them important focal points of international conflict. Economic growth spurred population

CHAPTER OUTLINE

THE ENLIGHTENMENT

EUROPEAN STATES IN THE AGE OF ENLIGHTENMENT

THE WIDENING WORLD OF COMMERCE AND WARFARE

ECONOMIC EXPANSION AND SOCIAL CHANGE

KEY TERMS

philosophes

Voltaire

Adam Smith

Jean-Jacques Rousseau

salons

enlightened despotism

Frederick the Great

Maria Theresa

Catherine the Great

Seven Years' War

slave trade

agricultural revolution

putting-out system

Online Study Center

This icon will direct you to interactive map and primary source activities on the website **college.hmco.com/ pic/noble5e**

growth, which in turn stimulated industry and trade. As the century closed, Europe was on the threshold of truly revolutionary changes in politics and production that had their roots in the intellectual, economic, and social ferment of eighteenth-century life.

FOCUS QUESTIONS

What were the most important notions in Enlightenment thought, and what were some of the intellectual, social, and political conditions that favored its development?

To what extent did the activities of "enlightened despots" reflect Enlightenment precepts, and to what extent did they reflect traditional concerns of state power?

How did warfare itself, and the causes of war, change in the eighteenth century?

How was European agriculture transformed in this era, and what further transformations did it bring in its wake?

THE ENLIGHTENMENT

What were the most important notions in Enlightenment thought, and what were some of the intellectual, social, and political conditions that favored its development?

The Enlightenment was an intellectual movement that applied to political and social thought the confidence in the intelligibility of natural law that Newton and other scientists had recently achieved. Following Descartes and Locke, Enlightenment thinkers believed that human beings could discern and work in concert with the laws of nature for the betterment of human life. Perhaps the most significant effect of this confidence was the questioning of traditional social and political bonds. A belief grew that society must be grounded on rational foundations to be determined by humans, not arbitrary foundations determined by tradition and justified by religious authority.

The Enlightenment was simultaneously a social and cultural movement: Enlightenment thought was debated in increasingly widespread publications, such as newspapers. There were new opportunities for exchanging views in literary societies, salons, and cafés. These new means of sharing information shaped the potential radicalism of the Enlightenment by helping to ensure that informed public opinion would become a new force in political and cultural life. Given this broad base, Enlightenment thinking was certain to challenge the very foundations of social and political order.

VOLTAIRE: THE QUINTESSENTIAL PHILOSOPHE

A wide range of thinkers participated in the Enlightenment. In France they were known as **philosophes** (fee-low-ZOHFS), a term meaning not a formal philosopher but rather a thinker and critic. The most famous of the philosophes was **Voltaire** (1694–1778). A prolific writer, critic, and reformer, Voltaire was lionized by admirers throughout Europe, including several rulers. Born François-Marie Arouet to a middle-class family, he took the pen name Voltaire in 1718, after one of his early plays was a critical success. Like many philosophes, Voltaire moved in courtly circles but was often on its margins. His mockery of the regent for the young French king earned him a year's imprisonment in 1717, and an exchange of insults with a leading courtier some years later led to enforced exile in Great Britain for two years.

After returning from Britain, Voltaire published his first major philosophical work. *Lettres philosophiques*

philosophes   French term referring to thinkers and critics of the Enlightenment era, including Voltaire and Rousseau.

Voltaire   French writer, critic, and reformer who embodied the spirit of eighteenth-century rationalism: its confidence, its increasingly practical bent, its wit and sophistication.

(*Philosophical Letters*, 1734) revealed the influence of his British sojourn and helped to popularize Newton's achievement. To confidence in the laws governing nature Voltaire added cautious confidence in humans' attempts to discern truth. From Locke's work (see page 494) he was persuaded to trust human educability tempered by awareness of the finite nature of the human mind. These elements gave Voltaire's philosophy both its passionate conviction and its sensible practicality.

Voltaire portrayed Great Britain as a more rational society than France. He was particularly impressed with the relative religious and intellectual toleration evident across the Channel. The British government had a more workable set of institutions; the economy was less crippled by the remnants of feudal privilege, and education was not in the hands of the church. Voltaire was one of many French thinkers who singled out the Catholic Church as the archenemy of progressive thought. Philosophes constantly collided with the church's negative views of human nature and resented its control over most education and its still strong sway in political life. Typical of Voltaire's castigation of the church is his stinging satire of the clerics who condemned Galileo: "I desire that there be engraved on the door of your holy office: Here seven cardinals assisted by minor brethren had the master of thought of Italy thrown into prison at the age of seventy, made him fast on bread and water, because he instructed the human race."

After the publication of his audacious *Letters*, Voltaire was again forced into exile from Paris, and he resided for some years in the country home of a woman with whom he shared a remarkable intellectual and emotional relationship: Emilie, marquise du Châtelet (shot-uh-LAY) (1706–1749). Châtelet was a mathematician and a scientist. She prepared a French translation of Newton's *Principia* while Voltaire worked on his own various writings, which included a commentary on Newton's work. Because of Châtelet's tutelage, Voltaire became more knowledgeable about the sciences and more serious in his efforts to apply scientific rationality to human affairs. He was devastated by her sudden death in 1749.

Shortly afterward he accepted the invitation of the king of Prussia, Frederick II, to visit Berlin. His stay was stormy and brief because of disagreements with other court philosophers. He resided for a time in Geneva, until his criticisms of the city's moral codes forced yet another exile on him. He spent most of the last twenty years of his life at his estates on the Franco-Swiss border, where he could be relatively free from interference by any government. These were productive years. He produced his best-known satirical novelette, *Candide*, in 1758. It criticized aristocratic privilege and the power of clerics as well as the naiveté of philosophers who

took "natural law" to mean that the world was already operating as it should.

Voltaire believed that only by struggle are the accumulated habits of centuries overturned. This belief led to his political activities. He became involved in several celebrated legal cases in which individuals were pitted against the authority of the church, which was still backed by the authority of the state. In pursuit of justice in these cases and in relentless criticism of the church, Voltaire added a stream of straightforward political pamphlets to his literary output. He also worked closer to home, initiating agricultural reform on his estates and working to improve the status of peasants in the vicinity.

Voltaire died in Paris in May 1778, after a triumphal welcome for the staging of one of his plays. By then he was no longer leader of the Enlightenment in strictly intellectual terms. Thinkers and writers more radical than Voltaire had become prominent during his long life and had dismissed some of his beliefs, such as the notion that a monarch could introduce reform. But Voltaire had provided a crucial stimulus to French thought with his *Philosophical Letters*. His importance lies also in his embodiment of the critical spirit of eighteenth-century rationalism: its confidence, its increasingly practical bent,

1715–1774	Reign of Louis XV in France
1722–1742	Walpole first British "prime minister"
1734	Voltaire, *Philosophical Letters*
1740–1748	War of the Austrian Succession
1740–1780	Reign of Maria Theresa of Austria
1740–1786	Reign of Frederick the Great of Prussia
1746	Battle of Culloden
1748	Montesquieu, *The Spirit of the Laws* Hume, *Essay Concerning Human Understanding*
1751–1765	Diderot, *Encyclopedia*
1756–1763	Seven Years' War
1758	Voltaire, *Candide*
1762	Rousseau, *The Social Contract*
1762–1796	Reign of Catherine the Great of Russia
1772	First partition of Poland
1776	Smith, *The Wealth of Nations*
1780–1790	Reign of Joseph II of Austria
1792	Wollstonecraft, *A Vindication of the Rights of Woman*

its wit and sophistication. Until the end of his life, Voltaire remained a bridge between the increasingly diverse body of Enlightenment thought and the literate elite audience.

THE VARIETY OF ENLIGHTENMENT THOUGHT

Differences among philosophes grew as the century progressed. In the matter of religion, for example, there was virtual unanimity of opposition to the Catholic Church among French thinkers, but no unanimity about God. Voltaire was a theist—believing firmly in God, creator of the universe, but not a specifically Christian God. To some later thinkers, God was irrelevant—the creator of the world, but a world that ran continuously according to established laws. Some philosophes were atheists, arguing that a universe operating according to discoverable laws needs no higher purpose and no divine presence to explain, run, or justify its existence. In Protestant areas of Europe, in contrast to France, Enlightenment thought was often less hostile to Christianity.

Montesquieu Questions about social and political order, as well as about human rationality, also were pondered. Charles de Secondat (1689–1755), baron of Montesquieu (mawn-tess-KYUH), a French judge and legal philosopher, combined the belief that human institutions must be rational with Locke's assumption of human educability. Montesquieu's treatise *De L'Esprit des lois* (*The Spirit of the Laws,* 1748) was published in twenty-two printings within two years. In it Montesquieu maintained that laws were not meant to be ar-

Voltaire Visits Frederick the Great of Prussia
Voltaire leans forward, at left, to discuss a point of philosophy with Frederick. Skill at witty conversation enabled philosophes such as Voltaire to advance fundamental criticisms of society even to elite audiences. *(Bildarchiv Preussischer Kulturbesitz/Art Resource, NY)*

bitrary rules but derived naturally from human society: the more evolved a society was, the more liberal were its laws. This notion that progress is possible within society and government deflated Europeans' pretensions with regard to other societies, for a variety of laws could be equally "rational" given different conditions. Montesquieu is perhaps best known to Americans as the advocate of the separation of legislative, executive, and judicial powers that later became enshrined in the U.S. Constitution. To Montesquieu this scheme seemed to parallel in human government the balance of forces observable in nature; moreover, the arrangement seemed best to guarantee liberty.

Adam Smith and David Hume   Enlightenment philosophers also investigated the "laws" of economic life. In France economic thinkers known as *physiocrats* proposed ending "artificial" control over land use in order to free productive capacity and permit the flow of produce to market. Their target was traditional forms of land tenure, including collective control of village lands by peasants and seigneurial rights over land and labor by landlords. The freeing of restrictions on agriculture, manufacture, and trade was proposed by the Scotsman **Adam Smith** in his treatise *An Inquiry into the Nature and Causes of the Wealth of Nations* (1776).

Smith (1723–1790), a professor at the University of Glasgow, is best known in modern times as the originator of "laissez-faire" economics. *Laissez faire,* or "let it run on its own," assumes that an economy will regulate itself, without interference by government and, of more concern to Smith, without the monopolies and other economic privileges common in his day. Smith's schema for economic growth was not merely a rigid application of natural law to economics. His ideas grew out of an optimistic view of human nature and rationality that was heavily indebted to Locke. Humans, Smith believed, have drives and passions that they can direct and govern by means of reason and inherent mutual sympathy. Thus, Smith suggested, in seeking their own achievement and well-being, people are often "led by an invisible hand" simultaneously to benefit society as a whole.

Throughout the century, philosophers of various stripes disagreed about the nature and the limits of human reason. Smith's countryman and friend David Hume (1711–1776) was perhaps the most radical in his critique of the human capacity for knowing. He was the archskeptic, taking Locke's view of the limitations on pure reason to the point of doubting the efficacy of any sensory data. His major exposition of these views, *Essay Concerning Human Understanding* (1748), led to important innovations later in the century in the work of the

German philosopher Immanuel Kant. At the time, though, Hume's arguments were almost contrary to the prevailing spirit that embraced empirical knowledge. Hume himself separated this work from his other efforts in moral, political, and economic philosophy, which were more in tune with contemporary views.

The Encyclopedia   Mainstream confidence in empirical knowledge and in the intelligibility of the world is evident in the production of the *Encyclopédie* (*Encyclopedia*). This seventeen-volume compendium of knowledge, criticism, and philosophy was assembled by leading philosophes in France and published there between 1751 and 1765. The volumes were designed to contain state-of-the-art knowledge about arts, sciences, technology, and philosophy. The guiding philosophy of the project, set forth by its chief editor, Denis Diderot (DEED-uh-row) (1713–1784), was a belief in the advancement of human happiness through the advancement of knowledge. The *Encyclopedia* was a history of the march of knowledge as well as a compendium of known achievements. It was revolutionary in that it not only intrigued and inspired intellectuals but also assisted thousands of government officials and professionals.

The encyclopedia project illustrates the political context of Enlightenment thought as well as its philosophical premises. The Catholic Church placed the work on the *Index of Prohibited Books,* and the French government might have barred its publication but for the fact that the official who would have made the decision was himself drawn to Enlightenment thinking. Many other officials, however, worked to suppress it. By the late 1750s, losses in wars overseas had made French officials highly sensitive to political challenges of any kind. Thus, like Voltaire, the major contributors to the *Encyclopedia* were admired by certain segments of the elite and persecuted by others in their official functions.

Gender Inequalities   The *Encyclopedia* reflects the complexities and limitations of Enlightenment thought on another score—the position of women. One might expect that the Enlightenment penchant for challenging received knowledge and traditional hierarchies would lead to arguments for the essential equality of women with men and thus for extending women's rights. Indeed, some contributors blamed women's inequality with men not on inherent gender differences but rather on the customs and laws that had kept women from education and the development of their abilities. However, other contributors blamed women, and not society, for their plight, or they argued that women had talents that fit them only for the domestic sphere.

Both positions were represented in Enlightenment thought as a whole. The assumption of the natural

Adam Smith   Scottish economist who developed the doctrine of "laissez faire" in his treatise *The Wealth of Nations* (1776).

ROUSSEAU DISCUSSES THE BENEFITS OF SUBMITTING TO THE GENERAL WILL

In this excerpt from his Social Contract, *Rousseau describes the relationship of individuals to the general will. Notice the wider-ranging benefits Rousseau believes men will enjoy in society as he envisions it. Rousseau is clearly interested in intellectual, moral, and emotional well-being.*

I assume that men reach a point where the obstacles to their preservation in a state of nature prove greater than the strength that each man has to preserve himself in that state. Beyond this point, the primitive condition cannot endure, for then the human race will perish if it does not change its mode of existence. . . .

"How to find a form of association which will defend the person and goods of each member with the collective force of all, and under which each individual, while uniting himself with the others, obeys no one but himself, and remains as free as before." This is the fundamental problem to which the social contract holds the solution. . . .

The passing from the state of nature to the civil society produces a remarkable change in man; it puts justice as a rule of conduct in the place of instinct, and gives his actions the moral quality they previously lacked. . . . And although in civil society man surrenders some of the advantages that belong to the state of nature, he gains in return far greater ones; his faculties are so exercised and developed, his mind is so enlarged, his sentiments so ennobled, and his whole spirit so elevated that . . . he should constantly bless the happy hour that lifted him for ever from the state of nature and from a stupid, limited animal made a creature of intelligence and a man. . . .

For every individual as a man may have a private will contrary to, or different from, the general will

that he has as a citizen. His private interest may speak with a very different voice from that of the public interest; his absolute and naturally independent existence may make him regard what he owes to the common cause as a gratuitous contribution, the loss of which would be less painful for others than the payment is onerous for him; and fancying that the artificial person which constitutes the state is a mere fictitious entity (since it is not a man), he might seek to enjoy the rights of a citizen without doing the duties of a subject. The growth of this kind of injustice would bring about the ruin of the body politic.

Hence, in order that the social pact shall not be an empty formula, it is tacitly implied in that commitment—which alone can give force to all others—that whoever refuses to obey the general will shall be constrained to do so by the whole body, which means nothing other than that he shall be forced to be free; for this is the necessary condition which, by giving each citizen to the nation, secures him against all personal dependence, it is the condition which shapes both the design and the working of the political machine, and which alone bestows justice on civil contracts—without it, such contracts would be absurd, tyrannical and liable to the grossest abuse.

QUESTIONS

1. What benefits will citizens find in society as Rousseau envisions it?
2. In what ways is Rousseau concerned with freedom?

Source: Jean-Jacques Rousseau, *The Social Contract*, translated by Maurice Cranston. Reprinted by permission of PFD on behalf of The Estate of Maurice Cranston. Copyright © 1968 by Maurice Cranston.

---

equality of all people provided a powerful ground for arguing the equality of women with men. Some thinkers, such as Mary Astell (1666–1731), challenged Locke's separation of family life from the public world of free, contractual relationships. "If absolute authority be not necessary in a state," she reasoned, "how comes it to be so in a family?" Most such thinkers advocated increased education for women, if only to make them more fit to raise enlightened children. By 1800 the most radical thinkers were advocating full citizenship rights for women and equal rights to property, along with enhanced education.

The best-known proponent of those views was an Englishwoman, Mary Wollstonecraft (1759–1797), who wrote *A Vindication of the Rights of Woman* (1792). She assumed that most elite women would devote themselves to domestic duties, but she argued that without the responsibilities of citizenship, the leavening of education, and economic independence, women could be neither fully formed individuals nor worthy of their duties. "[F]or how can a being be generous who has nothing of its own? Or virtuous, who is not free?" she asked.[1] Working women, she concluded, needed political and economic rights simply to survive.

Rousseau   A more limited view of women's capacities was one element in the influential writings of **Jean-Jacques Rousseau** (1712–1778). Like Locke, Rousseau (roo-SO) could conceive of the free individual only as male, and he grounded both his scorn of the old order and his novel political ideas in an arbitrary division of gender roles. Rousseau's view of women was linked to a critique of the artificiality of elite, cosmopolitan society in which Enlightenment thought was then flourishing, and in which aristocratic women were fully involved. Rousseau believed in the educability of men but was as concerned with issues of character and emotional life as with cognitive knowledge. Society—particularly the artificial courtly society—was corrupting, he believed. The true citizen had to cultivate virtue and sensibility, not manners, taste, or refinement. Rousseau designated women as guarantors of the "natural" virtues of children and as nurturers of the emotional life and character of men—but not as fully formed beings in their own right.

Rousseau's emphasis on the education and virtue of citizens was the underpinning of his larger political vision, set forth in *Du Contrat social* (*The Social Contract*, 1762). He imagined an egalitarian republic—possible particularly in small states such as his native Geneva—in which men would consent to be governed because the government would determine and act in accordance with the "general will" of the citizens. The "general will" was not majority opinion but rather what each citizen *would* want if he were fully informed and were acting in accordance with his highest nature. The "general will" became apparent whenever the citizens met as a body and made collective decisions, and it could be imposed on all inhabitants. (See the box "The Written Record: Rousseau Discusses the Benefits of Submitting to the General Will.") This was a breathtaking vision of direct democracy—but one with ominous possibilities, for Rousseau rejected the institutional checks on state authority proposed by Locke and Montesquieu.

Rousseau's emphasis on private emotional life anticipated the romanticism of the early nineteenth century. It also reflected Rousseau's own experience as the son of a humble family, always sensing himself an outcast in the sophisticated world of Parisian salons. He had a love-hate relationship with this life, remaining attached to several aristocratic women patrons even as he criticized their influence. His own personal life did not match his prescriptions for others. He completely neglected to give his four children the nurture and education that he argued were vital; indeed, he abandoned them all to a foundling home. He was nevertheless influential as a critic of an elite society still dominated by status, patronage, and privilege. Rousseau's work reflects to an extreme degree the tensions in Enlightenment thought generally: it was part of elite culture as well as its principal critic.

THE GROWTH OF PUBLIC OPINION

It is impossible to appreciate the significance of the Enlightenment without understanding the degree to which it was a part of public life. Most of the philosophes came from modest backgrounds. They influenced the privileged elite of their day because of the social and political environment in which their ideas were elaborated. Indeed, the clearest distinguishing feature of the Enlightenment may be the creation of an informed body of public opinion that stood apart from court society.

The Reading Public   Increased literacy and access to books and other printed materials are an important part of the story. Perhaps more important, the kinds of reading that people favored began to change. We know from inventories made of people's belongings at the time of their deaths (required for inheritance laws) that books in the homes of ordinary people were no longer just traditional works such as devotional literature. Ordinary people now read secular and contemporary philosophical works. As the availability of such works increased, reading itself evolved from a reverential encounter with old ideas to a critical encounter with new ideas. Solitary reading for reflection and pleasure became more widespread.

New kinds of reading material were available. Regularly published periodicals in Great Britain, France, and Italy served as important means for the spread of enlightened opinion in the form of reviews, essays, and published correspondence. Some of these journals had been in existence since the second half of the seventeenth century, when they had begun as a means to circulate the new scientific work. Now subscribers included Americans anxious to keep up with intellectual life in Europe. In addition to newsletters and journals, newspapers, which were regularly published even in small cities throughout western and central Europe, circulated ideas. Newspapers were uniquely responsive to their readers. They began to carry advertisements, which both produced revenue for papers and widened readers' exposure to their own communities. Even more important was the inauguration of letters to the editor. Newspapers thus became venues for the often rapid exchange of news and opinions.

Habits of reading and responding to written material changed not only because of this increased and changing reading matter but also because of changes in

Jean-Jacques Rousseau   French philosophe who imagined an egalitarian society governed by the "general will" in *The Social Contract* and was a sharp critic of aristocratic society.

The Growth of the Book Trade

Book ownership dramatically increased in the eighteenth century, and a wide range of secular works—from racy novelettes to philosophical tracts—was available in print. In this rendering of a bookshop, shipments of books have arrived from around Europe. Notice the artist's optimism in the great variety of persons, from the peasant with a scythe to a white-robed cleric, who are drawn to the shop by "Minerva" (the Roman goddess of wisdom). *(Musée des Beaux-Arts de Dijon)*

the social environment. In the eighteenth century, forerunners of the modern lending libraries made their debut. In Paris, for a fee, one could join a *salle de lecture* (sahl-duh-lek-TOOR) (literally, a "reading room") where the latest works were available to any member. Booksellers, whose numbers increased dramatically, found ways to meet readers' demands for inexpensive access to reading matter. One might pay for the right to read a book in the bookshop itself. Newspapers were available in such shops and in cafés. In short, new sites encouraged people to see themselves not just as readers but as members of a reading public.

The Salons Among the most famous and most important of these venues were the Parisian **salons,** regular gatherings in private homes, where Voltaire and others read their works in progress aloud and discussed them. Several Parisian women—mostly wealthy, but of modest social status—invited courtiers, bureaucrats, and intellectuals to meet in their homes at regular times each week. The *salonnières* (sal-on-YAIR) (salon leaders) themselves read widely in order to facilitate the exchange of ideas among their guests. This mediating function was crucial to the success of the salons. Manners and polite conversation had been a defining feature of aristocratic life since the seventeenth century, but they had largely been means of displaying status and safeguarding honor. The leadership of the salonnières and the protected environment they provided away from court life enabled a further evolution of "polite society" to occur: anyone with appropriate manners could participate in conversation as an equal. The assumption of equality in turn enabled conversation to turn away from maintaining the status quo to questioning it.

salons   Regular gatherings in eighteenth-century Parisian private homes, where Voltaire and other philosophes read and discussed their works; the exchange of ideas was facilitated by female *salonnières* (salon leaders).

The influence of salons was extended by the wide correspondence networks the salonnières maintained. Perhaps the most famous salonnière in her day, Marie-Thérèse Geoffrin (zhoh-FRAN) (1699–1777) corresponded with Catherine the Great, the reform-minded empress of Russia, as well as with philosophes outside Paris and with interested would-be members of her circle. The ambassador of Naples regularly attended her salon while in Paris and exchanged weekly letters with her when home in Italy. He reflected on the importance of salon leaders such as Geoffrin when he wrote from Naples lamenting, "[Our gatherings here] are getting farther away from the character and tone of those of France, despite all [our] efforts. . . . There is no way to make Naples resemble Paris unless we find a woman to guide us, organize us, *Geoffrinise* us."[2]

Various clubs, local academies, and learned and secret societies, such as Masonic lodges, copied some features of the salons of Paris. Hardly any municipality was without a private society that functioned both as a forum for political and philosophical discussion and as an elite social club. Here mingled doctors, lawyers, local officials—some of whom enjoyed the fruits of the political system in offices and patronage. In Scotland universities were flourishing centers of Enlightenment thought, but political clubs in Glasgow and Edinburgh enriched debate and the development of ideas.

Ideas circulated beyond the membership of the multitude of clubs, in turn, by means of print. Newsletters reporting the goings-on at salons in Paris were produced by some participants. The exchange and spread of Enlightenment ideas, regardless of the method used, encouraged a type of far-reaching political debate that had never before existed, except possibly in seventeenth-century England. The greatest impact of the Enlightenment, particularly in France, was not the creation of any specific program for political or social change. Rather its supreme legacy was an informed body of public opinion that could generate change.

ART IN THE AGE OF REASON

The Enlightenment reverberated throughout all aspects of cultural life. Just as the market for books and the reading public expanded, so did the audience for works of art in the growing leisured urban circles of Paris and other great cities. The modern cultured public—a public of concertgoers and art gallery enthusiasts—began to make its first appearance and constituted another arena in which public opinion was shaped. The brilliant and sophisticated courts around Europe continued to sponsor composers, musicians, and painters by providing both patronage and audiences. Yet some performances of concerts and operas began to take place in theaters and halls outside the courts in venues more accessible to the public.

Beginning in 1737 one section of the Louvre (LOO-vruh) palace in Paris was devoted annually to public exhibitions of painting and sculpture (though by royally sponsored and approved artists). In both France and Britain, public discussion of art began to take place in published reviews and criticisms: the role of art critic was born. Works of art were also sold by public means, such as auctions. As works became more available, demand grew and production increased.

In subject matter and style these various art forms exhibited greater variety than works in preceding centuries had shown. We can nevertheless discern certain patterns and tendencies in both the content and the form of eighteenth-century European art. Late baroque painters contributed to an exploration of private life and emotion sometimes called the "cult of sensibility." Frequently they depicted private scenes of upper-class life, especially moments of intimate conversation or flirtation.

The cult of sensibility was fostered by literature as well. The private life of emotion was nurtured by increased literacy, greater access to books, and the need to retreat from the elaborate artifice of court life. The novel became an increasingly important genre as a means of exploring social problems and human relationships. In English literature the novels of Samuel Richardson (1689–1761)—*Pamela* (1740) and *Clarissa* (1747–1748)—explored personal psychology and passion. Other novelists, such as Daniel Defoe in *Robinson Crusoe* (1717), used realism for purposes of social commentary.

Rousseau followed Richardson's lead in structuring his own novels, *La Nouvelle Héloïse* (1761) and *Emile* (1762). The cult of sensibility was not mere entertainment; it also carried the political and philosophical message that honest emotion was a "natural" virtue and that courtly manners, by contrast, were irrational and degrading. The enormous popularity of Rousseau's novels, for example, came from the fact that their intense emotional appeal was simultaneously felt to be uplifting.

A revival of classical subjects and styles after the middle of the century evoked what were thought to be the pure and timeless values of classical heroes. This revival revealed the influence of Enlightenment thought because the artists assumed the educability of their audience by means of example. Classical revival architecture illustrated a belief in order, symmetry, and proportion. Americans are familiar with its evocations because it has been the architecture of their republic, but even churches were built in this style in eighteenth-century Europe. The classical movement in music reflected both the cult of sensibility and the classicizing

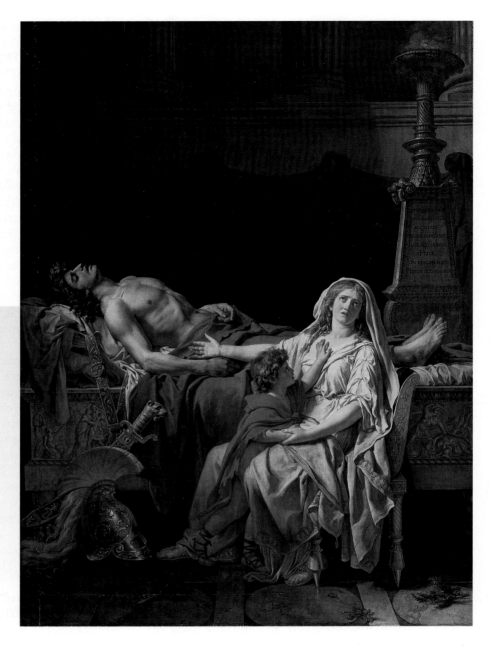

The Moralizing Message of Neoclassical Art

The French painter Jacques-Louis David portrays the mourning of the Trojan hero Hector by his wife, Andromache. This kind of art tried to depict and encourage virtuous feelings. David was well known for depicting his subjects with simple gestures—such as the extended arm of Andromache here—that were intended to portray sincere emotion.

(Private Collection/The Stapleton Collection/ Bridgeman Art Library International)

styles in the visual arts. Embodied in the works of Austrians Franz Josef Haydn (1732–1809) and Wolfgang Amadeus Mozart (1756–1791), this movement saw the clarification of musical structures, such as the modern sonata and symphony, and enabled melody to take center stage.

Another trend in art and literature was a fascination with nature and with the seemingly "natural" in human culture—less "developed" or more historically distant societies. One of the most popular printed works in the middle of the century was the alleged translation of the poems of Ossian (AHSH-un), a third-century Scots Highland poet. Early English, German, Norse, and other folktales were also "discovered" (in some cases invented) and published, some in several editions during the century. Folk life, other cultures, and untamed nature itself thus began to be celebrated at the very time they were being more definitively conquered. (See the feature "The Visual Record: Gardens.") Ossian, for example, was celebrated just as the Scottish Highlands were being punished and pacified by the English after the clans' support for a rival claimant to the English throne. Once purged of any threat, the exotic image of another culture (even the folk culture of one's own society) could be a spur to the imagination. Thus the remote became romantic, offering a sense of distance from which to measure one's own sophistication and superiority.

═══════════ S E C T I O N   S U M M A R Y ═══════════

- The "Enlightenment" was an intellectual movement that brought confidence in human reason and the workings of natural law from the sciences into political and social thought.

- A wide range of thinkers, known as philosophes, contributed to Enlightenment thought; opinions about religion, the limits of human reason, the equality of the sexes, and other issues were energetically debated.

- Enlightenment ideas were spread by publications such as newspapers and were discussed in cafés and salons; an informed body of public opinion independent of government and the court was created for the first time.

- Art became more accessible to the public; works of art became more thematically varied than before, though many explored "natural" emotion.

EUROPEAN STATES IN THE AGE OF ENLIGHTENMENT

To what extent did the activities of "enlightened despots" reflect Enlightenment precepts, and to what extent did they reflect traditional concerns of state power?

Mindful of the lessons to be learned from the civil war in England and eager to repeat the achievements of Louis XIV, European rulers in the eighteenth century continued their efforts to govern with greater effectiveness. Some, like the rulers of Prussia and Russia, were encouraged in their efforts by Enlightenment ideas that stressed the need for reforms in law, economy, and government. Like Voltaire, they believed that monarchs could be agents for change. In Austria significant reforms, including the abolition of serfdom, were enacted. The changes were uneven, however, and at times owed as much to traditional efforts at better government as to "enlightened" opinion.

In all cases, rulers' efforts to govern more effectively meant continual readjustments in relationships with traditional elites. Whether or not elites had formal roles in the governing process by means of established institutions such as the English Parliament, royal governments everywhere depended on their participation. However limited their "enlightened" policies, monarchs were changing their views of themselves and their public images from self-aggrandizing absolutist to diligent servant of the state. In this way, monarchs actually undermined their dynastic claims to rule by re-founding their regimes on a utilitarian basis. The state was increasingly seen as separate from the ruler, with dramatic consequences for the future.

FRANCE DURING THE ENLIGHTENMENT

It is one of the seeming paradoxes of the era of the Enlightenment that critical thought about society and politics flourished in France, an autocratic state. Yet France was blessed with a well-educated elite, a tradi-

tion of scientific inquiry, and a legacy of cultured court life that, since the early days of Louis XIV, had become the model for all Europe (see pages 495–498). French was the international intellectual language, and France was the most fertile center of cultural life. Both Adam Smith and David Hume, for example, spent portions of their careers in Paris and were welcomed into Parisian salons. In fact, the French capital was an environment that encouraged debate and dissent precisely because of the juxtaposition of the vibrant new intellectual climate with the institutional rigidities of its political system. In France access to power was wholly through patronage and privilege, a system that excluded many talented and productive members of the elite.

The French state continued to embody fundamental contradictions. As under Louis XIV, the Crown sponsored scientific research, subsidized commerce and exploration, and tried to rationalize the royal administration. Royal administrators tried to chip away at the privileges, accrued since the Middle Ages, that hampered effective government—such as the exemption most nobles enjoyed from taxation. However, the Crown also continued to claim the right to govern autocratically, and the king was supported both ideologically and institutionally by the Catholic Church. A merchant in the bustling port of Bordeaux might be glad of the royal navy's protection of the colonies, and of the Crown's efforts to build better roads for trade within France. However, with his fellow Masons, he would fume when church officials publicly burned the works of Rousseau and be continually frustrated over his exclusion from any formal role in the political process.

The problems facing the French government were made worse by two circumstances: first, the strength of

Gardens

What is a garden? Like most of the art forms that we see habitually, the garden is difficult to analyze or even to think of as an art form. Like the buildings they surround, however, gardens have much to tell us about human habits and values. Let us examine these eighteenth-century gardens for evidence of contemporaries' attitudes toward nature and their relationship with it.

Look at the two English-style gardens illustrated here. The first is next to the Governor's Mansion in Williamsburg, the capital of the English colony of Virginia. Construction of this garden began at the end of the seventeenth century; the photograph shows the restored gardens that tourists may visit today. The second garden, from the private estate of West Wycombe in England, looks very different—much more like a natural landscape. The engraving reproduced here dates from the 1770s. The two gardens represent distinct epochs in the development of the garden, hence the differences between them. However, each of these gardens in its own way celebrates human domination of nature.

This symbolic domination of nature is more obvious to us in the Williamsburg garden. The lawns and hedges are trimmed in precise geometrical shapes and are laid out, with the walkways, in straight lines. This "palace garden" was a small English variant of the classical garden developed in France—most spectacularly at the Versailles Palace—and then imitated throughout Europe during the seventeenth century. The garden at Versailles is so vast that at many points, all of nature visible to the eye is nature disciplined by humans.

We can think of such gardens as pieces of architecture, because that is how they were originally conceived. The design originated in the enclosed courtyard gardens of the homes of classical antiquity. The straight lines and square shapes of these gardens mimic the buildings they are attached to. In fact, these seventeenth- and eighteenth-century gardens were usually laid out as an extension of the buildings themselves. Notice the wide staircase that descends from the central axis of the Governor's Mansion into the central walkway of the garden. Other architectural details, such as the benches positioned at the ends of various walkways, add to the sense of

the garden as an exterior room. The garden symbolizes the taming of nature into a pleasing vision of order and regularity.

However, the later eighteenth-century garden represents even greater confidence in the human relationship with nature, although it does not appear to do so at first glance. The extensive garden at first seems to be nature itself plus a few added details, such as the statuary, and a few improvements, such as the grass kept trim by the workers in the foreground. Our familiarity with such landscapes—in our own suburban yards—keeps us from immediately perceiving how contrived such a landscape is. Nature, however, does not intersperse dense stands of trees or clumps of shrubbery with green expanses of lawns. Nor does nature conveniently leave portions of a hillside bare of trees to provide a view of the water from a palatial house on the hill (to the left). Note also that the waterfall cascading over rocks and statuary flows from an artificial lake, neatly bordered by a path.

This kind of garden reflects Enlightenment optimism about humans' ability to understand and work with nature. Such gardens were asymmetrical: Paths were usually curved, and lakes and ponds were irregularly shaped, as they would be in nature. Trees and shrubs were allowed to maintain their natural form. Nevertheless, this landscaping conveys a powerful message of confidence and order. Humans cannot bend or distort nature to their own ends, but they can live in harmony with it as they manage it and enjoy its beneficence. People were freed from regarding nature as hostile and needing to be fought. In this garden, one lives with nature but improves on it. The workers cutting the grass do not detract from the engraving but rather make the scene more compelling.

This brand of landscape gardening appeared in the English colonies across the Atlantic by the end of the eighteenth century. One of the best examples is at Monticello, Thomas Jefferson's Virginia estate, first designed in the 1770s and constructed and improved over the remainder of Jefferson's life (1743–1826). If you tour Monticello, you will notice a curving garden path bordered by flowers in season, with mature trees scattered here and there. Jefferson planned every inch of this largely random-looking outdoor space,

Governor's Mansion and Formal Gardens at Williamsburg, Virginia
(© Robert Llewellyn)

Landscape Garden at West Wycombe, England *(Courtesy of the Trustees of the British Museum)*

just as he planned the regimented fruit and vegetable garden that borders it. The older, classical style of the Williamsburg garden is partly explained by its earlier date and also because this more aggressively controlling style lasted longer in the American colonies than in Europe, perhaps because "nature" seemed more wild and more formidable in the New World.

QUESTIONS

1. How do the two gardens depicted here reflect two different visions of human power over nature?
2. What explains the evolution of styles, over the eighteenth century, in this art form?

Online Study Center
Improve Your Grade Visual Record Activities

the privileged elites' defense of their privileges, and second, mounting government debt from foreign wars. Fiscal reform was increasingly urgent, yet entrenched elites stood in the way of change. Louis XIV was followed on the throne by his 5-year-old great-grandson, Louis XV (r. 1715–1774). During the regency early in his reign, the supreme law courts, the parlements, reclaimed the right of remonstrance—that is, the right to object to royal edicts and thus to exercise some control over the enactment of law. Throughout Louis XV's reign, his administration often locked horns with the parlements, particularly as royal ministers tried various schemes to cope with financial crises.

The power of the parlements came not only from their routine role in government but also from the fact that parlementaires were all legally noble and owned their offices just as a great nobleman owned his country estate. In addition, the parlements were the only institutions that could legitimately check royal power. As such, the parlements were often supported in their opposition to royal policies by the weight of public opinion. On the one hand, enlightened opinion believed in the rationality of doing away with privileges such as the ownership of offices. On the other hand, the role of consultative bodies and the separation of powers touted by Montesquieu, himself a parlementaire, were much prized. And even our Bordeaux merchant, who had little in common with privileged officeholders, might nevertheless see the parlementaires' resistance as his best protection from royal tyranny. The parlementaires, however, usually used their power for protecting the status quo.

Further hampering reform efforts was the character of the king himself. Louis XV displayed none of the kingly qualities of his great-grandfather. He was neither pleasant nor affable, and he was lazy. By the end of his reign, he was roundly despised. He did not give the "rationality" of royal government a good name. By the late 1760s the weight of government debt from foreign wars finally forced the king into action. He threw his support behind the reforming schemes of his chancellor, Nicolas de Maupeou (mo-POO), who dissolved the parlements early in 1771 and created new law courts whose judges would not enjoy independent power.

The Crown lost control of reform when Louis died soon after, in 1774. His 20-year-old grandson, Louis XVI, well-meaning but insecure, allowed the complete restoration of the parlements. Further reform efforts, sponsored by the king and several talented ministers, came to nothing because of parlementary opposition. Not surprisingly, from about the middle of the century, there had been calls to revive the Estates General, the representative assembly last convened in 1614, as well as for the establishment of new councils such as provincial representative assemblies. By the time an Estates General was finally called in the wake of further financial problems in 1788, the enlightened elites' habit of carrying on political analysis and criticism outside the actual corridors of power, as well as their accumulated mistrust of the Crown, had created a volatile situation.

MONARCHY AND CONSTITUTIONAL GOVERNMENT IN GREAT BRITAIN

After the deaths of William (d. 1702) and Mary (d. 1694), the British crown passed to Mary's sister, Anne (r. 1702–1714), and then to a collateral line descended from Elizabeth Stuart (d. 1662), sister of the beheaded Charles I. Elizabeth had married Frederick, elector of the Palatinate (and had reigned with him briefly in Bohemia at the outset of the Thirty Years' War; see page 471), and her descendants were Germans, now electors of Hanover. The new British sovereign in 1714, George I (r. 1714–1727), was both a foreigner and a man of mediocre abilities. Moreover, his claim to the throne was immediately contested by Catholic descendants of James II (see page 504), who attempted to depose him in 1715 and later his son, George II (r. 1727–1760), in 1745.

The 1745 Invasion The 1745 attempt to depose the Hanoverian kings was more nearly successful. The son of the Stuart claimant (called the "pretender") to the throne, Charles (known in legend as Bonnie Prince Charlie), landed on the west coast of Scotland, with French assistance. He led his forces south into England. Most of the British army and George II himself were on the Continent, fighting in the War of the Austrian Succession (see page 572). Scotland had been formally united with England in 1707 (hence the term *Great Britain* after that time), and Charles had found some support among Scots dissatisfied with the economic and political results of that union.

But the vast majority of Britons, Scottish or English, did not want the civil war that Charles's challenge inevitably meant, especially on behalf of a Catholic pretender who relied on support from Britain's great rival, France. Charles's army, made up mostly of poor Highland clansmen, was destroyed at the Battle of Culloden (cull-UH-dun) in April 1746 by British army units hastily returned from abroad. Charles fled back to France, and the British government used the failed uprising as justification for the brutal and forceful integration of the still-remote Scottish Highlands into the British state.

Traditional practices, from wearing tartans to playing bagpipes, were forbidden. Control of land was redistributed to break the social and economic bonds of clan society. Thousands of Highlanders died at the battle itself, in prisons or on deportation ships, or by deliberate extermination at the hands of British troops after the battle.

Parliamentary Politics Despite this serious challenge to the new dynasty and the harsh response it occasioned, the British state, overall, enjoyed a period of relative stability as well as innovation in the eighteenth century. The civil war of the seventeenth century had reaffirmed both the need for a strong monarchy and the role of Parliament in defending elite interests. The power of Parliament had recently been reinforced by the Act of Settlement, by which the German Protestant heir to Queen Anne had been chosen in 1701. By excluding the Catholic Stuarts from the throne and establishing the line of succession, this document reasserted that Parliament determined the legitimacy of the monarchy. In fact, the act claimed greater parliamentary authority over foreign and domestic policy in the aftermath of William's constant involvement in war (see page 500).

In the eighteenth century, cooperation evolved further between monarchy and Parliament as Parliament became a more sophisticated and secure institution. Political parties—that is, distinct groups within the elite favoring certain foreign and domestic policies— came into existence. Two groups, the Whigs and the Tories, had begun to form during the reign of Charles II (d. 1685). The Whigs (named derisively by their opponents with a Scottish term for horse thieves) had resisted Charles's pro-French policies and his efforts to tolerate Catholicism. They had wholly opposed his

brother and successor, James II. Initially, the Whigs favored an aggressive foreign policy against continental opponents, particularly France. The Tories (whose name was also a taunt, referring to Irish cattle rustlers) tended to be staunch Anglicans uninterested in Protestant anti-Catholic agitation. They leaned toward a conservative view of their own role, favoring isolationism in foreign affairs and deference toward monarchical authority. Whigs generally represented the interests of the great aristocrats or wealthy merchants or gentry. Tories more often represented the interests of provincial gentry and the traditional concerns of landholding and local administration.

The Whigs were the dominant influence in government through most of the century to 1770. William and Mary, as well as Queen Anne, favored Whig religious and foreign policies. The loyalty of many Tories was called into question by their support for a Stuart, not Hanoverian, succession at Anne's death in 1714. The long Whig dominance of government was also ensured by the talents of Robert Walpole, a member of Parliament who functioned virtually as a prime minister from 1722 to 1742.

Walpole (1676–1745) was from a minor gentry family and was brought into government in 1714 with other Whig ministers in George I's new regime. An extremely talented politician, he took advantage of the mistakes of other ministers over the years and, in 1722,

Political Satire in England
This gruesome image, showing England being disemboweled by members of the government, criticizes the government's acceptance of a treaty with France. Satirical images such as this one were increasingly part of the lively and more open political life in eighteenth-century England. *(Courtesy of the Trustees of the British Museum)*

became both the first lord of the treasury and chancellor of the exchequer. No post or title of "prime minister" yet existed, but the great contribution of Walpole's tenure was to create that office in fact, if not officially. He chose to maintain peace abroad when and where he could and thus presided over a period of recovery and relative prosperity that enhanced the stability of government.

Initially, Walpole was helped in his role as go-between for king and Parliament by George I's own limitations. The king rarely attended meetings of his own council of ministers and, in any case, was hampered by his limited command of English. Gradually, the Privy Council of the king became something resembling a modern cabinet dominated by a prime minister. By the end of the century the notions of "loyal opposition" to the Crown within Parliament and parliamentary responsibility for policy had taken root.

In some respects, the maturation of political life in Parliament resembled the lively political debates in the salons of Paris. In both cases, political life was being legitimized on a new basis. In England, however, that legitimation was enshrined in a legislative institution, which made it especially effective and resilient.

Efforts at Parliamentary Reform

Parliament was not yet in any sense representative of the British population, however. Because of strict property qualifications, only about 200,000 adult men could vote. In addition, representation was very uneven, heavily favoring traditional landed wealth. Some constituencies with only a few dozen voters sent members to Parliament. Many of these "pocket boroughs" were under the control of (in the pockets of) powerful local families who could intimidate the local electorate, particularly in the absence of secret ballots.

Movements for reform of representation in Parliament began in the late 1760s as professionals, such as doctors and lawyers, with movable (as opposed to landed) property and merchants in booming but underrepresented cities began to demand the vote. As the burden of taxation grew—the result of the recently concluded Seven Years' War (discussed later in this chapter)—these groups felt increasingly deprived of representation. Indeed, many felt kinship and sympathy with the American colonists who opposed increased taxation by the British government on these same grounds and revolted in 1775.

However, the reform movement faltered over the issue of religion. In 1780 a tentative effort by Parliament to extend some civil rights to British Catholics provoked rioting in London (known as the Gordon Riots, after one of the leaders). The riots lasted for eight days and claimed three hundred lives. Pressure for parliamentary reform had been building as Britain met with

reversals in its war against the American rebels, but this specter of a popular movement out of control temporarily ended the drive for reform by disenfranchised elites.

"ENLIGHTENED" MONARCHY

Arbitrary monarchical power might seem antithetical to Enlightenment thought. After all, the Enlightenment stressed the reasonableness of human beings and their capacity to discern and act in accord with natural law. Yet monarchy seemed an ideal instrument of reform to Voltaire and to many of his contemporaries. The work of curtailing the influence of the church, reforming legal codes, and eliminating barriers to economic activity might be done more efficiently by a powerful monarch than by other available means. Historians have labeled a number of rulers of this era "enlightened despots" because of the arbitrary nature of their power and the enlightened or reformist uses to which they put it.

Scandinavia Enlightened despotism aptly describes certain developments in the Scandinavian kingdoms in the late eighteenth century. In Denmark the Crown had governed without significant challenge from the landholding nobility since the mid-seventeenth century. The nobility, however, like its counterparts in eastern Europe, had guaranteed its supremacy by means of ironclad domination of the peasantry. In 1784 a reform-minded group of nobles, led by the young crown prince Frederick (governing on behalf of his mentally ill father), began to apply Enlightenment remedies to the kingdom's economic problems. The reformers encouraged freer trade and sought, above all, to improve agriculture by elevating the status of the peasantry. With improved legal status and with land reform, which enabled some peasants to own the land they worked for the first time, agricultural productivity in Denmark rose dramatically. These reforms constitute some of the clearest achievements of any of the "enlightened" rulers.

In Sweden in 1772, Gustav III (r. 1771–1796) staged a coup with army support that overturned the dominance of the Swedish parliament, the Diet. In contrast to Denmark, Sweden had a relatively unbroken tradition of noble involvement in government, stemming in part from its marginal economy and the consequent interest of the nobility in participation in the Crown's aggressive foreign policy. Since Sweden's eclipse as a major

---

enlightened despotism Term for the reform-oriented rule of eighteenth-century monarchs. Enlightened despots applied Enlightenment remedies to economic problems and encouraged education and legal reform, but did not dismantle elites' privileges or share their own power.

power after the Great Northern War (see page 512), factions of the Diet, not unlike the rudimentary political parties in Great Britain, had fought over the reins of government. After reasserting his control, Gustav III began an ambitious program of reform of the government. Bureaucrats more loyal to parliamentary patrons than to the Crown were replaced, restrictions on trade in grain and other economic controls were liberalized, the legal system was rationalized, the death penalty was strictly limited, and legal torture was abolished.

Despite his abilities, Gustav III suffered the consequences of the contradictory position of advancing reform by autocratic means in a kingdom with a strong tradition of representative government. Gustav eventually tried to deflect the criticisms of the nobility by reviving grandiose—but completely unrealistic—schemes for the reconquest of Baltic territory. In 1796 he was mortally wounded by an assassin hired by disgruntled nobles.

Prussia Another claimant to the title "enlightened despot" was Frederick II of Prussia (r. 1740–1786), known as **Frederick the Great.** Much of the time, Frederick resided in his imperial electorate of Brandenburg, near its capital, Berlin. His scattered states, which he extended by seizing new lands, are referred to as Prussia rather than Brandenburg-Prussia because members of his family were now kings of Prussia thanks to their ambitions and the weakness of the Polish state, of which Prussia had once been a dependent duchy. In many ways, the Prussian state *was* its military victories, for Frederick's bold moves and the policies of his father, grandfather, and great-grandfather committed the state's resources to a military presence of dramatic proportions. Prussia was on the European stage at all only because of that driving commitment.

The institutions that constituted the state and linked the various provinces under one administration were dominated by the needs of the military. Frederick II's father, Frederick William (r. 1713–1740), had added an efficient provincial recruiting system to the state's central institutions, which he also further consolidated. But in many other respects, the Prussian state was in its infancy. There was no tradition of political participation—even by elites—and little chance of cultivating any. Nor was there any political or social room for maneuver at the lower part of the social scale. The rulers of Prussia had long ago given in to the aristocracy's demand for tighter control over peasant labor on their own lands in return for their support of the monarchy. The rulers relied on the nobles for local administration and army commands. Thus the kinds of social, judicial, or political reforms that Frederick could hope to carry out without undermining his own power were starkly limited.

Frederick tried to modernize agricultural methods and simultaneously to improve the condition of the peasants, but he met stiff resistance from the noble landholders. He did succeed in abolishing serfdom in some regions. He tried to stimulate the economy by sponsoring state industries and trading monopolies, but too few resources and too little initiative from the tightly controlled merchant communities stymied his plans. Simplifying and codifying the inherited jumble of local laws was a goal of every ruler. A law code published in 1794, after Frederick's death, was partly the product of his efforts.

Frederick's views of the role of Enlightenment thought reflect the limitations of his situation. One doesn't have to lead a frontal assault on prejudices consecrated by time, he believed; instead, one must be tolerant of superstition because it will always have a hold on the masses. Perhaps his most distinctive "enlightened" characteristic was the seriousness with which he took his task as ruler. He was energetic and disciplined to a fault. In his book *Anti-Machiavel* (1741), he argued that a ruler has a moral obligation to work for the betterment of the state. He styled himself as the "first servant" or steward of the state. However superficial this claim may appear, Frederick compares favorably with Louis XV of France, who, having a far more wealthy and flexible society to work with, did much less.

ENLIGHTENMENT AND TRADITION: THE CASE OF AUSTRIA

One of the most effective rulers of the eighteenth century was the Habsburg ruler **Maria Theresa** of Austria (r. 1740–1780). A devout Catholic, she was guided more by traditional concerns for effective rule and compassion for her subjects than by Enlightenment ideas. After surviving the near dismemberment of Austrian territories in the War of the Austrian Succession (see page 572), she embarked on an energetic program of reform to remedy the weaknesses in the state that the war had revealed. "Austria," it must be remembered, is a term of convenience; the state was a very medieval-looking hodgepodge that included present-day Austria, the kingdoms of Bohemia and Hungary, the Austrian Netherlands, and lands in northern Italy. In addition, since the sixteenth century a male member of the Habsburg family had almost always been elected emperor of the Holy Roman Empire.

Frederick the Great Autocratic king of Prussia who transformed the country into a major military power and also sponsored "enlightened" reforms.

Maria Theresa Habsburg archduchess of Austria and queen of Hungary and Bohemia who reformed and centralized the administration of her Austrian and Bohemian lands.

Maria Theresa streamlined and centralized administration, finances, and defense, particularly in Bohemia and Austria, where she was able to exercise her authority relatively unchecked, compared with her other domains. Above all, she reformed the assessment and collection of taxes to tap the wealth of her subjects more effectively and thus better defend all her domains. She improved her subjects' access to justice and limited the exploitation of serfs by landlords. She made primary schooling universal and compulsory, in order better to train peasants for the army. Although the policy was far from fully implemented at the time of her death (only about half of Austrian children were in school, and far fewer in Hungary and elsewhere), hers was the first European state with so ambitious an education policy. Maria Theresa accomplished all of this without being particularly "enlightened" personally. For example, she had a traditional fear of freedom of the press and cherished orthodoxy in religious matters.

Maria Theresa's policies were implemented by a group of ministers, bureaucrats, and officers who shared her concern for effective government and defense, and who were well versed in "enlightened" ideas for reform. The diverse character of the Habsburg lands meant that some members of the governing elite came from the Netherlands and from Italy, where sympathy for the Enlightenment was well rooted by comparison with the relatively poorer and more rural society of the Austrian hinterland. Moreover, the language of the Habsburg court was French (Maria Theresa spoke it fluently); thus no amount of local censorship—which, in any case, Maria Theresa relaxed—could prevent the governing class from reading and absorbing Enlightenment philosophy in its original language.

Maria Theresa was followed on the throne by her two sons, Joseph II (r. 1780–1790) and Leopold II (r. 1790–1792). Each son counted himself a follower of the Enlightenment, and each, as was the family custom, served a period of "apprenticeship" governing Habsburg territories where he could attempt to implement reform. After his mother's death, Joseph II carried out a variety of bold initiatives that she had not attempted, including freedom of the press, significant freedom of religion, and the abolition of serfdom in Habsburg lands. During his ten-year reign, the political climate in Vienna began to resemble that in Paris, London, and other capitals where political life was no longer confined to the royal court.

Maria Theresa in Uniform

Maria Theresa, in military dress, at a tournament held to celebrate a victory in war in the 1740s. Like other rulers of her day, Maria Theresa often appeared in uniform, rather than fancy court dress, to symbolize her seriousness as a ruler.

(Erich Lessing/Art Resource, NY)

Online Study Center **Improve Your Grade**
Primary Source: Joseph II, Religious Toleration,
and the Austrian Jews

Like Frederick the Great, Joseph regarded himself as a servant of the state. Also like Frederick, he was limited in his reform program by the economic and social rigidities of the society he ruled. Austria had only a small middle class to insist on reform, and Joseph could not directly assault the privileges of great landholders, on whose wealth the state depended. In addition, Joseph was by temperament an inflexible autocrat, whose methods antagonized many of these powerful subjects. Joseph's policies provoked simmering opposition, even open revolt, and some of his reforms were repealed even before his death. His more able brother, Leopold, had implemented many reforms while ruling as grand duke in Tuscany (Italy) before assuming the throne in 1790. Much of his two-year reign was spent dexterously saving reforms enacted by his mother and brother in the face of mounting opposition.

CATHERINE THE GREAT AND THE EMPIRE OF RUSSIA

Another ruler with a claim to the title "enlightened despot" was Catherine, empress of Russia (r. 1762–1796). **Catherine the Great,** as she came to be called, was the true heir of Peter the Great in her abilities, policies, and ambitions. Her determination and political acumen were obvious early in her life at the Russian court, where she had been brought from her native Germany in 1745. Brutally treated by her husband, Tsar Peter III, Catherine engineered a coup in which he was killed, then ruled alone for more than thirty years.

Like any successful ruler of her age, Catherine counted territorial aggrandizement among her chief achievements. With regard to the major European powers, Russia tended to ally with Britain (with which it had important trading connections, including the provision of timber for British shipbuilding) and with Austria (against their common nemesis, the Ottoman Empire), and against France, Poland, and Prussia. In 1768 Catherine initiated a war against the Ottoman Turks from which Russia gained much of the Crimean coast. She also continued Peter's efforts to dominate the weakened Poland. She was aided in this goal by Frederick the Great, who proposed the deliberate partitioning of Poland to satisfy his own territorial ambitions as well as those of his competitors, Russia and Austria. In 1772 portions of Poland were gobbled up in

the first of three successive "grabs" of territory (see **MAP 18.1**). Warsaw eventually landed in Prussian hands, but Catherine gained all of Belarus, Ukraine, and modern Lithuania—which had constituted the duchy of Lithuania.

Nevertheless, Catherine counted herself a sincere follower of the Enlightenment. While young, she had received an education that bore the strong stamp of the Enlightenment. Like Frederick, she attempted to take an active role in the European intellectual community, corresponding with Voltaire over the course of many years and acting as patron to the encyclopedist Diderot. One of Catherine's boldest political moves was the secularization of church lands. Although Peter the Great had extended government control of the Russian Orthodox Church, he had not touched church lands. Catherine also licensed private publishing houses and permitted a burgeoning periodical press. The number of books published in Russia tripled during her reign. This enriched cultural life was one of the principal causes of the flowering of Russian literature that began in the early nineteenth century.

The stamp of the Enlightenment on Catherine's policies is also clearly visible in her attempts at legal reform. In 1767 she convened a legislative commission and provided it with a guiding document, the *Instruction,* which she had penned. The commission was remarkable because it included representatives of all classes, including peasants, and provided a place for the airing of general grievances. Catherine hoped for a general codification of law as well as reforms such as the abolition of torture and capital punishment—reforms that made the *Instruction* radical enough to be banned from publication in other countries. She did not propose changing the legal status of serfs, however, and class differences made the commission unworkable in the end. Most legal reforms were accomplished piecemeal and favored the interests of landed gentry.

Online Study Center **Improve Your Grade**
Primary Source: Catherine the Great's Grand
Instruction to the Legislative Commission

Like the Austrian rulers, Catherine undertook far-reaching administrative reform to create more effective local units of government. Here again, political imperatives were fundamental, and reforms in local government strengthened the hand of the gentry. The legal subjection of peasants in serfdom was also extended as a matter of state policy to help win the allegiance of landholders in newly acquired areas—such as Ukrainian territory gained in the partition of Poland. Gentry in general and court favorites in particular, on whom the stability of her government depended, were rewarded with estates and serfs to work them.

In Russia, as in Prussia and Austria, oppression of the peasantry was perpetuated because the monarch

Catherine the Great   Empress of Russia who, through an astute policy of wars and alliances, expanded her country's borders. An "enlightened despot," she advanced the Westernizing reforms begun by Peter the Great.

MAP 18.1 The Partition of Poland and the Expansion of Russia

Catherine the Great acquired present-day Lithuania, Belarus, and Ukraine, which had once constituted the duchy of Lithuania, part of the multi-ethnic Polish kingdom.

wanted to ensure the allegiance of the elites who lived from the peasants' labor. Catherine particularly valued the cooperation of elites because the Russian state was in a formative stage in another sense as well. It was trying to incorporate new peoples, such as the Tatars in the Crimea, and to manage its relationships with border peoples such as the Cossacks. Catherine's reign was marked by one of the most massive and best-organized peasant rebellions of the century. Occurring in 1773, the rebellion expressed the grievances of the thousands of peasants who joined its ranks and called for the abolition of serfdom. The revolt took its name, however, from its Cossack leader, Emelian Pugachev (poo-guh-CHOFF) (d. 1775), and reflected the dissatisfaction

with the Russian government of this semi-autonomous people.

The dramatic dilemmas faced by Catherine illustrate both the promise and the costs of state formation throughout Europe. State consolidation permitted the imposition of internal peace, coordinated economic policy, and reform of justice, but it came at the price of greater—in some cases much greater—control and coercion of the population. Thus we can see from the alternative perspective of Russia the importance of the political sphere that was opening up in France and was being consolidated in England. It was in that environment, rather than in Russia, that the Enlightenment philosophy could find its most fertile ground.

========================== S E C T I O N   S U M M A R Y ==========================

- In France, the royal government tried unsuccessfully to eliminate the privileges of nobility, which limited state revenue and kept most people shut out of the political process.

- The Parliament in England was securely established as a part of government; political parties, representing differing interests among the elite, began to develop.

- Maria Theresa of Austria, though a traditional ruler philosophically, improved government, defense, and

public welfare in her lands; her sons continued her reforms.

- "Enlightened despots," such as Frederick the Great in Prussia, ruled autocratically but used their power for some reforms in law, education, and public welfare.

- Catherine the Great expanded Russian territory and sponsored limited "enlightened" reforms.

THE WIDENING WORLD OF COMMERCE AND WARFARE

How did warfare itself, and the causes of war, change in the eighteenth century?

In the eighteenth century a new constellation of states emerged to dominate politics in Europe. Alongside the traditional powers of England, France, and Austria were Prussia in central Europe and Russia to the east (see Map 18.1); these five states would dominate European politics until the twentieth century. Certain characteristics common to all these states account for their dominance. None is more crucial than their various abilities to field effective armies. In the eighteenth century most wars were launched to satisfy traditional territorial ambitions. Now, however, the increasing significance of overseas trade and colonization also made international expansion an important source of conflict, particularly between England and France. As warfare widened in scope, governments increasingly focused on recruiting and maintaining large navies and armies, with increasingly devastating effects on ordinary people.

THE CAUSES AND COSTS OF WARFARE

The large and small states of Europe continued to make war on one another for both strategic and dynastic reasons. States fought over territory that had obvious economic and strategic value, including territory within Europe and, increasingly, profitable colonies abroad. Dynastic claims, however, were still major causes of war. Indeed, the fundamental instability caused by hereditary rule accounts for many of the major wars of the eighteenth century. The century opened with the War of the Spanish Succession, and later the succession of the Austrian Habsburgs provoked a continent-wide war. Often these conflicts were carried out in arbitrary ways that reflected a dynastic, rather

than wholly strategic, view of territory. Although rational and defensible "national" borders were important, collecting isolated bits of territory was also still the norm. The wars between European powers thus became extremely complex strategically. France, for example, might choose to strike a blow against Austria by invading an Italian state in order to use the conquered Italian territory as a bargaining chip in eventual negotiations. Wars were preceded and carried out with complex systems of alliances and were followed by the adjustments of many borders and the changing control of small, scattered territories. Rulers of lesser states in Germany and Italy, particularly, remained important as allies and as potential rivals of the Great Powers. The rise of Prussia, after all, had demonstrated the benefits of zealous ambition.

The state of military technology, tactics, and organization shaped the outcomes of conflicts as well as the character of the leading states themselves. In the eighteenth century weapons and tactics became increasingly refined. More reliable muskets were introduced. A bayonet that could slip over a musket barrel without blocking the muzzle was invented. Coordinated use of bayonets required even more careful drill of troops than did volley fire alone to ensure disciplined action in the face of enemy fire and charges. Artillery and cavalry forces also were subjected to greater standardization of training and discipline in action. Increased discipline of forces meant that commanders could exercise meaningful control over a battle for the first time. But such battles were not necessarily decisive, especially when waged against a comparable force. Indeed, training now was so costly that commanders were at times ironically reluctant to hazard their fine troops in battle at all.

In addition, wars could still be won or lost not on the battlefield but on the supply line. Incentive still existed to bleed civilian populations and exploit the countryside. Moreover, when supply lines were disrupted and soldiers not equipped or fed, the armies of a major power could be vulnerable to smaller, less disciplined armies of minor states. Finally, even supplies, training, and sophisticated tactics could not guarantee success. Not until 1746, at Culloden, could the British army decisively defeat the fierce charge and hand-to-hand fighting of Highland clansmen by holding its position and using disciplined volley fire and bayonet tactics. Warfare became increasingly professional but was still an uncertain business with unpredictable results, despite its staggering cost.

One sure result of the new equipment, discipline, and high costs was that war became an ever greater burden on a state's resources and administration. It became increasingly difficult for small states, such as Sweden, to compete with the forces that others could mount. Small and relatively poor states, such as Prussia, that were able to support large forces did so by means of an extraordinary bending of civil society to the economic and social needs of the army. In Prussia twice as many people were in the armed forces, proportionally, as in other states, and a staggering 80 percent of its meager state revenue went to sustain the army.

Warfare on this scale also represented an increased burden on common people. Most states introduced some form of conscription in the eighteenth century. Although the very poor often volunteered for army service to improve their lives, conscription of peasants (throughout Europe but particularly in Prussia and Russia) imposed a significant burden on peasant communities and a sacrifice of productive members to the state. Governments everywhere supplemented volunteers and conscripts with mercenaries and even criminals, as necessary, to fill the ranks without tapping the wealthier elements of the community. Thus common soldiers were increasingly seen not as members of society but as its rejects. Said Frederick II, "useful hard-working people should [not be conscripted but rather] be guarded as the apple of one's eye," and a French war minister agreed that armies had to consist of the "scum of people and of all those for whom society has no use."[3] Brutality became an accepted tool for governments to use to manage such groups of men, and the army increasingly became an instrument of social control used to contain individuals who otherwise might disrupt their own communities.

THE POWER OF AUSTRIA AND PRUSSIA

Major wars during the mid-eighteenth century decided the balance of power in German-speaking Europe for the next hundred years. Prussia emerged as the equal of

Austria in the region. The first of these wars, now known as the War of the Austrian Succession, began shortly after the death of the emperor Charles VI in 1740. Charles died without a male heir, and his daughter, Maria Theresa, succeeded him. Charles VI had worked to shore up his daughter's position as his heir (versus other female relatives who also had claims) by means of an act called the Pragmatic Sanction, which he had painstakingly persuaded allies and potential opponents to accept. When Charles VI died, rival heiresses and their husbands challenged Maria Theresa for control of her various lands. They were supported by France, the Habsburgs' perennial rival.

The Austrian lands were threatened with dismemberment. Indeed, Charles had negotiated away the wealthy Bohemian province of Silesia (sigh-LEE-zhee-uh), promising it to Prussia in return for acceptance of his heir (see Map 18.1), and had not left his armies or his treasury well equipped to fight a war to defend it. When Frederick the Great's troops marched into Silesia in 1740, Maria Theresa's rivals saw their chance and invaded other Habsburg territories.

Maria Theresa proved a more tenacious opponent than anyone had anticipated, and she was helped by Great Britain, which saw the possibility of gains against its colonial rival, France. Fighting eventually spread throughout Habsburg territories, including the Netherlands and in Italy, as well as abroad to British and French colonies. In a preliminary peace signed in 1745, Frederick the Great was confirmed in possession of Silesia, but the throne of the Holy Roman Empire was returned to the Habsburgs—given to Maria Theresa's husband, Francis (Franz) I (r. 1745–1765). A final treaty in 1748 ended all the fighting that had continued since 1745, mostly by France and Britain overseas. The Austrian state had survived dismemberment, but Maria Theresa now embarked on the administrative and military reforms necessary to make her state less vulnerable in the future. Prussia, because of the annexation of Silesia and the psychological imprint of victory, emerged as a power of virtually equal rank to the Habsburgs.

The unprecedented threat that Austria now felt from Prussia led to a revolution in alliances across Europe. To isolate Prussia, Maria Theresa agreed to an alliance with France, the Habsburgs' long-standing enemy. Sweden and Russia, with territory to gain at Prussia's expense, joined as well.

Frederick the Great initiated what came to be known as the **Seven Years' War** in 1756, hoping to prevent consolidation of the new alliances. Instead, he found that he had started a war against overwhelming odds. What saved him in part was limited English aid. The English, engaged with France in the overseas con-

Seven Years' War (1756–1763) The first major war between European nations (Britain and France) started and fought largely in their overseas empires.

flict that Americans call the French and Indian War, wanted France to be heavily committed on the Continent. Prussia managed to emerge intact—though strained economically and demographically. Prussia and Austria were confirmed as the two states of European rank in German-speaking Europe. Yet their narrow escapes from being reduced to second-class status reveal how fragile even successful states could be; Prussia's emergence as a major power, particularly, was by no means assured.

THE ATLANTIC WORLD: EXPANDING COMMERCE AND THE SLAVE TRADE

The importance of international trade and colonial possessions to the states of western Europe grew enormously in the eighteenth century (see **MAP 18.2**). Between 1715 and 1785 Britain's trade with North America rose from 19 to 34 percent of its total trade, and its trade with Asia and Africa rose from 7 to 19 percent of the total. By the end of the century more than half of all British trade was carried on outside Europe; for France the figure was more than a third.

European commercial and colonial energies were concentrated in the Atlantic world in the eighteenth century because the profits were greatest there. The population of British North America grew from about 250,000 in 1700 to about 1.7 million by 1760. The densely settled New England colonies provided a market for manufactured goods from the mother country, although they produced little by way of raw materials or bulk goods on which traders could make a profit. The colonies of Maryland and Virginia produced tobacco, the Carolinas rice and indigo (a dyestuff). England re-exported all three throughout Europe at considerable profit.

The French in New France, only 56,000 in 1740, were vastly outnumbered by British colonists. Nevertheless, the French had successfully expanded their control of territory in Canada. Settlements sprang up between the outposts of Montreal and Quebec on the St. Lawrence River. Despite resistance, the French extended their fur trapping—the source of most of the profits New France generated—west and north along the Great Lakes, consolidating their hold by building forts at strategic points. They penetrated as far as the modern Canadian province of Manitoba, where they cut into the British trade run out of Hudson Bay. The French also contested the mouth of the St. Lawrence River and the Gulf of St. Lawrence with the British. The British held Nova Scotia and Newfoundland, the French controlled parts of Cape Breton Island, and both states fished the surrounding waters.

The commercial importance of these North American holdings, as well as those in Asia, was dwarfed by the European states' Caribbean possessions, however.

The British held Jamaica, Barbados, and the Leeward Islands; the French, Guadeloupe and Martinique; the Spanish, Cuba and Santo Domingo; and the Dutch, a few small islands. Sugar produced on plantations by slave labor was the major source of profits, along with other cash crops such as coffee, indigo, and cochineal (another dyestuff). The concentration of shipping to this region indicates the region's importance in the European trading system. For example, by the 1760s the British China trade occupied seven or eight ships. In the 1730s British trade with Jamaica alone drew three hundred ships.

The Treatment of Slaves on Caribbean Plantations

These images of the brutal treatment of slaves on West Indian plantations come from a report published in England designed to convince the British public of the horrors of slavery. At top, a husband and wife are violently separated after being sold to different slave owners. At bottom, a mouthpiece and neck guard are used to prevent escape. The treatment of slaves described here is also documented in other surviving accounts from the eighteenth century.
(New York Public Library/Art Resource, NY)

MAP 18.2 The Atlantic Economy, ca. 1750

The triangle trade linked Europe, Africa, and European colonies in the Americas. The most important component of this trade for Europe was the plantation agriculture of the Caribbean islands, which depended on enslaved Africans for labor.

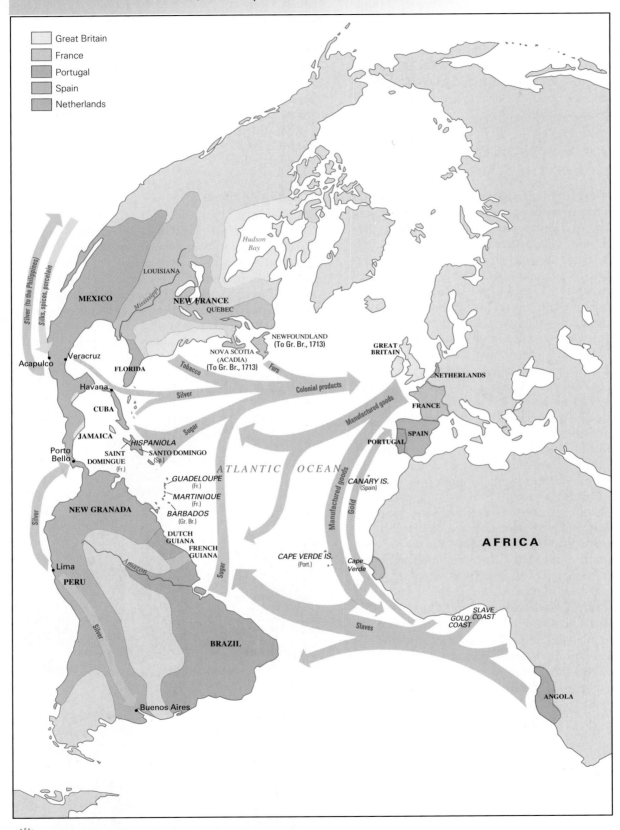

Great Britain
France
Portugal
Spain
Netherlands

Silver (to the Philippines)
Silks, spices, porcelain

Hudson Bay

LOUISIANA

MEXICO

NEW FRANCE
QUEBEC

NEWFOUNDLAND
(To Gr. Br., 1713)

NOVA SCOTIA
(ACADIA)
(To Gr. Br., 1713)

GREAT BRITAIN

Acapulco
Veracruz

Tobacco

FLORIDA

Furs

NETHERLANDS

Havana

Silver

Colonial products

Manufactured goods

CUBA

FRANCE

Sugar

JAMAICA

SPAIN

HISPANIOLA

PORTUGAL

Porto Bello

SAINT DOMINGUE
(Fr.)

SANTO DOMINGO
(Sp.)

ATLANTIC OCEAN

GUADELOUPE
(Fr.)

Manufactured goods

CANARY IS.
(Spain)

NEW GRANADA

MARTINIQUE
(Fr.)

BARBADOS
(Gr. Br.)

Silver

Gold

DUTCH GUIANA

FRENCH GUIANA

AFRICA

Lima

Amazon

Sugar

CAPE VERDE IS.
(Port.)

Cape Verde

PERU

Silver

SLAVE COAST

GOLD COAST

Slaves

BRAZIL

ANGOLA

Buenos Aires

THE GLOBAL RECORD

AN AFRICAN RECALLS THE HORRORS OF THE SLAVE SHIP

Olaudah Equiano (ca. 1750–1797) was an Ibo from the Niger region of West Africa. He first experienced slavery as a boy when kidnapped from his village by other Africans, but nothing prepared him for the brutality of the Europeans who bought and shipped him to Barbados, in the British West Indies. His narration of the horrors of the "Middle Passage" between Africa and the Americas may represent a composite story of others' experiences as well as his own. Nevertheless, his account remains one of the few written records by an African survivor of a slave ship.

The first object which saluted my eyes when I arrived on the [African] coast was the sea and a slave ship, which was then riding at anchor, and waiting for its cargo. . . . When I was carried on board I was immediately handled, and tossed up, to see if I were sound, by some of the crew. . . . When I looked around the ship . . . and saw . . . a multitude of black people of every description chained together, every one of their countenances expressing dejection and sorrow, I no longer doubted of my fate. . . .

I was not long suffered to indulge my grief; I was soon put down under the decks, and there I received such a salutation in the nostrils as I had never experienced in my life; so that with the loathsomeness of the stench . . . I became so sick and low that I was not able to eat. . . . I now wished for the last friend, death, to relieve me; but soon, to my grief, two of the white men offered me eatables; and, on my refusing to eat, one of them held me fast by the hands and laid me across, I think, the windlass, and tied my feet while the other flogged me severely.

One day, when we had a smooth sea and a moderate wind, two of my wearied countrymen, who were chained together . . . , preferring death to such a life of misery, somehow made through the nettings and jumped into the sea; immediately another dejected fellow who [was ill and so not in irons] followed their example; and I believe many more would very soon have done the same, if they had not been prevented by the ship's crew who were instantly alarmed. Those of us that were the most active were in a minute put down under the deck; and there was such a noise and confusion amongst the people of the ship as I have never heard before, to stop her, and get the boat to go after the slaves. However, two of the wretches were drowned, but they got the other and afterwards flogged him unmercifully for thus attempting to prefer death to slavery. In this manner we continued to undergo more hardships than I can now relate; hardships which are inseparable from this accursed trade.

QUESTIONS

1. What particular horrors of the Middle Passage seem to stand out in Equiano's mind? What is the significance of these vignettes?

2. What clues in this excerpt reveal the audience Equiano had in mind for his narrative?

Source: The Interesting Narrative of the Life of Olaudah Equiano, or Gustavus Vassa, the African (London, 1793); reprinted in David Northrup, ed., *The Atlantic Slave Trade* (Boston: Houghton Mifflin, 2002), pp. 68–70.

The economic dependence of the colonies on slave labor meant that the colonies were tied to their home countries not with a two-way commercial exchange but with a three-way, or "triangle," trade (see Map 18.2). Certain European manufactures were shipped to ports in western Africa, where they were traded for slaves. Captive Africans were transported to South America, the Caribbean, or North America, where planters bought and paid for them with profits from their sugar and tobacco plantations. (See the box "The Global Record: An African Recalls the Horrors of the Slave Ship.") Sugar and tobacco were then shipped back to the mother country to be re-exported at great profit throughout Europe.

This plantation economy in the Caribbean was vulnerable to slave revolts, as well as to competition among the Europeans. Often wars over control of the islands significantly disrupted production and lessened profits for the European planters on the islands and for their trading partners back in Europe. The growing demands by Europeans for sugar and other products kept the plantation system expanding, despite these challenges, throughout the eighteenth century. The **slave trade** grew dramatically as a result. Approximately five times as many Africans—perhaps as many as seven million people—were forcibly transported to the Americas as slaves in the eighteenth century as in the seventeenth.

slave trade   Europeans' trade with Africa in which involuntary laborers were shipped to the Americas to be sold to owners of, especially, sugar plantations. The trade reached its peak in the eighteenth century, when approximately seven million Africans were shipped across the Atlantic.

MAP 18.3 British Gains in North America

The British colonies on the Atlantic coast were effective staging posts for the armies that ousted the French from North America by 1763. However, taxes imposed on the colonies to pay the costs of the Seven Years' War helped spark revolt—the American Revolution—a decade later.

The slave trade became an increasingly specialized form of oceangoing commerce (for example, slave traders throughout Europe adopted a standardized ship design) and, at the same time, one increasingly linked to the rest of European commerce by complex trade and financial ties. In England, London merchants who imported Asian goods, exported European manufactures, or distributed Caribbean sugar could provide credit for slave traders based in the northern city of Liverpool to fund their journeys to Africa and then the Americas.

GREAT BRITAIN AND FRANCE: WARS OVERSEAS

The growth and the proximity of French and British settlements in North America ensured conflict (see **MAP 18.3**). The Caribbean and the coasts of Central and South America were strategic flashpoints as well. At the beginning of the eighteenth century, several substantial islands remained unclaimed by any power.

The British were making incursions along the coastline of Central America claimed by Spain and were trying to break into the monopoly of trade between Spain and its vast possessions in the region. Public opinion in both Britain and France became increasingly sensitive to colonial issues. For the first time, tensions abroad fueled major conflicts between two European states.

During this century England became the dominant naval power in Europe. Its navy protected its far-flung trading networks, its merchant fleet, and the coast of England itself. England's strategic interests on the Continent lay in promoting a variety of powers there, none of which (or no combination of which) posed too great a threat to England or to its widespread trading system. A second, dynastic consideration in continental affairs was the electorate of Hanover, the large principality in western Germany that was the native territory of the Hanoverian kings of England. Early in the century especially, the interests of this German territory were a significant factor in British foreign policy. Unable to field a large army, given their maritime interests, the British sought protection for Hanover in alliances and subsidies for allies' armies on the Continent and paid for these ventures with the profits on trade.

Conflict between England and France in colonial regions played out in three major phases. The first two were concurrent with the major land wars in Europe: the War of the Austrian Succession (1740–1748) and the Seven Years' War (1756–1763). The third phase coincided with the rebellion of British colonies in North America—the American Revolution—beginning in the 1770s. France was inevitably more committed to affairs on the Continent than were the British. The French were able to hold their own successfully in both arenas during the 1740s, but by 1763, though pre-eminent on the Continent, they had lost many of their colonial possessions to the English.

In the 1740s France was heavily involved in the War of the Austrian Succession, while Britain vied with Spain for certain Caribbean territories. Both France and England also tested each other's strength in scattered colonial fighting, which produced a few well-balanced gains and losses. Their conquests were traded back when peace was made in 1748.

Tension was renewed almost immediately at many of the strategic points in North America. French and British naval forces harassed each other's shipping in the Gulf of St. Lawrence. The French reinforced their encirclement of British colonies with more forts along the Great Lakes and the Ohio River. When British troops (at one point led by the colonial commander George Washington) attempted to strike at these forts beginning in 1754, open fighting between the French and the English began.

The Death of General Wolfe at Quebec

General Wolfe commanded British troops that in 1759 defeated the French at Quebec in Canada. Wolfe's death at the battle was memorialized ten years later by American-born artist Benjamin West. This image became widely popular after West sold cheap engraved versions. Notice West's sympathetic treatment of the Native American earnestly focused, like his British allies, on the death of the commander. *(National Gallery of Canada, Ottawa. Transfer from the Canadian War Memorials)*

In India, meanwhile, both the French and the British attempted to strengthen their commercial footholds by making military and political alliances with local Indian rulers. The disintegration of the Mogul Empire heightened competition among regional Indian rulers and sparked a new level of ambition on the part of the European powers with interests in Asia. A British attack on a French convoy provoked a declaration of war by France in May 1756, three months before fighting in the Seven Years' War broke out in Europe. For the first time, a major war between European nations had started and would be fought in their empires, signifying a profound change in the relation of these nations to the world.

The French had already committed themselves to an alliance with Austria and were increasingly involved on the Continent after Frederick II initiated war there in August 1756. Slowly, the drain of sustaining war both on the Continent and abroad began to tell, and Britain scored major victories against French forces after an initial period of balanced successes and failures. The French lost a number of fortresses on the Mississippi and Ohio Rivers and on the Great Lakes, and then they also lost the interior of Canada with the fall of Quebec and of Montreal in 1759 and 1760, respectively (see Map 18.3).

In the Caribbean, the British seized Guadeloupe, a vital sugar-producing island. Superior resources in India enabled the British to take several French outposts there, including Pondicherry (pon-dih-CHAIR-ee), the most important. The cost of involvement on so many fronts meant that French troops were short of money and supplies. They were particularly vulnerable to both supply and personnel shortages—especially in North America—because they were weaker than the British at sea and because New France remained sparsely settled and dependent on the mother country for food.

By the terms of the Peace of Paris in 1763, France regained Guadeloupe, the most profitable of its American colonies, although Britain gained control of several smaller, previously neutral Caribbean islands to add to its own sugar-producing colonies of Jamaica and Barbados. In India, France retained many of its trading stations but lost its political and military clout. British power in India was dramatically enhanced not only by French losses but also by victories over Indian rulers who had allied with the French. In the interior, Britain now controlled lands that had never before been under the control of any European power. British political rule in India, as opposed to merely a mercantile presence, began at this time. The British also held Canada. They emerged from the Seven Years' War as the preeminent world power among European states. The dramatic gains led some Britons to speak of the "British Empire" overseas that all preceding generations had lived within and taken for granted.

SECTION SUMMARY

- States recruited soldiers and equipped and trained their armies better than ever before, making war more costly and more demanding on their populations.

- Prussia fought two major wars and emerged as the equal of Austria in German-speaking Europe.

- The involvement of European states in international trade and overseas colonization grew markedly in the eighteenth century.

- Approximately seven million Africans were forcibly transported to work on plantations producing cash crops in the Americas.

- Britain and France fought over colonial possessions around the world; Britain won many of France's colonies by the end of the Seven Years' War in 1763.

ECONOMIC EXPANSION AND SOCIAL CHANGE

How was European agriculture transformed in this era, and what further transformations did it bring in its wake?

The eighteenth century was an era of dramatic change, although that change was not always apparent to those who lived through it. The intellectual and cultural ferment of the Enlightenment laid the groundwork for domestic political changes to come, just as British victories in the Seven Years' War shifted the balance of power abroad. More subtle and potentially more profound changes were occurring in the European countryside, however. Population, production, and consumption were beginning to grow beyond the bounds that all preceding generations had lived within and taken for granted.

MORE FOOD AND MORE PEOPLE

Throughout European history, a delicate balance had existed between available food and numbers of people to feed. Population growth had accompanied increases in the amount of land under cultivation. From time to time, however, population growth surpassed the ability of the land to produce food, and people became malnourished and prey to disease. In 1348 the epidemic outbreak of the plague known as the Black Death struck just such a vulnerable population in decline.

Europeans had few options for increasing the productivity of the land. Peasants safeguarded its fertility by alternately cultivating some portions while letting others lie fallow or using them as pasture. Manure provided fertilizer, but during the winter months livestock could not be kept alive in large numbers. Limited food for livestock meant limited fertilizer, which in turn meant limited production of food for both humans and animals.

After a devastating decline in the fourteenth century, the European population experienced a pro-

longed recovery, and in the eighteenth century the balance that had previously been reached began to be exceeded for the first time. The cause was not a decline in infant mortality, which remained as high as ever. Even Queen Anne of England outlived every one of the seventeen children she bore (and all but one of them died in infancy). Instead, population growth occurred because of a decline in the death rate for adults and a simultaneous increase in the birthrate in some areas owing to earlier marriages.

Adults began to live longer partly because of a decline in the incidence of plague. However, the primary reason adults were living longer, despite the presence of various epidemic diseases, was that they were better nourished and thus better able to resist disease. More and different kinds of food began to be produced. The increase in the food supply also meant that more new families could be started.

Food production increased because of the introduction of new crops and other changes in agricultural practices. The cumulative effect of these changes was so

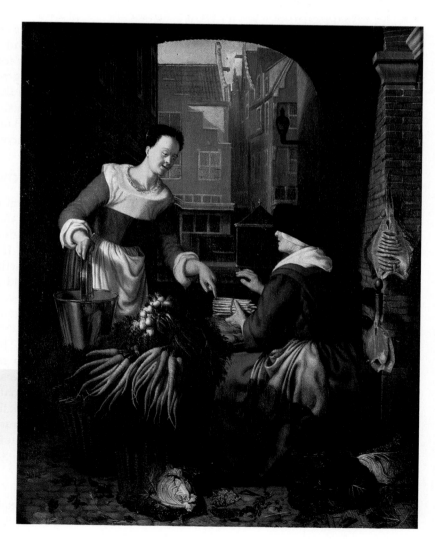

Gérard Dou: The Vegetable Seller
The specialization of agriculture meant that a more varied diet was available to increasing numbers of Europeans. *(Musée des Beaux-Arts, Nimes/Giraudon/Art Resource, NY)*

dramatic that historians have called them an **agricultural revolution.** The new crops included fodder, such as clover, legumes, and turnips, which did not deplete the soil and could be fed to livestock over the winter. The greater availability of animal manure in turn boosted grain production. In addition, the nutrient-dense potato was introduced from the Americas in the sixteenth century. It could feed more people per acre than could grain. In certain areas, farming families produced potatoes to feed themselves while they grew grain to be sold and shipped elsewhere.

More food being produced meant more food available for purchase. The opportunity to buy food freed up land and labor. A family that could purchase food might decide to convert its farm to specialized use, such as raising dairy cattle. In such a case, many families might be supported by a piece of land that had previously supported only one. Over a generation or two, a number of children might share the inheritance of what had previously been a single farm, yet each could make a living from his or her share, and population could grow as it had not done before.

Farmers had known about and experimented with many of the crops used for fodder for centuries. However, the widespread planting of these crops, as well as other changes, was long in coming and happened in scattered areas, because a farmer had to have control over land in order to implement change. In the traditional open-field system, peasants had split up all the land in each community so that each family might have a piece of each field. Making effective changes was hard when an entire community had to act together. Most important, changing agriculture required capital for seed and fertilizer and for the greater number of people and animals needed to cultivate the new crops. Only prosperous farmers had spare capital. Few were inclined to take risks with the production of food and to trust the workings of the market. The bad condition of roads was reason enough not to rely on distant markets.

Yet where both decent roads and growing urban markets existed, some farmers—even entire villages working together—were willing to produce for urban populations. Capital cities, such as London and Amsterdam, and trading centers, such as Glasgow and Bordeaux, were booming. These growing cities demanded not only grain but also specialized produce such as dairy products and fruits and vegetables. Thus farmers had an incentive to make changes. Urbanization and improved transportation networks also encouraged agriculture because human waste produced by city dwellers—known as "night soil"—could be collected and distributed in the surrounding agricultural regions as fertilizer. By the late eighteenth century, pockets of intensive, diversified agriculture existed in England, northern France, the Rhineland in Germany, the Po Valley in Italy, and Catalonia in Spain.

In some areas, changes in agriculture were accompanied by a shift in power in the countryside. Wealthy landlords began to invest in change in order to reap the profits of producing for the new markets. Where the traditional authority of the village to regulate agriculture was weak, peasants were vulnerable. In England a combination of weak village structure and the attraction of urban markets created a climate that encouraged landlords to treat land speculatively. To make their holdings more profitable, they raised the rents that farmers paid. They changed cultivation patterns on the land that they controlled directly. They appropriated the village common lands, a process known as "enclosure," and used them for cash crops such as sheep (raised for their wool) or beef cattle.

Thus, although the agricultural revolution increased the food supply to sustain more people in Europe generally, it did not create general prosperity. The growth of population did not mean that most people were better off. Indeed, many rural people were driven off the land or made destitute by the loss of the resources of common lands. Peasants in eastern Europe produced grain for export to the growing urban centers in western Europe, but usually by traditional methods. In both eastern and western Europe, the power and profits of landlords were a major force in structuring the rural economy.

THE GROWTH OF INDUSTRY

Agricultural changes led to changes in other areas of economic and social life. As more food was grown with less labor, that labor was freed to take on other productive work. If enough people could be kept employed making useful commodities, the nonagricultural population could continue to grow. If population grew, more and more consumers would be born, and the demand for more goods would help continue the cycle of population growth, changes in production, and economic expansion. This is precisely what happened in the eighteenth century. A combination of forces increased the numbers of people who worked at producing a few essential materials and products (see **MAP 18.4**).

Especially significant was the expansion in the **putting-out system.** Also known as cottage industry, putting out involved the production in the countryside

agricultural revolution Dramatic increase in food production from the sixteenth to eighteenth centuries, brought about by changes in agricultural practices and cultivation of new crops. The agricultural revolution allowed the population of Europe to expand beyond historic limits.

putting-out system Sometimes called "cottage industry," the production in country homes of items like thread and cloth by spinners and weavers for an entrepreneur who furnished raw materials and sold the finished product.

MAP 18.4   Population and Production in Eighteenth-Century Europe

The growth of cottage industry helped to support a growing population. With changes in agriculture, more land-poor workers were available in the countryside to accept work as spinners, knitters, and weavers.

Online Study Center Improve Your Grade
Interactive Map: Population and Production in Eighteenth-Century Europe

of thread and cloth by spinners and weavers working in their own homes for an entrepreneur who bought raw materials and "put them out" to be finished by individual workers. The putting-out system expanded in the eighteenth century as the agricultural economy was transformed. All agricultural work was seasonal, demanding intensive effort and many hands at certain times but not others. The labor demands of the new crops meant that an even larger number of people might periodically need work away from the fields to make ends meet. Rural poverty, whether as a result of traditional or new agricultural methods, made manufacturing work in the home attractive to more and more people.

Overseas trade also stimulated the expansion of production by spurring the demand in Europe's colonies for cloth and other finished products and increasing the demand at home for manufactured items, such as nails to build the ships that carried the trade. The production of cloth also expanded because heightened demand led to changes in the way cloth was made. Wool was increasingly combined with other fibers to make less expensive fabrics. By the end of the century, wholly cotton fabrics were being made cheaply in Europe from cotton grown in America by slave labor.

Steady innovation in textile production allowed woven goods to be aimed at broader markets. In the Middle Ages, weavers produced luxury-quality cloth, and their profits came not from demand, which was relatively low, but from the high price that affluent consumers paid. In the eighteenth century, cloth production became a spur to a transformed industrial economy because cheaper kinds of cloth were made for mass consumption. Producing in great quantities became important, and innovations that promoted productivity were welcomed.

A crucial innovation was increased mechanization. The invention of machines to spin thread in the late eighteenth century brought a marked increase in the rate of production. Machines likewise brought profound changes to the lives of rural workers who had been juggling agricultural and textile work according to season and need. The selected areas of England, France, and the Low Countries where the new technologies were introduced stood, by the end of the century, on the verge of a massive industrial transformation that would have unprecedented social consequences.

CONTROL AND RESISTANCE

The economic changes of the century produced both resistance and adaptation by ordinary people and a variety of responses by state authorities. Sometimes ordinary people coped in ways that revealed their desperation. In many cities numbers of abandoned children rose greatly because urban families, particularly recent immigrants from the countryside, could not support all their offspring. The major cities of Europe put increasing resources into police forces and city lighting schemes. Charitable institutions run by cities, churches, and central governments expanded. By 1789, for example, there were more than two thousand *hôpitaux* (oh-pee-TOE)—poorhouses for the destitute and ill—in France. The poor received food and shelter but were forced to work for the city or to live in poorhouses against their will. Men were sometimes taken out of poorhouses and forced to become soldiers.

On the high seas, states responded to the increasing value of trade with a campaign to suppress piracy. Piracy had been a way of life for hundreds of Europeans and colonial settlers since the sixteenth century. Indentured servants fleeing their obligations, runaway slaves, out-of-work laborers, and adventurers could take up the pirating life, which at least offered autonomy and a chance of some comforts. From the earliest days of exploration, European rulers had authorized men known as privateers to commit acts of war against specific targets. The Crown took little risk and was spared the cost of arming the ships but shared in the plunder. True piracy—outright robbery on the high seas—was illegal, but in practice the difference between piracy and privateering was negligible. As governments and merchants grew to prefer regular trade over the irregular profits of plunder, and as national navies developed in the late

seventeenth century, a concerted effort to eliminate piracy began.

Life on the seas became an increasingly vital part of western European economic life in the eighteenth century. English-speaking seamen alone numbered about thirty thousand around the middle of the century. Sea life began to resemble life on land in the amount of compulsion it entailed. Sailors in port were always vulnerable to forcible enlistment in the navy by impressment gangs, particularly during wartime. A drowsy sailor sleeping off a rowdy night could wake up to find himself aboard a navy ship. Press gangs operated throughout England and not just in major ports, for authorities were as interested in controlling "vagrancy" as in staffing the navy. Merchant captains occasionally filled their crews by such means, particularly when sailing unpopular routes.

Like soldiers in the growing eighteenth-century armies, sailors in the merchant marine as well as the navy could be subjected to brutal discipline and appalling conditions. Merchant seamen attempted to improve their lot by trying to regulate their relationship with ships' captains. Contracts for pay on merchant ships became more regularized, and seamen often negotiated their terms very carefully, including, for example, details about how rations were to be allotted. Sailors might even take bold collective action aboard ship. The modern term for a work stoppage, *strike,* comes from the sailing expression "to strike sail," meaning to loosen the sails so that they cannot fill with wind. Its use dates from the eighteenth century, from "strikes" of sailors protesting unfair shipboard conditions.

Seafaring men were an unusually large and somewhat self-conscious community of wage workers. Not until industrialization came into full swing a century later would a similar group of workers exist within Europe itself (see Chapter 21). But economic and political protests by ordinary people on the Continent also showed interesting parallel changes. Peasant revolts in the past had ranged from small-scale actions against local tax collectors to massive uprisings that only an army could suppress. The goals of peasant rebels were usually immediate and practical. For example, they aimed not to eliminate taxation altogether but perhaps to protest the collection of a particularly burdensome local tax. The political rationale behind such actions was not a hope that the system would disappear but rather a hope that it would operate more fairly, as it presumably had in the past. In cases where peasants did articulate a revolutionary vision, it was usually a utopian one—a political system with no kings, landlords, taxes, or state of any kind.

Peasant revolts continued to follow these patterns in the eighteenth century but in certain cases, peasants, like sailors, began to confront authority in new ways. For example, they might attack landlords' power, such as forced labor and compulsory use of landlords' mills, and they used new weapons to do so. They increasingly marshaled legal devices to maintain control over their land and to thwart landlords' efforts to enclose fields and cultivate cash crops. This change, though subtle, was important because it represented an effort to bring permanent structural change to the system and was not simply a temporary redress of grievances. In part, this trend toward "enlightened" revolt reflects increased access to information and the circulation of ideas about reform. A major peasant rebellion following bad harvests in Austrian lands, for example, specifically protested the delay in implementing changes—the subject of earnest debate among elites—in compulsory labor by peasants.

SECTION SUMMARY

- The introduction of new crops and changes in cultivation led to increases in food production and what has been called the "agricultural revolution."

- Changes in agriculture enabled the European population to grow beyond previous limits.

- Industrial production, especially of cloth, increased because more people were available for the work, markets for the products expanded, and new technologies arose to meet the demand.

- Most increased production occurred within the "putting-out system," in which goods were made in individual homes with materials provided by an entrepreneur who later sold the finished product.

- Soldiers, sailors, and peasants found new ways to resist the burdens of forced labor, brutal conditions, and heavy taxation.

CHAPTER SUMMARY

Online Study Center **ACE the Test**

What were the most important notions in Enlightenment thought, and what were some of the intellectual, social, and political conditions that favored its development?

To what extent did the activities of "enlightened despots" reflect Enlightenment precepts, and to what extent did they reflect traditional concerns of state power?

How did warfare itself, and the causes of war, change in the eighteenth century?

How was European agriculture transformed in this era, and what further transformations did it bring in its wake?

The Enlightenment was an intellectual movement that applied to political and social thought the confidence in the intelligibility of natural law that Newton and other scientists had recently achieved. Prominent thinkers, called "philosophes," included influential individuals such as Voltaire and Rousseau. But the Enlightenment was also a more general movement and one of its features was the growth of an informed body of public opinion outside the realm of government. The revolutionary potential of Enlightenment thought came from belief in its rationality and from the fact that it was both critical of its society and fashionable for educated elites to practice.

European rulers in the eighteenth century continued their efforts to govern with greater effectiveness; some self-consciously borrowed Enlightenment ideas to guide their policies, though they remained unwilling to share governing power. In France, although it was the center of the Enlightenment, the Crown failed to eliminate the privileges of nobility and could not adequately tap the wealth of the kingdom. In England,

Parliament's role in government was securely established in this century, and new elites wanted to be represented in it.

Though some rulers were inspired by precepts of the Enlightenment, all were guided by traditional concerns of dynastic aggrandizement and strategic advantage. After dramatic expansion of trade, colonization, and the plantation system, conflict over colonial possessions became increasingly important, particularly between England and France. Partly as a result of growing commerce, the European economy was expanding, the population was growing beyond previous limits, and the system of production was being restructured.

LOOKING AHEAD

Many of these economic developments occurred incrementally over many decades and were not yet recognized for the fundamental changes they were. For example, the full economic and strategic impact of British colonial gains would not be felt until the next century.

The most visible change would happen first in politics, where goals and expectations nurtured by Enlightenment philosophy clashed with the rigid structure of the French state and triggered the French Revolution.

KEY TERMS

philosophes (p. 552)

Voltaire (p. 552)

Adam Smith (p. 555)

Jean-Jacques Rousseau (p. 557)

salons (p. 558)

enlightened despotism (p. 566)

Frederick the Great (p. 567)

Maria Theresa (p. 567)

Catherine the Great (p. 569)

Seven Years' War (p. 572)

slave trade (p. 575)

agricultural revolution (p. 580)

putting-out system (p. 580)

Online Study Center
Improve Your Grade Flashcards

SUGGESTED READING

Anderson, M. S. *Europe in the Eighteenth Century, 1713–1783.* 4th ed. 2000. A general history covering political, economic, social, and cultural developments.

Black, Jeremy. *European Warfare, 1660–1815.* 1994. One of several recent books by this military historian known particularly for his studies of the seventeenth and eighteenth centuries.

Cipolla, Carlo. *Before the Industrial Revolution.* 1976. A comprehensive treatment of the development of the European economy and technology through this period.

Colley, Linda. *Britons: Forging the Nation, 1707–1837.* 1992. A history of the British that emphasizes the interrelationships of political, social, and cultural history.

Goodman, Dena. *The Republic of Letters: A Cultural History of the French Enlightenment.* 1994. Useful for understanding the social context of the Enlightenment, especially the role of women as salon leaders.

Kennedy, Paul. *The Rise and Fall of British Naval Mastery.* 1976. A comprehensive work on the rise of British sea power from the sixteenth century to modern times.

Porter, Roy. *The Enlightenment.* 1990. A brief introduction.

Roche, Daniel. *France in the Enlightenment.* 1998. A study of state and society in France by an eminent French scholar.

NOTES

1. Moira Ferguson, ed., *First Feminists: British Women Writers, 1578–1799* (Bloomington: Indiana University Press, 1985), p. 426.

2. Quoted in Dena Goodman, *The Republic of Letters: A Cultural History of the French Enlightenment* (Ithaca, N.Y.: Cornell University Press, 1994), p. 89.

3. Quoted in M. S. Anderson, *Europe in the Eighteenth Century, 1713–1783,* 3d ed. (London: Longman, 1987), pp. 218–219.

19

AN AGE OF REVOLUTION, 1789–1815

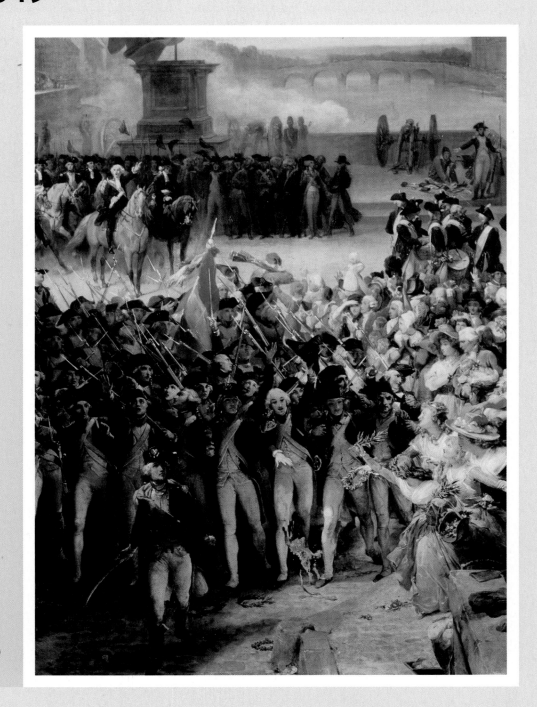

A French Citizen Army
The National Guard of
Paris leaves to join the
army, September 1792
(detail). *(Photos12.com-ARJ)*

These militiamen marching off to defend France against the invader in September 1792 appear to be heroes already. Adoring women in the crowd hand them laurel wreaths as they pass; the men march by, resolute and triumphant. Symbols of the ongoing revolution stand out as well: the prominent tricolor flag, the tricolor cockade in each man's hat. In fact, that September France's citizen armies for the first time defeated the army of a foreign monarch poised to breach its borders and snuff out its revolution. The painting celebrates this triumph about to happen and thereby inspires confidence in the Revolution and pride in its citizen-soldiers.

Today the French Revolution is considered the initiation of modern European as well as modern French history. The most powerful monarch in Europe was forced to accept constitutional limits to his power by subjects convinced of their right to demand them. Eventually, the king was overthrown and executed, and the monarchy abolished. Events in France reverberated throughout Europe because the overthrow of one absolute monarchy threatened fellow royals elsewhere. Revolutionary fervor on the part of ordinary soldiers enabled France's armies unexpectedly to best many of their opponents. By the late 1790s the armies of France would be led in outright conquest of other European states by one of the most talented generals in European history: Napoleon Bonaparte. He brought to the continental European nations that his armies eventually conquered a mixture of imperial aggression and revolutionary change. Europe was transformed both by the shifting balance of power and by the spread of revolutionary ideas.

Understanding the French Revolution means understanding not only its origins but also its complicated course of events and their significance. Challenges to the power of the king were not new, but the Revolution overthrew his right to rule at all. The notion that the people constituted the nation, were responsible as citizens, and had some right to representation in government became irresistible. Louis XVI was transformed from the divinely appointed father of his people to an enemy of the people, worthy only of execution. Central to the Revolution was the complex process by which public opinion was shaped and, in turn, shaped events. Change was driven

CHAPTER OUTLINE

THE BEGINNINGS OF REVOLUTION, 1775–1789

THE PHASES OF THE REVOLUTION, 1789–1799

THE NAPOLEONIC ERA AND THE LEGACY OF REVOLUTION, 1799–1815

KEY TERMS

Third Estate

National Assembly

Tennis Court Oath

Declaration of the Rights of Man and the Citizen

sans-culottes

Jacobins

Maximilien Robespierre

the Terror

Society of Revolutionary Republican Women

Directory

Napoleon Bonaparte

Civil Code

François Toussaint-Louverture

Online Study Center

This icon will direct you to interactive map and primary source activities on the website **college.hmco.com/pic/noble5e**

in part by the power of symbols—flags, rallying cries, inspiring art—to challenge an old political order and legitimize a new one.

FOCUS QUESTIONS

What factors led to the beginning of revolution in France in 1789?

Why did several phases of revolutionary change occur after 1789 and what were the characteristics of each phase?

What impact did the Revolution and Napoleonic rule have on France, the rest of Europe, and the wider world?

THE BEGINNINGS OF REVOLUTION, 1775–1789

What factors led to the beginning of revolution in France in 1789?

am a citizen of the world," wrote John Paul Jones, captain in the fledgling U.S. Navy, in 1778. He was writing to a Scottish aristocrat, apologizing for raiding the lord's estate while marauding along the British coast during the American Revolution. Jones (1747–1792), born a Scotsman himself, was one of the thousands of cosmopolitan Europeans who were familiar with European cultures on both sides of the Atlantic. As a sailor, Jones literally knew his way around the Atlantic world, but he was a "citizen of the world" in another sense as well. The Scotsman replied to Jones, surprised by the raid, since he was sympathetic to the American colonists; he was a man of "liberal sentiments" like Jones himself.[1] Both Jones and the Scottish lord felt they belonged to an international society of gentlemen who recognized certain Enlightenment principles regarding just and rational government.

In the Atlantic world of the late eighteenth century, both practical links of commerce and shared ideals about "liberty" were important shaping forces. The strategic interests of the great European powers were also always involved. Thus when the American colonists actively resisted British rule and then in 1776 declared their independence from Britain, the consequences were widespread and varied: British trading interests were challenged, French appetites for gains at British expense were whetted, and illusive notions about "liberty" seemed more plausible. The victory of the American colonies in 1783, followed by the creation of the U.S. Constitution in 1787, further heightened the appeal of liberal ideas elsewhere. Attempts at liberal reform were mounted in several states, including Ireland, the Netherlands, and Poland. However, the American Revolution had the most direct impact on later events in France because the French had been directly involved in the American effort.

REVOLUTIONARY MOVEMENTS IN EUROPE

While the British government was facing the revolt of the American colonies, it also confronted trouble closer to home. Like many Americans, many Britons had divided loyalties, and many who did favor armed force to subdue the rebellion were convinced that the war was being mismanaged. The prosecution of the war against the American colonies proceeded amid calls for reform of the ministerial government. The American rebellion also had ripple effects in other parts of Europe.

Ireland A reform movement also sprang up in Ireland in 1779. The reformers demanded greater autonomy from Britain. Like the Americans, Irish elites—mostly of English or Scottish origin—felt like disadvantaged junior partners in the British Empire. They objected to British policies that favored British imperial interests over those of the Irish ruling class: for example, the exclusion of Irish ports in favor of English and Scottish ones and the granting of political rights to Irish Catholics so that they might fight in Britain's overseas armies.

Protestant Irish landlords and elite families in towns, threatened by such policies, expressed their opposition not only in parliamentary debates but also in military defiance. Following the example of the American rebels, they set up a system of locally sponsored voluntary militia to resist British troops if necessary. The Volunteer Movement was neutralized when greater parliamentary autonomy for Ireland was granted in 1782, following the repeal of many restrictions on Irish commerce. Unlike the Americans, the Irish elites faced an internal challenge to their own authority—the Catholic population whom they had for centuries dominated. That challenge forced them to reach an accommodation with the British government.

The Netherlands Meanwhile, a political crisis with constitutional overtones was also brewing in the Netherlands. The United Provinces (the Netherlands) was governed by a narrow oligarchy of old merchant families, particularly in Amsterdam, and a military governor, the "stadtholder," from the princely House of Orange. The interests of the merchants and of the stadtholder frequently conflicted. Tensions between them deepened during the American Revolution, as merchants favored trade with the colonists and the prince favored maintaining an English alliance.

The conflict changed character when the representatives of the various cities, calling themselves the Dutch "Patriot" Party, defended their positions on the grounds of traditional balance of power within the Netherlands as well as with wider claims to American-style "liberty." The challenge to traditional political arrangements widened when middling urban dwellers, including newly wealthy traders and professionals, long disenfranchised by the closed merchant oligarchies, demanded "liberty," too—that is, political enfranchisement within the cities—and briefly took over the Patriot movement. Just as many Irish rebels accepted the concessions of 1782, the Patriot oligarchs in the Netherlands did nothing to resist an invasion in 1787 that restored the power of the stadtholder, the prince of Orange, and thereby ended the challenge to their own control of urban government.

Both the Irish volunteers and the Dutch Patriots, though members of very limited movements, echoed the American rebels in practical and ideological ways. Both were influenced by the economic and political consequences of Britain's relationship with its colonies. Both were inspired by the success of the American rebels and their thoroughgoing claims for political self-determination.

Poland Desire for political reform flared in Poland as well during this period. Reform along lines suggested by Enlightenment precepts was accepted as a necessity by Polish leaders after the first partition of Poland in 1772 had left the remnant state without some of its wealthiest territories (see Map 18.1 on page 570). Beginning in 1788, however, reforming gentry in the *Sejm* (representative assembly) went further; they established a commission to write a constitution, following the American example. The resulting document, known as the May 3 (1791) Constitution, was the first codified constitution in Europe; it was read and admired by George Washington.

Poles thus established a constitutional monarchy in which representatives of major towns as well as gentry and nobility could sit as deputies. The *liberum veto*, or individual veto power, which had allowed great nobles to obstruct royal authority, was abolished. However, Catherine the Great, empress of Russia, would not tolerate a constitutional government operating so close

1775–1783	American Revolutionary War
1779–1782	Irish Volunteer Movement
1788	U.S. Constitution ratified; Reform movement begins in Poland; "Patriot" movement ends in the Netherlands
1789	French Estates General meets at Versailles (May); Third Estate declares itself the National Assembly (June); Storming of the Bastille (July)
1791	Polish constitution French king Louis XVI captured attempting to flee (June) Slave revolt begins in Saint Domingue
1792	France declares war on Austria; revolutionary wars begin (April); Louis XVI arrested; France declared a republic (August–September)
1793	Louis XVI guillotined
1793–1794	Reign of Terror in France
1799	Napoleon seizes power in France
1801	Concordat with pope
1804	Napoleon crowned emperor Napoleonic Civil Code Independence of Haiti (Saint Domingue) declared
1805	Battle of Trafalgar; Battle of Austerlitz
1806	Dissolution of Holy Roman Empire
1812	French invasion of Russia
1814	Napoleon abdicates and is exiled French monarchy restored
1815	Hundred Days (February–June) Battle of Waterloo

to her own autocratic regime; she ordered an invasion of Poland in 1792. The unsuccessful defense of Poland was led by, among others, a Polish veteran of the American Revolution, Tadeusz Kosciuszko (tah-DAY-oosh kos-USE-ko) (1746–1817). The second, more extensive partition of Poland followed, to be answered in turn in 1794 by a widespread insurrection against Russian rule, spearheaded by Kosciuszko. The uprising was mercilessly suppressed by an alliance of Russian and Prussian troops. Unlike the U.S. Constitution from which they drew inspiration, the Poles' constitutional experiment was doomed by the power of its neighbors.

THE AMERICAN REVOLUTION AND THE KINGDOM OF FRANCE

As Britain's greatest commercial and political rival, France naturally was drawn into Britain's struggle with its North American colonies. In the Seven Years' War (1756–1763), the French had lost many of their colonial settlements and trading outposts to the English (see page 578). Stung by this outcome, certain French courtiers and ministers pressed for an aggressive colonial policy that would regain for France some of the riches in trade that Britain now threatened to monopolize. The American Revolution seemed to offer the perfect opportunity. The French extended covert aid to the Americans from the very beginning of the conflict in 1775. After the first major defeat of British troops by the Americans—at the Battle of Saratoga in 1777—France formally recognized the independent United States and committed troops as well as funds to the American cause. John Paul Jones's famous ship, the *Bonhomme Richard* (bon-OHM ree-SHARD), was purchased and outfitted by the French government, as were many other American naval vessels. French support was decisive. In 1781 the French fleet kept reinforcements from reaching the British force besieged by George Washington at Yorktown. The American victory at Yorktown effectively ended the war; the colonies' independence was formally recognized by the Treaty of Paris in 1783.

The consequences for France of its American alliance were momentous. Aid for the Americans saddled France with a debt of about 1 billion *livres* (pounds), which represented as much as one-quarter of the total debt that the French government was trying to service. A less tangible impact of the American Revolution came from the direct participation of about nine thousand French soldiers, sailors, and aristocrats. The best known is the Marquis de Lafayette, who became an aide to George Washington and helped command American troops. For many humble men, the war was simply employment. For others, it was a quest of sorts. For them, the promise of the Enlightenment—belief in human rationality, natural rights, and universal laws by which society should be organized—was brought to life in America.

Exposure to the American conflict occurred at the French court, too. Beginning in 1775, a permanent American mission to Versailles lobbied hard for aid and later managed the flow of that assistance. The chief emissary of the Americans was Benjamin Franklin (1706–1790), a philosophe by French standards whose writings and scientific experiments were already known to European elites. His talents—among them, a skillful exploitation of a simple, Quaker-like demeanor—succeeded in promoting the idealization of America at the French court.

The U.S. Constitution, the various state constitutions, and the debates surrounding their ratification were all published in Paris and much discussed in salons and at court, where lively debate about reform of French institutions had been going on for decades. America became the prototype of the rational republic—the embodiment of Enlightenment philosophy. It was hailed as the place where the irrationalities of inherited privilege did not prevail. A British observer, Arthur Young (1741–1820), believed that "the American revolution has laid the foundation of another in France, if [the French] government does not take care of itself."[2]

By the mid-1780s there was no longer a question of whether the French regime would experience reform but rather a question of what form the reform would take. The royal government was almost bankrupt. A significant minority of the politically active elite was convinced of the fundamental irrationality of France's system of government. Nevertheless, a dissatisfied elite and a financial crisis—even fanned by a successful revolt elsewhere—do not necessarily lead to revolution. Why did the French government—the *Ancien Régime* (ahn-SYEN ray-ZHEEM) or "Old Regime," as it became known after the Revolution—not "take care of itself"?

THE CRISIS OF THE OLD REGIME

The Old Regime was brought to the point of crisis in the late 1780s by three factors: (1) heavy debts that dwarfed an antiquated system for collecting revenue; (2) institutional constraints on the monarchy that defended privileged interests; and (3) public opinion that envisioned thoroughgoing reform and pushed the monarchy in that direction. Another factor was the ineptitude of the king, Louis XVI (r. 1774–1793).

Louis came to the throne in 1774, a year before the American Revolution began. He was a kind, well-meaning man better suited to be a petty bureaucrat than a king. The queen, the Austrian Marie Antoinette (1755–1793), was regarded with suspicion by the many who despised the "unnatural" alliance with Austria the marriage had sealed. She, too, was politically inept, unable to negotiate the complexities of court life and widely rumored to be selfishly wasteful of royal resources despite the realm's financial crises.

The fiscal crisis of the monarchy had been a long time in the making and was an outgrowth of the system by which the greatest wealth was protected by traditional privileges. At the top of the social and political pyramid were the nobles, a legal grouping that included warriors and royal officials. In France nobility conferred exemption from much taxation. Thus the royal government could not directly tax its wealthiest subjects.

This situation existed throughout much of Europe, a legacy of the individual contractual relation-

The Common People Crushed by Privilege

In this contemporary cartoon, a nobleman in military dress and a clergyman crush a commoner under the rock of burdensome taxes and forced labor *(corvées)*. The victim's situation reflects that of the peasantry, but his stylish clothes would allow affluent townspeople to identify with him. *(Musée Carnavalet, Paris/ Giraudon/Art Resource, NY)*

ships that had formed the political and economic framework of medieval Europe. Unique to France, however, was the strength of the institutions that defended this system. Of particular importance were the royal law courts, the parlements (par-luh-MAWHN), which claimed a right of judicial review over royal edicts. All the parlementaires—well-educated lawyers and judges— were noble and loudly defended the traditional privileges of all nobles. Louis XV (d. 1774), near the end of his life, had successfully undermined the power of the parlements by a bold series of moves. Louis XVI, immediately after coming to the throne, buckled under pressure and restored the parlements to full strength.

Deficit financing had been a way of life for the monarchy for centuries. After early efforts at reform, Louis XIV (d. 1715) had reverted to common fundraising expedients such as selling offices, which only added to the weight of privileged investment in the old order. England had established a national bank to free its government from the problem, but the comparable French effort early in the century had been undercapitalized and had failed. Late in the 1780s, under Louis XVI, one-fourth of the annual operating expenses of the government was borrowed, and half of all government expenditure went to paying interest on its debt. Short-term economic crises, such as disastrous harvests, added to the cumulative problem of government finance.

The king employed able finance ministers who tried to institute fundamental reforms, such as replacing the tangle of taxes with a simpler system in which all would pay and eliminating local tariffs, which were stifling commerce. The parlements and many courtiers and aristocrats, as well as ordinary people, resisted these policies. Peasants and townsfolk did not trust the "free market" (free from traditional trade controls) for grain; most feared that speculators would buy up the grain supply and people would starve. Trying to implement such reforms in times of grain shortage almost guaranteed their failure. Moreover, many supported the parlements simply because they were the only institution capable of standing up to the monarchy. Yet not all members of the elite joined the parlements in opposing reform. The imprint of "enlightened" public opinion was apparent in the thinking of some courtiers and thousands of educated commoners who believed that the government and the economy had to change and openly debated the nature and extent of reform needed.

In 1787 the king called an "Assembly of Notables"— an ad hoc group of elites—to support him in facing down the parlements and proceeding with some changes. He found little support even among men known to be sympathetic to reform. Some did not support particular proposals, and many were reluctant to allow the monarchy free rein. Others, reflecting the influence of the American Revolution, maintained that a "constitutional" body such as the Estates General, which had not been called since 1614, needed to make these decisions.

Ironically, nobles and clergy who were opposed to reform supported the call for the Estates General, too, confident they could control its deliberations. The three Estates met and voted separately by "order"—clergy (First Estate), nobles (Second Estate), and commoners (**Third Estate**). The combined votes of the clergy and nobles would presumably nullify whatever the Third Estate might propose.

THE ESTATES GENERAL

In 1788 mounting pressure from common people as well as courtiers led Louis to summon the Estates General. On Louis's orders, deputies were to be elected by local assemblies, which were chosen in turn by wide male suffrage. Louis mistakenly assumed he had widespread support in the provinces and wished to tap it by means of this grass-roots voting. Louis also agreed that the Third Estate should have twice as many deputies as the other two Estates, but he did not authorize voting by head rather than by order, which would have brought about the dominance of the Third Estate. Nevertheless, the king hoped that the specter of drastic proposals put forth by the Third Estate would frighten the aristocrats and clergy into accepting some of his reforms.

Louis's situation was precarious when the Estates General convened in May 1789. Already a groundswell of sentiment confirmed the legitimacy of the Estates General and the authority of the Third Estate to enact change. Political pamphlets abounded arguing that the Third Estate deserved enhanced power because it carried the mandate of the people. The most important of these was *What Is the Third Estate?* (1789) by Joseph Emmanuel Sieyès (1748–1836), a church official from the diocese of Chartres. The sympathies of Abbé Sieyès (say-EZ), as he was known, were with the Third Estate: his career had stalled because he was not noble. Sieyès argued that the Third Estate represented the nation because it did not reflect special privilege.

Among the deputies of the first two Estates—clergy and nobility—were men, such as the Marquis de Lafayette (1757–1834), who were sympathetic to reform. In the Third Estate, a large majority of deputies reflected the most radical political thought possible for men of their standing. Most were lawyers and other professionals who were functionaries in the government but, like Sieyès, of low social rank. They frequented provincial academies, salons, and political societies. They were convinced of the validity of their viewpoints and determined on reform, and they had little stake in the system as it was. When this group convened and met with resistance from the First and Second Estates and from Louis himself, they seized the reins of government and a revolution began.

1789: A REVOLUTION BEGINS

As soon as the three Estates convened at the royal palace at Versailles, conflicts surfaced. The ineptness of the Crown was immediately clear. On the first day of the meetings in May, Louis and his ministers failed to introduce a program of reforms for the deputies to consider. This failure raised doubt about the monarchy's commitment to reform. More important, it allowed the political initiative to pass to the Third Estate. The deputies challenged the Crown's insistence that the three Estates meet and vote separately. Deputies to the Third Estate refused to be certified (that is, to have their credentials officially recognized) as members of only the Third Estate rather than as members of the Estates General as a whole.

For six weeks the Estates General was unable to meet officially, and the king did nothing to break the impasse. During this interlude, the determination of the deputies of the Third Estate strengthened. More and more deputies were won over to the notion that the three Estates must begin in the most systematic way: France must have a written constitution.

The National Assembly By the middle of June, more than thirty reformist members of the clergy were sitting jointly with the Third Estate, which had invited all deputies from all three Estates to meet and be certified together. On June 17 the Third Estate simply declared itself the **National Assembly** of France. At first the king did nothing, but when the deputies arrived to meet on the morning of June 20, they discovered they had been locked out of the hall. Undaunted, they assembled instead in a nearby indoor tennis court and produced the document that has come to be known as the **Tennis Court Oath.** It was a collective pledge to meet until a written constitution had been achieved. Only one deputy refused to support it. Sure of their mandate, the deputies had assumed the reins of government.

The king continued to handle the situation with both ill-timed self-assertion and feeble attempts at compromise. As more and more deputies from the First and Second Estates joined the National Assembly, Louis "ordered" the remaining loyal deputies to join it, too. Simultaneously, however, he ordered troops to come to Paris. He feared disorder in the wake of the recent disturbances throughout France and believed that any challenge to the legitimacy of arbitrary monarchical authority would be disastrous.

National Assembly Legislative body formed in France in June 1789, when members of the Third Estate in the Estates General, joined by some deputies from the clergy, declared themselves the representatives of the nation.

Tennis Court Oath Pledge signed by all but one deputy of the National Assembly in France on June 20, 1789, to meet until a constitution was drafted.

Third Estate In France, the common people, as distinct from the nobles (First Estate) and clergy (Second Estate), in the representative body the Estates General.

The Tennis Court Oath

It was raining on June 20, 1789, when the deputies found themselves barred from their meeting hall and sought shelter in the royal tennis court. Their defiance created one of the turning points of the Revolution; the significance was recognized several years later by the creator of this painting. *(Réunion des Musées Nationaux/Art Resource, NY)*

Louis's appeal for armed assistance provoked unrest in the capital. Paris, with a population of about 600,000, was one of the largest cities in Europe. It was the political nerve center of the nation—the site of the publishing industry, salons, the homes of parlementaires and royal ministers. It was also a working city, with thousands of laborers of all trades plus thousands more—perhaps one-tenth of the inhabitants—jobless recent immigrants from the countryside. The city was both extremely volatile and extremely important to the stability of royal power. The king's call for troops aroused Parisians' suspicions. Some assumed a plot was afoot to starve Paris and destroy the National Assembly. Already they considered the Assembly to be a guarantor of acceptable government.

The Storming of the Bastille It took little—the announcement of the dismissal of a reformist finance minister—for Paris to erupt in demonstrations and looting. Crowds besieged City Hall and the royal armory, where they seized thousands of weapons. A popular militia formed as citizens armed themselves. Armed crowds assailed other sites of royal authority, including the huge fortified prison, the Bastille, on the

morning of July 14. The Bastille now held only a handful of petty criminals, but it still remained a potent symbol of royal power and, it was assumed, held large supplies of arms. Like the troops at the armory, the garrison at the Bastille had received no firm orders to fire on the crowds if necessary. The garrison commander at first mounted a hesitant defense, then decided to surrender after citizens managed to secure cannon and drag them to face the prison. Most of the garrison were allowed to go free, although the commander and several officers were murdered by the crowd.

The citizens' victory was a great embarrassment to royal authority. The king immediately had to embrace the popular movement. He came to Paris and in front of crowds at City Hall donned the red and blue cockade worn by the militia and ordinary folk as a badge of resolve and defiance. This symbolic action signaled the reversal of the Old Regime—politics would now be based on new principles.

Encouraged by events in Paris, inhabitants of cities and towns around France staged similar uprisings. In many areas, the machinery of royal government completely broke down. City councils, officials, and even parlementaires were thrown out of office. Popular

Women's March on Versailles, October 1789

Parisian marketwomen marched the 12 miles to the king's palace at Versailles, some provisioning themselves with tools or weapons as they left the capital.

(Réunion des Musées Nationaux/Art Resource, NY)

militias took control of the streets. A simultaneous wave of uprisings shook the countryside. Most of them were the result of food shortages, but their timing added momentum to the more strictly political protests in cities.

Toward Constitutional Government These events forced the members of the National Assembly to work energetically on the constitution and to pass legislation to satisfy popular protests against economic and political privileges. On August 4 the Assembly issued a set of decrees abolishing the remnants of powers that landlords had enjoyed since the Middle Ages, including the right to co-opt peasant labor and the bondage of serfdom itself. Although largely symbolic, because serfdom and forced labor had been eliminated in much of France, these changes represented a dramatic inroad into the property rights of the elite as they had been traditionally construed. The repeals were hailed as the "end of feudalism." A blow was also struck at established religion by eliminating the tithe, the forced payment of one-tenth of a person's income to the church. At the end of August, the Assembly issued the **Declaration of the Rights of Man and the Citizen.** It was a

bold assertion of the foundations of a newly conceived government, closely modeled on portions of the U.S. Constitution. Its preamble declared "that [since] the ignorance, neglect or contempt of the rights of man are the sole cause of public calamities and the corruption of governments," the deputies were "determined to set forth in a solemn declaration the natural, inalienable and sacred rights of man."[3]

In September the deputies debated the king's role in a new constitutional government. Monarchists favored a government rather like England's, with a two-house legislature, including an upper house representing the hereditary aristocracy and a royal right to veto legislation. More radical deputies favored a single legislative chamber and no veto power for the king. After deliberation, the Assembly reached a compromise. The king was given a three-year suspensive veto—the power to suspend legislation for the sitting of two legislatures. This was still a formidable amount of power but a drastic curtailment of his formerly absolute sovereignty.

The Women's March to Versailles Again Louis resorted to troops. This time he called them directly to Versailles, where the Assembly sat. News of the troops' arrival provoked outrage, which heightened with the threat of another grain shortage. Early on the morning of October 5, women in the Paris street markets saw the empty grocers' stalls and took immediate collective action. "We want bread!" they shouted at the steps of City

Declaration of the Rights of Man and the Citizen Document issued by the National Assembly of France in August 1789. Modeled on the U.S. Constitution, it asserted "the natural, inalienable and sacred rights of man."

Hall. Because they were responsible for procuring their families' food, women often led protests over bread shortages. This protest, however, went far beyond the ordinary. A crowd of thousands gathered and decided to walk all the way to Versailles, accompanied by the popular militia (now called the "National Guard"), to petition the king directly for sustenance.

Online Study Center **Improve Your Grade**
Primary Source: Popular Revolution: The Women of Paris March on Versailles

At Versailles, a joint delegation of the women and deputies from the National Assembly was dispatched to see the king. Some of the women fell at the feet of the king with their tales of hardship, certain that the "father of the people" would alleviate their suffering. He did order stored grain supplies distributed in Paris, and he agreed to accept the constitutional role that the Assembly had voted for him.

The king also agreed to return to Paris to reassure the people and was escorted back to the capital by both popular militia and bread protesters. The king was now in the hands of his people. Already, dramatic change had occurred as a result of a complex dynamic among the three Estates, the Crown, and the people of Paris. The king was still assumed to be the fatherly guardian of his people's well-being, but his powers were now limited and his authority badly shaken. The Assembly had begun to govern in the name of the "nation" and so far had the support of the people.

= S E C T I O N   S U M M A R Y =

- Inspired by events in America, elites in Ireland, the Netherlands, and Poland pushed for greater political liberty.

- France's support for the American colonies against Great Britain increased French government debt and exposed French soldiers and courtiers to revolutionary ideas.

- By the late 1780s, French royal government was in crisis owing to bankruptcy, institutions that impeded reform, and agitation for reform within elite society.

- The French Revolution began in 1789 when the Estates General convened and commoners in the Third Estate claimed a mandate to write a constitution and enact major changes in law.

- French citizens, led by the Parisians, formed popular militias, attacked royal fortresses, and marched to Versailles to confront the king.

THE PHASES OF THE REVOLUTION, 1789–1799

Why did several phases of revolutionary change occur after 1789 and what were the characteristics of each phase?

The French Revolution was a complicated affair. It was a series of changes, in a sense a series of revolutions, driven not by one group of people but by several groups. Even among elites convinced of the need for reform, the range of opinion was wide. The people of Paris continued to be an important force for change. Country people also became active, primarily in resisting changes forced on them by the central government.

All of the wrangling within France was complicated by foreign reaction to events there. Managing war to defend the revolution soon became a routine burden for the fragile revolutionary governments. In addition, they had to cope with the continuing problems that had precipitated the Revolution in the first place, including the government's chronic indebtedness and recurrent grain shortages. Finally, the Revolution itself was an issue in that, once the traditional arrangements of royal government had been altered, momentum for further change was unleashed.

THE FIRST PHASE COMPLETED, 1789–1791

At the end of 1789 Paris was in ferment, but for a time forward progress blunted the threat of disastrous divisions between king and Assembly and between either of them and the people of Paris. The capital continued to be the center of lively political debate. Salons continued to meet; academies and private societies proliferated. Deputies to the Assembly swelled the ranks of these societies or helped to found new ones. Several would be important throughout the Revolution—particularly the Jacobin (JACK-oh-bin) Club, named for the monastic order whose buildings the members used as a meeting hall.

These clubs represented the gamut of revolutionary opinion. Some, in which ordinary Parisians were well represented, focused on economic policies that would directly benefit common people. Women were active in a few of the more radical groups. Monarchists dominated other clubs. At first similar to the salons and debating societies of the Enlightenment era, the clubs quickly became sources of political pressure on the government. A bevy of popular newspapers also contributed to the vigorous political life in the capital.

The broad front of revolutionary consensus began to break apart as the Assembly forged ahead with decisions about the constitution and with policies necessary to remedy France's still-desperate financial situation. The largest portion of the untapped wealth of the nation lay with the Catholic Church, an obvious target of anticlerical reformers. The deputies did not propose to dismantle the church, but they did make sweeping changes: They kept church buildings intact and retained the clergy as salaried officials of the state. They abolished all monasteries and pensioned the monks and nuns to permit them to continue as nurses and teachers where possible. With the depleted treasury in mind, the Assembly seized most of the vast lands of the church and declared them national property (*biens nationaux*) to be sold for revenue.

However, revenue was needed faster than the property could be inventoried and sold, so government bonds (*assignats* [ah-see-NYAH]) were issued against the eventual sale of church lands. Unfortunately, in the cash-strapped economy, the bonds were treated like money, their value became inflated, and the government never realized the hoped-for profits. A greater problem was the political divisiveness generated by the restructuring of the church. Many members of the lower clergy, living as they did near ordinary citizens, were among the most reform-minded of the deputies. These clergy were willing to go along with many changes, but the required oath of loyalty to the state made a mockery of clerical independence.

The Civil Constitution of the Clergy, as these measures were called, was passed by the Assembly in July 1790 because the clerical deputies opposing it were outvoted. More than half of the churchmen did take the oath of loyalty. Those who refused, concentrated among the higher clergy, were in theory thrown out of their offices. A year later (April 1791) the pope declared that clergy who had taken the oath were suspended from their offices. Antirevolutionary sentiment grew among thousands of French people, particularly in outlying regions, to whom the church was still vital as a source of charity and a center of community life. This religious opposition worked to undermine the legitimacy of the new government.

Meanwhile, the Assembly proceeded with administrative and judicial reform. The deputies abolished the medieval provinces as administrative districts and replaced them with uniform *départements* (departments). They declared that local officials would be elected—a revolutionary dispersal of power that had previously belonged to the king.

As work on the constitution drew to a close in the spring of 1791, the king decided that he had had enough. Royal authority, as he knew it, had been virtually dismantled and Louis himself was now a virtual prisoner in the Tuileries (TWEE-lair-ee) Palace in central Paris. The king and a few loyal aides worked out a plan to flee France and on June 20, 1791, he and the members of his immediate family set out in disguise. However, the party was stopped—and recognized—in the town of Varennes (vah-REN) near the eastern border of the kingdom.

Louis and his family were returned to Paris and held under lightly disguised house arrest. The circumstances of his flight were quickly discovered. He and the queen had sent money abroad ahead of themselves. He had left behind a document that condemned the constitution and revealed his intention was to invade France with Austrian troops, if necessary. Thus, in July 1791, just as the Assembly was completing its proposal for a constitutional monarchy, the constitution it had created began to seem unworkable because the monarch was not to be trusted.

Editorials and protests against the monarchy increased. In one incident known as the Massacre of the Champ (Field) de Mars (SHOM duh MARSS), government troops led by Lafayette fired on citizens at an antimonarchy demonstration that certain Parisian clubs had organized; about fifty men and women died. This inflammatory incident heightened tensions between moderate reformers satisfied with the constitutional monarchy, such as Lafayette, and outspoken republicans who wanted to eliminate the monarchy altogether.

Nevertheless, on September 14 the king swore to uphold the constitution. He had no choice. The event became an occasion for celebration, but the tension between the interests of the Parisians and the provisions of the new constitution could not be glossed over. Though a liberal document for its day, the constitution reflected the views of the elite deputies who had created it. The right to vote, based on a minimal property qualification, was given to about half of all adult men. However, these men only chose electors, for whom the property qualifications were higher. The electors in turn chose deputies to national bodies as well as local officials. Although in theory any eligible voter could be an elected deputy or official, the fact that elite electors determined every officeholder meant that few ordinary citizens would become deputies or local administrators. A new Declaration of Rights accompanied the constitution that reflected a fear of the masses that had not existed when the Declaration of the Rights of Man and the Citizen was first promulgated in 1789. Freedom of the press and freedom of assembly, for example, were not fully guaranteed.

Further, the constitution granted neither political rights nor legal equality to women, nor did the Assembly pass laws beneficial to women, such as legalizing divorce or mandating female education. Educated women had joined some of the Parisian clubs and had attempted to influence the Assembly. A Declaration of the Rights of Woman was drafted by a woman named Olympe de Gouges (oh-LAMP duh GOOZH) to draw attention to the treatment of women in the new constitution.

Online Study Center **Improve Your Grade**
Primary Source: A French Woman Broadens the Revolution: Declaration of the Rights of Woman and Citizen

Very soon after the constitution was implemented, the fragility of the new system became clear. The National Assembly declared that its members could not serve in the first assembly to be elected under the constitution. Thus the members of the newly elected Legislative Assembly, which began to meet in October 1791, lacked any of the cohesiveness that would have come from collective experience. Also, unlike the previous National Assembly, they did not represent a broad range of opinion but were mostly republicans.

In fact, the Legislative Assembly was dominated by republican members of the Jacobin Club. They were known as Girondins (zhih-ron-DEHN), after the region in southwestern France from which many of the club's leaders came. The policies of these new deputies and continued pressure from the ordinary citizens of Paris would cause the constitutional monarchy to collapse in less than a year.

THE SECOND PHASE AND FOREIGN WAR, 1791–1793

An additional pressure on the new regime soon arose: a threat of foreign invasion and a war to respond to the threat. Aristocratic émigrés, including the king's brothers, had taken refuge in nearby German states and were planning to invade France. The emperor and other German rulers did little actively to aid the plotters. Austria and Prussia, however, in the Declaration of Pillnitz of August 1791, declared, as a concession to the émigrés, that they would intervene if necessary to support the monarchy in France.

The threat of invasion, when coupled with distrust of the royal family, seemed more real to the revolutionaries in Paris than it may actually have been. Indeed, many deputies hoped for war. They assumed that the outcome would be a French defeat, which would lead to a popular uprising that would rid them, at last, of the monarchy. In April 1792, under pressure from the

The French Revolution

May 5, 1789	Estates General meets in Versailles
June 17, 1789	Third Estate declares itself the National Assembly
June 20, 1789	Tennis Court Oath
July 14, 1789	Storming of the Bastille
August 27, 1789	Declaration of the Rights of Man and the Citizen
October 5–6, 1789	Women's march on Versailles Louis XVI returns to Paris
July 1790	Civil Constitution of the Clergy
June 1791	Louis XVI captured attempting to flee
August 1791	Declaration of Pillnitz
September 1791	New constitution implemented
October 1791	Legislative Assembly begins to meet
April 1792	France declares war on Austria
August 10, 1792	Storming of the Tuileries; Louis XVI arrested
September 21, 1792	National Convention declares France a republic
January 21, 1793	Louis XVI guillotined
May 1793	First Law of the Maximum
July 1793	Terror inaugurated
July 1794	Robespierre guillotined; Terror ends
October 1795	Directory established
November 1799	Napoleon seizes power

Assembly, Louis XVI declared war against Austria. From this point on, foreign war would be an ongoing factor in the Revolution.

At first the war was a disaster for France. The army had not been reorganized into an effective fighting force after the loss of many aristocratic officers and the addition of newly self-aware citizens. On one occasion troops insisted on putting an officer's command to a vote. Early defeats further emboldened critics of the monarchy. Under the direction of the Girondins, the Legislative Assembly began to press for the deportation of priests who had been leading demonstrations against the government. The Assembly abolished the personal guard of the king and summoned provincial National Guardsmen to Paris.

Louis XVI in 1792
The king, though a kindly man, had neither the character nor the convictions necessary to refashion royal authority symbolically as the Revolution proceeded. When Parisian crowds forced him to wear the "liberty cap," the monarchy was close to collapse.
(Metropolitan Museum of Art, The Elisha Whittelsey Collection, The Elisha Whittelsey Fund, 1962 [62.520.333]. Image © The Metropolitan Museum of Art)

The king's resistance to these measures, as well as fears of acute grain shortages owing to a poor harvest and the needs of the armies, created further unrest. Crowds staged boisterous marches near the royal palace, physically confronted the king, and forced him to don the "liberty cap," a symbol of republicanism. The king's authority and prestige were now thoroughly undermined.

By July 1792 tensions had become acute. The grain shortage was severe, Austrian and Prussian troops committed to saving the royal family were threatening to invade, and, most important, Parisian citizens were better organized and more determined than ever before. In each of the forty-eight "sections"—administrative wards—of Paris, a miniature popular assembly thrashed out all the events and issues of the day just as deputies in the nationwide Legislative Assembly did. Derisively

called **sans-culottes** (sahn–koo-LOT) ("without knee pants") because they could not afford elite fashions, the ordinary Parisians in the section assemblies included shopkeepers, artisans, and laborers. Their political organization enhanced their influence with the Assembly, the clubs, and Parisian newspapers. By late July most sections of the city had approved a petition calling for the exile of the king, the election of new city officials, the exemption of the poor from taxation, and other radical measures.

In August the sans-culottes took matters into their own hands. On the night of August 9, after careful preparations, representatives of the section assemblies constituted themselves as a new city government with the aim of "saving the state." The next day, August 10, they assaulted the Tuileries Palace, where the royal family was living. In the bloody confrontation, hundreds of royal guards and citizens died. The king and his family were imprisoned in one of the fortified towers in the city, under guard of the popularly controlled city government.

The storming of the Tuileries inaugurated the second major phase of the Revolution: the establishment of republican government in place of the monarchy. By their intimidating numbers, the people of Paris now controlled the Legislative Assembly. Some deputies fled. Those who remained agreed under pressure to dissolve the Assembly and make way for another body to be elected by universal manhood suffrage. On September 20 that assembly, known as the National Convention, began to meet. The next day the Convention declared the end of the monarchy and set to work crafting a constitution for the new republic.

Coincidentally, that same September day, French forces won their first genuine victory over the allied Austrian and Prussian invasion forces. Though not a decisive battle, it was a profound psychological triumph. A citizen army had defeated the professional force of a ruling prince. The victory bolstered the republican government and encouraged it to put more energy into the wars. Indeed, maintaining armies in the field became a weighty factor in the delicate equilibrium of revolutionary government. The new republican regime let it be known that its armies were not merely for self-defense but for the liberation of all peoples in the "name of the French Nation."

The Convention faced the divisive issue of what to do with the king. Some of the king's correspondence, discovered after the storming of the Tuileries, provided the pretext for charges of treason. The Convention held a trial for him, which lasted from December 11, 1792, to January 15, 1793. He was found guilty of treason by an overwhelming vote (683 to 39); the republican government would not compromise with monarchy. Less

sans-culottes   Ordinary citizens of revolutionary Paris, whose derisive nickname referred to their inability to afford fashionable knee pants ("culottes").

lopsided was the sentence: Louis was condemned to death by a narrow majority, 387 to 334.

The consequences for the king were immediate. On January 21, 1793, Louis mounted the scaffold in a public square near the Tuileries and was beheaded. The execution split the ranks of the Convention and soon resulted in the breakdown of the institution itself.

THE FALTERING REPUBLIC AND THE TERROR, 1793–1794

In February 1793 the republic was at war with virtually every state in Europe; the only exceptions were the Scandinavian kingdoms and Russia. Moreover, the regime faced massive and widespread counterrevolutionary uprisings within France. Vigilance against internal and external enemies became a top priority. The Convention established an executive body, the Committee of Public Safety. In theory, this executive council was answerable to the Convention as a whole. As the months passed, however, it acted with greater and greater autonomy not only to institute policies but also to eradicate enemies. The broadly based republican government represented by the Convention began to disintegrate.

Robespierre and the Committee for Public Safety
In June 1793, pushed by the Parisian sections, a group of extreme Jacobins purged the Girondin deputies from the Convention, arresting many of them. The Girondins were republicans who favored an activist government in the people's behalf, but they were less radical than their fellow Jacobins who now moved against them, less insistent on central control of the Revolution, and less willing to share power with the citizens of Paris. After the purge, the Convention still met, but most authority lay with the Committee of Public Safety.

Now, new uprisings against the regime began as revolts by Girondin sympathizers added to counterrevolutionary revolts by peasants and aristocrats. As resistance to the government mounted and the foreign threat continued, a dramatic event in Paris led the Committee of Public Safety officially to adopt a policy of political repression. A well-known figure of the Revolution, Jean Paul Marat (1743–1793), publisher of a radical republican newspaper very popular with ordinary Parisians, was murdered on July 13 by Charlotte Corday (1768–1793), a young aristocratic woman who had asked to meet with him. Shortly afterward, a longtime member of the Jacobin Club, **Maximilien Robespierre** (ROBES-pee-air) (1758–1794), joined the

Committee and called for "Terror"—the systematic repression of internal enemies. He was not alone in his views. Members of the section assemblies of Paris led demonstrations to pressure the government into making Terror the order of the day.

Since the previous autumn the guillotine had been at work against identified enemies of the regime, but now a more energetic apparatus of Terror was instituted. A Law of Suspects was passed that allowed citizens to be arrested simply on vague suspicion of counterrevolutionary sympathies. Revolutionary tribunals and an oversight committee made arbitrary arrests and rendered summary judgments. In October a steady stream of executions began, beginning with the queen, imprisoned since the storming of the Tuileries the year before. The imprisoned Girondin deputies followed, and then the beheadings continued relentlessly. Paris witnessed about 2,600 executions from 1793 to 1794.

Around France the verdicts of revolutionary tribunals led to approximately 14,000 executions. Another 10,000 to 12,000 people died in prison. Ten thousand or more were killed, usually by summary execution, after the defeat of counterrevolutionary uprisings. For example, 2,000 people were summarily executed in Lyon when a Girondin revolt collapsed there in October. The aim of **the Terror** was not merely to stifle active resistance; it was also to silence simple dissent. The victims in Paris included not only aristocrats or former deputies but also sans-culottes. The radical Jacobins wanted to seize control of the Revolution from the Parisian citizens who had lifted them to power.

Robespierre embodied all the contradictions of the policy of Terror. He was an austere, almost prim man who lived very modestly—a model, of sorts, of the virtuous, disinterested citizen. His unbending loyalty to his political principles earned him the nickname "the Incorruptible." The policies followed by the government during the year of his greatest influence, from July 1793 to July 1794, included generous, rational, and humane actions to benefit ordinary citizens as well as the atrocities of official Terror. (See the box "The Written Record: Robespierre Justifies Terror Against Enemies of the Revolution.") Indeed, the Terror notwithstanding, the government of the Committee of Public Safety was effective in providing direction for the nation at a critical time. In August 1793 it instituted the first mass conscription of citizens into the army (*levée en masse* [leh-VAY ohn MAHSS]), and a consistently effective popular army came into existence. In the autumn of 1793 this army won impressive victories. In May the

---

Jacobins   In revolutionary France, a republican political club named for a monastic order.

Maximilien Robespierre   French lawyer and revolutionary leader, influential member of the Committee of Public Safety (1793–1794); advocated Terror to suppress internal dissent.

the Terror   Systematic repression of internal enemies undertaken by French revolutionary government from 1793 to 1794. Approximately fourteen thousand people were executed, including aristocrats, Girondins, and sans-culottes.

ROBESPIERRE JUSTIFIES TERROR AGAINST ENEMIES OF THE REVOLUTION

In this excerpt from a speech before the National Convention in December 1793, Robespierre justifies the revolutionary government's need to act in a vigorous manner in order to defend itself from challenges within and without.

The defenders of the Republic must adopt Caesar's maxim, for they believe that "nothing has been done so long as anything remains to be done." Enough dangers still face us to engage all our efforts. It has not fully extended the valor of our Republican soldiers to conquer a few Englishmen and a few traitors. A task no less important, and one more difficult, now awaits us: to sustain an energy sufficient to defeat the constant intrigues of all the enemies of our freedom and to bring to a triumphant realization the principles that must be the cornerstone of public welfare.... Revolution is the war waged by liberty against its enemies; a constitution is that which crowns the edifice of freedom once victory has been won and the nation is at peace. The revolutionary government has to summon extraordinary activity to its aid precisely because it is at war. It is subjected to less binding and less uniform regulations, because the circumstances in which it finds itself are tempestuous and shifting, above all because it is compelled to deploy, swiftly and incessantly, new resources to meet new and pressing dangers. The principal concern of a constitutional government is civil liberty; that of a revolutionary government, public liberty. [A] revolutionary government is obliged to defend the state itself against the factions that assail it from every quarter. To good citizens revolutionary government owes the full protection of the state; to the enemies of the people it owes only death....

Is a revolutionary government the less just and the less legitimate because it must be more vigorous in its actions and freer in its movement than ordinary government? No! For it rests on the most sacred of all laws, the safety of the people, and on necessity, which is the most indisputable of all rights. It also has its rules, all based on justice and on public order. It has nothing in common with anarchy or disorder; on the contrary, its purpose is to repress them and to establish and consolidate the rule of law. It has nothing in common with arbitrary rule; it is public interest which governs it and not the whims of private individuals.

QUESTIONS

1. How does Robespierre describe the differences between constitutional and revolutionary government?

2. How does Robespierre defend the legitimacy of revolutionary government?

Source: Reprinted with permission of Scribner, an imprint of Simon & Schuster Adult Publishing Group, from *Robespierre,* edited by George Rudé. Copyright © 1967 by Prentice-Hall, Inc., copyright renewed © 1995 by George Rudé. All rights reserved.

Convention had instituted the Law of the Maximum, which controlled the price of grain so that city people could afford their staple food—bread. In September the Committee extended the law to apply to other necessary commodities. Extensive plans were made for a system of free and universal primary education. Slavery in the French colonies was abolished in February 1794. Divorce, first legalized in 1792, was made easier for women to obtain.

Social Reforms in the Name of Reason In the name of "reason," traditional rituals and rhythms of life were changed. One reform of long-term significance was the introduction of the metric system of weights and measures. Although people continued to use the old, familiar measures for a very long time, the change was eventually accomplished, leading the way for standardization throughout Europe. Equally "rational" but not as successful was the elimination of the traditional calendar; weeks and months were replaced by uniform thirty-day months and *decadi* (ten-day weeks with one day of rest), and all saints' days and Christian holidays were eliminated. The years had already been changed—Year I had been declared with the founding of the republic in the autumn of 1792.

Churches were rededicated as "temples of reason." Believing that outright atheism left people with no basis for personal or national morality, Robespierre sought instead to promote a cult of the Supreme Being. The new public festivals were solemn civic ceremonies intended to ritualize and legitimize the new political order. But the French people generally resented the elimination of the traditional calendar and the attacks on the church. In the countryside massive peasant uprisings protested the loss of poor relief, community life, and familiar ritual.

Divorce law and economic regulation were a boon, especially to urban women, but women's participation in section assemblies and in all organized political activity—which had been energetic and widespread—was banned in October 1793. The particular target of the regime was the **Society of Revolutionary Republican Women,** a powerful club representing the interests of female sans-culottes. By banning women from political life, the regime helped to ground its legitimacy, since the seemingly "natural" exclusion of women might make the new system of government appear part of the "natural" order. (See the feature "The Visual Record: Political Symbols.") Outlawing women's clubs and barring women from section assemblies also eliminated a source of popular power, from which the regime was now trying to distance itself.

The End of the Terror The Committee and members of the Convention were divided over religious and other policies, but the main policy differences concerned economic matters: how far to go to assist the poor, the unemployed, and the landless. Several of the moderate critics of Robespierre and his allies were guillotined for disagreeing about policy and for doubting the continuing need for the Terror itself. Their deaths helped precipitate the end of the Terror by causing Robespierre's power base to shrink so much that it had no further legitimacy.

Deputies to the Convention finally dared to move against Robespierre in July 1794. French armies had scored a major victory over Austrian troops on June 26, so there was no longer any need for the emergency status that the Terror had thrived on. In late July the Convention voted to arrest Robespierre, the head of the revolutionary tribunal in Paris, and their closest associates and allies in the city government. On July 28 and 29 Robespierre and the others—about a hundred in all—were guillotined, and the Terror ended.

THE THERMIDORIAN REACTION AND THE DIRECTORY, 1794–1799

After the death of Robespierre, the Convention reclaimed the executive powers that the Committee of Public Safety had seized. It dismantled the apparatus of the Terror, repealed the Law of Suspects, and forced the revolutionary tribunals to adopt ordinary legal procedures. The Convention also passed into law some measures, such as expanded public education, that had been proposed the preceding year but not enacted. This post-Terror phase of the Revolution is called the "Thermidorian Reaction" because it began in the revolutionary month of Thermidor (July 19–August 17).

Lacking the weapons of the Terror, the Convention was unable to enforce controls on the supply and price of bread. Thus economic difficulties and a hard winter produced famine by the spring of 1795. The people of Paris tried to retain influence with the new government. In May crowds marched on the Convention chanting "Bread and the Constitution of '93," referring to the republican constitution drafted by the Convention but never implemented because of the Terror. The demonstrations were met with force and were dispersed.

Members of the Convention remained fearful of a renewed, popularly supported Terror, on the one hand, or a royalist uprising, on the other. Counterrevolutionary uprisings had erupted in the fall of 1794, and landings on French territory by émigré forces occurred the following spring. The Convention drafted a new constitution that limited popular participation in government, as had the first constitution of 1791. The new plan allowed fairly widespread (but not universal) male suffrage, but only for electors, who would choose deputies for the two houses of the legislature. The property qualifications for being an elector were very high, so all but elite citizens were effectively disenfranchised. The Convention also decreed, at the last minute, that two-thirds of its members must serve in the new legislature, regardless of the outcome of elections. Although this maneuver enhanced the stability of the new regime, it undermined the credibility of the new vote.

Governance under the provisions of the new constitution, beginning in the fall of 1795, was called the **Directory,** for the executive council of five men chosen by the upper house of the new legislature. To avoid the concentration of authority that had produced the Terror, the members of the Convention had tried to enshrine separation of powers in the new system. However, the governments under the Directory were never free from outside plots or from their own extraconstitutional maneuvering.

The most spectacular challenge was an attempted coup by the "Conspiracy of Equals," a group of extreme Jacobins who wanted to restore popular government and aggressive economic and social policy on behalf of the common people. The conspiracy ended with arrests and executions in 1797. When elections in 1797 and 1798 returned many royalist as well as Jacobin deputies, the Directory abrogated the constitution: many "undesirable" deputies were arrested, sent into exile, or denied seats.

The armies of the republic did enjoy some spectacular successes during these years, for the first time carrying the fighting—and the effects of the Revolution—onto foreign soil. French armies conquered the Dutch in 1795. In 1796–1797 French armies led by the

Society of Revolutionary Republican Women In revolutionary Paris, a powerful political club that represented the interests of female sans-culottes.

Directory French revolutionary government from 1795 to 1799, consisting of an executive council of five men chosen by the upper house of the legislature.

Political Symbols

During the French Revolution, thousands of illustrations in support of various revolutionary (or counterrevolutionary) ideas were reproduced on posters, on handbills, and in pamphlets. Some satirized their subjects, such as Marie Antoinette, or celebrated revolutionary milestones, such as the fall of the Bastille. The etching here of the woman armed with a pike, dating from 1792, falls into this category. Other pictures, such as the representation from 1795 of Liberty as a young woman wearing the liberty cap, symbolized or reinforced various revolutionary ideals.*

Political images like these are an invaluable though problematic source for historians. Let us examine these two images of women and consider how French people during the Revolution might have responded to them. To understand what they meant to contemporaries, we must know something about the other images that these would have been compared to. We must also view the images in the context of the events of the Revolution itself. Immediately, then, we are presented with an interpretive agenda. How ordinary and acceptable was this image of an armed woman? If women were not citizens coequal with men, how could a woman be a symbol of liberty? What, in short, do these political images reveal about the spectrum of political life in their society?

The woman holding the pike stares determinedly at the viewer. Many details confirm what the original caption announced: This is a French woman who has become free. In her hat she wears one of the symbols of revolutionary nationhood: the tricolor cockade. The badge around her waist celebrates a defining moment for the revolutionary nation: the fall of the Bastille. Her pike itself is inscribed with the words "Liberty or death."

The woman appears to be serving not merely as a symbol of free women. She comes close to being the generic image of a free citizen, willing and

An Armed Citizen, ca. 1792
(Bibliothèque nationale de France)

able to fight for liberty—an astonishing symbolic possibility in a time when women were not yet treated equally under the law or granted the same political rights as the men of their class. Other images prevalent at the time echo this possibility. Many contemporary representations of the women's march on Versailles in 1789 show women carrying arms, active in advancing the Revolution. By the time this image was created (most likely in 1792), many other demonstrations and violent

*This discussion draws on the work of Joan Landes, "Representing the Body Politic: The Paradox of Gender in the Graphic Politics of the French Revolution," and Darlene Gay Levy and Harriet B. Applewhite, "Women and Militant Citizenship in Revolutionary Paris," in Sara E. Melzer and Leslie W. Rabine, eds., Rebel Daughters: Women and the French Revolution (New York: Oxford University Press, 1992), pp. 15–37, 79–101.

confrontations by ordinary people had resulted in the creation of dozens of popular prints and engravings that showed women acting in the same ways as men.

Repeatedly during 1792, women proposed to the revolutionary government that they be granted the right to bear arms. Their request was denied, but it was not dismissed out of hand. There was debate, and the issue was in effect tabled. Nevertheless, women's actions in the Revolution had created at least the possibility of envisaging citizenship with a female face.

The image of Liberty from 1795 does not reflect the actions of women but rather represents their exclusion from political participation. It is one of a number of images of Liberty that portray this ideal as a passive, innocent woman, here garbed in ancient dress, surrounded by a glow that in the past had been reserved for saints. Liberty here is envisaged as a pure and lofty goal, symbolized as a pure young woman.

Late in 1793, during the Terror, women were excluded from formal participation in politics with the disbanding of women's organizations. Nor did they gain political rights under the Directory, which re-established some of the limited gains of the first phase of the Revolution. The justification offered for their exclusion in 1793 was borrowed from Jean-Jacques Rousseau: it is contrary to nature for women to be in public life (see page 557). Women "belong" in the private world of the family, where they will nurture male citizens. Women embody ideal qualities such as patience and self-sacrifice; they are not fully formed beings capable of action in their own right.

Such notions made it easy to use images of women to embody ideals for public purposes. A woman could represent liberty precisely because actual women were not able to be political players.

The two images shown here thus demonstrate that political symbols can have varying relationships to "reality." The pike-bearing citizen is the more "real." Her image reflects the way of thinking about politics that became possible for the first time because of their actions. The other woman reflects not the attributes of actual women but an ideal type spawned by the use of arbitrary gender distinctions to legitimize political power. In these images we can see modern political life taking

Liberty as a Young Woman, ca. 1795 *(S. P. Avery Collection, Miriam and Ira D. Wallach Division of Arts, Prints, and Photographs, The New York Public Library, Astor, Lenox, and Tilden Foundations/Art Resource, NY)*

shape: the sophistication of its symbolic language, the importance of abstract ideas such as liberty and nationhood—as well as the grounding of much political life in rigid distinctions between public and private, male and female.

QUESTIONS

1. What circumstances explain the 1792 image of a woman as an armed citizen?

2. How would an idealized image of a young woman be useful as a symbol of liberty?

Online Study Center
   Improve Your Grade Visual Record Activities

young general Napoleon Bonaparte wrested control of northern Italy from the Austrians. Both regions were transformed into "sister" republics, governed by local revolutionaries but under French protection. By 1799, however, conditions had once again reached a critical juncture. The demands of the war effort, together with rising prices and the continued decline in the value of the assignats, brought the government again to the brink of bankruptcy. The government also seemed to be losing control of the French countryside; there were continued royalist uprisings, local political vendettas between moderates and Jacobins, and outright banditry.

Members of the Directory had often turned to sympathetic army commanders to suppress dissent and to carry out arrests and purges of the legislature. They now invited General Bonaparte to help them form a government that they could more strictly control. Two members of the Directory plotted with Napoleon and his brother, Lucien Bonaparte, to seize power on November 9, 1799.

SECTION SUMMARY

- The phases of the French Revolution were shaped by elites' desires for change, demands of common people, and the need to defend France against foreign monarchs.

- Between 1789 and 1791, the National Assembly wrote a constitution, seized and sold church property, ended traditional obligations of peasants, and reorganized local government.

- In 1791, the constitution was implemented and a Legislative Assembly elected.

- In 1792, Parisian citizens overthrew the monarchy; the Convention, elected by universal manhood suffrage, governed the republic.

- Control of the government passed to the Committee of Public Safety, which defended France from foreign invasion and gave economic assistance to common people but also implemented a policy of official Terror in which thousands of French people were killed.

- After the Terror, suffrage was again restricted, but the government of the Directory could not bring stability.

THE NAPOLEONIC ERA AND THE LEGACY OF REVOLUTION, 1799–1815

What impact did the Revolution and Napoleonic rule have on France, the rest of Europe, and the wider world?

Talented, charming, and ruthless, Napoleon Bonaparte (1769–1821) was the kind of person who gives rise to myths. His audacity, determination, and personal magnetism enabled him to profit from the political instability and confusion in France and to establish himself in power. Once in power, he temporarily stabilized the political scene by fixing in law the more conservative gains of the Revolution. He also used his power and his remarkable abilities as a general to continue wars of conquest against France's neighbors, which helped deflect political tensions at home.

Napoleon's troops in effect exported the Revolution as they conquered most of Europe. In most states that came under French control, law codes were reformed, governing elites were opened to talent, and public works were upgraded. Yet French conquest also meant domination, pure and simple, and involvement in France's rivalry with Britain. The Napoleonic era left Europe an ambiguous legacy—war and its enormous costs, yet also revolution and its impetus to positive change.

NAPOLEON: FROM SOLDIER TO EMPEROR, 1799–1804

Napoleon was from Corsica, a Mediterranean island that had passed from Genoese to French control in the eighteenth century. The second son of a large gentry family, he was educated at military academies in France, and he married the politically well-connected widow Joséphine de Beauharnais (1763–1814), whose aristocratic husband had been a victim of the Terror.

Napoleon steered a careful course through the political turmoil of the Revolution. By 1799 his military victories had won him much praise and fame. He had

Napoleon Bonaparte French general who took part in a coup in 1799 against the Directory, Napoleon consolidated power as first consul and ruled as emperor from 1804 to 1815.

demonstrated his reliability and ruthlessness in 1795 when he ordered troops guarding the Convention to fire on a Parisian crowd. He had capped his successful Italian campaign of 1796–1797 with an invasion of Egypt in an attempt to strike at British influence and trade connections in the eastern Mediterranean. The Egyptian campaign failed in its goals, but individual spectacular victories during the campaign ensured Napoleon's military reputation. In addition, Napoleon had demonstrated his widening ambitions. He had taken leading scientists and skilled administrators with him to Egypt in order to export the seeming benefits of French civilization—and to install a more lasting bureaucratic authority.

Napoleon's partners in the new government after the November 1799 coup soon learned of his great political ambition and skill. In theory, the new system was to be a streamlined version of the Directory: Napoleon was to be first among equals in a three-man executive—"First Consul," according to borrowed Roman termi-

nology. But Napoleon quickly asserted his primacy among them and began not only to dominate executive functions but also to bypass the authority of the regime's various legislative bodies.

Perhaps most important to the success of his increasingly authoritarian rule was his effort to include men of many political stripes—Jacobins, reforming liberals, even former Old Regime bureaucrats—among his ministers, advisers, and bureaucrats. He welcomed many exiles back to France, including all but the most ardent royalists. He thus stabilized his regime by healing some of the rifts among ruling elites. Napoleon combined toleration with ruthlessness, however. Between 1800 and 1804 he imprisoned, executed, or exiled dozens of individuals for alleged Jacobin agitation or royalist sympathies, including a prince of the royal family, whom he had kidnapped and coldly murdered.

Under Napoleon's regime, any semblance of free political life ended. Legislative bodies lost all initiative in the governing process, becoming rubber stamps for the

Napoleon Crossing the Alps

This stirring portrait by the great neoclassical painter Jacques-Louis David memorializes Napoleon's 1796 crossing of the Alps before his victorious Italian campaign, as a general under the Directory. In part because it was executed in 1801–1802, the painting depicts the moment heroically rather than realistically. (In truth, Napoleon wisely crossed the Alps on a sure-footed mule, not a stallion.) Napoleon, as First Consul, wanted images of himself that would justify his increasingly ambitious claims to power. (*Réunion des Musées Nationaux/ Art Resource, NY*)

MAP 19.1 **Napoleonic Europe, ca. 1810**
France dominated continental Europe after Napoleon's victories.

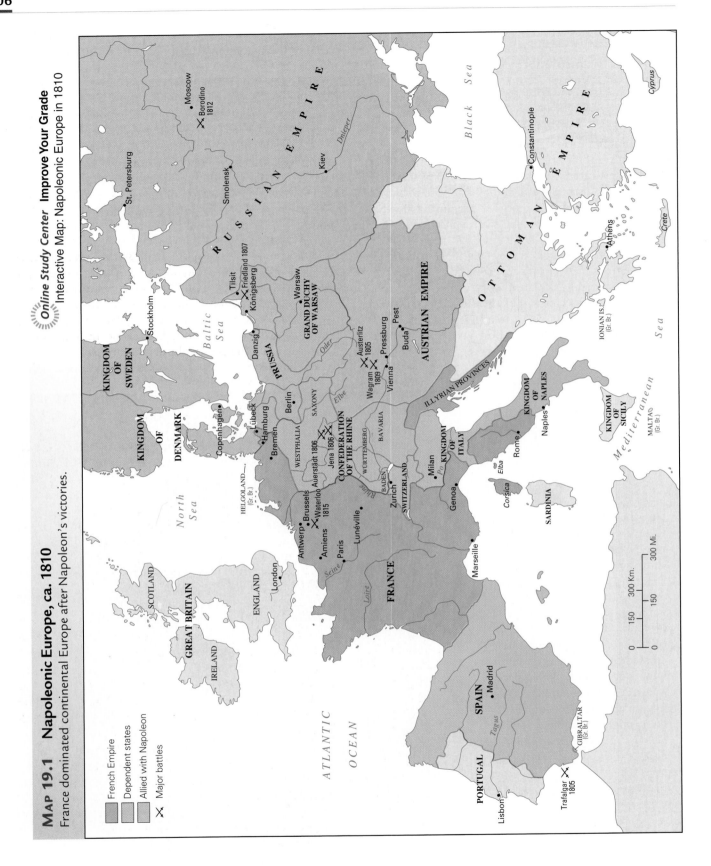

French Empire

Dependent states

Allied with Napoleon

X Major battles

consuls' policies. In any case, there were no meaningful elections. Voters chose only candidates for a kind of pool of potential legislators, from which occasional replacements were chosen by members of the Senate, an advisory body entirely appointed by Napoleon himself. Political clubs were banned; the vibrant press of the revolutionary years wilted under heavy censorship. Napoleon also further centralized the administrative system, set up by the first wave of revolutionaries in 1789, by establishing the office of prefect to govern the départements. All prefects and their subordinates were appointed by Napoleon, thus extending the range of his power and undermining autonomous local government.

Certain administrative changes that enhanced central control, such as for tax collection, were more uniformly positive in their effects. Napoleon oversaw the establishment of the Bank of France, modeled on the Bank of England. The bank provided capital for investment and helped the state stabilize the French currency. Perhaps the most important achievement early in his regime was the Concordat of 1801. The aim of this treaty with the pope was to solve the problem of church-state relations that for years had provoked counterrevolutionary rebellions. The agreement allowed for the resumption of Catholic worship and the continued support of the clergy by the state, but also accepted the more dramatic changes accomplished by the Revolution. Church lands that had been sold were guaranteed to their new owners. Although Catholicism was recognized as the "religion of the majority of Frenchmen," Protestant churches also were allowed, and their clergy were paid. Later, Napoleon granted new rights to Jews as well.

The law code that Napoleon established in 1804 was much like his accommodation with the church in its limited acceptance of revolutionary gains. His **Civil Code** (also known as the *code napoléon*, or Napoleonic Code) honored the revolutionary legacy in its guarantee of equality before the law and its requirement for the taxation of all social classes; it also enshrined modern forms of property ownership and civil contracts. Neither the code nor Napoleon's political regime fostered individual rights, especially for women. Fathers' control over their families was enhanced. Divorce was no longer permitted except in rare instances. Women lost all property rights when they married, and they generally faced legal domination by fathers and husbands.

Napoleon was careful, though, to avoid heavy-handed displays of power. He cleverly sought ratification of each stage of his assumption of power through national plebiscites (referendums in which all eligible voters could vote for or against proposals)—one plebiscite

for a new constitution in 1800 and another when he claimed consulship for life in 1802. He approached his final political coup—declaring himself emperor—with similar dexterity. Long before he claimed the imperial title, Napoleon had begun to sponsor an active court life appropriate to imperial pretensions. The empire was proclaimed in May 1804 with the approval of the Senate; it was also endorsed by another plebiscite. Napoleon rewarded members of his family and certain favorites with noble titles that carried no legal privilege but signaled social and political distinctions of great importance. Old nobles were allowed to use their titles on this basis.

Many members of the elite, whatever their persuasions, tolerated Napoleon's claims to power because he safeguarded fundamental revolutionary gains yet reconfirmed their status. War soon resumed against political and economic enemies—principally Britain, Austria, and Russia—and for a time Napoleon's success on the battlefield continued. Because military glory was central to the political purpose and self-esteem of elites, Napoleon's early successes as emperor further enhanced his power.

CONQUERING EUROPE, 1805–1810

Napoleon maintained relatively peaceful relations with other nations while he consolidated power at home, but the truces did not last. Tensions with the British quickly re-escalated when Britain resumed aggression against French shipping in 1803, and Napoleon countered by seizing Hanover, the ancestral German home of the English king. England was at war at sea with Spain and the Netherlands, which Napoleon had forced to enter the fray. Napoleon began to gather a large French force on the northern coast of France; his objective was to invade England.

The British fleet, commanded by Horatio Nelson (1758–1805), intercepted the combined French and Spanish fleets that were to have been the invasion flotilla and inflicted a devastating defeat off Cape Trafalgar in southern Spain (see **MAP 19.1**) on October 21, 1805. The victory ensured British mastery of the seas and, in the long run, contributed to Napoleon's demise. In the short run, the defeat at Trafalgar paled for the French beside Napoleon's impressive victories on land. Even as the French admirals were preparing for battle, Napoleon had abandoned the plans to invade England and in August had begun to march his army east through Germany to confront the great continental powers, Austria and Russia.

In December 1805, Napoleon's army routed a combined Austrian and Russian force near Austerlitz (AW-stir-lits), north of Vienna (see Map 19.1). The Battle of Austerlitz was Napoleon's most spectacular victory.

Civil Code Law code established under Napoleon in 1804 that included limited acceptance of revolutionary gains, such as a guarantee of equality before the law and taxation of all social classes.

Austria sued for peace. In further battles in 1806, French forces defeated Prussian as well as Russian armies once again. Prussia was virtually dismembered, but Napoleon tried to remake Russia into a contented ally. His hold on central Europe would not be secure with a hostile Russia, nor would the anti-British economic system that he envisioned—the Continental System (see page 609)—be workable without Russian participation.

French forces were still trying to prevail in Spain, which had been a client state since its defeat by revolutionary armies in 1795 but was resisting outright rule by a French-imposed king. In 1808, however, Napoleon turned his attention to more fully subduing Austria. After another loss to French forces in July 1809, Austria, like Russia, accepted French political and economic hegemony in a sort of alliance. By 1810 Napoleon had transformed most of Europe into allied or dependent states (see Map 19.1). The only exceptions were Britain and the parts of Spain and Portugal that continued, with British help, to resist France.

The states least affected by French hegemony were its reluctant allies: Austria, Russia, and the Scandinavian countries. Denmark allied with France in 1807 only for help in fending off British naval supremacy in the Baltic. Sweden reluctantly made peace in 1810 after losing control of Finland to Napoleon's ally, Russia, and only minimally participated in the Continental

System. At the other extreme were territories that had been incorporated into France. These included the Austrian Netherlands, territory along the Rhineland, and sections of Italy that bordered France. These regions were occupied by French troops and were treated as though they were départements of France itself.

In most other areas, some form of French-controlled government was in place, usually headed by a member of Napoleon's family. In both northern Italy and the Netherlands, where "sister" republics had been established after French conquests under the Directory, Napoleon imposed monarchies. Rulers were also installed in the kingdom of Naples and in Spain. Western German states of the Holy Roman Empire that had allied with Napoleon against Austria were organized into the Confederation of the Rhine, with Napoleon as its "Protector." After a thousand years, the Holy Roman Empire ceased to exist. Two further states were created, largely out of the defeated Prussia's territory: the kingdom of Westphalia in western Germany and the Grand Duchy of Warsaw in the east (see Map 19.1).

Napoleon's domination of these various regions had complex, and at times contradictory, consequences. On the one hand, Napoleonic armies essentially exported the French Revolution, in that French domination brought with it the Napoleonic Civil Code, and with it political and economic reform akin to that of the

"And It Cannot Be Changed"
This horrifying scene of an execution of rebels against French rule in Spain was one of a series of etchings by Madrid artist Francisco Goya. In the 1810 series, titled "The Disasters of War," Goya was severely critical of French actions, as well as of barbarities committed by the British-backed Spaniards.
(Foto Marburg/Art Resource, NY)

early phases of the Revolution. Equality before the law was decreed following the French example. This meant the end of noble exemption from taxation in the many areas where it existed. In general, the complex snarl of medieval taxes and tolls was replaced with straightforward property taxes that were universally applied. As a consequence, tax revenues rose dramatically—by 50 percent in the kingdom of Italy, for example. Serfdom and forced labor also were abolished, as they had been in France in August 1789.

In most Catholic regions the church was subjected to the terms of the Concordat of 1801. The tithe was abolished, church property was seized and sold, and religious orders were dissolved. Although Catholicism remained the state-supported religion in these areas, Protestantism was tolerated, and Jews were granted rights of citizenship. Secular education, at least for males, was encouraged.

On the other hand, Napoleon would allow in the empire only those aspects of France's revolutionary legacy that he tolerated in France itself. Just as he had suppressed any meaningful participatory government in France, so too did he suppress it in conquered regions. This came as a blow in states such as the Netherlands, which had experienced its own democratizing "Patriot" movement and which had enjoyed republican self-government after invasion by French armies during the Revolution itself. Throughout Napoleon's empire, many of the benefits of streamlined administration and taxation were offset by the drain of continual warfare. Deficits rose three- and fourfold, despite increased revenues. And throughout Europe Napoleon randomly allotted lands to reward his greatest generals and ministers, thereby exempting those lands from taxation and control by his own bureaucracy.

If true self-government was not allowed, a broad segment of the elite in all regions was nevertheless won over to cooperation with Napoleon by being welcomed into his bureaucracy or into the large multinational army, called the *Grande Armée* (grawnd are-MAY). Their loyalty was cemented when they bought confiscated church lands.

The impact of Napoleon's Continental System was equally mixed. Under this system the Continent was in theory closed to all British shipping and goods. The effects were widespread but uneven, and smuggling to evade controls on British goods became a major enterprise. Regions heavily involved in trade with Britain or its colonies or dependent on British shipping suffered in the new system, as did overseas trade in general when Britain gained dominance of the seas after Trafalgar. However, the closing of the Continent to British trade, combined with increases in demand to supply Napoleon's armies, spurred the development of continental industries, at least in the short run.

DEFEAT AND ABDICATION, 1812–1815

Whatever its achievements, Napoleon's empire was ultimately precarious because of the hostility of Austria and Russia, as well as the belligerence of Britain. Russia was a particularly weak link in the chain of alliances and subject states because Russian landowners and merchants were angered when their vital trade in timber for the British navy was interrupted and when supplies of luxury goods, brought in British ships, began to dwindle. A century of close alliances with German ruling houses made alliance with a French ruler an extremely difficult political option for Tsar Alexander I.

It was Napoleon, however, who ended the alliance by provoking a breach with Russia. He suddenly backed away from an arrangement to marry one of Alexander's sisters and accepted an Austrian princess instead. (He had reluctantly divorced Joséphine because their marriage had not produced an heir.) Also, he seized lands in Germany belonging to a member of Alexander's family. When Alexander threatened rupture of the alliance if the lands were not returned, Napoleon mounted an invasion. Advisers warned him about the magnitude of the task he seemed so eager to undertake—particularly about winter fighting in Russia—but their alarms went unheard.

Napoleon's previous military successes had stemmed from a combination of strategic innovations and pure audacity. Napoleon divided his forces into independent corps. Each corps included infantry, cavalry, and artillery. Organized in these workable units, his armies could travel quickly by several separate routes and converge in massive force to face the enemy. Leadership on the battlefield came from a loyal and extremely talented officer corps that had grown up since army commands had been thrown open to nonaristocrats during the Revolution. The final ingredient in the success formula was the high morale of French troops. Since the first victory of the revolutionary armies in September 1792, citizen-soldiers had proved their worth. Complicated troop movements and bravery on the battlefield were possible when troops felt they were fighting for their *nation*, not merely their ruling dynasty. Napoleon's reputation as a winning general added a further measure of self-confidence.

The campaign against Russia began in June 1812. It was a spectacular failure. Napoleon had gathered a force of about 700,000 men—about half from France and half from allied states—a force twice as large as Russia's. But the strategy of quickly moving independent corps and assembling massive forces could not be implemented: simply mustering so many men along the border was already the equivalent of gathering them for battle. Bold victories had often enabled Napoleon's troops to live off the countryside while they waited for supplies to catch up to the front line. But when the enemy attacked supply lines, the distances traveled were very great, the countryside was impoverished, or battles were not decisive, Napoleon's ambitious strategies proved futile. In varying degrees, these conditions prevailed in Russia.

By the time the French faced the Russians in the principal battle of the Russian campaign—at Borodino (bore-uh-DEE-no), west of Moscow (see Map 19.1)—the Grande Armée had been on the march for two and a half months and stood at less than half its original strength. After the indecisive but bloody battle, the French occupied and pillaged Moscow but found scarcely enough food and supplies to sustain them. When Napoleon finally retreated from Moscow late in October, the fate of the French forces was all but sealed. As they retreated, the soldiers who had not died in battle died of exposure or starvation or were picked off by Russian peasants when they wandered away from their units. Of the original 700,000 troops of the Grand Armée, fewer than 100,000 made it out of Russia.

Napoleon left his army before it was fully out of Russia to counter a coup attempt in Paris. The collapse of his reign had begun, spurred by a coincidental defeat in Spain. Since 1808 Spain had been largely under French domination, with Napoleon's brother, Joseph, as king. A rebel Cortes (national representative assembly), however, continued to meet in territory that the French did not control, and British troops supported resistance to the French. In 1812, as Napoleon was advancing against Russia, the collapse of French control accelerated. By the time Napoleon reached Paris at the turn of the new year, Joseph had been expelled from Spain, and an Anglo-Spanish force led by the duke of Wellington was poised to invade France.

Napoleon lost his last chance to stave off a coalition of all major powers against him when he refused an Austrian offer of peace for the return of conquered Austrian territories. With Britain willing to subsidize the allied armies, Tsar Alexander determined to destroy Napoleon, and the Austrians now anxious to share the spoils, Napoleon's empire began to crumble. Imperial forces—many now raw recruits—were crushed in the massive "Battle of Nations" in Germany in October 1813. The allies invaded France and forced Napoleon to abdicate on April 6, 1814.

Napoleon was exiled to the island of Elba, off France's Mediterranean coast. He was installed as the island's ruler and was given an income drawn on the French treasury. Meanwhile, however, the restored French king was having his own troubles. Louis XVIII (r. 1814–1824) was the brother of the executed Louis XVI (he took the number eighteen out of respect for Louis XVI's son, who had died in prison in 1795). The new monarch had been out of the country and out of touch with its circumstances since the beginning of the Revolution. In addition to the delicate task of establishing his own legitimacy, he faced enormous practical problems, including pensioning off thousands of soldiers now unemployed and still loyal to Napoleon.

Napoleon, bored and almost penniless in his island kingdom (the promised French pension never materialized), took advantage of the circumstances and returned surreptitiously to France on February 26, 1815. His small band of attendants was joined by the soldiers sent by the king to halt his progress. Louis XVIII abandoned Paris to the returned emperor.

Napoleon's triumphant return lasted only one hundred days, however. Though many soldiers welcomed his return, many members of the elite were reluctant to throw in their lot with Napoleon again, and many ordinary French citizens were disenchanted, especially since the defeat in Russia, with the high costs, in conscription and taxation, of his armies. In any case, Napoleon's reappearance galvanized the divided allies, who had been haggling over a peace settlement, into unity. Napoleon tried to strike first, but he lost against English and Prussian troops in his first major battle, at Waterloo (in modern Belgium; see Map 19.1) on June 18, 1815. When Napoleon arrived in Paris after the defeat, he discovered the government in the hands of an ad hoc committee that included the Marquis de Lafayette. Under pressure, he abdicated once again. This time he was exiled to the tiny, remote island of St. Helena in the South Atlantic, where he died in 1821.

THE LEGACY OF REVOLUTION FOR FRANCE AND THE WORLD

The process of change in France between 1789 and 1815 was so complex that it is easy to overlook the overall impact of the Revolution. Superficially, the changes seemed to come full circle—with first Louis XVI on the throne, then Napoleon as emperor, and then Louis XVIII on the throne. Even though the monarchy was restored, however, the Revolution had discredited absolute monarchy in theory and practice.

France   Louis XVIII had to recognize the right of "the people," however narrowly defined, to participate in government and to enjoy due process of law. Another critical legacy of the Revolution and the Napoleonic era was a centralized political system of départements rather than a patchwork of provinces. For the first time, a single code of law applied to all French people. Most officials—from département administrators to city mayors—were appointed by the central government until the late twentieth century. The conscientious attention of the government, at various stages of the Revolution, to advances for France generally reflects the positive side of this centralization. The government sponsored national scientific societies, a national library and archives, and a system of teachers' colleges and universities. Particularly under Napoleon, canal- and road-building projects improved transport systems.

Napoleon's legacy, like that of the Revolution itself, was mixed. His self-serving reconciliation of aristocratic pretensions with the opening of careers to men of talent ensured the long-term success of revolutionary principles from which the elite as a whole profited. His reconciliation of the state with the Catholic Church helped to stabilize his regime and cemented some revolutionary gains. The restored monarchy could not renege on these gains. Yet whatever his achievements, Napoleon's overthrow of constitutional principles worsened the problem of political instability. His brief return to power in 1815 reflects the degree to which his power had always been rooted in military adventurism and in the loyalty of soldiers and officers. Similarly, the swiftness of his collapse suggests that although the empire under Napoleon may have seemed an enduring solution to the political instability of the late 1790s, it was no more secure than any of the other revolutionary governments.

Although Louis XVIII acknowledged the principle of constitutionalism at the end of the Revolution, his regime rested on fragile footing. Indeed, the fragility of new political systems was one of the most profound legacies of the Revolution. There was division over policies, but even greater division over legitimacy—that is, the acceptance by a significant portion of the politically active citizenry of a particular government's right to rule. Before the Revolution started, notions about political legitimacy had undergone a significant shift. The deputies who declared themselves to be the National Assembly in June 1789 already believed that they had a right to do so. In their view, they represented "the nation," and their voice had legitimacy for that reason. These deputies brought to Versailles not only their individual convictions that "reason" should be applied to the political system but also their experience in social settings where those ideas were well received. In their salons, clubs, and literary societies, they had experienced the familiarity, trust, and sense of community that are essential to effective political action.

The deputies' attempt to transplant their sense of community into national politics, however, was not wholly successful. The National Assembly had scarcely been inaugurated when its deputies guaranteed its failure by disqualifying themselves from standing for office under the new constitution. The king also actively undermined the system because he disagreed with it in principle. The British parliamentary system, by comparison, though every bit as elitist as the narrowest of the representative systems during the French Revolution, had a long history as a workable institution for lords, wealthy commoners, and rulers. This shared experience was an important counterweight to differences over fundamental issues, so that Parliament as an institution both survived political crises and helped resolve them. The Revolution thus left a powerful yet ambiguous legacy for France. Politics was established on new principles, yet still lacking were the practical means to achieve the promise inherent in those principles.

Europe France's continental conquests were the least enduring of the changes of the revolutionary era. Nevertheless, French domination of Europe had certain lasting effects: elites were exposed to modern bureaucratic management, and equality under the law transformed social and political relationships. The breaking down of ancient political divisions provided important practical grounding for later cooperation among elites in nationalist movements. In Napoleon's kingdom of Italy, for example, a tax collector from Florence for the first time worked side by side with one from Milan.

Naturally, the most important legacy of the French Revolution, as of the American, was the very success of the Revolution. The most powerful absolute monarchy in Europe had succumbed to the demands of its people for dramatic social and political reforms. Throughout Europe in the nineteenth century, ruling dynasties faced revolutionary movements that demanded constitutional government, among other changes, and resorted to force to achieve it.

The most important legacy of the revolutionary wars, however, was the change in warfare itself made possible by the citizen armies of the French. Citizen-soldiers who identified closely with their nation, even when conscripts, proved able to maneuver and attack on the battlefield in ways that the brutishly disciplined poor conscripts in royal armies would not. In response, other states tried to build competing armies; the mass national armies that fought the world wars of the twentieth century were the result.

Europe and Its Colonies European colonies overseas felt the impact of the Revolution and subsequent European wars in several ways. The British tried to take advantage of Napoleon's preoccupation with continental affairs by seizing French colonies and the colonies of the French-dominated Dutch. In 1806 they seized the Dutch colony of Cape Town—crucial for support of trade around Africa—as well as French bases along the African coast. In 1811 they grabbed the island of Java. In the Caribbean, the French sugar-producing islands of Martinique and Guadeloupe were particularly vulnerable to English sea power. On the most

NAPOLEON'S LETTER TO TOUSSAINT-LOUVERTURE

In November 1801, Napoleon sent this letter to the governor of the colony of Saint Domingue, Toussaint-Louverture. Toussaint, a former slave, had commanded an army, composed largely of ex-slaves, which had restored order in Saint Domingue following a complicated civil war. As he mentions in the letter, Napoleon had dispatched a force to reestablish French control of the formerly profitable colony. Although Toussaint was captured and later died in a French prison, Napoleon's forces were not successful in reestablishing French control.

To Citizen General Toussaint Louverture, commander in chief of the armies of Saint-Domingue,

Peace with England and with other powers in Europe [now] enables France to pay attention to its colony of Saint-Domingue. We are sending General Leclerc, our brother-in-law, to serve as captain general and governor of the colony. He is accompanied by forces suitable to make the sovereignty of France respected. In these circumstances, it pleases us to hope that you will demonstrate to us and to all of France the sincerity of the sentiments that you have continually expressed in your letters to us. We hold you in very high esteem and it pleases us to acknowledge the great service you have rendered to the French people. . . . Called by your talents and by the force of circumstance to command, you have ended civil war. . . . The constitution you have made contains many good things but also things which are contrary to the dignity and the sovereignty of the French people, of which the people of Saint-Domingue form only a part. The circumstances in which you found yourself, surrounded on all sides by enemies, perhaps made some provisions of the constitution necessary and legitimate. But, happily, now that things have changed you will be able to render homage to the sovereignty of the Nation of which you are one of the most illustrious citizens. . . . Any contrary conduct . . . would lead you to lose the many rights you have earned to the recognition and the benefits of the Republic [and] would bring you to the edge of a precipice which, in swallowing you up, would contribute to the misery of the brave blacks, whose courage we admire and whose rebellion we would be sorry to have to punish.

Help the new captain general with your counsel, your influence and your talents. What could you want? The freedom of blacks? You know that in every country we have entered we have given liberty to the people who did not have it. Do you want respect, honors and fortune? . . . Given the services you have rendered and our esteem for you, you cannot be in doubt that respect, honors and fortune await you.

Make known to the peoples of Saint-Domingue that our concerns for their well-being were often impotent because of the demands of war that we faced. But now, peace and the force of our government will assure them prosperity and liberty. Tell them that if liberty is to them the most important right, that it cannot be enjoyed without the title of "French citizen" and that all acts contrary to the nation, and contrary to the obedience they owe its government and to its representative, the captain general, will be crimes against the national sovereignty. . . . And you, General, consider that if you are the first man of color to have arrived at such a pinnacle of power . . . you are also, before God and before us, responsible for their good conduct. . . .

QUESTIONS

1. What, in your opinion, was Napoleon trying to accomplish with this letter?

2. How would Toussaint-Louverture have interpreted Napoleon's words?

Source: Paul Rossier, ed., *Lettres du Général Leclerc* (Paris: Société de l'Histoire des Colonies Françaises, 1937). Translated by Kristen B. Neuschel.

productive of the French-controlled Caribbean islands, Saint Domingue (SAHN dome-ANGUE), the Revolution inspired a successful rebellion by the enslaved plantation workers.

The National Assembly in Paris had delayed abolishing slavery in French colonies, despite the moral appeal of such a move, because of pressure from the white planters and out of fear that the financially strapped French government would lose some of its profitable sugar trade. But the example of revolutionary daring in Paris and confusion about ruling authority as the Assembly and the king wrangled did not go unnoticed in the colonies—in either plantation mansions or slave quarters. White planters on Saint Domingue simply hoped for political and economic "liberty" from the French government and its mercantilist trade policies. White planter rule was challenged, in turn, by wealthy people of mixed European and African descent who wanted equal citizenship, hitherto denied them. A civil war broke out between these upper classes and was fol-

Haitian Leader Toussaint-Louverture

Son of an educated slave, Toussaint-Louverture had himself been freed in 1777 but took on a leadership role when the slave revolt began on Saint Domingue in 1791. His military skill and political acumen were vital to the success of the revolt and to ruling the island's diverse population afterward.   *(Stock Montage, Inc.)*

lowed by a full-fledged slave rebellion, beginning in 1791. Britain sent aid to the rebels when it went to war against the French revolutionary government in 1793. Only when the republic was declared in Paris and the Convention abolished slavery did the rebels abandon alliances with France's enemies and attempt to govern in concert with the mother country.

Although it recovered other colonies from the British, France never regained control of Saint Domingue. Led by a former slave, **François Dominique Toussaint-Louverture** (too-SAHN–loo-ver-TOUR) (1743–1803), the new government of the island tried to run its own affairs, though without formally declaring independence from France. (See the box

François Toussaint-Louverture   Former slave who governed the island of Saint Domingue (Haiti) as an independent state after the slave revolt of 1791.

"The Global Record: Napoleon's Letter to Toussaint-Louverture.") Napoleon decided to tighten control of the profitable colonies by reinstituting slavery and ousting the independent government of Saint Domingue. In 1802 French forces fought their way onto the island. They captured Toussaint-Louverture, who died shortly thereafter in prison. But in 1803 another rebellion, provoked by the threat of renewed slavery, expelled French forces for good. A former aide of Toussaint's declared the independence of the colony under the name Haiti—the island's Native American name—on January 1, 1804.

The French Revolution and Napoleonic rule, and the example of the Haitian revolution, had a notable impact on Spanish colonies in the Americas. Like other American colonies, the Spanish colonies wanted to loosen the closed economic relationships with the mother country. In addition, the liberal ideas that had helped spawn the French Revolution spurred moves toward independence in Spanish America. Because of the confusion of authority in Spain, some of these colonies were already governing themselves independently in all but name. Echoes of radical republican ideology and of the Haitian experience were present in two major rebellions in Mexico; participants espoused the end of slavery and championed the interests of the poor against local and Spanish elites. The leaders of these self-declared revolutions were executed (in 1811 and 1815), and their movements were crushed by local elites in alliance with Spanish troops. The efforts of local elites to become self-governing—the attempted liberal revolutions—were little more successful. Only Argentina and Paraguay broke away from Spain at this time.

But as in Europe, a legacy remained of both limited and more radical revolutionary activity. Slave rebellions rocked British Caribbean islands in subsequent decades. In some regions dominated by plantations, such as some British possessions and the Spanish island of Cuba, planters were reluctant to disturb the prevailing order with any liberal political demands on the mother country.

THE VIEW FROM BRITAIN

Today the city of Paris is dotted with public monuments that celebrate Napoleon's victories. In London another hero and other victories are celebrated. In Trafalgar Square stands a statue of Lord Nelson, the British naval commander whose fleet destroyed a combined French and Spanish navy in 1805. Horatio Nelson was a brilliant tactician, whose innovations in maneuvering ships in the battle line resulted in stunning victories at Trafalgar and, in 1798, at the Nile Delta, which limited French ambitions in Egypt and the eastern Mediterranean. Trafalgar looms large in British history because it ensured British mastery of

The Battle of Trafalgar

Admiral Nelson's bold strategy of dividing his fleet to break through the line of the French-Spanish fleet at Trafalgar resembled Napoleon's successful strategies in land warfare. Nelson's maneuver isolated portions of the enemy fleet, which could then be attacked in strength. Nelson's intense naval engagements, like Napoleon's battles, caused many casualties, even for the victorious side. *(The Bridgeman Art Library)*

the seas, which then forced Napoleon into economic policies that strained French ties to France's allies and satellites. Virtually unchallenged sea power enabled the British to seize colonies formerly ruled by France and its allies.

Britain's maritime supremacy and seizure of French possessions expanded British trading networks overseas—though in some cases only temporarily—and closer to home, particularly in the Mediterranean. As long as the British had been involved in trade with India, the Mediterranean had been important for economic and strategic reasons because it lay at the end of the land route for trade from the Indian Ocean. Especially after Napoleon's aggression in Egypt in the 1790s, the British redoubled their efforts to control strategic outposts in the Mediterranean.

The British economy would expand dramatically in the nineteenth century as industrial production soared. The roots for growth were laid in this period in the countryside of Britain, where changes in agriculture and in production were occurring. These roots were also laid in Britain's overseas possessions as tighter control of foreign sources of raw materials, notably raw Indian cotton, meant rising fortunes back in Britain. In regions of India, the East India Company was increasing its political domination, and hence its economic stranglehold on Indian commodities. The export of Indian cotton rose significantly during the revolutionary period as part of an expanding trading system that included China, the source of tea.

However, economic expansion was not the sole motive for British aggression. In fact, economic expansion was often a byproduct of increased British control of particular regions or sea-lanes, and the reasons for it were as much strategic as economic. But British elites were sure that strategic domination was a desirable step, wherever it could be achieved, and whether or not every conquest had direct economic payoffs. One Scotsman spoke for many when he said that Britain needed an empire to ensure its greatness and that an empire of the sea was an effective counterweight to Napoleon's empire on land. Much as the French were at that mo-

ment exporting features of their own political system, the British, he said, could export their constitution wherever they conquered territory.

Thus England and France were engaged in similar phases of expansion in this period. In both, desire for both power and profit drove policy. In each, myths about heroes and about the supposed benefits of domination masked the state's self-interest. For both, the effects of conquest would become a fundamental shaping force in the nineteenth century.

SECTION SUMMARY

- General Napoleon Bonaparte and two other men seized power from the Directory in a coup in 1799; Napoleon carefully expanded his power and finally declared himself emperor of France in 1804.

- Napoleon's law code and his agreement with the Catholic Church made permanent some of the key changes from the first phase of the Revolution.

- Napoleon recruited former royal officials, old nobility, and recent revolutionaries into his government, thereby resolving some of the political tensions that had resulted from the Revolution.

- The costs associated with Napoleon's foreign conquests resulted in the overthrow of his regime and contributed to the long-term problems of the French government.

- The export of revolution by French armies brought economic costs from war itself and from Napoleon's continental trading system but also political reform that led, in many cases, to further political liberty.

- In the Americas, the French Revolution inspired movements for independence from colonial rule; in Haiti, slaves and free persons without political rights allied to successfully overthrow French rule.

CHAPTER SUMMARY

Online Study Center **ACE the Test**

What factors led to the beginning of revolution in France in 1789?

Why did several phases of revolutionary change occur after 1789 and what were the characteristics of each phase?

What impact did the Revolution and Napoleonic rule have on France, the rest of Europe, and the wider world?

The French Revolution was a watershed in European history because it successfully challenged the principles of hereditary rule and political privilege by which all European states had hitherto been governed. The Revolution began when a financial crisis forced the monarchy to confront the desire for political reform by a segment of the French elite. Political philosophy emerging from the Enlightenment and the example of the American Revolution moved the French reformers to action. In

its initial phase the French Revolution established the principle of constitutional government and ended many of the traditional political privileges of the Old Regime.

Then, because of the intransigence of the king, the threat of foreign invasion, and the actions of republican legislators and Parisian citizens, the Revolution moved in more radical directions. Its most extremist phase, the Terror, produced the most effective legislation for ordinary citizens but also the worst violence of the Revolution. A period of unstable conservative rule that followed the Terror ended when Napoleon seized power.

Although Napoleonic rule solidified some of the gains of the Revolution, it also subjected France and most of Europe to the great costs of wars of conquest. After Napoleon the French monarchy was restored, but henceforth its power would not be absolute—and the people would not be refused a voice in government—as a result of the Revolution. The impact of events in France also continued beyond its borders; political and legal reform had been imposed in many parts of Europe and even, in more limited ways, had been embraced in European colonies.

LOOKING AHEAD

Hereditary rule and traditional social hierarchies remained in place in much of Europe, but they would not be secure in the future. The legacy of revolutionary change would prove impossible to contain in France or anywhere else.

KEY TERMS

 Online Study Center   **Improve Your Grade**   Flashcards

Third Estate (p. 592)

National Assembly (p. 592)

Tennis Court Oath (p. 592)

Declaration of the Rights of Man and the Citizen (p. 594)

sans-culottes (p. 598)

Jacobins (p. 599)

Maximilien Robespierre (p. 599)

the Terror (p. 599)

Society of Revolutionary Republican Women (p. 601)

Directory (p. 601)

Napoleon Bonaparte (p. 604)

Civil Code (p. 607)

François Toussaint-Louverture (p. 613)

SUGGESTED READING

Baker, Keith Michael. *Inventing the French Revolution.* 1990. A series of essays situating the Revolution amid the dramatic changes in eighteenth-century political culture.

Hunt, Lynn. *The French Revolution and Human Rights: A Brief Documentary History.* 1996. A well-presented short collection of documents, useful for a greater understanding of the impact of the Revolution on the development of human rights.

Jordan, D. P. *The King's Trial.* 1979. An engaging study of Louis XVI's trial and its importance for the Revolution.

Landes, Joan. *Women and the Public Sphere in the Age of the French Revolution.* 1988. An analysis of the uses of gender ideology to fashion the new political world of the revolutionaries.

Langley, Lester D. *The Americas in the Age of Revolution, 1750–1850.* 1996. A survey of all the American states and colonies and the impact of the Atlantic revolutions.

Popkin, Jeremy. *A Short History of the French Revolution.* 1995. A compact and readable recent synthesis of research.

NOTES

1. Quoted in Samuel Eliot Morrison, *John Paul Jones: A Sailor's Biography* (Boston: Little, Brown, 1959), pp. 149–154.

2. Quoted in Owen Connelly, *The French Revolution and the Napoleonic Era* (New York: Holt, Rinehart, and Winston, 1979), p. 32.

3. James Harvey Robinson, *Readings in European History* (Boston: Ginn, 1906), p. 409.

20

THE INDUSTRIAL TRANSFORMATION OF EUROPE, 1750–1850

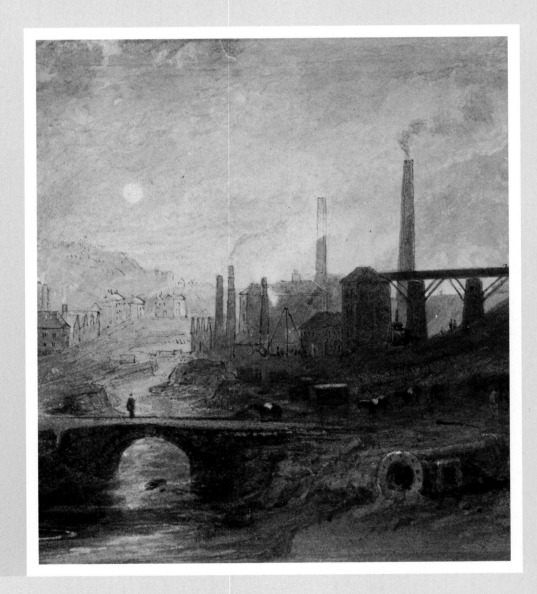

George Robertson:
Nat-Y-Glo Iron Works
*(National Museums & Galleries
of Wales)*

s the French Revolution gave way to the fires of war in continental Europe, across the Channel fires from factory chimneys in England's industrializing cities blurred the distinction between day and night with their constant flames, smoke, and smog. The painting on the left depicts Shropshire, England, in 1788, a region previously renowned for its natural beauty. Industrial activity had already transformed its landscape beyond recognition. Abraham Darby (1676–1717) and his descendants built one of the largest and most important concentrations of ironworks in Shropshire because it contained the ideal combination of coal and iron deposits. The dramatic rise in the use of new machinery throughout Britain, which led to previously unheard-of levels in the production of iron and textiles, struck contemporaries. In the 1830s the French socialist Louis Blanqui (blahn-KEE) (see page 661) proposed a descriptive term, suggesting that just as France had recently experienced a political revolution, so Britain was undergoing an "industrial revolution." Eventually, that expression entered the general vocabulary to describe the advances in production that occurred first in England and then dominated most of western Europe by the end of the nineteenth century. Many economic historians now emphasize how gradual and cumulative the changes were and question the appropriateness of the term *revolution*. Indeed, although mechanization transformed Europe, it did so unevenly. Great Britain offered a model of economic change because it was the first to industrialize; each nation subsequently took its own path and pace in a continuous process of economic transformation.

Industrial development left its mark on just about every sphere of human activity. Scientific and rational methods altered production processes, removing them from the home—where entire families had often participated—to less personal workshops and factories. Significant numbers of workers left farming to enter mining and manufacturing, and major portions of the population moved from rural to urban environments. Machines replaced or supplemented manual labor.[1]

Industrial development transformed Europe socially, culturally, physically. Mechanical production often meant that skilled artisans lost not only their livelihood, but their craft identity as well; it also drew women and children out of the home and into factories. New modes of production

CHAPTER OUTLINE

PRECONDITIONS FOR INDUSTRIALIZATION

NEW MODES OF PRODUCTION

SOCIAL, CULTURAL, AND ENVIRONMENTAL IMPACTS

RESPONSES TO INDUSTRIALIZATION

KEY TERMS

industrialization	primogeniture
mass production	urbanization
steam engine	proletariat
factories	friendly societies
entrepreneurs	Luddites

Online Study Center

This icon will direct you to interactive map and primary source activities on the website **college.hmco.com/pic/noble5e**

offered unprecedented opportunities for manufacturers, merchants, and entrepreneurs to create and amass wealth at levels previously unimaginable. Mechanization also caused pollution and environmental destruction. Miners in search of coal, iron ore, and other minerals cut deep gashes into the earth. The rapid growth of cities resulted in crowded slums, poor sanitation, filth, and visible poverty.

Industrialization simultaneously created unprecedented advancement and opportunity as well as unprecedented hardships and social problems. The social gap between the rich and the working poor increased. The latter, with a growing sense of solidarity, struggled to protect and advance their interests.

FOCUS QUESTIONS

What factors allowed Europe to industrialize before the rest of the world?

Which inventions appear to have been the most important in launching industrialization?

What impact did industrialization have on the environment and on social classes?

What did workers gain and lose as a result of industrialization, and how did they respond?

PRECONDITIONS FOR INDUSTRIALIZATION

What factors allowed Europe to industrialize before the rest of the world?

Industrialization—the substitution of human and animal power by mineral power—required a massive shift of labor and capital resources from agriculture to manufacturing and services. Europe, and especially Great Britain, were endowed with a unique combination of conditions—geographic, cultural, economic, demographic—that made this shift and its timing possible. Industrialization did not simply consist of mechanization. It consisted of, and required, simultaneous growth in commerce, population, and agricultural production. An entrepreneurial spirit and government support for banking and trading were required so that capital could be accumulated for investment in industry. Population growth increased pressure to supply manufactured goods at a faster pace. It also required more efficient food production. As farmers applied new scientific methods to cultivation, less labor was required for food production, thus allowing migration to towns and cities.

WHY EUROPE?

A unique set of circumstances in Europe favored its potential for rapid economic development. Centralized state power and the development of due legal process re-

duced the risks of highway robbery and the confiscation of wealth that merchants accumulated from trade. Such security was nonexistent in other parts of the world, such as the Ottoman Empire, where sultans and corrupt officials could grab wealth on a whim. Hence in the West, accumulating wealth was a worthwhile endeavor.

Compared with Asia, Europe exhibited far greater cultural, political, and social diversity. Challenges to dominant religious and political powers that had come from the Reformation, Counter-Reformation, and the Enlightenment promoted innovation. Toleration for such freedom was a rarity in Asia, where large territories tended to be dominated by a single ruler and faith. International competition among European states drove them to try to outdo one another. Governments actively encouraged industries and commerce to enrich their countries and make them more powerful than their neighbors. None of these factors alone explains why industrialization occurred, but their combination facilitated the process as well as its timing.[2] The industrialization of Europe radically transformed power relationships between the industrial West and nonindustrial Africa, Asia, and South America. By 1900 the West had overwhelmed the other regions with its economic and military power. (See the box "The Global Record: Alexis de Tocqueville's Thoughts on Colonization.")

industrialization A system of mass production of goods in which specialization and mechanization made manufacturing efficient and profitable.

Transformations Accompanying Industrialization

A number of other transformations favored economic innovation in Europe. Improved agricultural techniques dramatically increased food production. Rather than leaving a portion of their land fallow when crops depleted the soil, farmers learned to rotate them, use fertilizers, and plant new crops from the Americas—such as the potato and maize—that not only flourished in poor soil, but replenished the soil with nitrogen. New, more efficient plows enabled farmers to cultivate more land than ever before with less labor. Most important, the new crops and the more efficient cultivation of traditional ones increased the capacity to feed a growing population and freed many people to go to the city and work in the industries. Until these changes began occurring in the eighteenth century, food production required the work of 80 percent of the European population.

Population growth also helped promote industrialization. The first spurt in growth occurred in the mid-eighteenth century, before the effects of industrialization could be widely felt. Thereafter the population of Europe increased dramatically throughout the industrial era, doubling between 1750 and 1850. This growth was partly due to a lowering of the death rate. Infant mortality had been very high from illness and disease, such as gastrointestinal disorders from poor food, smallpox, diphtheria, and tuberculosis. Although none of these diseases had been medically conquered, slow improvement in sanitation and food intake after 1750 enabled children to better resist them. New employment opportunities led to earlier marriages and thus higher fertility. This growing population supplied the labor force for the new industries and provided the large surge in consumers of various industrial goods.

In the countryside industrialization was foreshadowed by a form of production that had developed beginning in the seventeenth century—the putting-out system, or cottage industry. During the winter and at other slack times, peasants took in handwork such as spinning, weaving, or dyeing. Often they were marginal agriculturists, frequently women, who on a part-time basis could augment the family income. Entrepreneurs discovered that some individuals were better than others at specific tasks. Rather than have one household process the wool through all the steps of production until it was a finished piece, the entrepreneur would buy wool produced by one family, then take it to another to spin, a third to dye, a fourth to weave, and so on. Although cottage industry, through its specialization, was an important contributor to industrialization in some regions, that was not the case everywhere.

1712	Newcomen invents steam-operated water pump
1733	Kay invents flying shuttle
1750–1800	Three million Africans are brought to the Americas as slaves
1753	First steam engine in the Americas
1760s	Hargreaves invents spinning jenny
1765	Watt improves steam engine with separate condenser
1769	Arkwright patents water frame for spinning
1785	Cartwright patents power loom
1793	Whitney invents cotton gin
1804	Jacquard invents automatic loom
1811–1812	Luddites organize
1825	Börsig builds first steam engine in Germany
1831, 1834	Workers' uprising in Lyon
1832	Cholera epidemic
1834	Creation of German customs union, the Zollverein
1844	Workers' uprising in Silesia
1851	Majority of Britain's population becomes urban

A less ambiguous prerequisite for industry was a good transportation network. Transportation improved significantly in the eighteenth century, particularly in response to expanding markets for agricultural and manufactured products. Better roads were built; new coaches and carriages could travel faster and carry heavier loads. Government and private companies built canals linking rivers to each other or to lakes. Road- and canal-building hastened and cheapened transportation, facilitating the movement of raw materials to factories and finished goods to local and distant markets. In Great Britain these transformations occurred simultaneously with industrialization; on the Continent they were actual precursors to economic change.

Britain, the first to industrialize, was the dominant political power throughout the nineteenth century. The rest of Europe admired Britain and regarded it not only as an economic model but also as a political and cultural one.

ALEXIS DE TOCQUEVILLE'S THOUGHTS ON COLONIZATION

The French military conquest of Algeria, beginning in 1830, provides an example of how economic modernization gave Europeans a sense of superiority and changed their relationship with the rest of the world. Charles X, king of France, sent the French military to the town of Algiers in response to a perceived insult from the dey (Algerian governor). The military conquest took seventeen years. Alexis de Tocqueville (1805–1859), member of the French parliament and author of the famous Democracy in America, *like many Europeans, thought that industrial progress not only enabled but legitimized the military and economic takeover of undeveloped regions inhabited by people of color. He also argued that white settlement would facilitate military conquest. In the first excerpt below, Tocqueville shares his awe at the vibrancy of urban culture in Algiers, and he describes how the French have begun to tear down and rebuild sections of the town. In the second excerpt, he portrays an example of what already had occurred in the French military occupation of Algeria and warns against it.*

From "Notes on the Voyage to Algeria in 1841"

First appearance of [Algiers]: I have never seen anything like it. Prodigious mix of races and costumes, Arab, Kabyle, Moor, Negro, Mahonais, . . . French. Each of these races, tossed together in a space much too tight to contain them, speaks its language, wears its attire, displays different mores. This whole world moves about with an activity that seems feverish. The entire lower town seems in a state of destruction and reconstruction. On all sides, one sees nothing but recent ruins, buildings going up; one hears nothing but the noise of the hammer. It is Cincinnati transported onto the soil of Africa.

The French are substituting broad arcaded streets for the Moors' tortuous little alleys. This is a necessity of our civilization. But they are also substituting their architecture for that of the Moors, and this is wrong; for the latter is very appropriate to the needs of the country, and besides, it is charming. . . .

From "First Report on Algeria," 1847

The indigenous towns were invaded, turned upside down, and sacked by our administration even more than by our arms. . . . In the vicinity of Algiers itself, the very fertile areas were torn from the hands of the Arabs and given to Europeans who, not being able or not wanting to cultivate them themselves, rented them to these same indigenous people, who thus became the mere farmers of the domains that had belonged to their fathers. Elsewhere, tribes or factions of tribes that were not hostile to us, or even more who had fought with us and sometimes without us, were pushed off their territory. We accepted conditions we did not fulfill, we promised indemnities we did not pay, thus allowing our honor to suffer even more than the interests of these indigenous peoples. . . .

Muslim society in Africa was not uncivilized; it was merely a backward and imperfect civilization. There existed within it a large number of pious foundations, whose object was to provide for the needs of charity or for public instruction. We laid our hands on these revenues everywhere, partly diverting them from their former uses; we reduced the charitable establishments and let the schools decay, we disbanded seminaries. Around us knowledge has been extinguished, and recruitment of men of religion and men of law has ceased; that is to say, we have made Muslim society much more miserable, more disordered, more ignorant, and more barbarous than it had been before knowing us. . . .

It is not along the road of our European civilization that they must, for the present, be pushed, but in the direction proper to them; we must demand of them things that suit their ways, and not those contrary to them. Individual property, industry, and sedentary dwelling [as opposed to nomadic lifestyle] are in no way contrary to the religion of Muhammad. Arabs know or have known these things elsewhere; they are known and appreciated by some in Algeria itself. Why do we despair of making them familiar to a greater number? . . . Islam is not absolutely impenetrable to enlightenment.

. . . If our arms have decimated certain tribes, there are others whom our commerce has enriched and strengthened considerably, and who feel and understand this. Everywhere the prices that the indigenous people can get for their wares and their labor have increased greatly by our presence. In addition, our agriculturalists gladly make use of indigenous manpower. The European needs the Arab to make his lands valuable; the Arab needs the European to obtain a high salary.

QUESTIONS

1. How does Tocqueville react to Algerian culture? Why does he compare Algiers with Cincinnati? How are the French attempting to remake Algeria in their own image?

2. What are Tocqueville's assumptions about economic modernization in Algeria, and its appropriateness for indigenous culture?

Source: Alexis de Tocqueville, *Writings on Empire and Slavery*, ed. and trans. Jennifer Pitts (Baltimore: Johns Hopkins University Press), pp. 36, 140, 142, 145.

First Railroad, from Manchester to Liverpool, England

The engineer George Stephenson (1781–1848) first built engines that could pull coal at mines, then in 1821 he constructed the first "locomotive" for public transportation. Four years later the first regular railroad line, connecting Manchester with Liverpool, was erected.   *(Private Collection/Bridgeman Art Libraryl)*

BRITAIN'S LEAD IN INDUSTRIAL INNOVATION

Britain led the way industrially for many reasons. It was the first European country to have a standard currency, tax, and tariff system. Although Britain was by no means an egalitarian society, it accommodated some movement between the classes. Ideas and experiments were readily communicated among entrepreneurs, workers, and scientists.

In addition, England had gained an increasing share of international trade since the seventeenth century. This trade provided capital for investment in industrial plants. The world trade network also ensured that Britain had a market beyond its borders, and because total demand was relatively high, mass manufacture was feasible. The international trade network also enabled Britain to import raw materials for its industry, the most important of which was cotton.

Earlier than its competitors, Britain had a national banking system that could finance industries in areas where private funding fell short. In addition to numerous London banks lending mainly in the capital, six hundred provincial banks serviced the economy by

1810. The banking system reflected the growth of the economy as much as it contributed to it. Banking could flourish because Britons had wide experience in trade, had accumulated considerable amounts of wealth, and had found a constant demand for credit.

Geographically, Britain was also fortunate. Coal and iron were located close to each other (see **MAP 20.1**). Because Britain is a relatively narrow island, virtually all of it has easy access to the sea—no part of the country is more than 70 miles from the coast. This was a strategic advantage, for water was by far the cheapest means of transportation. Compared with the Continent, Britain had few tolls, and moving goods was relatively easy and inexpensive.

On the whole, British workers were better off than their continental counterparts. They were more skilled, earned higher wages, and had discretionary income to spend on the manufactured goods now for sale. But because labor was more costly than on the Continent, British business owners had an incentive to find labor-saving devices and reduce the number of workers needed for production.

The population of Great Britain increased by 8 percent in each decade from 1750 to 1800, in part as a result of industrial growth. This swelling population, in turn, expanded the market for goods. The most rapid growth occurred in the countryside, causing a steady movement of people from rural to urban areas. The presence of this work force was another contributing factor in Britain's readiness for change.

Britain was far more open to dissent than were other European countries at the time. The lack of conformity was reflected in religion and also in a willingness to try new methods of production. In fact, the two often went together. A large proportion of British entrepreneurs was Quaker or belonged to one of the dissenting (non-Anglican) religious groups. Perhaps dissenters were accustomed to questioning authority and treading new paths. They were also well educated and, as a result of common religious bonds, inclined to provide mutual aid, including financial support.

Plentiful harvests in the years 1715 to 1750 also favored Britain and influenced the timing of industrial change. Farmers with good earnings could afford to

order the new manufactured iron plows, and demand for industrial goods generally rose with population growth, improvements to the transportation system, and the growing availability of capital for investment. Thus each change triggered more change; the cumulative effect was staggering.

═══ S E C T I O N   S U M M A R Y ═══

● Europe, and especially Great Britain, was endowed with rich iron and coal deposits, one of the most important factors that gave them the lead in industrialization.

● Population growth in the eighteenth century inspired greater efficiency in agricultural production, which in turn created a surplus labor force available for industrial production in urban areas and created a market for mass-produced goods.

● Toleration of religious diversity and dissent, especially in Great Britain, helped inspire innovation and an entrepreneurial spirit.

● The expansion of trade from the seventeenth century onward created new sources of raw materials for manufacture, such as cotton.

● Merchants brought raw materials to the countryside for processing, leading to the development of cottage industry (the putting-out system), the division of labor, and specialization of tasks.

● Centralized governments supported national banks and encouraged commerce, which in turn led to improved transportation.

British Cotton Manufacture

Machines simultaneously performed various functions. The carding machine (*front left*) separated cotton fibers, readying them for spinning. The roving machine (*front right*) wound the cotton onto spools. The drawing machine (*rear left*) wove patterns into the cloth. Rich in machines, this factory needed relatively few employees; most were women and children. *(The Granger Collection, New York)*

NEW MODES OF PRODUCTION

Which inventions appear to have been the most important in launching industrialization?

Several important technological advances powered European industry, and breakthroughs in one field often led to breakthroughs in others. Major technological innovations first transformed textiles and iron. At first limited to the British Isles, industry spread to the Continent, a development that occurred unevenly in various regions and at different times.

ADVANCES IN THE COTTON INDUSTRY

A series of inventions in the eighteenth century led to the **mass production** of textiles. One of the earliest was the flying shuttle, introduced in Britain in 1733 by John Kay (1704–1764). (A shuttle carries the thread

back and forth on a loom.) Kay's flying shuttle accelerated the weaving process to such an extent that it increased the demand for thread. This need was met in the 1760s by James Hargreaves (1720–1778), who invented the spinning jenny, a device that spun thread from wool or cotton. Improvements in spinning thread, such as the mule of Samuel Crompton (1753–1827), made the spinning jenny increasingly efficient, and by 1812 one jenny could produce as much yarn as two hundred hand spinners. In 1769 Richard Arkwright (1732–1792), a barber and wigmaker, patented the water frame, a machine capable of simultaneously spinning many threads. It was installed in a single establishment with three hundred employees, forming the first modern factory. The frame was originally powered by waterfall, but in 1780s Arkwright began operating it with a steam engine. This mode of production created a glut of thread for hand weavers, which then

mass production   System in which great numbers of people work in centralized, mechanized factories to produce large quantities of goods. The steam engine led to mass-produced textiles.

A FRENCH WOMAN GOES TO WORK

The new cotton mills presented several obstacles to women workers. They had to negotiate the machinery while wearing the petticoats and aprons that custom required. Such dress could catch in the machinery, causing broken limbs and loss of a job, if not of life. At work and on their way to and from work in the British mills or at the less mechanized garment workshops of France, women had to pass dangerous places, where some experienced sexual harassment. Suzanne Voilquin (ca. 1801–ca. 1876) went to work to help her family after her mother had died. She took a job not at a mill or a factory, as was common in England, but as an embroiderer in a small workshop in Paris. In this selection she writes of her experiences as a young woman from about 1823 to 1825.

We had to be at our looms at seven o'clock sharp and, even before setting out on the long race to get there on time, we had to carry out all our little household duties as quickly as we could. If certain details made us late, Mrs. Martin [her employer] would accept no excuses and offer no reprieve. We had to pay in kind, that is to say, make good those few minutes at the end of the day's work. When our days were prolonged in this way, I had a horrible fear of meeting on my return one of those contemptible men who make a game of accosting young working women and frightening them with disgraceful remarks. When this happened, my nerves were always on edge and I lacked all physical courage. It was quite otherwise with . . . Adrienne [her younger sister]. She would say to me, . . . "Dear Sister, aren't I here?" (She was barely fifteen.) "If the occasion arises, why then you'll see that *a person's worth is not measured in years!*" And indeed, one evening, she gave me positive proof. Around nine o'clock . . . we were stopped by the vulgar words and filthy gestures of some poor wretch. As always, I stood there trembling and unable to speak

before this reviler. Adrienne, on the contrary, experienced a moment of sublime energy. She managed to find such a tone of resolve, while brandishing an enormous key before his eyes, that he backed away, and, when we reached the corner of the main street, we were delivered from his insolent remarks.

Mrs. Martin seemed satisfied with our work, and we were accepted as regular employees. And so, at the end of the first week, we were very proud to deposit on our father's mantelpiece the eighteen francs we earned as wages. It was the same each week, for he had made himself the provisioner of our little group.

That cruel year was brought to an end by an accident that nearly caused my sister the loss of her right hand. My father's wail when he thought his child had been maimed for life was heart-rending. He cried!

. . . Around this time, my father wanted to marry us off. . . . The widower whom my father begged me to marry was fairly well established but neither handsome nor pleasant nor witty. Moreover, he came with a son twelve or thirteen years old, a charming Parisian street urchin who had been very badly raised. As a result, my mind, my senses, my whole being rebelled against the thought of such a match.

QUESTIONS

1. What is Suzanne Voilquin's attitude toward work? What hardships does she face?

2. What does this excerpt tell you about family relations? Why does Suzanne's father want to "marry her off"?

Source: Suzanne Voilquin, "Recollections of a Daughter of the People," in Mark Traugott, ed. and trans., *The French Worker: Autobiographies from the Early Industrial Era,* pp. 112–113. Copyright © 1993 The Regents of the University of California. Reprinted by permission of The University of California Press.

led to the development of the power loom by Richard Cartwright in 1785. These innovations in turn increased the demand for raw cotton, inspiring American Eli Whitney (1765–1825) to invent the cotton gin, which sped up the removal of seeds from raw cotton. These innovations mechanized cotton manufacturing, moving most production from the home to factories. The industry's output increased 130-fold between 1770 and 1841.

The cotton manufacturing industry in Great Britain was an important departure from traditional production. For the first time in history a staple industry was based on a natural resource that was not domestically produced—Britain imported cotton from the U.S. South. Manufactured cotton became so cheap that it competed effectively with all handmade textiles. Comfortable and easy to wash, the popularity of cotton may have improved public health as well, for it enabled people to own several changes of clothing and keep them clean. Everyone was eager to buy British cottons. The higher demand for raw material put pressure on cotton growers in the U.S. South, who opened up new land. Whitney's cotton gin not only massively increased cotton production and the profitability of the United States' southern plantation economy; it also made slave labor more attractive.

Between 1750 and 1800 approximately three million Africans were forcibly transported to the New World, causing an enormous demographic loss to Africa. At least 10 percent of the captives died in the Middle Passage while being transported to the Americas, and an unknown number died in the wars triggered by slavers. Since predominantly young men were enslaved, villages were often left without their most productive workers and became vulnerable to famine, which also may have decimated the population.

The slave economy in the Americas influenced Britain's economy in several ways. Slave-produced sugar in the West Indies and cotton in the American South shifted Britain's trade patterns from Asia to the Atlantic. The sophisticated administrative skills that went into organizing and operating the slave trade provided invaluable management experience to the more conventional sectors of the British economy. It also benefited enormously from the sugar and cotton produced by slaves.

The cotton trade, and later, other products, linked the economies of various nations and peoples. No longer, as in preindustrial trade, were all goods locally made, nor did the consumers have personal contact with the producers of goods they purchased. Increasingly, specialization became the norm. Those most skilled performed a particular function efficiently and productively. The results were high production and low prices for finished textile products. Hand sewing and needlework, usually done by young women, completed the garment-making process. (See the box "The Written Record: A French Woman Goes to Work.")

IRON, STEAM, AND FACTORIES

Coal, a new energy source, fueled industrial production. Traditionally, smelters used charcoal to extract iron from ore. Eventually, however, the source of charcoal—wood—became depleted in Britain. Coal offered an alternative fuel, and it was plentiful. But it contained impurities, particularly sulfur, which contaminated the materials with which it came into contact. In 1708 the English ironmaster Abraham Darby discovered that coal in a blast furnace could smelt iron without these attending complications. His discovery triggered the iron industry's use of coal. In 1777 the introduction of a steam engine to operate the blast furnace considerably increased efficiency. In 1783 a steam engine was first used to drive a forge hammer to shape the iron; three years later steam-driven rollers flattened the iron into sheets. With these innovations, the output of the English iron industry doubled between 1788 and 1796 and again in the following eight years.

The greater supply of iron stimulated other changes. Wooden machines, which wore out rapidly, were replaced by relatively cheap and durable iron machines.

The new machines opened the door to further advances. Improvements in manufacturing methods and techniques increased the production of a large variety of goods, usually at lower prices. Industrial change started with cotton, but breakthroughs in the use of iron and coal continued and sustained these changes.

Before the age of industry, humans, animals, wind, and water provided the power sources for production. Humans and animals were limited in their capacities to drive the large mills needed to grind grain or cut wood. Wind was unreliable because it was not constant. Water-driven mills depended on the seasons—streams dried up in the summer and froze in the winter. And water mills could be placed only where a strong current of water flowed downward. Clearly the infant industries needed a power source that was constant and not confined to riverbanks. The **steam engine,** invented and improved on in Britain, met that need and stoked Britain's industrial growth. As late as the 1860s, traditional sources of energy still supplied more than half of the manufacturing needs in Great Britain and the United States. But the steam engine was clearly the wave of the future.

The steam engine was first used to pump water out of coal mines. As mining shafts were dug ever deeper through groundwater, drainage became a critical factor. In 1712 Thomas Newcomen (1663–1729) invented a steam-operated water pump. Its use spread rapidly. James Watt (1736–1819) improved on the Newcomen engine, making it twice as efficient in energy output. Eventually, by developing a separate condenser, Watt devised an engine that could power a variety of machines. Thus steam engines could operate mills that had previously been powered by water or wind.

The steam engine made it practical and commonplace to organize work in a factory. Locating a manufacturing plant where it was most convenient eliminated the expense of transporting raw materials to be worked on at a natural but fixed power source such as a waterfall. The central factory also reinforced work discipline. These **factories** were large, austere edifices, sometimes inspired by military architecture and therefore resembling barracks. With the introduction of blast furnaces and other heat-producing manufacturing methods, the tall factory chimney became a common sight on the industrial landscape.

The steam engine powered a dramatic growth in production. It increased the force of blast furnaces and the mechanical power of machinery used to forge iron

steam engine   The steam engine provided mechanized power for manufacturing and made factories and mass production possible.

factories   Centralized workplaces where a number of people cooperate to mass-produce goods. The steam engine as a central power source in factories led to huge productivity increases.

The Jacquard Loom
Joseph-Marie Jacquard invented this loom in 1804. The pasteboard punch cards controlled the action of the loom to create complex designs automatically, making it possible for amateur weavers to produce highly prized fabrics. The punch card was an important precursor to computing hardware and programming. The looms' cards were interchangeable. They could also be stolen—an early instance of software piracy. *(Private Collection)*

and to produce equipment for spinning and weaving. Assisted by machines, workers were enormously more productive than when they depended solely on hand-operated tools. In 1700 spinning 100 pounds of cotton took 50,000 worker-hours; by 1825 it took only 135 worker-hours—a 370-fold increase in productivity capacity per worker.

INVENTORS AND ENTREPRENEURS

Inventions triggered the industrial age, and the continued flow of new ones sustained it. Rather than cling to traditional methods, many **entrepreneurs** persistently challenged tradition and attempted to find new ways of improving production. In this age of invention, innovation was prized as never before.

The early inventors and industrialists came from a variety of backgrounds. Many came from the merchant class, since the possession of capital was a distinct advantage in launching an industrial enterprise. In 1804, Frenchman Joseph-Marie Jacquard (1752–1834), the son of a weaver, invented the Jacquard loom, which used a punched-card system to automate complex silk weaving. Within his lifetime industrialists in France and England adopted his loom, which later became the model for early computers using punched cards.

Entrepreneurs such as Arkwright and Watt pioneered innovations and became famous, but most of those who advanced the cause of industrial production were not particularly inventive. They just replicated methods of production that had proved profitable to others. Truly successful entrepreneurs, however, seemed to share one attribute: they were driven by a nearly insatiable appetite for innovation, work, and profit.

Entrepreneurs took the financial risk of investing in new types of enterprises. Most industrialists ran a single plant by themselves or with a partner, but even in the early stages, some ran several plants. In 1788

entrepreneurs People who assume the risks of organizing and investing in new business ventures, inventions, and innovations.

Richard Arkwright and his partners ran eight mills. Some enterprises were vertically integrated, controlling production at many stages. The Peels in Britain owned operations ranging from spinning to printing and even banking. The entrepreneurs' dynamism and boldness fostered the growth of the British industrial system, making that small nation the workshop of the world.

THE SPREAD OF INDUSTRY TO THE CONTINENT

The ideas and methods that were changing industry in Britain spread to the Continent by direct contact and by emulation. Visitors came to Britain, studied local methods of production, and returned home to set up blast furnaces and spinning works inspired by British design. The German engineer August Börsig (BEUR-sick) (1804–1854), after studying steam engines in Britain, built the first German steam engine in 1825 and the first German locomotive in 1842. Some visitors even resorted to industrial espionage, smuggling blueprints of machines out of Britain. Despite a British law

that forbade local artisans to emigrate, some did leave, including entrepreneurs who helped set up industrial plants in France and Belgium. By the 1820s British technicians were all over Europe—in Belgium, France, Germany, and Austria.

France   In the eighteenth century, France had seemed a more likely candidate for economic growth than Britain. France's overseas trade was growing faster than Britain's, and in 1780 its industrial output was also greater. In the nineteenth century, however, British industry boomed and Britain became the workshop of the world. French production changed more slowly. Why?

Historians have suggested several reasons. The wars and revolutions of the late eighteenth century slowed economic growth and cut France off from the flow of information and new techniques from Britain. Moreover, in the 1790s, revolutionary legislation relieved some of the peasants' misery. Thus peasants were not forced off the land by poor conditions as they were in Britain, where they provided cheap and ready labor for industry. Further, the Napoleonic Code of 1804

The Börsig Ironworks in the 1840s

August Börsig, an artisan, founded these ironworks in Berlin. The factory expanded to meet the needs of the burgeoning German rail system. By the time of Börsig's death in 1854, his factory had built five hundred locomotives.   *(Bildarchiv Preussischer Kulturbesitz/Art Resource, NY)*

MAP 20.2   Continental Industrialization, ca. 1850

Industry was still sparse on the Continent, but important regions had developed near major coal deposits in Liège, the Ruhr, and Silesia.

Online Study Center   **Improve Your Grade**   Interactive Map: Continental Industrialization, ca. 1850

abolished **primogeniture,** so that when a peasant died, all of his children, at least in principle, enjoyed equal inheritance.

Population figures suggest another reason for France's relatively slow economic growth. Between 1800 and 1914 the population of France grew at half the average rate experienced by the rest of the Continent. In Britain during this period, much of the labor that left the land and worked the factories and mills came from the rural population explosion. But no such phenomenon occurred in the French countryside, and thus the labor force in France was not poised for industrial growth.

Traditionally, France had produced high-quality luxury goods, and French entrepreneurs who sought to emulate British accomplishments faced serious difficulties. Iron and coal deposits in France were not close

together (see **MAP 20.2**). Because labor was still quite cheap, many goods could be manufactured inexpensively by hand; thus the incentive to invest in laborsaving devices was absent. Soon, however, French manufacturers found themselves facing British competition. By being the first to industrialize, the British had the advantage of being able to manufacture goods and to corner markets efficiently and relatively cheaply. The French were the first to feel the negative effects of being industrial latecomers.

German States   The Napoleonic invasions of Germany caused considerable destruction, but they also brought some positive economic benefits. The example of revolutionary change in France led to important socioeconomic changes in the German states. Restrictive guilds declined. The French occupiers suppressed many tariffs and taxes that had hindered trade between German states; they also reduced the number of

primogeniture   A legal inheritance system that provided the firstborn, usually the firstborn son, the right to inherit all the family land and farm.

separate states, established a single unified legal system, and introduced a single standard of measurement based on the metric system. These changes remained intact after 1815.

Government in the German states played an important role in the adoption of improved methods of manufacturing. Eager for industrial development, the Prussian state sent an official to Britain to observe the puddling process (the method by which iron is freed of carbon) and bring that expertise back home. The Prussian government promoted industrial growth by investing in a transportation network to carry raw materials for processing and finished goods to their markets. To spur both trade and industrial growth, Prussia took the lead in creating a customs union, the *Zollverein* (TZOLL-fair-eyn), which abolished tariffs among its members. By 1834 a German market embracing eighteen German states with a population of 23 million had been created. The Zollverein was an important step toward the later unification of Germany into a single nation-state.

German industrial growth accelerated dramatically in the 1850s. Massive expenditures on railways created a large demand for metal, which pressured German manufacturers to enlarge their plant capacities and increase efficiency. The German states were not yet politically unified, but the German middle classes saw economic growth as the means by which their country could win a prominent place among Europe's nation-states.

Germany's growth was phenomenal. It successfully emulated Britain and overtook France's rate of economic growth. Toward the end of the nineteenth century Germany pioneered in the electrical engineering and chemical industries. If France experienced the disadvantages of being a latecomer to industrialization, Germany reaped the benefits of that status. The Germans were able to avoid costly and inefficient early experimentation and adopted the latest, proven methods; moreover, Germany entered fields that Britain had neglected.

Eastern and Southern Europe Even by the end of the century, however, progress remained slow in many areas of Europe. As long as Russia retained serfdom (until 1861), it would lack the mobile labor force needed for industrial growth. And until late in the century, the ruling Russian aristocracy hesitated to adopt an economic system in which wealth was not based on labor-intensive agriculture. In Austria, Bohemia was the only important industrial center; otherwise, Austria remained heavily agrarian (see Map 20.2).

The impoverished southern Mediterranean countries experienced little economic growth. With mostly poor soil, their agriculture yielded only a meager surplus. Spain, lacking coal and access to other energy sources, could not easily diversify its economic base. Some industry emerged in Catalonia, especially around Barcelona, but it was limited in scope and did not have much impact on the rest of the country. The Italian peninsula was still industrially underdeveloped in the middle of the nineteenth century. There were modest advances, but growth was too slow to have a measurable positive impact on the Italian economy. In 1871, 61 percent of the population of Italy was still agrarian.

Although by midcentury only a few European nations had experienced industrialization to any great extent, many more would do so by the end of the century, pressured by vigorous competition from their more advanced neighbors (see **FIGURE 20.1**). Economic

FIGURE 20.1   The Increase in Gross National Product per Capita in Principal European Countries, 1830–1913
The countries that industrialized rapidly—such as the United Kingdom in particular, and also Belgium, France, and Germany—experienced dramatic increases in per capita income during the nineteenth century. Other countries, such as Greece and Portugal, economically trailed the industrial leaders, and per capita income there remained essentially flat. *(Source: Norman J. G. Pounds, An Historical Geography of Europe, 1800–1914 [New York: Cambridge University Press, 1985], p. 32. Used by permission of the publisher.)*

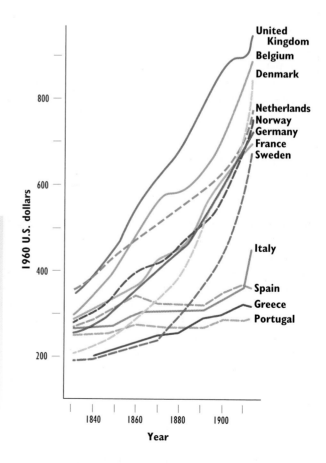

modernization had political and international implications as well, for industrialized nations had the backing of military might and superiority. Compared with the rest of the world, the European continent in the nineteenth century had acquired a distinct material culture that was increasingly based on machine manufacture or was in the process of becoming so. The possession of

"skillful industry," one Victorian writer exulted, was "ever a proof of superior civilization." Although only some regions of Europe were industrialized, many Europeans came to view themselves as obviously "superior," while deeming all other races inferior (see the box on page 622).

═══════════════ S E C T I O N   S U M M A R Y ═══════════════

- The influx of raw cotton into Britain, innovations that sped up the processes of spinning and weaving, as well as the mechanical removal of cotton seeds, led the revolution in textile production.

- The introduction of the blast furnace and steam engine doubled iron production at the end of the eighteenth century, leading to the production of less expensive and more durable machines, such as those used for textiles. Steam-driven machines led to the centralization of production into factories.

- The innovations that came with industrial production also depended upon entrepreneurs who were hungry for profits and willing to take investment risks.

- The pace of industrialization varied among nations and changed the nature of competition among them; the material culture produced by machine manufacture led Europeans to view themselves as a superior civilization with the military capability for colonial conquest.

SOCIAL, CULTURAL, AND ENVIRONMENTAL IMPACTS

What impact did industrialization have on the environment and on social classes?

Industry changed the traditional methods of agriculture, commerce, trade, and manufacture. It also transformed people's lives, individually and collectively. It altered how they made a livelihood, where and how they lived, even how they thought of themselves. Because industry required new specialized skills, the range of occupations that people adopted expanded dramatically.

The advent of industry transformed the way society functioned. Until the eighteenth century, power and influence derived from hereditary privilege, which meant aristocratic birth and land. The aristocracy did not disappear overnight. From the late eighteenth century on, however, it was challenged by a rising class of people whose wealth was self-made and whose influence was based on economic contributions to society rather than on bloodlines. Increased social mobility opened opportunities even for some workers. Industrialization transformed both the social and the natural environment. Cities experienced extraordinary growth as a result of industrialization. Europeans faced not only urban problems but also the dangerous pollution of their air and water.

URBANIZATION AND ITS DISCONTENTS

A sociologist at the end of the nineteenth century observed, "The most remarkable social phenomenon of the present century is the concentration of population in cities."[3] The number and size of cities grew as never before. The major impetus for urban growth was the concentration of industry in cities and the resulting need of large numbers of urban workers and their families for goods and services (see **MAP 20.3**).

Industrialization was not the only catalyst. France provides many examples of urban growth with little industry. Increased commercial, trading, and administrative functions led to the growth of cities in countries that had not yet witnessed much industrialization, such as France, Holland, Italy, and Switzerland. Urban growth in some places was explosive. In the entire eighteenth century, London grew by only 200,000; but in the first half of the nineteenth century, it grew by 1.4 million, more than doubling its size. Census figures show that by 1851 Britain was a predominantly urban society, the first country to have as many people living in cities as in the countryside. For Germany that date

MAP 20.3   Cities Reaching Population Level of 100,000 by 1750, 1800, and 1850

In 1750 the largest cities owed their existence primarily to commerce, but industrialization caused populations to concentrate more in cities. England, the leading industrial nation, contained many of the largest cities.   *(Source: Data from Tertius Chandler, Four Thousand Years of Urban Growth: An Historical Census [Lewistown, N.Y.: St. David's University Press, 1987], pp. 22–24.)*

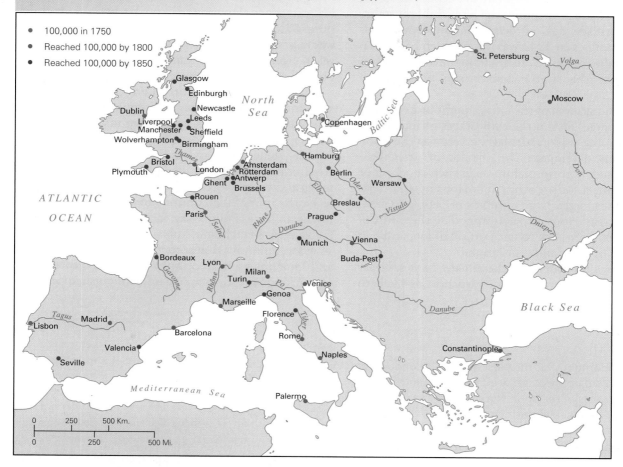

was 1891, and for France it was not until 1931. Although the proportion of people who were urban varied from place to place, the trend was clear and has continued.

As the pace of industry in part governed the growth of cities, **urbanization** in turn fueled it. Large cities provided convenient markets for goods and for a manufacturing labor pool. The concentration of people encouraged the exchange of ideas. A large city was likely to have scientific societies and laboratories where engineers and scientists could share new ideas and new inventions that would encourage industrial production. After midcentury, scientific and technological breakthroughs made in urban environments increasingly drove industrialization.

urbanization   Term related to the growth of cities, largely connected to the industrialization of the late eighteenth and nineteenth centuries.

Cities pulled in people from near and far; larger cities attracted migrants from great distances. The medium-sized French town of Saint-Etienne (sen-et-YEN) drew resettlers from the nearby mountains, whereas Paris drew from the entire country. Industrial centers even attracted people from beyond the nation's borders. The Irish arrived in large numbers to work in the factories of Lancashire, in northwestern England; Belgians came for mine work in northern France; and Poles sought employment in the Ruhr Valley of western Germany. Industrial activity stimulated the growth of world trade and shipping across the seas, taking merchant sailors far from home. Many large cities were marked by heterogeneous populations, which included people with different native languages, religions, and national origins, and increasingly, of different races. Africans and Asians inhabited port cities such as Amsterdam, Marseille, and Liverpool.

With the growth of cities came a multitude of urban ills, causing mortality rates to climb in cities. In the 1840s Britain as a whole had a death rate of 22 per thousand, but Liverpool averaged 39.2 and Manchester 33.1. In France national mortality rates were around 22 per thousand, but in some French cities the rate was as high as 35 per thousand. Social inequality in the face of death was startling. Including the high child mortality rate, the average age at death among upper-class Liverpool families in 1842 was 35; for members of laborers' families it was 15. In 1800 boys living in urban slums were 8 inches shorter than the sons of rich urban dwellers.

The rapid growth of the cities caught local authorities unprepared, and in the early stages of industrialization, city life was particularly severe for the poor. Urban slums developed. The squalor of St. Giles—London's most notorious slum—had such shock value that it became a tourist attraction. Housing shortages in many cities forced large numbers of people to cram into small areas. Houses to accommodate the influx of workers were built back to back on small lots and had insufficient lighting and ventilation.

Overcrowding worsened the already poor sanitary conditions. A single privy in a courtyard was likely to serve dozens of tenants—in some notorious cases in Britain and France, a few hundred. Waste from the privy might contaminate nearby wells, or drain through open sewers to a nearby river, which was likely to be the local source of drinking water. Some tenants lacked toilets and relieved themselves in the streets. In the 1830s people living in the poorest sections of Glasgow stored human waste in heaps alongside their houses and sold it as manure. Water in the cities was scarce and filthy. Piped water was reserved for the rich. The poor had to supply themselves from public fountains or wells and were often obliged to carry water a considerable distance.

The dizzying pace of urban growth made it impossible for cities to provide basic sanitary facilities. The causes of many diseases, such as typhus and tuberculosis, were unknown; the dirt, dampness, and darkness of crowded tenements and polluted streets created the conditions that fostered disease. Social reformers and medical experts, moreover, decried what they perceived to be the immoral conditions in which families lived. Physician James Philips Kay, for example, who practiced medicine in Manchester, England, wrote in 1832 of how "A whole family is often accommodated on a single bed, and sometimes a heap of filthy straw and a covering of old sacking hide them in one undistinguished heap, de-

St. Giles

This neighborhood was the most notorious London slum. Visual portrayals such as this one did not necessarily exaggerate slum conditions, but did help create negative images of the poor. Note the implied promiscuousness of the disheveled couple, and the indifferent attitude of the mother (who might be single) toward her infant. Note as well the class differences this image portrays: the disapproving middle-class women standing off to the side on the right often ventured into slums for charitable works, one of the few excuses respectable women had to be in public.

(From Thomas Beames, The Rookeries of London. Photo: Harvard Imaging Service)

PIERDON.

based alike by penury, want of economy and dissolute habits. Frequently, the inspectors found [that] . . . more than one family lived in a damp cellar, containing only one room, in whose pestilential atmosphere from twelve to sixteen persons were crowded. To these fertile sources of disease were sometimes added the keeping of pigs and other animals in the house, with other nuisances of the most revolting character."[4] Such descriptions contributed to the growing perceptions, as well as material reality, of class differences.

In manufacturing towns factory chimneys spewed soot, and everything was covered with dirt and grime. Smoke was a major ingredient of the famous London fog, which not only reduced visibility but posed serious health risks. Refuse, including the rotting corpses of dogs and horses, littered city streets. In 1858 the stench from sewage and other rot was so putrid that the British House of Commons was forced to suspend its sessions.

It is not surprising that cholera, a highly infectious disease transmitted through contaminated water, swept London and other European urban centers. In the 1830s one of the first epidemics of modern times struck Europe, killing 100,000 in France, 50,000 in Britain, and 238,000 in Russia. Typhoid fever, also an acute infectious disease, struck mostly the poor but did not spare the privileged. Queen Victoria of Great Britain nearly died of it; her husband, Prince Albert, did.

THE WORKING CLASSES AND THEIR LOT

In 1842 a middle-class observer traveling in industrial Lancashire noted that around the mills and factories there had developed a "population [that] like the system to which it belongs is NEW . . . hourly increasing in breadth and strength."[5] A French countess, using the pen name Daniel Stern, wrote in the 1830s and 1840s about the emergence of "a class apart, as if it were a nation within the nation," working in factories and mines, called "by a new name: the industrial **proletariat**."[6] Originally used to designate the poorest propertyless wretches in Roman society, the term *proletariat* became synonymous with the class of workers developing in the burgeoning factories. What distinguished this growing class throughout the nineteenth century was that it was relatively unskilled and totally dependent on the factory owners for its livelihood. Even lowly apprentices of earlier eras never occupied such a precarious status because guild rules and traditions protected them from arbitrariness; the guild system also made it possible for apprentices to become journeymen and then master artisans, owning their own tools and working on their own time and on their own premises. Improvement in

proletariat   Karl Marx's term for the new class of industrial workers who owned none of the means of production and were dependent on factory owners for their livelihoods.

status and owning the means of production would never be a possibility for the new proletariat.

As industry advanced and spread, more and more people depended on it for a livelihood. In the putting-out system, during an agricultural downturn, a cottager could spend more time on hand labor; when demand for piecework slacked off, the cottager could devote more time to cultivating the land. But people living in industrial cities had no such backup. And neither skilled nor unskilled workers were assured of regular employment: any downturn in the economy translated into layoffs or job losses. In addition, the introduction of new industries often devastated laborers in older forms of production. The mechanization of cotton production reduced the earning power of weavers. Cheap cotton production also drove down workers' wages in other textiles with higher production costs, such as linen, because of competition.

Most factory work was dirty and laborious and took place in grim plants with heavy, noisy machinery. Sixteen-hour workdays were common. Child labor was widespread. With no safety provisions, the workers were prone to accidents. Few factory owners protected their workers against dangerous substances or circumstances. Mercury used in hat manufacturing gradually poisoned the hatmakers and often led to dementia, hence the term *mad hatters*. Lead used in paints and pottery also had a devastating impact on workers' health.

Smaller than boys, and often underfed, young girls especially suffered poor health from heavy labor. In 1842, 18-year-old Ann Eggley, a mineworker since the age of 7, hauled carriages loaded with ore weighing 800 pounds for twelve hours a day. She testified to a parliamentary commission that, so worn out from her work, upon coming home, she often fell asleep before even going to bed. Isabel Wilson, another mineworker, testified that she had given birth to ten children and had suffered five miscarriages. These women were overworked, exhausted, and vulnerable to disease, and they faced premature death.

Did industrialization improve the workers' lot? Until the mid-nineteenth century, information about workers' standard of living, measured by income and expenses, is incomplete. The best evidence comes from Britain, where an average family of five needed at least 21 shillings a week to fend off poverty. Skilled workers, who were in demand, might earn as much as 30 shillings a week, but most workers were unskilled. And even skilled workers enjoyed little security: if they became less productive because of illness or old age, their wages fell. Women and children usually had to pitch in. Even when women were the main breadwinners, they almost never received wages sufficient to meet the needs of their own subsistence, let alone those of an entire family. Regardless of what work they performed,

Children Toiling in Mines
Able to crawl in narrow mine shafts, many children were employed underground. In this woodcut, a woman joins a child in his labor. Often whole families worked together and were paid a fixed price for the amount of coal extracted. *(Hulton Archive/Getty Images)*

women always earned a fraction of men's wages. Employers based women's wages on the assumption that they supplemented the income of a husband or father.

Incomes were so low that workers normally spent between two-thirds and three-fourths of their budget on food. Those who lived in rural areas might raise chickens or pigs or have a plot of potatoes. Bread was the largest single item consumed, varying between one and two pounds a day per person. A little bacon or other meat gave flavor to the soup in which people dipped their bread or potatoes, but meat was rarely consumed as a main course. Because men were the chief breadwinners and tended to have the most strenuous occupations, they received the choice piece of meat and the largest amount of food. Women and children ate what remained.

From the beginning, industrialization increased society's wealth, but historians continue to debate whether and at what point it benefited workers. "Optimist" historians argue that some of the new wealth trickled down to the lower levels of society. "Pessimist" historians say that a downward flow did not necessarily occur. Statistics suggest that by the 1840s workers' lives in Britain did improve. Their real income rose by 40 percent between 1800 and 1850 because of relatively low prices of many basic goods. As the cost of cloth declined, the dress of working-class people noticeably improved. On the Continent, the lot of workers improved a little later than in Britain, but the process followed the same pattern. Nonetheless, the general trend in real wages meant little when workers were unemployed and when they lived in crowded conditions, or during a major economic downturn such as occurred in the 1840s.

INDUSTRIALIZATION AND THE FAMILY

Industrialization dramatically changed the character of family and household among both the working and middle classes. Mechanization and removal of work from the home created job segregation on the basis of gender and age. The best-paying jobs went to men; they became factory supervisors and ran machinery such as the jenny. The textile industries especially employed children and women in the lowliest positions, where they tended machines, tied broken threads, and performed menial tasks. Women generally received from 30 to 50 percent of men's wages, children from 5 to 25 percent.

Factory work often undermined the ability of working women to take care of their children. As farmers or cottagers, women had been able to work and supervise their children simultaneously. The factory, however, often separated mothers from their children. It was not uncommon for an older child, sometimes only 5 or 6 years old, to be entrusted with the care of younger siblings.

Urban and rural women sometimes resorted to more dangerous methods of child-care. In both England and on the Continent many mothers sent their children to wet nurses in the countryside, where—if they survived—they stayed for up to two years. The mortality of these babies was high, as they were often neglected. In France and Italy, the poorest of mothers—especially single mothers—abandoned their infants at foundling homes, which in turn sent them out to be wet nursed. In many cases baby-farming was no more than a camouflaged form of infanticide. Mothers who kept their children, but were obliged to leave them unwatched at home during factory hours, sometimes pacified them with mixtures of opium, readily available from the local apothecary.

Because of the many demands on them, women often had sporadic work patterns. Young women might work before marriage or before giving birth, stay home until the children were older, and then return to work. Factory work had a harsh impact on women's lives, but it should be remembered that relatively few women were in the wage market—by 1850 only about a quarter in both Britain and France. Of that quarter, few worked in factories; far more were in agriculture, crafts industries (which still flourished despite poor working conditions), and domestic service. Some sectors of industry, such as textiles, employed a large proportion of women. Other sectors, such as the metal and mining industries, were heavily male-dominated.

Online Study Center **Improve Your Grade**
Primary Source: "Sweated Labor": A Poor Woman's Fate

The textile industry found employment for children once they were over the age of 5 or 6. Their size and agility made them useful for certain jobs, such as reaching under machines to pick up loose cotton. Because of their small hands they were also hired as "doffers," taking bobbins off frames and replacing them. Elizabeth Bentley began work as a doffer in 1815 at the age of 6. At the age of 23, when she testified before a parliamentary commission, she was "considerably

The Iron Forge

This painting from the late eighteenth century by Joseph Wright of Derby suggests the pride, dignity, and independence of the preindustrial forger, whose work not only allowed him to support his family but also blended with his unregimented everyday life. This romanticized portrayal starkly contrasts with the factory labor that would replace small-scale iron forgery.

(Broadlands Trust, Hampshire, UK/The Bridgeman Art Library)

deformed . . . in consequence of this labor." She normally worked from 6:00 A.M. to 7:00 P.M., but for six months worked sixteen-hour days, beginning at 5:00 A.M. She told the commission that children were strapped if they arrived late. She had only forty minutes at noon to eat, but said "I had not much to eat, and the little I had I could not eat it, my appetite was so poor, and being covered with dust; and it was no use taking it home, I could not eat it. . . ."[7] Child labor certainly did not start with the industrial transformation; it had always existed. The stern industrial discipline imposed on the very young, however, was new. Children were subject to the clock, closely supervised and prevented from taking long breaks or mixing work and play—as had been possible in an earlier era. Although children commonly worked in British textile industries, overall less than 10 percent of working children were employed in industrial work. Most were in agriculture or the service sector.

In some cases industrialization meant a transformation in the authority structure of workers' households; women's wage-earning capacity outside the home might undermine the influence of the male as head of the household. Most women did not, however, experience emancipation in factory or mine work because their low wages were not sufficient to support their independence. Even young women who left the countryside for factory work in towns and cities usually sent their wages back to their families. Moreover, as in the putting-out system, whole families were often hired as a group to perform a specific function. Contemporaries sometimes denounced industry for dissolving family bonds, but the family often remained an effective work unit.

If not participating in the wage market, wives and children contributed in other ways to the household budget—by making clothes, raising a pig, tending a potato patch, and performing daily household chores. Grandparents often moved from the country to live with the family and take care of the children. When industrial workers married, they frequently settled with their spouses on the same street or in the same neighborhood as their own parents. Thus although industry had the potential to break up traditional family structures, the historical evidence shows that the family generally adjusted and survived the challenges posed by the new economic system.

Industrial capitalism also gave rise to a new middle class or bourgeoisie, whose wealth derived from the capitalistic activities of trade, finance, and manufacturing. Previously the wives and daughters of small shopkeepers readily performed tasks such as bookkeeping or serving customers because the businesses were in or near the home. But as small businesses became public companies, women ceased participating. Family life came to reflect these new economic realities, justified and reinforced by a new set of cultural values. In more than any other social class, new family values based on gender distinctions became just as important a signifier of class identity as wealth itself. As Catherine Hall has noted in the history of middle-class private life in the nineteenth century, "A man's dignity lay in his occupation; a woman's gentility was destroyed if she had one."[8] The nineteenth-century world of market capitalism made wealth—rather than aristocratic bloodlines—the sign of success and power. Conspicuous consumption on homes, home furnishings, and clothing offered visible proof of success.

With business affairs removed from the home and enough wealth that women's employment was not required, motherhood and women's devotion to it became more idealized in the middle class than it ever had been in the past. Women developed a "cult of domesticity" in which they devoted themselves to their children and to home décor—or supervised servants who did—as men became preoccupied with work and with male sociability. While bourgeois men and women did not always live up to these ideals, they did generally embrace them as a prescription appropriate for family life in the new industrial world. These ideals also became a basis for judgment of those who did not live up to them—the lower classes and errant women of all classes.

THE LAND, THE WATER, AND THE AIR

Industrialization seriously disturbed the environment, transforming the surface of the earth, the water, and the air. To run the new machinery, coal was mined in increasing amounts (see **TABLE 20.1**). Iron and other minerals were also in great demand. The exploitation of coal ushered in the modern age of energy use, in which massive amounts of nonrenewable resources are consumed.

TABLE 20.1

Coal Production in Industrializing Nations

	Millions of Tons	Kilograms per Inhabitant
1700	4	26
1750	7	16
1800	16	76
1830	30	120
1860	129	390

Source: Based on B. R. Mitchell, "Statistical Appendix, 1700–1914," in *The Fontana Economic History of Europe,* ed. Carlo Cippola, vol. 4 (London: Collins, 1973), pp. 747, 770; and Norman J. G. Pounds, *An Historical Geography of Europe, 1500–1840* (New York: Cambridge University Press, 1979), pp. 268–269.

To extract coal and other minerals, miners dug deep tunnels, removing millions of tons of earth, rock, and other debris. This material, plus slag and other waste from the factories, was heaped up in mounds that at times covered acres of land, creating new geological formations.

With axes and saws people cut down trees, depleting forests to supply the wood needed to build shafts for coal, iron, and tin mines, or to make the charcoal necessary for glassmaking. Between 1750 and 1900 industrial and agricultural needs led to the clearing of 50 percent of all the forests ever cleared. Many of Europe's major forests disappeared or were seriously diminished. Deforestation in turn sped up soil erosion.

Industry changed the physical environment in which people lived. Forests, lakes, rivers, and air—as well as people themselves—showed the harmful effects of industry. Centrifugal pumps drained large marshes in the Fenland in eastern England. A contemporary lamented, "The wind which, in the autumn of 1851 was curling the blue water of the lake, in the autumn of 1853 was blowing in the same place over fields of yellow corn." Smoke and soot darkened the skies, intensifying the fog over London and other cities. Foul odors from factories could be detected at several miles' distance. Alkali, used for making glass, when released into the atmosphere killed trees for several miles around. Factories dumped waste ash into rivers, changing their channels and making them considerably shallower. Because of pollution from industrial and human waste, by 1850 no fish could survive in the lower Thames River. The Calder River in northern England was so thickly polluted that an irate Englishman used its water as ink when he wrote to the health board in 1868 to make his point about the river's condition. He also noted that readers of his letter would miss one dimension of the situation—the river's stench. Not merely unpleasant, these various pollutants caused cancer and lung diseases, though the connection between pollutants and disease was not yet understood.

A Changing Sense of Time

In agrarian societies time was measured in terms of natural occurrences, such as sunrise and sunset, or the time it might take to milk a cow. With industrialization, punctuality became essential. Shifts of labor had to be rotated to keep the smelters going; they could not stop, or the molten iron would harden at the bottom of the hearths. The interactive nature of industrial production, in which workers with differing specialties each performed a particular task in finishing a product, made it necessary for employees to be at the factory at an appointed time. Factory rules often reflected an obsession with the efficient use of time. In some workplaces, those arriving two minutes late lost an hour's wages, and after more than two minutes they were locked out until the first break. Idleness, and even conversation between workers, could be cause for dismissal.

Clocks were installed in church towers and municipal buildings as early as the fourteenth century, but they were not very reliable until the eighteenth century. Watches were commonly owned by men of property and even by some artisans. By the mid-nineteenth century, at least in Britain, as the price of watches dropped, many workers could afford them. And even when workers did not own timepieces, they were intensely aware of time. Those who ignored time were fined or fired from their jobs. People listened for the church bell or factory whistle or asked a neighbor or passerby for the time. Western societies increasingly regularized and internalized the sense of time.

SECTION SUMMARY

- Industrialization, as well as commerce and the growth of administrative bureaucracy, caused urbanization; rapid growth of cities created overcrowding and unsanitary conditions, facilitating the spread of infectious diseases.

- Industrialization ultimately raised living standards, but its early stages disrupted workers' lives by mechanizing traditional forms of production, which rendered some artisanal skills obsolete and caused systematic poverty.

- By removing production from the home, industrialization often forced women and children into low-paying factory jobs; it also reshaped middle-class families by making gender roles more distinct.

- Industrial production, particularly the consumption of nonrenewable resources such as coal, transformed the environment and polluted the earth, water, and air.

- Mechanical modes of production transformed the sense of time; they allowed work to be organized in long shifts that required discipline and rigid punctuality.

RESPONSES TO INDUSTRIALIZATION

What did workers gain and lose as a result of industrialization, and how did they respond?

People living at subsistence levels in urban slums offered visible and disquieting evidence of industrialization's social consequences. As middle-class reformers wondered how to contend with social ills, the working classes developed their own sense of a common interest and fate. The result was a resounding cry for political and social democracy that began in the first half of the nineteenth century and became increasingly insistent—and sometimes violent.

THE GROWTH OF WORKING-CLASS SOLIDARITY

Hardest hit by economic changes, workers sought to improve their conditions by organizing and articulating their needs. In the preindustrial economy, artisans and craftsmen lived in an accepted hierarchy with prescribed rules. They began by serving for a certain number of years as apprentices to a master, next became journeymen, and finally with hard work and good fortune became masters of their trades. As tradesmen with common interests, they tended to band together into brotherhoods, promising one another help and trying to improve their working conditions.

With industrialization, guilds declined. Unlike the skilled handicrafts that required years of apprenticeship, few aspects of industrial production demanded extensive training. The system of dependence between apprentice and master became irrelevant. Guilds trying to protect their members often resisted new technologies and came to be seen as a hindrance to economic development. Liberals viewed guilds as constraints on trade and on the free flow of labor. For this reason, the French abolished guilds and all workers' coalitions during the Revolution of 1789. Throughout the eighteenth century, the British Parliament passed various acts against "combinations" by workmen.

While guilds faded in importance, the solidarity and language born of the guild continued to shape workers' attitudes throughout much of the nineteenth century. New experiences also reinforced the sense of belonging to a group and sharing common aspirations.

Cultural forces such as shared religious practice further fostered workers' sense of solidarity. Religious sects flourished in an environment of despair punctuated by hopes of deliverance. Some historians believe that the growth of Methodism in England in the 1790s

(see page 654) was a response to grim economic conditions. Emphasis on equality before God fueled the sense of injustice in a world where a privileged few lived in luxury while others were condemned to work along with their children for a pittance. Joanna, a self-proclaimed prophet active in the 1810s in England, announced both salvation and the coming of a new world of material well-being. In France workers believed the new society would come about by their martyrdom; like Jesus, the workers would suffer, and from their suffering would emerge a new, better society. Ideas of social justice were linked in the countryside with religious broadsides speaking of "Jesus the worker." Religious themes and language continued to be important in labor organization for many years.

Other cultural and social factors created bonds among workers. Housing became increasingly segregated by class. Thus urban workers lived close together, in similar conditions of squalor and hardship, either in the center of cities or in the outlying areas near factories. They grew close by spending their leisure time together, drinking in pubs, attending theaters and new forms of popular entertainment such as the circus, or watching traditional blood sports such as boxing or cockfights. Sports became popular as both spectator and participatory events in the 1880s. Soccer, which developed in England at this time, drew players and fans overwhelmingly from the working classes.

Social institutions also encouraged class unity. In the eighteenth century, both husband and wife were usually in the same craft. By 1900 it became more common for workers to marry across their crafts, thereby strengthening the sense of solidarity that encompassed the working classes as a whole.

Faced with the uncertainties of unemployment and job-related accidents, in addition to disease and other natural catastrophes, workers formed so-called **friendly societies** in which they pooled their resources to provide mutual aid. These societies, descendants of benefit organizations of the Middle Ages and Renaissance, combined business activity with feasts, drinking bouts, and other social functions.

Friendly societies had existed as early as the seventeenth century, but they became increasingly popular and important after industrialization. Their strength in a region often reflected the degree to which the area

friendly societies Nineteenth-century organizations formed by workers; members pooled their resources to provide mutual aid.

Leisure Activity for the Working Poor

Some harsh forms of entertainment turned up in the industrial period. Scores of working-class spectators came to see the celebrated dog "Billy" kill a hundred rats at one time at the Westminster Pit in London in 1822. *(The British Library)*

was industrialized. Initially organized to provide aid for workers in a particular trade, they soon included members from several crafts. In time they federated into national organizations, so that a worker who moved to a new town could continue membership in the new locale. Connected by common membership in friendly societies, workers expressed a feeling of group solidarity beyond their individual occupations. Though far from solidified, a self-conscious working class was in the making.

COLLECTIVE ACTION

Militant and in some cases violent action strengthened workers' solidarity. Since they did not have the vote, they could not express their grievances through official political channels, and their frustrated efforts to improve their own work and living conditions underscored their common plight.

In the face of hardships, artisans organized for collective action. In 1811 and 1812 British hand weavers, in reaction against mechanized looms, organized in groups claiming to be led by a mythical General Ned Ludd. In the name of economic justice and to protect

their livelihood, the **Luddites,** as the general's followers were called, smashed machines or threatened to do so. German weavers went on machine-crushing campaigns in the 1830s and 1840s.

Online Study Center **Improve Your Grade**
Primary Source: Yorkshire Luddites Threaten the Owner of a Mechanized Factory

In Lyon, France, in 1831 and 1834, workers led insurrections to demand fair wages for piecework. Angered when the silk merchants lowered the amount they would pay, the workers marched in the streets bearing banners proclaiming "Live Working or Die Fighting." The government sent troops to restore order to the riot-torn city. Although conditions of the silk trade had been the immediate impetus for the uprising, the workers appealed for help to their fellow workers in other trades, who joined in the protests.

Labor agitation in much of Europe increased in the 1840s. A major strike wave involving twenty thousand workers broke out in Paris in 1840. In the summer of

Luddites Organized groups of British workers who smashed machines that threatened their livelihood. The name comes from their mythical leader, General Ned Ludd.

Union Membership Certificates

Though for the most part illegal, trade unions, often in the form of "brotherhoods" and mutual aid societies, existed in Europe from the beginning of the nineteenth century. But governments greatly restricted their power. The British Parliament, for example, gave unions legal status in 1825. However, it prohibited them from interfering with production, thus crippling their power to bargain effectively for improved wages or working conditions. Workers in other countries faced more severe restrictions.

In Britain, local unions of engineers began forming in the 1780s. In 1826, the Journeymen Steam Engine Makers' Society (JSEMS) organized and became one of the important early British unions. But to exert effective power, unions needed to organize on the national rather than on a local level, and to include more than one craft or trade. In 1851, William Allan, general secretary of the JSEMS, formed the national Amalgamated Society of Engineers, Machinists, Millwrights, Smiths, and Pattern Makers. By 1852, it had almost 11,000 members, and by 1866 its membership tripled.

This union represented skilled workers and professionals, a "labor aristocracy" that earned high enough wages to be able to afford the mem-

Unionization Certificate: Membership in the Amalgamated Society of Engineers   *(The Art Archive)*

BE UNITED AND INDUSTRIOUS

AMALGAMATED SOCIETY OF ENGINEERS, MACHINISTS, MILLWRIGHTS, SMITHS, AND PATTERN MAKERS.

bership dues. It did not include those who worked at unskilled jobs for low wages, who could have most benefited from membership. The Amalgamated Society of Engineers provided various forms of relief to its members, such as insurance for unemployment, sickness, disability, and accidents, and benefits for funerals.

Pictured here is an elaborate membership certificate for the Society. Note the wide array of symbolism and allegory on which it draws, with images of classical antiquity, Greek mythology, and the modern material culture of the nineteenth century. What do these symbols represent, and what did they mean to the union members? Surely they imbued a sense of pride, dignity, and an assured place in the industrial progress of Great Britain—all reinforced and justified by the timeless ideals of the classical past and of contemporary religion.

The angelic winged figure hovering above the symmetrical structure is the "Goddess of Fame." The dove, with the olive branch of peace in its beak, represents the Holy Spirit. Together these otherworldly beings connect the works of this professional union to the heavens. The goddess stands upon a Cornucopia of Plenty, which connotes the fruit of honest and industrious labor. With heavenly authority, she simultaneously crowns an iron smith (left) and an engineer (right) each with a laurel wreath. The iron smith represents the body and the physical strength of manual labor, while the engineer represents the mind and its capacity for innovation.

Mars, the god of war, asks the smith to repair his sword—but, as a further sign of the peaceful intent of the union's production, the latter refuses. Clio, the Muse of history, presents a design to the engineer, which he willingly accepts, perhaps signifying the historical progress of innovation. Between Mars and Clio are the portraits of three inventors: Samuel Crompton (left), inventor of the mule jenny; James Watt (middle), whose improvement to the steam engine allowed its use for machines; and Richard Arkwright (right), who invented the spinning frame. The two kneeling figures next to Mars and Clio illustrate Aesop's fable, "The Bundle of Sticks," in which a father teaches his sons that sticks cannot be broken when tied together; they are breakable only when separated. The fable

thus represents the strength that unity brings to workers.

Below the portrait is a large bird with majestic red and gold plumage—the phoenix of classical mythology rising from its ashes. After living for hundreds of years, it burned to ashes on a funeral pyre in a flame ignited by the sun and fanned by its flapping wings. But it rises from the ashes, reborn to live through another cycle.

The base of this altar-like structure houses five branches of the iron trade that surround, at the bottom center, James Watt's rotating engine. Note how the labor performed here is very different from that of the unskilled industrial work in large factories, such as that portrayed in the background on the left. The train calls to mind the modern age of industry and transport, while the ship on the right conjures up commerce and trade. The rose, thistle, and shamrock symbolize the United Kingdom, as they are the emblems, respectively, of England, Scotland, and Ireland.

QUESTIONS

1. Which types of workers are depicted on this certificate and which workers are excluded?

2. How are religion, science, and industry combined here? How do these symbols evoke Christianity as well as classical antiquity?

3. In what ways would these symbols and allegories inspire pride, dignity, and a sense of unity among the workers who held membership certificates? How is gender represented in this image, and what is its significance?

Online Study Center
Improve Your Grade Visual Record Activities

1842 an industrial downturn in England led to massive unemployment and rioting. During the summer of 1844 in Silesia, in eastern Prussia, linen hand-loom weavers, desperate because of worsening conditions brought on by competition from machine-made cotton fabrics, attacked the homes of the wealthy. In 1855 in Barcelona, the government tried to dissolve unions, and fifty thousand workers went on strike, carrying placards that warned "Association or Death."

Workers had to conform to severe discipline and rigid rules not only in the workplace but also away from it. Workers in some factories were forbidden to read certain newspapers, had to attend religious services, and could marry only with the owners' permission. Workers resisted these attempts at control and resented employers' intrusiveness.

Workers' actions in the early nineteenth century clearly showed that they wanted both freedom from intrusive regulation by their employers and the security of employment at a decent wage. Unions provided a means to these goals. (See the feature "The Visual Record: Union Membership Certificates.")

Many of the friendly societies struggled to improve their members' working conditions, acting very much as labor unions would. They organized strikes and provided support to members during work stoppages. The advantages offered by unions were well understood—by both sides. Unions were illegal in Britain until 1825, in Prussia until 1859, and in France until the 1860s. As a French workers' paper declared in 1847, "If workers came together and organized . . . nothing would be able to stop them." An organized force could threaten to withhold labor if the employer did not grant decent wages and acceptable conditions. Unions made workers a countervailing force to factory owners.

The process of unionization was difficult. By 1850 many countries had passed laws supporting employers against workers. Censorship and the use of force against organized strikes were not uncommon. Population growth made it difficult for workers to withhold labor lest they be replaced by others only too willing to take their places. Foreign workers—for example, the Irish who streamed into England and the Belgians and Italians who migrated to France—were often desperate for work and not well informed about local conditions.

In many countries workers formed unions illegally. Although there were early attempts in Britain to organize unions on a national basis, most were centered on a single craft or a single industry. Because labor unions originated in the crafts tradition, the earliest members were skilled craftsmen who organized to protect their livelihoods from the challenge that industrialization posed. These craftsmen were usually literate and long-time residents of their communities. They provided the labor movement with much of its leadership and organization. Skilled craft workers also played a strong role

in developing a sense of class-consciousness. The language and institutions that they had developed over decades, and sometimes over centuries, became the common heritage of workers in general.

Workers looked to political action as the means to improve their situations. In the 1830s and 1840s British and French workers agitated for the right to vote; they saw voting as a way to put themselves on equal footing with the privileged and to win better conditions. Their disappointment at their failure to win political representation strengthened their class solidarity against the wealthy, privileged upper classes. Politically, organized workers played a major role in the revolutions that would rock Europe in 1848 (see pages 671–677), sometimes helping to instigate the uprisings, often influencing their course. However vague their ideas, European workers showed that their organizations were legitimate representatives of the people and that the lot of the worker should be the concern of government. In general, workers upheld the ideal of a moral economy—one in which all who labored got a just wage and every person was assured a minimum level of well-being.

The working classes were never a monolithic group. They consisted of people with varying skills, responsibilities, and incomes. Artisans with valuable skills were the segment that employers most respected and favored in pay and in working conditions. In contrast, unskilled workers were poorly paid, harshly treated, and often given only temporary work. Many skilled workers looked with contempt on the unskilled.

The industrial workplace usually segregated men and women, but when they did work side by side, it created little solidarity between them. Men worried that women were undermining their earning power by accepting lower wages. They often excluded women from their unions. Men even went on strike to force employers to discharge women.

Nor was there solidarity across nationalities. Foreign workers were heartily despised. British workers were hostile toward the Irish, the French toward the Belgian and Italian immigrants. The hostility often led to anti-immigrant riots. Many forces fostered dissension among the working classes in the nineteenth century. Nevertheless, shared economic, material, and cultural experiences broadened and deepened workers' sense of a shared fate and common goals.

By the mid-nineteenth century, the middle classes had developed a clear fear of workers and viewed them as a single class that threatened society. It was not unusual for members of the elite to refer to workers as "the swinish multitude" or, as the title of a popular English book put it, *The Great Unwashed* (1868). In France reference was alternately made to "the dangerous classes" and "the laboring classes." Not just workers but even the privileged seemed to see relations between the groups as a form of class war.

SECTION SUMMARY

- As guilds declined (or were prohibited), new worker solidarities based on religion, language, a sense of social justice, and shared experiences provided the foundation for the emergence of trade unions.

- Workers at times resorted to violence in their effort to preserve more traditional modes of production and protect their right to work.

- Friendly societies and unions sought to provide health, accident, unemployment, and funeral benefits.

- Professional unionization faced the obstacles of government repression as well as the diversity of the labor force itself: skilled workers versus the unskilled; men versus women; nationals versus foreigners.

CHAPTER SUMMARY

Online Study Center **ACE the Test**

What factors allowed Europe to industrialize before the rest of the world?

Which inventions appear to have been the most important in launching industrialization?

What impact did industrialization have on the environment and on social classes?

What did workers gain and lose as a result of industrialization, and how did they respond?

Industrial transformation altered the face of Europe. This process, which started around 1750 in parts of England, spread by 1850 to the Continent. The proximity of coal and iron, the relative ease of domestic transportation, a culture open to innovation and entrepreneurship, and the existence of an already relatively dynamic economy help explain why Britain was the first nation to industrialize, and why industrialization spread to much of Europe. The new industrial economy changed power relations within Europe and altered the relationship of Europe to the rest of the world.

A number of key inventions gave impetus to industrialization. The desire for more efficient cotton production led to John Kay's flying shuttle, which so increased the production of weaving that it created a shortage of thread. James Hargreave's spinning jenny and Samuel Crompton's mule more than met the need for thread production, further inspiring the invention of power looms. The use of coal to process iron made possible the creation of iron machinery that could be powered by James Watt's steam engine, as well as stronger blast furnaces that could, in turn, improve iron processing.

The extraction and use of energy resources such as coal transformed the landscape and polluted the air and water. Industry also changed the nature of work for large numbers of Europeans. A decreasing number of people worked in agriculture, and more entered manufacturing, where machines replaced human energy. For the first time European cities grew to more than one million inhabitants.

Industrialization ultimately raised the standard of living across social classes, but in the short term a large portion of the lower classes suffered low wages, geographical displacement, periodic unemployment, and overcrowding in the cramped, unsanitary housing of fast-growing towns and cities. The amassing of workers in factories and urban areas called attention to their potential power. Eager to improve their lives, workers began to organize into associations that were more broadly based and therefore more powerful than those of the past. As workers began to think of themselves as a class, the dominant elites within society began to perceive them as such. The new proletarian class, shaped by industrialization, was a growing force that would challenge the existing order throughout the nineteenth century and much of the next.

LOOKING AHEAD

Industrialization began in England prior to the French Revolution of 1789 and the Napoleonic Wars that ensued. As industrialization spread to the Continent in the first half of the nineteenth century, its impacts unfolded in a distinct political context: the effort to return to and uphold the stable monarchical and hierarchical order that existed prior to 1789. But economic change and the new ideologies it produced, coupled with the persistent memory of eighteenth-century revolution, thwarted that effort. The new social classes to which industrial capitalism gave rise—the proletariat and bourgeoisie—promoted social reform and revolution, making a complete return to the past impossible. To these reactionary, reformist, and revolutionary efforts we now turn.

KEY TERMS

industrialization (p. 620)

mass production (p. 625)

steam engine (p. 627)

factories (p. 627)

entrepreneurs (p. 628)

primogeniture (p. 630)

urbanization (p. 633)

friendly societies (p. 640)

proletariat (p. 635)

Luddites (p. 641)

Online Study Center **Improve Your Grade** Flashcards

SUGGESTED READING

Clark, Anna. *The Struggle for the Breeches: Gender and the Making of the British Working Class.* 1995. An examination of the role of working women and gender conflicts in domestic life, work, and politics.

Fuchs, Rachel. *Gender and Poverty in Nineteenth Century Europe.* 2005. A fascinating study of the challenges facing women in daily experiences of birth, sex, and death in this era of enduring change.

Hopkins, Eric. *Industrialisation and Society.* 2000. A survey that considers the social and political impact of industry on British society.

Landes, David S. *The Wealth and Poverty of Nations.* 1999. Explores why Europe industrialized as compared with the rest of the world.

Mokyr, Joel. *The Lever of Riches: Technological Creativity and Economic Progress.* 1990. A comparative study of Western and Chinese technology, emphasizing cultural elements as explanations for the industrialization of the West.

Sylla, Richard, and Gianni Toniolo, eds. *Patterns of European Industrialization.* 1991. A comparative perspective on the patterns of industrialization.

Thompson, E. P. *The Making of the English Working Class.* 1963. Emphasizes the cultural factors that encouraged the development of working-class consciousness in England.

NOTES

1. Phyllis Deane, *The First Industrial Revolution* (Cambridge: Cambridge University Press, 1965), p. 1.

2. These ideas are provocatively developed in E. L. Jones, *The European Miracle: Environments, Economies and Geopolitics of Europe and Asia* (Cambridge: Cambridge University Press, 1981).

3. Adna Ferrin Weber, *The Growth of Cities in the Nineteenth Century: A Study in Statistics* (New York: Macmillan, 1899; repr., Ithaca, N.Y.: Cornell University Press, 1963), p. 1.

4. J. P. Kay, *The Moral and Physical Condition of the Working Classes Employed in the Cotton Manufacture in Manchester* (London: James Ridgway, 1832), pp. 6, 14–15, 19.

5. Cooke Taylor, *Notes of a Tour in the Manufacturing Districts of Lancashire, in a Series of Letters to His Grace the Archbishop of Dublin* (London, 1842), pp. 4–6, quoted in E. P. Thompson, *The Making of the English Working Class* (New York: Vintage, 1963), p. 191.

6. Marie de Flavigny d'Agoult [Daniel Stern], *Histoire de la Révolution de 1848*, 2d ed., vol. 1 (Paris, 1862), p. 7, quoted in Theodore S. Hamerow, *The Birth of a New Europe: State and Society in the Nineteenth Century* (Chapel Hill: University of North Carolina Press, 1983), pp. 206–207.

7. House of Commons, *Sessional Papers, 1831–32*, hearing of 4 June 1932, vol. 15, pp. 195–197.

8. Catherine Hall, "The Sweet Delights of Home," in *A History of Private Life: From the Fires of Revolution to the Great War*, ed. Michelle Perrot (Cambridge: Belknap Press, 1990), p. 74.

21

RESTORATION, REFORM, AND REVOLUTION, 1814–1848

Barricades in Vienna, Austria, May 1848
(Historical Museum Vienna/The Art Archive)

I n 1848 Europe experienced a revolutionary wave, unprecedented in over a half century since the heady days of the French Revolution. These revolutions erupted in protest against the reactionary regimes established after the fall of Napoleon.

Workers, artisans, and even members of the middle classes poured into the streets to challenge authoritarian rulers and the militaries that tried to repress rebellion. They built street barricades to defend themselves and to trap and attack military troops. Barricades, long a part of urban insurrectionary history, had almost become an art form. Revolutionaries systematically tore the paving stones from streets and beams from the façades of houses. To build the barricade, they confiscated passing omnibuses, carriages, and carts to pile rubble, along with empty barrels and casks. The barricades they built sometimes rose as high as nine feet.

In addition to its material reality, the painting at the left represents the spirit present at the barricades, as well as in the revolutions as a whole. Its mixture of social classes and genders shows the inclusive camaraderie in conquering the streets, as even fraternizing soldiers listen attentively to the speaker atop the rubble. The neatly piled shovels and signs of meal preparation suggest a systematic order in the midst of a chaos that is only apparent. The figure hung in effigy reminds the viewer of the seriousness of the event. Scenes such as this burst forth in major cities throughout western and eastern Europe.

The revolutions of 1848 had their ideological origins in the irrepressible forces unleashed in the Revolution of 1789. With the end of the Napoleonic Wars in 1815, the victorious Great Powers—Austria, Great Britain, Prussia, and Russia—tried to re-establish as much of the old European state system as possible. The international arrangements they carved out at the Congress of Vienna were soon shaken by outbreaks of nationalist fervor. Nationalists aimed either to create larger political units, as in Italy and Germany, or to win independence from foreign rule, as in Greece. In addition to nationalism, which had in part been sparked by Napoleonic reforms, other new ideologies such as romanticism, liberalism, and socialism, born of the French Revolution, prevented a complete restoration of the old order. (An ideology is a structured, organized set of ideas that reflects a group's thinking about life or society.) Even after the success of counterrevolution in 1848, the

CHAPTER OUTLINE

THE CONGRESS OF VIENNA, 1814–1815

IDEOLOGICAL CONFRONTATIONS

RESTORATION, REFORM, AND REACTION

THE REVOLUTIONS OF 1848

KEY TERMS

Congress of Vienna	socialism
conservatism	Marxism
romanticism	July Revolution
nationalism	Great Reform Bill
liberalism	Chartism
laissez faire	Decembrists
utilitarianism	Frankfurt Assembly

Online Study Center

This icon will direct you to interactive map and primary source activities on the website **college.hmco.com/pic/noble5e**

ideologies that helped promote revolution continued to shape development in the second half of the century.

The conservatism of European rulers and their opposition to change after 1815 were also at odds with the new dynamism of European society. Between 1800 and 1850 Europe's population increased by nearly 50 percent, from around 190 million to 280 million. Population growth and surging industrialization had turned small towns into large cities. The rapid growth of factory manufacturing reshaped class structures and the lives of workers. Romanticism, liberalism, and other systems of thought were redefining the relationship of the individual to society and the concept of human rights. Sporadic outbreaks of collective violence reached a crescendo when the revolutions of 1848 swept most of Europe, undermining the established order in state after state.

As revolution swept through Europe, a similar pattern took place: after the first exhilarating moments of emancipation from authoritarian monarchies, conflict, disappointment, and failure allowed the forces of reaction and repression to take control. Revolutionaries did not win all their goals, and in many cases the forces of order crushed them. Yet by midcentury major intellectual, social, and political changes had occurred.

FOCUS QUESTIONS

What were the goals and results of the Congress of Vienna?

What major ideologies developed in the first half of the nineteenth century?

How did the restorations that followed the Napoleonic era give way to reform?

What were the main causes of the revolutions of 1848, and what roles did nationalism, liberalism, and socialism play in inciting and sustaining revolution?

THE CONGRESS OF VIENNA, 1814–1815

What were the goals and results of the Congress of Vienna?

The defeat of Napoleon put an end to French dominance in Europe. In September 1814 the victorious Great Powers—Austria, Great Britain, Prussia, and Russia—convened an international conference, the **Congress of Vienna,** to negotiate the terms of peace. The victors sought to draw territorial boundaries advantageous to themselves and to provide long-term stability on the European continent. Having faced a powerful France, which had mobilized popular forces with revolutionary principles, the victors decided to erect an international system that would remove such threats. One method was to restore the European order that had existed before the French Revolution. Thus, following principles of "legitimacy and compensation," they redrew the map of Europe (see **MAP 21.1**). Rulers who had been overthrown were restored to their thrones. The eldest surviving brother of Louis XVI of France became King Louis XVIII. In Spain Ferdinand VII was restored to the throne from which Napoleon had toppled him and his father. The restoration, however, was not so complete as its proponents claimed. After the French Revolution certain new realities had to be recognized. For example, Napoleon had consolidated the German and Italian states; the process was acknowledged in the former with the creation of a loose German Confederation. In Italy the number of independent states had shrunk to nine. Also, unlike earlier French kings, Louis XVIII could not rule as an absolute monarch.

Negotiations at the Congress of Vienna strengthened the territories bordering France, enlarged Prussia and created the kingdom of Piedmont-Sardinia, joined Belgium to Holland, and provided the victors with spoils and compensation for territories bartered away. Austria received Venetia and Lombardy in northern Italy to strengthen its position and to compensate for the loss of Belgium (to the Netherlands) and parts of Poland (to Russia). Prussia was also allowed annexations in compensation for giving up parts of Poland. England acquired a number of colonies and naval out-

Congress of Vienna   Conference called by the Great Powers after Napoleon's defeat. They sought long-term stability as they drew new territorial boundaries and restored some of the rulers who had been overthrown.

Metternich
A consummate statesman and aristocrat, the Austrian prince Metternich tried to quell revolution at home and abroad. Some called his era the Metternichean age. (*The Royal Collection © 2006 Her Majesty Queen Elizabeth II*)

posts. Thus with one hand these conservative statesmen swore their loyalty to the prerevolutionary past, and with the other they redrew national boundaries with no consideration for the inhabitants whose territories changed.

The leading personality at the Congress of Vienna was the Austrian foreign minister, Prince Clemens von Metternich (MEH-ter-nick) (1773–1859). An aristocrat in exile from the Rhineland, which had been annexed by revolutionary France, he had gone into the service of the Habsburg empire and risen to become its highest official. Personal charm, tact, and representation of a state that for the time being was satisfied with its territories made Metternich seem a disinterested statesman. His influence at the congress was great.

Because it was Napoleon's belligerent imperialism that had brought the powers together in Vienna, France was at first treated as an enemy at the conference. By the end, however, France was included as one of the five Great Powers jointly known as the "Concert of Europe." The Concert continued to function for nearly forty years, meeting and resolving international crises and preventing any major European war from breaking out. Underlying the states' cooperation was the principle of a common European destiny.

SECTION SUMMARY

- At the Congress of Vienna (1814–1815), Austria, Great Britain, Prussia, and Russia, having defeated Napoleon, redrew territorial boundaries for their own advantage and to create stability.

- Rulers who had been overthrown by Napoleon were restored to their thrones.

- France, with its monarchy restored, became one of the five Great Powers known as the "Concert of Europe."

- The principle of a common European destiny lay at the basis of international cooperation; stability was maintained for nearly forty years.

MAP 21.1 Europe in 1815

Intent on regaining the security and stability of prerevolutionary years, the Great Powers redrew the map of Europe at the Congress of Vienna.

Kingdom of Prussia
Austrian Empire
Boundary of German Confederation

RUSSIAN EMPIRE

Moscow

Kiev

Dnieper

St. Petersburg

Riga

FINLAND

Stockholm

Baltic Sea

Vistula

Danzig

Warsaw
KINGDOM OF
POLAND
(Russia)

Cracow

GALICIA

UKRAINE

BESSARABIA

MOLDAVIA

WALLACHIA

Danube

BULGARIA

SERBIA

BOSNIA

HUNGARY

Pest

Buda

AUSTRIAN EMPIRE

CROATIA

Vienna

Troppau

Prague

BOHEMIA

SAXONY

Berlin

KINGDOM OF PRUSSIA

Elbe

HANOVER

DENMARK

SCHLESWIG

HOLSTEIN

Copenhagen

KINGDOM OF
SWEDEN AND
NORWAY

Oslo

North Sea

SCOTLAND

Manchester

ENGLAND

London

Dublin

IRELAND

UNITED KINGDOM
OF GREAT BRITAIN
AND IRELAND

Amsterdam

KINGDOM OF THE
NETHERLANDS

Waterloo

Luxembourg

Cologne

Rhine

Frankfurt

BAVARIA

WÜRTTEMBERG

Munich

BADEN

ALSACE

LORRAINE

SWITZERLAND

PIEDMONT

FRANCE

Paris

Seine

Loire

Marseille

Rhône

Ebro

SPAIN

Madrid

PORTUGAL

GIBRALTAR
(Gr. Br.)

ATLANTIC
OCEAN

LOMBARDY

VENETIA

Milan

Venice

PARMA

MODENA

LUCCA

TUSCANY

PAPAL
STATES

Rome

ELBA

CORSICA
(Fr.)

SARDINIA

KINGDOM OF
SARDINIA

NAPLES

KINGDOM
OF THE
TWO SICILIES

SICILY

MALTA
(Gr. Br.)

Mediterranean
Sea

OTTOMAN EMPIRE

Constantinople

Black Sea

ALBANIA

GREECE

Athens

0   200   400 Km.
0   200   400 Mi.

IDEOLOGICAL CONFRONTATIONS

What major ideologies developed in the first half of the nineteenth century?

The international and domestic political system established in 1815 was modified by a series of challenges, even revolts, culminating in revolutions throughout Europe in 1848. The order established in 1815 was inspired by conservatism. Its challengers advocated competing ideologies: romanticism, nationalism, liberalism, and socialism.

CONSERVATISM

The architects of the restoration justified their policies with doctrines based on the ideology of **conservatism,** emphasizing the need to preserve the existing order of monarchies, aristocracy, and an established church. As a coherent movement, conservatism sprang up during and after the French Revolution to resist the forces of change. Before the American and French Revolutions, the existing political institutions appeared to be permanent. When the old order faced serious challenges in the late eighteenth and early nineteenth centuries, an ideology justifying traditional authority emerged.

Edmund Burke (1729–1797), a British statesman and political theorist, launched one of the first intellectual assaults on the French Revolution. The revolutionary National Assembly had asserted that ancient prerogatives were superseded by the rights of man and principles of human equality based on appeals to natural law. In *Reflections on the Revolution in France* (1790), Burke countered that such claims were abstract and dangerous and that the belief in human equality undermined the social order. Government should be anchored in tradition, he argued. No matter how poorly the French monarchy and its institutions had served the nation, they should be preserved; their very longevity proved their usefulness. Burke's writings were widely read and influential on the Continent.

Reaction against the French Revolution also inspired a moral and religious conservatism. One of the most popular authors of this new morality was Hannah More (1745–1833), who with her four sisters ran a prosperous school. More saw piety as a rampart against rebellion. In a series of pamphlets titled *Cheap Repository Tracts,* she advocated the acceptance of the existing order and the solace of religious faith. Costing

but a penny, the moral tracts were often handed out by the rich together with alms or food to the poor. More was the first writer in history to sell over a million copies; within three years her sales doubled. Conservative values thus spread to a very large audience in both Britain and the United States, where one of her works appeared in thirty editions.

A more extreme version of conservatism was the counterrevolutionary or "ultraroyalist" ideology. Unlike Burke, who was willing to tolerate some change, counterrevolutionaries wanted to restore society to its prerevolutionary condition. The most extreme counterrevolutionaries were those who personally experienced the revolutionary upheavals. Count Joseph de Maistre (MESS-treh) (1753–1821), a Savoyard (from the Franco-Italian border region) nobleman whose estates were occupied by the invading French, described monarchy as a God-given form of government in his *Considerations on France* (1796). Any attempt to abolish or even limit it was a violation of divine law. According to de Maistre and his fellow reactionaries, only the authority of church and state could prevent human beings from falling into evil ways. De Maistre advocated stern government control, including the generous use of the death penalty, to keep people loyal to throne and altar.

Conservative ideas were not limited to intellectual circles; at times they had mass appeal, even for the peasantry. Especially in bourgeois and aristocratic circles, conservatism extended to private life, and placed priority on family stability, with a strict separation of gender roles and a strong sense of patriarchy, in which the husband and father held exclusive authority. Conservatism was also influenced by **romanticism,** with its glorification of the past, taste for pageantry, and belief in the organic unity of society.

ROMANTICISM

The long-lived romantic movement had emerged in the 1760s as a rebellion against rationalism and persisted until the 1840s. It was primarily a movement in the arts. Writers, painters, composers, and others consciously rebelled against the Enlightenment and its rationalist values. In contrast to the philosophes and their emphasis on reason (see Chapter 18), the romantics praised

conservatism   Ideology underlying the order established in Europe in 1815, which afterward emphasized support for the existing order of monarchy, aristocracy, and an established church.

romanticism   Cultural movement, prevalent from the 1760s to 1840s, that rebelled against rationalism and its Enlightenment values and prized sentiment.

Lord Byron in Albanian Costume

The British romantic poet had himself painted in exotic garb. Romantics were attracted to what were believed to be the mysteries of the East, representing a truer, more authentic existence. *(Courtesy of the National Portrait Gallery, London)*

emotion and feeling. Jean-Jacques Rousseau's strong appeal to sentiment was taken up by the German writer Johann Wolfgang von Goethe (GOE-teh) (1749–1832), who declared, "Feeling is everything." Goethe's *Sorrows of Young Werther* (1774), the most widely read book of the era—Napoleon had a copy by his bedside—depicted the passions of the hero, who, depressed over unrequited love, kills himself. Many young men dressed in "Werther clothes"—tight black pants, long blue jacket, and buff yellow leather vest—which exemplified the clothing of tradesmen and provided a visual protest by young intellectuals against the frivolous dress of the upper classes. In some cases they emulated the tragic hero by committing suicide.

Whereas the Enlightenment had studied nature for the principles it could impart, the romantics worshiped nature for its inherent beauty. The German composer Ludwig van Beethoven (1770–1827) wrote his *Pastoral Symphony* in praise of idyllic nature, depicting the passions one might feel in contemplating its loveliness and serenity. The English poets William Wordsworth (1770–1850) and Samuel Taylor Coleridge (1772–1834)

treated untamed wilderness as a particular subject of wonder. Fellow Englishman Joseph Mallord William Turner (1775–1851) displayed the raw passions of the sea in such paintings as *Fire at Sea* (1834) and *Snowstorm: Steamboat off a Harbour's Mouth* (1842). Before painting the latter, Turner is said to have tied himself to a ship's mast and braved a snowstorm for four hours.

In pursuit of the authentic and the ancient, of feeling rather than rationality, many romantics rediscovered religion. In some areas of Europe, popular religion had anticipated the artists' and intellectuals' romantic sensibilities. France experienced a revival of Catholicism. In the German states, pietism, which had emerged in the seventeenth and eighteenth centuries, stressed the personal relationship between the individual and God, unimpeded by theological formalities or religious authorities. The influence of pietism, with its emphasis on spirituality and emotion, spread throughout central Europe in schools and churches.

In England emotionalism in religion expressed itself in the popularity of Methodism. Founded in the 1730s by the English preacher John Wesley (1703–1791), this movement emphasized salvation by a faith made active in one's life, a method of living. Appealing especially to the poor and desperate, Methodism by the 1790s had gained seventy thousand members; within a generation it quadrupled its flock.

The classicism of the Enlightenment had required an audience well versed in the traditional texts. Since the mid-eighteenth century, however, the reading public had grown to include people without access to elite culture. Appeals to emotion and sentiment were congenial to these new audiences, and a new interest developed in folklore and rustic life. Franz Schubert (1797–1828) composed over 600 songs that echo the simplicity of folk tunes, and Frédéric Chopin (1810–1849) composed works influenced by the peasant music of his native Poland.

Whereas the philosophes had decried the Middle Ages, the romantics celebrated the medieval period. Painters frequently took Gothic buildings or ruins as their theme. Architects imitated the Gothic style in both private and public buildings. Sir Walter Scott (1771–1832) in Scotland and Victor Hugo (U-go) (1802–1885) in France recaptured chivalry and the age of faith in such popular works as *Ivanhoe* (1819) and *The Hunchback of Notre Dame* (1831). Thus romanticism also had a liberal and nationalistic appeal.

The romantics sought displacement not only in time but also in place. The exotic had great appeal to them. Recently conquered Algeria in North Africa provided exotic scenes for French painters, among them Eugène Delacroix (de-la-KRWAH) (1798–1863) and Jean Ingres (AENG-reh) (1780–1867). Senegal, in West Africa, which the French recovered from the British in 1815, offered the setting for Théodore Géricault's powerful *Raft of the "Medusa."* (See the feature "The Visual Record: Raft of the 'Medusa.'")

Romanticism exalted mythical figures as embodiments of human energy and passion. In the dramatic poem *Faust,* Goethe retold the legend of a man who sells his soul to the Devil in exchange for worldly success. Several composers set that story to powerful music. In the poetic drama *Prometheus Unbound,* the English romantic poet Percy Bysshe Shelley (1792–1822) celebrated Prometheus, who, according to Greek mythology stole fire from the gods and gave it to human beings. In much the same spirit, many romantics lionized Napoleon, who had overthrown kings and states. Delacroix, who witnessed the July Revolution of 1830 in Paris (see page 663), celebrated the heroism and passion of the revolutionaries in his huge canvas *Liberty Leading the People* (1830).

Romantics often challenged existing power relations, including relations between the sexes. The French writer Amandine-Aurore Dupin (1804–1876), better known by her pen name, George Sand (SAN), spoke for the emancipation of women from the oppressive supervision of their husbands, fathers, and brothers. In her personal life Sand practiced the freedom she preached, dressing like a man, smoking cigars, and openly pursuing affairs with a number of well-known artists. The English writer Mary Ann Evans (1819–1892), like George Sand, adopted a male pseudonym, George Eliot. She conducted her life in a nonconformist manner, living with a married man. The use of male pen names by both writers attests to the hostility that intellectual women still faced.

After the French Revolution nobles and monarchs ceased sponsoring art on a grand scale and were expected to conduct their lives soberly. Cut off from royal patronage, artists had to depend on members of the new middle classes to buy paintings and books and attend plays and musical performances. If earning a livelihood had often been difficult for artists in the past, it now became even more so. Forced to live marginally, they cultivated the image of the artist as unconventional. In their lifestyles and their work, they deliberately rejected the norms of society. The romantic period gave rise to the notion of the starving genius, alienated from society and loyal only to his all-consuming art.

Romantics of many stripes declared their determination to overthrow the smug present and create a new world. Victor Hugo called for "no more rules, no more models" to constrain the human imagination. Romantic painters and musicians consciously turned their backs on the classical tradition in both subject matter and style. The English poet George Gordon, Lord Byron (1788–1824), declared war on kings, on established religion, and on the international order. A nationalist as well as a romantic, he died while fighting for the independence of Greece.

NATIONALISM

The ideology of nationalism emerged in, and partly shaped, this era. **Nationalism** is the belief that people derive their identity from their nation and owe it their primary loyalty. A list of criteria for nationhood is likely to include a common language, religion, and political authority, as well as common traditions and shared historical experiences. Some nineteenth-century nationalists found any one of those criteria sufficient. Others insisted that all of them had to be present before a group could consider itself a nation.

In an era that saw the undermining of traditional religious values, nationalism offered a new locus of faith. To people who experienced the social turmoil brought about by the erosion of the old order, nationalism held out the promise of a new community. Nationalism became an ideal espoused as strongly as religion. The Italian nationalist Giuseppe Mazzini (mat-SEE-nee) (1805–1872) declared that nationalism was "a faith and mission" ordained by God. The Polish romantic poet and nationalist Adam Mickiewicz (MISS-kyev-ich) (1798–1855) compared perpetually carved-up Poland to the crucified Christ. The religious intensity of nationalism helps explain its widespread appeal.

Many forces shaped nationalism. Its earliest manifestation, cultural nationalism, had its origins in Rousseau's concept of the "general will" constituting the sovereign nation, greater than the sum of its parts. Johann Gottfried Herder (1744–1833), Rousseau's German disciple, elaborated on his mentor's ideas, declaring that every people has a "national spirit." To explore the unique nature of this spirit, intellectuals all over Europe began collecting local folk poems, songs, and tales. In an effort to document the spirit of the German people, the Grimm brothers, Jacob (1785–1863) and Wilhelm (1786–1859), compiled fairy tales and published them between 1812 and 1818; among the better known are "Little Red Riding Hood" and "Snow White."

Political nationalism, born in the era of the French Revolution, injected urgency and passion into the new ideology. French aristocrats resisted taxation by claiming that they embodied the rights of "the nation" and could not be taxed without its consent. Thus the concept of nation was given general currency. When revolutionary France was attacked by neighboring countries, which were ruled by kings and dukes, the Legislative Assembly called on the French people to rise and save the nation. The kingdom of France had become a nation of citizens who had a stake in its destiny. In reaction to the French threat, intellectuals in Germany and Italy embraced the

nationalism Belief that people derive their identity from their nation and owe it their primary loyalty. The criteria for nationhood typically included a common language, religion, and political authority, as well as common traditions and shared historical experiences.

Raft of the "Medusa"

In September 1816 the French were shocked at the news of the disaster that had befallen the government ship *Méduse* (Medusa) as it headed for Senegal in West Africa the previous July. Including the ship's crew, 400 passengers had boarded the vessel.

The captain of the ship was a nobleman, Duroys de Chaumareys (du-RWAH duh sho-mah-RAY), whom the restoration government had appointed solely on the basis of his family and political connections. Inexperienced as a seaman, the captain clumsily ran his ship aground on the Mauritanian coast, off West Africa, on July 2. The *Medusa* had only 6 lifeboats, capable of carrying a total of 250 people. For the rest of the passengers, a raft was rigged with planks, beams, and ropes. The captain and his officers forcibly took over the lifeboats, abandoning 150 passengers, including one woman, to the less secure raft. With no navigational tools and insufficient food and water, the passengers of the raft were at the mercy of stormy seas and a brutal sun. Anger at officers for having abandoned them led seamen on the raft to murder some of their superiors. By the third day, driven by thirst and hunger, some passengers ate their dead companions—killed by exposure or drowned by huge waves. On the sixth day the strongest among the survivors, fearing that their rations were dwindling, banded together and murdered the weaker ones. On the thirteenth day the French frigate *Argus* spotted the raft and rescued 15 survivors. Five died soon after, leaving only 10 survivors out of the raft's original 150 passengers.

Although the government tried to suppress information about the event, the French press exposed the incompetence and cowardice of Captain de Chaumareys. The event was understood to reflect the weakness of the regime that had appointed him. The selfish act of the captain and his fellow officers suggested the narrow class interest of the restoration government, favoring aristocracy at the cost of the common people.

The French painter Théodore Géricault (1791–1824) befriended the ship's surgeon, Henri Savigny, one of the lucky ten who survived the harrowing experience on the raft. In addition to press reports, Géricault (jair-ih-KO) thus had a direct eyewitness account of the event. The painter shared Savigny's sense of outrage against the government for having appointed the incompetent captain and for having treated the survivors callously. (At one point the government arrested Savigny for publicizing the tragedy.) The light prison sentence imposed on the captain was another source of grievance.

Since 1815 the French government had sought to bring distinction to itself by displaying art in salon expositions. That of 1819 was intended to be larger and more glorious than any previous one. Among its paintings was Géricault's huge canvas—the largest in that year's exposition—measuring 16 feet high by 24 feet wide and innocently titled "Scene of Shipwreck." Carelessly, the regime had wanted to gain glory for itself by exhibiting this impressive artwork while at the same time keeping hidden its real subject. But the stratagem failed; everyone recognized the painting to be the *Raft of the "Medusa"* and an attack on the Bourbon regime.

The painting, reproduced here, depicts the moment the survivors spotted the frigate *Argus*, barely visible on the horizon. Notice the figure of an African standing at the fore of the raft, waving a red and white cloth to attract the ship's attention. In this painting the nobility and symbol of hope the African symbolizes is an attack on the slave trade, which Britain had abolished but which France was still engaged in. By including the African, the artist was implicitly criticizing the restoration regime for sanctioning commerce in humans. Just as the *Argus* is coming to the rescue of the shipwrecked, the painting appears to suggest, so Africans will see the day when their enslavement will be ended.

Historians often regard the *Raft of the "Medusa"* as the most important painting of French romanticism, and it includes nearly all the major themes of the movement. By locating the scene off the coast of Africa, Géricault incorporated an element of exoticism. Nature—cruel and unforgiving—is central to the scene, reflected in the turbulent sea, dark clouds, and imperiled raft. The canvas includes an extraordinary range of passions. Observe, for example, the inconsolable grief of the figure at the bottom left, a father cradling the dead body of his son. Other figures express despair and terror, and still others limitless hope. The painting evokes the dark passions lurking in the human heart. Although it does not show the scenes of insanity,

Géricault: Raft of the "Medusa"   *(Erich Lessing/Art Resource, NY)*

murder, and cannibalism that the survivors had witnessed, they undoubtedly came to the minds of the viewers, who were familiar with the tragic events. The painting is a powerful indictment of Enlightenment faith in humans as creatures of reason and balance.

Romantic artists wanted to engage the passions of those viewing, reading, or hearing their works. *Raft of the "Medusa"* purposely stages the events in the foreground in order to pull viewers into the picture and make them participants in the drama. They thus share in the alternating feelings of terror and hope that swept the raft.

The fate of the painting and the artist followed a romantic script. When Géricault started the painting, he intended it as an indictment of the restoration government. He poured energy into it in an effort to take his mind off a disastrous love affair. As his work proceeded, he came to see the painting as an allegory of larger human passions and concerns. Yet when it was displayed, much to his disappointment, the painting was understood mainly in political terms. Disillusioned by this reaction, Géricault thereafter painted no major works. He grew sickly, rarely bestirred himself, and died of bone tuberculosis in 1824 at age 33. He illustrates the romantics' view of a heroic life—the genius who performs a major feat and then dies young, before realizing his potential. To the romantics, human intent and effort often appeared thwarted by larger forces. This painting, originally meant to criticize the regime, was purchased after Géricault's death by the restoration government and hung in France's national museum, the Louvre.

QUESTIONS

1. What elements in the subject matter and style of this painting typify romanticism?

2. Why was this painting seen as a brutal critique of the French restoration government? What had been the artist's intent?

Online Study Center
Improve Your Grade Visual Record Activities

spirit of nationalism. In Germany the philosopher Johann Gottlieb Fichte (FISH-te) (1762–1814) delivered his series of *Addresses to the German Nation* after the Prussian defeat at Jena, calling on all Germans to stand firm against Napoleon. He argued that Germans were endowed with a special genius that had to be safeguarded for the well-being of all humankind. Italian writer Vittorio Alfieri (1749–1803) insisted that, as the descendants and heirs of ancient Rome, Italians, not France, should lead the peoples of Europe.

For the most part, however, after the French Revolution and the Napoleonic era, early-nineteenth-century nationalism was generous and cosmopolitan in its outlook. Herder and Mazzini believed that each of Europe's peoples was destined to achieve nationhood by forming its own political identity and that the nations of Europe would then live peacefully side by side. The members of dedicated nationalist groups such as Young Germany and Young Italy were also members of Young Europe. Many nationalists in the 1830s and 1840s were likewise committed to the ideal of a "Europe of free peoples." Victor Hugo even envisioned a "European republic" with its own parliament.

It is important to remember, however, that although many intellectuals found nationalism attractive, in the first half of the nineteenth century most people felt stronger local and regional affinities than national identities. Only after several decades of propaganda by nationalists and governments did Europeans begin to imagine themselves as part of a national rather than local community, and only then could they think of dying for their nations.

LIBERALISM

Liberalism was a direct descendant of the Enlightenment's critique of eighteenth-century absolutism. Nineteenth-century liberals believed that individual freedom was best safeguarded by reducing government powers to a minimum. They wanted to impose constitutional limits on government, to establish the rule of law, to sweep away all restrictions on individual enterprise—specifically, state regulation of the economy—and to ensure a voice in government for men of property and education. Liberalism was influenced by romanticism, with its emphasis on individual freedom and the imperative of the human personality to develop to its full potential. Liberalism was also affected by nationalism, especially in multinational autocratic states such as Austria, Russia, and the Ottoman Empire, in which free institutions could be established only if political inde-

pendence were wrested from, respectively, Vienna, St. Petersburg, and Istanbul. (Nationalism challenged the established order in the first half of the century, but in the second half conservatives were to use nationalism as a means to stabilize their rule.)

Economic Liberalism   Liberalism was both an economic and a political theory. In 1776 Adam Smith (1723–1790), the influential Scottish economist, published *An Inquiry into the Nature and Causes of the Wealth of Nations.* Smith advocated freeing national economies from the fetters of the state. Under the mercantilist system, prevalent throughout Europe until about 1800, the state regulated the prices and conditions of manufacture. Smith argued for letting the free forces of the marketplace shape economic decisions. He believed that economics was subject to basic unalterable laws that could be discerned and applied in the same fashion as natural laws. Chief among them, in Smith's view, was the compatibility of economic self-interest and the general good. He argued that entrepreneurs who lower prices sell more products, thus increasing their own profits *and* providing the community with affordable wares. In this way an individual's drive for profit benefits society as a whole. The economy is driven as if "by an invisible hand." This competitive drive for profits, Smith predicted, would expand the "wealth of nations." In France advocates of nonintervention by government in the economy were called supporters of *laissez faire* (meaning "to leave alone, to let run on its own").

Smith and his disciples formed what came to be known as the school of classical economy, emphasizing the importance of laissez faire. Smith had been relatively optimistic about the capacities of the free market. Those who followed him, and who witnessed the negative results of industrial capitalism, developed gloomier views. Thomas Malthus (1766–1834), a parson, published in 1798 *An Essay on the Principle of Population,* which suggested that the rate of population growth was much higher than the rate of food production. Unless people had fewer children, they would suffer starvation. By their failure to exercise sexual restraint, the poor, Malthus declared, "are themselves the cause of their own poverty." The laws of economics suggested to Malthus that factory owners could not improve their workers' lot by increasing wages or providing charity because higher living standards would lead to more births, which in turn would depress wages and bring greater misery. He therefore advocated abstinence (birth control was considered sinful and unnatural) and thought couples

liberalism   Nineteenth-century economic and political theory that called for reducing government powers to a minimum. Liberals sought to eliminate state regulation of the economy and ensure a voice in government for men of property and education.

laissez faire   French term meaning "to leave alone," to advocate freeing national economies from the fetters of the state and allowing supply and demand to shape the marketplace.

should marry only when they could afford to raise children. Malthus himself had twelve.

David Ricardo (1772–1823) made his fortune in the stock market, retired young, and wrote on economics; his best-known work was *Principles of Political Economy* (1817). Ricardo argued that the only way capitalists could make profits in a competitive market would be to pay the lowest wages possible. The "iron law of wages" seemed to provide, as had Malthus, scientific justification for the exploitation of workers.

Even supporters of laissez faire had some reservations about the market economy. In France in the first half of the nineteenth century, commentators on the factory system, including industrialists, expressed fear that factory work would undermine the stability of family life and hence of society itself. Contrary to Malthus, they hoped philanthropic intervention would resolve the problems they had identified.

Even some of the British classical economists doubted the wisdom of allowing the market economy to operate entirely without regulation and of trusting it to provide for human happiness. Smith warned that the market tended to form monopolies, and he suggested that government intervene to prevent this occurrence. According to Smith, the marketplace could not provide for all human needs; the government needed to supply education, road systems, and an equitable system of justice.

Political Liberalism John Stuart Mill (1806–1873), the leading British economic and political thinker at midcentury, initially voiced strong support for laissez-faire economics in the first edition of his *Principles of Political Economy* (1848). In subsequent editions, however, he noted that the free market could not address every human need, and he argued that the state had an obligation to relieve human misery. Toward the end of his life, Mill seemed to be leaning toward socialism.

Mill's about-face reflected and presaged changing attitudes among the proponents of laissez faire. In the face of unsanitary urban conditions, child labor, stark inequities in wealth, and other alarming results of industrialization, at least some liberals around midcentury called on the state to intervene in areas of concern that would have been unthinkable a half century earlier. In the tradition of the Enlightenment and the French Revolution, French liberals in the nineteenth century continued to see human liberty—the freedom to pursue happiness—as founded on natural law. Their English counterparts were less theoretical in outlook. Jeremy Bentham (1748–1832) argued that the purpose of government is to provide "the greatest happiness of the greatest number" and that governments should be judged on that basis. Bentham and his disciples believed that the test of government is its usefulness; thus his theory is known as **utilitarianism.**

John Stuart Mill, a disciple of Bentham, was the foremost proponent of political liberalism, seeing it as guaranteeing the development of a free society. In his essay *On Liberty,* one of the fundamental documents of nineteenth-century liberalism, Mill argued for the free circulation of ideas—even false ideas. For in the free marketplace of ideas, false ideas will be defeated, and truth vindicated, in open debate. Mill also asserted that all members of society should have equal access to freedom. Influenced by his wife, Harriet Taylor Mill (1807–1856), he wrote in *On the Subjection of Women* (1861) that women should be permitted to vote and should have access to equal educational opportunities and the professions. Such equality not only would be just but also would have the advantage of "doubling the mass of mental faculties available for the higher service of humanity." Mill, the foremost male proponent of women's rights in his generation, helped win a broader audience for the principle of equality between the sexes.

Despite Mill's influence, many liberals, especially in the early nineteenth century, feared the masses and therefore vigorously opposed democracy. They feared that the common people, uneducated and supposedly gullible, would easily be swayed by demagogues who might become despotic or who, in a desire to curry favor with the poor, might attack the privileges of the wealthy. The French liberal Benjamin Constant denounced democracy as "the vulgarization of despotism"; the vote, he declared, should be reserved for the affluent and educated. When less fortunate Frenchmen denounced the property requirements that prevented them from voting, the liberal statesman François Guizot (1787–1874) smugly replied, "Get rich."

Guizot's comment reflects attitudes associated with the bourgeoisie, a social class that came of age in the nineteenth century. The word *bourgeois* derives from *burgers,* a term that referred to a group of people who gained wealth and civic identity from urban occupations beginning in the twelfth and thirteenth centuries. This class fully developed in the nineteenth century. If unsympathetic to extending suffrage to the lower classes, the *bourgeoisie* championed liberalism because it justified its own right to participate in governance. Economic liberalism was also attractive to merchants and manufacturers, who wished to gather wealth without state interference. The basic tenets of liberalism—the belief in the sanctity of human rights, of the freedoms of speech and of association, and of the rule of law and equality before the law—eventually

utilitarianism Political theory of Jeremy Bentham, who argued that the purpose of government is to provide "the greatest happiness of the greatest number" and that the test of government is its usefulness.

became widely accepted, even among conservatives and socialists who originally opposed them.

SOCIALISM

A fundamental element in the pursuit of happiness according to liberals was the ability to accumulate property. Socialists, on the other hand, believed that the "social" ownership of property, unlike private ownership, would benefit society as a whole. The notion that human happiness can best be ensured by the common ownership of property had been suggested in earlier times by individuals as different as the Greek philosopher Plato (427?–347 B.C.) and Sir Thomas More (1478–1535), the English author of *Utopia*. In the 1820s, troubled by the harsh condition of the working classes, thinkers in Britain and France began to espouse new theories to address the social ills produced by industrial capitalism. During the first half of the nineteenth century, most workers were still artisans, even in industrializing England, where manufacturing was increasingly large scale. Only in a later era would **socialism** address the issues raised by industry.

Early Socialist Thinkers In 1796, during the French Revolution, Gracchus Babeuf (GRAH-kus bah-BOEF) (1760–1797), a minor civil servant, participated in the Conspiracy of Equals (see page 601). He believed political equality was meaningless without economic equality. Babeuf advocated revolution to bring about a "communist" society—a society in which all property would be owned in common and private property would be abolished. Work would be provided for everyone; medical services and education would be free to all. Upon the discovery of his plot, Babeuf was guillotined, but his theories and his example of conspiratorial revolutionary action would influence later socialists.

Several other important French thinkers made contributions to European socialism. Henri de Saint-Simon (saen–see-MON) (1760–1825), a French aristocrat, emphasized the need "to ameliorate as promptly and as quickly as possible the moral and physical existence of the most numerous class." The state, he declared, should ensure the welfare of the masses. He argued, furthermore, that technical experts rather than an elite derived from birth should govern the state and formulate economic policies.

Another vital contribution to socialist thought came from thinkers who tried to imagine an ideal world. They were later derisively dismissed as builders of utopias, fantasy worlds (the Greek word *utopia* means "nowhere"). Their schemes varied, but they

shared the view that property should be owned in common and used for the common good. They also believed that society should rest on principles of cooperation rather than on competitive individualism.

One of the earliest and most notable utopians was the Welsh mill owner Robert Owen (1771–1859). Beginning in 1800 he ran a prosperous cotton mill in New Lanark, Scotland. He also provided generously for his workers, guaranteeing them jobs and their children a decent education. In his writings Owen suggested the establishment of self-governing communities owning the means of production. Essentials would be distributed to all members according to their needs. His ideas for the new society also included equal rights for women. Owen received little support from fellow manufacturers and political leaders, and his own attempt in 1824 to establish an ideal society in the United States at New Harmony, Indiana, ended in failure after four years.

Another influential contributor to early socialist theory was the Frenchman Charles Fourier (foor-YAY) (1772–1837). A clerk and salesman, Fourier wrote out in great detail his vision of the ideal future society. It would consist of cooperative organizations called "phalansteries," each with sixteen hundred inhabitants who would live in harmony with nature and with one another. Everyone would be assured gainful employment, which would be made enjoyable by rotating jobs. Because cooperative communes often faced the issue of who would carry out the distasteful tasks, everyone would share the pleasant *and* unpleasant work.

Fourier had an important female following because of his belief in the equality of the sexes, and some of these women tried to put his ideas into action. In Belgium the activist Zoé Gatti de Gamond (1806–1854) cofounded a phalanstery for women. She believed that if women could be assured of economic well-being, other rights would follow. Also inspired by Fourier, Flora Tristan (1801–1844) was an effective advocate for workers' rights. In her book *Union Ouvrière* (*Workers' Union*), she suggested that all workers should contribute funds to establish a "Workers' Palace" in every town. In the palace, the sick and disabled would have shelter, and the workers' children could receive a free education. Crossing France on foot, she spread the word of workers' solidarity and self-help.

There were other approaches. The French socialist journalist Louis Blanc (BLAHN) (1811–1882) thought that by securing the vote, the common people could win control over the state and require it to serve their needs. Once the workers controlled the state by the ballot, the state in turn would establish social workshops in which the workers would be responsible for produc-

---

socialism Nineteenth-century economic and social doctrine and political movement that advocated the "social" or state ownership of property in order to create a more just system.

Karl Marx
Through his writings and agitation, Marx transformed the socialism of his day and created an ideology that helped shape the nineteenth and twentieth centuries.
(Corbis)

tion and for supervision of business matters. Society should be established according to the maxim, "Let each produce according to his aptitudes and strength; let each consume according to his need."

Blanc's contemporary Louis Blanqui (1805–1882) suggested a more violent mode of action. He advocated seizure of the state by a small, dedicated band of men who would establish equality for all through communism. His ideas strengthened the notion of class warfare. The thought and example of Blanqui and the other socialists would have a major influence on the thinking of the most important socialist of the nineteenth century, Karl Marx.

Marxism   Karl Marx (1818–1883), the son of a lawyer, grew up in the Rhineland, in western Germany, an industrializing area that was particularly open to political ideas and agitation. As a young man, Marx studied philosophy at the University of Berlin and joined a group known as the "Young Hegelians," self-declared disciples of the idealist philosopher G. W. F. Hegel (1770–1831). Hegel taught that reality is mainly based on the ability of the mind to conceive of it. Marx, by contrast, was a materialist, believing that material realities impose themselves on the mind.

In 1842–1843 Marx edited a newspaper that spoke out for freedom and democracy in Germany. The following year, in Paris, he met several of the French socialist writers.

Because of his radical journalism, Marx was exiled from the Rhineland and lived briefly in Paris, then Brussels. In 1849 he settled in London, where he lived for the rest of his life, dedicated to establishing his ideas on what he viewed as scientific bases. In 1848 Marx and Friedrich Engels (1820–1895) published the *Communist Manifesto*. A pamphlet written for the Communist League, a group of Germans living in exile, the Manifesto made an appeal to the working classes of the world. The league deliberately called itself "Communist" rather than "Socialist." Communism was a revolutionary program, bent on changing property relations by violence; socialism was associated with more peaceful means of transformation. The pamphlet

laid out Marx's basic ideas. "The history of all hitherto existing society," he said, "is the history of class struggles." In this pamphlet, Marx and Engels called on the proletariat to rise—"You have nothing to lose but your chains"—and create a society that would end the exploitation of man by man. The idea of an international workers' movement contrasted with the dominant currents of capitalism and nationalism.

A number of political and polemical works flowed from Marx's pen, but most of them remained unpublished during his lifetime. The first volume of his major work, *Capital*, was published in 1867; subsequent volumes appeared posthumously. **Marxism,** the body of Marx's thought, is complex and sometimes contradictory, but certain basic concepts resound throughout and were embraced by Marx's followers.

Marx agreed with Hegel and many of his contemporaries that human history has a direction and a goal. Hegel believed that the goal was the realization of the

Marxism   The "scientific socialism" of Karl Marx and Friedrich Engels, which stated that the working class inevitably would rebel against the capitalist owners and build a communist society.

world spirit. Marx believed that it was the abolition of capitalism, the victory of the proletariat, the disappearance of the state, and the ultimate liberation of all humankind.

Whereas Hegel thought that ideas govern the world, Marx insisted that material conditions determine it. Hegel said that history evolves by the "dialectic": a principle, say despotism, has within it ideas that oppose it; in the struggle between despotism and its opposite, a higher ideal emerges—freedom, the ultimate goal of history. Following Hegel, Marx posited a world of change but insisted that it was embedded in material conditions, not in a clash of ideas. Hence the process of history was grounded on the notion of "dialectical materialism." Ideas, to Marx, were but a reflection of the material world.

Marx grouped human beings into classes based on their relationship to the means of production. Capitalists constituted a class because they owned the means of production. Workers were a separate class—the proletariat—because they did not own any of the means of production and their income came only from wage labor. Because these two classes had different relationships to the means of production, they had different—in fact, antagonistic—interests and were destined (Marx believed) to engage in a class struggle.

Online Study Center **Improve Your Grade**
Primary Source: Working Men of All Countries Unite!

Some of Marx's contemporaries lamented the increasing hostility between workers and capitalists. Marx, however, saw the conflict as necessary to advance human history, and he sought to validate his thesis by the study of the past. In the Middle Ages, he pointed out, the feudal class dominated society but eventually lost the struggle to the commercial classes. Now, in turn, the capitalists were destined to be defeated by the rising proletariat. Thus industrial capitalism, he argued, was a necessary, if painful, economic stage through which humankind had to traverse on its way to liberation.

In his study of history and economics, Marx found not only justification for but irrefutable proof of the "scientific" basis of his ideas. Capitalism was itself creating the forces that would supplant it. The large industrial plants necessitated an ever greater work force with a growing sense of class interest. The inherently competitive nature of capitalism would inevitably drive an increasing number of enterprises out of business, and a form of monopoly capitalism would emerge, abusive of both consumers and workers. Ever more savage competition would force businesses to fail, creating widespread unemployment. Angered and frustrated by their lot, workers would overthrow the system that had abused them for so long: "The knell of private property has sounded. The expropriators will be expropriated." Workers would take power and, to solidify their rule, would temporarily exercise the "dictatorship of the proletariat." Once that had taken place, the state would wither away. With the coming to power of the proletariat, the history of class war would end and the ideal society would prevail. In the absences of classes and struggles between them, history would end.

Marx's study of economics and history proved to him that the coming of socialism was not only desirable, but inevitable. The laws of history dictated that capitalism, having created the rising proletariat, would collapse. By labeling his brand of socialism as scientific, Marx gave it the aura it needed to become the faith of millions of people. To declare ideas scientific in the nineteenth century, when science was held in such high esteem, was to ensure their popularity.

SECTION SUMMARY

- From 1815 to 1848, conservatism provided the ideological foundations for restored monarchies and social hierarchy; the ideologies of romanticism, nationalism, liberalism, and socialism challenged that order.

- Romanticism was based on feeling and passion rather than on reason; it inspired the arts, but also revived religion and challenged the existing political order through its influence on nationalism.

- Nationalism—the identification with one's nation based on shared language, culture, political authority, and historical past—began to emerge in the first half of the nineteenth century.

- The economic and political theory of liberalism originated with and justified middle-class interests and stressed individual freedoms.

- Socialist ideologies—"utopian" and "scientific"— emerged in response to the harsh conditions of the working classes and offered an alternative to capitalism.

RESTORATION, REFORM, AND REACTION

How did the restorations that followed the Napoleonic era give way to reform?

Despite the new ideologies that emerged to challenge the existing order, efforts at restoration appeared successful until at least 1830. Indeed, in central and eastern Europe, from the German states to Russia and the Ottoman Empire, the political systems established in 1815 would persist virtually unchanged until midcentury. In western Europe, however, important transformations would occur by the 1830s as reaction gave way to reform. Then in 1848 widespread revolutions would break out on much of the Continent. The language of liberalism and nationalism, and even the newer idiom of socialism, would be heard on the barricades, in popular assemblies, and in parliamentary halls.

WESTERN EUROPE: FROM REACTION TO LIBERALISM, 1815–1830

Most of Europe until the 1830s experienced the heavy hand of reaction. Then western Europe saw more liberal regimes come into their own. Revolution and the threat of revolution helped dismantle the worst features of the restored regimes. The more liberal western European states faced continuing discontents of various sorts—mainly social and political—which they managed to negotiate with varying degrees of success.

France   The most dramatic restoration of the older order occurred in France. The restored Bourbons turned the clock back, not to 1789 but closer to 1791, when the country had briefly enjoyed a constitutional monarchy. Moreover, it maintained the Napoleonic Code with its provisions of legal equality. The Bourbon constitution provided for a parliament with an elected lower house, the Chamber of Deputies, and an appointed upper house, the Chamber of Peers. Although suffrage to the Chamber of Deputies was limited to a small elite of men with landed property—only 100,000 voters, about 0.2 percent of the population—this constitution was a concession to representative government that had not existed in the Old Regime (see page 590). Louis XVIII (r. 1814–1824) stands out among European rulers because he realized that it would be necessary to compromise on the principles of popular sovereignty proclaimed by the French Revolution. He intended to "popularize the monarchy" and "royalize the nation."

A moderate, Louis was succeeded by his ultrareactionary brother, Charles X (r. 1824–1830), who alienated the middle classes. More general disenchantment came with an economic downturn in 1827, marked by poor harvests and increased unemployment in the cities. Discontent brought to Parliament a liberal majority that refused to accept the reactionary ministers the king appointed. On July 26, 1830, after the humiliating defeat of his party at the polls, the king issued a set of decrees suspending freedom of the press, dissolving the Chamber of Deputies, and stiffening property qualifications for voters in subsequent elections. The king appeared to be engineering a coup against the existing political system.

The first to protest were the Parisian journalists and typesetters, directly threatened by the censorship laws. On July 28 others joined the protest and began erecting barricades across many streets. After killing several hundred protesters, the king's forces lost control of the city. This **July Revolution,** also known as "the three glorious days," drove the king into exile.

Alarmed by the crowds' clamor for a republic, the liberal opposition—consisting of some of the leading newspaper editors and sympathetic deputies—quickly drafted the duke of Orléans, Louis Philippe (r. 1830–1848), known for his liberal opinions, to occupy the throne.

Great Britain   Compared with the rest of Europe, Great Britain enjoyed considerable constitutional guarantees and a parliamentary regime. Yet liberals and radicals found their government retrograde and repressive. Traumatized by the French Revolution, the ruling class clung to the past, certain that advocates for change were Jacobins in disguise. Change seemed to invite revolution.

Social unrest beset Britain as it faced serious economic dislocation. The arrival of peace in 1815 led to a sudden drop in government expenditures, the return into the economy of several hundred thousand men who had been away at war, financial disarray, and plummeting prices. The poor and the middle classes were especially incensed over the clear economic advantages that the landed classes, dominating Parliament, had secured for themselves. In 1815 the Parliament passed legislation—known as the Corn Laws—that imposed high tariffs on various forms of imported grain. These

July Revolution   Uprising in Paris in July 1830 that forced King Charles X to abdicate and signaled a victory for constitutional reform over an absolute monarchy.

"Peterloo" Massacre
In August 1819 at St. Peter's Fields in Manchester, England, a crowd demanding parliamentary reform was charged by government troops, leading to bloodshed. Many English people derided the event and called it "Peterloo." *(The National Archives, Public Record Office)*

laws shielded landowning grain producers from international competition and allowed them to reap huge profits at the expense of consumers. All these issues caused various forms of protest.

In August 1819, sixty thousand people gathered in St. Peter's Fields in Manchester to demand universal suffrage for men and women alike, an annual Parliament, and other democratic reforms. The crowd was peaceful and unarmed, yet mounted soldiers charged, killing eleven and wounding four hundred. Using military force against the people as if against the French at Waterloo was seen as wrong, and the confrontation was branded "the battle of Peterloo," or more often "the Peterloo Massacre." The British public was shocked by this use of violence against peaceful demonstrators; Parliament responded by passing the so-called Six Acts, which outlawed freedom of assembly and effectively imposed censorship. Through much of the 1820s Britain appeared resistant to reform until news of revolution across the Channel in 1830 brought about change.

Spain and Its Colonies Spain, under the Napoleonic occupation, had in 1812 elected a national parliament, the Cortes. It issued a democratic constitution that provided for universal manhood suffrage and a unicameral legislature with control over government policy. Supporters and admirers of the constitution in

Spain were known as "friends of liberty," and the term *liberal* was coined. But in 1814, Ferdinand VII (r. 1808, 1814–1833), the Bourbon king of Spain whom Napoleon had ousted, returned to power. Though he promised to respect the liberal 1812 constitution, Ferdinand believed in the divine right of kings and was hostile to the new order. With support from the aristocracy and from segments of the general population still loyal to the call of throne and altar, Ferdinand had liberals arrested or driven into exile.

Ferdinand's plan to restore Spain to its earlier prominence included a reassertion of control over its American colonies. The Spanish dominions had grown restless in the eighteenth century, for they had witnessed the advent of an independent United States and the French occupation of Spain itself. Spain's emboldened colonies had refused to recognize the Napoleonic regime in Madrid and became increasingly self-reliant. Their attitude did not change when French control of Spain ended. Ferdinand refused to compromise with the overseas territories. Instead, he gathered an army to subdue them. Some liberal junior officers, declaring the army's loyalty to the constitution of 1812, won support from the rank and file, who balked at going overseas. This military mutiny coincided with a sympathetic provincial uprising to produce the "revolution of 1820," the first major assault on the European order established in 1815 at the Congress of Vienna. Ferdinand appealed to the European powers for help. France intervened on his behalf and crushed the uprising.

Ferdinand restored his reactionary regime but could not regain Spain's American colonies. The British, sympathetic to the cause of Latin American independence and eager for commercial access to the region, opposed reconquest, and their naval dominance of the seas kept Spain in its place. The United States, meanwhile, had recognized the independence of the Latin American republics and wished to see their independence maintained. In 1823 President James Monroe issued the statement known as the Monroe Doctrine, prohibiting European colonization or intervention in the affairs of independent republics in the Americas. Of course, the United States had no military muscle to back this proclamation, but the British navy effectively enforced it. By 1825 all of Spain's colonies on the mainland in Central and South America had won their freedom.

The newly independent states patterned their regimes on models of Spanish liberalism; all had constitutions stipulating separation of powers and guaranteeing human rights. Brazil, the Portuguese empire in the Americas, was a monarchy for most of the rest of the nineteenth century, as was Mexico for a short time, but all the other states became republics, opting for what was then an unusual form of government. Although most of the Latin regimes eventually became dictatorships, they continued to pay lip service to liberal values.

WESTERN EUROPE, 1830–1848

For the political systems of western Europe, the 1830s marked a time of modification. The threat, and occasionally the sting, of revolt produced more liberal regimes, but except for Britain and Spain, most governments were unable to stem the tide of discontent, which became revolution in 1848.

France and the July Monarchy   As a result of the 1830 revolution in Paris, a more liberal regime was installed in France. Louis Philippe proclaimed himself "King of the French," thus acknowledging that he reigned at the behest of the people. Freedom of the press was reinstated. Suffrage was extended to twice as many voters as before, 200,000 men. The July Monarchy, named after the month in which it was established by revolution, justified itself by celebrating the great Revolution of 1789. On the site where the Bastille had been razed in 1789, the government erected a large column with the names of the victims of the July 1830 revolution, thus suggesting a continuity between those who had fought tyranny in 1789 and 1830.

Identification with the Revolution appeared to legitimize the regime but also had the potential to subvert it. Fearful that the cult of revolution would encourage vio-

lence against the new monarchy, the regime censored artistic production, promoting only works that extolled the period from 1789 to 1791, when the revolutionaries had attempted to found a constitutional monarchy. Now that the revolution of 1830 had established a constitutional monarchy, the regime was suggesting, any further uprisings were illegitimate. If the July Monarchy turned out not to be as liberal as its founders had hoped, foreign visitors coming from more authoritarian societies were nonetheless impressed by France's apparently liberal institutions. (See the box "The Global Record: A Moroccan Describes French Freedom of the Press.") Many French liberals, however, saw the regime as a travesty of the hopes and promises it had represented on coming to power in 1830.

British Reforms   The major political problem facing Britain in the early nineteenth century was the composition of Parliament, which did not reflect the dramatic population shifts that had occurred since the seventeenth century. Industrialization had transformed mere villages into major cities—Manchester, Birmingham, Leeds, Sheffield—but those cities had no representation in Parliament. Localities that had lost population, however, were still represented. In districts known as "pocket boroughs," single individuals owned the right to a seat in Parliament. In districts known as "rotten boroughs," a handful of voters elected a representative.

News of the July 1830 revolution in Paris encouraged British liberals to push for reform. Fearing the same fate as the hapless Charles X, some conservatives silently yielded. The government introduced a reform bill abolishing or reducing representation for sparsely populated areas while granting seats for the populous and unrepresented cities. The bill also widened the franchise by lowering property qualifications to include many middle-class men. Following a prolonged, bitter political battle between the government and middle classes on one side and the aristocracy on the other, the House of Lords finally passed what came to be known as the **Great Reform Bill** of 1832.

The reform was not particularly radical. Only the upper layers of the male middle class were enfranchised, or one in seven adult men. Yet despite its shortcomings, the reform demonstrated the willingness of the political leaders to acknowledge the increasing economic importance of manufacturing. Parliament became a more representative forum whose makeup better reflected the shift of economic power from agricultural landowners to the industrial and commercial classes. The bill passed as a result of nationwide agitation, evidence that the

Great Reform Bill   British law that broadened the franchise and provided parliamentary seats for new urban areas that had not previously been represented.

A MOROCCAN DESCRIBES FRENCH FREEDOM OF THE PRESS

In 1845–1846 a Moroccan diplomatic mission visited Paris. The ambassador's secretary, Muhammad as-Saffar (d. 1881), wrote an account of the visit. Impressed by many aspects of French society, he praises France's press in the following passage. The "Sultan" as-Saffar refers to is King Louis Philippe. To this Moroccan observer, the extent to which the French enjoyed constitutional government was striking.

The people of Paris, like all the French indeed, like all of [Europe] are eager to know the latest news and events that are taking place in other parts [of the world]. For this purpose they have the gazette.[In] these papers ... they write all the news that has reached them that day about events in their own country and in other lands both near and far.

This is the way it is done. The owner of a newspaper dispatches his people to collect everything they see or hear in the way of important events or unusual happenings. Among the places where they collect the news are the two Chambers, the Great and the Small, where they come together to make their laws. When the members of the Chamber meet to deliberate, the men of the gazette sit nearby and write down everything that is said, for all debating and ratifying of laws is matter for the gazette and is known to everyone. No one can prevent them from doing this....

... [I]f someone has an idea about a subject but he is not a member of the press, he may write about it in the gazette and make it known to others, so that the leaders of opinion learn about it. If the idea is worthy they may follow it, and if its author was out of favor it may bring him recognition.

No person in France is prohibited from expressing his opinion or from writing it and printing it, on condition that he does not violate the law. ...

In the newspapers they write rejoinders to the men of the two Chambers about the laws they are making. If their Sultan demands gifts from the notables or goes against the law in any way, they write about that too, saying that he is a tyrant and in the wrong. He cannot confront them or cause them harm. Also, if someone behaves out of the ordinary, they write about that too, making it common knowledge among people of every rank. If his deeds were admirable, they praise and delight in him, lauding his example; but if he behaved badly, they revile him to discourage the like.

Moreover, if someone is being oppressed by another, they write about that too, so that everyone will know the story from both sides just as it happened, until it is decided in court. One can also read in it what their courts have decided.

QUESTIONS

1. Based on the diplomat's reaction to the French system, what can you deduce about freedom of the press and the expression of public opinion in Morocco?

2. Do you think this observer has a positive opinion of the French press? Why or why not?

Source: Susan Gilson Miller, ed. and trans., *Disorienting Encounters: Travels of a Moroccan Scholar in France in 1845–1846; The Voyage of Muhammad as-Saffar.* Copyright © 1992 Regents of the University of California. Reprinted by permission of the University of California Press Books in the format Textbook via Copyright Clearance Center.

---

political system could respond to grievances and bring about reform peacefully.

A series of colonial reforms also showed Parliament's willingness to adapt to changing circumstances. Opposition to slavery had been voiced since the 1780s. (See the box "The Written Record: A Plea to Abolish Slavery in the British Colonies.") Slavery, the very opposite of human freedom, was an affront to liberal principles. Moreover, its persistence threatened the empire—in 1831 sixty thousand slaves rebelled in Jamaica. Parliament heeded the call for change and in 1833 abolished slavery throughout the British Empire.

In addition, the British began to review their imperial administration. Their control over Canada had been challenged in an uprising in 1837. London sent out a fact-finding mission headed by Lord Durham (1806–1848). As a result of the *Durham Report,* the British government promulgated self-government for Canada in 1839 and 1841. Eventually all the British colonies with a majority of white settlers were given similar rights of self-rule. The idea of self-government for nonwhites in the colonies was not yet imagined.

Reforms solidified Britain's influence overseas. In Canada they reduced opposition to British rule. The antislavery campaign led to the extension of British power into Africa. Having abolished the slave trade in 1807, the British worked to compel other nations to end the trade. With the largest navy in the world, Britain was well equipped to patrol the coast of West Africa to suppress the traffic in humans and hinder its

A PLEA TO ABOLISH SLAVERY IN THE BRITISH COLONIES

Among the causes that British reformers embraced was the abolition of slavery. The slave trade had been abolished in 1807; one more step was left—ending in the colonies the institution of slavery itself. In this petition to Parliament in 1823, the Society for the Mitigation and Gradual Abolition of Slavery Throughout the British Dominions explains the harsh and degrading nature of the institution. Trading in slaves had been abolished as immoral and unnatural; here the petitioners remind Parliament that holding slaves is no less abhorrent. Under the pressure of this type of agitation, Parliament in 1833 abolished slavery in the British Empire.

In the colonies of Great Britain there are at this moment upwards of 800,000 human beings in a state of degrading personal slavery.

These unhappy persons, whether young or old, male or female, are the absolute property of their master, who may sell or transfer them at his pleasure, and who may also regulate according to his discretion (within certain limits) the measure of their labour, their food, and their punishment.

Many of the slaves are (and all may be) branded like cattle, by means of a hot iron, on the shoulder or other conspicuous part of the body, with the initials of their master's name; and thus bear about them in indelible characters the proof of their debased and servile state. . . .

It can hardly be alleged that any man can have a right to obtain his fellow creatures in a state so miserable and degrading as has been described. And the absence of such right will be still more apparent, if we consider how these slaves were originally obtained.

They, or their parents, were the victims of the Slave Trade. They were obtained, not by lawful means, or under any colourable pretext, but by the most undisguised rapine, and the most atrocious fraud. Torn from their homes and from every dear relation in life, barbarously manacled, driven like herds of cattle to the sea-shore, crowded into the potential holds of slaveships, they were transported to our colonies and there sold in bondage. . . .

The Government and Legislature of this country have on various occasions, and in the most solemn and unequivocal terms denounced the Slave Trade as immoral, inhuman, and unjust; but the legal perpetuation of that state of slavery, which has been produced by it, is surely, in its principle, no less immoral, inhuman and unjust, than the trade itself. . . .

QUESTIONS

1. Why would the British Parliament abolish the slave trade but allow slavery to continue in its colonies?

2. Why did it take ten years from the time of this petition for slavery to be abolished? What changes occurred in the British Parliament that might explain the timing of abolition?

Source: Reprinted in *Circular Letters of the Society for the Mitigation and Gradual Abolition of Slavery Throughout the British Dominions* (April 1823).

---

colonial rivals from benefiting from the trade. Needing bases for these patrols, the British established a number of minor settlements in West Africa, and thereby became the predominant European power along the coast. Although unimportant when acquired, these possessions foreshadowed the increasing European intrusion into African affairs.

Parliament's reforming zeal stimulated support for **Chartism,** a movement for political democracy as a means for social change. In 1838 political radicals with working-class support drew up a "people's charter," a petition calling for universal male suffrage, electoral districts with equal population, salaries and the abolition of property qualifications for members of Parliament, the secret ballot, and annual general elections. The Chartists hoped that giving workers the vote would end the dominance of the much smaller upper classes in Parliament and ensure an improvement in the workers' lot.

Chartism won wide support among men and women in the working classes, sparking demonstrations and petition drives of unprecedented size—millions signed the petition. Women participated to a larger extent than in any other political movement of the day, founding over a hundred female Chartist chapters. Some Chartists, especially female members, asked

Chartism   Nineteenth-century British political movement calling for universal male suffrage, electoral districts with equal population, salaries and the abolition of property qualifications for members of Parliament, the secret ballot, and annual general elections.

for women's suffrage, but this demand failed to gain overall adherence from the membership. Winning mass support during particularly hard economic years, Chartism lost followers during a temporary economic upswing. The movement also fell under the sway of advocates of violence, who scared off many artisans and potential middle-class supporters. Chartism failed as a political movement; yet it drew public attention to an integrated democratic program whose main provisions (except for yearly elections) would be adopted piecemeal over the next half century.

In 1839 urban businessmen founded the Anti–Corn Law League for the purpose of abolishing the Corn Law of 1815, which kept the price of grain high. The Corn Law was unpopular with manufacturers, who knew that low food prices would allow them to pay low wages. It was also unpopular with workers, who wanted bread at a price they could afford. The anti–Corn Law movement proved more effective than Chartism because it had the support of the middle classes. Alarmed by the threat of famine after the poor harvest of 1845, Parliament repealed the Corn Law in 1846.

In the end this action did not affect the price of grain. Nevertheless, repeal of the Corn Law was a milestone in British history, demonstrating the extent to which organized groups could bring about economic improvements. A popular, mass organization had been able to shape public policy—a far cry from the days of Peterloo, when the government had not only ignored the public but attacked it with bayonets fixed.

THE ABSOLUTIST STATES OF CENTRAL AND EASTERN EUROPE, 1815–1848

Having seen the turmoil unleashed by the French Revolution and suffered at the hands of the Grande Armée, the states of central and eastern Europe were particularly committed to maintaining absolute government. In contrast to many parts of western Europe, which saw important political changes in the 1830s, the absolutist states were able to preserve themselves essentially unchanged until 1848—and in some cases even beyond.

The Austrian Empire   The Austrian Empire's far-flung territories seemed to its Habsburg rulers to require a firm hand (see Map 21.1). Liberalism, which challenged imperial power, could not be countenanced. Nor, in this multinational empire, could nationalism be tolerated. The emperor, Francis I (r. 1792–1835), was opposed to any change; his motto was "Rule and change nothing." Prince Metternich, Francis's chief minister, viewed the French Revolution of 1789 and its aftermath as a disaster and believed his task was to hold the line against the threat of revolution. Quick to interpret protests or the desire for change as a threat to the fundamental order, Metternich established a network of secret police and informers to spy on the imperial subjects and keep them in check.

The German States   In most of the German states, the political order was authoritarian and inflexible. The states of Baden, Württemberg, and Bavaria had granted their subjects constitutions, although effective power remained in the hands of the ruling houses. The king of Prussia had repeatedly promised a constitution, but none had materialized. A representative Diet would not meet there until 1847. Prussia was ruled by an alliance of the king and the *Junkers* (YUNG-kurz), the landowning aristocrats who staffed the officer corps and the bureaucracy. The efficiency of the officer corps and the bureaucracy earned admiration throughout Europe. But by liberal standards, Prussia's political institutions seemed outdated.

Throughout the German states, the urban middle classes, intellectuals, journalists, university professors, and students were frustrated with the existing system. They were disappointed by the lack of free institutions and the failure of the patriotic wars against Napoleon to create a united Germany. University students formed *Burschenschaften* (BOOR-shen-shaft-en), or brotherhoods, whose slogan was "Honor, Liberty, Fatherland." Metternich reacted swiftly in July 1819 with the Carlsbad Decrees; these decrees established close supervision over the universities, censorship of the press, and dissolution of the youth groups. Wholesale persecution of liberals and nationalists followed. The Prussian king dismissed his more enlightened officials.

Renewed nationalist agitation swept the German states in the 1840s. A mass outpouring of patriotic sentiment erupted in response to possible French ambitions on the Rhine during a diplomatic crisis in 1840. Two patriotic songs were penned: "The Watch on the Rhine" and *"Deutschland, Deutschland über alles"* ("Germany, Germany Above All"); the latter became Germany's national anthem half a century later. German rulers, who in the past had been reluctant to support the national idea, now attempted to co-opt it. Cologne's unfinished cathedral, for example, became a symbol of German enthusiasm; from all over Germany donations poured in to finish it. These events suggested a broadening base for nationhood, which potentially could replace the existing system of a fragmented Germany. But with minor exceptions, the system established in 1815 prevailed until 1848.

Italian States   By the end of Napoleon's reign, Italy consisted of eight political states. Austria exercised considerable power over Italy through its possession of its northern territories, Lombardy and Venetia.

Austria also had dynastic ties to several ruling houses in the central part of the peninsula, and had political alliances with the papacy. The only ruling house free of Austrian ties—and hence eventually looked to by nationalists as a possible rallying point for the independence of the peninsula—was the Savoy dynasty of Piedmont-Sardinia. But it was in Austria's interest to maintain disunity.

Many Italian governments—notably the papacy, the kingdom of Naples, and the central Italian duchies—imposed repressive policies, knowing that they could count on Austrian assistance to squelch any uprising. Indeed, Metternich did crush rebellions that were intended to bring about freer institutions and a unified Italy. His interventions generated hatred of Austria among Italian liberals and nationalists.

Russia   By far the most autocratic of the European states was tsarist Russia. Alexander I (r. 1801–1825) was an enigmatic character who puzzled his contemporaries. His domestic policy vacillated between liberalism and reaction; his foreign policy wavered between brutal power politics and apparently selfless idealism. When the Congress of Vienna gave additional Polish lands to the tsar, establishing the kingdom of Poland, he demonstrated his liberalism to the world (and curried favor with his new subjects) by granting Poland a liberal constitution. But he offered no such constitution to his own people. Within a few years, moreover, he violated the same Polish constitution he had approved, by refusing to call the Diet into session. His planned efforts to abolish serfdom between 1803 and 1812 also failed. As much as he desired freedom for them, he was unwilling to impose the necessary policies toward that end because they would be detrimental to the interests and privileges of the landed gentry.

Toward the end of his rule, Alexander became increasingly authoritarian and repressive, probably in response to growing opposition. Myriad groups—Russian military officers who had served in western Europe, Russian Freemasons who had corresponded with Masonic lodges in western Europe, and Russian intellectuals who read Western liberal political tracts—had warmed to the ideals of individual freedom and constitutionalism. These groups formed secret societies with varying agendas. Some envisioned Russia as a republic, others as a constitutional monarchy, but all shared a commitment to the abolition of serfdom and the establishment of a freer society.

Alexander died in December 1825, without designating which of his brothers would succeed him. Taking advantage of the confusion, the military conspirators declared in favor of the older brother, Constantine, in the belief that he favored a constitutional government. The younger brother, Nicholas, claimed to be the legal heir. The St. Petersburg garrison rallied to the conspirators' cause. Taking their cue from the Spanish uprising of 1820, the officers believed that the military could bring about change on its own.

The "Decembrist uprising," as it is known, quickly failed. The military revolt in the Russian capital was badly coordinated with uprisings planned in the countryside, and Nicholas moved quickly to crush the rebellion. He had the leaders, called the **Decembrists,** executed, sent to Siberia, or exiled. In spite of its tragic end, throughout the nineteenth century the Decembrist uprising served as an inspiration to Russians resisting tsarist oppression.

Coming to the throne under such circumstances, Nicholas I (r. 1825–1855) was obsessed with the danger of revolution and determined to suppress all challenges to his authority. The declared goal of his rule was to uphold "orthodoxy, autocracy, and nationality." Nicholas created a stern, centralized bureaucracy to control all facets of Russian life. He originated the modern Russian secret police, called the "Third Section"; a state within the state, it was above the law. Believing in the divine right of monarchs, Nicholas refused to accept limits to his imperial powers. The tsar supported the primacy of the Russian Orthodox Church within Russian society; the church in turn upheld the powers of the state. Nicholas also used nationalism to strengthen the state, exalting the country's past and trying to "Russify" non-Russian peoples. After a nationalist rebellion in 1831 in Poland attempted to shake loose Russian control, Nicholas abrogated the kingdom's constitution and tried to impose the Russian language on its Polish subjects.

Russia's single most overwhelming problem was serfdom. Economically, serfdom had little to recommend it; free labor was far more efficient. Moreover, the serfs' dissatisfaction with their lot threatened public safety. Nicholas's thirty-year reign was checkered with over six hundred peasant uprisings, half of them put down by the military. Nicholas understood that serfdom had to be abolished for Russia's own good, but also he believed emancipation would only sow further disorder. Except for a few minor reforms, he did nothing. Nicholas's death, followed by Russia's defeat in the Crimean War (see pages 682–684), eventually brought to an end the institution that had held nearly half of the Russian people in bondage.

Ottoman Empire and Greek Independence

In its sheer mass, the Ottoman Empire continued to be a world empire. It extended over three continents. In Africa it ran across the whole North African coast. In

Decembrists   Group of Russian military officers, later viewed as martyrs, who led the unsuccessful December 1825 rebellion seeking to install a constitutional monarchy.

Europe it stretched from Dalmatia (on the Adriatic coast) to Istanbul. In Asia it extended from Mesopotamia (present-day Iraq) to Anatolia (present-day Turkey). But it was an empire in decline, seriously challenged from inside by nationalist movements and from outside by foreign threats.

The Ottoman bureaucracy, once the mainstay of the government, had fallen into decay. In the past officials had been recruited and advanced by merit; now lacking funds, Constantinople sold government offices. Tax collectors ruthlessly squeezed the peasantry. By the eighteenth century, the Janissaries, formerly an elite military force, had become an undisciplined band that menaced the peoples of the Ottoman Empire—especially those located at great distances from the close control of the capital. The reform-minded Sultan Selim III (r. 1789–1807) sought to curb the army, but rebellious Janissaries killed him. They then forced the new ruler, Mahmud II (r. 1808–1839), to retract most of the previous improvements. The worst features of the declining empire were restored.

Mehemet Ali
Painted by the famed British artist Sir David Wilkie, this portrait depicts the Egyptian leader at the height of his powers. Mehemet challenged the Ottoman Empire, winning for Egypt virtual independence and bringing Syria under his control.
(Tate Gallery, London/Art Resource, NY)

The ideas of nationalism and liberty that triggered changes in western Europe also stirred the peoples of the Balkans. Most of the Ottoman Empire was inhabited by Muslims, but in the Balkans Christians were in the majority. Ottoman officials usually treated religious minorities such as Jews and Orthodox Christians with tolerance. But the Christian subject peoples found in their religion a means of collectively resisting a harsh and at times capricious rule. Some Christian peoples in the Balkans looked back nostalgically to earlier eras—the Greeks to their great Classical civilization or the Serbs to their era of self-rule.

The Serbs were the first people to revolt successfully against Ottoman rule. A poor, mountainous region, Serbia suffered greatly from the rapaciousness of the Janissaries. In protest, a revolt broke out in 1804. At first the Ottomans were able to contain the insurrection, but in 1815 they had to recognize one of its leaders, Milosh Obrenovich (r. 1815–1839), as governor and allow the formation of a national assembly. In 1830, under pressure from Russia, which took an interest in fellow Slavs and members of the Orthodox faith, Constantinople recognized Milosh as hereditary ruler over an autonomous Serbia.

The Greeks' struggle led to complete independence from Ottoman rule. Greeks served as administrators throughout the Ottoman lands and, as merchants and seafarers, traveled widely throughout the Mediterranean world and beyond. They had encountered the ideas of the French Revolution and, in the 1790s, were affected by the nationalism spreading in Europe. Adamantios Koraïs (KOOR-ay-iss) (1748–1833), an educator living in revolutionary Paris, reformed written Greek to make it more consonant with ancient Greek by removing foreign accretions. Koraïs created a new, more elegant Greek and edited Greek classics to connect his fellow countrymen with their ancient and illustrious past. Greek cultural nationalism found an echo among some intellectuals. The *Philike Hetairia* (Society of Friends), a conspiratorial group founded in 1814, dedicated itself to restoring Greek independence by political means.

Greek peasants were not particularly interested in politics, but they were hostile to the Ottoman Turks, who had accumulated vast landholdings at their expense. This in part motivated Greek peasants to join the anti-Turkish revolt that began in 1821 and lasted several years. By 1827 the Ottomans, aided by their vassal Mehemet Ali (1769–1849) of Egypt, controlled most of the Balkan peninsula. The rest of Europe, excited by the idea of an independent Greece restored to its past greatness, widely supported the Greek movement for freedom. The Great Powers intervened in 1827, sending their navies to intercept supplies intended for the Ottoman forces. At Navarino Bay, in the southwest of the Peloponnesus, the Ottoman navy fired on the allies, who returned fire and sank the Turkish ships. The destruction of Ottoman power ensured the independence of Greece. In 1830 an international agreement spelled out Greek independence.

Losing influence in the Balkans, the Ottoman Empire also faced challenges elsewhere. In Egypt Mehemet Ali, nominally subordinate to Constantinople, actually ruled Egypt as if it were independent. He wrested Syria away in 1831 and threatened to march against his overlord, the sultan. Britain and Russia, concerned that an Ottoman collapse would upset the region's balance of power, intervened on the empire's behalf. Constantinople won back Syria but in 1841 had to acknowledge Mehemet Ali as the hereditary ruler of Egypt. The survival of the Ottoman Empire was beginning to depend on the goodwill—or self-interest—of the Great Powers.

=========== S E C T I O N   S U M M A R Y ===========

- Between 1815 and 1830, the restored governments in western Europe encountered periodic social discontent, which they managed to negotiate with various degrees of success, often through repressive measures.

- In July 1830, the French responded to reactionary measures taken by their king with revolution, which marked the beginning of more serious opposition to other regimes.

- British liberals responded to France's July Revolution by redrawing the voting districts to reflect the growth of cities, widening the franchise to include the middle classes, and loosening colonial rule over white settler populations.

- Having suffered more directly from Napoleonic invasions, rulers in central and eastern Europe remained determined to preserve absolute political power from 1815 to 1848.

- The 1825 "Decembrist uprising" in Russia challenged the power of Nicholas I; the memory of its brutal repression would inspire resistance to tsarist oppression throughout the nineteenth century.

- National movements from within and foreign threats from without challenged the religiously diverse Ottoman Empire, already in decay because of its corrupt bureaucracy; Serbs and Greeks successfully revolted against Ottoman rule.

THE REVOLUTIONS OF 1848

What were the main causes of the revolutions of 1848, and what roles did nationalism, liberalism, and socialism play in inciting and sustaining revolution?

From France in the west to Poland in the east, at least fifty separate revolts and uprisings shook the Continent in 1848, the most extensive outbreak of popular violence in nineteenth-century Europe (see **MAP 21.2**). The revolt had an impact far beyond Europe's borders. Inspired by the example of the European revolutions, Brazilians rose up against their government. In Bogota, Colombia, church bells rang, and in New York public demonstrations enthusiastically greeted the announcement of a republic in France. And as a result of the Parisian revolution, slaves in French colonies were finally emancipated.

The revolutions of 1848 also brought women into the political arena, creating new opportunities to criticize their legal status. In France, feminist clubs and newspapers proliferated as they never had before. In central, eastern, and southeastern Europe, revolution gave women political experience that promoted an emancipatory consciousness among them. The revolutions produced a long list of eloquent feminists throughout Europe who made various demands through their newspapers, magazines, and in their political participation. But just as had happened in the French Revolution of 1789, revolutionary governments eventually excluded women from politics, censored their newspapers, and disbanded their clubs.

ROOTS OF REBELLION

At no time since 1800 had so many Europeans been involved in collective action. Many reasons account for this widespread outbreak of discontent. In the countryside, restrictions in access to land such as enclosure frustrated peasants. Although in the past many had enjoyed free access to village commons, these were coming increasingly under private control, or the peasants faced competition for their use. Formerly a peasant might have grazed sheep in the commons, but now a

MAP 21.2   Major Uprisings and Reforms, 1848–1849

In no other year had as many revolts broken out simultaneously. In many cases the revolutions led to reforms and new constitutions.

Online Study Center **Improve Your Grade** Interactive Map: Major Uprisings and Reforms, 1848–1849

peasant's two or three animals competed with herds of sometimes hundreds of sheep owned by a rich farmer. Also, the poor once had relatively free access to forests to forage for firewood, but the limitation of this right also now led to frequent conflicts.

Points of friction were made worse by growing populations that put pressure on available resources. In the urban environment a crisis erupted in the handicrafts industry, which dominated city economies. Urban artisans were being undercut by the putting-out system or cottage industry, in which capitalists had goods produced in the countryside by cottagers—part-time artisans who supported themselves as well through agriculture and were thus willing to work for lower wages. Crises in the crafts hurt the journeymen who wanted to be masters; they had to serve far longer apprenticeships and in many cases could never expect promotion. Where the guild system still existed, it was in decline, unable to protect the economic interests of artisans anxious about their futures.

These developing concerns came to a crisis point as a result of the economic depression of 1845–1846. In 1845 a crop disaster, including the spread of potato blight, destroyed the basic food of the poor in northern Europe. The Irish suffered the most catastrophically from this blight: one million starved to death between 1844 and 1851. The poor harvests doubled the price of food from the 1840 level. An industrial downturn accompanied these agricultural disasters, creating massive unemployment. Municipal and national governments seemed unable to deal with the crowding, disease, and unsanitary conditions that were worsening already high tensions in the cities, the sites of national governments. The call to overthrow the existing regimes resonated not only because of discontent, but because new ideologies had created hope for change, as well as a vision for what it should be. The insurrections disoriented the established political and administrative elites, and they found they could not count on their traditional sources of support.

The revolutions of 1848 were sparked by the revolution in Paris in February. News of the fall of Louis Philippe triggered a ripple effect, spreading turbulence to over fifty localities in Europe. In France the revolution was for political and social rights, particularly the right to work. In several other countries, another issue was added to the combustible situation—nationalism. Once revolution in the German states broke out, the demands arose for national unification. National unity also became a goal throughout the Italian peninsula; northern Italians also desired independence from the Habsburg empire. In other Habsburg lands the cry went out for national independence: the Hungarians, Poles, and Czechs all wanted to be masters of their own destinies and free from Vienna's control.

LIBERALS: FROM SUCCESS TO DEFEAT

The revolutions of 1848 went through a number of stages. In the first stage liberal demands for more political freedoms such as the right to vote joined with popular demands for social and economic justice. In France the victors declared a republic, which provided basic constitutional freedoms and granted universal male suffrage (the first European regime to do so). The provisional government attempted to solve the problem of widespread unemployment by creating jobs through a system of "national workshops." Inspired by the example of Paris, crowds in Vienna demonstrated and petitioned the emperor. Having lost control over the capital, Metternich resigned and fled to England. On March 15, 1848, the Austrian imperial court, faced with continued agitation by students and

workers, announced its willingness to issue a constitution. Even more important was Austria's decision to abolish serfdom. Some had feared a serf uprising, but the relatively generous terms of the emancipation mollified the peasantry.

News of the February uprising in Paris also acted as a catalyst for change in the German states. The forces of change seemed irresistible. As the king of Württemberg observed, "I cannot mount on horseback against ideas." The wisest course appeared to be compromise. He and many of his fellow dukes and princes changed their governments by dismissing their cabinets and instituting constitutions.

Up to this point Prussia was conspicuous for being untouched by the revolutionary wave. But when news of Metternich's fall in Vienna reached Berlin on March 16, middle-class liberals and artisans demonstrated for reforms. King Friedrich Wilhelm IV (r. 1840–1861), who initially opposed the revolutionaries' demands for political liberties and a unified nation, chose appeasement. The king surprised his subjects on March 21 by announcing support for a united, free, constitutional Germany. He appointed as chief minister a liberal

King Friedrich Wilhelm IV Announcing His Devotion to German Unity
This print, distributed by the thousands, shows the grateful people—well-dressed middle-class citizens and humble artisans united in their purpose—acclaiming the king (*center*) on horseback. The black, red, and gold flags, the symbol of German unity since the Napoleonic Wars, are prominently displayed. (*Germanisches National Museum Nuremberg*)

Rhenish businessman, who in a ceremonial march through Berlin symbolically walked ahead of the king (see illustration on page 673). Representative government was introduced, and suffrage was extended, though it was still restricted to men of property. No longer the exclusive preserve of the aristocracy, the government was opened to men from the liberal professions and the business classes. As in Austria, the German countryside was appeased by reducing some of the feudal arrangements that still existed in many areas.

The second stage of the revolution marked a breakdown in the unity that had initially formed against the old regimes. With the enemy defeated or compliant, the middle classes, peasants, and workers discovered that they no longer shared a common goal. In France the peasants, who at least had not opposed the revolution, by April 1848 were hostile to the new republic. They decried the additional taxes that had to be levied to pay for the national workshops supporting unemployed urban workers. Armed with the vote, the peasants elected conservative landowners, lawyers, and notaries—a group nearly identical to the pre-1848 deputies. In June the new parliament decided to terminate the costly national workshops. The workers, in despair, revolted. The government carried out a bloody repression, killing 3,000 and arresting 15,000. The re-election of conservative forces revealed that universal suffrage could serve as a means to mobilize moderate public opinion against radicalism in Paris. The advent of railroads allowed the government to muster military support from outside the city. Thereafter it would be far more difficult for radical Parisian crowds to dictate policies to the rest of the country.

The propertied classes, feeling menaced by the poor, looked to authority for security. Of the several candidates for president in 1848, Louis Napoleon (1808–1873), a nephew of Napoleon Bonaparte, appealed to the largest cross section of the population.

Ballots, Not Bullets

This print from 1848 encourages the revolutionary on the barricades to put away his rifle and trust the democratic process. Pointing to the rifle, our French revolutionary announces, "This is for the external enemy." "As for the internal ones," he says, indicating the election urn, "this is how one fights them loyally."

(Harlingue-Viollet/Getty Images)

The middle class was attracted by the promise of authority and order. Peasants, disillusioned by the tax policies of the republic, remained loyal to the memory of Napoleonic glory. Workers embittered by the government's repression of the June uprisings were impressed by Louis Napoleon's vaguely socialistic program. Louis Napoleon was elected president. Three years later he dissolved the National Assembly by force and established a personal dictatorship. In 1852 he declared himself Emperor Napoleon III.

In Austria and Germany the middle classes became wary of the lower classes; the class conflict in Paris intensified their concern. Once the peasants had won their freedom from feudal dues in Germany and from serfdom in the Austrian Empire, they were no longer interested in what was occurring in the capital. Thus the alliance in favor of change disappeared, and it could not even serve as a bulwark against the return of conservative forces. In Austria the reactionary forces around the court, led by General Windischgrätz, reconquered Vienna in October 1848 for the emperor and suspended the liberals' constitution. In December the king of Prussia, who had appeared to bow to liberal opinion, regained his courage and dismissed the elected assembly. Most of the liberal forces were spent and overcome by the end of the year.

THE NATIONALIST IMPULSE

The revolutions did not break out because of nationalism, but once they erupted, the nationalist cause helped shape the outcome in several regions. Faced with internal turmoil, Prussia and Austria—which both opposed German unification lest it undermine their power—could not prevent the question of a united Germany from coming to the fore. In March 1848 a self-appointed national committee invited five hundred prominent German liberals to convene in Frankfurt to begin the process of unifying the German states into a single nation. In addition to fulfilling a long-standing liberal dream, a united Germany would consolidate the liberal victory over absolutism. The gathering called for suffrage based on property qualifications, thus excluding most Germans from the political process and alienating them from the evolving new order. The first all-German elected legislature met in May 1848 in Frankfurt to pursue unification. It faced the thorny issue of which regions should be included and which excluded in this new Germany. The most ambitious plan envisioned a *Grossdeutschland* (Grose-doyt-shlant), or large Germany, consisting of all the members of the German Confederation, including the German-speaking parts of Austria and the German parts of Bohemia. Such a solution would include many non-Germans, including Poles, Czechs, and Danes. The proponents of *Kleindeutschland* (Kline-doyt-shlant), or small Germany, which would exclude Austria and its possessions, saw their solution as a more likely scenario, although it would exclude many Germans. The proposal of a small Germany succeeded in the end, largely because the reassertion of Austrian imperial power in the fall of 1848 put the non-German areas under Vienna's control out of reach.

The Prussian reassertion of royal power, though partial, was a signal for other German rulers in late 1848 to dismiss their liberal ministers. The moment for liberalism and national unification to triumph had passed by the time the **Frankfurt Assembly** drew up a constitution in the spring of 1849. Having opted for the *Kleindeutsch* solution, the parliament offered the throne to Friedrich Wilhelm IV, king of Prussia. Although the king was not a liberal, he ruled the largest state within the designated empire. If power could promote and protect German unity, he possessed it in the form of the Prussian army. But Friedrich Wilhelm feared that accepting the throne would lead to war with Austria. Believing in the principle of monarchy, he also did not want an office offered by representatives of the people, and so he refused the offer. Lacking an alternative plan, most members of the Frankfurt Assembly went home. A rump parliament and a series of uprisings in favor of German unity were crushed by the Prussian army. So German unification failed. Liberalism alone was unable to bring about German unity; other means would be required to do so.

In Italy, too, nationalist aspirations emerged once a revolt triggered by social and economic grievances had broken out. In the years before 1848 nationalists and liberals hoped somehow to see their program of a united and free Italy implemented. News of the Paris uprising in February galvanized revolutions in Italy. Italians under Austrian rule forced the Austrians to evacuate their Italian possessions. Revolts and mass protests in several Italian states led rulers to grant, or at least promise, a constitution. The king of Piedmont, Charles Albert (r. 1831–1849), granted his people a constitution, the *Statuto*. Charles Albert hoped to play a major part in unifying Italy. In Austrian Italy the middle classes, although eager to be free of foreign rule, feared radical elements among the laborers. They believed that annexation to nearby Piedmont would provide security from both Austria and the troublesome lower classes. The king of Piedmont decided to unite Italy under his throne if doing so would prevent the spread of radicalism to his kingdom. On March 24, 1848, he declared war on Austria but was defeated in July and had to sue for an armistice. The continued spread of nationalist and revolutionary sentiment

Frankfurt Assembly Popularly elected national assembly that attempted to create a unified German state.

Constitutional Government in Denmark

On March 21, 1848, fifteen thousand Danes, inspired by the example of Paris, marched on the palace to demand constitutional rights. Unlike the protests at the French capital, however, this event was peaceful and led to the establishment of a constitutional government. This painting honors the new parliament that came into being after the liberal constitution was adopted in 1849. *(Photo, Statens Museum for Kunst, Copenhagen)*

tempted Charles Albert to declare war on Austria once again, in March 1849. The outcome for Piedmont was even worse than it had been a year earlier. Within six days its army was defeated. Humiliated, Charles Albert resigned his throne to his son, Victor Emmanuel II (r. 1849–1878). The Austrians quickly reconquered their lost provinces and reinstated their puppet governments. The dream of a united Italy was dashed.

In the multinational empire of the Habsburgs, nationalism manifested itself in the form of demands for national independence from foreign rule. With Austria's power temporarily weakened as a result of revolution in Vienna, nationalist revolts broke out not only in Italy, but simultaneously in Hungary, the Czech lands, and Croatia. The Austrian emperor yielded in Hungary, giving it virtual independence; it was joined to the empire solely by personal union to the ruler.

Constitutional government was established in Hungary, but participation in the political process was limited to Magyars, who were the single largest ethnic group, constituting 40 percent of the population. The other nationalities in Hungary—Romanians, Slovaks, Croats, and Slovenes—preferred the more distant rule of Austrian Vienna to Magyar authority. The Czech lands also witnessed agitation, but there and elsewhere the tide favoring the nationalists turned. The revolt against the empire was not coordinated, and the nationalisms were often in conflict with one another. Once the emperor re-established his power in Vienna, he could move against his rebellious subjects. The Austrian Empire practiced a policy of divide and rule; it re-established its authority in Italy, bombarded Prague into submission, and with Russian help brought Hungary to heel. If the nationalist fires had been quenched, the dangers nationalism posed to the survival of the Habsburg empire were also revealed.

Three major countries escaped the large sweep of revolutions that washed across Europe. In Great Britain the government had proven capable of adjusting to some of the major popular demands, averting the need for revolution. In Russia the repressive tsarist system prevented any defiance from escalating into an opposition mass movement. Spain was also spared. General Ramón Narváez (Nar-va-yes) (1799–1868) brutally ran the country from 1844 to 1851. When he was on his deathbed, the priest asked him whether he forgave his enemies. He answered, "I have no enemies. I have shot them all!"

SECTION SUMMARY

- Across the Continent, the roots for revolution lay in increasingly restricted resources among rural peasants and urban workers; the economic depression of 1845–1846 made this situation into a crisis.

- The liberal impulse to revolution at first united middle classes, peasants, and workers in demands for political freedoms and economic justice.

- Once regimes gave into the challenge or were overturned, the goals of different social classes conflicted; the divisions between them opened the path to reaction and repression.

- Liberal revolution in eastern and central Europe inspired movements of national unification in the German states and in Italy, Hungary, the Czech lands, and Croatia, all at the expense of the Austrian Empire.

- Although counterrevolutionary forces temporarily defeated both the liberal and nationalistic impulses behind the revolutions of 1848, experiments born of these events suggested new modes of political organization that would later come to fruition.

CHAPTER SUMMARY

Online Study Center **ACE the Test**

What were the goals and results of the Congress of Vienna?

What major ideologies developed in the first half of the nineteenth century?

How did the restorations that followed the Napoleonic era give way to reform?

What were the main causes of the revolutions of 1848, and what roles did nationalism, liberalism, and socialism play in inciting and sustaining revolution?

n 1814 and 1815, after more than twenty-two years of war, the powers that finally defeated Napoleon—Great Britain, Austria, Prussia, and Russia—sought to restore the prerevolutionary Old Regime to Europe. The Congress of Vienna sought to establish international stability by creating a balance of power. To that end, the Great Powers even brought the vanquished nation of France—with its Bourbon monarchy restored—into the Concert of Europe on equal footing.

In reaction to the revolutionary challenges of the past, a conservative ideology developed that asserted human beings were neither equal nor rational and were incapable of governing themselves. The artistic and literary movement of romanticism also rejected the Enlightenment past, by privileging passion and emotion over human reason, and helped fuel a religious revival. But romanticism also increased the appeal of nationalism, a new awareness of one's cultural past and national identity—a sentiment that would ultimately destabilize the restored order. The legacy of the Enlightenment and French Revolution, moreover, could not be extinguished completely, particularly as industrial capitalism developed. Liberalism, which advocated individual freedom in laissez-faire economics and in political rights, advanced middle-class interests. Socialism, in both its "utopian" and "scientific" varieties, addressed the social injustices wrought by capitalism.

By 1830, the restored order had already shown cracks that led to revolution and reform. The July Revolution of 1830 in France replaced its reactionary king with a more liberal one. That event sparked reform in Britain, which extended the vote to the middle classes. Eastern European regimes remained more autocratic, but nationalist and liberal sentiments developed nonetheless between 1820 and 1848.

The main causes of the 1848 revolutions were economic and ideological. By the 1840s, even though industrialization had only begun on the Continent, capitalist development had already transformed modes of production and displaced, or threatened to displace, many workers. The growing middle classes, still disenfranchised in most of Europe, sought more political freedom. In February 1848, revolutionaries in France demanded universal manhood suffrage and solutions to unemployment, setting off by their example revolutions elsewhere. Central and eastern Europeans demanded representative governments; but nationalism also raised the issue of *which* peoples the governments would represent. Most of the aspirations of the 1848 revolutions failed to be realized as authoritarian regimes regained the upper hand by 1851.

LOOKING AHEAD

Although the revolutionary and nationalistic movements of 1848–1849 were crushed, and the republics proclaimed in France, Germany, Hungary, and Italy did not last, this time, as opposed to 1815, the re-established monarchs knew that they could not simply return to the past. Rulers could no longer govern without considering public opinion; constitutions would become the norm in the second half of the century. Nationalism, too, would become a permanent feature in European politics, one that rulers of nation-states and empires could no longer ignore. In the next chapter, we will turn to these nationalist movements.

KEY TERMS

Congress of Vienna (p. 650)

conservatism (p. 653)

romanticism (p. 653)

nationalism (p. 655)

liberalism (p. 658)

laissez faire (p. 658)

utilitarianism (p. 659)

socialism (p. 660)

Marxism (p. 661)

July Revolution (p. 663)

Great Reform Bill (p. 665)

Chartism (p. 667)

Decembrists (p. 669)

Frankfurt Assembly (p. 675)

Online Study Center
Improve Your Grade Flashcards

SUGGESTED READING

Broers, Michael. *Europe After Napoleon: Revolution, Reaction, and Romanticism, 1815–1848.* 1996. Evaluates the era from the point of view of the participants.

Harsin, Jill. *Barricades: The War on the Streets in Revolutionary Paris, 1830–1848.* 2002. An insightful account of how the optimism for reform in 1830 helped produce the disillusion and anger of 1848.

Hobsbawm, E. J. *The Age of Revolution, 1789–1848.* 1962. Presents compelling arguments that the era was dominated by two simultaneous revolutions, the French Revolution and the industrial transformation.

Johnson, Paul. *The Birth of the Modern World Society, 1815–1830.* 1991. A weighty but readable book providing a panoramic view of the era; includes biographical sketches of some of the major figures of the time.

Laven, David, and Lucy Riall, eds. *Napoleon's Legacy: Problems of Government in Restoration Europe.* 2000. Essays on the restoration experience in different European countries.

Sperber, Jonathan. *The European Revolutions, 1848–1851.* 1994. The best up-to-date synthesis, which includes some new emphases, such as the role of rural and religious discontent in shaping the revolts.

Wheen, Francis. *Karl Marx: A Life.* 2000. A lively biography that, in addition to discussing Marxian thought, emphasizes the man's personal life.

22

NATIONALISM AND POLITICAL REFORM, 1850–1880

Wilhelm I at Versailles
Wilhelm is proclaimed ruler of the German Empire, 1871. *(Bismarck Museum/akg-images)*

The ceremonial occasion depicted in the painting on the left is a monumental one for European and world history: the crowned heads of different German states, without the benefit of a parliament or popular vote, proclaim the unification of all their states under one nation. On the podium, standing just behind the newly declared kaiser, Wilhelm I, is Crown Prince Friedrich Wilhelm (later Kaiser Friedrich III). To the kaiser's left, with his arm upraised, is the grand duke of Baden. In the middle of the scene, resplendent in his white uniform, is Bismarck, the political architect of German unification. On the right nearby is Field Marshal Helmuth von Moltke (fon molt-KEH), the military genius who provided the series of military victories allowing Prussia to unify Germany under its aegis. The location of this ceremony also has profound symbolism as well as irony: four months after delivering a humiliating defeat to France, a unified Germany was proclaimed in the famed Hall of Mirrors in the grandiose palace of Versailles, the former seat of French kings and royal court.

Germany had become a united nation by war. In the generation after 1850 the contours of European politics changed—new states appeared on the map, and within their national borders a good number of states reformed their political institutions. To meet the demand for popular participation in government so forcefully expressed in 1848, every European state except the Ottoman and Russian Empires found it necessary to have a parliament. Rare before midcentury, such institutions became common thereafter. No longer was the demand for popular participation seen as a threat to the existing political and social order. In fact, popular participation, or the appearance of it, gave the existing order a legitimacy it had not enjoyed since before the French Revolution. Nationalism flourished during this period, emerging as a decisive force throughout the West—in European affairs as well as in the United States, where it promoted territorial expansion and fired a determination to preserve the Union.

These political transformations occurred in an era of unprecedented economic growth and prosperity. Industrial production expanded the economy; the discovery of gold in California in 1848 led to the expansion of credit (since currencies were backed by gold), which in turn led to the

KEY TERMS

Realpolitik	Compromise of 1867
congress system	Young Turks
risorgimento	*mir*
trasformismo	manifest destiny
Otto von Bismarck	Second Reform Bill
February Patent	Paris Commune

Online Study Center

This icon will direct you to interactive map and primary source activities on the website **college.hmco.com/pic/noble5e**

founding of new banks and mass investments in growing industries. The standard of living rose significantly in industrializing nations. Between 1850 and 1880 industrial production increased by 90 percent in Great Britain and by 50 percent in France. The middle classes expanded dramatically.

In the first half of the century, international relations had been dominated by the congress system, in which representatives of the major European states met periodically to refine and preserve the balance of power. This system collapsed in the second half of the century, as political leaders pursued the narrow nationalist interests of their respective states. Instead of negotiating with one another, a new generation of leaders employed brute military force—or the threat of its use—to resolve international conflicts. The new age was dominated not by ideals but by force, announced Bismarck, the main practitioner of what became known as *Realpolitik,* a policy in which war became a regular instrument of statecraft.

FOCUS QUESTIONS

How did the Crimean War affect international relations?

How did political leaders in Piedmont harness the forces of nationalism to achieve Italian national unity?

What events led to the unification of Germany and what was the character of the new German nation?

How did the Austrian, Ottoman, and Russian Empires deal with the challenges they faced?

How were the United States and Canada transformed during this period?

How did western European states create democracies?

THE CHANGING NATURE OF INTERNATIONAL RELATIONS

How did the Crimean War affect international relations?

The Crimean War and its aftermath shaped European international relations for several decades. Following the 1815 Congress of Vienna (see Chapter 21), European states attempted, through the **congress system,** to work out their differences by negotiation, avoiding situations in which one state triumphed at the cost of another. The Crimean War and subsequent realignments raised mutual suspicions, leading nations to act in their own self-interests and to ignore the concerns of the other major players in the international system. This reorientation facilitated the emergence of nation-states at the expense of traditional empires.

Realpolitik   Style of governing that uses all means, including war, to expand the influence and power of a state.

congress system   System of European international relations in the first half of the nineteenth century in which the major European states cooperated to preserve the balance of power.

THE CRIMEAN WAR, 1854–1856

The Crimean War had many causes. Principally, however, it had to do with Russia claiming the right to protect Orthodox Christians within the predominantly Muslim Ottoman Empire. This claim led to war between Russia and the Ottoman Empire in 1853, resulting in a Russian victory. The defeat of the Ottoman Empire made it more vulnerable to further Russian incursions.

British and French statesmen had considerable interest in the conflict. Britain had long feared that the collapse of the Ottoman Empire would lead Russia to seek territorial gains in the Mediterranean. Such a move would challenge Britain's naval supremacy in that region. An explosion of public sentiment against Russia's aggressiveness also obliged the British government to consider military action. Meanwhile, the French emperor, Napoleon III, believed that successful war against Russia would provide the opportunity to redraw European borders. He hoped that a new order would lead to increased French power and influence. Napoleon also imagined that fighting side by side with Britain could lay the foundation for Anglo-French friendship. And so England and France rushed to defend the Ottoman Empire and declared war on Russia in March 1854.

The war was poorly fought on all sides. Leadership was woefully inadequate, and five times more casualties resulted from disease than from enemy fire. Although the Russians had a standing army of a million men, their poor communications and supply systems prevented them from ever fielding more than a quarter of their forces. In Britain, the press and members of Parliament denounced their side's inadequate materiel and incompetent leadership. For the first time, the press played an active role in reporting war; the new technologies of the telegraph and photography brought to readers at home the gruesome realities of battle. One of the few heroic figures to emerge from this conflict was the English nurse Florence Nightingale (1820–1910), who organized a nursing service to care for the British sick and wounded. Later her wartime experience allowed her to pioneer nursing as a professional calling. (See the box "The Written Record: Florence Nightingale in the Crimean War.")

CHRONOLOGY

1851	Louis Napoleon's coup d'état
1854–1856	Crimean War
1860	Italy united under Piedmontese rule
1861	Great Reforms in Russia
1861–1865	U.S. Civil War
1862	Bismarck appointed minister president of Prussia
1864	Austria and Prussia attack Denmark and occupy Schleswig-Holstein
1866	Austro-Prussian War
	Abolition of estate system in Sweden
1867	Second Reform Bill in England
	North America Act creates Canadian federation
	Austro-Hungarian compromise
1870	Franco-Prussian War
	Rome, joined to Italy, becomes its capital
	Declaration of French Third Republic
1871	Unification of German Empire
	Paris Commune
1876	Bulgarian horrors
1878	Congress of Berlin

After almost two years of fighting in the Balkans and the Crimean peninsula, Russia abandoned the key fortress of Sevastopol in September 1855. Militarily defeated, the Russians also were alarmed at Austria's posture. Tsar Nicholas I had expected Austrian assistance in the war in return for his help in crushing the Hungarian rebellion in 1849. Instead, Austria's leaders not only withheld aid but even threatened to join the Western alliance.

The Crimean conflict killed three-quarters of a million people—more than any European war between the

Florence Nightingale

This photograph was taken in 1856, shortly after Nightingale returned to England from the Crimean War. Her privileged background provided the official connections that helped her nursing services succeed. *(Courtesy, Florence Nightingale Museum, St. Thomas' Hospital, London. Photo: London Metropolitan Archives)*

Crimean War
This photograph shows the interior of the Sevastopol fortress after it had been battered into surrender. The Crimean War was the first conflict to be documented by photographers. *(Courtesy of the Board of Trustees of the Victoria & Albert Museum)*

end of the Napoleonic Wars and World War I. It was a particularly futile, senseless war whose most important consequence was political: it unleashed dramatic new changes in the international order that allowed for the emergence of the new nation-states.

THE CONGRESS OF PARIS, 1856

The former combatants met in Paris in February 1856 to work out a peace treaty. Their decisions—which pleased no one—shaped relations among European states for the next half century. Russian statesmen were especially discontented, as their country was forbidden to have a fleet in the Black Sea. Nor did French leaders feel that their nation had benefited, other than the prestige of holding the congress in Paris. The north Italian state of Piedmont, which had joined the allies, only gained a vague statement about the unsatisfactory nature of Italy's existing situation. Prussia was invited to attend the congress only as an afterthought and hence also felt slighted.

Although the war seemed to have sustained the integrity of the Ottoman Empire, the peace settlement weakened it indirectly by dictating reforms in the treatment of its Christian populations. These reforms impaired the empire's ability to repress the growing nationalist movements in the Balkans. British political leaders, galled by the heavy sacrifices of the war, moved toward isolationism in foreign policy. Austrian policymakers had hoped Britain and France would aid them in preserving the Habsburg empire; instead, these powers, angry that Austria had not helped in the war, offered no assistance—a stance that would further weaken Habsburg imperial hegemony. At the time the peace treaty was signed, few people foresaw the enormous results that would flow from it.

By and large, the decisions reached in Paris would be disregarded or unilaterally revised as competition and rivalry between the major powers destabilized the international system. This new international climate also allowed new states to take shape without international sanction.

THE WRITTEN RECORD

FLORENCE NIGHTINGALE IN THE CRIMEAN WAR

Florence Nightingale used her influential family connections to win an appointment to the Crimean battlefield. Once there, she organized nursing for the wounded and was able to secure additional personnel and medical supplies for her hospital. Women were supposed to be sheltered from the harsh realities of the outside world, but as this letter indicates, Nightingale was not spared war in its cruelest aspects.

We have no room for corpses in the wards. The Surgeons pass on to the next, an excision of the shoulder-joint—beautifully performed and going on well—[cannon] ball lodged just in the head of the joint, and fracture starred all round. The next poor fellow has two stumps for arms—and the next has lost an arm and leg. As for the balls, they go in where they like, and do as much harm as they can in passing. That is the only rule they have. The next case has one eye put out, and paralysis of the iris of the other. He can neither see nor understand. But all who can walk come into us for Tobacco, but I tell them that we have not a bit to put into our own mouths. Not a sponge, nor a rag of linen, not anything have I left. Everything is gone to make slings and stump pillows and shirts. These poor fellows have not had a clean shirt nor been washed for two months before they came here, and the state in which they arrive from the transport is literally crawl-ing. I hope in a few days we shall establish a little cleanliness. But we have not a basin nor a towel nor a bit of soap nor a broom—I have ordered 300 scrubbing brushes. But one half the Barrack is so sadly out of repair that it is impossible to use a drop of water on the stone floors, which are all laid upon rotten wood, and would give our men fever in no time. . . .

I am getting a screen now for the Amputations, for when one poor fellow, who is to be amputated tomorrow, sees his comrade today die under the knife it makes an impression—and diminishes his chance. But, anyway, among these exhausted frames the mortality of the operations is frightful.

QUESTIONS

1. How did Florence Nightingale's presence on the Crimean battlefield defy Victorian middle-class gender roles? How did it reaffirm them?

2. What does her description convey about the impact that modern technology had on warfare by 1854?

Source: Letter to Dr. William Bowman, November 14, 1854, in *"I Have Done My Duty": Florence Nightingale in the Crimean War, 1854–56,* ed. Sue M. Goldie (Iowa City: University of Iowa Press, 1987), pp. 37–38.

S E C T I O N   S U M M A R Y

- The Crimean War of 1854–1856 marked the end the spirit of cooperation that had resulted from the Congress of Vienna in 1815.

- The Crimean War was caused by the Russian defeat of the Ottomans in 1853, British fear of Russian influence in the Mediterranean, and Napoleon III's desire to increase French influence.

- The 1856 Congress of Paris humiliated Russia and restricted its military access to the Black Sea. The postwar settlement dictated reforms in the treatment of Christians in the Ottoman Empire, which, in turn, impaired the Ottoman ability to repress nationalist movements in the Balkans.

ITALIAN UNIFICATION, 1859–1870

How did political leaders in Piedmont harness the forces of nationalism to achieve Italian national unity?

n Metternich's memorable phrase, Italy at midcentury was nothing but a "geographic expression." The revolution of 1848 (see pages 671–677) had revealed an interest in national unification, but the attempt had failed. Within a dozen years, however, what many believed to be impossible would come to pass. Idealists such as Giuseppe Mazzini (see page 655) had preached that Italy would be unified not by its rulers but by its people, who would rise and establish a free republic. Instead, the deed was done by royalty, by war, and with the help of a foreign state. Although ideals were not absent from the process of unification, cynical manipulation and scheming also came into play.

Since the late eighteenth century, some Italians had been calling for a *risorgimento* (ree-sor-djee-MEN-toe), a political and cultural renewal of Italy. By the mid-nineteenth century, the idea was actively supported by a small, elite group consisting of the educated middle class, urban property owners, and members of the professions. For merchants, industrialists, and professionals, a unified state would provide a larger stage on which to pursue their ambitions.

CAVOUR PLOTS UNIFICATION

After the failed 1848 revolution, most Italian rulers resorted to repression. Only the northern Italian kingdom of Piedmont kept the liberal constitution adopted during the 1848 revolution, and it welcomed political refugees from other Italian states. Not only politically but economically, it was a beacon to the rest of Italy, establishing modern banks and laying half the rail lines on the peninsula.

The statesman who was to catapult Piedmont into a position of leadership in the dramatic events leading to Italian unification was Count Camillo di Cavour (1810–1861). The son of a Piedmontese nobleman and high government official, he grew up speaking French, the language of the royal court and formal education in Piedmont, and mastered Italian only as an adult. Cosmopolitan in his interests, Cavour knew more about Britain and France than about Italy. He was sympathetic to the aspirations of the middle class and saw in Britain and France models of what Italy ought to become, a liberal and economically advanced society.

Short, fat, and nearsighted, Cavour hardly cut a heroic figure. Yet he was ambitious, hard-working, and driven to succeed. A well-known journalist and the editor of the newspaper *Risorgimento*, he joined the government in 1850. Two years later King Victor Emmanuel appointed him prime minister. Cavour shared the enthusiasm of the middle classes for an Italian nation, but his vision did not include the entire Italian peninsula, only its north and center, which then could dominate the rest of Italy in a loose federation. Unifying the north and center would first require ousting Austria from the northern provinces. The failures of 1848 had taught Cavour that this task would require foreign help, especially French assistance.

When the Crimean War broke out in 1854, Cavour steered Piedmont to the allied side, hoping to advance his cause. He sent twenty thousand troops to the Crimea,

one-tenth of whom died. This act gained him a seat at the Congress of Paris, where his presence boosted the kingdom's prestige—and where he and Napoleon III had an opportunity to meet and size up each other.

Napoleon III favored the cause of Italian liberation from Austrian rule and some form of unification of the peninsula. Austria had been France's traditional opponent; destroying Austria's power in Italy might strengthen France. Thus in July 1858 the French emperor and the Piedmontese prime minister met secretly at Plombières (plom-bee-YAIR), a French spa, to discuss how Italian unity could be achieved. They agreed that Piedmont would stir up trouble in one of Austria's Italian territories in an effort to goad the Austrians into war. France would help the Piedmontese expel Austria from the northern provinces of Lombardy and Venetia, and the new Piedmont, doubled in size, would become part of a confederation under the papacy. In exchange, the French emperor demanded the Piedmontese provinces of Nice and Savoy, which bordered France.

War between Austria and Piedmont broke out in April 1859. By June the combined Piedmontese and French forces had routed the Austrians at Magenta and Solferino (see **MAP 22.1**). So bloody were these battles that the color magenta was named after the deep red of the soaked battlefield. The horrors of this war also inspired the founding of the Red Cross.

Shocked by the bloodshed he had witnessed, Napoleon III decided to end the fighting instead of pressing on. Prussian mobilization on behalf of Austria also alarmed him. In addition, his plan for Italy began to unravel. Several states in central Italy expressed a desire to be annexed to Piedmont, which would have resulted in an independent state much larger than Napoleon III had anticipated. These factors led him to betray Cavour; he made an agreement with the Austrians, which gave Lombardy to Piedmont, but allowed Venetia to remain within the Austrian Empire.

UNIFICATION ACHIEVED, 1860

Napoleon's betrayal outraged Cavour, but unexpected events in the south also changed his vision of national unification. The centuries-old misgovernment of the kingdom of Naples led to an uprising in Sicily in April 1860. The revolutionary firebrand Giuseppe Garibaldi (1807–1882), a rival of Cavour, set sail for Sicily in May 1860 with but a thousand poorly armed, red-shirted followers to help the island overthrow its Bourbon ruler. Winning that struggle, Garibaldi's forces crossed to the mainland in August. Victory followed victory, and enthusiasm for Garibaldi grew. His army swelled to 57,000 men, and he won the entire kingdom of Naples.

Threatened by the advance of Garibaldi's power and fearing its reach into the Papal States, Cavour sent his army into the area in September 1860. Although

risorgimento Italian term, beginning in the late eighteenth century, for the political and cultural renewal of Italy. It later came to be associated with Italian unification.

MAP 22.1 The Unification of Italy, 1859–1870

Piedmontese leadership under Cavour in the north, and nationalist fervor inspired by Garibaldi in the south, united Italy.

Garibaldi was a republican, he was convinced that Italy could best achieve unity under the king of Piedmont, and he willingly submitted the southern part of Italy, which he controlled, to the king, Victor Emmanuel II (r. 1849–1878). Thus by November 1860 Italy had been united under Piedmontese rule (see Map 22.1). The territories that had come under Piedmont's control affirmed their desire to be part of the new Italy through plebiscites based on universal male suffrage. The 1848 constitution of Piedmont became the constitution of the newly united Italy. Cavour lived to relish his handiwork for only a few months, as he died of an undiagnosed illness in May 1861. His last words were "Italy is made—all is safe."

Still to be joined to the new state were Austrian-held Venetia in the northeast and Rome and its environs, held

Garibaldi Leading His "Red Shirts" to Victory over the Neapolitan Army, May 1860

Garibaldi's conquests in the south and Cavour's in the north opened the way for Italian unification. *(Museo di Risorgimento, Milan/Scala/Art Resource, NY)*

by the pope with the support of a French garrison. But within a decade, a favorable international situation enabled the fledgling country to acquire both key areas. Upon its defeat in the Austro-Prussian War in 1866, Austria ceded Venetia to Italy. Then the Franco-Prussian War forced the French to evacuate Rome, which they had occupied since 1849. Rome was joined to Italy and became its capital in 1870. With that event unification was complete.

THE PROBLEMS OF A UNIFIED ITALY

National unity had been achieved, but it was frail. The uprisings that Garibaldi had led in the south were motivated more by hatred of the Bourbons than by fervor for national unification. And once the union was achieved, the north behaved like a conquering state—sending its officials to the south, raising taxes, and imposing its laws. In 1861, rebellion broke out among disbanded Neapolitan soldiers and brigands. Civil war ensued for five years, producing more casualties than the entire effort of unification.

Other major divisions remained. In 1861 only 2.5 percent of the population spoke the national language, Florentine Italian. Economics also divided the country. The north was far more industrialized than the rural south. In the south child mortality was higher, life expectancy was lower, and illiteracy was close to 90 percent. The two regions seemed to belong to two different nations. Piedmont imposed strong central control, resolutely refusing a federal system of government, which many Italians in an earlier era had hoped for. This choice reflected Piedmont's fear that any other form of government might lead to disintegration of the new state. Piedmont wanted to save the new Italian state from a fate similar to that of the United States, whose federal system of government led to secessionism and the Civil War in early 1861 (see page 700).

Piedmont imposed its constitution on unified Italy, which limited suffrage to men of property and education—less than 2 percent of the population. Further, as prime minister, Cavour created and manipulated parliamentary majorities in favor of his cabinet, reversing the logic behind the parliamentary system in which cabinets were supposed to represent, and answer to, freely elected legislative bodies. He cajoled and bribed parliamentarians, transforming previous foes into supporters. This system of manipulation, known as *trasformismo* (trass-for-MEES-mo), would characterize Italian government for the next several decades. Nevertheless, the new unified Italy was a liberal state that guaranteed legal equality and freedom of association, and provided more freedom for its citizens than the Italian people had seen for centuries.

The Catholic Church remained hostile to the new Italian state. The popes, left to rule a tiny domain—a few square blocks around the papal palace known as the Vatican—considered themselves prisoners. They denounced anyone who participated in elections. Thus many Italian Catholics refused to recognize the new state for decades, thwarting its legitimacy. With its 27 million people in 1870, Italy was the sixth most populous European nation. It was too small to be a great power and too large to accept being a small state. Italian statesmen found it difficult to define their country's role in international politics, and they lacked a firm consensus on Italy's future.

SECTION SUMMARY

- As prime minister of the northern Italian kingdom of Piedmont, Cavour plotted with Napoleon III to wage war against Austria so that he could unify northern and central Italy.

- Napoleon, betraying Cavour, ended the war before the Austrians were completely expelled from northern Italy.

- When rebellion broke out in the south, Giuseppe Garibaldi and his army overthrew the kingdom of Naples and then willingly submitted the southern part of Italy to Piedmont. Complete unification was achieved by 1870.

- The newly unified Italy was a liberal state that guaranteed freedom and equality; but stark economic and cultural differences between north and south, opposition of the Catholic Church, and the imposition of central control from Piedmont made national unity frail.

GERMAN UNIFICATION, 1850–1871

What events led to the unification of Germany and what was the character of the new German nation?

Like Italy, Germany had long been a collection of states. Since 1815 the thirty-eight German states had been loosely organized in the German Confederation. Like Piedmont in Italy, one German state, powerful Prussia, led the unification movement. And just as Italy had in Cavour a strong leader who imposed his will, so did German unification have a ruthless and cunning champion: **Otto von Bismarck,** minister president of Prussia. But whereas Cavour, for all his wiliness, was committed to establishing a liberal state, Bismarck was wedded to autocratic rule.

The revolutionaries of 1848 had failed in their attempt to achieve German unification when the king of Prussia refused to accept a throne offered by the elected Frankfurt Assembly. As the painting at the beginning of this chapter illustrates, German unification was ratified not by the ballot, as it was in Italy, but by the acclamation of the crowned heads of Germany. The nation was united by the use of military force and the imposition of Prussian absolutism over the whole country.

THE RISE OF BISMARCK

Austria under Metternich had always treated Prussia as a privileged junior partner. After Metternich's fall in 1848, however, rivalry erupted between the two German states. Each tried to manipulate for its own benefit the desire for national unity that had become manifest during the revolution of 1848.

In March 1850 representatives from a number of German states met to consider unification under Prussian sponsorship. Austria opposed such a union and, with Russian support, threatened war. Since the

---

trasformismo System of political manipulation used by Count Camillo di Cavour (1810–1861), Piedmont's prime minister, to create majorities in parliament to support his cabinet.

Otto von Bismarck Nineteenth-century German statesman who, through a series of aggressive wars, united Germany. Germany became the dominant power in Europe under his administration.

Prussian military was not strong enough to challenge Austria, Prussia agreed to abandon the plan for unification and to accept Austrian leadership in Germany. But a decade later, the new Prussian king, Wilhelm I (r. 1861–1888), was determined to strengthen Prussia by expanding the size and effectiveness of the army. The parliament, however, refused to approve funding for a military build-up. The conflict was not simply about the budget; it was an issue of who should govern the country—the king or the elected representatives. To get his way, the king appointed Count Otto von Bismarck as minister president.

Bismarck was a Junker, a Prussian aristocrat known for his reactionary views, who had opposed the liberal movement in 1848. As Prussian emissary to the German Confederation, he had challenged Austrian primacy. Devoted to his monarch, Bismarck sought to heighten Prussian power in Germany and throughout Europe. He faced down the parliament, telling the Budget Commission in 1862, "The position of Prussia in Germany will be decided not by its liberalism but by its power . . . not through speeches and majority decisions are the great questions of the day decided—that was the mistake of 1848 and 1849—but by iron and blood."[1]

Bismarck tried to win over the liberals by suggesting that with military force at its disposal, Prussia could lead German unification. But the liberals continued to resist, and the parliament voted against the military reforms. Unfazed, Bismarck carried out the military measures anyway and ordered the collection of the necessary taxes. The citizens acquiesced and paid to upgrade their army. Prussia would not yield to parliamentarism as Britain had.

German liberals faced a dilemma: which did they value more—the goal of nationhood or the principles of liberty? Fellow liberals elsewhere lived in existing nation-states in which statehood had preceded the development of liberalism. In Italy unification had been led by the liberal state of Piedmont. That was not the case in Germany, where the natural leader, Prussia, had a long tradition of militarism and authoritarianism. To oppose Bismarck effectively, German liberals knew they would have to join with the working classes, but they feared the workers and forestalled such an alliance. Germany appeared embarked on an illiberal course.

Bismarck ingeniously exploited the weakness of the liberals and the growing desire for German unification. During the Franco-Austrian War of 1859, which launched Italian unification, Germans had feared that the French would attack across the Rhine River. Many came to believe that only a strong, united Germany could give its inhabitants security. Prussia had already led the important move toward economic unification with the *Zollverein*, a customs union that included most German states, but excluded Austria. Founded in 1834, the customs union had become more extensive with the passage of time; even states that were politically hostile to Prussia joined the union to protect their economic interests. Economic unity led to all-German professional and cultural associations that surpassed state boundaries; it was an indispensable stage in the process toward political unity. By 1860, the idea of a united Germany had gained a substantial appeal.

PRUSSIAN WARS AND GERMAN UNITY

Having built up the military and established the supremacy of royal power in Prussia, Bismarck was ready to enlarge its role in Germany—and he believed that war against Austria was the only means to do so. Conflicts over the provinces of Schleswig (SHLES-vik) and Holstein (HOLL-shteyn) served as a pretext (see **MAP 22.2**). In 1864, Prussia and Austria had successfully gone to war against Denmark to secure the independence of these two German-speaking provinces. Bismarck then used disputes over their joint administration as an excuse for war against Austria. Prussia attacked Austrian-administered Holstein in June 1866, launching the Austro-Prussian War. After a scant seven weeks, the newly reformed Prussian army won a decisive victory in the Battle of Sadowa (SAH-doe-wah). Prussia's industrial superiority had enabled it to equip its soldiers with the new breech-loading rifles. These "needle guns" allowed troops to fire from a prone position, while the Austrians, with their muzzle loaders, had to stand up to shoot. With military victory, Prussia annexed its smaller neighbors, which had supported Austria. In Bismarck's scheme this enlarged Prussia would dominate the newly formed North German Confederation, comprising all the states north of the Main (MINE) River. From now on, Austria was excluded from German affairs.

The triumph of Sadowa made Bismarck a popular hero. Elections held on the day of the battle returned a conservative pro-Bismarck majority to the Prussian parliament. The legislature, including a large number of liberals mesmerized by the military victory, voted to legalize retroactively the illegal taxes that had been levied since 1862 to upgrade the military. In compromising their principles, liberals rationalized that national unity ought to be gained first, with liberal constitutional institutions secured later. Their optimism proved to be a miscalculation.

The unification of Germany, like that of Italy, was facilitated by a favorable international situation. The Crimean War had estranged Russia from Austria, once allies. Although it would have been opportune for France to intervene on the Austrian side, the French emperor had been lulled into inaction by vague Prussian promises of support for French plans to annex Luxembourg. Once the war was won, Bismarck reneged on these promises. France was left with the problem of a strong,

MAP 22.2   The Unification of Germany, 1866–1871

A series of military victories made it possible for Prussia to unite the German states under its domain.

Legend:
- Prussia before 1866
- Conquered by Prussia in Austro-Prussian War, 1866
- Austrian territories excluded from North German Confederation, 1867
- Joined with Prussia to form North German Confederation, 1867
- South German states joining with Prussia to form German Empire, 1871
- Won by Prussia in Franco-Prussian War, 1871

✕ Major battles
— German Confederation boundary, 1815–1866
— Bismarck's German Empire, 1871

Online Study Center **Improve Your Grade** Interactive Map: The Unification of Germany, 1866–1871

enlarged Prussia on its eastern border, which threatened France's position as a Great Power. British leaders likewise did not intervene in the unification process. Disillusioned by the results of the Crimean War, they were in an isolationist mood. Moreover, Britain's government was sympathetic to the rise of a fellow Protestant power.

Bismarck's design was almost complete. Only the southern German states remained outside the North German Confederation. He obliged them to sign a military treaty with Prussia and established a customs parliament for all the members of the Zollverein (the customs union), including the southern German states. The southern states, which were Catholic and sympathetic to Austria, were reluctant to see German unity advance any further. Only some dramatic event could remove their resistance.

THE FRANCO-PRUSSIAN WAR AND UNIFICATION, 1870–1871

French leaders were also determined to prevent German unity. Moreover, since the mid-seventeenth century, French security had relied on a weak and divided Germany.

Both Berlin and Paris anticipated war, which came soon enough, precipitated by a crisis over the Spanish succession. In 1868 a military coup had overthrown the Spanish queen Isabella, and the provisional government offered the throne to a Catholic member of the Hohenzollerns (HO-en-tsoll-ernz), the reigning Prussian monarch's family. The French viewed this candidacy as an unacceptable expansion of Prussian power and influence. Fearing a two-front war with Prussia in the east and Spain in the south, they insisted that the Hohenzollerns refuse the proffered throne. As passions heated, Bismarck was elated at the prospect of war, but King Wilhelm was not. On July 12, 1870, Wilhelm engineered the withdrawal of the young prince's candidacy for the Spanish throne, removing the cause for war. Bismarck was bitterly disappointed.

Not content with this diplomatic victory, the French pushed their luck further. On July 13 the French ambassador met the king of Prussia at Ems and demanded guarantees that no Hohenzollern would ever again be a candidate for the Spanish throne. Unable to provide any more concessions without a serious loss of prestige, the Prussian king refused the French petition.

Wilhelm telegraphed an account of his meeting to Bismarck. The chancellor immediately seized the opportunity this message provided. He edited what became known as the Ems dispatch, making the exchange between king and ambassador seem more curt than it actually had been; then he released it to the press. As he hoped, the French interpreted the report as a deliberate snub to their ambassador and overreacted. Napoleon III was deluged with emotional demands that he avenge the imagined slight to French national honor. On July 15 he declared war.

The Prussians led a well-planned campaign. An army of 384,000 Prussians was rushed by rail to confront a force of 270,000 Frenchmen. The French had the advantage of better rifles, but the Prussians were equipped with heavier cannon, which could pulverize French positions from a distance. Within a few weeks Prussia won a decisive victory at Sedan (seh-DAEN), taking the French emperor prisoner on September 2. The French continued the struggle, despite difficult odds. Infuriated by the continuation of the war, the Prussians resorted to extreme measures. They took hostages and burned down whole villages, and then laid siege to Paris, starving and bombarding its beleaguered population.

Throughout Germany the outbreak of the war aroused general enthusiasm for the Prussian cause. Exploiting this popular feeling, Bismarck called on leaders of the southern German states to accept the unification of Germany under the Prussian king. Reluctant princes, such as the king of Bavaria, were bought off with bribes. On January 18, 1871, the German princes met in the Hall of Mirrors at the palace of Versailles, symbol of past French greatness. There they acclaimed the Prussian king as Kaiser Wilhelm I, German emperor.

In May 1871 the Treaty of Frankfurt established the peace terms (see Map 22.1). France was forced to give up the industrially rich provinces of Alsace and Lorraine and to pay Germany a heavy indemnity of five billion francs. These harsh terms embittered the French, leading many to desire revenge and establishing a formidable barrier to future Franco-German relations.

THE CHARACTER OF THE NEW GERMANY

German unity had been won through a series of wars—against Denmark in 1864, Austria in 1866, and France in 1870. The military had played a key role in forging German unity, and it remained a dominant force in the new nation. Italian unity had been sanctioned by plebiscites and a vote by an elected assembly accepting the popular verdict. The founding act of the new German state, as the opening illustration to this chapter shows, was the acclamation of the German emperor by German rulers on the soil of a defeated neighbor. Thus the rulers placed themselves above elected assemblies and popular sanction.

On the surface, the constitution of the new Germany was remarkably democratic. It provided for an upper, appointed house, the *Bundesrat* (BOON-tes-raht), representing the individual German states, and a lower house, the *Reichstag* (RYSH-stak), which was elected by universal manhood suffrage. The latter might seem a surprising concession from Bismarck, the authoritarian aristocrat. But he knew the liberals lacked mass support and had confidence that he would be able to create majorities that could be manipulated for his purposes.

The authoritarianism of Prussia was projected onto all of Germany. The king of Prussia occupied the post of emperor, and the chancellor and other cabinet members were responsible only to him, and not to parliament. Only the emperor could make foreign policy and war, command the army, and interpret the constitution.

The emergence of a strong, united Germany shattered the European balance of power. In February 1871 the British political leader Benjamin Disraeli observed that the unification of Germany was a "greater political event than the French revolution of last century. . . . There is not a diplomatic tradition which has not been swept away. You have a new world. . . . The balance of power has been entirely destroyed."[2] Germany had become the dominant power on the Continent.

━━━━━ S E C T I O N   S U M M A R Y ━━━━━

- German unity resulted from a series of wars—against Denmark in 1864, Austria in 1866, and France in 1870.

- Under the leadership of Otto von Bismarck, Prussia reformed and expanded its army, leading to victory in war. To build up the army, Bismarck levied taxes and recruited troops without the approval of parliament.

- The Zollverein, a customs union that included most German states, but excluded Austria, helped

advance support for national unification under Prussia.

- Despite a liberal constitution that granted universal manhood suffrage, Prussian authoritarianism dominated Germany.

- With unification, Germany became the dominant power on the Continent, shattering the European balance of power.

PRECARIOUS EMPIRES

How did the Austrian, Ottoman, and Russian Empires deal with the challenges they faced?

The three large empires of central and eastern Europe, battered by aggressive behavior from other European states and challenged by internal tensions, attempted to weather the endless crises they confronted. The Austrian, Ottoman, and Russian Empires labored to fortify their regimes with political reforms, but only Austria tried to accommodate democratic impulses by establishing a parliament. The Ottoman sultans and the Russian tsars clung tenaciously to their autocratic traditions.

THE DUAL MONARCHY IN AUSTRIA-HUNGARY

Emperor Franz Joseph (r. 1848–1916) had come to the Austrian throne as an 18-year-old in that year of crisis, 1848. He was a well-meaning monarch who took his duties seriously. His upbringing was German, he lived in German-speaking Vienna, and he headed an army and a bureaucracy that was mostly German. But Franz Joseph was markedly cosmopolitan. He spoke several of his subjects' languages and thought of himself as the emperor of all his peoples. A much-loved, regal figure, Franz Joseph provided a visible symbol of the state. He lacked imagination, however, and did little more than try to conserve a disintegrating empire coping with the modern forces of liberalism and nationalism.

After the war with Piedmont and France (see page 686), Austrian statesmen sensed the vulnerability of their empire. To give the government credibility, in February 1861 Franz Joseph issued what became known as the **February Patent,** which guaranteed civil

liberties and provided for local self-government and a parliament elected by eligible males.

The need to safeguard the remaining territories was clear. By 1866 the Austrian Habsburgs were no longer a German or an Italian power (Venetia had been handed over to a united Italy). The strongest challenge to Habsburg rule came from Hungary, where the Magyars insisted on self-rule, a claim based on age-old rights and Vienna's initial acceptance of autonomy in 1848. Since Magyar cooperation was crucial for the well-being of the Habsburg empire, the government entered into lengthy negotiations with Magyar leaders in 1867. The outcome was the **Compromise of 1867.** The agreement divided the Habsburg holdings into Austria in the west and Hungary in the east (see **MAP 22.3**). Each was independent, but they were linked by the person of the emperor of Austria, Franz Joseph, who was also king of Hungary. Hungary had full internal autonomy and participated jointly in imperial affairs—state finance, defense, and foreign relations. The new state created in 1867 was known as the dual monarchy of Austria-Hungary.

Online Study Center **Improve Your Grade**
Primary Source: The Dual Monarchy Is Born: The Austro-Hungarian Augleich

The compromise confirmed Magyar dominance in Hungary. Although numerically a minority, the Magyars controlled the Hungarian parliament, the army, the bureaucracy, and other state institutions. They opposed self-rule of other ethnic groups in the kingdom who spoke different languages: the Croats, Serbs,

February Patent   Enactment issued in 1861 by the Austrian emperor Franz Joseph that established a constitutional monarchy in the old Austrian Empire.

Compromise of 1867   Agreement that divided the Habsburg empire into Austria in the west and Hungary in the east, a dual monarchy under Emperor Franz Joseph called Austria-Hungary.

RUSSIA

GALICIA

POLAND

SILESIA

MORAVIA

Prague

BOHEMIA

GERMAN
STATES

BAVARIA

Vienna

AUSTRIA

SALZBURG

TYROL

SWITZERLAND

CARINTHIA

LOMBARDY

VENETIA

Po

ITALIAN
STATES

Adriatic Sea

Budapest

HUNGARY

Tisza

TRANSYLVANIA

ROMANIA

OTTOMAN   EMPIRE

Danube

Danube

CROATIA-SLAVONIA

BOSNIA
Sarajevo

ILLYRIA

SERBIA

100 Mi.

100 Km.

50

50

0

0

Germans

Hungarians

Italians

Romanians

Poles

Czechs

Carpatho-Ukrainians
(Ruthenians)

Serbs and Croats

Slovaks

Slovenes

Habsburg Monarchy
boundaries

Kingdom of Hungary
boundaries

MAP 22.3   Austria-Hungary in 1878

The Compromise of 1867 produced the dual monarchy of Austria-Hungary. A state of many languages and ethnicities, the Austro-Hungarian Empire occupied Bosnia in 1878, bringing more dissatisfied peoples under its rule. Tensions in the Balkans would lead to the outbreak of world war in 1914.

Slovaks, Romanians. They also attempted a policy of Magyarization—teaching only Magyar in the schools, conducting all government business in Magyar, and giving access to government positions only to those fully assimilated in Magyar culture. This arrangement created frustrations and resistance among the various nationalities under their rule.

The terms of the compromise also gave the Hungarians a voice in imperial foreign policy. The Magyars feared that Slavic groups outside the empire, who planned to form independent states or had already done so, would inspire fellow Slavs in Austria-Hungary to revolt. To prevent that, the Hungarians favored an expansionist foreign policy in the Balkans, which the monarchy embraced (see Map 22.3). Having lost its influence in Germany, Austria-Hungary saw the Balkans as an area in which it could assert itself. The policy was fraught with risks and, by bringing more discontented Slavs into the empire, led to hostilities with other states.

THE AILING OTTOMAN EMPIRE

At midcentury the Ottoman Empire was still one of the largest European powers, but it faced unrest within its borders and threats from the expansionist designs of its neighbors. The ailing empire was commonly referred to as "the sick man of Europe." Over the next twenty-five years the empire shed some of its territory and modernized its government, but nothing could save it from decline in the face of nationalist uprisings in its Balkan possessions.

Western-Style Reform   As early as the 1840s, the Ottoman Empire had begun various reform movements to bring more security to its subjects. Emulating Western institutions, the reforms introduced security of property, equity in taxation, and equality before the law regardless of religion. Government officials—who previously had been free to collect taxes arbitrarily, sending the required amount to the central government and keeping the rest—were given fixed salaries and subjected to regular inspections.

These reforms were strengthened after the Crimean War by further imperial edicts. Many young intellectu-

als were impatient with the pace of change, however, and critical of the sultan. Unable freely to express their opinions at home, some went into exile in Paris and London in the late 1860s. Their hosts called them the **Young Turks,** an expression that became synonymous with activists for change and improvement.

The failure to hold on to its empire caused further dissatisfaction with Ottoman rule among its people, and in the spring of 1876 rioters demanded and won the establishment of constitutional government. Within a year, however, the new sultan, Abdul Hamid II (r. 1876–1909), dismissed the constitutional government and reverted to personal rule. Part of the administration's problem was financial. The easy terms of foreign credit lured the sultan into taking out huge loans to finance extravagant projects. In spite of drought and famine, the authorities raised taxes to pay debts, fostering widespread discontent.

Balkan Nationalism   Nationalist fervor further intensified opposition to the government. The central administration had lost control over its provincial officials, who were often corrupt and tyrannical. Christians, the majority population in the Balkans, blamed their suffering on Islamic rule, and many were inspired by the 1821 Greek war of independence and the revolutions of 1848 to seek their own independence.

The Romanians, who lived mainly in the adjoining provinces of Moldavia in the north and Wallachia (vall-AK-yah) in the south, began to express nationalist sentiments in the late eighteenth century. These sentiments were nurtured by Western-educated students, who claimed for their countrymen illustrious descent from Roman settlers of antiquity. News of the 1848 revolution in Paris helped trigger a revolt in both provinces by those demanding unification and independence. This uprising was quickly crushed by the Turks.

Upon Russia's defeat in the Crimean War, the Congress of Paris in 1856 removed Russia's right of protection over Moldavia and Wallachia and provided for a referendum to determine their future. In 1859 the two provinces chose a local military officer, Alexander Cuza (r. 1859–1866), as the ruler of each territory. In 1862 the Ottoman Empire recognized the union of the two principalities in the single, autonomous state of Romania. The Congress of Berlin in 1878 recognized Romania's full independence. Thus, in less than a quarter century, two provinces of the Ottoman Empire had gained full sovereignty.

The path to independence was much more violent for the Bulgarians. Revolutionary committees—

Young Turks   Young intellectuals who wanted to transform the Ottoman Empire into a more modern, Westernized state. The expression has subsequently come to designate any group of activists pushing for political change.

encouraged by Serbia and Russia—spread propaganda and agitated against Ottoman rule. An uprising in Bulgaria broke out in May 1876. The Christian rebels attacked not only symbols of Ottoman authority but also peaceable Muslim Turks living in their midst. The imperial army, aided by local Turkish volunteers, quickly re-established Ottoman authority. Incensed by the massacre of fellow Muslims, the volunteers resorted to mass killing, looting, and burning of Christian villages. The "Bulgarian horrors" shocked Europe and made the continuation of Turkish rule unacceptable.

Russia, which saw itself as the protector of the Slavic peoples, reacted to the Bulgarian horrors by declaring war on the Ottoman Empire in April 1877. At first progress was slow; then the Russians broke through the Turkish lines and forced the sultan to sue for peace. The resulting Treaty of San Stefano, signed in March 1878, created a huge, independent Bulgaria as essentially a Russian protectorate.

Nationalistic Uprising in Bulgaria

In this 1879 lithograph, Bulgaria is depicted in the form of a maiden—protected by the Russian eagle, breaking her chains, and winning liberty from the Ottoman Empire. *(St. Cyril and Methodius National Library, Sofia)*

The Congress of Berlin, 1878   The British, Austrians, and French were shocked at the extent to which the San Stefano treaty favored Russia. Under their pressure, the European Great Powers met in Berlin in 1878 to reconsider the treaty and re-establish a balance of power. The Congress of Berlin returned part of the Bulgarian territory to the Ottomans. It also removed Bosnia and Herzegovina from Ottoman rule. Henceforth Austria-Hungary administered these provinces (see Map 24.4 on page 765). The sultan was forced to acknowledge the legal independence of Serbia, Montenegro, and Romania and the autonomy of Bulgaria.

Thus Turkey was plundered not only by its enemies but also by powers that had intervened on its behalf. When France complained that it received no compensation, it was given the chance to grab Tunisia, another land under Ottoman rule. Russia was given the Bessarabian provinces that Romania had acquired in 1856. The devious work of the Congress of Berlin reflected the power politics that now characterized international affairs. Statesmen shamelessly used force against both foe and friend for the aggrandizement of their own states. Neither morality nor international law restrained ambition. While the Great Powers attempted to appease one another to maintain peace in the short run, the settlement of 1878 led to further instability in the Balkans, which ultimately became the principal cause of the First World War.

RUSSIA AND THE GREAT REFORMS

Russia's defeat in the Crimean War and its distrust of the Western powers forced the tsar to consider ways of strengthening Russia by restructuring its institutions. Beginning in 1861, a series of measures known collectively as the Great Reforms began to change the face of Russia.

The Abolition of Serfdom   Already by the 1840s concern about the archaic nature and structure of Russian government was mounting. Many officials lamented the tendency of a timid bureaucracy to lie to and mislead the public. Defeat in the Crimean War widened the critique of Russian institutions. The chief problem that needed resolution was serfdom. Educated opinion had long denounced serfdom as immoral, but it also presented clear disadvantages in both the domestic and international domains.

Serfdom held Russia back in its competition with the rest of the world. Defeat in the Crimean War by Britain and France suggested that soldiers with a stake in their society fought harder than men bound to lifetime servitude. In addition, the victorious Western states had won in part because their industrial might translated into more and better guns, ammunition, and transportation. Industrial progress required a mobile labor force, not one tied to the soil by serfdom.

A Critique of Russian Serfdom

The French artist Gustave Doré reveals how landowners inhumanely viewed their serfs as mere property that could be won and lost with a draw of the cards.

(Miriam and Ira D. Wallach Division of Art, Prints and Photographs, The New York Public Library, Astor, Lenox and Tilden Foundations/Art Resource, NY)

With a free labor force, rural populations, as in the West, could become the abundant labor supply that drove industrial production. Many educated Russians felt that the defeat in the Crimea had revealed Russia's general backwardness. To catch up with the West, they argued, Russia needed to shed its timeworn institutions, particularly serfdom.

The new tsar, Alexander II (r. 1855–1881), feared that if serfdom were not abolished from above, it would be overthrown by a serf rebellion that would destroy the aristocracy itself. In April 1861 he issued a decree freeing the serfs. With one stroke of a pen, he emancipated 22 million people from a system that allowed them to be bought and sold, separated from their families, and treated in the cruelest ways imaginable. Emancipation represented a compromise with the gentry, who had reluctantly agreed to liberate its serfs. They nonetheless insisted on compensation. As a result, the newly liberated peasants had to reimburse the government with mortgage payments lasting fifty years. The peasants received some land, but its value was vastly overrated and its quantity insufficient for peasant families. To make ends meet, most freed peasants continued working for their former masters.

The local commune, or *mir* (also the name of the Russian space station first launched in 1986), handled the mortgage payments and taxes that the central government imposed on the peasants. The mir (MEER) determined how the land was to be used, and it paid collectively for the mortgages and taxes on the land. As a consequence, the commune was reluctant for the peasants to leave the land, and they could do so only with its permission. Freed from serfdom, the peasants still suffered many constraints. In fact, the emancipation declaration was accompanied by massive peasant uprisings that had to be put down by force.

Online Study Center **Improve Your Grade**
Primary Source: Post-Emancipation Problems for Russian Peasants

The tsar and his advisers feared the large mass of uneducated peasants as a potential source of anarchy and rebellion. They depended on the mir to preserve control even though the commune system had some inherent economic disadvantages. Since increased productivity benefited the commune as much as the

mir Russian peasant commune. After Tsar Alexander II freed the serfs in 1861, the mir determined land use and paid the government mortgages and taxes.

individual peasant, there was little incentive for peasants to improve their land, and agricultural yields remained low. The mir system of organization also, however, helped promote the collective consciousness that later contributed to peasant revolutionary mentality.

Alexander remained wedded to the principles of autocracy. His aim in abolishing serfdom and introducing other reforms was to modernize and strengthen Russia and stabilize his divinely mandated rule. Like most Russians, Alexander believed that only the firm hand of autocracy could hold together a large, ethnically diverse country. The peasant uprisings that accompanied emancipation only confirmed his beliefs. Clearly, however, the sudden freedom of 22 million illiterate peasants threatened to overwhelm existing institutions, and some changes had to be made. Although he surrendered no powers, Alexander did institute a number of reforms, altering the government and the judicial and military systems so they could deal more effectively with the totally remodeled Russian society.

Government Reform Government reform had paramount importance. Between 1800 and 1850 the Russian population had increased from 36 million to 59 million, and administering this vast country had become more and more difficult. Overcentralized, with a poorly trained civil service, the government was unable to cope effectively with the problems of its people. Emancipation of the serfs greatly exacerbated this situation. To address these problems, an 1864 law created village or regional governments, or *zemstvos* (SEMST-vose), which gave Russians the authority and the opportunity to use initiative in local matters.

The zemstvos were largely controlled by the gentry and not particularly democratic. They were forbidden to debate political issues, and their decisions could be overridden or ignored by local officials appointed by the tsar. Some hoped that zemstvos could become the basis for self-government at the national level and looked for the creation of an all-Russian zemstvo, but the tsar firmly

squelched such hopes. He jealously continued to insist and depend on an undivided and undiminished autocracy. Nonetheless, the zemstvos were a viable attempt to modernize an overburdened central government and created an important precedent for self-government.

The tsar also created an independent judiciary that ensured equality before the law, public jury trials, and uniform sentences. Russian political leaders recognized that growth in commerce and industry required public confidence in the judiciary and the rule of law. Businessmen would no longer fear arbitrary intervention by capricious officials and could develop enterprises in greater security.

In addition, censorship of the press was abolished. Under the previous tsar, Nicholas I, all ideas that did not conform to government policy were censored. Such censorship prevented the central government from being well informed about public opinion or about the effects of its policies on the country. Under Alexander openness in the press was viewed as a remedy for corruption and misuse of power.

Reform also extended to the Russian army. Its structure and methods became more Western. Military service, previously limited to peasants, became the obligation of all Russian men, who submitted to a lottery. Those with an "unlucky" number entered the service. In an effort to make military service more attractive, the length of service was drastically cut and corporal punishment was abolished. Access to the officer corps was to be by merit rather than by social connection. The Ministry of War also improved the system of reserves, enabling Russia to mobilize a larger army with more modern weapons in case of war.

The Great Reforms represented considerable change for Russia. They abolished serfdom, created local self-government, established the rule of law, and made army service more humane. But above the change, the tsarist regime remained autocratic and repressive, flexible only to the degree that its rulers had the will and wisdom to be.

═══ S E C T I O N   S U M M A R Y ═══

- Internal tensions and aggressive behavior of the European powers, as well as nationalist aspirations in the Balkan provinces, forced the Austrian, Ottoman, and Russian Empires to reform.

- Loss of the Italian territories and Magyar desire for self-rule in Hungary resulted in the Compromise of 1867, which divided Habsburg territories into the dual monarchy of Austria-Hungary.

- The Ottoman Empire became weakened by nationalist uprisings in its Balkan possessions, making it prey to Western imperialistic ambitions.

- The Congress of Berlin in 1878 reduced Russia's influence in Bulgaria. It also became the occasion for a feeding frenzy on the ailing Ottoman Empire. Territorial shifts such as the transfer of Bosnia and Herzegovina to Austrian administration created conditions for further instability and war in the Balkans.

- Russia undertook a series of reforms beginning in 1861: the abolition of serfdom, establishment of local governments, equality before the law, abolition of press censorship, and improvements in military service.

MAP 22.4 U.S. Expansion Through 1853

In just eight years, from 1845 to 1853, the United States increased its territory by a third. The principle of manifest destiny appeared to be fulfilled, as the United States now stretched from the Atlantic to the Pacific.

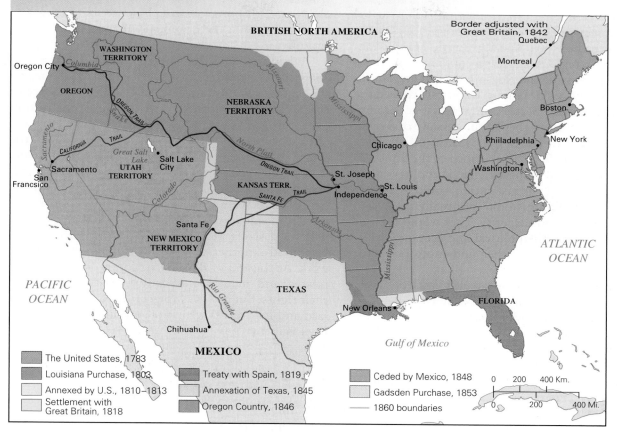

THE EMERGENCE OF NEW POLITICAL FORMS IN THE UNITED STATES AND CANADA, 1840–1880

How were the United States and Canada transformed during this period?

Across the sea, a new power emerged in these years, the United States. It enlarged its territories, strengthened its national government, and broadened its democracy by including a large category of people previously excluded from the political process—African Americans. But these achievements were the result of the bloodiest conflict in U.S. history, the Civil War.

TERRITORIAL EXPANSION AND SLAVERY

In the early years of its existence, the United States was confined to the land east of the Mississippi River, but in the nineteenth century it gained much territory through westward expansion (see **MAP 22.4**). In 1803 President Thomas Jefferson secured the Louisiana Pur-

chase from the French, which nearly doubled the size of the United States. In 1819 Florida was acquired from Spain. Some Americans looked even farther west and began to insist that the United States had a **manifest destiny** to occupy the whole North American continent from coast to coast.

The U.S. government used the settlements of American citizens in Mexican- and British-held territories as pretexts for expansion. In 1845 Congress voted to annex Texas, which had gained independence from Mexico in 1836. As a result of negotiation with Britain,

> **manifest destiny** Coined in 1845 for the belief that the United States was destined to occupy the North American continent from coast to coast. It justified war with Mexico and the U.S. acquisition of California and the Southwest.

the United States in 1846 acquired the Oregon Country south of the forty-ninth parallel. Declaring war on Mexico that same year, and quickly winning, the United States added California and the Southwest in 1848. Manifest destiny or not, the United States now spanned the continent from the Atlantic to the Pacific.

Serious sectional clashes began in the 1820s, especially between the North and the South. Many issues divided the two regions, notably a conflict between the industrial interests of the North and the agrarian interests of the South. The issue of slavery sharpened the divide. As the United States annexed new territories, the question of whether they would be slave or free divided the nation. The North opposed the extension of the "peculiar institution," while much of the South favored it. Southerners believed that if the new areas were closed to slavery, the institution would weaken in the South; slaveholding would eventually disappear, and with it Southern prosperity. They would then be unable to withstand the political and economic pressure of an economically richer and more populous North.

Americans passionately debated the issue of slavery for decades. In November 1860 Illinois Republican Abraham Lincoln (1809–1865) was elected president in a highly contested four-way race. Lincoln opposed the spread of slavery beyond its existing borders and hence appeared to threaten its future in the South. For many Southerners his election to the highest office was the final straw.

Beginning in December 1860, most Southern state legislatures voted to secede from the Union, forming in February 1861 the Confederate States of America. The South defined its cause as defending states' rights, claiming that the people of each state had the right to determine their destiny, free from what they viewed as the tyranny of the national government. The Southern states seized federal funds and property, and in April 1861 the Confederates bombarded federally held Fort Sumter, South Carolina. Lincoln was determined to preserve the Union and to put down the insurrection. The long-dreaded Civil War had begun.

CIVIL WAR AND NATIONAL UNITY, 1861–1865

The North had many advantages. It had nearly three times as many people as the South, a strong industrial base that could supply an endless stream of weapons, and a far more extensive rail system for transporting men and materiel to the front. Although blue and gray armies clashed in a number of important military engagements, the North effectively blockaded the South, leading it, toward the end of the war, to be desperately short of men, money, and supplies.

During the war, Lincoln's government took measures that centralized power in Washington, changing the nation from a loose federation of states to a more centrally governed entity. The federal government intruded into areas of life from which it had before been absent, establishing, for example, national banking and railroad systems. The word *national* came into increasing use.

When the main Confederate army surrendered in 1865, the principle of state sovereignty, proclaimed by the South, was roundly defeated. With the passage of the Thirteenth Amendment to the U.S. Constitution the same year, slaves, previously considered property, were declared to be free. The North occupied the South in an attempt to "reconstruct" it. Reconstruction included efforts to root out the Confederate leadership and ensure full civil and political rights for the newly emancipated African Americans. The government also embarked on a short-lived campaign to provide freed slaves with enough land to ensure them a livelihood—another example of federal authority at work. At the end of Reconstruction, federal power retreated and many states denied African Americans their rights. But certainly the nation was more centralized and its citizens were more enfranchised after the Civil War than before.

THE CREATION OF A CANADIAN NATION

Just north of the United States, in Canada, some similar processes unfolded during the 1800s that also resulted in a larger, freer, and more centralized society. Though Canada was spared a civil war, a popular uprising did occur as citizens chafed under the oligarchical grip of British colonial rule, in which authority was in the hands of a few families. Lord Durham, the new governor, suggested in 1839 a series of reforms (see page 666) that in the end were implemented, uniting Upper and Lower Canada and providing for an elected assembly and a government responsible to it. The British North America Act in 1867 created a federal system of government, with each province exercising considerable autonomy. With the purchase of the Northwest Territories from the private Hudson's Bay Company in 1869 and the gradual attachment of other provinces, Canada gained in size. By 1871 the country stretched from the Maritime Provinces in the east to the Pacific Ocean in the west (see **MAP 22.5**). The building of a transcontinental railroad in the 1880s helped unite the huge nation. By the end of the nineteenth century, Canada was virtually self-governing, having full control over all its affairs, except for defense and foreign affairs.

MAP 22.5 Dominion of Canada, 1873

By 1873 Canada had become a vast nation with the addition of the western territories. Like the United States, Canada reached from the Atlantic to the Pacific.

=== S E C T I O N   S U M M A R Y ===

- Through war and land purchases, by 1848 the United States spanned the North American continent.

- The United States experienced a civil war between North and South from 1861 to 1865, resulting in the abolition of slavery and an extension of federal powers at the expense of states' rights.

- By 1871 Canada also spanned the continent from east to west. The British North America Act of 1867 created a federal system of government that gave significant autonomy to each province, yet maintained Canada's unity as a nation.

THE DEVELOPMENT OF WESTERN DEMOCRACIES

How did western European states create democracies?

In the generation after 1850 Britain, France, and several smaller states in northern Europe made major strides forward in creating democratic political systems and cultures. Although universal manhood suffrage had been instituted only in France, all these countries' governments were responsible to elected representatives of the voters. Lincoln had spoken of the United States enjoying "government of the people, by the people, for the people." As a result of a series of political reforms, many European countries took up the process of attaining these goals.

VICTORIAN BRITAIN

The mid-nineteenth century was a period of exceptional wealth and security for Britain, as the population as a whole began to share in the economic benefits of industrialization. Britain enjoyed both social and political peace. The political system was not challenged as it had been in the generation after the Napoleonic Wars. A self-assured, even smug, elite—merchants, industrialists, and landowners—developed a political system reflecting liberal values.

A JAPANESE VIEW OF THE BRITISH PARLIAMENT

In 1862 the Japanese government sent its first diplomatic mission to Europe. Accompanying the delegation was a young translator, Fukuzawa Yukichi (1835–1901). Intrigued by what he saw and eager to interest his fellow Japanese in the West, Fukuzawa published several books. In fact, all books about the West in Japan came to be known as "Fukuzawa-bon." Toward the end of his life, in his Autobiography, *he described how, while in London, he had tried to understand the workings of the British Parliament.*

Of political situations at that time, I tried to learn as much as I could from various persons that I met in London . . . though it was often difficult to understand things clearly as I was as yet unfamiliar with the history of Europe. . . . A perplexing institution was representative government. When I asked a gentleman what the "election law" was and what kind of an institution the Parliament really was, he simply replied with a smile, meaning I suppose that no intelligent person was expected to ask such questions. But these were the things most difficult of all for me to understand. In this connection, I learned that there were different political parties—the Liberal and the Conservative—who were always "fighting" against each other in the government.

For some time it was beyond my comprehension to understand what they were "fighting" for, and what was meant, anyway, by "fighting" in peace time. "This man and that man are 'enemies' in the House," they would tell me. But these "enemies" were to be seen at the same table, eating and drinking with each other. I felt as if I could not make much out of this. It took me a long time, with some tedious thinking, before I could gather a general notion of these separate mysterious facts. In some of the more complicated matters, I might achieve an understanding five or ten days after they were explained to me. But all in all, I learned much from this initial tour of Europe.

QUESTIONS

1. Why might the Japanese visitor have been puzzled by the use of the words *fighting* and *enemies* in this context?

2. Would Japanese readers have obtained a good idea of the British parliamentary system based on this report?

Source: The Autobiography of Fukuzawa Yukichi, trans. Eiichi Kiyooka (Tokyo: Hokuseida Press, 1948), pp. 138, 143–144.

Although suffrage was still restricted to propertied Christian men before the 1850s, the parliamentary system was firmly established, with government clearly responsible to the electorate. The importance of Parliament was symbolized by the new building in which it met, finished in 1850 and of unprecedented splendor and size. The form of government developed in its halls after midcentury aroused the curiosity and envy of much of the world. (See the box "The Global Record: A Japanese View of the British Parliament.")

In the twenty years after 1846 five different political parties vied for power. Depending on the issue, parties and factions coalesced to support particular policies. After 1867, however, a clear two-party system emerged: Liberal and Conservative (Tory), both with strong leadership. This development gave the electorate a distinct choice. The Conservatives were committed to preserving traditional institutions and practices, whereas the Liberals were more open to change.

Two strong-minded individuals headed these parties and dominated British political life for over a generation: William E. Gladstone (1809–1898), a Liberal, and Benjamin Disraeli (1804–1881), a Conservative. Gladstone came from a family of industrialists and married into the aristocracy; Disraeli was the son of a Jewish man of letters who had converted to Christianity. His father's conversion made his career possible—before the 1850s Jews were barred from Parliament. Both Gladstone and Disraeli were master debaters; Parliament and the press hung on their every word. Each was capable of making speeches lasting five hours or more and of conducting debates that kept the house in session until 4:00 A.M. The rivalry between the two men thrilled the nation and made politics a popular pastime.

The Conservatives' electoral base came from the landed classes, from Anglicans, and from England, rather than the rest of the United Kingdom (consisting of Scotland, Wales, and Ireland). The Liberals' base came from the middle classes, from Christian groups other than the Church of England, and from Scotland and Wales. In the House of Commons both parties had a large number of members from the landed aristocracy, but cabinet members were increasingly chosen for political competence rather than family background. Aristocratic birth was no longer a requirement for reaching the pinnacle of power, as Gladstone and Disraeli so clearly illustrated.

Disraeli and Gladstone: Victorian Political Rivals

This 1868 cartoon from *Punch* magazine captures the politicians' personalities. Disraeli was known as vain and theatrical, while Gladstone was dour and moralistic. *(Mary Evans Picture Library)*

The competition for power between the Liberals and the Conservatives led to an extension of suffrage in 1867. The **Second Reform Bill** lowered property qualifications for the vote, thus extending it from 1.4 million to 2.5 million people out of a population of 22 million. The bill also equalized electoral districts, which gave new urban areas better representation. Although some in Parliament feared that these changes would lead to the masses capturing political power—"a leap into the dark," one member called it—in fact no radical change ensued. Extending the vote to clerks, artisans, and other skilled workers made them feel more a part of society and thus bolstered the existing system rather than undermining it. John Stuart Mill, then a member of Parliament, along with his colleague and wife, Harriet Taylor Mill (1807–1856), championed the cause of women's suffrage, but he had few allies in Parliament, and that effort failed.

Second Reform Bill   British legislation that extended suffrage to clerks, artisans, and other skilled workers by lowering property qualifications.

As the extension of voting rights increased the size of the electorate, parties became larger and stronger. Strong party systems meant alternation of power between the Liberals and the Conservatives. With an obvious majority and minority party, the monarch could no longer play favorites in choosing a prime minister. The leader of the majority party had to be asked to form a government. Thus even though Queen Victoria (r. 1837–1901) detested Gladstone, she had to ask him to form governments when the Liberals won parliamentary elections. (See the feature "The Visual Record: An Engraving of the British Royal Family.")

The creation of a broad-based electorate also meant that politicians had to make clear appeals to the public and its interests. In the past, oratory had been limited to the halls of Parliament, but after the electoral reforms, it occurred in the public arena as well. Public election campaigns became part of the political scene in Britain as they increasingly had to appeal to the common man. The adoption of the secret ballot in 1872 protected lower-class voters from intimidation by their employers, landowners, or other social superiors. In 1874 the first two working-class members of Parliament were elected, sitting as Liberals. Although their victory represented a very modest gain for workers' representation, it presaged the increasingly democratic turn England was to take.

FRANCE: FROM EMPIRE TO REPUBLIC

France took a more tumultuous path to parliamentary democracy than Britain. Revolutions and wars overthrew existing political systems and inaugurated new ones. Each time the French seemed to have democracy within reach, the opportunity slipped away.

The constitution of the Second French Republic provided for a single four-year presidential term. Frustrated by this limitation of power, Louis Napoleon engineered a coup d'état in 1851 to extend his presidency to a ten-year term. The following year he called for a plebiscite to confirm him as Napoleon III (r. 1852–1870), emperor of the French. Both of these moves were resisted in the countryside, particularly in the south, but massive repression defeated all opposition.

In the rest of the country huge majorities of voters endorsed first the prolonged presidency and then the imperial title. The new emperor seemed different from his predecessors. He believed in the principle of popular sovereignty (he maintained universal male suffrage, introduced in 1848), he did not pretend to reign by divine right, and he repeatedly tested his right to rule by an appeal to the popular vote. He seemed to combine order and authority with the promises of the Revolution—equality before the law, careers open to talent, and the abolition of hereditary rights.

An Engraving of the British Royal Family

This illustration of the British royal family might have been that of any upper-middle-class family. Queen Victoria is plainly dressed; her husband, Prince Albert, wears a dark business suit; the children are clothed in simple outfits. The simplicity conveyed by the family extends to the image of the rest of England, depicted as a quaint farm with a grouping of common people. Notice the crown hovering over this idyllic pastoral scene.

Illustrations of this type familiarized the British with their monarch. Surrounded by her husband and children, the queen focuses her gaze not on the viewer—a British subject—but on her children. It is her husband, the prince, who, protective of his family, gazes outward. In the past, representations of the monarchy had suggested power and intimidation. The aura of the close-knit, nuclear royal family suggested a serenity that was reassuring to British subjects. It also offered a model for the family and gender very much like those to which middle-class families aspired.

Victoria cultivated the image of herself as contented mother, but in reality she resented much about motherhood. She complained of the extent to which her pregnancies interfered with her daily routines and prevented her from traveling and from being with her beloved Albert. She lamented, "I think our sex a most unenviable one." She described childbearing as an "annoyance" that made her feel "so pinned down—one's wings clipped." She also refused to romanticize birthing, seeing it as an animal-like act that reduced a woman to "a cow or a dog." For the births of her seventh and eighth children, she resorted to the uncommon practice of using chloroform to alleviate the pain of labor—the first public figure to do so openly. Even after their infancy, Victoria continued to describe her children as "an awful plague and anxiety" who showed no gratitude. But such views were expressed privately, and the public never suspected Victoria's ambivalence about motherhood.

Despite her complaints, the highly moral image of Victoria's family life contrasted with that of her predecessors. Her grandfather George III (r. 1760–1820) had been plagued with bouts of insanity. Her uncle George IV (r. 1820–1830) was a notorious philanderer. George IV and his brothers, the duke of Clarence (later to be William IV [r. 1830–1837]) and the duke of Kent (Victoria's father), were bigamists. They fathered a large brood of children out of wedlock and were implicated in numerous public scandals.

Public outrage at the excesses of Victoria's predecessors had produced a call to abolish the institution of monarchy. Given the disrepute into which the monarchy had fallen and the rise of republican sentiment, the crowning of a woman in 1837 may have substantially lessened antimonarchical sentiment. Victoria, as a young, seemingly frail woman coming to the throne at age 18, lent a certain gallantry to the royal household. Moreover, as a female monarch, she was seen as less of a threat to constitutional liberties.

The image of Victoria shown here intentionally contrasts her reign with those of her predecessors. The simple terms in which she and her family are depicted appealed to the growing middle class of the second half of the nineteenth century. The portrayal also fit the emerging democratic spirit—and electoral power—of the lower classes. Henceforth, monarchs would not be able to ignore public opinion. This image marks a historical departure in other ways. Victoria is surrounded by four of her children (eventually she would have nine). Her royal predecessors had died without leaving any legitimate direct heirs, thus endangering the regular succession to the throne. This engraving sent the message that the royal line was assured. British people wary of a female ruler could find solace, not only from her husband's confident gaze outward, but in knowing that Victoria would be succeeded by one of her sons.

Unlike Victoria's uncles and father who were wastrels and bankrupts, the queen and her husband lived frugally by royal standards and conducted an exemplary family life. Royal wealth increased under Prince Albert's careful administration. Instead of being subject to various debtors, the British royal house became one of the wealthiest and most prominent landowners in Great Britain. It is most telling that by the time of her death in 1901, Victoria had considerably strengthened the institution of monarchy, having restored confidence in and respect for it.

Under Victoria's rule, Britain completed the process of becoming a constitutional monarchy.

ILLUSTRATED BOOK OF BRITISH SONG.

Illustration from the *Illustrated Book of British Song*

The queen cultivated the image of being above politics and a symbol of national unity. Fellow monarchs in central and eastern Europe exercised greater power, but after World War I they were all toppled. In Britain, monarchy in its constitutional form endured. Victoria established a pattern of public and private behavior by which members of subsequent generations of the British royal family were to be judged. This portrayal of the royal family also suggests the important role that visual imagery played in creating public support for state power in the nineteenth century.

QUESTIONS

1. Why did it make sense for the British royal family to have itself portrayed so simplistically? What values does this engraving communicate to British subjects?

2. How does this engraving exemplify the importance of visual imagery in conveying the meaning of monarchy to British subjects?

Online Study Center
Improve Your Grade Visual Record Activities

Most Frenchmen, including urban workers and peasants, generally enjoyed better living standards as a result of economic growth in the 1850s and 1860s. Louis Napoleon, in his youth the author of a book on pauperism, introduced measures congenial to labor. Workers won limited rights to strike, and labor unions were virtually legalized. The emperor expressed his desire to improve the workers' lot, and the government initiated a few concrete measures, such as providing some public housing. Although slum clearance during the rebuilding of Paris drove many from their homes to the outskirts of the city, it did provide healthier conditions for those who stayed behind, and the ambitious urban projects provided work for many (see page 723). Other public works projects, such as ports, roads, railroads, and monumental public buildings, also created jobs. Railroad mileage in France increased tenfold, enabling peasants to market their harvests more widely. If some peasants had initially opposed Louis Napoleon, most supported him once he was in power. Not only were they a cautious group, preferring stable authority, but they saw in the emperor—the heir to the great Napoleon—an incarnation of national glory.

Not all the French supported the emperor; many republicans could not forget that he had usurped the constitution of 1848. In protest, some had gone into exile, including the poet Victor Hugo. In an attempt to win over the opposition, Napoleon made some concessions in 1860, easing censorship and making his government more accountable to the parliament. But instead of winning him new support, liberalization allowed the expression of mounting opposition.

A number of issues—including opposition to policies of free trade, widespread hostility toward the influence of the Catholic Church, and the desire for more extensive freedom of expression and assembly—helped forge a republican alliance of the middle classes and workers. This alliance was strongest in the large cities and in some southern regions notorious for their opposition to central government control. Republicanism was better organized than in earlier years and had a more explicit program. Moreover, its proponents were now better prepared to take over the government, if the opportunity arose.

By 1869 the regime of Napoleon III, which declared itself a "liberal empire," had evolved into a constitutional monarchy, responsible to the parliament. In a plebiscite in May 1870, Frenchmen supported the liberal empire by a vote of five to one. It might have endured had Napoleon III not rashly declared war against Prussia two months later in a huff over the supposedly insulting Ems dispatch (see page 692). Rapid defeat at the hands of Bismarck brought down the empire. In September, at news of the emperor's capture, the republican opposition in the parliament declared a republic. It continued the war but had to sign an armistice in January 1871.

The leader of the new government was an old prime minister of Louis Philippe, Adolphe Thiers (tee-YAIR) (1797–1877). Before signing a definitive peace, the provisional government held elections. The liberals, known as republicans since they favored a republic, were identified with continuing the war; the conservatives, mostly royalists, favored peace. Mainly because of their position on this issue, the royalists won a majority from a country discouraged by defeat.

The new regime had no time to establish itself before a workers' uprising in the spring of 1871 shook France, while reminding the rest of Europe of revolutionary dangers. The uprising was called the **Paris Commune**—a name referring to the municipal government that harked back to 1792 to 1794, when the Paris crowds had dictated to the national government. The Commune insisted on its right to local rule. Radicals and conservatives greeted the Commune as a workers' revolt intended to establish a workers' government. Marx described it as the "bold champion of the emancipation of labor." Women took an active part, fighting on the barricades, pouring scalding water on soldiers, posting revolutionary broadsides. Louise Michel (1830–1905) was a schoolteacher who became famous for her leadership in active fighting and for her agitation for socialism and women's rights.

Online Study Center **Improve Your Grade**
Primary Source: An Eyewitness Account of the Paris Commune

Although labor discontent played a role in the Paris Commune, other forces also contributed, notably the earlier Prussian siege of Paris during the Franco-Prussian War. Paris had become radicalized during the siege: the rich had evacuated the city, leaving a power vacuum quickly filled by the lower classes. Parisians suffered much because of the siege, and angered that their economic needs went unmet and their courage against the Prussians unnoticed, they rose up against the new French government. Food was the paramount issue sparking the massive women's participation in the uprising. The Commune, composed largely of artisans, now governed the city.

In March 1871 the Commune declared itself free to carry out policies independent of the central government, temporarily located in Versailles. Its goals were quite moderate: it sought free universal education, a fairer taxation system, a minimum wage, and disestablishment of the official Catholic Church. But this was too radical for the conservative French government, which sent in the army. It suppressed the Commune,

Paris Commune Parisian workers' uprising intended to establish a workers' government under home rule. It was violently suppressed by the army of the conservative French government.

massacring 25,000 people, arresting 40,000, and deporting several thousand more.

The crushing of the Paris Commune and some of its sister communes in southern France, which had also asserted local autonomy, signified the increasing power of centralized government. One mark of the emerging modern state was its capacity to squelch popular revolts that, in the past, had constituted serious threats. Western Europe would not again witness a popular uprising of this magnitude.

Despite its brutality, the suppression of the Commune reassured many Frenchmen. The question now at hand was what form the new government would take. The monarchist majority in the democratically elected parliament offered the throne to the Bourbon pretender. However, he insisted he would become king only if the *tricouleur*—the blue, white, and red flag of the Revolution, which long since had become a cherished national symbol—were discarded and replaced by the white flag of the house of Bourbon. This was unacceptable, so France remained a republic. The republic, as Thiers put it, "is the regime which divides us the least."

By 1875 the parliament had approved a set of basic laws that became the constitution of the Third Republic. Ironically, a monarchist parliament had created a liberal, democratic parliamentary regime. A century after the French Revolution, the republican system of government in France was firmly launched.

SCANDINAVIA AND THE LOW COUNTRIES

France and especially Britain served as models of parliamentary democracy for the smaller states in northern Europe. Denmark, Sweden, Norway, Holland, and Belgium recast their political institutions at midcentury. Several of the states were affected by the revolutions of 1848. That year Denmark saw a peaceful protest demanding enlarged political participation (see page 676), Sweden saw minor riots, and the king of the Netherlands (after 1830 Holland and the Netherlands refer to the same country) feared that his country would be affected by revolution as in the neighboring German states. In Copenhagen King Frederick VII (r. 1848–1863), who had no stomach for a confrontation, yielded and accepted a constitution providing for parliamentary government. "Now I can sleep as long as I like," he is reputed to have said.

Sweden's parliamentary system, established in the Middle Ages, had representation by estates—noble, clergy, burgher, and peasant. The 11,000 nobles were given the same weight as the 2.5 million to 3 million peasants. After the riots of 1848 liberal aristocrats recognized that abolition of the estates system would best preserve their privileges, removing the major issue that had provoked popular resentments. With some delays, this conviction was finally carried out in 1866. The estates were replaced by a parliament with two houses. The upper house was restricted to the wealthiest landowners and the lower house to men of property, providing the vote to 20 percent of adult men. Although the king was not constitutionally obligated to choose a government reflecting parliamentary currents, he usually did so in an effort to avoid conflict.

Norway had been joined to Sweden in 1814 under the Swedish king, but it had a separate parliament and made its own laws. Swedish rule rankled the Norwegians, however, and in the 1850s the Norwegian Liberal Party began to insist that the king should not have the final word in governance. Instead, they argued, the parliament, representative of the Norwegian people, should be supreme. In 1883 the principle that government officials are responsible to parliament won out. In 1905 Norway peacefully separated from Sweden and became an independent state.

In the Netherlands, as a result of the revolutions of 1848, the king recognized the need to strengthen support for his crown by acceding to liberals' demands for parliamentary government. By midcentury, government officials in the Netherlands were responsible to the parliament rather than to the king. A new constitution guaranteed the principles of freedom of speech, assembly, and religion.

Belgium had enjoyed a liberal constitution from the time it became an independent state after its revolution in 1830, but because no strong party system materialized, the king was able to appoint to government whomever he pleased. In the 1840s the liberals organized, and the king, reluctantly, had to invite them to govern in 1848. The new government reduced property qualifications for voting, thus increasing the electorate. Contrary to the conservative backlashes that rescinded reform following the revolutions of 1848 elsewhere, the sweeping reforms in northern European states became the basis for their evolution into full democracies. For full democracy to take hold, the electorate had to be broadened. These years witnessed much agitation for universal male suffrage. Property qualifications, wherever they were instituted, were questioned and resisted. For instance, in Sweden the stipulation that a man had to earn 800 crowns a year to be a voter unleashed a pamphlet war: What if a man earned only 799 crowns? Did that make him less qualified? What if a man qualified one year but, through no fault of his own—for instance, because of a natural disaster—did not earn that much the following year? Should he then be barred from voting? In the 1880s Belgium saw a mass movement in favor of universal suffrage. The letters "SU," standing for universal suffrage in French, became emblematic of the masses' hope for a better life. Although suffrage still remained limited in these countries, it was only a matter of time before democracy would be achieved.

═══ S E C T I O N S U M M A R Y ═══

- By the late 1860s, a two-party system emerged in Britain: Conservative (Tory) and Liberal.

- The Second Reform Bill (1867) in Britain extended the vote and equalized voting districts, giving significantly more representation to urban areas.

- War and revolution continued to shape France's path to democracy. The French Second Republic, born of revolution, gave way to the authoritarian rule of Louis Napoleon, who became Napoleon III in 1852.

- The Franco-Prussian War of 1870–1871 ended the Second Empire of Napoleon III and gave birth to the French Third Republic.

- France and Britain provided both positive and negative models for change in northern Europe. Denmark, Sweden, Norway, the Netherlands, and Belgium peacefully established governments responsible to parliaments rather than to their kings, providing the basis for their evolution toward full democracies.

CHAPTER SUMMARY

Online Study Center **ACE the Test**

How did the Crimean War affect international relations?

How did political leaders in Piedmont harness the forces of nationalism to achieve Italian national unity?

What events led to the unification of Germany and what was the character of the new German nation?

How did the Austrian, Ottoman, and Russian Empires deal with the challenges they faced?

How were the United States and Canada transformed during this period?

How did western European states create democracies?

iberal nationalists in the early nineteenth century had believed that Europe would be freer and more peaceful if each people had a separate nation, if the power between those nations could be balanced. The Crimean War proved them wrong. The Great Powers became rival states in pursuit of their own self-interests, largely at the expense of the Ottoman Empire. The postwar peace settlement impaired Ottoman efforts to repress nationalist movements in the Balkans.

The Crimean War and its aftermath also created an international climate that permitted the emergence of two newly unified nation-states, Italy and Germany. In the case of Italy, unification occurred through the leadership of Cavour in Piedmont. After waging war against Austria to acquire the northern provinces (with partial success), Cavour brought the revolutionary national movement of the south, led by Garibaldi, under the centralized control of Piedmont. Plebiscites and an elected assembly sanctioned Italian unification.

Germany, through a series of wars, became unified under the authoritarian, centralized control of Prussia. Bismarck annexed the northern German states after defeating Austria. After Prussia's victory in war against France, Bismarck was able to press the southern states into unity with the north. This process lent the German state, even with parliamentary rule, an authoritarian and militaristic character. The rulers of the German states accepted unification by acclamation rather than through consent from the German people.

The Austrian and Ottoman Empires faced the daunting challenges of nationalistic movements seeking to break away from their rule. In the effort to keep their empires intact, rulers offered various reforms from above, modeled on the West; but at the same time they attempted to exert centralized rule to suppress breakaway movements. Austria compromised by establishing a dual monarchy with Hungary. But the empire then turned its aggressive ambitions toward the Balkans in order to exert control over Slavic people. These ambitions further challenged the Ottoman Empire, already weakened by defeat in war against Russia in 1853. The 1856 Congress of Paris and subsequent Balkan wars led to the creation of the independent and sovereign states of Romania and Bulgaria, formerly Ottoman provinces.

Russia, considering itself a protector of Slavic peoples, took advantage of the Ottoman Empire's weakness to wage war against it, further fueling Balkan nationalism and extending its influence there. In the face of its own domestic ills, Russia instituted major reforms on a Western model; nonetheless it remained autocratic, repressive, and inflexible.

Canada and the United States also faced challenges in the effort to govern vast expanses of territory with divergent regional needs under the auspices of representative government. The crisis of the American Civil War restored a federal government, albeit with tightened central control, and at the same time extended political participation. Canada more peacefully achieved a federalized government that permitted provincial autonomy and fostered democracy.

Britain, France, and several northern European states became increasingly democratic, answerable to a growing electorate. Britain successfully and peacefully extended suffrage and maintained its monarchy. In France the crushing of the Paris Commune spelled doom for those who wanted a nation of decentralized self-governing units. Indeed, strong, centralized governments increasingly became the norm. In other states, parliaments had only limited powers; but once they were in place, they gradually gained more power and expanded the electorate. Parliaments gave governments the appearance of legitimacy through the consent of their peoples. Hence all European rulers, except those of the Ottoman and Russian Empires, found it necessary to have a parliament.

LOOKING AHEAD

Two major changes that liberals had agitated for in 1848 had become a reality: freer political institutions and the organization of nation-states. Although neither of these changes was fully implemented everywhere, both appeared to have been generally established. Many Europeans—at least those who embraced these ideals as progress—could easily believe that they were living in an age of optimism.

KEY TERMS

Realpolitik (p. 682)

congress system (p. 682)

risorgimento (p. 686)

trasformismo (p. 689)

Otto von Bismarck (p. 689)

February Patent (p. 693)

Compromise of 1867 (p. 693)

Young Turks (p. 695)

mir (p. 697)

manifest destiny (p. 699)

Second Reform Bill (p. 703)

Paris Commune (p. 706)

Online Study Center
Improve Your Grade Flashcards

SUGGESTED READING

Alter, Peter. *The German Question and Europe: A History.* 2000. Explains the international context within which German unity was possible and its impact on European diplomacy.

Blackbourn, David. *The Long Nineteenth Century: A History of Germany, 1780–1918.* 1998. Particularly strong on the social aspects and consequences of German unification.

Eichner, Carolyn J. *Surmounting the Barricades: Women in the Paris Commune.* 2004. A study of three important revolutionary leaders and the intersection of feminism with social and political events.

Lewis, Bernard. *The Emergence of Modern Turkey.* 2001. The foremost historian on Turkey and the modern Middle East provides an important survey of the Ottoman Empire.

Lincoln, W. Bruce. *Great Reforms.* 1990. Shows the reforms to be part of a general program of modernization.

Matthew, Colin, ed. *The Nineteenth Century: The British Isles, 1815–1901.* 2000. An up-to-date collection of articles on major themes in British history.

NOTES

1. Quoted in Otto Pflanze, *Bismarck and the Development of Germany,* vol. 1 (Princeton, N.J.: Princeton University Press, 1990), p. 184.

2. Quoted in William Flavelle Monypenny and George Earle Buckle, *The Life of Benjamin Disraeli: Earl of Beaconsfield,* vol. 2 (London: John Murray, 1929), pp. 473–474.

23

THE AGE OF OPTIMISM, 1850–1880

Felix Valloton:
Le bon marché
(Private Collection)

The first department store in Paris, which served as a model for others in France and abroad, Le bon marché (the "good buy") opened its doors in the 1850s. The store bought goods in mass quantities and thus could sell them at low prices. Constructed of glass and iron, Le bon marché represented the new, modern age. It combined under one roof a large range of products that previously had been available only in separate specialty shops—a timesaving convenience in an increasingly harried age. The store also had a large catalog sales department for customers too busy or distant to shop in person. Filled with toys, bed linens, furniture, crystal, and other items, the department store was a symbol of the new opulence of the middle classes.

This new type of store would not have been possible in an earlier age. It serves as a summary of the various technological and social changes that the more prosperous regions of the West experienced as industrialization advanced in the second half of the nineteenth century. Industrial innovation had lowered the price of glass and steel, so that these new, huge commercial emporiums could be built at reasonable cost. Railroads brought into the city large quantities of increasingly mass-produced goods, as well as out-of-town customers. In town, trams and omnibuses transported shoppers to the store. The penny press provided advertising for the department store, which in turn supported the emergence of this new medium. The expansion of the postal system facilitated catalog sales and the mailing of parcels to customers. And the higher incomes available to many people allowed them to purchase more than just the necessities. A phenomenon began that would become predominant in the West a century later—the consumer society.

As industrialization spread throughout western Europe, rising productivity brought greater wealth to more social groups and nations. This wealth not only led to more consumer spending; it also changed attitudes. The second half of the nineteenth century was an era shaped to a large extent by the growing middle classes, who were filled with optimism and convinced they were living in an age of progress. John Stuart Mill proclaimed that in his era "the general tendency is and will continue to be . . . one of improvement—a tendency towards a better and happier state." Across the Channel in France, the social thinker Auguste Comte (1798–1857) concurred, confidently stating,

CHAPTER OUTLINE

INDUSTRIAL GROWTH AND ACCELERATION

SOCIAL IMPACTS OF ECONOMIC GROWTH

URBAN PROBLEMS AND SOLUTIONS

SOCIAL AND POLITICAL INITIATIVES

CULTURE IN AN AGE OF OPTIMISM

KEY TERMS

second industrial revolution

bourgeois century

professionalization

Victorian morality

separate spheres

solidarism

social Catholics

positivism

Darwinism

Social Darwinism

impressionist

Online Study Center

This icon will direct you to interactive map and primary source activities on the website **college.hmco.com/ pic/noble5e**

"Human development brings . . . an ever growing amelioration." The successful application of science and technology to social problems gave many men and women confidence in the human ability to improve the world. People controlled their environments to a degree never before possible. On farms they increased the fertility of the soil; to the burgeoning cities they brought greater order. Scientists used new methods to study and combat disease. Public authorities founded schools, trained teachers, and reduced illiteracy. Transportation and communication rapidly improved.

Not all of society benefited from the fruits of progress. The new wealth was far from equally shared. Eastern and southern Europe changed little, and even in the western regions a large part of the population still lived in great misery. If some cities carried out ambitious programs of urban renewal, others continued to neglect slums. Public sanitation programs did not affect the majority of Europeans who lived in rural areas. Despite spectacular advances in science, much of the population maintained a traditional belief in divine intervention. Many intellectuals strongly denounced the materialism and smugness of the age, stressing the meanness and ignorance that lay just beneath the surface.

It was the ascendant middle classes in western Europe who set the tone of the age. Their optimism was all the greater because the ultimate effects of the social and technological changes taking place in Europe were not yet known. Of the major processes that unfolded between 1850 and 1880, many were still in their infancy in 1880. What lay beyond the horizon would certainly be even more wonderful, or so many believed.

FOCUS QUESTIONS

What technological changes led to the expansion of the European economy after the mid-nineteenth century?

How did the economic expansion affect the various social classes, and city versus rural areas, differently?

What problems did urbanization create, and what were the solutions?

How and why did the state increasingly intervene in people's everyday lives?

What new scientific, intellectual, and cultural trends emerged in this period, and what impact did they have on systems of belief?

INDUSTRIAL GROWTH AND ACCELERATION

What technological changes led to the expansion of the European economy after the mid-nineteenth century?

Beginning in the 1850s, western Europe experienced an unprecedented level of economic expansion. Manufacturers created new products and harnessed new sources of energy. An enlarged banking system provided more abundant credit to fund this expansion. Scientific research was systematically employed to improve methods of manufacture. A revolution in transportation speedily delivered goods and services to distant places. Technological innovation profoundly changed the daily lives of many Europeans.

THE "SECOND INDUSTRIAL REVOLUTION"

The interrelated cluster of economic changes that began in the generation after 1850 is often called the **second industrial revolution.** It was characterized by a significant speedup in production and by the introduction of new materials such as mass-produced steel, synthetic dyes, and aluminum. Manufacturers replaced the traditional steam engine with stronger

second industrial revolution   Interrelated economic changes after 1850 that included new products, new methods of manufacture, and new materials such as mass-produced steel, synthetic dyes, and aluminum.

steam-powered turbines or with machines powered by new forms of energy—petroleum and electricity.

The invention of new products and methods of manufacture spurred this industrial expansion. The second half of the nineteenth century has often been called the "age of steel." In 1856 Sir Henry Bessemer (1813–1898) discovered a method that produced in twenty minutes the same amount of steel previously produced in twenty-four hours. In the next two decades, further advances in England and France made steel production even more efficient. The results were dramatic. In Great Britain steel production increased fourfold, and by the 1880s, its price fell by 50 percent. Greater steel production made possible the expansion of the rail system, the creation of a steamship fleet, and an explosive growth in the building industry. Steel, once a rare alloy used only for the finest swords and knives, became the material that defined the age.

Significant changes in the supply of credit further stimulated economic expansion. Discovery of gold in California and Australia led to the inflow of huge amounts of the precious metal to Europe, expanding the supply of money and credit. This led to the establishment of the modern banking system.

Each advance made possible additional changes. Increased wealth and credit accelerated further expansion of industrial plants and the financing of an ambitious infrastructure of roads, railroads, and steamships, which in turn boosted trade. Between 1850 and 1870 the value of world trade increased by 260 percent.

By the 1880s important scientific discoveries fueled industrial improvements. Electricity began to be more widely used, replacing coal as a source of energy. Synthetic dyes revolutionized the textile industry, as did alkali in the manufacture of soap and glass. Dynamite, invented by the Swedish chemist Alfred Nobel (no-BELL) (1833–1896) in the 1860s, made it possible to level hills and blast tunnels through mountains, facilitating construction. Nobel's will established a prestigious prize in his name to honor significant contributions to science and peace.

TRANSPORTATION AND COMMUNICATION

The rail system grew dramatically in the middle decades of the nineteenth century. By 1880 total European railroad mileage reached 102,000 (see **MAP 23.1**). In 1888 the Orient Express line opened, linking Constantinople to Vienna and thus to the rest of Europe. Speed also conquered distance. By midcentury trains ran 50 miles per hour, ten times as fast as when they were invented. The cost of rail transport steadily decreased, allowing for its greater use. Between 1850 and 1880 in Germany, the number of rail passengers increased tenfold and the volume of goods eightyfold. In France and Great Britain the increases were nearly as impressive.

CHRONOLOGY

1813	Gas streetlamps in London
1820s	Omnibuses introduced in France
1830	Lyell founds the principles of modern geology
1831	Faraday discovers electromagnetic induction
1833	Telegraph invented
1840	Penny stamp introduced
1848	England adopts first national health legislation
1850s	Age of clipper ships
	Trams added to public transportation systems
1851	Crystal Palace
1852–1870	Rebuilding of Paris
1859	Darwin, *On the Origin of Species*
1863	Europe's first underground railroad, in London
1864	Pope Pius IX issues *Syllabus of Errors*
1865	Transoceanic telegraph cable installed
	Lister initiates antiseptic surgery
	University of Zurich admits women
1869	Opening of Suez Canal
	Mendeleev produces periodic table of elements
1874	Impressionist exhibition
1875	Bell invents telephone
	Electric lights in Paris
1881	Pasteur proposes germ theory of disease
1891	Pope Leo XIII issues *Rerum novarum*

Ocean transportation was also revolutionized. In 1869 the French built the Suez Canal across Egyptian territory, linking the Mediterranean to the Red Sea and the Indian Ocean. The canal reduced by 40 percent the thirty-five-day journey between London and Bombay. More efficient carriers—such as the clipper ship and the steamship—were developed. By 1880 European shipping carried nearly three times the cargo it had thirty years earlier.

The optimism born of conquering vast distances was reflected in a popular novel by the French writer Jules Verne (DJOOL VAIRN) (1828–1905), *Around the*

The Suez Canal

Opened in 1869, the canal cut through one hundred miles of Egyptian desert to enable passage between the Mediterranean and the Red Seas. It reduced by half the voyage from Europe to India and the rest of Asia, and particularly benefited Britain. The Suez Canal exemplified the speeding up of transportation and communication in the second half of the nineteenth century. *(akg-images)*

World in Eighty Days (1873). The hero, Phineas Fogg, travels by balloon, llama, and ostrich, as well as by the modern steam locomotive and steamship, to accomplish in eighty days a feat that, only thirty years earlier, would have taken at least eleven months. In 1889 the New York newspaper the *World,* in a publicity gambit to increase readership, sent its reporter Nellie Bly (1867–1922) on an around-the-world trip to see if she could beat Phineas Fogg's record. Readers breathlessly kept up with reports of her progress. She circled the globe in 72 days, 6 hours, 11 minutes, and 14 seconds. Such was the impact of the steamship, the locomotive, the Suez Canal—and the newspaper.

Along with the new speed, advances in refrigeration changed food transport. Formerly, refrigeration could be achieved only with natural ice, cut from frozen ponds and lakes, but this changed in the 1870s with the introduction of mechanical ice-making machines. By the 1880s dairy products and meat were being transported vast distances by rail and even across the seas by ship. Thanks to these advances, the surplus food of the Americas and Australia, rich in grasslands, could offer Europe a cheaper and far more varied diet.

Regular postal service was also a child of the new era of improved transportation. In 1840 Britain instituted a postage system based on standard rates. Replacing the earlier practice in which the recipient paid for the delivery of a letter, the British system enabled the sender to buy a stamp—priced at just one penny—and drop the letter into a mailbox. It was collected, transported speedily by the new railroads, and delivered. The efficiency and low cost of mail led to a huge increase in use.

The reformed postal service and transoceanic telegraphs revolutionized the exchange of information. The telegraph was invented in the early 1830s, and by the 1860s, telegraph wire had been laid on both the European and North American continents; the two continents were then connected via the transatlantic cable. By the 1870s, telegraph lines extended 650,000 miles, connecting twenty thousand towns and villages around the world.

MAP 23.1   European Rails, 1850 and 1880

During the mid-nineteenth century, European states built railroads at an increasing rate, creating a dense network by the 1880s.   *(Adapted from Norman J. G. Pounds,* An Historical Geography of Europe, 1800–1914 *[New York: Cambridge University Press, 1985]. Used by permission of the publisher.)*

— Railroads in 1850
— Railroads added by 1880

Online Study Center   Improve Your Grade   Interactive Map: European Rails, 1850–1880

The telegraph had many uses. Newspapers prided themselves on being "wired" and so able to give their readers the latest news. Governments found the telegraph useful in collecting information and issuing orders to subordinates, better assuring imperial authority over distant territories. In the 1840s it took ten weeks for a message and a reply to go from London to Bombay and back. Thirty years later the exchange took four minutes.

The telegraph was also a tool of warfare. The first conflict in which it played a crucial role was the Crimean War. The British and French high commands in London and Paris were able to communicate with their officers in the Crimea, directing operations from afar. It was also the first war whose unfolding events could be communicated immediately through the telegraph to newspapers at home. Charles Dickens described the telegraph as "of all our modern wonders the most wonderful." Even more than improved transportation, it transformed the world into an instant, global village. As the governor of New York said at a commemorative event, "Men speak to one another now, though separated by the width of the earth, with lightning's speed and as if standing face to face."

To the telegraph was added another instant form of communication. In 1875 the American Alexander Graham Bell (1847–1922) invented a machine capable of transmitting the human voice by electrical impulses; in 1879 the first telephones were installed in Germany; two years later they appeared in France. At first a curiosity, used to listen to a musical or theatrical production at a distance, the phone entered the homes of the elite and became a new form of interpersonal communication.

═══════════ S E C T I O N   S U M M A R Y ═══════════

- After 1850, steam-powered turbines and new sources of energy, such as petroleum and electricity, increased the pace and quantity of industrial production.

- New methods of steel production made possible the expansion of railroads, the construction of steamships, and explosive growth in the building industry.

- Built by the French in 1869, the Suez Canal helped revolutionize ocean transportation by cutting travel time to India and other parts of Asia nearly in half, while ships as well became more efficient.

- The telegraph, telephone, and standardized mail systems sped up communications and collapsed global distances of time and space.

SOCIAL IMPACTS OF ECONOMIC GROWTH

How did the economic expansion affect the various social classes, and city versus rural areas, differently?

Industrial advances transformed the traditional structure of European society. Fewer people worked the land; more worked in manufacturing and services. The social and political influence of the aristocracy waned as wealth became far less dependent on landed property ownership. To varying degrees, this influence now had to be shared with the growing middle classes. Generally, life for both industrial and farm workers improved in this period. However, great disparities persisted, and many people continued to suffer from profound deprivation.

THE DECLINING ARISTOCRACY

Always a small, exclusive group, the European aristocracy in the nineteenth century represented less than 1 percent of the population. Many of noble birth were quite poor and economically indistinguishable from their non-noble neighbors. Others owned vast estates and were fabulously wealthy.

Distinctions between aristocrats and members of the upper middle class became increasingly blurred. Noble families in financial straits often married their children to the offspring of wealthy merchants. And many nobles who previously had shunned manufacture participated in the new economy by becoming industrialists and bankers. Idle members of the nobility were now somewhat rare. Although many aristocrats still enjoyed a lavish lifestyle, others had adopted the habits of successful business people.

The power of the aristocracy had surprisingly persisted through much of the nineteenth century despite the theories of egalitarianism sweeping Europe in the aftermath of the French Revolution and the rapidly changing social structure engendered by industrialization. In Prussia some of the wealthiest industrialists came from the highest aristocracy. The heavily aristocratic officer corps played an important role in running the Prussian state and unified Germany. In France about 20 to 25 percent of officers and many diplomats were aristocrats. In Britain officers, diplomats, and high-ranking civil servants were usually of noble birth. In Austria and Russia, aristocratic origin was the norm for government service.

Nonetheless, nobles no longer asserted privileges based exclusively on birth. In most European states, such claims had become anachronisms.

THE EXPANDING MIDDLE CLASSES

Up to the eighteenth century, society had been divided into legally separate orders on the basis of birth. In the nineteenth century, it became more customary to classify people by their economic functions. The "middle class" belonged neither to the nobility nor to the peasantry nor to the industrial working class. It included such people as wealthy manufacturers, country physicians, and bank tellers. Given this diversity, it has become common to use the plural and think of all these people as forming the "middle classes." Another term frequently used to describe these people is *bourgeois*.

The nineteenth century has often been described as the **bourgeois century,** because, especially in western Europe, the middle classes expanded dramatically and had an enormous social and cultural influence. More trade and manufacture meant more entrepreneurs and managers, while the increasingly complex society called for more engineers, lawyers, accountants, and bankers. New standards of comfort and health demanded more merchants and doctors. Urban improvements in the generation after 1850 created a need for architects and contractors, among other professionals.

The middle and lower levels of middle-class society grew most rapidly. In the 1870s about 10 percent of urban working-class people reached lower-middle-class status by becoming storekeepers, lower civil servants, clerks, or salespeople. Faster growth occurred for white-collar workers than for their blue-collar counterparts. As industries matured, the increasing use of machinery and better industrial organization created a greater need for clerks and bureaucrats rather than laborers. Large import-export businesses, insurance companies, and department stores provided opportunities of this kind. So did the expansion of government services.

The social impact of job growth was great. The men and women staffing these new positions often came from modest backgrounds. For the son or daughter of peasants to become village postmaster, schoolteacher, or clerk in a major firm signified social ascension, however modest. Accessibility to its ranks was certainly one of the strengths of the bourgeoisie, an ever growing group whose promise of social respectability and material comfort exercised a compelling force of attraction over the lower classes.

A widening subgroup of the middle classes consisted of members of the professions, those whose prestige rested on the claim of exclusive expertise in a particular field. In the early nineteenth century, requirements for exercising a profession, though they varied by country, became more stringent. Medical doctors, for instance, began requiring specialized education to distinguish themselves from herbalists, midwives, bonesetters, healers, and other competitors, and they insisted on their exclusive right to exercise their profession. Doctors controlled access to their ranks by establishing powerful professional associations.

Similarly other professions such as law, architecture, and engineering encouraged **professionalization**

Interior of a Danish Middle-Class Home
With its stuffed furniture, lace curtains and tablecloths, and gilt-edged framed paintings, this meticulously decorated living room contrasted sharply with the grimy exterior of the industrial city from which it provided a sheltered escape.   *(National Museum of Denmark)*

through the adoption of common requirements and standards of expertise. By midcentury either professional associations or the state itself accredited members of the professions. Women had limited access to these professions; typically their opportunities were confined to lower teaching positions. After the Crimean War, as a result of Florence Nightingale's efforts (see page 683), nursing became an increasingly popular profession for women. Even so, the dominant culture generally opposed middle-class women's salaried employment outside the home.

The growing role of the state in society led to bureaucratic expansion. Civil servants were increasingly subjected to educational requirements and had to pass civil service exams, sharply reducing the role that patronage played in the assignment of government positions.

bourgeois century   Characterization of the nineteenth century. Having expanded dramatically with industrialization, the bourgeoisie helped shape western European society.

professionalization   Standardization of requirements and regulation of expertise, especially in medicine, law, architecture, and engineering.

MIDDLE-CLASS LIFESTYLES

The standard of living among the middle classes varied considerably, ranging from the wealthy entrepreneur who bought a château, or built one, to the low-level clerk who dwelled in a modest apartment. All lived in new standards of comfort. Their homes increasingly had running water, upholstered furniture, and enough space to provide separate sleeping and living quarters. They owned several changes of clothing and consumed a varied diet that included meat and dairy products, sugar, coffee, and tea. They read books and subscribed to newspapers and journals. Having at least one servant was a requisite for anyone who wished to be counted among the middle classes in the mid-nineteenth century.

By 1900 servants were still common among bourgeois households, but their number was declining in proportion to the population as a whole. As service industries developed, the need for servants decreased.

With the growth of cab services, for instance, a family could dispense with a coachman and groom. Toward the end of the century, domestics' wages rose as competing forms of employment vied for their service, and households below the upper layers of the bourgeoisie found it difficult to afford domestic help.

The need to escape the relentless stimulation of crowded cities gave rise to resort towns throughout Europe, devoted principally to the amusement of the well-off. Water cures—bathing in hot springs and drinking the mineral waters thought to have special attributes—became fashionable, as did gambling in resorts such as Baden-Baden in Germany and Vichy in France. For the first time, tourism became big business. Thomas Cook (1808–1892), an Englishman, organized tours to the Crystal Palace exhibition of 1851 in London, the largest world exposition, which highlighted industrial accomplishments. Discovering the large market for guided travel, Cook began running tours in England and on the Continent. Middle-class wealth and leisure time led

The Crystal Palace
Built in 1851, this building was the largest glass and steel structure of its time. Site of the first great international exposition, the Crystal Palace displayed the inventiveness and opulence of the age. *(Courtesy of the Trustees of the British Museum)*

to the construction of more hotels, restaurants, and cafés.

The middle classes shared certain attitudes about the conduct of their lives. They believed their successes were due not to birth but to talent and effort. They wanted to be judged by their merits, and they expected their members to abide by strict moral principles. Their lives were supposed to be disciplined, especially with regard to sex and drink. The age was called "Victorian" because the middle classes in Britain saw in the queen who reigned for two-thirds of the century a reflection of their own values. (See the feature "The Visual Record: An Engraving of the British Royal Family" on pages 704–705 in Chapter 22.) **Victorian morality,** widely preached but not always practiced, was often viewed as hypocritical by social critics. Yet as the middle classes came to dominate society, their values became the social norms. Public drunkenness was discouraged, and anti-alcohol movements vigorously campaigned against drinking. Public festivals were regulated, making them more respectable and less rowdy.

In spite of their differences in education, wealth, and social standing, most of the bourgeoisie resembled one another in dress, habits of speech, and deportment. Bourgeois men dressed somberly, in dark colors, avoiding any outward signs of luxury. Their clothing fit closely and lacked decoration—a symbolic adjustment to the machine age, in which elaborate dress hampered activity. It also reflected a conscious attempt to emphasize achievement-oriented attitudes, and new standards for what constituted honorable manhood. Through dress and other fashionable tastes, middle classes distinguished themselves from what they viewed as a decadent and effeminate nobility.

Bourgeois conventions regarding women's dress were the opposite of men's, further reinforcing gender distinctions—women's dress became the material symbol of male success. Extravagant amounts of colorful fabrics used to fashion huge, beribboned hoop dresses reflected the newfound wealth of the middle classes and confirmed their view of women as ornaments whose lives were to be limited to the home and made easier by servants. The language and paraphernalia of idealized domesticity dominated this era. While the man was out in the secular world earning a living and advancing his career, the bourgeois woman was supposed to provide her family with an orderly, comfortable shelter from the storms of daily life. In 1861, London housewife Isabella Mary Mayson Beeton published *Mrs. Beeton's Book of Household Management*, which provided British middle-class women with advice on running their households. This book reflected middle-class values in fostering discipline, frugality, and cleanliness. The ideal woman decorated the rooms, changed the curtains with the seasons and styles, supervised the servants, kept the accounts, oversaw the children's homework and religious education, and involved herself in charitable works. In Britain this book was outsold only by the Bible. In the decades around mid-century, the notion of two **separate spheres**—one male and public, the other female and private—reached its height.

In spite of the relatively passive role assigned to bourgeois women, many were very active. Some helped their husbands or fathers in the office, the business, or the writing of scientific treatises. Others achieved success on their own terms, running their own businesses, writing, painting, or teaching. Though advice books prescribed a world of separate spheres, in practice the boundaries between them were not always rigid.

The expectation that middle-class women would be married and taken care of by their husbands led to the provision of inferior education for girls and young women, which sharply limited their options. Even bright and intellectually curious young girls most often could not receive as good an education as their brothers, nor as a consequence could they pursue as interesting a career.

Some liberals insisted that sexual difference should not constitute the basis for denying equal rights to women. Proponents of women's rights demanded equal access to education and the professions. Slowly, secondary and university education was made available to young women. On the European continent the University of Zurich was the first university to admit women, in 1865. Although British universities admitted women, they did not initially grant them degrees. Oxford and Cambridge did not grant degrees to women until after World War I. In spite of discriminatory laws, harassment by male students, and initial obstruction by professional and accrediting groups, a few female doctors and lawyers practiced in England by the 1870s and on the Continent in the following decades.

Women more easily penetrated the lower levels of middle-class occupations. Expanding school systems, civil services, and businesses provided new employment opportunities for them. By the 1890s two-thirds of primary school teachers in England and half the post office staff in France were women. By 1914 nearly half a million women worked as shop assistants in England. Some new technologies created jobs that became heavily feminized, such as the positions of typist and telephone operator.

Victorian morality Nineteenth-century ethos wherein the strict moral principles of the dominant middle class became the social norm. The middle classes saw in Queen Victoria a reflection of their own values.

separate spheres Notion of two distinct sets of roles—one male and public, the other female and private. While the man was out in the world advancing his career, the bourgeois woman was to run her home.

Ladies' Bicycling Fashion

This new mode of transportation suggested possibilities for female emancipation. Free on her bicycle, the young woman is contrasted with the man, who rides only a tricycle.

(From Karin Helm [ed.], Rosinen aus der Gartenlaube [Gütersloh: Signum Verlag, n.d.]. Reproduced with permission.)

Telephone Operators in London

New technologies opened up new employment opportunities for women. Telephone operators formed a completely feminized profession. *(Roger-Viollet/Getty Images)*

THE WORKERS' LOT

The increased prosperity and greater productivity of the period gradually improved the conditions of both female and male workers in the generation after 1850. Their wages and standards of living rose, and they enjoyed more job security. In Britain the earning power of the average worker rose by one-third between 1850 and 1875. For the first time, workers were able to put money aside to tide them over in hard times.

Legislation gradually reduced the length of the workweek. The British workweek, typically 73 hours in the 1840s, was reduced to 56 hours in 1874. In France it was reduced to 10 hours a day, in Germany to 11. But these improvements were accompanied by an increased emphasis on efficiency in the workplace. Fewer informal breaks were allowed as industrialists insisted on greater worker productivity. New machines increased the tempo of work, frequently leading to exhaustion and accidents.

As workers had more time and money, they had greater access to leisure activities that previously had been limited to the upper classes. Expanded rail connections enabled workers to visit resort towns. New music and dance halls, popular theaters, and other forms of public entertainment sprang up to claim workers' increased spending money.

Although most workers believed that their lot had improved, they were also aware that a vast gulf remained between them and the middle and upper classes. In the 1880s in the northern French industrial city of Lille, the combined property of twenty thousand workers equaled the estate of one average industrialist. Life expectancies still varied dramatically according to income. In Bordeaux in 1853, the life expectancy of a male bourgeois was twenty years greater than that of a male laborer.

The disparity between rich and poor was especially striking in the case of domestics, one of the most common sources of employment for women. Servants led tiring and restricted lives under the close supervision of their employers. Their hours were overly long, as they often worked six and a half days a week. Housed in either the basement or the attic, servants experienced extremes of cold, heat, and humidity. Sometimes they were subjected to physical or sexual abuse by the master of the house, his sons, or the head of the domestic staff. And yet, for impoverished rural women with little chance of finding better work, domestic service was a risky but often necessary option. It provided free housing, food, and clothing and sometimes allowed a servant to save an annual sum that might reach one-third to one-half of a worker's yearly wages. These savings often served as a dowry and could enable a young woman to marry advantageously.

Although a few members of the working class managed to enter the lower levels of the middle classes, most remained mired in the same occupations as their grandparents. Poverty was still pervasive. In the 1880s about one-third of Londoners were living at or below the subsistence level. Workers more commonly suffered from industrial and urban diseases, such as tuberculosis. Compared with the healthier, better-fed, and better-housed middle classes, the workers continued living in shabby and crowded conditions.

THE TRANSFORMATION OF THE COUNTRYSIDE

Before the nineteenth century, the countryside had hardly changed, but beginning at midcentury it transformed radically. Especially in western Europe, an increasing number of people left the land. In 1850, 20 percent of the British people worked in agriculture; by 1881 they constituted only 11 percent of the population. The decrease in the number of agricultural workers led in many places to labor shortages and therefore higher wages for farm hands.

The food supply grew significantly as agricultural methods became more efficient. Not only was more land cultivated, but the yield per acre increased. In 1760 an agricultural worker in England could feed himself and one other person; by 1841 he could feed himself and 2.7 others. The population of Europe nearly doubled between 1800 and 1880, and yet it was better nourished than ever before.

Higher yields were the result of an increased use of manure, augmented in the 1870s by saltpeter imported from Chile and, beginning in the 1880s, by chemical fertilizers manufactured in Europe. Innovations in tools also improved productivity. The sickle, which required the laborer to crouch to cut grass or wheat, was replaced by the long-handled scythe, which allowed the field hand to stand and use the full weight of the body to swing the instrument through the grain. This new method increased efficiency fourfold. In the 1850s steam-driven threshing machinery was introduced in some parts of western Europe. Organizational techniques borrowed from industrial labor, including specialization and regular schedules, also contributed to greater productivity on the land.

Steam-Powered Thresher
This image shows the thresher being operated in the French countryside in 1860. Its loud noise and relentlessly rhythmic speed changed the pace and sensibility of rural labor, and sometimes prolonged the hours demanded of workers. It would be decades before this kind of technology became a common sight in Europe, but it was a harbinger of the change coming to the rural world. *(Bibliothèque nationale de France)*

Economic growth and new and expanded technologies began to break through the insularity of rural life. Improved roads and dramatically expanded rail lines enabled farmers to extend their markets nationally and internationally. They also brought teachers into the villages, making school systems national. Local dialects, and in some cases even distinct languages that peasants had spoken for generations, were replaced by a standardized national language. Local provincial costumes became less common as styles fashionable in the cities spread to the countryside via mail order catalogs. The farm girls who went to the cities to work as domestic servants returned to their villages with urban and middle-class ideals. The military draft brought the young men of the village into contact with urban folk and further spread urban values to the countryside.

Many rural regions, however, suffered from modernization. The growth of urban manufacturing caused rural cottage industry to decline, depriving agricultural workers of the supplementary income on which they previously relied during slack seasons. In many cases railroads bringing goods made elsewhere wiped out some of the local markets on which cottage industries had depended. The steamship brought freight such as grain from distant Canada and Argentina, which often undersold wheat grown in Europe. The resultant crisis caused millions to emigrate; they left the land for towns and cities or even migrated across the seas to the Americas and Australia (see page 747).

These trends had a striking effect in the rural areas of western Europe. Eastern Europe, in contrast, was hardly touched by them. In Russia agriculture remained backward; the average yield per acre in 1880 was one-quarter that in Great Britain. The land sheltered a large surplus population that was underemployed and contributed little to the rural economy. In the Balkans, most peasants were landless and heavily indebted.

===== S E C T I O N   S U M M A R Y =====

- As landed wealth declined in economic importance during the second half of the nineteenth century, so too did the power and influence of the old aristocracy.

- New technologies of the second industrial revolution and the expansion of commerce, government bureaucracy, and the professions dramatically increased the size and influence of the middle classes.

- The middle class (bourgeoisie) helped instill the notion of separate spheres for men and women, but many women defied their prescribed role and sought the right to higher education and entry into the professions.

- Standards of living rose among workers who generally had better diets and more leisure time; stark class disparities of wealth and living conditions nonetheless persisted.

- New agricultural methods and technologies greatly increased agricultural production. But modernization also created competition for agricultural and cottage industry products, forcing migration from the countryside.

URBAN PROBLEMS AND SOLUTIONS

What problems did urbanization create, and what were the solutions?

Epidemics, crowding, crime, and traffic jams were among the many problems that accompanied explosive urban growth in the nineteenth century. In the second half of the century, city governments more aggressively tackled these problems by developing public health measures and urban planning. They provided amenities such as streetlights, public transportation, and water and sewer systems, and they established large, more efficient police forces. Cities gradually became safer and more pleasant places to live, although for a long time city dwellers continued to suffer high mortality rates.

CITY PLANNING AND URBAN RENOVATION

Most of Europe's cities, originating in the Middle Ages as walled enclaves, had grown haphazardly into major industrial centers. Their narrow, crooked streets could not accommodate the increased trade and daily movement of goods and people, and traffic snarls were common. City officials began to recognize that broad, straight avenues would help relieve the congestion and also bring sunlight and fresh air into the narrow and

Pissarro: L'avenue de l'Opéra, Sunlight, Winter Morning

Camille Pissarro, one of the leading impressionists, portrayed the broad new Parisian avenue designed by Baron Haussmann. The avenue leads to the new opera in the background, also planned during the Second Empire. Note the active pedestrian as well as equestrian traffic.   *(Musée Saint-Denis, Reims/Giraudon/Art Resource, NY)*

perpetually dank lanes and alleys. (See the feature "The Visual Record: The Modern City and Photography" on pages 734–735.)

The most extensive program of urban rebuilding took place in midcentury Paris. Over a period of eighteen years Napoleon III and his aide Baron Georges Haussmann (1809–1891) transformed Paris from a dirty medieval city to a beautiful modern one (see **Map 23.2**). Haussmann and his engineers carved broad, straight avenues through what had been overcrowded areas. They built visually elegant, if uniform, apartment houses on the new tree-lined avenues. Public monu-

ments and buildings, such as the new opera house, enhanced the city. The urban renewal program drove tens of thousands of the poorest Parisians to the outskirts of the city, leading to greater social segregation than had previously existed.

Haussmann's extensive work in Paris served as a model for other cities, and although none was rebuilt as extensively, many underwent significant improvements. The cities of Europe began to display an expansive grace and sense of order, supporting the belief of the middle classes that theirs was an age of progress.

MAP 23.2 Haussmann's Paris, 1850–1870

During the reign of Napoleon III, Baron Georges Haussmann reshaped the city of Paris, replacing its narrow medieval streets with a system of broad avenues and public parks and encircling the city with a railway.

— City walls

① Wall of Philippe Auguste (1180–1210)

② Tollhouse Wall (1784–1791), razed by Haussmann to rebuild as boulevards

③ Fortress Wall (1841–1845)

▨ Paris before 1860

⬚ Expanded city limits established in 1860

▨ Public parks opened during Second Empire

— Streets constructed by Haussmann

— Other streets

┼┼┼ Railway system created by Haussmann during Second Empire

Source: *Encyclopedia Universalis*

THE INTRODUCTION OF PUBLIC SERVICES

Beginning at midcentury, government at the central and local levels helped make cities more livable by legislating sanitary reforms and providing public transportation and lighting. Medical practitioners in the 1820s had observed that disease and higher mortality were related to dirt and lack of clean air, water, and sunshine. Since diseases spreading from the poorer quarters of town threatened the rich and powerful, there was a general interest in improving public health by clearing slums, broadening streets, and supplying clean air and water to the cities.

Reform began in England with the Public Health Bill of 1848. This legislation established national standards for urban sanitation and required cities to regulate the installation of sewers and the disposal of refuse.

The 1875 Health Act mandated certain basic health standards for water and drainage. Armed with these laws, cities and towns took the initiative: Birmingham cleared 50 acres of slums in the 1870s, for example.

London was also a leader in supplying public water, a service later adopted by Paris and many other cities. Berlin had a municipal water system in 1850, but it would be several decades before clean water was available in every household. In Paris, which typically led France in innovations, 60 percent of the houses had running water in 1882. The French capital did not have a unitary sewer system until the 1890s, however. As running water in the home became a standard rather than a luxury, bathing became more common. The English upper classes had learned the habit of frequent bathing from their colonial experience in India; on the

Continent it did not become the custom until about the third quarter of the nineteenth century.

All these changes had a direct impact on the lives of city dwellers. Between the 1840s and 1880, London's death rate fell from 26 per thousand to 20 per thousand. During the same period, the rate in Paris declined from 29.3 per thousand to 23.7 per thousand. The incidence of diseases associated with filthy living conditions also fell; improved water supplies sharply reduced the prevalence of waterborne diseases such as cholera and typhoid.

Other improvements also contributed to a better quality of life. With the introduction of urban transportation, city dwellers no longer had to live within walking distance of their workplaces. An early example of public transportation was the French omnibus service of the 1820s—a system of horse-drawn carriages available to the public on fixed routes. In the 1850s the tram was introduced. A carriage drawn on a rail line by horses, a tram could pull larger loads of passengers faster than the omnibus. Because of the many rail stations in London and the difficulty of getting from one station to another in time to make a connection, London built an underground railway in 1863, the predecessor of the subway system. Techno-logical improvements made the bicycle a serious means of transportation. By the mid-1880s nearly 100,000 bicycles were being pedaled around Great Britain; by 1900 France had 1 million bicycles.

Improvements in public transportation and urban renewal projects led workers to move out of the inner city and into the less dense and less expensive suburbs. This trend in turn led to a decrease in urban population density and eventually helped make the city a healthier place to live.

Gaslights also improved city life, making it easier and safer to be outside at night. (Prior to gaslights, city dwellers depended mainly on moonlight or, rarely, expensive and time-consuming oil lamps—which had to be lit one at a time.) In 1813 London was the first city to be illuminated by gas; Berlin followed in 1816. Electrical lights were introduced in Paris in 1875, although they were not common until the end of the century.

Cities also significantly expanded police forces to impose order, control criminal activity, and discourage behavior deemed undesirable, such as dumping garbage on the street, relieving oneself in public, and carousing late at night. In 1850 London was the best-policed city in Europe, with a 5,000-man force. Paris had around 3,000 police officers.

━━━━━━━━ S E C T I O N   S U M M A R Y ━━━━━━━━

- Rapid population growth occurred in cities that had originally been constructed in haphazard fashion; to cope with the problems of growth, city officials began programs of urban rebuilding.

- The most notable example of urban renewal was that of Haussmann in Paris, which became a model in cities elsewhere.

- Central and local governments introduced sanitary reforms to combat disease, such as installing sewers, regulating the disposal of refuse, and supplying public water.

- Improvement in public transportation allowed workers to leave the overcrowded conditions in urban centers, further contributing to improved health.

SOCIAL AND POLITICAL INITIATIVES

How and why did the state increasingly intervene in people's everyday lives?

Several institutions and groups emerged to tackle the unequal distribution of wealth and critical urban problems that followed in the wake of economic growth. The state intervened in the economy in new ways. Private charitable groups, which had existed for decades, continued to administer to a few of the poor, and new charities developed. Socialist political parties, exclusively dedicated to improving the workers' lot, gained in numbers and strength.

STATE INTERVENTION IN WELFARE

The difficult conditions industry imposed on workers led to debates in several countries about the need for the state to protect the workers. The growing militancy of organized labor also forced authorities to consider ways to meet the workers' needs. While some rejected government intervention in the free operation of market forces, others argued that the laws of supply and demand had caused the exploitation of many who ought to have been protected—especially very young children and pregnant women. Britain led the way with the Factory Acts, regulating child and female labor. Similar acts were passed later in Prussia and France. In much of Europe, however, the state did little to improve the welfare of the working class. In eastern Europe, where industry was still in its infancy, workers had no protection.

Fear of social upheaval, a desire to prevent depopulation, and the rising strength of socialist political parties prompted some governments to act. In France moderate bourgeois liberals attempted to defuse class war by advocating **solidarism.** Solidarism insisted on the mutual responsibility of classes and individuals for one another's well-being. Guided by such sentiments, French republicans passed a number of laws toward the end of the century that improved the lot of the working class. In newly unified Germany, the government wanted to impress workers with state benefits so they would abandon the growing Socialist Party and back the kaiser's authoritarian government. Thus in the 1880s the new German government, under the leadership of Chancellor Otto von Bismarck, provided a comprehensive welfare plan that included health insurance and old-age pensions.

Apart from state initiatives, upper- and middle-class individuals, inspired by pity and religious teachings, also became concerned about conditions among the poor. Women especially engaged in charity and social reform. In Sweden by the 1880s, women had founded shelters for the destitute, old-age homes, a children's hospital, an asylum for the mentally handicapped, and various societies to promote female industry. As many as half a million English women involved themselves in charities or efforts to enact social legislation. Among them was Josephine Grey Butler (1828–1906), who fought for the education of impoverished women. She also waged a fierce battle against the harsh laws directed against prostitutes. The Contagious Diseases Acts (beginning in 1864) empowered the police to arrest any woman suspected of prostitution and to force her to be examined for venereal disease. Largely as a result of Butler's efforts, these acts were repealed in 1886. Annie Wood Besant (1847–1933) became an active social reformer on behalf of the poor. Arguing that poor women suffered from excessive childbearing and that their children died too often because of their poverty, she and Charles Bradlaugh (1833–1891) republished a pamphlet that contained information on birth control. British authorities called the publication pornographic and brought Besant and Bradlaugh to trial in 1877. After being found guilty, Bradlaugh and Besant won the case on appeal. In 1888 Besant turned her attention to protecting the health of young women workers, and in 1893 she went to India to establish schools for girls, educate widows, and agitate for Indian home rule.

Religious sentiment in the second half of the century inspired a number of Christians, lay and clerical, to emphasize the church's need to address social issues. Pope Leo XIII (r. 1878–1903) reflected this trend and re-

inforced it among Catholics when in 1891 he issued his encyclical *Rerum novarum* (Of New Things), which defined the moral responsibility of Christians for the well-being of the poor. He declared, "Rich men and masters should remember this—that to exercise pressure for the sake of gain upon the indigent and the destitute and to make one's profit out of the need of another is condemned by all laws, human and divine." His message was taken up in France, Italy, and Spain among activists who became known as **social Catholics.** In England Protestants founded the Salvation Army to assist the poor in 1878. Religious groups also hoped to win converts to their faith through the assistance they provided.

Increasingly, municipalities, volunteer groups, and churches accepted responsibility for the well-being of others by providing cheap housing, advice, material assistance, and medical aid. In many cases these pioneering efforts were later taken over by the state—a first step toward the development of the twentieth-century welfare state.

EDUCATIONAL AND CULTURAL OPPORTUNITIES

At the beginning of the nineteenth century, governments took little responsibility for providing education. Some upper-class children were educated with private tutors, and others attended elite schools. All schools were segregated by social class and charged tuition. A few charity schools offered minimal education for the poor. In England the Second Reform Bill of 1867 made public education a national priority. This legislation reduced the tax-based voting qualification, extending suffrage to better-off workers, and prompted a movement to ensure that the new voters were educated. The English government provided significant subsidies for education, set educational standards, and established a national inspection system to enforce them. France joined England in establishing mandatory primary school education in the 1880s for boys and girls.

In addition to the skills of reading, writing, and arithmetic, public education also taught discipline. By insisting on punctuality and obliging students to carry out repetitive tasks, schools formed youth to fit into the emerging industrial society. The obedience and respect for authority learned at school shaped the soldiers and factory workers of the future. And regardless of political inclination, each regime took advantage of its control of the educational system to inculcate the love of one's country and of its form of government.

Secondary education was, on the whole, available only to the privileged few in the upper-middle classes, giving them access to the universities and the profes-

---

solidarism   A policy that emphasized the mutual responsibility of classes and individuals for one another's well-being and led to the passage of laws and benefits to improve the lot of the working class.

social Catholics   Catholics in western Europe who believed that society bore responsibility for the well-being of the poor.

sions. A small fraction of the lower middle class attended universities, and the children of workers and peasants were totally absent.

Other public institutions made culture available to the masses in new ways. Between 1840 and 1880 the number of large libraries in Europe increased from forty to five hundred. The French national public library, the *Bibliothèque nationale,* was established in Paris in the 1860s. This iron and glass building, radical for its time, was an impressive monument to the desire to make reading available to an expanded public. Many provincial cities, as well as the glittering capitals of Europe, were endowed with new libraries. Traveling libraries allowed books to reach rural populations.

Museums and art galleries, which in the previous century had been open to only a select few, gradually became accessible to the general public. After the Revolution of 1789, the Louvre in Paris became the first museum to open to the public. Other European countries lagged behind in making their cultural heritages available to the masses, but even the poorer classes gained access to these temples of culture by the late nineteenth century.

═══════ S E C T I O N   S U M M A R Y ═══════

- Some European governments responded to the threat of growing worker militancy and socialist politics through measures of social reform, such as protective labor legislation for women and children, health insurance, and old-age pensions.

- Municipalities, churches, and other charitable groups offered numerous forms of assistance to the poor, some of which the state eventually took over.

- The extension of voting rights led, in France and England, to the establishment of free and mandatory primary education whose goal was to instill love of country, discipline, and obedience to authority, as well as basic skills.

- Public libraries, museums, and art galleries provided further access to education and helped build national cultures.

CULTURE IN AN AGE OF OPTIMISM

What new scientific, intellectual, and cultural trends emerged in this period, and what impact did they have on systems of belief?

The improving economic and material conditions of the second half of the nineteenth century buoyed European thinkers. Many believed that men and women were becoming more enlightened, and they expressed faith in humankind's ability to transform the world with a parade of scientific and technological breakthroughs. The world seemed knowable and perfectible. This faith advanced secularism while it undermined the certainties of traditional religion. The arts reflected these new values, emphasizing realism and science—as well as an underlying foreboding about the dark side of this "age of optimism."

DARWIN AND EVOLUTION

By midcentury most thinkers accepted the notion of the change and transformation of society—and, by analogy, of the natural environment. The French thinker Auguste Comte (oh-GOOST KONT) championed the notion that human development—human history—proceeded through distinct and irreversible stages. Human progress, inscribed in the laws of nature, leads inexorably upward to the final and highest stage of development, the "positive"—or scientific—stage. Widely read throughout Europe and Latin America, Comte's writings helped bolster the era's faith in science, and the very progress science made seemed to confirm its precepts. Comte's philosophy, known as **positivism,** dominated the era. Whereas the romantics had emphasized feeling, the positivists upheld the significance of what could be measured and verified. They were confident that scientific methods would ensure the continued progress of humanity.

Although evolution in the biological realm had been suggested as early as the end of the eighteenth century, Charles Darwin (1809–1882) was the first to offer a systematic explanation of the process. As the naturalist on an official British scientific expedition in the 1830s, he had visited the Galápagos Islands off the western coast of South America. On these islands he found species similar to but very different from those on the mainland. Could they be the results of separate creations? Or was it more likely that in varying environments they had

positivism   Philosophy of the French thinker Auguste Comte who asserted that human history progressed through distinct and irreversible stages, leading to the final and highest stage of development, the positive—or scientific—stage.

DARWIN'S BASIC LAWS OF EVOLUTION

Writing in an age of vast transformations, Darwin could imagine the mutability of all nature, including species, over time. And like his contemporaries, he could imagine that evolution would lead to improvement, to increasing "perfection" of various species. A religious man who lost much of his faith as a result of his scientific investigations, Darwin was anxious to reassure Christians, hence his attempt to portray evolution as part of God's divine plan.

Nothing at first can appear more difficult to believe than that the more complex organs and instincts have been perfected, not by means superior to, though analogous with, human reason, but by the accumulation of innumerable slight variations, each good for the individual possessor. Nevertheless, this difficulty, though appearing to our imagination insuperably great, cannot be considered real if we admit the following propositions, namely, that all parts of the organisation and instincts offer, at least, individual differences—that there is a struggle for existence leading to the preservation of profitable deviations of structure or instinct—and, lastly, that gradations in the state of perfection of each organ may have existed, each good of its kind. The truth of these propositions cannot, I think, be disputed. . . .

As geology plainly proclaims that each land has undergone great physical changes, we might have expected to find that organic beings have varied under nature, in the same way as they have varied under domestication. And if there has been any variability under nature, it would be an unaccountable fact if natural selection had not come into play. . . .

There is grandeur in this view of life, with its several powers, having been originally breathed by the Creator into a few forms or into one; and that, whilst this planet has gone cycling on according to the fixed law of gravity, from so simple a beginning endless forms most beautiful and most wonderful have been, and are being evolved.

QUESTIONS

1. What role does natural selection play in Darwin's theory, and what is the logic behind it?
2. How and why does Darwin attempt to reconcile his theory with religion?

Source: Charles Darwin, *On the Origin of Species by Means of Natural Selection*, 6th ed., vol. 2 (1872; repr., New York: Appleton, 1923), pp. 267–268, 279, 305–306.

adapted differently? Darwin proposed that closely related species compete for food and living space. In this struggle, those in each species that are better adapted to the environment have the advantage over the others and hence are more likely to survive. In the "struggle for existence," only the fittest endure. Those surviving, Darwin surmised, pass on the positive traits to their offspring. He called the mechanism that explained the evolution and development of new species "natural selection," a process that he proposed was imperceptible but continuous. Darwin's observations in the Galápagos Islands became the basis for *On the Origin of Species by Means of Natural Selection* (1859), the most important scientific work of the nineteenth century. (See the box "The Written Record: Darwin's Basic Laws of Evolution.")

Darwin's theory that evolution in nature was inevitable echoes the nineteenth-century conviction that the present represented an ever more developed stage of the past. Many viewed his work as confirmation that societies—like species—were preordained to evolve toward progressively higher stages. Darwin at first avoided the question of whether human beings, too, are affected by the laws of evolution. The notion of human evolution would throw into question humanity's uniqueness and its separation from the rest of creation by its possession (in the Christian view) of a soul. But Darwin finally did confront the issue in *The Descent of Man* (1871), in which he presented evidence that humanity, too, is subject to these natural laws. The recognition that human beings are members of the animal kingdom like other species disturbed him, and the admission, he wrote, "is like confessing a murder." Nonetheless, for Darwin scientific evidence took precedence over all other considerations.

These assertions shocked Christians, and some denounced the new scientific findings. Some argued that science and faith belonged to two different worlds. Others claimed that there was no reason why God could not have created the world through natural forces. In the long run, however, **Darwinism** seemed to undermine

Darwinism Influential theory of biological evolution, first put forth by Charles Darwin. He proposed that all forms of life continuously develop through natural selection, whereby those that are better adapted to the environment have the advantage and are more likely to survive and pass on their beneficial traits to their offspring.

the certainties of religious orthodoxies; many found them incompatible with scientific discovery.

Some contemporaries took Darwin's theories beyond biology and applied them to human social development. Social Darwinists argued that human societies evolve in the same way as plants and animals. According to their logic, human societies—races, classes, nations—like species, were destined to compete for survival, and some would be condemned to fade away. And from these harsh laws, a better humanity would evolve. The British social theorist Herbert Spencer (1820–1903), who coined the expression "survival of the fittest," believed that society should be established in such a way that the strongest and most resourceful would survive. The weak, poor, and improvident were not worthy of survival, and if the state helped them survive—for instance, by providing welfare—it would only perpetuate the unfit. Poverty was a sign of biological inferiority, wealth a sign of success in the struggle for survival. In Europe and the United States (where Spencer was extremely popular, selling hundreds of thousands of books), **Social Darwinism** was thus used to justify callousness toward the poor at home and toward imperial conquest abroad. The European subjugation of Africans and Asians through colonization offered confirmation for Social Darwinists of white racial superiority. People of color were seen as poorly endowed to compete in the race for survival (see Chapter 24).

PHYSICS, CHEMISTRY, AND MEDICINE

Dramatic scientific breakthroughs occurred in the nineteenth century, confirming the prevalent belief that human beings could understand and control nature. Since the seventeenth century, scientists had attempted to study nature by careful observation, seeking its regularities and developing theories to explain what they had observed. The scientific method of experimental testing yielded major breakthroughs. In physics, laws regarding electricity and magnetism were articulated by Michael Faraday (1791–1867) and James Clerk Maxwell (1831–1879) in the 1830s and 1850s, respectively. Their work established the field of electrical science. In the 1840s Hermann von Helmholtz (1821–1894) in Germany and James Joule (1818–1889) in Great Britain defined the nature of energy in the laws of thermodynamics. In chemistry, new elements were discovered almost every year. In 1869 Russian chemist Dmitri Mendeleev (men-del-LAY-ef) (1834–1907) developed the periodic table, in which the elements are arranged by their atomic weight. He left blank spaces

for elements still unknown but that he was confident existed. Within ten years, three of these elements were discovered, affirming the belief that scientific knowledge not only can be experimentally tested but also has predictive value. Such triumphs further enhanced science's prestige.

Science also became increasingly specialized. In the eighteenth century, the scientist had been a learned amateur practicing a hobby. In the nineteenth century, as the state and industry became more involved in promoting scientific research, the scientist became a professional employed by a university, a hospital, or some other institution. Scientific journals and meetings of scientific associations disseminated new discoveries and theories. Around midcentury a number of important breakthroughs occurred in medicine. Before the development of anesthesia, surgical intervention was limited. With only alcohol to dull the patient's pain, even the swiftest surgeons could perform only modest surgical procedures. In the 1840s, however, the introduction of ether and then chloroform allowed people to undergo more extensive surgery. It also was used to relieve pain in more routine procedures and in childbirth; Queen Victoria asked for chloroform when in labor.

Increasingly, physicians applied the scientific experimental method to medicine, and as a result they became concerned with discovering the origins of diseases and not just their treatment. Louis Pasteur (1822–1895) achieved notable breakthroughs when he discovered that microbes, small organisms invisible to the naked eye, cause various diseases. Pasteur found that heating milk to a certain temperature kills disease-carrying organisms. This process, called pasteurization, reduced the incidence of gastrointestinal illnesses that were particularly harmful to children. Pasteur initiated other advances as well in the prevention of disease. Vaccination against smallpox had started in England in the eighteenth century, but Pasteur invented vaccines for other diseases and was able to explain the process by which the body, inoculated with a weak form of bacilli, developed antibodies that successfully overcame more serious infections. In England the surgeon Joseph Lister (1827–1912) developed an effective disinfectant, carbolic acid, to kill the germs that cause gangrene and other infections in surgical patients. Lister's development of germ-free procedures transformed the science of surgery. By reducing the patient's risk, more ambitious surgery could be attempted. Eventually midwives and doctors, by washing their hands and sterilizing their instruments, began to reduce the incidence of the puerperal, or "childbed," fever that killed so many women after childbirth. The increasingly scientific base of medicine and its visible success in combating disease improved its reputation.

Social Darwinism   Theory of social evolution that states that human societies evolve in the same way as plants and animals, and that the weak, poor, and improvident are not worthy of survival.

BIRTH OF THE SOCIAL SCIENCES

The scientific method, so dramatically effective in uncovering the mysteries of nature, could, it was thought, also be applied to the workings of society.

No field in the human sciences flourished as much in the nineteenth century as that of history. In an era undergoing vast transformations, many people became interested in change over time, particularly with regard to their own national histories. The father of modern historical writing is the German Leopold von Ranke (fon RANG-key) (1795–1886). Departing from the tradition of earlier historians, who explained the past as the ongoing fulfillment of an overarching purpose—divine will, the liberation of humanity, or some other goal—Ranke insisted that the role of the historian was to "show how things actually were." Like a scientist, the historian must be objective and dispassionate. By viewing humankind of all eras and environments on their own terms, and not those of others, historians could arrive at a better understanding of humanity.

This perspective transformed the study of history into a discipline with recognizable common standards of evidence. Historians studied and interpreted original (or "primary") sources; they collected and published their findings; they founded professional organizations and published major journals.

Other social sciences also developed in this period. Anthropology, the comparative study of people in different societies, had been the subject of speculative literature for hundreds of years. Increased contacts with non-European societies in the nineteenth century—the effect of burgeoning trade, exploration, and missionary activities—stimulated anthropological curiosity. In 1844 the Society of Ethnology was founded in Paris, followed by the Anthropological Society (1859). London, Berlin, and Vienna quickly followed suit, establishing similar societies in the 1860s. Anthropologists speculated on the causes of the perceived differences among human races, mainly attributing the variations to their physical structures. They offered apparent "scientific" backing to the era's racism, explaining that non-Europeans were condemned to an existence inferior to the white races.

The main anthropological theorist in Britain was Edward Tylor (1832–1917), the son of a brass manufacturer. Through his travels Tylor came into contact with non-European peoples, who aroused his curiosity. Strongly influenced by the evolutionary doctrines of his day, Tylor believed that the various societies of humankind were subject to discoverable scientific laws. Tylor posited that if one could travel back in time, one would find humankind increasingly unsophisticated. So, too, the farther one traveled from Europe, the more primitive humankind became. Thus, according to his view, the contemporary African was at a level of development similar to that of Europeans in an earlier era.

Tylor was not technically a racist, since he argued that the conditions of non-Europeans were not due to biology but rather were a function of their institutions. Eventually they would "evolve" and become akin to Europeans. Like racists, however, evolutionists believed in European superiority. Anthropology gave "scientific" sanction to the idea of a single European people, sharing either a similar biological structure or a common stage of social development, which distinguished them from non-Europeans.

The term *sociology* was coined by Auguste Comte. A number of ambitious thinkers, among them the English "social philosopher" Herbert Spencer (see page 729), had considered how individuals are affected by the society in which they live. In the 1840s various social reformers published detailed statistical investigations revealing relationships between, for instance, income, disease, and death rates. A few decades later the theoretical principles underlying sociology were spelled out. Among the first researchers to do so was Emile Durkheim (DIRK-hime) (1858–1917), who insisted that sociology was a verifiable science. His disciples, and the journal he founded, ensured the success of sociology as a professionalized discipline.

Whereas in the past history, anthropology, and sociology were the purview of amateurs, now professional historians, anthropologists, and sociologists were engaged full-time in research and teaching at universities or research institutes. Professionalization and specialization led to significant advances in several disciplines, but it also led to the fragmentation and compartmentalization of knowledge. People of broad learning and expertise became far less common.

THE CHALLENGE TO RELIGION

The scientific claims of the era clashed with some fundamental religious precepts. Although most Europeans continued to be strongly influenced by traditional religious beliefs, they appeared less confident than in earlier eras.

Religion had assumed increased importance as a bulwark of order in the wake of the 1848 revolutions. In France Napoleon III gave the Catholic Church new powers over education, and the bourgeoisie flocked to worship. In Spain moderates who had been anticlerical (opposed to the clergy) began to support the church, and in 1851 they signed a concordat (an agreement with the papacy) declaring Roman Catholicism "the only religion of the Spanish nation." In Austria in 1855, the state surrendered powers it had acquired in the 1780s, returning to bishops full control over the clergy, the seminaries, and the administration of marriage laws.

In 1848 the papacy had been nearly overthrown by revolution, and in 1860 it lost most of its domains to Italy. Thus Pope Pius IX became a sworn enemy of liberalism. In 1864, he issued the *Syllabus of Errors,* in which he condemned a long list of faults that included "progress," "liberalism," and "modern civilization." To establish full control over the clergy and believers, the Lateran Council in 1870 issued the controversial doctrine of papal infallibility, which declared that the pope, when speaking officially on matters of faith and morals, is incapable of error. This doctrine became a target of anticlerical opinion.

The political alliance the Catholic Church struck with reactionary forces meant that when new political groups came to power, they moved against the church. In Italy, since the church had discouraged national unification, conflict raged between the church and the new state. In Germany Catholics had either held on to their regional loyalties or favored unification under Austrian auspices. When Protestant Prussia unified Germany, Chancellor Bismarck viewed the Catholics with suspicion as unpatriotic and launched a campaign against them, the *Kulturkampf* (KOOL-toor-kampf) ("cultural struggle"). Bismarck expelled the Jesuits and attempted to establish state control over the Catholic schools and appointment of bishops. Not satisfied, he seized church property and imprisoned or exiled eighteen hundred priests.

In France the republicans, who finally won the upper hand over the monarchists in 1879, bitterly resented the church's support of the monarchist party. Strongly influenced by Comte's ideas of positivism, republicans believed that France would not be a free country until the power of the church was diminished and its nonscientific or antiscientific disposition was overcome. The republican regime reduced the role of the church in education as well as some other clerical privileges.

Greater tolerance, or perhaps indifference to religion in general, led to more acceptance of religious diversity. In 1854 and 1871 England opened university admission and teaching posts at all universities to non-Anglicans. In France, too, the position of religious minorities improved. Some of the highest officials of the Second Empire were Protestants, as were some early leaders of the Third Republic and some important business leaders and scientists.

Legal emancipation of Jews, started in France in 1791, subsequently spread to the rest of the Continent. The British allowed Jews to hold seats in the House of Commons in 1858, and in the House of Lords the following decade. In the 1860s Germany and Austria-Hungary granted Jews the rights of citizenship. Although some Jews occupied high office in France and Italy, they had to convert to Christianity before they could aspire to such positions in Germany and Austria-Hungary. In other fields such as banking and commerce, access was easier.

Social discrimination continued, however—most of European society refused to accept Jews as social equals.

In the expanding economy of western Europe, where the condition of most people was improving, the enhanced opportunity of a previously despised minority aroused relatively little attention. In other parts of Europe, Jews were not so fortunate. In eastern Europe, they incurred resentment when they moved into commerce, industry, and the professions. Outbreaks of violence against them, called *pogroms,* occurred in Bucharest, the capital of Romania, in 1866 and in the Russian seaport of Odessa in 1871. Although economic rivalries may have fueled anti-Jewish feelings, they do not completely explain it. In most cases anti-Jewish sentiment occurred in the areas of Europe least exposed to liberal ideas of human equality and human rights.

As the continued anti-Semitism demonstrates, science by no means always led to increased tolerance; nor did it necessarily weaken religious fervor. Church attendance continued to be high, especially in rural areas. French people reported frequent sightings of the Virgin Mary. In 1858 a shepherd girl claimed to have seen and spoken with her at Lourdes (LOORD), which became an especially important shrine whose waters were reputed to heal the lame and the sick. In 1872 construction of a rail line allowed 100,000 people a year to visit the town.

CULTURE IN THE AGE OF MATERIAL CHANGE

The era's admiration of technology and science and its idolization of progress were reflected in the arts. Some artists optimistically believed they could more accurately portray reality by adopting the methods of the scientist, objectively depicting their subjects. A minority, however, were disillusioned by the materialism of the age and warned against its loss of values.

Photography had a direct impact on painting. Various experiments in the late eighteenth century, plus the inventions of the Frenchman Louis Daguerre (dah-GAIR) (1789–1851), made the camera relatively usable by the 1830s. Its widespread use began in the 1890s with the introduction of celluloid film and American George Eastman's (1854–1932) invention of the Kodak camera, which became mass-produced. Unlike painting and sculpture, photography was affordable for the public. Photographic services were in high demand; by the 1860s, thirty thousand people in Paris made a living from photography and allied fields. (See "The Visual Record: The Modern City and Photography.")

The ability of photography to depict a scene with exactitude had a significant impact on art. On the one hand, it encouraged many artists to be true to reality, to reproduce on the canvas a visual image akin to that of a photograph. On the other hand, some artists felt that such realism was no longer necessary in their sphere.

Courbet: The Stone Breakers

This realistic 1849 painting depicts the rough existence of manual laborers. The bleakness of the subject matter and the style in which it was carried out characterized much of the realist school of art. *(Staatliche Kunstsammlungen, Dresden/The Bridgeman Art Library)*

However, the great majority of the public, which now had wide access to museum exhibitions, was accustomed to photographic accuracy and desired art that was representative and intelligible. Realistic works of art met this need, at least superficially.

Many artists discarded myths and symbols to portray the world as it actually was, or at least as it appeared to them—a world without illusions, everyday life in all its grimness. The realist painter Gustave Courbet (koor-BAY) (1819–1877) proclaimed himself "without ideals and without religion." His fellow Frenchman Jean-François Millet (mil-LAY) (1814–1875) held a similar opinion. Instead of romanticizing peasants in the manner of earlier artists, he painted the harsh physical conditions under which they labored. In England the so-called pre-Raphaelites took as their model those painters prior to Raphael in Renaissance Italy, who had depicted the realistic simplicity of nature. In painting historical scenes, these artists meticulously researched the landscape, architecture, fauna, and costumes of their subjects.

Photography and artistic realism also helped inspire their counterpoint in less realistic representations. On April 15, 1874, six French artists—Edgar Degas (1834–1917), Claude Monet (1840–1926), Camille Pissarro (1830–1903), Auguste Renoir (1840–1919), Alfred Sisley (1839–1899), and Berthe Morisot (1841–1895)— opened an exhibition in Paris that a critic disparagingly called **impressionist,** after the title of one of Monet's paintings, *Impression: Sunrise.* The impressionists were influenced by new theories of physics that claimed images were transmitted to the brain as small light particles that the brain then reconstituted. The impressionists wanted their paintings to capture what things looked like before the brain "distorted" them. Many of these painters unconventionally left their studios to paint objects exactly as they looked outdoors when light hit them at a certain angle. Monet, for example, emphasized outdoor painting and the need for spontaneity—for reproducing subjects without preconceptions about how earlier artists had depicted them— and seeking to show exactly how the colors and shapes struck the eye. Monet was particularly interested in creating multiple paintings of the same scene—from different viewpoints, under different weather conditions, at different times of day—to underscore that no single "correct" depiction could possibly capture a subject.

Online Study Center **Improve Your Grade**
Primary Source: Impressionism Defined

impressionist Late-nineteenth-century style of painting pioneered by the French artists Degas, Monet, Pissarro, Renoir, Sisley, and Morisot.

A CHINESE OFFICIAL'S VIEWS OF EUROPEAN MATERIAL PROGRESS

Educated in European universities, Ku Hung-Ming rose to become a high official in the Chinese court. His essays were penned under the impact of the European military intervention in China during the Boxer Rebellion in 1900. Ku denounced European notions of superiority over Asia by arguing that material progress was not an appropriate measure of a civilization's value.

In order to estimate the value of a civilization, it seems to me, the question we must finally ask is not what great cities, what magnificent houses, what fine roads it has built and is able to build; what beautiful and comfortable furniture, what clever and useful implements, tools and instruments it has made and is able to make; no, not even what institutions, what arts and sciences it has invested: the question we must ask, in order to estimate the value of a civilization—is what type of humanity, what kind of men and women it has been able to produce. In fact, the man and woman,—the type of human beings—which a civilization produces, it is this which shows the essence, the personality, so to speak, the soul of that civilization. Now if the men and women of a civilization show the essence, the personality and soul of that civilization, the language which the men and women in that civilization speak, shows the essence, the personality, the soul of the men and women of that civilization. . . .

To Europeans, and especially to unthinking practical Englishmen, who are accustomed to take what modern political economists call "the standard of living" as the test of the moral culture of or civilization of a people, the actual life of the Chinese and of the people of the East at the present day, will no doubt appear very sordid and undesirable. But the standard of living by itself is not a proper test of the civilization of a people. The standard of living in America at the present day, is, I believe, much higher than it is in Germany. But although the son of an American millionaire, who regards the simple and comparatively low standard of living among the professors of a German University, may doubt the value of the education in such a University, yet no educated man, I believe, who has traveled in both countries, will admit that the Germans are a less civilized people than the Americans.

QUESTIONS

1. How does the Chinese official define civilization? How does his view differ from the European view?
2. What is Ku Hung-Ming's idea of a hierarchy of civilization?
3. According to the ideas in this reading, what is the connection between progress and civilization?

Source: Ku Hung-Ming, *The Spirit of the Chinese People*, 2d ed. (Beijing: Commercial Press, 1922), pp. 1, 144–145.

The school of realism also influenced literature, especially the novel. In realist novels, life was not glorified or infused with mythical elements; the stark existence of daily life was seen as a suitable subject. Charles Dickens (1812–1870), who came from a poor background and had personally experienced the inhumanity of the London underworld, wrote novels depicting the lot of the poor with humor and sympathy. The appalling social conditions he described helped educate his large middle-class audience on the state of the poor.

Another realist, the French novelist Gustave Flaubert (flo-BEAR) (1821–1880), consciously debunked the romanticism of his elders. His famous novel, *Madame Bovary*, describes middle-class life as bleak, boring, and meaningless. The heroine seeks to escape the narrow confines of provincial life by adulterous and disastrous affairs.

Emile Zola (1840–1902), another Frenchman, belonged to the naturalist school of literature. The writer, he declared, should record and represent human behavior scientifically. He described his own work as sim-

ilar to "the analysis that surgeons make on cadavers." Zola's Rougon-Macquart (roo-ZHON–mah-KAR) series, which includes the novels *Nana* and *Germinal*, describes in detail the experience of several generations of a family. His major theme is the impact of environment and heredity on his characters' lives of degradation and vice, in which they seem locked in a Darwinian struggle for survival: some are doomed by the laws of biology to succeed, others to succumb.

The Russian novelist Leo Tolstoy (1828–1910) brought a new perspective to the historical novel in *War and Peace*. Instead of a heroic approach to battle, he showed individuals trapped by forces beyond their control. Small and insignificant events as well as major ones seemed to govern human destiny. Another Russian novelist often associated with the realist school, Feodor Dostoyevsky (1821–1881), aimed to portray realistically the psychological dimensions of his characters in novels such as *Crime and Punishment* (1866), *The Idiot* (1868), and *The Brothers Karamazov* (1879–1880).

The Modern City and Photography

This photo of Piccadilly Square in Manchester documents the modernization of the nineteenth-century city and at the same time conveys the sense of immediacy that photography provided as a new means of representation.

Taken in the 1880s, this photo* shows evidence of the great progress that had taken place in photography since its invention half a century earlier. In 1839 Louis Daguerre publicized the method of fixing an image on silvered copperplate. At first the cameras and equipment were so cumbersome that photography was confined to studios. Thus the only images were portraits of people and the occasional still life. As the camera became simpler, photographers could leave the studio and take pictures outdoors. The introduction of the dry plate method in the 1870s made film far more sensitive to light, reducing exposure time to a fraction of a second. Now a photograph could capture movement without reducing it to a blur, as in this bustling city scene.

Originally photography had been regarded as a more exact, and less expensive, form of illustration and so was influenced by the conventions of painting. Because of the slowness of taking pictures and the obvious presence of the photographer with bulky equipment, most early photographs, even outdoor shots, were staged. But soon thereafter, thanks to technical innovations, photographers could capture a scene even without the cooperation of the subject. None of the subjects in this photo has eye contact with the camera. In fact, they seem unaware of the photographer as they go about their daily business.

This photo also conveys important visual information about the emerging modern city. A vibrant textile city, Manchester had a population that more than doubled to 600,000 inhabitants between 1830 and 1900. Piccadilly was its commercial center. As the photo here shows, it had been built as a large open square intended for the easy movement of pedestrians and wagons. City planners of the nineteenth century created squares and broad, straight avenues feeding into them, such as suggested here. Replacing old slums and narrow alleys, broad avenues eased the flow of traffic and admitted fresh air and sunlight. The square contained fancy stores with dwellings situated on the upper floors behind the elegantly crafted façades.

Piccadilly, the commercial center of Manchester, had warehouses and offices where buyers purchased textiles that they would in turn sell to retail consumers. As seen in this photo, Piccadilly Square, as a commercial center, required public transportation to move people quickly on the broad new avenues. Notice the rails for the horse-drawn tramway that had been introduced as early as the 1820s. They were the first means of mass transportation within the city. Trams on rails reduced friction and allowed a horse to pull a far greater load. In this case the tram, located in the center of the photo, is a double-decker.

The large modern city required ease of communication at night as well as in the daytime. Street lighting not only provided that convenience but also made the streets more secure by making potential crime more visible. Streetlamps became the norm in large cities, especially in the better neighborhoods. The elegant gaslights viewable in the photo of Piccadilly Square were replaced a few years later by electric lamps that were cheaper to operate and allowed for the spread of city lighting.

An industrial town, Manchester was not a particularly pleasant city to live in. Visitors complained of its grime, pollution, and foul smells. Many members of the commercial classes lived in wealthy suburbs and commuted by tram to work in the center. Sometime after this picture was taken, the horse-drawn tram was replaced by the electric tram, which could transport more people faster than its predecessor. Its lower cost also meant that it was accessible to most workers. With the advent of the electric tram, workers also began to move to the suburbs, making the center less crowded.

If the modern photograph was different from a painting, photography still adhered to some of the traditions of painting—notably composition. The photographer composed this image by making choices, for example, as to what to put in the foreground. Our eye centers on the harried merchant crossing the well-ordered street with its backdrop of amenities.

Compare this photograph with Camille Pissarro's *L'avenue de l'Opéra, Sunlight, Winter Morning* on page 723. Paris, known as the "city of light," was very different from Manchester, though like that industrial city, the new boulevards resulting from "Hausmannization" allowed for a larger and speedier flow of traffic and commerce. Pissarro also

*The advice of Thomas Prasch in the choice of this photo is gratefully acknowledged.

Piccadilly Square, Manchester, ca. 1886   *(Topham Picturepoint/The Image Works)*

conveys in this painting the bustle—and perhaps alienation—some felt in modern life. Note the predominance of solitary figures in both the painting and the photograph. Wide boulevards meant that pedestrians did not "run into each other" and socialize as readily as they had on narrow streets. Indeed, Pissarro and other impressionist painters disdained the modernization of cities and turned instead to the suburbs and rural landscapes, leaving the documentation of urban change to photographers. Pissarro thought Paris had become "ill" from all of its changes.

The chemical and optical breakthroughs that made the camera such an effective new tool were implemented by inventors in cities such as London, Paris, and Berlin. Photographers in turn took pictures of some of the great technical feats of their era, such as the Eiffel Tower. The modern aspects of the city, such as the scene in this photo, were frequent subjects for the photographer's lens. Before the end of the century, photographs such as this were commonly used on postcards. The producers and consumers of postcards were more fascinated by the reality of representation rather than the beauty of particular sites, as postcards geared toward tourism would later embrace.

QUESTIONS

1. How did modernization—urbanization, commercialization, the design of cities, and modern means of transportation—change people's sensual experience and perceptions?

2. In its replication of "reality," how did photography both record and create our understanding of the past? How did it both replicate traditional art and create new ways of seeing?

Online Study Center
Improve Your Grade Visual Record Activities

Although this era generally celebrated material progress, a number of intellectuals reacted against it. They were alarmed by the prospect of the popular masses achieving political power through winning the vote and by mass production and consumption. They denounced the smug and the self-satisfied, who saw happiness in acquisition and consumption. Some condemned the age in severe terms. Dostoyevsky railed against the materialism and egotism of the West, branding its civilization as driven by "trade, shipping, markets, factories." In Britain—the nation that seemed to embody progress—the historian Thomas Carlyle (1795–1881) berated his age as one not of progress but of selfishness. He saw parliamentarianism as a sham, and he called for a strong leader to save the nation from endless debates and compromises. Unlike most of his contemporaries, who saw in material plenty a sign of progress, Carlyle saw the era as one of decline, bereft of spiritual values.

Another Englishman, John Ruskin (1819–1900), looked back to the Middle Ages as an ideal era in which people exercised a fine sense of craftsmanship instead of producing with machines. People then supposedly had a better sense of community and labored for the common good rather than out of a sense of selfish individualism. Ruskin was one of the founders of the arts and crafts movement, which aimed to produce goods for daily use with an eye for beauty and originality. "Industry without art is brutality," Ruskin warned.

In France republicans saw in the ostentation of the Second Empire a sign of depravity and decline. The 1870–1871 defeat in war and the insurrection of the Paris Commune contributed to the mood of pessimism among many intellectuals. Flaubert detested his own age, seeing it as petty and mean. The characters in Zola's Rougon-Macquart novels slide steadily downward as each generation's mental faculties, social positions, and morals degenerate. Some people abroad also were unimpressed with developments in Europe. (See the box "The Global Record: A Chinese Official's Views of European Material Progress.")

Not all were optimistic in this age of optimism. If many people celebrated what they viewed as an age of progress, others claimed that under the outer trappings of material comfort lay a frightening ignorance of aesthetic, moral, and spiritual values.

SECTION SUMMARY

- Darwin's theory of evolution reinforced the belief among some of the inevitability of human progress; others found the placement of human beings in the same category as animal species profoundly disturbing.

- Social Darwinists applied Darwin's theories to human society in order to justify inequality, racial hierarchies, and "survival of the fittest."

- The application of the scientific method (experimentation) led to scientific breakthroughs, transforming fields such as physics (especially electrical science), chemistry, and medicine.

- The scientific method also transformed the study of human society, professionalizing the fields of history, anthropology, and sociology.

- Scientific discoveries and theories undermined religious belief among some people; others, however, reacted to the harshness of the material world by embracing religion more fervently.

- Science and technology infused the arts with a new emphasis on realism and on the importance of visual representations.

HAPTER SUMMARY

Online Study Center **ACE the Test**

What technological changes led to the expansion of the European economy after the mid-nineteenth century?

How did the economic expansion affect the various social classes, and city versus rural areas, differently?

What problems did urbanization create, and what were the solutions?

How and why did the state increasingly intervene in people's everyday lives?

What new scientific, intellectual, and cultural trends emerged in this period, and what impact did they have on systems of belief?

During the second half of the nineteenth century, the cluster of technological innovations known as the second industrial revolution—mass-produced steel, synthetic dyes, new forms of energy such as petroleum and electricity, and the speedup in production—created for many Westerners an era of unprecedented material plenty. The expansion of railroads, advances in shipping, the standardization of postal service, and the inventions of the telegraph and telephone collapsed distances of time and space, and brought Europe further into a global economy.

Economic changes transformed the class structure of many European countries: the middle classes expanded and their values and tastes defined the second half of the century, while the aristocracy declined in power. Many rural and urban laborers still lived in poverty. Agricultural workers left the countryside, and cities continued their rapid growth, giving rise to overcrowding, traffic jams, and pollution and facilitating the spread of contagious diseases.

To address problems of urban growth, local governments established services such as street lighting and public transportation. They, along with charities, also took measures to improve public health and provide advice and material assistance. In both the countryside and the cities, governments provided new services, such as public education and cultural institutions.

Intellectual and cultural currents reflected material changes and the confidence they inspired. In addition to new breakthroughs in the sciences, scientific methods were applied to the study of human behavior. Novelists and painters aimed to dissect like scientists the world around them, adopting realism in the arts. Some intellectuals, however, were repulsed by the crass self-satisfaction of the bourgeoisie, and they despised their age's worship of industry and materialism.

LOOKING AHEAD

Progress, as Europeans were to learn in a later era, was two-edged: the very forces that improved life for many also threatened it. The same breakthroughs in chemistry that led to the development of artificial fertilizers also provided more powerful military explosives. The expansion of education and the reduction of illiteracy lessened ignorance but created a public that could more easily absorb messages of hate against a rival nation or against religious or ethnic minorities at home. In the shadows of material progress lurked new forces that would ultimately undermine the comforts, self-assurance, and peace of this age.

KEY TERMS

second industrial revolution (p. 712)

bourgeois century (p. 717)

professionalization (p. 717)

Victorian morality (p. 719)

separate spheres (p. 719)

solidarism (p. 726)

social Catholics (p. 726)

positivism (p. 727)

Darwinism (p. 728)

Social Darwinism (p. 729)

impressionist (p. 732)

Online Study Center
Improve Your Grade Flashcards

SUGGESTED READING

Browne, Janet. *Charles Darwin: The Power of Place.* 2005. A highly readable biography that surveys debates between scientists and churchmen over evolutionary theory.

Cannadine, David. *The Rise and Fall of Class in Britain.* 1999. Reveals the importance of class in nineteenth-century British society.

Clark, Linda L. *The Rise of Professional Women in France.* 2000. A fine study delineating the increasing role of women in the professions, especially public administration.

Goodman, David, and Colin Chant, eds. *European Cities and Technology Reader.* 1999. Emphasizes the importance of technological breakthroughs in the modernization of cities.

Hobsbawm, Eric J. *The Age of Capital, 1848–1875.* 1979. Particularly strong on social and economic developments.

Nord, Philip. *Impressionists and Politics.* 2000. Sets the French impressionists in their political and social contexts.

Standage, Tom. *The Victorian Internet.* 1998. A brief, popular history of the telegraph.

24

ESCALATING TENSIONS, 1880–1914

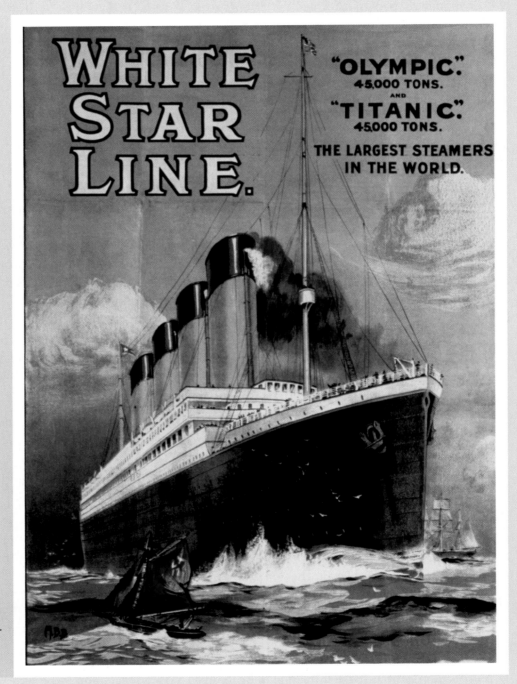

The "Unsinkable"
Titanic
The *Titanic* proudly announces its maiden voyage.
(Corbis)

n April 1912 the *Titanic*, the largest and most technologically advanced passenger ship ever built, sailed from Southampton, England, for New York. Its owners, the White Star Line, boasted that the building of this majestic vessel testified to "the progress of mankind" and would "rank high in the achievements of the twentieth century." Hailed as "virtually unsinkable," on the night of April 12 the *Titanic* struck an iceberg south of Newfoundland and rapidly sank. More than 1,500 of the 2,100 people aboard perished in the icy North Atlantic waters. The overconfident captain had not taken warnings of icebergs in the ship's path seriously enough.

Two years later European society was hit by a major disaster—the outbreak of a world war. That such a disaster would end the era called by contemporaries the *belle époque* (BELL eh-POK), or "beautiful epoch," was as unimaginable as the *Titanic*'s fate. The booming economy had been expanding opportunities for many. Parliamentary government continued to spread, and more nations seemed to be adapting to democracy as suffrage was extended. Yet hand in hand with these trends of apparent progress appeared troubling tendencies. Under the surface were forces threatening the stability of European society, which is why, in 1914, a lone assassin's bullet could set off a series of reactions that brought a whole era to a tragic close.

In the decades prior to 1914, governing became more complex as nations grew larger. The population of Europe jumped from 330 million in 1880 to 460 million by the outbreak of war. A larger population coupled with extended suffrage meant that more men participated in the political system, but it became harder to reach a consensus. The example of democracy in some countries led to discontent in the autocracies that failed to move toward freer institutions. Where freer institutions did exist, those excluded from them—women, ethnic minorities, and the poor—became ever more resentful.

Intellectuals revolted against what they viewed as the smug self-assuredness of earlier years. They no longer felt certain that the world was knowable, stable, or subject to mastery by rational human beings. Some jettisoned rationality and instead glorified emotion, irrationality, and in some

CHAPTER OUTLINE

THE NEW IMPERIALISM AND THE SPREAD OF EUROPE'S POPULATION

FROM OPTIMISM TO ANXIETY: POLITICS AND CULTURE

VULNERABLE DEMOCRACIES

AUTOCRACIES IN CRISIS

THE COMING WAR

KEY TERMS

new imperialism	suffragists
Second International	*Weltpolitik*
anti-Semitism	Bolsheviks
Zionism	Triple Alliance
Sigmund Freud	Triple Entente
avant-garde	

Online Study Center

This icon will direct you to interactive map and primary source activities on the website **college.hmco.com/pic/noble5e**

cases violence. The works of painters and writers seemed to anticipate the impending destruction of world order.

The anxieties and tensions that beset many Europeans took a variety of forms. Ethnic minorities became targets of hatred. European states embarked on a race for empire throughout the world, forcibly putting non-Europeans under white domination. On the Continent states felt increasingly insecure, worried that they would be subject to attack. They established standing armies, shifted alliances, drafted war plans, and, in the end, went to war.

FOCUS QUESTIONS

What were the main motivations for European imperialism?

In what ways did the worldview of intellectuals living in the belle époque differ from that of a generation earlier?

What factors made parliamentary rule in Great Britain, France, and Italy dysfunctional?

What various crises weakened autocratic rule in Germany, Russia, and the Ottoman Empire?

What responsibility did each of the Great Powers have for the outbreak of war in 1914?

THE NEW IMPERIALISM AND THE SPREAD OF EUROPE'S POPULATION

What were the main motivations for European imperialism?

Part of Europe's self-confidence during the period from the 1880s to 1914 was based on the unchallenged sway it held over the rest of the globe. Europeans brought under political control large swaths of land across the seas and also marked the globe by massive migrations.

The age of empire building that started in Europe in the sixteenth century seemed to have ended by 1750. Then, in the 1880s, the European states launched a new era of expansionism, conquering an unprecedented amount of territory. In only twenty-five years Europeans subjugated 500 million people—one-half of the world's non-European population. European expansion was also manifest in a massive movement of people: between 1870 and 1914, 55 million Europeans moved overseas, mainly to Australia, the United States, Canada, and Argentina.

This era of ambitious conquest is often called the **new imperialism,** to differentiate it from the earlier stage of empire building. Whereas the earlier imperialism focused on the Americas, nineteenth-century imperialism centered on Africa and Asia. And unlike the colonizing of the earlier period, the new imperialism occurred in an age of mass participation in politics and was accompanied by expressions of popular enthusiasm.

new imperialism Era of European overseas expansion launched in the 1880s. Europeans subjugated 500 million people in Africa and Asia.

ECONOMIC AND SOCIAL MOTIVES

The desire for huge markets and the hope for profit—much of it illusory—stirred an interest in empire. Colonies, it was believed, would provide eager buyers for European goods that would stimulate production at home. Yet colonies did not represent large markets for the metropolitan countries. In 1914 France's colonies represented only 12 percent of its foreign trade. Great Britain's trade with its colonies represented a considerable one-third of its foreign trade, but most of that was with the settlement colonies, such as Canada and Australia, not with those acquired in the era of the new imperialism. As for Germany, colonial trade represented less than 1 percent of its exports. Even protective tariffs imposed on colonies failed to secure trade monopolies. Far more than their colonies, France, Germany, and Great Britain continued to be one another's best customers.

Lack of profitability, however, mattered little to many proponents of empire. Some of them, known as social imperialists, argued that possession of an empire could resolve social as well as economic issues. An empire could be an outlet for a variety of domestic frustrations, especially for those nations concerned about overpopulation. German and Italian imperialists often argued that their nations needed colonies in which to resettle their multiplying poor. Once the overseas territories were acquired, however, few Europeans found them attractive for settlement.

NATIONALISTIC MOTIVES

To a large extent, empire building was triggered by the desire to assert national power. At the end of the nineteenth century, two major powers emerged, Russia and the United States. Compared with these giants, western European nations seemed small and insignificant, and many of their leaders believed that to compete effectively on the world stage, they needed to become large territorial entities. Empires would enable them to achieve that goal.

The British Empire, with India as its crown jewel, constituted the largest, most powerful, and apparently wealthiest of all the European domains. It was the envy of Europe. Although the real source of Britain's wealth and power was the country's industrial economy, many people believed that its success came from its vast empire. And so the British example stimulated other nations to carve out empires. Their activities in turn triggered British anxieties. Britain and France unleashed a scramble for Africa and Asia; in Asia Britain also competed with Russia.

France, defeated by Prussia in 1870, found in its colonies proof that it was still a Great Power. Germany and Italy, which formed their national identities relatively late, cast a jealous eye on the British and French empires and decided that if they were to be counted as Great Powers, they too would need overseas colonies. Belgium's King Leopold II (r. 1876–1909) spun out various plans to acquire colonies to compensate for his nation's small size. And Britain, anxious at the emergence of rival economic and political powers in the late nineteenth century, found in its colonies a guarantee for the future.

In the race for colonies, worldwide strategic concerns stimulated expansion. Because the Suez Canal ensured the route to India, the British established a protectorate over Egypt in 1882. Beginning in the next decade, they feared that a rival power might threaten their position by encroaching on the Nile. They consequently established control over the Nile Valley all the way south to Uganda (see **MAP 24.1**). Russia, fearing a British takeover in central Asia, expanded toward Afghanistan, while the British movement northwestward to Afghanistan had a similar motivation—to prevent Russia from encroaching on India. The "great game" played by Russia and Britain in central Asia ended only in 1907, with the signing of the Anglo-Russian Entente.

Much of this expansion was driven by the desire to control the often-turbulent frontiers of newly acquired areas. Once those frontiers had been brought under control, there were, of course, new frontiers that had to be subdued. As a Russian foreign minister said of such an incentive for expansion, "The chief difficulty is to know where to stop." The imperial powers rarely did.

CHRONOLOGY

1873	Three Emperors' League
1882	Britain seizes Egypt
	Triple Alliance of Germany, Italy, and Austria-Hungary
1884	Three Emperors' League renewed
1890	Kaiser Wilhelm II dismisses Bismarck as chancellor
1894	Franco-Russian Alliance
	Beginning of the Dreyfus affair
1900	King of Italy assassinated
1903	Emmeline Pankhurst founds the Women's Social and Political Union
1904	Anglo-French Entente
1905	Einstein proposes theory of relativity
	Revolution in Russia
1907	Anglo-Russian Entente
1908	Young Turk rebellion in Ottoman Empire
1911	Italy colonizes Libya
	Second Moroccan crisis
June 28, 1914	Assassination of Archduke Franz Ferdinand
August 4, 1914	With the entry of Britain, Europe is at war

The bitter rivalry among the Great Powers helps explain the division of the globe, but it also protected some regions from falling under European domination, especially in parts of Asia. Most of China survived because the European powers held one another's ambitions in check. No state alone could conquer all of China; none would allow the others to do so either.

OTHER IDEOLOGICAL MOTIVES

In addition to the search for profit and nationalistic pride, Europeans developed a strong rationalization for imperialism. Because Europeans had gained technological and scientific know-how, many imperialists believed it was Europe's duty to develop Africa and Asia for the benefit of colonizer and colonized. Railroads, telegraphs, hospitals, and schools would transform colonial peoples by opening them to what were seen as the beneficent influences of Europe. If necessary, these changes would be realized by force.

MAP 24.1   Africa in 1914

European powers in the late nineteenth century conquered most of Africa. Only
Liberia and Ethiopia were left unoccupied at the start of World War I.

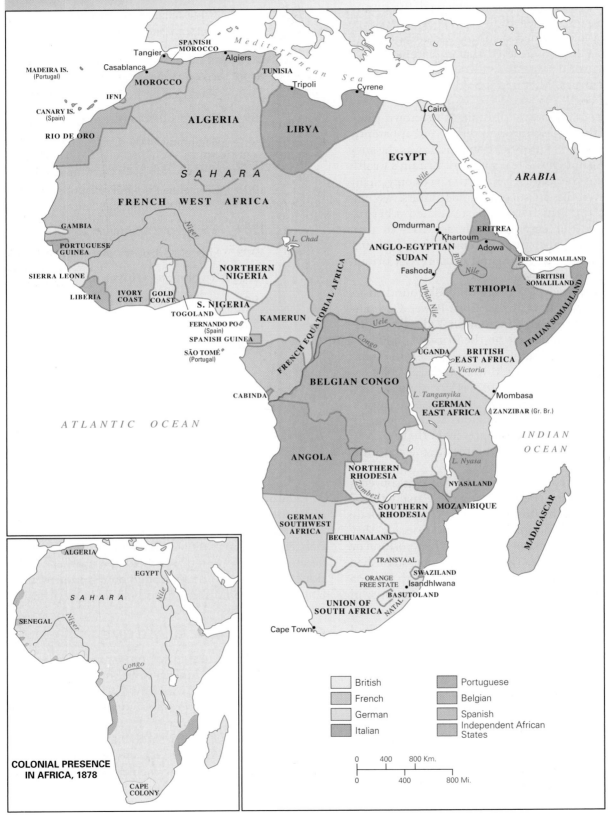

SPANISH MOROCCO
Tangier
Casablanca
MADEIRA IS.
(Portugal)
MOROCCO
IFNI
CANARY IS.
(Spain)
RIO DE ORO
ALGIERS
Algiers
TUNISIA
Tripoli
Cyrene
Mediterranean Sea
Cairo
ALGERIA
LIBYA
EGYPT
ARABIA
SAHARA
Red Sea
Nile
FRENCH   WEST   AFRICA
GAMBIA
PORTUGUESE GUINEA
SIERRA LEONE
LIBERIA
IVORY COAST
GOLD COAST
NORTHERN NIGERIA
Niger
L. Chad
Omdurman
Khartoum
ERITREA
Adowa
ANGLO-EGYPTIAN SUDAN
Fashoda
FRENCH SOMALILAND
BRITISH SOMALILAND
ETHIOPIA
Blue Nile
White Nile
ITALIAN SOMALILAND
TOGOLAND
S. NIGERIA
FERNANDO PO (Spain)
SPANISH GUINEA
SÃO TOMÉ (Portugal)
KAMERUN
FRENCH EQUATORIAL AFRICA
Uele
Congo
UGANDA
BRITISH EAST AFRICA
L. Victoria
CABINDA
BELGIAN CONGO
L. Tanganyika
Mombasa
GERMAN EAST AFRICA
ZANZIBAR (Gr. Br.)
ATLANTIC   OCEAN
INDIAN OCEAN
ANGOLA
NORTHERN RHODESIA
L. Nyasa
NYASALAND
Zambezi
MOZAMBIQUE
SOUTHERN RHODESIA
MADAGASCAR
GERMAN SOUTHWEST AFRICA
BECHUANALAND
TRANSVAAL
SWAZILAND
ORANGE FREE STATE
Isandhlwana
BASUTOLAND
NATAL
UNION OF SOUTH AFRICA
Cape Town

COLONIAL PRESENCE IN AFRICA, 1878
ALGERIA
EGYPT
SAHARA
Nile
SENEGAL
Niger
Congo
CAPE COLONY

British
French
German
Italian
Portuguese
Belgian
Spanish
Independent African States

0   400   800 Km.
0   400   800 Mi.

Online Study Center **Improve Your Grade** Interactive Map: Africa in 1914

At the same time that Europeans were making substantial material progress as a result of industrialization, their wide-scale expansion overseas brought them into contact with Africans and Asians who had traditional economies. They assumed that the dramatic disparity between their own material culture and that of colonial peoples was proof of their own innate superiority. They viewed Africans and Asians as primitive, inferior peoples, still in their evolutionary "infancy."

Influenced by Darwin and his theory of the struggle for survival (see pages 727–729), many argued that just as competition among species existed in nature, so did groups of humans struggle for survival. Dubbed "Social Darwinists," these thinkers envisioned a world of fierce competition. They believed that the most serious struggle was among the races and, further, that the outcome was predetermined: the white race was destined to succeed, the nonwhites to succumb.

Many Europeans paternalistically believed they had a duty to "develop" these "infant" peoples. The British bard of imperialism, Rudyard Kipling (1865–1936), celebrated this view in his poem "White Man's Burden" (1899):

> Take up the White Man's burden—
> Send forth the best ye breed—
> Go bind your sons to exile
> To serve your captives' need.

Each nation was certain that providence had chosen it for a colonial mission. France, its leaders announced, had a civilizing mission to fulfill in the world; Prime Minister Ferry (feh-REE) declared it the duty of his country "to civilize the inferior races." Although European states were colonial rivals, they also believed they were engaged in a joint mission overseas. Empire building underscored the belief in a common European destiny, as opposed to the ascribed savagery and backwardness of non-Europeans.

Colonial acquisitions triggered public support for further expansion of the empire—support that was expressed by the founding of various colonial societies. Britain's Primrose League, which lobbied for empire as well as other patriotic goals, had 1 million members.

Dutch Colonial Officials in the Dutch East Indies
In this club in an outpost of empire (in present-day Indonesia), the comforts of European bourgeois life were lovingly re-created. Absent from this photo are the countless Indonesian servants who were part of the colonial officials' lives.
(Royal Tropical Institute, Amsterdam)

Though more limited in size, Germany, France, and Italy had similar organizations. Colonial societies generally drew their membership from the professional middle classes—civil servants, professors, and journalists—who were quite open to nationalist arguments. These societies produced a steady stream of propaganda favoring empire building.

Much of the literature celebrating empire building described it in masculine terms. European men were seen as proving their virility by going overseas, conquering, and running empires. They contrasted their manliness with the supposed effeminacy of the colonial peoples. And in building empires, Europeans asserted their manliness in comparison with their wives, sisters, or mothers. Women were to stay home; if later they came overseas, it was as helpmates to male colonial officials or as missionaries. Believing that they would have a positive influence on the world, women missionaries, either as members of a religious order or joining their husbands, went to the colonies to spread Western religions and European values. A few women heroically explored distant lands; the Englishwoman Mary Kingsley (1862–1900) went on two exploration trips into Africa. Her popular books focused British interest on overseas territories, but they in no way shook the established view that empire was a man's enterprise.

CONQUEST, ADMINISTRATION, AND WESTERNIZATION

Industrialization gave Europeans the means to conquer overseas territories. They manufactured rapid-fire weapons. Their steam-driven gunboats and oceangoing vessels effectively projected power overseas. Telegraphic communications tied the whole world into a single network, allowing Europeans to gather information and coordinate military and political decision making. Such advantages made Europeans virtually invincible in a colonial conflict. One remarkable exception was the 1896 Italian defeat in Adowa at the hands of an Ethiopian force that was not only superior in numbers but better armed.

Conquest was often brutal. In September 1898 British-led forces at the Battle of Omdurman slaughtered 20,000 Sudanese. From 1904 to 1908 an uprising in southwest Africa against German rule led to the killing of an estimated 60,000 of the Herero people. The German general, who had expressly given an order to exterminate the whole population, was awarded a medal by Kaiser Wilhelm II.

Colonial governments could be brutally insensitive to the needs of the indigenous peoples. (See the box "The Global Record: Chief Montshiwa Petitions Queen Victoria.") To save administrative costs in the 1890s, France put large tracts of land in the French Congo under the control of private rubber companies, which systematically and savagely coerced the local people to collect the sap of the rubber trees. When the scandal broke in Paris, the concessionary companies were abolished, and the French state re-established its control. The most notorious example of exploitation, terror, and mass killings was connected with the Belgian Congo. Leopold II of Belgium had acquired it as a personal empire. It was his private domain, and he was not accountable to anyone for his actions there. To his shame, Leopold mercilessly exploited the Congo and its people. An international chorus of condemnation finally forced the king to surrender his empire and put it under the administration of the Belgian government, which abolished some of the worst features of Leopold's rule.

Imperialism also spread Western technologies, institutions, and values. By 1914 Great Britain had built 40,000 miles of rail lines in India—nearly twice as much as in Britain. In India and Egypt, the British erected hydraulic systems that irrigated previously arid lands. Colonials built cities often modeled on the European grid system. In some cases they were graced with large, tree-lined avenues, and some neighborhoods were equipped with running water and modern sanitation. Schools, patterned after those in Europe, taught the imperial language and spread Western ideas and scientific knowledge—though only to a small percentage of the local population.

The European empire builders created political units that had never existed before. In many parts of Africa they ignored tribal and indigenous differences, which had serious repercussions in the postcolonial world. Although there had been many efforts in the past to join the whole Indian subcontinent under a single authority, the British were the first to accomplish this feat (see **MAP 24.2**). Through a common administration, rail network, and trade, Britain gave Indians the sense of a common condition, leading in 1885 to the founding of the India Congress Party. The Congress Party platform included the demand for constitutional government, representative assemblies, and the rule of law—concepts all based on Western theory and practice. Though initially demanding reforms within the British colonial system, the Congress Party eventually became India's major nationalist group.

In contact with the colonizers, intellectuals in colonial societies adopted a European ideology, nationalism. Nationalism was one of the major values Europeans successfully exported to their overseas possessions. Indians, having studied in British schools or visited Britain, were most likely to be nationalists. They founded a movement, known as "Young India," harking back to "Young Italy" and other European nationalist movements founded during the mid-1800s (see page 658).

CHIEF MONTSHIWA PETITIONS QUEEN VICTORIA

In 1885 Bechuanaland, in southern Africa, became a British protectorate. The Bechuana leaders saw British protection as a means to prevent takeover by the Boers, Dutch-speaking white settlers who were aggressively expanding in South Africa. The British were cavalier about their responsibilities, however, and a few years later allowed the British South Africa Company, a particularly exploitive enterprise, to take control of Bechuanaland. In protest, Chief Montshiwa (1815–1896), a major chief of the Baralong people, petitioned Queen Victoria for redress. His petition was supported by missionary lobbying, and most of Bechuanaland was saved from the clutches of the company.

Mafeking, 16 August 1895

To the Queen of England and Her Ministers:

We send greetings and pray that you are all living nicely. You will know us; we are not strangers. We have been your children since 1885.

Your Government has been good, and under it we have received much blessing, prosperity, and peace. . . .

We Baralong are very astonished because we hear that the Queen's Government wants to give away our country in the Protectorate to the Chartered Company; we mean the B[ritish] S[outh] A[frica] Company.

Our land there is a good land, our fathers lived in it and buried in it, and we keep all our cattle in it.

What will we do if you give our land away? My people are increasing very fast and are filling the land.

We keep all the laws of the great Queen; we have fought for her; we have always been the friends of her people; we are not idle; we build houses; we plough many gardens; we sow. . . .

Why are you tired of ruling us? Why do you want to throw us away? We do not fight against your laws. We keep them and are living nicely.

Our words are No: No. The Queen's Government must not give my people's land in the Protectorate to the Chartered Company. . . .

Peace to you all, we greet you;
Please send a good word back.
I am etc,

Montshiwa

QUESTIONS

1. What are Chief Montshiwa's grievances?

2. Why did the missionaries lend their support to the chief?

3. How does Montshiwa view the relationship between his people and the queen?

Source: S. M. Molema, *Montshiwa, 1815–1896* (Cape Town: G. Struik, 1966), pp. 181–182.

Similarly, in French Algeria before World War I, a movement named "Young Algerians" sprang up.

It was to be several decades before nationalism successfully challenged the European empires. In the meantime, Europeans took great satisfaction in their achievements overseas, confirming their sense of themselves as agents of progress, building a new and better world. Europeans arrogantly believed that they knew what was best for other people, and they accepted force as a means of implementing their ideas. Such attitudes may have colored the increasingly caustic relations between European states.

The ties of empire affected metropolitan cultures. The Hindi word for *bandit* became the English word *thug;* the Hindi number five, denoting the five ingredients necessary for a particular drink, became *punch.* Scenes from the colonial world often were the themes of European art, such as Paul Gauguin's paintings of Tahiti and advertising posters for products as different as soap and whiskey. (See the feature "The Visual Record: Empire and Advertising" on pages 750–751.) After the turn of the century, Pablo Picasso's cubism reflected his growing familiarity with African art. In running the largest empire in the world, the British emphasized the need to develop masculine virtues. They cultivated competitive sports and stern schooling, which, they believed, would develop "character" and leadership. To administer their overseas colonies, Europeans developed sophisticated means of gathering and managing information that benefited metropolitan societies. A growing number of people from the colonies also came to live in European cities. By 1900 some former colonial subjects, despite various forms of discrimination, had become full participants in the lives of their host countries; two Indians won election to the British Parliament in the 1890s.

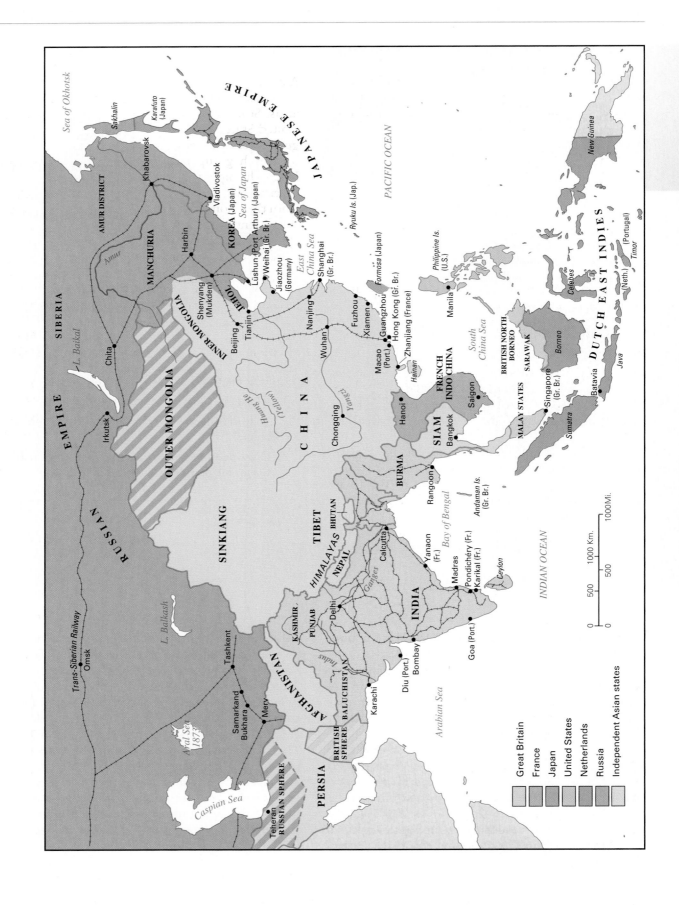

Sea of Okhotsk

JAPANESE EMPIRE

PACIFIC OCEAN

Sakhalin

Karafuto (Japan)

Khabarovsk

AMUR DISTRICT

Vladivostok

Amur

SIBERIA

MANCHURIA

Harbin

KOREA (Japan)

Sea of Japan

Lüshun (Port Arthur) (Japan)

Weihai (Gr. Br.)

JEHOL

Shenyang (Mukden)

Beijing

Tianjin

Jiaozhou (Germany)

Shanghai (Gr. Br.)

East China Sea

Formosa (Japan)

Ryuku Is. (Jap.)

New Guinea

Timor (Portugal)

Philippine Is. (U.S.)

Manila

DUTCH EAST INDIES

Celebes

BRITISH NORTH BORNEO

SARAWAK

Borneo

Java

Batavia

Sumatra

Singapore (Gr. Br.)

MALAY STATES

South China Sea

Saigon

FRENCH INDO CHINA

Hanoi

SIAM

Bangkok

Macao (Port.)

Zhanjiang (France)

Hainan

Hong Kong (Gr. Br.)

Guangzhou

Xiamen

Fuzhou

Nanjing

Wuhan

Chongqing

Yangzi

C H I N A

Yellow

Huang He

SINKIANG

INNER MONGOLIA

OUTER MONGOLIA

Chita

Irkutsk

L. Baikal

RUSSIAN EMPIRE

Trans-Siberian Railway

Omsk

L. Balkash

Aral Sea 1873

Tashkent

Samarkand

Bukhara

Merv

Caspian Sea

Teheran

RUSSIAN SPHERE

PERSIA

AFGHANISTAN

BRITISH SPHERE

BALUCHISTAN

Karachi

Indus

KASHMIR

PUNJAB

Delhi

NEPAL

BHUTAN

TIBET

HIMALAYAS

BURMA

Rangoon

Calcutta

Ganges

INDIA

Yanaon (Fr.)

Madras

Pondichéry (Fr.)

Karikal (Fr.)

Ceylon

Bay of Bengal

Andaman Is. (Gr. Br.)

Goa (Port.)

Bombay

Diu (Port.)

Arabian Sea

INDIAN OCEAN

1000 Mi.

1000 Km.

500

500

0

0

Great Britain

France

Japan

United States

Netherlands

Russia

Independent Asian states

OVERSEAS MIGRATIONS AND THE SPREAD OF EUROPEAN VALUES

The nineteenth century saw a phenomenal expansion in European overseas migrations, adding to Europe's impact on other societies (see **MAP 24.3**). Europeans had always migrated. They left villages for towns or, in the case of migrant farm laborers, traveled from village to village as the seasons changed and different crops needed to be harvested. With the expansion of European power abroad beginning in the sixteenth century, Europeans migrated overseas. Between the sixteenth and eighteenth centuries, around 6 million people left Europe. These numbers pale, however, when compared with the nineteenth-century figures. Between 1870 and 1914, 55 million Europeans left the Continent for the Americas, Australia, and New Zealand.

Certain European groups migrated to specific areas. Scandinavians settled in the upper midwestern United States, Italians in Argentina, Germans in Paraguay, Britons in South Africa, and Portuguese in Brazil, with each group leaving its imprint on its adopted land. The upper Midwest was known as "the great desert," but Scandinavians used farming techniques from their homelands to cultivate these dry lands. German Mennonites settled in Kansas and brought with them a strain of wheat that became the basis of the state's prosperity. Immigrants had a similar impact on urban areas. Durban, South Africa, looks like an English city, and some towns in Paraguay resemble Alpine villages of southern Germany. The Germans who came to Milwaukee, Wisconsin, made it a city of beer and strong socialist convictions, reminiscent of home.

Emigration scattered peoples and extended cultures overseas. The settlers consumed many European goods and in turn produced for the European market, increasing the centrality of Europe in the world economy. The migrations around the globe reinforced imperial conquest, further putting Europe's stamp on peoples and societies abroad.

Petersen: Emigrants Preparing to Depart
Edward Petersen's 1890 painting depicts Danish emigrants preparing to leave their homeland. Between 1860 and 1914, 300,000 people emigrated from the small country of Denmark, most of them to the United States.   *(Courtesy of the Aarhus Kunstmuseum. Reproduced with permission of Thomas, Poul, and Ole Hein Pedersen, Aarhus.)*

MAP 24.3　European Migrations, 1820–1910

Throughout the nineteenth century, millions of Europeans left home for overseas, most headed for the United States. *(Source: The Times Atlas of World History, 3d ed. (Times Books). Reprinted by permission of HarperCollins Publishers, Ltd. © HarperCollins Publishers, Ltd. Some data from Eric Hobsbawm, The Age of Empire, 1875–1914 [New York: Pantheon, 1987].)*

Online Study Center **Improve Your Grade** Interactive Map: European Migrations, 1820–1910

═══════════ S E C T I O N　S U M M A R Y ═══════════

- Although the quest for commercial profit helped motivate imperialism, the colonies, for the most part, did not become large markets of the colonizing powers.

- Growing nationalism, rivalry among the Great Powers, and the need to protect the frontiers of already acquired colonies also generated empire building.

- Technological superiority, strong public support, notions of racial and cultural superiority, and a "civilizing mission" justified colonial conquest in the minds of Europeans.

- Industrialization produced powerful weaponry that made colonial conquest possible; European powers brought Western technologies, and methods of administration and education, to the colonized, as well as Western ideologies such as nationalism.

- Colonial cultures influenced metropolitan societies through art, advertising, linguistic practices, and immigration.

- Between 1870 and 1914, 55 million Europeans migrated to the Americas, Australia, and New Zealand, reinforcing Europe's global impact.

FROM OPTIMISM TO ANXIETY: POLITICS AND CULTURE

In what ways did the worldview of intellectuals living in the belle époque differ from that of a generation earlier?

Any of the beliefs and institutions that had seemed so solid in the "age of optimism" found themselves under attack in the next generation. Forces hostile to liberalism became increasingly vocal. In the arts and philosophy, the earlier confidence was replaced by doubt, relativism, and a desire to flee the routines of everyday life.

THE EROSION OF THE LIBERAL CONSENSUS

In 1850 liberals assumed that with the passage of time more and more people would be won over to their worldview. By 1900, however, liberalism faced serious challenges. Various ideas and movements—some new, some rooted in the past—chipped away at the liberal consensus. Prominent among these were socialism, anarchism, a new political right, racism, and anti-Semitism.

The undermining of the liberal consensus began among liberals themselves, who, in the face of changing circumstances, retreated from some of their basic tenets. For example, one of the principal emphases of liberalism had always been free trade. But under the pressure of economic competition, liberals supported tariffs at home and created closed markets in their empires.

Historically, liberals had typically stood for an expansion of civil liberties, yet they saw nothing wrong or inconsistent in continuing to deny women both the vote and free access to education and professional advancement. In the face of labor agitation, many liberals no longer unconditionally supported civil liberties for workers and favored instead the violent crushing of strikes.

Similarly, liberals had always upheld the sanctity of private property, but under the pressure of events, they abandoned this principle as an absolute goal. To ensure workers' safety, they placed limits on employers' liberties by passing legislation requiring them to improve working conditions. In some countries, some liberals supported progressive income taxes, which other liberals perceived as a serious invasion of private property. When it became clear that a free market was unable to meet many human needs, welfare programs were instituted in several countries. These reforms were intended to strengthen the state by winning support from the masses and by fostering the growth of a healthy population through limited aid to mothers and children. In the effort to address real-life problems of the day, however, liberals encountered a paradox at the heart of their ideology: creating rights for one group (such as workers or women) infringed on those of others (such as employers or men). Whatever action liberals took seemed to reveal a willingness to breach fundamental principles.

THE GROWTH OF SOCIALISM AND ANARCHISM

Among the groups challenging the power and liberal ideology of the middle classes were the socialist parties, both Marxist and non-Marxist, whose goal was to win the support of workers by espousing their causes. Socialists varied in their notions of how their goals should be achieved: some favored pursuing objectives gradually and peacefully; others were dedicated to a violent overthrow of capitalist society.

Socialism   In Britain, socialists founded the Fabian Society in 1884, named after the Roman general noted for winning by avoiding open, pitched battles. The Fabians criticized the capitalist system as inefficient, wasteful, and unjust. They believed that by gradual, democratic means, Parliament could transfer factories and land from the private sector to the state, which would manage them for the benefit of society as a whole. More efficient and more just, socialism would come into being not through class war but through enlightened ideas. This gradualist approach became the hallmark of British socialism; it shaped the ideology of the Labour Party that would gain electoral success in the 1920s.

In Germany various strands of socialism came together when a single united party was formed in 1875. But within a few years a debate that divided socialism in general broke up the German party: could socialism come about by gradual democratic means, or, as Marx had contended, would it require a violent revolution? The German socialist leader Eduard Bernstein (1850–1932), who had visited England and had soaked up the influence of the Fabians, argued for gradualism in a book with the telling English title *Evolutionary Socialism* (1898). Marx had been wrong, said Bernstein, to suggest that capitalism necessarily led to the increasing wretchedness of the working class. The capitalist economy had in fact expanded and been able to provide for steadily improved conditions. Workers would not need to seize power by some cataclysmic act. Rather, by

Empire and Advertising

In 1822 Joseph Huntley opened a small bakery in Reading, England. It was located near a coaching inn on the busy road between London and Bath. From a handbasket, he sold biscuits to hungry coach travelers passing through. In 1832, Huntley's son, who had an ironmongery across from the bakery, began producing tin boxes for the biscuits, which allowed them to "retain their freshness for years" and to travel worldwide without breaking. The bakery expanded rapidly. George Palmer joined the business in 1841; five years later they purchased a former silk factory of 5,000 square feet that occupied more than half an acre. From this point on, Huntley & Palmers mass-produced their biscuits. By 1898, Huntley & Palmers was the largest biscuit manufacturer in the world; more than 5,000 men and women produced biscuits in a cluster of factory buildings that then occupied 24 acres and had become a "small city" unto itself.*

The image depicted here, a trade card advertising the Huntley & Palmers product, portrays a British hunting party in India around the turn of the nineteenth century. This card and the story behind the company it represents illustrate several themes inherent to nineteenth-century Western civilization: industrial capitalism, the modernization in transportation, global commerce, and most poignantly, the interaction between imperialism and advertising.

The expansion of Huntley & Palmers in the second half of the century could not have occurred without the "second industrial revolution" (see pages 712–713). Improved modes of transportation, improved metal production for packaging, the building of the Suez Canal, and the expansion of empire brought Huntley & Palmers biscuits to ever greater distances. Export to the British colonies began in the 1840s. By 1874 the company could boast that "seldom a ship sails from England that does not bear within [its] ribs a Reading biscuit." By the end of the nineteenth century, Huntley & Palmers had sales representatives in China, Japan, India, South Africa, and North and South America. Ten percent of all its exports went to Britain's most important colony, India. Foreign

companies produced biscuits under the Huntley & Palmers license in India, France, New Zealand, and Australia. The company increasingly relied on raw materials imported from overseas—eggs came from Ireland, coconuts came from Barbados and the West Indies, and cocoa came from West Africa.

An important reason for Huntley & Palmers' success lay in advertising. In addition to newspaper advertisements, handbills and posters placarded urban surfaces. Particularly pervasive were trade cards, usually 4 x 6 inches in size, such as the one presented here. Huntley & Palmers produced hundreds of these trade cards, with colorful images on the front and a description of their latest products on the back. They showed not only how the biscuits could be found all over the world, but how they were transported, such as by camel, hot air balloon, elephant, and ship. Retailers distributed the cards, which were so appealing that they became collectors' items.

The card shown here depicts a tiger hunt in India, to which only those who had power and authority—royalty and senior imperial officials—were given the honor of attending. Members of the hunting party sit atop the crates in which 10-pound tins of Huntley & Palmers' biscuits have been shipped, transported by a British-built railroad, and then carried on elephants. Retaining their civilized British custom, the hunters take their tea break after killing tigers, whose carcasses hang from the elephants. The Indians serve not only as their guides, but also as servants to them, performing functions women would perform at home. The relationship the colonizer had to native men was one that effeminized the latter. The scene also suggests the successful and safe insertion of British civilization into an exotic, adventurous, and potentially dangerous context.

In addition to cards, images such as this were placed on the biscuit tins themselves and on calendars, on posters, and in catalogs. Advertisements that included colonial themes conveyed the message that biscuits could bring a "taste of home" to British who found themselves almost anywhere on the globe; they also made imperialism seem safe, adventurous, and appealing.

The colonies themselves were also targets of advertising, especially since they provided such important markets. Advertisements appeared in Indian

---

*Most of the historical information on Huntley & Palmers comes from "The Huntley & Palmers Collection" on the Reading Museum website, at <http://www.huntleyandpalmers.org.uk>.

Trade Card Advertising
Huntley & Palmers
Biscuits *(The Robert Opie
Collection)*

street markets from the mid-nineteenth century. One image from 1902, indeed, depicts an Indian market located in a narrow shadowy street where two upper-class British ladies negotiate with a turbaned figure. Once again, the portrayal suggests potential danger lurking in the shadows; but a tin of Huntley & Palmers biscuits is displayed on the stall, with more stacked in the background, bringing a sense of safety and familiarity to an otherwise strange scene. This 1902 image was used for trade cards as well as for pocket calendars that were placed inside the tins as a promotional gift.

Similar images on the tins made them into collectable objects that are of great value today. One of the most elaborate is an "Arabian Nights" tin from 1888 featuring the adventures of Ali Baba and his encounter with the forty thieves. Folk tales and stories such as these—and the distribution of images depicting such figures in exotic dress—influenced European perceptions of the Muslim world.

Huntley & Palmers iconography turned ordinary objects—trade cards, tins, calendars—into vehicles that carried multiple messages about imperial domination into the homes of ordinary people in Europe and around the globe. The images showed that Huntley & Palmers biscuits could accompany civilized British men (and occasionally women) into sites of potential danger. The biscuit represented all that was civilized about the British—from its mass production and distribution, to its ability to preserve the habit of tea time—and it offered symbolic proof of British capacity to tame nature and establish order over the "uncivilized." For consumers at home and abroad, Huntley & Palmers represented the success of British imperial dominance.

Huntley & Palmers became so associated with the export business that in 1953 a cartoon depicted their tins of biscuits arriving by spaceship to curious aliens on the planet Mars. So dependent was the company for its success on the British Empire, post–World War II decolonization was one of the factors that caused its closure in 1972.

QUESTIONS

1. What role did the British Empire play in the success of companies such as Huntley & Palmers? What role, in turn, did such a company play in the British experience of empire?

2. How did advertising contribute to the shaping of national, ethnic, and gender identities?

Online Study Center
Improve Your Grade Visual Record Activities

Jean Jaurès

An ideological moderate, the French socialist leader Jean Jaurès (Zhaw-REZ) (1859–1914) was one of France's greatest orators. Much of his socialism was based on ethical notions about social justice, rather than on Marxist doctrine. Here Jaurès addresses a social gathering in 1913. On the eve of World War I, he was assassinated for his efforts to prevent war.

(Roger-Viollet/Getty Images)

piecemeal democratic action, they could win more power and legislate on behalf of their interests. Since he argued for a revision of Marxist theory, Bernstein was labeled a "revisionist." Opposing him in this great debate was the party theoretician, Karl Kautsky (KOUT-skee) (1854–1938). Kautsky insisted that nothing short of a revolution would institute socialism.

Like most other socialists in Europe, the German socialists rejected revisionism and claimed to embrace the doctrine of a violent proletarian revolution. In fact, however, they pursued revisionist policies. Socialists in practice had become another parliamentary party that hoped to reach its goals through legislation.

Despite internal divisions, European socialists also attempted to make their movement international, with some success. In 1864 Marx helped found the Interna-

tional Workers' Association, known as the First International. It was followed by a more robust **Second International,** in 1889. The International met yearly and debated issues of concern to socialists in general, including the worsening relations among European states. As early as 1893 the International urged European states to resolve their conflicts by mandatory arbitration. In 1907, sensing impending war, the International called on workers to strike and refuse military service in case of international conflict.

Anarchism   Another movement that sought to liberate the downtrodden was anarchism, which proclaimed that humans could be free only when the state had been abolished. According to anarchist theory, in a stateless society people would naturally join together in communes and share the fruits of their labor. Some anarchists believed they could achieve their goal by educating people. Others were more impatient and hoped to speed up the process by making direct attacks on existing authority.

The Russian nobleman Michael Bakunin (bah-KOO-neen) (1814–1876), frustrated at the authoritarianism of his homeland, became a lifelong anarchist. He challenged tsarism at home and participated in the 1848 revolutions throughout Europe. He viewed all governments as repressive and declared unilateral war on them: "The passion for destruction is also a creative passion." His ideas were particularly influential in Italy, Spain, and parts of France, especially among the artisan classes.

Many anarchists of this period wanted to bring about the new society by "propaganda of the deed." An attack on the bastions of power, these anarchists believed, could bring about the dissolution of the state. They formed secret terrorist organizations that assassinated heads of state or those close to them. Between 1894 and 1901 anarchists killed a president of France, a prime minister of Spain, an empress of Austria, a king of Italy, and a president of the United States. These murders fixed the popular image of anarchism as a violence-prone ideology. Such "deeds," moreover, produced no particular improvement in the lives of the working-class people on whose behalf they had been undertaken.

Without accepting the anarchists' methods, some in the labor movement shared their hostility toward parliamentary institutions. A working-class program, labor activists argued, could be implemented only by a pure workers' movement, such as unionization. Workers should shun the political arena and concentrate on direct action. According to this line of thought, known

Second International   International socialist organization founded in 1889 that met yearly to debate issues of broad concern. It called for workers to strike and refuse military service.

as "syndicalism" (after the French word for unions), workers would amass their power in unions and at the right moment carry out a general strike, crippling capitalist society and bringing it down. Syndicalism was particularly popular in Mediterranean countries, where its more militant form, anarcho-syndicalism, radicalized labor and made a sizable number of workers hostile to parliamentary government.

THE NEW RIGHT, RACISM, AND ANTI-SEMITISM

The traditional opponents of liberalism on the political right were the conservatives, wedded to preserving the existing order. Beginning in the 1880s, however, a "new right" emerged that was populist and demagogic. Although conservatives had been wary of nationalism, the new right embraced it. Alienated by democracy and social egalitarianism, many in this new right rejected doctrines of human equality and embraced racist ideologies.

Many Europeans believed that human races were not only different physiologically, but also differently endowed in intelligence and other qualities (see page 730). At midcentury the Frenchman Arthur de Gobineau (1816–1882) published his *Essay on the Inequality of Human Races,* declaring that race "dominates all other problems and is the key to it." Biologists and early anthropologists made similar statements, thus giving racism a "scientific" aura. Throughout the second half of the nineteenth century, race was thought to be the principal explanation for the differences that were discovered among human groupings.

These racist ideas helped fuel **anti-Semitism.** For centuries Jews had been the object of suspicion and bigotry. Originally, the basis of the prejudice was religious. As early as the Middle Ages, however, the argument emerged that "Jewish blood" was different. And with the popularization of pseudoscientific racist thinking in the nineteenth century, Jews were commonly viewed as a separate, inferior race, unworthy of the same rights as the majority of the population.

Historically, Christians had relegated the Jews in their midst to marginal positions. In the Middle Ages, when land was the basis of wealth and prestige, Jews were prohibited from owning land, and had thus been confined to urban trades, among which was moneylending. They incurred high risks by lending money: they often were not paid back and faced unsympathetic courts when they tried to collect their debts. To counteract these risks, Jewish moneylenders charged high interest rates that earned them their unpopular reputation as usurers.

The emancipation of the Jews, which began in France with the Revolution and spread to Germany and Austria by the 1860s, provided them with unprecedented opportunities. Some members of society found it hard to adjust to the prominence that some Jews gained. Because their increased social standing and success were concurrent with the wrenching social transformations brought by industrialization and urbanization, anti-Semites pointed to the Jews as the perpetrators of these unsettling changes.

Many people perceived Jews as prototypical of the new capitalist class. Although most of them were of modest means, Jews often became the brunt of resentment toward the rich. Earlier in the century many anti-Semites were socialists, speaking on behalf of the working class. Later they came from among the petite bourgeoisie—small shopkeepers and artisans—who felt threatened by economic change.

Political movements based on anti-Semitism were founded in the 1880s. They depicted Jews as dangerous and wicked and called for their exclusion from the political arena and from certain professions. In some cases proponents suggested that Jews be expelled from the state. Karl Lueger (1844–1928) was elected mayor of Vienna on an anti-Semitic platform. In Berlin the emperor's chaplain, Adolf Stöcker (SHTOE-kur) (1835–1909), founded an anti-Semitic party, hoping to make political inroads among the working-class supporters of socialism. In France Edouard Drumont (1844–1917) published one of the bestsellers of the second half of the nineteenth century, *Jewish France,* in which he blamed all the nation's misfortunes on the Jews.

In Russia organized *pogroms,* or mass attacks, killed two thousand Jews in the 1880s and one thousand in 1905, frightening two million into exile, mostly to the United States. Russian Jews lived under social as well as legal disabilities. Condemned to second-class citizenship, they won full emancipation only with the Bolshevik Revolution of 1917.

In the face of growing hostility, some Jews speculated that they would be safe only in their own nation. The Austrian Jewish journalist Theodore Herzl (HER-tsl) (1860–1904), outraged by the Dreyfus affair in France, in which a Jewish officer was imprisoned on trumped-up charges of treason (see pages 758–759), founded the Zionist movement. He advocated establishing a Jewish state in the Jews' ancient homeland of Palestine. In the beginning, the Zionist movement won a following only in eastern Europe, where the Jews were particularly ill-treated, but by 1948 **Zionism** culminated in the creation of the state of Israel.

anti-Semitism Centuries-old prejudice against and demonization of Jews that became virulent in the 1880s with the emergence of the ultranationalist and racist ideologies and political movements.

Zionism Nationalist Jewish movement beginning in the late nineteenth century. In face of anti-Semitism, Zionism advocated establishing a Jewish state in the Jews' ancient homeland of Palestine.

IRRATIONALITY AND UNCERTAINTY

In contrast to the confidence in reason and science that had prevailed at midcentury, the era starting in the 1880s was characterized by a sense of irrationality and uncertainty—in philosophy, in the arts, even in religion. The positivism of the earlier era had emphasized the surface reality of "progress" but had ignored the emotional and intuitive aspects of life. By the 1890s a neo-romantic mood, emphasizing emotion and feeling, stirred major intellectual movements. The spotlight was no longer on reason, but on instinct.

Philosophy In philosophy the tension between reason and emotion was vividly expressed in the work of the German philosopher Friedrich Nietzsche (FREED-reesh NEET-sheh) (1844–1900), who proclaimed that rationality had led humankind into a meaningless abyss. Reason would not resolve human problems, nor would any preconceived ideas. "God is dead," Nietzsche announced. With no God, humankind was free of all outside constraints, free to overthrow all conventions. Nietzsche admonished his readers to challenge existing institutions and accepted truths and to create new ones.

The French philosopher Henri Bergson (BERK-sohn) (1859–1940) argued that science—and indeed life—must be interpreted not rationally but intuitively. "Science," Bergson declared, "can teach us nothing of the truth; it can only serve as a rule of action." Humans could best understand meaningful truths—such as those of religion, literature, and art—by relying on their feelings.

Social Sciences Various disciplines of knowledge subscribed to the notion that human beings are often irrational, motivated by deep-seated instinctive forces. The Austro-Hungarian **Sigmund Freud** (1856–1939) founded psychoanalysis, a method of treating psychic disorders by exploring the unconscious. Freud believed that people were motivated not only by observed reality but also by their unconscious feelings and emotions. Whereas earlier physicians had described the frequently diagnosed women's illness of "hysteria" as a physical ailment, Freud saw its roots as psychological, the result of unresolved inner conflicts. He stressed that irrational forces played a significant role in human behavior.

Online Study Center **Improve Your Grade**
Primary Source: The Interpretation of Dreams: Psychoanalysis Is Born

The social theorist Gaetano Mosca (1858–1941) pessimistically argued that the desire to dominate is a basic part of human nature. In his book *Elements of Political Science* (1891), he posited that in all societies—even democratic ones—an elite minority rules over the majority. Beneath slogans touting the public good lies selfish ambition, and the thirst for power is never slaked—a poor prognosis for socialist ideals. Thus, as did Freud, Mosca suggested that surface appearances are deceptive and that irrational forces guide human behavior.

Arts In the arts, the idea of being *avant-garde*—French for "forefront"—took hold among creative people. Breaking the taboos of society and the conventions of one's craft seemed to be signs of artistic creativity. Artistic movements proclaimed idiosyncratic manifestoes and constantly called for the rejection of existing forms of expression and the creation of new ones. The symbolists in France and in Italy, the expressionists in Germany, the futurists in Italy, and the secessionists in Austria all reflected the sense that they were living through a fractured period.

In protest against the mass culture of their day, artists focused on images that were unique. Unlike earlier art, which had a clear message, the art of this era did not. Many artists no longer believed their role was to portray or spread ideals. Rather, they tended to be introspective and even self-absorbed. The public at large found it difficult to decipher the meaning of the new art, but a number of patrons supported the avant-garde artists' talent and insight.

Unlike the realists who preceded them, artists in the 1890s surrendered to neo-romanticism, trying to investigate and express inner forces. As the French painter Paul Gauguin (1848–1903) noted, the purpose of painting is to communicate not how things look but the emotions they convey. The Russian Wassily Kandinsky (vass-IH-lee kan-DIN-skee) (1866–1944) asked viewers of his art to "look at the picture as a graphic representation of a mood and not as a representation of objects." Artists appeared to be examining the hidden anxieties of society. The Frenchman Gustave Moreau (mo-RO) (1826–1898) displayed monsters—creations of nightmare and byproducts of the unconscious. The Norwegian painter Edvard Munch (MOONGK) (1863–1944) emphasized scenes of violence, fear, and sheer horror.

Religion and Science The era of uncertainty undermined both religious belief and confidence in science. Although large numbers of people still held traditional religious beliefs, indifference to organized

---

Sigmund Freud Austrian founder of psychoanalysis, a method of treating psychic disorders by exploring the unconscious, based on the belief that people are motivated by unconscious feelings and drives.

avant-garde French for "forefront," the term refers to early-twentieth-century artists who inspired unconventional techniques, considered themselves precursors of new styles, and called for the rejection of existing forms of expression.

Munch: The Scream
Painted in 1893, this work reflects the fear and horror that some intellectuals experienced at the end of the nineteenth century.
(Nasjonalgalleriet, Oslo/Art Resource, NY. © 2002 Artists Rights Society [ARS], New York/ADAGP, Paris)

religion spread. In urban areas of western Europe, church attendance declined, while various forms and practices of mysticism—such as séances—became more widespread. Some people were attracted to Eastern religions such as Buddhism and Hinduism, perhaps reflecting a loss of faith in Western culture itself.

Scientists of this period questioned long-held commonsense beliefs. During the last week of the century, the German physicist Max Planck (1858–1947) suggested that light and other kinds of electromagnetic radiation, such as radio waves, which had always been considered continuous trains of waves, actually consist of individual packages of well-defined energy, which he called "quanta." In 1905 Albert Einstein (1879–1955) proposed the theory of relativity, which required a drastic change in fundamental ideas about space and time. To the three dimensions of space—length, breadth, and width—was added a complicating fourth dimension, that of time. The new ideas were not easily grasped. The old concept of a fixed cause tied to a fixed effect did not hold, because even though things happen predictably, they also happen randomly.

SECTION SUMMARY

- The liberal ideology of the early nineteenth century could not address economic and social practicalities by the century's end. Civil and political liberties, some concluded, could not apply to everyone.

- Two strands of socialism emerged by the end of the nineteenth century: one that advocated violent revolution, and another—revisionism—that argued change could come through gradual, democratic means. The latter became more dominant.

- A "new right" of the late nineteenth century embraced nationalism and rejected democracy and the notion of human equality. It also adopted racist and anti-Semitic ideologies.

- By the 1890s a neo-romantic mood emphasized the validity of feeling and emotion, while irrationality and uncertainty permeated philosophy, the social sciences, the arts, religion, and science itself.

VULNERABLE DEMOCRACIES

What factors made parliamentary rule in Great Britain, France, and Italy dysfunctional?

By the end of the nineteenth century, most of Europe's political systems floundered in crisis. The major powers with democratic institutions—Great Britain, France, and Italy—confronted volatile public opinion and had difficulty winning a broad consensus for their policies. They struggled with new challenges emerging from an expanded electorate that was at times frustrated by the failure of the system to respond to its demands. Turning away from the democratic precept of resolving differences through the ballot and legislation, many people—both in government and out—were willing to resort to extraparliamentary means, including violence, to see their interests prevail.

GREAT BRITAIN

In Great Britain the Reform Bill of 1884 extended the vote to two of every three adult men, doubling suffrage to five million. The appeal of this enlarged electorate tempted politicians to make demagogic promises, which were often broken later, to the exasperation of their constituents. Representing a population with more diverse interests and values, members of Parliament found compromise more difficult. Unable to resolve issues peacefully, the British government uncharacteristically resorted to the use of force.

As in earlier periods, the problem of Ireland persisted. The Irish seethed under alien British rule. In 1886, Prime Minister William Gladstone (GLAD-sten) proposed autonomy, or "home rule," for Ireland. But many opposed this plan. If Ireland, a predominantly Catholic country, ruled itself, the local Protestant majority in Ulster (the northeast part of the island) would be overwhelmed by Catholic control. "Home rule is Rome rule," chanted the supporters of Ulster Protestantism. In addition, many opposed changing the existing relationship between England and its neighboring possession. With considerable political maneuvering, the Liberals finally pushed a home-rule bill through the House of Commons in 1911, but it was obstructed in the House of Lords and was not slated to go into effect until September 1914.

Passage of the home-rule bill did not resolve the Irish problem. Many segments of British society showed they were willing to resort to extralegal and even violent means. Fearing Catholic domination, Protestants in northern Ireland armed themselves in their determination to resist home rule. Catholic groups took up arms, too, insisting on the unity of the island. The Conservative Party in Britain, which opposed home rule, called on Ulster Protestants to revolt. British officers threatened to resign their commissions rather than fight Ulster. The behavior of the Conservatives and the army indicated a breakdown of order and authority—a disregard for tradition by two of its major bulwarks. Only the outbreak of world war in 1914 delayed a showdown over Ireland, and then by only a few years.

Irish home rule was not the only issue that eroded civility in the British Parliament. Liberals, who dominated the House of Commons from 1906, committed themselves to an impressive array of social reforms, such as old-age pensions. To finance such measures, the feisty chancellor of the exchequer, David Lloyd George (1863–1945), proposed raising income taxes and death duties, and levying a tax on landed wealth. A bill with these measures easily passed the House of Commons in 1909 but was stymied in the upper chamber, where many members were prominent landowners.

The House of Lords technically had the power to amend or reject a bill passed by Commons, but for nearly 250 years it had been tacitly understood that the Lords did not have the right to reject a money bill. Nonetheless, motivated by economic self-interest and personal spite against the Liberals, a majority in the House of Lords disregarded convention and voted against the bill. Lloyd George expressed his outrage that a handful of magnates in the upper chamber—sitting there not by election but by hereditary right—could thwart the will of the people. A major constitutional crisis ensued.

In 1911 the government sponsored a bill to limit the legislative power in the House of Lords to a suspensive veto—meaning that any bill defeated there would simply be suspended for a predetermined period, such as two years. The House of Lords initially refused to pass the bill, but finally conceded when the king threatened to appoint four hundred new lords.

During the debate over the bill, Conservatives resorted to brawling and refused to let the prime minister speak. It was the first time in British parliamentary history that such a breach of conduct had occurred. The British Parliament, considered the model for supporters of free institutions, had shown itself unable to resolve issues in a civil manner.

Violence also appeared in another unexpected place: the women's suffrage movement. Most liberal males, when speaking of the need to extend human liberty, had

A Suffragist Attempts to Chain Herself to the Gates of Buckingham Palace, London, 1914
In their effort to win the vote, women resorted to civil disobedience, and police often violently intervened.
(Popperfoto/Retrofile.com)

excluded women because they thought public affairs an inappropriate arena for them. Women were supposed to restrict their concerns to motherhood; they were insufficiently educated and lacking in the capacity for rational and independent thought that voting required. In 1903 Emmeline Pankhurst (1858–1928) and her two daughters founded the Women's Social and Political Union, whose goal was immediate suffrage.

Angered and frustrated by their lack of progress, the **suffragists** (often referred to by contemporaries as "suffragettes"), led by the Pankhursts, began a more militant program of protest in 1906. They disrupted the proceedings in Parliament, broke windows at the prime minister's residence, slashed canvases at the National Gallery, burned down empty houses, dropped acid into mailboxes, and threw bombs. They even threatened the lives of the prime minister and the king. In 1913, Emily Wilding Davidson sacrificed her life to the cause of female suffrage when, before thousands of spectators at the Derby, she threw herself in front of

the king's horse. These acts of violence and tragedy drew condemnation, but they also brought world-wide attention to the cause.

But these acts also incurred severe punishment. Suffragists who were arrested often engaged in hunger strikes, which provoked the authorities to force-feed them—an extremely painful and humiliating procedure that amounts to torture. Female protesters were also physically attacked by male thugs. (See the box "The Written Record: Pankhurst Testifies on Women's Rights.") That women would resort to violence, and that men inside and outside government would retaliate in kind, demonstrated how widespread the cult of force had become.

FRANCE

The Third Republic, founded in 1870 after France's humiliating military defeat at the hands of the Prussians, also struggled with an ongoing series of crises. Challenged by enemies on the political left and right who continually called for the abolition of democracy, the regime found itself buffeted from all sides.

suffragists   Activists who, beginning in the late nineteenth century, organized to win the vote for women and adopted increasingly violent tactics. Also called "suffragettes."

PANKHURST TESTIFIES ON WOMEN'S RIGHTS

In 1908 the suffragists, led by Emmeline Pankhurst, issued a handbill calling on the people of London to "rush" Parliament and win the vote for women. The legal authorities interpreted their action as a violation of the peace, and several suffragists, including Pankhurst, were put on trial. They put up a spirited defense, in which Pankhurst movingly explained her motives for leading the suffragist cause.

I want you to realise how we women feel; because we are women, because we are not men, we need some legitimate influence to bear upon our law-makers. Now, we have tried every way. We have presented larger petitions than were ever presented for any other reform, we have succeeded in holding greater public meetings than men have ever had for any reform, in spite of the difficulty which women have in throwing off their natural diffidence, that desire to escape publicity which we have inherited from generations of our foremothers; we have broken through that. We have faced hostile mobs at street corners, because we were told that we could not have that representation for our taxes which men have won unless we converted the whole of the country to our side. Because we have done this, we have been misrepresented, we have been ridiculed, we have had contempt poured upon us. The ignorant mob at the street corner has been incited to offer us violence, which we have faced unarmed and unprotected by the safeguards which Cabinet Ministers have. We know that we need the protection of the vote even more than men have needed it. . . .

We believe that if we get the vote it will mean better conditions for our unfortunate sisters. We know what the condition of the woman worker is . . . and we have been driven to the conclusion that only through legislation can any improvement be effected, and that that legislation can never be effected until we have the same power as men have to bring pressure to bear upon our representatives and upon Governments to give us the necessary legislation. . . .

I should never be here if I had the same kind of power that the very meanest and commonest of men have—the same power that the wife-beater has, the same power that the drunkard has. I should never be here if I had that power, and I speak for all the women who have come before you and other magistrates. . . .

If you had power to send us to prison, not for six months, but for six years, for sixteen years, or for the whole of our lives, the Government must not think that they can stop this agitation. It will go on. . . .

We are here not because we are law-breakers; we are here in our efforts to become lawmakers.

QUESTIONS

1. What is the logic behind Pankhurst's comment that women need the "protection of the vote" even more than men? What is her main argument here for why women should get the vote?

2. Do you think women were justified in breaking laws in order to obtain their goal? Why or why not? How did their behavior compare with that of men, both within and outside of the British Parliament?

Source: F. W. Pethick Lawrence, ed., *The Trial of the Suffragette Leaders* (London: The Women's Press, 1909), pp. 21–24.

This situation resulted in part from the French government's lack of strong leadership. The need to build coalitions among the several parties in the parliament rewarded those politicians who had moderate, and often mediocre, programs. Firm ideas and commitments had little purchase, and the prime minister offered conciliation more often than he did leadership. In addition, supporters of the republic actually found lackluster leadership appealing. They continued to fear that a strong leader might—as Louis Napoleon had in 1851—exploit his support to make himself dictator.

The regime lurched from one crisis to another. The most notorious was the Dreyfus affair. In October 1894 Captain Alfred Dreyfus (1859–1935) of the French army was arrested and charged with passing military secrets to the German embassy. Dreyfus (DRY-fooss) seems to have attracted suspicion because he was the only Jewish officer on the general staff. The evidence was flimsy—a handwritten letter that some thought Dreyfus had penned, although other experts testified that the handwriting was not that of the young officer.

This letter, and materials that later turned out to be forged, led the French army to court-martial Dreyfus and sentence him to life imprisonment on Devil's Island off the coast of South America. By March 1896 the general staff had evidence that another officer, Major Esterhazy, was actually the spy. But to reopen the case would be to admit the army had made an error, and the general staff refused to do this.

By late 1897, when the apparent miscarriage of justice became widely known, French society split over "the affair." The political left argued for reopening the case. The army and its supporters—right-wing politicians, royalists, and zealous Catholics—argued that the decision should stand. They believed the army, as a bulwark against internal and foreign threats, should be above the law, and the fate of a single man—guilty or innocent—was immaterial. From the outset, Dreyfus was the target of virulent anti-Semitism.

The affair unleashed a swirl of controversy and rioting, which led the government to order a retrial in 1899. But the court again found Dreyfus guilty—this time with "extenuating circumstances" and the recommendation that he be pardoned. Finally, in 1906, Dreyfus was fully exonerated.

The strong encouragement many Catholics gave to those who supported the original verdict confirmed the republicans' belief that the church was a menace to the regime. The politicians who backed Dreyfus—anticlericals—were voted into the parliament. In 1905 they passed a law separating church and state, thus ending the privileged position the Catholic Church had enjoyed. Violent language and physical confrontations on both sides accompanied this division. Catholics trying to prevent state officials from entering churches to take required inventories sometimes resorted to force, using weapons or, in one case, a bear chained to the church. Armed soldiers broke down church doors and dragged priests away.

Labor problems also triggered repeated confrontations with the government. Increased labor militancy produced long, drawn-out strikes, which in 1904 alone led to the loss of four million workdays. Rural workers agitated as well, particularly in the Midi, the south of France. This region suffered from a crisis in the wine industry caused by a disease that attacked the vines, competition from cheap foreign wines, and fraud. The region witnessed increased rural proletarianization as landholdings became concentrated in fewer hands. Rural militancy led to a revolt in 1907. Troops were sent in; they killed dozens and won for the Radical regime the title "government of assassins."

ITALY

Italy, the third major power in Europe to adopt parliamentary government, also had grave problems. Although unification took place in 1860, genuine national unity proved elusive. As in the past, the south especially challenged the central government. Assertive regionalism, crime, and poverty made this area resistant to most government programs.

The parliamentary system established in 1860 was unrepresentative and far from democratic. Property qualifications limited suffrage to less than 3 percent of the population. And as a result of the persistence

of *trasformismo* (see page 689)—the practice by which government corrupted and co-opted the opposition—electoral choice was short-circuited.

Between 1870 and 1890 the Italian government introduced some important reforms, but the relatively low standard of living failed to improve. In the fifty years after unification, the population increased from 25 million to 35 million, and the country had limited resources to deal with such growth. In the south a few wealthy landowners held large private estates, while the majority of the peasants were landless and forced to work the land for minimum wages. In the north industrialization had started, but the region was not rich in coal or iron. To be competitive, industry paid very low wages, and the workers lived in abject misery.

Conditions on the land and in the factories led to widespread protests. In 1893 a Sicilian labor movement

Riots in Italian Parliament
Party strife and conflicts between individuals in the Italian parliament were so severe that often they degenerated into fisticuffs. This illustration catches a particularly violent moment of a parliamentary debate. *(Madeline Grimoldi)*

won the adherence of 300,000 members, who seized land and attacked government offices. The government responded with massive force and declared martial law. As unrest spread throughout the peninsula in 1896, the government placed half of the provinces under military rule. A cycle of violence and repression gripped the nation. In this turbulent atmosphere, an anarchist killed King Umberto I on July 29, 1900.

After the turn of the century, a new prime minister, Giovanni Giolitti (jo-VAH-nee jo-LEE-tee) (1842–1928), tried to end the upheaval. He used government force more sparingly and showed a spirit of cooperation toward the workers. Seeking to divert attention from domestic ills and appeal to nationalist fervor, Giolitti launched an attack on Libya in 1911, wresting it from the ailing Ottoman Empire. The territory was arid and bereft of economic promise, but its conquest was championed as a test of national virility and the foundation of national greatness. The imperialists proudly proclaimed force the arbiter of the nation's future.

The government also returned to the use of force for its domestic problems when, in June 1914, a national strike led to rioting and workers' seizing power in several municipalities. In northern Italy, workers proclaimed an independent republic. It took 100,000 government troops ten days to restore order. The workers' brazen defiance led some nationalist right-wing extremists to form groups of "volunteers for the defense of order," anticipating the vigilante thugs who were to make up the early bands of Italian fascism.

============ S E C T I O N   S U M M A R Y ============

- Democratic governments in western Europe experienced crises that led to forceful repression. The British resorted to violence or uncivil behavior over the issues of Irish home rule, a constitutional crisis over social reform, and women's suffrage.

- Democracy in the French republic was threatened by the nation-splitting Dreyfus affair, the role of the Catholic Church, and labor militancy.

- Regionalism, poverty, social strife, violence, and unrepresentative government challenged Italy's efforts at parliamentary democracy.

AUTOCRACIES IN CRISIS

What various crises weakened autocratic rule in Germany, Russia, and the Ottoman Empire?

Four major autocracies dominated central and eastern Europe: Germany, Austria-Hungary, the Ottoman Empire, and Russia. If the democracies encountered difficulties in these years, the autocracies faced even more vehement opposition. Although many groups in the parliamentary regimes grew impatient at the slowness of change, theoretically at least they could believe that someday their goals would be realized. Not so in the autocracies. In authoritarian states, the demands for more democracy grew louder. Protesters resorted to violence and governments in turn used force to maintain themselves.

The severity of autocratic rule varied from state to state, ranging from the absolutism of the Ottoman Empire to the semiparliamentary regime of Germany; but in all of the states, the ruler had the final political say. Resistance to the autocracies included broad popular challenges to the German imperial system, discontent among ethnic minorities in the nearly ungovernable empire of Austria-Hungary, and revolution and war in the Russian and Ottoman Empires.

GERMANY

Although Germany had a parliament, the government was answerable to the kaiser, not the people's electoral representatives. To rule effectively, Chancellor Otto von Bismarck maneuvered and intrigued to quell opposition. In the face of socialist growth, he used an attempt to assassinate the emperor as the excuse to ban the Socialist Party in 1879. He also turned against the Catholics, who were lukewarm toward Protestant Prussia, persecuting them and their institutions. These measures, however, did not prevent the growth of the Socialist and Catholic Center Parties.

Unfortunately for Bismarck, whose tenure in office depended on the goodwill of the emperor, Wilhelm I died in 1888, to be succeeded first by his son, Friedrich, who ruled only a few months, and then by his grandson, Wilhelm II (r. 1888–1918). The young Kaiser Wilhelm intended to rule as well as reign, but he was ill fit to govern. Convinced of his own infallibility, he bothered to learn very little. Born with a crippled hand,

Wilhelm II
The German emperor liked to be viewed in a heroic and military posture. His crippled left hand is turned away from the viewer. *(Landesarchiv Berlin)*

Wilhelm seemed to want to compensate for this infirmity by appearing forceful, even brutal. He hated any hint of limitation to his power, announcing, "There is only one ruler in the Reich and I am he. I tolerate no other." A restless individual, Wilhelm changed uniforms eight times daily and traveled ceaselessly among his seventy-five castles and palaces. Intimidated by Bismarck and dismayed by his domestic and foreign policies, the kaiser dismissed him.

Wilhelm II was determined to make Germany a world power whose foreign policy would have a global impact. He wanted Germany to have colonies, a navy, and major influence among the Great Powers. This policy, *Weltpolitik,* or "world politics," greatly troubled Germany's neighbors. They were wary of a new, assertive power in central Europe, especially given the kaiser's bombastic threats. Within Germany, however, Weltpolitik won support. Steel manufacturers and shipbuilders received lucrative contracts; workers, in some industries at least, seemed assured of employment.

Weltpolitik Meaning "world politics," the term describes the policy pursued, with nationalistic appeals and bombastic threats, by Kaiser Wilhelm II to make Germany a world power.

Although the nationalist appeals impressed many Germans, the nation could not be easily managed. The emperor's autocratic style was challenged, and his behavior was increasingly viewed as irresponsible. In the elections of 1912 one-third of all Germans voted for Socialist Party candidates. Thus the largest single party in the Reichstag challenged both the capitalist system and autocracy. Labor militancy also reached new heights. In 1912 one million workers—a record number—went on strike. More and more Germans pressed for a government accountable to the people's elected representatives.

The emperor could not tolerate criticism of his behavior. He frequently talked about using the military to crush socialists and the parliament, ideas that were echoed in the officer corps and in government circles. To some observers it seemed likely that the days of German autocracy were numbered—or that the army and the people would come to blows.

AUSTRIA-HUNGARY

A series of crises also wracked the neighboring Austro-Hungarian Empire. In an age of intense nationalism, a multinational empire was an anomaly, as the emperor Franz Joseph (r. 1848–1916) himself acknowledged. Despite the Compromise of 1867 (see page 693) that regulated the relationship between Austria and Hungary, conflict grew, particularly over control of their joint army. Hungary increasingly saw its interests as separate from Austria's and probably would have broken loose from the dual monarchy had world war not occurred.

In the Hungarian half of the empire, the Magyar rule faced growing challenges. Other nationalities opposed Magyarization—the imposition of the Magyar language and institutions—and insisted on the right to use their own languages in their schools and administrations. The Hungarian government censored and imprisoned nationalist leaders. The Austrian half of the empire treated minority nationalities less harshly, but the government was equally strife-ridden.

There were no easy solutions to the many conflicts the empire faced. Hoping to dilute the influence of nationalist middle-class intellectuals, the Habsburg government introduced universal male suffrage in 1907. The result backfired. The extended suffrage produced a parliament that included thirty ethnically based political parties, making a workable majority nearly impossible to achieve. The empire became even more difficult to govern.

The virulence of debate based on nationality and class divisions grew to unprecedented extremes. Within the parliament, deputies threw inkwells at each other, rang sleigh bells, and sounded bugles. Parliament ceased to be relevant. By 1914 the emperor had dissolved it and several regional assemblies. Austria was being ruled by decree. Emperor Franz Joseph feared that the empire would not survive him.

OTTOMAN EMPIRE

In the generation before 1914, no political system in Europe suffered from so advanced a case of dissolution as the Ottoman Empire, undermined by both secessionist movements within its borders and aggression from other European powers. Sultan Abdul Hamid II (r. 1876–1909) ruled the country as a despot and authorized mass carnage against those who contested his rule, earning him the title "the Great Assassin."

Young, Western-educated Turks—the so-called Young Turks—disgusted at one-man rule and the continuing loss of territory and influence, overthrew Abdul Hamid in a coup in July 1908. They set up a government responsible to an elected parliament. The Young Turks hoped to stem the loss of territory by establishing firmer central control, but their efforts had the opposite effect. The various nationalities of the empire resented the imposition of Turkish education and administration. Renewed agitation broke out in Macedonia, in Albania, and among the Armenians. The government carried out severely repressive measures to end the unrest, massacring thousands of Armenians.

To foreign powers, the moment seemed propitious to plunder the weakened empire. In 1911 Italy occupied Libya, an Ottoman province. Greece, Bulgaria, and Serbia—impatient to enlarge their territories—formed an alliance, the Balkan League. In 1912 the League waged a successful war against the empire. Albania became independent, and Macedonia was partitioned among members of the League. This war stripped the empire of most of its European possessions.

RUSSIA

The Great Reforms of the 1860s, intended to resolve Russia's problems, instead unleashed new forces because they coincided with major social changes. Tsarist rule became even more difficult.

The needs of a modernizing country led to an increase in the number of universities and students. The newly educated Russian youths almost instantly began an ardent, sustained critique of autocracy. In the absence of a sizable middle class upholding liberal, advanced ideas, university students and graduates, who came to be known as the *intelligentsia,* saw it as their mission to transform Russia.

In the 1870s university youths by the thousands organized a populist movement, hoping to bring change to the countryside. These young idealists, both men and women, intended to educate the peasants and make them more politically aware. But they met with suspicion from the peasantry and repression by the government. Large numbers of populists were arrested and put on trial. Frustrated at the difficulty of bringing about change from below, disaffected radicals formed the People's Will, which turned to murdering public officials to hasten the day of revolution.

In response, the regime intensified repression. But it also sought to broaden its public support. In 1881 Tsar Alexander II decided to create an advisory committee that some thought would eventually lead to a parliamentary form of government. In March 1881, as he was about to sign the decree establishing this committee, the tsar was assassinated by members of the People's Will.

The new ruler, Tsar Alexander III (r. 1881–1894), who had witnessed the assassination, blamed it on his father's leniency. He thus decided to make the government even more autocratic. He weakened his father's reforms and in the process reduced local self-rule.

When Alexander's son, Nicholas II (r. 1894–1917), succeeded to the throne in 1894, he too was determined to maintain autocratic rule. However, he lacked the methodical, consistent temperament such a pledge required, as well as the forcefulness to establish a coherent policy for his troubled country.

Serious problems had accumulated that threatened the stability of the regime. Conditions worsened in the countryside as explosive population growth increased pressure on the land. Despite the abolition of serfdom, the peasants were not free to come and go as they pleased. Agriculture remained inefficient, far inferior to that of western Europe. Between 1861 and 1914 the peasant population grew by 50 percent, but it acquired only 10 percent more land. In 1891 famine broke out in twenty provinces, killing a quarter of a million people.

Although Russia remained largely agrarian, there were pockets of industrial growth. Some factories and mining concerns were unusually large, with as many as six thousand employees. When workers grew incensed at their condition and insistent on winning the same rights and protection as workers in western Europe, they engaged in massive strikes that crippled industry.

Political dissatisfaction with the autocracy grew among all social classes—the slowly expanding middle classes and aristocrats demanded the right to political participation. Various revolutionary groups committed to socialism flourished. Socialist Revolutionaries, heirs to the People's Will, emerged as a political force in the 1890s. They believed that the peasants would bring socialism to Russia.

In 1898 the Russian Social Democratic Party was founded. A Marxist party, it promoted the industrial

Workers' Demonstration in Moscow, 1905

In 1905 workers as well as peasants protested against the Russian autocracy. To bring the revolution under control, Nicholas II was obliged to grant several concessions. *(Novosti)*

working class as the harbinger of socialism. In 1903 that party split into the Menshevik and Bolshevik factions. The Mensheviks insisted that Russia had to go through the stages of history Marx had outlined—to witness the full development of capitalism and its subsequent collapse before the socialists could come to power. The Bolsheviks, a minority group, were led by Vladimir Ilich Lenin (1870–1924), a zealous revolutionary and Marxist. Rather than wait for historical forces to undermine capitalism, he insisted that a revolutionary cadre could seize power on behalf of the working class. Lenin favored a small, disciplined, conspiratorial party, like the People's Will, while the Mensheviks favored a more open, democratic party.

But popular opposition to tsarism soon grew in the face of Russian military ineptitude in the war against Japan, which broke out in February 1904 in a dispute over control of northern Korea. An economic slowdown heightened social tensions, and antagonism to the tsarist regime escalated.

Beginning in January 1905 a series of demonstrations, strikes, and other acts of collective violence erupted. Together they were dubbed "the revolution of

1905." On a Sunday of that month 400,000 workers gathered in front of the tsar's St. Petersburg palace. Rather than hear their demands, officials ordered soldiers to fire on them, resulting in 150 deaths and hundreds more wounded. "Bloody Sunday" inflamed the populace. The tsar, instead of being viewed as an understanding, paternal authority, had become the murderer of his people. Unrest spread to most of the country. The regime's prestige deteriorated further with reports of increasing losses in the war with Japan. By September 1905 Russia had to sue for peace and admit defeat. Challenged in the capital, where independent workers' councils called *soviets* had sprung up, the government also lost control over the countryside, the site of widespread peasant uprisings.

Fearing for his regime, Nicholas hoped to disarm the opposition by meeting some of its demands. He granted major constitutional and civil liberties, including freedom of religion, speech, assembly, and association. At the end of October the tsar established an elective assembly, the Duma, with restricted male suffrage and limited political power. It quickly became the arena for criticism of autocracy. Nicholas responded to the criticism by suspending the Duma and changing its electoral base and rules of operation. Even many conservatives were disillusioned with his breach of the

Bolsheviks Faction of the Russian Socialist Democratic Party led by Marxist Vladimir Ilich Lenin (1870–1924), who insisted that an exclusive revolutionary cadre could seize power on behalf of the working class.

promise he had made in 1905 to establish constitutionalism and parliamentarianism.

Poor social conditions continued to fuel opposition to the tsar. Although the government reduced the peasants' financial obligations, weakened the power of the commune, or *mir* (see pages 696–698), and ex-tended local self-rule to the peasants, these changes did little to alleviate rural poverty. Labor unrest also mounted. In 1912, 725,000 industrial workers went on strike; that number doubled in the first half of 1914. On the eve of the outbreak of the First World War, barricades were rising in the workers' neighborhoods.

SECTION SUMMARY

- In Germany after 1890, Wilhelm II's aggressive foreign policy menaced other European powers; his repressive, irresponsible, and autocratic governing style created widespread opposition to his rule.

- Parliamentary rule in Austria-Hungary failed because of ongoing conflicts between the two monarchies as well as between the multiple nationalities within each.

- The Ottoman Empire continued to suffer from both secessionist movements within its borders and aggression from other European powers; by 1912 the empire had lost most of its European possessions.

- In Russia, the emergence of revolutionary socialist groups, deteriorating conditions of peasants, worker discontent, and defeat in war with Japan fueled opposition to tsarist rule. The revolution of 1905 and subsequent reforms failed to stem the regime's problems.

THE COMING WAR

What responsibility did each of the Great Powers have for the outbreak of war in 1914?

Instability and upheaval characterized international relations in the years between 1880 and 1914. But the outbreak of war was by no means inevitable. Common sense dictated against it, and some intelligent people predicted that in the new modern era, war would become so destructive that it would be unthinkable. Finally, no European state wanted a war, although the Great Powers carried on policies that brought them to its brink.

POWER ALIGNMENTS

Germany enjoyed an unchallenged position in the international order of the 1870s and 1880s. It was united in an alliance with the two other eastern conservative states—Russia and Austria-Hungary—in the Three Emperors' League, formed in 1873 and renewed by treaty in 1884. It also formed part of the **Triple Alliance** with Austria and Italy. France stood alone, without allies. Britain, with little interest in continental affairs, appeared to be enjoying a "splendid isolation."

However, Germany's alliance system was not free from problems. Two of its allies, Austria-Hungary and Russia, were at loggerheads over control of the Balkans. How could Germany be the friend of both? Wary of ap-parent German preference for Austria, Bismarck signed the Reinsurance Treaty in 1887, assuring Russia that Germany would not honor its alliance with Austria if the latter attacked Russia. After Bismarck's resignation in 1890, Kaiser Wilhelm allowed the Reinsurance Treaty to lapse. Alarmed, the Russians turned to France and, in January 1894, signed the Franco-Russian Alliance, by which each side pledged to help the other should either be attacked by Germany.

The Great Powers on the Continent were now divided into two alliances, the Triple Alliance and the Franco-Russian Alliance. Britain formally belonged to neither, but if it favored any side, it would be the German-led alliance because of colonial rivalries with France over Africa and with Russia over Asia.

In the 1890s Germany lost British goodwill. Launching his Weltpolitik, Wilhelm II built up the German navy. An island nation dependent on international trade for its economic survival, Britain had developed a navy second to none—and it saw the German naval buildup as a threat to its security.

In the face of a mounting German menace, France and Britain decided to reconcile their differences. In 1904 they signed an understanding, or *entente*, resolving their rivalries in Egypt. In 1907 Great Britain and Russia regulated their competition for influence in Persia (present-day Iran) with the Anglo-Russian Entente. Europe was now loosely divided into a new configura-

Triple Alliance Military alliance established in 1882 among Germany, Austria-Hungary, and Italy to counter the Franco-Russian Alliance (later the Triple Entente).

tion of two groups: the Triple Alliance of Germany, Austria-Hungary, and Italy, and the **Triple Entente** of Great Britain, France, and Russia.

THE MOMENTUM TOWARD WAR

Only through a series of crises did these alignments solidify to the point where their members were willing to go to war to save them. In 1905 and again in 1911, France and Germany nearly went to war over their respective interests in Morocco; both instances left Germany with the appearance of unreasonable aggressiveness. Meanwhile, the unstable situation in the Balkans sharpened tensions between Austria and Russia.

The heightened international tensions forced the European states to increase their arms expenditures, which in turn increased their sense of insecurity. In 1906 Britain introduced a new class of ships with the launching of the *Dreadnought*. Powered by steam turbines, it was the fastest ship afloat; heavily armored, it could not be sunk easily, and its 12-inch guns made it a menace on the seas. The British had thought the Germans incapable of building equivalent ships. But they did, wiping out British supremacy. Older British ships could now easily be sunk by German dreadnoughts. No longer able to depend on its past supremacy, Britain felt less secure than at any time since the Napoleonic Wars, and it continued an expensive and feverish naval race with Germany.

In Germany the growing war-making capacity of Russia created great anxieties. The Japanese defeat of the tsarist empire in 1905 had revealed the Russian military to be inferior—a lumbering giant, slow to mobilize and maneuver. As a result, Germany had not been particularly afraid of its eastern neighbor. But stung by its humiliation in 1905, Russia quickly rebuilt its army and planned an extensive rail network in the west, which would, in the event of war, be used for military purposes. Germany now felt encircled by a hostile Russia to the east and an equally unfriendly France to the west, and by 1912 some military officers and government officials began thinking about a preventive war. If war was inevitable, many Germans argued, it should occur before Russia became even stronger.

Many political leaders viewed the escalating arms race as a form of madness. Between 1904 and 1913 French and Russian arms expenditures increased by 80 percent, those of Germany by 120 percent, those of Austria-Hungary by 50 percent, and those of Italy by 100 percent. British foreign secretary Sir Edward Grey (1862–1933) warned that if the arms race continued, "it will submerge civilization."

But on the whole, warfare was not greatly feared. The Western powers had not experienced a major conflict since the Crimean War (1854–1856). Most policymakers believed that the next war would be short. The wars that had so dramatically changed the borders of European states in the second half of the nineteenth century, notably the Austro-Prussian War of 1866 and the Franco-Prussian War of 1870, had been decided within a few weeks. Because few imagined that the next war would be either long or brutal, Europe's leaders did not make a major effort to prevent it.

The territorial rivalry between Austria and Russia triggered international disaster. For decades enmity had been growing between the two empires over control of the Balkans (see **MAP 24.4**). In 1903, following a

MAP 24.4 The Balkans in 1914
By 1914 the Ottoman Empire was much diminished, containing virtually no European territory. Political boundaries did not follow nationality lines. Serbia was committed to unite all Serbs at the expense of the Austro-Hungarian Empire.

Triple Entente Military alliance between Great Britain, France, and Russia, completed in 1907, countering the Triple Alliance.

bloody military coup that killed the king and queen of Serbia, a pro-Russian party took control of the Serbian government. In 1908 Russia, still not recovered from its defeat in 1905, was surprised when Austria unilaterally declared the annexation of the province of Bosnia (which it had administered since the Congress of Berlin in 1878; see page 696). Austria's action thwarted Serbia's ambition of annexing Bosnia, which had many Serb inhabitants. Fearing war, Russia had to accept diplomatic defeat and abandoned its ally, Serbia. But Russia was determined not to cave in again.

Undeterred, Serbia spread anti-Austrian propaganda and sought to unify under its banner Slavs living in the Balkans—including those under Austrian rule.

As a result, many Austrian officials were convinced that the survival of the Austro-Hungarian Empire required the destruction of Serbia. Talk of an attack on Serbia filled the Austrian court in 1914.

On June 28, 1914, the heir to the Habsburg throne, Archduke Franz Ferdinand, visited Sarajevo in Austrian-ruled Bosnia. A young Bosnian-Serb nationalist hostile to Austrian rule, who had been trained and armed by a Serb terrorist group called the Black Hand, assassinated the archduke and his wife.

The assassination of the heir to the throne provided Austria with an ideal pretext for military action. The German kaiser, fearing that failure to support Vienna would lead to Austrian collapse and a Germany bereft of

The Shot Heard Round the World
The young Serb nationalist Gavril Princip shoots Franz Ferdinand, the heir to the Austro-Hungarian throne, and his consort. The assassination led to the outbreak of World War I. *(Österreichische National-bibliothek, Vienna)*

any allies, urged Austria to attack Serbia. On July 23 Austria issued an ultimatum to Serbia, deliberately worded in such a way as to be unacceptable. When Serbia refused the ultimatum, Austria declared war on July 28.

Perceived self-interest motivated each state's behavior in the ensuing crisis. Russia's status as a Great Power required that it not allow its client state, Serbia, to be humiliated, much less obliterated. In the past the French government had acted as a brake on Russian ambitions in the Balkans. On the eve of the war in 1914, France counseled restraint, but it did not withhold its promise of aid. Since 1911 France had increasingly feared isolation in the face of what it perceived as growing German aggression. Its only ally on the Continent was Russia. To remain a Great Power, France needed to preserve its friendship with Russia and help that country maintain its own Great Power status.

Germany could not allow Austria, its only ally, to be destroyed. Its leaders may also have seen the crisis as a propitious moment to begin a war that was going to occur anyway. The Germans no doubt thought it expedient to strike before the Entente powers, especially Russia, became stronger. After declaring war on Russia, Germany then invaded France through Belgium to prevent it from coming to Russia's aid. The British, concerned for their ally France and outraged by the violation of Belgian neutrality (to which all the Great Powers had been signatories since 1839), on August 4 declared war on Germany. Europe was at war. Eventually so would be much of the world.

SECTION SUMMARY

- By 1907, Europe was loosely divided into the Triple Alliance of Germany, Austria-Hungary, and Italy, and the Triple Entente of Great Britain, France, and Russia.

- Mounting crises solidified the alliances: France and Germany came into conflict over Morocco; all the countries, but especially Britain and Germany, engaged in an arms race; rivalry over the Balkans between Russia and Austria intensified when the latter annexed Bosnia.

- Anti-Austrian sentiments in Serbia led to the assassination of the Austrian archduke Franz Ferdinand, provoking Austria to declare war on Serbia; the system of alliances then brought all of the Great Powers into war.

CHAPTER SUMMARY

Online Study Center **ACE the Test**

What were the main motivations for European imperialism?

In what ways did the worldview of intellectuals living in the belle époque differ from that of a generation earlier?

What factors made parliamentary rule in Great Britain, France, and Italy dysfunctional?

What various crises weakened autocratic rule in Germany, Russia, and the Ottoman Empire?

What responsibility did each of the Great Powers have for the outbreak of war in 1914?

In the decades prior to 1914, Europe appeared to dominate the globe. With the intention of acquiring new sources of wealth, trade, and the trappings of international power and prestige, Europeans forcibly conquered most of Africa and much of Asia. They also conceived of their mission as one that brought civilization to inferior peoples. They introduced both technology and Western education to the colonized subjects.

The scramble to build empires reflected growing competition among the Great Powers, but it also produced anxiety and tensions over them.

Between 1880 and 1914, more Europeans than ever before enjoyed material advantages and improved standards of living. Many intellectuals, however, abandoned the optimism of the generation that preceded them and saw in materialism and democracy the evidence of decline and decadence. Freud and Bergson and artists such as Munch and Moreau suggested that a hidden, irrational dimension of life lurked beneath the tranquil surface. Among the new nationalist right, fear of mass society gave way to racist and anti-Semitic ideologies.

In Western democracies, improved conditions also led to rising expectations. People grew more demanding, insisting in sometimes violent ways on their political and economic rights. Although mass movements such as socialism and women's suffrage generally used peaceful means in their campaigns to change society, some of their members advocated and employed force. Anarchism appeared to stalk Europe. States readily used force in efforts to quell various protest movements, even resorting to martial law.

In central and eastern Europe, similar problems emerged. Added to the mix of extremist ideologies and movements that opposed autocratic rule were the apparently unsolvable conflicts between national and ethnic groups. Everywhere in Europe, domestic ills raised the stakes in competition for overseas empire; at the same time the traditional empires of Austria-Hungary and Turkey were threatened with dissolution.

Every European power had some responsibility for feeding the international tensions that led to the outbreak of war in 1914. France and Germany clashed over Morocco; Austria and Russia competed for influence over the Balkans; Britain and Germany raced each other to build warships. The *Weltpolitik* of Wilhelm II menaced France and Britain. Among European thinkers and leaders, force had become widely accepted as the means to an end; all the powers (except Britain) built up large standing armies with millions of men and lethal modern equipment. As rising tensions tightened the alliance system, Europe divided into two armed camps. Some leaders—notably those of Austria-Hungary and Germany—favored war over negotiation in July 1914.

LOOKING AHEAD

If some leaders still feared war, more dreaded the consequences of not fighting, believing that war would save their regimes from the internal and external challenges they faced. Few could foresee the dire consequences of such a choice. Europe's very success in technological advancement and empire building would make this war a prolonged conflagration that would involve most of the world.

KEY TERMS

new imperialism (p. 740)

Second International (p. 752)

anti-Semitism (p. 753)

Zionism (p. 753)

Sigmund Freud (p. 754)

avant-garde (p. 754)

suffragists (p. 757)

Weltpolitik (p. 761)

Bolsheviks (p. 763)

Triple Alliance (p. 764)

Triple Entente (p. 765)

Online Study Center
Improve Your Grade Flashcards

SUGGESTED READING

Burrow, J. W. *The Crisis of Reason: European Thought, 1848–1914.* 2000. A strong emphasis on individual intellectuals and their contributions.

Carrère d'Encaussé, Hélène. *Nicholas II.* 2000. A biography of the tsar, set within the context of an increasingly difficult country to govern.

Hochschild, Adam. *King Leopold's Ghost.* 1998. A dramatic account of Leopold II's brutal rule over the Congo.

Jay, Mike, and Michael Neve, eds. *1900: A Fin-de-Siècle Reader.* 1999. A rich collection of documents on how people imagined the new century.

Johnson, Martin P. *The Dreyfus Affair.* 1999. A brisk review of the major events shaping the affair.

Joll, James. *The Origins of the First World War.* 1984. A clear, concise, readable history tracing how strategic interests and nationalist passions led to the outbreak of war.

Levine, Philippa, ed. *Gender and Empire.* 2004. A collection of essays that examine how gender, and particularly male domination, influenced British imperialism.

Schorske, Carl E. *Fin de Siècle Vienna: Politics and Culture.* 1980. A critically acclaimed work on the arts and social and political thought in the Habsburg capital at the turn of the century.

25

WAR AND REVOLUTION, 1914–1919

770

ud. It was not what soldiers had in mind when they headed off to war in August 1914 amid visions of glory, gallantry—and quick victory. But after heavy rain and constant shelling, mud was a fact of life for those fighting on the western front—Belgium and northern France—during the fall of 1917. The mud was so pervasive, in fact, that soldiers literally drowned in it. These Canadian troops are holding the line on November 14, 1917, at the end of the Battle of Passchendaele (PAH-shun-dale), a British-led assault that began late in July. That assault pushed the Germans back a mere 5 miles—at the cost of 300,000 lives. There was no end to the war in sight.

Some had thought a major war impossible in rational, civilized Europe. Others had devoutly wished for war—precisely to break out of the stifling bourgeois conventions of rational, civilized Europe. When war actually began early in August 1914, the European mood was generally enthusiastic, even festive. No one was prepared for what this war would bring, including the hellish scenes of mud, smoke, artillery craters, blasted trees, decaying bodies, and ruined buildings that came to frame the daily experience of those on the western front. A far wider and more destructive war would follow within a generation, but it was World War I, known to contemporaries as "the Great War," that shattered the old European order, with its comfortable assumptions of superiority, rationality, and progress. After this war, neither Westerners nor non-Westerners could still believe in the privileged place of Western civilization in quite the same way.

The war that began in August was supposed to be over by Christmas. The British government promised "business as usual." But the fighting bogged down in a stalemate during the fall of 1914, then continued for four more years. By the time it ended, in November 1918, the war had strained the whole fabric of life, affecting everything from economic organization to literary vocabulary, from journalistic techniques to the role of women.

Partly because the war grew to become the first "world war," it proved the beginning of the end of European hegemony. The intervention of the United States in 1917 affected the military balance and seemed to give the war more idealistic and democratic purposes. The geographic reach of the

CHAPTER OUTLINE

THE UNFORESEEN STALEMATE, 1914–1917

THE EXPERIENCE OF TOTAL WAR

THE TWO RUSSIAN REVOLUTIONS OF 1917

THE NEW WAR AND THE ALLIED VICTORY, 1917–1918

THE OUTCOME AND THE IMPACT

KEY TERMS

Sacred Union

British blockade

total war

Kriegsrohstoffabteilung (KRA)

Petrograd Soviet

provisional government

Vladimir Lenin

Fourteen Points

Treaty of Brest-Litovsk

"stab in the back" myth

Treaty of Versailles

League of Nations

Online Study Center

This icon will direct you to interactive map and primary source activities on the website **college.hmco.com/pic/noble5e**

war was itself unprecedented, especially after the intervention of the Ottoman Empire spread the fighting to the Middle East. Because of European colonial networks, the war also involved many other non-Europeans in combat or support roles. Although the old colonialism continued into the postwar era, the war nourished the forces that would later overthrow it.

Because of all the strains it entailed, the war had many unintended consequences. Revolutions dramatically changed the political landscape first in Russia, then in Germany. The Habsburg and Ottoman Empires collapsed. So when the victors met early in 1919 to shape the peace, they confronted a situation that could not have been foreseen in 1914. Their effort to determine the contours of the postwar world, and thus the immediate meaning of the war, left much unresolved.

FOCUS QUESTIONS

How and why had the course of the war by 1917 defied the expectations that had surrounded the beginning of fighting in August 1914?

Why did this prove a total war, making necessary new forms of socioeconomic coordination and even systematic propaganda?

Why did the first revolution in Russia pave the way for a second, spearheaded by the Bolsheviks?

Why did Germany and its allies end up losing the war even after forcing Russia to make a separate peace by early 1918?

What factors shaped the peace settlement that the victors imposed on Germany and its allies in 1919–1920?

THE UNFORESEEN STALEMATE, 1914–1917

How and why had the course of the war by 1917 defied the expectations that had surrounded the beginning of fighting in August 1914?

When the war began in August 1914, enthusiasm and high morale, based on expectations of quick victory, marked both sides. But fighting on the crucial western front led to a stalemate by the end of 1914, and the brutal encounters of 1916 made it clear that this was not the sort of war most had expected. By early 1917 the difficulties of the war experience brought to the surface underlying questions about what all the fighting was for—and whether it was worth the price.

AUGUST 1914: THE DOMESTIC AND MILITARY SETTING

Although some, including Helmuth von Moltke (MOLT-kuh) (1848–1916), chief of the German general staff, worried that this would prove a long, destructive war testing the very fabric of Western civilization, the outbreak of fighting early in August produced a wave of euphoria and a remarkable degree of domestic unity. To many, war came almost as a relief; at last, the issues that had produced intermittent crisis for the past decade would find a definitive solution. Especially among educated young people, this settling of accounts seemed to offer the prospect of renewal, even a kind of redemption, for themselves and their societies. The war promised an escape from the stifling bourgeois world and, in response to the common danger, an end to the bickering and divisiveness of everyday politics.

An unexpected display of patriotism from the socialist left reinforced the sense of domestic unity and high morale. Forgetting their customary rhetoric about international proletarian solidarity, socialist parties rallied to their respective national war efforts almost everywhere in Europe. To socialists and workers, national defense against a more backward aggressor seemed essential to the eventual creation of socialism. French Socialists had to defend France's democratic republic against autocratic and militaristic Germany; German Socialists had to defend German institutions, and the strong socialist organizations that had proven possible within them, against repressive tsarist Russia. When, on August 4, the German Socialist Party delegation in the Reichstag voted with the other parties to give the government the budgetary authority to wage war, it was clear that the Second International had failed in its long-standing commitment to keep the workers of Europe from slaughtering each other.

In France, the government had planned, as a precaution, to arrest roughly one thousand trade union and socialist leaders in the event of war, but no such arrests were necessary. The order of the day was **Sacred Union,** which meant that French leaders from across the political spectrum agreed to cooperate for the duration of the war. Rather than seek to sabotage the war, Socialist leaders joined the new government of national defense. Germany enjoyed a comparable "Fortress Truce," including an agreement to suspend labor conflict during the war, although no Socialist was invited to join the war cabinet.

In 1914 the forces of the Triple Entente outnumbered those of Germany and Austria-Hungary. Russia had an army of over 1 million men, the largest in Europe, and France had 700,000. Britain, which did not introduce conscription until 1916, had about 250,000. Germany led the Central Powers with 850,000; Austria-Hungary contributed 450,000. Though outnumbered, the Central Powers had potential advantages in equipment, coordination, and speed over their more dispersed adversaries. The outcome was hardly a foregone conclusion in August 1914.

After the fighting began, a second group of nations intervened one by one, expanding the war's scope and complicating the strategic alternatives. In November 1914 the Ottoman Empire, fearful of Russia, joined the Central Powers, thereby extending the war along the Russo-Turkish border and on to Mesopotamia and the approaches to the Suez Canal in the Middle East. For Arabs disaffected with Ottoman Turkish rule, the war presented an opportunity to take up arms—with the active support of Britain and France. Italy, after dickering with both sides, committed itself to the Entente in the Treaty of London of April 1915. This secret agreement specified the territories Italy would receive—primarily the Italian-speaking areas still within Austria-Hungary—in the event of Entente victory. In September 1915 Bulgaria entered the war on the side of the Central Powers, seeking territorial advantages at the expense of Serbia, which had defeated Bulgaria in the Second Balkan War in 1913. Finally, in August 1916, Romania intervened on the side of the Entente, hoping to gain Transylvania, then part of Hungary.

Thus the war was fought on a variety of fronts (see **MAP 25.1**). This fact, combined with uncertainties about the role of sea power, led to ongoing debate among military decision makers about strategic priorities. Some expected that Britain and Germany would quickly be drawn into a decisive naval battle. But

Sacred Union An agreement between leaders of different French political groups to cooperate during World War I.

August 1914	Fighting begins
September 1914	French forces hold off the German assault at the Marne
August–September 1914	German victories repel Russian invasion on eastern front
May 1915	Italy declares war on Austria-Hungary
February–December 1916	Battle of Verdun
July–November 1916	Battle of the Somme
January 1917	Germans resume unrestricted submarine warfare
March 1917	First Russian revolution: fall of the tsar
April 1917	U.S. declaration of war
July 1917	German Reichstag war aims resolution
November 1917	Second Russian revolution: the Bolsheviks take power
March 1918	Treaty of Brest-Litovsk between Germany and Russia
March–July 1918	Germany's last western offensive
June 1918	Initial outbreak of the "Spanish flu"
July 1918	Second Battle of the Marne
November 1918	Armistice: fighting ends
January 1919	Paris Peace Conference convenes
June 1919	Victors impose Treaty of Versailles on Germany

though Britain promptly instituted an effective naval blockade on imports to Germany, the great showdown on the seas never materialized. Even the most significant naval encounter between them, the Battle of Jutland in 1916, was inconclusive. Despite the naval rivalry of the prewar years, World War I proved fundamentally a land war.

Germany faced not only the long-anticipated two-front war against Russia in the east and France and Britain in the west; it also had to look to the southeast, given the precarious situation of its ally Austria-Hungary, which was fighting Serbia and Russia, then also Italy and Romania as well. On the eastern front, Germany was largely successful, forcing first Russia, then Romania, to seek a separate peace by mid-1918. But it was the western front that proved decisive.

MAP 25.1 Major Fronts of World War I

Although World War I included engagements in East Asia and the Middle East, it was essentially a European conflict, encompassing fighting on a number of fronts.

Moscow

Treaty of Brest-Litovsk, March 1918

RUSSIA

Petrograd (St. Petersburg)

Helsinki

FINLAND

ESTONIA

LATVIA

Riga

COURLAND

LITHUANIA

Masurian Lakes 1914

Tannenberg 1914

E. PRUSSIA

Warsaw

POLAND

MAY 1915

Farthest Russian Advance, 1914

Kiev

UKRAINE

Armistice line, December 1917

Dnieper

Don

Black Sea

Brest-Litovsk

GALICIA

Vistula

Oder

Berlin

GERMANY

Elbe

Kiel

DENMARK

Jutland 1916

British blockade line

North Sea

NORWAY

SWEDEN

Baltic Sea

NETHERLANDS

Louvain

BELGIUM

LUXEMBOURG

Rhine

SWITZERLAND

AUSTRIA-HUNGARY

Vienna

TRANSYLVANIA

ROMANIA

Bucharest

SERBIA

Danube

Sarajevo

MONTENEGRO

ALBANIA

BULGARIA

Balkan Front

GREECE

1917-1918

1916

1915

Dardanelles

Constantinople

OTTOMAN EMPIRE

Gallipoli 1915

Black Sea

Mediterranean Sea

Caporetto 1917

AUG. 1917

MAR. 1918

Italian Front

ITALY

Rome

Western Front

Seine

Paris

FRANCE

Bordeaux

Loire

Rhône

GREAT BRITAIN

London

IRELAND

ATLANTIC OCEAN

SPAIN

300 Mi.

300 Km.

150

150

0

0

Triple Entente and Its Allies
Central Powers
Neutral nations
Farthest German-Austrian advance
Major battles
Battle lines

No Trenches in Sight
Spirits were high early in August 1914, as soldiers like these in Paris marched off to war. None foresaw what fighting this war would be like. None grasped the long-term impact the war would have.
(Giraudon/Art Resource, NY)

INTO THE NIGHTMARE, 1914–1916

With the lessons of the wars of German unification in mind, both sides had planned for a short war based on rapid offensives. According to the Schlieffen (SHLEE-fyn) Plan, drafted in 1905, Germany would concentrate first on France, devoting but one-eighth of its forces to containing the Russians, who would need longer to mobilize. After taking just six weeks to defeat France, Germany would focus on Russia. French strategy, crafted by commander-in-chief Joseph Joffre (JOFF-ruh) (1852–1931), similarly relied on rapid offensives. The boys would be home by Christmas—or so it was thought.

Although German troops encountered more opposition than expected from the formerly neutral Belgians, they moved swiftly through Belgium into northern France during August. By the first week of September they had reached the Marne River, threatening Paris and forcing the French government to retreat south to Bordeaux (bor-DOH). But French and British troops counterattacked from September 6 to 10, forcing the Germans to fall back and begin digging in along the Aisne (ENN) River. By holding off the German offensive at this first Battle of the Marne, the Entente had undercut the Schlieffen Plan—and with it, it turned out, any chance of a speedy victory by either side.

During the rest of the fall of 1914, each side tried—unsuccessfully—to outflank the other. When, by the end of November, active fighting ceased for the winter, a military front of about 300 miles had been established, all the way from Switzerland to the coast of the North Sea in Belgium (see Map 25.2 on page 788). This line failed to shift more than 10 miles in either direction over the next three years. The result of the first six weeks of fighting on the western front was not a gallant victory but a grim and unforeseen stalemate.

Virtually from the start, the war took a fiercely destructive turn. In northern France in September 1914, the Germans fired on the famed Gothic cathedral at Reims (RAANZ), severely damaging its roof and nave, because they believed—apparently correctly—that the French were using one of its towers as an observation post. If such a catastrophe could happen to one of the great monuments in Europe, what else might this war bring?

The two sides were forced to settle into a war of attrition relying on an elaborate network of defensive trenches. Although separated by as much as 5 miles in some places, enemy trenches were sometimes within shouting distance, so there was occasionally banter back and forth, even attempts to entertain the other side. But the trenches quickly became almost unimaginably gruesome—filthy, ridden with rats and lice, noisy and smoky from artillery fire, and foul-smelling, partly from the odor of decaying bodies.

Online Study Center **Improve Your Grade**
Primary Source: The World of the Trenches:
 A Deadly Life

As defensive instruments, however, the trenches proved quite effective. Each side quickly learned to take advantage of barbed wire, mines, and especially machine guns to defend its positions. A mass of barbed wire, 3 to 5 feet high and 30 yards wide, guarded a typical trench. The machine gun had been developed before the war as an offensive weapon; few foresaw the decided advantage it would give the defense. But with machine guns, soldiers could defend trenches even against massive assaults—and inflict heavy casualties on the attackers.

In 1916 the British sent the first shipment of tanks to France as an antidote to the machine gun, but, as skeptics had warned, tanks proved too ungainly and unreliable to be widely effective. Although the French used them to advantage in the decisive Allied offensive in 1918, tanks were not crucial to the outcome of the war.

Despite the advantages of defensive trenches, neither side could give up the vision of a decisive offensive. Thus the troops were periodically called on to go "over the top" and then across "no man's land" to assault the dug-in enemy. Again and again, however, such offensives proved futile, producing incredibly heavy casualties: "Whole regiments gambled away eternity for ten yards of wasteland."[1]

For the soldiers on the western front, the war became a nightmarish experience in a hellish landscape. Bombardment by new, heavier forms of artillery scarred the terrain with craters, which became muddy, turning the landscape into a near swamp. Beginning early in 1915, tear gas, chlorine gas, and finally mustard gas found use on both sides. Although the development of gas masks significantly reduced the impact of this menacing new chemical warfare, the threat of poison gas added another nightmarish element to the experience of those who fought the war.

The notions of patriotism, comradeship, duty, and glory that had been prevalent in 1914 gradually dissolved as soldiers experienced the horrors of this war. A French soldier, questioning his own reactions after battle in 1916, responded with sarcasm and irony: "What sublime emotion inspires you at the moment of assault? I thought of nothing other than dragging my feet out of the mud encasing them. What did you feel after surviving the attack? I grumbled because I would have to remain several days more without *pinard* [wine]. Is not one's first act to kneel down and thank God? No. One relieves oneself."[2]

Although the Germans had been denied their quick victory in the west, by the end of 1914 they occupied much of Belgium and almost one-tenth of France, including major industrial areas and mines producing most of France's coal and iron. On the eastern front, as well, the Germans won some substantial advantages in 1914—but not a decisive victory.

Trench Warfare
Grim though they were, the trenches proved effective for defensive purposes. Here a British soldier guards a trench at Ovillers, on the Somme, in July 1916. *(Courtesy of the Trustees of the Imperial War Museum)*

The first season of fighting suggested that the pattern in the east would not be trench warfare but rapid movement across a vast but thinly held front. When hostilities began in August, the Russians mustered more quickly than anticipated, confronting an outnumbered German force in a menacing, if reckless, invasion of East Prussia. But by mid-September German forces under General Paul von Hindenburg (1847–1934) and his chief of staff, General Erich Ludendorff (1865–1937), repelled the Russian advance, taking a huge number of prisoners and seriously demoralizing the Russians.

As a result of this victory, Hindenburg and Ludendorff emerged as heroes, and they would play major roles in German public life thereafter. Hindenburg became chief of staff of the entire German army in August 1916, but the able and energetic Ludendorff proved the key figure as this duo gradually assumed undisputed control of the whole German war effort, both military and domestic.

SEEKING A BREAKTHROUGH, 1915–1917

After the campaigns of 1915 proved inconclusive, German leaders decided to concentrate in 1916 on a massive offensive against the great French fortress at Verdun, intending to inflict a definitive defeat on France. To assault the fortress, the Germans gathered 1,220 pieces of artillery for attack along an 8-mile front. Included were thirteen "Big Bertha" siege guns, weapons so large that nine tractors were required to position each of them; a crane was necessary to insert the shell, which weighed over a ton. The level of heavy artillery firepower that the Germans applied at Verdun was unprecedented in the history of warfare.

German forces attacked on February 21, taking the outer defenses of the fortress, and appeared poised for victory. The tide turned, however, when General Philippe Pétain (puh-TANH) (1856–1951) assumed control of the French defense. Pétain had the patience and skill necessary to organize supply networks for a long siege. Furthermore, he proved able, through considerate treatment, to inspire affection and confidence among his men. By mid-July the French army had repelled the German offensive, although only in December did the French retake the outer defenses of the fortress. The French had held firm in what would prove the war's longest, most trying battle—one that killed over 700,000 people.

To relieve pressure on Verdun, the British led a major attack at the Somme River on July 1, 1916. On that day alone the British suffered almost 60,000 casualties, including 21,000 killed. Fighting continued into the fall, but the offensive proved futile in the end. One-third of those involved, or over 1 million soldiers, ended up dead, missing, or wounded.

Dominated by the devastating battles at Verdun and the Somme, the campaigns of 1916 finally extinguished the high spirits of the summer of 1914. Both sides suffered huge losses—apparently for nothing. By the end of 1916, the front had shifted only a few miles from its location at the beginning of the year.

In light of the frustrating outcome so far, the French turned to new military leadership, replacing Joffre as commander-in-chief with Robert Nivelle (1856–1924), who promptly sought to prove himself with a new offensive during the spring of 1917. Persisting even as it became clear that this effort had no chance of success, Nivelle provoked increasing resistance among French soldiers, some of whom were refusing to follow orders by the end of April.

With the French war effort in danger of collapse, the French government replaced Nivelle with General Pétain, the hero of the defense of Verdun. Pétain reestablished discipline by adopting a conciliatory approach—improving food and rest, visiting the troops in the field, offering encouragement, even dealing relatively mercifully with the resisters themselves. To be sure, many of the soldiers who had participated in this near mutiny were court-martialed, and over 3,400 were convicted. But of the 554 sentenced to death, only 49 were actually executed.

After the failure of the Nivelle offensive, the initiative fell to the British under General Douglas Haig (1861–1928), who was convinced, despite skepticism in the British cabinet, that Nivelle's offensive had failed simply because of tactical mistakes. Beginning near Ypres (EE-pray) in Belgium on July 31, 1917, and continuing until November, the British attacked. As before, the effort yielded only minimal territorial gains—about 50 square miles—at a horrifying cost, including 300,000 British and Canadian casualties. Known as the Battle of Passchendaele, the British offensive of 1917 ranks with the Battles of Verdun and the Somme as the bloodiest of the war.

1917 AS A TURNING POINT

Meanwhile, the Germans decided to concentrate on the eastern front in 1917 in an effort to knock Russia out of the war. This intensified German military pressure helped spark revolution in Russia, and in December 1917 Russia's new revolutionary regime asked for a separate peace (see page 787). The defeat of Russia freed the Germans at last to concentrate on the west, but by this time France and Britain had a new ally.

On April 6, 1917, the United States entered the war on the side of the Entente, in response to Germany's controversial use of submarines. Germany did not have enough surface ships to respond to Britain's naval blockade, whether by attacking the British fleet directly or by mounting a comparable blockade of the British

Isles. So the Germans decided to use submarines to interfere with shipping to Britain. Submarines, however, were too vulnerable to be able to surface and confiscate goods, so the Germans had to settle for sinking suspect ships with torpedoes. In February 1915 they declared the waters around the British Isles a war zone and served notice that they would torpedo not only enemy ships but also neutral ships carrying goods to Britain.

The German response was harsh, but so was the **British blockade,** which violated earlier international agreements about the rights of neutral shipping and the scope of wartime blockades. The British had agreed that only military goods such as munitions and certain raw materials, not such everyday goods as food and clothing, were to be subject to confiscation. Yet in blockading Germany, the British refused to make this distinction, prompting the sarcastic German quip that Britannia not only rules the waves but waives the rules.[3]

In May 1915 a German sub torpedoed the *Lusitania*, a British passenger liner, killing almost 1,200 people and producing widespread indignation. Partly because 128 of those killed were Americans, U.S. president Woodrow Wilson issued a severe warning, which contributed to the German decision in September 1915 to pull back from unrestricted submarine warfare. But as German suffering under the British blockade increased, pressure mounted on Berlin to put the subs back into action.

The issue provoked bitter debate. Chancellor Theobald von Bethmann-Hollweg (BETT-mahn–HOHL-veg) (1856–1921) and the civilian authorities opposed resumption, fearing it would provoke the United States to enter the war. But Ludendorff and the military finally prevailed, arguing that even if the United States did intervene, U.S. troops could not get to Europe in time to have a major impact. Germany announced it would resume unrestricted submarine warfare on January 31, 1917, and the United States responded with a declaration of war on April 6.

Many on both sides doubted that U.S. intervention would make a pivotal difference; most assumed—correctly—that it would take at least a year for the American presence to materialize in force. Still, the entry of the United States gave the Entente at least the promise of more fighting power. And the United States seemed capable of renewing the sense of purpose on the Entente side, showing that the war had a meaning that could justify the unexpected costs and sacrifice.

═══════ S E C T I O N   S U M M A R Y ═══════

- Although the war was fought on a variety of fronts and even expanded beyond Europe, it was the fighting on the western front, in a relatively small chunk of Belgium and northern France, that proved decisive.

- At the outset, each side expected a short war of rapid offensives, but the struggle on the western front produced only a stalemate, based on defensive trench warfare, by the end of 1914.

- The defensive trenches proved so difficult to attack, especially because of barbed wire and the machine gun.

- Massive assaults during 1916–1917 failed to produce the intended breakthrough for either side, though they resulted in horrifying numbers of casualties.

- Though the United States declared war in 1917 in response to Germany's resumption of unrestricted submarine warfare, it was not equipped to make an immediate difference on European battlefields.

THE EXPERIENCE OF TOTAL WAR

Why did this prove a total war, making necessary new forms of socioeconomic coordination and even systematic propaganda?

As the war dragged on, the distinction between the military and civilian spheres blurred. Suffering increased on the home front, and unprecedented governmental mobilization of society proved necessary to wage war on the scale that had come to be required. Because it became "total" in this way, the war decisively altered not only the old political and diplomatic order, but also culture, society, and the patterns of everyday life.

HARDSHIP ON THE HOME FRONT

The war meant food shortages, and thus malnutrition, for ordinary people in the belligerent countries, although Britain and France, with their more favorable

British blockade   Britain's naval blockade of Germany during World War I; it seriously impeded the German war effort.

geographic positions, suffered considerably less than others. Germany was especially vulnerable, and the British naval blockade exacerbated an already dire situation. With military needs taking priority, the Germans encountered shortages of the chemical fertilizers, farm machinery, and draft animals necessary for agricultural production. The government began rationing bread, meat, and fats during 1915. The increasing scarcity of food produced sharp increases in diseases such as rickets and tuberculosis and in infant and childhood mortality rates.

The need to pay for the war produced economic dislocations as well. Government borrowing covered some of the cost for the short term, but to underwrite the rest, governments all over Europe found it more palatable to inflate the currency, by printing more money, than to raise taxes. The notion that the enemy would be made to pay once victory had been won seemed to justify this decision. But this way of financing the war meant rising prices and severe erosion of purchasing power for ordinary people all over Europe. In France and Germany, the labor truces of 1914 gave way to increasing strike activity during 1916.

With an especially severe winter in 1916–1917 adding to the misery, there were serious instances of domestic disorder, including strikes and food riots, in many parts of Europe during 1917. In Italy, major strikes developed in Turin and other cities over wages and access to foodstuffs. The revolution that overthrew the tsarist autocracy in Russia that same year began with comparable protests over wartime food shortages.

The strains of war even fanned the flames in Ireland, where an uneasy truce over the home-rule controversy accompanied the British decision for war in 1914. Partly because of German efforts to stir up domestic trouble for Britain, unrest built up again in Ireland, culminating in the Easter Rebellion in Dublin in 1916. The brutality with which British forces crushed the uprising intensified demands for full independence—precisely what Britain would be forced to yield to the Irish republic shortly after the war.

Moreover, new technologies made civilians more vulnerable to wartime violence. Although bombing from aircraft began with an immediate military aim—to destroy industrial targets or to provide tactical support for other military units—it quickly became clear that night bombing, especially, might demoralize civilian populations. In 1915 German airplanes began bombing English cities, provoking British retaliation against cities in western Germany. These raids had little effect on the course of the war, but they showed that new technologies could make warfare more destructive even for civilians.

DOMESTIC MOBILIZATION

Once it became clear that the war would not be over quickly, leaders on both sides realized that the outcome would not be determined on the battlefield alone. Victory required mobilizing all of the nation's resources and energies. So World War I became a **total war,** involving the entire society.

The British naval blockade on Germany, which made no distinction between military and nonmilitary goods, was a stratagem characteristic of total war. The blockade would not affect Germany's immediate strength on the battlefield, but it could damage Germany's long-term war-making capacity. The blockade was effective partly because Germany had not made adequate preparations—including stockpiling—for a protracted war of attrition.

In peacetime, Germany had depended on imports of food, fats, oils, and chemicals, including the nitrates needed for ammunition. With the onset of war, these goods were immediately in short supply, as was labor. Thus Germany seemed to need stringent economic coordination and control. By the end of 1916, the country had coordinated all aspects of economic life for the war effort. Under the supervision of the military, state agencies, big business, and the trade unions were brought into close collaboration. The new system included rationing, price controls, and compulsory labor arbitration, as well as a national service law enabling the military to channel workers into jobs deemed vital to the war effort.

The Germans did not hesitate to exploit the economy of occupied Belgium, requisitioning foodstuffs even to the point of causing starvation among the Belgians themselves. They forced sixty-two thousand Belgians to work in German factories under conditions of virtual slave labor. By the time this practice was stopped in February 1917, nearly a thousand Belgian workers had died in German labor camps.

The body coordinating Germany's war economy was the **Kriegsrohstoffabteilung (KRA)** (kreegs-roh-stoff-AHB-ty-loong), or "War Raw Materials Office." Led initially by the able Jewish industrialist Walther Rathenau (RAT-un-ow) (1867–1922), this agency came to symbolize the unprecedented coordination of the German economy. Recognizing that Germany lacked the raw materials for a long war, Rathenau devised an imaginative program that included the development of synthetic substitute products and the creation of new mixed (private and government) companies to

total war   The concept, first associated with World War I, that war requires the mobilization of all a nation's resources and energies.

Kriegsrohstoffabteilung (KRA)   The "War Raw Materials Office" that coordinated Germany's World War I economy.

allocate raw materials. The KRA's effort was remarkably successful—a model for later economic planning and coordination in Germany and elsewhere.

Although Germany presented the most dramatic example, this sort of domestic coordination was evident everywhere. In Britain, the central figure was David Lloyd George (1863–1945), appointed to the newly created post of minister of munitions in 1915. During his year in office, ninety-five new factories opened, soon overcoming the shortage of guns and ammunition that had impeded the British war effort until then. His performance made Lloyd George seem the one person who could organize Britain for victory. Succeeding Herbert Asquith as prime minister in December 1916, he would direct the British war effort to its victorious conclusion.

Accelerating Socioeconomic Change

Everywhere the war effort quickened the long-term socioeconomic change associated with industrialization. Government orders for war materiel fueled industrial expansion. The needs of war spawned new technologies—advances in food processing and medical treatment, for example—that would carry over into peacetime.

With so many men needed for military service, women were called on to assume new economic roles—such as running farms in France, or working in the new munitions factories in Britain. During the course of the war, the number of women employed in Britain rose from 3.25 million to 5 million. In Italy, 200,000 women had war-related jobs by 1917. Women also played indispensable roles at the front, especially in nursing units.

The expanded opportunities of wartime intensified the debate over the sociopolitical role of women that the movement for women's suffrage had stimulated. The outbreak of war led some antiwar feminists to argue that women would be better able than men to prevent wars, which were essentially masculine undertakings. Women should have full access to public life, not because they could be expected to respond as men did but because they had a distinctive—and valuable—role to play. At the same time, by giving women jobs and the opportunity to do many of the same things men did, the war undermined the stereotypes that had long justified restrictions on women's political roles and life choices.

For many women, doing a difficult job well, serving their country in this emergency situation, afforded a new sense of accomplishment, as well as a new taste of independence. Women were now much more likely to have their own residences and to go out on their own, eating in restaurants, even smoking and drinking. Yet while many seized new opportunities and learned new skills, women frequently had to combine paid employ-

Working Women and the War
All over Europe, governments recruited women to work in munitions factories. This Russian government poster uses an image of working women to rally support for the war. The text reads, "Everything for the war effort! Subscribe to the war loans at 5½ percent." *(Eileen Tweedy/The Art Archive)*

ment with housework and child rearing, and those who left home—to serve in nursing units, for example—often felt guilty about neglecting their traditional family roles.

Online Study Center **Improve Your Grade**
Primary Source: A British Feminist Analyzes the Impact of the War on Women

Propaganda and the "Mobilization of Enthusiasm"

Because the domestic front was crucial to sustaining a long war of attrition, it became ever more important to shore up civilian morale as the war dragged on. The result was what the historian Elie Halévy called the "mobilization of enthusiasm"—the manipulation of collective passions by governments on an unprecedented scale.

Devastation at Louvain

Unexpected destruction at the outset of the war fanned the flames of hatred and changed the stakes of the conflict. Located in the path of the first German advance, the Belgian city of Louvain was particularly hard-hit.   *(Courtesy of the Trustees of the Imperial War Museum)*

Every country instituted extensive censorship, even of soldiers' letters from the front. Because of concerns about civilian morale, the French press carried no news of the Battle of Verdun, with its horrifying numbers of casualties. In addition, systematic propaganda included not only patriotic themes but also attempts to discredit the enemy, even through outright falsification of the news. British anti-German propaganda helped draw the United States into the war in 1917.

At the outset of the war, the brutal behavior of the German armies in Belgium made it easy for the French and the British to demonize the Germans. Having expected to pass through neutral Belgium unopposed, the Germans were infuriated by the Belgian resistance they encountered. At Louvain late in August 1914 they responded to alleged Belgian sniping by shooting a

number of hostages and setting the town on fire, destroying the famous old university library. This episode led the *London Times* to characterize the Germans as "Huns," a reference to the central Asian tribe that began invading Europe in the fourth century. Stories about German soldiers eating Belgian babies began to circulate.

In October 1914 ninety-three German intellectuals, artists, and scientists signed a manifesto, addressed to "the world of culture," justifying Germany's conduct in Belgium and its larger purposes in the war. As passions heated up, major intellectuals on both sides—from the German theologian Adolf von Harnack (1851–1930) to the French philosopher Henri Bergson (1859–1941)— began denigrating the culture of the enemy and claiming a monopoly of virtue for their own side.

As the war dragged on, some came to believe that real peace with an adversary so evil, so abnormally different, was simply not possible. There must be no compromise but rather total victory, no matter what the cost. At the same time, however, war-weariness produced a countervailing tendency to seek a "white peace," a peace without victory for either side. But in 1917, as Europeans began earnestly debating war aims, the Russian Revolution and the intervention of the United States changed the war's meaning for all the belligerents.

S E C T I O N   S U M M A R Y

- Partly because of the advent of new technologies, the war threatened civilian populations in unforeseen ways.

- The unexpected length of the war forced domestic mobilization, both to maintain civilian morale and to enhance the production necessary to sustain the military effort.

- Britain's naval blockade of Germany forced German leaders to adopt innovative, highly centralized forms of socioeconomic coordination, partly to spearhead the development of substitute products.

- Domestic mobilization accelerated socioeconomic change, especially by enhancing employment opportunities for women.

- Systematic attempts to discredit the enemy, by intellectuals as well as governments, made it harder to envision the scope for a lasting peace.

THE TWO RUSSIAN REVOLUTIONS OF 1917

Why did the first revolution in Russia pave the way for a second, spearheaded by the Bolsheviks?

Strained by war, the old European order cracked first in Russia in 1917. Initially the overthrow of the tsarist autocracy seemed to lay the foundations for parliamentary democracy. But by the end of the year, the Bolsheviks, the smallest and most extreme of Russia's major socialist parties, had taken power, an outcome that was hardly conceivable when the revolution began.

THE WARTIME CRISIS OF THE RUSSIAN AUTOCRACY

The Russian army performed better than many had expected; as late as June 1916, it mounted a successful offensive against Austria-Hungary. Russia had industrialized sufficiently by 1914 to sustain a modern war, at least for a while, and the country's war production increased significantly by 1916. But even early in 1915, perhaps a fourth of Russia's newly conscripted troops were sent to the front without weapons; they were told to pick up rifles and supplies from the dead. Moreover, Russia suffered from problems of leadership and organization that made it less prepared for a long war than the other belligerents.

In August 1915, Tsar Nicholas II (1868–1918) assumed personal command of the army, but his absence from the capital only accelerated the deterioration in government and deepened the divisions within the ruling clique. With the tsar away, the illiterate but charismatic Siberian "holy man" Grigori Rasputin (ca. 1872–1916) emerged as the key political power within the circle of the German-born Empress Alexandra (1872–1918). He won her confidence because of his alleged ability to control the bleeding of her hemophiliac son, Alexis, the heir to the throne. Led by Rasputin, those around the empress made a shambles of the state administration. Many educated Russians, appalled at what was happening, assumed—incorrectly—that pro-German elements at court were responsible for the eclipse of the tsar and the increasing governmental chaos. Asked one Duma deputy of the government's performance, "Is this stupidity, or is it treason?"

Finally, late in December 1916, Rasputin was assassinated by aristocrats seeking to save the autocracy from these apparently pro-German influences. This act indicated how desperate the situation had become, but eliminating Rasputin made little difference.

By the end of 1916, the difficulties of war had combined with the strains of rapid wartime industrialization to produce a revolutionary situation in Russia. The country's urban population had mushroomed, and now, partly because of transport problems, the cities faced severe food shortages. Strikes and demonstrations spread from Petrograd (the former St. Petersburg—

a name abandoned as too German at the start of the war) to other cities during the first two months of 1917. In March renewed demonstrations in Petrograd, spearheaded by women protesting the lack of bread and coal, led to revolution.

THE MARCH REVOLUTION AND THE FATE OF THE PROVISIONAL GOVERNMENT

At first, the agitation that began in Petrograd on March 8, 1917, appeared to be just another bread riot. Even when it turned into a wave of strikes, the revolutionary parties (see page 763) expected it to be crushed by government troops. But when they were called out to help the police break up the demonstrations, the soldiers generally avoided firing at the strikers. Within days, they were sharing weapons and ammunition with the workers; the government's troops were joining what was now becoming a revolution.

Late in the afternoon of March 12, leaders of the strike committees, delegates elected by factory workers, and representatives of the socialist parties formed a *soviet*, or council, following the example of the revolution of 1905, when such soviets had first appeared. Regiments of the Petrograd garrison also began electing representatives, soon to be admitted to the **Petrograd Soviet,** which officially became the Council of Workers' and Soldiers' Deputies. This soviet was now the ruling power in the Russian capital. It had been elected and was genuinely representative—though of a limited constituency of workers and soldiers. Following the lead of Petrograd, Russians elsewhere promptly began forming soviets, so that over 350 local units were represented when the first All-Russian Council of Soviets met in Petrograd in April. The overwhelming majority of their representatives were Mensheviks and Socialist Revolutionaries; about one-sixth were Bolsheviks.

On March 14 a committee of the Duma, recognizing that the tsar's authority had been lost for good, persuaded Nicholas to abdicate, then formed a new **provisional government.** This government was to be strictly temporary, paving the way for an elected constituent assembly, which would write a constitution and establish fully legitimate governmental institutions.

Considering the strains that had produced the revolution of 1905 after the Russo-Japanese War, it was hardly surprising that the autocratic system would shatter now, in light of this far more trying war and the resulting governmental disarray. Russia had apparently

experienced, at last, the bourgeois political revolution necessary to develop a Western-style parliamentary democracy. Even from an orthodox Marxist perspective, the immediate priority was to help consolidate the new democratic order, which would then provide the framework for the longer-term pursuit of socialism.

Although the fall of the tsarist government produced widespread relief, Russia's new leaders faced difficult questions about priorities. Should they focus their efforts on revitalizing the Russian war effort? Or, given the widespread war-weariness in the country, should they focus on domestic political reform? For now, the Petrograd Soviet was prepared to give the provisional government a chance to govern. But the soviet was a potential rival for power if the new government failed to address Russia's immediate problems.

The provisional government took important steps toward democracy, establishing universal suffrage, civil liberties, autonomy for ethnic minorities, and labor legislation, including provision for an eight-hour workday. But the government failed in two key areas, fostering discontents that the Bolsheviks soon exploited. First, it persisted in fighting the war. Second, it dragged its feet on agrarian reform.

The provisional government's determination to renew the war effort stemmed from concern about Russia's obligations to its allies, its national honor and position among the great powers. The long-standing goal of Russian diplomacy—an outlet to the Mediterranean Sea through the Dardanelles—seemed within reach if Russia could continue the war and contribute to an Entente victory. The educated, well-to-do Russians who led the new government expected that ordinary citizens, now free, would fight with renewed enthusiasm, like the armies that had grown from the French Revolution over a century before. These leaders failed to grasp how desperate the situation of ordinary people had become.

Although the March revolution began in the cities, the peasantry soon moved into action as well, seizing land, sometimes burning the houses of their landlords. By midsummer, a full-scale peasant war seemed to be developing in the countryside, and calls for agrarian reform became increasingly urgent. Partly from expediency, partly from genuine concern for social justice, the provisional government promised a major redistribution of land. But it insisted that the reform be carried out legally—not by the present provisional government, but by a duly elected constituent assembly.

Calling elections would thus seem to have been the first priority. The new political leaders kept putting it off, however, waiting for the situation to cool off. But playing for time was a luxury they could ill afford. As unrest grew in the countryside, the authority of the provisional government diminished and the soviets gained in stature. But what role were the soviets to play?

Petrograd Soviet   The *soviet* (council) of leaders of strike committees and army regiments elected in March 1917, when Petrograd's workers protested in response to severe wartime food and coal shortages.

provisional government   The body that ruled Russia from March to November 1917, in the wake of the revolution that overthrew the tsarist regime.

Lenin as Leader
Although he was in exile during much of 1917, Lenin's leadership was crucial to the Bolshevik success in Russia. He is shown here addressing a May Day rally in Red Square, Moscow, on May 1, 1919.
(ITAR-TASS/Sovfoto)

THE BOLSHEVIKS COME TO POWER

In the immediate aftermath of the March revolution, the Bolsheviks had not seemed to differ substantially from their rivals within the socialist movement, at least on matters of immediate concern—the war, land reform, and the character of the revolution itself. But the situation began to change in April when Lenin, assisted by the German military, returned from exile in Switzerland. The Germans assumed—correctly, it turned out—that the Bolsheviks would help undermine the Russian war effort. Largely through the force of Lenin's leadership, the Bolsheviks soon took the initiative within the still-developing revolution in Russia.

Early Years Under Lenin Born Vladimir Ilich Ulianov, **Vladimir Lenin** (1870–1924) came from a comfortable upper-middle-class family. He was university-educated and trained as a lawyer. But after an older brother was executed in 1887 for participating in a plot against the tsar's life, Lenin followed him into revolutionary activity. Arrested for the first time in 1895, he

Vladimir Lenin Russian revolutionary and leader of the Bolsheviks since 1903, he masterminded the November 1917 revolution that overthrew the provisional government and led to a communist regime in Russia.

was confined to Siberia until 1900. He then lived in exile abroad for almost the entire period before his return to Russia in 1917.

The Bolshevik Party was identified with Lenin from its beginning in 1903, when it emerged from the schism in Russian Marxist socialism. Because of his emphases, Bolshevism came to mean discipline, organization, and a special leadership role for a revolutionary vanguard. Lenin proved effective because he was a stern and somewhat forbidding figure, disciplined, fiercely intelligent, sometimes ruthless. As a Bolshevik colleague put it, Lenin was "the one indisputable leader . . . a man of iron will, inexhaustible energy, combining a fanatical faith in the movement, in the cause, with an equal faith in himself."[4]

Still, Lenin's reading of the situation when he returned to Petrograd in April astonished even many Bolsheviks. He argued that the revolution was about to pass from the present bourgeois-democratic stage to a socialist phase, involving proletarian dictatorship in the form of government by the soviets. So the Bolsheviks should begin actively opposing the provisional government, especially by denouncing the war as fundamentally imperialist and by demanding the distribution of land from the large estates to the peasants. This latter measure had long been identified with the Socialist Revolutionaries; most Bolsheviks had envisioned collectivization and nationalization instead.

As Lenin saw it, the strains of war had made all of Europe ripe for revolution. A revolution in Russia would provide the spark to ignite a wider proletarian revolution, especially in Germany. He did not envision backward Russia seeking to create socialism on its own. Although some remained skeptical of Lenin's strategy, he promptly won over most of his fellow Bolsheviks. And thus the Bolsheviks began actively seeking wider support by promising peace, land, and bread.

The Bolshevik Revolution   In April 1917 moderate socialists still had majority support in the soviets, so the Bolsheviks sought to build support gradually, postponing any decisive test of strength. But events escaped the control of the Bolshevik leadership in mid-July when impatient workers, largely Bolshevik in sympathy, took to the streets of Petrograd on their own. The Petrograd Soviet refused to support the uprising, and the provisional government had no difficulty getting military units to put it down, killing two hundred in the process. Though the uprising had developed spontaneously, Bolshevik leaders felt compelled to offer public support, and this gave the government an excuse to crack down on the Bolshevik leadership. Lenin managed to escape to Finland, but a number of his colleagues were arrested and jailed.

With the Bolsheviks on the defensive, counterrevolutionary elements in the Russian military decided to seize the initiative with a march on Petrograd in September. To resist this attempted coup, the provisional government, now led by the young Socialist Revolutionary Alexander Kerensky (1881–1970), had to rely on whoever could offer help, including the Bolsheviks. And thanks to Bolshevik propaganda, the soldiers under the command of the counterrevolutionaries refused to fight against the upholders of the revolution in Petrograd. Thus the coup was thwarted. Within days, the Bolsheviks won their first clear-cut majority in the Petrograd Soviet, then shortly gained majorities in most of the other soviets as well.

During the fall of 1917, the situation became increasingly volatile, eluding control by anyone. People looted food from shops; peasants seized land, sometimes murdering their landlords. Desertions and the murder of officers increased within the Russian military.

With the Bolsheviks now the dominant power in the soviets, and with the government's control diminishing, Lenin, from his hideout in Finland, urged the Bolshevik central committee to prepare for armed insurrection. Although some found this step too risky, the majority accepted Lenin's argument that the provisional government would continue dragging its feet,

inadvertently giving right-wing officers time for another coup.

Because Lenin remained in hiding, the task of organizing the seizure of power fell to Leon Trotsky (1870–1940), who skillfully modified Lenin's aggressive strategy. Lenin wanted the Bolsheviks to rise in their own name, in opposition to the provisional government, but Trotsky linked the insurrection to the cause of the soviets and played up its defensive character against the ongoing danger of a counterrevolutionary coup. With the political center at an impasse, the only alternative to such a coup seemed to be a Bolshevik initiative to preserve the Petrograd Soviet, by now the sole viable institutional embodiment of the revolution and its promise. Trotsky's interpretation led people who wanted simply to defend the soviet to support the Bolshevik action.

During the night of November 9, armed Bolsheviks and regular army regiments occupied key points in Petrograd, including railroad stations, post offices, telephone exchanges, power stations, and the national bank. Able to muster only token resistance, the provisional government collapsed. Kerensky escaped and mounted a futile effort to rally troops at the front for a counterattack. In contrast to the March revolution, which had taken about a week, the Bolsheviks took over the capital, overthrowing the Kerensky government, literally overnight and almost without bloodshed.

But though the Bolsheviks enjoyed considerable support in the network of soviets, it was not clear that they could extend their control across the whole Russian Empire. Moreover, from their own perspective, the revolution's immediate prospects, and its potential wider impact, were bound up with the course of the war. Would the Bolshevik Revolution in Russia prove the spark for revolution elsewhere in war-weary Europe, as Lenin anticipated?

THE RUSSIAN REVOLUTION AND THE WAR

Having stood for peace throughout the revolution, the Bolsheviks promptly moved to get Russia out of the war, agreeing to an armistice with Germany in December 1917. They hoped that Russia's withdrawal would speed the collapse of the war effort on all sides and that this, in turn, would intensify the movement toward revolution elsewhere in Europe. The Russian Revolution was but a chapter in this larger story. As Lenin noted to Trotsky, "If it were necessary for us to go under to assure the success of the German revolution, we should have to do it. The German revolution is vastly more important than ours." Indeed, said Lenin to the Bolsheviks' party congress of March 1918, "It is an absolute truth that we will go under without the German revolution."[5]

After assuming control in November, the Bolsheviks published the tsarist government's secret agreements specifying how the spoils were to be divided in the event of a Russian victory. They hoped to inflame revolutionary sentiment elsewhere by demonstrating that the war had been, all along, an imperialist offensive on behalf of capitalist interests. This Bolshevik initiative added fuel to the controversy already developing in all the belligerent countries over the war's purpose and significance.

=========== S E C T I O N   S U M M A R Y ===========

- The strains of war led to a revolution that ended the tsarist order in Russia in March 1917.

- Although the soviet, or workers' and soldiers' council, was a major force in Petrograd, the first Russian revolution of 1917 was not intended to produce a socialist system.

- The provisional government proved ineffective because it dragged its feet on land reform and insisted on maintaining the war effort.

- Due partly to the leadership of Lenin and Trotsky, the Bolsheviks were able to seize the initiative and take power from the provisional government in November 1917.

- The Bolsheviks envisioned their takeover as a spark to revolution elsewhere in war-torn Europe.

THE NEW WAR AND THE ALLIED VICTORY, 1917–1918

Why did Germany and its allies end up losing the war even after forcing Russia to make a separate peace by early 1918?

Because the stakes of the war changed during 1917, the eventual outcome included consequences that Europeans could not have foreseen in 1914. German defeat brought revolution against the monarchy and the beginning of a new democracy. Austro-Hungarian defeat brought the collapse of the Habsburg monarchy and thus the opportunity for its national minorities to form nations of their own. As the old European order fell, grandiose new visions competed to shape the postwar world.

THE DEBATE OVER WAR AIMS

The French and British governments publicly welcomed the March revolution in Russia, partly because they expected Russia's military performance to improve under new leadership, but also because the change of regime seemed to have highly favorable psychological implications. With Russia no longer an autocracy, the war could be portrayed—and experienced—as a crusade for democracy. At the same time, the March revolution could only sow confusion among the many Germans who had understood their own war effort as a matter of self-defense against reactionary Russia. But the November revolution required a deeper reconsideration by all the belligerents.

Allied war aims agreements, such as the Treaty of London that brought Italy into the war in 1915, had remained secret until the Bolsheviks published the tsarist documents. Products of old-style diplomacy, those agreements had been made by a restricted foreign policy elite; even members of the elected parliaments generally did not know their contents. The debate over war aims that developed in 1917 thus became a debate over decision making as well. Many assumed that a more democratic approach to foreign policy would minimize the chances of war, since the people would not agree to wars for dynastic or business interests. In addition, there were exhortations for all the parties in the present war to renounce annexations and settle for a white peace. It was time to call the whole thing off and bring the soldiers home.

Seeking to counter such sentiments, especially the Russian contention that the war was not worth continuing, the idealistic U.S. president, Woodrow Wilson (1856–1924), insisted on the great potential significance of an Allied victory. In his State of the Union speech of January 1918, and in several declarations thereafter, Wilson developed the **Fourteen Points** that he proposed should guide the new international order.

Fourteen Points Proposals by U.S. president Woodrow Wilson to guide the new international order that would follow an Allied victory in World War I.

Notable among them were open diplomacy, free trade, reduced armaments, self-determination for nationalities, a league of nations, and a recasting of the colonial system to ensure equal rights for the indigenous populations.

Online Study Center **Improve Your Grade**
Primary Source: A New Diplomacy:
The Fourteen Points

Lenin and Wilson, then, offered radically different interpretations of the war, with radically different implications for present priorities. Yet, compared with the old diplomacy, they had something in common. Together, they seemed to represent a whole new approach to international relations—and the possibility of a more peaceful world. Thus they found an eager audience among the war-weary peoples of Europe.

Despite the strains of the war, Sacred Union in France did not weaken substantially until April 1917, with General Nivelle's disastrous offensive. But then, as near mutiny began to develop within the army, rank-and-file pressures forced socialist leaders to demand clarification, and perhaps revision, of French war aims. Suddenly the French government was under pressure to suggest that the war had idealistic and democratic purposes. Doubts about the government's goals were threatening to turn into active opposition to the war.

The same pressures were at work in Germany. Antiwar sentiment grew steadily within the Social Democratic Party (SPD) until the antiwar faction split off and formed the Independent Socialist Party (USPD) in April 1917. A large-scale debate over war aims, linked to considerations of domestic political reform, developed in the Reichstag by the summer of 1917. On July 19, a solid 60 percent majority passed a new war aims resolution, which affirmed that Germany's purposes were solely defensive, that Germany had no territorial ambitions. Germany, too, seemed open to a white peace.

But just as the dramatic events of 1917 interjected new pressures for moderation and peace, pressures in the opposite direction also mounted as the war dragged on. It seemed to some that this war was only the beginning of a new era of cutthroat international competition; the old rules would no longer apply. War aims grew more grandiose as nations tried to gain the leverage for success in the contentious postwar world.

The shape of the current war convinced top German officials that Germany's geography and dependence on imports made it especially vulnerable in a long war. So Germany had to seize the present opportunity to conquer the means to fight the next war on a more favorable footing. Responding in February 1918 to calls for a white peace, General Ludendorff stressed that "if Germany makes peace without profit, it has lost the war." Germany, insisted Ludendorff, must win the mil-

itary and economic basis for future security—to "enable us to contemplate confidently some future defensive war."[6] Many German officials believed that Germany could achieve parity with Britain, and thus the basis for security and peace, only if it maintained control of the Belgian coast. German expansion into Russian Poland and up the Baltic coast of Lithuania and Latvia seemed essential as well.

When, in response to the Russian request for an armistice, Germany was able to dictate the peace terms, as specified in the **Treaty of Brest-Litovsk** of March 1918, it became clear how radically annexationist Germany's war aims had become. European Russia was to be largely dismembered, leaving Germany in direct or indirect control of 27 percent of Russia's European territory, 40 percent of its population, and 75 percent of its iron and coal. All the Reichstag parties except the Socialists accepted the terms of the treaty, which, in fact, produced a renewed determination to push on to victory.

France, less vulnerable geographically than Germany, tended to be more modest. But news of the terms the Germans had imposed at Brest-Litovsk inflamed the French, reinforcing their determination to fight on to an unqualified victory. Only thus could France secure the advantages necessary to ward off an ongoing German menace.

THE RENEWAL OF THE FRENCH WAR EFFORT

The domestic division in France that followed the failure of Nivelle's offensive reached its peak during the fall of 1917. In November, with pressure for a white peace intensifying and France's ability to continue fighting in doubt, President Raymond Poincaré (1860–1934) called on Georges Clemenceau (1841–1929) to lead a new government. The 76-year-old Clemenceau (klem-ahn-SOH) was known as a "hawk"; his appointment portended a stepped-up prosecution of the war. His message was simple as he appeared before the Chamber of Deputies on November 20, 1917: "If you ask me about my war aims, I reply: my aim is to be victorious." For the remainder of the war, France was under the virtual dictatorship of Clemenceau and his cabinet.

Clemenceau moved decisively on both the domestic and military fronts. By cracking down on the antiwar movement—imprisoning antiwar leaders, suppressing defeatist newspapers—he stiffened morale on the home front. Understanding that lack of coordination between French and British military leaders had hampered the Allied effort on the battlefield, Clemenceau persuaded the British to accept the French general Ferdinand Foch

Treaty of Brest-Litovsk Harsh peace terms that Germany imposed on Russia in March 1918.

(FOHSH) (1851–1929) as the first supreme commander of all Allied forces in the west. In choosing Foch, known for his commitment to aggressive offensives, Clemenceau was pointedly bypassing Pétain, whom he found too passive, even defeatist. After some initial friction, Clemenceau let Foch have his way on the military level, and the two proved an effective leadership combination.

THE GERMAN GAMBLE, 1918

As the military campaigns of 1918 began, Germany seemed in a relatively favorable position: Russia had been knocked out of the war, and American troops were yet to arrive. Moderates in Germany wanted to seize the opportunity to work out a compromise peace while there was still a chance. But military leaders persuaded Kaiser Wilhelm II that Germany could win a definitive victory on the western front if it struck quickly, before U.S. help became significant. Since Germany would be out of reserves by summer, the alternative to decisive victory in the west would be total German defeat.

The German gamble almost succeeded. From March to June 1918, German forces seized the initiative with four months of sustained and effective attacks. By May 30 they had again reached the Marne, where they had been held in 1914. Paris, only 37 miles away, had to be evacuated once more (see **MAP 25.2**). As late as mid-

July, Ludendorff remained confident of victory, but by mid-August it was becoming clear that Germany lacked the manpower to exploit the successes of the offensive.

The German advance had caused mutual suspicion between the French and the British at first, but under Foch's leadership the Western allies eventually managed more effective coordination. By mid-1918 American involvement was also becoming a factor. On June 4, over a year after the U.S. declaration of war, American troops went into action for the first time, bolstering French forces along the Marne. This was a small operation, in which the Americans' performance was amateurish when compared with that of their battle-seasoned allies. But as the Allied counterattack proceeded, 250,000 U.S. troops were arriving per month, considerably boosting Allied morale and battlefield strength.

By June 1918 Europe was experiencing the first outbreak of a virulent new influenza virus, promptly dubbed the "Spanish flu," though it had originated in South Africa. Because of their inferior diets, German soldiers proved far more susceptible to the disease than their adversaries, a fact that significantly affected Germany's combat performance during the crucial summer of 1918.

Germany lost the initiative for good during the second Battle of the Marne, which began on July 15 with yet another German attack. Foch launched a sustained

MAP 25.2 Stalemate and Decision on the Western Front
On the western front, in northern France and Belgium, trench warfare developed and the best-known battles of the war were fought. Notable sites include Verdun, Passchendaele, and the Marne and Somme Rivers.

counterattack on July 18, using tanks to good advantage, and maintained the momentum thereafter. By early August the whole western front began to roll back. With astonishing suddenness, the outcome was no longer in doubt, although most expected the war to drag on into 1919. Few realized how desperate Germany's situation had become.

Meanwhile, Germany's allies began falling one by one. In the Balkans an Allied offensive broke through the German-Bulgarian line in September, prompting the Bulgarians to ask for an armistice. The Turkish military effort collapsed in October. With the defeat of Russia in 1917, German troops joined the Austrians on the Italian front, breaking through the Italian line at Caporetto late in 1917 and almost inflicting a decisive defeat. But after retreating, the Italians managed to regroup and hold—and eventually to drive the Austrians back. The Italian victory at Vittorio Veneto forced Austria's unconditional surrender on November 3, 1918. But by this point the armies of the Habsburg empire were disintegrating along nationality lines. And the impending collapse of this centuries-old empire gave its various national minorities the chance to form states of their own.

MILITARY DEFEAT AND POLITICAL CHANGE IN GERMANY

By late September it was clear to Ludendorff that his armies could not stop the Allied advance. On September 29 he informed the government that to avoid invasion, Germany would have to seek an immediate armistice. Hoping to secure favorable peace terms and to foist responsibility for the defeat onto the parliamentary politicians, Hindenburg and Ludendorff asked that a government based on greater popular support be formed. A leading moderate, Prince Max von Baden (BAH-dyn) (1867–1929), became chancellor, and he promptly replaced Ludendorff with General Wilhelm Groener (GREU-nur) (1867–1939), who seemed more democratic in orientation. By now it was clear that ending the war could not be separated from the push for political change in Germany, especially because it was widely assumed that a more democratic Germany could expect more favorable peace terms.

After securing a written request for an armistice from Hindenburg, Prince Max sent a peace note to President Wilson early in October, asking for an armistice based on Wilson's Fourteen Points. During the month that followed, Prince Max engineered a series of measures, passed by the Reichstag and approved by the emperor, that reformed the constitution, abolishing the three-class voting system in Prussia and making the chancellor responsible to the Reichstag. At last Germany had a constitutional monarchy. Not completely satisfied, President Wilson encouraged speculation that Germany could expect better peace terms if Wilhelm II were to abdicate and Germany became a republic.

But a far more radical outcome seemed possible during late 1918 and early 1919. As negotiations for an armistice proceeded in October, the continuing war effort produced instances of mutiny in the navy and breaches of discipline in the army. By early November workers' and soldiers' councils were being formed all over Germany, just as in Russia the year before. On November 7, antiwar socialists in Munich led an uprising of workers and soldiers that expelled the king of Bavaria and proclaimed a new Bavarian republic. Its provisional government promptly sought its own peace negotiations with the Allies. On November 9, thousands of workers took to the streets of Berlin to demand immediate peace, and the authorities could not muster enough military resources to move against them.

The senior army leadership grew concerned that the collapse of government authority would undermine the ability of officers even to march their troops home. So Hindenburg and Groener persuaded the emperor to abdicate. Having lost the support of the army, Wilhelm II accepted the inevitable and left for exile in the Netherlands.

With the German right, including the military, in disarray, and with the centrist parties discredited by their support for what had become an annexationist war, the initiative passed to the socialists. They, at least, had been in the forefront of the movement for peace. But the socialists had divided in 1917, mostly over the question of response to the war. The mainstream of the SPD, by supporting the war for so long, had irrevocably alienated the party's leftist socialist wing. The most militant of these leftist socialists, led by Karl Liebknecht (1871–1919) and Rosa Luxemburg (1870–1919), envisioned using the workers' and soldiers' councils as the basis for a full-scale revolution, more or less on the Bolshevik model.

The SPD, on the other hand, clung to its reformist heritage and insisted on working within parliamentary institutions. Party leaders argued that a Bolshevik-style revolution was neither appropriate nor necessary under the circumstances. So SPD moderates proclaimed a parliamentary republic on November 9, just hours before the revolutionaries proclaimed a soviet-style republic. The next day the soldiers' and workers' councils in Berlin elected a provisional executive committee, to be led by the moderate socialist Friedrich Ebert (A-bairt) (1871–1925). As the new republic sought to consolidate itself, the radical leftists continued to promote further revolution.

Birth from military defeat was especially disabling for the new republic because the German people were so little prepared for defeat when it came. Vigorous censorship had kept the public in the dark about Germany's real situation, so the request for an armistice early in October came as a shock. At no time during the war had Germany been invaded from the west, and by mid-1918 the German army had seemed on the brink of victory. It appeared inconceivable that Germany had

lost a military decision, plain and simple. Thus the **"stab in the back" myth,** the notion that political intrigue and revolution at home had sabotaged the German military effort, developed to explain what otherwise seemed an inexplicable defeat. This notion would prove a heavy burden for Germany's new democracy to bear.

S E C T I O N   S U M M A R Y

- By 1917, the will to continue the war was flagging on both sides, as some began to question war aims and even to call for a "white peace."

- The idealism of U.S. president Wilson, with his Fourteen Points, suggested to Europeans that the war might indeed be worth fighting to a victorious conclusion.

- The harsh Treaty of Brest-Litovsk that Germany imposed on Russia reflected changes in German war aims.

- The leadership combination of Clemenceau and Foch was crucial to the renewal of the French war effort.

- Germany's gamble on one last massive offensive during the summer of 1918 almost succeeded, but, led by France, the Allies began forcing the Germans back, prompting Germany to ask for an armistice.

- German leaders decided to turn from Wilhelm II's imperial regime toward democracy, partly in an effort to secure more favorable peace terms.

THE OUTCOME AND THE IMPACT

What factors shaped the peace settlement that the victors imposed on Germany and its allies in 1919–1920?

After the armistice officially ended the fighting on November 11, 1918, it was up to the war's four victors—France, Britain, Italy, and the United States—to establish the terms of peace and, it was to be hoped, a new basis for order at the same time. But the peacemakers had to deal with a radically new political and territorial situation. Revolution had undermined, or threatened to undermine, the old political order in much of Europe. And the war had come to involve non-European powers and peoples in unprecedented ways. After all that had happened since August 1914, it was not clear what a restoration of peace and order would require. But it was evident that Europe would no longer dominate world affairs in quite the way it had.

THE COSTS OF WAR

Raw casualty figures do not begin to convey the war's human toll, but they afford some sense of its magnitude. Estimates differ, but it is generally agreed that from 10 million to 13 million military men lost their lives, with another 20 million wounded. In addition, between 7 million and 10 million civilians died as a result of the war and its hardships. In the defeated countries especially, food shortages and malnutrition continued well after the end of the fighting. Thus the Spanish flu that had affected the balance on the battlefield early in the summer of 1918 returned with particularly devastating results during the fall. The influenza pandemic killed perhaps 40 million people worldwide.

Germany suffered the highest number of military casualties, but France suffered the most in proportional terms. Two million Germans were killed, with another 4 million wounded. Military deaths per capita for France were roughly 15 percent higher than for Germany—and twice as severe as for Britain. Of 8 million Frenchmen mobilized, over 5 million were killed or wounded. Roughly 1.5 million French soldiers, or 10 percent of the active male population, were killed—and this in a country already concerned about demographic decline. The other belligerents suffered less, but still in great numbers. Among the military personnel killed were 2 million Russians, 500,000 Italians, and 114,000 Americans.

Economic costs were heavy as well. In addition to the privations suffered during the years of war, Euro-

"stab in the back" myth The notion, widely held among Germans after their unexpected loss in World War I, that political intrigue and revolution at home had sabotaged the German military effort.

peans found themselves reeling from inflation and saddled with debt, especially to the United States, once the war was over. Although the immediate transition to a peacetime economy did not prove as difficult as many had feared, the war and its aftermath produced an economic disequilibrium that lingered, helping to produce a worldwide depression by the 1930s.

THE SEARCH FOR PEACE IN A REVOLUTIONARY ERA

The war had begun because of an unmanageable nationality problem in Austria-Hungary, and it led not simply to military defeat for Austria-Hungary but to the breakup of the Habsburg system (see **MAP 25.3**). In east-central Europe, the end of the war brought bright hopes for self-determination to peoples like the Czechs, Slovaks, Poles, Serbs, and Croats. Even before the peacemakers opened deliberations in January 1919, some of these ethnic groups had begun creating a new order on their own. For example, a popular movement of Czechs and Slovaks established a Czechoslovak republic on October 29, 1918, and a new Yugoslavia and an independent Hungary similarly emerged from indigenous movements. Czechoslovakia and Yugoslavia were made up of different ethnic groups that found cooperation advantageous now but that might well disagree in the future. Moreover, many of these countries lacked traditions of self-government, and they had reason to feud among themselves. With the Habsburg system no longer imposing one form of stability, a power vacuum seemed likely in this potentially volatile part of Europe.

The Bolshevik Revolution in Russia immeasurably complicated the situation. The unsettled conditions in Germany and the former Habsburg territories seemed to invite the spread of revolution—precisely according to Lenin's script. Shortly after taking power, Lenin and his party had begun calling themselves "communists," partly to jettison the provincial Russian term *bolshevik*, but especially to underline their departure from the old reformist socialism of the Second International. In adopting "communism," they wanted to make it clear that they stood for a revolutionary alternative, and they actively sought to inspire revolution elsewhere.

Outside Russia, the greatest communist success was in Hungary, where a communist regime under Béla Kun (1885–1937) governed Budapest and other parts of the country from March to August 1919, when it was put down by Allied-sponsored forces. At about the same time, communist republics lasted for months in the Slovak part of Czechoslovakia and in the important German state of Bavaria. Even in Italy, which had shared in the victory, socialists infatuated with the Bolshevik example claimed that the substantial labor unrest during 1919 and 1920 was the beginning of full-scale revolution.

Meanwhile, fears that the Russian Revolution might spread had fueled foreign intervention in Russia itself beginning in June 1918, when 24,000 French and British troops landed at Murmansk, in northern Russia. As long as the war with Germany lasted, military concerns helped justify this course, but after the armistice of November 1918, the intervention became overtly anticommunist, intended to help topple the new regime and undercut its efforts to export revolution.

Further complicating the postwar situation were the defeat and dissolution of the Turkish Ottoman Empire, which had controlled much of the Middle East in 1914. The Arab revolt against the Turks that developed in the Arabian peninsula in 1916 did not achieve its major military aims, though it caused some disruption to the Turkish war effort. Its success was due partly to the collaboration of a young British officer, T. E. Lawrence (1888–1935), who proved an effective military leader and an impassioned advocate of the Arab cause. The support that Britain had offered the Arabs suggested that independence, perhaps even a single Arab kingdom, might follow from a defeat of the Ottoman Empire.

But British policy toward the Arabs was uncertain and contradictory. Concerned about the Suez Canal, the British government sought to tighten its control in Egypt by declaring it a protectorate in 1914, triggering increased anti-British sentiment in the region. The secret Sykes-Picot Agreement of May 1916, named for the British and French diplomats who negotiated it, projected a division of the Ottoman territories of the Middle East into colonial spheres of influence. France would control Syria and Lebanon, while Britain would rule Palestine and Mesopotamia, or present-day Iraq.

Potentially complicating the situation in the region was Zionism, the movement to establish a Jewish state in Palestine. Led by Chaim Weizmann (1874–1952), a remarkable Russian-born British chemist, the Zionists reached an important milestone when British foreign secretary Arthur Balfour (1848–1930) cautiously announced, in the Balfour Declaration of November 1917, that the British government "looked with favor" on the prospect of a "Jewish home" in Palestine. At this point Jews were only 10 percent of the population in Palestine. British leaders sympathetic to Zionism saw no conflict in simultaneously embracing the cause of the Arabs against the Ottoman Turks. Indeed, Arabs and Jews, each seeking self-determination, could be expected to collaborate.

In the heat of war, the British established their policy for the former Ottoman territories without careful study. Thus they made promises and agreements that were not entirely compatible. After the war, the victors' efforts to install a new order in the Middle East would create fresh conflicts.

MAP 25.3 The Impact of the War: The Territorial Settlement in Europe and the Middle East

The defeat of Russia, Austria-Hungary, Germany, and Ottoman Turkey opened the way to major changes in the map of east-central Europe and the Middle East. A number of new nations emerged in east-central Europe, while in the Arab world the end of Ottoman rule meant not independence but new roles for European powers.

Legend:
- Boundaries of German, Russian, and Austro-Hungarian empires in 1914
- Areas lost by Austro-Hungarian Empire
- Areas lost by Russian Empire
- Areas lost by German Empire
- Areas lost by Bulgaria
- Areas lost by Ottoman Empire
- Demilitarized Zones
- Boundaries of 1926
- Areas controlled under mandates from the League of Nations, 1920

An Arab in Paris
Prince Faisal (*foreground*) attended the Paris Peace Conference, where he lobbied for the creation of an independent Arab kingdom from part of the former Ottoman Turkish holdings in the Middle East. Among his supporters was the British officer T. E. Lawrence (*middle row, second from the right*), on his way to legend as "Lawrence of Arabia." *(Courtesy of the Trustees of the Imperial War Museum)*

THE PEACE SETTLEMENT

The peace conference took place in Paris, beginning in January 1919. Its labors led to separate treaties with each of the five defeated states. The first and most significant was the **Treaty of Versailles** with Germany, signed in the Hall of Mirrors of the Versailles Palace on June 28, 1919. Treaties were also worked out, in turn, with Austria, Bulgaria, Hungary, and finally Turkey, in August 1920.

The Participants   This was to be a dictated, not a negotiated, peace. Germany and its allies were excluded, as was revolutionary Russia. The passions unleashed by the long war had dissolved the possibility of a more conciliatory outcome, a genuinely negotiated peace. Having won the war, France, Britain, the United States, and Italy were to call the shots on their own. However, spokesmen for many groups—from Slovaks and Croats to Arabs, Jews, and pan-Africanists—were in Paris as well, seeking a hearing for their respective causes. Both the Arab Prince Faisal (1885–1933), who would later become king of Iraq, and Colonel T. E. Lawrence were on hand to plead for an independent Arab kingdom. (See the box "The Global Record: Prince Faisal at the

Peace Conference.") The African American leader W. E. B. Du Bois (doo BOYS) (1868–1963), who took his Ph.D. at Harvard in 1895, led a major pan-African congress in Paris concurrently with the peace conference.

The fundamental challenge for the peacemakers was to reconcile the conflicting visions of the postwar world that had emerged by the end of the war. U.S. president Wilson represented the promise of a new order that could give this terrible war a lasting meaning. As he toured parts of Europe on his way to the peace conference, Wilson was greeted as a hero. Clemenceau, in contrast, was a hard-liner concerned with French security and dismissive of Wilsonian ideals. Since becoming prime minister in 1917, he had stressed that only permanent French military superiority over Germany, and not some utopian league of nations, could guarantee a lasting peace. The negotiations at Paris centered on this fundamental difference between Wilson and Clemenceau. Although Britain's Lloyd George took a hard line on certain issues, he also sought to mediate, helping engineer the somewhat awkward compromise that resulted. When, after the peace conference, he encountered criticism for the outcome, Lloyd George replied, "I think I did as well as might be expected, seated as I was between Jesus Christ and Napoleon Bonaparte."[7]

Treaty of Versailles   Peace treaty that the victors in World War I imposed on a defeated Germany in 1919.

Shifting Powers In Article 231 of the final treaty, the peacemakers sought to establish a moral basis for their treatment of Germany by assigning responsibility for the war to Germany and its allies. The Germans were required to pay reparations to reimburse the victors for the costs of the war, although the actual amount was not established until 1921. The determination to make the loser pay was one of the factors militating against a compromise peace on both sides by 1917.

Germany was also forced to dismantle much of its military apparatus. The army was to be limited to a hundred thousand men, all volunteers. The treaty severely restricted the size of the German navy as well, and Germany was forbidden to manufacture or possess military aircraft, submarines, tanks, heavy artillery, or poison gas.

France took back Alsace and Lorraine, the provinces it had lost to Germany in 1871 (see Map 25.3). But for France, the crucial security provision of the peace settlement was the treatment of the adjacent Rhineland section of Germany itself. For fifteen years Allied troops were to occupy the west bank of the Rhine River in Germany—the usual military occupation of a defeated adversary. But this would only be temporary. The long-term advantage for France was to be the permanent demilitarization of all German territory west of the Rhine and a strip of 50 kilometers along its east bank. Germany was to maintain no troops on this part of its own soil; in the event of hostilities French forces would be able to march into Germany unopposed.

French interests also helped shape the settlement in east-central Europe. Wilsonian principles called for self-determination, but in this area of great ethnic complexity, ethnic differences were not readily sorted out geographically. This made it easier for the French to bring their own strategic concerns to bear on the situation. To ensure that Germany would again face potential enemies from both the east and the west, French leaders envisioned building a network of allies in east-central Europe. The first was the new Poland, created from Polish territories formerly in the German, Russian, and Austro-Hungarian Empires. That network might come to include Czechoslovakia, Yugoslavia, and Romania as well. These states would be weak enough to remain under French influence but, taken together, strong enough to replace Russia as a significant force against Germany.

Partly as a result of French priorities, Poland, Czechoslovakia, Yugoslavia, and Romania ended up as large as possible, either by combining ethnic groups or by incorporating minorities that, on ethnic grounds, belonged with neighboring states. The new Czechoslovakia included not only Czechs and Slovaks but also numerous Germans and Magyars. Indeed, Germans, mostly from the old Bohemia, made up 22 percent of the population of Czechoslovakia. By contrast, Austria, Hungary, and Bulgaria, as defeated powers, found themselves diminished (see **MAP 25.4**). What remained of Austria, the German part of the old Habsburg empire, was prohibited from choosing to join Germany, an obvious violation of the Wilsonian principle of self-determination.

Desires to contain revolutionary Russia were also at work in the settlement in east-central Europe. A band of states in east-central Europe, led by France, could serve not only as a check to Germany but also as a shield against the Russian threat. Romania's aggrandizement came partly at the expense of the Russian Empire, as did the creation of the new Poland. Finland, Latvia, Estonia, and Lithuania, all part of the Russian Empire for over a century, became independent states (see Map 25.3).

PRINCE FAISAL AT THE PEACE CONFERENCE

With the war nearing its end in October 1918, British authorities, in line with provisions of the Sykes-Picot Agreement, permitted Faisal ibn-Husayn (1885–1933) to set up a provisional Arab state, with its capital at Damascus. As head of a delegation from this area to the Paris Peace Conference, Faisal claimed to speak for all Arab Asia, but some on the Arabian peninsula challenged his claim. In the memorandum of January 1919 that follows, he outlined the Arab position, mixing pride and assertiveness with a recognition that the Arabs would continue to need the support and help of Western powers. After the peace was concluded, Faisal found himself caught up in British and French rivalries as he was installed as king—first of Syria, then of Iraq (Mesopotamia). But his efforts were central to the eventual achievement of Arab independence in the Middle East.

We believe that our ideal of Arab unity in Asia is justified beyond need of argument. If argument is required, we would point to the general principles accepted by the Allies when the United States joined them, to our splendid past, to the tenacity with which our race has for 600 years resisted Turkish attempts to absorb us, and, in a lesser degree, to what we tried our best to do in this war as one of the Allies. . . .

The various provinces of Arab Asia—Syria, Irak [sic], Jezireh, Hedjaz, Nejd, Yemen—are very different economically and socially, and it is impossible to constrain them into one frame of government.

We believe that Syria, an agricultural and industrial area thickly peopled with sedentary classes, is sufficiently advanced politically to manage her own internal affairs. We feel also that foreign technical advice and help will be a most valuable factor in our national growth. We are willing to pay for this help in cash; we cannot sacrifice for it any part of the freedom we have just won for ourselves by force of arms.

. . . The world wishes to exploit Mesopotamia rapidly, and we therefore believe that the system of government there will have to be buttressed by the men and material resources of a great foreign Power. We ask, however, that the Government be Arab, in principle and spirit, the selective rather than the elective principle being necessarily followed in the neglected districts, until time makes the broader basis possible. . . .

In Palestine the enormous majority of the people are Arabs. The Jews are very close to the Arabs in blood, and there is no conflict of character between the two races. In principles we are absolutely at one. Nevertheless, the Arabs cannot risk assuming the responsibility of holding level the scales in the clash of races and religions that have, in this one province, so often involved the world in difficulties. They would wish for the effective super-position of a great trustee, so long as a representative local administration commended itself by actively promoting the material prosperity of the country. . . .

In our opinion, if our independence be conceded and our local competence established, the natural influences of race, language, and interest will soon draw us together into one people; but for this the Great Powers will have to ensure us open internal frontiers, common railways and telegraphs, and uniform systems of education. To achieve this they must lay aside the thought of individual profits, and of their old jealousies. In a word, we ask you not to force your whole civilisation upon us, but to help us to pick out what serves us from your experience. In return we can offer you little but gratitude.

QUESTIONS

1. How does Prince Faisal assess the prospects for unity among the diverse Arab peoples of Asia?

2. What role does Prince Faisal envision for the Western powers in Arab Asia?

Source: J. C. Hurewitz, *Diplomacy in the Near and Middle East: A Documentary Record: 1914–1956,* vol. 2 (Princeton, N.J.: D. Van Nostrand, 1956), pp. 38–39. Reprinted by Archive Editions, UK, 1987.

The territorial settlement cost Germany almost 15 percent of its prewar territory, but German bitterness over the peace terms stemmed above all from a sense of betrayal. In requesting an armistice, German authorities had appealed to Wilson, who had not emphasized war guilt and reparations. He seemed to be saying that the whole prewar international system, not one side or the other, had been responsible for the current conflict. Yet the peacemakers now placed the primary blame on Germany, so for Germans the terms of the peace greatly intensified the sting of defeat.

A New International Order? Wilson had been forced to compromise with French interests in dealing with east-central Europe, but he achieved a potentially significant success in exchange—the establishment of a **League of Nations,** embodying the widespread hope

League of Nations An international organization established at the end of World War I without the membership of the United States. Though its covenant called for the peaceful settlement of disputes and for sanctions against a member that went to war in violation of League provisions, it failed to prevent the escalating violence that culminated in World War II.

MAP 25.4 Ethnicity in East-Central Europe, 1919
Ethnic diversity made it hard to create homogeneous nation-states in east-central Europe. The new states that emerged after World War I mixed ethnic groups, and ethnic tensions would contribute to future problems.

Albanian	Macedonian
Bosnian	Polish
Bulgarian	Romanian
Croatian	Russian, Belorussian, and Ukrainian
Czech	Serbian
German	Slovakian
Hungarian	Slovenian

0 50 100 Km.

0 50 100 Mi.

Online Study Center **Improve Your Grade**
Interactive Map: Ethnicity in East-Central Europe, 1919

for a new international order. (See the box "The Written Record: The Covenant of the League of Nations.") According to the League covenant worked out by April, disputes among member states were to be settled no longer by war but by mechanisms established by the new assembly. Other members were to participate in sanctions, from economic blockade to military action, against a member that went to war in violation of League provisions.

How could Wilsonian hopes for a new international order be squared with the imperialist system, which seemed utterly at odds with the ideal of self-determination? Elites among the colonial peoples had tended to support the war efforts of their imperial rulers, but often in the hope of winning greater autonomy or even independence. The Indian leader Mohandas Gandhi (GAHN-dee) (1869–1948), who had been educated in the West and admitted to the English bar in 1889, even helped recruit Indians to fight on the British side. But his aim was to speed Indian independence, and he led demonstrations that embarrassed the British during the war. (See the box "The Global Record: Gandhi Advocates Nonviolence" on page 842 in Chapter 27.)

Colonial peoples participated directly in the war on both sides. In sub-Saharan Africa, for example, German-led Africans fought against Africans under British or French command. France brought colonial subjects from West and North Africa into front-line service during the war. But one result was an expansion of political consciousness that led more of those subject to European imperialism to question the whole system.

The hope that support for the Western powers in wartime would eventually be rewarded led China and Siam (now Thailand) to associate with the Allied side in 1917, in an effort to enhance their international stature. Each was seeking to restore full sovereignty in the face of increasing Western influence. China sent 200,000 people to work in France to help ease France's wartime labor shortage.

At the peace conference, spokesmen for the non-Western world tended to be moderate in their demands. And prodded by Wilson, the peacemakers made some concessions. German colonies and Ottoman territories were not simply taken over by the victors, in the old-fashioned way, but were placed under the authority of the League. The League then assigned them as mandates to one of the victorious powers, which was to report to the League annually on conditions in the area in question. Classes of mandates varied, based on how prepared for sovereignty the area was judged to be. In devising this system, the Western powers formally recognized for the first time that non-Western peoples under Western control had rights of their own and, in principle, were progressing toward independence.

Still, the mandate approach to the colonial question was a halting departure at best. Although Britain granted considerable sovereignty to Iraq in 1932, the victorious powers generally operated as before, assimilating the new territories into their existing systems of colonial possessions. After the hopes for independence raised in the Arab world during the war, this outcome produced a sense of betrayal among Arab leaders.

The Chinese similarly felt betrayed. Despite China's contributions to the Allied war effort, the victors acquiesced in special rights for Japan in China, causing a renewed sense of humiliation among Chinese elites and provoking popular demonstrations and a boycott of

THE WRITTEN RECORD

THE COVENANT OF THE LEAGUE OF NATIONS

In its very first part, before treating defeated Germany, the Treaty of Versailles established a new "League of Nations," outlining its aims and procedures as well as the obligations of its members. With this bold experiment, the war's victors sought to organize international relations on a radically new basis. The League's overriding aim was to settle international disputes without resort to war. But the League was also to fulfill an international responsibility, newly recognized here, for the gradual departure from colonialism. Although it instilled great hope at first, the League's inability to prevent aggression and war became clear during the 1930s. Even so, its failure prompted a still more determined effort to order international affairs with the creation of the United Nations in the aftermath of World War II.

The High Contracting Parties,

In order to promote international co-operation and to achieve international peace and security by the acceptance of obligations not to resort to war, by the prescription of open, just and honourable relations between nations, by the firm establishment of the understandings of international law as the actual rule of conduct among Governments, and by the maintenance of justice and a scrupulous respect for all treaty obligations in the dealings of organised peoples with one another,

Agree to this Covenant of the League of Nations. . . .

Article 12.

The Members of the League agree that if there should arise between them any dispute likely to lead to a rupture, they will submit the matter either to arbitration or to inquiry by the Council, and they agree in no case to resort to war until three months after the award by the arbitrators or the report by the Council. . . .

Article 16.

Should any Member of the League resort to war in disregard of its covenants under Articles 12, 13, or 15, it shall *ipso facto* be deemed to have committed an act of war against all other Members of the League, which hereby undertake immediately to subject it to the severance of all trade or financial relations, the prohibition of all intercourse between their nations and the nationals of the covenant-breaking State, and the prevention of all financial, commercial, or personal intercourse between the nationals of the covenant-breaking State and the nationals of any other State, whether a Member of the League or not. . . .

Article 22.

To those colonies and territories which as a consequence of the late war have ceased to be under the sovereignty of the States which formerly governed them and which are inhabited by peoples not yet able to stand by themselves under the strenuous conditions of the modern world, there should be applied the principle that the well-being and development of such peoples form a sacred trust of civilisation and that securities for the performance of this trust should be embodied in this Covenant.

The best method of giving practical effect to this principle is that the tutelage of such peoples should be entrusted to advanced nations who by reason of their resources, their experience or their geographical position can best undertake this responsibility, and who are willing to accept it, and that this tutelage should be exercised by them as Mandatories on behalf of the League.

QUESTIONS

1. How did the League of Nations expect to minimize the resort to war?

2. On what grounds did the League assume responsibility for overseeing the development of the former colonies of the defeated German and Ottoman Empires?

Source: The Treaties of Peace, 1919–1923, vol. 1 (New York: The Carnegie Endowment for International Peace, 1924), pp. 10, 14, 17, 19.

Japanese goods. Although Western leaders were allowing a non-Western power, Japan, access to the imperial club, they were hardly departing from imperialism. For Chinese, Arabs, and others, the West appeared hypocritical. Those whose political consciousness had been raised by the war came to believe not only that colonialism should end, but that the colonial peoples would themselves have to take the lead in ending it.

The incongruities of the postwar settlement prompted Marshal Foch to proclaim, "This is not peace. It is an armistice for twenty years."[8] Would the principal victors have the resolve, and the capacity, to preserve the new order they had established at Paris? Debate over the American role promptly developed in the United States as President Wilson sought Senate ratification of the Versailles treaty, which entailed U.S.

membership in the League of Nations as well as commitments to France and Britain. Wilson's opponents worried that League membership would compromise U.S. sovereignty, but other nations managed to overcome such concerns and join the new organization. American reluctance stemmed especially from the isolationist backlash that was developing against the U.S. intervention in the European war. Late in 1919, at the height of the debate, Wilson suffered a disabling stroke. The Senate then refused to ratify the peace treaty, thereby keeping the United States out of the League of Nations.

American disengagement stemmed partly from doubts about the wisdom of the peace settlement that quickly developed in both Britain and the United States. During the peace conference, a member of the British delegation, the economist John Maynard Keynes (KAINZ) (1883–1946), resigned to write *The Economic Consequences of the Peace* (1920), which helped undermine confidence in the whole settlement. Keynes charged that the shortsighted, vindictive policy of the French, by crippling Germany with a punishing reparations burden, threatened the European economy and thus the long-term peace of Europe. For some, then, the challenge was not to enforce the Versailles treaty but to revise it. This lack of consensus about the legitimacy of the peace made it especially hard to anticipate the longer-term consequences of the war.

THE CULTURAL IMPACT OF THE GREAT WAR

Coming after a century of relative peace and apparent progress, this long and brutal war ended up shaking Europe's social and cultural foundations. The number of casualties, the advent of terrifying new weapons, and the destruction of famous old monuments—all gave the war an apocalyptic aura that heightened its psychological impact.

The war touched virtually everyone, but it marked for life those who had experienced the nightmare of the trenches. At first, traditional notions of glory, heroism, and patriotic duty combined with images of fellowship and regeneration to enable the soldiers to make a certain sense of their wartime experience. But as the war dragged on, such sentiments gradually eroded, giving way, in many cases, to resignation and cynicism. (See the feature "The Visual Record: Max Beckmann's *The Night*.") But others, such as the young German soldier and writer Ernst Jünger (1895–1998), lauded the war as the catalyst for a welcome new era of steel, hardness, discipline, organization, and machine precision.

After the war, many of those who had fought it felt a sense of ironic betrayal. Their prewar upbringing, the values and assumptions they had inherited, had not equipped them to make sense of what they had lived through. But the effort to find meaning involved not only the survivors but also the families and friends of those killed or maimed. There was much effort to recast traditional, often-religious categories and images for the near-universal experience of bereavement, which transcended national and class divisions.

Beginning in the late 1920s a wave of writings about the war appeared. Many were memoirs, such as *Goodbye to All That* by the English writer Robert Graves (1895–1985) and *Testament of Youth* by Vera Brittain (1893–1970), who had served as a British army nurse at the front. But easily the most famous retrospective was the novel *All Quiet on the Western Front* (1929) by the German Erich Maria Remarque (1898–1970); it sold 2.5 million copies in twenty-five languages in its first eighteen months in print. Remarque provided a gripping portrait of the experience of ordinary soldiers on the western front, but his book also reflected the disillusionment that had come to surround the memory of the war by the late 1920s. Not only were many dead or maimed for life, but all the sacrifices seemed to have been largely in vain, a sentiment that fueled determination to avoid another war in the future.

The novel forms of warfare introduced during World War I intensified fears of renewed war. Thanks to modern technology, which had been central to the West's confident belief in progress, Europeans had now experienced machine-gun fire, poison gas attacks, and the terror-bombing of civilians from airplanes. A generation later, to be sure, the advent of the nuclear age occasioned a measure of terror hardly imaginable earlier, but the experience of World War I was the turning point, the end of an earlier innocence.

What followed from the war, most fundamentally, was a new sense that Western civilization was neither as secure nor as superior as it had seemed. The celebrated French poet Paul Valéry (1871–1945), speaking at Oxford shortly after the war, observed that "we modern civilizations have learned to recognize that we are mortal like the others. We had heard . . . of whole worlds vanished, of empires foundered. . . . Elam, Nineveh, Babylon were vague and splendid names; the total ruin of these worlds, for us, meant as little as did their existence. But France, England, Russia . . . these names, too, are splendid. . . . And now we see that the abyss of history is deep enough to bury all the world. We feel that a civilization is as fragile as a life."[9] Valéry went on to warn that the coming transition to peace would be even more difficult and disorienting than the war itself. So traumatic might be the convulsion that Europe might lose its leadership and be shown up for what it was in fact—a pathetically small corner of the world, a mere cape on the Asiatic landmass. Astounding words for a European, yet even Valéry, for all his foresight, could not anticipate what Europe would experience in the decades to follow.

Severini: Armoured Train
In this painting from 1915, the Italian futurist Gino Severini (1883–1966) conveys the hard, steel-like imagery and the sense of disciplined modern efficiency that became associated with war, making it attractive to some young Europeans.
(Richard S. Zeisler Collection, New York/ The Bridgeman Art Library. © 2001 Artists Rights Society [ARS], New York/ADAGP, Paris)

─── S E C T I O N   S U M M A R Y ───

- Although Germany suffered the highest number of wartime casualties, France's losses in proportional terms were 15 percent higher—and twice as high as Britain's.

- The breakup of the Habsburg and Ottoman Empires, together with the defeat of Russia and Germany, raised hopes for self-determination among formerly subject peoples but also complicated the challenges of peacemaking.

- The peace settlement represented an awkward compromise between Wilson's idealistic principles and Clemenceau's hardheaded concern for long-term French interests.

- The harsh peace terms imposed on Germany not only inflamed German opinion but also seemed counterproductive to many elsewhere, thereby compromising the moral force of the peace settlement.

- Britain and France divided the Arab parts of the former Ottoman Empire according to the secret Sykes-Picot Agreement of 1916.

Max Beckmann's *The Night*

"One of the most disagreeable images which the art of our century has to show," wrote the noted art historian and critic John Russell in 1981 of the painting we see here.* Max Beckmann (1884–1950) painted *The Night* during 1918–1919, as Germany was suffering military defeat, experiencing political turmoil, and encountering extreme economic hardship. And surely this unprecedented and disturbing image reflects that difficult combination of circumstances. But what are the sources of the imagery we see here, and what does this painting tell us about the war's cultural impact?

The young Beckmann established himself as an innovative painter before the war, working within the idiom of German expressionism. Emerging as a formal movement in 1905, expressionism became the major German contribution to the avant-garde in the visual arts. Expressionists like Ernst Ludwig Kirchner, Ernst Haeckel, and Franz Marc used unnatural colors and deformed natural appearance to convey emotion and to provoke a psychological response in the viewer. In much of their work they sought an appropriately innovative response to the uncanniness, even the menace, of modern life—and especially the modern urban world, at once enticing and threatening.

Like so many of the educated youth of his generation, Beckmann initially welcomed the war as a source of renewal. Indeed he was especially fascinated with its potentially cataclysmic effects, in light of his quasi-Nietzschean faith in the scope for a more intense form of life through struggle and suffering. After volunteering for service in the fall of 1914, he was assigned to the German medical corps. Working in a field hospital on the western front in 1915, Beckmann still found something grandly apocalyptic in the death, the suffering, the wounded bodies. Indeed, he welcomed the chance to observe all that up close; it inspired notes and sketches to be used as material for his art. At the same time, he began to envision conveying his ideas through images recalling the scourging of Christ.

But Beckmann's beliefs were being shaken, and his drawings during 1915 depicted suffering, pain, and death with ever greater intensity. That summer he suffered a nervous breakdown and was sent back to Germany to recuperate. In 1917 he was finally discharged from the army as unfit for further service.

Beckmann turned back to painting in an effort to convey his increasingly disillusioning experience of the war. Like many expressionist artists, he had been influenced by late Gothic German painting, and *The Night* uses certain formal elements from that earlier tradition. Note especially the color—pure but thin, even sour—and the space—shallow and confined, with the figures almost piled atop one another. Beckmann also adapted the religious themes of German Gothic—not, however, as a believer. Rather, he valued their familiarity, as images of suffering, combined with suggestions of cruelty and guilt. Such familiar images seemed to offer the means to create the new, utterly unfamiliar imagery that, Beckmann felt, was necessary to convey what human beings had come to feel as a result of the war and its aftermath.

Here is how Beckmann put it at the end of 1918, precisely as he was working on *The Night:*

> The stronger my determination grows to grasp the unutterable things of this world, the deeper and more powerful the emotion burning inside me about our existence, the tighter I keep my mouth shut and the harder I try to capture the terrible, thrilling monster of life's vitality and to confine it, to beat it down and to strangle it with crystal-clear, razor-sharp lines and planes. . . . We must be a part of all the misery which is coming. We have to surrender our heart and our nerves, we must abandon ourselves to the horrible cries of pain of a poor deluded people.[†]

On the immediate level, *The Night* conveys a scene of violence, torture, and suffering, for three of the figures have apparently broken into a family's home (complete with dog and phonograph) in order to torture, rape, and perhaps kidnap or murder. Yet the complex interplay between the figures suggests that we cannot easily distinguish perpetrators from victims.

*John Russell, *The Meanings of Modern Art* (New York: Harper & Row, 1981), p. 95.

†Max Beckmann, "Creative Credo," in *Art in Theory, 1900–1990: An Anthology of Changing Ideas,* edited by Charles Harrison and Paul Wood (Oxford: Blackwell, 1993), pp. 267–268.

Beckmann: The Night
(Erich Lessing/Art Resource, NY)

The suffering figure on the left seems to be Beckmann himself, in the pose of the suffering Christ, yet his bandaged torturer may suggest the wounded to whom Beckmann had earlier ministered on the battlefield. In performing his medical duties, he had become haunted with the ambiguity between causing and relieving suffering, especially, perhaps, because he had initially observed the suffering of the wounded with the combination of voyeuristic excitement and clinical detachment we noted earlier. His initial attitude had been symptomatic of the somewhat cavalier attitude with which so many of the educated of his generation had gone off to war.

Another of the torturers is patterned after a blind figure in a fourteenth-century Italian fresco—yet is also made to look like Lenin and/or a contemporary German worker. With bourgeois and proletarian seemingly both implicated in gratuitous violence, there seems no scope for political redemption. Yet neither is the family's home a safe refuge from the violence of politics and war. We all seem to be at once perpetrators and victims, caught in a claustrophobic space, with no place to escape, and little if any scope for action. We are even a hell unto ourselves.

Through this combination of images suggesting suffering and guilt, but seemingly precluding any hope of redemption, "Beckmann achieves," as Reinhard Spieler has put it, "a form which transcends commentary on his own time: the corrup-

tion and cruelty of postwar society is raised to a general and timeless level of human experience, to eternal night, to humanity's hell on earth."[‡]

The Night conveys not simply the disarray of a moment—the German experience of defeat and revolutionary violence—but a changed sensibility; in the wake of World War I the world could never be the same. Although he was determined to avoid sentimentality or collective self-pity, Beckmann still thought that we might hope, through art, to come to terms with all that recent historical experience had revealed. But it had come to seem that we could do so only through "one of the most disagreeable images" in modern art.

QUESTIONS

1. Why does Beckmann place this combination of interconnected figures in such a shallow, confined space?

2. What relationship between the private domestic sphere and the public political sphere does Beckmann seem to be depicting in *The Night?*

[‡]Reinhard Spieler, *Max Beckmann, 1884–1950: The Path to Myth* (Cologne: Taschen, 1995), p. 38.

Online Study Center
Improve Your Grade Visual Record Activities

How and why had the course of the war by 1917 defied the expectations that had surrounded the beginning of fighting in August 1914?

Why did this prove a total war, making necessary new forms of socioeconomic coordination and even systematic propaganda?

Why did the first revolution in Russia pave the way for a second, spearheaded by the Bolsheviks?

Why did Germany and its allies end up losing the war even after forcing Russia to make a separate peace by early 1918?

What factors shaped the peace settlement that the victors imposed on Germany and its allies in 1919–1920?

The war that began in August 1914 was supposed to be over in a few months, but after the French held at the first Battle of the Marne in September, it bogged down in a stalemate on the western front, thanks partly to the unforeseen effectiveness of defensive trenches. The massive assaults of 1916–1917 yielded horrifying numbers of casualties—but not the intended breakthrough for either side.

Because it was so much longer and more difficult than expected, this first "world war" proved a total war, calling forth new forms of socioeconomic coordination and even systematic propaganda. Partly as a result, the war accelerated processes, from economic coordination to technological development to women's suffrage, that many deemed progressive.

But the war also caused cracks in the old order, first and most dramatically in Russia, where war-weariness led to a revolution overthrowing the tsarist regime early in 1917. Although this was not a socialist revolution, it paved the way by the end of 1917 to a second revolution, spearheaded by the Bolsheviks, who represented the more extreme wing of Russian Marxism. Although their own tactical prowess was also a factor, they were able to seize the initiative especially because of the mistakes of the provisional government, which kept Russia in the war and balked at systematic land reform. In taking power, the Bolsheviks were seeking not simply to control Russia but to spark the wider revolution they believed essential if a viable new socialist order was to be created.

Although war-weariness on both sides prompted calls for a white peace by 1917, the defection of revolutionary Russia and the intervention of the United States dramatically altered the lineup—and even the potential stakes and meaning of the war. In 1918, Germany mounted a last-ditch offensive in the west that came close to succeeding. But France had toughened under Georges Clemenceau, and a lack of food, provisions, and manpower was fatally weakening the German effort by that point. U.S. intervention gave the anti-German coalition the long-term advantage in any case. Although it entailed far more sacrifice than anyone had expected at the outset, the war reached a definitive outcome with the defeat of Germany and its allies by November 1918.

Conflicting aspirations among the victors led to an awkward peace settlement. Whereas Woodrow Wilson envisioned a new era in world affairs, based on national self-determination and a new League of Nations, Clemenceau was concerned to cement French superiority on the European continent in the face of Germany's greater long-term demographic, economic, and military potential. Such security considerations even compromised the principle of self-determination at the peace conference. But the harshness of the Treaty of Versailles, which produced much resentment even outside Germany, led some observers to doubt the peace could last for long.

LOOKING AHEAD

In destroying the Habsburg empire and the imperial regime in Germany, the war seemed to have overcome the problems that had caused it in the first place. But the future remained uncertain, even after the major provisions of the peace settlement were established in 1919. Did the victors have the unity and will to enforce the peace? Despite a widespread desire to return to normal, many people sensed how radically the world had changed—and that it could never be the same again. Troubling new uncertainties mixed with exciting new possibilities as Europe and the West looked to the future.

EY TERMS

Online Study Center **Improve Your Grade** Flashcards

Sacred Union (p. 773)

British blockade (p. 778)

total war (p. 779)

Kriegsrohstoffabteilung (KRA) (p. 779)

Petrograd Soviet (p. 783)

provisional government (p. 783)

Vladimir Lenin (p. 784)

Fourteen Points (p. 786)

Treaty of Brest-Litovsk (p. 787)

"stab in the back" myth (p. 790)

Treaty of Versailles (p. 793)

League of Nations (p. 795)

SUGGESTED READING

Beckett, Ian F. W. *The Great War, 1914–1918.* 2001. A thematically organized treatment; especially good on the global dimensions of the conflict.

Boemke, Manfred F., Gerald D. Feldman, and Elisabeth Glaser, eds. *The Treaty of Versailles: A Reassessment After 75 Years.* 1998. Scholars from a number of countries reassess all aspects of the treaty in a major collection of essays.

Chickering, Roger. *Imperial Germany and the Great War, 1914–1918.* 1998. A balanced, comprehensive introduction to the German war effort and experience; especially good on the interpenetration of military and sociopolitical concerns.

Ellis, John. *Eye-Deep in Hell: Trench Warfare in World War I.* 1989. A compelling account of life and death in the trenches, covering topics from trench construction to eating, drinking, and sex; includes striking photographs.

Figes, Orlando. *A People's Tragedy: The Russian Revolution, 1891–1924.* 1997. A lengthy, comprehensive, and gripping account of the revolutionary trajectory, from the famine of 1891 to the death of Lenin in 1924. Seeks to reveal the complexity of the whole process, its many episodes and forms of agency.

Fitzpatrick, Sheila. *The Russian Revolution, 1917–1932.* 2d ed. 1994. An ideal introductory work that places the events of 1917 in the sweep of Russian history.

Holquist, Peter. *Making War, Forging Revolution: Russia's Continuum of Crisis, 1914–1921.* 2002. By focusing on a particular region, this work shows how the Bolsheviks used the tools of mobilization and coercion already called forth by the war in their effort to reshape Russian society.

Keegan, John. *The First World War.* 1999. A comprehensive and accessible study by a widely read military historian.

Morrow, John H., Jr. *The Great War: An Imperial History.* 2004. A clear and balanced chronological account that incorporates the European colonial networks in

showing how the war was fought—and in assessing its consequences.

Sharp, Alan. *The Versailles Settlement: Peacemaking in Paris, 1919.* 1991. A brief, clear, and balanced overview that seeks to do justice to the magnitude of the task the peacemakers faced.

Winter, J. M. *The Experience of World War I.* 1989. A beautifully illustrated work that proceeds via concentric circles from politicians to generals to soldiers to civilians, then to the war's longer-term effects.

Winter, Jay. *Sites of Memory, Sites of Mourning.* 1995. Using an effective comparative approach, a leading authority argues that Europeans relied on relatively traditional means of making sense of the bloodletting of World War I.

NOTES

1. Thus wrote the German poet Ivan Goll in 1917; quoted in Modris Eksteins, *Rites of Spring: The Great War and the Birth of the Modern Age* (Boston: Houghton Mifflin, 1989), p. 144.

2. The remarks of Raymond Joubert, as quoted in John Ellis, *Eye-Deep in Hell: Trench Warfare in World War I* (Baltimore: Johns Hopkins University Press, 1989), p. 104.

3. Brian Bond, *War and Society in Europe, 1870–1970* (New York: Oxford University Press, 1986), p. 114.

4. A. N. Potresov, quoted in Richard Pipes, *The Russian Revolution* (New York: Random House, Vintage, 1991), p. 348.

5. Both statements are quoted in Koppel S. Pinson, *Modern Germany: Its History and Civilization,* 2d ed. (New York: Macmillan, 1966), p. 337.

6. Quoted in Arno J. Mayer, *Political Origins of the New Diplomacy, 1917–18* (New York: Random House, Vintage, 1970), p. 135.

7. Quoted in Walter Arnstein, *Britain Yesterday and Today: 1830 to the Present,* 6th ed. (Lexington, Mass.: D. C. Heath, 1992), p. 266.

8. Quoted in P. M. H. Bell, *The Origins of the Second World War* (London and New York: Longman, 1986), p. 14.

9. Paul Valéry, *Variety,* 1st series (New York: Harcourt, Brace, 1938), pp. 3–4.

26

THE ILLUSION OF STABILITY, 1919–1930

Kees van Dongen: Au cabaret nègre (detail)

(Christie's Images)

804

I n 1925 Josephine Baker (1906–1975), a black entertainer from St. Louis, moved from the chorus lines of New York to the bistros of Paris, where she quickly became a singing and dancing sensation. Also a favorite in Germany, she was the most famous of the African American entertainers who took the cultural capitals of Europe by storm during the 1920s. After the disillusioning experience of war, many Europeans found a valuable infusion of vitality in Baker's jazz music, exotic costumes, and "savage," uninhibited dancing (see the poster on page 821).

The European attraction to African Americans as primitive, vital, and sensual reflected a good deal of racial stereotyping, but there really *was* something fresh and uninhibited about American culture, especially its African American variant. And even as they played to those stereotypes, black performers like Baker had great fun ironically subverting them. Many realized they could enjoy opportunities in parts of Europe that were still denied them in the United States. Baker herself was a woman of great sophistication who became a French citizen in 1937, participated in progressive causes, and was decorated for her secret intelligence work in the anti-Nazi resistance during World War II.

The prominence of African Americans in European popular culture was part of a wider infatuation with things American as Europeans embraced the new during the 1920s. Lacking the cultural baggage of Europe, America seemed to offer revitalization and modernity at the same time. With so many old conventions shattered by the war, the ideal of being "modern" became widespread among Europeans, affecting everything from sex education to furniture design. "Modern" meant no-nonsense efficiency, mass production, and a vital popular culture, expressed in jazz, movies, sport, and even advertising. (See the feature "The Visual Record: Advertising" on pages 822–823.)

But Europeans themselves had pioneered modernism in many areas of the arts and sciences, and innovation continued after the war. Paris held its own as an international cultural center, hosting a decorative arts exhibition in 1925 that produced art deco, the sleek, "modernistic" style that helped give the decade its distinctive flavor. And in the unsettled conditions of

CHAPTER OUTLINE

THE WEST AND THE WORLD AFTER THE GREAT WAR

COMMUNISM, FASCISM, AND THE NEW POLITICAL SPECTRUM

TOWARD MASS SOCIETY

WEIMAR GERMANY AND THE TRIALS OF THE NEW DEMOCRACIES

THE SEARCH FOR MEANING IN A DISORDERED WORLD

KEY TERMS

Maginot Line

fascism

Comintern (Third, or Communist, International)

New Economic Policy (NEP)

Joseph Stalin

Benito Mussolini

Matteotti murder

corporativism, corporative state

Gustav Stresemann

Treaty of Locarno

surrealism

Bauhaus

Online Study Center

This icon will direct you to interactive map and primary source activities on the website **college.hmco.com/ pic/noble5e**

postwar Germany, Berlin emerged to rival Paris for cultural leadership during what Germans called "the Golden Twenties." Innovations ranged from avant-garde drama to a sophisticated cabaret scene with a prominent homosexual dimension.

Still, there was something dizzying, even un-nerving, about the eager embrace of the new during the 1920s. The war had accelerated the long-term modernization process toward large industries, cities, and bureaucracies, and toward mass politics, society, and culture. That process was positive, even liberating, in certain respects, but it was also disruptive and disturbing. Some Europeans viewed the vogue of black American entertainers as a symptom of decadence that would only undermine further the best of European civilization. In this sense, the postwar sense of release and excitement combined with an anxious longing for stability, for a return to order. Even in embracing the new, many were seeking a new basis for order and security.

Although the immediate disruptions of war-time carried over to 1923, a more hopeful era of relative prosperity and international conciliation followed, continuing until 1929. But there was much that called into question the ideal of a "world safe for democracy" that had surrounded the end of the war. Revolutionary Russia remained an uncertain force, even as it began seeking to build social-ism on its own. In Italy, the democracy that had emerged in the nineteenth century gave way to the first regime to call itself fascist, and some of the new democracies in east-central Europe did not survive the decade. The postwar efforts at economic resta-bilization, apparently successful for a while, masked growing strains in the international economy. In one sphere after another, postwar restabilization was fragile—and could quickly unravel.

FOCUS QUESTIONS

How did the differing priorities of Britain and France affect international relations during the 1920s?

Why did Italy turn from parliamentary democracy to fascism even after sharing in the victory in World War I?

Why, and on what basis, did sexuality, gender roles, and the "new woman" provoke so much concern during this period?

What factors made the future of the new German democracy so uncertain during the 1920s?

How did cultural and intellectual leaders differ over the place of "tradition" as they sought to suggest how to come to terms with the new situation of the 1920s?

THE WEST AND THE WORLD AFTER THE GREAT WAR

How did the differing priorities of Britain and France affect international relations during the 1920s?

Although the United States and Japan were becoming important, the major international players before 1914 had been the European powers, who had apportioned much of the non-Western world in imperial networks. But the war and the peace had weakened—and to some extent discredited—the Europeans, who now found themselves saddled with foreign debts and unbalanced economies. Though the United States pulled back from a direct po-litical role in Europe in 1919, it became far more active in world affairs, helping to engineer major conferences on arms limitation and international economic relations during the 1920s. But in crucial respects, the shape of the postwar international order still depended on Europeans. And colonial concerns continued to affect the balance of power in Europe, where it fell to the two major victors in the war, France and Britain, to enforce the controversial peace settlement.

The Erosion of European Power

Emerging from the war as the principal power in East Asia was a non-Western country, Japan, whose claims to the German bases in the region and to special rights in China were formally recognized at the Paris Peace Conference. With the Washington treaty of 1922, Japan won naval parity with Britain and the United States in East Asia. The Western nations were recognizing Japan as a peer, a great power—even a threat. Aspects of the Washington agreements were intended to block Japanese expansion in East Asia. If a new international system was to emerge, it would not be centered in Europe to the extent the old one had been.

As the old Europe lost prestige, President Wilson's ideals of self-determination and democracy were greeted enthusiastically outside the West—in China, for example. At the same time, the Russian revolutionary model appealed to those in the colonial world seeking to understand the mainsprings of Western imperialism—and the means of overcoming it. To some Chinese intellectuals by the early 1920s, Leninism was attractive because it showed the scope for mass mobilization by a revolutionary vanguard.

Non-Western elites were learning to pick and choose from among the elements of the Western tradition. In the 1920s, ever greater numbers of colonial subjects were traveling to western Europe, often for education. Paris was a favored destination, partly because France made an effort to assimilate its colonial peoples. Although those educated in Europe were subject to Westernization, that did not necessarily make them more supportive of Western rule. Many began not only to question colonialism but also to take a fresh look at their own traditions, asking how they might serve the quest for a postcolonial order.

By the 1920s, a generation of anticolonialist, nationalist intellectuals was emerging to lead the non-Western world. Some were more radical than others, but most agreed that the challenge was to learn from the West and to modernize, but without simply copying the West and losing distinctive cultural identities. It was imperative to sift through tradition, determining what needed to be changed and what was worth preserving. The pioneering Chinese nationalist Sun Yixien (Sun Yat-sen, 1866–1925) was typical in recognizing the need to adopt the science and technology of the West. But China, he insisted, could do so in its own way, without sacrificing its unique cultural and political traditions. (See the box "The Global Record: Sun Yixien on Chinese Nationalism.")

As the greatest imperial power, Britain was especially vulnerable to the growing anticolonial sentiment. The struggle to hang on to its empire drew British energies away from the problems of Europe after the peace settlement.

In light of the strong Indian support for the British war effort, the British government promised in 1917 to extend the scope for Indian involvement in the colonial administration in India. Growing expectations as the war was ending provoked episodes of violence against the British, whose troops retaliated brutally in April 1919, firing indiscriminately into an unarmed crowd. This Amritsar Massacre helped galvanize India's independence movement, even though the British, seeking conciliation in the aftermath, extended self-rule by entrusting certain less essential government services to Indians. Another milestone was reached in 1921, when Mohandas Gandhi, the British-educated leader of the Indian independence movement, shed his European clothes in favor of simple Indian attire. But it was on the basis of Western egalitarianism, not some indigenous value, that Gandhi demanded political rights for the "untouchables," the

March 1919	Founding of the Italian fascist movement
November 1920	Russian civil war ends
March 1921	New Economic Policy announced at Russian Communist Party congress
October 1922	Mussolini becomes Italian prime minister
January 1923	French-led occupation of the Ruhr
November 1923	Peak of inflation in Germany
January 1924	First Labour government in Britain
	Death of Lenin
August 1924	Acceptance of the Dawes Plan on German reparations
October 1925	Treaty of Locarno
May 1926	Pilsudski's coup d'état in Poland
	Beginning of general strike in Britain
May 1927	Lindbergh completes first transatlantic solo flight
January 1929	Stalin forces banishment of Trotsky from Soviet Union
April 1929	Soviets adopt first economic Five-Year Plan
August 1929	Acceptance of the Young Plan on German reparations
October 1929	Death of Stresemann

Reinforcing Imperialist Rule

In response to episodes of anti-colonialist violence in Amritsar, India, early in 1919, the British brutally cracked down, most notably in the massacre of April 1919. Here British authorities enforce a decree in the wake of the beating of a female British doctor on this road—forcing any Indian using the road to crawl along it. *(National Army Museum, London)*

lowest group in India's long-standing caste system. (See the box "The Global Record: Gandhi Advocates Nonviolence" on page 842 in Chapter 27.)

Online Study Center **Improve Your Grade**
Primary Source: An Indian Nationalist Condemns the British Empire

In Egypt a full-scale anti-British insurrection broke out in 1919. After British troops suppressed the rebellion, British authorities offered to grant moderate concessions, as in India. But Egyptian nationalists demanded independence, which was finally granted in 1922. Egypt gradually evolved into a constitutional monarchy, with representative government and universal suffrage. But Britain retained a predominant influence in Egypt until the nationalist revolution of 1952 (see page 929).

At the same time, nationalism was growing among West Africans who had studied in England. In March 1919 Western-educated Africans in the Gold Coast asked the British governor to establish representative institutions so that Africans could at least be consulted about governmental affairs. The West African National Congress, formed in 1920, made similar demands. The British agreed to new constitutions for Nigeria in 1923 and the Gold Coast in 1925 that took significant steps in that direction. They also agreed to build more schools, though they tended to promote practical education, including African languages and agriculture, whereas the African leaders wanted students to learn the Western classics that "made gentlemen." Such conflicting priorities indicate the complexities of the relationships between colonial rulers and the emerging elites among the colonized peoples.

THE GLOBAL RECORD

SUN YIXIEN ON CHINESE NATIONALISM

Sun Yixien (Sun Yat-sen), widely regarded as the father of modern China, founded the Guomindang (Kuomintang), the Chinese nationalist movement, in 1912. Educated by Western missionaries in China, he lived in the United States for extended periods and came to admire the West in important respects. But he insisted that China, to make the best use of what the West offered, had to reconnect with its own unique traditions. Variations on this argument would be heard for decades as the rest of the world sought to come to terms with the seemingly more advanced West. The following passages are from an influential series of lectures that Sun Yixien presented in China in the early 1920s.

What is the standing of our nation in the world? In comparison with other nations we have the greatest population and the oldest culture, of four thousand years' duration. We ought to be advancing in line with the nations of Europe and America. But the Chinese people have only family and clan groups; there is no national spirit. Consequently, in spite of four hundred million people gathered together in one China, we are in fact but a sheet of loose sand. We are the poorest and weakest state in the world, occupying the lowest position in international affairs; the rest of mankind is the carving knife and the serving dish, while we are the fish and the meat. Our position now is extremely perilous; if we do not earnestly promote nationalism and weld together our four hundred millions into a strong nation, we face a tragedy—the loss of our country and the destruction of our race. To ward off this danger, we must espouse nationalism and employ the national spirit to save the country. . . .

But even if we succeed in reviving our ancient morality, learning, and powers, we will still not be able, in this modern world, to advance China to a first place among the nations. . . . [W]e will still need to learn the strong points of Europe and America before we can progress at an equal rate with them. Unless we do study the best from foreign countries, we will go backward. With our own fine foundation of knowledge and our age-long culture, with our own native intelligence besides, we should be able to acquire all the best things from abroad. The strongest point of the West is its science. . . .

As soon as we learn Western machinery we can use it anytime, anywhere; electric lights, for example, can be installed and used in any kind of Chinese house. But Western social customs and sentiments are different from ours in innumerable points; if, without regard to customs and popular feelings in China, we try to apply Western methods of social control as we would Western machinery—in a hard and fast way—we shall be making a serious mistake. . . .

. . . For the governmental machinery of the United States and France still has many defects, and does not satisfy the desires of the people nor give them a complete measure of happiness. So we in our proposed reconstruction must not think that if we imitate the West of today we shall reach the last stage of progress and be perfectly contented. . . .

Only in recent times has Western culture advanced beyond ours, and the passion for this new civilization has stimulated our revolution. Now that the revolution is a reality, we naturally desire to see China excel the West and build up the newest and most progressive state in the world. We certainly possess the qualifications necessary to reach this ideal, but we must not merely imitate the democratic systems of the West.

QUESTIONS

1. Why does Sun Yixien think China, despite its ancient and sophisticated culture, has fallen behind the West?

2. On what grounds does Sun Yixien consider it necessary for China to study Western culture, as opposed to relying on its own traditions?

Source: Sun Yat-sen, *San Min Chu I: The Three Principles of the People* (Taipei, Taiwan: China Cultural Service, 1953), pp. 5, 46, 109–113, 136, 138–139.

ENFORCING THE VERSAILLES SETTLEMENT

It was up to France and Britain to make sure the new international order worked, but it was not clear that either had the will and resources to do so. Cooperation between them was essential, yet sometimes their differences—in geography, in values, and in perceptions—seemed to doom them to work at cross-purposes.

France was the dominant power on the European continent after World War I, and until well into the 1930s it boasted the strongest army in the world. Yet even in the early 1920s a sense of artificiality surrounded France's image of strength—thus the shrillness and the defensiveness that came to mark French thinking and French policy.

In light of Germany's larger population and stronger industrial base, France's long-term security seemed to require certain measures to tip the scales in its favor. By imposing German disarmament and the demilitarization of the Rhineland, the Versailles treaty gave France immediate military advantages. Yet how long could these measures be maintained, once the passions of war had died down and Germany no longer seemed such a threat? France had hoped for British help in enforcing the treaty, but Britain was pulling back from the Continent to concentrate on its empire, just as it had after other major European wars.

In particular, the British wanted to avoid getting dragged into the uncertain situation in east-central Europe, where its own national interests did not seem to be at stake. Yet the French, to replace their earlier link with Russia, promptly developed an alliance system with several of the new or expanded states of the region, including Poland, Czechoslovakia, Romania, and Yugoslavia. France's ties to east-central Europe made the British especially wary of binding agreements with the French.

At first, France felt confident enough to take strong steps even without British support. In response to German foot-dragging in paying reparations, Prime Minister Raymond Poincaré decided to get tough in January 1923. Declaring the Germans in default, he sent French troops at the head of an international force to occupy the Ruhr industrial area and force German compliance. But the move backfired. The Germans adopted a policy of passive resistance in response, and the costs of the occupation more than offset the increase in reparations that France received. The French government ended up having to raise taxes to pay for the venture. Moreover, the move alienated the British, whose lack of support bordered on active hostility.

British leaders now viewed French policy as unnecessarily vindictive and bellicose, and they increasingly saw the Versailles treaty as counterproductive. Instead, they placed great store in the League of Nations and in the international arms reduction effort gaining momentum by the later 1920s. So France found itself with ever less support from its wartime allies as it sought to enforce the peace settlement. The Ruhr occupation of 1923 proved the last time the French dared to go it alone.

From that point on, France gradually lost the advantages it had gained by defeating Germany, and self-confidence gave way to defensiveness and resignation. The defensive mentality found physical embodiment in the **Maginot Line**, a system of fortifications on the country's eastern border. Remembering the defensive warfare of World War I and determined to preclude the sort of invasion France had suffered in 1914, the military convinced France's political leaders to adopt a defensive strategy based on a fortified line. Construction began in 1929, and the Maginot (MAH-zhih-noh) system reached preliminary completion in 1935, when it extended along France's border with Germany from Switzerland to the border with Belgium.

This defensive system was not consistent with the other major strands of French policy, especially its alliances with states in east-central Europe. If France emphasized defense behind an impregnable system of forts, what good were French security guarantees to such new allies as Poland and Czechoslovakia?

Still, the situation remained fluid during the 1920s. In France, as in Britain, national elections in 1924 produced a victory for the moderate left, ending a period of conservative nationalist dominance since the war. In each country, international relations became a major issue in the elections, and the outcome heralded a more conciliatory tack, especially in relations with Germany.

=== SECTION SUMMARY ===

- Although the prewar European colonial system remained largely in place after the war, Wilsonian ideals of self-determination spurred anticolonial sentiment in the colonized world.

- On the basis of their study in the West, intellectuals from Europe's colonies sought to combine Western values with indigenous traditions as they began spearheading the anticolonial struggle.

- More vulnerable geographically, France was initially more determined than Britain to keep Germany limited by strictly enforcing the Versailles settlement.

- France's confident, even aggressive, posture gradually gave way to the defensiveness of the "Maginot mentality," evident in the decision to build a series of defensive fortifications.

Maginot Line A 200-mile system of elaborate permanent fortifications on France's eastern border, named for war minister André Maginot and built primarily during the 1930s. It was a defense against German frontal assault; in 1940 the Germans invaded by flanking the line.

COMMUNISM, FASCISM, AND THE NEW POLITICAL SPECTRUM

Why did Italy turn from parliamentary democracy to fascism even after sharing in the victory in World War I?

In making their revolution in 1917, the Russian Bolsheviks had expected to spark wider revolution. Hopes—and fears—that the revolution would spread were palpable in the immediate postwar period. The Russian Communists initially enjoyed extraordinary prestige on the European left; but as the nature of Leninist communism became clearer, some Marxists grew skeptical or hostile, and the Russian model eventually produced a damaging split in international socialism. By the end of the 1920s revolution elsewhere was nowhere in sight, and it seemed that, for the foreseeable future, the communist regime in Russia would have to go it alone.

By then, a new and unexpected political movement had emerged in Italy, expanding the political spectrum in a different direction. This was the first **fascism,** which brought Benito Mussolini to power in 1922. Emerging directly from the war, Italian fascism was violent and antidemocratic—and thus disturbing to many. Stressing national solidarity and discipline, the fascists were hostile not only to liberal individualism and the parliamentary system, but also to Marxist socialism, with its emphasis on class struggle and the special role of the working class. Claiming to offer a modern alternative to both, Italian fascism quickly attracted the attention of those in other countries who were disillusioned with parliamentary politics and hostile to the Marxist left. The interplay of communism and fascism, as new political experiments, added to the uncertainties of the novel postwar world.

CHANGING PRIORITIES IN COMMUNIST RUSSIA, 1918–1921

Even after leading the revolution that toppled the provisional government in November 1917, the Bolsheviks could not claim majority support in Russia. When the long-delayed elections to select a constituent assembly were held a few weeks after the revolution, the Socialist Revolutionaries won a clear majority, while the Bolsheviks ended up with fewer than one-quarter of the seats. But the Bolsheviks dispersed the assembly by force

fascism   A violent, antidemocratic movement founded by Benito Mussolini in Italy in 1919. The term is widely used to encompass Hitler's Nazi regime in Germany and other movements stressing disciplined national solidarity and hostile to liberal individualism, the parliamentary system, and Marxist socialism.

when it met in January 1918. And over the next three years the Communists, as the Bolsheviks renamed themselves, gradually consolidated their power, establishing a centralized and nondemocratic regime. Power lay not with the soviets, nor with some coalition of socialist parties, but solely with the Communist Party.

Civil War   During its first years, the new communist regime encountered a genuine emergency that especially seemed to require such a monopoly of power. During 1918 to 1920, in what became a brutal civil war, the communist "Reds" battled counterrevolutionary "Whites," people who had been dispossessed by the revolution or who had grown disillusioned with the Communist Party. Moreover, foreigners eager to topple the communist regime began to intervene militarily. At the same time, several of the non-Russian nationalities of the old Russian Empire sought to take advantage of the unsettled situation to free themselves from Russian and communist control. Appointed "People's Commissar for War" in April 1918, Leon Trotsky forged a loyal and disciplined Red Army in an effort to master the difficult situation.

A series of thrusts, involving troops from fourteen countries at one time or another, struck at Russia from a variety of points along its huge border. The Whites and the foreign troops never managed a coordinated strategy, but the dogged counterrevolutionary assault seriously threatened the young communist regime and the territorial basis of the state it had inherited from the tsarist autocracy. In the final analysis, however, the Whites proved unable to rally much popular support. Peasants feared, plausibly enough, that a White victory would mean a restoration of the old order, including the return of their newly won lands to the former landlords. By the end of active fighting in November 1920, the communist regime had not only survived but regained most of the territory it had lost early in the civil war (see **MAP 26.1**).

The need to launch the new communist regime in this way, fighting counterrevolutionaries supported by foreign troops, inevitably affected Communists' perceptions and priorities. Separatist sentiment might continue to feed counterrevolutionary efforts, so the new regime exerted careful control over the non-Russian nationalities. Thus, when the Union of Soviet Socialist Republics (USSR) was organized in December 1922, it

Boundary of the Russian Empire 1914
Boundary of area controlled by the Bolsheviks August 1918
Boundary of area controlled by the Bolsheviks October 1919
Boundary of Soviet territory March 1921
Boundary of area controlled by the anti-Bolshevik forces May 1920
White Russian armies
Non-Russian anti-Bolshevik forces

MAP 26.1   Foreign Intervention and Civil War in Revolutionary Russia, 1918–1920

By mid-1918 the new communist regime was under attack from many sides, by both foreign troops and anticommunist Russians. Bolshevik-held territory shrank during 1919, but over the next year the Red Army managed to regain much of what had been lost and to secure the new communist state. Anton Denikin, Alexander Kolchak, and Nicholas Yudenich commanded the most significant counterrevolutionary forces.

(Source: Adapted from The Times Atlas of World History, 3d ed. *Reprinted by permission of HarperCollins Publishers Ltd. © HarperCollins Publishers Ltd.)*

was only nominally a federation of autonomous republics; strong centralization from the communist regime's new capital in Moscow was the rule from the start.

The Comintern In March 1919, while fighting the civil war, the Russian Communists founded the Third, or Communist, International—widely known as the **Comintern**—to make clear their break with the seemingly discredited strategies of the Second International. Through the Comintern, the Russian Communists expected to translate their success in Russia into leadership of the international socialist movement. However, many old-line Marxists elsewhere were not prepared to admit that the leadership of European socialism had passed to the Communist rulers of backward Russia. As early as 1919, the German Karl Kautsky (1854–1938), who had been the leading spokesman for orthodox Marxism after the death of Friedrich Engels in 1895, harshly criticized Leninist communism as a heretical departure that would lead to despotism and severely damage international socialism.

From its founding in March 1919 until the spring of 1920, as a wave of leftist political agitation and labor unrest swept Europe, the Comintern actively promoted the wider revolution that Lenin had envisioned. Seeking to win mass support, the organization accented leftist solidarity and reached out to the rank and file in the labor unions. By the spring of 1920, however, it seemed clear that further revolution was not imminent. Thus Comintern leaders began focusing on a more protracted revolutionary struggle.

The Russians felt that poor organization and planning had undermined the wider revolutionary possibil-

Comintern (Third, or Communist, International) An association founded in March 1919 by the Communists (formerly Bolsheviks) to translate their success in Russia into leadership of the international socialist movement.

ity in Europe during 1919 and 1920. The Comintern would cut through all the revolutionary romanticism to show what the Leninist strategy, or communism, meant in fact. The Russians themselves would have to call the shots because what communism meant, above all, was tight organization and discipline.

The second Comintern congress, during the summer of 1920, devised twenty-one conditions for Comintern affiliation. Most notably, any socialist party seeking membership had to accept the Comintern's authority, adopt a centralized organization, and purge its reformists. By early 1921, the Comintern's aggressive claim to leadership had split the international socialist movement, for the Comintern attracted some, but not all, of the members of the existing socialist parties. Those who now called themselves "communists" accepted the Leninist model and affiliated with the Comintern. Those who retained the "socialist" label rejected Comintern leadership; they still claimed to be Marxists but declined to embrace the Bolshevik strategy for taking power.

At first, many European socialists had difficulty assessing the Comintern objectively. The Russian Communists enjoyed great prestige because they had made a real revolution, while elsewhere socialists had talked and compromised, even getting swept up in wartime patriotism. When the French Socialist Party debated Comintern membership at its national congress in December 1920, about 70 percent of the delegates voted to join and accept the twenty-one points, while a minority walked out to form a new socialist party. But as the implications of Comintern membership became clearer over the next few years, the balance shifted in favor of the socialists. Membership in the French Communist Party, which stood at 131,000 in 1921, declined to 28,000 by 1932.

Late in 1923 the Comintern finally concluded that revolution elsewhere could not be expected any time soon. The immediate enemy was not capitalism or the bourgeoisie, but the socialists, the Communists' rivals for working-class support. The Communists' incessant criticism of the socialists, whom they eventually dubbed "social fascists," demoralized and weakened the European left, especially in the face of the growing threat of fascism by the early 1930s. The schism on the left remained an essential fact of European political life for half a century.

FROM LENIN TO STALIN, 1921–1929

To win the civil war, the communist regime had adopted a policy of "war communism," a rough-and-ready controlled economy in which food and supplies were commandeered for the Red Army. At the beginning of 1921, the economy was in crisis. Industrial production equaled only about one-fifth the 1913 total,

Rivals for the Soviet Leadership

In July 1926 in Moscow, Soviet leaders carry the coffin of Feliks Dzerzhinsky, the first head of the secret police. Among them are Trotsky (*with glasses, center left*), Stalin (*right foreground*), and Bukharin (*with mustache, at far right*), rivals for the Soviet leadership after Lenin's death. The winner, Stalin, would eventually have his two competitors killed.

(David King Collection)

workers in key factories went on strike, and peasants were resisting further requisitions of grain. In March 1921 sailors at the Kronstadt naval base near Petrograd mutinied, suffering considerable loss of life as governmental control was reestablished.

With the very survival of the revolution in question, Lenin replaced war communism with the **New Economic Policy (NEP)** in March 1921. Although transport, banking, heavy industry, and wholesale commerce remained under state control, the NEP restored considerable scope for private enterprise, especially in the retail sector and in agriculture. Peasants could again sell some of their harvest. The economy quickly began to revive and by 1927 was producing at prewar levels.

Online Study Center **Improve Your Grade**
Primary Source: A Revolutionary Retreat: The New Economic Policy

But what about the longer term? If revolution elsewhere was not on the immediate horizon, could the Soviet Union—relatively backward economically and scarred by over a decade of upheaval—build a genuinely socialist order on its own? Certain measures were obvious: The new regime engineered rapid improvements in literacy, for example. But the Marxist understanding of

historical progress required industrialization, and so debate focused on how to promote industrial development under Soviet conditions.

This debate about priorities became intertwined with questions about the leadership of the new regime. Lenin suffered the first of a series of strokes in May 1922 and then died in January 1924, setting off a struggle among his possible successors. Leon Trotsky, an effective organizer and powerful thinker, was by most measures Lenin's heir apparent. Although he favored tighter economic controls to speed industrial development, Trotsky insisted that the top priority should be spreading the revolution to other countries.

In contrast, Nikolai Bukharin (1888–1938) wanted to concentrate on the gradual development of the Soviet Union, based on a more open and conciliatory strategy. Rather than tightening controls to squeeze a surplus from agricultural producers, the government should promote purchasing power by allowing producers to profit. By the time of his death Lenin had apparently begun thinking along the same lines. And he had come to have considerable misgivings about the man who would win this struggle to direct the fragile new Soviet regime, **Joseph Stalin** (1879–1953).

Stalin was born Josef Djugashvili into a lower-class family in Georgia, in the Caucasus region. As an ethnic

New Economic Policy (NEP)   A Russian economic liberalization measure aimed at reviving an economy in crisis. The NEP restored considerable scope for private enterprise and allowed peasants to sell some of their harvest.

Joseph Stalin   Soviet dictator who jettisoned the New Economic Policy and instituted a program of crash industrialization and agricultural collectivization. He concluded the Nazi-Soviet Pact in 1939 but joined the Allies after the German invasion of the Soviet Union in 1941.

Georgian, he did not learn to speak Russian until he was 11 years old. From the position of party secretary, which he had assumed in 1922, Stalin established his control within the Soviet system by 1929. Though he lacked Trotsky's charisma and knew little of economics, he was highly intelligent and proved a master of backstage political maneuvering. Stalin first outmaneuvered Trotsky and his allies, removing them from positions of power and forcing Trotsky himself into exile in 1929. Bitterly critical of Stalin to the end, Trotsky was finally murdered by Stalin's agents in Mexico in 1940. Stalin's victory over those like Bukharin was more gradual, but ultimately just as complete. And his victory proved decisive for the fate of Soviet communism.

By the later 1920s, those who believed in the communist experiment were growing disillusioned with the compromises of the NEP. It was time for the Soviet Union to push ahead to a new order, leaving capitalism behind altogether. Even if revolution was not imminent elsewhere, the Soviet Union could seize the lead and build "socialism in one country." Genuine enthusiasm greeted the regime's turn to centralized economic planning in 1927 and its subsequent adoption of the first Five-Year Plan early in 1929. Central planning led to a program of crash industrialization, favoring heavy industry, by the end of that year. But this new, more radical direction was not fully thought through, and it soon caused incredible suffering.

To buy the necessary plant and equipment, the state seemed to require better control of agricultural output than had been possible under the NEP. The key was to squeeze the agricultural surplus from the peasantry on terms more favorable to the government. By forcing peasants into large, state-controlled collective farms, government leaders could more readily extract the surplus, which would then be sold abroad, earning the money to finance factories, dams, and power plants.

Stalin's effort to mobilize society for the great task of rapid industrialization affected the whole shape of the regime—including cultural and artistic policy. During the 1920s, the possibility of building a new socialist society in the Soviet Union had attracted a number of modernist artists, who assumed that artistic innovation went hand in hand with radical socioeconomic transformation. These artists wanted to make art more socially useful and more central to the lives of ordinary people. With Soviet cultural officials welcoming their experiments, such Soviet artists as Vladimir Tatlin (1885–1956) and Alexander Rodchenko (1891–1956) developed striking new cultural forms.

But in 1929 Soviet officials began mobilizing the cultural realm to serve the grandiose task of building socialism in one country. No longer welcoming experiment and innovation, they demanded "socialist real-

Tatlin: Monument to the Third International
Vladimir Tatlin created this model for a monument to the Third International, or Comintern, during 1919 and 1920. He envisioned a revolving structure of glass and iron; it would be twice as tall as the later Empire State Building. Although the monument was never built, Tatlin's bold, dynamic form symbolizes the utopian aspirations of the early years of the communist experiment in Russia. *(David King Collection)*

ism," which portrayed the achievements of the ongoing Soviet revolution in an inspiring, heroic light. Modernism, in contrast, they denounced as decadent and counterrevolutionary.

In retrospect, it is clear that a Stalinist revolution within the Soviet regime had begun by 1930, but where it was to lead was by no means certain—not even to Stalin himself. Still, the Soviet Union was pulling back, going its own way by the end of the 1920s. For the foreseeable future, the presence of a revolutionary regime in the old Russia would apparently be less disruptive for the rest of Europe than it had first appeared.

THE CRISIS OF LIBERAL ITALY AND THE CREATION OF FASCISM, 1919–1925

Fascism emerged directly from the Italian experience of World War I, which proved especially controversial because the Italians could have avoided it altogether. No one attacked Italy in 1914, and the country could have received significant territorial benefits just by remaining neutral. Yet it seemed to many, including leading intellectuals and educated young people, that Italy could not stand idly by in a European war, especially one involving Austria-Hungary, which still controlled significant Italian-speaking areas. To participate in this major war would be the test of Italy's maturity as a nation. In May 1915 Italy finally intervened on the side of the Triple Entente. The government's decision stemmed not from vague visions of renewal but from the commitment of tangible territorial gains that France and Britain made to Italy with the secret Treaty of London.

Despite the near collapse of the Italian armies late in 1917, Italy lasted out the war and contributed to the victory over Austria-Hungary. Supporters of the war felt that this success could lead to a thoroughgoing renewal of Italian public life. Yet many Italians had been skeptical of claims for the war from the outset, and the fact that it proved so much more difficult than expected hardly won them over. To socialists, Catholics, and many left-leaning liberals, intervention itself had been a tragic mistake. Thus, despite Italy's participation in the victory, division over the war's significance immensely complicated the postwar Italian political situation.

Their skepticism was only confirmed when Italy did not secure all the gains it sought at the Paris Peace Conference. Italy got most of what it had been promised in the Treaty of London, but appetites increased with the dissolution of the Austro-Hungarian Empire. To some Italians, the disappointing outcome of the peace conference simply confirmed that the war had been a mistake, its benefits not worth the costs. But others were outraged at what seemed a denigration of the Italian contribution by France, Britain, and the United States. The outcome fanned resentment not only of Italy's allies but also of the country's political leaders, who seemed too weak to deliver on what they had pledged.

The leaders of Italy's parliamentary democracy also failed to renew the country's political system in light of the war experience. To be sure, in a spirit of democratic reform, Italy adopted proportional representation to replace the old system of small, single-member constituencies in 1919. The new system meant a greater premium on mass parties and party discipline at the expense of the one-to-one bargaining that had character-ized the earlier *trasformismo*. But the new multiparty system quickly reached an impasse—partly because of the stance of the Italian Socialist Party.

Italian Socialism   In contrast to the French and German parties, the Italian Socialists had never supported the war, and they did not accept the notion that the war experience could yield political renewal in the aftermath. So rather than reaching out to idealistic but discontented war veterans, Socialist leaders talked of imitating the Bolshevik Revolution. And the Italian situation seemed at least potentially revolutionary during 1919 and 1920, when a wave of strikes culminated in a series of factory occupations. But despite their revolutionary rhetoric, Italy's Socialist leaders did not understand the practical aspects of Leninism and did not carry out the planning and organization that might have produced an Italian revolution.

The established parliamentary system was at an impasse, and the Socialist Party seemed at once too inflexible and too romantic to lead some sort of radical transformation. It was in this context that fascism emerged, claiming to offer a third way. It was bound to oppose the Socialists and the socialist working class because of conflict over the meaning of the war and the kind of transformation Italy needed. And this antisocialist posture made fascism open to exploitation by reactionary interests. By early 1921 landowners in northern and central Italy were footing the bill as bands of young fascists drove around the countryside in trucks, beating up workers and burning down socialist meeting halls. But fascist spokesmen claimed to offer something other than mere reaction—a new politics that all Italians, including the workers, would eventually find superior.

At the same time, important sectors of Italian industry, which had grown rapidly thanks to wartime government orders, looked with apprehension toward the more competitive international economy that loomed after the war. With its relative lack of capital and raw materials, Italy seemed to face an especially difficult situation. Nationalist thinkers and business spokesmen questioned the capacity of the parliamentary system to provide the vigorous leadership that Italy needed. Prone to short-term bickering and partisanship, ordinary politicians lacked the vision to pursue Italy's international economic interests and the will to impose the necessary discipline on the domestic level. Thus the government's response to the labor unrest of 1919 and 1920 was hesitant and weak.

Postwar Italy, then, witnessed widespread discontent with established forms of politics, but those discontented were socially disparate, and their aims were not entirely compatible. Some had been socialists before the war, others nationalists hostile to socialism.

Benito Mussolini

The founder of fascism is shown with other fascist leaders in 1922, as he becomes prime minister of Italy. Standing at Mussolini's right (with beard) is Italo Balbo, later a pioneering aviator and fascist Italy's air force minister.   *(Corbis)*

While some envisioned a more intense kind of mass politics, others thought the masses already had too much power. Still, these discontented groups agreed on the need for an alternative to both parliamentary politics and Marxist socialism. And all found the germs of that alternative in the Italian war experience.

The Rise of Mussolini   The person who seemed able to translate these aspirations into a new political force was **Benito Mussolini** (1883–1945), who had been a prominent socialist journalist before the war. Indeed, he was so talented that he was made editor of the Socialist Party's national newspaper in 1912, when he was only 29 years old. At that point many saw him as the fresh face needed to revitalize Italian socialism.

His concern with renewal made Mussolini an unorthodox socialist even before 1914, and he was prominent among those on the Italian left who began calling for Italian intervention once the war began. The fact that socialists in France, Germany, and elsewhere had immediately rallied to their respective national war efforts

raised new questions about conventional socialism, based on international proletarian solidarity. But the Italian Socialist Party refused to follow his call for intervention, remaining neutralist and aloof, so Mussolini found himself cut off from his earlier constituency.

However, through his new newspaper, *Il popolo d'Italia* (*The People of Italy*), Mussolini helped rally the disparate groups that advocated Italian participation in the war. He saw military service once Italy intervened, and after the war he seemed a credible spokesman for those who wanted to translate the war experience into a new form of politics. Amid growing political unrest, he founded the fascist movement in March 1919, taking the term *fascism* from the ancient Roman *fasces,* a bundle of rods surrounding an ax carried on state occasions as a symbol of power and unity.

But fascism found little success at first. And even as it gathered force in violent reaction against the socialist labor organizations by 1921, the movement's direction was uncertain. Although young fascist militants wanted to replace the established parliamentary system with a new political order, Mussolini seemed to be using fascism as his personal instrument to achieve power

Benito Mussolini   Founder of the fascist movement and subsequently dictator within the Italian fascist regime.

within the existing system. When his maneuvering finally won him the prime minister's post in October 1922, it was not at all clear that a change of regime, or a one-party dictatorship, was at hand.

At that point, Mussolini, like most Italians, emphasized normalization and legality. Fascism had apparently been absorbed within the political system, perhaps to provide an infusion of youthful vitality after the war. With Mussolini as prime minister, there would be changes, but not revolutionary changes. Government would become more vigorous and efficient; the swollen Italian bureaucracy would be streamlined; the trains would run on time. But those who had envisioned more sweeping change were frustrated that nothing more had come of fascism than this.

A crisis in 1924 forced Mussolini's hand. In June the moderate socialist Giacomo Matteotti (mah-tay-OH-tee) rose in parliament to denounce the renewed fascist violence that had accompanied recent national elections. His murder by fascist thugs shortly thereafter produced a great public outcry, though the responsibility of Mussolini and his government was unclear. Many establishment figures who had tolerated Mussolini as the man who could keep order now deserted him. A growing chorus called for his resignation. The crisis surrounding the **Matteotti murder** proved pivotal for the fascist regime.

Mussolini sought at first to be conciliatory, but more radical fascists saw the crisis as an opportunity to end the compromise with the old liberal order and to begin creating a whole new political system. The crisis came to a head on December 31, 1924, when thirty-three militants called on Mussolini to demand that he make up his mind. In their view, the way out of the crisis was not to delimit the scope of fascism but to expand it. Mussolini was not an ordinary prime minister but the leader of fascism, *Il Duce* (eel DOO-chay). In that role he would have to accept responsibility even for his movement's violent excesses and finally begin implementing a full-scale fascist revolution.

Mussolini committed himself to this more radical course in a speech to the Chamber of Deputies a few days later, on January 3, 1925. Defiantly claiming the "full political, moral, and historical responsibility for all that has happened," including "all the acts of violence," he promised to accelerate the transformation that he claimed to have initiated with his agitation for intervention in 1914 and 1915.[1] And now began the creation of a new fascist state, although the compromises continued and the direction was never as clear as committed fascists desired.

INNOVATION AND COMPROMISE IN FASCIST ITALY, 1925–1930

Early in 1925, the fascist government began to undermine the existing democratic system by imprisoning or exiling opposition leaders and outlawing nonfascist parties and labor unions. But fascism was not seeking simply a conventional monopoly of political power; the new fascist state was to be totalitarian, all-encompassing, limitless in its reach. Under the old liberal regime, the fascists charged, the state had been too weak to promote the national interest, and Italian society had been too fragmented to achieve its full potential. So Mussolini's regime both expanded the state's sovereignty and mobilized society to create a deeper sense of national identity and shared purpose. To settle labor disputes, a new system of labor judges replaced the right to strike, which, the fascists claimed, had fostered neither productivity nor long-term working-class interests. New organizations—for youth, for women, for leisure-time activities—were to make possible new forms of public participation.

The centerpiece of the new fascist state was **corporativism,** which entailed mobilizing people as producers, through organization of the workplace. Groupings based on occupation, or economic function, were gradually to replace parliament as the basis for political participation and decision making. Beginning in 1926, corporativist institutions were established in stages until a Chamber of Fasces and Corporations at last replaced the old Chamber of Deputies in 1939.

Especially through this **corporative state,** the fascists claimed to be fulfilling their grandiose mission and providing the world with a third way, beyond both outmoded democracy and misguided communism. The practice of corporativism never lived up to such rhetoric, but the effort to devise new forms of political participation and decision making was central to fascism's self-understanding and its quest for legitimacy. And that effort attracted much attention abroad, especially with the Great Depression of the 1930s.

Online Study Center **Improve Your Grade**
Primary Source: The Fascist "Corporative State"

Despite the commitment to a new regime, however, fascism continued to compromise with pre-existing elites and institutions. The accommodation was especially evident in the arrangements with the Catholic Church that Mussolini worked out in 1929, formally ending the dispute between the church and the Italian state that had festered since national unification in

---

Matteotti murder The 1924 killing by fascist thugs of Italian moderate socialist Giacomo Matteotti; the public outcry following the murder eventually led Mussolini to commit to a more radical direction, which included the creation of a new, fascist form of state.

corporativism, corporative state The system established in fascist Italy beginning in 1926 that sought to involve people in public life not as citizens but as producers, through their roles in the economy.

1870. With the Lateran Pact, Mussolini restored a measure of sovereignty to the Vatican; with the Concordat, he gave the church significant roles in public education and marriage law.

This settlement of an old and thorny dispute afforded Mussolini a good deal of prestige among nonfascists at home and abroad. But compromise with the church displeased many committed fascists, who complained that giving this powerful, autonomous institution a role in Italian public life compromised fascism's totalitarian ideal. Such complaints led to a partial crackdown on Catholic youth organizations in 1931, as Mussolini continued trying to juggle traditionalist compromise and revolutionary pretension.

By the end of the 1920s, then, it remained unclear whether Italian fascism was a form of restoration or a form of revolution. It had restored order in Italy, overcoming the labor unrest of the immediate postwar years, but it was order on a new, antidemocratic basis. Yet the fascists claimed to be implementing a revolution of their own at the same time. Fascism could be violent and disruptive, dictatorial and repressive, but Mussolini's regime seemed dynamic and innovative. Though its ultimate direction remained nebulous, fascism attracted those elsewhere who were discontented with liberal democracy and Marxist socialism. It thus fed the volatility and ideological polarization that marked the European political order after World War I.

═══ SECTION SUMMARY ═══

- The question of whether to affiliate with the new Communist International (Comintern), established by the Russian Communists in 1919, split Marxist socialist parties throughout the world.

- The struggle for the Soviet leadership with the death of Lenin became intertwined with questions about communist priorities in the wake of the New Economic Policy adopted in 1921.

- A Stalinist revolution within the Soviet communist experiment had begun by 1930, but where it would lead was not at all clear.

- The fascist reaction against both liberalism and socialism reflected deep divisions in Italy over the significance of the Italian war effort.

- Once Mussolini committed himself to a decisively postliberal direction, the fascists fastened upon corporativism as the basis for a new, specifically fascist form of state.

TOWARD MASS SOCIETY

Why, and on what basis, did sexuality, gender roles, and the "new woman" provoke so much concern during this period?

After a few years of wild economic swings just after the war, Europe enjoyed renewed prosperity by the later 1920s. Common involvement in the war had blurred class lines and accelerated the trend toward what contemporaries began to call "mass society." As the new prosperity spread the fruits of industrialization more widely, ordinary people increasingly set the cultural tone, partly through new mass media such as film and radio. To some, the advent of mass society portended a welcome revitalization of culture and a more authentic kind of democracy, whereas others saw only a debasement of cultural standards and a susceptibility to populist demagoguery. But though the contours of mass society now became evident, social change did not keep up with the promise of—and the requirements for—democratic politics.

ECONOMIC READJUSTMENT AND THE NEW PROSPERITY

In their effort to return to normal, governments were quick to dismantle wartime planning and control mechanisms. But the needs of war had stimulated innovations that helped fuel the renewed economic growth of the 1920s. The civilian air industry, for example, developed rapidly during the decade by taking advantage of wartime work on aviation for military purposes. More generally, newer industries such as chemicals, electricity, and advanced machinery led the way to a new prosperity in the 1920s, which significantly altered patterns of life in the more industrialized parts of the West. The automobile, a luxury plaything for the wealthy before the war, began to be mass-produced in western Europe. In France, automobile production shot up dramatically, from 40,000 in 1920 to 254,000 in 1929.

But the heady pace masked problems that lay beneath the relative prosperity of the 1920s, even in victorious Britain and France. While new industries prospered, old ones declined in the face of new technologies and stronger foreign competition. In Britain, the sectors responsible for Britain's earlier industrial pre-eminence—textiles, coal, shipbuilding, and iron and steel—now had trouble competing. Rather than investing in new technologies, companies in these industries demanded government protection and imposed lower wages and longer hours on their workers. At the same time, British labor unions resisted the mechanization necessary to make these older industries more competitive.

Rather than realistically assessing Britain's prospects in the new international economy, British leaders sought to return to the prewar situation, based on the gold standard, with London the world's financial center. For many Britons, the government's announcement in 1925 that the British pound was again freely convertible to gold at 1914 exchange rates was the long-awaited indication that normality had returned at last. Yet the return to 1914 exchange rates overvalued the pound relative to the U.S. dollar, making British goods more expensive on export markets and making it still more difficult for aging British industries to compete.

The structural decline of older industries was clearest in Britain, but inflation and its psychological impact was most prominent in Germany and France. By the summer of 1923, Germany's response to the French occupation of the Ruhr had transformed an already serious inflationary problem, stemming from wartime deficit spending, into one of the great hyperinflations in history. At its height in November, when it took 4.2 trillion marks to equal a dollar, Germans were forced to cart wheelbarrows of paper money to stores to buy ordinary grocery items. By the end of 1923, the government managed to stabilize prices through currency reform and drastically reduced government spending—a combination that elicited greater cooperation from the victors. But the rampant inflation, and the readjustment necessary to control it, had wiped out the life savings of ordinary people while profiting speculators and those in debt, including some large industrialists. This inequity left scars that remained even as Germany enjoyed a measure of prosperity in the years that followed.

Inflation was less dramatic in France, but there, too, it affected perceptions and priorities in significant ways. For over a century, from the Napoleonic era to the outbreak of war in 1914, the value of the French franc had remained stable. But the war started France on an inflationary cycle that shattered the security of its many small savers—those, such as teachers and shopkeepers, who had been the backbone of the Third Republic. To repay war debts and rebuild war-damaged industries, the French government continued to run budget deficits, and thereby cause inflation, even after 1918. Runaway inflation threatened during 1925 and 1926, but the franc was finally restabilized in 1928, though at only about one-fifth its prewar value.

On the international level, war debts and reparations strained the financial system, creating problems with the financing of trade. But in the course of the 1920s, experts made adjustments that seemed to be returning the international exchange system to equilibrium. Only in retrospect, after the international capitalist system fell into crisis late in 1929, did it become clear how potent those strains were—and how inadequate the efforts at readjustment.

WORK, LEISURE, AND THE NEW POPULAR CULTURE

The wartime spur to industrialization produced a large increase in the industrial labor force all over Europe, and a good deal of labor unrest accompanied the transition to peacetime. Some of that agitation challenged factory discipline and authority relationships. Seeking to re-establish authority on a new basis for the competitive postwar world, business advocates fostered a new cult of efficiency and productivity, partly by adapting Taylorism and Fordism, influential American ideas about mass production. On the basis of his "time-and-motion" studies of factory labor, Frederick W. Taylor (1856–1915) argued that breaking down assembly-line production into small, repetitive tasks was the key to maximizing worker efficiency. In contrast, Henry Ford (1863–1947) linked the gospel of mass production to mass consumption. In exchange for accepting the discipline of the assembly line, the workers should be paid well enough to be able to buy the products they produced—even automobiles. Sharing in the prosperity that mass production made possible, factory workers would be loyal to the companies that employed them. Not all Europeans, however, welcomed the new ideas from America. In the new cult of efficiency and mass production, some saw an unwelcome sameness and a debasement of cultural standards.

Changing Roles for Women   In light of the major role women had played in the wartime labor force, the demand for women's suffrage proved irresistible in Britain, Germany, and much of Europe, though not yet in France or Italy. In Britain, where calls for women's suffrage had earlier met with controversy (see page 757), the right to vote was readily conceded in 1918, though at first only to women over 30. By now women no longer seemed a threat to the political system. And in fact British women, once they could vote, simply flowed into the existing parties, countering earlier hopes—and

The Sensational Josephine Baker

After moving from the United States to Paris in 1925, Baker quickly created a sensation as a cabaret dancer and singer. Her exotic costumes played on the European association of Africa with the wild and uninhibited. This poster advertises her appearance at the Folies-Bergère, a famed Parisian music hall.   *(The Granger Collection, New York)*

fears—that a specifically feminist political agenda would follow from women's suffrage.

Although there was much discussion of the "new woman," especially in Germany, the wider place of women in society and politics was uncertain during the 1920s, as the new sense of openness clashed with the desire to return to normal. (See the feature "The Visual Record: Advertising.") Female employment remained higher than before the war, but many women—willingly or not—returned home, yielding their jobs to the returning soldiers. The need to replace the men killed in the war lent renewed force to the traditional notion that women served society, and fulfilled themselves, by marrying and rearing families. More generally, some men found the emancipated "new woman" threatening, and after all the disruptions of war, male leaders sometimes assumed that the very stability of the political sphere depended on conventional gender roles. Still, the decade's innovative impulse brought into the public arena subjects—largely taboo before the war— that might portend changes in gender roles later on. The desire to be "modern" produced, for example, a more open, unsentimental, even scientific discussion of sexuality and reproduction.

The new "rationalization of sexuality" fed demands that governments provide access to sex counseling, birth control, and even abortion as they assumed ever greater responsibilities for promoting social health. This trend was especially prominent in Germany, although German innovators learned from experiments in the new Soviet Union and from the birth control movement that Margaret Sanger (1883–1966) was spearheading in the United States.

The more open and tolerant attitude toward sexuality affected popular entertainment—for example, Josephine Baker's dancing and costumes, which would have been unthinkable before the war. Another result was the emergence of a more visible gay subculture, prominent especially in the vibrant cabaret scene in Berlin during the 1920s.

Prosperity and the Culture of Leisure

Mass consumption followed from the mass production that created the new prosperity of the 1920s. As it became possible to mass-produce the products of the second industrial transformation, more people could afford automobiles, electrical gadgets such as radios and phonographs, and clothing of synthetic fabrics, developed through innovations in chemistry. First came rayon, produced in small quantities since 1891 but mass-produced beginning in the 1920s. In this new artificial form, silk, long one of the trappings of wealth, was now within the means of ordinary people.

Advertising

A sleek new automobile. A stylish "new woman" who'd adore a Christmas gift of jewelry. These images from the 1920s catch our eye even today, but why? The designs look "modern" somehow, and they convey particular messages about efficiency and the good life. What do such advertisements tell us about the changes at work in Western culture after World War I?

Advertising in one form or another is as old as civilization itself. But the advent of printing expanded possibilities, and the second industrial revolution led to a big boost in advertising by the 1890s, as ads for new products like bicycles and sewing machines appeared in newspapers and magazines. But it was during the 1920s that modern advertising came into its own. As mass consumption grew, advertising budgets expanded dramatically, and professional ad agencies emerged to study tastes and determine how to shape the desires of consumers. Moreover, the advent of commercial radio in 1920 opened a whole new set of possibilities, including the scope for musical jingles.

Mass consumption required advertising to show people what to want. And during the 1920s, ad agencies began offering images of the good life, seeking to define the popular sense of what it meant to be "modern." They often drew from the United States, which stood for efficiency and a fast-paced life of fun, pleasure, and consumerist abundance. So eager were the Germans to follow the U.S. lead in advertising that they adopted the term *sex appeal*, leaving it untranslated.

The new products featured in the print and broadcast media ran the gamut from automobiles to cosmetics, from rayon apparel to chewing gum. When the Wrigley Company of Chicago opened a factory in Germany in 1925, chewing gum quickly became associated with Americanization—and its use increased dramatically. But luxury goods were prominent as well, as in elegant ads such as the two shown here. Even for the many who could not afford expensive jewelry or the six-cylinder Opel, images of the good life stimulated the desire to buy less costly versions. Automobile consumption rose sharply during the 1920s, thanks also to the new techniques of mass production that Henry Ford had pioneered in the United States.

Although advertising served the economic interests of business by stimulating consumption, many began to view it as an art form as well. Far more attention was paid to its design, so the advertising "look" of the 1920s differed dramatically from anything seen before. As in the examples here, the new ads were often self-consciously modern, using simplified typefaces and stylized images suggesting the sleek efficiency and precision of the new machine age. The jewelry ad features an elegant contemporary typeface, and the German automobile ad of 1928 relies on crisp, bold forms and a clean, modern design.

The new prominence of advertising raised issues that were debated all over, but especially in Weimar Germany, where conditions remained unsettled even as a measure of prosperity returned by 1924. From cultural standards to gender roles, much was being called into question, and the wider implications of advertising were central to the "culture wars" of the period.

At an international advertising congress in Berlin in 1929, critics charged that advertising was furthering the debasement of standards already associated with mass culture and Americanization. Defenders countered that advertising was rejuvenating the mainstream culture, which had grown either stale and conventional or overblown and elitist. The fact that advertising served a commercial purpose need not mean cultural debasement. On the contrary, they argued, this new meshing of the best design with popular culture was healthy. In 1928 G. F. Hartlaub, a leading German art dealer, summed up a widespread view when he observed that advertising was a "truly social, collective, mass art, the only one we now have. It shapes the visual habits of that anonymous collectivity, the public. Little by little an artistic attitude is hammered into the mass soul by billboards."*

A particular advertising target was the "new woman," with her bobbed hair, short skirts, and freer lifestyle. But the image of women in advertisements was controversial, especially in Weimar Germany. Partly because of the simplification of female attire, images of the new woman in popular magazines provoked much concern about the "masculinization" of women by the mid-1920s. Some men found such images aggressive, even threatening.

---

*Quoted in John Willett, *Art and Politics in the Weimar Period: The New Sobriety, 1917–1933* (New York: Pantheon, 1978), p. 137. Translation modified slightly.

Jewelry Ad, 1920s: "Wear jewelry—
It makes you a winner. And it's the
ideal Christmas gift." *(akg-images)*

Car Ad, 1928: The Six-Cylinder Opel Hits the Jackpot
*(From Bärbel Schrader and Jürgen Schebera, The "Golden" Twenties: Art
and Literature in the Weimar Republic [New Haven: Yale University
Press, 1990]. Reproduced with permission.)*

Yet at the same time, advertising often assumed women to be master consumers—or perhaps merely mindless shoppers. In the holiday advertisement here, the woman is chic and liberated in one sense, but she is urged to drape herself with jewelry—to indulge in conventional ornamentation. This was also an age that claimed to value efficiency purified of ornament, as with the stripped-down typeface in the automobile ad. So though gender differentiation and women's roles were very much at issue in advertising, the relationship between portrayals of the new woman and genuine liberation remained uncertain.

Despite tensions and contradictions, advertising helped bring new issues to center stage after World War I. Although the ads of the 1920s assumed a prosperity that proved fleeting, the cultural change proved enduring. Eye-catching images of the sleek, the chic, the new—all bathed in "sex appeal"—became the staples of twentieth-century advertising, bound up with the new culture of mass consumption.

QUESTIONS

1. What factors led to the upsurge in advertising during the 1920s?

2. What seems specifically modern about the images we see here?

Online Study Center
Improve Your Grade Visual Record Activities

Innovation in Cinema
This poster advertises Fritz Lang's 1926 film *Metropolis*, which explored the dehumanization and exploitation of the modern city. *(Schulz-Neudamm, Metropolis, 1926. Lithograph, 83" × 36½". Gift of Universum-Film-Aktiengesellschaft. Photograph © 1997 The Museum of Modern Art, New York/Art Resource, NY)*

With the eight-hour workday increasingly the norm, growing attention was devoted to leisure as a positive source of human fulfillment—for everyone, not just the wealthy. European beach resorts grew crowded as more people had the time, and the means, to take vacations. An explosion of interest in soccer among Europeans paralleled the growth of professional baseball and college football in the United States. Huge stadiums were built across Europe.

The growth of leisure was linked to the development of mass media and mass culture. During the early 1920s radio became a commercial venture, reaching a mass audience in Europe, as in the United States and Canada. Although movies had begun to emerge as vehicles of popular entertainment even before the war, they came into their own during the 1920s, when the names of film stars became household words for the first time.

Exploiting the new popular fascination with air travel, the American Charles Lindbergh (1902–1974) captured the European imagination in 1927 with the first solo flight across the Atlantic. Lindbergh's feat epitomized the affirmative side of the decade—the sense that there were new worlds to conquer and that there still were heroes to admire, despite the ironies of the war and the ambiguities of the peace.

SOCIETY AND POLITICS IN THE VICTORIOUS DEMOCRACIES

France and Britain seemed the best positioned of the major European countries to take advantage of renewed peace and stability to confront the sociopolitical problems of the postwar era. And during the 1920s, each seemed to return to normal. But was normal good enough, in light of the rupture of the war and the challenges of the emerging mass society?

France Victory in the Great War seemed to belie France's prewar concerns about decadence and decline. In the immediate aftermath of the war, Clemenceau and other French leaders were confident in dealing with radical labor unrest and aggressive in translating the battlefield victory into a dominant position on the European continent. But the tremendous loss of French lives had produced a new fear—that France could not withstand another such challenge. The renewed confidence thus proved hollow.

Although some in prewar France had worried about falling behind rapidly industrializing Germany, victory seemed to have vindicated France's more cautious, balanced economy, with its blend of industry and agriculture. Thus the prewar mistrust of rapid industrial development continued. Rather than foster a program of economic modernization that might have promoted genuine security, the French pulled back even from the measure of state responsibility for the economy that had developed during the war.

To be sure, in France, as elsewhere, the 1920s was a decade of relative prosperity. Led by the oil and electricity industries, the economy grew at an annual rate of 4.6 percent between 1923 and 1929, double the prewar rate. Industrial production by 1929 was 40 percent higher than it had been in 1913. But, with the exception of Britain, other Western economies grew more rapidly during the 1920s, and the opportunity that growth afforded to modernize the French economy was not seized. Although government grants helped reconstruct almost eight thousand factories, most were simply rebuilt as they had been before the war. Moreover, the working class benefited little from the relative prosperity of the 1920s. Housing remained poor, wages failed to keep up with inflation, and France continued to lag behind other countries in social legislation.

Great Britain   Britain, too, made certain adjustments after the war but missed the chance to make others. The government's handling of the Easter Rebellion in Ireland in 1916 (see page 779) intensified anti-British feeling and fed further violence. But the British finally forged at least a provisional resolution. The first step was to partition Ireland, creating a separate Ulster, or Northern Ireland, from those counties with Protestant majorities. Ulster then remained under the British crown when a new independent Republic of Ireland was established in the larger, majority-Catholic part of the island in 1922.

The British political system remained stable between the wars, although the Labour Party supplanted the Liberals to become the dominant alternative to the Conservatives by the early 1920s. The Labour Party even got a brief taste of power when Ramsay MacDonald (1866–1937) formed Britain's first Labour government in January 1924. The coming of Labour to power resulted in a significant expansion of the governmental elite to incorporate those, like MacDonald himself, with genuinely working-class backgrounds.

However, it was the Conservative leader, Stanley Baldwin (1867–1947), who set the tone for British politics between the wars in three stints as prime minister from 1923 to 1937. Although he was the wealthy son of a steel manufacturer, Baldwin deliberately departed from the old aristocratic style of British Conservative politics. More down-to-earth and pragmatic than his predecessors, he was the first British prime minister to use radio effectively, and he made an effort to foster good relations with workers. Yet Baldwin's era was one of growing social tension.

With exports declining, unemployment remained high in Britain throughout the interwar period, never falling below 10 percent. The coal industry, though still the country's largest employer, had become a particular trouble spot in the British economy. As coal exports declined, British mine owners became ever more aggressive in their dealings with labor, finally, in 1926, insisting on a longer workday and a wage cut of 13 percent to restore competitiveness. The result was a coal miners' strike in May that promptly turned into a general strike, involving almost all of organized labor—about four million workers—in the most notable display of trade-union solidarity Britain had ever seen. For nine days the economy stood at a virtual standstill. But threats of arrest and a growing public backlash forced the union leadership to accept a compromise. The miners continued the strike on their own, but they finally returned to work six months later at considerably lower wages.

Although for somewhat different reasons, Britain and France both failed during the 1920s to take advantage of what would soon seem, in retrospect, to have been a precious opportunity to adjust their economies, heal social wounds, and create more genuinely democratic political systems. The lost opportunity would mean growing social tensions once the relative prosperity of the decade had ended.

======= S E C T I O N   S U M M A R Y =======

- The inflation that resulted from the war and its aftermath had long-term psychological consequences, most dramatically in Germany, but also in France.

- Adapting influential American ideas about mass production, business leaders throughout much of Europe fostered a new cult of efficiency and productivity as they sought to adjust to the more competitive postwar world economy.

- Although there was much discussion of the "new woman," reflecting a new sense of openness after the war, women were pulled in traditional as well as modernizing directions during the 1920s.

- Mass production yielded mass consumption, the growth of leisure, and the popularity of new media like movies and radio.

- Victory bred a certain complacency in Britain and France, each of which failed to take advantage of what would seem, in retrospect, to have been a precious opportunity to adjust their economies and deepen their democracies.

WEIMAR GERMANY AND THE TRIALS OF THE NEW DEMOCRACIES

What factors made the future of the new German democracy so uncertain during the 1920s?

The war was supposed to have paved the way for democracy, and new democracies emerged in Germany, Poland, and elsewhere in Europe. But almost everywhere they led tortured lives and soon gave way to more authoritarian forms of government. So the postwar decade did not see the extension of the political democracy that optimistic observers associated with the emerging mass society.

The most significant test took place in Germany, where a new democracy emerged from the republic proclaimed in November 1918. Elections in January 1919 produced a constituent assembly that convened in Weimar, a town associated with what seemed the most humane German cultural traditions. The assembly gave this new Weimar Republic, as it came to be called, Germany's first fully democratic constitution. But the Weimar democracy had great difficulty establishing its legitimacy, and it was suffering serious strains by 1930.

DEMOCRACY ABORTED IN EAST-CENTRAL EUROPE

New democracies were established in much of central and eastern Europe after the war, but except in Czechoslovakia and Finland, the practice of parliamentary government did not match the initial promise. Democracy seemed divisive and ineffective, so one country after another adopted a more authoritarian alternative during the 1920s and early 1930s.

Poland offers the most dramatic example. Although its democratic constitution of 1921 established a cabinet responsible to a parliamentary majority, the parliament fragmented into so many parties that instability proved endemic from the start. Poland had fourteen different ministries from November 1918 to May 1926, when Marshal Josef Pilsudski led a coup d'état that replaced parliamentary government with an authoritarian regime stressing national unity. This suppression of democracy came as a relief to many Poles—and was welcomed even by the trade unions. After Pilsudski's death in 1935, a group of colonels ruled Poland until the country was conquered by Nazi Germany in 1939.

Democracy proved hard to manage in east-central Europe partly because of the economic difficulties resulting from the breakup of the Habsburg system. New national borders meant new economic barriers that disrupted long-standing economic relationships. Industrial centers such as Vienna and Budapest found themselves cut off from their traditional markets and sources of raw materials. In what was now Poland, Silesians had long been oriented toward Germany, Galicians toward Vienna, and those in eastern Poland toward Russia. Thus the new Polish nation-state was hardly a cohesive economic unit.

The countries of east-central Europe remained overwhelmingly agrarian, and this, too, proved unconducive to democracy. Land reform that accompanied the transition to democracy made small properties the norm in much of the region. But because these units were often too small to be efficient, agricultural output actually decreased after land was redistributed, most dramatically in Romania and Yugoslavia. When agricultural prices declined in the late 1920s, many peasants had no choice but to sell out to larger landowners. What had seemed a progressive and democratic reform thus failed to provide a stable agrarian smallholder base for democracy.

GERMANY'S CAUTIOUS REVOLUTION, 1919–1920

Meanwhile, in Germany, the Weimar Republic began under particularly difficult circumstances. Born of military defeat, it was promptly forced to take responsibility for the harsh Treaty of Versailles in 1919. During its first years, moreover, the regime encountered severe economic dislocation, culminating in the hyperinflation of 1923, as well as ideological polarization that threatened to tear the country apart.

Although Germany had strong military and authoritarian traditions, the initial threat to the new democracy came not from the right, disoriented and discredited, but from the left, stimulated by the Russian example. Those seeking further revolution, and those who feared it, could easily equate the proclamation of a German republic with the first revolution in Russia; as in Russia, the new, more democratic order could prove a mere prelude to communist revolution. Even after Karl Liebknecht and Rosa Luxemburg were captured and murdered in Berlin in January 1915, a serious chance of further revolution persisted through May 1919, and communist revolutionary agitation continued to flare up until the end of 1923.

As it turned out, there was no further revolution, partly because the parallel between Germany and Russia carried only so far. The new German government had made peace, whereas the leaders of the provisional government in Russia had sought to continue the war. Furthermore, those who ended up controlling the councils that sprang up in Germany during the fall of 1918 favored political democracy, not communist revolution; therefore, they supported the provisional government.

Even so, the revolutionary minority constituted a credible threat. And the new government made repression of the extreme left a priority—even if it meant leaving in place some of the institutions and personnel of the old imperial system. In November 1918, at the birth of the new republic, the moderate socialist leader Friedrich Ebert had agreed with General Wilhelm Groener, the new army head, to preserve the old imperial officer corps to help prevent further revolution. But when the regular army, weakened by war and defeat, proved unable to control radical agitation in Berlin in December, it seemed the republic would have to take extraordinary measures to defend itself from the revolutionary left. With the support of Ebert and Groener, Gustav Noske (1868–1946), the minister of national defense, began to organize "Free Corps," volunteer paramilitary groups to be used against the revolutionaries. Noske, who was a socialist, but one long supportive of the military, noted that "somebody will have to be the bloodhound—I won't shirk the responsibility."[2]

During the first five months of 1919, the government unleashed the Free Corps to crush leftist movements all over Germany, often with wanton brutality. In relying on right-wing paramilitary groups, the republic's leaders were playing with fire, but the immediate threat at this point came from the left. In 1920, however, the government faced a right-wing coup attempt, the Kapp Putsch. The army declined to defend the republic, but the government managed to survive thanks largely to a general strike by leftist workers. The republic's early leaders had to juggle both extremes because, as one of them put it, the Weimar Republic was "a candle burning at both ends."

Though sporadic street fighting by paramilitary groups continued, the republic survived its traumatic birth and achieved an uneasy stability by 1924. But Germany's postwar revolution had remained confined to the political level. There was no program to break up the cartels, with their concentrations of economic power. Even on the level of government personnel, continuity was more striking than change. There was no effort to build a loyal republican army, and no attempt to purge the bureaucracy and the judiciary of antidemocratic elements from the old imperial order. When right-wing extremists assassinated prominent leaders, such as the Jewish industrialist Walther Rathenau in 1922, the courts often proved unwilling to prosecute those responsible.

In light of the republic's eventual failure, the willingness of its early leaders to leave intact so much from the old order has made them easy targets of criticism. It can be argued, however, that the course they followed—heading off the extreme left, reassuring the established elites, and playing for time—was the republic's best chance for success. The new regime might establish its legitimacy by inertia, much like the Third Republic in France, which had similarly been born of defeat. Even lacking the sentimental fervor that had earlier surrounded democratic ideals, Germans might gradually become "republicans of reason," recognizing that this regime could be a framework for prosperity and renewed German prominence in international affairs. In the event of an early crisis, however, a republic consolidating itself in this cautious way might well find fewer defenders than opponents.

The constituent assembly elections of January 1919 took place before the peace conference had produced the widely detested Treaty of Versailles. When the first regular parliamentary elections finally were held in June 1920, the three moderate parties that had led the new government, and that had been forced to accept the treaty, suffered a major defeat, together dropping from 76 to 47 percent of the seats. These were the parties most committed to democratic institutions, but they were never again to achieve a parliamentary majority.

The 1920 elections revealed the problems of polarization and lack of consensus that would bedevil, and eventually ruin, the Weimar Republic. Because the electorate found it difficult to agree, or even to compromise, Germany settled into a multiparty system that led to unstable coalition government. And the strength, or potential strength, of the extremes immeasurably complicated political life for those trying to make the new democracy work. On the left, the Communist Party constantly criticized the more moderate Socialist Party for supporting the republic. On the right, the Nationalist Party (DNVP) played on nationalist resentments and fears of the extreme left—but the result was similarly to dilute support for the new republic. To the right even of the Nationalists were Adolf Hitler's National Socialists, or Nazis, who were noisy and often violent, but they attracted little electoral support before 1930.

GUSTAV STRESEMANN AND THE SCOPE FOR GRADUAL CONSOLIDATION

All was not necessarily lost for the republic when the three moderate, pro-Weimar parties were defeated in 1920. Germans who were unsupportive or hostile at first might be gradually won over. After the death of President Ebert in 1925, Paul von Hindenburg, the emperor's field marshal, was elected president. Depending on the circumstances, having a conservative military leader from the old order in this role could prove

Hopes for Peace

Foreign ministers Aristide Briand (*left*) of France and Gustav Stresemann of Germany spearheaded the improved international relations that bred optimism during the late 1920s. *(Corbis)*

advantageous, or damaging, for the future of democracy. As long as there was scope for consolidation, Hindenburg's presidency might help persuade skeptics that the new regime was legitimate and a worthy object of German patriotism. But when crisis came by 1930, Hindenburg was quick to give up on parliamentary government—with devastating results.

The individual who best exemplified the possibility of winning converts to the Weimar Republic was **Gustav Stresemann** (STRAY-zuh-mahn) (1878–1929), the leader of the German People's Party (DVP), a conservative party that did not support the republic at the outset. But it was relatively flexible and offered at least the possibility of broadening the republic's base of support. As chancellor, and especially as foreign minister, Stresemann proved the republic's leading statesman.

Stresemann's background and instincts were not democratic, but by the end of 1920 Germany's postwar political volatility had convinced him that if the new republic should go under, the outcome would not be the conservative monarchy he preferred but the triumph of the extreme left. Moreover, it had become clear that the new democratic republic was not likely to be revolutionary on the socioeconomic level. It made sense, then, to work actively to make the new regime succeed. From within this framework Germany could pursue its international aims, negotiating modifications of the Versailles treaty and returning to great power status.

Stresemann became chancellor in August 1923, when inflation was raging out of control. Within months his government managed to get the German economy functioning effectively again, partly because the French agreed that an international commission should review the reparations question, specifying realistic amounts based on Germany's ability to pay. During the summer of 1924, a commission led by the American financier Charles G. Dawes produced the Dawes Plan, which remained in force until 1929. The plan worked well by pinpointing revenue sources, lowering payments, providing loans, and securing the stability of the German currency. With the expiration of the Dawes Plan in 1929, the Young Plan, conceived by American businessman Owen D. Young, removed Allied controls over the German economy and specified that Germany pay reparations until 1988. The annual amount was less than Germany had been paying, so it was expected that this plan constituted a permanent, and reasonable, settlement.

Quite apart from the immediate economic issue, Stresemann understood that better relations with France had to be a priority if Germany was to return to great power status. French foreign minister Aristide Briand (bree-AHN) (1862–1932) shared Stresemann's desire for improved relations, and together they engineered a new, more conciliatory spirit in international affairs. Its most substantial fruit was the **Treaty of Locarno** of 1925. France and Germany accepted the postwar border between the two countries, which meant that Germany gave up any claim to Alsace-Lorraine. France, for its part, renounced the sort of direct military intervention in Germany that it had attempted with the Ruhr invasion of 1923 and agreed to begin withdrawing troops from the Rhineland ahead of schedule. Germany freely accepted France's key advantage, the demilitarization of the Rhineland, and Britain and Italy now explicitly guaranteed the measure.

By accepting the status quo in the west, Stresemann was freeing Germany to concentrate on eastern Europe, where he envisioned gradual but substantial revision in the territorial settlement that had resulted

Gustav Stresemann German statesman of the Weimar Republic, he secured a reduction of Germany's reparations payments and negotiated the Treaty of Locarno, paving the way for Germany's entry into the League of Nations in 1926.

Treaty of Locarno The 1925 treaty in which Germany, again recognized as a diplomatic equal, freely agreed with France, Britain, and Italy to accept key aspects of the Versailles peace settlement.

from the war. Especially with the creation of Poland, that settlement had come partly at Germany's expense. Stresemann, then, was pursuing German interests, not subordinating them to some larger European vision. But he was willing to compromise and, for the most part, to play by the rules as he did so.

With the Locarno treaty, the victors accepted Germany as a diplomatic equal for the first time since the war. Germany's return to good graces culminated in its entry into the League of Nations in 1926. The new spirit of reconciliation was widely welcomed. Indeed, Stresemann and Briand were joint winners of the Nobel Peace Prize for 1926.

Still, those to the right in Germany continually exploited German resentments by criticizing Stresemann's compromises with Germany's former enemies—in accepting the Dawes and Young Plans, for example. Even when successful from Stresemann's own perspective, these negotiations cost his party electoral support. The controversy that surrounded Stresemann, a German conservative pursuing conventional national interests, indicates how volatile the German political situation remained, even with the improved economic and diplomatic climate of the later 1920s. Still, Strese-

mann's diplomatic successes were considerable, and his death in October 1929, at the age of 51, was a severe blow to the republic.

AN UNCERTAIN BALANCE SHEET

Although Weimar Germany was better off in 1929 than it had been in 1923, the political consensus remained weak, the political party system remained fragmented, and unstable coalition government remained the rule. Although the immediate threat from the extreme left had been overcome, many German conservatives continued to fear that the unstable Weimar democracy would eventually open the way to a socialist or communist regime.

The Weimar Republic epitomized the overall European situation during the 1920s. As long as prosperity and international cooperation continued, the new democracy in Germany might endure, even come to thrive. But the new institutions in Germany, like the wider framework of prosperity and stability, were fragile indeed. At the first opportunity, antidemocratic elites, taking advantage of their access to President Hindenburg, would begin plotting to replace the Weimar Republic with a more authoritarian alternative.

═══════ S E C T I O N   S U M M A R Y ═══════

- Although new democracies were established in central and eastern Europe after the war, parliamentary government proved divisive and ineffective in much of the region, so one country after another adopted a more authoritarian alternative.

- Germany's democratic political revolution was not accompanied by major changes in socioeconomic relations—or even in the administrative structures inherited from Wilhelm II's government.

- Because of polarization and lack of consensus in the electorate, the Weimar Republic quickly fell into a

multiparty system that led to unstable coalition government.

- A conservative monarchist by instinct, Gustav Stresemann rallied to the Weimar Republic because he found it the best framework for restoring Germany to prosperity and international influence—and for heading off leftist revolution.

- Although many Germans continued to resent the peace settlement, the Treaty of Locarno of 1925 seemed to suggest a hopeful new spirit of reconciliation between France and Germany.

THE SEARCH FOR MEANING IN A DISORDERED WORLD

How did cultural and intellectual leaders differ over the place of "tradition" as they sought to suggest how to come to terms with the new situation of the 1920s?

or all its vitality, the new culture of the 1920s had something brittle about it. The forces that produced a sense of openness, liberation, and innovation were disruptive and disturbing at the same time.

Perhaps the frenetic pace only masked a deeper sense that things had started to come apart and might well get worse. The era called forth some notable diagnoses and prescriptions, but, not surprisingly, they differed dramatically.

ANXIETY, ALIENATION, AND DISILLUSIONMENT

Concern about the dangers of the emerging mass civilization was especially clear in the *Revolt of the Masses* (1930), by the influential Spanish thinker José Ortega y Gasset (1883–1955). In his view, contemporary experience had shown that ordinary people, incapable of creating standards, remained content with the least common denominator. Communism and fascism indicated the violent, intolerant, and ultimately barbaric quality of the new mass age. But Ortega found the same tendencies in American-style democracy. The fact that much of Europe seemed to be moving toward the mass politics and culture of the United States was a symptom of the deeper problem, not a solution.

Concern with cultural decline was part of a wider pessimism about the condition of the West, which stood in stark contrast to the belief in progress, and the attendant confidence in Western superiority, that had been essential to Western self-understanding before 1914. The German thinker Oswald Spengler (1880–1936) made concern with decline almost fashionable with his bestseller of the immediate postwar years, *The Decline of the West* (1918), which offered a cyclical theory purporting to explain how spirituality and creativity were giving way to a materialistic mass-based culture in the West.

To Sigmund Freud (1856–1939), the eruption of violence and hatred during the war and afterward indicated a deep, instinctual problem in the human makeup (see page 754). In his gloomy essay *Civilization and Its Discontents* (1930), Freud suggested that the progress of civilization requires individuals to bottle up their aggressive instincts, which are directed inward as guilt, but which may erupt in violent outbursts. This notion raised questions not only about the scope for continued progress but also about the plausibility of the Wilsonian ideals that had surrounded the end of the war. Perhaps, with civilization growing more complex, the Great War had been only the beginning of a new era of hatred and violence.

The sense that something incomprehensible, even nightmarish, haunted modern civilization, with its ever more complex bureaucracies, technologies, and cities, found vivid expression in the work of the Czech Jewish writer Franz Kafka (1883–1924), most notably in the novels *The Trial* and *The Castle,* published posthumously in the mid-1920s. In a world that claimed to be increasingly rational, Kafka's individual is the lonely, fragile plaything of forces utterly beyond reason, comprehension, and control. In such a world, the quest for law, or meaning, or God, is futile, ridiculous.

Especially in the unsettled conditions of Weimar Germany, the anxiety of the 1920s tended to take extreme forms, from irrational activism to a preoccupation with death. Suicides among students increased dramatically. Youthful alienation prompted the novelist Jakob Wassermann (1873–1934) to caution German young people in 1932 that not all action is good simply because it is action, that feeling is not always better than reason and discipline, and that youth is not in itself a badge of superiority.

RECASTING THE TRADITION

Expressions of disillusionment revealed something about human experience in the unsettled new world, but they were sometimes morbid and self-indulgent. Other cultural leaders sought to be more positive; the challenge was not to give vent to new anxieties but to find antidotes to them. One direction was to recast traditional categories—in the arts, in religion, in politics—to make them relevant to contemporary experience. Although not all were optimistic about human prospects, many found such a renewal of tradition to be the best hope for responding to the disarray of the postwar world.

Among artists, even those who had been prominent in the modernist avant-garde before the war now pulled back from headlong experimentation and sought to pull things back together, though on a new basis. In music, composers as different as Igor Stravinsky (1882–1971) and Paul Hindemith (1895–1963) adapted earlier styles, although often in a somewhat ironic spirit, as they sought to weave new means of expression into familiar forms. The overall tendency toward neoclassicism during the period was an effort to give musical composition a renewed basis of order.

One of the most striking responses to the anxieties of this increasingly secular age was a wave of neo-orthodox religious thinking, most prominent in Protestants like the German-Swiss theologian Karl Barth (1886–1968). In his *Epistle to the Romans* (1919), Barth reacted against the liberal theology, the attempt to marry religious categories to secular progress, that had become prominent by the later nineteenth century. The war, especially, had seemed to shatter the liberal notion that the hand of God was at work in history, and Barth emphasized the radical cleft between God and our human, historical world, sunken in sin. Recalling the arguments of Augustine and Luther, he portrayed humanity as utterly lost, capable only of a difficult relationship with God, through faith, grace, and revelation.

With democracy faring poorly in parts of Europe, and with fascism and communism claiming to offer superior alternatives, some sought to make new sense of the liberal democratic tradition. In Italy, Benedetto Croce (CROH-chay) (1866–1952) agreed with critics that the old justifications, based on natural law or util-

THE WRITTEN RECORD

TRADITION AND WOMEN: THE CONDITIONS OF INDEPENDENCE

Speaking in 1928 about the situation of women writers, the British novelist Virginia Woolf raised questions that were relevant to all women seeking the opportunity to realize their potential. Indeed, her reflections about the value of difference and the need for particular traditions inspired those seeking equal opportunity for decades to come. And her question about why we know so little about women's lives in the past helped stimulate later historians to investigate the experiences of ordinary people.

Woman . . . pervades poetry from cover to cover; she is all but absent from history. . . . Occasionally an individual woman is mentioned, an Elizabeth, or a Mary; a queen or a great lady. But by no possible means could middle-class women with nothing but brains and character at their command have taken part in any one of the great movements which, brought together, constitute the historian's view of the past. . . . What one wants . . . is a mass of information; at what age did she marry; how many children had she as a rule; what was her house like; had she a room to herself; did she do the cooking; would she be likely to have a servant? All these facts lie somewhere, presumably, in parish registers and account books; the life of the average Elizabethan woman must be scattered about somewhere, could one collect it and make a book of it. It would be ambitious beyond my daring, I thought, looking about the shelves for books that were not there, to suggest to the students of those famous colleges that they should rewrite history, though I own that it often seems a little queer as it is, unreal, lop-sided. . . .

But whatever effect discouragement and criticism had upon their writing—and I believe they had a very great effect—that was unimportant compared with the other difficulty which faced them (I was still considering those early nineteenth-century novelists) when they came to set their thoughts on paper—that is that they had no tradition behind them, or one so short and partial that it was of little help. For we think back through our mothers if we are women. It is useless to go to the great men writers for help, however much one may go to them for pleasure. . . .

. . . Women have sat indoors all these millions of years, so that by this time the very walls are permeated by their creative force, which has, indeed, so overcharged the capacity of bricks and mortar that it must needs harness itself to pens and brushes and business and politics. But this creative power differs greatly from the creative power of men. And one must conclude that it would be a thousand pities if it were hindered or wasted, for it was won by centuries of the most drastic discipline, and there is nothing to take its place. It would be a thousand pities if women wrote like men, or lived like men, or looked like men. . . . Ought not education to bring out and fortify the differences rather than the similarities?

QUESTIONS

1. Why does Woolf find something "lop-sided" about the body of historical writing available in her own time, and how does she believe the problem might be overcome?

2. Why does Woolf suggest that education ought to nurture a distinctive female voice?

Source: Virginia Woolf, *A Room of One's Own* (San Diego: Harcourt Brace Jovanovich, Harvest/HBJ, 1989), pp. 43–45, 76, 87–88.

---

itarianism, were deeply inadequate, but he also became one of Europe's most influential antifascists. The most significant innovations in modern thought, he argued, show us why democratic values, institutions, and practices are precisely what we need. We human beings are free, creative agents of a history that we make as best we can, without quite understanding what will result from what we do. Humility, tolerance, and equal access to political participation are essential to the process whereby the world is endlessly remade.

The new political challenges also stimulated fresh thinking within the Marxist tradition. By showing that Marxism could encompass consciousness as well as economic relationships, the Hungarian Georg Lukács (LOO-kash) (1885–1971) invited a far more sophisticated Marxist analysis of capitalist culture than had been possible before. Lukács accented the progressive role of realistic fiction and attacked the disordered fictional world of Kafka, which seemed to abandon all hope for human understanding of the forces of history. Though more eclectic, the Institute for Social Research, founded in Frankfurt, Germany, in 1923, gave rise to an influential tradition of criticism of capitalist civilization in what came to be known as the Frankfurt

School. These innovations helped give the Marxist tradition a new lease on life in the West, even as it was developing in unforeseen ways in the Soviet Union.

THE SEARCH FOR A NEW TRADITION

While some intellectuals sought renewal from within the European tradition, others insisted that a more radical break was needed—but also that the elements for a viable new cultural tradition were available.

Reflecting on the situation of women writers in 1928, the British novelist Virginia Woolf (1882–1941) showed how women in the past had suffered from the absence of a tradition of writing by women. By the 1920s, women had made important strides, but Woolf suggested that further advance required a more self-conscious effort by women to develop their own tradition. Most basically, women needed greater financial independence so that they could have the time for scholarship, the leisure for cultivated conversation and travel, and the privacy of "a room of one's own." Woolf also envisioned a new sort of historical inquiry, focusing on how ordinary women lived their lives, that could show contemporary women where they came from—and thus deepen their sense of identity. (See the box "The Written Record: Tradition and Women: The Conditions of Independence.")

A very different effort to establish a new tradition developed in Paris, where the poet André Breton (1896–1966) spearheaded the surrealist movement in literature and the visual arts. **Surrealism** grew directly from Dada, an artistic movement that had emerged in neutral Zurich, Switzerland, and elsewhere during the war. Radically hostile to the war, Dada artists developed shocking, sometimes nihilistic forms to deal with a reality that now seemed senseless and out of control. Some made collages from gutter trash; others indulged

in nonsense or relied on chance to guide their art. By the early 1920s, however, the surrealists felt it was time to create a new and deeper basis of order after the willful disordering of Dada. Having learned from Freud about the subconscious, they sought to adapt Dada's novel techniques—especially the use of chance—to gain access to the subconscious mind, which they believed contains a deeper truth, without the overlay of logic, reason, and conscious control.

But other artists, seeking to embrace the modern industrial world in a more positive spirit, found surrealism merely escapist. Among them was Walter Gropius (1883–1969), a pioneering modernist architect and leader of an influential German art school, the **Bauhaus,** during the 1920s. Gropius held that it was possible to establish new forms of culture, even a new tradition, that could be affirmative and reassuring in the face of the postwar cultural disarray. Rather than putting up familiar neoclassical or neo-Gothic buildings, "feigning a culture that has long since disappeared," society had to face up to the kind of civilization it had become—industrial, technological, efficient, urban, mass-based. If people chose carefully from among the elements of this new machine-based civilization, they could again have a culture that worked, an "integrated pattern for living."[3]

This "constructive," pro-modern impulse was particularly prominent in Germany, but it could be found all over—in the modernists of the Russian Revolution, in the French painter Fernand Léger (leh-ZHAY) (1881–1955), in the Swiss architect Le Corbusier (luh cor-BOO-zee-ay) (1887–1965). Whereas many of their contemporaries were at best ambivalent about the masses, these artists sought to bring high art and mass society together in the interests of both. And they welcomed the new patterns of life that seemed to be emerging in the modern world of mass production and fast-paced cities.

SECTION SUMMARY

- The shock of the war produced a sense of disillusionment and even decline that took many forms in the culture of the 1920s.

- Some accented the scope for recasting traditions during the 1920s, but others insisted on the need to form new traditions if the era's challenges were to be met.

- The contrast between surrealism and the German Bauhaus suggested a wider disagreement over

whether Western culture was excessively rational or not rational enough.

- Whereas some, like Ortega y Gasset, were at best ambivalent about the advent of modern mass society, others welcomed it and sought to devise cultural forms that seemed more appropriate to a mass machine age.

surrealism   A literary and artistic movement that emerged in Paris in the early 1920s, it sought to explore the subconscious, which it believed to hold something liberating for human beings.

Bauhaus   An influential German art school, founded in 1919, that sought to adopt contemporary materials to develop new forms of architecture, design, and urban planning in response to the cultural uncertainty that followed World War I.

The Bauhaus Building, Dessau
The Bauhaus, an influential but controversial German art school, was established in Weimar in 1919 and then moved to Dessau in 1925. Walter Gropius, its founding director, spearheaded the design of its headquarters building. Constructed in 1925–1926, it immediately became a symbol of the Weimar modernism that some admired and others detested.   *(Vanni/Art Resource, NY)*

CHAPTER SUMMARY

Online Study Center **ACE the Test**

How did the differing priorities of Britain and France affect international relations during the 1920s?

Why did Italy turn from parliamentary democracy to fascism even after sharing in the victory in World War I?

Why, and on what basis, did sexuality, gender roles, and the "new woman" provoke so much concern during this period?

What factors made the future of the new German democracy so uncertain during the 1920s?

How did cultural and intellectual leaders differ over the place of "tradition" as they sought to suggest how to come to terms with the new situation of the 1920s?

n the wake of the most destructive war in history, questions about the new international framework, established at the peace conference of 1919–1920, were bound to be central. Although they bore the major responsibility for enforcing the peace, France and Britain seemed to drift apart as the British, preoccupied with colonial concerns, distanced themselves from politics on the Continent. Whereas France was willing to intervene actively to enforce the Versailles treaty, Britain placed greater faith in reconciliation and the new League of Nations.

The threat of leftist revolution was a major factor in the emergence of fascism in Italy, although the fascists claimed to offer a "third way," a modern alternative to *both* Marxist socialism and liberal democracy. Once Mussolini committed himself to a decisively postliberal direction, the fascists fastened upon corporativism as the basis for a new, specifically fascist form of state. Corporativism, they claimed, offered a way of transcending the class divisions accented by Marxism while also involving people in public life in more constant and direct ways than democratic institutions had made possible.

The war had seemingly enhanced opportunities for women, and a new sense of openness and possibility carried into the postwar period. During the 1920s sexuality, reproductive choices, gender roles, and family life were open to discussion as never before in the West. But in light of demographic losses and the seemingly brutalizing effects of the war, women encountered considerable pressure to conform to traditional roles of mothering and nurturing. Although the image of the liberated "new woman" was central to the era, women themselves were sometimes torn between conflicting roles and expectations.

Germany's Weimar Republic provided the central test of the bright hopes for democracy that marked the beginning of the postwar era. Yet the new German democracy was launched under the difficult circumstances of defeat, harsh peace terms, and ongoing revolutionary unrest. Moreover, the limits of political consensus in Germany meant a fragmented electorate, a complicated multiparty system, and a reliance on unstable coalition governments. Although the improved economic and diplomatic situation by 1925 enhanced the prospects for democracy, the Weimar Republic remained fragile and vulnerable.

In light of the cultural disruptions of the war and its aftermath, many intellectuals insisted that certain traditions could be recast to provide the sense of direction that people needed. But there was wide disagreement over which traditions were relevant. Whereas some pointed to religion, others fastened upon Marxism. Still others found it essential to return to more accessible forms in the arts, turning from the avant-garde experiment that had marked the immediate prewar period. At the same time, however, figures as disparate as Virginia Woolf, André Breton, and Walter Gropius insisted that the means were available to develop *new* traditions, more appropriate to the needs and possibilities of the postwar world.

LOOKING AHEAD

Despite the ferment that marked the years since World War I, Europe seemed on its way to restabilization by early 1929. Of the three most volatile of the major countries, Italy and Germany seemed to be settling down, and the Soviet Union, though embarking on an unprecedented experiment in socioeconomic engineering, was by this point looking inward, not actively seeking to export revolution. But the Great Depression, growing from the strains in the postwar economic restabilization, was just around the corner. When the decade of the 1920s is taken on its own terms, it is clear that the vitality, the renewed prosperity, and the diplomatic goodwill were all real. But so were the unresolved problems that made the 1920s a prelude to the more difficult 1930s, when the notion that postwar Europe had returned to normal came to seem but a fairy tale.

KEY TERMS

Maginot Line (p. 810)

fascism (p. 811)

Comintern (Third, or Communist,
    International) (p. 813)

New Economic Policy (NEP) (p. 814)

Joseph Stalin (p. 814)

Benito Mussolini (p. 817)

Matteotti murder (p. 818)

corporativism, corporative state (p. 818)

Gustav Stresemann (p. 828)

Treaty of Locarno (p. 828)

surrealism (p. 832)

Bauhaus (p. 832)

Online Study Center
Improve Your Grade Flashcards

SUGGESTED READING

Bush, Barbara. *Imperialism, Race, and Resistance: Africa and Britain, 1919–1945*. 1999. Focuses on western and southern Africa; probes the changing nature of British colonial rule in light of growing resistance during the pivotal interwar period.

De Grazia, Victoria. *Irresistible Empire: America's Advance Through Twentieth-Century Europe*. 2005. An illuminating account of the impact of the American business ethos—from Rotary Clubs to chain stores to advertising—on twentieth-century Europe, including key steps during the 1920s.

Gay, Peter. *Weimar Culture: The Outsider as Insider*. 1970. An influential study providing a good sense of the conflicting impulses—the embrace of modernity, the nostalgia for wholeness, the sense of foreboding—that made German culture so intense and vital during the 1920s.

Gentile, Emilio. *The Sacralization of Politics in Fascist Italy*. 1996. An engaging account of the rituals, symbols, and myths that, beginning in Italy during the 1920s, fed the first overtly totalitarian experiment.

Kolb, Eberhard. *The Weimar Republic*. 1988. Provides a good overall survey, then pinpoints the recent trends in research and the questions at issue among historians of the period.

Pedersen, Susan. *Family, Dependence, and the Origins of the Welfare State: Britain and France, 1914–1945*. 1993. An effective comparative study showing how concerns about gender roles and family relations helped shape discussion and policy as government assumed greater responsibility for social welfare. Detailed but readable; a landmark in the new gender history.

Peukert, Detlev. *The Weimar Republic: The Crisis of Classical Modernity*. 1992. An influential interpretive study, accenting the strains stemming from the rapid modernization of the 1920s. Stresses the loss of political legitimacy even before the onset of the Depression.

Stites, Richard. *Revolutionary Dreams: Utopian Visions and Experimental Life in the Russian Revolution*. 1989. A vivid account of the utopian aspirations that gave the new communist regime emotional force from 1917 to 1930.

Tucker, Robert C. *Stalin as Revolutionary, 1879–1929: A Study in History and Personality*. 1973. A pioneering account of Stalin's early years and rise to power, probing the sources of the elements of character and personality that helped shape his subsequent rule.

Wright, Jonathan. *Gustav Stresemann: Weimar's Greatest Statesman*. 2002. A balanced study showing that Stresemann's willingness to play by the democratic rules was important in giving Weimar democracy a chance.

NOTES

1. Benito Mussolini, speech to the Italian Chamber of Deputies, January 3, 1925, from Charles F. Delzell, ed., *Mediterranean Fascism, 1919–1945* (New York: Harper & Row, 1970), pp. 59–60.

2. Quoted in Robert G. L. Waite, *Vanguard of Nazism: The Free Corps Movement in Postwar Germany, 1918–1923* (New York: W. W. Norton, 1969), pp. 14–15.

3. Walter Gropius, *Scope of Total Architecture* (New York: Collier Books, 1962), pp. 15, 67.

27

THE TORTURED DECADE, 1930–1939

¡No pasarán! ("They shall not pass") Defending the democratic republic during the Spanish civil war. *(Biblioteca Nacional, Madrid)*

"They shall not pass," proclaimed the charismatic Spanish communist Dolores Ibarruri (ee-bah-RUHR-ee) (1895–1989), whose impassioned speeches and radio broadcasts helped inspire the heroic defense of Madrid during the civil war that gripped Spain, and captured the attention of the world, during the later 1930s. Known as *La Pasionaria*—the passion flower—Ibarruri became a living legend for her role in defending the Spanish republic against the antidemocratic Nationalists seeking to overthrow it. But the Republican side lost, and she spent thirty-eight years in exile before returning to Spain in 1977, after the end of the military dictatorship that had resulted from the Spanish civil war.

In her effort to rally the Republican side, Ibarruri stressed the political power of women, and indeed women were prominent in the citizen militias defending Madrid and other Spanish cities. Women fought for the republic partly because it seemed to open new opportunities for them, especially as it became more radical by 1936. But just as some women welcomed the new direction, others became politically active on the opposing Nationalist side—to support the church, to combat divorce, to defend a separate sphere for women as the guardians of private life and family values.

The ideological polarization that characterized the Spanish civil war reflected the expanding reach of politics in the 1930s, when economic depression and the challenge from new, antidemocratic governments immeasurably complicated the European situation. The mechanisms used to realign the international economy after World War I had seemed effective for most of the 1920s, but by 1929 they were beginning to backfire, helping to trigger the Great Depression. During the early 1930s the economic crisis intensified sociopolitical strains all over the Western world—and beyond, heightening anti-Western feeling. In Germany the Depression helped undermine the Weimar Republic and opened the way for the new Nazi regime under Adolf Hitler, whose policies led through a series of diplomatic crises to a new European war.

German Nazism paralleled Italian fascism in its reliance on a single charismatic leader, its willingness to use violence, and its hostility to both parliamentary democracy and Marxist socialism. But Nazism emphasized racism

CHAPTER OUTLINE

THE GREAT DEPRESSION

THE STALINIST REVOLUTION IN THE SOVIET UNION

HITLER AND NAZISM IN GERMANY

FASCIST CHALLENGE AND ANTIFASCIST RESPONSE, 1934–1939

THE COMING OF WORLD WAR II, 1935–1939

KEY TERMS

collectivization

show trials

gulag

Adolf Hitler

National Socialist (Nazi) Party

Schutzstaffel (SS)

Kristallnacht (Crystal Night)

"euthanasia" program

popular front

Rome-Berlin Axis

remilitarization of the Rhineland

appeasement

Nazi-Soviet Pact

Online Study Center

This icon will direct you to interactive map and primary source activities on the website **college.hmco.com/pic/noble5e**

and anti-Semitism in a way that Italian fascism did not, and it more radically transformed its society.

At the same time, Stalin's communist regime in the Soviet Union seemed to converge, in some ways, with these new fascist regimes—especially with German Nazism. So though they expressed widely different aims, Stalinism and Nazism are sometimes lumped together as instances of "totalitarianism." Both apparently sought control over all aspects of society, partly through the use of secret police agencies. But on closer inspection, the forms of coercion and violence in the Soviet and German regimes by the later 1930s were quite different, and the extent to which each can be understood as an instance of totalitarianism remains controversial.

Fascism, Nazism, and communism seemed able to sidestep—or surmount—the ills of the Depression, yet they stood opposed to the parliamentary democracy that had long seemed the direction of progressive political change. So the democratic movement appeared to lose its momentum in the face of the political and economic challenges of the 1930s. The defeat, by early 1939, of the democratic republic in Spain by the authoritarian Nationalists seemed to exemplify the political direction of the decade.

FOCUS QUESTIONS

With what array of measures did governments respond to the Great Depression?

Why did the Stalinist attempt to build "socialism in one country" lead to the "terror-famine" of 1932–1933 and the "great terror" of 1937–1938?

Through what measures did the Nazi regime claim to be improving the quality of the German population?

Why did the "popular front" strategy prove counterproductive in both France and Spain?

Why did the other countries not stop Hitler's Germany before it was strong enough to start a new European war in 1939?

THE GREAT DEPRESSION

With what array of measures did governments respond to the Great Depression?

If any single event can be said to have triggered the world economic crisis of the early 1930s, it was the stock market crash of October 1929 in the United States. But that crash had such an impact only because the new international economic order after World War I was extremely fragile. By October 1929, in fact, production was already declining in all the major Western countries except France.

The economies of Germany and the states of east-central Europe remained particularly vulnerable after the war, and in the increasingly interdependent economic world, their weaknesses magnified problems that started elsewhere. The crash of the U.S. stock market led to a restriction of credit in central Europe, which triggered a more general contraction in production and trade. Facing cruel dilemmas, policymakers proved unable to master the situation for the first few years of the crisis.

CAUSES OF THE DEPRESSION

Certain economic sectors, especially coal mining and agriculture, were already suffering severe problems by the mid-1920s, well before the stock market crash. British coal exports fell partly because oil and hydro-electricity were rapidly developing as alternatives. Unemployment in Britain was never less than 10 percent even in the best of times between the wars. In agriculture high prices worldwide during the war produced oversupply, which, in turn, led to a sharp drop in prices once the war was over. During the later 1920s, bumper harvests of grain and rice in many parts of the world renewed the downward pressure on prices. The result of low agricultural prices was a diminished demand for industrial goods, which impeded growth in the world economy.

Throughout the 1920s, finance ministers and central bankers had difficulty juggling the economic imbalances created by the war, centering on war debts to the United States and German reparations obligations to France, Britain, and Belgium. The strains in the system finally caught up with policymakers by 1929, when an international restriction of credit forced an end to the international economic cooperation that had been attempted throughout the decade.

The shaky postwar economic system depended on U.S. bank loans to Germany, funneled partly by international agreements but also drawn by high interest rates. By 1928, however, U.S. investors were rapidly withdrawing their capital from Germany in search of the higher returns that could be made in the booming U.S. stock market. This shift tightened credit in Germany. Then the crash of the overpriced U.S. market in October 1929 deepened the problem by forcing suddenly strapped American investors to pull still more of their funds out of Germany. This process continued over the next two years, weakening the major banks in Germany and the other countries of central Europe, which were closely tied to the German economy. In May 1931 the bankruptcy of Vienna's most powerful bank, the Credit-Anstalt, made it clear that a crisis of potentially catastrophic proportions was in progress.

Despite attempts at adjustment on the international level, fears of bank failure or currency devaluation led to runs on the banks and currencies of Germany and central Europe. To maintain the value of the domestic currency in world markets, and thereby to resist the withdrawal of capital, government policymakers raised interest rates. This measure was not sufficient to stem the capital hemorrhage, but by restricting credit still more, it further dampened domestic economic activity.

Finally, the Germans seemed to have no choice but to freeze foreign assets—that is, to cease allowing conversion of assets held in German marks to other currencies. In this atmosphere, investors seeking the safest place for their capital tried to cash in currency for gold—or for British pounds, which could then be converted to gold. Europe's flight to gold, however, soon put such pressure on the British currency that Britain was forced to devalue the pound and sever it from the gold standard in September 1931. This proved the definitive end of the worldwide system of economic exchange based on the gold standard that had gradually crystallized during the nineteenth century.

The absence of a single standard of exchange, combined with various currency restrictions, made foreign trade more difficult, thereby diminishing it further. So did the scramble for tariff protection that proved a widespread response to the developing crisis. Crucial was the U.S. Smoot-Hawley Tariff Act of June 1930, which raised taxes on imports by 50 to 100 percent,

CHRONOLOGY

October 1929	U.S. stock market crash helps trigger Great Depression
December 1929	Forced collectivization in Soviet agriculture begins
June 1930	Smoot-Hawley Tariff Act (U.S.)
May 1931	Bankruptcy of Vienna's Credit-Anstalt
January 1933	Hitler becomes German chancellor
December 1934	Assassination of Kirov
March 1935	Hitler announces rearmament
October 1935	Italy invades Ethiopia
March 1936	Germany remilitarizes the Rhineland
May 1936	Blum becomes French popular front prime minister
July 1936	Spanish civil war begins
March 1938	Third Moscow show trial; Bukharin and others convicted and executed
	Anschluss: Germany absorbs Austria
September 1938	"Appeasement": Munich conference ends Sudetenland crisis
November 1938	Crystal Night pogrom
March 1939	Dismemberment of Czechoslovakia
May 1939	Pact of Steel binds fascist Italy and Nazi Germany
August 23, 1939	Nazi-Soviet Pact
September 1, 1939	Germany invades Poland
September 3, 1939	Britain and France declare war on Germany

forcing other nations to take comparable steps. Even Britain, long a bastion of free trade, adopted a peacetime tariff for the first time in nearly a century with the Import Duties Act of 1932, which imposed a 10 percent tax on most imports.

The decline of trade spread depression throughout the world economic system. By 1933 most major European countries were able to export no more than two-thirds, and in some cases as little as one-third, of the amount they had sold in 1929. At the same time, losses from international bank failures contracted credit and purchasing power and furthered the downward spiral, until by 1932 the European economies had shrunk to a little over half their 1929 size. This was the astonishing outcome of the short-lived prosperity of the 1920s.

Unemployment in Britain
The Depression hit Britain hard—and its effects continued to be felt throughout the 1930s. These unemployed shipyard workers from Jarrow, in northeastern England, are marching to London in 1936 to present a protest petition. *(Hulton Archive/Getty Images)*

CONSEQUENCES AND RESPONSES

The Depression was essentially a radical contraction in economic activity; with less being produced and sold, demand for labor declined sharply. In Germany industrial production by early 1933 was only half what it had been in 1929, and roughly six million Germans, or one-third of the labor force, were unemployed.

Although its timing and severity varied, the Depression profoundly affected the lives of ordinary people throughout the Western world and beyond. Unemployment produced widespread malnutrition, which led, in turn, to sharp increases in such diseases as tuberculosis, scarlet fever, and rickets. The decline in employment opportunities helped produce a backlash against the ideal of the "new woman," working outside the home, which had been a prominent aspect of the new freedom of the 1920s in Germany and elsewhere. Even those men and women who hung on to jobs suffered from growing insecurity. In his aptly titled *Little Man, What Now?* (1932), the German novelist Hans Fallada (1893–1947) explored the effects of the Depression on members of the lower middle class—store clerks, shop owners, civil servants. Such people were first resentful, then resigned, as their dreams of security, of "order and cleanliness," fell apart.

During the first years of the Depression, central bankers everywhere sought to balance budgets in order to reassure investors and stabilize currencies. With economies contracting and tax revenues declining, the only way to balance the budget was to sharply reduce government spending. In addition, governments responded to the decline in exports by forcing wages down, seeking to enhance competitiveness abroad. But by cutting purchasing power at home, both these measures reinforced the slowdown in economic activity.

Economic policymakers based their responses on the "classical" economic model that had developed from the ideas of Adam Smith in the eighteenth century (see page 658). According to this model, a benign "invisible hand" ensured that a free-market price for labor, for capital, and for goods and services would produce an ongoing tendency toward economic equilibrium. A downturn in the business cycle was a normal and necessary adjustment; government interference would only upset this self-adjusting mechanism.

By 1932, however, it was clear that the conventional response was not working, and governments began seeking more actively to stimulate the economy. Although the British economist John Maynard Keynes would outline the rationale for governmental intervention in technical economic terms in 1936, governments could only experiment, and strategies varied widely. (See the box "The Written Record: The Government's Role in Managing a Free-Market Economy.") In the United States, Franklin D. Roosevelt (1882–1945) defeated the incumbent president, Herbert Hoover, in 1932 with the promise of a New Deal—a commitment to increase government spending to restore purchasing power. In fascist Italy, a state agency created to infuse capital into failing companies proved a reasonably effective basis for collaboration between government and business. In Germany, economics minister Hjalmar Schacht (1877–1970) mounted an energetic assault on the economic problem after Hitler came to power in 1933. Government measures sealed off the German mark from international

THE GOVERNMENT'S ROLE IN MANAGING A FREE-MARKET ECONOMY

In 1936, at the height of the Depression, the British economist John Maynard Keynes published The General Theory of Employment, Interest and Money, *which proved the most influential work in economics of the twentieth century. While recognizing the advantages of a free-market economy, Keynes noted that capitalism seemed to entail a built-in tendency toward unemployment, dramatically evident in the Depression. Thus some people were attracted to socialist or statist alternatives, which might include, for example, the wholesale nationalization of industry. But Keynes insisted that a more active role for government in managing the capitalist economy could overcome the tendency toward unemployment while preserving a democratic framework and the advantages of a market economy. Government could manage the economy especially through the "socialization of investment"— absorbing money through taxation and spending it to stimulate the economy toward full employment.*

The outstanding faults of the economic society in which we live are its failure to provide for full employment and its arbitrary and inequitable distribution of wealth and incomes. . . .

. . . I conceive, therefore, that a somewhat comprehensive socialisation of investment will prove the only means of securing an approximation to full employment; though this need not exclude all manner of compromises and of devices by which public authority will co-operate with private initiative. But beyond this no obvious case is made out for a system of State Socialism which would embrace most of the economic life of the community. It is not the ownership of the instruments of production which it is important for the State to assume. If the State is able to determine the aggregate amount of resources devoted to augmenting the instruments and the basic rate of reward to those who own them, it will have accomplished all that is necessary. Moreover, the necessary measures of socialisation can be introduced gradually and without a break in the general traditions of society. . . .

. . . The central controls necessary to ensure full employment will, of course, involve a large extension of the traditional functions of government. Furthermore, the modern classical theory has itself called attention to various conditions in which the free play of economic forces may need to be curbed or guided. But there will still remain a wide field for the exercise of private initiative and responsibility. Within this field the traditional advantages of individualism will still hold good.

Let us stop for a moment to remind ourselves what these advantages are. They are partly advantages of efficiency—the advantages of decentralisation and of the play of self-interest. . . .

Whilst, therefore, the enlargement of the functions of government, involved in the task of adjusting to one another the propensity to consume and inducement to invest, would seem to a nineteenth-century publicist or to a contemporary American financier to be a terrific encroachment on individualism, I defend it, on the contrary, both as the only practicable means of avoiding the destruction of existing economic forms in their entirety and as the condition of the successful functioning of individual initiative. . . .

The authoritarian state systems of to-day seem to solve the problem of unemployment at the expense of efficiency and of freedom. It is certain that the world will not much longer tolerate the unemployment which, apart from brief intervals of excitement, is associated—and, in my opinion, inevitably associated—with present-day capitalistic individualism. But it may be possible by a right analysis of the problem to cure the disease whilst preserving efficiency and freedom.

QUESTIONS

1. Why does Keynes argue for a considerably expanded role for government in coordinating the capitalist economy?

2. In what sense is Keynes trying to save free-market capitalism in light of the Depression and the appeal of the alternatives emerging in Italy, Germany, and the Soviet Union?

Source: John Maynard Keynes, *The General Theory of Employment, Interest and Money* (New York: Harcourt, Brace & World, n.d.), pp. 372, 378–381. Reprinted by permission of J. S. Dring.

---

fluctuations, stimulated public spending—partly on rearmament—and kept wages low. By 1935 Germany was back to full employment. This success added tremendously to Hitler's popularity.

High unemployment in Norway, Sweden, and Denmark helped Social Democrats win power in all three of these Scandinavian countries by the mid-1930s. The new left-leaning governments responded to the economic

GANDHI ADVOCATES NONVIOLENCE

Mohandas Gandhi, a successful English-educated lawyer, emerged as a major force in the movement for Indian independence just after World War I. Calling first for a strategy of noncooperation with the British colonial overlords, Gandhi gradually developed a philosophy of nonviolent civil disobedience, which won widespread sympathy for the cause of Indian independence. The following excerpts from articles published in 1935 and 1939—years notable for outbreaks of violence elsewhere—explain the significance of nonviolence to Gandhi's overall strategy.

Non-violence to be a creed has to be all-pervasive. I cannot be non-violent about one activity of mine and violent about others. That would be a policy, not a life-force. That being so, I cannot be indifferent about the war that Italy is now waging against Abyssinia. . . . India has an unbroken tradition of non-violence from times immemorial. But at no time in her ancient history, as far as I know it, has it had complete non-violence in action pervading the whole land. Nevertheless, it is my unshakeable belief that her destiny is to deliver the message of non-violence to mankind. . . .

. . . India as a nation is not non-violent in the full sense of the term. . . . Her non-violence is that of the weak. . . . She lacks the ability to offer physical resistance. She has no consciousness of strength. She is conscious only of her weakness. If she were otherwise, there would be no communal problems, nor political. If she were non-violent in the consciousness of her strength, Englishmen would lose their role of distrustful conquerors. We may talk politically as we like and often legitimately blame the English rulers. But if we, as Indians, could but for a moment visualize ourselves as a strong people disdaining to strike, we should cease to fear Englishmen whether as soldiers, traders or administrators, and they to distrust us. Therefore if we became truly non-violent we should carry Englishmen with us in all we might do. In other words, we being millions would be the greatest moral force in the world, and Italy would listen to our friendly word. . . .

. . . [W]hen society is deliberately constructed in accordance with the law of non-violence, its structure will be different in material particulars from what it is today. But I cannot say in advance what the government based wholly on non-violence will be like.

What is happening today is disregard of the law of non-violence and enthronement of violence as if it were an eternal law. The democracies, therefore, that we see at work in England, America and France are only so called, because they are no less based on violence than Nazi Germany, Fascist Italy or even Soviet Russia. The only difference is that the violence of the last three is much better organized than that of the three democratic powers. Nevertheless we see today a mad race for outdoing one another in the matter of armaments. And if and when the clash comes, as it is bound to come one day, the democracies win, they will do so only because they will have the backing of their peoples who imagine that they have a voice in their own government whereas in the other three cases the peoples might rebel against their own dictatorships.

Holding the view that without the recognition of non-violence on a national scale there is no such thing as a constitutional or democratic government, I devote my energy to the propagation of non-violence as the law of our life—individual, social, political, national and international. I fancy that I have seen the light, though dimly. I write cautiously, for I do not profess to know the whole of the Law. If I know the successes of my experiments, I know also my failures. But the successes are enough to fill me with undying hope. I have often said that if one takes care of the means, the end will take care of itself. Non-violence is the means, the end for every nation is complete independence.

QUESTIONS

1. What is the difference between "strong" and "weak" nonviolence in Gandhi's thinking?

2. Why does Gandhi play down the difference between the democracies and the dictatorships of the West?

Source: Raghavan Iyer, ed., *The Essential Writings of Mahatma Gandhi* (Delhi: Oxford University Press, 1991), pp. 245–247, 262–263. Copyright © 1991 by Navajivan Trust. Reprinted by permission of Navajivan Trust.

crisis not by a frontal assault on capitalism but by pioneering the "welfare state," providing such benefits as health care, unemployment insurance, and family allowances. To pay for the new welfare safety net, the Scandinavian countries adopted a high level of progressive taxation and pared military expenditures to a minimum. The turn to a welfare state eased the immediate human costs of the Depression and helped restore production by stimulating demand. At the same time, the Scandinavian model attracted much admiration as a "third way" between free-market capitalism and the various dictatorial extremes.

In the other European democracies the Depression proved more intractable. Although Britain saw some recovery by the mid-1930s, it was especially the rearmament of the later 1930s, financed by borrowing, or deficit spending, that got the British economy growing again. France, less dependent on international trade, experienced the consequences of the world crisis only gradually. But by the early 1930s, France, too, was suffering its effects, which lingered to the end of the decade, helping to poison the political atmosphere.

THE IMPACT BEYOND THE WEST

The radical restriction of international trade meant a sharp decline in demand for the basic commodities that colonial and other regions exported to the industrialized West. Economic strains fed nationalist, anti-Western sentiments in colonial nations. The increase in misery among rural villagers in India, for example, spread the movement for national independence from urban elites to the rural masses. In this context Mohandas Gandhi, who had become known by 1920 for advocating noncooperation with the British, became the first leader to win a mass following throughout the Indian subcontinent (see pages 897 and 901). Encouraging villagers to boycott British goods, Gandhi accented simplicity, self-reliance, and an overall strategy of nonviolent civil disobedience based on Indian traditions. (See the box "The Global Record: Gandhi Advocates Nonviolence.")

In Japan, the strains of the Great Depression helped produce precisely the turn to imperialist violence that Gandhi sought to counter. Densely populated yet lacking raw materials, Japan was particularly dependent on international trade and reacted strongly as increasing tariffs elsewhere cut sharply into Japanese exports. Led by young army officers who were already eager for a less subservient form of Westernization, Japan turned to aggressive imperialism. As justification, the Japanese began arguing that they were spearheading a wider struggle to free East Asia from Western imperialism. (See the box "The Global Record: Japan's 'Pan-Asian' Mission" on page 887 in Chapter 28.) Attacking in 1931, Japanese forces quickly reduced Manchuria to a puppet state, but the Japanese met stubborn resistance when they began seeking to extend this conquest to the rest of China in 1937.

Japanese pressure indirectly advanced the rise of the Chinese communist movement, led by Mao Zedong (Mao Tse-tung, 1893–1976). Securing a base in the Yanan district in 1936, Mao began seeking to apply Marxism-Leninism to China through land reform and other measures to link the Communist Party elite to the Chinese peasantry. Mao was notable among those adapting Western ideas to build an indigenous movement that would at once overcome Western imperialism and create an alternative to Western liberal capitalism.

━━━━━━━━ S E C T I O N   S U M M A R Y ━━━━━━━━

- The new international economic interdependence after World War I entailed strains that were difficult to understand at the time—and that eventually helped produce the Great Depression.

- The effort to respond to the economic downturn through the principles of classical economics only deepened the crisis.

- The new regimes of the extreme left and right won greater prestige in some circles because they seemed

to be surviving the global economic crisis more successfully than the capitalist democracies.

- Gradually the democratic governments began trying out more innovative, interventionist responses to the Depression.

- By restricting imports into the industrialized West, the Depression hurt the non-Western world and helped fuel anticolonialist sentiment.

THE STALINIST REVOLUTION IN THE SOVIET UNION

Why did the Stalinist attempt to build "socialism in one country" lead to the "terror-famine" of 1932–1933 and the "great terror" of 1937–1938?

Seeking to build "socialism in one country," Joseph Stalin led the Soviet Union during the 1930s through an astounding transformation that mixed achievement with brutality and terror in often tragic ways. The resulting governmental system, which gave Stalin unprecedented power, proved crucial

to the outcome of the great experiment that had begun with the Russian Revolution of 1917. But whether the fateful turn of the 1930s had been implicit in the Leninist revolutionary model all along or stemmed mostly from unforeseen circumstances and Stalin's idiosyncratic personality remains uncertain.

Collectivization in Soviet Agriculture
At the "New Life" collective farm, not far from Moscow, women stand for the morning roll call. The Soviet collectivization effort of the 1930s rested in important measure on the forced mobilization of peasant women.
(Endeavor Group UK)

CRASH INDUSTRIALIZATION AND FORCED COLLECTIVIZATION

Stalin's program of rapid industrialization based on forced **collectivization** in agriculture began in earnest at the beginning of 1930. It entailed an assault on the better-off peasants, or *kulaks,* who were often sent to labor camps in Siberia while their lands were taken over by the government. The remaining peasants were herded into new government-controlled collective farms. So unpopular was this measure that many peasants simply killed their livestock or smashed their farm implements rather than have them collectivized. During the first two months of 1930, as many as fourteen million head of cattle were slaughtered, resulting in an orgy of meat eating and a shortage of draft animals. By 1934 the number of cattle in the Soviet Union was barely half what it had been in 1928.

Online Study Center **Improve Your Grade**
Primary Source: Collectivization in the Soviet Union: A Peasant's Report

Collectivization served, as intended, to squeeze from the peasantry the resources needed to finance industrialization, but it was carried out with extreme brutality. What was being squeezed was not merely a surplus—the state's extractions cut into subsistence. So while Soviet agricultural exports increased after 1930,

large numbers of peasants starved to death. The great famine that developed during 1932–1933 resulted in between five million and six million deaths, over half of them in Ukraine. This "terror-famine" went unrecorded in the Soviet press, and the Soviets refused help from international relief agencies.

By 1937 almost all Soviet agriculture took place on collective farms—or on state farms set up in areas not previously under agriculture. However, restrictions on private plots and livestock ownership were eased slightly after 1933, and partly as a result, agriculture rebounded and living standards began to rise. By the late 1930s, moreover, significant increases in industrial output had established solid foundations in heavy industry, including the bases for military production.

In pursuing this program, Stalin played up the great historical drama surrounding the Soviet experiment, with its incredible targets and goals. Suggestions by some that the pace could not be maintained only proved grist for Stalin's mill: "No, comrades," he told a workers' conference early in 1931, "the tempo must not be reduced. On the contrary, we must increase it as much as is within our powers and capabilities. . . . To slow the tempo would mean falling behind. And those who fall behind get beaten. . . . Do you want our socialist fatherland to be beaten and to lose its independence? . . . We are fifty or a hundred years behind the advanced countries. We must make good this distance in ten years. Either we do this or they will crush us."[1]

Soviet propaganda, including art in the official socialist realist style, glorified the achievements of the

collectivization Soviet program under Stalin that reshaped agriculture by forcing peasants into government-controlled collective farms in order to better finance rapid industrialization.

new Soviet industrial and agricultural workers. "Stakhanovism (stah-KAH-nov-izm)," named for a coal miner who had heroically exceeded his production quota in 1935, became the term for the prodigious economic achievements that the regime valued as it proclaimed the superiority of the communist system.

But whatever its successes, this forced development program created many inefficiencies and entailed tremendous human costs. The Soviet Union could probably have done at least as well, with much less suffering, through other strategies of industrial development. Moreover, Stalin's program departed from certain socialist principles—egalitarianism in wages, for example—that the regime had taken very seriously during the late 1920s. By 1931, bureaucratic managers, concerned simply with maximizing output, were openly favoring workers in certain industries. Collective bargaining and the right to strike had vanished from the workers' arsenal.

FROM OPPOSITION TO TERROR, 1932–1938

Stalin's radical course, with its brutality and uncertain economic justification, quickly provoked opposition. During the summer of 1932, a group centered on M. N. Ryutin (ree-YOU-tin) (1890–1937) circulated among party leaders a two-hundred-page tract calling for a retreat from Stalin's economic program and a return to democracy within the party. It advocated readmitting those who had been expelled—including Stalin's archenemy, Leon Trotsky. Moreover, the document strongly condemned Stalin personally, describing him as "the evil genius of the Russian Revolution, who, motivated by a personal desire for power and revenge, brought the Revolution to the verge of ruin."[2]

Stalin promptly had Ryutin and his associates ousted from the party, then arrested and imprisoned. But especially as the international situation grew menacing during the 1930s, Stalin became ever more preoccupied with the scope for further opposition. Both Germany and Japan exhibited expansionist aims that might threaten Soviet territories. Trotsky from exile might work with foreign agents and Soviet dissidents to sabotage the Soviet development effort.

In December 1934 the assassination of Sergei Kirov (KIH-roff) (1888–1934), party leader of Leningrad (the former Petrograd), indicated the potential for violence. But whether Stalin was actually responsible for the assassination, or simply felt vulnerable because of it, remains uncertain. In any case, the determination to root out "wreckers," those assumed to be sabotaging the great Soviet experiment, led gradually to purges, **show trials,** and even a kind of terror, with several categories

of citizens vulnerable to arbitrary arrest by the secret police. By the time it wound down, early in 1939, this "great terror" had significantly changed the communist regime—and Soviet society. But though the bare facts are clear, what to make of them is not.

In the three Moscow show trials, which took place during a twenty-month period from 1936 to 1938, noted Bolsheviks, including Nikolai Bukharin and major functionaries such as Genrikh Yagoda, recently removed as chief of the secret police, confessed to a series of sensational trumped-up charges: that they had been behind the assassination of Kirov, that they would like to have killed Stalin, that they constituted an "anti-Soviet, Trotskyite center," spying for Germany and Japan and preparing to sabotage Soviet industry in the event of war. Almost all the accused, including Bukharin and others who had been central to the 1917 revolution, were convicted and executed. Soviet authorities did not dare risk public trial for the few who refused, even in the face of torture, to play their assigned roles and confess. Among them was Ryutin, who was shot in secret early in 1937.

During 1937 a purge wiped out much of the top ranks of the army, with half the entire officer corps shot or imprisoned in response to unfounded charges of spying and treason. The Communist Party underwent several purges, culminating in the great purge of 1937 and 1938. Of the roughly two thousand delegates to the 1934 congress of the Communist Party, over half were shot during the next few years. The most prominent were especially vulnerable. Indeed, 114 of the 139 central committee members elected at the 1934 party congress had been shot or sent to a forced labor camp by 1939.

The first such camps were established under Lenin in 1918, during the civil war, but the camp system expanded exponentially under Stalin during the 1930s, coming to play a major economic role. This network of forced labor camps—there were eventually at least 476 of them—became known as the **gulag,** originally an acronym for "main camp administration."

Although considerable controversy remains over the number of victims of the Stalinist revolution, the totals are staggering. According to one influential high-end estimate, 8.5 million of the approximately 160 million people in the Soviet Union were arrested during 1937 and 1938, and of these perhaps 1 million were executed by shooting. Half of those belonging to the Communist Party—1.2 million people—were arrested; of these, 600,000 were executed, and most of the rest died in gulag camps. Altogether, the terror surrounding the several purges resulted in as many as 8 million deaths. Estimates of the death toll from all of Stalin's

show trials   Trials staged for ideological and propaganda reasons in the USSR.

gulag   An acronym for "main camp administration," it was a network of forced labor camps for political prisoners in the Soviet Union.

policies of the 1930s, including the forced collectivizations, range as high as 20 million.

COMMUNISM AND STALINISM

What was going on in this bizarre and lethal combination of episodes? Obviously Stalinism was one possible outcome of Leninist communism, but was it the logical, even the inevitable, outcome? Leninism had accented centralized authority and the scope for human will to force events, so it may have created a framework in which Stalinism was likely to emerge. Yet Stalin's personal idiosyncrasies and growing paranoia seem to have been crucial for the Soviet system to develop as it did. But though he ended up the regime's undisputed leader, Stalin was part of a wider dynamic.

It was long assumed that Stalin was pursuing a coordinated policy of terror to create a system of total control. Yet recent research has shown that he was often merely improvising, responding to a situation that had become chaotic, out of control, as the Communists tried to carry through a revolution in a backward country. No one had ever attempted this sort of forced industrialization based on a centrally planned economy. At once idealistic, inexperienced, and suspicious, the regime's leaders really believed that failures must be due to sabotage—that "wreckers" were seeking to undermine the heroic Soviet experiment. Moreover, though Stalin tended to blow them out of proportion, there were genuine threats to the Soviet regime and his own leadership by the mid-1930s.

Whereas the terror was long viewed as almost random, it is now clearer that those in the upper and middle reaches of the Soviet system were the most vulnerable. Top officials encouraged ordinary workers to provide information about plant managers and local party officials who seemed incompetent or corrupt. And whether to serve the revolution or to vent personal resentments, such workers often took the initiative in denouncing their superiors, thereby playing important roles in the dynamic that developed.

But what explains the "confessions" that invariably resulted from the bizarre show trials? The accused sometimes succumbed to torture, and to threats to their families. But some, at least, offered false confessions because they believed that in doing so they were still serving the communist cause. All along, the revolution had required a willingness to compromise personal scruples, including "bourgeois" concerns about personal honor and dignity. Even though false, these confessions could help the communist regime ward off the genuine dangers it faced. So in confessing, the accused would be serving the long-term cause, which they believed to be bigger than Stalin and the issues of the moment. What some could not see—or admit—was that the triumph of Stalinism was fatally compromising the original revolutionary vision.

Although much was unplanned and even out of control, Stalin's ultimate responsibility for the lethal dynamic of the later 1930s is undeniable. At the height of the terror, he personally approved lists for execution, and he took advantage of the chain of events to crush all actual or imagined opposition. By 1939 Stalin loyalists constituted the entire party leadership.

Even as some turned away in disillusionment or despair, others found the regime's ruthlessness in rooting out its apparent enemies evidence of its ongoing revolutionary purpose. And whereas Stalin was not a charismatic leader like Hitler or Mussolini, he was coming for many to embody the ongoing promise of the communist experiment.

━━━━━━━ S E C T I O N S U M M A R Y ━━━━━━━

- Forced collectivization was a way—ultimately a brutal way—of extracting the agricultural surplus from the peasantry to finance rapid industrialization in the Soviet Union.

- The *gulag,* the network of forced labor camps, expanded dramatically with the Stalinist revolution of the 1930s—and especially with the "great terror" of 1937–1938.

- Soviet leaders really believed that failures must be due to sabotage—that "wreckers" were seeking to undermine the heroic communist experiment.

- Although Stalin's ultimate responsibility is clear, the great terror of 1937–1938 grew not from some conscious design but from a momentum that spun out of control.

- Stemming from an effort to root out "wreckers," the terror especially affected those in the upper and middle reaches of the Soviet system.

HITLER AND NAZISM IN GERMANY

Through what measures did the Nazi regime claim to be improving the quality of the German population?

Beset with problems from the start, the Weimar Republic lay gravely wounded by 1932. Various antidemocratic groups competed to replace it. The winner was the Nazi movement, led by **Adolf Hitler,** who became chancellor in January 1933. It was especially Hitler's new regime in Germany that made the 1930s so tortured, for Hitler not only radically transformed German society but fundamentally altered the power balance in Europe.

Nazism took inspiration from Italian fascism, but Hitler's regime proved more dynamic—and more troubling—than Mussolini's. Nazism was not conventionally revolutionary, in the sense of mounting a frontal challenge to the existing socioeconomic order. Some of its themes were traditionalist and even antimodernizing. But in the final analysis Nazism was anything but conservative. Indeed, it constituted a direct assault on what had long been held as the best of Western civilization.

THE EMERGENCE OF NAZISM AND THE CRISIS OF THE WEIMAR REPUBLIC

The **National Socialist German Workers' (Nazi) Party** (NSDAP) emerged from the turbulent situation in Munich just after the war. A center of leftist agitation, the city also became a hotbed of the radical right, nurturing a number of new nationalist, militantly anticommunist political groups. One of them, a workers' party founded under the aegis of the right-wing Thule Society early in 1919, attracted the attention of Adolf Hitler, who soon gave it his personal stamp.

Adolf Hitler (1889–1945) had been born not German but Austrian, the son of a middling government official. As a young man he had gone to Vienna, hoping to become an artist, but he failed to gain admission to the Viennese Academy of Fine Arts. By 1913 he had become a German nationalist hostile to the multinational Habsburg empire, and he emigrated to Germany to escape service in the Austrian army. He was not opposed to military service per se, however, and

when war broke out in 1914, he immediately volunteered for service in the German army.

Corporal Hitler experienced firsthand the fighting at the front and, as a courier, performed bravely and effectively. Indeed, he was in a field hospital being treated for gas poisoning when the war ended. Although his fellow soldiers considered him quirky and introverted, Hitler found the war experience crucial; it was during the war, he said later, that he "found himself."

Following his release from the hospital, Hitler worked for the army in routine surveillance of extremist groups in Munich. In this role he joined the infant German Workers' Party late in 1919. When his first political speech at a rally in February 1920 proved a resounding success, Hitler began to believe he could play a special political role. From this point, he gradually developed the confidence to lead a new nationalist, anticommunist, and anti-Weimar movement.

But Hitler jumped the gun in November 1923 when, with Erich Ludendorff at his side, he led the Beer Hall Putsch in Munich, an abortive attempt to launch a march on Berlin to overthrow the republic. On trial after this effort failed, Hitler gained greater national visibility as he denounced the Versailles treaty and the Weimar government. Still, *Mein Kampf* (*My Battle*), the political tract that he wrote while in prison during 1924, sold poorly. To most, Hitler was simply a right-wing rabble-rouser whose views were not worth taking seriously.

His failure in 1923 convinced Hitler that he should exploit the existing political system, but not challenge it directly, in his quest for power on the national level. Yet Hitler did not view the NSDAP as just another political party, playing by the same rules as the others within the Weimar system. Thus, most notably, the Nazi Party maintained a paramilitary arm, the *Sturmabteilung* (SA), which provoked a good deal of antileftist street violence. Still, the Nazis remained confined to the margins of national politics even as late as 1928, when they attracted only 2.6 percent of the vote in elections to the Reichstag.

The onset of the economic depression by the end of 1929 produced problems that the Weimar democracy could not handle—and that radically changed the German political framework. The pivotal issue was unemployment insurance, which became a tremendous financial burden for the government as unemployment grew. The governing coalition fell apart over the issue in March 1930, and this proved to be the end of normal parliamentary government in Weimar Germany.

Adolf Hitler German dictator whose aggressive foreign policy led to World War II and whose policies of anti-Semitism and racial purity led to the murder of millions.

National Socialist (Nazi) Party The political party that grew from the movement that German dictator Adolf Hitler made his vehicle to power.

President Paul von Hindenburg called on Heinrich Brüning (1885–1970), an expert on economics from the Catholic Center Party, to become chancellor. Brüning was to spearhead a hard-nosed, deflationary economic program intended to stimulate exports by lowering prices. Like most of the German middle classes, Brüning feared inflation, disliked unemployment insurance, and believed that Germany could not afford public works projects to pump up demand—the obvious alternative to his deflationary policy. But when he presented his program to the Reichstag, he encountered opposition not only from those on the left but also from conservatives, eager to undermine the republic altogether. As a result, Brüning could get no parliamentary majority. Rather than resigning or seeking a compromise, he invoked Article 48, the emergency provision of the Weimar constitution, which enabled him to govern under presidential decree.

When this expedient provoked strenuous protests, Brüning dissolved the Reichstag and scheduled new elections for September 1930. At this point there was still some chance that a more conciliatory tack would have enabled the chancellor to build a new parliamentary majority—and save parliamentary government. The Socialists were seeking to be more cooperative in the face of the deepening economic crisis and the prospect of new parliamentary elections, which, under these difficult circumstances, seemed to invite trouble. However, Brüning persisted, believing the electorate would vindicate him.

In fact, the outcome of the elections of September 1930 was disastrous—for Brüning, and ultimately for Germany as well. While two of the democratic, pro-Weimar parties lost heavily, the two extremes, the Communists and the Nazis, improved their totals considerably. Indeed, this was a major breakthrough for the Nazis, whose share of the vote jumped from 2.6 percent to 18.3 percent of the total.

Brüning continued to govern, still relying on President Hindenburg and Article 48 rather than majority support in the Reichstag. But his program of raising taxes and decreasing government spending failed to revive the economy. Meanwhile, the growth of the political extremes helped fuel an intensification of the political violence and street fighting that had bedeviled the Weimar Republic from the beginning. As scuffles between Nazis and Communists sometimes approached pitched battles, the inability of the government to keep order further damaged the prestige of the republic. And as the crisis deepened in 1932, conservative fears of a Marxist outcome played into Hitler's hands.

By this point, conservatives close to Hindenburg sensed the chance to replace the fragmented parliamentary system with some form of authoritarian government. A new, tougher regime would not only attack the economic crisis but also stiffen governmental resistance

against the apparent threat from the extreme left. In May 1932 those advisers finally persuaded Hindenburg to dump Brüning, and two of them, Franz von Papen (PAH-pin) (1878–1969) and General Kurt von Schleicher (SHLY-shur) (1882–1934), each got a chance to govern in the months that followed. But neither succeeded, partly because of the daring strategy Hitler adopted.

When, following the ouster of Brüning, new elections were held in July 1932, the Nazis won 37.3 percent of the vote and the Communists 14.3 percent. Together, the two extremes controlled a majority of the seats in the Reichstag. Hitler, as the leader of what was now the Reichstag's largest party, refused to join any coalition—unless he could lead it as chancellor. Meanwhile, the authoritarian conservatives around President Hindenburg wanted to take advantage of the Nazis' mass support for antidemocratic purposes. Finally, in January 1933, with government at an impasse, Papen lined up a new coalition that he proposed to Hindenburg to replace Schleicher's government. Hitler would be chancellor, Papen himself vice chancellor, and Alfred Hugenberg (1865–1951), the leader of the Nationalist Party, finance minister. For months, Hindenburg had resisted giving Hitler a chance to govern, but he felt this combination might work to establish a parliamentary majority, to box out the left and to contain Nazism. So Hindenburg named Hitler Germany's chancellor on January 30, 1933.

It became clear virtually at once that the outcome of the crisis was a dramatic change of regime, the triumph of Hitler and Nazism. But though the Nazis had always wanted to destroy the Weimar Republic, they were not directly responsible for overthrowing it. The rise of Nazism was more a symptom than a cause of the crisis of Weimar democracy.

In one sense, the Weimar Republic collapsed from within, largely because the German people disagreed fundamentally about priorities after the war—and then again with the onset of the Depression. Thus the new democracy produced unstable government based on multiparty coalitions, and it fell into virtual paralysis when faced with the economic crisis by 1930. At the same time, however, those around Hindenburg were particularly quick to begin undercutting democratic government in 1930, as the economic crisis seemed to intensify the threat from the extreme left.

With unemployment growing during the first years of the 1930s, both the Nazis and the Communists gained electoral support, but the Germans voting for the Nazis were not simply those most threatened economically. Nor did the Nazi Party appeal primarily to the uneducated or socially marginal. Rather, the party served as a focus of opposition for those alienated from the Weimar Republic itself. Although the Nazis did relatively poorly among Catholics and industrial workers, they put together a broad, fairly diverse base of electoral support, ranging from artisans and small shop-keepers to university students and civil servants. But though Hitler was clearly anti-Weimar, anticommunist, and anti-Versailles, his positive program remained vague; those who voted for the Nazis were not clear what they might be getting. In light of economic depression and political impasse, however, it seemed time to try something new.

THE CONSOLIDATION OF HITLER'S POWER, 1933–1934

When Hitler became chancellor, it was not obvious that a change of regime was beginning. Like his predecessors, he could govern only with the president's approval, and governmental institutions like the army, the judiciary, and the diplomatic corps, though hardly bastions of democracy, were not in the hands of committed Nazis. But even though an element of caution and cultivated ambiguity remained, a revolution quickly began, creating a new regime, the Third Reich.

On February 23, just weeks after Hitler became chancellor, a fire engulfed the Reichstag building in Berlin. It was set by a young Dutch communist acting on his own, but it seemed to suggest that a communist uprising was imminent. This sense of emergency gave Hitler an excuse to restrict civil liberties and imprison leftist leaders, including the entire Communist parliamentary delegation. Even in this atmosphere of crisis, the Nazis could not win a majority in the Reichstag elections of March 5. But support from the Nationalists and the Catholic Center Party enabled the Nazis to win Reichstag approval for an enabling act granting Hitler the power to make laws on his own for the next four years, bypassing both the Reichstag and the president.

Although the Weimar Republic was never formally abolished, the laws that followed fundamentally altered government, politics, and public life in Germany. The other parties were either outlawed or persuaded to dissolve, so that in July 1933 the Nazi Party was declared the only legal party. When President Hindenburg died in August 1934, the offices of chancellor and president were merged, and Germany had just one leader, Adolf Hitler, holding unprecedented power. Members of the German armed forces now swore loyalty to him personally.

Hitler and Children
Adolf Hitler was often portrayed as the friend of children. This photograph accompanied a story for an elementary school reader that described how Hitler, told it was this young girl's birthday, picked her from a crowd of well-wishers to treat her "to cake and strawberries with thick, sweet cream." *(Bayerisches Staatsbibliotek, Munich)*

During this period of power consolidation, Hitler acted decisively but carefully, generally accenting normalization. To be sure, his methods occasionally gave conservatives pause, most notably when he had several hundred people murdered in the "blood purge" of June 30, 1934. But this purge was directed especially against the SA, led by Ernst Röhm (1887–1934), who had had pretensions of controlling the army. His removal seemed evidence that Hitler was taming the radical elements in his own movement. In fact, however, this purge led to the ascendancy of the *Schutzstaffel* (SS), the select Nazi elite, led by Heinrich Himmler (1900–1945). Linked to the Gestapo, the secret political police, the SS became the institutional basis for the most troubling aspects of Nazism.

HITLER'S WORLDVIEW AND THE DYNAMICS OF NAZI PRACTICE

In achieving the chancellorship and in expanding his power thereafter, Hitler showed himself an adept politician, but he was hardly a mere opportunist, seeking to amass power for its own sake. Power was only the instrument for the grandiose transformation he believed necessary. And the most troubling aspects of Nazism, from personal dictatorship to the eventual effort to exterminate the Jews of Europe, stemmed from an overall vision of the world that radiated from Hitler himself. It had coalesced in Hitler's mind by about 1924.

This is not to say that Hitler was an original thinker or that his ideas were true—or even plausible. But he sought to make systematic sense of things, and the most disturbing features of his political activity stemmed directly from the resulting worldview. His most committed followers shared certain of his ideas, although fanatical loyalty to Hitler himself was more important for some of them. The central components of Hitler's thinking—geopolitics, biological racism, anti-Semitism, and Social Darwinism—were by no means specifically German. They could be found all over the Western world by the early twentieth century.

Geopolitics claimed to offer a scientific understanding of world power relationships based on geographical determinism. In his writings of the 1920s, Hitler warned that Germany faced imminent decline unless it confronted its geopolitical limitations. To remain fully sovereign in the emerging new era of global superpowers like the United States, Germany would have to act quickly to expand its territory. Otherwise it would end up like Switzerland or the Netherlands.

For decades German imperialists had argued about whether Germany was better advised to seek overseas colonies or to expand its reach in Europe. As Hitler saw it, Germany's failure to make a clear choice had led to its defeat in World War I. Now choice was imperative, and current geopolitical thinking suggested the direction for expansion. Far-flung empires relying on naval support were said to be in decline. The future lay with land-based states—unified, geographically contiguous, with the space necessary for self-sufficiency. By expanding eastward into Poland and the Soviet Union, Germany could conquer the living space, or *Lebensraum*, necessary for agricultural-industrial balance—and ultimately for self-sufficiency.

Though limited and mechanistic, this geopolitical way of thinking is at least comprehensible, in light of the German vulnerabilities that had become evident during World War I. The other three strands of Hitler's worldview were much less plausible, though each had become prominent during the second half of the nineteenth century. Biological racism insisted that built-in racial characteristics determine what is most important about any individual. Anti-Semitism went beyond racism in claiming that Jews had played, and continued to play, a special and negative role in history. The fact that the Jews were dispersed and often landless indicated that they were different—and parasitical. Finally, Social Darwinism, especially in its German incarnation, accented the positive role of struggle—not among individuals, as in a prominent American strand, but among racial groups.

The dominant current of racist thinking labeled the "Aryans" as healthy, creative, superior. Originally the Sanskrit term for "noble," *Aryan* gradually came to indicate the ancient language assumed to have been the common source of the modern Indo-European languages. An Aryan was simply a speaker of one of those languages. By the late nineteenth century, however, the term had become supremely ill defined. In much racist thinking, Germanic peoples were somehow especially Aryan, but race mixing had produced impurity—and thus degeneration. Success in struggle with the other races was the ultimate measure of vitality, the only proof of racial superiority for the future.

Hitler brought these themes together by emphasizing that humanity is not special, but simply part of nature, subject to the same laws of struggle and selection as the other animal species. Humanitarian ideals are thus dangerous illusions. As he put it to a group of officer cadets in 1944:

> Nature is always teaching us . . . that she is governed by the principle of selection: that victory is to the strong and that the weak must go to the wall. She teaches us that what may seem cruel to us, because it affects us personally or because we have been brought up in ignorance of her laws, is nevertheless often essential if a higher way of life

Schutzstaffel (SS) Specially selected Nazi elite, entrusted with the most sensitive ideological tasks of the Nazi regime—and responsible for many of its worst atrocities.

is to be attained. Nature . . . knows nothing of the notion of humanitarianism, which signifies that the weak must at all costs be protected and preserved even at the expense of the strong.

Nature does not see in weakness any extenuating reasons . . . on the contrary, weakness calls for condemnation.[3]

To Hitler, the Jews were not simply another of the races involved in this endless struggle. Rather, as landless parasites, they embodied the principles—from humanitarianism to class struggle—that were antithetical to the healthy natural struggle among racial groups. "Jewishness" was bound up with the negative, critical intellect that dared suggest things ought to be not natural but just, even that it was up to human beings to change the world, to make it just. The Jews were the virus keeping the community from a healthy natural footing. Marxist communism, embodying divisive class struggle as well as utopian humanitarian ideals, was fundamentally Jewish.

The central features of Nazism in practice, from personal dictatorship to the extermination of the Jews, followed from Hitler's view of the world. First, the racial community must organize itself politically for this ceaseless struggle. Individuals are but instruments for the success of the racial community. Parliamentary democracy, reflecting short-term individual interests, fosters selfish materialism and division, thereby weakening that community. The political order must rest instead on a charismatic leader, united with the whole people through bonds of common blood.

NAZI AIMS AND GERMAN SOCIETY

Although Hitler's worldview provided the underlying momentum for the Nazi regime, it did not specify a consistent program that could be implemented all at once. Moreover, the regime sometimes found it necessary to adopt short-term expedients that conflicted with its long-term aims. Thus it was possible for Germans living under Nazi rule in the 1930s to embrace aspects of Nazism in practice without seeing where it was all leading.

To create a genuine racial community, or *Volksgemeinschaft*, it was necessary to unify society and instill Nazi values, thereby making the individual feel part of the whole—and ultimately an instrument to serve the whole. This entailed more or less forced participation in an array of Nazi groupings, from the Women's Organization to the Hitler Youth, from the Labor Front to the Strength Through Joy leisure-time organization. Common participation meant shared experiences such as weekend hikes and a weekly one-dish meal. Even the most ordinary, once-private activities took on a public or political dimension. Moreover, the Nazis devised unprecedented ways to stage-manage public life, using rituals like the Hitler salute, symbols like the swastika, new media like radio and film, and carefully orchestrated party rallies—all in an effort to foster this sense of belonging. (See the feature "The Visual Record: Film as Propaganda.")

Online Study Center **Improve Your Grade**
Primary Source: Nazi Recreation: Summer Camps for Girls

The Response of the German People The Nazi regime enjoyed considerable popular support, but even after Hitler was well entrenched in power, most Germans did not grasp the regime's deeper dynamic. Some welcomed the sense of unity, the feeling of belonging and participation, especially after what had seemed the alienation and divisiveness of the Weimar years. Moreover, Hitler himself was immensely popular, partly because of his personal charisma, partly because his apparently decisive leadership was a welcome departure from the near paralysis of the Weimar parliamentary system. But most important, before the coming of war in 1939, he seemed to go from success to success, surmounting the Depression and repudiating the major terms of the hated Versailles treaty.

Hitler's propaganda minister, Joseph Goebbels (1897–1945), played on these successes to create a "Hitler myth," which made Hitler seem at once a hero and a man of the people, even the embodiment of healthy German ideals against the excesses and corruption that could be attributed to the Nazi Party. This myth became central to the Nazi regime, but it merely provided a façade behind which the real Hitler could pursue partially hidden, longer-term aims. These aims were not publicized directly because the German people did not seem ready for them. In this sense, then, support for Hitler and his regime was broad but shallow during the 1930s.

Moreover, resistance increased as the regime became more intrusive. Youth gangs actively opposed the official Hitler Youth organization as it became more overbearing and militaristic by the late 1930s. But people resisted especially by minimizing their involvement with the regime, retreating into the private realm, in response to the Nazi attempt to make everything public.

Did such people feel constantly under threat of the Gestapo, the secret police? In principle, the Gestapo could interpret the will of the *Führer*, or leader, and decide whether any individual citizen was "guilty" or not. And the Gestapo was not concerned about due process; on occasion it simply bypassed the regular court system. But the Gestapo did not terrorize Germans at random. Its victims were generally members of specific groups, people suspected of active opposition, or people who protected those the Gestapo had targeted.

Film as Propaganda

One of the extraordinary pieces of evidence from the Nazi period is *Triumph of the Will,* a documentary film on the sixth Nazi Party rally, which took place from September 4 to 10, 1934, in the historic city of Nuremberg, by this time the official site for such party rallies. Directed by a talented young woman named Leni Riefenstahl (1902–2003), *Triumph of the Will* has long been recognized as one of the most compelling propaganda films ever made. What can we learn from this film about how the Nazis understood and used propaganda? What was the Nazi regime trying to convey in sponsoring the film, with the particular images it contained?

A sense of the scope for political propaganda was one of the defining features of the Nazi movement virtually from its inception. In his quest for power Hitler allotted an especially significant role to his future propaganda minister, Joseph Goebbels. Both Hitler and Goebbels saw that new media and carefully orchestrated events might be used to shape the political views of masses of people.

The Nazi Party held the first of what would become annual conventions in Nuremberg in 1927. From the start, these meetings were rallies of the faithful, intended to give the Nazi movement a sense of cohesion and common purpose; but they increasingly became carefully staged propaganda spectacles, with banners and searchlights, parades and speeches. When, by 1934, the regime had completed the task of immediate power consolidation, it seemed time to seize the potential of the film medium to carry the spectacle beyond those present in Nuremberg. The intention to make a film thus influenced the staging of the 1934 rally. Film would transform the six-day event into a single potent work of art.

When Hitler came to power, Goebbels, as propaganda minister, assumed control of the German film industry, and he was particularly jealous of his prerogatives in this sphere. If there was to be a film of one of the Nuremberg rallies, he assumed that he would be in charge. So he objected strenuously when Hitler decided that Riefenstahl, who was not even a party member, should film the 1934 rally.

Already popular as an actress, Riefenstahl had established her own filmmaking company in 1931, before she turned 30. Her first film won the admiration of Hitler, who sought her out and eventually proposed that she direct the film of the party rally.

Although she was an artist with no special interest in politics, Riefenstahl, like many Germans, believed at this point that Hitler might be able to revive Germany's fortunes. So despite considerable reluctance, she bowed to Hitler's persistence and agreed to do the film—though only after she was guaranteed final control over editing. Her relations with Goebbels remained strained, but Hitler continued to support her as she made *Triumph of the Will.*

Riefenstahl developed the 107-minute film by editing 61 hours of footage that covered everything from Hitler's arrival and motorcade to the closing parades and speeches. As depicted on film, the party rally does not convey an overt ideological message. We hear Hitler simply trumpeting German renewal, not attacking Jews or glorifying conquest. Most striking in Riefenstahl's portrayal are the unity and epic monumentality that Nazism had apparently brought to Germany thanks to Hitler's leadership.

The film opens as Hitler emerges from dramatic cloud formations to arrive by airplane, descending from the sky like a god. He appears throughout the film as an almost superhuman figure, even, as in the shot shown here, as inspired, possessed, uncanny. Above all, he is a creator who shapes reality by blending will and art, forging masses of anonymous individuals into one people, one racial community, ready for anything. Those individuals seem, from one perspective, to lose their individuality in a monolithic mass, as in the shot of the parade grounds. But their sense of involvement in grandiose purposes charges them emotionally, even gives them a kind of ecstasy. The symbols, the massed banners, the ritualistic show of conformity, all strengthened this sense of participation in the new people's community. But unity and community were not ends in themselves; the film exalted military values and depicted a disciplined society organized for war.

Triumph of the Will extended participation in the spectacle to those who were not actually present in Nuremberg. Because the film chiseled the sprawling event into a work of art, seeing the film was in some ways more effective than being there. The Nazis looked for every means possible to involve the whole society in ritualistic spectacles that could promote a sense of belonging and unity. In addition to film, they made effective use of radio, even subsidizing the purchase of radio sets, or "people's

. . . and the Disciplined, Tightly Knit Community of Followers *(Both photos from the Museum of Modern Art/Film Stills Archive)*

As seen in *Triumph of the Will*, the Leader . . .

receivers." Such new media were to help ordinary Germans feel a more meaningful kind of belonging than Weimar democracy made possible. But this was only an emotional involvement, not the active participation of free citizens invited to make rational choices.

Triumph of the Will had its premiere in March 1935, with Hitler in the audience. It won several prizes in Germany and abroad but enjoyed only mixed success with the German public, especially outside the large cities. For some, it was altogether too artistic, and the Nazi regime did not use it widely for overt propaganda purposes. Still, the Nazis commissioned no other film about Hitler, for

Triumph of the Will captured the way he wanted to be seen. Indeed, Hitler praised the film as an "incomparable glorification of the power and beauty of our Movement."

QUESTIONS

1. Why did Hitler feel it so important to film a Nazi party rally—and even to plan the rally with the filming in mind?

2. What relationship between Hitler and the Nazi movement does *Triumph of the Will* convey?

Online Study Center
Improve Your Grade Visual Record Activities

Women, Family, and Reproduction Moreover, changes and contradictions in Nazi goals allowed considerable space for personal choice. During the struggle for power, the Nazis had emphasized the woman's role as wife and mother and deplored the ongoing emancipation of women. Once Hitler came to power, concerns about unemployment reinforced these views. Almost immediately Hitler's government began offering interest-free loans to help couples set up housekeeping if the woman agreed to leave the labor force. Such efforts to increase the German birthrate reinforced the emphasis on child rearing in Nazi women's organizations. Nonetheless, the size of the family continued to decrease in Germany as elsewhere in the industrialized world during the 1930s.

Beginning in 1936, when rapid rearmament began to produce labor shortages, the regime did an about-face and began seeking to attract women back to the workplace, especially into jobs central to military preparation. These efforts were not notably successful, and by 1940 the military was calling for the conscription of women into war industries.

Further, the Nazis valued the family only insofar as it was congruent with the "health" of the racial community. They were determined to promote that health by actually implementing radical eugenics measures that had been discussed, but not seriously implemented, during the Weimar years. The Nazi regime encouraged childbearing and large families on the part of those considered fit, while silmultaneously discouraging those considered unfit from having children. In pursuit of these goals, the regime regulated marriage, essentially politicized the family, and compromised traditional family values again and again.

Just months after coming to power in 1933, Hitler brushed aside the objections of Vice Chancellor Franz von Papen, a Catholic, and engineered a law mandating the compulsory sterilization of persons suffering from certain allegedly hereditary diseases. Medical personnel sterilized some 400,000 people, the vast majority of them "Aryan" Germans, during the Nazi years.

Nazi Policy Toward the Jews Eugenics was essentially one of two prongs of the Nazis' radical population policy. The other sought ethnic homogeneity, especially through measures directed against Germany's small Jewish minority. Although the regime began immediately to single out the Jews, Nazi Jewish policy remained an improvised hodgepodge prior to World War II. Within weeks after Hitler became chancellor in 1933, new restrictions limited Jewish participation in the civil service, in the professions, and in German cultural life—and quickly drew censure from the League of Nations. The Nuremberg Laws, announced at a party rally in 1935, included prohibition of sexual relations and marriage between Jews and non-Jewish Germans. Beginning in 1938,

the Jews had to carry special identification cards and to add "Sarah" or "Israel" to their given names.

Online Study Center **Improve Your Grade**
Primary Source: The Centerpiece of Nazi Racial Legislation: The Nuremberg Laws

But though Hitler and other Nazi leaders claimed periodically to be seeking a definitive solution to Germany's "Jewish problem," the dominant objective during the 1930s was to force German Jews to emigrate. About 60,000 of Germany's 550,000 Jews left the country during 1933 and 1934, and perhaps 25 percent had gotten out by 1938. The fact that the regime stripped emigrating Jews of their assets made emigration more difficult. Potential host countries, concerned about unemployment during the Depression, were especially unwilling to take in substantial numbers of Jews if they were penniless.

On November 9, 1938, using the assassination of a German diplomat in Paris as a pretext, the Nazis staged the *Kristallnacht* (Crystal Night) pogrom, during which almost all the synagogues in Germany and about seven thousand Jewish-owned stores were destroyed. Between 30,000 and 50,000 relatively prosperous Jews were arrested and forced to emigrate after their property was confiscated. Although the German public had generally acquiesced in the earlier restrictions on Jews, this pogrom, with its wanton violation of private property, shocked many Germans.

Concentration camps—supplementary detention centers—had become a feature of the Nazi regime virtually at once, but prior to 1938 they were used primarily to hold political prisoners. As part of the Crystal Night pogrom, about 35,000 Jews were rounded up and sent to the camps, but most were soon released as long as they could document their intention to emigrate. When World War II began in 1939, the total camp population was about 25,000. The systematic physical extermination of the Jews began only during World War II.

Euthanasia and Nazi Preparation for War
However, the killing of others deemed superfluous or threatening to the racial community began earlier, with the so-called **euthanasia program** initiated under volunteer medical teams in 1939. Its aim was to eliminate chronic mental patients, the incurably ill, and people with severe physical handicaps. Those subject to

Kristallnacht **(Crystal Night)** Organized Nazi assault on Jewish businesses and synagogues during the night of November 9–10, 1938, following the assassination of a German diplomat in Paris.

"euthanasia" program The Nazi program of systematically killing people deemed superfluous or threatening to Germany's racial health because of their physical or mental disabilities.

such treatment were overwhelmingly ethnic Germans, not Jews or foreigners. Although the regime did all it could to make it appear the victims had died naturally, a public outcry developed, especially among relatives and church leaders by 1941, when the program was largely discontinued. But by then it had claimed 100,000 lives and seems essentially to have achieved its initial objectives.

This "euthanasia" program was based on the sense, fundamental to radical Nazism, that war was the norm and readiness for war the essential societal imperative. In war, societies send individuals to their deaths and, on the battlefield, make difficult distinctions among the wounded, letting some die in order to save those most likely to survive and return to battle. Struggle necessitates selection, which requires overcoming humanitarian scruples—especially the notion that "weakness" calls for special protection. Thus it was desirable to kill even ethnic Germans who were deemed unfit, as "life unworthy of life."

Preparation for war was the core of Nazism in practice. The conquest of living space in the east would make possible a more advantageous agricultural-industrial balance. The result would be not only the self-sufficiency necessary for sovereignty but also the land-rootedness necessary for racial health. Such a war of conquest would strike not only the allegedly inferior Slavic peoples of the region but also detested communism, centered in the Soviet Union.

The point of domestic reorganization was to marshal the community's energies and resources for war. Because German business interests generally seemed congruent with Nazi purposes, Nazi aims did not appear to require some revolutionary assault on business elites or the capitalist economy. But the Nazis had their own road to travel, and beginning in 1936 they proved quite prepared to bend the economy, and to coordinate big business, to serve their longer-term aims of war-making.

The Nazi drive toward war during the 1930s transformed international relations in Europe. The responses of the other European powers, as they sought to deal with Hitler, reflected the increasingly polarized political context of the period. Before considering the fortunes of Hitler's foreign policy, we must consider fascism as a wider phenomenon—and the efforts of the democracies, on the one hand, and the Soviet Union, on the other, to come to terms with it.

═══════════════ S E C T I O N   S U M M A R Y ═══════════════

- The Nazis did not directly overthrow the Weimar Republic but ended up the beneficiaries when it reached an impasse during 1930–1933.

- The central components of Hitler's thinking—geopolitics, biological racism, anti-Semitism, and Social Darwinism—were neither original with Hitler nor specifically German.

- Among ordinary Germans, support for Hitler and his regime was broad but shallow during the 1930s.

- A radical eugenics program, entailing forced sterilization and eventually the actual killing of those deemed unfit, was central to Nazi action on the domestic level during the 1930s.

- During the 1930s the Nazis began stripping German Jews of citizenship rights as part of a haphazard effort to encourage—or force—Jews to emigrate.

FASCIST CHALLENGE AND ANTIFASCIST RESPONSE, 1934–1939

Why did the "popular front" strategy prove counterproductive in both France and Spain?

ommunism, fascism, and Nazism all repudiated the parliamentary democracy that had been the West's political norm. Each seemed subject to violence and excess, yet each had features that some found attractive, especially in light of the difficult socioeconomic circumstances of the 1930s. But communists and adherents of the various forms of fascism were bitterly hostile to each other, and the very presence of these new political systems caused polarization all over Europe.

Beginning in 1934 communists sought to join with anyone who would work with them to defend the democratic framework against further fascist assaults. Without democracy, the very survival of communist parties was in doubt. This effort led to new antifascist coalition governments in Spain and France. In each case, however, the Depression restricted maneuvering room, and these governments ended up furthering the polarization they were seeking to avoid. By mid-1940, democracy had fallen in Spain, after a brutal civil war, and even in France, in the wake of military defeat.

EUROPEAN FASCISM AND THE POPULAR FRONT RESPONSE

Although some across Europe who were disaffected with democracy and hostile to communism found genuine fascism attractive, the line between fascism and conservative authoritarianism blurred in the volatile political climate of the 1930s. To many, any retreat from democracy appeared a step toward fascism.

In east-central Europe, political distinctions became especially problematic. Movements like the Arrow Cross in Hungary and the Legion of the Archangel Michael in Romania modeled themselves on the Italian and German prototypes, but they never achieved political power. Those who controlled the antidemocratic governments in Hungary and Romania, as in Poland, Bulgaria, and Yugoslavia, were authoritarian traditionalists, not fascists. Still, many government leaders in the region welcomed the closer economic ties with Germany that Hitler's economics minister, Hjalmar Schacht, engineered. The difference between authoritarianism and fascism remained clearest in Austria, where Catholic conservatives undermined democracy during 1933 and 1934. They were actively hostile to the growing pro-Nazi agitation in Austria, partly because they wanted to keep Austria independent.

In France various nationalist, anticommunist, and anti-Semitic leagues gathered momentum during the early 1930s. They covered a spectrum from monarchism to outspoken pro-fascism, but together they constituted at least a potential threat to French democracy. In February 1934, right-wing demonstrations against the Chamber of Deputies provoked a bloody clash with police and forced a change of ministry. As it began to seem that even France might be vulnerable, those from the center and left of the political spectrum began to consider collaborating to resist fascism. The communists, especially, took the initiative by promoting **popular fronts** of all those seeking to preserve democracy.

This was a dramatic change in strategy for international communism. Even as Hitler was closing in on the German chancellorship in the early 1930s, German Communists, following Comintern policy, continued to attack their socialist rivals rather than seek a unified response to Nazism. From the communist perspective, fascism represented the crisis phase of monopoly capi-

Ideological Confrontation

At a major international exhibition in Paris in 1937, the new antidemocratic political regimes made bold propaganda statements. With a sculpture from fascist Italy's pavilion in the foreground, we look across the Seine River to a classic representation of the ideological warfare of the 1930s: the Soviet Pavilion, on the left, facing the German Pavilion, on the right. Crowning the Soviet building is the noted sculpture by Vera Muchina, *Worker and Collective Farmer.* (*AP/Wide World Photos*)

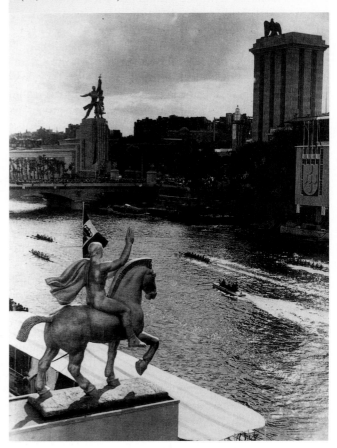

talism, so a Nazi government would actually be useful to strip away the democratic façade hiding class oppression in Germany. But by 1934 the threat of fascism seemed so pressing that Communists began actively promoting electoral alliances and governing coalitions with socialists and even liberal democrats to resist its further spread. From 1934 until 1939, Communists everywhere consistently pursued this "popular front" strategy.

By the 1930s, however, it was becoming ever harder to know what was fascist, what was dangerous, what might lead where. As fears intensified, perceptions became as important as realities. Popular front governments, intended to preserve democracy against what appeared to be fascism, could seem to conservatives to

popular front A term for antifascist electoral alliances and governing coalitions that communists promoted from 1934 until 1939 to resist the further spread of fascism.

be leaning too far to the left. Ideological polarization made democracy extraordinarily difficult. The archetypal example proved to be Spain, where a tragedy of classical proportions was played out.

FROM DEMOCRACY TO CIVIL WAR IN SPAIN, 1931–1939

Spain became a center of attention in the 1930s, when its promising new parliamentary democracy, launched in 1931, led to civil war in 1936 and the triumph of a repressive authoritarian regime in 1939. An earlier effort at constitutional monarchy had fizzled by 1923, when King Alfonso XIII (1886–1941) supported a new military dictatorship. But growing opposition led first to the resignation of the dictator in 1930 and then, in April 1931, to the end of the monarchy and the proclamation of a republic. The elections for a constituent assembly that followed in June produced a solid victory for a coalition of liberal democrats and Socialists, as well as much hope for substantial reform.

A significant agrarian reform law was passed in 1932, but partly because of the difficult economic context, the new government was slow to implement it. Feeling betrayed, Socialists and agricultural workers became increasingly radical, producing growing upheaval in the countryside. Radicalism on the left made it harder for the moderates to govern and, at the same time, stimulated conservatives to become more politically active.

A right-wing coalition known as the CEDA, led by José Maria Gil Robles (heel ROH-blayce) (1898–1980), grew in strength, becoming the largest party in parliament with the elections of November 1933. In light of its parliamentary strength, the CEDA had a plausible claim to a government role, but it was kept from participation in government until October 1934. It seemed to the left, in the ideologically charged atmosphere of the time, that the growing role of the CEDA was a prelude to fascism. To let the CEDA into the government would be to hand the republic over to its enemies.

A strong Catholic from the traditional Spanish right, Gil Robles refused to endorse the democratic republic as a form of government, but he and the CEDA were willing to work within it. So the Spanish left may have been too quick to see the CEDA as fascist—and to react when the CEDA finally got its government role. However, Mussolini and Hitler had each come to power more or less legally, from within parliamentary institutions. The German left had been criticized for its passive response to the advent of Hitler; the Spanish left wanted to avoid the same mistake.

Thus, when the CEDA finally got a role in the government, the left responded during the fall of 1934 with quasi-revolutionary uprisings in Catalonia and Asturias, where a miners' commune was put down only after two weeks of heavy fighting. In the aftermath,

the right-leaning government of 1935 began undoing some of the reforms of the left-leaning government of 1931–1933, though still legally, within the framework of the parliamentary republic.

In February 1936 a popular front coalition to ward off fascism won a narrow electoral victory, sufficient for an absolute majority in parliament. As would be true in France a few months later, electoral victory produced popular expectations that went well beyond the essentially defensive purposes of the popular front. Hoping to win back the leftist rank and file and head off what seemed a dangerous attempt at revolution, the new popular front government began to implement a progressive program, now including the land reform that had been promised but not implemented earlier. It was too late, however, to undercut the growing radicalization of the masses.

A wave of land seizures began in March 1936, followed by the most extensive strike movement in Spanish history, which by June was becoming clearly revolutionary in character. To many, the government's inability to keep order had become the immediate issue. By the early summer of 1936, leaders of the democratic republic had become isolated between the extremes of left and right, each preparing an extralegal solution.

Finally, in mid-July, several army officers initiated a military uprising against the government. Soon led by General Francisco Franco (1892–1975), these Nationalist insurgents took control of substantial parts of Spain. But elsewhere they failed to overcome the resistance of the Republicans, or Loyalists, those determined to defend the republic. So the result was not the intended military takeover but a brutal civil war (see **MAP 27.1**). The substantial Italian fascist and Nazi German intervention on the Nationalist side by the end of 1936 intensified the war's ideological ramifications. At the same time, the remarkable, often heroic resistance of the Loyalists captured the imagination of the world. Indeed, forty thousand volunteers came from abroad to fight to preserve the Spanish republic.

It proved a war of stunning brutality on both sides. Loyalist anticlericalism led to the murder of twelve bishops and perhaps one-eighth of the parish clergy in Spain. On the other side, the German bombing of the Basque town of Guernica (gair-NEE-kah, in Spanish; GWAIR-nee-kah, as customarily rendered in English) on a crowded market day in April 1937, represented unforgettably in Pablo Picasso's painting, came to symbolize the violence and suffering of the whole era (see the painting on page 859).

Republican Loyalists assumed that Franco and the Nationalists represented another instance of fascism. In fact, however, Franco was no fascist, but rather a traditional military man whose leadership role did not rest on personal charisma. He was an authoritarian emphasizing discipline, order, and Spain's Catholic traditions.

MAP 27.1 The Spanish Civil War, 1936–1939

The Nationalist insurgents quickly took over most of northern and eastern Spain in 1936 and then gradually expanded their territory. The fall of Madrid early in 1939 marked the end of the fighting. The revolutionary effort of 1936 and 1937 within the Republican zone was centered in Barcelona. *(Source: Adapted from* The Times Atlas of World History, *3d ed. Reprinted by permission of HarperCollins Publishers Ltd. © HarperCollins Publishers Ltd.)*

Still, in their effort to rally support during the civil war, Franco's forces found it expedient to take advantage of the appeal of the Falange (fah-LAHN-hay), a genuinely fascist movement that had emerged under the leadership of the charismatic young José Antonio Primo de Rivera (1903–1936). Although extremely weak at the time of the elections in February 1936, the Falange grew rapidly in opposition to the leftist radicalism that followed the popular front victory. As street fighting between left and right intensified that spring, the republic arrested José Antonio, as he was called, and he was in prison when the civil war began.

José Antonio decided that his best hope was alliance with the military. Although he was contemptuous of their shortsighted conservatism, he felt that their very absence of ideas afforded an opening for the Falange to provide direction, a genuine alternative. But it worked out the other way. In November 1936, the republican government tried and executed José Antonio for conspiring to overthrow the republic. The Nationalists promptly began invoking his memory, and using other trappings of the Falange, to increase their popular appeal.

Meanwhile, the republic's leaders had to fight a civil war while dealing with continuing revolution in their own ranks. Developing especially in Catalonia from the uprisings of 1936, that revolution was not communist but anarcho-syndicalist in orientation. The Communists, true to popular front principles, insisted that this was no time for such "infantile leftist" revolutionary experiments. What mattered, throughout the Republican zone, was the factory discipline necessary to produce essential war materiel. As a consequence, the Communists, under Stalin's orders, were instrumental in putting down the anarchist revolution in Catalonia in June 1937.

Under these extraordinary circumstances, the Communists, at first a distinct minority on the Spanish left, gradually gained ascendancy on the Republican side, partly because they were disciplined and effective, partly because Soviet assistance enhanced their prestige. However, this single-minded prosecution of the civil war did not prove enough to defeat the military insurgency, despite the considerable heroism on the Loyalist side. The war ended with the fall of Madrid to the Nationalists in March 1939. General Franco's authoritarian regime governed Spain until his death in 1975.

Picasso: Guernica

Created for the Spanish Pavilion at the famed 1937 Paris Exhibition, Picasso's painting conveys horror and outrage—his response to the German bombing of Guernica on a crowded market day in 1937, during the Spanish civil war. Picasso's stark, elemental imagery helped define this era of violence and suffering for the generations that followed.   *(Pablo Picasso, Guernica [1937, May–early June]. Oil on canvas. Art Resource, NY. © 2002 Artists Rights Society [ARS], New York/ADAGP, Paris)*

In Spain, as in Weimar Germany, the lack of consensus in a new republic made parliamentary democracy difficult, and the wider ideological framework magnified the difficulties. With the political boiling point so low, the left and the right each saw the other in extreme terms and assumed that extraordinary response to the other was necessary. Thus the left tended to view even conservatives operating within a parliamentary framework as "fascist," and both sides were relatively quick to give up on a democratic republic that seemed to be tilting too far in the wrong direction.

FRANCE IN THE ERA OF THE POPULAR FRONT

In France, as in Spain, concern to arrest the spread of fascism led to a popular front coalition, here including Socialists, Communists, and Radicals, that governed the country from 1936 to 1938. Although it did not lead to civil war, the popular front was central to the French experience of the 1930s, producing polarization and resignation and undermining confidence in the Third Republic.

Beginning in 1934, the French Communists took the initiative in approaching first the Socialists, then the Radicals, to develop a popular front coalition against fascism. In reaching out to the Radicals, the Commu-

nists stressed French patriotism and made no demand for significant economic reforms. Stalin gave this effort a major push in 1935 when, in a stunning change in the communist line, he stressed the legitimacy of national defense and explicitly endorsed French rearmament.

In the elections of April and May 1936, the popular front won a sizable majority in the Chamber of Deputies, putting the Socialists' leader, Léon Blum (1872–1950), in line to become France's first Socialist prime minister. The Communists pledged full support of the new Blum government, but to avoid fanning fears, they did not participate directly. However, despite the popular front's moderate and essentially defensive aims, the situation quickly began to polarize after the elections.

Fearing that the new Blum government would be forced to devalue the French currency, and thereby diminish the value of assets denominated in francs, French investors immediately began moving their capital abroad. At the same time, the popular front victory produced a wave of enthusiasm among workers that escaped the control of popular front leaders and culminated in a spontaneous strike movement, the largest France had ever seen. By early June it had spread to all major industries nationwide. Although the workers' demands—for collective bargaining, a forty-hour work-week, and paid vacations—were not extraordinary, the movement involved sit-down strikes as well as the normal walkouts and thus seemed quasi-revolutionary in character. The major trade union confederation, the Communists, and most Socialists, including Blum himself, saw the strikes as a danger to the popular front, with its more modest aims of defending the republic, and eagerly pursued a settlement.

That settlement, the Matignon (mah-tin-YON) Agreement of June 8, 1936, was a major victory for the French working class. Having been genuinely frightened by the strikes and now reassured that the popular front government would at least uphold the law, French industrialists were willing to make significant concessions. So the workers got collective bargaining, elected shop stewards, and wage increases as a direct result of Matignon, then a forty-hour week and paid vacations in a reform package promptly passed by the parliament.

In the enthusiasm of the summer of 1936, other reforms were enacted as well, but after that the popular front was forced onto the defensive. Two problems undermined its energy and cohesion: the noncooperation of French business and the Spanish civil war. The cautious response of Blum, the Socialist prime minister, is striking in each case, but he faced a situation with little maneuvering room.

From the outset Blum stressed that he had no mandate for revolution, and as France's first Socialist prime minister, he felt it essential to prove that a Socialist could govern responsibly. Thus Blum did not respond energetically to the capital flight, even though it produced serious currency and budgetary difficulties. Perhaps, as critics suggest, he should have acted more aggressively to overhaul the French banking and credit system. But Blum shied away from any such drastic measures, both to prove he could be moderate and to avoid antagonizing business.

Blum was also uncertain as he faced the dilemmas surrounding the Spanish civil war. The key question was whether the French government should help the beleaguered Spanish republic, at least by sending supplies. Although he initially favored such help, Blum changed his mind under pressure from three sides. The Conservative government of Stanley Baldwin in Britain was against it. So was the French right; some even suggested that French intervention would provoke a comparable civil war in France. Moreover, the Radicals in his own coalition were generally opposed to helping the Spanish republic, so intervention would jeopardize the cohesion of the popular front itself.

Thus, rather than help supply the Spanish republic, Blum promoted a nonintervention agreement among the major powers, including Italy and Germany. Many Socialists and Communists disliked Blum's cautious policy, especially as it became clear that Mussolini and Hitler were violating their hands-off pledges. As Blum stuck to nonintervention, the moral force of the popular front dissolved.

In 1938 a new government under the Radical Edouard Daladier (dah-lah-dee-YAY) (1884–1970), still nominally a creature of the popular front, began dismantling some of the key gains of 1936, even attacking the forty-hour week. Citing productivity and national security concerns, Daladier adopted pro-business policies and succeeded in attracting capital back to France. But workers, watching the gains they had won in 1936 slip away, felt betrayed. At the same time, businessmen and conservatives began blaming the workers' gains—such as the five-day week—for slowing French rearmament. Although such charges were not entirely fair, they indicated how poisoned the atmosphere in France had become in the wake of the popular front.

As France began to face the possibility of a new war, the popular front was widely blamed for French weakness. When war came at last, resignation and division were prevalent, in contrast with the patriotic unity and high spirits of 1914. It was partly for that reason that France was so easily defeated by Germany in 1940. And when France fell, the democratic Third Republic fell with it.

━━━━━━ S E C T I O N   S U M M A R Y ━━━━━━

- In light of the ideological polarization of the 1930s, many people found it difficult to distinguish between conservative authoritarianism and fascism.

- In a dramatic change in their international strategy, the Communists in 1934 began promoting "popular fronts," which were to bring together all those seeking to preserve democracy against the threat of fascism.

- The wider ideological framework magnified the difficulties of parliamentary democracy in Spain, contributing to the polarization that soon led to civil war.

- Although he sometimes exploited the trappings of fascism, General Franco was not a fascist but an authoritarian Catholic traditionalist.

- Although it was intended to preserve the Third Republic, the popular front experiment in France produced a backlash and was widely blamed for French weakness as war again loomed by the end of the 1930s.

THE COMING OF WORLD WAR II, 1935–1939

Why did the other countries not stop Hitler's Germany before it was strong enough to start a new European war in 1939?

Even as the Great Depression added to their burdens, Western leaders faced the challenge of maintaining the peace during the 1930s. But despite the promising adjustments of the 1920s, many of the problems that accompanied the World War I peace settlement were still in place when Hitler came to power. And Hitler had consistently trumpeted his intention to overturn that settlement. What scope was there for peaceful revision? Could the threat of war stop Hitler? By the last years of the 1930s, these questions tortured the Western world as Hitler went from one success to another, raising the possibility of a new and more destructive war. And the power balance rested on the responses not only of the Western democracies, but of fascist Italy and the communist Soviet Union as well.

THE REORIENTATION OF FASCIST ITALY

During its first decade in power, Benito Mussolini's fascist regime in Italy concentrated on domestic reconstruction, especially the effort to mobilize people through their roles as producers within a new corporative state (see page 861). But though corporativist institutions were gradually constructed, with great rhetorical fanfare, they bogged down in bureaucratic meddling. Corporativism proved more the vehicle for regimentation than for a more direct kind of participation. Mussolini offered assurances that, despite the necessary compromises, fascism's corporativist revolution was continuing, but many committed fascists were sharply critical of the new system. Fascism seemed to have stalled, partly as the result of compromise with prefascist elites and institutions, and partly as the result of its own internal contradictions.

Mussolini was never merely the instrument of the established elites, but neither was he a consistent ideologue like Hitler. By the early 1930s, he sometimes seemed satisfied with ritual, spectacle, and the growing cult of his own infallibility as he juggled the contending forces in fascist Italy. But the limitations he had encountered on the domestic level increasingly frustrated him. On the international level, in contrast, the new context after Hitler came to power offered some welcome space for maneuver.

Though Italy, like Germany, remained dissatisfied with the territorial status quo, it was not obvious that fascist Italy and Nazi Germany had to end up in the same camp. For one thing, Italy was anxious to preserve an independent Austria as a buffer with Germany, whereas many Germans and Austrians favored the unification of the two countries. Such a greater Germany might then threaten the gains Italy had won at the peace conference at Austria's expense. When, in 1934, Germany seemed poised to absorb Austria, Mussolini helped force Hitler to back down. He even warned that Nazism, with its racist orientation, posed a significant threat to the best of European civilization.

As it began to appear that France and Britain might have to work with the Soviet Union to check Hitler's Germany, French and British conservatives pushed for good relations with Mussolini's Italy to provide ideological balance. So Italy was well positioned to play off both sides as Hitler began shaking things up on the international level. In 1935, just after Hitler announced significant rearmament measures, unilaterally repudiating provisions of the Versailles treaty for the first time, Mussolini hosted a meeting with the French and British prime ministers at Stresa, in northern Italy. In an overt warning to Hitler's Germany, the three powers agreed to resist "any unilateral repudiation of treaties which may endanger the peace of Europe."

However, Mussolini was already preparing to extend Italy's possessions in East Africa to encompass Ethiopia (formerly called Abyssinia). He assumed that the French and British, who needed his support against Hitler, would not offer significant opposition. Ethiopia had become a League of Nations member in 1923—sponsored by Italy, but opposed by Britain and France because it still practiced slavery. After a border incident, Italian troops invaded in October 1935, prompting the League to announce sanctions against Italy.

These sanctions were applied haphazardly, largely because France and Britain wanted to avoid damaging their longer-term relations with Italy. In any case, the sanctions did not deter Mussolini, whose forces prevailed through the use of aircraft and poison gas by May 1936. But they did make Italy receptive to German overtures in the aftermath of its victory. And the victory made Mussolini more restless. Rather than seeking to play again the role of European balancer, he sent Italian troops and materiel to aid the Nationalists in the Spanish civil war, thereby further alienating democratic opinion elsewhere.

Conservatives in Britain and France continued to push for accommodation with Italy, hoping to revive the "Stresa front" against Hitler. Some even defended Italian imperialism in East Africa. But Italy continued its drift toward Germany. Late in 1936 Mussolini spoke of a new **Rome-Berlin Axis** for the first time. During 1937 and 1938 he and Hitler exchanged visits. Finally, in May 1939, Italy joined Germany in an open-ended military alliance, the Pact of Steel, but Mussolini made it clear that Italy could not be ready for a major European war before 1943.

Partly to strengthen this developing relationship, fascist Italy adopted anti-Semitic racial laws, even though Italian fascism had not originally been anti-Semitic. Indeed, the party had attracted Jewish Italians to its membership in about the same proportion as non-Jews. Although the imperial venture in Ethiopia had been popular among the Italian people, the seeming subservience to Nazi Germany displeased even many fascists. Such opposition helped keep Mussolini from intervention when war broke out in September 1939.

RESTORING GERMAN SOVEREIGNTY, 1935–1936

During his first years in power, through 1936, Hitler could be understood as merely restoring German sovereignty, revising a postwar settlement that had been misconceived in the first place. However uncouth and abrasive he might seem, it was hard to find a basis for opposing him. Yet with the beginning of rearmament in 1935, and especially with the **remilitarization of the Rhineland** in March 1936, Hitler fundamentally reversed the power balance established in France's favor at the peace conference.

France's special advantage had been the demilitarization of the entire German territory west of the Rhine River and a 50-kilometer strip on the east bank. The measure had been reaffirmed at Locarno in 1925, now with Germany's free agreement, and it was guaranteed by Britain and Italy. Yet on a Saturday morning in March 1936, that advantage disappeared as German troops moved into the forbidden area. The French and British acquiesced, uncertain of what else to do. After all, Hitler was only restoring Germany to full sovereignty.

But Hitler was not likely to stop there. As a result of the war and the peace, three new countries—Austria, Czechoslovakia, and Poland—bordered Germany (see **MAP 27.2**). In each, the peace settlement had left trouble spots involving the status of ethnic Germans; in each, the status quo was open to question.

AUSTRIA, CZECHOSLOVAKIA, AND APPEASEMENT

As early as 1934, Hitler had moved to encompass his homeland, Austria, but strenuous opposition from Italy led him to back down. The developing understanding with Mussolini by 1936 enabled Hitler to focus again on Austria—initiating the second, more radical phase of his prewar foreign policy. On a pretext in March 1938, German troops moved into Austria, which was promptly incorporated into Germany. This time Mussolini was willing to acquiesce, and Hitler was genuinely grateful.

The Treaty of Versailles had explicitly prohibited this *Anschluss,* or unity of Austria with Germany, though that prohibition violated the principle of self-determination. It was widely believed in the West, no doubt correctly, that most Austrians favored unity with Germany now that the Habsburg empire had broken up. The *Anschluss* could thus be justified as revising a misconceived aspect of the peace settlement.

Czechoslovakia presented quite a different situation. Although it had preserved democratic institutions, the country included restive minorities of Magyars, Ruthenians, Poles, and—concentrated especially in the Sudetenland, along the German and Austrian borders—about 3.25 million Germans. After having been part of the dominant nationality in the old Habsburg empire, those Germans were frustrated with their minority status in the new Czechoslovakia. Worse, they seemed to suffer disproportionately from the Depression. Hitler's agents actively stirred up their resentments.

Leading the West's response, when Hitler began making an issue of Czechoslovakia, was Neville Chamberlain (1869-1940), who followed Stanley Baldwin as Britain's prime minister in May 1937. An intelligent, vigorous, and public-spirited man from the progressive wing of the Conservative Party, Chamberlain has long been derided as the architect of the **"appeasement"** of Hitler at the Munich conference of 1938, which settled the crisis over Czechoslovakia. Trumpeted as the key to peace, the Munich agreement proved but a step to the war that broke out less than a year later. Yet though it failed, Chamberlain's policy of appeasement stemmed not from cowardice or mere drift, and certainly not from some unspoken pro-Nazi sentiment.

Rather than let events spin out of control, as seemed to have happened in 1914, Chamberlain sought to

Rome-Berlin Axis Alliance between Hitler's Nazi Germany and Mussolini's fascist Italy, which began informally in 1936, then was cemented by an open-ended military alliance, the Pact of Steel, in 1939.

remilitarization of the Rhineland The reoccupation of Germany's Rhineland territory by German troops in March 1936, in clear violation of the Treaty of Versailles.

appeasement The policy employed by Britain's prime minister, Neville Chamberlain, to defuse the 1938 crisis with Germany's Adolf Hitler. Chamberlain acquiesced to Hitler's demands to annex the Sudetenland portion of Czechoslovakia, but this proved merely a step toward the war that broke out less than a year later.

MAP 27.2   The Expansion of Nazi Germany, 1936–1939

Especially with the remilitarization of the Rhineland in 1936, Hitler's Germany began moving, step by step, to alter the European power balance. In September 1939 the Soviet Union also began annexing territory, capitalizing on its agreement with Germany the month before.

Online Study Center **Improve Your Grade** Interactive Map: The Growth of Nazi Germany, 1933–1939

master the difficult international situation through creative bargaining. Surely, he felt, the excesses of Hitler's policy resulted from the mistakes of Versailles; redo the settlement on a more realistic basis, and Germany would behave responsibly. The key was to pinpoint the sources of Germany's frustrations and, as Chamberlain put it, "to remove the danger spots one by one."

Moreover, in Britain as elsewhere, there were some who saw Hitler's resurgent Germany as a bulwark against communism, which might spread into east-central Europe—especially in the event of another war. Indeed, the victor in another war might well be the revolutionary left. To prevent such an outcome was worth a few concessions to Hitler.

The Czechs, led by Eduard Beneš (BAY-naish) (1884–1948), made some attempt to liberalize their nationality policy. But by April 1938 they were becoming ever less sympathetic to Sudeten German demands for

The Illusion of Peace

Neville Chamberlain, returning home to Britain from Munich to a hero's welcome, waves the peace declaration that was supposed to have brought "peace in our time." This was late September 1938. Less than a year later, Europe was again at war. *(Hulton Archive/ Getty Images)*

autonomy, especially as German bullying came to accompany them. Tensions between Czechoslovakia and Germany mounted, and by late September 1938 war appeared imminent, despite Chamberlain's efforts to mediate. Both the French and the British began mobilizing, with French troops manning the Maginot Line for the first time.

A 1924 treaty bound France to come to the aid of Czechoslovakia in the event of aggression. Moreover, the Soviet Union, according to a treaty of 1935, was bound to assist Czechoslovakia if the French did so. And throughout the crisis, the Soviets pushed for a strong stand in defense of Czechoslovakia against German aggression. For both ideological and military reasons, however, the British and French were reluctant to line up for war on the side of the Soviet Union. The value of the Soviet military was uncertain, at best, at a time when the Soviet officer corps had just been purged.

By September, Hitler seemed eager to smash the Czechs by force, but when Mussolini proposed a four-power conference, he was persuaded to talk again. At Munich late in September, Britain, France, Italy, and Germany settled the matter, with Czechoslovakia—and the Soviet Union—excluded. Determined not to risk war over what seemed Czech intransigence, the Brit-

ish ended up agreeing to what Hitler had wanted all along—not merely autonomy for the Sudeten Germans but German annexation of the Sudetenland.

The Munich agreement specified that all Sudeten areas with German majorities be transferred to Germany. Plebiscites were to be held in areas with large German minorities, and Hitler pledged to respect the sovereignty of the now diminished Czechoslovak state. Chamberlain and his French counterpart, Edouard Daladier, each returned home to a hero's welcome, having transformed what had seemed certain war to, in Chamberlain's soon-to-be-notorious phrase, "peace in our time."

Rather than settle the nationality questions bedeviling Czechoslovakia, the Munich agreement only provoked further unrest. Poland and Hungary, eager to exploit the new weakness of Czechoslovakia, agitated successfully to annex disputed areas with large numbers of their respective nationalities. Then unrest stemming from Slovak separatism afforded a pretext for Germany to send troops into Prague in March 1939. The Slovak areas were spun off as a separate nation, while the Czech areas became the Protectorate of Bohemia and Moravia. Less than six months after the Munich conference, most of what had been Czechoslovakia had landed firmly within the Nazi orbit (see Map 27.2). It was no longer possible to justify Hitler's actions as an effort to unite all Germans in one state.

POLAND, THE NAZI-SOVIET PACT, AND THE COMING OF WAR

With Poland, the German grievance was still more serious, for the new Polish state had been created partly at German expense. Especially galling to Germans was the Polish corridor, which cut off East Prussia from the bulk of Germany in order to give Poland access to the sea. The city of Danzig (now Gdansk, in Poland), historically Polish but part of Germany before World War I, was left a "free city," supervised by the League of Nations.

Disillusioned by Hitler's dismemberment of Czechoslovakia and angered by the Germans' menacing rhetoric regarding Poland, Chamberlain announced on March 31, 1939, that Britain and France would intervene militarily should Poland's independence be threatened. Chamberlain was not only abandoning the policy of appeasement; he was making a clear commitment to the Continent, of the sort that British governments had resisted since 1919. He could do so partly because Britain was rapidly rearming. By early 1940, in fact, Britain was spending nearly as large a share of its national income on the military as Germany was.

Chamberlain's assertive statement was not enough to deter Hitler, who seems to have been determined to settle the Polish question by force. In an effort to localize the conflict, however, Hitler continued to insist that German aims were limited and reasonable. Germany simply wanted Danzig and German transit across the corridor; it was the Polish stance that was rigid and unreasonable. Hitler apparently believed that Polish stubbornness would alienate the British and French, undercutting their support. And as the crisis developed by mid-1939, doubts were increasingly expressed, on all sides, that the British and French were really prepared to aid Poland militarily—that they had the will "to die for Danzig."

Although they had been lukewarm to Soviet proposals for a military alliance, Britain and France began to negotiate with the Soviet Union more seriously during the spring and summer of 1939. But reservations about the value of a Soviet alliance continued to gnaw at Western leaders. For one thing, Soviet troops could gain access to Germany only by moving through Poland or Romania. But each had territory gained at the expense of Russia in the postwar settlement, so the British and French, suspicious of Soviet designs, were reluctant to insist that Soviet troops be allowed to pass through either country.

Even as negotiations between the Soviet Union and the democracies continued, the Soviets came to their own agreement with Nazi Germany on August 23, 1939, in a pact that astonished the world. Each side had been denouncing the other, and although Hitler had explored the possibility of Soviet neutrality in May, serious negotiations began only that August, when the Soviets got the clear signal that a German invasion of Poland was inevitable. It now appeared that no Soviet alliance with Britain and France could prevent war. Under these circumstances, a nonaggression pact with Germany seemed better to serve Soviet interests than a problematic war on the side of Britain and France. So the Soviets agreed with the Germans that each would remain neutral in the event that either became involved in a war with some other nation.

The Soviet flip-flop stemmed partly from disillusionment with the British and French response to the accelerating threat of Nazism. The democracies seemed no more trustworthy, and potentially no less hostile, than Nazi Germany. But the Soviets were playing their own double game. A secret protocol to the **Nazi-Soviet Pact** apportioned major areas of east-central Europe between the Soviet Union and Germany. As a result, the Soviets soon regained much of what they had lost after World War I, when Poland, Finland, and other states had been created or aggrandized with territories that had been part of the tsarist empire.

The Nazi-Soviet Pact seemed to give Hitler the free hand he wanted in Poland. With the dramatic change in alignment, the democracies were surely much less likely to intervene. But Chamberlain, again determined to avoid the hesitations of 1914, publicly reaffirmed the British guarantee to Poland on August 25. Britain would indeed intervene if Germany attacked. And after Hitler ordered the German invasion of Poland on September 1, the British and French responded with declarations of war on September 3.

With each step on the path to war, Hitler had vacillated between apparent reasonableness and wanton aggressiveness. Sometimes he accented the plausibility of his demands in light of problems with the postwar settlement; sometimes he seemed to be actively seeking war. Even in invading Poland, he apparently still hoped to localize hostilities. But he was certainly willing to risk a more general European war, and the deepest thrust of his policy was toward an all-out war of conquest—first against Poland, but ultimately against the Soviet Union. War was essential to the Nazi vision, and only when the assault on Poland became a full-scale war did the underlying purposes of Nazism become clear.

SECTION SUMMARY

- In light of the ideological polarization of the period, even the efforts to check Hitler by Britain and France, the major European democracies, depended partly on their relations with fascist Italy and the Soviet Union.

- Germany's remilitarization of the Rhineland in March 1936 prompted no military response by France and Britain, even though Germany's move removed the trump card that France had won with the Versailles treaty.

- In "appeasing" Hitler, Neville Chamberlain was not simply caving in but was seeking, through creative diplomacy, to remove the present sources of international hostility.

- Disillusioned by Hitler's course after the Munich agreement of September 1938, Chamberlain announced in March 1939 that Britain and France would intervene militarily should Germany threaten Poland's independence.

- Although they came to terms with Hitler's Germany in 1939 partly from mistrust of Britain and France, the Soviets quickly pursued their own aggressive aims in north-central Europe.

Nazi-Soviet Pact Surprise agreement between the Soviet Union and Nazi Germany in August 1939 that each would remain neutral if the other went to war against some other nation.

With what array of measures did governments respond to the Great Depression?

Why did the Stalinist attempt to build "socialism in one country" lead to the "terror-famine" of 1932–1933 and the "great terror" of 1937–1938?

Through what measures did the Nazi regime claim to be improving the quality of the German population?

Why did the "popular front" strategy prove counterproductive in both France and Spain?

Why did the other countries not stop Hitler's Germany before it was strong enough to start a new European war in 1939?

The Great Depression caught decision makers in the democracies unprepared. Reflecting conventional economic thinking, their initial response was to keep government budgets balanced. But this required cutting government spending on such measures as unemployment benefits, which not only added to the human misery but also intensified the economic contraction. The further effort to protect domestic economies through higher tariffs also worsened the downturn by restricting global trade. Only after several years, and for quite disparate reasons, did governments begin increasing spending and thereby stimulating renewed economic growth.

Stalin sought to rekindle the Russian revolutionary experiment by attempting to build "socialism in one country." The essential prerequisite was rapid industrialization, to be financed by squeezing the peasantry through forced collectivization in agriculture. Both the collectivization itself and the ensuing extractions of agricultural produce were extremely brutal, culminating in the "terror-famine" of 1932–1933. Partly because of its brutality, and partly because its economic results were mixed at best, the Stalinist departure produced opposition even from within the Communist Party. Seeking to root out those who might be sabotaging the great Soviet experiment, Communist leaders embarked on a series of purges and show trials, but their effort gradually spun out of control, producing the "great terror" of 1937–1938.

Population engineering, based on eugenics—on the one hand, racism and anti-Semitism, on the other—was central to the Nazis' domestic program. Determined to implement radical eugenics measures that had been discussed but not implemented under the Weimar Republic, the regime launched a program of forced sterilization in 1933. By the eve of World War II, German medical personnel were actually killing mental patients, the terminally ill, and others deemed unfit. Even as they sought to "improve" the "Aryan" population through such eugenics measures, the Nazis also sought ethnic homogeneity, especially by stripping German Jews of citizenship rights in an effort to force emigration.

Hitler's consolidation of power in Germany and the apparent threat of fascism in France in 1934 prompted leaders of the Comintern to make resistance to the further spread of fascism their top priority. To that end, communists spearheaded the formation of "popular fronts" with socialists and others concerned to preserve democratic institutions. But though it produced electoral successes in 1936 in Spain and France, the strategy proved polarizing. Popular front electoral victories produced radical pressures that the new popular front governments had trouble containing. Those pressures eventually produced a backlash from the right. Partly as a result, democracy was defeated in both Spain and France by 1940.

Hitler's aggressive foreign policy provided an unprecedented challenge to the European order, but the leading democracies, Britain and France, were slow to respond. Eagerness to avoid another war affected their reactions, as did the ideological polarization of the decade. But up to a point, Hitler's steps could seem legitimate, in terms of principles of national sovereignty and ethnic self-determination that had been compromised to Germany's disadvantage at the Paris Peace Conference. In 1939, when Hitler's further steps could no longer be justified in such terms, the democracies, led by Britain, at last began to stiffen. But Hitler was determined to crush Poland. The Nazi-Soviet Pact seemed to make the intervention of Britain and France unlikely, but the Nazi leader was more than willing to risk another European war.

Looking Ahead

During the 1930s the democracies had to respond to three novel regimes—Italian fascism, German Nazism, and Stalinist communism—that did not play by the expected rules. Although they involved ordinary people in new ways, each of the three regimes concentrated power in the hands of dictators. Thus they were at once dynamic and unpredictable—and thus, in part, the hesitancy and uncertainty of the democracies in dealing with them. The hesitations of the democracies during the 1930s tended to confirm the view of the three dictators that democracy was weak, decadent, passé. Such contempt inclined Mussolini and Hitler to ever greater recklessness and persuaded Stalin finally to make his own deal with the Nazis in August 1939. When Germany invaded Poland on September 1, Hitler believed the democracies would let him have his way. It was hardly clear that this would end up another European war, let alone the most destructive, cataclysmic war the world had ever seen.

Key Terms

Online Study Center **Improve Your Grade** Flashcards

collectivization (p. 844)

show trials (p. 845)

gulag (p. 845)

Adolf Hitler (p. 847)

National Socialist (Nazi) Party (p. 847)

Schutzstaffel (SS) (p. 850)

Kristallnacht (Crystal Night) (p. 854)

"euthanasia" program (p. 854)

popular front (p. 856)

Rome-Berlin Axis (p. 862)

remilitarization of the Rhineland (p. 862)

appeasement (p. 862)

Nazi-Soviet Pact (p. 865)

Suggested Reading

Applebaum, Anne. *Gulag: A History*. 2003. A major survey of the Soviet camp network, based on extensive new research. Comprehensive, but sensitive and accessible.

Bell, P. M. H. *The Origins of the Second World War in Europe.* 2d ed. 1997. A well-organized and fair-minded survey.

Burleigh, Michael. *The Third Reich: A New History*. 2000. A lengthy reinterpretation by a major authority who uses the notions of totalitarianism and political religion to place the Nazi experience within the wider context of the era.

Fitzpatrick, Sheila. *Everyday Stalinism, Ordinary Life in Extraordinary Times: Soviet Russia in the 1930s.* 1999. An engaging, balanced account of urban life in the Soviet Union in the context of the upheavals of the 1930s.

Kershaw, Ian. *Hitler,* vol. 1, *1889–1936, Hubris,* and vol. 2, *1936–1945, Nemesis.* 1999, 2000. Thorough and readable, the most important biography of Hitler.

Northrop, Douglas. *Veiled Empire: Gender and Power in Stalinist Central Asia.* 2004. Examines the anomalies that resulted as the Communists sought to bring their revolution to Uzbekistan, in Soviet central Asia, by reforming Muslim gender relations.

Paxton, Robert O. *The Anatomy of Fascism.* 2004. Comes to an effective conclusion based on a careful account of the actual trajectories of the major fascist movements and regimes.

Roberts, David D. *The Totalitarian Experiment in Twentieth-Century Europe.* 2006. Seeks to reassess the historically specific common elements in the Soviet communist, Italian fascist, and Nazi German experiments of the interwar period.

Watt, Donald Cameron. *How War Came: The Immediate Origins of the Second World War, 1938–1939.* 1989. A detailed but readable narrative account, based on thorough research.

Weber, Eugen. *The Hollow Years: France in the 1930s.* 1994. A lively account of French life and manners during a decade that led to humiliation and defeat.

Notes

1. Quoted in Martin McCauley, *The Soviet Union Since 1917* (London and New York: Longman, 1981), pp. 72-73.

2. Quoted in Robert Conquest, *The Great Terror: A Reassessment* (New York: Oxford University Press, 1990), p. 24.

3. Quoted in Helmut Krausnick et al., *Anatomy of the SS State* (New York: Walker, 1968), p. 13.

28

The Era of the Second World War, 1939–1949

Atomic Bombing of Nagasaki, August 9, 1945
When this photo was taken, from an observation plane 6 miles up, thirty-five thousand people on the ground had already died. *(By courtesy of the Trustees of the Imperial War Museum)*

"The effects could well be called unprecedented, magnificent, beautiful, stupendous and terrifying. No man-made phenomenon of such tremendous power had ever occurred before. . . . Thirty seconds after the explosion came first, the air blast pressing hard against the people and things, to be followed almost immediately by the strong, sustained, awesome roar which warned of doomsday and made us feel that we puny things were blasphemous to dare tamper with the forces heretofore reserved to The Almighty."[1]

So wrote Brigadier General Thomas F. Farrell, who had just witnessed the birth of the atomic age. On July 16, 1945, watching from a shelter 10,000 yards away, Farrell had seen the first explosion of an atomic bomb at a remote, top-secret U.S. government testing ground near Alamogordo, New Mexico. Such a weapon had been little more than a theoretical possibility when World War II began, and it required a remarkable concentration of effort, centered first in Britain, then in the United States, to make possible the awesome spectacle that confronted General Farrell. Exceeding most expectations, the test revealed a weapon of unprecedented power and destructiveness.

Within weeks, the United States dropped two other atomic bombs—first on Hiroshima, then on Nagasaki—to force the surrender of Japan in August 1945. Thus ended the Second World War, the conflict that had begun six long years earlier with the German invasion of Poland. At first Germany enjoyed remarkable success, prompting Italy to intervene and encouraging Japanese aggressiveness as well. But Britain held on even after its ally, France, fell to Germany in 1940. Then the war changed character in 1941 when Germany attacked the Soviet Union and Japan attacked the United States.

Britain, the United States, and the Soviet Union quickly came together in a "Grand Alliance," which spearheaded the victorious struggle against the Axis powers—Germany, Italy, and Japan. In Europe, the Soviet victory in a brutal land war with Germany proved decisive. In East Asia and the Pacific, the Americans gradually prevailed against Japan. The American use of the atomic bomb to end the war was the final stage in an escalation of violence that made World War II the most destructive war in history. What the

CHAPTER OUTLINE

THE VICTORY OF NAZI GERMANY, 1939–1941

THE ASSAULT ON THE SOVIET UNION AND THE NAZI NEW ORDER

A GLOBAL WAR, 1941–1944

THE SHAPE OF THE ALLIED VICTORY, 1944–1945

INTO THE POSTWAR WORLD

KEY TERMS

Vichy France
Charles de Gaulle
Winston Churchill
Auschwitz-Birkenau
Stalingrad
"the Great Patriotic War"
Franklin Delano Roosevelt

Lend-Lease Act
D-Day
Yalta conference
United Nations
Potsdam conference
Nuremberg trials
"iron curtain"
cold war
Truman Doctrine

Online Study Center
This icon will direct you to interactive map and primary source activities on the website **college.hmco.com/pic/noble5e**

advent of this terrifying new weapon would mean for the future remained unclear in the war's immediate aftermath.

The ironic outcome of the Second World War was a new cold war between two of the victors, the United States and the Soviet Union. Emerging from the war with far greater power and prestige, each assumed a world role that would have been hard to imagine just a few years earlier. By the end of the 1940s, these two new superpowers had divided Europe into competing spheres of influence. Indeed, the competition between the United States and the Soviet Union almost immediately became global in scope, creating a bipolar world. And the cold war between them was especially terrifying because, seeking military advantage, they raced to stockpile ever more destructive nuclear weapons. Thus the threat of nuclear annihilation helped define the cold war era.

World War II led to the defeat of Italy, Germany, and Japan and in this sense resolved the conflicts that had caused it. But the experience of this particular war changed the world forever. Before finally meeting defeat, the Nazis were sufficiently successful to begin implementing their "new order" in Europe, especially in the territories they conquered to the east. As part of this effort, in what has become known as the Holocaust, they began systematically murdering Jews in extermi-

nation camps, eventually killing as many as six million. The most destructive of the camps was at Auschwitz (OWSH-vits), in what had been Poland. Often paired after the war, Auschwitz and Hiroshima came to stand for the incredible new forms of death and destruction that the war had spawned—and that continued to haunt the world long after it had ended, posing new questions about the meaning of Western civilization.

FOCUS QUESTIONS

What were the outcomes of the war as of late spring 1941, before the German invasion of the Soviet Union and before the intervention of the United States?

What was the place of the Holocaust in the Nazi effort to begin constructing a "new order" in eastern Europe?

How did the Grand Alliance of Britain, the United States, and the Soviet Union come together against the Axis powers?

How did the Allies manage to defeat Nazi Germany in World War II, after Germany's remarkable initial successes?

What was the relationship between the Allied victory in World War II and the coming of the cold war?

THE VICTORY OF NAZI GERMANY, 1939–1941

What were the outcomes of the war as of late spring 1941, before the German invasion of the Soviet Union and before the intervention of the United States?

nstead of the enthusiasm evident in 1914, the German invasion of Poland on September 1, 1939, produced a grim sense of foreboding, even in Germany. Well-publicized incidents such as the German bombing of civilians during the Spanish civil war and the Italian use of poison gas in Ethiopia suggested that the frightening new technologies introduced in World War I would now be used on a far greater scale. The new conflict would be a much uglier war, more directly involving civilians.

Still, as in 1914, there were hopes that this war could be localized and brief—that it would not become a "world war." Hitler and the Germans envisioned a *Blitzkrieg*, or "lightning war," and the initial outcome seemed to confirm these expectations. Poland fell quickly, and Hitler publicly offered peace to Britain and France, seriously thinking that might be the end of it. The British and French refused to call off the war, but from 1939 through 1941 the Nazis won victory after victory, establishing the foundation for their new order in Europe.

INITIAL CONQUESTS AND "PHONY WAR"

The Polish army was large enough to have given the Germans a serious battle. But in adapting the technological innovations of World War I, Germany had developed a new military strategy based on rapid mobility. This Blitzkrieg strategy employed swift, highly concentrated offensives based on mobile tanks covered with concentrated air support, including dive-bombers that struck just ahead of the tanks. In Poland this strategy proved decisive. The French could offer only token help, and the last Polish unit surrendered on October 2, barely a month after the fighting had begun. The speed of the German victory stunned the world.

Meanwhile, the Soviets began cashing in on the pact they had made with Nazi Germany a few weeks before. It offered a precious opportunity to undo provisions of the World War I settlement that had significantly diminished the western territories of the former Russian Empire. On September 17, with the German victory in Poland assured, Stalin sent Soviet forces westward to share in the spoils. Soon Poland was again divided between Germany and Russia, just as most of it had been before 1914. The Baltic states of Estonia, Latvia, and Lithuania soon fell as well.

When Finland proved less pliable, the Soviets invaded in November 1939. In the ensuing "Winter War," the Finns held out bravely, and the Soviets managed to prevail by March 1940 only by taking heavy casualties. The difficult course of the war in Finland seemed to confirm suspicions that Stalin's purge during the mid-1930s had substantially weakened the Soviet army. Still, by midsummer 1940, the Soviet Union had regained much of the territory it had lost during the upheavals that followed the revolution of 1917.

In the west, little happened during the strained winter of 1939–1940, known as the "Phony War." Then, on April 9, 1940, the Germans attacked Norway and Denmark in a surprise move to preempt a British and French scheme to cut off the major route for the shipment of Swedish iron ore to Germany. Denmark fell almost at once, while the staunch resistance in Norway was effectively broken by the end of April. The stage was set for the German assault on France.

THE FALL OF FRANCE, 1940

The war in the west began in earnest on May 10, 1940, when Germany attacked France and the Low Countries. The Germans launched their assault on France through the Ardennes Forest, above the northern end of the Maginot Line—terrain so difficult the French had discounted the possibility of an enemy strike there (see page 810). As in 1914, northern France quickly became the focus of a major war pitting French forces and

CHRONOLOGY

September 1, 1939	Germany invades Poland
1939–1940	Soviets wage "Winter War" against Finland
1940	Germany attacks Denmark and Norway (April)
	Germany attacks the Netherlands, Belgium, and France (May 10)
1941	Germany attacks the Soviet Union (June 22)
	Churchill and Roosevelt agree to the Atlantic Charter (August)
December 7, 1941	Japan attacks Pearl Harbor
August 1942–February 1943	Battle of Stalingrad
November 1942	Allied landings in North Africa
1943	Warsaw ghetto revolt (April–May)
	Soviet victory in Battle of Kursk-Orel (July)
	Allied landings in Sicily; fall of Mussolini; Italy asks for an armistice (July)
	Teheran conference (November)
June 6, 1944	D-Day: Allied landings in Normandy
February 1945	Yalta conference
May 7–8, 1945	Germany surrenders
June 1945	Founding of the United Nations
July–August 1945	Potsdam conference
August 6, 1945	U.S. atomic bombing of Hiroshima
August 15, 1945	Japan announces surrender
March 1947	Truman Doctrine
June 1948–May 1949	Berlin blockade and airlift
August 1949	First Soviet atomic bomb
September 1949	Founding of the Federal Republic in West Germany

their British allies against invading Germans. But this time, in startling contrast to World War I, the Battle of France was over in less than six weeks, a humiliating defeat for the French.

The problem for France was not lack of men and materiel, but strategy. Germany had only a slight numerical

871

MAP 28.1   World War II: European Theaters

Much of Europe saw fighting during World War II, although different fronts were important at different times. What proved decisive was the fighting that ensued in the vast expanse of the Soviet Union after the Germans invaded in June 1941.

advantage in tanks but used mobile tanks and dive-bombers to mount rapid, highly concentrated offensives. Anticipating another long, defensive war, France had dispersed its tanks among infantry units along a broad front. Once the German tank column broke through the French lines, it quickly cut through northern France and moved toward the North Sea. France's poor showing convinced the British that rather than commit troops and planes to a hopeless battle in France, they should get out and regroup for a longer global war. Finally, in early June, 200,000 British troops—as well as 130,000 French—escaped German encirclement and capture through a difficult evacuation at Dunkirk (see **MAP 28.1**).

By mid-June, Germany had won a decisive victory. As the French military collapsed, the French cabinet resigned, to be replaced by a new government under Marshal Philippe Pétain, who had led the successful French effort in the Battle of Verdun during World War I. Pétain's government first asked for an armistice and then engineered a change of regime. The French parliament voted by an overwhelming majority to give Pétain exceptional powers, including the power to draw up a new constitution. So ended the parliamentary democracy of the Third Republic, which seemed responsible for France's weakness. The republic gave way to the more authoritarian **Vichy** (VEE-shee) regime, named after the resort city to which the government retreated as the Germans moved into Paris. The end of the fighting in France resulted in a kind of antidemocratic revolution, but one in which the French people, stunned by military defeat, at first acquiesced.

According to the armistice agreement, the French government was not only to cease hostilities but also to collaborate with the victorious Germans. French resistance began immediately, however. In a radio broadcast from London on June 18, **Charles de Gaulle** (1890–1970), the youngest general in the French army, called

Vichy France   Authoritarian French government, headquartered in the town of Vichy, that followed the Third Republic after France's defeat by Nazi Germany in 1940. The government collaborated with the victorious Germans, who occupied Paris.

Charles de Gaulle   The youngest general in the French army, he called on French forces to follow his lead and continue the fight against Nazi Germany after the fall of France in June 1940.

on French forces to rally to him to continue the fight against Nazi Germany. The military forces stationed in the French colonies, as well as the French troops that had been evacuated at Dunkirk, could form the nucleus of a new French army. Under the present circumstances of military defeat and political change, de Gaulle's appeal seemed quixotic at best. Most French colonies went along with what seemed the legitimate French government at Vichy—to which de Gaulle was a traitor. Yet a new Free French force grew from de Gaulle's remarkable appeal, and its subsequent role in the war compensated, in some measure, for France's humiliating defeat in 1940.

WINSTON CHURCHILL AND THE BATTLE OF BRITAIN

With the defeat of France, Hitler seems to have expected that Britain, now apparently vulnerable to German invasion, would come to terms. And certainly some prominent Britons questioned the wisdom of remaining at war. But the British war effort found a new and effective champion in **Winston Churchill** (1874–1965), who replaced Neville Chamberlain as prime minister on May 10, when the German invasion of western Europe began. Although Churchill had been prominent in British public life for years, his career to this point had not been noteworthy for either judgment or success. He was obstinate, difficult, something of a curmudgeon. Yet he rose to the wartime challenge, becoming one of the notable leaders of the modern era. In speeches to the House of Commons during the remainder of 1940, he inspired his nation with perhaps the most memorable words of the war. Though some found a negotiated settlement with Germany even more sensible in light of the outcome in France, Churchill's dogged promise of "blood, toil, tears, and sweat" helped rally the British people, so that later he could say, without exaggeration, that "this was their finest hour."

Online Study Center   **Improve Your Grade**
Primary Source: "This Was Their Finest Hour"

After the fall of France, Churchill's Britain promptly moved to full mobilization for a protracted war. Indeed, Britain developed the most thoroughly coordinated war economy of all the belligerents, producing more tanks, aircraft, and machine guns than Germany did between 1940 and 1942. The National Service Act of 1941 subjected men ages 18 to 50 and women ages 20 to 30 to military or civilian war service. The upper age limits were subsequently raised to meet the demand for labor. Almost 70 percent of the three million

Winston Churchill   British prime minister during World War II, his courage and decisiveness made him widely seen as one of modern Britain's greatest leaders.

people added to the British work force during the war were women.

Britain, then, intended to continue the fight even after France fell. Hitler weighed his options and decided to attack. In light of British naval superiority, he hoped to rely on aerial bombardment to knock the British out of the war without an actual invasion. The ensuing Battle of Britain culminated in the nightly bombing of London from September 7 through November 2, 1940, killing fifteen thousand people and destroying thousands of buildings. But the British held. Ordinary people holed up in cellars and subway stations, while the fighter planes of the Royal Air Force fought back effectively, inflicting heavy losses against German aircraft over Britain.

Although the bombing continued into 1941, the British had withstood the worst the Germans could deliver, and Hitler began looking to the east, his ultimate objective all along. In December 1940 he ordered preparations for Operation Barbarossa, the assault on the Soviet Union. Rather than continuing the attack on Britain directly, Germany would use submarines to cut off shipping—and thus the supplies the British needed for a long war. Once Germany had defeated the Soviet Union, it would enjoy the geopolitical basis for world power, while Britain, as an island nation relying on a dispersed empire, would sooner or later be forced to come to terms.

ITALIAN INTERVENTION AND THE SPREAD OF THE WAR

Lacking sufficient domestic support, and unready for a major war, Mussolini could only look on as the war began in 1939. But as the Battle of France neared its end, it seemed safe for Italy to intervene, sharing in the spoils of what appeared certain victory. Thus in June 1940 Italy entered the war, expecting to secure territorial advantages in the Mediterranean, starting with Corsica, Nice, and Tunisia, at the expense of France. Italy also hoped eventually to supplant Britain in the region—and even to take the Suez Canal.

Although Hitler and Mussolini got along reasonably well, their relationship was sensitive. When Hitler seemed to be proceeding without Italy during the first year of the war, Mussolini grew determined to show his independence. Finally, in October 1940, he ordered Italian forces to attack Greece. But the Greeks mounted a strong resistance, thanks partly to the help of British forces from North Africa.

Meanwhile, Germany had established its hegemony in much of east-central Europe without military force, often by exploiting grievances over the outcome of the Paris Peace Conference in 1919. In November 1940 Romania and Hungary joined the Axis camp, and Bulgaria followed a few months later. But in March 1941, just after Yugoslavia had similarly committed to

British Resistance
At the height of the German bombing of Britain in 1940, Winston Churchill and his wife, Clementine, survey the damage in London.
(Hulton Archive/Getty Images)

the Axis, a coup overthrew the pro-Axis government in Yugoslavia, and the new Yugoslav government prepared to aid the Allies.

By this point Hitler had decided it was expedient to push into the Balkans with German troops, both to reinforce the Italians and to consolidate Axis control of the area. As the war's geographic extent expanded, its stakes increased, yet the Germans continued to meet every challenge. By the end of May 1941 they had taken Yugoslavia and Greece (see Map 28.1).

At the same time, the war was spreading to North Africa and the Middle East because of European colonial ties. The native peoples of the area sought to take advantage of the conflict among the Europeans to pursue their own independence. Iraq and Syria became involved as the Germans, operating from Syria, which was administered by Vichy France, aided anti-British

Arab nationalists in Iraq. But most important proved to be North Africa, where Libya, an Italian colony since 1912, lay adjacent to Egypt, where the British presence remained strong.

In September 1940 the Italian army drove 65 miles into Egypt, initiating almost three years of fighting across the North African desert. A British counter-offensive from December 1940 to February 1941 drove the Italians back 340 miles into Libya, prompting Germany to send some of its forces from the Balkans into North Africa. Under General Erwin Rommel (1891–1944), the famous "Desert Fox," Axis forces won remarkable victories in North Africa from February to May 1941. But successful though they had been, the German forays into North Africa and the Balkans had delayed the crucial attack on the Soviet Union.

SECTION SUMMARY

- In implementing its innovative *Blitzkrieg* strategy, Germany employed rapid, highly concentrated offensives that combined tanks and airpower to great effect.

- After Poland fell quickly, Hitler offered peace to Britain and France, seriously thinking that this particular war might be over.

- Once German victory in Poland was assured, the Soviet Union began sharing the spoils and, by mid-summer 1940, had regained much of the territory lost during the upheavals that followed the Russian Revolution.

- In dramatic contrast with World War I, France in 1940 fell to German invasion in less than six weeks.

- The defeat of France led to the end of the Third Republic and the advent of the authoritarian Vichy regime, which, according to the armistice agreement, was obliged to collaborate with Nazi Germany.

- Inspired by Churchill's determined leadership, the British withstood the sustained German air assault during the second half of 1940 and finally forced Hitler to alter his overall strategy.

THE ASSAULT ON THE SOVIET UNION AND THE NAZI NEW ORDER

What was the place of the Holocaust in the Nazi effort to begin constructing a "new order" in eastern Europe?

erman troops invaded the Soviet Union on June 22, 1941, initiating what proved to be the decisive confrontation of World War II. Although the Nazis enjoyed the expected successes for a while, the Soviets eventually prevailed, spearheading the Allied victory in Europe. Supplies from their new Allies—Britain and eventually the United States—aided the Soviet cause, but the surprising strength of the Soviet military effort was the most important factor in the eventual outcome. In the process, the Soviets suffered incredible casualties, and after they gained the

initiative, they proceeded with particular brutality as they forced the invading Germans back into Germany.

In doing so, the Soviets were responding to the unprecedented form of warfare that the Nazis had unleashed. While preparing for the attack on the Soviet Union, Hitler had made it clear to the Nazi leadership that this was to be no ordinary military engagement but a war of racial-ideological extermination. The Germans penetrated well into the Soviet Union, reaching the apex of their power late in 1942. German conquests by that point enabled Hitler to begin constructing the

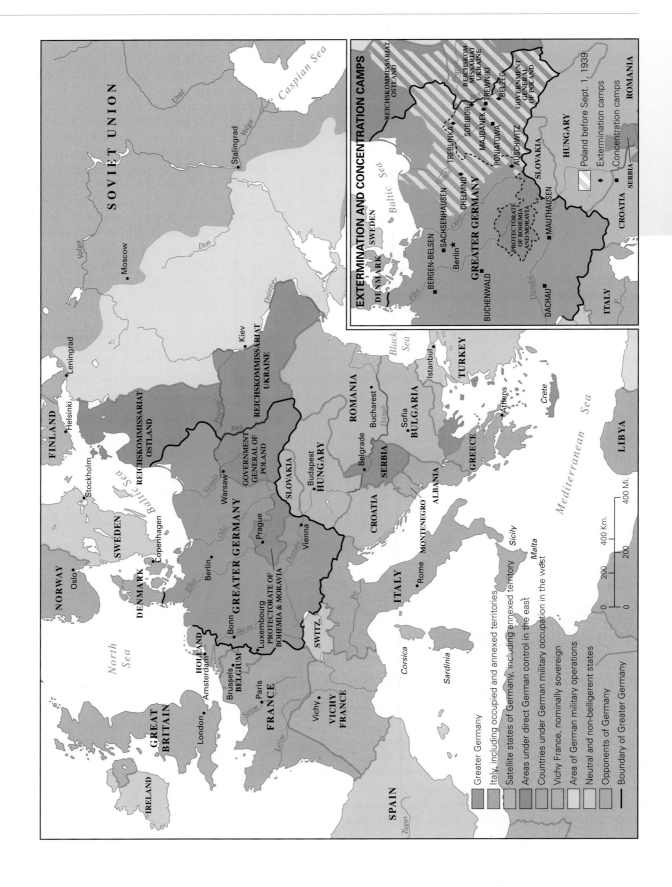

EXTERMINATION AND CONCENTRATION CAMPS

Poland before Sept. 1, 1939

◆ Extermination camps

■ Concentration camps

Greater Germany

Italy, including occupied and annexed territories

Satellite states of Germany, including annexed territory

Areas under direct German control in the east

Countries under German military occupation in the west

Vichy France, nominally sovereign

Area of German military operations

Neutral and non-belligerent states

Opponents of Greater Germany

Boundary of Greater Germany

MAP 28.2   The Nazi New Order in Europe, 1942

At the zenith of its power in 1942, Nazi Germany controlled much of Europe. Concerned most immediately with winning the war, the Nazis sought to coordinate the economies of their satellite states and conquered territories. But they also began establishing what was supposed to be an enduring new order in eastern Europe. The inset shows the locations of the major Nazi concentration camps and the six extermination camps the Nazis constructed in what had been Poland.

Forgive me, comrade . . .

On June 23, 1941, the day after Nazi Germany attacked the Soviet Union, the *London Daily Mail* published this cartoon depicting Hitler's betrayal of his 1939 pact with Stalin.   (Daily Mail, *London, 23 June 1941.* Reprinted with permission of Solo Syndication Limited)

—by Illingworth.

new, race-based European order he had dreamed of. Although in western Europe the Nazis generally sought the collaboration of local leaders, in the Soviet Union, as in Poland, the new order meant brutal subjugation of local populations. As part of this process, the Nazis began systematically killing Jews, first by shooting, then by mass-gassing them in specially constructed death camps.

AN AMBIGUOUS OUTCOME, 1941–1942

In ordering preparations for Operation Barbarossa in December 1940, Hitler decided to risk attacking the Soviet Union before knocking Britain out of the war. Then he invaded the Balkans and North Africa in what may have been an unnecessary diversion. In retrospect, it is easy to pinpoint that combination as his fatal mistake. But in light of the Soviet purges of the 1930s and what seemed the poor performance of the Soviet army against Finland, Hitler had reason to believe the Soviet Union would crack relatively easily. Western military experts had come to similar conclusions, estimating that German forces would need but six weeks to take Moscow. And if Germany were to defeat the Soviet Union with another Blitzkrieg, it could gain control of the oil and other resources required for a longer war against Britain and, if necessary, the United States.

Attacking the Soviet Union on June 22, 1941, German forces achieved notable successes during the first month of fighting, partly because Stalin was so unprepared for this German betrayal. Ignoring warnings of an impending German assault, he had continued to live up to his end of the 1939 bargain with Hitler, even supplying the Germans with oil and grain. After the attack, Russia's defenses were at first totally disorganized, and by late November German forces were within 20 miles of Moscow.

But the Germans were ill-equipped for Russian weather, and as an early and severe winter descended, the German offensive bogged down. In December the Soviets mounted a formidable surprise counterattack

near Moscow. The German Blitzkrieg, which had seemed a sure thing in July, had failed. Germany might still prevail, but a different strategy would be required.

Although their initial assault had stalled, the Germans still had the advantage. German forces failed to take the key city of Leningrad in 1941, but they cut it off by blockade and, until early 1944, kept it under siege with relentless bombing and shelling. During the summer of 1942, they mounted another offensive, moving more deeply into the Soviet Union than before, reaching Stalingrad in November. But this proved the deepest penetration of German forces—and the zenith of Nazi power in Europe.

HITLER'S NEW ORDER

By the summer of 1942, Nazi Germany dominated the European continent as no power had before (see **MAP 28.2**). German military successes allowed the Nazi regime to begin building a new order in the territories under German domination. Satellite states in Slovakia and Croatia, and client governments in Romania and Hungary, owed their existence to Nazi Germany and readily adapted themselves to the Nazi system. Elsewhere in the Nazi orbit, some countries proved eager collaborators; others did their best to resist; still others were given no opportunity to collaborate but were ruthlessly subjugated instead.

The Nazis' immediate aim was simply to exploit the conquered territories to serve the continuing war effort. Precisely as envisioned, access to the resources of so much of Europe made Germany considerably less vulnerable to naval blockade than during World War I. France proved a particularly valuable source of raw materials; by 1943, for example, 75 percent of French iron ore went to German factories.

But the deeper purposes of the war were also clear in the way the Nazis treated the territories under their control, especially in the difference between east and west. Western Europe experienced plenty of atrocities, but Nazi victory there still led to something like conventional military occupation. The Germans tried to enlist the cooperation of local authorities in countries like Denmark, the Netherlands, and France, though with mixed results. And whereas the Nazis exploited the economy of France, for example, it never became clear what role France might play in Europe after a Nazi victory. However, in Poland and later in the conquered parts of the Soviet Union, there was no pretense of cooperation, and it was immediately clear what the Nazi order would entail.

After the conquest of Poland, the Germans annexed the western part of the country outright and promptly executed, jailed, or expelled members of the Polish elite—professionals, journalists, business leaders, and priests. The Nazis prohibited the Poles from entering the professions and restricted even their right to marry. All the Polish schools and most of the churches were simply closed.

In the rest of Poland, known as the General Government, Nazi policy was slightly less brutal at first. Most churches remained open, and Poles were allowed to practice the professions, but the Nazis closed most schools above the fourth grade, as well as libraries, theaters, and museums, as they sought to root out every expression of Polish culture. Some Poles in this area were forced into slave labor, but a final decision as to whether the Polish population was to be exterminated, enslaved, or shipped off to Siberia was postponed—to be made after the wider war had been won.

With the conquest of Poland, Nazi leaders proclaimed that a new era of monumental resettlement in eastern Europe had begun for Germany. Germans selected for their racial characteristics were now resettled in the part of Poland annexed to Germany. Most were ethnic Germans who had been living outside Germany.

During the fall of 1942, Heinrich Himmler's *Schutzstaffel* (SS), the select Nazi elite, began to arrest and expel peasants from the rest of Poland to make way for further German resettlement. By 1943 perhaps one million Germans had been moved into what had been Poland.

After the assault on the Soviet Union, Hitler made it clear that eastern Europe as far as the Ural Mountains was to be opened for German settlement. War veterans were to be given priority, partly because the German settlers would have to be tough to resist the Slavs, who would be concentrated east of the Urals. To prepare for German colonization, Himmler told SS leaders that Germany would have to exterminate thirty million Slavs in the Soviet Union. After the German invasion, the SS promptly began executing prisoners of war, as well as any Soviet leaders they could find. However, the Nazis expected that several generations would be required for the resettlement of European Russia.

THE HOLOCAUST

Conquest of the east also opened the way to a more radical solution to the "Jewish problem" than the Nazis had contemplated before. Under the cover of war, they began actually killing the Jews within their orbit. Thus began the process, and the experience, that has come to be known as the Holocaust.

When and why this radical policy was chosen remains controversial. Although prewar Nazi rhetoric occasionally suggested the possibility of actual physical extermination, talk of a "final solution to the Jewish problem" seemed to mean forced emigration. Although the precise chain of events that led to a more radical approach will no doubt remain uncertain, it was surely bound up with the fortunes of the war.

The Ghettos   The conquest of Poland, with a Jewish population of 3.3 million, gave the Nazis control over a far greater number of Jews than ever before. In 1940, as part of their effort to create a new order, the Nazis began confining Polish Jews to ghettos set up in Warsaw and five other cities. Although much brutality and many deaths accompanied this process, the Nazis had not yet adopted a policy of systematic killing. Indeed, at first no one knew what was to become of these Jews. At this point Nazi authorities were concentrating on removing, or even killing, non-Jewish Poles to make way for German resettlement into former Polish lands. The fate of the Jews would be decided later.

Online Study Center **Improve Your Grade**
Primary Source: The Ghettoization of the Jews: Prelude to the Final Solution

After the defeat of France, Himmler and the SS made tentative plans to develop a kind of superghetto for perhaps four million Jews on the island of Madagascar, at that point still a French colony, once the war had been won. However, as the Polish ghettos grew more crowded and difficult to manage, Nazi officials in Poland began pressing for a more immediate solution.

The SS Plan for Annihilation   At the same time, Hitler made it clear that the invasion of the Soviet Union would launch something new, a racial-ideological war of annihilation. Accompanying the military forces were specially trained SS units, essentially mobile killing squads, assigned to get rid of Communist Party officials and adult male Jews. But soon some began murdering Jewish women and children as well. By late November 1941, the Nazis had killed 136,000 Jews, most by shooting, in the invaded Soviet territories. But this mode of killing proved both inefficient and psychologically burdensome—even for these specially trained killers. Their experience in the Soviet Union combined with the problems in the Polish ghettos to lead Nazi leaders to begin seeking a more systematic and impersonal method of mass extermination by late summer 1941.

The most likely scenario is that Hitler settled on physical extermination of the Jews in the thrill of what seemed impending victory over the Soviet Union. At the end of July 1941, Reinhard Heydrich of the SS began developing a detailed plan, and by the fall the Nazis were sending German and Austrian Jews to the ghettos in Poland and actively impeding further Jewish emigration from Europe.

Heydrich explained his plan for the extermination of the Jews in January 1942 at a conference of high-ranking officials at Wannsee, a suburb of Berlin. The conference had been postponed from early December, and by January the operation had already begun. The Nazis took advantage of the personnel and the methods—especially the use of poison gas—that had proven effective during the "euthanasia" campaign of 1939 through 1941 in Germany (see pages 854–855). By March 1942 they had constructed several extermination camps with gas chambers and crematoria, intended to kill large numbers of Jews and dispose of their bodies as efficiently as possible. Now they began full-scale mass killing, targeting first the Polish Jews who had already been confined to ghettos. The Nazis brutally suppressed attempts at resistance, like the Warsaw ghetto uprising of April and May 1943.

The End of the Warsaw Ghetto
In April 1943 the sixty thousand Jews remaining in the Warsaw ghetto revolted rather than face shipment to the extermination camps. Many died in the ensuing fighting; others perished as the Germans set fire to the ghetto. Almost all the rest were captured and sent to their deaths at Treblinka. Before it was put down in May, the uprising killed at least three hundred Germans.   *(AP/Wide World Photos)*

Nazi Death Camps During the war the Nazis constructed six full-scale death camps, although not all were operating at peak capacity at the same time. All six were located in what had been Poland (see inset, Map 28.2). Horrifying though they were, the concentration camps in Germany, such as Dachau, Buchenwald, and Bergen-Belsen, were not extermination camps, although many Jews died in them late in the war.

The largest of the six death camps was the **Auschwitz-Birkenau** complex, which became the principal extermination center in 1943. The Nazis shipped Jews from all over Europe to Auschwitz, which was killing about twelve thousand people a day at the height of its operation in 1944. Auschwitz was one of two extermination camps that included affiliated slave-labor factories, in which Jews considered most able to work were often literally worked to death. Among the companies profiting from the arrangement were two of Germany's best known, Krupp and IG Farben.

The Jews typically arrived at one of the camps crammed into cattle cars on special trains. SS medical doctors subjected new arrivals to "selection," picking some for labor assignments and sending the others, including most women and children, to the gas chambers. Camp personnel made every effort to deceive the Jews who were about to be killed, to lead them to believe they were to be showered and deloused. Even in camps without forced-labor factories, Jews were compelled to do much of the dirty work of the extermination operation. But under the brutal conditions of the camps, those initially assigned to work inevitably weakened; most were then deemed unfit and put to death.

Secrecy Surrounding the Camps The Nazis took every precaution to hide what was going on in the death camps. The SS personnel involved were sworn to silence. Himmler insisted that if secrecy was to be maintained, the operation would have to be quick—and total, to include women and children, "so that no Jews will remain to take revenge on our sons and grandsons." Himmler constantly sought to accelerate the process, even though it required labor and transport facilities desperately needed for the war effort. Indeed, as the fortunes of war turned against Germany, the extermination of the Jews became a kind of end in itself.

Himmler and the other major SS officials, such as Rudolf Höss (HOESS), the commandant at Auschwitz, or Adolf Eichmann (IKE-mahn), who organized the transport of the Jews to the camps, were not simply sadists who enjoyed humiliating their victims. Rather, they took satisfaction in doing what they believed was their duty without flinching, without signs of weakness. Addressing a group of SS members in 1943, Himmler portrayed the extermination of the Jews as a difficult "historical task" that they, the Nazi elite, must do for their racial community: "Most of you know what it means to see a hundred corpses piled up, or five hundred, or a thousand. To have gone through this and—except for cases of human weakness—to have remained decent, that has made us tough. This is an unwritten, never to be written, page of glory in our history."[2]

However, as Himmler's casual reference to "cases of human weakness" suggests, a minority of camp guards and others failed to live up to this image and indulged in wanton cruelty toward their helpless victims. For some, the extermination process became the occasion to act out sadistic fantasies. But though this dimension is surely horrifying, the bureaucratic, factory-like nature of the extermination process has seemed still more troubling in some respects, for it raises questions about the nature of modern rationality itself. The mass killing of Jews required the expertise of scientists, doctors, and lawyers; it required the bureaucratic organization of the modern state—all to provide the most efficient means to a monstrous end.

Despite the overriding emphasis on secrecy, reports of the genocide reached the West almost immediately in 1942. At first, however, most tended to discount them as wartime propaganda of the sort that had circulated during World War I, when stories about Germans eating Belgian babies whipped up war fever. Skepticism about extermination reports was easier because there were a few concentration camps, like Theresienstadt (teh-REZ-ay-en-shtat) in the former Czechoslovakia, that housed Jews who had been selected for special treatment. These camps were not used for extermination and were not secret; the Red Cross was even allowed to inspect Theresienstadt several times. Those outside, and the German people as well, were led to believe that all the Jews were being interned, for the duration of the war, in camps like these, much as Japanese Americans were being interned in camps in the western United States at the same time. But even as the evidence grew, Allied governments, citing military priorities, refused pleas from Jewish leaders in 1944 to bomb the rail line into Auschwitz.

An Array of Victims The Nazis' policy of actually murdering persons deemed undesirable or superfluous did not start with, and was not limited to, the Jews. First came the "euthanasia" program in Germany, and the war afforded the Nazis the chance to do away with an array of other "undesirables," including Poles, Sinti and Roma ("Gypsies"), communists, homosexuals, and vagrants. The Nazis also systematically killed perhaps 2 million Soviet prisoners of war. So the most radical

Auschwitz-Birkenau The largest of Nazi Germany's six extermination camps, all of which were located in what had been Poland.

and appalling aspect of Nazism did not stem from anti-Semitism alone. This must not be forgotten, but neither must the fact that the Jews constituted by far the largest group of victims—perhaps 5.7 to 6 million, almost two-thirds of the Jews in Europe. (See the feature "The Visual Record: Holocaust Snapshots.")

COLLABORATION IN NAZI EUROPE

In rounding up Jews for extermination, and in establishing their new order in Europe, the Nazis found willing collaborators among some of the countries within their orbit. Several of them found collaboration with the victorious Nazi regime the best way to pursue their own nationalist agendas. Croatia, earlier part of the new state of Yugoslavia, was eager to round up Jews and Gypsies, as well as to attack Serbs, as part of its effort to establish itself as a nation-state. But national circumstances varied across Europe, and so did degrees of collaboration. In Denmark, Norway, and the Netherlands, the Nazis thought racial kinship would matter, but they never found sufficient support to make possible genuinely independent collaborationist governments. Denmark did especially well at resisting the German effort to round up Jews, as did Italy and Bulgaria.

Vichy France was somewhere in the middle, and thus it has remained particularly controversial. When the Vichy regime was launched during the summer of 1940, Marshal Pétain, its 84-year-old chief of state, enjoyed widespread support. Pétain promised to maximize French sovereignty and shield his people from the worst aspects of Nazi occupation. At the same time, the Vichy government claimed to be implementing its own "national revolution," returning France to authority, discipline, and tradition after the shambles of the Third Republic. Vichy's revolution was anti-Semitic and hostile to the left, so it seemed compatible, up to a point, with Nazism. And at first Germany seemed likely to win the war. Thus, Pétain's second-in-command, Pierre Laval (1883–1945), was willing to collaborate actively with the Nazis. The Vichy regime ended up doing much of the Nazis' dirty work for them—rounding up workers for forced shipment to German factories, hunting down members of the anti-German resistance, and picking up Jews to be sent to the Nazi extermination camps.

After the war, Pétain, Laval, and others were found guilty of treason by the new French government. Because of his advanced age, Pétain was merely imprisoned, while Laval and others were executed. Despite the contributions of de Gaulle's Free French and the French resistance, the shame of Vichy collaboration continued to haunt France, deepening the humiliation of the defeat in 1940.

TOWARD THE SOVIET TRIUMPH

The import of what happened elsewhere in Europe depended on the outcome of the main event, the German invasion of the Soviet Union. Although the German Sixth Army, numbering almost 300,000 men, reached Stalingrad by late 1942, the Germans could not achieve a knockout. The Soviets managed to defend the city in what was arguably the pivotal military engagement of World War II. While some Soviet troops fought street by street, house by house, others counterattacked, encircling the attacking German force. Hitler refused a strategic retreat, but his doggedness backfired. By the end of January 1943, the Soviets had captured what remained of the German force, about 100,000 men, very few of whom survived to return to Germany. Perhaps 240,000 German soldiers died in the Battle of **Stalingrad** or as prisoners afterward. But the price to the Soviets for their victory was far greater: a million Soviet soldiers and civilians died at Stalingrad.

Although the Germans resumed the offensive on several fronts during the summer of 1943, the Soviets won the tank battle of Kursk-Orel in July, and from then on Stalin's Red Army moved relentlessly westward, forcing the Germans to retreat. By February 1944 Soviet troops had pushed the Germans back to the Polish border, and the outcome of the war was no longer in doubt.

The Soviet victory on what proved the decisive front of World War II was incredible, in light of the upheavals of the 1930s and the low esteem in which most held the Soviet military in 1941. Portraying the struggle as **"the Great Patriotic War"** for national defense, Stalin managed to rally the Soviet people as the Germans attacked. Rather than emphasize communist themes, he recalled the heroic defenses mounted against invaders in tsarist times, including the resistance to Napoleon in 1812. But though the Soviets ultimately prevailed, the cost in death, destruction, and suffering was almost unimaginable. For example, by the time Soviet forces finally broke the siege of Leningrad in January 1944, a million people in the city had died, most from starvation, freezing, or disease. And the Soviets won on the battlefield partly by taking incredible numbers of casualties.

The invading Germans gained access to major areas of Soviet industry and oil supply, and by the end of 1941 the country's industrial output had been cut in half. Yet the Soviet Union was able to weather this blow and go

Stalingrad   Decisive World War II battle in which Soviet forces launched repeated counterattacks on Germany's Sixth Army, stopping it from advancing farther and finally forcing it to surrender.

"the Great Patriotic War"   Term for World War II devised by Joseph Stalin to rally Soviet citizens against the German invasion.

Holocaust Snapshots

What are we to make of these pictures? In one sense, they appear to be ordinary snapshots of the sort that became popular between the wars, as inexpensive cameras became common consumer items for the first time. But these photographs are hardly ordinary; they depict disturbing aspects of the Nazi effort to exterminate the Jews between 1941 and 1945. So we wonder who took these pictures—and why. Why did these particular images seem worth preserving? What do such photographs tell us about the mentality that made possible the monstrous process that we have come to know as the Holocaust?

More than 50 percent of the victims of the Holocaust died in the six extermination camps, the camps with systematic gassing facilities. Almost a quarter died from such factors as malnutrition, disease, or exhaustion while in transit, in the ghettos, or in the labor or concentration camps. The rest—more than one quarter of the victims—were killed individually, mostly by shooting, up close.

These photos, and many others like them, were taken by members of Hamburg-based Reserve Battalion 101 of the "order police," made famous through the somewhat conflicting accounts of Christopher R. Browning and Daniel Jonah Goldhagen.[3] This local branch of the complex German police system was sent to assist in the removal of Jews from a remote section of Poland in July 1942. Only upon arriving in the village of Józefów did these ordinary policemen find that their first task was to shoot large numbers of defenseless Jews one by one. When given their collective charge, these men were offered a chance to pull back from the actual murder of Jews. But the vast majority did what they were told—why?

We know that the men of Battalion 101 had not been specially selected and trained for such a task. Indeed, they were unprepared and surprised when, upon arriving in Józefów, they learned what they were there to do. Browning suggests that many of the men felt that they had to be tough, following orders based on government policy, whatever it entailed. Moreover, they did not want to appear weak or leave the dirty work to their comrades. Others tried not to think about what they were doing or masked it through heavy drinking.

But photographs like these suggest a further step. Ordinary Germans took them not so that they could forget, obviously, but precisely to remember and commemorate their participation. Indeed, the very act of taking the photographs was essential to their dehumanization and humiliation of the Jews. Notice the photo on the left, taken during the liquidation of the ghetto at Lukow, Poland, probably in the fall of 1942. Three of the four police officers are looking directly at the camera. Some of the officers have stern facial expressions, as if they are trying to convey their toughness and power. Others, such as the officer at far left, smile broadly for the camera. The Jews, meanwhile, are humiliated by being forced to kneel and raise their hands above their heads.

In the other photograph, Jews are shown digging their own graves. Unlike the one taken at Lukow, no officers appear in this photo and no one is posing for the camera. Yet somehow even this image seemed worth preserving in a snapshot.

What did these Germans find so memorable about what they were doing? We may first assume that sheer anti-Semitism was the key, a notion that Goldhagen wholeheartedly supports. He argues that these photographs manifest a virulent anti-Semitism endemic in German society even before the rise of Nazism. But most experts deny that German anti-Semitism had been especially pronounced before Hitler came to power, so something more complex was surely at work in the minds of these policemen. Especially as the Nazi revolution yielded an apocalyptic war of race, ideology, and annihilation, the Nazi regime's ongoing campaign to demonize the Jews affected the responses to the Jews by ordinary Germans. The Jews came to seem not merely superfluous, but alien and threatening.

Thus the key variable was not anti-Semitism per se but the momentum of the Nazi revolution itself. By 1942 a sense of the extraordinariness of the overall Nazi enterprise had produced an altered frame of mind in many reaches of German society. For example, a doctor involved in the earlier "euthanasia" program, Friedrich Mennecke, sought, in his letters to his wife, to chronicle for posterity this, "the greatest of times" in which he was privileged to participate.[4] In the same vein, historians Michael Burleigh and Wolfgang Wippermann found, as central to the Holocaust, "the group intoxication with violence and the prospect of going outside the limits of received moral norms."[5]

The ongoing Nazi revolution caught up even the members of Reserve Battalion 101 in essential

Lukow, Poland, July 1942   *(Yad Vashem Film and Photo Archive)*

Lomazy, Poland, August 1942   *(Courtesy, ZstL, Ludwigsburg, Germany)*

roles. So those who took, and kept, and perhaps showed off these photographs were not merely ordinary human beings, or even ordinary Germans, but ordinary *Nazified* Germans. To some extent they, too, believed themselves to be involved in an enterprise that was grandiose, unprecedented, and of world-historical import. They did not merely follow orders but came to experience the "extraordinary exhilaration" that Saul Friedländer found central to the overall extermination process.[6] Partly as a result, they sometimes fell into the gratuitous cruelty evident in many of the photographs they took. Most of these men would not have been capable of such cruelty under ordinary circumstances.

When the veterans of police Battalion 101 were put on trial in the 1960s, one of them, Erwin Graffman, noted that only after the fact had it occurred to him that the killing had been wrong.[7] When acting, he had believed in the essential rightness of the wider Nazi revolution. The participation of such people is not to be explained simply through universal, ahistorical mechanisms, as if "we all could have done it." Those operating from within the framework of the Nazi revolution were especially likely to have treated the Jews as they did, not just killing them, but often humiliating them—and finding something memorable in the process.

Thus, for these perpetrators, the import of capturing the extraordinary enterprise through snapshots. But twenty years later, those who took them found it almost impossible to explain what had been their mindset at the time. As Browning noted, "it was a different time and place, as if they

had been on another political planet, and the political values and vocabulary of the 1960s were useless in explaining the situation in which they had found themselves in 1942."[8] Yet these haunting images remain.

QUESTIONS

1. What, beyond sheer anti-Semitism, seems to have stimulated the policemen of Battalion 101 to preserve these scenes for posterity?

2. Does Erwin Graffman seem credible, or merely self-serving, when he says that, at the time these photographs were taken, he genuinely believed what he was doing was right?

Online Study Center
Improve Your Grade Visual Record Activities

883

Stalingrad, November 1942
From September 1942 until the German surrender early in February 1943, this city on the Volga River saw some of the heaviest fighting of World War II. The Soviet victory, in the face of incredible casualties, was arguably the turning point of the war in Europe. *(Sovfoto/Eastfoto)*

on to triumph. Outside help contributed, but only 5 to 15 percent of Soviet supplies came from the West. Between 1939 and 1941, Soviet leaders had begun building a new industrial base east of the Urals. And when the Germans invaded in 1941, the plant and equipment of 1,500 enterprises were dismantled and shipped by rail for reassembly farther east, out of reach of German attack. Then, beginning in 1942, thousands of brand-new factories were constructed in eastern regions as well.

Moreover, the earlier purges of the armed forces proved to have done less long-term damage than outside observers had expected. If anything, the removal of so many in the top ranks of the military hierarchy made it easier for talented young officers like Georgi Zhukov (1896–1974), who would become the country's top military commander, to rise quickly into major leadership positions.

When the United States entered the war in December 1941, the Soviets were fighting for survival. They immediately began pressuring the United States and Britain to open another front in Europe, preferably by landing in northern France, where an Allied assault could be expected to have the greatest impact. But the Allies did not invade northern France and open a major second front until June 1944. By then the Soviets had turned the tide in Europe on their own.

═══════════ S E C T I O N   S U M M A R Y ═══════════

- Although the German invasion of the Soviet Union in 1941 failed to bring the expected quick victory, the Germans drove still further into the country in 1942—but then met defeat at the Battle of Stalingrad.

- Brutal though it was, Nazi policy in northern and western Europe approached something like conventional military occupation, whereas in the conquered territories of the east, first and most dramatically in the former Poland, the Nazis engaged in radical population engineering as they began constructing a race-based "new order."

- By the end of 1941, the Holocaust became a systematic program as the Nazis decided to kill Jews and others by adapting the methods developed through the "euthanasia" program.

- Although the Jews constituted by far the largest group of victims, the Nazis also killed an array of others, from homosexuals to Soviet prisoners of war.

- After defeating the Germans at Kursk-Orel in July 1943, the Soviets began steadily advancing toward Germany, thereby turning the tide in Europe well before the U.S.-British landing in northern France opened a major second front in June 1944.

A GLOBAL WAR, 1941–1944

How did the Grand Alliance of Britain, the United States, and the Soviet Union come together against the Axis powers?

World War II proved unprecedented in its level of violence partly because it eclipsed even World War I in its geographical reach. The European colonial presence quickly drew the war to North Africa and the Middle East. But the war's early results in Europe also altered the power balance in East Asia and the Pacific, where the Russians and the Japanese had long been antagonists. During the 1930s, the United States had also become involved in friction with Japan. By 1941 President **Franklin Delano Roosevelt** was openly favoring the anti-Axis cause, though it took a surprise attack by the Japanese in December 1941 to bring the United States into the war.

JAPAN AND THE ORIGINS OF THE PACIFIC WAR

As a densely populated island nation lacking the raw materials essential for industry, Japan had been especially concerned about foreign trade and spheres of economic influence as it modernized after 1868. By the interwar period, the Japanese had become unusually reliant on exports of textiles and other products. During the Depression of the 1930s, when countries all over the world adopted protectionist policies, Japan suffered from increasing tariffs against its exports. This situation tilted the balance in Japanese ruling circles from free-trade proponents to those who favored a military-imperialist solution.

To gain economic hegemony by force, Japan could choose either of two directions. The northern strategy, concentrating on China, would risk Soviet opposition as well as strong local resistance. The southern strategy, focusing on southeast Asia and the East Indies, would encounter the imperial presence of Britain, France, the Netherlands, and the United States.

Japan opted for the northern strategy in 1931, when it took control of Manchuria, in northeastern China. But the Japanese attempt to conquer the rest of China, beginning in 1937, led only to an impasse by 1940. Japanese aggression in China drew the increasing hostility of the United States, a strong supporter of the Chinese nationalist leader Jiang Jieshi (Chiang Kaishek) (1887–1975), as well as the active opposition of the Soviet Union. Clashes with Soviet troops along the border between Mongolia and Manchuria led to significant defeats for the Japanese in 1938 and 1939. The combination of China and the Soviet Union seemed more than Japan could handle.

By 1941, Germany's victories in Europe had seriously weakened Britain, France, and the Netherlands, the major European colonial powers in southeast Asia and the East Indies. The time seemed right for Japan to shift to a southern strategy. To keep the Soviets at bay, Japan agreed to a neutrality pact with the Soviet Union in April 1941. Rather than worry about China and the areas of dispute with the Soviet Union, the Japanese would seek control of southeast Asia, a region rich in such raw materials as oil, rubber, and tin—precisely what Japan lacked.

Japan had already joined with Nazi Germany and fascist Italy in an anticommunist agreement in 1936. In September 1940, the three agreed to a formal military alliance. For the Germans, alliance with Japan was useful to help discourage U.S. intervention in the European war. Japan, for its part, could expect the major share of the spoils of the European empires in Asia. However, diplomatic and military coordination between Germany and Japan remained minimal.

The United States began imposing embargoes on certain exports to Japan in 1938, in response to the Japanese aggression in China. After Japan had assumed control of Indochina, nominally held by Vichy France, by the summer of 1941, the United States imposed total sanctions, and the British and Dutch followed, forcing Japan to begin rapidly drawing down its oil reserves. Conquest of the oil fields of the Dutch East Indies now seemed a matter of life and death to the Japanese.

These economic sanctions heightened the determination of Japanese leaders to press forward aggressively now, when the country's likely enemies were weakened or distracted. But the Japanese did not expect to achieve a definitive victory over the United States in a long, drawn-out war. Rather, they anticipated, first, that their initial successes would enable them to grab the resources to sustain a longer war if necessary, and, second, that Germany would defeat Britain, leading the United States to accept a compromise peace allowing the Japanese what they wanted—a secure sphere of economic hegemony in southeast Asia.

Some Japanese leaders—diplomats, businessmen, naval officers, and even the emperor and some of his circle—were dismayed by the prospect of war with the United States. But as the influence of the military grew

Franklin Delano Roosevelt U.S. president who served from 1933 to 1945, through the Great Depression of the 1930s and most of World War II.

MAP 28.3   The War in East Asia and the Pacific

After a series of conquests in 1941 and 1942, the Japanese were forced gradually to fall back before advancing U.S. forces. When the war abruptly ended in August 1945, however, the Japanese still controlled much of the territory they had conquered.

Online Study Center   **Improve Your Grade**   Interactive Map: World War II in the Pacific

during the 1930s, it became ever more difficult for those opposing Japan's new imperialist direction to make themselves heard. By 1941, a conformist confidence in victory was demanded, and dissenters dared not speak out for fear of being labeled traitors.

The Japanese finally provoked a showdown on December 7, 1941, with a surprise attack on Pearl Harbor, a U.S. naval base in Hawaii. The next day, Japanese forces seized Hong Kong and Malaya, both British colonies, and Wake Island and the Philippines, both under U.S. control. The United States promptly declared war; in response, Hitler kept an earlier promise

to Japan and declared war on the United States. World War II was now unprecedented in its geographic scope (see **MAP 28.3**).

Much like their German counterparts, Japanese forces got off to a remarkably good start. By the summer of 1942, Japan had taken Thailand, the Dutch East Indies, the Philippines, and the Malay Peninsula. Having won much of what they had been seeking, the Japanese began devising the Greater East Asia Co-Prosperity Sphere, their own "new order" in the conquered territories. (See the box "The Global Record: Japan's 'Pan-Asian' Mission.")

JAPAN'S "PAN-ASIAN" MISSION

With the coming of war against the Western powers in 1941, the Japanese could claim to be freeing Asians from Western imperialism and establishing a new economic order in East Asia and the Pacific. This selection from an essay titled "Our Present War and Its Cultural Significance," written just after the bombing of Pearl Harbor by the well-known author Nagayo Yoshio (1888–1961), accents Japan's anti-Western mission in the region. Yoshio understood, especially from his country's recent experience in China, that Asians might find Japanese hegemony just as oppressive as Western domination. Although it served Japan's own economic interests and was often applied brutally, Japanese "pan-Asianism" helped fuel the reaction against Western imperialism in Asia and the Pacific, with lasting results after the war.

Whenever Japan has faced a powerful enemy it has been the *yamato damashii* [Japanese national spirit] which provided the basis of our courage. Now that we can talk in retrospect of the Sino-Japanese War, I am afraid our national spirit has not been given a proper chance to be aroused, due to the deplorable fact that we had to fight with China, our sister nation, with no foreseeable conclusion to look forward to.... While desperately fighting with a country which we made our enemy only reluctantly we were trying to find out a principle, an ethic based upon a new view of the world, which would justify our course of action.... The China incident was not only insufficient to fulfill this goal but also met with insurmountable obstacles. Consequently, time and opportunity ripened to declare war against the United States and England....

... We would have nothing to say for ourselves if we were merely to follow the examples of the imperialistic and capitalistic exploitation of Greater East-Asia by Europe and the United States....

... It is true that the science of war is one manifestation of a nation's culture. But from this time on we have to realize the increasing responsibility on our part if we are to deserve the respect of the people of East-Asian countries as their leaders, in the sphere of culture in general (not only the mere fusion and continuance of Western and Oriental cultures but something surpassing and elevating them while making the most out of them) such as the formation of national character, refinement, intellect, training to become a world citizen, etc. ...

The sense of awe and respect with which the Orientals have held the white race, especially the Anglo-Saxons, for three hundred years is deep-rooted almost beyond our imagination. It is our task to realize this fact and deal with this servility at its root, find out why the white people became the objects of such reverence. It goes without saying that we cannot conclude simplemindedly that their shrewdness is the cause. Also we have to be very careful not to impose the *hakko ichiu* [the gathering of the whole world under one roof] spirit arbitrarily upon the Asians. If we make this kind of mistake we might antagonize those who could have become our compatriots and thus might also blaspheme our Imperial rule....

To sum up, we have finally witnessed the dawn of a new principle which we had been searching for over ten years.... The phrase "Greater East-Asian Co-prosperity Sphere" is no longer a mere abstract idea.

QUESTIONS

1. Why, according to the author, did the Japanese effort in China sow confusion about Japan's wider aims?

2. What role was Japan to play in southeast Asia if it was *not* merely to replace Western imperialistic exploitation with another form?

Source: "Our Present War and Its Cultural Significance" by Nagayo Yashio, translated by Mitsuko Iriye, in *Modern Asia and Africa*, edited by William H. McNeill and Mitsuko Iriye (New York: Oxford University Press, 1971), pp. 232–236.

THE UNITED STATES IN EUROPE AND THE PACIFIC

During the first years of the war in Europe, the United States did not have armed forces commensurate with its economic strength; in 1940, in fact, its army was smaller than Belgium's. But the United States could be a supplier in the short term and, if it chose to intervene, a major player over the longer term. With the Lend-Lease Act of March 1941, intended to provide war materiel without the economic dislocations of World War I, the United States lined up on the side of Britain against the Axis powers. In August 1941 a meeting between Churchill and Roosevelt aboard a cruiser off the coast of Newfoundland produced the Atlantic Charter, the first tentative agreement about the aims

Lend-Lease Act Act by the U.S. Congress authorizing President Franklin Roosevelt to lend or lease weapons or other aid to countries the president designated.

and ideals that were to guide the anti-Axis war effort. The Americans extended lend-lease to the Soviet Union the next month.

But though Roosevelt was deeply committed to the anti-Axis cause, isolationist sentiment remained strong in the United States. The Japanese attack on Pearl Harbor in December inflamed American opinion and enabled Roosevelt at last to bring his country into the war as an active belligerent. By May 1942 the United States had joined with Britain and the Soviet Union in a formal military alliance against the Axis powers.

The two democracies had joined with Stalin's Soviet Union in a marriage of expediency, and mutual suspicions marked the relationship from the start. Initially, Britain and the United States feared that the Soviet Union might even seek a separate peace, as Russia had in World War I. The Soviets, for their part, worried that these newfound allies, with their long-standing anticommunism, might hold back from full commitment or even seek to undermine the Soviet Union.

In response to pressure from Stalin, Britain and the United States agreed to open a second front in Europe as soon as possible. But the Nazis dominated the Continent, so opening such a front required landing troops from the outside. It proved far more difficult to mount an effective assault on Europe than either Churchill or Roosevelt anticipated in 1942. The resulting delays furthered Stalin's suspicions that his allies were only too eager to have the Soviets do the bulk of the fighting against Nazi Germany—and weaken themselves in the process.

The United States agreed with its new allies to give priority to the war in Europe. But because it had to respond to the direct Japanese assault in the Pacific, the United States was not prepared to act militarily in Europe right away. What it could do, however, was supply the British with the ships needed to overcome German submarines, which seriously threatened shipping to Britain by 1942.

In the Pacific theater, in contrast, it was immediately clear that the United States would bear the brunt of the fighting against Japan. Although the Japanese went from one success to another during the first months of the war, they lacked the long-term resources to exploit their initial victories. In May 1942 the Battle of Coral Sea—off New Guinea, north of Australia—ended in a stalemate, stopping the string of Japanese successes. Then in June, the United States defeated the Japanese navy for the first time in the Battle of Midway, northwest of Hawaii. After the United States stopped attempted Japanese advances in the Solomon Islands and New Guinea early in 1943, U.S. forces began steadily advancing across the islands of the Pacific toward Japan (see Map 28.3).

THE SEARCH FOR A SECOND FRONT IN EUROPE

As the Soviet army fought the Germans in the Soviet Union, the United States and Britain tried to determine how they could help tip the scales in Europe, now an almost impregnable German fortress. Stalin kept urging a direct assault across the English Channel, which, if successful, would have the greatest immediate impact. Churchill, however, advocated attacking the underbelly of the Axis empire by way of the Mediterranean, which would first require winning control of North Africa. And it was that strategy the Allies tried first, starting in 1942.

By May 1943, step one of Churchill's plan had succeeded, but North Africa was valuable only as a staging ground for an Allied attempt to penetrate Europe from the south (see Map 28.1). Meeting at the Moroccan city of Casablanca in January 1943, Churchill and Roosevelt agreed that British and American forces would proceed from North Africa to Sicily and on up through Italy. The Soviets, still pushing for an invasion across the English Channel into France, objected that the Germans could easily block an Allied advance through the long, mountainous Italian peninsula.

Crossing from North Africa, Allied troops landed in Sicily in July 1943, prompting the arrest of Mussolini and the collapse of the fascist regime. Supported by King Victor Emmanuel III, the Italian military commander, Pietro Badoglio (bah-DOHL-yo), formed a new government to seek an armistice. Meanwhile, Allied forces moved on to the Italian mainland, but the Germans quickly occupied much of Italy in response. They even managed a daring rescue of Mussolini and promptly re-established him as puppet leader of a new rump republic in northern Italy, now under German control. Just as the Soviets had warned, the Germans sought to block the Italian peninsula, and it was not until nine months later, in June 1944, that the Allies reached Rome. So Churchill's strategy of assaulting Europe from the south proved less than decisive.

Only when Churchill, Roosevelt, and Stalin met for the first time, at Teheran, Iran, in November 1943, did they agree that the next step would be to invade western Europe from Britain. Preparations had been underway since early 1942, but the operation was complex and hazardous in the extreme. Finally, Allied troops crossed the English Channel to make an amphibious landing on the beaches of Normandy, in northern France, on June 6, 1944, known to history as **D-Day.** Partly by deceiving the Germans seeking to defend the area, they were quickly able to consolidate their positions.

D-Day The complex Allied amphibious landings in Normandy, France, on June 6, 1944, that opened a second major European front in World War II.

The success of the D-Day invasion opened a major second front in Europe at last. Now American-led forces from the west and Soviet forces from the east worked systematically toward Germany. The one substantial German counterattack in the west, the Battle of the Bulge in December 1944, slowed the Allies' advance, but on March 7, 1945, Allied troops crossed the Rhine River (see Map 28.1).

By June 1944, when Allied forces landed at Normandy, Soviet forces had already crossed the 1939 border with Poland as they moved steadily westward. But in August the Soviets stopped before reaching Warsaw, allowing the Nazis to crush a notable uprising by the Polish resistance from August to October. The Polish Home Army, as it was called, was seeking to liberate Warsaw on its own, without waiting for the Soviets, who seemed likely to impose communism on Poland. In putting down the uprising, the German occupying forces suffered ten thousand casualties, then destroyed much of the city in retaliation. Meanwhile, the major Soviet thrust began cutting south, through Romania, which surrendered in August, and on into the Danube Valley in Hungary and Yugoslavia during the fall. The Soviets resumed their advance, taking Warsaw and moving westward toward Germany, only in January 1945.

Now, with the defeat of Germany simply a matter of time, Allied concern shifted to the postwar order. Churchill, especially, worried about the implications of the Soviet advances in east-central Europe and the Balkans. As a supplement to the D-Day landings, he wanted to strike from Italy through Yugoslavia into east-central Europe. But the Americans resisted; Churchill's priorities, they felt, reflected old-fashioned concerns over spheres of influence that were no longer appropriate. So the Allies concentrated instead on a secondary landing in southern France in August 1944. This assault, in which Free French forces were prominent, led quickly to the liberation of Paris. But because the Allies made both their landings in France, and not in southeastern Europe, the Western democracies were involved only in the liberation of western Europe. It was the Soviets who drove the Germans from east-central Europe and the Balkans. This fact, and the resulting geographic distribution of military strength, fundamentally affected the postwar order in Europe.

D-Day, 1944

Allied forces land at Normandy, early in the morning of June 6, 1944, at last opening a major second front in Europe. *(National Archives, Washington)*

- Japan turned to a more aggressive, expansionist foreign policy during the 1930s largely because its economy, heavily dependent on exports, proved especially vulnerable during the Great Depression.

- Although Japan and Nazi Germany each had reasons for a military alliance with the other, diplomatic and military coordination between them was minimal during World War II.

- Delays in opening a major second front in Europe furthered Stalin's suspicions that Britain and the United States were happy to let the Soviets bear the brunt of the burden in the fight against Nazi Germany.

- After the Allied invasion of Italy failed to make a conclusive difference on the continental level, Churchill, Roosevelt, and Stalin agreed in November 1943 that, as the next step, the democracies would invade western Europe from Britain.

- In making their continental landings in Italy and France, the Western democracies left it to the Soviets to drive the German forces from east-central Europe and the Balkans.

THE SHAPE OF THE ALLIED VICTORY, 1944–1945

How did the Allies manage to defeat Nazi Germany in World War II, after Germany's remarkable initial successes?

The leaders of the Soviet Union, Britain, and the United States sought to mold that postwar order at two notable conferences in 1945. Even as they brought different aspirations for the postwar world, they had to deal together with the legacy of a war of unprecedented violence and destruction. At the same time, they also had to face the hard military realities that had resulted from the fighting so far: each country had armies in certain places but not in others. The result was an informal division of Europe into spheres of influence among the victors.

The most serious question the Allies faced concerned Germany, which was widely held responsible for the two world wars, as well as for Nazism with all its atrocities—including the concentration and extermination camps, discovered with shock and horror by the advancing Allied armies in 1945. Germany was to be forced to surrender unconditionally; there would be no negotiation or armistice. But what should be done with the country over the longer term?

In the Pacific theater, as in Europe, the way the war ended had major implications for the postwar world. The United States decided to use the atomic bomb, a weapon so destructive that it forced a quick Japanese surrender. The suddenness of the ending helped determine the fate of the European empires in Asia.

THE YALTA CONFERENCE: SHAPING THE POSTWAR WORLD

When Stalin, Roosevelt, and Churchill met at Yalta, a Soviet Black Sea resort, in February 1945, Allied victory was assured, and the three leaders accomplished a great deal. Yet controversy has long surrounded the **Yalta conference.** Western critics have charged that the concessions made there to Stalin consigned east-central Europe to communist domination and opened the way to the dangerous cold war of the next forty years. At the time, however, the anticipation of victory produced a relatively cooperative spirit among the Allies. Thus they firmed up plans for military occupation of Germany in separate zones, for joint occupation of Berlin, and for an Allied Control Council, composed of the military commanders-in-chief, which would make policy for all of Germany by unanimous agreement.

Each of the Allies had special concerns, but each got much of what it was seeking at Yalta. Roosevelt was eager for Soviet help against Japan as soon as possible, and he won Soviet commitment to an agreement tentatively worked out earlier. In exchange for territorial concessions in Asia and the Pacific, Stalin agreed to declare war on Japan within three months of the German surrender.

Churchill, meanwhile, worried about the future of Europe in light of the American intention, which Roosevelt announced at Yalta, to maintain occupation troops in Europe for only two years after the war. To help balance Soviet power on the Continent, Churchill felt it essential to restore France as a great power. To this end, he urged that France be granted a share in the occupation of Germany and a permanent seat on the Security Council of the proposed new international organization,

Yalta conference 1945 meeting between Stalin, Roosevelt, and Churchill in which they began outlining plans for the postwar order, including the military occupation of Germany.

The Big Three at Yalta

With victory over Nazi Germany assured, Churchill, Roosevelt, and Stalin were in reasonably good spirits when they met at Yalta, a Black Sea resort in the Soviet Union, in February 1945. Important sources of friction among them were evident at the meeting, but the differences that led to the cold war did not seem paramount at this point. The Yalta conference proved to be the last meeting of the three leaders. *(F.D.R. Library)*

the **United Nations** (see page 898). Roosevelt agreed, even though he had little use for Charles de Gaulle or what he viewed as the pretensions of the French.

It seemed to the Americans that both Britain and the Soviet Union remained too wedded to traditional conceptions of national interest as they sought to shape the postwar world. Hence one of Roosevelt's major priorities was to secure British and Soviet commitment to the United Nations before the three allies began to disagree over particular issues. He won that commitment at Yalta, but only by giving in to Churchill on the sensitive matter of British colonies.

Because anti-imperial sentiment worked to Japan's advantage in Asia, the United States had pestered Britain on the colonial issue since early in the war. Roosevelt even asked Churchill in 1941 about British intentions in India. So prickly was Churchill that he proclaimed in 1942, "I have not become the King's First Minister in order to preside over the liquidation of the British Empire." The parties agreed at Yalta that the British Empire would be exempt from an anticipated measure to bring former colonies under United Nations trusteeship after the war.

Although it was not the only question on the table, the future of the former Axis territories was central to the seaside deliberations. By the time of the conference, those territories were already being divided into

spheres of influence among the Allies, and in light of the location of Allied troops, the eventual alignment was probably inevitable. In Italy, where U.S. and British troops held sway, the two democracies had successfully resisted Stalin's claim for a share in the administration. In east-central Europe, however, the Soviet army was in control. Still, the United States, with its vision of a new world order, objected to spheres of influence and insisted that democratic principles be applied everywhere. At Yalta this American priority led to an awkward compromise over east-central Europe: the new governments in the area were to be both democratic and friendly to the Soviet Union.

Most important to the Soviets was Poland, with its crucial location between the Soviet Union and Germany. Although they insisted that communists lead the new Polish government at the outset, the Soviets compromised by allowing a role for the noncommunist Polish government-in-exile in London and by promising free elections down the road. The Allies agreed that Poland would gain substantial German territory to its west to make up for the eastern territory it had already lost to the USSR (see **Map 28.4**).

In addition, the United States and Britain were to have a role in committees set up to engineer the transition to democracy in the rest of east-central Europe. However, only the Soviets had troops in the area, and those committees proved essentially powerless. The sources of future tension were already at work at Yalta, but they generally remained hidden by the high spirits of approaching victory.

United Nations International organization of nations founded in 1945 to encourage peace, cooperation, and recognition of human rights.

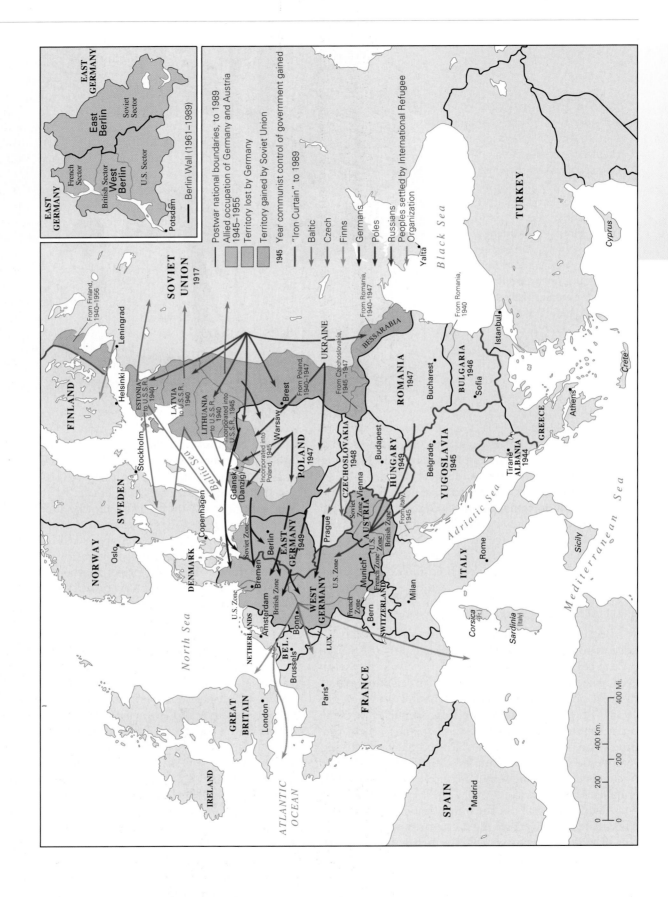

MAP 28.4 The Impact of World War II in Europe

As a result of World War II the Soviet Union expanded its western borders and Poland shifted westward at the expense of Germany. Territorial changes added to the wartime disruption and produced a flood of refugees. The cold war division of Europe did not depend on immediate territorial changes, but soon Germany itself came to be divided on east-west lines.

Online Study Center **Improve Your Grade**
Interactive Map: The Impact of World War II in Europe

VICTORY IN EUROPE

Although the tide had turned in 1943, Germany managed to continue the war by exploiting its conquered territories and by more effectively allocating its domestic resources for war production. Thanks partly to the efforts of armaments minister Albert Speer, war production grew sharply between 1941 and 1944, so Germany had plenty of weapons even as the war was ending. The Germans even proved able to withstand the systematic bombing of cities that the British, especially, had thought might prove decisive.

Beginning in 1942, British-led bombing attacks destroyed an average of half the built-up area of seventy German cities, sometimes producing huge firestorms. The bombing of the historic city of Dresden in February 1945 killed at least sixty thousand civilians in the most destructive air assault of the war in Europe. But despite this widespread destruction, such bombing did not undermine morale or disrupt production to the extent expected. Even in the face of steady Allied bombing, Germany increased its war production during 1943 and 1944.

But Germany encountered two crucial bottlenecks that finally crippled its military effort: it was running out of both oil and military personnel. Despite making effective use of synthetics, the Nazi war machine depended heavily on oil from Romania. And although the terror bombing of cities did not have the anticipated impact, the more precisely targeted bombing favored by U.S. strategists significantly affected the outcome. In May 1944 the United States began bombing oil fields in Romania and refineries and synthetic oil plants in Germany. Then, late in August 1944, Soviet troops crossed into Romania, taking control of the oil fields. Soon Germany lacked enough fuel even to train pilots. So serious were the bottlenecks by 1945 that the German air force could not use all the aircraft that German industry was producing.

Soviet troops moving westward finally met U.S. troops moving eastward at the Elbe River in Germany on April 26, 1945. With his regime now thoroughly defeated and much of his country in ruins, Hitler committed suicide in his underground military head-

The Soviet Victory in Europe

After forcing the Germans back for almost two years, Soviet troops reached Berlin in April 1945. After a day of heavy fighting and bombardment, the Soviets took the Reichstag building, in the heart of the devastated German capital, on April 30. Here two Soviet sergeants, Yegorov and Kantariya, plant the Soviet flag atop the Reichstag, symbolizing the Soviet victory in the decisive encounter of World War II in Europe. *(ITAR-TASS/Sovfoto)* quarters in Berlin on April 30, 1945. The war in Europe finally ended with the German surrender to General Dwight D. Eisenhower (1890–1969) at Reims, France, on May 7 and to Marshal Zhukov at Berlin on May 8. The world celebrated the end of the fighting in Europe, but an element of uncertainty surrounded the Allied victory. East-West differences were increasingly coming to the fore within the anti-German alliance.

THE POTSDAM CONFERENCE AND THE QUESTION OF GERMANY

The immediate question for the victorious Allies was the fate of Germany, which they confronted at the last of their notable wartime conferences, at **Potsdam,** just outside Berlin, from July 17 to August 2, 1945. The circumstances were dramatically different from those at Yalta just months before. With Hitler dead and Germany defeated, no common military aim provided unity. And of the three Allied leaders who had been at Yalta, only Stalin remained. President Roosevelt had died in April, so his successor, Harry Truman (1884–1972), represented the United States. In Britain, Churchill's Conservatives lost the general election during the first days of the conference, so Clement Attlee (1883–1967), the new Labour prime minister, assumed the leadership of the British delegation.

At Potsdam the Allies had to determine how to implement their earlier agreements about Germany, which, devastated by bombing and devoid of a government, depended on the Allied occupying forces even for its day-to-day survival. For a time, U.S. policymakers had even considered destroying Germany's industrial capacity in perpetuity. However, cooler heads understood that the deindustrialization, or "pastoralization," of Germany would not be in anyone's economic interests. Moreover, as the democracies grew increasingly suspicious about Soviet intentions, an economically healthy Germany seemed necessary to help in the balance against the Soviet Union.

For their part, the Soviets had reason to take a much harder line against Germany. Having been ravaged by invading German forces twice within living memory, the Soviet Union wanted to weaken Germany both territorially and economically. And of the three victors, the Soviets had suffered a greatly disproportionate share of the wartime destruction and economic loss, so they also sought to exploit the remaining resources of Germany by exacting heavy reparations. Moreover, the British and the Americans accepted the

Soviet proposal that Germany's eastern border with Poland be shifted substantially westward, to the line formed by the Oder and Neisse (NYE-suh) Rivers. But just as Poland gained at the expense of Germany, the Soviet Union kept a substantial slice of what had been eastern Poland (see Map 28.4).

Each of the three Allies had responsibility for administering a particular zone of occupation, but they were supposed to coordinate their activities in a common policy toward Germany. This effort was to include de-Nazification, demilitarization, and an assault on concentrations of economic power—to root out what seemed to have been the sources of Germany's anti-democratic and aggressive tendencies. But East-West disagreements over economic policy soon undermined the pretense of joint government.

THE ATOMIC BOMB AND THE CAPITULATION OF JAPAN

In the Pacific, Japan had been forced onto the defensive by September 1943, and though it mounted two major counterattacks during 1944, the Japanese navy was crippled by shortages of ships and fuel by the end of the year. However, as the situation grew more desperate for Japan, Japanese ground soldiers battled ever more fiercely, often fighting to the death or taking their own lives rather than surrendering. Beginning late in 1944, aircraft pilots practiced *kamikaze* (kah-mih-KAH-zee), suicidally crashing planes filled with explosives into U.S. targets. The Japanese used this tactic especially as the Americans sought to take Okinawa in the spring of 1945. The U.S. forces finally prevailed in June, but only after the most bitter combat of the Pacific war (see Map 28.3).

In conquering Okinawa, American forces got close enough for air raids on the Japanese home islands. But though the United States was now clearly in control, it seemed likely that an actual invasion of Japan would be necessary to force a Japanese surrender. Some estimated that, because the Japanese could be expected to fight even more desperately to defend their own soil, invasion might well cost the United States one million additional casualties. It was especially for this reason that the Americans decided to try to end the war in an altogether different way—by using an atomic bomb.

In 1939 scientists in several countries, including Germany, had started to advise their governments that new, immensely destructive weapons based on thermonuclear fission were theoretically possible. The German economics ministry began seeking uranium as early as 1939, but Hitler promoted jet- and rocket-propelled terror weaponry instead, especially the V-2 rocket bombs that the Germans began showering on England in the fall of 1944. Still, fear that the Nazis were developing

Potsdam conference A July–August 1945 meeting held at Potsdam, Germany, between the USSR, the United States, and Great Britain to implement their earlier agreements concerning the treatment of defeated Germany.

atomic weapons lurked behind the Allied effort to produce the ultra-lethal bomb as quickly as possible.

Although the British were the first to initiate an atomic weapons program, by late 1941 the Americans were building on what they knew of British findings to develop their own crash program, known as the Manhattan Project. Constructing an atomic bomb proved far more difficult and costly than most had expected in 1941, and it took a concerted effort by the United States to have atomic weapons ready for use by mid-1945.

Online Study Center **Improve Your Grade**
Primary Source: Witness to the Birth of the Atomic Age

The U.S. decision to use the atomic bomb on Japanese civilians has been one of the most controversial of modern history. The decision fell to the new president, Harry Truman, who had known nothing of the bomb project when Roosevelt died in April 1945. During the next few months, Truman listened to spirited disagreement among American policymakers. Was it necessary actually to drop the bomb to force the Japanese to surrender? Since the ultimate victory of the United States was not in doubt, some argued that it would be enough simply to demonstrate the new weapon to the Japanese in a test firing.

By July, when the Allies met at Potsdam, the United States was prepared to use the bomb. But President Truman first warned Japan that if it did not surrender at once, it would be subjected to destruction immeasurably greater than Germany had just suffered. The Japanese ignored the warning, although the United States had begun area-bombing Japanese cities a few months before. The bombing of Tokyo in March produced a firestorm that gutted one-fourth of the city and killed over 80,000 people. In light of the Japanese refusal to surrender, the use of the atomic bomb seemed to Truman to be the logical next step.

At 8:15 on the morning of August 6, 1945, from a height of 32,000 feet above the Japanese city of Hiroshima, an American pilot released the first atomic bomb to be used against an enemy target. The bomb exploded after 45 seconds, 2,000 feet above the ground, killing 80,000 people outright and leaving tens of thousands more to die in the aftermath. Three days later, on August 9, the Americans exploded a second atomic bomb over Nagasaki, killing perhaps 50,000 people. Although sectors of the Japanese military held out for continued resistance, Emperor Hirohito (hee-roh-HEE-toh) (1901–1989) finally announced Japan's surrender on August 15. The bombing of civilians had discredited the Japanese military, which not only had proved unable to defend the country but had systematically misled the Japanese people about their country's prospects.

The war in the Pacific ended more suddenly than had seemed possible just a few months earlier (see Map 28.3). This worked in favor of the various national liberation or decolonization movements that had developed in Asia during the war, for the Europeans had little opportunity to re-establish their dominance in the colonial territories they had earlier lost to the Japanese. In the Dutch East Indies, the Japanese had encouraged anticolonial sentiment, even helping local nationalists create patriotic militias. After the war, the Dutch were never able to reassert their control against this Indonesian nationalist movement. But though the war had severely weakened the old Western imperialism in Asia and the Pacific, what would replace it remained unclear.

DEATH, DISRUPTION, AND THE QUESTION OF GUILT

World War II left as many as 60 million people dead—three times as many as World War I. About that same number were left homeless for some length of time, or found themselves forced onto the mercies of others as refugees. The Soviet Union, Poland and Germany suffered by far the highest casualty figures; for each, the figure was considerably higher than in World War I. An appalling 23 million Soviet citizens died, of whom 12 million to 13 million were civilians. Poland lost over 6 million, the vast majority civilians, including perhaps 3 million Jews. Germany lost 5 million to 6 million, including perhaps 2 million civilians.

In contrast, casualty rates for Italy, Britain, and France were lower than in World War I. Italy suffered 200,000 military and 200,000 civilian deaths. Total British losses, including civilians, numbered 450,000, to which must be added 120,000 from the British Empire. Despite its quick defeat, France lost more lives than Britain because of the ravages of German occupation: the 350,000 deaths among French civilians considerably exceeded the British figure, closer to 100,000.

The United States lost 300,000 servicemen and 5,000 civilians. Figures for Japan are problematic, partly because the Japanese claim that 300,000 of those who surrendered to the Soviets in 1945 have remained unaccounted for. Apart from this number, 1.74 million Japanese servicemen died from 1941 to 1945, more from hunger and disease than from combat, and 300,000 civilians died in Japan, most from U.S. bombing.

During the war, Jews, Poles, and others deemed undesirable by the Nazis had been rounded up and shipped to ghettos or camps, where the great majority had died. Of those Jews who were still alive when the Nazi camps were liberated, almost half died within a few weeks. Even those who managed to return home sometimes faced pogroms during the difficult months that followed; forty Jews were killed in the worst of them, at Kielce (KYEL-tsuh), Poland, in 1946.

Late in the war, as German forces in the east retreated, ethnic Germans living in Poland, Czechoslovakia, Hungary, and elsewhere in east-central Europe began seeking refuge in Germany. They were fleeing the Soviet advance but also seeking to escape the growing wave of anti-German resentment in those countries. Once the war was over, the Poles began expelling ethnic Germans from the historically German areas that were now to become Polish. These Germans were sometimes sent to detention camps, and when they were shipped out, it was often in cattle cars. According to some estimates, as many as two million died in the process. At the same time, the uprooting of Poles that had begun during the war continued as Poles were systematically forced from the Polish territories incorporated into the Soviet Union.

In Czechoslovakia the government expelled 3.5 million Germans from the Sudetenland area by 1947. All told, at least 7 million German refugees moved west into the shrunken territory of the new Germany by 1947. They were among the 16 million Europeans who were permanently uprooted and transplanted during the war and its immediate wake. And the process continued at a diminished rate thereafter. By 1958 perhaps 10 million Germans had either left or been forced out of the new Poland, leaving only about 1 million Germans still living there.

As the end of the war approached, Europeans began attempting to assess guilt and to punish those responsible for the disasters of the era. In the climate of violence, resistance forces in France, Italy, and elsewhere often subjected fascists and collaborators to summary justice, sometimes through quick trials in ad hoc courts. In Italy this process led to 15,000 executions, in France 10,000. French women accused of sleeping with German soldiers were shamed by having their heads shaved.

The most sensitive confrontation with the recent past took place in Germany, where the occupying powers imposed a systematic program of de-Nazification. In the western zones, German citizens were required to attend lectures on the virtues of democracy and to view the corpses of the victims of Nazism. In this context, the Allies determined to identify and bring to justice those responsible for the crimes of Hitler's regime. This effort led to the **Nuremberg trials** of 1945 and 1946, the most famous of a number of war crimes trials held in Germany and the occupied countries after the war.

Although Hitler, Himmler, and Goebbels had committed suicide, the occupying authorities apprehended for trial twenty-four individuals who had played important but very different roles in Hitler's Third Reich. All but three were convicted of war crimes and "crimes against humanity." Twelve were sentenced to death; of those, two committed suicide, and the other ten were executed.

Questions about their legitimacy dogged the Nuremberg trials from the start. To a considerable extent the accused were being judged according to law made after the fact. The notion of "crimes against humanity" remained vague. Moreover, even insofar as a measure of international law was in force, it was arguably binding only on states, not individuals. But in light of the unprecedented atrocities of the Nazi regime, there was widespread agreement among the victors that the Nazi leaders could not be treated simply as defeated adversaries.

═══════ S E C T I O N   S U M M A R Y ═══════

- The future of east-central Europe was but one of the items on the agenda at Yalta, where each of the Big Three achieved some of its major aims concerning the shape of the postwar world.

- As a result of the agreements at Yalta and Potsdam, the reconstituted Poland was shifted substantially westward at the expense of Germany.

- Although the terror bombing of cities did not undermine the German war effort, the more precisely targeted bombing of industrial and military targets hastened Germany's defeat, especially by cutting off oil supplies.

- Because the war in the Pacific ended so suddenly, as the result of the atomic bombing of Japan by the United States, the Europeans had little opportunity to re-establish their dominance in the colonial territories they had earlier lost to the Japanese.

- Of the twenty-four Germans charged with war crimes and "crimes against humanity" in the Nuremberg trials of 1945 and 1946, twenty-one were convicted, of whom twelve were sentenced to death.

Nuremberg trials   The war crimes trials conducted in Nuremberg, Germany. Most of the twenty-four defendants were convicted of war crimes and "crimes against humanity."

INTO THE POSTWAR WORLD

What was the relationship between the Allied victory in World War II and the coming of the cold war?

Even after the fighting stopped in 1945, remarkable changes continued as the forces unleashed by the war played themselves out. In a number of war-torn countries, the legacies of wartime resistance movements helped shape the political order and priorities for beginning anew. At the same time, differences between the Soviets and the Western democracies began to undermine the wartime alliance, soon producing the division of Germany and a bipolar Europe. Thus the conclusion of World War II led directly to the danger of a third world war, which might involve nuclear weapons and thus prove immeasurably more destructive than the last.

In addition to the dramatic changes in Europe, the wider effects of the war brought to the forefront a whole new set of issues, from anticolonialism to the Arab-Israeli conflict to the spread of communism in the non-Western world. These issues would remain central for decades. By 1949, however, it was already possible to discern the contours of the new postwar world, a world with new sources of hope but also with conflicts and dangers hardly imaginable ten years earlier.

RESISTANCE AND RENEWAL

Though the Nazis had found some willing collaborators, the great majority of those living under German occupation came to despise the Nazis as their brutality became ever clearer. Nazi rule meant pillage, forced labor in Germany, and the random killing of hostages in reprisal for resistance activity. In one extreme case, the Germans destroyed the Czech village of Lidice (LIH-dyit-seh), killing all its inhabitants, in retaliation for the assassination of SS security chief Reinhard Heydrich in 1942.

Clandestine movements of resistance to the occupying Nazi forces gradually developed all over Europe. In western Europe, resistance was especially prominent in France and, beginning in 1943, northern Italy, which was subjected to German occupation after the Allies defeated Mussolini's regime. But the anti-German resistance was strongest in Yugoslavia, Poland, and the occupied portions of the Soviet Union, where full-scale guerrilla war against the Germans and their collaborators produced the highest civilian casualties of World War II. The Polish resistance achieved some notable successes in sabotaging roads and railroads, although it met disastrous defeat when it sought to tackle the Germans head-on in Warsaw in 1944.

The role of the resistance proved most significant in Yugoslavia, where the Croatian Marxist Josip Broz, taking the pseudonym Tito (1892–1980), forged the opponents of the Axis powers into a broadly based guerrilla army. Its initial foe was the inflated Croatian state that the Germans, early in 1941, carved from Yugoslavia and entrusted to the pro-Axis Croatian separatist movement, the Ustashe (oo-STAH-zhiy). But Tito's forces soon came up against a rival resistance movement, led by Serb officers, that tended to be pro-Serb, monarchist, and anticommunist. By 1943 Tito led 250,000 men and women in what had become a vicious civil war, one that deepened ethnic divisions and left a legacy of bitterness. Tito's forces prevailed, enabling him to create a communist-led government in Yugoslavia late in the war.

In France and Italy as well, communists played leading roles in the wartime resistance movements. As a result, the Communist Party in each country overcame the disarray that followed from the Nazi-Soviet Pact of 1939, and after the war each enjoyed a level of prestige that would have been unthinkable earlier.

In the French case, the indigenous resistance, with its significant communist component, generally worked well with de Gaulle and the Free French, operating outside France until August 1944. Still, de Gaulle took pains to cement his own leadership in the overall struggle. Among the measures to this end, he decreed women's suffrage for France, partly because women were playing a major role in the resistance. After the liberation of France in 1944, he sought to control a potentially volatile situation by disarming the resistance as quickly as possible.

The western European resistance movements are easily romanticized, their extent and importance overstated. Compared with regular troops, resistance forces were poorly trained, equipped, and disciplined. In France fewer than 30 percent of the nearly 400,000 active resisters had firearms in 1944. But though the Allies never tried to use them in a systematic way, the resistance movements made at least some military contribution, especially through sabotage. And they boosted national self-esteem for the longer term, helping countries humiliated by defeat and occupation make a fresh start after the war.

But had governments and institutions outside Germany done all they could—especially as the dimensions of the Nazi exterminations began to come into focus? For example, President Roosevelt, in the face of appeals from Jewish groups, declined to try to disrupt the Nazi killing machine by bombing the rail lines to Auschwitz. As he saw it, the way to save as many Jews as possible was to win the war as quickly as possible.

Especially controversial has been the response of Pope Pius XII (r. 1939–1958), who declined to take the moral high ground and denounce Nazi atrocities explicitly. He felt that he could not censure the Nazis without also censuring the Soviets, at that point allies in the anti-Nazi cause. He also feared for the fortunes of the Catholic Church as an institution in areas under German control, including Rome itself during the pivotal nine months from September 1943 to June 1944. The mission of the church was not merely to save lives but above all to save souls—and for that the institution was essential. Many felt, however, that stronger moral leadership by the Catholic Church would have stiffened resistance to the Nazis, stimulated aid to individual Jews, and enhanced the overall self-confidence of the West as it faced the post-Holocaust future.

CONFLICTING VISIONS AND THE COMING OF THE COLD WAR

Starting with the Atlantic Charter conference of 1941, Roosevelt had sought to ensure that the common effort against the Axis powers would lead to a firmer basis for peace, to be framed through a new international organization after the war. At a conference at Dumbarton Oaks in Washington, D.C., in September 1944, the United States proposed the structure for a new "United Nations." Meeting in San Francisco from April to June 1945, delegates from almost fifty anti-Axis countries translated that proposal into a charter for the new organization. As Roosevelt had envisioned, the major powers were given a privileged position in the organization as permanent members of the Security Council, each with veto power. To dramatize its departure from the Geneva-based League of Nations, which the United States had refused to join, the United Nations was headquartered in New York. In July 1945 the U.S. Senate approved U.S. membership in the international body almost unanimously.

By the end of the war, several international meetings had used the United Nations title. In July 1944 the United Nations Monetary and Financial Conference at Bretton Woods, New Hampshire, brought together delegates from forty-four nations to deal with problems of currency and exchange rates. Although it produced only recommendations subject to ratification by the individual countries, the conference indicated a new determination to cooperate on the international level after the failures of the interwar period. The outcome of the conference, the Bretton Woods Agreement, laid the foundation for international economic exchange in the noncommunist world for the crucial quarter century of economic recovery after the war. In addition, the conference gave birth to the International Monetary Fund and the International Bank for Reconstruction and Development, which played major roles in the decades that followed.

Whereas the United States envisioned a world order based on the ongoing cooperation of the three victors, the Soviet Union had a different agenda. Its top priority was to create a buffer zone of friendly states in east-central Europe, especially as a bulwark against Germany. While seeking this sphere of influence in east-central Europe, Stalin gave the British a free hand to settle the civil war between communists and anticommunists in Greece, and he did not push for revolution in western Europe. The strong communist parties that had emerged from the resistance movements in Italy and France were directed by Moscow to work within broad-based democratic fronts rather than try to take power. Although no formal deal was made, Stalin saw this moderate position in western and southern Europe as a tacit exchange with the West for a free hand in east-central Europe.

THE DIVISION OF GERMANY

The site of greatest potential stress between the Soviets and the democracies was Germany. At first, the Western Allies were concerned especially to root out the sources of Germany's antidemocratic, aggressive behavior, but that concern faded as communism, not Nazism, came to seem the immediate menace. And it was especially conflict over Germany that cemented the developing division of Europe. Neither the democracies nor the Soviets lived up to all their agreements concerning Germany, but in light of the fundamental differences in priorities, cooperation between the two sides was bound to be difficult at best.

Disagreements over economic policy proved the major source of the eventual split. At Potsdam, the West had accepted Soviet demands for German reparations, but rather than wait for payment, the Soviets began removing German factories and equipment for reassembly in the Soviet Union. To ensure that they got their due, the Soviets wanted access to the economic resources not simply of the Russian occupation zone but of the whole of Germany. The United States and Britain, in contrast, gave priority to economic reconstruction and quickly began integrating the economies of the Western zones for that purpose.

Friction developed from 1945 to 1948 as the West insisted on reduced reparations and a higher level of industrial production than the Soviets wanted. Finally, as part of their effort to spur economic recovery, the United States and Britain violated Allied agreements by introducing a new currency without Soviet consent. Stalin answered in June 1948 by blockading the city of Berlin, cutting its western sectors off from the main

Western occupation zones, almost 200 miles west (see Map 28.4). The Western Allies responded with a massive airlift that kept their sectors of Berlin supplied for almost a year, until May 1949, when the Soviets finally backed down.

By 1948 two separate German states began emerging from the Allied occupation zones. The Western occupying powers had begun restoring local government immediately after the war, to create the administrative framework necessary to provide public utilities and food distribution. Gradually a governing structure was built from the ground up in the Western zones, which were increasingly coordinated.

With Allied support, a "parliamentary council" of West German leaders met during 1948 and 1949 and produced a document that, when ratified in September 1949, became the "Basic Law" of a new Federal Republic of Germany, with its capital at Bonn. This founding document was termed simply the Basic Law, as opposed to the constitution, to emphasize the provisional character of the new West German state. To create a state limited to the west was not to foreclose the future reunification of Germany. But as it became clear that a new state was being created in the Western zones, the Soviets settled for a new state in their zone, in eastern Germany. Thus the Communist-led German Democratic Republic, with its capital in East Berlin, was born in October 1949.

THE "IRON CURTAIN" AND THE EMERGENCE OF A BIPOLAR WORLD

In east-central Europe, only Yugoslavia and Albania had achieved liberation on their own, and the communist leaders of their resistance movements had a plausible claim to political power. Elsewhere, the Soviet army had provided liberation, and the Soviet military presence remained the decisive political fact as the war ended. In much of the region, authoritarianism and collaboration had been the rule for a decade or more, so there was no possibility of returning to a clearly legitimate prewar political order. To be sure, each country had local political groups, some representing former governments in exile, that now claimed a governing role, but their standing in relation to the Soviet army was uncertain.

Under these circumstances, the Soviets were able to work with local communists to install new regimes, led by communists and friendly to the Soviet Union, in most of east-central Europe. But though Churchill warned as early as 1946 that an **"iron curtain"** was de-

scending from the Baltic to the Adriatic, the process of Soviet power consolidation was not easy, and it took place gradually, in discrete steps over several years. The Communist-led government of Poland held elections in January 1947—but rigged them to guarantee a favorable outcome. In Czechoslovakia the Communist Party anticipated serious losses in upcoming elections and so finally took power outright in 1948. By 1949 communist governments, relying on Soviet support, controlled Poland, Czechoslovakia, East Germany, Hungary, Romania, and Bulgaria, with Yugoslavia and Albania also communist but capable of a more independent line.

Communism might have spread still farther in Europe, and perhaps beyond, but the West drew the line at Greece. There, as in Yugoslavia, an indigenous, communist-led resistance movement had become strong enough to contend for political power by late 1944. But when it sought to oust the monarchical government that had just returned to Greece from exile, the British intervened, helping the monarchy put down the leftist uprising. Although Stalin gave the Greek communists little help, communist guerrilla activity continued, thanks partly to support from Tito's Yugoslavia. In 1946 a renewed communist insurgency escalated into civil war.

As U.S.-Soviet friction turned into a **cold war,** both countries began taking a more active interest in the Greek conflict, though Soviet intentions remained uncertain. After the financially strapped Labour government in Britain reduced its involvement early in 1947, the United States stepped in to support the Greek monarchy against the communists. American policymakers feared that communism would progress from the Balkans through Greece to the Middle East. Thus, in March 1947, President Truman announced the **Truman Doctrine,** which committed the United States to the "containment" of communism throughout the world. (See the box "The Written Record: 'Containment' as a Cold War Strategy.") American advisers now began re-equipping the anticommunist forces in Greece. Faced with this determined opposition from the West, Stalin again pulled back, but the Greek communists, with their strong indigenous support, were not defeated until 1949.

Thus the wartime marriage of expediency between the Soviet Union and the Western democracies gradually fell apart in the war's aftermath. Only in Austria,

"iron curtain"   Term used by Winston Churchill in a speech on March 5, 1946, to warn that, thanks to Soviet policy, a formidable de facto barrier was emerging in Europe, cutting the Soviet sphere off from the West and threatening the long-term division of the Continent.

cold war   The hostile standoff between the Soviet Union and the United States that began after World War II as Europe was divided into spheres of influence between the two superpowers and the United States vowed to resist the further spread of communism.

Truman Doctrine   The U.S. policy of containment, or limiting communist expansion, as outlined by President Harry Truman in 1947.

"CONTAINMENT" AS A COLD WAR STRATEGY

As a foreign service officer, George F. Kennan (1904–2005) emerged as the U.S. government's leading authority on the dynamics of Soviet foreign policy by the later 1940s. After analyzing Soviet postwar objectives in his now-famous "long telegram" from Moscow to the U.S. State Department in 1946, Kennan returned to the United States to become director of the State Department's Policy Planning Staff from 1947 to 1949. With hawks pondering a preemptive strike on the Soviet Union and doves stressing mutual accommodation, Kennan forcefully advocated a middle position, a strategy of "containment," in an article published anonymously in the journal Foreign Affairs *in 1947. And his views prevailed. An uncertain experiment when it began in 1947, containment proved successful— arguably for the reasons Kennan anticipated.*

[The Soviet Union] is under no ideological compulsion to accomplish its purposes in a hurry. . . . Thus the Kremlin has no compunction about retreating in the face of superior force. And being under the compulsion of no timetable, it does not get panicky under the necessity for such retreat. Its political action is a fluid stream which moves constantly, wherever it is permitted to move, toward a given goal. . . .

. . . The patient persistence by which it is animated means that it can be effectively countered not by sporadic acts which represent the momentary whims of democratic opinion but only by intelligent long-range policies on the part of Russia's adversaries— policies no less steady in their purpose, and no less variegated and resourceful in their application, than those of the Soviet Union itself.

In these circumstances it is clear that the main element of any United States policy toward the Soviet Union must be that of a long-term, patient but firm and vigilant containment of Russian expansive tendencies. It is important to note, however, that such a policy has nothing to do with outward histrionics: with threats or blustering or superfluous gestures of outward "toughness." While the Kremlin is basically flexible in its reaction to political realities, it is by no means unamenable to considerations of prestige. . . . It is a *sine qua non* of successful dealing with Russia that the foreign government in question should remain at all times cool and collected and that its demands on Russian policy should be put forward in such a manner as to leave the way open for a compliance not too detrimental to Russian prestige.

In the light of the above, it will be clearly seen that the Soviet pressure against the free institutions of the western world is something that can be contained by the adroit and vigilant application of counter-force at a series of constantly shifting geographical and political points, corresponding to the shifts and manœuvres of Soviet policy, but which cannot be charmed or talked out of existence. . . .

. . . Soviet power is only a crust concealing an amorphous mass of human beings among whom no independent organizational structure is tolerated. . . . If, consequently, anything were ever to occur to disrupt the unity and efficacy of the Party as a political instrument, Soviet Russia might be changed overnight from one of the strongest to one of the weakest and most pitiable of national societies. . . .

. . . It is . . . a question of the degree to which the United States can create among the peoples of the world generally the impression of a country which knows what it wants, which is coping successfully with the problems of its internal life and with the responsibilities of a World Power, and which has a spiritual vitality capable of holding its own among the major ideological currents of the time. To the extent that such an impression can be created and maintained, the aims of Russian Communism must appear sterile and quixotic, the hopes and enthusiasm of Moscow's supporters must wane, and added strain must be imposed on the Kremlin's foreign policies. For the palsied decrepitude of the capitalist world is the keystone of Communist philosophy. . . .

. . . The United States has it in its power to increase enormously the strains under which Soviet policy must operate, to force upon the Kremlin a far greater degree of moderation and circumspection than it has had to observe in recent years, and in this way to promote tendencies which must eventually find their outlet in either the break-up or the gradual mellowing of Soviet power.

QUESTIONS

1. What conception of the Soviet Union and its aims led Kennan to propose a policy of containment?

2. What would containment actually entail on a practical level as a response to Soviet moves?

3. Why did Kennan believe that the United States had to be unified, consistent, and principled in everything it did if it was eventually to prevail in the cold war?

Source: "X" [George F. Kennan], "The Sources of Soviet Conduct," *Foreign Affairs* 25, no. 4 (July 1947). Reprinted by permission of *Foreign Affairs.* Copyright 1947 by the Council on Foreign Relations, Inc.

jointly occupied by the Soviets and the Western democracies, were the former Allies able to arrange the postwar transition in a reasonably amicable way. The Soviets accepted the neutralization of a democratic Austria as the occupying powers left in 1955. Elsewhere, Europe was divided into two antagonistic power blocs.

The antagonism between the two superpowers became more menacing when the Soviets exploded their first atomic bomb in August 1949, intensifying the postwar arms race. By then, in fact, the United States was on its way to the more destructive hydrogen bomb. The split between these two nations, unmistakable by 1949, established the framework for world affairs for the next forty years.

THE WEST AND THE NEW WORLD AGENDA

At the same time, other dramatic changes around the world suggested that, with or without the cold war, the postwar political scene would be hard to manage. Events in India in 1947, in Israel in 1948, and in China in 1949 epitomized the wider new hopes and uncertainties spawned by World War II.

Independence in India Although the British, under U.S. pressure, had reluctantly promised independence for India in order to elicit Indian support during the war, British authorities and Indian leaders had continued to skirmish. Mohandas Gandhi (see pages 807 and 843) was twice jailed for resisting British demands and threatening a massive program of nonviolent resistance to British rule. But by 1946 the British lacked the will and the financial resources to maintain their control on the subcontinent. Thus Britain acquiesced as the new independent states of India and Pakistan emerged on August 15, 1947. Allowing independence to India, long the jewel of the British Empire, raised questions about Britain's role in the postwar world and portended a wider disintegration of the European colonial system. There would be new countries, many of them poor—and resentful of Western imperialism. What would that mean for the new world order, centering on the United Nations, that Roosevelt had envisioned?

The Creation of Israel Questions about the fate of the Jews, who had suffered so grievously during World War II, were inevitable as well. Almost two-thirds of the Jews of Europe had been killed, and many of the survivors either had no place to go or had decided that they could never again live as a minority in Europe. Many concluded that the Jews must have a homeland of their own. For decades such Zionist sentiment (see page 791) had centered on the biblical area of Israel, in what had become, after World War I, the British mandate of Palestine. Jewish immigration to the area accelerated during the interwar period, but it caused increasing friction between the Jews and the Palestinian Arabs.

Concerned about access to Middle Eastern oil, the British sought to cultivate good relations with the Arab world after the war. Thus they opposed further immigration of Jews to Palestine, as well as proposals to carve an independent Jewish state from the area. The United States, however, was considerably more sympathetic to the Zionist cause. As tensions built, Jewish terrorists blew up the British headquarters in Jerusalem,

Gandhi and Anticolonialism

An apostle of nonviolence, Mohandas Gandhi became one of the most admired individuals of the century as he spearheaded the movement for Indian independence. He is pictured (*center*) in December 1942 with the British statesman Sir Stafford Cripps (*left*), who had come to India to offer a plan for Indian self-government. Despite the good spirit evident here, Cripps's mission failed; Gandhi and his movement held out for full independence. *(Corbis)*

MAP 28.5   The Proposed Partition of Palestine and the Birth of the State of Israel

In November 1947 the United Nations offered a plan to partition the British mandate of Palestine, but complications immediately arose. The Jews of the area won their own state, Israel, but the Palestinian Arabs were left stateless. Thus tensions continued in the area.

Online Study Center   Improve Your Grade
Interactive Map: The Proposed Partition of Palestine and the Birth of the State of Israel

and the British decided to abandon what seemed a no-win situation. In September 1947 they announced their intention to withdraw from Palestine, leaving its future to the United Nations. In November the UN voted to partition Palestine, creating both a Jewish and a new Arab Palestinian state (see **MAP 28.5**).

Skirmishing between Jews and Arabs became full-scale war in December 1947, and in that context the Jews declared their independence as the new state of Israel on May 14, 1948. When the fighting ended in 1949, the Israelis had conquered more territory than had been envisioned in the original partition plan, and the remaining Arab territories fell to Egypt and Jordan, rather than forming an independent Palestinian state. Thus was born the new state of Israel, partly a product of the assault on the Jews during World War II. Yet it was born amid Arab hostility and Western concerns about oil, and so its long-term prospects remained uncertain.

Communism in China   In 1949 the communist insurgency in China under Mao Zedong (Mao Tse-tung) (see page 843) finally triumphed over the Chinese Nationalists under Jiang Jieshi (Chiang Kai-shek), who fled to the island of Taiwan. During the war, the Communists had done better than the Nationalists at identifying themselves with the Chinese cause against both Japanese and Western imperialism. And after their victory, the Chinese Communists enjoyed great prestige among other "national liberation" movements struggling against Western colonialists. To many in the West, however, the outcome in China by 1949 simply intensified fears that communism was poised to infect the unsettled postwar world.

SECTION SUMMARY

- Although it had spurned the League of Nations after World War I, the U.S. Senate approved U.S. membership in the United Nations almost unanimously in July 1945.

- Concerned primarily to win a secure sphere of influence in east-central Europe, especially as a bulwark against Germany, Stalin took a moderate position with regard to western Europe and did not seek to foment communist revolution.

- Disagreements over economic policy, especially, fed the split that led to the creation of two separate German states, one oriented toward the West, the other oriented toward the Soviet Union, in 1949.

- The communist challenge in Greece by 1947 prompted the Truman Doctrine, which committed the United States to the "containment" of communism throughout the world.

- The granting of independence to India in 1947, the creation of the state of Israel in 1948, and the communist takeover in China in 1949 indicated the new world agenda emerging after World War II.

CHAPTER SUMMARY

Online Study Center **ACE the Test**

What were the outcomes of the war as of late spring 1941, before the German invasion of the Soviet Union and before the intervention of the United States?

What was the place of the Holocaust in the Nazi effort to begin constructing a "new order" in eastern Europe?

How did the Grand Alliance of Britain, the United States, and the Soviet Union come together against the Axis powers?

How did the Allies manage to defeat Nazi Germany in World War II, after Germany's remarkable initial successes?

What was the relationship between the Allied victory in World War II and the coming of the cold war?

Using an effective new offensive strategy, Germany quickly defeated Poland in 1939, but Britain and France refused Hitler's peace overtures in the aftermath. After France fell to German invasion eight months later, the Third Republic gave way to the authoritarian Vichy regime, which was obliged to collaborate with Nazi Germany. When the British again refused to come to terms, Hitler launched a sustained air assault on Britain. The British withstood it, but Hitler remained confident of containing Britain over the longer term. Even when the reckless intervention of Italy forced Hitler's attention to North Africa and the Balkans, the Germans won further successes, which suggested that the Soviet Union would fall in a matter of weeks in the wake of Germany's invasion of June 1941.

In dealing with their conquered territories first in Poland, then in the Soviet Union, the Nazis were concerned with population engineering and ideology; Jewish policy was distinctly secondary. Even when Jews were confined to ghettos in Poland, there was no plan to kill them. But ghettoization produced problems of its own, so Nazi forces were instructed to shoot Soviet Jews once the invasion of the Soviet Union began. Such shooting also proved to be problematic, so gradually the Nazi leadership decided on a more systematic method—mass extermination by gassing, to start with the Jews in the ghettos in Poland. Such a program could be envisioned, and implemented, especially because of the precedent of the "euthanasia" program in Germany. Once it began, the process of mass killing developed a momentum of its own, especially as it became clear that Germany was likely to lose the war.

After a disastrous start in the face of German invasion, Soviet forces stiffened in the fall of 1941,

then, in December, mounted a formidable counterattack. That same month the United States declared war on Germany in the aftermath of the bombing of Pearl Harbor by the Japanese. Meanwhile, the British, having withstood the German air assault, were regrouping for a protracted war. Common hostility to the Axis powers brought Britain, the Soviet Union, and the United States together in a "Grand Alliance" early in 1942, but mutual suspicions between the democracies, on the one hand, and the Soviet Union, on the other, marked the relationship. Above all, Stalin worried that Britain and the United States were dragging their feet in opening a major second front on the European continent. By the time of the D-Day landings in France in June 1944, the Soviets were steadily forcing the Germans back on the eastern front.

Even after all the upheavals of the 1930s, the Soviets proved able to spearhead the Allied victory in Europe, though they suffered incredibly heavy casualties in the process. Stalin managed to rally the Soviet people, and the Soviet military and industrial effort proved more effective than outside observers had thought possible. But the efforts of the democracies in North Africa, Italy, and France contributed to the final victory as well. And American-led bombing of military and industrial targets, especially oil refining facilities, seriously compromised Germany's capacity to wage war by the end.

The Grand Alliance began unraveling soon after the war was over, especially because the priorities of the Soviets differed considerably from those of the two democracies. Having been invaded, and devastated, by German forces twice in a generation, the Soviets were determined to have friendly states on their

903

borders, especially in Poland. And having suffered from direct German military invasion as the other two victors had not, the Soviets were also determined to extract reparations from Germany, even including plant and equipment to be dismantled and carried back to the Soviet Union. By 1949 two competing German states had emerged, and Europe was clearly divided between East and West.

LOOKING AHEAD

Whereas there had been, for a while, some illusion of a "return to normal" after World War I, it was obvious after World War II that the old Europe was gone forever. As a result of the war, the two major fascist powers collapsed, and fascist forms of politics, with their hostility to democracy and their tendencies toward violence and war, stood discredited. But it was not clear whether Europe would be able to develop effective democratic political systems amid defeat and destruction. Indeed, much of Europe's proud culture, on the basis of which it had claimed to lead the world, lay in the ruins of war, apparently exhausted. What role could Europe play in Western civilization, and in the wider world, after all that had happened? What lessons had been learned, and what foundations for the future could be found, now in the shadow of the cold war?

KEY TERMS

Vichy France (p. 873)

Charles de Gaulle (p. 873)

Winston Churchill (p. 873)

Auschwitz-Birkenau (p. 880)

Stalingrad (p. 881)

"the Great Patriotic War" (p. 881)

Franklin Delano Roosevelt (p. 885)

Lend-Lease Act (p. 887)

D-Day (p. 888)

Yalta conference (p. 890)

United Nations (p. 891)

Potsdam conference (p. 894)

Nuremberg trials (p. 896)

"iron curtain" (p. 899)

cold war (p. 899)

Truman Doctrine (p. 899)

Online Study Center
Improve Your Grade Flashcards

SUGGESTED READING

Browning, Christopher R. *The Origins of the Final Solution: The Evolutions of Nazi Jewish Policy, September 1939–March 1942.* 2004. A leading expert's detailed but gripping account of the often haphazard steps that led to the Nazi program to exterminate the Jews.

Campbell, John, ed. *The Experience of World War II.* 1989. Focusing on the experience of those touched by the war, this collaborative volume covers everything from prisoners of war to the uses of the arts for propaganda purposes; large format, with superb illustrations and maps.

Gaddis, John Lewis. *The Cold War: A New History.* 2005. A comprehensive but accessible synthesis that finds the cold war to have been necessary to settle the contest between American democracy and Soviet communism in a definitive and desirable way.

Hilberg, Raul. *Perpetrators, Victims, Bystanders: The Jewish Catastrophe, 1933–1945.* 1992. The dean of Holocaust historians offers an accessible, compelling account by weaving capsule portraits delineating the many layers of involvement and responsibility at issue in the Holocaust.

Jackson, Julian. *The Fall of France: The Nazi Invasion of 1940.* 2003. After assessing causes and consequences from a variety of angles, this major study of a long-standing problem concludes that, in light of the anomalous Nazi determination to wage war, the fall of France was not a "strange defeat."

_____. *France: The Dark Years, 1940–1944.* 2001. A major reassessment of the Vichy period, set within the broader sweep of modern French history.

Keegan, John. *The Second World War.* 1989. A detailed but readable study featuring military operations; well illustrated.

Overy, Richard J. *Why the Allies Won.* 1995. Denying that the sheer weight of numbers made the outcome inevitable, this account focuses on the differences in political, economic, and even moral mobilization to explain why the Allies defeated the Axis powers.

Parker, R. A. C. *Struggle for Survival: The History of the Second World War.* 1990. An accessible, comprehensive, and well-balanced survey, especially good on debates over strategy and the wider implications of the strategies chosen.

Trachtenberg, Marc. *A Constructed Peace: The Making of the European Settlement, 1945–1963.* 1999. An original work that pushes beyond the long-standing cold war framework to argue that concerns about Germany and nuclear weapons were central to the postwar settlement.

Weinberg, Gerhard L. *A World at Arms: A Global History of World War II.* 1994. An enlightening global approach by a leading historian of the period that stresses the interrelationship among simultaneous events and decisions in the various theaters of the war around the world.

NOTES

1. From Farrell's full account as related by General Leslie Groves in his "Memorandum to the Secretary of War," dated July 18, 1945, in *The American Atom: A Documentary History of Nuclear Policies from the Discovery of Fission to the Present,* ed. Philip L. Cantelon, Richard G. Hewlett, and Robert C. Williams, 2d ed. (Philadelphia: University of Pennsylvania Press, 1991), pp. 56–57.

2. Quoted in Karl Dietrich Bracher, *The German Dictatorship: The Origins, Structure, and Effects of National Socialism,* trans. Jean Steinberg (New York: Praeger, 1970), p. 423.

3. Christopher R. Browning, *Ordinary Men: Reserve Police Battalion 101 and the Final Solution in Poland,* with a new afterward (New York: HarperCollins, 1998); Daniel Jonah Goldhagen, *Hitler's Willing Executioners: Ordinary Germans and the Holocaust* (New York: Random House [Vintage], 1997).

4. Michael Burleigh, *Death and Deliverance: "Euthanasia" in Germany, c. 1900–1945* (Cambridge: Cambridge University Press, 1994), p. 221.

5. Michael Burleigh and Wolfgang Wippermann, *The Racial State: Germany, 1933–1945* (Cambridge: Cambridge University Press, 1991), p. 98.

6. Martin Broszat and Saul Friedländer, "A Controversy About the Historicization of National Socialism," in Peter Baldwin, ed., *Reworking the Past: Hitler, the Holocaust, and the Historians' Debate* (Boston: Beacon Press, 1990), pp. 120–121.

7. Goldhagen, *Hitler's Willing Executioners,* pp. 279–280.

8. Browning, *Ordinary Men,* p. 72.

29

An Anxious Stability: The Age of the Cold War, 1949–1989

Berlin Wall, November 1989 East Germans stream through the dismantled Berlin Wall into West Berlin. *(Lionel Cironneau/AP/Wide World Photos)*

The atmosphere was festive, euphoric. Those who came to celebrate could hardly believe it was happening, for it had been unthinkable just a few months before. Yet happening it was, one of the defining events of the twentieth century, live on television. This was November 1989, and the Berlin Wall was coming down.

Erected to stop emigration from communist East Germany to the West in 1961, the wall had become an all-too-tangible symbol of the division of Europe, and much of the world, for more than four decades after World War II. The two superpowers that had emerged from the war, the Soviet Union and the United States, had settled into a cold war marked by ideological competition, an arms race, and nuclear stalemate.

As a physical barrier of concrete and barbed wire, the Berlin Wall had divided families and caused much human suffering. Indeed, 191 people died and 5,000 were arrested trying to cross it. But the East German government, desperate by 1989 to preserve its legitimacy, opened the wall on November 9 and began dismantling it within days. However, it proved too late. The communist regime in East Germany collapsed as part of a wider anticommunist revolution that finally enveloped even the Soviet Union in 1991. The anxious cold war era was suddenly over; virtually no one had foreseen its abrupt ending.

Although Berlin had been a particular hot spot, the cold war was global in scope. It seemed that confrontation between the Soviet Union and the United States might take place almost anywhere, sparking the cold war into a hot war threatening nuclear annihilation. And indeed confrontation came closest not over Berlin but over Soviet missiles in Cuba in 1962. That crisis was surmounted, and East-West relations alternately warmed and cooled during the quarter century that followed.

Both halves of Europe had to operate within the bipolar framework, but the Western and Soviet blocs confronted different challenges and evolved in different ways. The countries of western Europe adjusted to a diminished international role as they recognized their dependence on U.S. leadership and gradually lost their overseas colonies. The change in scale led many

CHAPTER OUTLINE

THE SEARCH FOR CULTURAL BEARINGS

PROSPERITY AND DEMOCRACY IN WESTERN EUROPE

THE COMMUNIST BLOC: FROM CONSOLIDATION TO STAGNATION

EUROPE, THE WEST, AND THE WORLD

THE COLLAPSE OF THE SOVIET SYSTEM, 1975–1991

KEY TERMS

existentialism

North Atlantic Treaty Organization (NATO)

welfare state

Konrad Adenauer

Willy Brandt

Margaret Thatcher

Warsaw Pact

Prague Spring

Suez crisis

European Economic Community (EEC)

Helsinki Accords

Solidarity

Mikhail Gorbachev

Online Study Center

This icon will direct you to interactive map and primary source activities on the website **college.hmco.com/pic/noble5e**

politicians and intellectuals to advocate some form of European union, which might eventually enable the western Europeans to deal with the superpowers on a more equal basis. On the domestic level, the immediate postwar situation was so unsettled that few western European countries could simply return to the prewar norm. Postwar reconstruction rested on a new consensus that government must play a more active role in promoting economic growth and social welfare. By the 1960s the promise of shared prosperity was realized to a remarkable extent. But changing circumstances by the early 1970s threatened the consensus that postwar prosperity had made possible.

Although the Soviet Union had suffered immensely in winning World War II, the communist regime emerged from the war with renewed legitimacy. During the 1950s and 1960s, the Soviet system achieved some significant successes, but its efforts to outgrow its Stalinist framework were halting. By 1980 the system was becoming rigid and stagnant. And thus the dramatic changes in the Soviet bloc that came to a head in 1989, leading to the opening of the Berlin Wall and, by 1991, to the end of communism in Europe. Only as it was ending, more than four decades after World War II, did observers realize that the anxious cold war era had been one of relative stability and peace.

FOCUS QUESTIONS

What seemed the most likely overall directions as western Europeans pondered priorities in light of all the disasters surrounding the era of the two world wars?

What factors led to the surprisingly rapid restoration of democracy in much of continental western Europe after World War II?

How did Soviet policy evolve after the death of Stalin in 1953?

How did the place of western Europe in world affairs change during the cold war era?

What led to the collapse of the communist system in the Soviet Union and its satellite states?

THE SEARCH FOR CULTURAL BEARINGS

What seemed the most likely overall directions as western Europeans pondered priorities in light of all the disasters surrounding the era of the two world wars?

The events from World War I to the cold war added up to an unprecedented period of disaster for Europe. Europeans were bound to ask what had gone wrong and what could be salvaged from the ruins of a culture that had made possible the most destructive wars in history, as well as fascism, totalitarianism, and the Holocaust. With so much discredited or called into question, Europeans faced an unprecedented period of experiment.

The cold war framework crucially shaped responses all over the Western world. Some embraced the Soviet Union or sought a renewed Marxism. Opposition to communism helped stimulate others to return to religious or classical traditions or to embrace new ideas associated with America's recent successes. In western Europe, at least, this effort to take stock led promptly to the renewed determination that helped produce the dramatically successful reconstruction of the postwar years. But the anxieties stemming from superpower rivalry, and especially the nuclear arms race, were bound to temper any renewed optimism.

ABSURDITY AND COMMITMENT IN EXISTENTIALISM

The postwar mood of exhaustion and despair found classic expression in the work of the Irish-born writer Samuel Beckett (1906–1989), especially in his plays *Waiting for Godot* (1952) and *Endgame* (1957). Through Beckett's characters, we see ourselves going through the motions, with nothing worth saying or doing, ludicrously manipulating the husks of a worn-out culture. The only redeeming element is the comic pathos we feel as we watch ourselves.

The same sense of anxiety and despair led to the vogue of **existentialism,** a movement that marked philosophy, the arts, and popular culture from the later 1940s until well into the 1950s. Existentialism developed from the ideas of the German thinker Martin Heidegger (1889–1976), especially *Being and Time* (1927), one of the most influential philosophical works of the century. Though it was a philosophy of sorts, existentialism was most significant as a broader cultural tendency, finding expression in novels and films. The existentialists explored what it means to be human in a world cast adrift from its cultural moorings, with no mutually accepted guideposts, standards, or values.

The most influential postwar existentialists were the Frenchmen Jean-Paul Sartre (SAH-truh) (1905–1980) and Albert Camus (kah-MOO) (1913–1960), each of whom had been involved in the French resistance, Camus in a particularly central role as editor of an underground newspaper. For both, an authentic human response to a world spinning out of control entails engagement, commitment, and responsibility—even though every action is fraught with risk.

Rather than accept the bleak, ludicrously comic vision of Beckett's plays, Camus sought to show how we might go on living in a positive, affirmative spirit, even in a world that seemed simply absurd in one sense, especially after the recent disasters in Europe. Conventional values like friendship and tolerance could be made usable again, based on the simple fact that we human beings are all caught up in this unmasterable situation together. People suffer and die, but as we come together to help as best we can, we might at least learn to stop killing one another.

Camus split from Sartre in a disagreement over the ongoing value of Marxism and the communist experiment in the Soviet Union. Though never an orthodox communist, Sartre found potential for human liberation in the working class, in communist political parties, even in the Soviet Union itself, which he saw as the strongest alternative to U.S. imperialism. By the 1950s he was portraying existentialism as fundamentally a way to revitalize Marxism.

Online Study Center **Improve Your Grade**
Primary Source: Existentialism Defined

By contrast, Camus, who had started as a communist in the 1930s, had grown disillusioned with communism even before the war, and his major political tract, *The Rebel* (1951), was partly an attack on Marxism and communism. Establishing new bases for human happiness and solidarity meant recognizing limits to

existentialism A philosophical and cultural movement, often associated with Jean-Paul Sartre and Albert Camus, for whom an authentic human response to an apparently meaningless universe entailed commitment and responsibility.

CHRONOLOGY

1947	India and Pakistan achieve independence
	Marshall Plan announced
1949	Formation of NATO
1951	Formation of the European Coal and Steel Community
1953	Death of Stalin
	Workers' revolt in East Germany
1955	West Germany joins NATO
	Warsaw Pact
1956	Khrushchev de-Stalinization speech
	Suez crisis
	Hungarian reform movement crushed
1957	*Sputnik I* launched
	Common Market established
1958	Beginning of Fifth Republic in France
1959	Bad Godesberg congress: reorientation of German socialism
1961	Berlin Wall erected
1962	Algerian independence from France
	Cuban missile crisis
1964	Ouster of Khrushchev
1968	Days of May uprising in France
	Prague Spring reform movement crushed
1969	Brandt becomes West German chancellor
1973	First OPEC oil crisis
1975	Communist victory in Vietnam
1978	Election of Pope John Paul II
1979	Thatcher becomes prime minister of Britain
1980	Formation of Solidarity in Poland
	Formation of independent Zimbabwe from Southern Rhodesia
1981	Mitterrand elected president of France
1982	Death of Brezhnev
1985	Gorbachev comes to power in the Soviet Union
1986	Chernobyl disaster
1989	Collapse of communism in east-central Europe
1991	Collapse of communism in the Soviet Union
	Dissolution of the Soviet Union

Sartre and de Beauvoir
Among the most influential intellectual couples of the century, Jean-Paul Sartre and Simone de Beauvoir emerged as leaders of French existentialism by the later 1940s. *(Corbis Sygma)*

what human beings could accomplish, limits even to our demands for freedom and justice. These were precisely the limits that the new political movements of the century had so disastrously overstepped. Communism, like fascism, was part of the problem, not the solution.

MARXISTS AND TRADITIONALISTS

Sartre was among the many European intellectuals who believed that Marxism had won a new lease on life from the wartime resistance. As they saw it, Marxism could be revamped for the West, without the Stalinist excesses of the Soviet Union. Marxism remained a significant strand in Western political culture throughout the cold war era, but it also attracted periodic waves of denunciation.

In Italy, as in France, the communists' major role in the resistance enhanced their prestige, preparing the way for the extraordinary posthumous influence of Antonio Gramsci (GRAHM-she) (1891–1937), a founder of the Italian Communist Party who had spent most of the fascist period in prison. His *Prison Notebooks,* published during the late 1940s, became influential throughout the world and helped make Marxism a powerful force in postwar Italian culture. Seeking to learn the lessons of the fascist triumph in Italy, Gramsci pointed Marxists toward a flexible political strategy, attuned to the special historical circumstances of each country. Thanks partly to Gramsci's legacy, Italy had the most innovative and important communist party outside the communist world for several decades after the war.

Loosely Marxist ideas were central to the renewal of political activism in the West by the late 1960s, although Marxism proved more effective as a critique of capitalism than as a blueprint for change. The best-known spokesman for a renewed radicalism on both sides of the Atlantic during the late 1960s and early 1970s was the German-born social thinker Herbert Marcuse (mar-KOO-zuh) (1898–1979), who explored the cultural mechanisms through which capitalism perpetuates itself in *One-Dimensional Man* (1964).

Even during the late 1940s, however, others, like Camus, denied that any recasting could overcome the inherent flaws in Marxism. Damaging revelations about the excesses of Stalinism during the 1930s seemed to confirm this view. Such writers as the Hungarian-born Arthur Koestler (KEST-lur) (1905–1983) who had believed in communism during the 1930s now denounced it as "the God that failed." Whatever its initial promise, Marxism anywhere would inevitably lead to the kind of tyranny that had developed in the Soviet Union. In his futuristic novel *Nineteen Eighty-Four,* published in 1949, the British intellectual George Orwell (1903–1950), long a partisan of leftist causes, chillingly portrayed the dehumanization that totalitarianism—and, by association, communism—seemed bound to entail.

By the mid-1970s, the disturbing portrait of the Soviet gulag, or forced-labor-camp system, by the exiled Soviet writer Alexander Solzhenitsyn (soul-zhen-EET-sin) (b. 1918) stimulated another wave of anticommunist thinking. And whether or not Marxism was necessarily Stalinist and repressive in implication, its relevance to the increasingly prosperous industrial democracies of western Europe was open to question. By the early 1980s, many had come to believe that the Marxist understanding of capitalism and class relations was simply passé.

Those hostile to Marxism often insisted that the West had to reconnect with older traditions if it were to avoid further horrors like those it had just been through. Especially in the first years after the war, many, like the French Catholic thinker Jacques Maritain (mar-eh-TAN) (1882–1973), held that only a return to religious traditions would suffice. For the American-born British writer T. S. Eliot (1888–1965), the essential return to tradition had to embrace family and locality, as well as religion. Without a return to tradition, Eliot warned, the West could expect more excesses such as fascism and totalitarianism in the future.

THE INTELLECTUAL MIGRATION AND AMERICANISM

The extraordinary migration of European artists and intellectuals to the United States to escape persecution during the 1930s and 1940s profoundly affected the cultural life of the postwar period. An array of luminaries arrived on American shores, from the composer Igor

Stravinsky to the theoretical physicist Albert Einstein, from the architect Walter Gropius to the radical social theorist Herbert Marcuse.

Before this cross-fertilization, American culture had remained somewhat provincial, sometimes proudly and self-consciously so. All the direct contact with these Europeans by the 1940s helped propel the United States into the Western cultural mainstream. No longer could "Western" culture be identified primarily with Europe. In some spheres—painting, for example—Americans were now confident enough to claim the leadership for the first time.

But the American abstract expressionism emerging by the later 1940s owed something to European existentialism, and it became possible only because so many of the most innovative European painters had come to New York, where the Americans had been able to learn their lessons firsthand. At the same time, European painters such as Jean Dubuffet (doo-boo-FAY) (1901–1985) in France and Francis Bacon (1910–1992) in Britain created new forms of their own—sometimes playful, sometimes brutal—as they sought the startling new visual imagery that seemed appropriate to Western culture after the era of fascism and war. Even in the United States, artists began reacting against the deep seriousness of abstract expressionism during the mid-1950s. One new direction led by the early 1960s to "pop art," which was "American" in a different sense, featuring the ordinary objects and mass-produced images of modern consumerist culture. (See the feature "The Visual Record: Pop Art.")

Some Europeans were eager to embrace what seemed distinctively American because America had remained relatively free of the political ideologies that seemed to have led Europe to totalitarianism and ruin. By the 1950s, there was much talk of "the end of ideology," with America indicating a healthier alternative combining technology, value-free social science, and scientific management. Whereas the old European way led either to mere theorizing, to political extremism, or to polarization and impasse, the American approach got results by tackling problems one at a time, so that they could be solved by managerial or technical experts.

Such Americanism fed the notion that Europe needed a clean break based on technological values. If such a break was necessary, however, what was to become of the European tradition, for centuries the center of gravity of the West and until recently dominant in the world? Did anything distinctively European remain, or was Europe doomed to lick its wounds in the shadow of America? These questions lurked in the background as Europeans faced the difficult task of economic and political restoration.

Dubuffet: Spinning Round

Seeking to depart from the European tradition of sophisticated, well-made art, Jean Dubuffet developed imagery that was at once crude and primitive, playful and whimsical. *(Tate Gallery, London/Art Resource, NY. © 2003 Artists Rights Society [ARS], New York/ADAGP, Paris)*

Pop Art

Hamburgers, comic strips, soup-can labels, familiar images of entertainment icons—such was the stuff of "pop art," which burst onto the New York art scene in the early 1960s and came to exert a widespread cultural influence. Indeed, with their imaginative renderings of familiar images and whimsical sculptures of everyday objects, artists like Andy Warhol (1928–1987), Roy Lichtenstein (1923–1997), and Claes Oldenburg (b. 1929) helped shape the experience of the later twentieth century. But was this serious art or simply a joke, a parody, a put-on? Were the pop artists poking fun at the triviality of modern society, or were they deepening our encounter with defining aspects of contemporary culture? Whatever their intent, what does this striking new art form tell us about the direction of Western culture in the decades after World War II?

The term *pop art* was coined in England in the 1950s, when a group of artists and critics became interested in bridging the cultural gap between "fine art" and the emerging popular culture of mass media and machine-produced images, of advertising and automobiles. Like everyone else, they associated that consumerist mass culture with America—the America of Hollywood, Detroit, and Madison Avenue. And they found it more vital than the conventional fine art of the period. The American pop artists were similarly fascinated by the impersonal, mass-produced, often expendable quality of the objects and images that have come to surround us.

Oldenburg: Floor Burger, 1962 *(Claes Oldenburg [American, b. 1929], Floor Burger, 1962. Canvas filled with foam rubber and cardboard boxes, painted with acrylic paint, 132.1 x 213.4 cm. Art Gallery of Ontario, Toronto. Reproduced with permission of Claes Oldenburg.)*

Pop art was part of a wider reaction against the deeply serious abstract expressionist painting that emerged in New York just after the Second World War. By the early 1950s, abstract expressionists like Jackson Pollock (1912–1956) and Mark Rothko (1903–1970) had created images of unprecedented power, whether seeking to forge an artistic identity in the face of nothingness or to transcend selfhood in a cosmic wholeness. In the mid-1950s, however, younger artists, "tired of the stink of artists' egos," began reacting against the self-importance of abstract expressionism. For these younger artists, art did not have to be a vehicle for the psychological expression of the artist or a quest for "the tragic and timeless." Although the reaction took several forms, pop art proved the most influential. The pop movement emerged especially in the United States, and it interested Europeans as typically American—fresh and fascinating or garish and vulgar, depending on one's point of view.

Whereas the abstract expressionists had sought to rise above the everyday world, Claes Oldenburg's sculptures played with the scale and context of the most ordinary objects—a mixer, a three-pronged plug, a lipstick, a hamburger—to deepen our involvement with the everyday things that surround us. In this sense, the aim of pop art was not simply to parody or satirize, but to affirm our relationship with the trappings of ordinary life. Hollywood, Detroit, and Madison Avenue were all right after all; indeed, they had become the centers of Western culture by the later twentieth century.

Though anonymous and impersonal, the modern world of mass production, mass consumption, and mass media is "popular" because its images and objects are accessible to us all. In fact, they bombard us from all directions, giving shared shape and definition to our everyday lives. This is our world, the pop artists were saying, and they were creating the art appropriate to our time. They invite us to relax and enjoy that world, but they also enhance our experience by making art from it, thereby awakening us to its novelty and vitality.

But some viewers have found an element of melancholy, nostalgia, even tragedy just beneath pop art's eye-catching surface. In a world of mass media and reproduced images, more of our experience becomes secondhand and literally superficial. Likewise, pop subjects, from fast food to billboards,

Warhol: Marilyn Diptych, 1962 *(Tate Gallery, London/Art Resource, NY. © Artists Rights Society [ARS],*
New York/ADAGP, Paris)

have no deeper meaning, no expressive personal agenda. With his multiplied image of Marilyn Monroe, Andy Warhol dealt not with the actress herself but with the obsessive familiarity of her image. He cultivated a deadpan, detached style that reflected the machine-made quality of his subject matter— the quality that made the images he started with so familiar in the first place. But even as, on one level, he embraced aspects of the new mass culture, Warhol was exploring precisely the emotional detachment—and the accompanying trivialization of emotion—at work in the culture that had produced the images he adapted. Especially in his paintings treating impersonal newspaper images of disaster and death, Warhol bore witness to our indifference—and perhaps to a cosmic meaninglessness as well. One expert has noted that "in Warhol's pictures of the material objects and other false idols that most of us worship, the pain lies just below the bright surfaces of the images and waits passively to engage us."*

The advent of pop art provoked a series of questions that remain unanswered: Is the embrace of the mass-produced and commercial, at the expense of traditional "fine art" values, a symptom of exhaustion or a healthy affirmation of contemporary popular culture, so bound up with the commercial world? Or is pop art perhaps a valuable comment on the emptiness of that culture, with its impersonal conformity, garish commercialism, and mechanical repetition? In the final analysis, were the pop artists abandoning the artist's lofty mission and giving in to the ordinary? Or were they the first to show us what "Western civilization" had come to mean by the late twentieth century?

QUESTIONS

1. Does pop art seem to be embracing, or poking fun at, the modern world of consumerism and advertising?

2. What is "popular" about pop art?

Online Study Center
Improve Your Grade Visual Record Activities

_____
* Eric Shanes, *Warhol* (New York: Portland House, 1991), p. 41.

═══════════ S E C T I O N   S U M M A R Y ═══════════

- Existentialism and the plays of Samuel Beckett expressed the sense of exhaustion and lack of bearings in Western culture after World War II.

- Cold war concerns helped fuel an often bitter debate between Marxists and anti-Marxists that continued, off and on, from the later 1940s well into the 1970s.

- Some held that a return to religious and other traditions offered the only antidote in light of the disasters surrounding the era of the two world wars.

- The migration of European artists and intellectuals to America profoundly affected cultural relations between America and western Europe, especially during the early years of the cold war era.

- As they sought a fresh start for Europe, many western Europeans sought to adapt what they took to be American practicality.

PROSPERITY AND DEMOCRACY IN WESTERN EUROPE

What factors led to the surprisingly rapid restoration of democracy in much of continental western Europe after World War II?

By 1941 democracy seemed to be dying on the European continent, yet it quickly revived in western Europe after World War II, taking root more easily than most had thought possible. The bipolar international framework helped. The United States actively encouraged democracy, and Europeans fearing the spread of communism were happy to follow the American lead. Success at economic reconstruction was important as well. Not only was there greater prosperity, but governments could afford to deliver on promises of enhanced security, social welfare, and equal opportunity. It also mattered that western Europeans learned from past mistakes.

ECONOMIC RECONSTRUCTION AND THE ATLANTIC ORIENTATION

It is hard to imagine how desperate the situation in much of western Europe had become by 1945. Major cities like Rotterdam, Hamburg, and Le Havre lay largely in ruins, and normal routines suffered radical disruption. Production had declined to perhaps 25 percent of the prewar level in Italy, to 20 percent in France, and to a mere 5 percent in southern Germany. Cigarettes, often gained through barter from American soldiers, served widely as a medium of exchange.

Although the U.S. commitment to assist European economic reconstruction was not originally a cold war measure, the developing cold war context added urgency to the American effort. The key was the Marshall Plan, which U.S. secretary of state General Marshall outlined in 1947 and which channeled $13.5 billion in aid to western Europe by 1951.

Online Study Center **Improve Your Grade**
Primary Source: An American Plan to Rebuild a Shattered Europe

Cold war concerns deepened the partnership in April 1949, when the United States spearheaded a military alliance, the **North Atlantic Treaty Organization (NATO),** that included much of western Europe. The Soviets were tightening their grip on their satellite states in east-central Europe, and the NATO alliance was intended to check any Soviet expansion westward. The Soviets had considerable superiority in conventional forces, which had ready access to western Europe, but U.S. nuclear superiority provided a balance. Indeed, the American nuclear guarantee to western Europe was the cornerstone of the NATO alliance.

On the economic level, the western Europeans quickly proved worthy partners. So impressive was the recovery in continental western Europe by the 1950s that some dubbed it an "economic miracle." Western Europeans took advantage of the need to rebuild by adopting up-to-date methods and technologies, though economic strategies differed from one country to the next. The new German government intervened in the economy only to ensure free competition. In France, by contrast, many were determined to use government to modernize the country, thereby overcoming the weakness that had led to defeat. So France adopted a flexible, pragmatic form of government-led economic

North Atlantic Treaty Organization (NATO)
An alliance for regional defense, created in 1949 by the United States, Canada, and western European nations, whose members agree to defend one another from attack by nonmember countries.

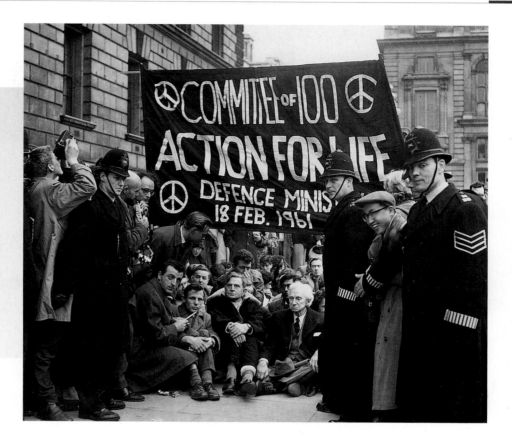

Ban the Bomb
As nuclear tension escalated during the 1950s, some people built air-raid shelters; others took to the streets in antinuclear protests. The protest movement was especially prominent in Britain, where the noted philosopher Bertrand Russell (1872–1970) played a central role. Here, at the right of those seated, he awaits arrest during a sit-in demonstration outside the British Defense Ministry. *(Hulton Archive/Getty Images)*

planning, spearheaded by the technocrat Jean Monnet (moh-NAY) (1888–1979). By 1951 French industrial production had returned to its prewar peak, and by 1957 it had risen to twice the level of 1938. Indeed, strong and sustained rates of economic growth were achieved throughout much of western Europe until the late 1960s, although Britain lagged considerably.

As part of the new postwar consensus, labor was supposed to be brought more fully into economic decision making. Thus, for example, the trade unions participated in the planning process in France. In Germany the codetermination law of 1951 provided for labor participation in management decisions in heavy industry, and labor representatives were given access to company books and full voting memberships on boards of directors. This measure ultimately made little difference in the functioning of the affected firms, but it helped head off any return to trade-union radicalism.

During the first years of rapid economic growth, the labor movement remained fairly passive in western Europe, even though wages stayed relatively low. By the 1960s, however, labor began demanding—generally with success—to share more fully in the new prosperity. Now, rather abruptly, much of western Europe took on the look of a consumer society, with widespread ownership of automobiles, televisions, and other household appliances.

SOCIAL WELFARE AND THE ISSUE OF GENDER

Western governments began to adopt social welfare measures late in the nineteenth century (see page 726), and by the 1940s some degree of governmental responsibility for unemployment insurance, workplace safety, and old-age pensions was widely accepted. Some Europeans, seeking renewal after the war, found attractive models in Sweden and Denmark, where the outlines of a **welfare state** had emerged by the 1930s. Sweden, especially, drew attention as a "middle way" that avoided the extremes of either Soviet Marxism, with its coercive statism, or American-style capitalism, with its brash commercialism and selfish individualism.

Sweden   Sweden's economy remained fundamentally capitalist, based on private ownership; even after World War II, its nationalized, or government-run, sector was not large by European standards. But the system of social insurance in Sweden was the most extensive in Europe, and the government worked actively with business to promote full employment and to steer the economy in directions deemed socially desirable. Moreover, the

welfare state   The concept, especially prevalent in Western countries after World War II, that government should adopt large-scale social welfare measures, while maintaining a primarily capitalistic economy.

Social Welfare in Sweden With the state playing a major role, Sweden proved a pioneer in responding to the family and children's issues that became increasingly prominent after World War II. Here children play at a day-care center in Stockholm in 1953. *(Roland Janson/Pressens Bild, Stockholm)*

welfare state came to mean a major role for the Swedish trade unions, which won relatively high wages for workers and even enjoyed a quasi-veto power over legislation.

At the same time, the Swedish government began playing a more active role in spheres of life that had formerly been private, from sexuality to child rearing. Thus, for example, drugstores were required to carry contraceptives beginning in 1946. Sweden was the first country to provide sex education in the public schools; optional beginning in 1942, it became compulsory in 1955. By 1979 the Swedes were limiting corporal punishment—the right to spank—and prohibiting the sale of war toys. This deprivatization of the family stemmed from a sense, especially pronounced in Sweden, that society is collectively responsible for the well-being of its children.

Britain Although the Swedish model was extreme in certain respects, most of western Europe moved in the same direction in an effort to restore consensus and establish the foundations for democratic renewal after the war. Even Britain, one of the war's major victors, quickly began constructing a welfare state, dumping Winston Churchill in the process.

Early in the war most Britons began to take it for granted that major socioeconomic changes would follow from victory. Greater collective responsibility for the well-being of all British citizens seemed appropriate in light of the shared hardships the war had imposed. Moreover, the successes of government planning and control during the wartime emergency sug-

gested that once the war was over, government could assume responsibility for the basic needs of the British people, guaranteeing full employment and providing a national health service. But the Labour Party, led by Clement Attlee (1883–1967), seemed better equipped to deliver on that promise than the Conservatives, whose leader, Churchill, was in fact quite hostile to welfare state notions. So when Britain held its first postwar elections, in July 1945, Churchill's Conservatives suffered a crushing loss to Labour, which promptly began creating the British welfare state.

Although some expected, and others feared, that the result would be a form of socialism, the new direction did not undermine the capitalist economic system. The Labour government nationalized some key industries, but 80 percent of the British work force remained employed in private firms in 1948. Moreover, even under Labour, the British government did not seek the kind of economic planning role that government was playing in France.

The core of the British departure was a set of government-sponsored social welfare measures that significantly affected the lives of ordinary people. These included old-age pensions; insurance against unemployment, sickness, and disability; and allowances for pregnancy, child rearing, widowhood, and burial. The heart of the system was free medical care, to be provided by the National Health Service, created in November 1946 and operating by 1948.

In Britain, as elsewhere, gender roles were inevitably at issue as government welfare measures were debated and adopted. Were married women to have access to the welfare system as individual citizens or as members of a family unit, responsible for child rearing and dependent on their husbands as breadwinners? Should government seek to enable women to be both mothers and workers, or should government help make it possible for mothers not to have to work outside the home?

As during the First World War, the percentage of women in the work force had increased significantly during World War II, but both women and men proved eager to embrace the security of traditional domestic patterns once the war was over. So the war did not change gender patterns of work even to the extent that World War I had done. In Britain women made up about 30 percent of the labor force in 1931, 31 percent in 1951. Thus the embrace of welfare measures took place at a time of renewed conservatism in conceptions of gender roles.

British feminists initially welcomed provisions of the British welfare state that recognized the special role of women as mothers. The government was to ease burdens by providing family allowances, to be paid directly to mothers of more than one child to enable them to stay home with their children. This seemed a more progressive step than the perpetual British trade-union demand for a "family wage," sufficient to enable the male breadwinner to support a family. But though women were now to be compensated directly for their role as mothers, the assumptions about gender roles remained essentially the same.

France   In France, which had refused even to grant women the vote after World War I, the very different situation after 1945 stimulated an especially innovative response to gender and family issues. After the experience of defeat, collaboration, and resistance, the French were determined to pursue both economic dynamism and individual justice. But they also remained concerned with population growth, so they combined incentives to encourage large families with measures to promote equal opportunity and economic independence for women.

As they expanded the role of government after the war, the French tended more than the British to assume that paid employment for women was healthy and desirable. New laws gave French women equal access to civil service jobs and guaranteed equal pay for equal work. At the same time, the French recognized that women had special needs as mothers, but also that husbands shared the responsibility for parenting. So the French system provided benefits for women during and after pregnancy and then family allowances that treated the two parents as equally essential. At the same time, the system viewed women as individual citizens, regardless of marital or economic status. Thus all were

equally entitled to pensions, health services, and job-related benefits.

Although female participation in the paid labor force declined just after the war, it began rising throughout the West during the 1950s, then accelerated during the 1960s, reaching new highs in the 1970s and 1980s. Thanks partly to the expansion of government, the greatest job growth was in the service sector—in social work, health care, and education, for example—and many of these new jobs went to women. From about 1960 to 1988, the percentage of women aged 25 to 34 in the labor force rose from 38 to 67 in Britain, from 42 to 75 in France, and from 49 to 87 in Germany.

These statistics reflect significant changes in women's lives, but even as their choices expanded in some respects, women became more deeply aware of enduring limits to their opportunities. Thus a new feminist movement emerged by the early 1970s, drawing intellectual inspiration from *The Second Sex,* a pioneering work published in 1949 by the French existentialist Simone de Beauvoir (1908–1986).

THE RESTORATION OF DEMOCRACY

Much of continental western Europe faced the challenge of rebuilding democracy after defeat and humiliation. With the developing cold war complicating the situation, the prospects for democracy were by no means certain in the late 1940s. Although the division of Germany weakened communism in the new Federal Republic, in France and Italy strong communist parties had emerged from the wartime resistance and claimed to point the way beyond conventional democracy altogether.

Germany   The new Federal Republic of Germany held its first election under the Basic Law in August 1949, launching what proved to be a stable and successful democracy. Partly to counter the Soviet Union, but also to avoid what seemed the disastrous mistake of the harsh peace settlement after World War I, the victors sought to help get West Germany back on its feet as quickly as possible. At the same time, West German political leaders, determined to avoid the mistakes of the Weimar years, now better understood the need to compromise, to take responsibility for governing the whole nation.

To prevent the instability that had plagued the Weimar Republic, the creators of the new government strengthened the chancellor in relation to the Bundestag, the lower house of parliament. In the same way, the Basic Law helped establish a stable party system by discouraging splinter parties and by empowering the courts to outlaw extremist parties. And the courts found reason to outlaw both the Communist Party and a Neo-Nazi Party during the formative years of the new German democracy.

Franco-German Cooperation

French president Charles de Gaulle (*left*) and West German chancellor Konrad Adenauer (*right*) draw an enthusiastic crowd in Bonn in September 1963. De Gaulle was in the West German capital for the first formal meeting after France and West Germany had signed a friendship treaty in January. Each of the two leaders strongly advocated the new cooperation between their countries, and that cooperation proved a cornerstone of the unprecedented peace and prosperity in western Europe after World War II. *(akg-images)*

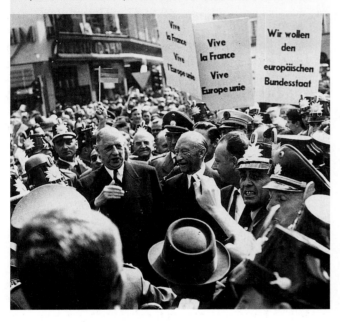

The West German republic proved more stable than the earlier Weimar Republic partly because the political party system was now considerably simpler. Two mass parties, the Christian Democratic Union (CDU) and the Social Democratic Party (SPD), were immediately predominant, although a third, the much smaller Free Democratic Party (FDP), proved important for coalition purposes.

Konrad Adenauer (1876–1967), head of the CDU, the largest party in 1949, immediately emerged as West Germany's leading statesman. A Catholic who had been mayor of Cologne under Weimar, he had withdrawn from active politics during the Nazi period, but he reemerged after the war to lead the council that drafted the Basic Law. As chancellor from 1949 to 1963, he oriented the new German democracy toward western Europe and the Atlantic bloc, led by the United States.

The new bipolar world confronted West Germany with a cruel choice. By accepting the bipolar framework, the country could become a full partner within the Atlantic bloc. But by straddling the fence instead, it could keep open the possibility that Germany could be reunified as a neutral and disarmed state. When the outbreak of war in Korea in 1950 intensified the cold war, the United States pressured West Germany to rearm and join the Western bloc. Although some West Germans resisted, Adenauer prevailed, committing the Federal Republic to NATO in 1955. Adenauer was eager to anchor the new Federal Republic to the West, partly to buttress the new democracy in West Germany, but also to cement U.S. support in the face of what seemed an ongoing Soviet threat to German security.

By the late 1950s the West German economy was recovering nicely, and the country was a valued member of the Western alliance. Adenauer's CDU seemed so potent that the other major party, the SPD, appeared to be consigned to permanent—and sterile—opposition. Frustrated with its outsider status, the SPD began to shed its Marxist trappings in an effort to widen its appeal. Prominent among those pushing in this direction was **Willy Brandt** (1913–1992), who became mayor of West Berlin in 1957, and who would become the party's leader in 1963. At its watershed national congress at Bad Godesberg in 1959, the party officially gave up talk of the class struggle and adopted a more moderate program.

Adenauer stepped down in 1963 at the age of 87, after fourteen years as chancellor. The contrast with Weimar, which had known twenty-one different cabinets in a comparable fourteen-year period, could not be more striking. The Adenauer years proved to Germans that democracy could mean effective government, economic prosperity, and foreign policy success. Still, Adenauer had become somewhat authoritarian by his later years, and it was arguable that West Germany had become overly reliant on him and his party.

During the years from 1963 to 1969, the CDU proved it could govern without Adenauer, and the SPD came to seem ever more respectable, even joining as the junior partner in a government coalition with the CDU in 1966. Finally, in October 1969, new parliamentary elections brought Brandt to the chancellorship, and the SPD became responsible for governing West Germany for the first time since the war.

Brandt sought to provide a genuine alternative to the CDU without undermining the consensus that had developed around the new regime since 1949. He wanted

Konrad Adenauer Leading statesman of post–World War II Germany who oriented the country toward western Europe and the United States and proved to Germans that democracy could mean effective government, economic prosperity, and foreign policy success.

Willy Brandt Social Democratic West German chancellor whose policy of opening to the East, or *Ostpolitik,* made possible closer economic ties between West and East Germany and helped ordinary citizens interact across the east-west border.

especially to improve relations between West Germany and the Soviet bloc, but this required a more independent foreign policy than Adenauer and his successors had followed. Under Adenauer, the Federal Republic had refused to deal with East Germany at all. So Brandt's opening to the East, or *Ostpolitik* (OST-po-luh-teek), was risky for a socialist chancellor seeking to prove his respectability. But he pursued it with skill and success.

In treaties with the Soviet Union, Czechoslovakia, and Poland during the early 1970s, West Germany accepted the main lines of the postwar settlement. This was to abandon any claim to the former German territory east of the Oder-Neisse line, now in Poland. Brandt also managed to improve relations with East Germany. After the two countries finally agreed to mutual diplomatic recognition, each was admitted to the United Nations in 1973. Brandt's overtures made possible closer economic ties between them, and even broader opportunities for ordinary citizens to interact across the east-west border. His *Ostpolitik* was widely popular and helped deepen the postwar consensus in West Germany.

France, Italy, and Southern Europe

In France and Italy, unlike West Germany, the communists constituted a potent force in light of their major roles in wartime resistance movements. The presence of Western troops in France and Italy gave the leverage to noncommunists, however, and Moscow directed the communists in both countries to settle for the moderate course of participation in broad political coalitions. But in each nation the United States intervened persistently to minimize the communists' role. Though support for the communists in France continued to grow until 1949, the French Communist Party settled into a particularly doctrinaire position, maintaining strict subservience to the Soviet Union, and found itself increasingly marginalized thereafter.

As the leader of the French resistance effort, Charles de Gaulle immediately assumed the dominant political role after the liberation of France in August 1944. But he withdrew, disillusioned, from active politics early in 1946, as the new Fourth Republic returned to the unstable multiparty coalitions that had marked the later years of the Third Republic. Still, governmental decision making changed significantly as the nonpolitical, technocratic side of the French state gained power in areas such as economic planning. And government technocrats survived the fall of the Fourth Republic in 1958, when de Gaulle returned to politics in a situation of crisis stemming from France's war to maintain control of Algeria (see page 930).

It was clear that de Gaulle's return signified a change of regime. After the French legislature gave him full powers for six months, his government drafted a new constitution, which was then approved by referendum in the fall of 1958. The result was the new Fifth Republic, which featured a stronger executive—and soon a president elected directly by the people and not dependent on the Chamber of Deputies. It was only in 1958, with the return of de Gaulle and the advent of the Fifth Republic, that government in postwar France began to assume definitive contours.

Italy's political challenge, after more than twenty years of fascism, was even more dramatic than France's. Shortly after the war, the Italians adopted a new democratic constitution and voted to end the monarchy, thereby making modern Italy a republic for the first time. But much depended on the balance of political forces, which quickly crystallized around the Christian Democratic Party (DC), oriented toward the Catholic Church, and the strong Communist Party. Many Italian moderates with little attachment to the church supported the Christian Democrats as the chief bulwark against communism. And though they consistently had to work with smaller parties to attain a parliamentary majority, the Christian Democrats promptly assumed the dominant role, which they maintained until the early 1990s.

The Communists continued to offer the major opposition, typically winning 25 to 35 percent of the vote in national elections. Taking their cue from Gramsci's writings, they adopted a proactive strategy to make their presence felt in Italian life and to demonstrate the superiority of their diagnoses and prescriptions. And they found considerable success as they organized profit-making cooperatives for sharecroppers, ran local and regional governments, and garnered the support of intellectuals, journalists, and publishers. But though they had proven capable of operating constructively within a democratic framework, their longer-term role remained unclear into the 1970s. What were the Communists trying to accomplish on the national level, and how long was it supposed to take? Could they function as part of a majority governing coalition within a democratic political system?

By the 1960s the new democracies in Germany, France, and Italy seemed firmly rooted, and during the 1970s Greece, Spain, and Portugal also established workable democracies after periods of dictatorial rule. Following the death of Francisco Franco in 1975, almost forty years after his triumph in the Spanish civil war, democracy returned to Spain more smoothly than most had dared hope. Franco ordained that a restoration of the monarchy would follow his death, and King Juan Carlos (b. 1938; r. 1975–) served as an effective catalyst in the transition to democracy. The new constitution of 1978 dismantled what was left of the Franco system so that, for example, Catholicism was no longer recognized as the official religion of the Spanish state.

New Discontents and New Directions

Even as democracy seemed to be thriving in western Europe, political disaffection began to threaten the consensus by the late 1960s. At that point western Europe was at the height of the new prosperity, so the discontent did not stem from immediate economic circumstances. A new radicalism similarly emerged in the United States during the 1960s. Although this American radicalism developed especially from the civil rights movement and from opposition to the U.S. war in Vietnam, a sense that ordinary people were not truly empowered by contemporary democratic institutions fed the new radicalism on both sides of the Atlantic.

Long in gestation, the American civil rights movement sought to overcome racial segregation and other limitations on the rights of African Americans in the United States. It gathered momentum during the 1950s, inspired partly by decolonization struggles elsewhere. A Baptist minister, Martin Luther King, Jr. (1929–1968), emerged as the movement's best-known leader after he spearheaded a successful bus boycott in Montgomery, Alabama, during 1955 and 1956. Professing the technique of nonviolence that Mohandas Gandhi had practiced in India (see the box "The Global Record: Gandhi Advocates Nonviolence" on page 842 in Chapter 27), King won widespread sympathy for the movement among American whites. In 1963 he led a mixed-race throng of 200,000 in a march on Washington, D.C., that helped produce the landmark Civil Rights Act of 1964 and other legislation ending segregation and overt forms of racial discrimination. Although discrimination and de facto segregation could still be found thereafter, the civil rights movement transformed American society and helped stimulate movements for change around the world for decades thereafter.

The most dramatic instance of radical protest in western Europe was the "Days of May" uprising of students and workers that shook France during May and June of 1968. The movement's aims were amorphous or utopian, and cooperation between students and workers proved sporadic. But the episode gave vent to growing discontent with the aloofness of the technocratic leaders and the unevenness of the modernization effort in de Gaulle's France. Despite the impressive economic growth, many ordinary people were coming to feel left out as public services were neglected and problems worsened in such areas as housing and education. French universities were a particular target, drawing protests and even full-scale takeovers by radical students.

Enrollment in French universities more than doubled between 1939 and 1960, then more than doubled again between 1960 and 1967. Apart from a few highly selective *grandes écoles*, the institutions of the state-run university system were open to anyone who passed a standard examination. To limit enrollments by restricting access did not seem politically feasible. Instead, the government tried to build to keep up with demand—thereby creating vast, impersonal institutions with professors increasingly inaccessible to students. But overcrowding persisted, and the value of a university degree diminished, leaving graduates with uncertain job prospects.

In Italy frustration with the stagnation of the political system bred radical labor unrest by 1969 and then a major wave of terrorism during the 1970s. By this time many radical young people found the Communists too caught up in the system to be genuinely innovative, yet still too weak to break the Christian Democrats' lock on power. Because the Italian Communists, unlike the German Social Democrats, never established their credibility as a national governing party, the Christian Democrats grew ever more entrenched, becoming increasingly arrogant and corrupt.

In Germany the Green movement formed by peace and environmental activists during the late 1970s took pains to avoid acting like a conventional party. Concerned that Germany, with its central location, would end up the devastated battleground in any superpower confrontation, the Greens opposed deployment of additional U.S. missiles on German soil and called for an alternative to the endless arms race. The SPD, as the governing party in an important NATO state, seemed unable to confront this issue and lost members as a result.

Prominent among the new political currents emerging by the early 1970s was the renewed feminist movement, which recalled the earlier movement for women's suffrage. This drive for "women's liberation" sought equal opportunities for women in education and employment. It was striking, for example, that despite major steps toward equal educational opportunity in postwar France, the country's prestigious engineering schools were still not admitting women in the late 1960s and would begin doing so only during the 1980s. But feminists also forced new issues onto the political stage as they worked, for example, to liberalize divorce and abortion laws.

As the established Marxist left seemed unable to deal persuasively with contemporary concerns, new coalitions developed around newly politicized issues such as abortion and the environment. The successes of this new left fed renewed hopes for a more systematic change in socioeconomic relations by the early 1980s, when revitalized socialist parties in France, Spain, and Italy marginalized the communists and, for a time, seemed poised to reorient government, even to spearhead that systematic change.

The pivotal case was France, where François Mitterrand (MEE-tuh-rahn) (1916–1996) was elected president in 1981, promising to create the first genuinely democratic socialism. Despite a vigorous start, how-

Thatcher's Conservative Revolution

As British prime minister from 1979 to 1990, Margaret Thatcher led an assault on the welfare state and a renewed embrace of free-market economics in Britain. Together with U.S. president Ronald Reagan, who greatly admired her, she came to symbolize the retreat from government that marked the 1980s. Thatcher is shown at a political rally in London in 1987.

(D. Hudson/Corbis Sygma)

ever, he gradually abandoned any talk of socialism in the face of economic and political pressures. By the end of the 1980s, he was questioning the relevance of long-standing socialist tenets and playing up the virtues of entrepreneurship, the profit mechanism, and free-market competition. Mitterrand realized that France, like the other industrial democracies, had to operate in an increasingly competitive international economy, which seemed to impose the same rules on all.

RETHINKING THE WELFARE STATE

In much of western Europe the reach of government continued to expand into the 1970s, when reforms in Italy, for example, made available a wider range of state services—from kindergarten and medical care to sports and recreational facilities—than ever before. But during the 1970s some began to question both the monetary costs of such measures and their implications for European competitiveness in the global economy.

Although much publicity surrounded the postwar British welfare state, by the early 1970s the percentage of the British economy devoted to public expenditure for welfare, housing, and education—18.2 percent—was about average for the industrialized nations of the West. Sweden had the highest figure at 23.7 percent, and by that point 40 percent of Sweden's national income was devoted to taxes to finance the system—the highest rate of taxation in the world. But pressures on the welfare state were especially striking in Sweden at the same time. Swedish opinion-makers grew increasingly doubtful that a welfare state could nurture the initiative and productivity needed for success in international economic competition. Sweden found itself less competitive, both because its wages were high and because it was not keeping abreast of technological developments.

In Britain a dramatic assault on the welfare state began developing at the same time, especially because the postwar British economy, having lagged behind the others of the industrialized West, suffered especially with the more difficult economic circumstances of the 1970s. Between 1968 and 1976, the country lost one million manufacturing jobs. By the mid-1970s this economic decline threatened to shatter Britain's postwar consensus around the welfare state, as the British people could not agree on how to apportion the pain of the necessary austerity measures.

During the 1970s each of Britain's two major political parties made a serious effort to come to grips with the situation, but neither succeeded, especially because neither could deal effectively with Britain's strong trade unions. But when the militantly conservative **Margaret Thatcher** (b. 1925) became prime minister in 1979, it was clear that Britain was embarking on a radically different course.

Thatcher insisted that Britain could reverse its economic decline only by fostering a new "enterprise culture," restoring the individual initiative that had been sapped, as she saw it, by decades of dependence on government. So her government made substantial cuts in taxes and corresponding cuts in spending for education, national health, and public housing. It also fostered privatization, selling off an array of state-owned firms from Rolls-Royce to British Airways. The government even sold public housing to tenants, at as much

Margaret Thatcher Conservative prime minister of Britain from 1979 to 1990, she promoted privatization and free enterprise at the expense of the welfare state and the British labor unions.

as 50 percent below market value, a measure that helped win considerable working-class support.

At the same time, several new laws curtailed trade-union power, and Thatcher refused to consult with union leaders as her predecessors had done since the war. A showdown was reached with the yearlong coal miners' strike of 1984–1985, one of the most bitter and violent European strikes of the century. Its failure in the face of government intransigence further discred-ited the labor movement and enhanced Thatcher's prestige.

Even critics admitted that Thatcher's policies had produced a significant change in British attitudes in favor of enterprise and competition. And Britain's economic performance certainly improved in the wake of the Thatcher revolution. But the gap between rich and poor widened, and the old industrial regions of the north were left ever farther behind.

═══════════ S E C T I O N   S U M M A R Y ═══════════

- The continuing American commitment to western Europe, on both the economic and military-diplomatic levels, helped provide a framework for democratic restoration.

- Government promises of enhanced social welfare and equality of opportunity were essential to a new social compact in the years of democratic reconstruction in western Europe.

- Konrad Adenauer led West Germany into the American-led Atlantic bloc as part of his effort to cement democratic institutions in the new West Germany.

- Discontent with the quality of democracy surfaced on both sides of the Atlantic by the 1960s, even before the economic downturn of the 1970s.

- The traditional socialist left and even the welfare state were on the defensive in many parts of western Europe by the 1980s.

THE COMMUNIST BLOC: FROM CONSOLIDATION TO STAGNATION

How did Soviet policy evolve after the death of Stalin in 1953?

By the late 1950s, policymakers in the West were increasingly concerned that the Soviet Union, though rigid and inhumane in important respects, might have significant advantages in the race with the capitalist democracies. Westerners worried especially about producing enough scientists and engineers to match the Soviets. With the Great Depression still in memory, some economists held that central planning might prove more efficient, and more likely to serve social justice, than capitalism. The sense that the communist system offered formidable competition added to the anxieties in the U.S.-led Atlantic bloc.

Nonetheless, the flawed political and economic order that had emerged under Stalin continued in the Soviet Union. And when it was imposed on the countries within the Soviet orbit after the war, it produced widespread resentment—and new dilemmas for Soviet leaders. Efforts to make communism more flexible after Stalin's death in 1953 proved sporadic at best. The Soviet suppression of the reform movement in Czechoslovakia during the "Prague Spring" of 1968 seemed to prove the inherent rigidity of the Soviet system.

DILEMMAS OF THE SOVIET SYSTEM IN POSTWAR EUROPE, 1949–1955

Even in victory, the Soviet Union had suffered enormously in the war with Nazi Germany. Especially in the more developed western part of the country, thousands of factories and even whole towns lay destroyed, and there were severe shortages of everything from labor to housing. Yet the developing cold war seemed to require that military spending remain high.

At the same time, the Soviet Union faced the challenge of solidifying the new system of satellite states it had put together in east-central Europe. Most of the region had no desirable interwar past to reclaim, and thus there was widespread sentiment for significant change. Even in Czechoslovakia, which had been the most prosperous and democratic state in the region, considerable nationalization of industry was completed even before the communist takeover in 1948. And whatever integration into the new Soviet bloc might mean politically, it was not clear in the late 1940s that it had to be economically disadvantageous over the long term.

The Soviet system seemed to have proved itself in standing up to the Nazis, and many believed that a socialist economic system could be made to work.

Partly in response to U.S. initiatives in western Europe, the Soviets sought to mold the new communist states into a secure, coordinated bloc of allies. In the economic sphere, the Soviets founded a new organization, COMECON, as part of their effort to lead the economies of the satellite states away from their earlier ties to the West and toward the Soviet Union (see **MAP 29.1**). In the military-diplomatic sphere, the Soviets countered NATO in 1955 by bringing the Soviet bloc countries together in a formal alliance, the **Warsaw Pact,** which provided for a joint military command and mutual military assistance.

From the start, Yugoslavia had been a point of vulnerability for the Soviet system. Communist-led partisans under Josip Tito had liberated Yugoslavia from the Axis on their own, and they had not needed the Red Army to begin constructing a new communist regime (see page 897). Tito was willing to work with the Soviets, but because he had his own legitimacy, he could be considerably more independent than those elsewhere whose power rested on Soviet support. Thus the Soviets deemed it essential to bring Tito to heel, lest his example encourage too much independence in the other communist states. When Soviet demands became intolerably meddlesome from the Yugoslav point of view, Tito broke with the Soviet Union altogether in 1948. Yugoslavia then began developing a more flexible socialist economic system, with greater scope for local initiatives.

Stalin's response to Tito's defection was a crackdown on potential opponents throughout the Soviet bloc. Though the terror did not approach the massive scale of 1937–1938 (see pages 845–846), again the secret police executed those suspected of deviation, inspiring fear even among the top leadership. As such repression proceeded in the satellite states, opposition strikes and demonstrations developed as well, finally reaching a crisis point in East Germany in 1953.

In East Berlin a workers' protest against a provision to increase output or face wage cuts promptly led to political demands, including free elections and the withdrawal of Soviet troops. Disturbances soon spread to the other East German cities. Though this spontaneous uprising was not well coordinated, Soviet military forces had to intervene to save the East German communist regime. But the East German protest helped stimulate strikes and antigovernment demonstrations elsewhere in the Soviet bloc as well, convincing Soviet leaders that something had to be done. However, at this point the leadership of the Soviet Union was again being sorted out, for Stalin had died early in 1953, a few months before the crisis in East Germany came to a head.

DE-STALINIZATION UNDER KHRUSHCHEV, 1955–1964

Although a struggle for succession followed Stalin's death, the political infighting involved a reasonable degree of give-and-take, as opposed to terror and violence. To be sure, the contestants quickly ganged up on the hated secret police chief, who was tried and executed within months, but this stemmed from their prior agreement to limit the role of the secret police. Moreover, although one of the eventual losers was sent to Siberia to run a power station and the other was made ambassador to Outer Mongolia, it was a major departure that the winner, Nikita Khrushchev (KROOSH-choff) (1894–1971), ordered neither of them exiled or executed.

Slightly crude, even something of a buffoon, Khrushchev outmaneuvered his rivals by 1955 partly because they repeatedly underestimated him. Although his period of leadership was brief, it was eventful indeed—and in some ways the Soviet system's best chance for renewal.

At a closed session of the Soviet Communist Party's twentieth national congress in February 1956, Khrushchev made a dramatic late-night speech denouncing the criminal excesses of the Stalinist system and the "cult of personality" that had developed around Stalin himself. Khrushchev's immediate aim was to undercut his hard-line rivals, but he also insisted that key features of Stalinism had amounted to an unnecessary deviation from Marxism-Leninism. So the advent of Khrushchev suggested that there might be liberalization and reform.

In the face of the East German uprising of 1953, the Soviets backed off from hard-line Stalinism in the satellite states, making room for more moderate communists they had previously shunned, such as the Hungarian Imre Nagy (NAHZH) (1896–1958). Khrushchev even sought to patch things up with Tito, exchanging visits with him in 1955 and 1956. In his speech to the party congress in 1956, Khrushchev suggested that different countries might take different routes to communism.

But could liberalization be contained within the larger framework of Soviet leadership, or were openness and innovation bound to threaten the system itself? The test case proved to be Hungary, where reformers led by the moderate communist Nagy had taken advantage of the liberalizing atmosphere by mid-1956 to begin dismantling collective farms and moving toward a multiparty political system. They even called for Soviet troops to withdraw, to enable Hungary to leave the Warsaw Pact and become neutral. These were not changes within the system, but challenges to the

Warsaw Pact Military-diplomatic alliance of Soviet bloc countries, created to counter NATO.

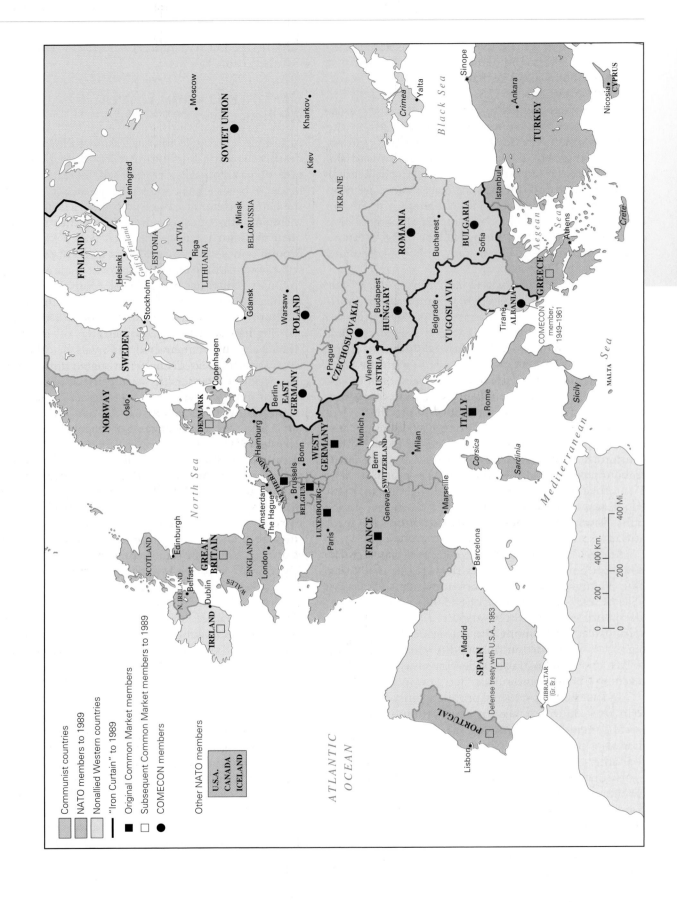

SOVIET UNION

• Moscow

• Leningrad

FINLAND

• Helsinki

Gulf of Finland

ESTONIA

LATVIA
• Riga

LITHUANIA

• Minsk
BELORUSSIA

UKRAINE

• Kiev

• Kharkov

Crimea

• Yalta

Black Sea

• Sinope

• Ankara

TURKEY

Nicosia • CYPRUS

SWEDEN

• Stockholm

NORWAY

• Oslo

DENMARK
Copenhagen

North Sea

• Gdansk

• Warsaw
POLAND

Prague •
CZECHOSLOVAKIA

Berlin •
EAST
GERMANY

Hamburg

• Bonn
WEST
GERMANY

Brussels •
BELGIUM
Amsterdam • NETHERLANDS
The Hague •
LUXEMBOURG

• Munich

Vienna •
AUSTRIA

Budapest •
HUNGARY

Bern •
SWITZERLAND

Geneva •

• Milan

ITALY

• Rome

Belgrade •
YUGOSLAVIA

ROMANIA
• Bucharest

BULGARIA
• Sofia

Tirane •
ALBANIA

Istanbul

GREECE

Athens •

Aegean
Sea

Crete

COMECON
member,
1949–1961

SCOTLAND
• Edinburgh

GREAT
BRITAIN
N. IRELAND
Belfast •
WALES
ENGLAND
London •
Dublin •
IRELAND

ATLANTIC
OCEAN

FRANCE

• Paris

• Marseille

Corsica

Sardinia

Mediterranean

Sicily

MALTA

Sea

SPAIN

• Madrid

• Barcelona

GIBRALTAR
(Gr. Br.)

Defense treaty with U.S.A., 1953

PORTUGAL

• Lisbon

400 Mi.

400 Km.

200

200

0

0

Communist countries

NATO members to 1989

Nonallied Western countries

"Iron Curtain" to 1989

Original Common Market members

Subsequent Common Market members to 1989

COMECON members

Other NATO members

U.S.A.
CANADA
ICELAND

MAP 29.1   Military Alliances and Multi-national Economic Groupings, 1949–1989
The cold war split was reflected especially in the two military alliances: NATO, formed in 1949, and the Warsaw Pact, formed in 1955. Each side also had its own multinational economic organization, but the membership of the EEC, or Common Market, was not identical to that of NATO. Although communist, Yugoslavia remained outside Soviet-led organizations, as did Albania for part of the period.

Online Study Center **Improve Your Grade**
Interactive Map: Military Alliances and Multinational Economic Groupings, 1949–1989

system itself. When a democratic coalition government was set up by November, the Soviets used tanks to crush the Hungarian reform movement. Thousands were killed during the fighting or subsequently executed, and 200,000 Hungarians fled to the West.

Yet even the crackdown in Hungary did not mean a return to the old days of Stalinist rigidity in the Soviet bloc. The Soviets understood that the system had to become more palatable, but liberalization was to be contained within certain limits. Above all, it could not challenge communist monopoly rule and the Warsaw Pact. After 1956 the satellites were granted greater leeway, and showed greater diversity, than had previously seemed possible. Hungary's new leader, János Kádár (1912–1989), collectivized agriculture more fully than before, but he also engineered a measure of economic decentralization, allowing scope for local initiatives and market mechanisms.

In East Germany, in contrast, Walter Ulbricht (1893–1973) concentrated on central planning and heavy industry in orthodox fashion. The East German economy became the most successful in the Soviet bloc, primarily because here the new communist regime fell heir to a skilled industrial labor force. Still, that economic growth was built on low wages, so East German workers were tempted to emigrate to West Germany as the West German economic miracle gleamed ever brighter during the 1950s. The special position of Berlin, in the heart of East Germany yet still divided among the occupying powers, made such emigration relatively easy, and 2.6 million East Germans left for the West between 1950 and 1962. With a population of only 17.1 million, East Germany could not afford to let this hemorrhaging continue. Thus, in August 1961 the Ulbricht regime erected the Berlin Wall, an ugly symbol of the cold war division of Europe.

FROM LIBERALIZATION TO STAGNATION

As a domestic leader, Khrushchev proved erratic, but he was an energetic innovator, willing to experiment. He jettisoned the worst features of the police state apparatus, including some of the infamous forced-labor camps, and offered several amnesties for prisoners. He also liberalized cultural life and gave workers greater freedom to move from one job to another. The economic planning apparatus was decentralized somewhat, affording more scope for local initiatives and placing greater emphasis on consumer goods. The government expanded medical and educational facilities and, between 1955 and 1964, doubled the nation's housing stock, substantially alleviating a severe housing shortage.

Even Khrushchev's claim in 1961 that the Soviet Union would surpass the Western standard of living within twenty years did not seem to be an idle boast. The Soviets had launched *Sputnik I* in 1957, assuming the lead in the ensuing space race, and they sent the first human into space in 1961. Such achievements suggested that even ordinary Soviet citizens had reason for optimism. More generally, the communist regimes throughout the Soviet bloc entered the 1960s with confidence after achieving excellent rates of economic growth during the 1950s.

Yet Khrushchev had made enemies with his erratic reform effort, and this led to his forced retirement in October 1964. After the unending experiment in the economy, his opponents wanted to consolidate, to return to stability and predictability. But not until 1968 did it become clear that the liberalization and innovation of the Khrushchev era were over.

By early 1968 a significant reform movement had developed within the Communist Party in Prague, the capital of Czechoslovakia. Determined to avoid the fate of the Hungarian effort in 1956, the reformers emphasized that Czechoslovakia was to remain a communist state and a full member of the Warsaw Pact. But within that framework, they felt, it should be possible to invite freer cultural expression, to democratize the Communist Party's procedures, and to broaden participation in public life.

However, efforts to reassure the Soviets alienated some of the movement's supporters, who stepped up their demands. As earlier in Hungary, the desire for change seemed to outstrip the intentions of the movement's organizers. Finally, in August 1968, Soviet leaders decided to crack down, sending Soviet tanks into Prague to crush the reform movement. This end of the **Prague Spring** closed the era of relative flexibility and

Prague Spring   The attempt by Czechoslovakian reformers in 1968 to gain freer cultural expression, democratization of Communist Party procedures, and broader participation in public life within the framework of a communist state.

The End of the Prague Spring

Moving tanks into Prague in August 1968, Soviet leaders ended the widely admired reform movement in Czechoslovakia. Though there were protests, as shown here on August 20, the outcome was a foregone conclusion once the Soviets decided to intervene. The ending of the Prague Spring proved a watershed for the fate of communism in Europe. *(Josef Kondelka/Magnum Photos)*

cautious innovation in the Soviet bloc that had begun in 1953.

A period of relative stagnation followed under Leonid Brezhnev (BREZH-nef) (1906–1982), a careful, consensus-seeking bureaucrat. In dealing with the United States, Brezhnev helped engineer significant moves toward arms control and an easing of tensions.

But despite this *détente*, the "Brezhnev Doctrine" made it clear that the Soviet Union would intervene as necessary to help established communist regimes remain in power. For the Soviet satellite states, there seemed to be no further hope of reform from within. But even as resignation marked the first years after 1968, forces soon emerged that undermined the whole communist system.

══════════ S E C T I O N   S U M M A R Y ══════════

- The imposition of Stalinist forms of governing in the new Soviet satellite states produced tensions that led the whole satellite system to a breaking point by 1953.

- Nikita Khrushchev's speech of February 1956 denouncing the excesses of Stalinism opened the way to a measure of liberalization and reform in the Soviet Union.

- The Soviet suppression of the Hungarian revolution in the fall of 1956 indicated a strict set of limits, but

the Soviet satellite states had some freedom to set their own course thereafter.

- The East German government erected the Berlin Wall in August 1961 to stop people from moving to West Berlin—and from there to other parts of West Germany.

- In light of the Soviet suppression of the Prague Spring reform movement in 1968, there seemed little scope for reforming the communist systems from within.

EUROPE, THE WEST, AND THE WORLD

How did the place of western Europe in world affairs change during the cold war era?

By the early 1950s, the old Europe seemed dwarfed by the two superpowers and, for the foreseeable future, divided by the conflict between them. The colonial networks that had manifested European predominance unraveled rapidly at the same time. One obvious response was some form of European integration. A unified Europe might eventually become a global superpower in its own right. Although the first steps toward European unity did not go as far as visionaries had hoped, a new group of leaders established lasting foundations by the late 1950s. Still, the cold war framework limited the new union's geographical extent and the scope of its activity for decades.

THE COLD WAR FRAMEWORK

That cold war tensions could produce dangerous military conflict quickly became clear as superpower divisions over Korea, which had been jointly liberated from the Japanese by the Americans and the Soviets, helped produce the complex Korean War (1950–1953). Although the United States had previously declared Korea outside the U.S. defense perimeter, it intervened in support of noncommunist South Korea in the face of an attempt by communist North Korea, encouraged by Stalin, to unify Korea as a communist state. The war was inconclusive, leaving the Korean peninsula divided more or less as before, but it prompted the United States to extend containment to the global level and to step up military production.

In retrospect, however, it is clear that the most intense phase of the cold war ended with Stalin's death in 1953. In his speech to the twentieth party congress in 1956, Khrushchev repudiated the previous Soviet tenet that the very existence of Western capitalist imperialism made a military showdown with the communist world inevitable. During a visit to the United States in 1959, he stressed that the ongoing competition between the two sides could be peaceful. However, despite summit conferences and sporadic efforts at better relations, friction between the Soviet Union and the United States continued to define the era.

Indeed, a new peak of tension was reached in October 1962, when the Soviets began placing missiles in Cuba, just 90 miles from the United States. Cuba had developed close ties with the Soviet Union after a 1959 revolution led by Fidel Castro (b. 1926). With Castro beginning to develop a communist system, a U.S.-supported force of Cuban exiles sought to invade Cuba and foment insurrection against the new regime in April 1961. This effort proved a fiasco, but it demonstrated to the Soviets that the new Cuban regime was vulnerable to overthrow from the United States.

Although the United States had placed offensive missiles in NATO member Turkey, adjacent to the Soviet Union, the Soviet attempt to base missiles in Cuba seemed an intolerable challenge to the U.S. administration. President John F. Kennedy (1917–1963) responded with a naval blockade of Cuba, and for several days the superpowers seemed on the verge of military confrontation. Finally, the Soviets agreed to withdraw their missiles in exchange for a U.S. promise not to seek to overthrow the communist government of Cuba. The Americans also agreed informally to remove their offensive missiles from Turkey. Khrushchev's willingness to retreat antagonized hard-liners in the Soviet military and contributed to his ouster from power two years later. Yet Khrushchev himself viewed the outcome in Cuba as a victory. By challenging the United States with missiles, the Soviets had helped secure the survival of the Cuban communist regime, which was now less vulnerable to overthrow by the United States. The Cuban missile crisis was the closest the superpowers came to direct, armed confrontation during the cold war period.

At the same time, it became increasingly clear that international communism was not the monolithic force it had once seemed. The most dramatic indication was the Sino-Soviet split, which developed during the 1950s as the Chinese Communist Party under Mao Zedong solidified its power. In the long struggle that led to their victory in 1949, the Chinese Communists had often had no choice but to go their own way, and during the 1940s especially, Stalin had been willing to subordinate any concern for their cause to Soviet national interests. After taking power in 1949, the Chinese Communists pursued their own path to development without worrying about the Soviet model. Not without reason, the Soviets feared that the independent, innovative Chinese might be prepared to challenge Soviet leadership in international communism. By the early 1960s, the Chinese Communists' path had become appealing to many in the non-Western world, though it attracted dissident communists in the West as well.

MAP 29.2 Decolonization, 1945–1980

During a thirty-five-year period after World War II, the European empires in Africa, Asia, and the Pacific gradually came apart as the former colonies became independent nations.

PACIFIC OCEAN

JAPAN

NORTH KOREA 1948

SOUTH KOREA 1948
From Japan

PHILIPPINES 1946

NORTH VIETNAM 1954

Unified 1974

SOUTH VIETNAM 1954

BRUNEI 1984
From Great Britain

INDONESIA 1949

CAMBODIA 1954

MALAYSIA 1963

SINGAPORE 1965

LAOS 1949

MYANMAR (BURMA) 1947

PAKISTAN 1947, BANGLADESH 1973

SRI LANKA (CEYLON) 1948

INDIA 1947

PAKISTAN 1947

INDIAN OCEAN

OMAN 1971

P.D.R. OF YEMEN 1967

DJIBOUTI 1977

SOMALIA 1960

MAURITIUS 1968
From Great Britain

KUWAIT 1961

BAHRAIN 1971

QATAR 1971

UNITED ARAB EMIRATES 1971

YEMEN 1946

IRAQ 1932

JORDAN 1946

ETHIOPIA 1941

KENYA 1963

MALAWI 1964

MADAGASCAR 1960

SYRIA 1944

CYPRUS 1960

LEBANON 1944

ISRAEL 1948

EGYPT 1922

SUDAN 1956

UGANDA 1962

TANZANIA 1964

ZAMBIA 1964

ZIMBABWE 1980

MOZAMBIQUE 1974

SWAZILAND 1968

LESOTHO 1966

MALTA 1964
From Great Britain

TUNISIA 1957

LIBYA 1951

CHAD 1960

CENTRAL AFRICAN REPUBLIC 1960

DEM. REP. OF CONGO 1960

RWANDA 1962

BURUNDI 1962

BOTSWANA 1966

SOUTH AFRICA (Republic 1961)

ITALY

ALGERIA 1962

NIGER 1960

NIGERIA 1960

CAMEROON 1960

GABON 1960

ANGOLA 1975

NAMIBIA 1985
From South Africa

FRANCE

MOROCCO 1956

MALI 1960

BURKINA FASO 1960

BENIN 1960

TOGO 1960

EQUATORIAL GUINEA 1968

REPUBLIC OF CONGO 1960

GREAT BRITAIN

SPAIN

PORTUGAL

MAURITANIA 1960

GUINEA 1958

CÔTE D'IVOIRE 1960

GHANA 1957

LIBERIA 1826

WESTERN SAHARA (Morocco) 1975

SENEGAL 1960

GAMBIA 1965

GUINEA-BISSAU 1974

SIERRA LEONE 1961

NETHERLANDS

BELGIUM

ATLANTIC OCEAN

Date is year independence was achieved.
Shading indicates former colonial power.

Great Britain
France
Netherlands
Italy
Belgium
Portugal
Spain
United States

| 0 | 500 | 1000 | 1500 Mi. |
| 0 | 500 | 1000 | 1500 Km. |

THE VARIETIES OF DECOLONIZATION

The advent of a new world configuration, with a circumscribed place for Europe, found dramatic expression in the rapid disintegration of the European colonial empires after World War II (see **MAP 29.2**). The war itself had been a major catalyst for independence movements throughout the world. In southeast Asia and the Pacific, quick Japanese conquests revealed the tenuous hold of France, the Netherlands, and Britain on their domains. And it was not colonial reconquest that marked the end of the war, but the atomic bomb and the victory of the United States, which took a dim view of conventional European colonialism.

New Nations in Asia   The effort of the Netherlands to regain control of the Dutch East Indies led to four years of military struggle against the Indonesian nationalist insurgency. Although most independent observers felt that the Dutch could not win, the Dutch were reluctant to relinquish control of the East Indies, which had been in their hands since the seventeenth century. Especially after the humiliations of defeat and occupation during World War II, many of the Dutch took pride in their imperial role. The struggle lasted from 1945 to 1949, when the Dutch finally had to yield as their former colony became independent Indonesia.

Unlike the Netherlands, Britain was still a great power in the twentieth century, and its empire had long seemed essential to its stature. But the structure of the British Empire had been evolving for decades before World War II. With the Statute of Westminster, passed by the British Parliament in 1931, such dominions as Canada, Australia, New Zealand, and South Africa became truly independent, controlling their own foreign policies and joining the League of Nations. This statute was essentially the founding document of the British Commonwealth of Nations. Though it initially encompassed only former British possessions dominated by people of European origin, the commonwealth provided the basis for relatively orderly decolonization after World War II.

In granting independence to India and Pakistan in 1947, the British understood that traditional colonial arrangements were ending, but they envisioned playing an ongoing leadership role by incorporating their former colonies into the British Commonwealth. However, the commonwealth idea proved to have little appeal for those winning independence, and the British Commonwealth proved to be little more than a voluntary cooperative association. Still, Britain was the most realistic of the European colonial powers, grasping the need to compromise and work with emerging national leaders in light of decolonization pressures.

The Suez Crisis   Nevertheless, even Britain decided to resist in 1956, when it provoked an international crisis over the status of the Suez Canal in Egypt (see Map 28.1 on page 872). Once a British protectorate, Egypt had remained under heavy British influence even after nominally becoming sovereign in 1922. But a revolution in 1952 produced a new government of Arab nationalists, led by the charismatic Colonel Gamal Abdel Nasser (1918–1970). In 1954 Britain agreed with Egypt to leave the Suez Canal zone within twenty months, though the zone was to be international, not Egyptian, and Britain was to retain special rights there in the event of war. In 1956, however, Nasser announced the nationalization of the canal, partly so that Egypt could use its revenues to finance public works projects.

Led by the Conservative Anthony Eden (1897–1977), Britain decided on a showdown. Eden won the support of Israel and France, each of which had reason to fear the pan-Arab nationalism that Nasser's Egypt was now spearheading. Israel had remained at odds with its Arab neighbors since its founding in 1948, and Nasser was helping the Arabs who were beginning to take up arms against French rule in Algeria.

Late in 1956 Britain, Israel, and France orchestrated a surprise attack on Egypt. After the Israelis invaded, the British and French bombed military targets, then landed troops to take the canal. But the troops met stubborn Egyptian resistance, and the British and French encountered decisive defeat in the diplomatic maneuvering that accompanied the outbreak of fighting. Both the United States and the Soviet Union opposed the Anglo-French-Israeli move, as did world opinion. The old European powers had sought to act on their own, by the old rules, but the outcome of this Suez crisis demonstrated how limited their reach had become.

The French in Vietnam   Still, the 1956 debacle did not convince France to abandon its struggle to retain Algeria. And that struggle proved the most wrenching experience that any European country was to have with decolonization. For the French the process started not in North Africa but in Indochina, in southeast Asia, during World War II.

Led by the communist Ho Chi Minh (1890–1969), the Indochinese anticolonialist movement gained strength resisting the Japanese during the war. Then, before the French could return, Ho established a political base in northern Vietnam in 1945. Although the French reestablished control in the South, negotiations between the French and the Vietnamese nationalists

Suez crisis   Crisis prompted by Egypt's nationalization of the British-owned Suez Canal. The effort of Britain, France, and Israel to seize the canal prompted a strong negative reaction in world opinion, forcing them to withdraw.

seemed at first to be moving toward some form of self-government for Vietnam. But in 1946 French authorities in Indochina deliberately provoked an incident to undercut negotiations and start hostilities. Eight years of difficult guerrilla war followed, creating a major drain on the French economy.

With its strongly anticolonialist posture, the United States was unsympathetic to the French cause at first. But the communist takeover in China in 1949 and the outbreak of war in Korea in 1950 made the French struggle in Indochina seem to be a battle in a larger war against communism in Asia. By 1954 the United States was covering 75 percent of the cost of the French effort in Indochina. Nonetheless, when the fall of the fortified area at Dien Bien Phu in May 1954 signaled a decisive French defeat, the United States decided to pull back and accept a negotiated settlement. Partly at the urging of its European allies, the United States had concluded that the Soviet threat in Europe must remain its principal concern.

France worked out the terms of independence for Vietnam in 1955. The solution, however, entailed a North-South partition to separate the communist and anticommunist forces, pending elections to unify the country. The anticommunist regime the United States sponsored in the South resisted holding the elections, so the country remained divided (see Map 29.2). With the Americans providing first advisers, then, beginning in 1964, active military support, South Vietnam sought unsuccessfully to defeat a guerrilla insurgency supported by the communist North. After finally defeating the United States and South Vietnam in 1975, the communist heirs of those who had fought the French assumed the leadership of a reunified Vietnam.

In France the defeat in Indochina in 1954 left a legacy of bitterness, especially among army officers, many of whom felt that French forces could have won had they not been undercut by politicians at home. When the outcome in Indochina emboldened Arab nationalists in North Africa to take up arms against the French colonial power, the French army was anxious for a second chance—and the French government was willing to give it to them. Algeria had been under French control since 1830, and it had a substantial minority of ethnic Europeans, totaling over a million, or 10 percent of the population.

The War in Algeria Although France gradually committed 500,000 troops to Algeria, the war bogged down into what threatened to become a lengthy stalemate, with increasing brutality on both sides. As it drained French lives and resources, the war became a highly contentious political issue in France. The situation came to a head during the spring of 1958, when the advent of a new ministry, rumored to favor a compromise settlement, led to violent demonstrations, engineered by the sectors of the French army in Algeria. Military intervention in France itself seemed likely to follow—and with it the danger of civil war.

It was at this moment of genuine emergency that Charles de Gaulle returned to lead the change to the Fifth Republic. Those determined to hold Algeria welcomed him as their savior. But de Gaulle fooled them, working out a compromise with the nationalist rebels that ended the war and made Algeria independent in 1962. Only de Gaulle could have engineered this outcome without provoking still deeper political division in France.

Independence in sub-Saharan Africa By the end of the 1950s, the colonialist impulse, which had still been significant immediately after World War II, was waning noticeably all over Europe. But resistance remained, though its forms varied considerably, as the colonies of sub-Saharan Africa continued to move toward independence. Outcomes depended on several factors: the number and intransigence of European settlers, the extent to which local elites had emerged, and the confidence of the Europeans that they could retain their influence if they agreed to independence. Of the major imperial powers in the region, Britain had done best at preparing local leaders for self-government and proved the most willing to work with indigenous elites. The two smallest countries, Belgium and Portugal, were less certain they could maintain their influence, and they proved the most reluctant to give up their imperial status.

The transition was smoothest in British West Africa, where the Gold Coast achieved independence as Ghana, first as a commonwealth dominion in 1957, then as a fully independent republic in 1960. Few British settlers lived in that part of Africa, and the small, relatively cohesive African elite favored a moderate transition, not revolution. Where British settlers were relatively numerous, however, the transition to independence was much more difficult. The very presence of Europeans had impeded the development of cohesive local elites, so movements for independence in those areas tended to become more radical, threatening the expropriation of European-held property. In Southern Rhodesia, unyielding European settlers resisted the British government's efforts to promote a compromise. A white supremacist government declared its independence from Britain in 1965, fueling a guerrilla war. The Africans won independence as Zimbabwe only in 1980.

The reaction against Eurocentrism that accompanied the turn from colonialism was not confined to those who had been subjected to European imperialism. There was also much interest among Westerners in the work of Frantz Fanon (1925–1961), a black intellectual from Martinique who became identified especially with the cause of the Algerian rebels. In *The Wretched of the Earth* (1961), Fanon found the West spir-

THE LEGACY OF EUROPEAN COLONIALISM

In the following passages from The Wretched of the Earth *(1961), Frantz Fanon probes the negative consequences of colonialism—for both colonizers and colonized—and tries to show why a radical, even violent break from colonialism was necessary. In his conclusion, he offers a stirring call to the colonized world to repudiate the West, whose claims to offer universal values he finds hypocritical in the extreme.*

The violence which has ruled over the ordering of the colonial world, which has ceaselessly drummed the rhythm for the destruction of native social forms and broken up without reserve the systems of reference of the economy, the customs of dress and external life, that same violence will be claimed and taken over by the native at the moment when, deciding to embody history in his own person, he surges into the forbidden quarters. . . .

. . . In the colonial context the settler only ends his work of breaking in the native when the latter admits loudly and intelligibly the supremacy of the white man's values. In the period of decolonization, the colonized masses mock at these very values, insult them, and vomit them up.

. . . All that the native has seen in his country is that they can freely arrest him, beat him, starve him: and no professor of ethics, no priest has ever come to be beaten in his place, nor to share their bread with him. As far as the native is concerned, morality is very concrete; it is to silence the settler's defiance, to break his flaunting violence—in a word, to put him out of the picture. . . .

. . . The colonialist bourgeoisie, in its narcissistic dialogue, expounded by the members of its universities, had in fact deeply implanted in the minds of the colonized intellectual that the essential qualities remain eternal in spite of all the blunders men may make: the essential qualities of the West, of course. . . . Now it so happens that during the struggle for liberation, at the moment that the native intellectual comes into touch again with his people, . . . [a]ll the Mediterranean values—the triumph of the human individual, of clarity, and of beauty . . . are revealed as worthless,

simply because they have nothing to do with the concrete conflict in which the people is engaged.

Individualism is the first to disappear. . . . The colonialist bourgeoisie had hammered into the native's mind the idea of a society of individuals where each person shuts himself up in his own subjectivity, and whose only wealth is individual thought. Now the native who has the opportunity to return to the people during the struggle for freedom will discover the falseness of this theory. The very forms of organization of the struggle will suggest to him a different vocabulary. Brother, sister, friend—these are words outlawed by the colonialist bourgeoisie, because for them my brother is my purse, my friend is part of my scheme for getting on. The native intellectual . . . will . . . discover the substance of village assemblies, the cohesion of people's committees, and the extraordinary fruitfulness of local meetings and groupments. Henceforward, the interests of one will be the interests of all, for in concrete fact *everyone* will be discovered by the troops, *everyone* will be massacred—or *everyone* will be saved. . . .

Leave this Europe where they are never done talking of Man yet murder men everywhere they find them. . . . For centuries they have stifled almost the whole of humanity in the name of a so-called spiritual experience. Look at them today swaying between atomic and spiritual disintegration. . . .

Come then, comrades, the European game has finally ended; we must find something different. We today can do everything, so long as we do not imitate Europe, so long as we are not obsessed by the desire to catch up with Europe.

QUESTIONS

1. On what basis does Fanon believe that even native intellectuals who have embraced Western values can be won back for the anticolonialist cause?

2. What Western value does Fanon claim is the first to be repudiated—and why?

Source: Frantz Fanon, *The Wretched of the Earth* (New York: Grove, 1968), pp. 40–47, 311–312.

itually exhausted and called on the peoples of the non-Western world to go their own way, based on their own values and traditions. (See the box "The Global Record: The Legacy of European Colonialism.")

The process of decolonization led to a remarkable transformation in the thirty-five years after World War II. Forms of colonial rule that had been taken for granted before World War I stood discredited, virtually

without defenders, by the late twentieth century. Europeans were now accepting the principle of national self-determination for non-Europeans. But decolonization hardly offered a neat and definitive solution. In formerly colonial territories, new political boundaries often stemmed from the ways Europeans had carved things up, rather than from indigenous ethnic or national patterns. Moreover, questions remained about the longer-term economic relationships between the Europeans and their former colonies.

ECONOMIC INTEGRATION AND THE ORIGINS OF THE EUROPEAN UNION

As the old colonialism increasingly fell into disrepute, many found in European unity the best prospect for the future. Although hopes for full-scale political unification were soon frustrated, the movement for European integration achieved significant successes in the economic sphere, especially through the European Economic Community, or Common Market, established in 1957.

The impetus for economic integration came especially from a new breed of "Eurocrats"—technocrats with a supranational, or pan-European, outlook. A notable example was Robert Schuman (1886–1963), a native of Lorraine, which had passed between France and Germany four times between 1870 and 1945. After serving as a German officer in World War I, he was elected to the French Chamber of Deputies in 1919 just after Lorraine was returned to France. As French foreign minister after World War II, Schuman was responsible for a 1950 plan to coordinate French and German production of coal and steel. The Schuman Plan quickly encompassed Italy, Belgium, the Netherlands, and Luxembourg to become the European Coal and Steel Community (ECSC) in 1951. Working closely with Schuman was Jean Monnet, who served as the ECSC's first president. From this position, he pushed for more thoroughgoing economic integration. The successes of the ECSC led the same six countries to agree to a wider "Common Market," officially known as the **European Economic Community (EEC),** in 1957.

After the merger of the governing institutions of the several European supranational organizations in 1967, the term *European Community* (EC) and later *European Union* (EU) came to indicate the institutional web that had emerged since the launching of the European Coal and Steel Community in 1951. Meanwhile, its membership gradually expanded, encompassing, during the cold war era, Denmark, Ireland, and Britain in 1973, Greece in 1981, and Spain and Portugal in 1986 (see Map 29.1). For newly democratic countries like Spain, Portugal, and Greece, Common Market membership became a pillar of the solidifying democratic consensus.

The immediate aim of the original EEC was to facilitate trade by eliminating customs duties between its member countries and by establishing common tariffs on imports from the rest of the world. For each member of the EEC, tariff reduction meant access to wider markets abroad, but also the risks of new competition in its own domestic market. However, the EEC proved advantageous to so many that tariff reduction proceeded well ahead of schedule. By 1968 the last internal tariffs had been eliminated.

With tariffs dropping, trade among the member countries nearly doubled between 1958 and 1962. For example, French exports of automobiles and chemicals to Germany increased more than eightfold. Partly because the increasing competition stimulated initiative and productivity, industrial production within the EEC increased at a robust annual rate of 7.6 percent during those years.

Despite these successes, vigorous debate accompanied the development of the EEC during the 1960s. To enable goods, capital, and labor to move freely among the member countries, some coordination of social and economic policy was required. But were the member states prepared to give up some of their own sovereignty to the Common Market to make that coordination possible?

In the mid-1960s French president de Gaulle forced some of the underlying uncertainties to the fore. Though he had willingly turned from the old colonialism, de Gaulle was not prepared to compromise French sovereignty, and he was not persuaded that supranational integration offered the best course for postwar Europe. With the end of the Algerian war in 1962, France began playing an assertively independent role in international affairs. Thus, for example, de Gaulle developed an independent French nuclear force, curtailed the French role in NATO, and recognized the communist People's Republic of China.

This determination to assert France's sovereignty led to friction between de Gaulle and the supranational Eurocrats of the Common Market. Matters came to a head in 1965, when a confrontation developed over agricultural policy. The immediate result was a compromise, but de Gaulle's tough stance served to check the increasing supranationalism evident in the EEC until then. As the economic context became more difficult during the 1970s, it became still harder to maintain the EEC's cohesion. So though the Common Market was an important departure, it did not overcome traditional national sovereignty or give western Europe a more muscular world role during the first decades after World War II.

THE ENERGY CRISIS AND THE CHANGING ECONOMIC FRAMEWORK

As the political situation in western Europe became more volatile by the early 1970s, events outside Europe made it clear how interdependent the world had become—and that the West did not hold all the trump cards. In the fall of 1973, Egypt and Syria attacked Is-

European Economic Community (EEC)
Common market formed by Belgium, France, West Germany, Italy, Luxembourg, and the Netherlands to promote free trade.

rael, seeking to recover the losses they had suffered in a brief war in 1967. Although the assault failed, the Arab nations of the oil-rich Middle East came together in the aftermath to retaliate against the Western bloc for supporting Israel. By restricting the output and distribution of the oil its members controlled, the Arab-led Organization of Petroleum Exporting Countries (OPEC) produced a sharp increase in oil prices and a severe economic disruption all over the industrialized world.

The 1970s proved to be an unprecedented period of "stagflation"—sharply reduced rates of growth combined with inflation and rising unemployment. The economic miracle was over, partly because the process soon to be known as globalization was now taking off. The European economies were subject to growing competition from non-Western countries, most notably Japan. In light of increasing global competition and rising unemployment, the labor movement was suddenly on the defensive throughout the industrialized West. And the changing circumstances inevitably strained the social compact that had enabled western Europe to make a fresh start after the war.

═══════ S E C T I O N   S U M M A R Y ═══════

- Dependent on the United States for their security, the western European countries had limited freedom of action in world affairs during the cold war era.

- Though the decolonization process varied considerably from case to case, the long-standing European colonial networks gradually dissolved after World War II.

- Desires to remove the sources of war and to enhance Europe's economic competitiveness fueled the movement toward European integration, including the

- formation of the European Economic Community (Common Market) in 1957.

- French president Charles de Gaulle envisioned a more independent role for Europe from within the cold war framework, but that role was to be based on French leadership, not European integration.

- The difficult economic circumstances of the 1970s raised questions about the long-term sustainability of welfare state measures.

THE COLLAPSE OF THE SOVIET SYSTEM, 1975–1991

What led to the collapse of the communist system in the Soviet Union and its satellite states?

Though the reasons were different, the Soviet Union also encountered economic stagnation during the 1970s. The deteriorating situation finally produced a major Soviet reform effort by the mid-1980s. At the same time, new forms of opposition developed in the satellite states after the crushing of the Prague reform movement in 1968. The intersection of these forces led to the unraveling of the satellite system in 1989, then to the collapse of the Soviet communist regime in 1991. This outcome stunned Western observers, who had come to take the anxious stability of the cold war framework for granted.

ECONOMIC STAGNATION IN THE SOVIET BLOC

The impressive rates of economic growth achieved in the Soviet Union and several of the satellite states continued into the 1960s. However, much of that success came from adding labor—women and underemployed peasants—to the industrial work force. By the end of the 1960s that process was reaching its limits, so increasingly the challenge for the Soviet bloc was to boost productivity through technological innovation.

By the late 1970s, however, the Soviets were falling seriously behind the West as a new technological revolution gathered force. The state-directed Soviet economy had proven quite capable of technological leadership when marshaling resources for a particular task was required. Thus, for example, the Soviets led the way in space travel. But continuing development in high technology demanded the freedom to experiment and exchange ideas and the flexibility to anticipate innovation and shift resources. In these areas, the Soviet system, with its direction from the top, proved too rigid. Moreover, as the Soviet system bogged down, the expense of the arms race with the United States dragged ever more seriously on the Soviet economy. Ordinary Soviet citizens grew increasingly frustrated as the communist economy proved erratic in providing the most basic consumer goods. Yet major functionaries now enjoyed access to special shops and other privileges.

Women's Work in the Soviet Union
This cartoon adapts the caryatid form from ancient sculpture to depict the special burdens that were coming to wear more heavily on women as the Soviet economy bogged down. Intended to commemorate International Women's Day, the image appeared in the Soviet magazine *Krokodil* in 1984.
(Krokodil Magazine, March 1984)

In satellite countries such as Poland and Hungary, the communist governments managed for a while to win mass support by borrowing from foreign banks to provide meat and other consumer goods at artificially low prices—"sausage-stuffing," some called it. But as the lending banks came to realize, by the end of the 1970s, that such loans were not being used to enhance productivity, these governments found it much harder to borrow. Thus they began having to impose greater austerity.

Throughout the Soviet bloc, frustration grew especially among women, who seemed to bear a disproportionate share of the burdens. Women were more likely to be employed outside the home in the communist countries than in the West. About 90 percent of adult women in the Soviet Union and East Germany had paid jobs outside the home by 1980. Yet not only were these women concentrated in jobs with low pay and prestige, but they also still bore the major responsibility for child-care, housework, and shopping. They had few of the labor-saving devices available in the West, and they often had to spend hours in line to buy ordinary consumer items. Dissatisfaction among women fed an underground protest movement that began developing in the Soviet bloc in the mid-1970s—an indication of the growing strains in the overall system.

THE CRISIS OF COMMUNISM IN THE SATELLITE STATES

For many intellectuals in the Soviet bloc, the Soviet suppression of the Prague Spring in 1968 ended any hope that communism could be made to work. The immediate outcome was a sense of hopelessness, but by the mid-1970s a new opposition movement had begun to take shape, especially in Hungary, Poland, and Czechoslovakia. It centered initially on underground (or *samizdat*) publications, privately circulated writings that enabled dissidents to share ideas critical of the regime.

In one sense, these dissidents realized, intellectuals and ordinary people alike were powerless in the face of heavy-handed communist government. But they came to believe they could make a difference simply by "living the truth," ceasing to participate in the empty rituals of communist rule. And mere individual honesty could have political potential especially because of the Helsinki Accords on human rights that the Soviet bloc countries had accepted in 1975.

The meeting of thirty-five countries in Helsinki, Finland, in 1975 was one of the most important fruits of the *Ostpolitik,* or opening to the East, that Willy Brandt began pursuing after becoming West Germany's chancellor in 1969 (see page 919). Eager to grasp Brandt's offer to regularize the status of East Germany and to confirm the western border of Poland, the Soviet bloc found it expedient to accept the detailed agreement on human rights included in the resulting **Helsinki Accords.**

Though merely symbolic in one sense, the human rights agreement proved a touchstone for initiatives that would help bring the whole Soviet system crashing down. Through various "Helsinki Watch" groups monitoring civil liberties, anticommunists in the satellite states managed to assume moral leadership. By demanding that the communist governments live up to their agreements, and by noting the gap between idealistic pretense and grim reality, opposition intellectuals began to cast doubts on the very legitimacy of the communist regimes.

The most significant such group was Charter 77, which emerged in Czechoslovakia in response to the arrest of a rock group called "The Plastic People of the Universe." Longhaired and anti-establishment like their counterparts in the West, the Plastic People were deemed filthy, obscene, and disrespectful of society by the repressive Czechoslovak regime. In 1977, protesting the crackdown on the group, 243 individuals signed "Charter 77"—using their own names and addresses, living the truth, acting as if they were free to register such an opinion.

A leader in Charter 77 was the writer Václav Havel (HA-vul) (b. 1936), who noted that, after 1968, the hope for change depended on people organizing themselves, outside the structures of the party-state, in diverse, independent social groupings. (See the box "The Written Record: Power from Below: Living the Truth.") Havel and a number of his associates were in and out of jail as the government sought to stave off this protest movement. Despite the efforts of Havel and his colleagues, government remained particularly repressive and ordinary people relatively passive in Czechoslovakia until the late 1980s. For quite different reasons, Hungary and Poland offered greater scope for change.

Even after the failed reform effort of 1956, Hungary proved the most innovative of the European communist countries. Partly because its government allowed small-scale initiatives outside the central planning apparatus, Hungary was able to respond more flexibly to the growing economic stagnation. By the mid-1980s various alternative forms of ownership were responsible for one-third of Hungary's economic output.

This openness to economic experimentation enabled reformers within the Hungarian Communist Party to gain the upper hand. Amid growing talk of "socialist pluralism," the Hungarian elections of 1985 intro-

duced an element of genuine democracy. Increasingly open to a variety of viewpoints, the Hungarian Communists gradually pulled back from their long-standing claim to a monopoly of power.

The reform effort that built gradually in Hungary stemmed especially from aspirations within the governing elite. More dramatic was the course of change in Poland, where workers and intellectuals, at odds even as recently as 1968, managed to come together during the 1970s. When Polish workers struck in 1976, in response to a cut in food subsidies, intellectuals formed a committee to defend them. This alliance had become possible because dissident intellectuals were coming to emphasize the importance of grass-roots efforts that challenged the logic of the communist system without attacking it directly.

An extra ingredient from an unexpected quarter also affected the situation in Poland, perhaps in a decisive way. In 1978 the College of Cardinals of the Roman Catholic Church departed from long tradition and, for the first time since 1522, elected a non-Italian pope. Even more startling was the fact that the new pope was from Poland, behind the iron curtain. He was Karol Cardinal Wojtyla (voy-TILL-ah) (1920–2005), the archbishop of Cracow, who took the name John Paul II.

After World War II, the Polish Catholic Church had been unique among the major churches of east-central Europe in maintaining and even enhancing its position. It worked just enough with the ruling Communists to be allowed to carve out a measure of autonomy. For many Poles, the church thus remained a tangible institutional alternative to communism and the focus of national self-consciousness in the face of Soviet domination. Thus the new pope's visit to Poland in 1979 had an electrifying effect on ordinary Poles, who took to the streets by the millions to greet him—and found they were not alone. This boost in self-confidence provided the catalyst for the founding of a new trade union, **Solidarity,** in August 1980.

Led by the remarkable shipyard electrician Lech Walesa (va-WEN-sah) (b. 1944), Solidarity emerged from labor discontent in the vast Lenin shipyard in Gdansk, on the Baltic Sea (see Map 29.1). Demanding the right to form their own independent unions, seventy thousand workers took over the shipyard, winning support both from their intellectual allies and from the Catholic Church. Support for Solidarity grew partly because the government, facing the crisis of its "sausage-stuffing" strategy, was cutting subsidies and raising food prices. But the new union developed such force because it placed moral demands first—independent

POWER FROM BELOW: LIVING THE TRUTH

Considering the scope for change in the communist world by the late 1970s, Václav Havel imagines a conformist grocer who routinely puts a sign in his window with the slogan "Workers of the world, unite!" simply because it is expected. That same grocer, says Havel, has the power to break the system, which rests on innumerable acts of everyday compliance. Havel finds this system "post-totalitarian" because it rests on neither the coercion nor the fanatical belief that, in some combination, had sustained the earlier totalitarian systems. At the same time, he senses that aspects of the "post-totalitarian" order reveal, in stark and garish terms, more general modern tendencies that are merely masked in the Western democracies. So the West did not offer an easy model; in fact, it might actually have something to learn from the forms of opposition that Havel saw emerging in the communist bloc.

The real meaning of the greengrocer's slogan has nothing to do with what the text of the slogan actually says. Even so, this real meaning is quite clear and generally comprehensible because the code is so familiar: the greengrocer declares his loyalty . . . in the only way the regime is capable of hearing; that is, by accepting the prescribed *ritual*, by accepting appearances as reality, by accepting the given rules of the game. In doing so, however, he has himself become a player in the game, thus making it possible for the game to go on, for it to exist in the first place. . . .

In the end, is not the greyness and emptiness of life in the post-totalitarian system only an inflated caricature of modern life in general? And do we not stand (although in the external measures of civilization, we are far behind) as a kind of warning to the West, revealing its own latent tendencies?

Let us now imagine that one day something in our greengrocer snaps and he stops putting up the slogans merely to ingratiate himself. He stops voting in elections he knows are a farce. He begins to say what he really thinks at political meetings. . . . He rejects the ritual and breaks the rules of the game. He discovers once more his suppressed identity and dignity. . . .

. . . By breaking the rules of the game, he has disrupted the game as such. He has exposed it as a mere game. He has shattered the world of appearance, the fundamental pillar of the system. . . . He has shown everyone that it *is* possible to live within the truth. Living within the lie can constitute the system only if it is universal. The principle must embrace and permeate everything. There are no terms whatsoever on which it can coexist with living within the truth, and therefore everyone who steps out of line *denies it in principle and threatens it in its entirety.* . . .

And since all genuine problems and matters of critical importance are hidden beneath a thick crust of lies, it is never quite clear when the proverbial last straw will fall, or what that straw will be. This . . . is why the regime prosecutes, almost as a reflex action preventively, even the most modest attempts to live within the truth.

. . . The crust presented by the life of lies is made of strange stuff. As long as it seals off hermetically the entire society, it appears to be made of stone. But the moment someone breaks through in one place, when one person cries out, "The emperor is naked!"—when a single person breaks the rules of the game, thus exposing it as a game—everything suddenly appears in another light and the whole crust seems then to be made of a tissue on the point of tearing and disintegrating uncontrollably. . . .

The post-totalitarian system is only one aspect . . . of this general inability of modern humanity to be the master of its own situation. The automatism of the post-totalitarian system is merely an extreme version of the global automatism of technological civilization. The human failure that it mirrors is only one variant of the general failure of modern humanity.

. . . It would appear that the traditional parliamentary democracies can offer no fundamental opposition to the automatism of technological civilization and the industrial-consumer society, for they, too, are being dragged helplessly along by it. People are manipulated in ways that are infinitely more subtle and refined than the brutal methods used in the post-totalitarian societies.

QUESTIONS

1. Why does Havel believe that small, everyday acts of conformity actually constitute the post-totalitarian system?

2. What relationship between the communist bloc and the Western democracies is Havel positing?

Source: Václav Havel et al., *The Power of the Powerless: Citizens Against the State in Central-Eastern Europe* (Armonk, N.Y.: M. E. Sharpe, 1985), pp. 31, 37–40, 42–43, 90–91. Reprinted by permission from M. E. Sharpe, Inc., Armonk, NY 10504.

Lech Walesa and Solidarity
A shipyard electrician, Walesa spearheaded the dissident Polish trade union, Solidarity, formed in 1980, and then emerged from prison to lead the movement that eventually undercut the communist regime in Poland in 1989. Here he addresses a rally during a strike at the Lenin shipyard in Gdansk in August 1988.

(Corbis Sygma)

labor organizations, the right to strike, and freedom of expression. Reflecting the wider opposition thinking in east-central Europe, Solidarity was not to be bought off with lower meat prices, even had the government been able to deliver them.

After over a year of negotiation, compromise, and broken promises, the tense situation came to a head in December 1981, when the government under General Wojciech Jaruzelski (yah-roo-ZELL-skee) (b. 1923) declared martial law and outlawed Solidarity, imprisoning its leaders. Strikes in protest were crushed by military force. So much for that, it seemed: another lost cause, another reform effort colliding with inflexible communist power, as in 1953, 1956, and 1968. But this time it was different, thanks especially to developments in the Soviet Union.

THE QUEST FOR REFORM IN THE SOVIET UNION

The death of Leonid Brezhnev in 1982 paved the way for a concerted reform effort that began in earnest when **Mikhail Gorbachev** (GOR-ba-choff) (b. 1931) became Soviet Communist Party secretary in 1985. Gorbachev's effort encompassed four intersecting initiatives: arms reduction; liberalization in the satellite states; *glasnost* (GLAHZ-nost), or "openness" to discussion and criticism; and *perestroika* (pair-es-TROY-kah), or economic "restructuring." This was to be a reform within the Soviet system. There was no thought of giving up the Communist Party's monopoly on power or embracing a free-market economy. The reformers still took it for granted that communism could point the way beyond Western capitalism, with its shallow consumerism. But they had to make communism work.

Gorbachev understood that "openness" was a prerequisite for "restructuring." The freedom to criticize was essential to check abuses of power, which, in turn, was necessary to overcome the cynicism of the workers and improve productivity. Openness was also imperative to gain the full participation of the country's most creative people, whose contributions were critical if the Soviet Union was to become competitive in advanced technology.

The main thrust of perestroika was to depart from the rigid economic planning mechanism by giving local managers more autonomy. But any restructuring was bound to encounter resistance, especially from those with careers tied to the central planning apparatus. And Gorbachev's program made only partial headway in this crucial sector.

Online Study Center **Improve Your Grade**
Primary Source: The Last Heir of Lenin Explains His Reform Plans: Perestroika and Glasnost

THE ANTICOMMUNIST REVOLUTION IN EAST-CENTRAL EUROPE

Meanwhile, in Poland, repression continued, as dramatized especially by the murder of the charismatic priest and Solidarity supporter Jerzy Popieluszko (pope-yeh-LUSH-koh) by the secret police in 1984. But Walesa

Mikhail Gorbachev   Soviet Communist Party secretary who attempted to reform the Soviet communist system through arms reduction; liberalization in the satellite states; *glasnost;* and *perestroika.*

remained a powerfully effective leader even from prison. He was able to keep his heterogeneous movement together as the ideas of Solidarity continued to spread underground. Then the advent of Gorbachev in 1985 changed the overall framework, for Gorbachev was convinced that restructuring the Soviet system required reform in the satellites as well. As the Polish economy, already in difficulty by 1980, reached a crisis in 1987, Solidarity began stepping up its efforts.

When proposed price increases were rejected in a referendum, the Polish government imposed them by fiat. Strikes demanding the relegalization of Solidarity followed during the spring of 1988. The government again responded with military force, but Solidarity-led strikes in August forced government leaders to send signals that they might be prepared to negotiate. With the economy nearing collapse, the government recognized that it could no longer govern on its own.

The negotiations that followed early in 1989 proved pivotal. When they began, Walesa and his advisers wanted primarily to regain legal status for Solidarity within the Communist-dominated system, still under Jaruzelski. In exchange, they assumed they would have to help legitimate a rigged election to approve painful but necessary economic measures. But as these "Round Table" negotiations proceeded, the government gave ever more in exchange for Solidarity's cooperation. Not only did it consent to legalize Solidarity, but it agreed to make the forthcoming elections free enough for the opposition genuinely to participate.

The elections of June 1989 produced an overwhelming repudiation of Poland's communist government. Even government leaders running unopposed failed to win election as voters crossed out their names. In the aftermath of the elections, President Jaruzelski was forced to give Solidarity a chance to lead. Not all members of the opposition felt it wise to accept government responsibility under such difficult economic circumstances, but finally Tadeusz Mazowiecki (mah-zo-VYETS-kee) (b. 1927), Walesa's choice and one of the movement's most distinguished intellectuals, agreed to form a government.

The chain of events in Poland culminated in one of the extraordinary events of modern history—the negotiated end of communist rule. That a communist government might give up power voluntarily had been utterly unforeseen. It happened partly because the Soviet Union under Gorbachev was seeking reform and thus had become much less likely to intervene militarily. It also helped that the Polish Catholic Church was available to act as mediator, hosting meetings, reminding both sides of their shared responsibilities in the difficult situation facing their country. By some accounts, General Jaruzelski, who seemed for most of the 1980s to be just another military strongman and Soviet lackey, had proved to be a national hero for his grace, perhaps even ingenuity, in yielding power to the opposition. But most important was the courage, the persistence, and the vision of Solidarity itself.

Although the Hungarians were already breaking out of the communist mold, it was especially the Polish example that suggested to others in the Soviet bloc that the whole system was open to challenge. During 1989 demands for reform and, increasingly, for an end to communist rule spread through east-central Europe by means of the domino effect that had preoccupied the Soviets from the start. By the end of that year, the Soviet satellite system was in ruins (see Map 30.1 on page 948).

By 1989 a number of grass-roots movements, involving especially young people, had emerged across the Soviet bloc to challenge governmental authority in indirect ways. Although they were indebted to older leaders like Havel, who had stressed the power of simply "living the truth," these movements fastened upon such new issues as disarmament, the treatment of the elderly, and environmental threats like nuclear power. And their modes of action often had an absurd, carnival-like dimension, such as traveling about in an open sightseeing bus. Precisely because it was not obviously subversive, such activity backed the regimes into uncomfortable corners—even made the authorities appear weak and flatfooted. The remaining legitimacy of the communist systems was dissipating.

A marked increase in illegal emigration from East Germany to the West had been one manifestation that the system was starting to unravel. During 1989 the reform-minded Hungarian Communists decided to stop impeding East Germans, many of whom vacationed in Hungary, from emigrating to the West at the Hungarian border with Austria. If the communist reformers in East Germany were to have any chance of turning the situation around, they had to relax restrictions on travel and even grant the right to emigrate. They began preparing to do both as part of a host of reforms intended to save the system. On November 9, 1989, the East German communist regime did the unthinkable and opened the Berlin Wall, which was promptly dismantled altogether. Germans now traveled freely back and forth between East and West. Although the fate of the Soviet Union itself remained uncertain, the opening of the wall signaled the end of the cold war. It was no longer a bipolar world.

By this point, discontented East Germans envisioned not simply reforming the communist system but ending it altogether. Within weeks it was clear that the rhythm of events was beyond the control of East

Germany's reform communists, who opened the way for German reunification in 1990. Despite some nervousness, the four postwar occupying powers—the United States, Britain, France, and the Soviet Union—gave their blessing as the Federal Republic incorporated the five East German states. The communist system in East Germany simply dissolved.

Although some in West Germany were hesitant about immediate reunification, especially because of the economic costs that seemed likely, West German chancellor Helmut Kohl (KOLE) (b. 1930) sought to complete the process as quickly as possible. By early 1990 the emigration of East Germans to the West had become a flood. West German law treated these Germans as citizens, entitled to social benefits, so their arrival in such numbers presented a considerable financial burden. It seemed imperative for West Germany to regularize the situation as quickly as possible, assuming responsibility for the East and restoring its economy.

The division of Germany, symbolized by the Berlin Wall, had been the central fact of the bipolar cold war world. Now Germany was a unified country for the first time since Nazism and the Second World War. What would it mean?

THE END OF THE SOVIET UNION

Meanwhile, in the Soviet Union, what began as a restructuring of the communist system became a struggle for survival of the system itself. The much-trumpeted glasnost produced greater freedom in Soviet culture and politics, but Gorbachev sought to avoid alienating hard-line Communists, so he compromised, watering down the economic reforms essential to perestroika. The result proved a set of half measures that only made things worse. Because so little was done to force the entrenched Soviet bureaucracy to go along, the pace of economic reform was lethargic. The essential structures of the command economy weakened, but free-market forms of exchange among producers, distributors, and consumers did not emerge to replace them.

In 1986 an accidental explosion at the Soviet nuclear power plant at Chernobyl, in Ukraine (see **MAP 29.3**), released two hundred times as much radiation as the atomic bombs dropped on Hiroshima and Nagasaki combined. The accident contaminated food supplies and forced the abandonment of villages and thousands of square miles of formerly productive land. The radioactivity released would eventually hasten the deaths of at least 100,000 Soviet citizens. Despite his commitment to openness, Gorbachev reverted to old-fashioned Soviet secrecy for several weeks after the accident, in an effort to minimize what had happened. As a result, the eventual toll was far greater than it need have been. The accident and its aftermath seemed stark manifestation

of all that was wrong with the Soviet system—its arrogance and secrecy, its premium on cutting corners to achieve targets imposed from above.

By the end of the 1980s, Soviet citizens felt betrayed by their earlier faith that Soviet communism was leading to a better future. A popular slogan spoke sarcastically of "seventy years on the road to nowhere." The economic situation was deteriorating, yet people were free to discuss alternatives as never before. As the discussion came to include once-unthinkable possibilities such as privatization and a market economy, it became clear that the whole communist system was in jeopardy.

By mid-1990, moreover, the union of Soviet republics itself tottered on the verge of collapse. Lithuania led the way in calling for outright independence. But the stakes were raised enormously when the Russian republic, the largest and most important in the USSR, followed Lithuania's lead. In June 1990 the newly elected chairman of Russia's parliament, Boris Yeltsin (b. 1931), persuaded the Russian republic to declare its sovereignty. Yeltsin had grown impatient with the slow pace of economic and political change, and by threatening that Russia might go its own way, he hoped to force Gorbachev's reform effort beyond the present impasse. As a further challenge to Gorbachev, Yeltsin dramatically resigned from the Communist Party during its televised national congress in July 1990. When, in June 1991, free elections in the Russian republic offered the first clear contest between communists determined to preserve the system and those seeking to replace it, the anticommunist Yeltsin was elected the republic's president by a surprising margin.

After tilting toward the hard-liners late in 1990, Gorbachev sought a return to reform after Yeltsin's dramatic election as Russia's president in June 1991. He even engineered a new party charter that jettisoned much of the Marxist-Leninist doctrine that had guided communist practice since the revolution. In August the hard-liners struck back with a coup that forced Gorbachev from power—but only for a few days. Yeltsin, supported by ordinary people in Moscow, stood up to the conspirators, while the secret police refused to follow orders to arrest Yeltsin and other opposition leaders. The coup quickly fizzled, but the episode galvanized the anticommunist movement and radically accelerated the pace of change.

Although Gorbachev was restored as head of the Soviet Union, the winner was Yeltsin, who quickly mounted an effort to dismantle the party apparatus before it could regroup. Anticommunist demonstrations across much of the Soviet Union toppled statues of Lenin and dissolved local party networks. In a referendum in December 1991, Ukraine, the second most populous Soviet republic, overwhelmingly voted for

MAP 29.3   **The Dissolution of the Soviet Union**

As crisis gripped the Soviet system by the late 1980s, the republics of the Soviet Union began declaring first their sovereignty, then their independence. Most of the fifteen republics that had made up the Soviet Union became part of a much looser confederation, the Commonwealth of Independent States, in 1991 and 1992.

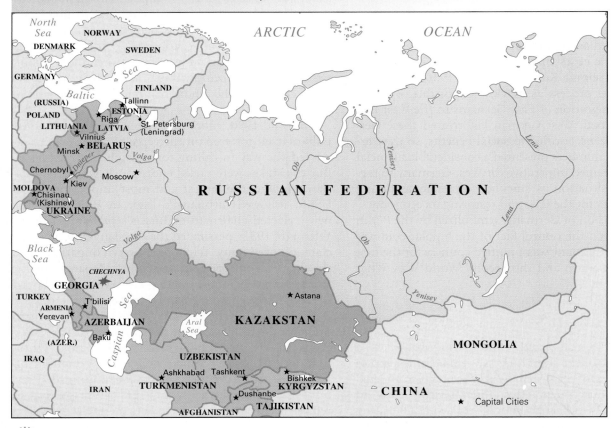

Online Study Center **Improve Your Grade**
Interactive Map: The Dissolution of the Soviet Union

independence. Not only the communist system but the Soviet Union itself was simply disintegrating. Late in December, Gorbachev finally resigned, paving the way for the official dissolution of the Soviet Union on January 1, 1992 (see Map 29.3). The European map again included Russia, as well as, in a matter of months, fourteen other sovereign states from what had been the Soviet Union.

One of the notable experiments in the history of the West, nourished by the hopes and ideals of generations, the communist regime in the Soviet Union had proved a resounding failure.

━━━━━ S E C T I O N   S U M M A R Y ━━━━━

- The economies of the Soviet bloc were encountering stagnation by the 1970s, especially because they proved less adept than the capitalist economies at technological innovation.

- Disparate factors converged in Poland to yield the trade union Solidarity, which proved decisive in un-

dermining the communist system not only in Poland but throughout the Soviet bloc.

- Seeking to overcome Soviet stagnation, Mikhail Gorbachev spearheaded a reform effort around *glasnost*, or "openness," and *perestroika*, or economic "restructuring," beginning in 1985.

- Changes in government policy in Poland and Hungary during 1989 produced a domino effect that led to the opening of the Berlin Wall and the fall of the communist regimes in east-central Europe.

- As Gorbachev's reform effort proved insufficient, the republics of the Soviet Union began pulling away, leading, by 1991, to the disintegration of the communist system and the breakup of the Soviet Union itself.

CHAPTER SUMMARY

Online Study Center **ACE the Test**

What seemed the most likely overall directions as western Europeans pondered priorities in light of all the disasters surrounding the era of the two world wars?

What factors led to the surprisingly rapid restoration of democracy in much of continental western Europe after World War II?

How did Soviet policy evolve after the death of Stalin in 1953?

How did the place of western Europe in world affairs change during the cold war era?

What led to the collapse of the communist system in the Soviet Union and its satellite states?

Western Europeans faced a situation of unprecedented cultural uncertainty as they pondered priorities in the wake of all that had befallen Europe from 1914 to 1949. Whereas some explored the loss of bearings, others called for a return to tradition, and still others found renewed possibilities in the Marxist tradition. At the same time, deeper interaction with the United States during and immediately after World War II led many to look to America for a more successful model, free of the ideological extremes that, it seemed, had helped lead Europe to disaster.

The United States sought to assist the rebuilding of western Europe, and partly because of American help, the western Europeans were able to restore their economies—and even surpass prewar production levels—with remarkable speed. And economic success greatly facilitated the restoration of democracy. At the same time, the shared experience of wartime led to a new social compact based on greater government responsibility for economic well-being and social welfare. By 1968, however, the Western democracies were beginning to experience unforeseen strains, some of which then deep-ened with the slowdown in economic growth during the 1970s.

In the Soviet bloc, Stalin's death in 1953 brought an end to the most repressive features of the communist system. Under his successor, Nikita Khrushchev, the Soviet Union seemed able to compete with the United States in areas from education to space travel. But the experiment with various forms of central planning in the Soviet bloc proved ever less successful. At the same time, the crushing of a series of opposition and reform efforts, from East Berlin in 1953 to Prague in 1968, suggested that the Soviets were prepared to intervene as necessary to keep their satellites on a communist path.

The bipolar cold war framework meant a diminished influence in world affairs for the states of western Europe. Even their own security, in the face of the potential Soviet threat, seemed to depend on the United States. At the same time, the western Europeans gradually gave up control of their remaining colonial possessions, though not without instances of fighting and bitterness, evident most notably in the French effort to retain Algeria. However, France joined with Germany in the first key steps toward European integration, and such leaders as Charles de Gaulle and Willy Brandt showed the scope for European initiatives from within the limiting cold war framework.

Even as they faced new economic and political strains by the 1970s, the nations of western Europe could take for granted a substantial measure of prosperity and political legitimacy. In the communist part of Europe, in contrast, growing economic stagnation fueled a much deeper form of political disaffection during the 1970s and 1980s. New modes of opposition arose in Poland and Czechoslovakia, while in Hungary and eventually in the Soviet Union itself, communist leaders sought to renew the system from within. But the crisis of Soviet-style communism proved too deep, and by the end of 1991 discontent had produced forces for change that led to the breakup of the Soviet Union and the unraveling of the communist system in Europe.

LOOKING AHEAD

Thus ended the cold war era. The immediate response in the West was euphoria, for the anxieties that had resulted from superpower rivalry seemed to vanish almost overnight. But what would follow remained unclear. Reformers in the former communist countries claimed to want individual freedom, political democracy, and free-market capitalism, but it would be necessary to build these on the ruins of the now-discredited communist system, a task never confronted before. And what sort of international order might replace the dangerous but stable bipolar framework that had stood since World War II?

KEY TERMS

existentialism (p. 909)

North Atlantic Treaty Organization (NATO) (p. 914)

welfare state (p. 915)

Konrad Adenauer (p. 918)

Willy Brandt (p. 918)

Margaret Thatcher (p. 921)

Warsaw Pact (p. 923)

Prague Spring (p. 925)

Suez crisis (p. 929)

European Economic Community (EEC) (p. 932)

Helsinki Accords (p. 935)

Solidarity (p. 935)

Mikhail Gorbachev (p. 937)

Online Study Center
Improve Your Grade Flashcards

SUGGESTED READING

Bark, Dennis L., and David R. Gress. *A History of West Germany*, vol. 1, *From Shadow to Substance, 1945–1963*, and vol. 2, *Democracy and Its Discontents, 1963–1991*. 2d ed. 1993. A favorable account of West Germany's democracy and its Atlantic and European roles in the face of ongoing suspicion and criticism.

Caute, David. *The Dancer Defects: The Struggle for Cultural Supremacy During the Cold War*. 2003. An engaging, comprehensive treatment of the efforts of both sides during the cold war to use culture for political advantage.

Crockatt, Richard. *The Fifty Years' War: The United States and the Soviet Union in World Politics, 1941–1991*. 1995. A balanced history of U.S.-Soviet relations, showing the global impact of their cold war rivalry.

Dedman, Martin J. *The Origins and Development of the European Union, 1945–95: A History of European Integration*. 1996. A concise and accessible introductory work.

Hitchcock, William I. *The Struggle for Europe: The Turbulent History of a Divided Continent, 1945–2002*. 2003. A highly regarded survey—comprehensive, balanced, and engaging.

Kenney, Padraic. *A Carnival of Revolution: Central Europe 1989*. 2002. A ground-level account of the diverse popular initiatives that helped undermine the legitimacy of communist systems in varied parts of the Soviet bloc.

Marwick, Arthur. *The Sixties: Cultural Revolution in Britain, France, Italy, and the United States, c. 1958–c. 1974*. 1998. A lengthy but gripping portrait of a pivotal decade.

Saxonberg, Steven. *The Fall: A Comparative Study of the End of Communism in Czechoslovakia, East Germany, Hungary, and Poland*. 2001. Contrasts the governmental initiatives in Poland and Hungary with the initiatives from below that undermined the communist regimes in Czechoslovakia and East Germany.

Schulze, Max-Stephan, ed. *Western Europe: Economic and Social Change Since 1945*. 1999. A superior collection of essays accenting economic change; some treat individual countries, others overarching topics.

Springhall, John. *Decolonization Since 1945: The Collapse of European Overseas Empires*. 2001. An accessible and comprehensive survey.

30

A CONTINUING EXPERIMENT: THE WEST AND THE WORLD SINCE 1989

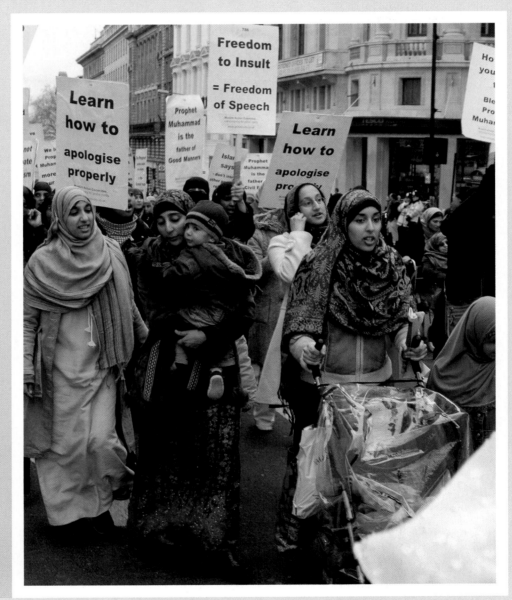

Cartoon Protest
On February 18, 2006, Muslims march through central London in an angry but peaceful protest against the publication in the Western press of cartoons seeming to caricature the prophet Muhammad. *(AP/Wide World Photos)*

The relationship between the West and the wider world was sorely tested early in 2006 as it gradually became known that the previous September a Danish newspaper, *Jyllands-Posten*, had published twelve cartoons depicting the Islamic prophet Muhammad, one wearing a turban in the shape of a bomb. The stated aim was to confront the fear, the sense of intimidation, that some claimed had resulted from the cultural interface with Muslims in European countries. Especially unsettling had been the brutal assassination, by a Dutch national of Moroccan descent, of Theo Van Gogh in the Netherlands in 2004. Van Gogh had been targeted for having made a film denouncing the treatment of women in Islamic societies.

The editor who invited the cartoons claimed that fears of violence against anyone perceived to be denigrating Islam were leading to self-censorship. The episode unfolded against a backdrop of increasing tensions in several European countries over the assimilation of immigrants, or the children or grandchildren of immigrants—and especially, it seemed, of those who professed Islam.

A number of predominantly Islamic nations promptly protested the Danish cartoons, but Denmark's prime minister refused to meet with their ambassadors, saying that he did not, and should not, have any control over what Danish newspapers published. But as news of the cartoons gradually became known, there was outrage across the Muslim world, including violence first against Danish interests, then against Europeans and Westerners more generally. Scores of people were killed. The cartoonists themselves received death threats and had to go into hiding.

Any depiction of the prophet Muhammad would have offended Muslims, who traditionally have been particularly concerned to ward off idolatry, the worship of images. Muslims had periodically protested a frieze dating from the 1930s in the U.S. Supreme Court, which included Muhammad, portrayed between Charlemagne and the Roman emperor Justinian, as one of eighteen "great lawgivers of history." But Muslims found the Danish cartoons gratuitously offensive.

Defenders of the cartoons stressed the Western values of free speech and a free press, and, as the controversy grew, a number of news outlets published one or more of the cartoons in solidarity with the now-beleaguered Danish publication. But others, especially in Britain and the United States, refused to

CHAPTER OUTLINE

THE UNCERTAIN INTERNATIONAL FRAMEWORK AFTER THE COLD WAR

THE CONTINUING EXPERIMENT WITH DEMOCRATIC CAPITALISM

LIFESTYLES AND IDENTITIES

THE WEST IN A GLOBAL AGE

QUESTIONING THE MEANING OF THE WEST

KEY TERMS

G-8 (Group of 8)
European Union (EU)
Maastricht agreements
euro
Common Agricultural Policy (CAP)
ethnic cleansing
unilateralism
Vladimir Putin

social market economy
World Health Organization (WHO)
information technology
World Trade Organization (WTO)
digital divide
nongovernmental organizations (NGOs)

Online Study Center

This icon will direct you to interactive map and primary source activities on the website **college.hmco.com/pic/noble5e**

republish them, stressing the wisdom of voluntary restraint. Whatever the formal freedom of the press, matters of taste, decorum, and responsibility were also at issue. Yet some charged that such refusal to republish, despite the undeniable news value of the cartoons, reflected not responsibility but plain fear.

Compounding the problem were charges of hypocrisy from both the Western and the Islamic worlds. Islamic spokespersons doubted that Western publications would have been equally open to cartoons about, for example, the Holocaust, or slavery in the American South. Conversely, it was widely noted that Christians and especially Jews had long been caricatured in the most grotesque terms in a number of Islamic countries.

Both defenders and critics of the cartoons noted limitations on freedom of speech in the West. Hitler's *Mein Kampf* could not be sold in Germany. It was illegal to deny the Holocaust in Germany and indeed in fourteen Western countries. Charges of hypocrisy produced pressure to get rid of such laws and embrace freedom of speech more consistently in the West.

Whatever was to be made of tensions between the West and the Islamic world, they played in complex ways against the process known as globalization, through which ever more of the world was drawn into the competitive market economy that had gradually spread from Europe over the previous millennium. It seemed to make the world more unified and homogeneous, yet it also produced a backlash, including the embrace of traditional cultural expressions like the headscarf worn by many Muslim women in Europe. But that backlash also included violence and terrorism.

Within the West itself, the end of the cold war led not to a new era of peace and stability but to unforeseen tensions, including ethnic and sectarian conflict in parts of Europe and splintering within the Western alliance. The former communist countries scrambled to institute Western-style democratic capitalism, and during the first decade of the twenty-first century many of them were accepted into the European Union (EU). But even in the established Western democracies, unprecedented economic and technological change raised new questions, some of which threatened to challenge the political consensus that had crystallized since World War II. Nervousness among Europeans about the pace of change even seemed, by 2005, to arrest the notable progress the EU had made since the mid-1980s.

FOCUS QUESTIONS

Why and how did the relationship between western Europe and the United States change after the end of the cold war?

What forces raised new questions about the effectiveness of Western-style democracy by the early years of the twenty-first century?

How did the changes bound up with globalization affect identities in the West?

What questions emerged as the West faced new crises all over the globe after the end of the cold war?

On what basis was the wider contemporary relevance of "Western civilization" being debated by the first decade of the twenty-first century?

THE UNCERTAIN INTERNATIONAL FRAMEWORK AFTER THE COLD WAR

Why and how did the relationship between western Europe and the United States change after the end of the cold war?

The disintegration of the Soviet system from 1989 to 1991 meant the swift, unexpected end of the bipolar cold war framework that had defined the era since World War II (see **MAP 30.1**). An immediate and troubling outcome was renewed ethnic conflict in parts of Europe. Although Czechoslovakia divided peacefully into two nations, the Czech and Slovak Republics, on January 1, 1993, ethnic concerns elsewhere produced violence and massive human rights violations. Violence also found expression in increased international terrorism by the early twenty-first century.

Although the need to respond to such problems unified the West up to a point, differences soon surfaced, differences that threatened to fragment the West as never before since World War II. At the same time, efforts to address the unforeseen problems of the post–cold war world raised questions about the respective roles of multinational entities such as the UN, NATO, and the EU.

NEW POWER RELATIONSHIPS IN THE WEST

That the end of the cold war had left the United States "the world's only superpower" quickly became a cliché, and the Americans continued to offer leadership through the framework they had established after World War II. Although NATO's role was less clear with the end of the Soviet threat, NATO expanded first in 1999, then in 2004, to encompass most of the former Soviet satellite states of eastern Europe, from Poland to Bulgaria. To the former communist countries, NATO membership meant the definitive repudiation of the cold war division of Europe.

Whereas the collapse of communism meant renewed pride and independence for the former satellite states, Russia felt humiliated as a onetime superpower that was now diminished in size, struggling economically, and far less influential in world affairs. But the West was anxious not to alienate the new Russia. Germany and France each developed strong bilateral relations with the former communist power. Moreover, Russia was invited to join the informal grouping of the world's seven largest economic powers (the United States, Japan, Germany, France, Britain, Italy, and Canada), which had begun meeting during the 1970s in an effort to coordinate economic policies. Although the size of the Russian economy did not warrant inclusion in this "Group of Seven," or G-7, it seemed worthwhile to give the new Russia a voice in what thus became the **G-8 (Group of 8)**.

Germany, which promptly reunified as communism collapsed, seemed a major beneficiary of the end of the cold war. Whereas some worried that the new Germany might return to bullying and aggressiveness, others—Germans and non-Germans alike—were eager to have Germany assume a stronger diplomatic role, and thus the responsibilities commensurate with its population and economic strength.

G-8 (Group of 8) Originally a Group of Seven, or G-7, this informal association of the world's seven largest economic powers (the United States, Japan, Germany, France, Britain, Italy, and Canada) began meeting during the 1970s in an effort to coordinate economic policies. After the fall of communism, the group added Russia.

1990	Reunification of Germany
1991	Beginning of fighting in Yugoslavia
	Maastricht agreements expand scope of European Union
1996	Peace in Bosnia
1997	Blair becomes prime minister of Britain
1998	UN establishes international criminal court in The Hague
1999	Euro launched as currency of European Union
	NATO bombing of Serbia in response to Serb policies in Kosovo
	Renewal of Russia's war with Chechnya
2000	Putin elected president of Russia
2001	Milosevic put on trial for war crimes at The Hague
	Terrorist attacks on United States
2003	U.S.- and British-led forces overthrow Saddam Hussein's regime in Iraq
	WTO meeting in Cancún, Mexico, breaks up amid protests
2004	EU adds ten new member countries, for a total of twenty-five
	Terrorist bombings on commuter trains in Madrid
2005	EU draft constitution rejected in referenda in France and the Netherlands
	Terrorist attack on the London public transportation system
	Angela Merkel becomes German chancellor
	Riots by Muslim youth in Paris and other French cities
2006	Demonstrations in France protesting new labor legislation

The Federal Republic officially moved its capital from provincial Bonn to Berlin in 1999, when a costly makeover of the old parliament (Reichstag) building had been completed. As it happened, precisely as the refurbished building was opened, German forces were involved in their first combat roles since World War II, participating in NATO air strikes responding to what seemed genocidal aggression in Yugoslavia. German chancellor Gerhard Schroeder, a socialist, insisted that Germany, in light of its recent history, could not turn away but indeed had a particular responsibility to respond. Still, though Germany contributed significantly

947

MAP 30.1 Europe in the Early Twenty-First Century

The reunification of Germany and the breakup of the Soviet Union, Yugoslavia, and Czechoslovakia fundamentally altered the map of Europe during the 1990s.

ICELAND

Reykjavík

ATLANTIC OCEAN

NORWAY

SWEDEN

FINLAND

RUSSIA

Moscow

St. Petersburg (Leningrad)

Lake Ladoga

Volga

Oslo

Stockholm

Helsinki

Tallinn

ESTONIA

Riga LATVIA

LITHUANIA

Vilnius

RUSSIA

BELARUS

Minsk

Kharkov

Donetsk

UKRAINE

Dnepropetrovsk

Dnieper

Kiev

Odessa

MOLDOVA

Chisinau

KAZAKHSTAN

Caspian Sea

Baku

AZERBAIJAN

AZER.

ARMENIA

Yerevan

GEORGIA

Tbilisi

IRAN

IRAQ

SYRIA

TURKEY

Ankara

Black Sea

Bucharest

ROMANIA

BULGARIA

Sofia

Kosovo UN Protectorate, 1999

SERBIA

Belgrade

MONT.

Podgorica

Skopje

ALBANIA F.Y.R. MACEDONIA

Tiranë

Istanbul

GREECE

Athens

Crete (Gr.)

Nicosia CYPRUS

North Sea

Faroe Islands (Den.)

Shetland Islands (U.K.)

UNITED KINGDOM

Glasgow

NORTHERN IRELAND

IRELAND

Dublin

London

DENMARK

Copenhagen

Gdansk

Hamburg

Elbe

Berlin

POLAND

Warsaw

Vistula

Prague

CZECH REPUBLIC

SLOVAKIA

Bratislava

Budapest

HUNGARY

Vienna

AUSTRIA

Zagreb

CROATIA

SLOVENIA

Ljubljana

BOSNIA & HERZEGOVINA

Sarajevo

SAN MARINO

San Marino

NETHERLANDS

The Hague

Amsterdam

BELGIUM

Brussels

GERMANY

Leipzig

Frankfurt

Bonn

Luxembourg

LUX.

Munich

LIECH.

Vaduz

SWITZ.

Zürich

Bern

Geneva

Stuttgart

Rhine

Danube

Po

Milan

Turin

ITALY

Naples

Rome

VATICAN CITY

Sardinia (It.)

Corsica (Fr.)

Sicily (It.)

MALTA

Valletta

Mediterranean Sea

FRANCE

Paris

Seine

Loire

Lyons

MONACO

Monaco

ANDORRA

Andorra la Vella

Barcelona

Balearic Islands (Sp.)

SPAIN

Madrid

Tagus

PORTUGAL

Lisbon

Porto

Gibraltar (U.K.)

MOROCCO

ALGERIA

TUNISIA

500 Mi.

500 Km.

250

250

0

0

The Democratic Reichstag, Berlin
The centerpiece of the renovation of the German parliament building, completed in 1999, was the addition of a glass dome, intended to manifest the openness of Germany's democracy as its capital moved from Bonn to Berlin. *(Reimer Wulf/ akg-images)*

to international peacekeeping efforts, many Germans remained reluctant to support an expanded international military role. German military spending remained low compared with that of the United States, Britain, and France. Germany had to lease planes from Ukraine to transport its troops to Afghanistan for peacekeeping in 2002.

THE EUROPEAN UNION

As the **European Union (EU)** continued to expand and deepen by the early twenty-first century, it became clear that it constituted one of the notable experiments in Western history. Though still very much in progress, that experiment had produced a complex web of institutional arrangements that was bizarre and complex in one sense, bold and innovative in another.

Origins of the Union   After the oil crises of the 1970s, and amid concern over lack of innovation and competitiveness, the twelve members of the European Community committed themselves in 1985 to creating a true single market with genuinely free competition by the end of 1992. Goods, services, and money would circulate freely among the member countries; manufacturing would conform to uniform product standards; and equal competition for government contracts would apply.

Meeting at Maastricht, in the Netherlands, in 1991, leaders of the member countries agreed to a new "Treaty on European Union," which, among other things, pro-

vided for a common policy on workers' rights and a common currency and central banking structure by 1999. Although the EU's members eventually ratified most of the **Maastricht agreements,** member countries could opt out of certain provisions. Even as the new common currency, the **euro,** was introduced in two major steps, in 1999 and 2002, four of the now-fifteen EU members, including Britain, remained outside the common currency mechanism. Still, the common currency facilitated a notable increase in supranational mergers and takeovers—a trend that threatened some but promised greater international competitiveness for European firms.

So successful was the EU that others clamored to join. In 2004 the EU added ten new member countries, eight of them recently communist, thereby increasing the membership to twenty-five. The lure of membership significantly strengthened democracy in the candidate states, for the EU insisted on democratic institutions and alignment with EU procedures as a condition of membership.

Structure and Organization   Although the EU made democracy a condition for membership, it had its own "democratic deficit": major decisions were made

Maastricht agreements   1991 agreements among member states of the European Union. They agreed to expand cooperation on social, foreign, judicial, and security matters and adopted a timetable for common economic policies.

euro   The common currency launched by the European Union in 1999 and 2002 to eliminate the cost of currency exchange and boost trade and economic interaction.

European Union (EU)   New name for the European Community after the Maastricht agreements of 1991. It consists of twenty-five member countries.

by an unelected elite of technical experts. By the early twenty-first century, the EU included a network of five interlocking core institutions, variously seated in Brussels, Strasbourg, Luxembourg, and Frankfurt. The executive branch was the Commission in Brussels, consisting of twenty appointed members, but with a professional staff of sixteen thousand. Charged to pursue the wider interests of the community, not to represent national interests, the Commission had considerable power to initiate and enforce EU legislation.

The legislative branch of the EU was the Council of Ministers, composed of ministers from the governments of the member countries. On routine matters, the Council voted by majority, weighted by the size of each country's population. More sensitive issues required unanimity; thus each member country had veto power. Especially as the EU prepared to expand, reformers sought to extend the role of majority rule and minimize the scope for veto.

EU membership entailed some loss of national sovereignty, thanks especially to the increasingly powerful role of the judicial branch, the European Court of Justice, headquartered in Luxembourg. In contrast, the power of the European Parliament, which had developed from the assembly of the European Coal and Steel Community, and which divided its time between Strasbourg and Brussels, was more potential than actual. Although it had some oversight over budget and expanding powers to block or amend legislation, the parliament remained the weakest of the core EU institutions.

The fifth core institution, the European Central Bank, headquartered in Frankfurt, was born with the commitment to a common monetary policy and currency in 1991. Like central banks everywhere, it sought to regulate the money supply and thereby to help the EU's economies function in a smooth and coordinated way.

By the early twenty-first century, "Europe" had become a kind of hybrid, at once a collection of sovereign states and a genuinely supranational entity, thanks to the gradual, incremental emergence of the EU over more than fifty years. In spheres such as trade, agriculture, and the environment, the EU was dominant; national governments had little freedom of action. But other spheres, such as defense, taxation, and criminal justice, remained mostly national prerogatives. The question was whether the EU would continue to expand its sphere of competence—and in what directions. For example, by 2006 there was not yet a true single market for services, though services accounted for 70 percent of economic activity in the EU. Thus reformers advocated that the EU specify uniform standards for professional qualifications.

The creation of an internal customs union, benign though it seemed, had never committed the EU to freer trade with nonmember countries—the United States, for example, or the developing nations of the non-Western world. Indeed, half the EU budget at the end of the 1990s went to the widely criticized **Common Agricultural Policy (CAP),** entailing subsidies to protect farmers from outside competition. Efforts by the EU Commission to lower price supports led to several massive demonstrations by French farmers during the 1990s. Political opposition to change remained strong, especially in France, so the scope for reform was uncertain at best.

The Constitution and New Member States

Especially with expansion coming in 2004, it seemed essential that the EU clarify and streamline its procedures through a formal constitution. But as questions about further expansion loomed, the EU's momentum was halted dramatically and unexpectedly when, in May 2005, French voters rejected the EU's new draft constitution in a referendum. It was the biggest check to European integration since the 1970s. Voters in the Netherlands followed suit shortly thereafter. Most of the EU's member states required approval of the constitution only by their elected parliaments, and such approval had, for the most part, been readily forthcoming. So the surprising setbacks in France and the Netherlands constituted a wake-up call; they indicated strains, doubts, and frustrations that could be found throughout Europe.

The rejection reflected a sense that the recent expansion had itself been too radical a step. But especially troubling was the prospect of further expansion to include not just Romania and Bulgaria, for example, but Turkey, Serbia, Albania, Ukraine, and others.

The case of Turkey, a key NATO member, was particularly controversial. Although it had a tradition of secular government, Turkey was a predominantly Islamic country at a time of growing tensions between Europe and the Islamic world and growing concerns about militant Islamic fundamentalism. Even as skeptical Europeans pointed to aspects of the Turkish constitution that were not congruent with EU norms, the Turks worked to make the adjustments necessary to meet those norms. Still, the Turkish candidacy raised questions about how far the EU was prepared to expand, even about the meaning of "Europe."

Matters of European and national identities were very much at issue in the 1995 referenda. "We want to stay Dutch" was one of the slogans used to mobilize voters against the constitution in the Netherlands.[1] The increasingly volatile issues surrounding immigration and assimilation heightened concerns. In its specific measures, the proposed EU constitution would have given more power to the European parliament and

Common Agricultural Policy (CAP) A major pillar of the European Union, it entailed subsidies to protect farmers from outside competition. The CAP was widely criticized by advocates of freer world trade.

Questioning the European Union
The upcoming French referendum on the proposed EU constitution prompted this French demonstrator to distribute posters during a protest in Paris on January 22, 2005. His first concern was simply to urge people to vote "no," but the smaller print on his poster, with such phrases as "no to privatization" and "defend public services," provides a sense of the stakes of the vote as some in France perceived it at that point. *(Charles Platiau/Reuters/Corbis)*

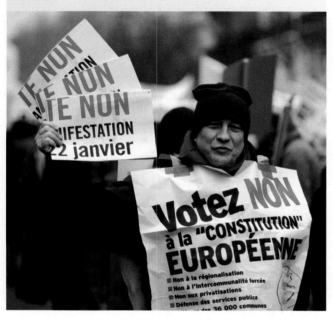

significantly restricted national veto power. So it proved controversial because it seemed to entail a further sacrifice of sovereignty to an ever larger and more diffuse entity.

Concerns about economic well-being were also at work; meshing with more general concerns about globalization was a sense that the recent eastward expansion of the EU had intensified competition from lower-wage countries. It was clear especially in France that those most vulnerable to economic change were the most likely to shift from approval of the EU to rejection of the new constitution.

Evidence of increasing economic nationalism among EU members also worried proponents of European integration. In 2006 the French government acted to facilitate a merger of two major firms in the French energy-utilities industry to head off a hostile takeover of one of the companies by an Italian firm. Further measures followed to make French firms harder for foreigners to acquire. But the Italian government had taken comparable measures to prevent the takeover of two Italian banks, as had the Spanish government in the wake of an acquisition attempt by a German firm.

Such measures reflected the notion that key firms in areas like utilities, transportation, and banking should be immune from foreign takeover, even if government-sanctioned near-monopoly on the national level was required. But such nationality was not supposed to matter in the EU economy; mergers were to be based on business decisions, not political criteria. Although some began to proclaim that "Europe is dead," it remained to be seen whether this wave of defensive measures by governments would seriously compromise the cohesion of the EU.

Although it was surely a setback, the rejection of the proposed constitution did not undermine the existing union, which continued as before. EU membership had played a major role in transforming the economies of once-poor countries like Greece, Ireland, Spain, and Portugal; comparable successes could apparently be expected for the new members from east-central Europe. And expansion to include Romania and Bulgaria remained likely, even if, in light of the new restiveness, still further expansion appeared unlikely for the foreseeable future.

ETHNIC CONFLICT AND PEACEKEEPING ROLES

As the members of the European Union struggled to create a supranational entity, forces in the opposite direction—subnational, religious, ethnic, tribal—grew more powerful in parts of the West, sometimes producing violent conflict. Beginning in 1969, the British had to use troops in Northern Ireland to keep order in the face of ongoing threats from Irish Catholics seeking the end of British rule and unification with the Republic of Ireland. The result was more than three decades of conflict between Protestants and Catholics that eluded definitive solution into the twenty-first century. A movement to separate French-speaking Quebec from the rest of Canada periodically achieved prominence, almost succeeding in 1995.

The War in Bosnia The most dramatic situation, however, was in postcommunist Yugoslavia, where ethnic and religious conflict led to the disintegration of the country in a series of brutal wars among Serbs, Croats, Bosnian Muslims, and ethnically Albanian Kosovars (see **MAP 30.2**). Defining events of the 1990s, these wars proved a major challenge for the new international order after the cold war.

Although much was made of ancient ethnic and religious differences once Yugoslavia began falling apart, the area had long traditions of pluralism and tolerance. Ethnic relations had been poisoned, however, by recent events, especially the civil war during World War II (see page 897). The situation had remained reasonably stable under Josip Tito's independent communist regime,

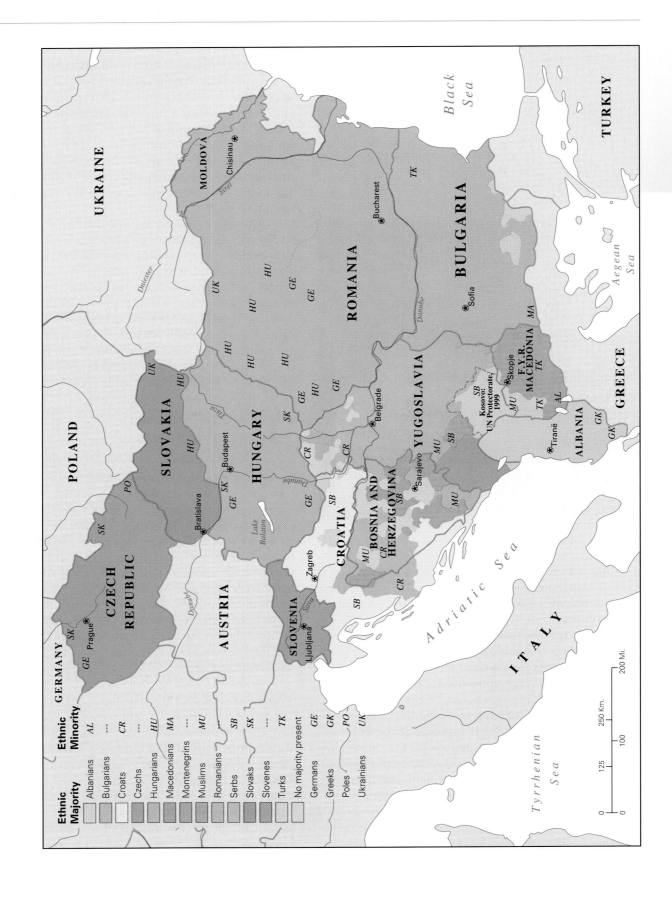

Ethnic Majority

	Albanians
	Bulgarians
	Croats
	Czechs
	Hungarians
	Macedonians
	Montenegrins
	Muslims
	Romanians
	Serbs
	Slovaks
	Slovenes
	Turks
	No majority present

Ethnic Minority

AL Albanians
— Bulgarians
CR Croats
— Czechs
HU Hungarians
MA Macedonians
— Montenegrins
MU Muslims
— Romanians
SB Serbs
SK Slovaks
— Slovenes
TK Turks
GE Germans
GK Greeks
PO Poles
UK Ukrainians

GERMANY
POLAND
UKRAINE
CZECH REPUBLIC
Prague *GE* *SK*
SLOVAKIA
SK *PO* *UK* *HU*
Bratislava *GE* *SK* *HU*
AUSTRIA
HUNGARY
Budapest
Lake Balaton
HU *SK* *GE* *HU* *GE* *HU* *GE* *HU*
UK *HU* *HU* *HU* *GE* *GE* *GE*
MOLDOVA
Chisinau
Dniester
Dniester
ROMANIA
Bucharest
Danube
BULGARIA
Sofia
Black Sea
TURKEY
Aegean Sea
GREECE
GK *GK*
ALBANIA
Tiranë *AL*
F.Y.R. MACEDONIA
Skopje *TK* *MA* *TK* *TK*
Kosovo: UN Protectorate, 1999 *SB* *MU*
YUGOSLAVIA
Belgrade *SB* *SB* *MU* *MU*
TK
BOSNIA AND HERZEGOVINA
Sarajevo *MU* *SB* *CR*
CROATIA
Zagreb *SB* *MU* *CR* *CR* *CR*
SLOVENIA
Ljubljana
Sava
Danube
Danube
Tisza
Adriatic Sea
ITALY
Tyrrhenian Sea

0   125   250 Km.
0   100   200 Mi.

MAP 30.2   Ethnic Conflict in the Balkans and East-Central Europe

Much of east-central Europe, and particularly the Balkans, has long been an area of complex ethnic mixture. The end of communist rule opened the way to ethnic conflict, most tragically in what had been Yugoslavia. This map shows ethnic distribution in the region in the mid-1990s.

which insisted on Yugoslav unity while affording some measure of regional autonomy. But within a few years of Tito's death in 1980, intellectuals concerned about cultural distinctiveness began undermining the wider Yugoslav identity that Tito had sought to foster.

After the fall of communism, Slovenia and Croatia declared themselves independent of Yugoslavia in May 1991. At the same time, the Serb leader of the remaining Yugoslavia, Slobodan Milosevic (mih-LOH-suh-vitch) (1941–2006), a former communist, embraced Serb nationalism at least partly to maintain his own power. His aim was to unite all the Serbs, two million of whom lived outside Serbia, mostly in Croatia and Bosnia-Herzegovina. He would start by taking over the substantial parts of Croatia with Serb majorities, then divide Bosnia-Herzegovina with Croatia.

Starting in 1991, Milosevic proceeded with extreme brutality, fostering **ethnic cleansing**—forced relocation or mass killing to rid the territory in question of non-Serb inhabitants. In the Bosnian capital, Sarajevo, a culturally diverse city long known for its tolerant, cosmopolitan atmosphere, more than 10,000 civilians, including 1,500 children, were killed by shelling and sniper fire during a Serb siege from 1992 to early 1996.

When a Serb mortar killed thirty-seven civilians in a marketplace in Sarajevo in August 1995, NATO forces responded with air strikes that led to peace accords and the end of fighting by early 1996. Although the peace agreement envisioned a unified Bosnian state, the contending Serbs, Croats, and Bosnian Muslims quickly began carving out separate spheres, violating agreements about repatriation and the rights of minorities. A decade later Bosnia remained an ethnically divided international protectorate, still dependent on the international peacekeeping force stationed there.

The War in Kosovo   The next phase of the Yugoslav tragedy centered on the province of Kosovo (KOH-soh-voh), which Serbs viewed as the cradle of

their nationhood (see Map 30.2). For complex historical reasons, however, Serbs had long constituted only a minority of its population. The majority were ethnically Albanian, and by the late 1980s they were talking independence—and sometimes mistreating the minority Serbs. As part of his effort to foster Serb nationalism, Milosevic countered by suspending autonomy for Kosovo within the Yugoslav confederation in 1991. The fissuring of Yugoslavia over the next few years emboldened the Kosovars, who had come to envision full independence, as opposed to mere autonomy within the Serbian part of what remained of Yugoslavia. By provoking Serb intransigence, they could expect to win international support as they demanded independence.

When Milosevic struck against the Kosovars in the spring of 1999, ruthlessly pursuing ethnic cleansing, the Western powers again intervened, first convening a meeting with Serb and Kosovar leaders on Kosovo's future. When the Serb-led remnant of Yugoslavia refused to sign, NATO made good on its threats to bomb Serbia in retaliation. The bombing, concentrated on such economic targets as bridges and power stations, continued for eleven weeks in late 1999.

Critics argued that it set a dubious precedent to attack Serbia for refusing a settlement that would have ceded territory and opened the rest of Serbia to quasi-occupation by NATO. No one denied that Kosovo was part of Serbia, so the NATO action was an overt interference in the internal affairs of a sovereign state. Even the notion that the operation was a humanitarian response to genocide seemed hypocritical to some, who asked why the international community had done nothing in response to the far more systematic genocide in Rwanda in 1994, when 800,000 people had been killed in a hundred days. Defenders countered that it was partly because of the soul-searching in the aftermath of Rwanda that the Western countries were now changing the rules and taking responsibility for concerted action.

Once the NATO bombing began, the Serbs intensified their ethnic cleansing of Kosovo, burning homes, forcing 800,000 refugees to flee into neighboring Macedonia and Albania. But the bombing finally led both the Serbs and the Kosovars to pull back from their more extreme demands, and Russia agreed to join in the multinational peacekeeping force in Kosovo in the aftermath. Still, the outcome bore little relationship to the multi-ethnic pluralism NATO had been seeking. As Kosovars came to dominate the now-ravaged territory, still nominally part of Serbia, the rule was ethnic separation, portending some sort of division. Moreover, the new Kosovo was dominated first by lawless gangs, then increasingly by criminal organizations that the peacekeepers proved powerless to control.

ethnic cleansing   An effort, through forced relocation or even mass killing, to remove an unwanted ethnic group from a particular geographical area. This tactic was implemented by Yugoslavian ruler Slobodan Milosevic to unite all Serbs.

The Shadow of Violence in the Balkans
Early in 2006 Dzevad Delic, a Bosnian Muslim, prays at the grave of his father, who was killed during the Serbian assault on Bosnia in the early 1990s. This is at the memorial center of Potocari, near Srebrenica, where the worst Serb atrocities against Bosnian Muslims occurred.   *(AP/Wide World Photos)*

War Crimes Tribunals   Authority over Kosovo was transferred to the UN, and talks to settle the province's future began early in 2006. With ethnic Albanians constituting 90 percent of Kosovo's 2 million people by this point, it was widely expected that the province would be made independent. The potential for renewed ethnic violence remained, so Serbia could only try to get the best deal possible for the remaining Serbs.

Although Milosevic was the first sitting head of state to be indicted for war crimes, he proved resilient, initially surviving his defeat in Kosovo in 1999. He lost the presidential election in September 2000, however, and the following year, under pressure from the international community, the Serbian government within the rump Yugoslav confederation turned him over to a UN war crimes tribunal in The Hague. There, as his trial dragged on, he died in prison in 2006. Meanwhile, those who led Serbia after Milosevic's defeat fought a difficult battle against systematic corruption and organized crime as they sought to make their country worthy of membership in the EU.

It was increasingly clear that if Serbia was to have any hope of such membership, it would have to be more helpful in the ongoing effort to apprehend the Bosnian Serb general Ratko Mladic (MLAH-ditch) for his own war crimes trial at The Hague. Charged with the slaughter of as many as 8,000 Bosnian Muslim men and boys when his forces took the town of Srebrenica

(shreb-reh-NEET-sah) in 1995, Mladic had been indicted but had managed to evade capture, most basically because he was still deemed a hero by many Serbs.

RESPONDING TO GLOBAL TERRORISM

Further complicating international relations after the cold war was an increase in the scale and extent of terrorism, sometimes pitting non-Westerners against the West. European venues ranged from Northern Ireland to the Basque region of northern Spain to the rebellious Russian republic of Chechnya to the subways of London. In the United States right-wing extremists bombed a federal government building in Oklahoma City in 1995, and U.S. embassies in Kenya and Tanzania were subjected to terrorist attacks in 1998.

With this new terror already erupting, a terrorist attack of unprecedented proportions shook the United States on September 11, 2001. Suicide hijackers seized four large airliners, crashing one into each of the towers of the World Trade Center in New York City and another into the Pentagon, just outside Washington, D.C. The fourth plane, apparently also headed for Washington, crashed in Pennsylvania. The World Trade Center crashes collapsed both towers, which had been among the world's most visible landmarks. The coordinated attacks claimed the lives of over three thousand people from eighty-two countries.

The United States proclaimed this assault an act of war, and the NATO alliance invoked Article 5 for the first time: the attack on one of its members was to be treated as an attack against all. U.S. leaders promptly assigned responsibility to al Qaeda, an international terrorist network led by the wealthy Saudi Arabian Osama bin Laden, who was living in exile in Afghanistan. There he and others of his network were protected by the Taliban regime, whose extreme, radically fundamentalist version of Islam they shared in certain respects.

Led by President George W. Bush, the United States initiated military action against the Taliban regime later in 2001. Several weeks of U.S. bombing enabled Afghan opposition forces to oust the Taliban and force al Qaeda onto the defensive. But bin Laden survived, and al Qaeda regrouped sufficiently to launch terrorist

Terror in New York City, September 11, 2001
With one of the twin towers of the World Trade Center burning from an attack at 8:45 A.M., a second hijacked plane crashed into the second tower less than an hour later. By the end of the morning, both towers had collapsed. *(Chao Soi Cheong/AP/Wide World Photos)*

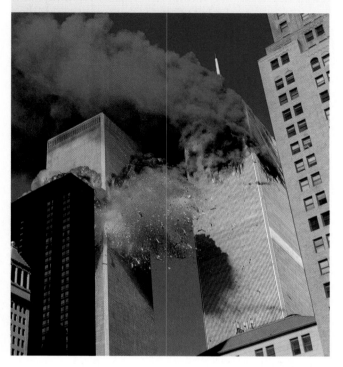

attacks against Western interests in Morocco and Saudi Arabia in 2002 and 2003. Then, in March 2004, the network struck in Europe for the first time with a series of terrorist bombings on commuter trains in Madrid that killed over 200 people.

But terror could be bred in Western countries as well. The suicide bombers who led a coordinated attack on the London public transportation system, killing 56, in July 2005 seemed to have been British citizens, Muslims of Pakistani descent, acting on their own. Whatever its sources, such terrorism posed an ongoing threat to Western security and complicated the West's relations with the non-Western world.

DIVISIONS OVER THE INVASION OF IRAQ

The United States won widespread support for its effort to root out international terrorist networks. But the Americans encountered formidable opposition in 2002 when the Bush administration began to call for the overthrow of Saddam Hussein's regime in Iraq. Saddam was charged with stockpiling chemical and bi-

ological weapons of mass destruction in violation of the UN peace agreement that followed the Persian Gulf War of 1991. In that war a broad, U.S.-led coalition defeated an Iraqi effort to conquer Kuwait. Iraq was also accused of developing a nuclear weapons program and supporting terrorist networks like al Qaeda. Moreover, Saddam had long tyrannized the Iraqi people.

As it began to appear that the United States might be prepared to act unilaterally, the Iraq issue became one of the most divisive in recent history, seriously straining Western relations. No one denied that the Iraqi regime was a brutal dictatorship that had developed, and even used, weapons of mass destruction in the past. But an array of countries, with France, Germany, Russia, and China in the forefront, insisted that UN weapons inspectors be given more time to assess Iraq's compliance with the peace terms. Moreover, they held that any punitive action in the event of noncompliance be directed by the UN Security Council, not the United States acting unilaterally.

Yet the Americans won a good deal of international support. Most notably, British prime minister Tony Blair, despite considerable opposition from within his own Labour government, made Britain a full partner of the United States. The governments of Italy, Spain, Denmark, Poland, Hungary, and the Czech Republic supported Bush's get-tough policy. Romania and Bulgaria cooperated, even letting their military bases be used as staging points for the ensuing U.S. assault on Iraq. Each hoped to gain not only NATO membership but also permanent American bases as the United States contemplated redeploying some of its forces in Europe in light of the changing international configuration. But even in countries whose governments supported U.S. policy, the public tended to be strongly opposed to a military showdown in Iraq.

When it became clear they could not win UN Security Council endorsement, the United States and Britain sent military forces into Iraq in March 2003 and toppled Saddam Hussein's regime within six weeks. The military success proved easier than most people had expected, but the tasks of reconstruction proved far more difficult than U.S. officials had envisioned. Although there were steps toward what might eventually prove genuine democracy, an anti-occupation insurgency developed after the United States declared active hostilities ended on May 1, 2003. Sectarian and ethnic violence further complicated the effort of Iraqi leaders to develop a workable new government.

In the aftermath of the invasion it had gradually become clear that Saddam Hussein's Iraq had not been actively developing weapons of mass destruction. In addition, evidence suggested that both the U.S. and British governments had relied to some extent on faulty intelligence or had used intelligence selectively to justify the invasion. And whereas no links between Saddam's regime and al Qaeda had been shown, the newly chaotic Iraq seemed a far more dangerous breeding ground for international terrorists than Saddam's Iraq had been.

In the Spanish elections that followed the terrorist bombings in Madrid of March 2004, voters elected the Socialist leader José Luis Rodríguez Zapatero, who charged that the U.S.-led occupation of Iraq was becoming a fiasco. He promptly followed through on an earlier pledge to withdraw the 1,300 Spanish troops from Iraq. But though some of America's European partners gradually pulled back, the coalition remained reasonably stable, despite the difficulties encountered.

U.S. UNILATERALISM

A major source of friction between the United States and Europe was growing U.S. unilateralism—the country's willingness, even determination, to go its own way in the world on the basis of what it took to be its own interests. As the world's military-diplomatic superpower, the United States was increasingly prone to such unilateralism during the 1990s, then moved more decisively in that direction in the aftermath of the terrorist attacks of September 2001. In pursuing its own course, the United States was departing from the multilateral international system that it had fostered since World War II. Foreshadowed in the Atlantic Charter of 1941 (see pages 887–888), multilateralism found expression in NATO, in the economic organizations growing from the Bretton Woods Agreement, and in a whole array of multilateral understandings and institutions governing matters such as arms control and war crimes.

While an overwhelming majority of nations—120, to be exact—supported the establishment of the UN's International Criminal Court in The Hague in 1998, the United States was among only 7 that opposed it. Then, as the court was being established, the United States sought an exemption for itself because it worried that American peacekeepers might be especially tempting targets of false accusations of war crimes. Such concerns were not groundless, and they indicated the unique problems the United States faced as the world's undisputed, and often resented, superpower. But many found it disturbing that the United States did not want to play by the same rules as the vast majority.

Some Europeans continued to look to the UN to check American hegemony, but others, including many non-Europeans, found a stronger European military and diplomatic presence the only potential balance to the United States. EU forces were prominent in peacekeeping missions in Macedonia, Bosnia, Kosovo, Afghanistan, and Congo. Yet the Europeans were much less willing than Americans to use force in the first place. As of early 2006, the United States was spending 3.4 percent of its gross domestic product (GDP) on defense, Europe 1.9 percent. Moreover, the Europeans were devoting only half as much of their defense spending to modernizing equipment and twice as much to pay and pensions. The Iraq War dramatized how far the U.S. military had outpaced even the British in technological capacities. Many experts found this gap between the Europeans and the Americans a threat to NATO, which might become simply useless as a battle-ready alliance.

Some suggested that Europeans had grown soft in their reliance on the United States since World War II. While they agreed that, in principle, the West must be prepared to fight on occasion, they were unwilling to pay if it meant cutting the welfare benefits they had come to expect. Moreover, Europeans could muster no unified military and diplomatic policy. It was attractive for a variety of reasons to let the United States shoulder the military burden in a dangerous world.

Still, some observers noted the scope for the United States and Europe to play complementary roles in world affairs. Americans were better at fighting wars, but Europeans might be better at preventing them. Precisely because they were not prone to threaten force, Europeans could play a constructive role of moral suasion, even if it was up to the Americans to provide the muscle.

═══════════ S E C T I O N   S U M M A R Y ═══════════

- The end of the cold war opened the way to a series of new issues that the West had to confront, even as it also changed power relationships within the West itself.

- The European Union expanded and gathered strength but also encountered unforeseen setbacks.

- Ethnic conflict contributed to the breakup of Yugoslavia in a series of wars that included major human rights violations and significant dilemmas for peacekeepers.

- International terrorism, often reflecting tensions between the West and the Islamic world, became a major concern throughout the Western world.

- Increasing U.S. unilateralism, evident most dramatically in the U.S.-led invasion of Iraq, alienated others in the West.

unilateralism Term describing the increasing willingness of the United States to go its own way in world affairs after the end of the cold war, and especially after the terrorist attacks on the United States in September 2001.

THE CONTINUING EXPERIMENT WITH DEMOCRATIC CAPITALISM

What forces raised new questions about the effectiveness of Western-style democracy by the early years of the twenty-first century?

Democracy had become the unchallenged norm in western Europe by the 1980s, and after the fall of communism the former Soviet bloc countries seemed eager to adopt the western European model. But though patterns in several of the former communist countries increasingly approximated those of the mature democracies of western Europe, disaffection and even some unforeseen new political and economic forms emerged as well. The problems of adjustment were especially dramatic, and even tragic, in Russia.

The mainstream tendency was toward democratic procedures, the rule of law, and an orderly alternation of competing political parties within a framework of stability, consensus, and tolerance. But even in the established democracies, technological change and globalization were altering the socioeconomic framework, producing new challenges for governments and even threatening the socioeconomic compact that had emerged after World War II.

THE POSTCOMMUNIST EXPERIMENT

The former communist countries had little experience with the give-and-take of democratic politics, and their fragile new political systems had to engineer the difficult transition to a free-market economy. With the economies close to chaos as the transition began, the effort led to unemployment, inflation, and widespread corruption. No longer could ordinary people count on the subsidized consumer goods or the welfare safety net the communist regimes had provided. While many suffered great hardship, some former communist functionaries quickly got rich by taking over state-owned companies.

The pattern of change and the degree of success varied considerably from country to country, though in per capita income the whole region continued to lag behind western Europe considerably. Still, by the mid-1990s, the transition to a market economy seemed to be working (see **Map 30.3**). Thanks partly to the lure of EU membership, most of the postcommunist countries made considerable progress toward mainstream democracy. Even the election of former Communists in Poland and Hungary during the mid-1990s did not compromise democracy or the market economy.

Still, the case of Poland manifested certain enduring strains and risks. On the one hand, the country by 2006 had experienced changes scarcely imaginable in 1989. A full member of both NATO and the EU, it was now numbered among Europe's new "big six," together with Germany, France, Britain, Italy, and Spain. GDP grew by 50 percent from 1990 to 2005, as Poland attracted considerable foreign investment.

But, on the other hand, the costs were high for those left out. In 2006 unemployment stood at 18 percent, ever more people were falling into poverty, and the gap between rich and poor was widening. The state was widely seen as weak, bloated, inefficient, and highly corrupt. Services were poor, and the tax system was full of loopholes. Low electoral turnouts manifested the widespread disillusionment with the new political class—and even doubts about democracy itself.

In Russia, where communism had far deeper roots than elsewhere in the former Soviet bloc, the transition from communism proved especially difficult. Although privatization proceeded rapidly, it mostly benefited former Communist Party functionaries, some of whom became instant multimillionaires. By the mid-1990s Russia had evolved a kind of "crony capitalism," with a small group of economic oligarchs manipulating much of the economy through dubious banking practices and outright extortion—and paying no taxes. After ten years the postcommunist Russian economy had shrunk to perhaps half its former size. Especially sobering were the demographic effects: Russians were dying young and having few children. By 2001 the population had dropped to 143 million—a decline of 6 million people in ten years.

The combination of economic stringency and governmental weakness produced a chilling increase in street crime, from muggings to auto theft. By the end of the 1990s, moreover, dozens of journalists, politicians, and business leaders had been murdered gangland style, with the killers never apprehended. Particularly appalling was the death of Galina Starovoitova (stah-ro-VOY-to-vah), a widely admired liberal legislator and potential presidential candidate who was gunned down outside her St. Petersburg apartment in 1998.

As Russia's president during the first postcommunist years, Boris Yeltsin seemed a committed reformer—surely the best hope for an orderly transition to democracy and a market economy. He enjoyed widespread support from the Western democracies, but among Russians the difficult circumstances produced disenchantment with reform, nostalgia for the stability of communism, and much resentment of the West.

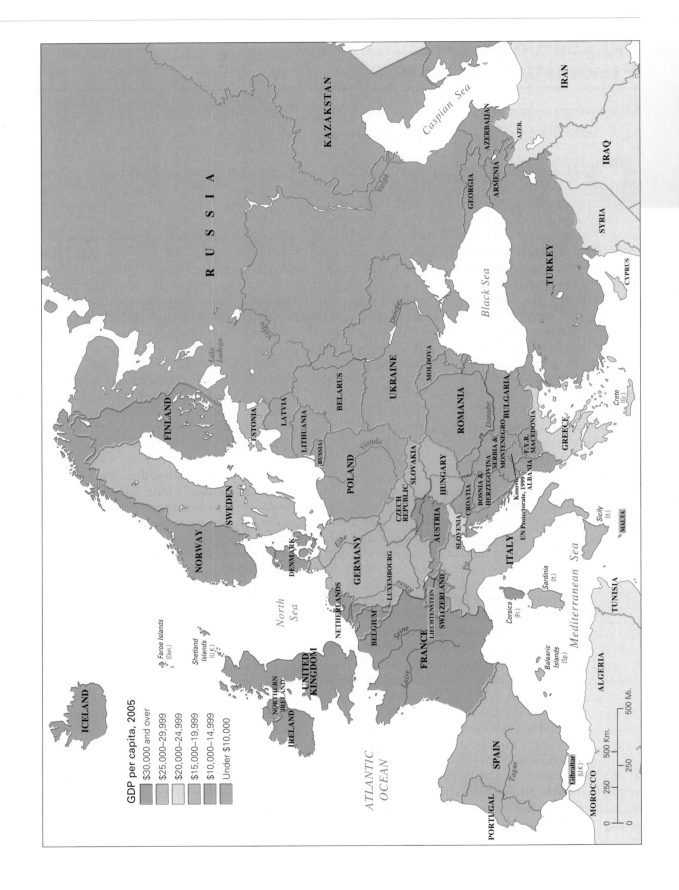

GDP per capita, 2005

- $30,000 and over
- $25,000–29,999
- $20,000–24,999
- $15,000–19,999
- $10,000–14,999
- Under $10,000

ICELAND

Faroe Islands
(Den.)

Shetland Islands
(U.K.)

NORTHERN IRELAND

IRELAND

UNITED KINGDOM

NORWAY

SWEDEN

FINLAND

North Sea

DENMARK

NETHERLANDS

BELGIUM

LUXEMBOURG

GERMANY

Elbe

ESTONIA

LATVIA

LITHUANIA

(RUSSIA)

POLAND

Vistula

BELARUS

UKRAINE

CZECH REPUBLIC

SLOVAKIA

HUNGARY

AUSTRIA

SLOVENIA

CROATIA

BOSNIA & HERZEGOVINA

SERBIA & MONTENEGRO

Kosovo
UN Protectorate, 1999

F.Y.R. MACEDONIA

ALBANIA

MOLDOVA

ROMANIA

Danube

BULGARIA

GREECE

Crete
(Gr.)

Sicily
(It.)

MALTA

ITALY

Po

Rhine

SWITZERLAND

LIECHTENSTEIN

FRANCE

Seine

Loire

ATLANTIC OCEAN

SPAIN

PORTUGAL

Tagus

Gibraltar
(U.K.)

MOROCCO

ALGERIA

TUNISIA

Balearic Islands
(Sp.)

Corsica
(Fr.)

Sardinia
(It.)

Mediterranean Sea

RUSSIA

Volga

Lake Ladoga

Dnieper

KAZAKSTAN

Caspian Sea

Black Sea

GEORGIA

ARMENIA

AZERBAIJAN

AZER.

TURKEY

CYPRUS

SYRIA

IRAQ

IRAN

0   250   500 Km.

0   250   500 Mi.

MAP 30.3   GDP per Capita in Europe, 2005
Gross domestic product (GDP) per capita is a widely recognized measure of national economic success. By 2005, this measure varied dramatically among the European countries, revealing the wide disparity in economic well-being across the Continent. The former communist countries continued to lag, even as some were growing at impressive rates. The U.S. figure was $42,000, and Canada's was $32,900.

As it sought to engineer the transition to democratic capitalism, the Yeltsin government had to deal with the attempted defection of Chechnya (CHECH-nyah), a small, largely Muslim republic located in the Caucasus (see Map 29.3 on page 940). Long restive under Russian control, the Chechens began demanding independence after the collapse of the Soviet Union in 1991, finally provoking war with Russia in 1994. In the aftermath of a compromise in 1996, Chechen hardliners oppressed the Russian minority, kidnapping and enslaving some, and even killed journalists and international aid workers. When Islamic militants began spreading the anti-Russian message from Chechnya to adjacent Dagestan, Russia renewed full-scale war with Chechnya in 1999.

This renewed confrontation made possible the rise of **Vladimir Putin** (POO-tin), who had been director of Russia's secret police, though he was virtually unknown in political circles. Calling for a tough stance on Chechnya, Putin was Yeltsin's choice for prime minister in 1999, and he immediately delivered on his promise to clear Dagestan of Chechen terrorists. Whereas most Russians had disliked the earlier confrontation with Chechnya, by now they had had enough—not only of Chechen defiance but also of Russian weakness. Putin's popularity soared as he talked tough and acted tougher. A brutal Russian assault late in 1999 left much of Chechnya, especially the capital, Grozny, in ruins.

In poor health and increasingly erratic, Yeltsin resigned at the end of 1999, essentially to make way for Putin, who was elected president early in 2000. Reelected in 2004, Putin remained quite popular among Russians. Still, outside observers tended to give his performance decidedly mixed marks. In the economic sphere, there was considerable evidence that, thanks partly to Putin's leadership, the post-Soviet decline had at last been reversed by 2006. Tax collection had improved, some well-run companies had emerged, and

Vladimir Putin   President of Russia since 2000, he strengthened the Russian state against the forces of disintegration that emerged after communism, but critics accused him of authoritarianism and excessive governmental secrecy.

the Russian middle class was clearly expanding. Especially as a result of high oil prices, life was much better for average Russians—perhaps better than ever before. But the political order suffered from secrecy and governmental inaccessibility. The media were increasingly concentrated and subject to restrictions and controls.

Especially contested was the relationship between state power and business power. A showdown between Putin and the economic barons led in 2003 to the arrest of Russia's richest person, Yukos Oil chief Mikhail Khodorkovsky (koh-dor-KOV-skee), who was given an eight-year sentence in Siberia for corruption and tax evasion. The company itself was essentially renationalized, thereby reversing the earlier, largely fraudulent privatization from which Khodorkovsky had benefited. Whereas some read the move as a welcome notice to such tycoons to start paying taxes, others charged that Putin was merely jealous of Khodorkovsky, who had been willing to act independently and who had been admired in the West as the embodiment of Russia's new capitalist spirit.

As itself an unprecedented experiment, the effort to move from communism to democratic capitalism made clearer what was required to make democratic capitalism work. The Russian case demonstrated that even a turn to free elections and a market economy could yield an exploitative and brutal "gangster capitalism." If democracy and a market economy were to be socially beneficial, a deeper consensus around civic responsibility and the rule of law was required. People had to be willing to pay taxes, and the state had to be strong enough to collect taxes, to limit corruption, and to sustain genuinely open markets and an orderly banking system. Merely getting government out of the way was not sufficient.

CONSENSUS IN THE ESTABLISHED DEMOCRACIES

During the half century since World War II, renewed prosperity came together with the new compact concerning economic and social welfare to sustain the Western democracies. At the same time, something like an orderly alternation of moderately conservative and moderately progressive parties or coalitions became the norm, or at least the direction, helping to sustain the democratic consensus. Even Italy, long notorious for the surface instability of its government, moved toward a system of alternating left-leaning and right-leaning coalitions after major scandals during the early 1990s undermined the long-standing political establishment.

Although the European left had won reforms that were now central to the consensus around democratic capitalism, by the 1990s it had abandoned much of what it had stood for in its earlier socialist forms—from class struggle and revolution to state ownership and a centrally planned economy. Though still nominally socialist, the German SPD, for example, could serve only as the mildly left-leaning alternative within the framework of capitalist democracy. When the Labour Party returned to power in Britain in 1997, the popular new prime minister, Tony Blair, did not offer a bold new program or reverse Margaret Thatcher's privatization measures of the 1980s. To be sure, he was more concerned to care for those worst-off and to enhance equality of opportunity. But he expressed admiration for her concerted effort to modernize the British economy, and he was no more sympathetic than she to trade-union efforts to protect jobs at the expense of productivity.

TWO MODELS OF DEMOCRATIC CAPITALISM

By the 1980s much of western Europe had caught up with the United States in standard of living, and it was increasingly clear that two models of democratic capitalism were at work—and to some extent in competition. The U.S. model, largely shared by Britain since the Thatcher years, placed greater emphasis on free enterprise and the market, whereas continental western Europe had evolved a **social market economy,** with greater commitment to security, consensus, and communitarian values. The European model provided a more substantial safety net—in health care, for example—as well as a stronger commitment to subsidized transportation and day care. Generous pensions, especially for government workers, had been one aspect of the postwar compact. By 2003 Italy and Austria were devoting 15 percent of their economies to public-sector pensions, the highest figures in Europe. Few Austrians worked past age 60.

In France by the mid-1990s, five-week paid vacations were mandatory, with the government sometimes subsidizing the cost of transportation to seaside or mountain resorts. Indeed, the French welfare system had emerged as a model. In 2000 the UN's **World Health Organization (WHO)** rated the French health-care system the world's best. Moreover, social services in France were delivered with less paperwork and intrusiveness than elsewhere.

In some respects, it was almost as if the Americans

and Europeans had passed in the night in the decades since World War II. In the United States, which had long prided itself on its egalitarianism vis-à-vis class-bound Europe, disparities between rich and poor had become greater than anywhere in the developed world by the early twenty-first century. In business firms, the ratio of executive compensation to worker salaries was dramatically higher in the United States than in Europe.

Perhaps still more significant was the difference in attitudes toward such disparities. Wary of extreme inequalities of income, Europeans tended to view unrestricted competition more as a threat than an opportunity. Whereas most Europeans found the inequalities and insecurities of American life unacceptable, Americans accented the scope for upward mobility that their system offered. As long as anyone could get rich, it did not matter that some were much richer than others. Americans were far more likely than Europeans to see themselves as moving up.

At the same time, Americans had grown more skeptical about government and its capacity to provide social services. Whereas 62 percent of those surveyed in Britain in 2002 said they would accept higher taxes for better services, less than 1 percent of those in the United States held this view. Friction over particular policies from pollution control to product testing reflected similar differences in priorities and values. The United States was more likely than Europe to rely on unfettered freedom, competition, and the market. Europe was more cautious—more willing to err on the side of health and the environment. Accustomed to a strong government role in society, Europeans had difficulty understanding how measures such as government-sponsored health care could cause such controversy among Americans.

By the 1990s the changing socioeconomic framework was producing new challenges for governments on both sides of the Atlantic. But continental western Europe seemed especially vulnerable because of the difficulties it encountered in squaring its social market model with increasing global competition.

NEW ECONOMIC COMPETITORS

During most of the 1990s the United States experienced remarkable prosperity as it asserted its leadership in the "new economy" revolving around **information technology.** The technological revolution encompassed everything from robotics to fiber optics but was based especially on the computer. Some new firms were able to exploit technology and start from scratch, while

social market economy   The socially oriented model of capitalism practiced in continental western Europe, providing a substantial safety net in health care and a commitment to public services such as transportation and day care.

World Health Organization (WHO)   Established as a specialized agency of the United Nations in 1948, it serves as the coordinating authority on international public health. It is headquartered in Geneva, Switzerland.

information technology   Term for the revolution in information availability and communications resulting from the late-twentieth-century development of personal computers and the Internet.

older competitors often faced problems of redundant workers or outmoded plants and equipment. In all cases, manufacturing jobs were lost, as competition forced the industrial sector to become more efficient through computers and automation. In the German steel industry, which had spearheaded a remarkable industrial transformation a century before, more than half the jobs disappeared during the 1970s and 1980s.

Just as the West became concerned with economic challenges from the Soviet Union in the 1950s, Japan by the later 1970s, and a wider array of East Asian "tigers" by the 1980s, it came to view China and to a lesser extent India as potential economic superpowers by the early twenty-first century. Although still nominally communist, China was increasingly willing to compete in the global economic marketplace and did well at manufacturing, thanks especially to a cheap, disciplined labor force. With its favorable trade balance, China came to hold such a large share of the U.S. national debt that it seemed capable, at least potentially, of compromising the independence of American foreign policy.

By the 1980s Italy had become Europe's leading producer of clothing and shoes, thanks primarily to the initiatives of small and medium-sized family firms. Having established a global presence in the 1980s, the well-known clothing retailer Benetton had exemplified Italy's success. Even in 1990, almost 90 percent of its output was being produced in Italy. By early 2006, however, that figure had fallen to 30 percent—and was expected to fall still further, to 10 percent, by 2010. Responding to global competition, Benetton was relying increasingly on Chinese suppliers, who offered low labor costs and rapidly improving production skills.

In 2003 France's Peugeot Citroën chose Trnava, a town in western Slovakia, for a site of a major automobile assembly plant, to start turning out cars in 2006. At the same time, the British firm MG Rover was making a major investment in Poland, and France's Renault was launching a new budget model at its factory in Romania. The former communist countries of east-central Europe were proving tremendously appealing to automakers elsewhere. Although the communist system had not proved competitive over the long term, it had left a reasonably good infrastructure, as well as a skilled and disciplined labor force costing only about 20 percent as much as the EU labor force.

By 2006, major carmakers in France, Germany, and Italy were being forced to cut costs—and thus jobs and benefits—at home in order to remain competitive in light of the much lower labor costs in east-central Europe. There was much sensitivity in western Europe that competition from new EU members in east-central Europe was causing downward pressure on living standards. But it was not only the new EU members that

were attracting such investment. Volkswagen was building new plants in Russia and China. Some were predicting that auto manufacture in western Europe would have ceased altogether in ten to fifteen years.

UNEMPLOYMENT AND ECONOMIC CHALLENGES IN WESTERN EUROPE

As global economic competition intensified, governments throughout western Europe found it more difficult to pay for all the benefits they had gradually come to promise. By the early 1990s some found the social compact all too generous—and unsustainable. Pension reform, labor legislation, and the costs of education became flash points across much of western Europe.

Falling birthrates and aging populations meant that relatively fewer workers would have to foot the pension and health-care bills for increasing numbers of older people. Although most agreed that reform was necessary, massive union-led demonstrations against government proposals to scale back pensions brought France almost to a halt in May 2003. Comparable protests greeted reform proposals in Germany, Italy, and Austria. As a result, little was done anywhere to address the problem.

Even with the renewed prosperity of the 1980s, unemployment in western Europe reached levels not seen since the Great Depression. During the 1990s high unemployment persisted in much of Europe, even as it declined to postwar lows in the United States. Most people attributed the difference in unemployment rates to the different structure of labor markets and, more generally, to the greater flexibility of the U.S. economy. As a result of laws, labor agreements, and the postwar consensus now in place, European workers who had jobs were more secure than their American counterparts. But European employers were less able to adapt to changing conditions by laying off workers or hiring new ones with different skills. Government reform efforts provoked strenuous protests.

Widespread demonstrations in France in the spring of 2006 forced the government to abandon legislation that would have adjusted labor laws to enable employers to fire, without cause, workers under 26 years of age within two years after hiring. It was thought that such flexibility would encourage employers to hire more younger workers, thereby reducing France's 22 percent employment rate among youth. Yet it was French youth, supported by France's trade unions, that led the protests. One poll indicated that 75 percent of French young people aspired to a civil service job, primarily because of the security such a job seemed to entail.

In Germany, the ongoing costs of assimilating the former communist East complicated reform efforts. By early 2006, Germany was still transferring 80 billion euros a year to the former East. As of that point, the subsidy to the East since reunification totaled 1.3 trillion euros overall. Yet young people continued to migrate from East to West, and the birthrate in the former East was even lower than in the West.

Upon becoming Germany's first female chancellor in November 2005, the conservative Angela Merkel sought the measures necessary to streamline the German economy. But Merkel led an unstable "grand coalition" of the two largest parties, her own conservatives and the socialists, in light of the near dead heat in the national elections that September. It remained to be seen whether her awkward coalition could muster the unified will and the political muscle to tackle Germany's problems in a concerted way.

The difficulties that Merkel faced seemed to suggest a certain political paralysis, not only in Germany but in Europe more widely. It was symptomatic that with the German electorate split and the postwar social compact eroding, an increasing number of private schools emerged in Germany—for those who could afford them. At the same time, a growing black market economy had come to constitute an estimated 15 percent of Germany's GDP by early 2006.

Although the extent of the problem varied from country to country, the increasingly obvious role of money in politics—needed to finance campaigns and win elections—raised doubts throughout the Western

world about the capacity of elected governments to pursue some common public interest. This tendency toward corruption yielded political cynicism—and declining voter turnouts—all over the Western world.

Whatever the patterns of divergence and convergence within the West, what was ultimately at issue, after its roughly two-hundred-year experiment with liberal capitalism, was the scope for creating and maintaining a genuine public sphere. It rested on the capacity for citizenship, as opposed to the mere pursuit of individual or group interests. It required a capacity for compromise and shared sacrifice. Conversely, a government worthy of public trust would be not a mere dispenser of favors but a shared responsibility of the entire citizenry. In terms of its sustaining commitments, the democracy that the West held up as a model for the non-Western world remained very much an experiment in progress.

IMMIGRATION, ASSIMILATION, AND THE NEW RIGHT

With the decline of socialism as a political alternative, and with the welfare state increasingly open to question, a new right gained prominence in much of Europe by the mid-1990s. Though differing considerably in priorities, respectability, and success, leaders such as José María Aznar in Spain, Jean-Marie Le Pen in France, Jörg Haider (HY-dur) in Austria, Gianfranco Fini (FEE-nee) in Italy, and Pim Fortyn (for-TOON) in the Netherlands tapped into political frustration and economic uncertainty. Some were absorbed into the mainstream, while others provoked renewed political division.

In addressing economic anxieties, the new conservatives sometimes articulated problems that mainstream politicians ignored, but they often disagreed among themselves—over the relative merits of free trade and protectionism, for example. On one issue, however, they were in clear agreement. This was the issue of assimilation, citizenship, and national identity as globalization proceeded and immigration increased. The arrival of refugees from the former Yugoslavia and other trouble spots during the 1990s added another dimension. Even figures like Le Pen and Haider, who typically won only 15 to 20 percent of the vote, articulated a wider sense among the public that immigrant communities were responsible not only for increasing crime but also for a weakening of the common values necessary to sustain society.

By the first years of the new millennium, concerns about national community, cultural diversity, and the meaning of citizenship were taking center stage all over Europe. It was striking that the Netherlands and Denmark, two small countries widely known for openness and tolerance, became flash points. But especially cen-

On Her Way to the Chancellorship
As leader of the German conservative party (Christian Democratic Union), Angela Merkel launches her campaign to become German chancellor in 2005. Her party won a narrow victory in the September elections, and she became chancellor as head of a broad coalition in November.   *(David Bathgate/Corbis)*

tral was France, proud of what had seemed its traditions of inclusiveness, and by 2006 home of the largest concentration of Muslims in western Europe, roughly 6 million, or 10 percent of the French population.

Most were recent immigrants or members of immigrant families established since World War II. Indeed, many French Muslims were French citizens, the second- or third-generation descendants of immigrants who had begun coming to France from Algeria and other former French African colonies in the 1950s when, as the postwar economic miracle gathered force, France needed workers. But beginning in the early 1970s, jobs had become increasingly scarce.

With open citizenship central to the French self-understanding, French law accorded citizenship automatically to second-generation immigrants, on the assumption that these offspring would be readily assimilated. However, the Muslim community in France had not been well assimilated, and by the end of the 1980s finger-pointing on all sides had begun. Whereas the French left defended cultural diversity and its compatibility with citizenship, the right complained that citizenship was being devalued as a mere convenience, requiring no real commitment to the national community. Critics such as Le Pen charged that many from recent immigrant families did not want to assimilate.

An especially symptomatic episode in 1989—the "affair of the scarves"—made it clear that the place of Muslims in France had become a central and volatile issue. Three teenaged Muslim girls were suspended from school on the grounds that, in wearing the traditional Muslim headscarf, they were violating a long-standing law banning religious displays in public schools. The girls insisted they were not seeking to flaunt their religion or to convert others; the point was simply that Islamic teaching required women to cover their heads in public as a sign of modesty. Yet in the eyes of some Westerners, that practice reflected the second-class status of women in Islamic civilization. To defend the right to wear the scarves was thus to condone the oppression of women.

An uncertain compromise resulted from this episode, but the issue continued to smolder, becoming more intense as the Muslim presence in France increased and tensions between Muslims and non-Muslims grew. Early in 2004 the French National Assembly passed, by an overwhelming margin, a new law to ban conspicuous religious displays in French public schools, hospitals, and other governmental buildings. Although large Christian crosses and Jewish yarmulkes, or skullcaps, were also at issue, the law seemed especially to target the headscarves traditionally worn by Muslim women. The law was passed despite massive protest marches, especially featuring Muslim women, in cities throughout France and in a number of major cities elsewhere.

Polls indicated that whereas 69 percent of the French backed the new law, these issues divided the French Muslim community. Muslim support for the ban on the headscarf reflected a fear of backlash against indications of Islamic separatism, but a genuine desire for assimilation was also at work. However, many Muslims were reluctant to accept full assimilation if it was to mean the gradual loss of their religious identity in France's secular society. At the same time, many non-Muslims supported the right of women to wear the scarf precisely on the grounds of pluralism, tolerance, and freedom of expression. Yet some of those opposing the new law sought not to preserve diversity but to keep Muslim girls in the public schools to expose them to secular influence and to promote long-term assimilation. In the short term, they argued, any law restricting religious expression would spawn separate Islamic schools, thereby deepening the divisions already evident in France.

By the first decade of the new century French Muslims were clustered in deteriorating high-rise ghetto suburbs ringing Paris and other cities. Whereas young Muslims were widely blamed for criminality, they complained of police harassment and job discrimination. Certainly they experienced very high rates of unemployment, well over 40 percent in many areas. And thus, it was feared, they were increasingly prone to militancy or Islamic fundamentalism.

As the police sought to crack down on crime, an incident late in October 2005 provoked a riot among Muslim youth in the ghetto suburb of Clichy-sous-Bois. During the next few days waves of looting and car-burning spread to cities throughout France. The rioting continued well into November, until the government declared a state of emergency and deployed sharply increased security forces. It was France's worst civil unrest since the Days of May demonstrations of 1968 (see page 920). President Jacques Chirac admitted that the riots had dramatized problems that had to be addressed vigorously and promptly. Some observers called for a form of affirmative action to bring French Muslims, or French citizens of North African descent, into positions of greater prominence in business, politics, and the media, spheres in which they were virtually absent.

But the problem was by no means confined to France. Germany started from a very different set of assumptions than France about assimilation and citizenship, yet ended up with many of the same problems. Germany had actively recruited foreign workers during the decades of economic boom and labor shortage that followed the war. At first these "guest workers" had been viewed not as immigrants but as temporary, almost migrant, laborers. But many of the 14 million guest workers let in from 1955 to 1973, especially the Turks, remained in Germany. Although their family patterns came to approximate those of the rest of the population, their birthrates were considerably higher. By the 1980s Germany had a large and increasingly settled population of non-Germans, many of them born and educated there.

In addition, the German Federal Republic had adopted a generous asylum law as one bit of atonement for the crimes of the Nazi period. With the turmoil surrounding the end of communism in the Soviet bloc, the newly reunified Germany found 60,000 new arrivals seeking asylum every month by 1993. At that point Germany had a large foreign population of 6.4 million, or roughly 8 percent of the population.

Germany's law governing citizenship for immigrants and their descendants reflected a long-standing German assumption that citizenship presupposed German ethnicity—or at least full assimilation. Thus ethnic Germans—more than a million of whom moved to Germany from the former Soviet bloc between 1988 and 1991—were immediately accorded German citizenship. But the many Turks, for example, who had been born in Germany were denied citizenship. Precisely because citizenship seemed to entail full assimilation, some Germans opposed it for "foreigners" out of respect for cultural diversity.

In 1999, however, the law was reworked to make naturalization much easier. In principle, citizenship was now available to almost everyone born in Germany or whose parents had resided and worked in Germany for at least eight years. But as of 2006, this formal change had not made the expected difference in practice. The Turks in Germany remained largely separate, as many Turks seemed to prefer to remain in Turkish ghettoes, having minimal contact with ethnic Germans. At the same time, many ethnic Germans remained wedded to the notion that belonging is based on descent, or ethnic origin. Even as access to citizenship on the national level became easier, some German states erected new barriers to naturalization during the first decade of the twenty-first century. And although citizenship was more accessible in light of the 1999 law, the national government concentrated not on liberaliz-

ing immigration rules but on tightening security and fostering the assimilation of those of non-German descent already in Germany. Thus, for example, a 2004 law required new immigrants to take German lessons.

Indeed, by the early twenty-first century, the tendency all over Europe was to push assimilation—the formation of national citizens. Whereas some conflated the impulse with racism, others insisted that, on the contrary, anyone could belong, regardless of race or ethnicity, but that belonging required a positive commitment, adopting the mainstream values of the national community, not holding to cultural differences.

In the wake of the assassination of Theo Van Gogh in 2004 and the controversy over the Danish cartoons of 2005, the Netherlands in 2006 adopted a law, the first of its kind anywhere, requiring that prospective immigrants take a "civic integration examination" testing their willingness to accept the tolerant openness of Dutch culture. The chairman of a leading Dutch Muslim organization defended the measure, suggesting that all immigrants needed to be prepared to embrace modernity.

The Dutch were in the forefront of a wider retreat from the multiculturalism that had been prevalent especially on the European left, and that had made the persistence of immigrant subcultures in European countries seem a virtue. A veteran, highly respected observer of the contemporary European scene, Jane Kramer, summed up the dilemma that seemed to face well-meaning Europeans as they came to grasp the implications of the cultural differences separating them from many in the immigrant communities in their midst. Noting that the Internet in the Netherlands was awash in hate-mail by Muslims, who often equated the pluralistic tolerance of the Netherlands with mere decadence, Kramer suggested that the Dutch were coming to recognize that democracy without assimilation might be a dangerous contradiction in terms. "But," she concluded, "like everybody else in Europe, they have no answer to the question What now?"[2]

═══════════ S E C T I O N   S U M M A R Y ═══════════

- Although the transition from communism to some variety of democratic capitalism proved difficult throughout the former Soviet bloc, it proved especially problematic in Russia.

- With the decline of the traditional left, accenting class division and anticapitalism, the established democracies tended toward a new level of consensus around some variety of a two-party framework.

- From within the wider democratic census, there was a split between much of continental western Europe,

with its "social market economy," and the United States, which had greater confidence in free-market capitalism and less confidence in government.

- Especially in continental western Europe, the challenges of globalization suggested the need for reforms—reforms that proved difficult to engineer through the democratic process.

- Concerns about the assimilation of immigrant communities in much of Europe strengthened the political right and raised newly volatile political issues.

LIFESTYLES AND IDENTITIES

How did the changes bound up with globalization affect identities in the West?

Even as matters of diversity and citizenship were becoming mainstream political concerns, they were very much bound up with wider issues of personal identity. And in that respect they intersected in complex ways with other potential influences on identity, from consumerism to religion to gender.

By the mid-1960s, the remarkable postwar economic growth had created a secular, consumerist society throughout much of the West, establishing patterns of life that continued into the twenty-first century, when cell phones and personal computers were commonplace. But changing lifestyles dictated new choices, and the new affluence challenged traditional sources of personal identity in unexpected ways, producing new concerns—and sometimes conflict. Important groups of non-Westerners rejected Western secular consumerism altogether. At the very least, it indicated a kind of decadence. For the various forms of Islamic fundamentalism, it was nothing less than an abomination.

SUPRANATIONAL, NATIONAL, AND SUBNATIONAL IDENTITIES

By the late 1980s consumerism and the widening impact of American popular culture—from blue jeans and American TV to shopping malls and theme parks—suggested a growing homogenization in the capitalist democracies. A Euro-Disneyland opened in France in 1992 and, after a slow start, proved increasingly popular. American fast-food chains such as McDonald's, adopting some European ways and even serving beer and wine, satisfied hungry locals in cities all over Europe.

But Americanization threatened long-standing European identities, and Europeans sometimes adopted special measures to preserve distinctiveness. The EU specified that EU television programming had to be at least 40 percent EU-made, while the French mandated that at least every third popular song played on the radio had to be French.

Prominent among European critics of Americanization was José Bové, the outspoken leader of France's small farmers. When he stood trial in 2000 for vandalizing a McDonald's restaurant in France, thirty thousand people turned out to demonstrate their support. Typically equating globalization with Americanization, Bové articulated a widespread concern for French distinctiveness and identity in the face of U.S. "cultural imperialism," as France seemed increasingly overrun by American films, television, music, even novels in French translation.

But were quotas and mandates really necessary to preserve distinctiveness? The American chain Starbucks, which had revolutionized the serving of coffee in the United States, found it hard to penetrate continental Europe, which had its own long traditions of coffee-making. Even as many were coming to assume that American pop culture was irresistible, it became clear that European viewers were increasingly picking local TV programming on their own, quite apart from quotas. Between 1996 and 2002, the number of hours of American TV programming fell 26 percent in Spain, 17 percent in Germany, and 9 percent in Italy. By 2003 every EU country was well above the 40 percent minimum for local programming, with the average at 62 percent.

Meanwhile, the growing prominence of the supranational EU, and doubts about the significance of national politics, nourished a renewed premium on subnational identities in such distinctive European regions as Flanders, Corsica, Scotland, and Catalonia. Flemings and Corsicans, Scots and Catalans, actively sought to preserve some measure of their distinct cultures and languages in the face of all the contemporary pressures toward standardization. In Britain Tony Blair fostered the "devolution" of powers from the central government in London to Scottish and Welsh assemblies in 1999.

National sentiment grew especially uncertain in Italy, which had had a relatively brief and problematic history as a unified nation. Although its movement for national unification had drawn widespread enthusiasm throughout the Western world in the nineteenth century (see pages 685–689), by the 1990s disillusionment with national politics made many Italians particularly eager to embrace the EU, while others turned in the opposite direction, renewing their identification with region or locality. Resentful of the national government's ties to the less prosperous south, a new political movement, the Northern League, emerged during the 1990s to push for the north to become an independent state. Whatever the seriousness of such literal separatism, the Northern League's persistent strength suggested that "Italian" was becoming less important as a basis of individual identity in Italy's prosperous north.

CLASS IDENTITIES AND TRADE UNIONS

The advent of a media-driven consumerist society produced greater homogeneity of experience and taste and a corresponding de-emphasis on class as a basis of identity. One symptom was the decline of the trade-union movement, long central to working-class identity and advancement.

Changing labor patterns reinforced the decline of organized labor, which was decidedly on the defensive throughout western Europe and the United States by the 1980s. The increasing danger of unemployment undercut the leverage of the unions. And as the economy grew more complex, workers were less likely to think of themselves as members of a single, unified working class.

Still, union membership varied considerably from country to country, and some unions found new ways of exerting influence. In a survey of union membership as a percentage of the work force in twelve industrialized countries in 2001, Denmark and Sweden had the highest figures—around 80 percent. The figures for Italy, Germany, and Britain were all around 30 percent. The lowest figures were in France (10 percent) and the United States (14 percent). Despite some much-publicized militancy in resisting government efforts at pension reform, the unions generally had moved beyond their earlier confrontational posture to an increasing pragmatism.

In Germany local union councils were more willing to make informal agreements with big companies that, while technically violating Germany's restrictive labor regulations, helped keep jobs in Germany. At the same time, some German-based multinational companies such as Volkswagen actively sought to head off trouble with German unions by agreeing to guidelines specifying how they would operate worldwide. By committing itself to offering its workers elsewhere proper pay and working conditions, as well as the right to unionize, Volkswagen was saying that it would not merely seek the lowest bidder, as globalization sometimes seemed to demand. In this respect, too, the unions were still making a difference.

ECONOMIC GROWTH AND ENVIRONMENTAL CONCERNS

The impact of rapid economic growth on the European landscape and cityscape provoked ever greater concern by the last third of the twentieth century. The number of automobiles in western Europe increased from 6 million in 1939 to 16 million by 1959 to 42 million by 1969. Almost overnight, traffic and air pollution fundamentally changed the face of Europe's old cities. In 1976 five statues that had supported the Eastern Portico of the Erectheum Temple on the Acropolis in Athens since the fifth century B.C. were replaced by replicas and put in a museum to save them from the rapid decay that air pollution was causing.

With the end of communist rule, it became obvious that the years of communism had produced environmental degradation on an appalling scale in the Soviet bloc. In the Soviet Union itself, the overproduction of cotton in central Asia, stemming from efforts to foster regional specialization, led to the desiccation of the Aral Sea, an ecological catastrophe. Even with the fall of communism, it was hard to break from the old, often polluting patterns because jobs and energy sources often depended on them. For years Ukraine could not afford to replace the remaining nuclear reactors at Chernobyl, despite safety and environmental risks that the 1986 accident had only worsened (see page 939). International aid finally enabled Ukraine to close the plant in 2000.

The greater affluence in western Europe made possible, and sometimes dictated, more creative responses to pollution and other environmental side effects of economic growth. Many cities adopted pedestrian-only zones to restrict automobile traffic, and some experimented with road-pricing measures in an effort to reduce traffic in central cities.

It was not only the urban environment that proved vulnerable to the byproducts of the new affluence. By the early 1980s acid rain had damaged one-third of the forests of West Germany, including the famous Black Forest of the southwest. Water pollution was a major problem from the Rhine to the Mediterranean to the Black Sea.

Differences in response to environmental concerns sometimes produced friction among Western countries or complicated the West's relations with the non-Western world. Especially symptomatic was the controversy over genetically altered foods, widely consumed in the United States since 1996. European concerns over safety led the EU to impose a moratorium on genetically modified products, including imports from the United States, in 1998. The United States considered the moratorium illegal under existing trade agreements and filed suit with the **World Trade Organization (WTO)** in 2003 to compel the EU to lift the moratorium.

In May 2003, on the eve of the annual G-8 meeting, U.S. president George W. Bush charged that European restrictions on genetically altered foods were undercutting efforts to provide food aid to Africa. The European example had led Africans to avoid investments in such crops. Moreover, some famine-ridden African countries

World Trade Organization (WTO) Growing from a multilateral trade agreement in 1947, it sought, with mixed success, to promote freer trade throughout the world. By the early twenty-first century WTO meetings tended to draw demonstrations by anti-globalization activists.

had refused U.S. food aid because of European-induced concerns about safety. Partly at issue was the fear that genetically modified crops might infiltrate native crops and thereby jeopardize African exports to Europe. Americans countered that Europeans were using a bogus issue to help limit U.S. food exports to Europe—and hurting African development in the process.

The United States had joined the other industrialized nations in signing the Kyoto agreement of 1997, designed to limit emissions of the "greenhouse gases" widely held by scientists to be causing global warming, with potentially catastrophic consequences. But questioning the scientific evidence and citing concerns about economic growth, the United States pulled out of the agreement in 2001, causing much resentment in Europe and elsewhere. With 5 percent of the world's population, the United States was responsible for 25 percent of the world's greenhouse gas emissions per year.

Still, global warming was increasingly recognized, in the United States as elsewhere, as a serious issue that had to be addressed promptly. The question was what needed to be done, and how to muster the political will to do it. New technologies might make it possible to reduce the emissions in question without compromising living standards in the developed world—or the chance for growth in the less-developed world.

RELIGIOUS IDENTITIES

Whereas religious affiliation and church or synagogue attendance remained relatively stable in the United States, Europeans abandoned churches in droves after the mid-1950s. As church attendance dropped, popular culture revolved less around religious festivals and holy days. Moreover, in assuming responsibility for social welfare, European governments had gradually taken over much of the charitable role that the churches had long played.

Seeking to change with the times, the Catholic Church undertook a notable modernization effort under the popular Pope John XXIII (r. 1958–1963). But under his more conservative successors, the church became caught up in controversy, especially over issues such as abortion that women had forced to the fore. By the 1990s its conservative social policy had put the Catholic Church on the defensive. Still, the active, highly visible role of Pope John Paul II (r. 1978–2005) in a variety of spheres attracted widespread admiration. His death in 2005 led to an enormous outpouring of affection.

In such traditionally Catholic countries as France, Italy, and Spain, many people considered themselves "cultural Catholics" and ignored church rulings they found inappropriate, especially those concerning sexuality, marriage, and gender roles. In referenda in 1974 and 1981, two-thirds of Italians defied the Vatican by voting to legalize divorce and approve abortion rights.

Even in heavily Catholic Ireland, the electorate approved, though narrowly, the legalization of divorce in 1995, after having defeated it overwhelmingly in a referendum just nine years before.

When surveys showed that 80 percent of Spaniards considered themselves Catholic by the twenty-first century, even the cardinal-bishop of Madrid admitted that for many, "Catholic" was not a way of life but merely a label, perhaps linked to national identity. Other surveys showed that whereas in 1975, the year of the dictator Francisco Franco's death, 61 percent of Spaniards reported regular church attendance, that figure had dropped to 19 percent by the early twenty-first century. Even 46 percent of those calling themselves Catholic admitted that they almost never went to church.

A survey of church attendance in eleven western European countries in 1999–2000 found Spain somewhere in the middle, with 25 percent of the population saying they had been to church at least once a month. Ireland had the highest rate of attendance (58 percent), followed by Italy (about 40 percent). The lowest rates were in Denmark (3 percent) and Sweden (4 percent). Other surveys suggested that such self-responses probably doubled the actual rate of church attendance. While religious affiliations weakened in western Europe, the Russian Orthodox Church experienced a notable revival after the collapse of communism and the breakup of the Soviet Union.

In parts of the West, religious and ethnic identities blurred, sometimes enhancing the potential for conflict. Even after the breakup of the wider Soviet Union gave independence to the predominantly Muslim central Asian republics, the remaining Russian Federation included more than twenty million Muslims, or about 15 percent of the overall population. In both absolute numbers and percentage terms, this was the largest Muslim population in Europe. Included were those who identified themselves as Muslims in cultural terms even if they did not practice the Islamic religion.

A significant Islamic revival among Russian Muslims followed the collapse of communism, producing increasing friction with the central authorities. In 2002 the interior ministry banned women from wearing headscarves in photos for official documents. The Russian supreme court upheld the ban in response to an appeal by Islamic women that it violated Russia's constitutionally guaranteed freedom of religion. At the same time, the Russian army refused to allow Muslim services on military bases.

FAMILY LIFE AND GENDER ROLES

The new affluence significantly affected demographic patterns, partly because contraception became more readily available. Indeed, the advent of the birth control pill, widely obtainable by the late 1960s, fostered a

MAP 30.4 World Population Trends, 2002–2015

This map shows populations in 2002, as well as projected average annual growth rates from 2002 to 2015, in countries throughout the world. In the developed countries of the West, populations are relatively high but growing slowly, if at all. Most of the world's population growth is occurring in the less developed countries outside the West.

(Source: Data from www.worldbank.org)

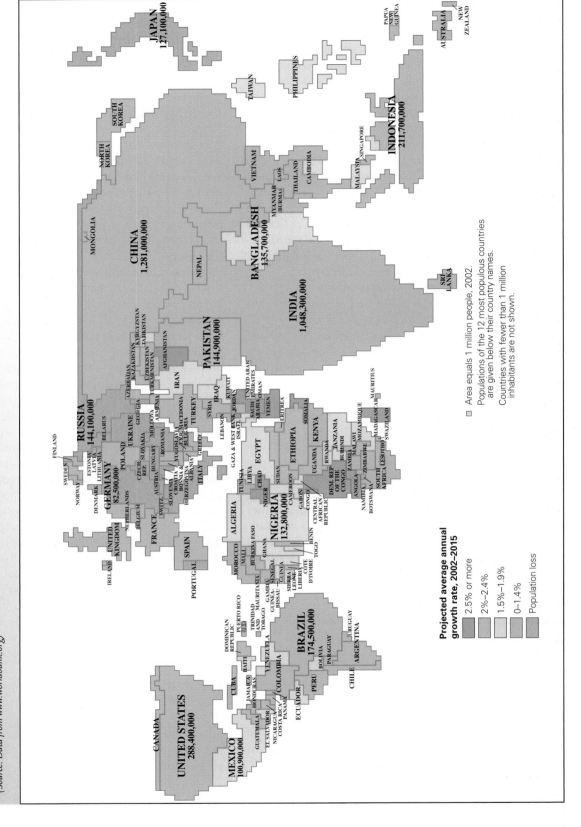

☐ Area equals 1 million people, 2002.

Populations of the 12 most populous countries are given below their country names.

Countries with fewer than 1 million inhabitants are not shown.

Projected average annual growth rate, 2002–2015

- 2.5% or more
- 2%–2.4%
- 1.5%–1.9%
- 0–1.4%
- Population loss

sexual revolution that was central to the emerging secular lifestyle. At the same time, falling birthrates meant an aging population, and thus all the concerns about paying for the pensions and other welfare measures central to the postwar social compact.

In western Europe, as in the United States, a remarkable baby boom had followed the end of World War II and carried into the early 1960s. But the birthrate declined rapidly thereafter, so family size had diminished markedly by 1990. In Italy the number of births in 1987 was barely half the number in 1964, when the postwar baby boom reached its peak. Between 1993 and 2003, Italy's population increased by but 0.01 percent, to 57.5 million, and it was expected to shrink to 56 million by 2010. By 1995 the population was not sustaining itself in a number of European countries (see **MAP 30.4**).

The feminist movement that had re-emerged in the late 1960s gradually expanded its focus beyond the quest for formal equality of opportunity. Examining subtle cultural obstacles to equality led feminists to the more general issue of gender—the way societies make sense of sexual difference and allocate social roles on that basis. By the late twentieth century, gender was central not only to public policy but also to private relationships and life choices in much of the Western world.

By the 1970s women sought measures such as government-subsidized day care that would enable them to combine paid employment with raising a family. At the same time, governments increasingly understood the value of policies to encourage both productive working parents and effective childhood development. Setting the pace was France, where the government began making quality day care available to all during the 1980s. Government subsidies kept costs within reach for ordinary working families. In addition, 95 percent of French children ages 3 to 6 were enrolled in the free public nursery schools available by the early 1990s. The figures for Italy (85 percent) and Germany (65 to 70 percent) were also relatively high, but Britain lagged behind (35 to 40 percent).

As some people saw it, the increasing reliance on child-care at once reflected and reinforced a decline in the socializing role of the traditional family. But the social changes at work were complex, and their longer-term implications for the well-being of parents, children, and society itself remained unclear. Some studies showed that an early day-care experience enhanced the socialization of children. Others cautioned against romanticizing the traditional nuclear family, which had been less prevalent than widely believed and not always successful in any case. Moreover, the responsibilities of parenting did not have to fall primarily on mothers. The biological difference in childbearing and nursing remained, however, and even committed feminists disagreed about whether parenting entailed a special role for women and, if so, about the policy implications that followed from it.

Although much remained contested or uncertain, the scope for greater sharing of parental responsibilities and the need for equal career opportunities across gender lines were widely recognized by the 1990s. The French model seemed to work well in combining child support with equal opportunity for paid employment. In simultaneously offering day care and allowances to concentrate on parenting, French government programs seemed to give French mothers a genuine choice as to whether to work outside the home. French family policy was widely popular; the key question by 2006 was whether France could afford it.

Also much at issue by the early twenty-first century were the rights of homosexual couples—to adopt children, for example, or to have their partnerships legally recognized as marriage. Whether married or not, were homosexual partners entitled to job benefits such as health care, which often were available to heterosexual couples?

The interrelationship of family, gender, sexuality, and personal self-realization, never static, was evolving in new ways—a crucial aspect of the ongoing experiment in the West.

═══════════ S E C T I O N   S U M M A R Y ═══════════

- The advent of a consumer society, increasingly on a global level, affected national, supranational, and subnational identities in complex, often unforeseen ways.

- The de-emphasis on class and class distinction as a basis of identity contributed to the decline of the trade-union movement.

- Economic growth seemed to have adverse effects on the environment, though there was disagreement over how best to respond.

- In the face of pressures toward secularization, the strength of religious identities varied considerably from country to country throughout the West.

- Affluence led to new ways of conceiving gender roles and family life.

NELSON MANDELA AND THE UNIVERSALITY OF HUMAN VALUES

For all the admiration that continued to surround those who had helped undermine Soviet-style communism, the most revered person in the West and the world at the beginning of the twenty-first century was surely the black South African Nelson Mandela (b. 1918). As a militant in the African National Congress, which was seeking to overcome the brutally segregationist apartheid system in South Africa, he spent twenty-seven years in prison. He was released in 1990 as part of a wider amnesty granted by South Africa's new president, F. W. De Klerk (b. 1936). Responding to international pressures, including effective trade sanctions, De Klerk wanted Mandela's help in restructuring the South African system. The two were central to the ensuing negotiations that repealed apartheid and began the transition to a nonracial democracy in South Africa. When the first elections were held under the new system in 1994, Mandela was elected president of South Africa. In this passage from the conclusion to his autobiography, he articulates the idealism that inspired his remarkable achievement and made him a symbol of shared human values to Westerners and non-Westerners alike.

On the day of the inauguration, I was overwhelmed with a sense of history. In the first decade of the twentieth century, a few years after the bitter Anglo-Boer War and before my own birth, the white-skinned peoples of South Africa patched up their differences and erected a system of racial domination against the dark-skinned peoples of their own land. The structure they created formed the basis of one of the harshest, most inhumane societies the world has ever known. Now, in the last decade of the twentieth century, and my own eighth decade as a man, that system had been overturned forever and replaced by one that recognized the rights and freedoms of all peoples regardless of the color of their skin.

That day had come about through the unimaginable sacrifices of thousands of my people, people whose suffering and courage can never be counted or repaid. I felt that day, as I have on so many other days, that I was simply the sum of all those African patriots who had gone before me. That long and noble line ended and now began again with me. I was pained that I was not able to thank them and that they were not able to see what their sacrifices had wrought. . . .

I never lost hope that this great transformation would occur. Not only because of the great heroes I have already cited, but because of the courage of the ordinary men and women of my country. I always knew that deep down in every human heart, there is mercy and generosity. No one is born hating another person because of the color of his skin, or his background, or his religion. People must learn to hate, and if they can learn to hate, they can be taught to love, for love comes more naturally to the human heart than its opposite. Even in the grimmest times in prison, when my comrades and I were pushed to our limits, I would see a glimmer of humanity in one of the guards, perhaps just for a second, but it was enough to reassure me and keep me going. . . .

I was not born with a hunger to be free. I was born free—free in every way that I could know. . . .

But then I slowly saw that not only was I not free, but my brothers and sisters were not free. I saw that it

THE WEST IN A GLOBAL AGE

What questions emerged as the West faced new crises all over the globe after the end of the cold war?

By the early twenty-first century, the West was part of a world that was, in one sense, dramatically less Eurocentric than it had been a century before, when European imperialism was at its peak. Events in the West competed for attention with OPEC oil prices, Chinese trade practices, and Iran's nuclear program. Decisions vitally affecting, or demanding the response of, the industrialized countries of the West might be made anywhere. Just as capital and information flowed more quickly than ever across national borders, so could epidemic diseases emerging in some distant forest or jungle. This was the reverse side of the new interconnectedness of a global world. A planetary culture, a threatened environment, an interdependent economy, and an increasing sense of international responsibility required people to think in global terms as never before. (See the box "The Global Record: Nelson Mandela and the Universality of Human Values.")

was not just my freedom that was curtailed, but the freedom of everyone who looked like I did. That is when I joined the African National Congress, and that is when the hunger for my own freedom became the greater hunger for the freedom of my people. It was this desire for the freedom of my people to live their lives with dignity and self-respect that animated my life, that transformed a frightened young man into a bold one, that drove a law-abiding attorney to become a criminal, that turned a family-loving husband into a man without a home, that forced a life-loving man to live like a monk. I am no more virtuous or self-sacrificing than the next man, but I found that I could not even enjoy the poor and limited freedoms I was allowed when I knew my people were not free. Freedom is indivisible; the chains on any one of my people were the chains on all of them, the chains on all of my people were the chains on me.

It was during those long and lonely years that my hunger for the freedom of my own people became a hunger for the freedom of all people, white and black. I knew as well as I knew anything that the oppressor must be liberated just as surely as the oppressed. A man who takes away another man's freedom is a prisoner of hatred, he is locked behind the bars of prejudice and narrow-mindedness. I am not truly free if I am taking away someone else's freedom, just as surely as I am not free when my freedom is taken from me. The oppressed and the oppressor alike are robbed of their humanity.

When I walked out of prison, that was my mission, to liberate the oppressed and the oppressor both. Some say that has now been achieved. But I know that that is not the case. The truth is that we are not yet free; we have merely achieved the freedom to be free, the right not to be oppressed. We have not taken the final step of our journey, but the first step on a longer and even more difficult road. For to be free is not merely to cast off one's chains, but to live in a way that respects and enhances the freedom of others. The true test of our devotion to freedom is just beginning.

. . . After climbing a great hill, one only finds that there are many more hills to climb. I have taken a moment here to rest, to steal a view of the glorious vista that surrounds me, to look back on the distance I have come. But I can rest only for a moment, for with freedom comes responsibilities, and I dare not linger, for my long walk is not yet ended.

QUESTIONS

1. In what sense is Mandela appealing to human values, as opposed to the values or special circumstances of a particular group?

2. Why does Mandela suggest that the struggle for freedom is essentially endless?

Source: Long Walk to Freedom by Nelson Mandela, pp. 541–544. Copyright © 1994 by Nelson Rolihlahla Mandela. Reprinted by permission of Little, Brown and Company (Inc.).

UNIFORMITY AND DIVERSITY IN THE "GLOBAL VILLAGE"

By the last decades of the twentieth century, a kind of global culture began to emerge for the first time. Indeed, talk of a single "global village" became commonplace. But just as "Americanization" produced concerns about preserving distinctiveness elsewhere in the West, "globalization" produced comparable concerns on a global level. Although the process promised a better life for many people in less developed countries, valuable diversity was seemingly being lost in an ever more uniform world. For instance, half of the world's 6,500 languages were expected to disappear during the twenty-first century.

Skyscrapers in booming Asian cities looked much like skyscrapers in the West. Indeed, they were often designed by the same architects. Businessmen in conservative Western dress made postwar Japan the world's second-largest economy. American firms transferred billing and even customer service operations to lower-cost India, even as India was becoming a major player in computer technology. "Americanization" made products such as Coca-Cola and McDonald's burgers familiar not just in Europe but worldwide. Especially among urban youth, a common style emerged that owed much to American popular culture. Meanwhile, for everyone from scientists to business leaders to airline pilots, English became the common language.

At work, however, was not simply Western or American cultural imperialism. What resulted in many spheres, from food to popular music, was not homogenization but a more complex kind of fusion, as elements from diverse cultures interpenetrated and enriched one another while retaining distinctive features. The British tourist board declared Indian curry to be the official British dish, testimony to the number of Indian restaurants in Britain—itself testimony to the enduring cultural impact of the Indian heritage on Britain.

Even multinational media conglomerates increasingly accented local content. When Viacom launched MTV in the 1980s, the producers assumed that since the pop music culture was universal, a single channel would succeed everywhere. But it quickly became evident that success required local variation. Between 2001 and 2003, MTV launched fourteen new channels, for a total of thirty-eight around the world. Each was tailored to local tastes, with no emphasis on an American link. One MTV executive observed, "we don't even call it an adaptation of American content: it's local content creation. . . . The American thing is irrelevant."[3] So whereas the advent of MTV had initially seemed to entail overt cultural imperialism, the program's evolution manifested—and contributed to—the more complex global cross-fertilization in process.

THE "NORTH-SOUTH" DIVIDE AND MUTUAL INTERDEPENDENCE

Beginning especially in the 1970s, western Europe and North America encountered formidable economic competition first from Japan and then from other countries of the East Asian Pacific rim. What increasingly mattered, as globalization proceeded, was the difference between the industrialized, relatively affluent "North" and the less developed "South," including much of Africa and Latin America, southern Asia, and the Middle East. Indeed, "North-South" tensions, resulting from demographic and economic patterns, quickly moved to center stage to replace the East-West tensions that had ended with the cold war. World population reached six billion in 1999, having doubled since 1960. This was the fastest rate of world population growth ever, and by the 1990s virtually all of that growth was in Africa, Asia, and Latin America (see Map 30.4).

As the population exploded in the less developed world, the gap between rich and poor nations widened. One aspect of this process, producing much concern by the early twenty-first century, was the growing **digital divide**—the disparity in access to the computing and Internet technologies that seemed essential to compete in the global economy. New technologies were not bridging, but rather widening, the gap between the richer and poorer nations of the world.

The West recognized some responsibility to assist economic development in the developing world, but individual countries differed considerably in the ways they claimed to be doing so. Whereas most Americans assumed that they led the world in foreign aid, the United States, among the twenty-one richest countries, actually devoted the smallest percentage of its overall economy to direct foreign aid as of 2002. The most generous countries—Denmark, Norway, and the Netherlands—gave almost seven times as much. But such direct aid was only one measure of the ways the developed world might assist development elsewhere. Also important were direct investment, trade policy, and a willingness to accept immigrants, who often sent money back to their countries of origin, thereby providing essential foreign exchange. As the least protectionist of the wealthy nations, the United States was most helpful on trade because its markets were more open to products from developing countries.

Growing concern about the environment intensified the sense of global interdependence and pointed to the need for international cooperation. Problems such as global warming, the loss of biodiversity, and the deterioration of the ozone layer were inherently supranational in scope. Yet environmental concerns also complicated relations between the industrialized nations and the rest of the world. Countries seeking to industrialize encountered environmental constraints that had not been at issue when the West industrialized. The challenge for the West was to foster protection of the environment in poorer regions of the globe without imposing unfair limitations on economic growth.

Also bringing home mutual interdependence was the rapid spread of disease with the intensification of contacts around the world. Moreover, there was evidence that new diseases were emerging more frequently as the world grew more crowded. The human population intruded into previously untouched jungles and forests, intensifying interaction among species that had formerly remained largely separated. The crowding of animals for food production also fed the genesis and spread of new diseases.

AIDS (acquired immune deficiency syndrome), a sexually transmitted disease caused by the HIV virus, had apparently spread from chimpanzees to humans in Africa earlier in the twentieth century, although it began to be recognized only in the late 1970s. It then spread throughout the world beginning in the 1980s. Particularly devastating in Africa, AIDS remained a major concern in the early twenty-first century.

In the late 1990s, West Nile virus and monkey pox appeared at almost the same time. SARS (severe acute

digital divide   A term for the disparity in access to the computing and Internet technologies that seemed essential to compete in the twenty-first-century global economy.

respiratory syndrome), a highly contagious and often fatal disease, was first reported in southern China in 2003, apparently contracted by a human being from a civet cat. The disease reached epidemic proportions in some areas of China and was carried elsewhere by travelers. The fact that Toronto, one of the most successful North American cities, was especially hard hit made clear the wider vulnerability of the West in this age of rapid transport and communication.

By 2006, there was much concern with "bird flu," a new strain of influenza virus first identified in Hong Kong in 1997. Cases involving humans were rare; as of early 2006, 170 people had been infected, of whom 92 had died. But this was an especially dangerous strain that might mutate further to facilitate the jump from birds to human populations. It might then produce a pandemic to rival the so-called Spanish flu, which killed perhaps forty million people in 1918 and 1919 (see page 790).

Seemingly under control at first, bird flu was eventually spread by migratory birds to southeast Asia and from there westward, reaching Turkey, then Africa and western Europe. When, in France in 2006, it infected a European poultry farm for the first time, 43 countries promptly banned the import of French poultry and foie gras, to the dismay of French producers. Officials of the UN's World Health Organization (WHO) stressed that they lacked the global infrastructure to head off the sort of pandemic that could develop.

The Controversy over Economic Globalization

Although many forces fed globalization, arguably the most potent, and increasingly controversial, was international capitalism itself. The capitalist ideal of free and open markets sounded appealing, and economic models, based on comparative advantage, could explain how everybody wins through expanded international economic exchange. The world economy was not a zero-sum game. But whatever the virtues of free global markets in principle, experience showed globalization to be a multi-edged sword, producing complex, often-contradictory results.

Indeed, globalization bred increasingly vocal opposition, fueled by concerns over fairness, exploitation, and the "Americanization" of the world. Critics charged that globalization was not helping the poorer nations to catch up, as theory would have it, but leaving them ever further behind. Meetings of the G-8 proved prominent targets of opposition, but at least as important was the network of supranational agencies, starting with the World Bank and the International Monetary Fund (IMF), that had developed from the Bretton Woods Agreement near the end of World War II (see page 898). Also central, especially in promoting free trade, was the World Trade Organization (WTO), which grew from a multilateral trade agreement in 1947.

These organizations had long drawn praise for helping to keep the world economy stable and growing. By the late 1990s, however, they had come to constitute a focal point for the growing concerns about accelerating economic globalization.

Meetings of the WTO in Seattle in 1999 and of the World Bank and IMF in Washington, D.C., in 2000 drew large demonstrations. Riots accompanied G-8 meetings in 2001 and 2003. Those protesting were often naive about economics and the benefits of free trade. But their protests raised significant questions about wages, working conditions, environmental impact, and international financial arrangements that were not always adequately addressed in the prevailing economic models. Most fundamentally at issue was whether it made sense to foster free trade and globalization without greater consistency in social and environmental policy. In the absence of common standards, free trade was not likely to be fair trade. The challenge was to find some balance between free trade and regulation within an increasingly global economy.

Heading Off Disease

As "bird flu" was becoming a major international concern, the disease struck a turkey farm in the Ain region in southeastern France, prompting many foreign countries to suspend French poultry imports. The French responded quickly. Here a veterinarian vaccinates a duck at a poultry farm in Horsarrieu, in southwestern France, on March 6, 2006.   *(AP/Wide World Photos)*

In September 2003 the WTO meeting in Cancún, Mexico, broke up amid much bitterness. A group of twenty-one poorer nations, led by Brazil, India, and China, walked out, accusing the United States and the EU of hypocrisy in calling for freer trade while still subsidizing their own farmers. By helping the richer countries export agricultural products at lower prices, such subsidies made it harder for poorer countries to develop their own crops and to sell them to the richer countries. West African cotton farmers suffered as the United States spent more than $3 billion a year on subsidies to 25,000 U.S. cotton growers, helping to make the United States the world's largest cotton exporter and depressing cotton prices worldwide. The United States claimed to be eager to cut farm subsidies, but only as part of a more systematic reduction that would also involve Japan and the EU, which was devoting 40 percent of its budget to such subsidies.

THE QUESTION OF GLOBAL RESPONSIBILITY

If people were forced to think in global terms as never before, how far did global responsibility extend in a world that remained divided into sovereign nation-states? The series of brutal, sometimes genocidal conflicts from Yugoslavia to Rwanda to Liberia that marked the post–cold war period fostered a growing sense of collective responsibility on the part of what was increasingly called "the international community." Amorphous though it was, that entity seemed to take on real existence by the end of the 1990s. But who or what constituted "the international community" and the conditions under which it should act remained uncertain.

Of course, a prominent international organization was already in place—the United Nations, the fruit of the hopes for a better world in light of World War II. By the 1990s no one denied that it had achieved significant successes in areas such as nutrition, health, and education. Kofi Annan (b. 1938) of Ghana, who became its secretary-general in 1997, was highly regarded worldwide. Indeed, he, together with the UN itself, was awarded the Nobel Peace Prize in 2001. But scandals surrounding the implementation of the UN's "oil-for-food" program in Iraq partly discredited the UN, especially among those skeptical about it in the first place. This program was initiated in 1996 to diminish the suffering of ordinary Iraqis in the wake of sanctions imposed on Iraq after its invasion of Kuwait in 1990. An exhaustive independent report made it clear that whereas the program had achieved considerable success, even saving lives, it had suffered from mismanagement and corruption. As an organization of 191 member states with diffuse lines of authority, the UN was simply not equipped to run so complicated a program without mishap.

More generally, UN forces were often overburdened as they took on the often-incompatible objectives of peacekeeping and humanitarian relief—sometimes in areas where there was no real peace to keep. And the organization's members, especially its leaders on the Security Council, were frequently divided about what should be done. The need to seem impartial sometimes paralyzed UN peacekeepers. In July 1995 four hundred Dutch troops failed to prevent the massacre of more than 7,000 Muslim men and boys in a UN "safe area" around Srebrenica, in Bosnia. But the UN Security Council had not allocated enough troops or weapons to protect the victims in any case, despite the secretary-general's pleas for additional resources.

Still, the UN was a visible presence even as concerns for national sovereignty compromised its ability to act. UN inspectors assumed the burden of policing Iraqi compliance with the peace that followed the Persian Gulf War of 1991. After ad hoc UN war crimes tribunals began dealing with the atrocities that had taken place in the Balkans and Rwanda, the UN established its permanent International Criminal Court (ICC) in The Hague in 1998. Its charge was to bring to justice those responsible for war crimes or crimes against humanity. And the UN was sufficiently credible that, for many people throughout the world, the lack of UN sanction undermined the legitimacy of the U.S.-led invasion and occupation of Iraq.

Whatever its center of gravity, the international community rested on the commitment and initiative of the rich Western countries, because only they had the means to act globally in response to natural or human-made disasters. Supplementing the efforts of governments was a network of **nongovernmental organizations (NGOs),** such as the Red Cross, Amnesty International, and Doctors Without Borders, that had emerged over the years to deal with humanitarian relief or human rights issues. Collectively they were a major presence on the international scene by the early twenty-first century and central to the international community.

But those seeking to provide aid or maintain peace were often forced to deal with semicriminal elements who diverted humanitarian aid to buy weapons or who took peacekeepers and aid workers hostage—or even killed them. In 1994, for the first time, more UN civilian aid workers (twenty-four) than peacekeeping soldiers were killed in the line of duty. And the death toll for aid workers rose rapidly during the decade.

The conflicts that developed in hot spots around the world after the cold war spawned an increasing sense that it was up to the Western-led international community to "do something." But do what—and at

nongovernmental organizations (NGOs)
Private, independent organizations designed to deal with humanitarian relief and human rights issues. Though unaffiliated with governments or the United Nations, they became central to the international community.

THE QUESTION OF WESTERN RESPONSIBILITY

The end of the cold war helped open the way to ethnic conflict, terrorism, and, in some areas, the breakdown of government as violent warlords fought for control. With the world more interconnected than ever before, it was increasingly assumed that "the international community," spearheaded by the rich countries of the West, ought to respond to tragedy anywhere. But quite apart from the difficult questions of leadership and coordination, it was not clear what level of risk, and expense, the West was prepared to assume. In the following excerpt, Brian Urquhart, born in Britain in 1919 and long a senior official of the United Nations, offers a pointed analysis of the issues that came to the fore as the West experimented with a more active response to tragedies around the world.

What is to be done when hundreds of thousands of people in a hitherto little-known region of the world are hounded from their homes, massacred, or starved to death in a brutal civil war, or even in a deliberate act of genocide? To our credit, we no longer turn away from the face of evil, but we still don't know how to control it. As the new century dawns, one of the biggest problems for international organizations and their member governments is to learn how to react to the great human emergencies that still seem to occur regularly in many parts of the world. . . .

The so-called "international community" is anything but a constitutional system. As far as it is organized at all, it is an institutional arrangement, unpredictable and slow to act. It usually responds only when disaster has already struck and when its members, usually in the UN Security Council, can agree to take action. Even then, since the UN has no standing forces or substantial resources of its own, its action, if it can be agreed upon, is likely to be too little and too late.

In his opening address to the General Assembly on September 20, 1999, Secretary-General Kofi Annan made an impassioned plea for UN intervention in cases of gross violations of human rights. The reactions of governments to Annan's remarks showed very clearly how far the world still has to go before evil can be systematically dealt with internationally. Most comments on Annan's speech were critical and stressed the paramount importance of national sovereignty; some even saw humanitarian intervention as a cloak for American or Western hegemony or neo-colonialism. Only a small minority of Western countries supported Sweden's position that the collective conscience of mankind demands action.

A new idea of "human security" has now taken its place alongside the much older concept of "international peace and security." It has emerged as the result of a vaguely defined and fitful international conscience on the part of the liberal democracies, and it has been encouraged both by the prodigious growth of nongovernmental organizations and by the communications revolution. However, the rules and the means for protecting human security are still tentative and controversial, not least because virtually any situation threatening human security is likely to raise questions of national sovereignty. No government wants to set up a system which may, at some point in the future, be invoked against itself.

. . . Humanitarian action as it emerged in the aftermath of World War II was principally concerned with refugee resettlement and the reconstruction of war-shattered countries. In those innocent days, humanitarian relief was seen as a nonpolitical activity, dictated by the needs of the afflicted and by the resources and expertise available to meet them. . . . That relatively nonpolitical concept of humanitarianism has come to a brutal end with the rising importance of warlords and the conflicts within states of the post–cold war world. The international sponsors of humanitarian aid are no longer dealing with more or less responsible governments. . . .

. . . "The whole aid community has been overtaken by a new reality," the IRC [International Rescue Committee] stated. "Humanitarianism has become a resource . . . and people are manipulating it as never before. Sometimes we just shouldn't show up for a disaster." . . .

QUESTIONS

1. Why did the West find it so difficult to respond to the sorts of disasters that came to the fore after the cold war?

2. Why did even humanitarian aid come to seem increasingly ineffective under certain circumstances?

Source: "In the Name of Humanity" by Brian Urquhart, *The New York Review of Books*, April 27, 2000, pp. 19–21. Reprinted with permission from *The New York Review of Books*. Copyright © 2000 NYREV, Inc.

what cost? What aims were realistic? During the first decade of the new century the international community was widely called upon to end the apparent ongoing genocide in the Darfur region of Sudan. But there was no consensus on what degree of response was appropriate or on how it should be coordinated. (See the box "The Written Record: The Question of Western Responsibility.")

═══════════ S E C T I O N   S U M M A R Y ═══════════

- Although globalization meant cultural homogeneity in one sense, it also produced unforeseen forms of cultural fusion and a deeper appreciation of cultural diversity.

- New diseases dramatized global interdependence even as the gap between the rich countries of the "North" and many of the poorer countries of the "South" seemed to widen.

- Economic globalization produced a backlash, often targeting multinational entities like the World Trade Organization, on the grounds that free trade was too often exploitative and unfair.

- Even as it increasingly felt responsible for dealing with disasters around the world, the West, leading "the international community," was often unsure how best to respond.

QUESTIONING THE MEANING OF THE WEST

On what basis was the wider contemporary relevance of "Western civilization" being debated by the first decade of the twenty-first century?

Although in one sense "globalization" meant "Westernization" to advocates and critics alike, its accelerating pace bred deeper uncertainty about what was specifically Western—about the meaning and value of the Western tradition. During the cold war, the West had offered two competing visions to the world. But with the fall of communism, one of them stood discredited, and democratic capitalism emerged the clear winner. As the end of the cold war also ended the division of Europe and removed the common adversary, the ties that had helped bind western Europe to the United States loosened. Indeed, the need to respond both to the challenges of the competitive global economy and to the increasingly volatile international environment occasioned friction and fragmentation within the West.

CULTURAL DIFFERENCES WITHIN THE WEST

Even on the cultural level, differences between Europeans and Americans seemed to be deepening by the early twenty-first century. As a corollary of religious differences between the two, the United States experienced periodic controversy over the teaching of Darwinian evolution in the public schools—controversy that would have been unthinkable in Europe. In the same way, homosexuality and abortion continued to stir greater controversy in America than they did in most of Europe.

In light of the disruptions and disasters of the twentieth century, the place of history became especially problematic in Europe. At the same time, the radical transformation in the half century since World War II in some ways cut Europeans off from their own traditions. The uneasy contemporary relationship with the past, especially the traumatic past of the earlier twentieth century, took especially pointed form in the neo-expressionist painting prominent in Germany and Italy by the late twentieth century.

For a generation after World War II European artists, unsure of their direction, had tended to follow the lead of New York. But by the late 1960s, the new generation that included such artists as the German Anselm Kiefer (b. 1945) and the Italian Sandro Chia (KEE-ah) (b. 1946) sought to confront the recent past—and thus the meaning of a tradition that now included fascism, total war, and the Holocaust. What did it mean to be German, Italian, or even European in light of this difficult past and the globalizing present and future? Wrestling with the interface of recent history and national identity, Kiefer and Chia conveyed the paradox and ambiguity that many felt as the rapidly changing West encountered the layers of its own cultural tradition.

The ongoing effort to come to terms with the recent past produced controversy and sometimes seemed to open old wounds, as earlier fascist or communist sympathies came under scrutiny. In Italy and France questions about collaboration and resistance during World War II produced periodic waves of bitterness. Even how to remember and commemorate the Holocaust produced much dispute, although Berlin's Holocaust memorial, opened in 2005, was one prominent indication of the widespread agreement that some such remembrance and commemoration was essential.

Kiefer: Osiris and Isis

The German artist Anselm Kiefer combined unusual materials to create haunting images that often suggested the horrors of recent history. In this work, dated 1985–1987, the interpenetrating layers of human culture include images of ruin and death, hope and resurrection. *(Anselm Kiefer,* Osiris und Isis, *1985–1987. Mixed media on canvas, 150" × 220½" × 6½". San Francisco Museum of Modern Art. Purchased through a gift of Jean Stein by exchange, the Mrs. Paul L. Wattis Fund, and the Doris and Don Fisher Fund. Photo: Ben Blackwell)*

COMMON VALUES AND THE PARADOX OF PLURALISM

The West was surely more willing than some of the non-Western world to embrace the messy, inconclusive openness, the ongoing give-and-take, associated with freedom of speech and freedom of religion. But did Western approaches enjoy some universal sanction, or was Western pluralism—including the right to religious freedom, even the right to ridicule someone else's religion—itself merely one value in a wider global pluralism?

Some observers noted that democracy rested on such rights, with the scope for diversity and the implication of tolerance that they implied. But arguably that notion was relevant only to the rules *within* democratic, pluralistic societies. It was surely symptomatic that the Netherlands and Denmark, as prominent examples of such societies, took extraordinary steps to establish that membership in their democratic societies required acceptance of precisely the messy, inconclusive openness that some outside the West found objectionable. But what expectations and even rules were required for a genuinely democratic society was only "half" the question. Was the West to take a further step and say to non-Western countries that Western-style pluralism was the ultimate value? Was Western democracy, revolving around "human rights," the one-size-fits-all model for the world, even to be imposed by force under certain circumstances?

To be sure, the UN convention on human rights was at least nominally accepted around the world. And non-Western figures from Mohandas Gandhi to Nelson

Postmodern Architecture

Three building complexes, one by an Italian working in Japan, another by an American working in Germany, and a third by a Spaniard working in Spain: they look dramatically different, yet they were built at roughly the same time. Do they have anything in common? In fact, each was rejecting earlier "modern" architecture, and each expressed what came to be known as "postmodernism" by the last two decades of the twentieth century.

Modernism in architecture, design, and urban planning had emerged especially during the 1920s from sources like the German Bauhaus, which turned resolutely from tradition to embrace the modern industrial age (see page 832). During the first two decades after World War II, this modernist approach triumphed at last, transforming cities throughout the world. Now known as "the international style," it reflected the wider self-understanding of the modern world, centered in the West. "Modern" meant rationality and efficiency, clarity and regularity, machine precision and mass culture. Ornament, decoration, symbolism, and historical reference had little or no place.

At issue, in fact, was not just a particular style of building but a new relationship with history. As modern, we seemed to be living on the cutting edge of history, in the eternal present, endlessly being cut off from our past. Henry Ford, widely taken as the personification of modernity in his time, put the matter directly: "History is bunk."

But by the 1960s, a reaction began to develop in architecture and urban planning, reflecting deeper thinking about history, about what it meant to be modern, and about the contemporary relationship with cultural traditions, including older buildings. In 1977 the architectural critic Charles Jencks, in his book *The Language of Post-Modern Architecture,* used the term "post-modernism" to characterize what now seemed to be a new movement or direction.

The earlier notion of modernity was coming to seem dubious in an emerging world of global interchange and plural perspectives. Memory, history, and the presence of the past were more, not less, important as accelerating technological change made possible instant communication and constant access to information across the globe. Yet there was sometimes irony, uncertainty, or paradox in the coexistence of old and new.

Postmodernist architects did not merely reject the earlier modernism, and certainly their aim was

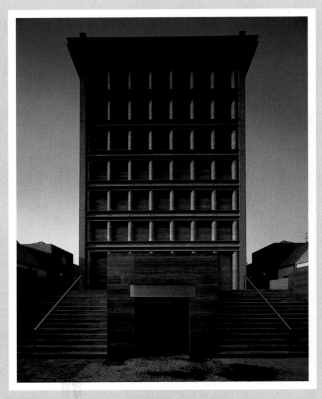

Aldo Rossi: Il Palazzo Hotel, Fukuoka, Japan
(Courtesy, Nacasa & Partners, Inc.)

not simply to revive previous styles such as classical or Gothic, though elements of them, as embodiments of our living history, might be incorporated in postmodern buildings. For example, look at the photo above of the Palazzo Hotel, designed by the Italian Aldo Rossi (1931–1997). Set in a Japanese city, the hotel clearly recalls Italian buildings, even those of the fascist period, themselves ambiguously modern, with references to the classical tradition and especially ancient Rome. For the façade, constructed of red marble and brick crossed with green steel moldings, Rossi combined contrasting materials, uncertain scale, and historical reference in a striking, even uncanny way.

Moreover, postmodernist architects were just as committed to modern techniques and materials as the modernists. They reacted, however, against the modernist pretense of a single right way, the rejection of ornament and history, and the reduction of architecture to function and the logic of machines. Postmodernists did not simply accept but actively celebrated messiness, variety, mixture, and complexity. The American Frank Gehry (b. 1929) suggested impermanence as well as postmodern pluralism in

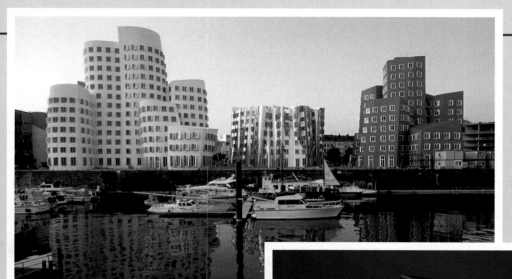

Frank Gehry: Der Neue Zollhof
(The New Customs House),
Düsseldorf, Germany
(*Thomas Mayer, photographer*)

Santiago Calatrava: City of Arts
and Sciences, Valencia, Spain
(Barbara Burg and Oliver Schuh, Palladium
Photodesign, Cologne, Germany)

his complex of three office buildings in Düsseldorf, Germany (above left). Notice how the project incorporates modernist elements—flat roofs, identical prefabricated windows—but provides remarkable variety and contrast by cladding one of the units in red brick, one in mirror-polished stainless steel, and the third in white plaster. At the same time, the uniform, angled windows contrast with the curved surfaces. None of the three is the right way; rather, they play evocatively against one another.

Santiago Calatrava (b. 1951) drew on an even wider frame of reference to create shapes that were never before part of our built environment. Calatrava used highly sculptured forms for the building shown here (above right)—the centerpiece of a science museum complex built in the bed of a diverted river in his native Valencia, Spain. Taking advantage of his engineering background, he created unexpected spaces and sculptural surfaces that went beyond tradition altogether. With structures suggesting bones and tendons, he conveyed the dynamics of movement, of folding, opening, and closing—even the opening and closing of an eye.

Dramatically different though they appear, these three architectural statements share the wider postmodern framework. Rossi invokes the past to resist change; Gehry plays with the past, even the recent modernist past, while suggesting impermanence; Calatrava transcends the present outcome of the past, but without the limitations, the particular discipline, that modernism imposed. Rather than submit to the logic of the machine, he felt free to experiment more boldly, devising radically new forms. Each of the three architects represents a strand in the wider, complex, and contradictory postmodernist approach to history and tradition, including the tradition of modernism itself.

QUESTIONS

1. In what sense are the buildings we see here recognizably *post*-modern, in the sense of consciously rejecting earlier modernist tenets?

2. How do Rossi, Gehry, and Calatrava differ in their approach to change and history?

Online Study Center
Improve Your Grade Visual Record Activities

Mandela were widely admired in the West, precisely as spokesmen for what seemed universal human values. But the UN human rights convention was engineered by the dominant powers under the very particular circumstances surrounding the end of World War II. Were freedom of speech, freedom of religion, and equality for women to be understood as genuinely universal "human rights," even if parts of the world had difficulty grasping them? Or was there a place for genuine cultural diversity on the global level, including, for example, the differential handling of gender relations and religious freedom?

Although they were contested even then, these issues seemed less troubling to the Western world a century before. The West set the standard, and spearheading "Westernization" even seemed a moral duty. But the events of the tumultuous century that followed shook the West's self-confidence. Reflecting on what seemed the special European or Western path "from Athens to Auschwitz," the noted German classicist Christian Meier insisted that the Holocaust marked the end of the notion that European civilization had a special role to play, even that Europe could understand itself in terms of a continuous and unified history.[4]

Yet even if the West had long since abandoned "the white man's burden" in its late nineteenth century forms, it was hardly prepared to embrace the mode of multiculturalism that meant a thoroughgoing cultural relativism, the notion that you have your practices and I have mine, that we live and let live and learn to appreciate and even celebrate the differences. On the contrary, the West held to the notion that ideals and institutions most fully developed in the West—democracy, human rights, notions of equality—are not only relevant for the West but somehow of universal value. The West still claimed to have a privileged template that enabled it to assess the practices—and the progress—of everybody else.

The question was where lines were to be drawn. Westerners of goodwill differed, for example, over the Muslim headscarf issue in France. Most defenders of the right to wear the headscarf in public schools were not claiming to discern some hidden wisdom in the traditional Islamic handling of gender; rather, they were insisting on the right to individual self-expression. The choice of women to wear the headscarf deserved respect—as, say, the disproportionate abortion of female fetuses in India did not. Pluralism and the embrace of diversity had their limits, even if there was disagreement over where lines should be drawn.

Arguably what distinguished the West at that point was precisely the growing recognition that some measure of such disagreement was inevitable, legitimate, and even healthy. During the first decade of the twenty-first century, the West was wrestling with matters of humanity and diversity, human rights and national sovereignty, as never before. Whereas "the West" had always been a continuing experiment, that experiment would now continue in a more self-conscious way.

WESTERN CIVILIZATION IN A POSTMODERN WORLD

By the end of the twentieth century, bitter debate had raged in the West for two decades and more over the legitimacy of "Western civilization" as a concept. Some critics highlighted the geographical imprecision of "the West" and claimed that the words *Western* and *civilization* had been juxtaposed simply to justify conquest and domination. Even among those who recognized a distinctive Western cultural tradition, some found it elitist and limiting. In their view, Western culture had defined itself around a group of artifacts—writings, paintings, monuments—that reflected the experience of a very restricted circle.

Others countered that imperialism and assumptions of superiority had not been confined to the West. Moreover, they continued, the West had been the source of ideas—the "rights of man," the scope for eliminating exploitation—that were now being eagerly embraced in the non-Western world. Even the charges of cultural elitism directed against the Western tradition stemmed from a democratic impulse that had itself grown from within that Western tradition. And by the last decades of the twentieth century, that impulse had prompted historians to focus on ordinary people and a far wider circle of cultural interpreters, thereby dramatically expanding the "canon"—the body of works considered worthy of our attention.

Questions about the Western tradition and its contemporary relevance were bound up with the advent of *postmodernism*, a term widely used by the early 1990s for a cultural orientation that had been gathering force for decades. (See the feature "The Visual Record: Postmodern Architecture.") Postmodernism reflected a certain conception of what *modernism* had meant, even a sense that modernism had defined an era that was ending. But what was ending—and how it was bound up with the debate over Western civilization—was not so clear.

Postmodernism emerged partly as confidence in the scope for a neutral, objective social science began to decline during the 1960s. That confidence had reflected the belief in reason that had emerged from the Scientific Revolution and the Enlightenment. Reason had seemed universal, not limited to any particular culture, and it was assumed to be applicable to the human as well as the natural world.

To apply reason seemed "modern," and the West, apparently having progressed by applying reason, had long understood itself to be in the forefront of modernity. Everyone else was scrambling to catch up through the universal process of modernization. Such was the

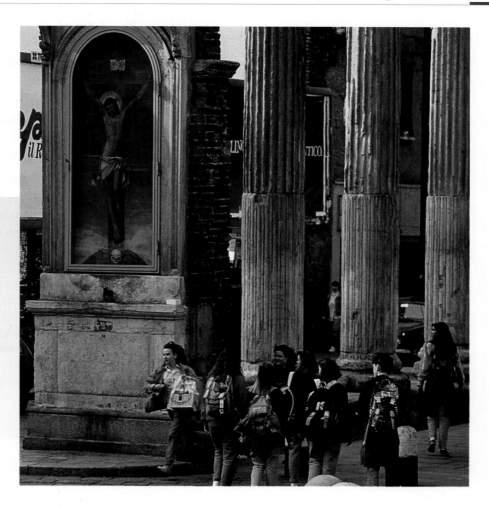

Old and New in Contemporary Europe
Especially with the transformation of Europe since World War II, new styles intersect with living artifacts from the past to form sometimes ironic combinations. Here, in a neighborhood in Milan, Italy, teenagers wearing blue jeans and backpacks seem oblivious to the legacies of Roman antiquity and Christianity that are prominent around them. *(© 1999, George Steinmetz)*

"master narrative" through which the West had understood its place in the world during the modern era.

But even as globalization proceeded during the late twentieth century, Western thinkers retreated from this long-standing master narrative. There was no question that capitalism had spread from Europe, but the West was not necessarily the model, the standard of development. Thus the growing interest in the non-Western world, the increasing respect for its diverse traditions, that came to mark Western culture by the last decades of the twentieth century.

Postmodernists questioned claims of certainty, objective truth, and intrinsic meaning in language, in works of art, and ultimately in all cultural expressions. Some held that such claims were assertions of privilege in what was essentially a political struggle for power—the power to set the wider social agenda. Especially in the United States, the postmodernist reaction led by the 1980s to the vogue of the French philosopher and historian Michel Foucault (foo-KOH) (1926–1984), who had sought to show that the power to specify what counts as knowledge was the key to social or political power. Since, from this perspective, all knowledge was suspect, Foucault's accents invited mistrust and disruption.

At the same time, however, an array of equally innovative thinkers, from the German Jürgen Habermas (b. 1929) to the American Richard Rorty (b. 1931), sought a more constructive orientation based on a renewed, no longer arrogant understanding of Western traditions, including the place of reason and democracy.

For those embracing this more constructive approach, the point was not to celebrate Western civilization but simply to understand it—as the framework that continued to shape the West and, less directly, the world. That tradition included much that might be criticized, and its present outcome entailed much that might be changed. Habermas, in particular, was a persistent and often radical critic of what he saw as the disparity between Western democratic ideals and contemporary social and political practices. But effective criticism had to rest on free inquiry and rational understanding, as opposed to prejudice or wishful thinking. The invitation to think freely about the Western tradition, to criticize and change it, rested on precisely that tradition; indeed, the scope for such criticism and change had been central to the Western belief in reason. That openness remained perhaps the West's most fundamental legacy.

S E C T I O N   S U M M A R Y

- Cultural differences between Europeans and Americans, as reflected, for example, in attitudes toward religion or the role of government, seemed to be deepening by the early twenty-first century.

- Even as encounters with the Muslim world, especially, brought home the distinctiveness of Western traditions, there was disagreement over the degree of multicultural pluralism that was healthy in a democratic society.

- Although the existence of universal human values was widely accepted in principle, it was not always clear how such values meshed with cultural pluralism and diversity on the global level.

- The advent of postmodernism suggested the end of the "modern" period, partly defined by the assumption that the West was in the forefront, playing a privileged role in world development.

- Even as the very legitimacy of "Western civilization" was debated in the West, intellectual leaders sought to show how Western notions of reason and democracy could be given renewed relevance.

CHAPTER SUMMARY

Online Study Center **ACE the Test**

Why and how did the relationship between western Europe and the United States change after the end of the cold war?

What forces raised new questions about the effectiveness of Western-style democracy by the early years of the twenty-first century?

How did the changes bound up with globalization affect identities in the West?

What questions emerged as the West faced new crises all over the globe after the end of the cold war?

On what basis was the wider contemporary relevance of "Western civilization" being debated by the first decade of the twenty-first century?

With the end of the cold war, the United States and the nations of western Europe no longer faced a common communist adversary, so close collaboration seemed less pressing to both sides. Greater freedom for Europe to set its own course provided a further impetus to the expansion and deepening of the European Union. And whereas the West was mostly united in response to increasing terrorism, Western nations split over the wisdom of the U.S.-led invasion of Iraq, which, to many Europeans, seemed to indicate an unwelcome unilateralism on the part of the United States.

Although democracy was the unquestioned norm, especially with the decline of the traditional left, a variety of changes posed new challenges for governments and the political order more generally. In light of aging populations and increasing global competition, western European countries found it ever harder to pay for the benefits promised as part of the postwar social compact.

Yet effort at reform provoked protests that led governments to back down. Adding to political volatility was growing concern over the assimilation of immigrants.

Increasing economic globalization expanded horizons but also affected the self-understanding of individuals in complex ways. Skeptical Europeans often equated globalization with Americanization and promoted various measures to preserve distinctiveness. However, people disagreed over whether what was to be preserved was "European," national, or local. Ways of understanding class, gender, and the place of religion also changed, though in some countries more than others.

An array of challenges, from new diseases to genocidal aggression, called for coordinated multinational responses. Although the UN played more visible roles after the cold war, it was an unwieldy organization whose effectiveness was sometimes limited. Even its specialized entities, such as the World Health Organization, sometimes lacked the resources and the clout to coordinate multinational responses to new problems. In dealing with politically inspired humanitarian crises in the non-Western world, the West found it difficult to develop a consistent and workable policy of intervention.

Changing relationships between the West and the non-Western world prompted new questions about the meaning and ongoing relevance of "Western civilization" as a concept. Some suggested that the whole "modern" conception of history, which had assumed a privileged leadership role for the West, had fallen away. But wider cultural encounters helped bring home the centrality of Western notions of openness and pluralism.

KEY TERMS

Online Study Center **Improve Your Grade** Flashcards

G-8 (Group of 8) (p. 947)

European Union (EU) (p. 949)

Maastricht agreements (p. 949)

euro (p. 949)

Common Agricultural Policy (CAP) (p. 950)

ethnic cleansing (p. 953)

unilateralism (p. 956)

Vladimir Putin (p. 959)

social market economy (p. 960)

World Health Organization (WHO) (p. 960)

information technology (p. 960)

World Trade Organization (WTO) (p. 966)

digital divide (p. 972)

nongovernmental organizations (NGOs) (p. 974)

SUGGESTED READING

Brubaker, Rogers. *Citizenship and Nationhood in France and Germany.* 1992. A lucid comparative study showing how very different conceptions of citizenship emerged in these two countries as a result of their contrasting historical experiences over the past two centuries.

Calleo, David P. *Rethinking Europe's Future.* 2001. Against a carefully drawn historical backdrop, this important work pinpoints the key issues in the evolving partnership between Europe and the United States and stresses the potential for a greater European contribution to world affairs.

Cohen, Daniel. *Globalization and Its Enemies.* 2006. A French writer's brief but probing and original analysis of the West's complex relations with the non-Western world in an age of globalization.

Fehrenbach, Heide, and Uta G. Poigner, eds. *Transactions, Transgressions, Transformations: American Culture in Western Europe and Japan.* 2000. A superior collection of essays reassessing the United States's cultural impact on Europe and Japan. Several of the essays treat film or popular music, while others are more comparative or synthetic in approach.

Garton Ash, Timothy. *Free World: America, Europe, and the Surprising Future of the West.* 2004. In the face of Western self-doubt, features the scope for the West to offer renewed global leadership, with Britain positioned to point the way by mediating between continental Europe and the United States.

Jack, Andrew. *Inside Putin's Russia.* 2004. While offering a balanced assessment of Putin's priorities and style of governance, questions whether Russia can have economic reform without more genuine democracy.

Judt, Tony. *Postwar: A History of Europe Since 1945.* 2005. A masterly and comprehensive survey by a leading expert on the period.

Lebovics, Herman. *Bringing the Empire Back Home: France in the Global Age.* Features the interplay of France's capital city, its provinces, and its former colonies in the ongoing consideration of what it means to be French in a changing European and global context.

McCormick, John. *Understanding the European Union: A Concise Introduction.* 1999. A clear introduction to the history, structure, and functioning of the central institutions of the EU.

Shawcross, William. *Deliver Us from Evil: Peacekeepers, Warlords, and a World of Endless Conflict.* 2000. Accents the limits and contradictions of the Western response to crises in areas lacking an indigenous political class.

NOTES

1. William Pfaff, "What's Left of the Union?" *New York Review of Books,* July 14, 2005, p. 27.

2. Jane Kramer, "The Dutch Model: Multiculturalism and Muslim Immigrants," *The New Yorker,* April 3, 2006, p. 67.

3. Quoted in *The Economist,* April 5, 2003, p. 59.

4. Christian Meier, *From Athens to Auschwitz: The Uses of History* (Cambridge, Mass.: Harvard University Press, 2005), pp. 170, 173.

GLOSSARY

This Glossary covers the complete text, Chapters 1 through 30.

absolutism   Extraordinary concentration of power in royal hands, achieved particularly by the kings of France, most notably **Louis XIV,** in the seventeenth century. Proponents argued that hereditary monarchy was the divinely ordained form of government. *(Ch. 16)*

Act of Supremacy (1534)   Act of the English Parliament during the Protestant Reformation that finalized the break with the Catholic Church by declaring the king to be head of the Church of England. Henry VIII required a public oath supporting the act, which Sir **Thomas More** refused to take; More was then executed for treason. *(Ch. 14)*

Adenauer, Konrad (1876–1967)   Leading statesman of post–World War II Germany. As chancellor (1949–1963), he oriented the country toward western Europe and the United States and proved to Germans that democracy could mean effective government, economic prosperity, and foreign policy success. *(Ch. 29)*

agricultural revolution   Dramatic increase in food production from the sixteenth to eighteenth centuries, brought about by changes in agricultural practices, cultivation of new crops, greater availability of animal manure, and introduction of the nutrient-rich potato from the Americas. *(Ch. 18)*

Alexander the Great (356–323 B.C.)   King of **Macedon** (r. 336–323) and conqueror of the **Persian Empire.** Son of **Philip II** of Macedon, Alexander was an ingenious warrior who, in the course of his conquests, spread Greek civilization to western Asia, Egypt, and India. His despotism and ruler-worship set a precedent for later monarchs, including many Roman emperors. *(Ch. 4)*

Alexandria   Mediterranean seaport in northern Egypt founded by **Alexander the Great** in 332 B.C. It was a thriving Hellenistic city with great harbors, marketplaces, banks, inns, courts, shipbuilding facilities, and a renowned library. *(Ch. 4)*

Amarna reform   Term for the ancient Egyptian king Amenhotep IV's seizure of power from temple priests by replacing the god Amun-Re with Aten and renaming himself Akhenaten. After Akhenaten's death, the Amun-Re cult regained power. *(Ch. 1)*

Anabaptists   Radical religious reformers in Germany and Switzerland during the Reformation. They rejected the practice of infant baptism, believing that baptism should occur only after confession of sin. They also believed that Christians should live apart in communities of the truly redeemed. Mennonites and Hutterites are their modern descendants. *(Ch. 14)*

Antigonids   Dynasty of Macedonian rulers founded in 276 B.C. by Antigonus Gonatas, grandson of Antigonus the One-Eyed, a general of **Alexander the Great.** The Antigonid dynasty lasted about 140 years, until the Roman conquest. *(Ch. 4)*

Antioch   Greatest of the cities founded by Seleucus, a general of **Alexander the Great.** Located near the present-day Turkish-Syrian border, it became one of the wealthiest and most luxurious of all eastern Mediterranean cities. *(Ch. 4)*

anti-Semitism   Centuries-old prejudice against and demonization of Jews. Anti-Semitism became virulent in Europe in the 1880s with the emergence of the ultranationalist and racist "new right" ideologies and political movements. An essential part of the Nazi worldview, it led to the Holocaust. *(Ch. 24)*

appeasement   The term for the policy employed by Britain's prime minister, Neville Chamberlain, to defuse the 1938 crisis with Germany's **Adolf Hitler.** Chamberlain acquiesced to Hitler's demands to annex the Sudetenland portion of Czechoslovakia, which proved a giant step toward the war that broke out less than a year later. *(Ch. 27)*

Aquinas, Thomas (1225–1274)   Dominican friar and theologian. In his two most famous works, *Summa Contra Gentiles* and *Summa Theologiae,* he distinguished between natural truth, or what a person could know by reasoning, and revealed truths, which can be known only through faith in God's revelation. No one before him had so rigorously followed the dialectical method of reasoning through a whole field of knowledge. *(Ch. 10)*

Archaic Greece   Period of ancient Greek history from around 700 to 500 B.C. Archaic Greece was characterized by artistic achievement, increased individualism amid communal solidarity, and a moving away from divine and toward abstract, mechanistic explanations. The Western philosophical tradition began during this period. *(Ch. 3)*

Arianism   Popular heresy advocated by the priest Arius (ca. 250–336), emphasizing that Jesus was the "first born of all creation." It sought to preserve and purify Christianity's monotheism by making Jesus slightly subordinate to the Father. It was condemned by the **Council of Nicaea.** *(Ch. 7)*

Aristotle (384–322 B.C.)   Ancient Greek philosopher, student of **Plato** and tutor of **Alexander the Great.** Aristotle emphasized the goal (*telos* in Greek) of change; in his view the entire cosmos is teleological, and every one of its parts has an essential purpose. Aristotle's scientific writings were the most influential philosophical classics of Greek and Roman civilization and remained so during the Middle Ages. *(Ch. 3)*

Armada (1588)   Massive fleet of Spanish warships sent against England by **Philip II** but defeated by the English navy and bad weather. The tactics used by the English helped set the future course of naval warfare. *(Ch. 15)*

Assyrians   Warlike people who ruled the ancient Near East during the first millennium B.C. Their innovations included using cavalry as their main striking force and having weapons and armor made of iron. *(Ch. 2)*

Augsburg Confession (1532)   Document written by Philipp Melanchthon (1497–1560), with the approval of **Martin Luther,** that became the most widely accepted statement of the Lutheran faith. It constitutes part of the creedal basis for today's Lutheran churches. *(Ch. 14)*

Augustine (354–430)   North African bishop and one of the most influential Christian thinkers. Augustine wrote that all people were sinners in need of God's redemption, that history is the struggle between those who call on divine grace and those who sin, and that learning was useful only to the extent that it equipped individuals to read and understand the Bible's message of salvation. *(Ch. 7)*

Augustus (63 B.C.–A.D. 14)   Honorific title of Gaius Julius Caesar Octavianus, grandnephew of **Julius Caesar** and first Roman emperor. After defeating Mark Antony and Cleopatra at the Battle of Actium (31 B.C.), Augustus ruled the empire for forty-five years. His rule laid the foundations of two hundred years of prosperous Roman peace. See also **Principate.** *(Ch. 6)*

Auschwitz-Birkenau   The largest and principal extermination center of Nazi Germany's six death camps, all of which were located in what had been Poland. The Nazis shipped Jews from all over Europe to Auschwitz, which killed about twelve thousand people a day at the height of its operation in 1944. *(Ch. 28)*

avant-garde   French for "forefront," the term refers to early-twentieth-century artists who, inspired by novel or unconventional techniques, considered themselves precursors of new styles. Avant-garde movements proclaimed idiosyncratic manifestos and constantly called for the rejection of existing forms of expression and the creation of new ones. *(Ch. 24)*

Aztecs   Amerindian people that dominated central Mexico from the fourteenth through the sixteenth centuries from their capital Tenochtitlán (present-day Mexico City). Weakened by exposure to virulent Old World diseases, they were conquered in 1521–1523 by Spanish forces led by **Hernán Cortés.** *(Ch. 13)*

Babylonian Captivity of the Papacy   Term used to describe the period from 1309 to 1378 when popes resided north of the Alps rather than in central Italy or Rome, where the pope was the bishop. The term refers to the period when the tribes of Israel lived in exile. *(Ch. 11)*

Bacon, Francis (1561–1626)   England's lord chancellor during the reign of James I and author of a utopian essay extolling science's benefits for a peaceful society and human happiness. His influential works encouraged the empirical method and inductive reasoning. See also **empirical method.** *(Ch. 17)*

baroque   Style of European art and architecture popular from the late sixteenth to early eighteenth century. Baroque artists, such as Peter Paul Rubens, modified Renaissance techniques, adding dynamism and emotional energy. Baroque painting used light to portray dramatic illusion, and baroque churches were both impressively grand and emotionally engaging. *(Ch. 15)*

Bauhaus   An influential German art school, founded in 1919, that sought to adopt contemporary materials to develop new forms of architecture, design, and urban planning in response to the cultural uncertainty that followed World War I. Though it arguably failed in its immediate German context, the Bauhaus helped shape the whole idea of "the modern" in the West and throughout the world for decades to come. *(Ch. 26)*

Bernard of Clairvaux (1090–1153)   Monk, church reformer, and influential adviser to kings and popes. Bernard believed that faith and divine inspiration were more important than dialectical reasoning. He was instrumental in the success of the Cistercian religious order. *(Ch. 10)*

Bismarck, Otto von (1815–1898)   Nineteenth-century German statesman. A Prussian aristocrat, Bismarck was the autocratic architect who, through a series of aggressive wars, united Germany and served as the nation's first chancellor. He administered an emperor-controlled country that became the dominant power in Europe. See also ***Realpolitik.*** *(Ch. 22)*

Black Death (1348–1351)   First of a series of epidemics, possibly bubonic plague, that raged in Europe and western Asia for three centuries. The Black Death killed about 60 percent of those infected. The huge population decline fueled the economic and social transformations of the late Middle Ages. *(Ch. 11)*

Bolsheviks   Members of a faction of the Russian Socialist Democratic Party led by **Vladimir Ilyich Lenin** (1870–1924), a zealous Marxist who insisted that a revolutionary cadre could seize power on behalf of the working class. The Bolsheviks gained control of Russia in November 1917. *(Ch. 24)*

Bonaparte, Napoleon.   See **Napoleon Bonaparte.**

bourgeois century   Characterization of the nineteenth century, especially the latter half. In western Europe, the bourgeois elites (middle classes), which had expanded dramatically in the wake of industrialization, helped fashion much of society. *(Ch. 23)*

Brandenburg-Prussia   Group of German territories, ruled by the Hohenzollern family, that became one of Europe's most powerful states in the seventeenth century. Its military strength was supported by its hereditary landowners, who were granted autonomy in their territories. *(Ch. 16)*

Brandt, Willy (1913–1992)   Socialist West German chancellor (r. 1969–1974). Brandt's widely popular policy of opening to the East, or *Ostpolitik,* made possible closer economic ties between West and East Germany and broader opportunities for ordinary citizens to interact across the east-west border. *(Ch. 29)*

Brest-Litovsk, Treaty of (1918)   Treaty in which Russia accepted its defeat by Germany and its allies in World War I. The treaty forced the Russians to cede much of European Russia to Germany. After Germany's defeat by the Allies later in the year, the **Bolsheviks** recaptured Ukraine and the Caucasus region. *(Ch. 25)*

British blockade Britain's naval blockade of Germany during World War I. By means of this tactic, which cut off supplies to Germany but which also violated several provisions of international law, the British seriously impeded the German war effort. *(Ch. 25)*

Caesar, Gaius Julius (63 B.C.– A.D. 14) Roman general gifted at war and politics. Named dictator in 49 B.C., he was assassinated by the members of the **senate** in 44 B.C. He introduced to Europe the calendar of 365¼ days. He was succeeded as ruler by his grandnephew Octavian (**Augustus**). Later Roman emperors were also called *caesar*. *(Ch. 5)*

caliphate Arab empire established by the successors of **Muhammad;** *caliph* means "successor to the prophet." The Umayyad caliphate, with its capital in Damascus, ruled from 661 to 750; the Abbasid caliphate, based in Baghdad, from 750 to 1258. *(Ch. 8)*

Calvin, John (1509–1564) Franco-Swiss theologian and founder of the Reformed Church in Geneva. Calvin's theological writings, most notably *Institutes of the Christian Religion* (1536), were widely disseminated and hugely influential. Calvin stressed the absolute power of God and the need for moral reform of the Christian community. *(Ch. 14)*

canon law Collection of orderly rules for the government of the Catholic Church, based on papal decrees and decisions of church councils. In 1140 the monk Gratian published the *Decretum,* the first systematic collection of canon law. *(Ch. 10)*

Carlowitz, Treaty of (1699) Treaty imposed by the European allies on a weakening Ottoman Empire. The Habsburgs, Venetians, Russians, and Poles gained territory and power at the Turks' expense. *(Ch. 16)*

Carolingian Renaissance Major revival of learning, combined with reform of religious and political institutions, that occurred under **Charlemagne** and his successors. The revival encompassed the founding of schools in religious institutions, production of textbooks, dissemination of early church teachings and of **canon law,** as well as secular reforms such as regularization of royal estates. *(Ch. 8)*

Catherine the Great (r. 1762–1796) Empress of Russia. Through an astute policy of wars and alliances, Catherine expanded her country's borders south to the Black Sea and west into Europe. An "enlightened despot," she advanced the Westernizing reforms begun by **Peter the Great.** *(Ch. 18)*

Cato the Censor (234–149 B.C.) Marcus Porcius Cato, Roman general and statesman. Known as Cato the Censor because he denounced luxury goods, he was the first Roman historian to write in Latin. *(Ch. 5)*

Charlemagne (r. 768–814) Frankish king, crowned emperor in 800. He carried out a program of legal and ecclesiastical reform, patronized learning, and revitalized the western Roman Empire. See also **Carolingian Renaissance.** *(Ch. 8)*

Charles V (r. 1519–1558) Holy Roman emperor and, as Charles I, king of Spain. His empire included Spain, Italy, the Low Countries, and Germany. Though he vigorously opposed the spread of Protestantism during the Reformation, he was forced to sign the Religious Peace of Augsburg in 1555, which acknowledged the right of German princes to choose the religion to be practiced in their territories, Lutheran or Catholic. Charles abdicated his imperial and royal titles the next year, ceding the empire to his brother Ferdinand and his Spanish possessions to his son **Philip II.** *(Ch. 14)*

Chartism Nineteenth-century British political movement whose goal was to transform Britain from an oligarchy to a democracy. The Chartists' demands were contained in the 1838 "people's charter," which called for universal male suffrage, electoral districts with equal population, salaries and the abolition of property qualifications for Members of Parliament, the secret ballot, and annual general elections. The movement failed, but most of its measures eventually became law. See also **Second Reform Bill.** *(Ch. 21)*

chivalry Initially, a medieval code of conduct for mounted warriors, focusing on military prowess, open-handed generosity, and earning a glorious reputation. Later it evolved into an elaborate set of rules governing relations between men and women. *(Ch. 10)*

Christianity Sect originally rooted in Judaism that emerged as a fully separate religion by around A.D. 200. Emphasizing belief in one God and the mission of his son, **Jesus of Nazareth,** as savior, Christianity offered salvation in the next world and a caring community in the present one. A messianic religion, Christianity emphasized Christ's return, leading to the beginning of a heavenly kingdom on earth. *(Ch. 6)*

Churchill, Winston (1874–1965) British prime minister (1940–1945; 1951–1955). As the leader of his country during World War II, Churchill's courage, decisiveness, memorable words, and boundless energy made him widely seen as one of Britain's greatest leaders of the twentieth century. See also **Yalta conference.** *(Ch. 28)*

Cicero, Marcus Tullius (106–43 B.C.) Philosopher, writer, and statesman who was Rome's greatest orator. He was crucial in making the Latin language a vessel for the heritage of Greek thought. *(Ch. 5)*

city-state State consisting of an independent city and the surrounding territory under its control. Early examples were the Sumerian city-states in the third millennium B.C. *(Ch. 1)*

civic humanism An ideology, championed by Florentine writers and public officials during the Renaissance, that emphasized their city's classical republican virtues and history. They argued that a moral and ethical value was intrinsic to public life. *(Ch. 12)*

Civil Code Law code established under Napoleon in 1804 that included limited acceptance of revolutionary gains, such as a guarantee of equality before the law and taxation of all social classes. Also known as the Napoleonic Code, it enshrined modern forms of property ownership and civil contracts, enhanced paternal control of families, outlawed divorce in most circumstances, and placed women under the legal domination of fathers and husbands. *(Ch. 19)*

Classical Greece   Period of ancient Greek history from about 480 to 323 B.C. Classical Greek culture emphasized public life as the central theme of art and literature, and its sculpture was the most anatomically precise yet. Classical Greece set many standards for modern Western culture. See also **demokratia.** *(Ch. 3)*

Cluny (Cluniacs)   A spiritual reform begun in 910 in central France. The movement emphasized strict adherence to the Benedictine Rule, as well as the ideas that the church should pray for the world without being deeply involved in it and must be free from lay control. *(Ch. 10)*

cold war   The hostile standoff between the Soviet Union and the United States that began after World War II, when communist governments, relying on Soviet support, took control of most of east-central Europe. The Soviets' first atomic bomb explosion in 1949 intensified the conflict, which shaped world affairs for the next forty years. *(Ch. 28)*

collectivization   The program that reshaped agriculture in the Soviet Union under **Joseph Stalin** during the early 1930s. By forcing peasants into government-controlled collective farms, the Soviet regime sought to take control of agricultural production in order better to finance rapid industrialization. *(Ch. 27)*

Columbian Exchange   Historians' term for the blending of cultures between the Old World and the New after Christopher Columbus's arrival in the New World in 1492. The Spanish and other Europeans brought their plants, domesticated animals, and diseases to the Americas. The Americas contributed New World crops, most notably maize (corn) and potatoes, transforming the Old World diet. *(Ch. 13)*

Comintern (Third, or Communist, International)   An association founded in March 1919 by the Communists (formerly **Bolsheviks**) to translate their success in Russia into leadership of the international socialist movement. Its program of tight organization and discipline under Russian leadership produced a schism between communists and socialists in Europe and throughout the world. *(Ch. 26)*

Common Agricultural Policy (CAP)   A major pillar of the **European Union,** accounting for half of its budget by 2000, the Common Agricultural Policy entailed subsidies to protect farmers from outside competition. The CAP was widely criticized by advocates of freer world trade. *(Ch. 30)*

communes   Form of government in Italian towns that rose in the eleventh century. Despite numerous local variations, communes involved common decision making by local notables, including both landed aristocrats and wealthy merchants or industrialists. *(Ch. 9)*

Compromise of 1867   Agreement that divided the Habsburg empire into Austria in the west and Hungary in the east, a dual monarchy under Emperor Franz Joseph called Austria-Hungary. The compromise confirmed Magyar dominance in Hungary. *(Ch. 22)*

conciliarists   These people argued that the pope was not a universal monarch, but rather the first among equals in the church. Thus, church councils had the right and duty to reform and correct even the pope. *(Ch. 11)*

congress system   System of European international relations in the first half of the nineteenth century in which the major European states cooperated to preserve the balance of power. This system disappeared as political leaders increasingly used force to pursue their narrow interests. *(Ch. 22)*

Congress of Vienna (1814–1815)   Conference called by the victorious powers—Austria, Great Britain, Prussia, and Russia—who defeated Napoleon. Guided by the Austrian foreign minister, Prince Metternich, the Great Powers drew new territorial boundaries advantageous to themselves. They also attempted to provide long-term stability on the European continent and restored some of the rulers who had been overthrown. See also **congress system.** *(Ch. 21)*

conservatism   Ideology underlying the order established in Europe in 1815. Conservatives emphasized resistance to change and preservation of the existing order of monarchy, aristocracy, and an established church. *(Ch. 21)*

Copernicus, Nicholas (1473–1543)   Polish astronomer who initiated the Scientific Revolution by proposing that the earth and other planets orbit the sun, a theory called the heliocentric, or sun-centered, system. See also **helio-centric theory.** *(Ch. 17)*

corporativism, corporative state   The system established in fascist Italy beginning in 1926 that sought to involve people in public life not as citizens but as producers, through their roles in the economy. A system based on such occupational groupings eventually replaced parliament as the basis of political representation in fascist Italy. *(Ch. 26)*

Cortés, Hernán (1485–1546)   Spanish commander who conquered the **Aztecs** and claimed the Valley of Mexico for Spain. Cortés had only five hundred men but was aided by an outbreak of smallpox and the help of Amerindian peoples eager to end Aztec control. *(Ch. 13)*

Cossacks   Originally the term (from a Russian word meaning "free man" or "adventurer") for peoples of Tatar origin who inhabited the hinterland of the Black and Caspian Seas. Their numbers swelled, after 1500, by peasants who fled serfdom in Poland-Lithuania and the growing Russian state. The Cossacks helped to provide a military buffer between the Polish-Lithuanian and Russian states and the Ottomans to the south, and they resisted Polish domination in the seventeenth century, but slowly lost their autonomy to the expanding Russian state in the eighteenth century. *(Ch. 16)*

Council of Constance (1414–1418)   Assembly convened by Holy Roman Emperor Sigismund to heal deep religious and civil divisions. The council declared that its rulings were binding even on the pope. Its selection of Pope Martin V ended the **Great Schism.** *(Ch. 11)*

Council of the Indies   Body established by the king of Spain in 1524 to oversee Spain's colonial possessions. Located at court, eventually in Madrid, it supervised all legal, administrative, and commercial activity in the colonies until the early eighteenth century. *(Ch. 13)*

Council of Nicaea (325)   History's first ecumenical, or "all-church," council, convened by the emperor Constantine. The council condemned **Arianism** and proclaimed key elements of the Nicene Creed, especially the doctrine that Christ was "one in being with the Father," co-equal and co-eternal. (*Ch. 7*)

Council of Trent (1545–1563)   Ecumenical council of the Roman Catholic Church during the Reformation. Though rejecting many Protestant positions, the council reformed and reorganized the church partly in response to Protestant criticisms. Its decrees reaffirmed and defined the basic tenets of Roman Catholicism for the next four hundred years. (*Ch. 14*)

covenant   As told in the Hebrew Bible, the pact God made with Abraham, the first patriarch of Israel. In return for the land of Canaan and the promise of becoming a great nation, the Israelites agreed to worship no other gods. (*Ch. 2*)

Cromwell, Oliver (1599–1658)   English Puritan general and statesman. A military genius and leader in the English civil war, Cromwell governed as Lord Protector during the Interregnum from 1653 to 1658. (*Ch. 16*)

Crusades   A series of largely unsuccessful wars waged by western European Christians to recapture the Holy Land from the Muslims and ensure the safety of Christian pilgrims to Jerusalem. Later, the term came to designate any military effort by Europeans against non-Christians. (*Ch. 9*)

Crystal Night (*Kristallnacht*)   Organized Nazi assault on Jewish businesses and synagogues during the night of November 9–10, 1938, following the assassination of a German diplomat in Paris. Almost all the synagogues in Germany and about seven thousand Jewish-owned stores were destroyed. The broken shop windows gave the episode its name. Although the German public generally deplored this wanton destruction of property, the Crystal Night pogrom initiated a more radical phase of Nazi anti-Jewish policy. (*Ch. 27*)

cuneiform   First writing system in Mesopotamia, consisting of wedge-shaped impressions in soft clay. Named from the Latin word for "wedge-shaped," it was developed about 3500–3100 B.C. (*Ch. 1*)

Darwinism   Profoundly influential theory of biological evolution, first put forth by Charles Darwin (1809–1882). He proposed that all forms of life continuously develop through natural selection, whereby those that are better adapted to the environment have the advantage and are more likely to survive and pass on their beneficial traits to their offspring. (*Ch. 23*)

D-Day   The complex Allied amphibious landings in Normandy, France, on June 6, 1944, that opened a second major European front in World War II. In the aftermath of this invasion, American-led forces in the west began moving toward Germany, complementing the Soviet effort, which was already forcing the Germans back on the eastern front. (*Ch. 28*)

Decembrists   Group of Russian military officers who led the December 1825 rebellion after the death of Tsar Alexander I, seeking to install a constitutional monarchy with Alexander's eldest brother, Constantine, as tsar. They were defeated and executed by Constantine's younger brother, Nicholas. The Decembrists were seen as martyrs by later Russian revolutionaries. (*Ch. 21*)

Declaration of the Rights of Man and the Citizen (1789)   Document issued by the **National Assembly** of France in August 1789. Modeled on the U.S. Constitution, the declaration set forth the basis for the new French government and asserted "the natural, inalienable and sacred rights of man." (*Ch. 19*)

De Gaulle, Charles (1890–1970)   The youngest general in the French army, he called on French forces to follow his lead and continue the fight against Nazi Germany after the fall of France in June 1940. As the leader of the new Free French force that emerged thereafter, he won renewed respect for France as a major power and sought to exercise political leadership after France's liberation in 1944. Though he retired from public life in 1946, disillusioned with politics, he returned in 1958 to spearhead the creation of the new Fifth Republic. He served as its president from 1958 to 1969. (*Ch. 28*)

demokratia   Term coined in Athens in the fifth century B.C. to describe the city's system of direct government. It means "the power (*kratos*) of the people (*demos*)." Athenian society pioneered today's key democratic principles, including freedom, equality, universal citizenship, and the rule of law. (*Ch. 3*)

Descartes, René (1596–1650)   French philosopher, scientist, and mathematician. Descartes emphasized skepticism and deductive reasoning in his most influential treatise, *Discourse on Method*. He offered the first alternative physical explanation of matter after the Copernican revolution. (*Ch. 17*)

digital divide   A term for the disparity in access to the computing and Internet technologies that seemed essential to compete in the twenty-first-century global economy. It was one way that new technologies were widening the gap between the world's haves and have-nots. (*Ch. 30*)

Directory   French revolutionary government from 1795 to 1799, consisting of an executive council of five men chosen by the upper house of the legislature. It was overthrown in a coup led by **Napoleon Bonaparte.** (*Ch. 19*)

Dominic de Guzman (1170–1221)   Spanish priest and founder of the spiritually influential Dominican mendicant order. The order was known for the irreproachable life of its members, its learning, and its desire to emulate the apostolic life of the early church by poverty and preaching. (*Ch. 10*)

Dutch East India Company   Commercially innovative Dutch company formed in 1602 that combined government management of trade with both public and private investment. The formation of the company created a permanent pool of capital to sustain trade and resulted in a dramatic expansion of commerce with Asia. (*Ch. 16*)

Edict of Milan (313)   Proclamation issued primarily by Emperor Constantine that made Christianity a legal religion in the Roman Empire. Constantine promoted the

Christian church, granting it tax immunities and relieving the clergy of military service. *(Ch. 7)*

Edict of Nantes (1598) Edict of Henry IV granting France's Protestants **(Huguenots)** the right to practice their faith and maintain defensive garrisons. They were also guaranteed access to schools, hospitals, royal appointments, and separate judicial institutions. The edict was revoked by **Louis XIV** in 1685. *(Ch. 15)*

Elizabeth I (r. 1558–1603) First woman to occupy the English throne successfully. Elizabeth's adroit rule brought stability to England after the turmoil of previous reigns. She firmly established Protestantism in England, encouraged English commerce, defended the nation against the Spanish **Armada,** and fostered the English Renaissance in poetry and drama. *(Ch. 15)*

empirical method Philosophical view developed by the seventeenth-century English philosophers **Francis Bacon** and **John Locke,** asserting that all knowledge is based on observation and experimentation and that general principles should be derived from particular facts. *(Ch. 17)*

encomienda A Spanish royal grant of protectorship over a group of Amerindians. The receivers of the grants (encomenderos) were obliged to Christianize the people under their charge, but instead most forced the natives to work as virtual slaves in mines and on Spanish lands. See also **Bartolomé de Las Casas.** *(Ch. 13)*

enlightened despotism Term for the reform-oriented rule of eighteenth-century monarchs such as **Frederick the Great,** Joseph II of Austria, and **Catherine the Great.** Enlightened despots applied Enlightenment remedies to economic problems, encouraged education and legal reform, and improved agricultural productivity by enabling some peasants to own the land they worked. *(Ch. 18)*

entrepreneurs People who assume the risks of organizing and investing in a new business venture. Entrepreneurship is closely connected with the inventions and innovations made during the industrial age. *(Ch. 20)*

Epicureans Adherents of the Athenian philosopher Epicurus (341–270 B.C.), who taught that the soul is made up of atoms that do not exist after death. Epicureans emphasized the avoidance of pain and the pursuit of intellectual pleasure. *(Ch. 4)*

Erasmus, Desiderius (1466–1536) Prominent Dutch humanist during the Renaissance, best known for his satire *Praise of Folly.* Erasmus's works reinterpreted Greek and Roman wisdom and emphasized tolerance, reason, and faith in the goodness and educability of the individual. *(Ch. 12)*

ethnic cleansing A term describing attempts to remove an unwanted ethnic group from an area, which can include forced relocation and mass killing. Beginning in 1991, this tactic was implemented by Yugoslavian ruler Slobodan Milosevic (b. 1941) to unite all Serbs, many of whom lived in neighboring Croatia, Bosnia-Herzegovina, and Kosovo. *(Ch. 30)*

Etruscans Inhabitants of twelve loosely confederated city-states north of Rome in Etruria that flourished in the seventh to sixth centuries B.C. They were conquered by the Romans by the early third century B.C. *(Ch. 5)*

euro The common currency launched by the **European Union** in 1999 to eliminate the cost of currency exchange and boost trade and economic interaction. As of January 1, 2002, it replaced the national currencies of the participating countries (the "Eurozone"). *(Ch. 30)*

European Economic Community (EEC) (1957–1967) Common market formed by Belgium, France, West Germany, Italy, Luxembourg, and the Netherlands to promote free trade. The EEC was replaced by the European Community (EC) in 1967. *(Ch. 29)*

European Union (EU) New name for the European Community after the **Maastricht agreements** of 1991. It consists of twenty-five member countries. See also **euro.** *(Ch. 30)*

"euthanasia" program The Nazi program of systematically killing people, overwhelmingly ethnic Germans, whom the Nazis deemed superfluous or threatening to the German racial health. Victims included chronic mental patients, the incurably ill, and people with severe physical handicaps. Initiated in 1939, the program had claimed 100,000 lives by the time it was discontinued in 1941. *(Ch. 27)*

existentialism A philosophical and cultural movement, influential from the late 1940s into the 1950s, that explored life in a world cast adrift from its cultural moorings. Highly influential were the Frenchmen Jean-Paul Sartre (1905–1980) and Albert Camus (1913–1960), for whom an authentic human response to an apparently meaningless universe entailed commitment and responsibility. *(Ch. 29)*

factories Centralized workplaces where a number of people cooperate to mass-produce goods. The first factories of industrializing Europe were made possible by the development of the **steam engine** as a central power source. The mechanized production of factories led to huge productivity increases in the nineteenth century. See also **industrialization; mass production.** *(Ch. 20)*

fascism A violent, antidemocratic movement founded by **Benito Mussolini** in Italy in 1919. The term is widely used to encompass Hitler's Nazi regime in Germany and other movements stressing disciplined national solidarity and hostile to liberal individualism, the parliamentary system, and Marxist socialism. *(Ch. 26)*

February Patent (1861) Enactment issued in February 1861 by the Austrian emperor Franz Joseph (r. 1848–1916) that established a constitutional monarchy in the old Austrian Empire. The patent guaranteed civil liberties and provided for local self-government and an elected parliament. *(Ch. 22)*

feudal revolution The societal change in tenth-century France from prince-dominated territories with loyal, reliable, but few vassals to the advent of many locally powerful magnates with numerous vassals whose fidelity was uncertain and who primarily provided military service. *(Ch. 9)*

Five Pillars The basic teachings of Islam: (1) the profession of faith, "There is no God but Allah and **Muhammad** is His Prophet"; (2) individual prayer five times daily, plus group prayers at noon on Friday; (3) the sunup-to-sundown fast during the month of Ramadan; (4) giving generous alms to the poor; and (5) pilgrimage to Mecca at least once in a person's lifetime. *(Ch. 8)*

Flavians Dynasty of the Roman emperors Vespasian (r. 69–79), Titus (r. 79–81), and Domitian (r. 81–96), whose rule was a time of relative peace and good government. Unlike the Julio-Claudians, the Flavians descended from Italian landowners, not old Roman nobility. Domitian persecuted the nobility and was assassinated. *(Ch. 6)*

Fourteen Points Proposals by U.S. president Woodrow Wilson (1856–1924) to guide the new international order that would follow an Allied victory in World War I. Specifics included open diplomacy, free trade, reduced armaments, self-determination for nationalities, and a league of nations. *(Ch. 25)*

Francis of Assisi (1181–1226) Italian monk and founder of a new order of friars ("brothers," from the Latin *fratres*). Francis was born wealthy but adopted a life based on the scriptural ideals of poverty, preaching, and service. His apostolate to the urban poor was highly popular. *(Ch. 10)*

Frankfurt Assembly (1848–1849) Popularly elected national assembly that attempted to create a unified German state. The assembly drew up a constitution and offered the German throne to Friedrich Wilhelm IV, king of Prussia, who declined, fearing a war with Austria and not wanting an office offered by representatives of the people. *(Ch. 21)*

Frederick the Great (r. 1740–1786) Autocratic king of Prussia who transformed the country into a major military power, acquired Polish Prussia, and waged three wars against Austria. He participated in and encouraged the study of philosophy, history, poetry, and French literature. *(Ch. 18)*

Freud, Sigmund (1856–1939) Austrian founder of psychoanalysis, a method of treating psychic disorders by exploring the unconscious. Freud believed that people were motivated in part by their unconscious feelings and drives. He helped call attention to the concept that irrational forces play a significant role in human behavior. *(Ch. 24)*

friendly societies Nineteenth-century organizations formed by workers; members pooled their resources to provide mutual aid. Combining business activity with feasts, drinking bouts, and other social functions, friendly societies promoted group solidarity and a sense of working-class identity. *(Ch. 20)*

G-8 (Group of 8) Originally a Group of Seven, or G-7, this informal association of the world's seven largest economic powers (the United States, Japan, Germany, France, Britain, Italy, and Canada) began meeting during the 1970s in an effort to coordinate economic policies. After the fall of communism, the group added Russia, thereby becoming the G-8. *(Ch. 30)*

Galilei, Galileo (1564–1642) Italian physicist and astronomer who provided evidence supporting the **heliocentric theory** of **Nicholas Copernicus** and helped develop the physics of mechanics. His publication of his astronomical observations and his subsequent condemnation by the Catholic Church spurred popular debate and greatly influenced the future of science. *(Ch. 17)*

gentry Class of wealthy, educated, and socially ambitious families in western Europe, especially England, whose political and economic power was greatly enhanced during the sixteenth century. They shared with traditional old-family warrior-aristocrats certain legal privileges, security of landownership, and a cooperative relationship with the monarchy. See also **price revolution.** *(Ch. 15)*

Glorious Revolution (1688) Bloodless English revolution in which Parliament replaced the Catholic King James II with William (of Orange) and his wife, Mary (James's Protestant daughter). Parliament imposed on the new sovereigns a Bill of Rights that confirmed Parliament's power and protected freedom of speech. *(Ch. 16)*

Golden Bull of 1356 Edict of Holy Roman Emperor Charles IV establishing the method of electing a new emperor. It acknowledged the political autonomy of Germany's seven regional princes. *(Ch. 11)*

Gorbachev, Mikhail (b. 1931) The Soviet Communist Party secretary who, beginning in 1985, attempted to reform the Soviet communist system through arms reduction; liberalization in the satellite states; *glasnost,* or "openness" to discussion and criticism; and *perestroika,* or economic "restructuring." Though widely admired in the West, these measures failed, and Gorbachev ended up presiding over the end of the Soviet communist regime. *(Ch. 29)*

Gothic Period in European architecture, sculpture, and painting from the twelfth to early sixteenth centuries. Gothic architecture was distinguished by the pointed arch, ribbed vault, and point support, which produced a building characterized by verticality and translucency. Examples are the Cathedral of Notre-Dame of Paris and the royal portal at Chartres Cathedral. *(Ch. 10)*

Gracchi Ancient Roman faction led by Tiberius Sempronius Gracchus (163–133 B.C.) and later his brother, Gaius (153–121), both of whom were killed by their political opponents. They challenged the conservative **senate** on behalf of the poor. *(Ch. 5)*

"the Great Patriotic War" Term for World War II devised by **Joseph Stalin** to rally Soviet citizens against the German invasion. Stalin appealed to Russian nationalism and recalled past heroic defenses of Russia rather than communist themes. *(Ch. 28)*

Great Reform Bill (1832) British law that broadened the franchise and provided parliamentary seats for new urban areas that had not previously been represented. The bill was a major victory for the government and middle classes over the aristocracy. *(Ch. 21)*

Great Schism (1378–1417) Period during which two, then three, rival popes claimed to rule the Christian

Church in the West. The schism ended when the **Council of Constance** deposed all three competing previous popes and elected Martin V as the new pope. *(Ch. 11)*

guilds Merchant groups and associations of crafts and trades established in European cities and towns beginning in the thirteenth century. Guilds expanded greatly during the later Middle Ages. They provided economic benefits, fostered a sense of community, and served as mutual assistance societies. *(Ch. 9)*

gulag Network of 476 forced labor camps for political prisoners in the Soviet Union. The *gulag* (an acronym for "main camp administration") was first used by Lenin in 1918 but was greatly expanded by **Joseph Stalin** in the 1930s. *(Ch. 27)*

Gutenberg, Johann (ca. 1399–1468) German inventor of movable metal type. His innovations led to the publication of the first printed book in Europe, the Gutenberg Bible, in the 1450s. Printed books and broadsheets played a critical role in disseminating the ideas of the Renaissance and the Reformation. *(Ch. 12)*

Hagia Sophia Largest Christian church ever built, constructed in Constantinople from 532 to 537 for the Roman emperor **Justinian.** The church consists of two intersecting rectangular basilicas that incorporate arches; the whole is surmounted by a huge dome. *(Ch. 7)*

Hanseatic League Late medieval association of over a hundred trading cities, centered on the German city of Lübeck. The league dominated coastal trade in northern Europe from the fourteenth to the fifteenth centuries, until Dutch, English, and south German merchants finally gained shares of the wool, grain, and fur trades. *(Ch. 11)*

heliocentric theory Theory advanced by **Nicholas Copernicus** that the earth and other planets orbit the sun. Supported by the scientific and mathematical discoveries of **Johannes Kepler** and **Galileo Galilei,** heliocentrism, which means "sun-centered," won acceptance by the end of the seventeenth century. *(Ch. 17)*

Hellenism Term used to designate ancient Greece's language, culture, and civilization, especially after **Alexander the Great** spread them to other parts of the Mediterranean, western Asia, and North Africa. *(Ch. 4)*

Helsinki Accords (1975) Agreements signed by thirty-five countries in Helsinki, Finland, that committed the signatories to recognize existing borders, to increase economic and environmental cooperation, and to promote freedom of expression, religion, and travel. Dissidents in Soviet bloc countries soon fastened on these provisions to highlight the lack of human rights and to discredit the ruling communist governments. *(Ch. 29)*

Henry VIII (r. 1509–1547) King of England. Initially a defender of traditional Christianity, Henry broke with the papacy over the issue of his divorce. He needed a divorce, he argued, in order to marry a younger woman who might be able to produce a male heir to the kingdom. As a result of the dispute, Henry supported Reformers in the English Church. *(Ch. 14)*

Henry "the Navigator," Prince (1394–1460) Portuguese prince and director of Portugal's exploration and colonization of Africa's western coast. The Portuguese quickly established trading stations in the region, laying the foundations for their overseas empire. *(Ch. 13)*

heresy An opinion that goes against religious or political doctrine and beliefs. *(Ch. 7)*

Herodotus (ca. 485–425 B.C.) Ancient Greek historian; with **Thucydides,** a founder of history-writing in the West. The word *history* comes from a word used by Herodotus, *historiai,* meaning "inquiries" or "research." In his history of the Persian Wars, Herodotus saw the fall of the Persian Empire as part of a perpetual cycle of the rise and fall of empires. *(Ch. 3)*

Hildegard of Bingen (1098–1179) German abbess who was perhaps the most profound psychological thinker of her age. More than anyone before her, Hildegard opened up for discussion the feminine aspects of divinity. She was also adept in music and biblical studies. *(Ch. 10)*

Hitler, Adolf (1889–1945) The German dictator who, after being legally named chancellor in 1933, militarized Germany and started World War II in 1939, leading the country to defeat in 1945. His enforcement of state-sponsored **anti-Semitism** and racial purity among German people led to the murder of millions. *(Ch. 27)*

Hittites Builders of a great empire in Anatolia in the Late Bronze Age, the Hittites fought Egypt to a standstill and made history's first peace treaty between equals. Hittite is the oldest recorded Indo-European language, the language group to which English belongs. *(Ch. 1)*

Hobbes, Thomas (1588–1679) English philosopher. In his treatise *Leviathan,* Hobbes asserted that people are made up of mechanistic appetites and so need a strong ruler to hold them in check. However, he also envisioned citizens as potentially equal and constrained neither by morality nor by natural obedience to authority. *(Ch. 17)*

Homer Greatest ancient Greek poet, credited as the author of the epics the *Iliad* and the *Odyssey,* both written during the eighth century B.C. His dramatic stories inspired, moved, and educated the Greeks. *(Ch. 2)*

hominids The primate family *Hominidae,* which includes humans. The modern human being, *Homo sapiens sapiens,* is the only species of this family still in existence. *(Ch. 1)*

hoplite phalanx Battlefield tactic of **Archaic Greece** that relied on a tightly ordered unit of heavily armed, pike-bearing infantrymen. It was the dominant military force in western Asia and the Mediterranean region until 197 B.C. *(Ch. 3)*

Huguenots French Protestants, followers of the teachings of **John Calvin.** Huguenots battled Catholics throughout the sixteenth and seventeenth centuries. Many emigrated to other western European countries and England's American colonies, especially after the revocation of the **Edict of Nantes.** French Protestants gained full religious freedom in the nineteenth century. *(Ch. 15)*

humanism Western European literary and cultural movement of the fourteenth and fifteenth centuries. Humanists emphasized the superiority of ancient Greek and Roman literature, history, and politics, and focused on learning and personal and public duty. See also **Desiderius Erasmus; Francesco Petrarch; Thomas More.** *(Ch. 12)*

Hundred Years' War (1337–1453)   Series of conflicts between the ruling families of France and England over territory in France and the succession to the French crown. Sporadic raids and battles devastated the French countryside and checked population growth. The inspirational leadership of **Joan of Arc** contributed to France's eventual success in expelling the English from nearly all of the disputed land. *(Ch. 11)*

hunter-gatherers   Food-collecting society in which people live by hunting, fishing, and gathering fruits and nuts, with no crops or livestock being raised for food. During the **Neolithic Revolution,** some hunter-gatherers developed agriculture. *(Ch. 1)*

Hus, Jan (ca. 1370–1415)   Czech religious reformer who strongly attacked clerical power and privileges and advocated reform of church practice. His execution for heresy at the **Council of Constance** provoked a civil war in Prague and Bohemia. *(Ch. 11)*

iconoclasm   Rejection of, or even the destruction of, religious images in worship. Iconoclasm was the official policy of the Byzantine Empire from 726 to 843 and played a role in the continuing estrangement of Byzantium from the West. *(Ch. 8)*

impressionist   Late-nineteenth-century style of painting pioneered by the French artists Degas, Monet, Pissarro, Renoir, Sisley, and Morisot. Influenced by new theories that images were transmitted to the brain as small light particles, which the brain then reconstituted, the impressionists sought to capture what things looked like before they were "distorted" by the brain. *(Ch. 23)*

Inca   A flourishing sixteenth-century empire administered from the mountains of Peru and extending from modern Ecuador to Chile. It was conquered for Spain by Francisco Pizzaro (1470–1541), aided by a smallpox epidemic and native peoples seeking to end Inca domination. *(Ch. 13)*

Index of Prohibited Books   A list of books banned by the Roman Catholic Church because of moral or doctrinal error. First announced in 1559, it was only sporadically enforced and had little effect. The Index was suppressed in 1966. *(Ch. 14)*

industrialization   Beginning in Britain in the later eighteenth century, a system of **mass production** of goods in which specialization and mechanization made manufacturing efficient and profitable. Early industrialization enabled Britain to become the dominant world power in the nineteenth century. See also **factories.** *(Ch. 20)*

information technology   Term for the revolution in information availability and communications resulting from the late-twentieth-century development of personal computers and the Internet. See also **digital divide.** *(Ch. 30)*

"iron curtain"   Term used by Winston Churchill in a speech on March 5, 1946, to warn that, thanks to Soviet policy, a formidable de facto barrier was emerging in Europe, cutting the Soviet sphere off from the West and threatening the long-term division of the Continent. Though the term was not coined by Churchill, his phrasing dramatically affected public opinion in the West. The "iron curtain" suggested both the division of Europe and Soviet culpability throughout the cold war period. *(Ch. 28)*

Israelites   People who settled on the eastern shore of the Mediterranean around 1200 B.C., or perhaps earlier. Their belief in one God directly influenced the faith of Christians, Muslims, and modern Jews. See also **monotheism.** *(Ch. 2)*

Ivan IV, "the Terrible" (r. 1533–1584)   First Russian ruler routinely to use the title "tsar" (Russian for "Caesar"), he presided over the expansion and centralization of the Russian state. Ivan continued Moscow's expansion, begun by his grandfather Ivan III, south and east against Mongol-controlled states. Under Ivan IV, Russians moved east across Siberia for the first time. Within his expanding empire, Ivan ruled as an autocrat; he was able to bypass noble participation and intensify the centralization of government by creating ranks of officials loyal only to himself. *(Ch. 15)*

Jacobins   In revolutionary France, a political club named for a monastic order. One of the most radical of republican groups, the Jacobins purged the Girondins, originally fellow members of the club, from the National Convention in 1793. Leaders of the **Terror,** such as **Maximilien Robespierre,** came from their ranks. *(Ch. 19)*

Jesus of Nazareth (ca. 4 B.C.–A.D. 30)   Founder of **Christianity.** A forceful preacher and reformer who, to his followers, was Christ, "the anointed one" (from the Greek *Christos*), foretold in the Hebrew Bible as the redeemer of Israel who would initiate the Kingdom of Heaven. The dynamism and popularity of his teachings led to a clash with Jewish and Roman authorities in Jerusalem and to his crucifixion by the Romans. *(Ch. 6)*

Joan of Arc (d. 1431)   Charismatic French military leader during the **Hundred Years' War.** A late medieval mystic, Joan heard "voices" telling her to assist in driving the English from France. She was captured and burned as a heretic by the English. Later she was canonized as Saint Joan, patron saint of France. *(Ch. 11)*

Julio-Claudians   Dynasty of Roman emperors founded by **Augustus** and ruling from A.D. 14 to 68. The succession consisted of Augustus's stepson Tiberius, great-grandson Caligula, grandnephew Claudius, and great-great-grandson Nero. For elite Romans, this era was one of decadence and scandal; for ordinary people, it was a time of stability and peace. *(Ch. 6)*

July Revolution (1830)   Uprising in Paris in July 1830 that forced King Charles X to abdicate and signaled a victory for constitutional reform over an absolute monarchy. The liberal Louis Philippe was proclaimed "King of the French," with limited powers, by the Chamber of Deputies. The revolution sparked democratic uprisings in Belgium, Germany, Italy, and Russian Poland and helped persuade British peers to vote for the **Great Reform Bill.** *(Ch. 21)*

justification by faith Doctrine professed by **Martin Luther** that Christians can be saved (justified) only by faith, a free gift of God, and not by penitential acts or good works. Luther's doctrine directly challenged the authority and fundamental practices of the Roman Catholic Church. *(Ch. 14)*

Justinian (r. 527–565) One of the greatest of all Rome's emperors. His comprehensive collection of Roman law is the most influential legal collection in human history. He built **Hagia Sophia,** reformed the imperial administration, and fought constant wars to expand the empire. *(Ch. 7)*

Kepler, Johannes (1571–1630) German astronomer. Kepler developed the three laws of planetary motion, known as Kepler's laws, which are still accepted, and mathematically confirmed the Copernican **heliocentric theory.** *(Ch. 17)*

Kriegsrohstoffabteilung (KRA) The "War Raw Materials Office" that coordinated Germany's World War I economy. The KRA produced synthetic substitute products and created new mixed (private and government) companies to allocate raw materials. This body served as a model for later economic planning and coordination in Germany and elsewhere. *(Ch. 25)*

Kristallnacht See **Crystal Night.**

laissez faire French term meaning "to leave alone," it was applied to the economic doctrine put forward by **Adam Smith** in 1776. Smith advocated freeing national economies from the fetters of the state and allowing supply and demand to shape the marketplace. Laissez-faire ideas contributed to the drive to lower tariffs in the nineteenth century. See also **liberalism.** *(Ch. 21)*

Las Casas, Bartolomé de (1474–1566) First bishop of Chiapas, in southern Mexico. A former *encomendero,* Las Casas passionately condemned the brutality of the Spanish conquests. In 1542 King Charles accepted Las Casas's criticisms, abolishing Indian slavery and greatly restricting the transfer of **encomiendas.** *(Ch. 13)*

Latin Indo-European language of ancient Rome and its empire, from which today's Romance languages developed. *(Ch. 5)*

laws of motion The natural laws of gravity, planetary motion, and inertia first laid out in the seventeenth century by **Isaac Newton.** Newton demonstrated that these laws apply to the solar system and could be used to predict the existence of an as-yet-unseen planet. *(Ch. 17)*

lay investiture Control of church appointments by laymen. Emperor Henry IV (1066–1106) and Pope Gregory VII (1073–1085) disputed who should have this authority in the Christian world. The 1122 Concordat of Worms stipulated that bishops could be invested by kings only after a free church election. *(Ch. 9)*

League of Nations (1919–1946) An international alliance established at the end of World War I without the membership of the United States. Though its covenant called for the peaceful settlement of disputes among member states and for sanctions against a member that went to war in violation of League provisions, it failed to prevent the escalating violence that culminated in World War II. *(Ch. 25)*

legion Innovative and highly successful ancient Roman battle formation. The legion included many flexible, adaptable, and semi-independent groups that broke their enemies' order with javelins at long range, then charged with sword and shield. *(Ch. 5)*

Lend-Lease Act (1941) Act by the U.S. Congress authorizing President **Franklin Delano Roosevelt** to lend or lease weapons or other aid to countries the president designated. A major declaration of American support for the threatened British, lend-lease was later extended to several other countries. *(Ch. 28)*

Lenin, Vladimir Ilyich (1870–1924) Russian revolutionary. Leader of the **Bolsheviks** since 1903, he masterminded the November 1917 revolution that overthrew the **provisional government** and led to a communist regime in Russia. See also **New Economic Policy.** *(Ch. 25)*

Leonardo da Vinci (1452–1519) A painter, engineer, and scientist, da Vinci rejected arguments and ideas based on imitation of the ancients. Rather, he advocated careful study of the natural world. *(Ch. 12)*

liberalism Nineteenth-century economic and political theory that called for reducing government powers to a minimum. Liberals worked to impose constitutional limits on government, establish the rule of law, eliminate state regulation of the economy, and ensure a voice in government for men of property and education. *(Ch. 21)*

linear perspective Revolutionary technique developed by early-fifteenth-century Florentine painters for representing three-dimensional objects on a two-dimensional plane. The technique is based in part on the observation that as parallel lines recede, they appear to converge. *(Ch. 12)*

Livia (58 B.C.–A.D. 29) Wife of **Augustus** and mother of Tiberius, his successor. As one of Augustus's main advisers, she intrigued to secure the succession for Tiberius and was suspected of poisoning several family members, including Augustus himself. *(Ch. 6)*

Locarno, Treaty of (1925) Treaty that introduced a new, more conciliatory spirit in international affairs. France and Germany accepted the postwar border between them, and Germany was again recognized as a diplomatic equal and entered the League of Nations in 1926. *(Ch. 26)*

Locke, John (1632–1704) English philosopher. In his influential *Two Treatises of Government,* Locke asserted that the state arises from a contract that individuals freely accept. Thus, rebellion against abuse of power is justified. In addition, Locke theorized that human knowledge is largely the product of experience. See also **empirical method.** *(Ch. 17)*

Louis XIV (r. 1643–1715) Longest-reigning ruler in European history, who imposed absolute rule on France and waged several wars attempting to dominate Europe. He was known as the Sun King, and his reign marked a great flowering of French culture. *(Ch. 16)*

Loyola, Ignatius (1491–1556) Spanish nobleman and founder of the Society of Jesus, or Jesuits, which has been called the vanguard of the Catholic reform movement. After papal approval of the order, the Jesuits focused primarily on educating Catholics and reconverting Protestants. *(Ch. 14)*

Luddites Organized groups of British workers formed in 1811–1812, who smashed machines and rioted to protest against industrialization, which they felt would threaten their livelihood. The name comes from their mythical leader, General Ned Ludd. *(Ch. 20)*

Luther, Martin (1483–1546) German theologian and religious reformer. Luther began the Protestant Reformation in 1517 with the publication of his *Ninety-Five Theses,* which challenged indulgences and Catholic teachings on penitential acts. His translation of the Bible into German in 1522 standardized the modern German language. See also **Augsburg Confession; justification by faith;** *sola scriptura*. *(Ch. 14)*

Maastricht agreements (1991) Agreements among twelve European Community countries at Maastricht, the Netherlands, to form the **European Union.** The member states agreed to expand cooperation on social, foreign, judicial, and security matters and adopted a timetable for a common policy on workers' rights, a common currency (the **euro**), and a common central banking structure. *(Ch. 30)*

Maccabees Traditionalist Jews led by the Hasmonean family, who in 168 B.C. revolted against Hellenizing laws and influences. Their success is celebrated today during the Jewish holiday of Hanukkah. *(Ch. 4)*

Macedon Weaker, less culturally advanced state on Greece's northern border. It was unified and led to power by **Philip II** and **Alexander the Great,** who became rulers of Greece. *(Ch. 4)*

Machiavelli, Niccolò (1469–1527) Florentine politician and political theorist. His most famous work, *The Prince,* describes the methods a prince can use to acquire and maintain power. Often misunderstood as a defender of despotism, Machiavelli emphasized that a successful ruler needed to anticipate and consider the consequences of his actions. *(Ch. 12)*

Magellan, Ferdinand (1480?–1521) Portuguese-born Spanish explorer who led the first expedition to sail around the world. After finding the South American passage to the Pacific Ocean, he sailed to the Philippines, where he was killed by natives. Survivors on one of his ships completed the circumnavigation. *(Ch. 13)*

Maginot Line A 200-mile system of elaborate permanent fortifications on France's eastern border, named for war minister André Maginot, and built primarily during the 1930s. It was a defense against German frontal assault; in 1940 the Germans invaded by flanking the line. *(Ch. 26)*

Magna Carta (1215) Momentous document that England's barons forced King John to sign. It required the king to respect the rights of feudal lords, not abuse his judicial powers, and consult the barons—in essence, it put the king under the law, not above it. *(Ch. 9)*

manifest destiny Term coined in 1845 for the belief that the expanding United States was destined to occupy the North American continent from coast to coast. The rhetoric of manifest destiny was invoked to justify war with Mexico in 1846 and the acquisition of California and the Southwest from Mexico in 1848. *(Ch. 22)*

manor In western Europe, a type of estate that developed under the Carolingians. One-quarter to one-half of the land was set aside as a reserve (or demesne), to be worked on behalf of the landlord; the remainder was divided into tenancies worked by individual peasants for their own support. *(Ch. 8)*

Maria Theresa (r. 1740–1780) Habsburg archduchess of Austria and queen of Hungary and Bohemia. After successfully defending her right to the Austrian throne against attacks by **Frederick the Great** and others, she reformed and centralized the administration of her Austrian and Bohemian lands. *(Ch. 18)*

Marina, Doña (Malintzin) (1501–1550) An Aztec by birth, she was sold to the Mayas and eventually became a translator and guide for the Spanish. After her critical role in the conquest, she married a Spaniard and lived as a Spanish noblewoman. *(Ch. 13)*

Marxism Political and economic theories of the two German philosophers and revolutionaries, Karl Marx (1818–1883) and Friedrich Engels (1820–1895), which they called scientific **socialism** and which gave birth to modern communism. Marxism argued that the oppressed working class should and inevitably would rebel against the capitalist owners and build a communist society. *(Ch. 21)*

mass production System in which great numbers of people work in centralized, mechanized **factories** to produce large quantities of goods; an essential feature of **industrialization.** A series of eighteenth-century inventions, culminating in the **steam engine,** enabled Britain to mass-produce textiles and benefit from the resulting increases in productivity. *(Ch. 20)*

Matteotti murder The 1924 killing by fascist thugs of Italian moderate socialist Giacomo Matteotti after he denounced the fascist violence accompanying national elections. The public outcry following the murder eventually led **Mussolini** to commit to a more radical direction, which included the creation of a new, fascist form of state. *(Ch. 26)*

mechanistic worldview Seventeenth-century philosophical view that saw the world as a machine that functions in strict obedience to physical laws, without purpose or will. Experience and reason were regarded as the standards of truth. *(Ch. 17)*

mercantilism Economic policy pursued by western European states in the seventeenth and eighteenth centuries, stressing self-sufficiency in manufactured goods, tight government control of trade to foster the domestic economy, protectionist policies, and the absolute value of bullion. *(Ch. 16)*

Minoans   Society that flourished between 2000 and 1375 B.C. on the Aegean island of Crete, where Greece's first civilization appeared. Their sophisticated culture and economy were administered from their magnificent palaces. See also **Mycenaeans.** *(Ch. 2)*

mir   Russian peasant commune. After Tsar Alexander II freed the serfs in 1861, the mir determined land use and paid the government mortgages and taxes. Peasants could leave the land only with the mir's permission. *(Ch. 22)*

monasticism   Ascetic way of life. Christian monasticism was founded by an Egyptian layman, Anthony (d. 356), who renounced all worldliness and pursued a life of prayer in the desert. A more communal form of monasticism was created by Pachomius (290–346), who wrote the first monastic Rule—a code for daily living in a monastic community. Monasticism quickly spread throughout the Christian world. *(Ch. 7)*

monotheism   Belief that there is only one God. The Hebrew Bible places this belief as originating about 2000–1500 B.C., when God commanded Abraham to give up Mesopotamian polytheism for belief in one God. *(Ch. 2)*

More, Thomas (1478–1535)   Chancellor of England under Henry VIII. More's best-known work, *Utopia,* was highly critical of contemporary European kingdoms. It describes a fictional land of peace and harmony that has outlawed private property and all forms of wealth. More was executed when he refused to take an oath to support the **Act of Supremacy.** See also **humanism.** *(Ch. 12)*

Muhammad (570–632)   Prophet and founder of Islam. In 610 he began to receive revelations commanding him to teach all people a new faith that called for an unquestioned belief in one god, Allah, and a deep commitment to social justice for believers. Before his death, he had converted most of Arabia. See also **Five Pillars; Quran.** *(Ch. 8)*

Mussolini, Benito (1883–1945)   Italian fascist dictator. Mussolini founded the fascist movement in 1919 and took power in 1922. He replaced Italy's parliamentary democracy with a **corporative state** and pursued an expansionist foreign policy. He concluded the Pact of Steel with **Adolf Hitler** in 1939 and took Italy into World War II in 1940. Deposed in 1943, he was killed by partisans in 1945. *(Ch. 26)*

Mycenaeans   Militaristic people from the Greek mainland who conquered the **Minoans** around 1550–1375 B.C. Mycenaean civilization was a center of Bronze Age culture until its destruction around 1100 B.C. *(Ch. 2)*

mystery religions   Popular Hellenistic cults featuring the initiation of worshipers into secret doctrines. Mystery religions replaced the traditional Greek religion of the Olympian gods. Some ancient Egyptian cults were recast as mystery religions, influencing early Christianity. *(Ch. 4)*

Napoleon Bonaparte (1769–1821)   Emperor of the French (r. 1804–1815). A French general who took part in a coup in 1799 against the **Directory,** Napoleon consolidated power as first consul and proclaimed himself emperor with the approval of a national plebiscite in 1804. His military conquests exported French revolutionary reforms to the rest of Europe. He was finally defeated and exiled in 1815. *(Ch. 19)*

National Assembly (1789–1791)   Legislative body formed in France in 1789 after the Third Estate insisted on being certified as members of the Estates General as a whole. The National Assembly drafted the **Declaration of the Rights of Man and the Citizen** and a constitution that called for a constitutional (not absolute) monarchy. *(Ch. 19)*

National Socialist (Nazi) Party   The political party that grew from the movement that German dictator **Adolf Hitler** made his vehicle to power. Originating from the radical right in Munich in 1919, the Nazi Party won voting support during the early 1930s, paving the way for Hitler to be named German chancellor in 1933. *(Ch. 27)*

nationalism   Belief arising in the eighteenth century that people derive their identity from their nation and owe it their primary loyalty. The criteria for nationhood typically included a common language, religion, and political authority, as well as common traditions and shared historical experiences. Nationalism was a major force in most of the revolutions of 1848 and in the subsequent unification of Italy and of Germany. *(Ch. 21)*

Nazi Party   See **Nationalist Socialist (Nazi) Party.**

Nazi-Soviet Pact (1939)   Surprise agreement between the Soviet Union and Nazi Germany in August 1939 that each would remain neutral if the other went to war with some other nation. The pact freed Germany to attack Poland a few days later without fear of Soviet reprisal. *(Ch. 27)*

Neo-Babylonians   Rulers of western Asia between 612 and 539 B.C. who elaborately rebuilt Babylon, creating the famous Hanging Gardens. They destroyed Jerusalem, deporting many Judeans in what is known as the Babylonian Captivity. *(Ch. 2)*

Neolithic Revolution   Human discovery and spread of agriculture, between about 13,000 and 5000 B.C. People first domesticated dogs and other animals and then learned how to cultivate crops. *(Ch. 1)*

New Economic Policy (NEP) (1921–1928)   A Russian economic liberalization measure aimed at reviving an economy in crisis. The NEP restored considerable scope for private enterprise and allowed peasants to sell some of their harvest. After initial economic success, it was eventually considered a threat to the socialist state and was replaced by state-controlled central planning. *(Ch. 26)*

new imperialism   Era of European overseas expansion launched in the 1880s. In the following decades, Europeans subjugated 500 million people in Africa and Asia—one half of the world's non-European population. *(Ch. 24)*

Newton, Isaac (1643–1727)   English physicist, mathematician, and natural philosopher. Newton's mathematical computation of the laws of gravity and planetary motion, which he combined with a fully developed theory of inertia, completed the explanation for motion initiated by **Nicholas Copernicus.** See also **laws of motion.** *(Ch. 17)*

nongovernmental organizations (NGOs)   A network of organizations unaffiliated with governments but central to the international community, such as the Red Cross, Amnesty International, and Doctors Without Borders, that had gradually emerged by the early twenty-first century to deal with humanitarian relief and human rights issues. *(Ch. 30)*

North Atlantic Treaty Organization (NATO) An alliance for regional defense, created in 1949 by the United States, Canada, and western European nations, whose members agree to defend one another from attack by non-member countries. Its original aim was to contain the Soviet Union. *(Ch. 29)*

Nuremberg trials The war crimes trials conducted in Nuremberg, Germany. Most of the twenty-four defendants were convicted of war crimes and "crimes against humanity." *(Ch. 28)*

On the Donation of Constantine Work by Lorenzo Valla (1407–1457) proving that the *Donation of Constantine* was not written at the time of the emperor Constantine. The forged *Donation* purported to record Constantine's transfer to the pope of jurisdiction over Rome and the western half of the empire. Valla's work undermined the papacy's claim to political rule in central Italy. *(Ch. 12)*

Orthodox The Catholic Christian faith of Byzantium. It differed from Roman Catholicism by its use of Greek instead of Latin, the inclusion of icons in worship, an adherence to the Greek Church Fathers, some differences in basic theology, and many differences in customs and practices. *(Ch. 8)*

papacy Name for the institution ruled by the bishop of Rome who, in Roman Catholic tradition, is the successor to Peter, the most prominent apostle. Since Peter was believed to be the leader of the original followers of Christ, his successors, the popes (from *papa* by the fourth century), were believed to be the leaders of the whole church. *(Ch. 7)*

Papal Monarchy Period during the twelfth and thirteenth centuries when the power of the Catholic Church was increasingly expanded and centralized in the hands of the popes, as papal policy focused on recovering lost lands and rights in central Italy. *(Ch. 9)*

Papal States Beginning in the eighth century, territories held by the popes in central Italy under the protection of the Frankish kings. *(Ch. 8)*

papyrus Paperlike writing material used by the ancient Egyptians, Greeks, and Romans. Made primarily in Egypt from the papyrus plant, it was durable, flexible, and easy to write on. *(Ch. 1)*

Paris Commune (1871) Parisian workers' uprising intended to establish a workers' government under home rule. Stemming from labor discontent and the radicalization of workers during the siege of Paris in the Franco-Prussian War, the commune was suppressed by the army of the conservative French government. *(Ch. 22)*

Parliament English legislative institution, consisting of a House of Lords and a House of Commons, whose ancestors were the royal courts that met in 1265 and 1295. The king considered the courts a device to win support for royal agendas; the barons viewed them as opportunities to play a real policymaking role in government. In the late sixteenth and early seventeenth centuries, Parliament used control over monies to bargain with the Crown over foreign and domestic policies, leading to resistance to and eventual deposition of Charles I. The power of Parliament within the government was definitively established when it forced William and Mary to accept its role in government in the Glorious Revolution (1688). See also **Glorious Revolution.** *(Ch. 16)*

parliaments Initially expanded meetings of the royal court intended to secure consensus for royal policies. *(Ch. 9)*

paterfamilias Oldest living male in an ancient Roman family, who had supreme legal power within the household. Only the paterfamilias could own property free and clear. *(Ch. 5)*

Paul of Tarsus (d. ca. 67) Christian apostle and saint. A Jew from Anatolia and a Roman citizen, Paul first persecuted the Christians but became a believer around A.D. 36. Paul taught that the life and resurrection of **Jesus of Nazareth** offered all humanity the hope of salvation through faith. Under Paul, **Christianity** began its complete separation from Judaism. *(Ch. 6)*

pax Romana Latin for "Roman peace," the term refers to the period of peace and prosperity in the Roman Empire from A.D. 69 to 180. During this time the emperors emphasized extending citizenship and spreading prosperity throughout the provinces, and Italy was no longer the tyrant of the Mediterranean. See also **Flavians.** *(Ch. 6)*

Peace of Westphalia (1648) Treaty that ended the **Thirty Years' War.** The principalities within the Holy Roman Empire were recognized as virtually autonomous, severely weakening the power of the emperor. Calvinism joined Catholicism and Lutheranism as tolerated faiths within the empire, and the treaty closed the age of religious wars. *(Ch. 15)*

Pericles Leader of fifth-century-B.C. Athens when **demokratia** became entrenched as the government and way of life. Distinguished for his oratory and honesty, he established Athens as a great center of art and literature as well as a great empire. *(Ch. 3)*

Persian Empire Vast, prosperous, and law-abiding West Asian empire, from about 550 B.C. to its conquest by **Alexander the Great** around 330 B.C. The relatively tolerant rule of the Persian emperors represented the greatest success yet of a universal kingship. The Persians also built the first great navy. *(Ch. 2)*

Peter the Great (r. 1682–1725) Russian tsar. Brilliant, energetic, and tyrannical, Peter revolutionized Russian society by his determined efforts to westernize his nation culturally, economically, and politically. He modernized the army and navy, secured seaports, and made Russia into a great power. *(Ch. 16)*

Petrarch, Francesco (1304–1374) Influential Italian poet, biographer, and humanist during the Renaissance. Petrarch advocated imitating the actions, values, and culture of the ancient Romans to reform the excesses of the present world. *(Ch. 12)*

Petrograd Soviet The *soviet* (council) of leaders of strike committees and army regiments elected in March 1917, when Petrograd's workers protested in response to severe wartime food and coal shortages. Central to the Bolshevik Revolution of 1917, the soviet eventually became the ruling power in the Russian capital—but only temporarily. *(Ch. 25)*

pharaoh Ancient Egyptians' title for their king, an absolute, all-powerful, and all-providing ruler. It was believed that the ruler represented the ancestors and guaranteed the fertility of the soil. *(Ch. 1)*

Philip II (r. 359–336 B.C.) King of **Macedon.** A brilliant soldier and statesman, Philip conquered the Greek world. He developed a well-trained, professional year-round army and mastered the technology of siegecraft. He was succeeded by his son, **Alexander the Great.** *(Ch. 4)*

Philip II (r. 1556–1598) King of Spain, son of **Charles V.** An avid Roman Catholic, he ruled Spain at the height of its influence. Philip dispatched the ill-fated **Armada** to invade England and attempted to quash the revolt of the Netherlands. *(Ch. 15)*

philosophes French term referring to thinkers and critics of the Enlightenment era, including **Voltaire** and Diderot. Philosophes applied to political and social thought the confidence in human reason and the intelligibility of natural law that **Isaac Newton** and other scientists had recently achieved. *(Ch. 18)*

Phoenicians Canaanites whose civilization flourished about 1050–750 B.C. in present-day coastal Syria, where they established major trading ports. Master sailors, they planted colonies around the Mediterranean, many of which, including Carthage, became independent states. The Phoenicians exported the civilization of western Asia—including the Phoenician alphabet, derived from Ugarit—to the Mediterranean world. *(Ch. 2)*

plantation system Agricultural practices developed by the fifteenth-century Portuguese to produce sugar on their island colonies in the Atlantic using involuntarily transported slaves from Africa. Portugal's prototype—wealthy absentee landlords and masses of forced labor producing cash crops on vast tracts of land—was the model for the New World plantation system. In seventeenth- and eighteenth-century French and English colonies in the Caribbean, large sugar plantations owned by wealthy, often absentee, landlords replaced smaller-scale independent farming. See also **slave trade.** *(Ch. 16)*

Plato (427–348 B.C.) Ancient Greek philosopher, student of **Socrates.** One of Western philosophy's greatest exponents of idealism, Plato believed that the senses are misleading and that truth can therefore be attained only by training the mind to overcome commonsense evidence. In the *Republic,* Plato describes an ideal state in which philosophers rule as kings, benevolently and unselfishly. *(Ch. 3)*

polis Term for an ancient Greek city-state, a system that reached its height around 700–300 B.C. The ideological and political organization of the polis emphasized equality and a shared community life for all citizens, not just the elite. *(Ch. 3)*

popular front A term for antifascist electoral alliances and governing coalitions that Communists promoted from 1934 until 1939 to resist the further spread of fascism. Popular front coalitions won control of government in both Spain and France during 1936. *(Ch. 27)*

positivism Philosophy of the French thinker Auguste Comte (1798–1857). Comte asserted that human history progressed through distinct and irreversible stages, leading inexorably upward to the final and highest stage of development, the positive—or scientific—stage. Positivism and its optimistic outlook for human progress were influential in both Europe and Latin America during the nineteenth century. *(Ch. 23)*

Potsdam conference A July–August 1945 meeting held at Potsdam, Germany, between the USSR, the United States, and Great Britain to implement their earlier agreements concerning the treatment of defeated Germany. Many of the agreements reached were later abandoned amid growing hostility between the USSR and the Western democracies. *(Ch. 28)*

Prague Spring The attempt by Czechoslovakian reformers in 1968 to gain freer cultural expression, democratization of Communist Party procedures, and broader participation in public life within the framework of a communist state. The forcible suppression of the movement by Soviet leaders seemed to signal the end of any hope for flexibility and openness within the Soviet sphere. *(Ch. 29)*

price revolution Steady rise in prices in the sixteenth and seventeenth centuries, resulting from population growth and the influx of precious metals from Spain's New World territories. As wages lost one-tenth to one-fourth of their value, people sought new work, protested against taxes, and attacked scapegoats. The price revolution concentrated wealth in fewer hands and contributed to the rise of a new **gentry** class. *(Ch. 15)*

primogeniture A legal inheritance system that provided the firstborn, usually the firstborn son, the right to inherit all the family land and farm. *(Ch. 20)*

Principate The constitutional monarchy of the Early Roman Empire, from 31 B.C. to A.D. 192. The term comes from *Princeps,* or "first citizen," an old title of respect used in the **senate.** See also **Augustus; Flavians.** *(Ch. 6)*

professionalization Establishment in the nineteenth century of common standards and requirements, especially in medicine, law, architecture, and engineering. Professionalization brought either government or self-regulation to vocations whose prestige rested on the claim of exclusive expertise in their fields. *(Ch. 23)*

proletariat Term used by Karl Marx to describe the new class of industrial workers who owned none of the means of production and were totally dependent on factory owners for their livelihoods. In Marxist thought, capitalists were destined to be overthrown by the proletariat. See also **Marxism.** *(Ch. 20)*

provisional government   The body that ruled Russia from March to November 1917, in the wake of the revolution that overthrew the tsarist regime. Originally intended to be a temporary step to an elected constituent assembly, its policies caused discontents that the **Bolsheviks** were quick to exploit. (Ch. 25)

Ptolemies   Dynasty of Egyptian kings who ruled from 304 to 30 B.C., founded by Ptolemy I, a Macedonian general of **Alexander the Great.** It was the wealthiest, most sophisticated, and longest lasting of the Hellenistic kingdoms. See also **Alexandria.** (Ch. 4)

Punic Wars (264–146 B.C.)   Three wars during which the Roman Empire eventually destroyed Carthage. The Romans later adopted the Carthaginians' plantation system using massive numbers of slaves. (Ch. 5)

Puritans   Radical Protestants in late-sixteenth- and seventeenth-century England. Puritans emphasized Bible reading, preaching, private scrutiny of conscience, and de-emphasized institutional ritual and clerical authority. Puritans became a majority in Parliament during the reign of Charles I and led the campaign against the king during the English Civil War. (Ch. 15)

Putin, Vladimir   Elected president of Russia early in 2000, he had been director of Russia's secret police before coming to political prominence as prime minister in 1999. He cracked down on the insurgency in Chechnya and, as president, proved more energetic in dealing with Russia's problems than his predecessor, Boris Yeltsin. (Ch. 30)

putting-out system   The production in country homes of thread and cloth by spinners and weavers for an entrepreneur who bought raw materials and "put them out" to be finished by individual workers. This cottage industry system expanded in eighteenth-century Europe as increased numbers of agricultural laborers needed more nonfarm work in off-seasons. (Ch. 18)

Quran   Islamic sacred writings, which **Muhammad** communicated in the form of "recitations," insisting that he was transmitting a direct revelation from Allah. After Muhammad's death, his followers arranged the recitations into 114 *Suras,* or chapters, containing legal and wisdom literature and moral teaching. (Ch. 8)

rabbinic Judaism   Main form of Judaism, which emerged during the first century A.D. under the leadership of the rabbis, the spiritual descendants of the Pharisees. Rabbinic Judaism amplified and interpreted the Hebrew Bible to clarify Jewish practice, elevated the oral law to equal authority with the written **Torah,** and enabled Judaism to evolve flexibly. (Ch. 6)

Realpolitik   Style of governing that uses all means, including war, to expand the influence and power of a state. The best-known practitioner of Realpolitik was Prussian chancellor **Otto von Bismarck.** (Ch. 22)

Reconquista   Wars of reconquest in the Iberian Peninsula from the eleventh to fifteenth centuries. Spanish and Portuguese rulers seized territories from the weakening Muslim regime. By awarding reconquered lands to their nobles,

Christian kings enhanced their own status and power. (Ch. 9)

remilitarization of the Rhineland   The reoccupation of Germany's Rhineland territory by German troops in March 1936, in clear violation of the **Treaty of Versailles.** When the French and British did not resist the German move, **Adolf Hitler** was emboldened to additional acts of aggression elsewhere. (Ch. 27)

Renaissance   Term derived from the French word for "rebirth" used to describe a period of intense creativity between 1350 and 1500 when cultural values were based on imitation of classical Greek and Roman norms. (Ch. 12)

res publica   Romans' concept of their republic, which uniquely influenced Western political institutions. *Res publica* is Latin for "public thing," as opposed to *res privata,* "private thing," as the Romans characterized monarchy. (Ch. 5)

risorgimento   Italian term, beginning in the late eighteenth century, for the political and cultural renewal of Italy. It later came to describe the political and military events that led to the unification of Italy in 1861. (Ch. 22)

Robespierre, Maximilien (1758–1794)   French lawyer and revolutionary leader. A **Jacobin** who joined the Committee of Public Safety in 1793, Robespierre called for the **Terror** to suppress internal dissent. (Ch. 19)

Romanesque   Meaning "in the Roman style," this nineteenth-century term characterized the transitional architecture and painting of the period between the waning of Carolingian art and the full emergence of **Gothic** art in the twelfth century. Distinctive features of Romanesque churches are their exuberant decoration and ornament. (Ch. 10)

romanticism   Artistic movement, prevalent from the 1760s to 1840s, that rebelled against rationalism. Writers, painters, and composers rejected the Enlightenment and its rationalist values, instead praising emotion and sensitivity, and worshiping nature for its inherent beauty. (Ch. 21)

Rome-Berlin Axis   Alliance between Hitler's Nazi Germany and Mussolini's fascist Italy. Beginning as an informal understanding by 1936, it was cemented by an anti-Comintern agreement and eventually by an open-ended military alliance, the Pact of Steel, in 1939. (Ch. 27)

Roosevelt, Franklin Delano (1882–1945)   U.S. president who served from 1933 to 1945, through the Great Depression of the 1930s and most of World War II. His New Deal program, including large public works projects, was an innovative response to the Depression. (Ch. 28)

Rousseau, Jean-Jacques (1712–1778)   French writer and philosopher. In his 1762 work, *The Social Contract,* Rousseau depicted a hypothetical state with direct democracy in which citizens have inalienable rights to wide-ranging liberties. He was influential as a critic of an elite society still dominated by status, patronage, and privilege. (Ch. 18)

Sacred Union   An agreement made between French leaders of different political groups to cooperate during World

War I. The French government had initially feared that the Socialists might sabotage the war, when, in fact, they were eager to join the new government of national defense. *(Ch. 25)*

salons Regular gatherings in eighteenth-century Parisian private homes, where **Voltaire** and other **philosophes** read and discussed their works in progress, with the exchange of ideas facilitated by female *salonnières* (salon leaders). Anyone with appropriate manners could participate as an equal, enabling conversation to shift from maintaining the status quo to questioning it. *(Ch. 18)*

sans-culottes Ordinary citizens of revolutionary Paris, whose derisive nickname referred to their inability to afford fashionable knee pants ("culottes"). Because of their effective political organization, they were able to influence the direction of the French Revolution through pressure on the government as well as direct action, such as to overthrow the monarchy in August 1792. *(Ch. 19)*

Sappho (fl. ca. 625 B.C.) Ancient Greek poet from the island of Lesbos. Sappho wrote odes, wedding songs, and hymns expressing intimate feelings, including love for other women. She wrote of female sexuality in a male-dominated culture. *(Ch. 3)*

Schutzstaffel (SS) Nazi elite troops, led by Heinrich Himmler. Linked to the Gestapo, the secret political police, the SS specialized in institutionalized terror tactics and were responsible for some of the worst atrocities of the Nazi regime. *(Ch. 27)*

second industrial revolution Interrelated economic changes that resulted in a significant speedup in production in western Europe after 1850. Key factors were the introduction of new products, new methods of manufacture, and new materials such as mass-produced steel, synthetic dyes, and aluminum. *(Ch. 23)*

Second International International socialist organization founded in 1889 that met yearly to debate issues of broad concern. Beginning in 1907, it called for workers to strike and to refuse military service in case of international conflict. *(Ch. 24)*

Second Reform Bill (1867) British legislation that extended suffrage by lowering property qualifications and set equal population requirements for all parliamentary districts. The legislation bolstered the existing system, as the newly enfranchised clerks, artisans, and other skilled workers felt more a part of society. *(Ch. 22)*

Seleucids Dynasty of rulers of Asia Minor from 312 to 64 B.C. Founded by Seleucus (ca. 358–281 B.C.), a general of **Alexander the Great,** the kingdom spread **Hellenism** by establishing seventy colonies throughout the Near East. *(Ch. 4)*

senate In the ancient Roman Republic and Empire, the powerful council of elders that advised the monarchs (Latin: *senatus,* from *senex,* "old man"). Romans spoke of the senate's *auctoritas,* a quasi-religious prestige. *(Ch. 5)*

separate spheres Notion, especially prevalent in the mid-nineteenth century, of two distinct sets of roles—one male and public, the other female and private. While the man was out in the world advancing his career, the bourgeois woman was to run her home, providing her family with an orderly, comfortable shelter. *(Ch. 23)*

Seven Years' War (1756–1763) The first major war between European nations started and fought largely in their overseas empires, the Seven Years' War was in part a conflict between Britain and France for control of overseas possessions. Britain emerged the decisive winner, partly because France was simultaneously fighting on the European continent, where France and Austria tried to contain Prussia. *(Ch. 18)*

show trials Trials staged for ideological and propaganda reasons in the USSR. In the most famous, orchestrated by **Joseph Stalin** from 1936 to 1938, major communist figures were made to confess to trumped-up charges and executed. These trials helped persuade Soviet citizens that a high-level conspiracy was responsible for the USSR's economic woes. *(Ch. 27)*

Sistine Chapel Chapel at the Vatican Palace commissioned by Pope Sixtus IV in 1475, best known for Michelangelo's magnificent paintings of the Creation and Last Judgment. The monument vividly captures the cultural, religious, and ideological program of the papacy. *(Ch. 12)*

slave trade Europeans' trade with Africa in which involuntary laborers were bought and shipped to the Americas to be sold primarily to owners of plantations where sugar and other commodities were produced. The trade reached its peak in the eighteenth century, when approximately 7 million Africans were shipped across the Atlantic. The slave trade was an integral part of the "triangle trade" by which Europe, Africa, and the Americas were connected. See also **plantation system.** *(Ch. 18)*

Smith, Adam (1723–1790) Scottish economist who developed the doctrine of *laissez faire.* In his treatise *The Wealth of Nations* (1776), Smith argued that an economy regulates itself better without interference by government and without monopolies and other economic privileges. Smith suggested that people's economic activities are often "led by an invisible hand" to benefit society as a whole. *(Ch. 18)*

social Catholics Catholics in western Europe who believed that society bore responsibility for the well-being of the poor. They were following the ideas set out in 1891 by Pope Leo XIII (r. 1878–1903) in his encyclical *Rerum novarum* (Of New Things). *(Ch. 23)*

Social Darwinism Theory of social evolution first articulated by Herbert Spencer (1820–1902). According to Social Darwinists, human societies evolve in the same way as plants and animals, and the weak, poor, and improvident are not worthy of survival. Social Darwinism was used to justify callousness toward the poor at home and imperialist conquest abroad. See also **Darwinism.** *(Ch. 23)*

social market economy The late-twentieth-century socially oriented model of capitalism practiced in continental western Europe, providing a substantial safety net in health care and a commitment to public services such as transportation and day care. It competed with the U.S.

model, shared by Britain, which emphasized free enterprise. *(Ch. 30)*

socialism   Nineteenth-century economic and social doctrine and political movement that opposed private ownership and control of the means of production. Socialists believed that the "social" or state ownership of property, unlike private ownership, would benefit society as a whole, creating a more just system. *(Ch. 21)*

Society of Jesus (Jesuits)   Founded in 1534 by **Ignatius Loyola** (1491-1556), the Jesuits soon became leaders in the Catholic Counter-Reformation. The Jesuits were famed for their schools and work as spiritual advisers. *(Ch. 14)*

Society of Revolutionary Republican Women   In revolutionary France, a powerful political club that represented the interests of female **sans-culottes.** The society was included in a general ban on political participation by women that the Committee of Public Safety instituted in October 1793. *(Ch. 19)*

Socrates (469-399 B.C.)   Ancient Greek philosopher, a founder of the Western philosophical tradition. Socrates changed the emphasis of philosophy from the natural world to human ethics. He believed that no one who truly understood goodness would ever choose to do evil. Accused of being an atheist and corrupting the young, Socrates was executed in 399. Socrates' teachings were recorded and transmitted by his students, including **Plato.** *(Ch. 3)*

sola scriptura   Doctrine put forward by **Martin Luther** in *On the Babylonian Captivity of the Church* (1520) that church authority had to be based on biblical teachings. In particular he argued that the sacraments of the Catholic Church—other than baptism and communion—were not found in the Bible. *(Ch. 14)*

solidarism   Late-nineteenth-century policy of conservative and liberal parties to blunt the appeal of socialism. Solidarism emphasized the mutual responsibility of classes and individuals for one another's well-being and led to the passage of laws and benefits to improve the lot of the working class. *(Ch. 23)*

Solidarity   A trade union formed from a movement of shipyard workers in communist Poland in 1980. It became the nucleus of widespread demands for change—including independent labor organizations, the right to strike, and freedom of expression. Though forced underground in 1981, the movement eventually proved crucial to the downfall of the communist regime in Poland. *(Ch. 29)*

Solon (ca. 630-560 B.C.)   Statesman of early Athens. Appointed to a one-year term as sole archon in 594 B.C., Solon transformed Greek society through mediation, moderation, respect for law, and measures that liberated the poor and downtrodden. His economic reforms sparked a commercial boom. *(Ch. 3)*

Spanish Inquisition   Church court that began in 1478 when King Ferdinand and Queen Isabella obtained papal approval to control the grand inquisitor. The Spanish Inquisition investigated and condemned many former Jews and Muslims who were believed to have insincerely con-

verted to Christianity. It became an important and lucrative instrument to expand state power. *(Ch. 11)*

"stab in the back" myth   The notion, widely held among Germans after their unexpected loss in World War I, that political intrigue and revolution at home had sabotaged the German military effort. It helped alienate Germans from their new democratic government. *(Ch. 25)*

Stalin, Joseph (1879-1953)   Soviet dictator. Secretary of the Communist Party since 1922, Stalin outmaneuvered his rivals after the death of Lenin to take control of the Soviet government by 1929. Stalin jettisoned the **New Economic Policy** and instituted a program of crash industrialization and agricultural **collectivization.** He concluded the **Nazi-Soviet Pact** in 1939 but joined the Allies after the German invasion of the Soviet Union in 1941. Victorious in World War II, Stalin sponsored the takeover of governments in eastern Europe by communist regimes, contributing to the development of the **cold war.** See also **"the Great Patriotic War"; gulag; Potsdam conference; show trials; Yalta conference.** *(Ch. 26)*

Stalingrad (1942-1943)   Decisive World War II battle. The Soviet Union, at immense cost in lives, launched repeated counterattacks on Germany's Sixth Army, stopping it from advancing farther and finally forcing it to surrender. The battle is often considered the turning point of World War II in Europe. *(Ch. 28)*

steam engine   Machine invented in England in its modern form by James Watt in 1777. The steam engine provided mechanized power for manufacturing and made **factories** and **mass production** possible. *(Ch. 20)*

Stoics   Believers in a philosophical system begun in Athens by Zeno (335-263 B.C.). Stoicism emphasized the pursuit of wisdom, the reliability of sensory experience, and freedom from all passion. Stoics focused on intentions as well as the results of actions. *(Ch. 4)*

Stresemann, Gustav (1878-1929)   German statesman of the Weimar Republic. Leader of the conservative German People's Party, Stresemann served briefly as chancellor in 1923, then as foreign secretary from 1923 to 1929. He secured a reduction of Germany's reparations payments and negotiated the **Treaty of Locarno,** paving the way for Germany's entry to the League of Nations in 1926. His death in 1929 was a blow to hopes for the development of democracy in Germany and peace in Europe. *(Ch. 26)*

Suez crisis (1956)   Crisis prompted by Egypt's nationalization of the British-owned Suez Canal. The effort of Britain, France, and Israel to seize the canal prompted a strong negative reaction in world opinion, forcing them to withdraw. The episode demonstrated the newly limited reach of the western European powers in world affairs. *(Ch. 29)*

suffragists   Activists who, beginning in the late nineteenth century, organized to win the vote for women. Adopting increasingly violent tactics, English suffragists (often referred to by contemporaries as "suffragettes") endured attacks by male thugs, were arrested, engaged in hunger strikes, and were force-fed. *(Ch. 24)*

Sumerians Dominant inhabitants of Mesopotamia in the third millennium B.C. They established the world's first civilization, thirty flourishing city-states with a common culture, commerce, and tendency to make war on one another. *(Ch. 1)*

summa An encyclopedic compendium of carefully arrayed knowledge on a particular subject. Examples are the two most famous works of **Thomas Aquinas,** the *Summa Contra Gentiles* and the *Summa Theologiae.* *(Ch. 10)*

surrealism A movement in literature and the visual arts that emerged in Paris in the early 1920s. Though indebted to dada and its mocking defiance of convention, surrealism sought to find something positive by exploring the realm of the subconscious, partly by following some of **Sigmund Freud**'s insights about access to the subconscious. *(Ch. 26)*

Tacitus, Cornelius (ca. A.D. 55–120) Roman historian of the "Silver Age." Tacitus lauded the simple virtues of the German tribes and expressed nostalgia for the Republic. His greatest works were *The Histories,* on the civil wars of A.D. 69, and *The Annals,* chronicling the emperors from Tiberius through Nero. *(Ch. 6)*

Tennis Court Oath (1789) Pledge signed by all but one Third Estate deputy of the Estates General of France on June 20, 1789. The deputies swore to continue to meet until a constitution was drafted. *(Ch. 19)*

Terror (1793–1794) Systematic repression of internal enemies undertaken by revolutionary tribunals across France at the urging of **Maximilien Robespierre.** Approximately fourteen thousand people were executed, including aristocrats, Girondins, and **sans-culottes.** The Terror ended with the arrest and execution of Robespierre in July 1794. *(Ch. 19)*

tetrarchy Government ruled by four leaders. Emperor Diocletian established a tetrarchy in about 293 to address the Roman Empire's political instability, huge size, and complexity, as well as to promote experienced men and provide an orderly imperial succession. *(Ch. 7)*

Thatcher, Margaret (b. 1925) As Conservative prime minister of Britain from 1979 to 1990, she spearheaded a number of measures to promote privatization and free enterprise at the expense of the welfare state and the British labor unions. So dramatic was the resulting change in direction that it is sometimes characterized as Thatcher's conservative revolution. *(Chs. 29, 30)*

third-century crisis Period from A.D. 235 to 284, when the Roman Empire suffered barbarian invasions, domestic economic problems, plague, assassinations, and urban decline. Attempting to fend off invasions at opposite fronts, the emperors devalued the currency, leading to massive inflation. *(Ch. 6)*

Third Estate In France, the common people, as distinct from the nobles (First Estate) and clergy (Second Estate). In the Estates General in 1789, it was presumed that the votes of the First and Second Estates would overrule those of the Third Estate, although the commoners vastly outnumbered the nobles and clergy. *(Ch. 19)*

Thirty Years' War (1618–1648) Destructive war, involving most European countries but fought in Germany, resulting from sixteenth-century religious tensions, regionalism versus centralizing forces, and dynastic and strategic rivalries between rulers. See also **Peace of Westphalia.** *(Ch. 15)*

Thucydides (ca. 455–397 B.C.) Ancient Greek historian; with **Herodotus,** a founder of history-writing in the West. A failed Athenian general, Thucydides made a careful study of the Peloponnesian War and prided himself on the accuracy of his account of the prolonged conflict. *(Ch. 3)*

Torah First five books of the Bible. Accepted as sacred by the Hebrews around 425 B.C., it relates the working out of God's pact, or **covenant,** with the Hebrews, his chosen people. *(Ch. 2)*

Tordesillas, Treaty of (1494) Treaty by which Pope Alexander VI divided the rights of colonization of the newly identified lands between Portugal and Spain. He had intended to give Africa to the Portuguese and the New World to Spain, but by a miscalculation Brazil remained in the Portuguese area. *(Ch. 13)*

total war The concept, first associated with World War I, that war requires the mobilization of all a nation's resources and energies. The unexpected need to wage total war during World War I accelerated social and economic processes, from technological development to women's suffrage. *(Ch. 25)*

Toussaint-Louverture, François (1743–1803) Former slave who governed the island of Saint Domingue (Haiti) as an independent state after the slave revolt of 1791. In 1802 French forces captured Toussaint-Louverture, who died in prison. *(Ch. 19)*

trading-post empire Commercial system developed by Portugal in the sixteenth century to dominate trade in the Indian Ocean through fortified, strategically placed naval bases. All merchants were expected to acquire export licenses and ship products through Portuguese ports. *(Ch. 13)*

tragedy Serious play with an unhappy ending. Greek tragedy emerged and reached its height in the fifth century B.C. in the works of Aeschylus, Sophocles, and Euripides. The essence of Greek tragedy is the nobility in the spectacle of a great man or woman failing because of a "fatal flaw," but learning from failure. *(Ch. 3)*

trasformismo System of political manipulation used by Count Camillo di Cavour (1810–1861), Piedmont's prime minister, to create majorities in parliament to support his cabinet. The practice of using cajolery and bribery to transform foes into supporters would continue to characterize Italian government in the late nineteenth century. *(Ch. 22)*

Triple Alliance Military alliance established in 1882 among Germany, Austria-Hungary, and Italy to counter the Franco-Russian Alliance (later the **Triple Entente**). The system of rival alliances contributed to the escalation of international tensions. *(Ch. 24)*

Triple Entente Military alliance between Great Britain, France, and Russia, completed in 1907, countering the

Triple Alliance. The system of rival alliances eventually brought all of Europe into World War I. *(Ch. 24)*

triumph   Elaborate procession through the streets of ancient Rome. Triumphs were voted by the **senate** to salute a general's victory over a foreign army. *(Ch. 5)*

Truman Doctrine   The U.S. policy of containment, or limiting communist expansion, as outlined by President Harry Truman in 1947. Intended most immediately to deter any communist designs on Greece or Turkey, the doctrine was used thereafter to support any country that the United States considered threatened by communism during the **cold war.** *(Ch. 28)*

unilateralism   Term describing the increasing willingness of the United States to go its own way in world affairs after the end of the cold war, and especially after the terrorist attack on the United States in September 2001. In pursuing its own course, the United States was departing from the multilateral international system that it had sought to foster since World War II. This departure alienated many Europeans. *(Ch. 30)*

United Nations   International organization of nations founded in 1945 to encourage peace, cooperation, and recognition of human rights. The major powers—China, France, Great Britain, the Soviet Union, and the United States—were given a privileged position as permanent members of the Security Council, each with veto power. *(Ch. 28)*

urbanization   Term related to the growth of cities, largely connected to the **industrialization** of the late eighteenth and nineteenth centuries. Cities aided industry by providing markets for goods and a concentrated source of workers. However, with urbanization came a host of new problems such as urban slums, lack of sanitation, and pollution. *(Ch. 20)*

utilitarianism   Political theory of Jeremy Bentham (1748–1832). Bentham argued that the purpose of government is to provide "the greatest happiness of the greatest number" and that the test of government is its usefulness. Democracy was implicit in Bentham's philosophy: the greatest number could ensure its own happiness only by voting for its rulers. *(Ch. 21)*

Vasco da Gama (1460?–1524)   Pioneering Portuguese explorer and trader whose voyage from 1497 to 1499 around the Cape of Good Hope to Mozambique and India inaugurated a four-hundred-year-long Portuguese presence in the Indian Ocean region. *(Ch. 13)*

vassals   Drawing on both Roman and Germanic customs, vassalage linked two men—lord and vassal—in an honorable, reciprocal bond based on loyalty and service. Eventually leading nobles and their vassals formed a social and political elite. *(Ch. 8)*

Versailles, Treaty of (1919)   Peace treaty that the victors in World War I imposed on a defeated Germany in 1919. The harsh terms of this dictated peace produced a sense of bitterness and betrayal in Germany. *(Ch. 25)*

Vichy France   The term for the repressive French government that followed the Third Republic after France's defeat by Nazi Germany in 1940. Headquartered in the resort town of Vichy, the government collaborated with the victorious Germans, who occupied Paris. *(Ch. 28)*

Victorian morality   Nineteenth-century ethos wherein the values of the dominant middle class, which emphasized strict moral principles, especially regarding sex and drink, became the social norms. In Queen Victoria, who reigned for two-thirds of the century, the middle classes saw a reflection of their own values. *(Ch. 23)*

Virgil   Roman poet whose works contributed to the Augustan renewal. In the *Eclogues,* Virgil (Publius Vergilius Maro, 70–19 B.C.) describes the blessings of peace under **Augustus;** in the *Georgics,* he glorifies Italian agriculture. His *Aeneid* mythologizes Rome and describes both the burden and glory of empire. *(Ch. 6)*

Visigoths   Germanic people who served as allied troops for the Romans. When threatened by the Huns, the Visigoths crossed the Danube and settled in the Balkans. Eventually they sacked Rome in 410 and expanded their rule to parts of Spain and southern France. *(Ch. 7)*

Voltaire (François-Marie Arouet, 1694–1778)   Prolific French writer, critic, and reformer who embodied the spirit of eighteenth-century rationalism: its confidence, its increasingly practical bent, its wit and sophistication. His satires and philosophical critiques targeted Christianity, intolerance, and tyranny. See also **philosophes.** *(Ch. 18)*

Vulgate Bible   Latin version of new translations of the Hebrew Scriptures and Greek New Testament written by Jerome (331–420) for Pope Damasus. It was called the Vulgate because it was the Bible for the "people" (*vulgus*), whose language was Latin. *(Ch. 7)*

Warsaw Pact (1955–1991)   Military-diplomatic alliance of Soviet bloc countries, created to counter NATO. The pact established a joint military command and mutual military assistance, as well as a new basis for the continuing presence of Soviet troops in the satellite states. See also **cold war.** *(Ch. 29)*

welfare state   The concept, especially prevalent in Western countries after World War II, that government should adopt large-scale social welfare measures, while maintaining a primarily capitalistic economy. Among the welfare measures usually adopted were a national health service, old-age pensions, and insurance against unemployment, sickness, and disability. *(Ch. 29)*

Weltpolitik   Meaning "world politics," the term describes the policy pursued by Kaiser Wilhelm II (r. 1888–1918) to make Germany a world power, with colonies, a navy, and major influence among the Great Powers. The kaiser implemented his ambitious agenda with nationalistic appeals and bombastic threats. *(Ch. 24)*

World Health Organization (WHO)   Established as a specialized agency of the United Nations in 1948, it serves as the coordinating authority on international public health. It is headquartered in Geneva, Switzerland. *(Ch. 30)*

World Trade Organization (WTO) Growing from a multilateral trade agreement in 1947, it sought, with mixed success, to promote freer trade throughout the world. By the end of the 1990s WTO meetings were drawing large demonstrations by anti-globalization activists, most notably in Seattle in 1999 and in Cancún, Mexico, in 2003. *(Ch. 30)*

Yalta conference The meeting in February 1945 at Yalta, a Soviet Black Sea resort, between Stalin, Roosevelt, and Churchill. With Allied victory assured, they began outlining plans for the postwar order, including the military occupation of Germany. See also **Potsdam conference.** *(Ch. 28)*

Young Turks Term describing the young intellectuals who wanted to transform the Ottoman Empire into a more modern, Westernized state. Self-exiled in the late 1860s in Paris and London, they overthrew the sultan and seized power in 1908. The expression has subsequently come to designate any group of activists pushing for political change. *(Ch. 22)*

Zionism Nationalist Jewish movement. In the late nineteenth century, faced with growing **anti-Semitism,** some Jews argued that they would be safe only in their own nation. Zionism advocated establishing a Jewish state in the Jews' ancient homeland of Palestine, an idea that became reality with the creation of Israel in 1948. *(Ch. 24)*

Zoroastrianism Religion founded about 1000–550 B.C. by the Persian prophet Zarathustra (*Zoroaster* in Greek). Zoroastrians believe in a supreme deity and a cosmic contest between good and evil within each individual. *(Ch. 2)*

Zwingli, Huldrych (1484–1531) Town preacher of Zurich, Zwingli became a leader of the urban reformation in Switzerland and southwest Germany, emphasizing the importance of the community in the salvation of individuals. *(Ch. 14)*

INDEX